# A PIRATE ANTHOLOGY

*A Collection of Swashbuckling Tales of Piracy, Buried Treasure & Adventure At Sea*

ROBERT LOUIS STEVENSON J. M. BARRIE
CHARLES DICKENS JACK LONDON
WASHINGTON IRVING EDGAR ALLAN POE
R. M. BALLANTYNE F. SCOTT FITZGERALD
ARTHUR CONAN DOYLE BRET HARTE
DANIEL DEFOE

# CONTENTS

# TREASURE ISLAND

ROBERT LOUIS STEVENSON

# I

# THE OLD BUCCANEER

# I

# THE OLD SEA-DOG AT THE "ADMIRAL BENBOW"

Quire Trelawney, Dr. Livesey, and the rest of these gentlemen having asked me to write down the whole particulars about Treasure Island, from the beginning to the end, keeping nothing back but the bearings of the island, and that only because there is still treasure not yet lifted, I take up my pen in the year of grace 17__ and go back to the time when my father kept the Admiral Benbow inn and the brown old seaman with the sabre cut first took up his lodging under our roof.

I remember him as if it were yesterday, as he came plodding to the inn door, his sea-chest following behind him in a hand-barrow—a tall, strong, heavy, nut-brown man, his tarry pigtail falling over the shoulder of his soiled blue coat, his hands ragged and scarred, with black, broken nails, and the sabre cut across one cheek, a dirty, livid white. I remember him looking round the cover and whistling to himself as he did so, and then breaking out in that old sea-song that he sang so often afterwards:

"Fifteen men on the dead man's chest—
Yo-ho-ho, and a bottle of rum!"

in the high, old tottering voice that seemed to have been tuned and broken at the capstan bars. Then he rapped on the door with a bit of stick like a handspike that he carried, and when my father appeared, called roughly for a glass of rum. This, when it was brought to him, he drank slowly, like a connoisseur, lingering on the taste and still looking about him at the cliffs and up at our signboard.

"This is a handy cove," says he at length; "and a pleasant sittyated grog-shop. Much company, mate?"

My father told him no, very little company, the more was the pity.

"Well, then," said he, "this is the berth for me. Here you, matey," he cried to the man who trundled the barrow; "bring up alongside and help up my chest. I'll stay here a bit," he continued. "I'm a plain man; rum and bacon and eggs is what I want, and that head up there for to watch ships off. What you mought call me? You mought call me captain. Oh, I see what you're at—there"; and he threw down three or four gold pieces on the threshold. "You can tell me when I've worked through that," says he, looking as fierce as a commander.

And indeed bad as his clothes were and coarsely as he spoke, he had none of the appearance of a man who sailed before the mast, but seemed like a mate or skipper accustomed to be obeyed or to strike. The man who came with the barrow told us the mail had set him down the morning before at the Royal George, that he had inquired what inns there were along the coast, and hearing ours well spoken of, I suppose, and described as lonely, had chosen it from the others for his place of residence. And that was all we could learn of our guest.

He was a very silent man by custom. All day he hung round the cove or upon the cliffs with a brass telescope; all evening he sat in a corner of the parlour next the fire and drank rum and water very strong. Mostly he would not speak when spoken to, only look up sudden and fierce and blow through his nose like a fog-horn; and we and the people who came about our house soon learned to let him be. Every day when he came back from his stroll he would ask if any seafaring men had gone by along the road. At first we thought it was the want of company of his own kind that made him ask this question, but at last we began to see he was desirous to avoid them. When a seaman did put up at the Admiral Benbow (as now and then some did, making by the coast road for Bristol) he would look in at him through the curtained door before he entered the parlour; and he was always sure to be as silent as a mouse when any such was present. For me, at least, there was no secret about the matter, for I was, in a way, a sharer in his alarms. He had taken me aside one day and promised me a silver fourpenny on the first of every month if I would only keep my "weather-eye open for a seafaring man with one leg" and let him know the moment he appeared. Often enough when the first of the month came round and I applied to him for my wage, he would only blow through his nose at me and stare me down, but before the week was out he was sure to think better of it, bring me my four-penny piece, and repeat his orders to look out for "the seafaring man with one leg."

How that personage haunted my dreams, I need scarcely tell you. On stormy nights, when the wind shook the four corners of the house and the surf roared along the cove and up the cliffs, I would see him in a thousand forms, and with a thousand diabolical expressions. Now the leg would be cut off at the knee, now at the hip; now he was a monstrous kind of a creature who had never had but the one leg, and that in the middle of his body. To see him leap and run and pursue me over hedge and ditch was the worst of nightmares. And altogether I paid pretty dear for my monthly fourpenny piece, in the shape of these abominable fancies.

But though I was so terrified by the idea of the seafaring man with one leg, I was far less afraid of the captain himself than anybody else who knew him. There were nights when he took a deal more rum and water than his head would carry; and then he would sometimes sit and sing his wicked, old, wild sea-songs, minding nobody; but sometimes he would call for glasses round and force all the trembling company to listen to his stories or bear a chorus to his singing. Often I have heard the house shaking with "Yo-ho-ho, and a bottle of rum," all the neighbours joining in for dear life, with the fear of death upon them, and each singing louder than the other to avoid remark. For in these fits he was the most overriding companion ever known; he would slap his hand on the table for silence all round; he would fly up in a passion of anger at a question, or sometimes because none was put, and so he judged the company was not following his story. Nor would he allow anyone to leave the inn till he had drunk himself sleepy and reeled off to bed.

His stories were what frightened people worst of all. Dreadful stories they were—about hanging, and walking the plank, and storms at sea, and the Dry Tortugas, and wild deeds and places on the Spanish Main. By his own account he must have lived his life among some of the wickedest men that God ever allowed upon the sea, and the language in which he told these stories shocked our plain country people almost as much as the crimes that he described. My father was always saying the inn would be ruined, for people would soon cease coming there to be tyrannized over and put down, and sent shivering to their beds; but I really believe his presence did us good. People were frightened at the time, but on looking back they rather liked it; it was a fine excitement in a quiet country life, and there was even a party of the younger men who pretended to admire him, calling him a "true sea-dog" and a "real old salt" and such like names, and saying there was the sort of man that made England terrible at sea.

In one way, indeed, he bade fair to ruin us, for he kept on staying week after week, and at last month after month, so that all the money had been long exhausted, and still my father never plucked up the heart to insist on having more. If ever he mentioned it, the captain blew through his nose so loudly that you might say he roared, and stared my poor father out of the room. I have seen him wringing his hands after such a rebuff, and I am sure the annoyance and the terror he lived in must have greatly hastened his early and unhappy death.

All the time he lived with us the captain made no change whatever in his dress but to buy some stockings from a hawker. One of the cocks of his hat having fallen down, he let it hang from that day forth, though it was a great annoyance when it blew. I remember the appearance of his coat, which he patched himself upstairs in his room, and which, before the end, was nothing but patches. He never wrote or received a letter, and he never spoke with any but the neighbours, and with these, for the most part, only when drunk on rum. The great sea-chest none of us had ever seen open.

He was only once crossed, and that was towards the end, when my poor father was far gone in a decline that took him off. Dr. Livesey came late one afternoon to see the patient, took a bit of dinner from my mother, and went into the parlour to smoke a pipe until his horse should come down from the hamlet, for we had no stabling at the old Benbow. I followed him in, and I remember observing the contrast the neat, bright doctor, with his powder as white as snow and his bright, black eyes and pleasant manners, made with the coltish country folk, and above all, with that filthy, heavy, bleared scarecrow of a pirate of ours, sitting, far gone in rum, with his arms on the table. Suddenly he—the captain, that is—began to pipe up his eternal song:

"Fifteen men on the dead man's chest—<br>
Yo-ho-ho, and a bottle of rum!<br>
Drink and the devil had done for the rest—<br>
Yo-ho-ho, and a bottle of rum!"

At first I had supposed "the dead man's chest" to be that identical big box of his upstairs in the front room, and the thought had been mingled in my nightmares with that of the one-legged seafaring man. But by this time we had all long ceased to pay any particular notice to the song; it was new, that night, to nobody but Dr. Livesey, and on him I observed it did not produce an agreeable effect, for he looked up for a moment quite angrily before he went on with his talk to old Taylor, the gardener, on a new cure for the rheumatics. In the meantime, the captain gradually brightened up at his own music, and at last flapped his hand upon the table before him in a way we all knew to mean silence. The voices stopped at once, all but Dr.

Livesey's; he went on as before speaking clear and kind and drawing briskly at his pipe between every word or two. The captain glared at him for a while, flapped his hand again, glared still harder, and at last broke out with a villainous, low oath, "Silence, there, between decks!"

"Were you addressing me, sir?" says the doctor; and when the ruffian had told him, with another oath, that this was so, "I have only one thing to say to you, sir," replies the doctor, "that if you keep on drinking rum, the world will soon be quit of a very dirty scoundrel!"

The old fellow's fury was awful. He sprang to his feet, drew and opened a sailor's clasp-knife, and balancing it open on the palm of his hand, threatened to pin the doctor to the wall.

The doctor never so much as moved. He spoke to him as before, over his shoulder and in the same tone of voice, rather high, so that all the room might hear, but perfectly calm and steady: "If you do not put that knife this instant in your pocket, I promise, upon my honour, you shall hang at the next assizes."

Then followed a battle of looks between them, but the captain soon knuckled under, put up his weapon, and resumed his seat, grumbling like a beaten dog.

"And now, sir," continued the doctor, "since I now know there's such a fellow in my district, you may count I'll have an eye upon you day and night. I'm not a doctor only; I'm a magistrate; and if I catch a breath of complaint against you, if it's only for a piece of incivility like tonight's, I'll take effectual means to have you hunted down and routed out of this. Let that suffice."

Soon after, Dr. Livesey's horse came to the door and he rode away, but the captain held his peace that evening, and for many evenings to come.

# ❧ 2 ❧

# BLACK DOG APPEARS AND DISAPPEARS

It was not very long after this that there occurred the first of the mysterious events that rid us at last of the captain, though not, as you will see, of his affairs. It was a bitter cold winter, with long, hard frosts and heavy gales; and it was plain from the first that my poor father was little likely to see the spring. He sank daily, and my mother and I had all the inn upon our hands, and were kept busy enough without paying much regard to our unpleasant guest.

It was one January morning, very early—a pinching, frosty morning—the cove all grey with hoar-frost, the ripple lapping softly on the stones, the sun still low and only touching the hilltops and shining far to seaward. The captain had risen earlier than usual and set out down the beach, his cutlass swinging under the broad skirts of the old blue coat, his brass telescope under his arm, his hat tilted back upon his head. I remember his breath hanging like smoke in his wake as he strode off, and the last sound I heard of him as he turned the big rock was a loud snort of indignation, as though his mind was still running upon Dr. Livesey.

Well, mother was upstairs with father and I was laying the breakfast-table against the captain's return when the parlour door opened and a man stepped in on whom I had never set my eyes before. He was a pale, tallowy creature, wanting two fingers of the left hand, and though he wore a cutlass, he did not look much like a fighter. I had always my eye open for seafaring men, with one leg or two, and I remember this one puzzled me. He was not sailorly, and yet he had a smack of the sea about him too.

I asked him what was for his service, and he said he would take rum; but as I was going out of the room to fetch it, he sat down upon a table and motioned me to draw near. I paused where I was, with my napkin in my hand.

"Come here, sonny," says he. "Come nearer here."

I took a step nearer.

"Is this here table for my mate Bill?" he asked with a kind of leer.

I told him I did not know his mate Bill, and this was for a person who stayed in our house whom we called the captain.

"Well," said he, "my mate Bill would be called the captain, as like as not. He has a cut on one cheek and a mighty pleasant way with him, particularly in drink, has my mate Bill. We'll put it, for argument like, that your captain has a cut on one cheek—and we'll put it, if you like, that that cheek's the right one. Ah, well! I told you. Now, is my mate Bill in this here house?"

I told him he was out walking.

"Which way, sonny? Which way is he gone?"

And when I had pointed out the rock and told him how the captain was likely to return, and how soon, and answered a few other questions, "Ah," said he, "this'll be as good as drink to my mate Bill."

The expression of his face as he said these words was not at all pleasant, and I had my own reasons for thinking that the stranger was mistaken, even supposing he meant what he said. But it was no affair of mine, I thought; and besides, it was difficult to know what to do. The stranger kept hanging about just inside the inn door, peering round the corner like a cat waiting for a mouse. Once I stepped out myself into the road, but he immediately called me back, and as I did not obey quick enough for his fancy, a most horrible change came over his tallowy face, and he ordered me in with an oath that made me jump. As soon as I was back again he returned to his former manner, half fawning, half sneering, patted me on the shoulder, told me I was a good boy and he had taken quite a fancy to me. "I have a son of my own," said he, "as like you as two blocks, and he's all the pride of my 'art. But the great thing for boys is discipline, sonny—discipline. Now, if you had sailed along of Bill, you wouldn't have stood there to be spoke to twice—not you. That was never Bill's way, nor the way of sich as sailed with him. And here, sure enough, is my mate Bill, with a spy-glass under his arm, bless his old 'art, to be sure. You and me'll just go back into the parlour, sonny, and get behind the door, and we'll give Bill a little surprise—bless his 'art, I say again."

So saying, the stranger backed along with me into the parlour and put me behind him in the corner so that we were both hidden by the open door. I was very uneasy and alarmed, as you may fancy, and it rather added to my fears to observe that the stranger was certainly frightened himself. He cleared the hilt of his cutlass and loosened the blade in the sheath; and all the time we were waiting there he kept swallowing as if he felt what we used to call a lump in the throat.

At last in strode the captain, slammed the door behind him, without looking to the right or left, and marched straight across the room to where his breakfast awaited him.

"Bill," said the stranger in a voice that I thought he had tried to make bold and big.

The captain spun round on his heel and fronted us; all the brown had gone out of his face, and even his nose was blue; he had the look of a man who sees a ghost, or the evil one, or something worse, if anything can be; and upon my word, I felt sorry to see him all in a moment turn so old and sick.

"Come, Bill, you know me; you know an old shipmate, Bill, surely," said the stranger.

The captain made a sort of gasp.

"Black Dog!" said he.

"And who else?" returned the other, getting more at his ease. "Black Dog as ever was, come for to see his old shipmate Billy, at the Admiral Benbow inn. Ah, Bill, Bill, we have seen a sight of times, us two, since I lost them two talons," holding up his mutilated hand.

"Now, look here," said the captain; "you've run me down; here I am; well, then, speak up; what is it?"

"That's you, Bill," returned Black Dog, "you're in the right of it, Billy. I'll have a glass of rum from this dear child here, as I've took such a liking to; and we'll sit down, if you please, and talk square, like old shipmates."

When I returned with the rum, they were already seated on either side of the captain's breakfast-table—Black Dog next to the door and sitting sideways so as to have one eye on his old shipmate and one, as I thought, on his retreat.

He bade me go and leave the door wide open. "None of your keyholes for me, sonny," he said; and I left them together and retired into the bar.

For a long time, though I certainly did my best to listen, I could hear nothing but a low gattling; but at last the voices began to grow higher, and I could pick up a word or two, mostly oaths, from the captain.

"No, no, no, no; and an end of it!" he cried once. And again, "If it comes to swinging, swing all, say I."

Then all of a sudden there was a tremendous explosion of oaths and other noises—the chair and table went over in a lump, a clash of steel followed, and then a cry of pain, and the next instant I saw Black Dog in full flight, and the captain hotly pursuing, both with drawn cutlasses, and the former streaming blood from the left shoulder. Just at the door the captain aimed at the fugitive one last tremendous cut, which would certainly have split him to the chine had it not been intercepted by our big signboard of Admiral Benbow. You may see the notch on the lower side of the frame to this day.

That blow was the last of the battle. Once out upon the road, Black Dog, in spite of his wound, showed a wonderful clean pair of heels and disappeared over the edge of the hill in half a minute. The captain, for his part, stood staring at the signboard like a bewildered man. Then he passed his hand over his eyes several times and at last turned back into the house.

"Jim," says he, "rum"; and as he spoke, he reeled a little, and caught himself with one hand against the wall.

"Are you hurt?" cried I.

"Rum," he repeated. "I must get away from here. Rum! Rum!"

I ran to fetch it, but I was quite unsteadied by all that had fallen out, and I broke one glass and fouled the tap, and while I was still getting in my own way, I heard a loud fall in the parlour, and running in, beheld the captain lying full length upon the floor. At the same instant my mother, alarmed by the cries and fighting, came running downstairs to help me. Between us we raised his head. He was breathing very loud and hard, but his eyes were closed and his face a horrible colour.

"Dear, deary me," cried my mother, "what a disgrace upon the house! And your poor father sick!"

In the meantime, we had no idea what to do to help the captain, nor any other thought but that he had got his death-hurt in the scuffle with the stranger. I got the rum, to be sure, and tried to put it down his throat, but his teeth were tightly shut and his jaws as strong as iron. It was a happy relief for us when the door opened and Doctor Livesey came in, on his visit to my father.

"Oh, doctor," we cried, "what shall we do? Where is he wounded?"

"Wounded? A fiddle-stick's end!" said the doctor. "No more wounded than you or I. The man has had a stroke, as I warned him. Now, Mrs. Hawkins, just you run upstairs to your husband and tell him, if possible, nothing about it. For my part, I must do my best to save this fellow's trebly worthless life; Jim, you get me a basin."

When I got back with the basin, the doctor had already ripped up the captain's sleeve and exposed his great sinewy arm. It was tattooed in several places. "Here's luck," "A fair wind," and "Billy Bones his fancy," were very neatly and clearly executed on the forearm; and up near the shoulder there was a sketch of a gallows and a man hanging from it—done, as I thought, with great spirit.

"Prophetic," said the doctor, touching this picture with his finger. "And now, Master Billy

Bones, if that be your name, we'll have a look at the colour of your blood. Jim," he said, "are you afraid of blood?"

"No, sir," said I.

"Well, then," said he, "you hold the basin"; and with that he took his lancet and opened a vein.

A great deal of blood was taken before the captain opened his eyes and looked mistily about him. First he recognized the doctor with an unmistakable frown; then his glance fell upon me, and he looked relieved. But suddenly his colour changed, and he tried to raise himself, crying, "Where's Black Dog?"

"There is no Black Dog here," said the doctor, "except what you have on your own back. You have been drinking rum; you have had a stroke, precisely as I told you; and I have just, very much against my own will, dragged you headforemost out of the grave. Now, Mr. Bones—"

"That's not my name," he interrupted.

"Much I care," returned the doctor. "It's the name of a buccaneer of my acquaintance; and I call you by it for the sake of shortness, and what I have to say to you is this; one glass of rum won't kill you, but if you take one you'll take another and another, and I stake my wig if you don't break off short, you'll die—do you understand that?—die, and go to your own place, like the man in the Bible. Come, now, make an effort. I'll help you to your bed for once."

Between us, with much trouble, we managed to hoist him upstairs, and laid him on his bed, where his head fell back on the pillow as if he were almost fainting.

"Now, mind you," said the doctor, "I clear my conscience—the name of rum for you is death."

And with that he went off to see my father, taking me with him by the arm.

"This is nothing," he said as soon as he had closed the door. "I have drawn blood enough to keep him quiet awhile; he should lie for a week where he is—that is the best thing for him and you; but another stroke would settle him."

## 3

# THE BLACK SPOT

About noon I stopped at the captain's door with some cooling drinks and medicines. He was lying very much as we had left him, only a little higher, and he seemed both weak and excited.

"Jim," he said, "you're the only one here that's worth anything, and you know I've been always good to you. Never a month but I've given you a silver fourpenny for yourself. And now you see, mate, I'm pretty low, and deserted by all; and Jim, you'll bring me one noggin of rum, now, won't you, matey?"

"The doctor—" I began.

But he broke in cursing the doctor, in a feeble voice but heartily. "Doctors is all swabs," he said; "and that doctor there, why, what do he know about seafaring men? I been in places hot as pitch, and mates dropping round with Yellow Jack, and the blessed land a-heaving like the sea with earthquakes—what to the doctor know of lands like that?—and I lived on rum, I tell you. It's been meat and drink, and man and wife, to me; and if I'm not to have my rum now I'm a poor old hulk on a lee shore, my blood'll be on you, Jim, and that doctor swab"; and he ran on again for a while with curses. "Look, Jim, how my fingers fidges," he continued in the pleading tone. "I can't keep 'em still, not I. I haven't had a drop this blessed day. That doctor's a fool, I tell you. If I don't have a dram o' rum, Jim, I'll have the horrors; I seen some on 'em already. I seen old Flint in the corner there, behind you; as plain as print, I seen him; and if I get the horrors, I'm a man that has lived rough, and I'll raise Cain. Your doctor hisself said one glass wouldn't hurt me. I'll give you a golden guinea for a noggin, Jim."

He was growing more and more excited, and this alarmed me for my father, who was very low that day and needed quiet; besides, I was reassured by the doctor's words, now quoted to me, and rather offended by the offer of a bribe.

"I want none of your money," said I, "but what you owe my father. I'll get you one glass, and no more."

When I brought it to him, he seized it greedily and drank it out.

"Aye, aye," said he, "that's some better, sure enough. And now, matey, did that doctor say how long I was to lie here in this old berth?"

"A week at least," said I.

"Thunder!" he cried. "A week! I can't do that; they'd have the black spot on me by then. The lubbers is going about to get the wind of me this blessed moment; lubbers as couldn't keep what they got, and want to nail what is another's. Is that seamanly behaviour, now, I want to know? But I'm a saving soul. I never wasted good money of mine, nor lost it neither; and I'll trick 'em again. I'm not afraid on 'em. I'll shake out another reef, matey, and daddle 'em again."

As he was thus speaking, he had risen from bed with great difficulty, holding to my shoulder with a grip that almost made me cry out, and moving his legs like so much dead weight. His words, spirited as they were in meaning, contrasted sadly with the weakness of the voice in which they were uttered. He paused when he had got into a sitting position on the edge.

"That doctor's done me," he murmured. "My ears is singing. Lay me back."

Before I could do much to help him he had fallen back again to his former place, where he lay for a while silent.

"Jim," he said at length, "you saw that seafaring man today?"

"Black Dog?" I asked.

"Ah! Black Dog," says he. "*He's* a bad un; but there's worse that put him on. Now, if I can't get away nohow, and they tip me the black spot, mind you, it's my old sea-chest they're after; you get on a horse—you can, can't you? Well, then, you get on a horse, and go to—well, yes, I will!—to that eternal doctor swab, and tell him to pipe all hands—magistrates and sich—and he'll lay 'em aboard at the Admiral Benbow—all old Flint's crew, man and boy, all on 'em that's left. I was first mate, I was, old Flint's first mate, and I'm the on'y one as knows the place. He gave it me at Savannah, when he lay a-dying, like as if I was to now, you see. But you won't peach unless they get the black spot on me, or unless you see that Black Dog again or a seafaring man with one leg, Jim—him above all."

"But what is the black spot, captain?" I asked.

"That's a summons, mate. I'll tell you if they get that. But you keep your weather-eye open, Jim, and I'll share with you equals, upon my honour."

He wandered a little longer, his voice growing weaker; but soon after I had given him his medicine, which he took like a child, with the remark, "If ever a seaman wanted drugs, it's me," he fell at last into a heavy, swoon-like sleep, in which I left him. What I should have done had all gone well I do not know. Probably I should have told the whole story to the doctor, for I was in mortal fear lest the captain should repent of his confessions and make an end of me. But as things fell out, my poor father died quite suddenly that evening, which put all other matters on one side. Our natural distress, the visits of the neighbours, the arranging of the funeral, and all the work of the inn to be carried on in the meanwhile kept me so busy that I had scarcely time to think of the captain, far less to be afraid of him.

He got downstairs next morning, to be sure, and had his meals as usual, though he ate little and had more, I am afraid, than his usual supply of rum, for he helped himself out of the bar, scowling and blowing through his nose, and no one dared to cross him. On the night before the funeral he was as drunk as ever; and it was shocking, in that house of mourning, to hear him singing away at his ugly old sea-song; but weak as he was, we were all in the fear of death for him, and the doctor was suddenly taken up with a case many miles away and was never near the house after my father's death. I have said the captain was weak, and indeed he seemed rather to grow weaker than regain his strength. He clambered up and down stairs, and went from the parlour to the bar and back again, and sometimes put his nose out of doors to smell the sea, holding on to the walls as he went for support and breathing hard and fast like a man on a steep mountain. He never particularly addressed me, and it is my belief he had as good as forgotten his confidences; but his temper was more flighty, and allowing for his bodily weakness, more violent than ever. He had an alarming way now when he was drunk of drawing his cutlass and laying it bare before him on the table. But with all that, he minded people less and seemed shut up in his own thoughts and rather wandering. Once, for instance, to our extreme wonder, he piped up to a different air, a kind of country love-song that he must have learned in his youth before he had begun to follow the sea.

So things passed until, the day after the funeral, and about three o'clock of a bitter, foggy, frosty afternoon, I was standing at the door for a moment, full of sad thoughts about my father, when I saw someone drawing slowly near along the road. He was plainly blind, for he tapped before him with a stick and wore a great green shade over his eyes and nose; and he was hunched, as if with age or weakness, and wore a huge old tattered sea-cloak with a hood that made him appear positively deformed. I never saw in my life a more dreadful-looking figure. He stopped a little from the inn, and raising his voice in an odd sing-song, addressed the air in front of him, "Will any kind friend inform a poor blind man, who has lost the precious sight of his eyes in the gracious defence of his native country, England—and God bless King George!—where or in what part of this country he may now be?"

"You are at the Admiral Benbow, Black Hill Cove, my good man," said I.

"I hear a voice," said he, "a young voice. Will you give me your hand, my kind young friend, and lead me in?"

I held out my hand, and the horrible, soft-spoken, eyeless creature gripped it in a moment like a vise. I was so much startled that I struggled to withdraw, but the blind man pulled me close up to him with a single action of his arm.

"Now, boy," he said, "take me in to the captain."

"Sir," said I, "upon my word I dare not."

"Oh," he sneered, "that's it! Take me in straight or I'll break your arm."

And he gave it, as he spoke, a wrench that made me cry out.

"Sir," said I, "it is for yourself I mean. The captain is not what he used to be. He sits with a drawn cutlass. Another gentleman—"

"Come, now, march," interrupted he; and I never heard a voice so cruel, and cold, and ugly as that blind man's. It cowed me more than the pain, and I began to obey him at once, walking straight in at the door and towards the parlour, where our sick old buccaneer was sitting, dazed with rum. The blind man clung close to me, holding me in one iron fist and leaning almost more of his weight on me than I could carry. "Lead me straight up to him, and when I'm in view, cry out, 'Here's a friend for you, Bill.' If you don't, I'll do this," and with that he gave me a twitch that I thought would have made me faint. Between this and that, I was so utterly terrified of the blind beggar that I forgot my terror of the captain, and as I opened the parlour door, cried out the words he had ordered in a trembling voice.

The poor captain raised his eyes, and at one look the rum went out of him and left him staring sober. The expression of his face was not so much of terror as of mortal sickness. He made a movement to rise, but I do not believe he had enough force left in his body.

"Now, Bill, sit where you are," said the beggar. "If I can't see, I can hear a finger stirring. Business is business. Hold out your left hand. Boy, take his left hand by the wrist and bring it near to my right."

We both obeyed him to the letter, and I saw him pass something from the hollow of the hand that held his stick into the palm of the captain's, which closed upon it instantly.

"And now that's done," said the blind man; and at the words he suddenly left hold of me, and with incredible accuracy and nimbleness, skipped out of the parlour and into the road, where, as I still stood motionless, I could hear his stick go tap-tap-tapping into the distance.

It was some time before either I or the captain seemed to gather our senses, but at length, and about at the same moment, I released his wrist, which I was still holding, and he drew in his hand and looked sharply into the palm.

"Ten o'clock!" he cried. "Six hours. We'll do them yet," and he sprang to his feet.

Even as he did so, he reeled, put his hand to his throat, stood swaying for a moment, and then, with a peculiar sound, fell from his whole height face foremost to the floor.

I ran to him at once, calling to my mother. But haste was all in vain. The captain had been struck dead by thundering apoplexy. It is a curious thing to understand, for I had certainly never liked the man, though of late I had begun to pity him, but as soon as I saw that he was dead, I burst into a flood of tears. It was the second death I had known, and the sorrow of the first was still fresh in my heart.

# 4

# THE SEA-CHEST

Lost no time, of course, in telling my mother all that I knew, and perhaps should have told her long before, and we saw ourselves at once in a difficult and dangerous position. Some of the man's money—if he had any—was certainly due to us, but it was not likely that our captain's shipmates, above all the two specimens seen by me, Black Dog and the blind beggar, would be inclined to give up their booty in payment of the dead man's debts. The captain's order to mount at once and ride for Doctor Livesey would have left my mother alone and unprotected, which was not to be thought of. Indeed, it seemed impossible for either of us to remain much longer in the house; the fall of coals in the kitchen grate, the very ticking of the clock, filled us with alarms. The neighbourhood, to our ears, seemed haunted by approaching footsteps; and what between the dead body of the captain on the parlour floor and the thought of that detestable blind beggar hovering near at hand and ready to return, there were moments when, as the saying goes, I jumped in my skin for terror. Something must speedily be resolved upon, and it occurred to us at last to go forth together and seek help in the neighbouring hamlet. No sooner said than done. Bare-headed as we were, we ran out at once in the gathering evening and the frosty fog.

The hamlet lay not many hundred yards away, though out of view, on the other side of the next cove; and what greatly encouraged me, it was in an opposite direction from that whence the blind man had made his appearance and whither he had presumably returned. We were not many minutes on the road, though we sometimes stopped to lay hold of each other and hearken. But there was no unusual sound—nothing but the low wash of the ripple and the croaking of the inmates of the wood.

It was already candle-light when we reached the hamlet, and I shall never forget how much I was cheered to see the yellow shine in doors and windows; but that, as it proved, was the best of the help we were likely to get in that quarter. For—you would have thought men would have been ashamed of themselves—no soul would consent to return with us to the Admiral Benbow. The more we told of our troubles, the more—man, woman, and child—they clung to the shelter of their houses. The name of Captain Flint, though it was strange to me, was well enough known to some there and carried a great weight of terror. Some of the men who had been to field-work on the far side of the Admiral Benbow remembered, besides, to have seen several strangers on the road, and taking them to be smugglers, to have bolted away; and one at least had seen a little lugger in what we called Kitt's Hole. For that matter, anyone who was a comrade of the captain's was enough to frighten them to death. And the short and the long of the matter was, that while we could get several who were willing enough to ride to Dr. Livesey's, which lay in another direction, not one would help us to defend the inn.

They say cowardice is infectious; but then argument is, on the other hand, a great emboldener; and so when each had said his say, my mother made them a speech. She would not, she declared, lose money that belonged to her fatherless boy; "If none of the rest of you dare," she said, "Jim and I dare. Back we will go, the way we came, and small thanks to you big, hulking, chicken-hearted men. We'll have that chest open, if we die for it. And I'll thank you for that bag, Mrs. Crossley, to bring back our lawful money in."

Of course I said I would go with my mother, and of course they all cried out at our foolhardiness, but even then not a man would go along with us. All they would do was to give me a loaded pistol lest we were attacked, and to promise to have horses ready saddled in case we were pursued on our return, while one lad was to ride forward to the doctor's in search of armed assistance.

My heart was beating finely when we two set forth in the cold night upon this dangerous venture. A full moon was beginning to rise and peered redly through the upper edges of the fog, and this increased our haste, for it was plain, before we came forth again, that all would be as bright as day, and our departure exposed to the eyes of any watchers. We slipped along the hedges, noiseless and swift, nor did we see or hear anything to increase our terrors, till, to our relief, the door of the Admiral Benbow had closed behind us.

I slipped the bolt at once, and we stood and panted for a moment in the dark, alone in the house with the dead captain's body. Then my mother got a candle in the bar, and holding each other's hands, we advanced into the parlour. He lay as we had left him, on his back, with his eyes open and one arm stretched out.

"Draw down the blind, Jim," whispered my mother; "they might come and watch outside. And now," said she when I had done so, "we have to get the key off *that*; and who's to touch it, I should like to know!" and she gave a kind of sob as she said the words.

I went down on my knees at once. On the floor close to his hand there was a little round of paper, blackened on the one side. I could not doubt that this was the *black spot*; and taking it up, I found written on the other side, in a very good, clear hand, this short message: "You have till ten tonight."

"He had till ten, Mother," said I; and just as I said it, our old clock began striking. This sudden noise startled us shockingly; but the news was good, for it was only six.

"Now, Jim," she said, "that key."

I felt in his pockets, one after another. A few small coins, a thimble, and some thread and big needles, a piece of pigtail tobacco bitten away at the end, his gully with the crooked handle, a pocket compass, and a tinder box were all that they contained, and I began to despair.

"Perhaps it's round his neck," suggested my mother.

Overcoming a strong repugnance, I tore open his shirt at the neck, and there, sure enough, hanging to a bit of tarry string, which I cut with his own gully, we found the key. At this triumph we were filled with hope and hurried upstairs without delay to the little room where he had slept so long and where his box had stood since the day of his arrival.

It was like any other seaman's chest on the outside, the initial "B" burned on the top of it with a hot iron, and the corners somewhat smashed and broken as by long, rough usage.

"Give me the key," said my mother; and though the lock was very stiff, she had turned it and thrown back the lid in a twinkling.

A strong smell of tobacco and tar rose from the interior, but nothing was to be seen on the top except a suit of very good clothes, carefully brushed and folded. They had never been worn, my mother said. Under that, the miscellany began—a quadrant, a tin canikin, several sticks of tobacco, two brace of very handsome pistols, a piece of bar silver, an old Spanish watch and some other trinkets of little value and mostly of foreign make, a pair of compasses mounted with brass, and five or six curious West Indian shells. I have often wondered since why he should have carried about these shells with him in his wandering, guilty, and hunted life.

In the meantime, we had found nothing of any value but the silver and the trinkets, and neither of these were in our way. Underneath there was an old boat-cloak, whitened with sea-salt on many a harbour-bar. My mother pulled it up with impatience, and there lay before us, the last things in the chest, a bundle tied up in oilcloth, and looking like papers, and a canvas bag that gave forth, at a touch, the jingle of gold.

"I'll show these rogues that I'm an honest woman," said my mother. "I'll have my dues, and not a farthing over. Hold Mrs. Crossley's bag." And she began to count over the amount of the captain's score from the sailor's bag into the one that I was holding.

It was a long, difficult business, for the coins were of all countries and sizes—doubloons, and louis d'ors, and guineas, and pieces of eight, and I know not what besides, all shaken together at random. The guineas, too, were about the scarcest, and it was with these only that my mother knew how to make her count.

When we were about half-way through, I suddenly put my hand upon her arm, for I had heard in the silent frosty air a sound that brought my heart into my mouth—the tap-tapping of the blind man's stick upon the frozen road. It drew nearer and nearer, while we sat holding our breath. Then it struck sharp on the inn door, and then we could hear the handle being turned and the bolt rattling as the wretched being tried to enter; and then there was a long time of silence both within and without. At last the tapping recommenced, and, to our indescribable joy and gratitude, died slowly away again until it ceased to be heard.

"Mother," said I, "take the whole and let's be going," for I was sure the bolted door must have seemed suspicious and would bring the whole hornet's nest about our ears, though how thankful I was that I had bolted it, none could tell who had never met that terrible blind man.

But my mother, frightened as she was, would not consent to take a fraction more than was due to her and was obstinately unwilling to be content with less. It was not yet seven, she said, by a long way; she knew her rights and she would have them; and she was still arguing with me when a little low whistle sounded a good way off upon the hill. That was enough, and more than enough, for both of us.

"I'll take what I have," she said, jumping to her feet.

"And I'll take this to square the count," said I, picking up the oilskin packet.

Next moment we were both groping downstairs, leaving the candle by the empty chest; and the next we had opened the door and were in full retreat. We had not started a moment too soon. The fog was rapidly dispersing; already the moon shone quite clear on the high ground on either side; and it was only in the exact bottom of the dell and round the tavern door that a thin veil still hung unbroken to conceal the first steps of our escape. Far less than half-way to the hamlet, very little beyond the bottom of the hill, we must come forth into the moonlight. Nor was this all, for the sound of several footsteps running came already to our ears, and as we looked back in their direction, a light tossing to and fro and still rapidly advancing showed that one of the newcomers carried a lantern.

"My dear," said my mother suddenly, "take the money and run on. I am going to faint."

This was certainly the end for both of us, I thought. How I cursed the cowardice of the neighbours; how I blamed my poor mother for her honesty and her greed, for her past foolhardiness and present weakness! We were just at the little bridge, by good fortune; and I helped her, tottering as she was, to the edge of the bank, where, sure enough, she gave a sigh and fell on my shoulder. I do not know how I found the strength to do it at all, and I am afraid it was roughly done, but I managed to drag her down the bank and a little way under the arch. Farther I could not move her, for the bridge was too low to let me do more than crawl below it. So there we had to stay—my mother almost entirely exposed and both of us within earshot of the inn.

## 5

# THE LAST OF THE BLIND MAN

My curiosity, in a sense, was stronger than my fear, for I could not remain where I was, but crept back to the bank again, whence, sheltering my head behind a bush of broom, I might command the road before our door. I was scarcely in position ere my enemies began to arrive, seven or eight of them, running hard, their feet beating out of time along the road and the man with the lantern some paces in front. Three men ran together, hand in hand; and I made out, even through the mist, that the middle man of this trio was the blind beggar. The next moment his voice showed me that I was right.

"Down with the door!" he cried.

"Aye, aye, sir!" answered two or three; and a rush was made upon the Admiral Benbow, the lantern-bearer following; and then I could see them pause, and hear speeches passed in a lower key, as if they were surprised to find the door open. But the pause was brief, for the blind man again issued his commands. His voice sounded louder and higher, as if he were afire with eagerness and rage.

"In, in, in!" he shouted, and cursed them for their delay.

Four or five of them obeyed at once, two remaining on the road with the formidable beggar. There was a pause, then a cry of surprise, and then a voice shouting from the house, "Bill's dead."

But the blind man swore at them again for their delay.

"Search him, some of you shirking lubbers, and the rest of you aloft and get the chest," he cried.

I could hear their feet rattling up our old stairs, so that the house must have shook with it. Promptly afterwards, fresh sounds of astonishment arose; the window of the captain's room was thrown open with a slam and a jingle of broken glass, and a man leaned out into the moonlight, head and shoulders, and addressed the blind beggar on the road below him.

"Pew," he cried, "they've been before us. Someone's turned the chest out alow and aloft."

"Is it there?" roared Pew.

"The money's there."

The blind man cursed the money.

"Flint's fist, I mean," he cried.

"We don't see it here nohow," returned the man.

"Here, you below there, is it on Bill?" cried the blind man again.

At that another fellow, probably him who had remained below to search the captain's body, came to the door of the inn. "Bill's been overhauled a'ready," said he; "nothin' left."

"It's these people of the inn—it's that boy. I wish I had put his eyes out!" cried the blind man, Pew. "There were no time ago—they had the door bolted when I tried it. Scatter, lads, and find 'em."

"Sure enough, they left their glim here," said the fellow from the window.

"Scatter and find 'em! Rout the house out!" reiterated Pew, striking with his stick upon the road.

Then there followed a great to-do through all our old inn, heavy feet pounding to and fro, furniture thrown over, doors kicked in, until the very rocks re-echoed and the men came out again, one after another, on the road and declared that we were nowhere to be found. And just the same whistle that had alarmed my mother and myself over the dead captain's money was once more clearly audible through the night, but this time twice repeated. I had thought it to be the blind man's trumpet, so to speak, summoning his crew to the assault, but I now found that it was a signal from the hillside towards the hamlet, and from its effect upon the buccaneers, a signal to warn them of approaching danger.

"There's Dirk again," said one. "Twice! We'll have to budge, mates."

"Budge, you skulk!" cried Pew. "Dirk was a fool and a coward from the first—you wouldn't mind him. They must be close by; they can't be far; you have your hands on it. Scatter and look for them, dogs! Oh, shiver my soul," he cried, "if I had eyes!"

This appeal seemed to produce some effect, for two of the fellows began to look here and there among the lumber, but half-heartedly, I thought, and with half an eye to their own danger all the time, while the rest stood irresolute on the road.

"You have your hands on thousands, you fools, and you hang a leg! You'd be as rich as kings if you could find it, and you know it's here, and you stand there skulking. There wasn't one of you dared face Bill, and I did it—a blind man! And I'm to lose my chance for you! I'm to be a poor, crawling beggar, sponging for rum, when I might be rolling in a coach! If you had the pluck of a weevil in a biscuit you would catch them still."

"Hang it, Pew, we've got the doubloons!" grumbled one.

"They might have hid the blessed thing," said another. "Take the Georges, Pew, and don't stand here squalling."

Squalling was the word for it; Pew's anger rose so high at these objections till at last, his passion completely taking the upper hand, he struck at them right and left in his blindness and his stick sounded heavily on more than one.

These, in their turn, cursed back at the blind miscreant, threatened him in horrid terms, and tried in vain to catch the stick and wrest it from his grasp.

This quarrel was the saving of us, for while it was still raging, another sound came from the top of the hill on the side of the hamlet—the tramp of horses galloping. Almost at the same time a pistol-shot, flash and report, came from the hedge side. And that was plainly the last signal of danger, for the buccaneers turned at once and ran, separating in every direction, one seaward along the cove, one slant across the hill, and so on, so that in half a minute not a sign of them remained but Pew. Him they had deserted, whether in sheer panic or out of revenge for his ill words and blows I know not; but there he remained behind, tapping up and down the road in a frenzy, and groping and calling for his comrades. Finally he took a wrong turn and ran a few steps past me, towards the hamlet, crying, "Johnny, Black Dog, Dirk," and other names, "you won't leave old Pew, mates—not old Pew!"

Just then the noise of horses topped the rise, and four or five riders came in sight in the moonlight and swept at full gallop down the slope.

At this Pew saw his error, turned with a scream, and ran straight for the ditch, into which he rolled. But he was on his feet again in a second and made another dash, now utterly bewildered, right under the nearest of the coming horses.

The rider tried to save him, but in vain. Down went Pew with a cry that rang high into the night; and the four hoofs trampled and spurned him and passed by. He fell on his side, then gently collapsed upon his face and moved no more.

I leaped to my feet and hailed the riders. They were pulling up, at any rate, horrified at the accident; and I soon saw what they were. One, tailing out behind the rest, was a lad that had gone from the hamlet to Dr. Livesey's; the rest were revenue officers, whom he had met by the way, and with whom he had had the intelligence to return at once. Some news of the lugger in Kitt's Hole had found its way to Supervisor Dance and set him forth that night in our direction, and to that circumstance my mother and I owed our preservation from death.

Pew was dead, stone dead. As for my mother, when we had carried her up to the hamlet, a little cold water and salts and that soon brought her back again, and she was none the worse for her terror, though she still continued to deplore the balance of the money. In the meantime the supervisor rode on, as fast as he could, to Kitt's Hole; but his men had to dismount and grope down the dingle, leading, and sometimes supporting, their horses, and in continual fear of ambushes; so it was no great matter for surprise that when they got down to the Hole the lugger was already under way, though still close in. He hailed her. A voice replied, telling him to keep out of the moonlight or he would get some lead in him, and at the same time a bullet whistled close by his arm. Soon after, the lugger doubled the point and disappeared. Mr. Dance stood there, as he said, "like a fish out of water," and all he could do was to dispatch a man to B—— to warn the cutter. "And that," said he, "is just about as good as nothing. They've got off clean, and there's an end. Only," he added, "I'm glad I trod on Master Pew's corns," for by this time he had heard my story.

I went back with him to the Admiral Benbow, and you cannot imagine a house in such a state of smash; the very clock had been thrown down by these fellows in their furious hunt after my mother and myself; and though nothing had actually been taken away except the captain's money-bag and a little silver from the till, I could see at once that we were ruined. Mr. Dance could make nothing of the scene.

"They got the money, you say? Well, then, Hawkins, what in fortune were they after? More money, I suppose?"

"No, sir; not money, I think," replied I. "In fact, sir, I believe I have the thing in my breast pocket; and to tell you the truth, I should like to get it put in safety."

"To be sure, boy; quite right," said he. "I'll take it, if you like."

"I thought perhaps Dr. Livesey—" I began.

"Perfectly right," he interrupted very cheerily, "perfectly right—a gentleman and a magistrate. And, now I come to think of it, I might as well ride round there myself and report to him or squire. Master Pew's dead, when all's done; not that I regret it, but he's dead, you see, and people will make it out against an officer of his Majesty's revenue, if make it out they can. Now, I'll tell you, Hawkins, if you like, I'll take you along."

I thanked him heartily for the offer, and we walked back to the hamlet where the horses were. By the time I had told mother of my purpose they were all in the saddle.

"Dogger," said Mr. Dance, "you have a good horse; take up this lad behind you."

As soon as I was mounted, holding on to Dogger's belt, the supervisor gave the word, and the party struck out at a bouncing trot on the road to Dr. Livesey's house.

## 6

# THE CAPTAIN'S PAPERS

We rode hard all the way till we drew up before Dr. Livesey's door. The house was all dark to the front.

Mr. Dance told me to jump down and knock, and Dogger gave me a stirrup to descend by. The door was opened almost at once by the maid.

"Is Dr. Livesey in?" I asked.

No, she said, he had come home in the afternoon but had gone up to the hall to dine and pass the evening with the squire.

"So there we go, boys," said Mr. Dance.

This time, as the distance was short, I did not mount, but ran with Dogger's stirrup-leather to the lodge gates and up the long, leafless, moonlit avenue to where the white line of the hall buildings looked on either hand on great old gardens. Here Mr. Dance dismounted, and taking me along with him, was admitted at a word into the house.

The servant led us down a matted passage and showed us at the end into a great library, all lined with bookcases and busts upon the top of them, where the squire and Dr. Livesey sat, pipe in hand, on either side of a bright fire.

I had never seen the squire so near at hand. He was a tall man, over six feet high, and broad in proportion, and he had a bluff, rough-and-ready face, all roughened and reddened and lined in his long travels. His eyebrows were very black, and moved readily, and this gave him a look of some temper, not bad, you would say, but quick and high.

"Come in, Mr. Dance," says he, very stately and condescending.

"Good evening, Dance," says the doctor with a nod. "And good evening to you, friend Jim. What good wind brings you here?"

The supervisor stood up straight and stiff and told his story like a lesson; and you should have seen how the two gentlemen leaned forward and looked at each other, and forgot to smoke in their surprise and interest. When they heard how my mother went back to the inn, Dr. Livesey fairly slapped his thigh, and the squire cried "Bravo!" and broke his long pipe against the grate. Long before it was done, Mr. Trelawney (that, you will remember, was the squire's name) had got up from his seat and was striding about the room, and the doctor, as if to hear the better, had taken off his powdered wig and sat there looking very strange indeed with his own close-cropped black poll.

At last Mr. Dance finished the story.

"Mr. Dance," said the squire, "you are a very noble fellow. And as for riding down that black, atrocious miscreant, I regard it as an act of virtue, sir, like stamping on a cockroach. This lad Hawkins is a trump, I perceive. Hawkins, will you ring that bell? Mr. Dance must have some ale."

"And so, Jim," said the doctor, "you have the thing that they were after, have you?"

"Here it is, sir," said I, and gave him the oilskin packet.

The doctor looked it all over, as if his fingers were itching to open it; but instead of doing that, he put it quietly in the pocket of his coat.

"Squire," said he, "when Dance has had his ale he must, of course, be off on his Majesty's service; but I mean to keep Jim Hawkins here to sleep at my house, and with your permission, I propose we should have up the cold pie and let him sup."

"As you will, Livesey," said the squire; "Hawkins has earned better than cold pie."

So a big pigeon pie was brought in and put on a sidetable, and I made a hearty supper, for I was as hungry as a hawk, while Mr. Dance was further complimented and at last dismissed.

"And now, squire," said the doctor.

"And now, Livesey," said the squire in the same breath.

"One at a time, one at a time," laughed Dr. Livesey. "You have heard of this Flint, I suppose?"

"Heard of him!" cried the squire. "Heard of him, you say! He was the bloodthirstiest buccaneer that sailed. Blackbeard was a child to Flint. The Spaniards were so prodigiously afraid of him that, I tell you, sir, I was sometimes proud he was an Englishman. I've seen his top-sails with these eyes, off Trinidad, and the cowardly son of a rum-puncheon that I sailed with put back—put back, sir, into Port of Spain."

"Well, I've heard of him myself, in England," said the doctor. "But the point is, had he money?"

"Money!" cried the squire. "Have you heard the story? What were these villains after but money? What do they care for but money? For what would they risk their rascal carcasses but money?"

"That we shall soon know," replied the doctor. "But you are so confoundedly hot-headed and exclamatory that I cannot get a word in. What I want to know is this: Supposing that I have here in my pocket some clue to where Flint buried his treasure, will that treasure amount to much?"

"Amount, sir!" cried the squire. "It will amount to this: If we have the clue you talk about, I fit out a ship in Bristol dock, and take you and Hawkins here along, and I'll have that treasure if I search a year."

"Very well," said the doctor. "Now, then, if Jim is agreeable, we'll open the packet"; and he laid it before him on the table.

The bundle was sewn together, and the doctor had to get out his instrument case and cut the stitches with his medical scissors. It contained two things—a book and a sealed paper.

"First of all we'll try the book," observed the doctor.

The squire and I were both peering over his shoulder as he opened it, for Dr. Livesey had kindly motioned me to come round from the side-table, where I had been eating, to enjoy the sport of the search. On the first page there were only some scraps of writing, such as a man with a pen in his hand might make for idleness or practice. One was the same as the tattoo mark, "Billy Bones his fancy"; then there was "Mr. W. Bones, mate," "No more rum," "Off

Palm Key he got itt," and some other snatches, mostly single words and unintelligible. I could not help wondering who it was that had "got itt," and what "itt" was that he got. A knife in his back as like as not.

"Not much instruction there," said Dr. Livesey as he passed on.

The next ten or twelve pages were filled with a curious series of entries. There was a date at one end of the line and at the other a sum of money, as in common account-books, but instead of explanatory writing, only a varying number of crosses between the two. On the 12th of June, 1745, for instance, a sum of seventy pounds had plainly become due to someone, and there was nothing but six crosses to explain the cause. In a few cases, to be sure, the name of a place would be added, as "Offe Caraccas," or a mere entry of latitude and longitude, as "62o 17′ 20″, 19o 2′ 40″."

The record lasted over nearly twenty years, the amount of the separate entries growing larger as time went on, and at the end a grand total had been made out after five or six wrong additions, and these words appended, "Bones, his pile."

"I can't make head or tail of this," said Dr. Livesey.

"The thing is as clear as noonday," cried the squire. "This is the black-hearted hound's account-book. These crosses stand for the names of ships or towns that they sank or plundered. The sums are the scoundrel's share, and where he feared an ambiguity, you see he added something clearer. 'Offe Caraccas,' now; you see, here was some unhappy vessel boarded off that coast. God help the poor souls that manned her—coral long ago."

"Right!" said the doctor. "See what it is to be a traveller. Right! And the amounts increase, you see, as he rose in rank."

There was little else in the volume but a few bearings of places noted in the blank leaves towards the end and a table for reducing French, English, and Spanish moneys to a common value.

"Thrifty man!" cried the doctor. "He wasn't the one to be cheated."

"And now," said the squire, "for the other."

The paper had been sealed in several places with a thimble by way of seal; the very thimble, perhaps, that I had found in the captain's pocket. The doctor opened the seals with great care, and there fell out the map of an island, with latitude and longitude, soundings, names of hills and bays and inlets, and every particular that would be needed to bring a ship to a safe anchorage upon its shores. It was about nine miles long and five across, shaped, you might say, like a fat dragon standing up, and had two fine land-locked harbours, and a hill in the centre part marked "The Spy-glass." There were several additions of a later date, but above all, three crosses of red ink—two on the north part of the island, one in the southwest—and beside this last, in the same red ink, and in a small, neat hand, very different from the captain's tottery characters, these words: "Bulk of treasure here."

Over on the back the same hand had written this further information:

*Tall tree, Spy-glass shoulder, bearing a point to the N. of N.N.E.*

*Skeleton Island E.S.E. and by E.*

*Ten feet.*

*The bar silver is in the north cache; you can find it by the trend of the east hummock, ten fathoms south of the black crag with the face on it.*

*The arms are easy found, in the sand-hill, N. point of north inlet cape, bearing E. and a quarter N.*

*J.F.*

That was all; but brief as it was, and to me incomprehensible, it filled the squire and Dr. Livesey with delight.

"Livesey," said the squire, "you will give up this wretched practice at once. Tomorrow I start for Bristol. In three weeks' time—three weeks!—two weeks—ten days—we'll have the best ship, sir, and the choicest crew in England. Hawkins shall come as cabin-boy. You'll make a famous cabin-boy, Hawkins. You, Livesey, are ship's doctor; I am admiral. We'll take Redruth, Joyce, and Hunter. We'll have favourable winds, a quick passage, and not the least difficulty in finding the spot, and money to eat, to roll in, to play duck and drake with ever after."

"Trelawney," said the doctor, "I'll go with you; and I'll go bail for it, so will Jim, and be a credit to the undertaking. There's only one man I'm afraid of."

"And who's that?" cried the squire. "Name the dog, sir!"

"You," replied the doctor; "for you cannot hold your tongue. We are not the only men who know of this paper. These fellows who attacked the inn tonight—bold, desperate blades, for sure—and the rest who stayed aboard that lugger, and more, I dare say, not far off, are, one and all, through thick and thin, bound that they'll get that money. We must none of us go alone till we get to sea. Jim and I shall stick together in the meanwhile; you'll take Joyce and Hunter when you ride to Bristol, and from first to last, not one of us must breathe a word of what we've found."

"Livesey," returned the squire, "you are always in the right of it. I'll be as silent as the grave."

## II

# THE SEA-COOK

## I

# I GO TO BRISTOL

It was longer than the squire imagined ere we were ready for the sea, and none of our first plans—not even Dr. Livesey's, of keeping me beside him—could be carried out as we intended. The doctor had to go to London for a physician to take charge of his practice; the squire was hard at work at Bristol; and I lived on at the hall under the charge of old Redruth, the gamekeeper, almost a prisoner, but full of sea-dreams and the most charming anticipations of strange islands and adventures. I brooded by the hour together over the map, all the details of which I well remembered. Sitting by the fire in the housekeeper's room, I approached that island in my fancy from every possible direction; I explored every acre of its surface; I climbed a thousand times to that tall hill they call the Spy-glass, and from the top enjoyed the most wonderful and changing prospects. Sometimes the isle was thick with savages, with whom we fought, sometimes full of dangerous animals that hunted us, but in all my fancies nothing occurred to me so strange and tragic as our actual adventures.

So the weeks passed on, till one fine day there came a letter addressed to Dr. Livesey, with this addition, "To be opened, in the case of his absence, by Tom Redruth or young Hawkins." Obeying this order, we found, or rather I found—for the gamekeeper was a poor hand at reading anything but print—the following important news:

*Old Anchor Inn, Bristol, March 1, 17—*

*Dear Livesey—As I do not know whether you are at the hall or still in London, I send this in double to both places.*

*The ship is bought and fitted. She lies at anchor, ready for sea. You never imagined a sweeter schooner—a child might sail her—two hundred tons; name, Hispaniola.*

*I got her through my old friend, Blandly, who has proved himself throughout the most surprising trump. The admirable fellow literally slaved in my interest, and so, I may say, did everyone in Bristol, as soon as they got wind of the port we sailed for—treasure, I mean.*

"Redruth," said I, interrupting the letter, "Dr. Livesey will not like that. The squire has been talking, after all."

"Well, who's a better right?" growled the gamekeeper. "A pretty rum go if squire ain't to talk for Dr. Livesey, I should think."

At that I gave up all attempts at commentary and read straight on:

*Blandly himself found the Hispaniola, and by the most admirable management got her for the merest trifle. There is a class of men in Bristol monstrously prejudiced against Blandly. They go the length of declaring that this honest creature would do anything for money, that the Hispaniola belonged to him, and that he sold it me absurdly high—the most transparent calumnies. None of them dare, however, to deny the merits of the ship.*

*So far there was not a hitch. The workpeople, to be sure—riggers and what not—were most annoyingly slow; but time cured that. It was the crew that troubled me.*

*I wished a round score of men—in case of natives, buccaneers, or the odious French—and I had the worry of the deuce itself to find so much as half a dozen, till the most remarkable stroke of fortune brought me the very man that I required.*

*I was standing on the dock, when, by the merest accident, I fell in talk with him. I found he was an old sailor, kept a public-house, knew all the seafaring men in Bristol, had lost his health ashore, and wanted a good berth as cook to get to sea again. He had hobbled down there that morning, he said, to get a smell of the salt.*

*I was monstrously touched—so would you have been—and, out of pure pity, I engaged him on the spot to be ship's cook. Long John Silver, he is called, and has lost a leg; but that I regarded as a recommendation, since he lost it in his country's service, under the immortal Hawke. He has no pension, Livesey. Imagine the abominable age we live in!*

*Well, sir, I thought I had only found a cook, but it was a crew I had discovered. Between Silver and myself we got together in a few days a company of the toughest old salts imaginable—not pretty to look at, but fellows, by their faces, of the most indomitable spirit. I declare we could fight a frigate.*

*Long John even got rid of two out of the six or seven I had already engaged. He showed me in a moment that they were just the sort of fresh-water swabs we had to fear in an adventure of importance.*

*I am in the most magnificent health and spirits, eating like a bull, sleeping like a tree, yet I shall not enjoy a moment till I hear my old tarpaulins tramping round the capstan. Seaward, ho! Hang the treasure! It's the glory of the sea that has turned my head. So now, Livesey, come post; do not lose an hour, if you respect me.*

*Let young Hawkins go at once to see his mother, with Redruth for a guard; and then both come full speed to Bristol.*

*John Trelawney*

*Postscript—I did not tell you that Blandly, who, by the way, is to send a consort after us if we don't turn up by the end of August, had found an admirable fellow for sailing master—a stiff man, which I regret, but in all other respects a treasure. Long John Silver unearthed a very competent man for a mate, a man named Arrow. I have a boatswain who pipes, Livesey; so things shall go man-o'-war fashion on board the good ship Hispaniola.*

*I forgot to tell you that Silver is a man of substance; I know of my own knowledge that he has a banker's account, which has never been overdrawn. He leaves his wife to manage the inn; and as she is a woman of colour, a pair of old bachelors like you and I may be excused for guessing that it is the wife, quite as much as the health, that sends him back to roving.*

*J. T.*

*P.P.S.—Hawkins may stay one night with his mother.*

*J. T.*

You can fancy the excitement into which that letter put me. I was half beside myself with glee; and if ever I despised a man, it was old Tom Redruth, who could do nothing but grumble and lament. Any of the under-gamekeepers would gladly have changed places with him; but such was not the squire's pleasure, and the squire's pleasure was like law among them all. Nobody but old Redruth would have dared so much as even to grumble.

The next morning he and I set out on foot for the Admiral Benbow, and there I found my mother in good health and spirits. The captain, who had so long been a cause of so much discomfort, was gone where the wicked cease from troubling. The squire had had everything repaired, and the public rooms and the sign repainted, and had added some furniture—above all a beautiful armchair for mother in the bar. He had found her a boy as an apprentice also so that she should not want help while I was gone.

It was on seeing that boy that I understood, for the first time, my situation. I had thought up to that moment of the adventures before me, not at all of the home that I was leaving; and now, at sight of this clumsy stranger, who was to stay here in my place beside my mother, I had my first attack of tears. I am afraid I led that boy a dog's life, for as he was new to the work, I had a hundred opportunities of setting him right and putting him down, and I was not slow to profit by them.

The night passed, and the next day, after dinner, Redruth and I were afoot again and on the road. I said good-bye to Mother and the cove where I had lived since I was born, and the dear old Admiral Benbow—since he was repainted, no longer quite so dear. One of my last thoughts was of the captain, who had so often strode along the beach with his cocked hat, his sabre-cut cheek, and his old brass telescope. Next moment we had turned the corner and my home was out of sight.

The mail picked us up about dusk at the Royal George on the heath. I was wedged in between Redruth and a stout old gentleman, and in spite of the swift motion and the cold night air, I must have dozed a great deal from the very first, and then slept like a log up hill and down dale through stage after stage, for when I was awakened at last it was by a punch in the ribs, and I opened my eyes to find that we were standing still before a large building in a city street and that the day had already broken a long time.

"Where are we?" I asked.

"Bristol," said Tom. "Get down."

Mr. Trelawney had taken up his residence at an inn far down the docks to superintend the work upon the schooner. Thither we had now to walk, and our way, to my great delight, lay along the quays and beside the great multitude of ships of all sizes and rigs and nations. In one, sailors were singing at their work, in another there were men aloft, high over my head, hanging to threads that seemed no thicker than a spider's. Though I had lived by the shore all my life, I seemed never to have been near the sea till then. The smell of tar and salt was something new. I saw the most wonderful figureheads, that had all been far over the ocean. I saw, besides, many old sailors, with rings in their ears, and whiskers curled in ringlets, and tarry pigtails, and their swaggering, clumsy sea-walk; and if I had seen as many kings or archbishops I could not have been more delighted.

And I was going to sea myself, to sea in a schooner, with a piping boatswain and pig-tailed singing seamen, to sea, bound for an unknown island, and to seek for buried treasure!

While I was still in this delightful dream, we came suddenly in front of a large inn and met Squire Trelawney, all dressed out like a sea-officer, in stout blue cloth, coming out of the door with a smile on his face and a capital imitation of a sailor's walk.

"Here you are," he cried, "and the doctor came last night from London. Bravo! The ship's company complete!"

"Oh, sir," cried I, "when do we sail?"

"Sail!" says he. "We sail tomorrow!"

## 2

# AT THE SIGN OF THE SPY-GLASS

When I had done breakfasting the squire gave me a note addressed to John Silver, at the sign of the Spy-glass, and told me I should easily find the place by following the line of the docks and keeping a bright lookout for a little tavern with a large brass telescope for sign. I set off, overjoyed at this opportunity to see some more of the ships and seamen, and picked my way among a great crowd of people and carts and bales, for the dock was now at its busiest, until I found the tavern in question.

It was a bright enough little place of entertainment. The sign was newly painted; the windows had neat red curtains; the floor was cleanly sanded. There was a street on each side and an open door on both, which made the large, low room pretty clear to see in, in spite of clouds of tobacco smoke.

The customers were mostly seafaring men, and they talked so loudly that I hung at the door, almost afraid to enter.

As I was waiting, a man came out of a side room, and at a glance I was sure he must be Long John. His left leg was cut off close by the hip, and under the left shoulder he carried a crutch, which he managed with wonderful dexterity, hopping about upon it like a bird. He was very tall and strong, with a face as big as a ham—plain and pale, but intelligent and smiling. Indeed, he seemed in the most cheerful spirits, whistling as he moved about among the tables, with a merry word or a slap on the shoulder for the more favoured of his guests.

Now, to tell you the truth, from the very first mention of Long John in Squire Trelawney's letter I had taken a fear in my mind that he might prove to be the very one-legged sailor whom I had watched for so long at the old Benbow. But one look at the man before me was enough. I had seen the captain, and Black Dog, and the blind man, Pew, and I thought I knew what a buccaneer was like—a very different creature, according to me, from this clean and pleasant-tempered landlord.

I plucked up courage at once, crossed the threshold, and walked right up to the man where he stood, propped on his crutch, talking to a customer.

"Mr. Silver, sir?" I asked, holding out the note.

"Yes, my lad," said he; "such is my name, to be sure. And who may you be?" And then as he saw the squire's letter, he seemed to me to give something almost like a start.

"Oh!" said he, quite loud, and offering his hand. "I see. You are our new cabin-boy; pleased I am to see you."

And he took my hand in his large firm grasp.

Just then one of the customers at the far side rose suddenly and made for the door. It was close by him, and he was out in the street in a moment. But his hurry had attracted my notice, and I recognized him at glance. It was the tallow-faced man, wanting two fingers, who had come first to the Admiral Benbow.

"Oh," I cried, "stop him! It's Black Dog!"

"I don't care two coppers who he is," cried Silver. "But he hasn't paid his score. Harry, run and catch him."

One of the others who was nearest the door leaped up and started in pursuit.

"If he were Admiral Hawke he shall pay his score," cried Silver; and then, relinquishing my hand, "Who did you say he was?" he asked. "Black what?"

"Dog, sir," said I. "Has Mr. Trelawney not told you of the buccaneers? He was one of them."

"So?" cried Silver. "In my house! Ben, run and help Harry. One of those swabs, was he? Was that you drinking with him, Morgan? Step up here."

The man whom he called Morgan—an old, grey-haired, mahogany-faced sailor—came forward pretty sheepishly, rolling his quid.

"Now, Morgan," said Long John very sternly, "you never clapped your eyes on that Black —Black Dog before, did you, now?"

"Not I, sir," said Morgan with a salute.

"You didn't know his name, did you?"

"No, sir."

"By the powers, Tom Morgan, it's as good for you!" exclaimed the landlord. "If you had been mixed up with the like of that, you would never have put another foot in my house, you may lay to that. And what was he saying to you?"

"I don't rightly know, sir," answered Morgan.

"Do you call that a head on your shoulders, or a blessed dead-eye?" cried Long John. "Don't rightly know, don't you! Perhaps you don't happen to rightly know who you was speaking to, perhaps? Come, now, what was he jawing—v'yages, cap'ns, ships? Pipe up! What was it?"

"We was a-talkin' of keel-hauling," answered Morgan.

"Keel-hauling, was you? And a mighty suitable thing, too, and you may lay to that. Get back to your place for a lubber, Tom."

And then, as Morgan rolled back to his seat, Silver added to me in a confidential whisper that was very flattering, as I thought, "He's quite an honest man, Tom Morgan, on'y stupid. And now," he ran on again, aloud, "let's see—Black Dog? No, I don't know the name, not I. Yet I kind of think I've—yes, I've seen the swab. He used to come here with a blind beggar, he used."

"That he did, you may be sure," said I. "I knew that blind man too. His name was Pew."

"It was!" cried Silver, now quite excited. "Pew! That were his name for certain. Ah, he looked a shark, he did! If we run down this Black Dog, now, there'll be news for Cap'n Trelawney! Ben's a good runner; few seamen run better than Ben. He should run him down, hand over hand, by the powers! He talked o' keel-hauling, did he? *I'll* keel-haul him!"

All the time he was jerking out these phrases he was stumping up and down the tavern on his crutch, slapping tables with his hand, and giving such a show of excitement as would have convinced an Old Bailey judge or a Bow Street runner. My suspicions had been thoroughly reawakened on finding Black Dog at the Spy-glass, and I watched the cook narrowly. But he was too deep, and too ready, and too clever for me, and by the time the two men had come back out of breath and confessed that they had lost the track in a crowd, and been scolded like thieves, I would have gone bail for the innocence of Long John Silver.

"See here, now, Hawkins," said he, "here's a blessed hard thing on a man like me, now, ain't it? There's Cap'n Trelawney—what's he to think? Here I have this confounded son of a Dutchman sitting in my own house drinking of my own rum! Here you comes and tells me of it plain; and here I let him give us all the slip before my blessed deadlights! Now, Hawkins, you do me justice with the cap'n. You're a lad, you are, but you're as smart as paint. I see that when you first come in. Now, here it is: What could I do, with this old timber I hobble on? When I was an A B master mariner I'd have come up alongside of him, hand over hand, and broached him to in a brace of old shakes, I would; but now—"

And then, all of a sudden, he stopped, and his jaw dropped as though he had remembered something.

"The score!" he burst out. "Three goes o' rum! Why, shiver my timbers, if I hadn't forgotten my score!"

And falling on a bench, he laughed until the tears ran down his cheeks. I could not help joining, and we laughed together, peal after peal, until the tavern rang again.

"Why, what a precious old sea-calf I am!" he said at last, wiping his cheeks. "You and me should get on well, Hawkins, for I'll take my davy I should be rated ship's boy. But come now, stand by to go about. This won't do. Dooty is dooty, messmates. I'll put on my old cockerel hat, and step along of you to Cap'n Trelawney, and report this here affair. For mind you, it's serious, young Hawkins; and neither you nor me's come out of it with what I should make so bold as to call credit. Nor you neither, says you; not smart—none of the pair of us smart. But dash my buttons! That was a good un about my score."

And he began to laugh again, and that so heartily, that though I did not see the joke as he did, I was again obliged to join him in his mirth.

On our little walk along the quays, he made himself the most interesting companion, telling me about the different ships that we passed by, their rig, tonnage, and nationality, explaining the work that was going forward—how one was discharging, another taking in cargo, and a third making ready for sea—and every now and then telling me some little anecdote of ships or seamen or repeating a nautical phrase till I had learned it perfectly. I began to see that here was one of the best of possible shipmates.

When we got to the inn, the squire and Dr. Livesey were seated together, finishing a quart of ale with a toast in it, before they should go aboard the schooner on a visit of inspection.

Long John told the story from first to last, with a great deal of spirit and the most perfect truth. "That was how it were, now, weren't it, Hawkins?" he would say, now and again, and I could always bear him entirely out.

The two gentlemen regretted that Black Dog had got away, but we all agreed there was nothing to be done, and after he had been complimented, Long John took up his crutch and departed.

"All hands aboard by four this afternoon," shouted the squire after him.

"Aye, aye, sir," cried the cook, in the passage.

"Well, squire," said Dr. Livesey, "I don't put much faith in your discoveries, as a general thing; but I will say this, John Silver suits me."

"The man's a perfect trump," declared the squire.

"And now," added the doctor, "Jim may come on board with us, may he not?"
"To be sure he may," says squire. "Take your hat, Hawkins, and we'll see the ship."

## 3

# POWDER AND ARMS

The *Hispaniola* lay some way out, and we went under the figureheads and round the sterns of many other ships, and their cables sometimes grated underneath our keel, and sometimes swung above us. At last, however, we got alongside, and were met and saluted as we stepped aboard by the mate, Mr. Arrow, a brown old sailor with earrings in his ears and a squint. He and the squire were very thick and friendly, but I soon observed that things were not the same between Mr. Trelawney and the captain.

This last was a sharp-looking man who seemed angry with everything on board and was soon to tell us why, for we had hardly got down into the cabin when a sailor followed us.

"Captain Smollett, sir, axing to speak with you," said he.

"I am always at the captain's orders. Show him in," said the squire.

The captain, who was close behind his messenger, entered at once and shut the door behind him.

"Well, Captain Smollett, what have you to say? All well, I hope; all shipshape and seaworthy?"

"Well, sir," said the captain, "better speak plain, I believe, even at the risk of offence. I don't like this cruise; I don't like the men; and I don't like my officer. That's short and sweet."

"Perhaps, sir, you don't like the ship?" inquired the squire, very angry, as I could see.

"I can't speak as to that, sir, not having seen her tried," said the captain. "She seems a clever craft; more I can't say."

"Possibly, sir, you may not like your employer, either?" says the squire.

But here Dr. Livesey cut in.

"Stay a bit," said he, "stay a bit. No use of such questions as that but to produce ill feeling. The captain has said too much or he has said too little, and I'm bound to say that I require an explanation of his words. You don't, you say, like this cruise. Now, why?"

"I was engaged, sir, on what we call sealed orders, to sail this ship for that gentleman where he should bid me," said the captain. "So far so good. But now I find that every man before the mast knows more than I do. I don't call that fair, now, do you?"

"No," said Dr. Livesey, "I don't."

"Next," said the captain, "I learn we are going after treasure—hear it from my own hands, mind you. Now, treasure is ticklish work; I don't like treasure voyages on any account, and I don't like them, above all, when they are secret and when (begging your pardon, Mr. Trelawney) the secret has been told to the parrot."

"Silver's parrot?" asked the squire.

"It's a way of speaking," said the captain. "Blabbed, I mean. It's my belief neither of you gentlemen know what you are about, but I'll tell you my way of it—life or death, and a close run."

"That is all clear, and, I dare say, true enough," replied Dr. Livesey. "We take the risk, but we are not so ignorant as you believe us. Next, you say you don't like the crew. Are they not good seamen?"

"I don't like them, sir," returned Captain Smollett. "And I think I should have had the choosing of my own hands, if you go to that."

"Perhaps you should," replied the doctor. "My friend should, perhaps, have taken you along with him; but the slight, if there be one, was unintentional. And you don't like Mr. Arrow?"

"I don't, sir. I believe he's a good seaman, but he's too free with the crew to be a good officer. A mate should keep himself to himself—shouldn't drink with the men before the mast!"

"Do you mean he drinks?" cried the squire.

"No, sir," replied the captain, "only that he's too familiar."

"Well, now, and the short and long of it, captain?" asked the doctor. "Tell us what you want."

"Well, gentlemen, are you determined to go on this cruise?"

"Like iron," answered the squire.

"Very good," said the captain. "Then, as you've heard me very patiently, saying things that I could not prove, hear me a few words more. They are putting the powder and the arms in the fore hold. Now, you have a good place under the cabin; why not put them there?—first point. Then, you are bringing four of your own people with you, and they tell me some of them are to be berthed forward. Why not give them the berths here beside the cabin?—second point."

"Any more?" asked Mr. Trelawney.

"One more," said the captain. "There's been too much blabbing already."

"Far too much," agreed the doctor.

"I'll tell you what I've heard myself," continued Captain Smollett: "that you have a map of an island, that there's crosses on the map to show where treasure is, and that the island lies —" And then he named the latitude and longitude exactly.

"I never told that," cried the squire, "to a soul!"

"The hands know it, sir," returned the captain.

"Livesey, that must have been you or Hawkins," cried the squire.

"It doesn't much matter who it was," replied the doctor. And I could see that neither he nor the captain paid much regard to Mr. Trelawney's protestations. Neither did I, to be sure, he was so loose a talker; yet in this case I believe he was really right and that nobody had told the situation of the island.

"Well, gentlemen," continued the captain, "I don't know who has this map; but I make it a point, it shall be kept secret even from me and Mr. Arrow. Otherwise I would ask you to let me resign."

"I see," said the doctor. "You wish us to keep this matter dark and to make a garrison of the stern part of the ship, manned with my friend's own people, and provided with all the arms and powder on board. In other words, you fear a mutiny."

"Sir," said Captain Smollett, "with no intention to take offence, I deny your right to put words into my mouth. No captain, sir, would be justified in going to sea at all if he had ground enough to say that. As for Mr. Arrow, I believe him thoroughly honest; some of the men are the same; all may be for what I know. But I am responsible for the ship's safety and the life of every man Jack aboard of her. I see things going, as I think, not quite right. And I ask you to take certain precautions or let me resign my berth. And that's all."

"Captain Smollett," began the doctor with a smile, "did ever you hear the fable of the mountain and the mouse? You'll excuse me, I dare say, but you remind me of that fable. When you came in here, I'll stake my wig, you meant more than this."

"Doctor," said the captain, "you are smart. When I came in here I meant to get discharged. I had no thought that Mr. Trelawney would hear a word."

"No more I would," cried the squire. "Had Livesey not been here I should have seen you to the deuce. As it is, I have heard you. I will do as you desire, but I think the worse of you."

"That's as you please, sir," said the captain. "You'll find I do my duty."

And with that he took his leave.

"Trelawney," said the doctor, "contrary to all my notions, I believed you have managed to get two honest men on board with you—that man and John Silver."

"Silver, if you like," cried the squire; "but as for that intolerable humbug, I declare I think his conduct unmanly, unsailorly, and downright un-English."

"Well," says the doctor, "we shall see."

When we came on deck, the men had begun already to take out the arms and powder, yo-ho-ing at their work, while the captain and Mr. Arrow stood by superintending.

The new arrangement was quite to my liking. The whole schooner had been overhauled; six berths had been made astern out of what had been the after-part of the main hold; and this set of cabins was only joined to the galley and forecastle by a sparred passage on the port side. It had been originally meant that the captain, Mr. Arrow, Hunter, Joyce, the doctor, and the squire were to occupy these six berths. Now Redruth and I were to get two of them and Mr. Arrow and the captain were to sleep on deck in the companion, which had been enlarged on each side till you might almost have called it a round-house. Very low it was still, of course; but there was room to swing two hammocks, and even the mate seemed pleased with the arrangement. Even he, perhaps, had been doubtful as to the crew, but that is only guess, for as you shall hear, we had not long the benefit of his opinion.

We were all hard at work, changing the powder and the berths, when the last man or two, and Long John along with them, came off in a shore-boat.

The cook came up the side like a monkey for cleverness, and as soon as he saw what was doing, "So ho, mates!" says he. "What's this?"

"We're a-changing of the powder, Jack," answers one.

"Why, by the powers," cried Long John, "if we do, we'll miss the morning tide!"

"My orders!" said the captain shortly. "You may go below, my man. Hands will want supper."

"Aye, aye, sir," answered the cook, and touching his forelock, he disappeared at once in the direction of his galley.

"That's a good man, captain," said the doctor.

"Very likely, sir," replied Captain Smollett. "Easy with that, men—easy," he ran on, to the fellows who were shifting the powder; and then suddenly observing me examining the swivel we carried amidships, a long brass nine, "Here you, ship's boy," he cried, "out o' that! Off with you to the cook and get some work."

And then as I was hurrying off I heard him say, quite loudly, to the doctor, "I'll have no favourites on my ship."

I assure you I was quite of the squire's way of thinking, and hated the captain deeply.

# ☙ 4 ❧
# THE VOYAGE

All that night we were in a great bustle getting things stowed in their place, and boatfuls of the squire's friends, Mr. Blandly and the like, coming off to wish him a good voyage and a safe return. We never had a night at the Admiral Benbow when I had half the work; and I was dog-tired when, a little before dawn, the boatswain sounded his pipe and the crew began to man the capstan-bars. I might have been twice as weary, yet I would not have left the deck, all was so new and interesting to me—the brief commands, the shrill note of the whistle, the men bustling to their places in the glimmer of the ship's lanterns.

"Now, Barbecue, tip us a stave," cried one voice.

"The old one," cried another.

"Aye, aye, mates," said Long John, who was standing by, with his crutch under his arm, and at once broke out in the air and words I knew so well:

"Fifteen men on the dead man's chest—"

And then the whole crew bore chorus:—

"Yo-ho-ho, and a bottle of rum!"

And at the third "Ho!" drove the bars before them with a will.

Even at that exciting moment it carried me back to the old Admiral Benbow in a second, and I seemed to hear the voice of the captain piping in the chorus. But soon the anchor was short up; soon it was hanging dripping at the bows; soon the sails began to draw, and the land and shipping to flit by on either side; and before I could lie down to snatch an hour of slumber the *Hispaniola* had begun her voyage to the Isle of Treasure.

I am not going to relate that voyage in detail. It was fairly prosperous. The ship proved to be a good ship, the crew were capable seamen, and the captain thoroughly understood his business. But before we came the length of Treasure Island, two or three things had happened which require to be known.

Mr. Arrow, first of all, turned out even worse than the captain had feared. He had no command among the men, and people did what they pleased with him. But that was by no means the worst of it, for after a day or two at sea he began to appear on deck with hazy eye, red cheeks, stuttering tongue, and other marks of drunkenness. Time after time he was ordered below in disgrace. Sometimes he fell and cut himself; sometimes he lay all day long in his little bunk at one side of the companion; sometimes for a day or two he would be almost sober and attend to his work at least passably.

In the meantime, we could never make out where he got the drink. That was the ship's mystery. Watch him as we pleased, we could do nothing to solve it; and when we asked him to his face, he would only laugh if he were drunk, and if he were sober deny solemnly that he ever tasted anything but water.

He was not only useless as an officer and a bad influence amongst the men, but it was plain that at this rate he must soon kill himself outright, so nobody was much surprised, nor very sorry, when one dark night, with a head sea, he disappeared entirely and was seen no more.

"Overboard!" said the captain. "Well, gentlemen, that saves the trouble of putting him in irons."

But there we were, without a mate; and it was necessary, of course, to advance one of the men. The boatswain, Job Anderson, was the likeliest man aboard, and though he kept his old title, he served in a way as mate. Mr. Trelawney had followed the sea, and his knowledge made him very useful, for he often took a watch himself in easy weather. And the coxswain, Israel Hands, was a careful, wily, old, experienced seaman who could be trusted at a pinch with almost anything.

He was a great confidant of Long John Silver, and so the mention of his name leads me on to speak of our ship's cook, Barbecue, as the men called him.

Aboard ship he carried his crutch by a lanyard round his neck, to have both hands as free as possible. It was something to see him wedge the foot of the crutch against a bulkhead, and propped against it, yielding to every movement of the ship, get on with his cooking like someone safe ashore. Still more strange was it to see him in the heaviest of weather cross the deck. He had a line or two rigged up to help him across the widest spaces—Long John's earrings, they were called; and he would hand himself from one place to another, now using the crutch, now trailing it alongside by the lanyard, as quickly as another man could walk. Yet some of the men who had sailed with him before expressed their pity to see him so reduced.

"He's no common man, Barbecue," said the coxswain to me. "He had good schooling in his young days and can speak like a book when so minded; and brave—a lion's nothing alongside of Long John! I seen him grapple four and knock their heads together—him unarmed."

All the crew respected and even obeyed him. He had a way of talking to each and doing everybody some particular service. To me he was unweariedly kind, and always glad to see me in the galley, which he kept as clean as a new pin, the dishes hanging up burnished and his parrot in a cage in one corner.

"Come away, Hawkins," he would say; "come and have a yarn with John. Nobody more welcome than yourself, my son. Sit you down and hear the news. Here's Cap'n Flint—I calls my parrot Cap'n Flint, after the famous buccaneer—here's Cap'n Flint predicting success to our v'yage. Wasn't you, cap'n?"

And the parrot would say, with great rapidity, "Pieces of eight! Pieces of eight! Pieces of eight!" till you wondered that it was not out of breath, or till John threw his handkerchief over the cage.

"Now, that bird," he would say, "is, maybe, two hundred years old, Hawkins—they live forever mostly; and if anybody's seen more wickedness, it must be the devil himself. She's sailed with England, the great Cap'n England, the pirate. She's been at Madagascar, and at

Malabar, and Surinam, and Providence, and Portobello. She was at the fishing up of the wrecked plate ships. It's there she learned 'Pieces of eight,' and little wonder; three hundred and fifty thousand of 'em, Hawkins! She was at the boarding of the viceroy of the Indies out of Goa, she was; and to look at her you would think she was a babby. But you smelt powder —didn't you, cap'n?"

"Stand by to go about," the parrot would scream.

"Ah, she's a handsome craft, she is," the cook would say, and give her sugar from his pocket, and then the bird would peck at the bars and swear straight on, passing belief for wickedness. "There," John would add, "you can't touch pitch and not be mucked, lad. Here's this poor old innocent bird o' mine swearing blue fire, and none the wiser, you may lay to that. She would swear the same, in a manner of speaking, before chaplain." And John would touch his forelock with a solemn way he had that made me think he was the best of men.

In the meantime, the squire and Captain Smollett were still on pretty distant terms with one another. The squire made no bones about the matter; he despised the captain. The captain, on his part, never spoke but when he was spoken to, and then sharp and short and dry, and not a word wasted. He owned, when driven into a corner, that he seemed to have been wrong about the crew, that some of them were as brisk as he wanted to see and all had behaved fairly well. As for the ship, he had taken a downright fancy to her. "She'll lie a point nearer the wind than a man has a right to expect of his own married wife, sir. But," he would add, "all I say is, we're not home again, and I don't like the cruise."

The squire, at this, would turn away and march up and down the deck, chin in air.

"A trifle more of that man," he would say, "and I shall explode."

We had some heavy weather, which only proved the qualities of the *Hispaniola*. Every man on board seemed well content, and they must have been hard to please if they had been otherwise, for it is my belief there was never a ship's company so spoiled since Noah put to sea. Double grog was going on the least excuse; there was duff on odd days, as, for instance, if the squire heard it was any man's birthday, and always a barrel of apples standing broached in the waist for anyone to help himself that had a fancy.

"Never knew good come of it yet," the captain said to Dr. Livesey. "Spoil forecastle hands, make devils. That's my belief."

But good did come of the apple barrel, as you shall hear, for if it had not been for that, we should have had no note of warning and might all have perished by the hand of treachery.

This was how it came about.

We had run up the trades to get the wind of the island we were after—I am not allowed to be more plain—and now we were running down for it with a bright lookout day and night. It was about the last day of our outward voyage by the largest computation; some time that night, or at latest before noon of the morrow, we should sight the Treasure Island. We were heading S.S.W. and had a steady breeze abeam and a quiet sea. The *Hispaniola* rolled steadily, dipping her bowsprit now and then with a whiff of spray. All was drawing alow and aloft; everyone was in the bravest spirits because we were now so near an end of the first part of our adventure.

Now, just after sundown, when all my work was over and I was on my way to my berth, it occurred to me that I should like an apple. I ran on deck. The watch was all forward looking out for the island. The man at the helm was watching the luff of the sail and whistling away gently to himself, and that was the only sound excepting the swish of the sea against the bows and around the sides of the ship.

In I got bodily into the apple barrel, and found there was scarce an apple left; but sitting down there in the dark, what with the sound of the waters and the rocking movement of the ship, I had either fallen asleep or was on the point of doing so when a heavy man sat down with rather a clash close by. The barrel shook as he leaned his shoulders against it, and I was just about to jump up when the man began to speak. It was Silver's voice, and before I had heard a dozen words, I would not have shown myself for all the world, but lay there, trembling and listening, in the extreme of fear and curiosity, for from these dozen words I understood that the lives of all the honest men aboard depended upon me alone.

## ✥ 5 ✥

# WHAT I HEARD IN THE APPLE BARREL

No, not I," said Silver. "Flint was cap'n; I was quartermaster, along of my timber leg. The same broadside I lost my leg, old Pew lost his deadlights. It was a master surgeon, him that ampytated me—out of college and all—Latin by the bucket, and what not; but he was hanged like a dog, and sun-dried like the rest, at Corso Castle. That was Roberts' men, that was, and comed of changing names to their ships—*Royal Fortune* and so on. Now, what a ship was christened, so let her stay, I says. So it was with the *Cassandra,* as brought us all safe home from Malabar, after England took the viceroy of the Indies; so it was with the old *Walrus,* Flint's old ship, as I've seen amuck with the red blood and fit to sink with gold."

"Ah!" cried another voice, that of the youngest hand on board, and evidently full of admiration. "He was the flower of the flock, was Flint!"

"Davis was a man too, by all accounts," said Silver. "I never sailed along of him; first with England, then with Flint, that's my story; and now here on my own account, in a manner of speaking. I laid by nine hundred safe, from England, and two thousand after Flint. That ain't bad for a man before the mast—all safe in bank. 'Tain't earning now, it's saving does it, you may lay to that. Where's all England's men now? I dunno. Where's Flint's? Why, most on 'em aboard here, and glad to get the duff—been begging before that, some on 'em. Old Pew, as had lost his sight, and might have thought shame, spends twelve hundred pound in a year, like a lord in Parliament. Where is he now? Well, he's dead now and under hatches; but for two year before that, shiver my timbers, the man was starving! He begged, and he stole, and he cut throats, and starved at that, by the powers!"

"Well, it ain't much use, after all," said the young seaman.

"'Tain't much use for fools, you may lay to it—that, nor nothing," cried Silver. "But now, you look here: you're young, you are, but you're as smart as paint. I see that when I set my eyes on you, and I'll talk to you like a man."

You may imagine how I felt when I heard this abominable old rogue addressing another in the very same words of flattery as he had used to myself. I think, if I had been able, that I would have killed him through the barrel. Meantime, he ran on, little supposing he was overheard.

"Here it is about gentlemen of fortune. They lives rough, and they risk swinging, but they eat and drink like fighting-cocks, and when a cruise is done, why, it's hundreds of pounds instead of hundreds of farthings in their pockets. Now, the most goes for rum and a good fling, and to sea again in their shirts. But that's not the course I lay. I puts it all away, some here, some there, and none too much anywheres, by reason of suspicion. I'm fifty, mark you; once back from this cruise, I set up gentleman in earnest. Time enough too, says you. Ah, but I've lived easy in the meantime, never denied myself o' nothing heart desires, and slep' soft and ate dainty all my days but when at sea. And how did I begin? Before the mast, like you!"

"Well," said the other, "but all the other money's gone now, ain't it? You daren't show face in Bristol after this."

"Why, where might you suppose it was?" asked Silver derisively.

"At Bristol, in banks and places," answered his companion.

"It were," said the cook; "it were when we weighed anchor. But my old missis has it all by now. And the Spy-glass is sold, lease and goodwill and rigging; and the old girl's off to meet me. I would tell you where, for I trust you, but it'd make jealousy among the mates."

"And can you trust your missis?" asked the other.

"Gentlemen of fortune," returned the cook, "usually trusts little among themselves, and right they are, you may lay to it. But I have a way with me, I have. When a mate brings a slip on his cable—one as knows me, I mean—it won't be in the same world with old John. There was some that was feared of Pew, and some that was feared of Flint; but Flint his own self was feared of me. Feared he was, and proud. They was the roughest crew afloat, was Flint's; the devil himself would have been feared to go to sea with them. Well now, I tell you, I'm not a boasting man, and you seen yourself how easy I keep company, but when I was quartermaster, *lambs* wasn't the word for Flint's old buccaneers. Ah, you may be sure of yourself in old John's ship."

"Well, I tell you now," replied the lad, "I didn't half a quarter like the job till I had this talk with you, John; but there's my hand on it now."

"And a brave lad you were, and smart too," answered Silver, shaking hands so heartily that all the barrel shook, "and a finer figurehead for a gentleman of fortune I never clapped my eyes on."

By this time I had begun to understand the meaning of their terms. By a "gentleman of fortune" they plainly meant neither more nor less than a common pirate, and the little scene that I had overheard was the last act in the corruption of one of the honest hands—perhaps of the last one left aboard. But on this point I was soon to be relieved, for Silver giving a little whistle, a third man strolled up and sat down by the party.

"Dick's square," said Silver.

"Oh, I know'd Dick was square," returned the voice of the coxswain, Israel Hands. "He's no fool, is Dick." And he turned his quid and spat. "But look here," he went on, "here's what I want to know, Barbecue: how long are we a-going to stand off and on like a blessed bumboat? I've had a'most enough o' Cap'n Smollett; he's hazed me long enough, by thunder! I want to go into that cabin, I do. I want their pickles and wines, and that."

"Israel," said Silver, "your head ain't much account, nor ever was. But you're able to hear, I reckon; leastways, your ears is big enough. Now, here's what I say: you'll berth forward, and you'll live hard, and you'll speak soft, and you'll keep sober till I give the word; and you may lay to that, my son."

"Well, I don't say no, do I?" growled the coxswain. "What I say is, when? That's what I say."

"When! By the powers!" cried Silver. "Well now, if you want to know, I'll tell you when.

The last moment I can manage, and that's when. Here's a first-rate seaman, Cap'n Smollett, sails the blessed ship for us. Here's this squire and doctor with a map and such—I don't know where it is, do I? No more do you, says you. Well then, I mean this squire and doctor shall find the stuff, and help us to get it aboard, by the powers. Then we'll see. If I was sure of you all, sons of double Dutchmen, I'd have Cap'n Smollett navigate us half-way back again before I struck."

"Why, we're all seamen aboard here, I should think," said the lad Dick.

"We're all forecastle hands, you mean," snapped Silver. "We can steer a course, but who's to set one? That's what all you gentlemen split on, first and last. If I had my way, I'd have Cap'n Smollett work us back into the trades at least; then we'd have no blessed miscalculations and a spoonful of water a day. But I know the sort you are. I'll finish with 'em at the island, as soon's the blunt's on board, and a pity it is. But you're never happy till you're drunk. Split my sides, I've a sick heart to sail with the likes of you!"

"Easy all, Long John," cried Israel. "Who's a-crossin' of you?"

"Why, how many tall ships, think ye, now, have I seen laid aboard? And how many brisk lads drying in the sun at Execution Dock?" cried Silver. "And all for this same hurry and hurry and hurry. You hear me? I seen a thing or two at sea, I have. If you would on'y lay your course, and a p'int to windward, you would ride in carriages, you would. But not you! I know you. You'll have your mouthful of rum tomorrow, and go hang."

"Everybody knowed you was a kind of a chapling, John; but there's others as could hand and steer as well as you," said Israel. "They liked a bit o' fun, they did. They wasn't so high and dry, nohow, but took their fling, like jolly companions every one."

"So?" says Silver. "Well, and where are they now? Pew was that sort, and he died a beggar-man. Flint was, and he died of rum at Savannah. Ah, they was a sweet crew, they was! On'y, where are they?"

"But," asked Dick, "when we do lay 'em athwart, what are we to do with 'em, anyhow?"

"There's the man for me!" cried the cook admiringly. "That's what I call business. Well, what would you think? Put 'em ashore like maroons? That would have been England's way. Or cut 'em down like that much pork? That would have been Flint's, or Billy Bones's."

"Billy was the man for that," said Israel. "'Dead men don't bite,' says he. Well, he's dead now hisself; he knows the long and short on it now; and if ever a rough hand come to port, it was Billy."

"Right you are," said Silver; "rough and ready. But mark you here, I'm an easy man—I'm quite the gentleman, says you; but this time it's serious. Dooty is dooty, mates. I give my vote —death. When I'm in Parlyment and riding in my coach, I don't want none of these sea-lawyers in the cabin a-coming home, unlooked for, like the devil at prayers. Wait is what I say; but when the time comes, why, let her rip!"

"John," cries the coxswain, "you're a man!"

"You'll say so, Israel when you see," said Silver. "Only one thing I claim—I claim Trelawney. I'll wring his calf's head off his body with these hands, Dick!" he added, breaking off. "You just jump up, like a sweet lad, and get me an apple, to wet my pipe like."

You may fancy the terror I was in! I should have leaped out and run for it if I had found the strength, but my limbs and heart alike misgave me. I heard Dick begin to rise, and then someone seemingly stopped him, and the voice of Hands exclaimed, "Oh, stow that! Don't you get sucking of that bilge, John. Let's have a go of the rum."

"Dick," said Silver, "I trust you. I've a gauge on the keg, mind. There's the key; you fill a pannikin and bring it up."

Terrified as I was, I could not help thinking to myself that this must have been how Mr. Arrow got the strong waters that destroyed him.

Dick was gone but a little while, and during his absence Israel spoke straight on in the cook's ear. It was but a word or two that I could catch, and yet I gathered some important news, for besides other scraps that tended to the same purpose, this whole clause was audible: "Not another man of them'll jine." Hence there were still faithful men on board.

When Dick returned, one after another of the trio took the pannikin and drank—one "To luck," another with a "Here's to old Flint," and Silver himself saying, in a kind of song, "Here's to ourselves, and hold your luff, plenty of prizes and plenty of duff."

Just then a sort of brightness fell upon me in the barrel, and looking up, I found the moon had risen and was silvering the mizzen-top and shining white on the luff of the fore-sail; and almost at the same time the voice of the lookout shouted, "Land ho!"

# 6

# COUNCIL OF WAR

There was a great rush of feet across the deck. I could hear people tumbling up from the cabin and the forecastle, and slipping in an instant outside my barrel, I dived behind the foresail, made a double towards the stern, and came out upon the open deck in time to join Hunter and Dr. Livesey in the rush for the weather bow.

There all hands were already congregated. A belt of fog had lifted almost simultaneously with the appearance of the moon. Away to the south-west of us we saw two low hills, about a couple of miles apart, and rising behind one of them a third and higher hill, whose peak was still buried in the fog. All three seemed sharp and conical in figure.

So much I saw, almost in a dream, for I had not yet recovered from my horrid fear of a minute or two before. And then I heard the voice of Captain Smollett issuing orders. The *Hispaniola* was laid a couple of points nearer the wind and now sailed a course that would just clear the island on the east.

"And now, men," said the captain, when all was sheeted home, "has any one of you ever seen that land ahead?"

"I have, sir," said Silver. "I've watered there with a trader I was cook in."

"The anchorage is on the south, behind an islet, I fancy?" asked the captain.

"Yes, sir; Skeleton Island they calls it. It were a main place for pirates once, and a hand we had on board knowed all their names for it. That hill to the nor'ard they calls the Fore-mast Hill; there are three hills in a row running south'ard—fore, main, and mizzen, sir. But the main—that's the big un, with the cloud on it—they usually calls the Spy-glass, by reason of a lookout they kept when they was in the anchorage cleaning, for it's there they cleaned their ships, sir, asking your pardon."

"I have a chart here," says Captain Smollett. "See if that's the place."

Long John's eyes burned in his head as he took the chart, but by the fresh look of the paper I knew he was doomed to disappointment. This was not the map we found in Billy Bones's chest, but an accurate copy, complete in all things—names and heights and soundings—with the single exception of the red crosses and the written notes. Sharp as must have been his annoyance, Silver had the strength of mind to hide it.

"Yes, sir," said he, "this is the spot, to be sure, and very prettily drawed out. Who might have done that, I wonder? The pirates were too ignorant, I reckon. Aye, here it is: 'Capt. Kidd's Anchorage'—just the name my shipmate called it. There's a strong current runs along the south, and then away nor'ard up the west coast. Right you was, sir," says he, "to haul your wind and keep the weather of the island. Leastways, if such was your intention as to enter and careen, and there ain't no better place for that in these waters."

"Thank you, my man," says Captain Smollett. "I'll ask you later on to give us a help. You may go."

I was surprised at the coolness with which John avowed his knowledge of the island, and I own I was half-frightened when I saw him drawing nearer to myself. He did not know, to be sure, that I had overheard his council from the apple barrel, and yet I had by this time taken such a horror of his cruelty, duplicity, and power that I could scarce conceal a shudder when he laid his hand upon my arm.

"Ah," says he, "this here is a sweet spot, this island—a sweet spot for a lad to get ashore on. You'll bathe, and you'll climb trees, and you'll hunt goats, you will; and you'll get aloft on them hills like a goat yourself. Why, it makes me young again. I was going to forget my timber leg, I was. It's a pleasant thing to be young and have ten toes, and you may lay to that. When you want to go a bit of exploring, you just ask old John, and he'll put up a snack for you to take along."

And clapping me in the friendliest way upon the shoulder, he hobbled off forward and went below.

Captain Smollett, the squire, and Dr. Livesey were talking together on the quarter-deck, and anxious as I was to tell them my story, I durst not interrupt them openly. While I was still casting about in my thoughts to find some probable excuse, Dr. Livesey called me to his side. He had left his pipe below, and being a slave to tobacco, had meant that I should fetch it; but as soon as I was near enough to speak and not to be overheard, I broke immediately, "Doctor, let me speak. Get the captain and squire down to the cabin, and then make some pretence to send for me. I have terrible news."

The doctor changed countenance a little, but next moment he was master of himself.

"Thank you, Jim," said he quite loudly, "that was all I wanted to know," as if he had asked me a question.

And with that he turned on his heel and rejoined the other two. They spoke together for a little, and though none of them started, or raised his voice, or so much as whistled, it was plain enough that Dr. Livesey had communicated my request, for the next thing that I heard was the captain giving an order to Job Anderson, and all hands were piped on deck.

"My lads," said Captain Smollett, "I've a word to say to you. This land that we have sighted is the place we have been sailing for. Mr. Trelawney, being a very open-handed gentleman, as we all know, has just asked me a word or two, and as I was able to tell him that every man on board had done his duty, alow and aloft, as I never ask to see it done better, why, he and I and the doctor are going below to the cabin to drink *your* health and luck, and you'll have grog served out for you to drink *our* health and luck. I'll tell you what I think of this: I think it handsome. And if you think as I do, you'll give a good sea-cheer for the gentleman that does it."

The cheer followed—that was a matter of course; but it rang out so full and hearty that I confess I could hardly believe these same men were plotting for our blood.

"One more cheer for Cap'n Smollett," cried Long John when the first had subsided.

And this also was given with a will.

On the top of that the three gentlemen went below, and not long after, word was sent forward that Jim Hawkins was wanted in the cabin.

I found them all three seated round the table, a bottle of Spanish wine and some raisins before them, and the doctor smoking away, with his wig on his lap, and that, I knew, was a sign that he was agitated. The stern window was open, for it was a warm night, and you could see the moon shining behind on the ship's wake.

"Now, Hawkins," said the squire, "you have something to say. Speak up."

I did as I was bid, and as short as I could make it, told the whole details of Silver's conversation. Nobody interrupted me till I was done, nor did any one of the three of them make so much as a movement, but they kept their eyes upon my face from first to last.

"Jim," said Dr. Livesey, "take a seat."

And they made me sit down at table beside them, poured me out a glass of wine, filled my hands with raisins, and all three, one after the other, and each with a bow, drank my good health, and their service to me, for my luck and courage.

"Now, captain," said the squire, "you were right, and I was wrong. I own myself an ass, and I await your orders."

"No more an ass than I, sir," returned the captain. "I never heard of a crew that meant to mutiny but what showed signs before, for any man that had an eye in his head to see the mischief and take steps according. But this crew," he added, "beats me."

"Captain," said the doctor, "with your permission, that's Silver. A very remarkable man."

"He'd look remarkably well from a yard-arm, sir," returned the captain. "But this is talk; this don't lead to anything. I see three or four points, and with Mr. Trelawney's permission, I'll name them."

"You, sir, are the captain. It is for you to speak," says Mr. Trelawney grandly.

"First point," began Mr. Smollett. "We must go on, because we can't turn back. If I gave the word to go about, they would rise at once. Second point, we have time before us—at least until this treasure's found. Third point, there are faithful hands. Now, sir, it's got to come to blows sooner or later, and what I propose is to take time by the forelock, as the saying is, and come to blows some fine day when they least expect it. We can count, I take it, on your own home servants, Mr. Trelawney?"

"As upon myself," declared the squire.

"Three," reckoned the captain; "ourselves make seven, counting Hawkins here. Now, about the honest hands?"

"Most likely Trelawney's own men," said the doctor; "those he had picked up for himself before he lit on Silver."

"Nay," replied the squire. "Hands was one of mine."

"I did think I could have trusted Hands," added the captain.

"And to think that they're all Englishmen!" broke out the squire. "Sir, I could find it in my heart to blow the ship up."

"Well, gentlemen," said the captain, "the best that I can say is not much. We must lay to, if you please, and keep a bright lookout. It's trying on a man, I know. It would be pleasanter to come to blows. But there's no help for it till we know our men. Lay to, and whistle for a wind, that's my view."

"Jim here," said the doctor, "can help us more than anyone. The men are not shy with him, and Jim is a noticing lad."

"Hawkins, I put prodigious faith in you," added the squire.

I began to feel pretty desperate at this, for I felt altogether helpless; and yet, by an odd train of circumstances, it was indeed through me that safety came. In the meantime, talk as we pleased, there were only seven out of the twenty-six on whom we knew we could rely; and out of these seven one was a boy, so that the grown men on our side were six to their nineteen.

# III

# MY SHORE ADVENTURE

# I

# HOW MY SHORE ADVENTURE BEGAN

The appearance of the island when I came on deck next morning was altogether changed. Although the breeze had now utterly ceased, we had made a great deal of way during the night and were now lying becalmed about half a mile to the south-east of the low eastern coast. Grey-coloured woods covered a large part of the surface. This even tint was indeed broken up by streaks of yellow sand-break in the lower lands, and by many tall trees of the pine family, out-topping the others—some singly, some in clumps; but the general colouring was uniform and sad. The hills ran up clear above the vegetation in spires of naked rock. All were strangely shaped, and the Spy-glass, which was by three or four hundred feet the tallest on the island, was likewise the strangest in configuration, running up sheer from almost every side and then suddenly cut off at the top like a pedestal to put a statue on.

The *Hispaniola* was rolling scuppers under in the ocean swell. The booms were tearing at the blocks, the rudder was banging to and fro, and the whole ship creaking, groaning, and jumping like a manufactory. I had to cling tight to the backstay, and the world turned giddily before my eyes, for though I was a good enough sailor when there was way on, this standing still and being rolled about like a bottle was a thing I never learned to stand without a qualm or so, above all in the morning, on an empty stomach.

Perhaps it was this—perhaps it was the look of the island, with its grey, melancholy woods, and wild stone spires, and the surf that we could both see and hear foaming and thundering on the steep beach—at least, although the sun shone bright and hot, and the shore birds were fishing and crying all around us, and you would have thought anyone would have been glad to get to land after being so long at sea, my heart sank, as the saying is, into my boots; and from the first look onward, I hated the very thought of Treasure Island.

We had a dreary morning's work before us, for there was no sign of any wind, and the boats had to be got out and manned, and the ship warped three or four miles round the corner of the island and up the narrow passage to the haven behind Skeleton Island. I volunteered for one of the boats, where I had, of course, no business. The heat was sweltering, and the men grumbled fiercely over their work. Anderson was in command of my boat, and instead of keeping the crew in order, he grumbled as loud as the worst.

"Well," he said with an oath, "it's not forever."

I thought this was a very bad sign, for up to that day the men had gone briskly and willingly about their business; but the very sight of the island had relaxed the cords of discipline.

All the way in, Long John stood by the steersman and conned the ship. He knew the passage like the palm of his hand, and though the man in the chains got everywhere more water than was down in the chart, John never hesitated once.

"There's a strong scour with the ebb," he said, "and this here passage has been dug out, in a manner of speaking, with a spade."

We brought up just where the anchor was in the chart, about a third of a mile from each shore, the mainland on one side and Skeleton Island on the other. The bottom was clean sand. The plunge of our anchor sent up clouds of birds wheeling and crying over the woods, but in less than a minute they were down again and all was once more silent.

The place was entirely land-locked, buried in woods, the trees coming right down to high-water mark, the shores mostly flat, and the hilltops standing round at a distance in a sort of amphitheatre, one here, one there. Two little rivers, or rather two swamps, emptied out into this pond, as you might call it; and the foliage round that part of the shore had a kind of poisonous brightness. From the ship we could see nothing of the house or stockade, for they were quite buried among trees; and if it had not been for the chart on the companion, we might have been the first that had ever anchored there since the island arose out of the seas.

There was not a breath of air moving, nor a sound but that of the surf booming half a mile away along the beaches and against the rocks outside. A peculiar stagnant smell hung over the anchorage—a smell of sodden leaves and rotting tree trunks. I observed the doctor sniffing and sniffing, like someone tasting a bad egg.

"I don't know about treasure," he said, "but I'll stake my wig there's fever here."

If the conduct of the men had been alarming in the boat, it became truly threatening when they had come aboard. They lay about the deck growling together in talk. The slightest order was received with a black look and grudgingly and carelessly obeyed. Even the honest hands must have caught the infection, for there was not one man aboard to mend another. Mutiny, it was plain, hung over us like a thunder-cloud.

And it was not only we of the cabin party who perceived the danger. Long John was hard at work going from group to group, spending himself in good advice, and as for example no man could have shown a better. He fairly outstripped himself in willingness and civility; he was all smiles to everyone. If an order were given, John would be on his crutch in an instant, with the cheeriest "Aye, aye, sir!" in the world; and when there was nothing else to do, he kept up one song after another, as if to conceal the discontent of the rest.

Of all the gloomy features of that gloomy afternoon, this obvious anxiety on the part of Long John appeared the worst.

We held a council in the cabin.

"Sir," said the captain, "if I risk another order, the whole ship'll come about our ears by the run. You see, sir, here it is. I get a rough answer, do I not? Well, if I speak back, pikes will be going in two shakes; if I don't, Silver will see there's something under that, and the game's up. Now, we've only one man to rely on."

"And who is that?" asked the squire.

"Silver, sir," returned the captain; "he's as anxious as you and I to smother things up. This is a tiff; he'd soon talk 'em out of it if he had the chance, and what I propose to do is to give him the chance. Let's allow the men an afternoon ashore. If they all go, why we'll fight the ship. If they none of them go, well then, we hold the cabin, and God defend the right. If some go, you mark my words, sir, Silver'll bring 'em aboard again as mild as lambs."

It was so decided; loaded pistols were served out to all the sure men; Hunter, Joyce, and Redruth were taken into our confidence and received the news with less surprise and a better spirit than we had looked for, and then the captain went on deck and addressed the crew.

"My lads," said he, "we've had a hot day and are all tired and out of sorts. A turn ashore'll hurt nobody—the boats are still in the water; you can take the gigs, and as many as please may go ashore for the afternoon. I'll fire a gun half an hour before sundown."

I believe the silly fellows must have thought they would break their shins over treasure as soon as they were landed, for they all came out of their sulks in a moment and gave a cheer that started the echo in a faraway hill and sent the birds once more flying and squalling round the anchorage.

The captain was too bright to be in the way. He whipped out of sight in a moment, leaving Silver to arrange the party, and I fancy it was as well he did so. Had he been on deck, he could no longer so much as have pretended not to understand the situation. It was as plain as day. Silver was the captain, and a mighty rebellious crew he had of it. The honest hands—and I was soon to see it proved that there were such on board—must have been very stupid fellows. Or rather, I suppose the truth was this, that all hands were disaffected by the example of the ringleaders—only some more, some less; and a few, being good fellows in the main, could neither be led nor driven any further. It is one thing to be idle and skulk and quite another to take a ship and murder a number of innocent men.

At last, however, the party was made up. Six fellows were to stay on board, and the remaining thirteen, including Silver, began to embark.

Then it was that there came into my head the first of the mad notions that contributed so much to save our lives. If six men were left by Silver, it was plain our party could not take and fight the ship; and since only six were left, it was equally plain that the cabin party had no present need of my assistance. It occurred to me at once to go ashore. In a jiffy I had slipped over the side and curled up in the fore-sheets of the nearest boat, and almost at the same moment she shoved off.

No one took notice of me, only the bow oar saying, "Is that you, Jim? Keep your head down." But Silver, from the other boat, looked sharply over and called out to know if that were me; and from that moment I began to regret what I had done.

The crews raced for the beach, but the boat I was in, having some start and being at once the lighter and the better manned, shot far ahead of her consort, and the bow had struck among the shore-side trees and I had caught a branch and swung myself out and plunged into the nearest thicket while Silver and the rest were still a hundred yards behind.

"Jim, Jim!" I heard him shouting.

But you may suppose I paid no heed; jumping, ducking, and breaking through, I ran straight before my nose till I could run no longer.

## 2

# THE FIRST BLOW

I was so pleased at having given the slip to Long John that I began to enjoy myself and look around me with some interest on the strange land that I was in.

I had crossed a marshy tract full of willows, bulrushes, and odd, outlandish, swampy trees; and I had now come out upon the skirts of an open piece of undulating, sandy country, about a mile long, dotted with a few pines and a great number of contorted trees, not unlike the oak in growth, but pale in the foliage, like willows. On the far side of the open stood one of the hills, with two quaint, craggy peaks shining vividly in the sun.

I now felt for the first time the joy of exploration. The isle was uninhabited; my shipmates I had left behind, and nothing lived in front of me but dumb brutes and fowls. I turned hither and thither among the trees. Here and there were flowering plants, unknown to me; here and there I saw snakes, and one raised his head from a ledge of rock and hissed at me with a noise not unlike the spinning of a top. Little did I suppose that he was a deadly enemy and that the noise was the famous rattle.

Then I came to a long thicket of these oak-like trees—live, or evergreen, oaks, I heard afterwards they should be called—which grew low along the sand like brambles, the boughs curiously twisted, the foliage compact, like thatch. The thicket stretched down from the top of one of the sandy knolls, spreading and growing taller as it went, until it reached the margin of the broad, reedy fen, through which the nearest of the little rivers soaked its way into the anchorage. The marsh was steaming in the strong sun, and the outline of the Spy-glass trembled through the haze.

All at once there began to go a sort of bustle among the bulrushes; a wild duck flew up with a quack, another followed, and soon over the whole surface of the marsh a great cloud of birds hung screaming and circling in the air. I judged at once that some of my shipmates must be drawing near along the borders of the fen. Nor was I deceived, for soon I heard the very distant and low tones of a human voice, which, as I continued to give ear, grew steadily louder and nearer.

This put me in a great fear, and I crawled under cover of the nearest live-oak and squatted there, hearkening, as silent as a mouse.

Another voice answered, and then the first voice, which I now recognized to be Silver's, once more took up the story and ran on for a long while in a stream, only now and again interrupted by the other. By the sound they must have been talking earnestly, and almost fiercely; but no distinct word came to my hearing.

At last the speakers seemed to have paused and perhaps to have sat down, for not only did they cease to draw any nearer, but the birds themselves began to grow more quiet and to settle again to their places in the swamp.

And now I began to feel that I was neglecting my business, that since I had been so foolhardy as to come ashore with these desperadoes, the least I could do was to overhear them at their councils, and that my plain and obvious duty was to draw as close as I could manage, under the favourable ambush of the crouching trees.

I could tell the direction of the speakers pretty exactly, not only by the sound of their voices but by the behaviour of the few birds that still hung in alarm above the heads of the intruders.

Crawling on all fours, I made steadily but slowly towards them, till at last, raising my head to an aperture among the leaves, I could see clear down into a little green dell beside the marsh, and closely set about with trees, where Long John Silver and another of the crew stood face to face in conversation.

The sun beat full upon them. Silver had thrown his hat beside him on the ground, and his great, smooth, blond face, all shining with heat, was lifted to the other man's in a kind of appeal.

"Mate," he was saying, "it's because I thinks gold dust of you—gold dust, and you may lay to that! If I hadn't took to you like pitch, do you think I'd have been here a-warning of you? All's up—you can't make nor mend; it's to save your neck that I'm a-speaking, and if one of the wild uns knew it, where'd I be, Tom—now, tell me, where'd I be?"

"Silver," said the other man—and I observed he was not only red in the face, but spoke as hoarse as a crow, and his voice shook too, like a taut rope—"Silver," says he, "you're old, and you're honest, or has the name for it; and you've money too, which lots of poor sailors hasn't; and you're brave, or I'm mistook. And will you tell me you'll let yourself be led away with that kind of a mess of swabs? Not you! As sure as God sees me, I'd sooner lose my hand. If I turn agin my dooty—"

And then all of a sudden he was interrupted by a noise. I had found one of the honest hands—well, here, at that same moment, came news of another. Far away out in the marsh there arose, all of a sudden, a sound like the cry of anger, then another on the back of it; and then one horrid, long-drawn scream. The rocks of the Spy-glass re-echoed it a score of times; the whole troop of marsh-birds rose again, darkening heaven, with a simultaneous whirr; and long after that death yell was still ringing in my brain, silence had re-established its empire, and only the rustle of the redescending birds and the boom of the distant surges disturbed the languor of the afternoon.

Tom had leaped at the sound, like a horse at the spur, but Silver had not winked an eye. He stood where he was, resting lightly on his crutch, watching his companion like a snake about to spring.

"John!" said the sailor, stretching out his hand.

"Hands off!" cried Silver, leaping back a yard, as it seemed to me, with the speed and security of a trained gymnast.

"Hands off, if you like, John Silver," said the other. "It's a black conscience that can make you feared of me. But in heaven's name, tell me, what was that?"

"That?" returned Silver, smiling away, but warier than ever, his eye a mere pin-point in his big face, but gleaming like a crumb of glass. "That? Oh, I reckon that'll be Alan."

And at this point Tom flashed out like a hero.

"Alan!" he cried. "Then rest his soul for a true seaman! And as for you, John Silver, long you've been a mate of mine, but you're mate of mine no more. If I die like a dog, I'll die in my dooty. You've killed Alan, have you? Kill me too, if you can. But I defies you."

And with that, this brave fellow turned his back directly on the cook and set off walking for the beach. But he was not destined to go far. With a cry John seized the branch of a tree, whipped the crutch out of his armpit, and sent that uncouth missile hurtling through the air. It struck poor Tom, point foremost, and with stunning violence, right between the shoulders in the middle of his back. His hands flew up, he gave a sort of gasp, and fell.

Whether he were injured much or little, none could ever tell. Like enough, to judge from the sound, his back was broken on the spot. But he had no time given him to recover. Silver, agile as a monkey even without leg or crutch, was on the top of him next moment and had twice buried his knife up to the hilt in that defenceless body. From my place of ambush, I could hear him pant aloud as he struck the blows.

I do not know what it rightly is to faint, but I do know that for the next little while the whole world swam away from before me in a whirling mist; Silver and the birds, and the tall Spy-glass hilltop, going round and round and topsy-turvy before my eyes, and all manner of bells ringing and distant voices shouting in my ear.

When I came again to myself the monster had pulled himself together, his crutch under his arm, his hat upon his head. Just before him Tom lay motionless upon the sward; but the murderer minded him not a whit, cleansing his blood-stained knife the while upon a wisp of grass. Everything else was unchanged, the sun still shining mercilessly on the steaming marsh and the tall pinnacle of the mountain, and I could scarce persuade myself that murder had been actually done and a human life cruelly cut short a moment since before my eyes.

But now John put his hand into his pocket, brought out a whistle, and blew upon it several modulated blasts that rang far across the heated air. I could not tell, of course, the meaning of the signal, but it instantly awoke my fears. More men would be coming. I might be discovered. They had already slain two of the honest people; after Tom and Alan, might not I come next?

Instantly I began to extricate myself and crawl back again, with what speed and silence I could manage, to the more open portion of the wood. As I did so, I could hear hails coming and going between the old buccaneer and his comrades, and this sound of danger lent me wings. As soon as I was clear of the thicket, I ran as I never ran before, scarce minding the direction of my flight, so long as it led me from the murderers; and as I ran, fear grew and grew upon me until it turned into a kind of frenzy.

Indeed, could anyone be more entirely lost than I? When the gun fired, how should I dare to go down to the boats among those fiends, still smoking from their crime? Would not the first of them who saw me wring my neck like a snipe's? Would not my absence itself be an evidence to them of my alarm, and therefore of my fatal knowledge? It was all over, I thought. Good-bye to the *Hispaniola*; good-bye to the squire, the doctor, and the captain! There was nothing left for me but death by starvation or death by the hands of the mutineers.

All this while, as I say, I was still running, and without taking any notice, I had drawn near to the foot of the little hill with the two peaks and had got into a part of the island where the live-oaks grew more widely apart and seemed more like forest trees in their bearing and dimensions. Mingled with these were a few scattered pines, some fifty, some nearer seventy, feet high. The air too smelt more freshly than down beside the marsh.

And here a fresh alarm brought me to a standstill with a thumping heart.

## 3

# THE MAN OF THE ISLAND

From the side of the hill, which was here steep and stony, a spout of gravel was dislodged and fell rattling and bounding through the trees. My eyes turned instinctively in that direction, and I saw a figure leap with great rapidity behind the trunk of a pine. What it was, whether bear or man or monkey, I could in no wise tell. It seemed dark and shaggy; more I knew not. But the terror of this new apparition brought me to a stand.

I was now, it seemed, cut off upon both sides; behind me the murderers, before me this lurking nondescript. And immediately I began to prefer the dangers that I knew to those I knew not. Silver himself appeared less terrible in contrast with this creature of the woods, and I turned on my heel, and looking sharply behind me over my shoulder, began to retrace my steps in the direction of the boats.

Instantly the figure reappeared, and making a wide circuit, began to head me off. I was tired, at any rate; but had I been as fresh as when I rose, I could see it was in vain for me to contend in speed with such an adversary. From trunk to trunk the creature flitted like a deer, running manlike on two legs, but unlike any man that I had ever seen, stooping almost double as it ran. Yet a man it was, I could no longer be in doubt about that.

I began to recall what I had heard of cannibals. I was within an ace of calling for help. But the mere fact that he was a man, however wild, had somewhat reassured me, and my fear of Silver began to revive in proportion. I stood still, therefore, and cast about for some method of escape; and as I was so thinking, the recollection of my pistol flashed into my mind. As soon as I remembered I was not defenceless, courage glowed again in my heart and I set my face resolutely for this man of the island and walked briskly towards him.

He was concealed by this time behind another tree trunk; but he must have been watching me closely, for as soon as I began to move in his direction he reappeared and took a step to meet me. Then he hesitated, drew back, came forward again, and at last, to my wonder and confusion, threw himself on his knees and held out his clasped hands in supplication.

At that I once more stopped.

"Who are you?" I asked.

"Ben Gunn," he answered, and his voice sounded hoarse and awkward, like a rusty lock. "I'm poor Ben Gunn, I am; and I haven't spoke with a Christian these three years."

I could now see that he was a white man like myself and that his features were even pleasing. His skin, wherever it was exposed, was burnt by the sun; even his lips were black, and his fair eyes looked quite startling in so dark a face. Of all the beggar-men that I had seen or fancied, he was the chief for raggedness. He was clothed with tatters of old ship's canvas and old sea-cloth, and this extraordinary patchwork was all held together by a system of the most various and incongruous fastenings, brass buttons, bits of stick, and loops of tarry gaskin. About his waist he wore an old brass-buckled leather belt, which was the one thing solid in his whole accoutrement.

"Three years!" I cried. "Were you shipwrecked?"

"Nay, mate," said he; "marooned."

I had heard the word, and I knew it stood for a horrible kind of punishment common enough among the buccaneers, in which the offender is put ashore with a little powder and shot and left behind on some desolate and distant island.

"Marooned three years agone," he continued, "and lived on goats since then, and berries, and oysters. Wherever a man is, says I, a man can do for himself. But, mate, my heart is sore for Christian diet. You mightn't happen to have a piece of cheese about you, now? No? Well, many's the long night I've dreamed of cheese—toasted, mostly—and woke up again, and here I were."

"If ever I can get aboard again," said I, "you shall have cheese by the stone."

All this time he had been feeling the stuff of my jacket, smoothing my hands, looking at my boots, and generally, in the intervals of his speech, showing a childish pleasure in the presence of a fellow creature. But at my last words he perked up into a kind of startled slyness.

"If ever you can get aboard again, says you?" he repeated. "Why, now, who's to hinder you?"

"Not you, I know," was my reply.

"And right you was," he cried. "Now you—what do you call yourself, mate?"

"Jim," I told him.

"Jim, Jim," says he, quite pleased apparently. "Well, now, Jim, I've lived that rough as you'd be ashamed to hear of. Now, for instance, you wouldn't think I had had a pious mother—to look at me?" he asked.

"Why, no, not in particular," I answered.

"Ah, well," said he, "but I had—remarkable pious. And I was a civil, pious boy, and could rattle off my catechism that fast, as you couldn't tell one word from another. And here's what it come to, Jim, and it begun with chuck-farthen on the blessed grave-stones! That's what it begun with, but it went further'n that; and so my mother told me, and predicked the whole, she did, the pious woman! But it were Providence that put me here. I've thought it all out in this here lonely island, and I'm back on piety. You don't catch me tasting rum so much, but just a thimbleful for luck, of course, the first chance I have. I'm bound I'll be good, and I see the way to. And, Jim"—looking all round him and lowering his voice to a whisper—"I'm rich."

I now felt sure that the poor fellow had gone crazy in his solitude, and I suppose I must have shown the feeling in my face, for he repeated the statement hotly: "Rich! Rich! I says. And I'll tell you what: I'll make a man of you, Jim. Ah, Jim, you'll bless your stars, you will, you was the first that found me!"

And at this there came suddenly a lowering shadow over his face, and he tightened his grasp upon my hand and raised a forefinger threateningly before my eyes.

"Now, Jim, you tell me true: that ain't Flint's ship?" he asked.

At this I had a happy inspiration. I began to believe that I had found an ally, and I answered him at once.

"It's not Flint's ship, and Flint is dead; but I'll tell you true, as you ask me—there are some of Flint's hands aboard; worse luck for the rest of us."

"Not a man—with one—leg?" he gasped.

"Silver?" I asked.

"Ah, Silver!" says he. "That were his name."

"He's the cook, and the ringleader too."

He was still holding me by the wrist, and at that he give it quite a wring.

"If you was sent by Long John," he said, "I'm as good as pork, and I know it. But where was you, do you suppose?"

I had made my mind up in a moment, and by way of answer told him the whole story of our voyage and the predicament in which we found ourselves. He heard me with the keenest interest, and when I had done he patted me on the head.

"You're a good lad, Jim," he said; "and you're all in a clove hitch, ain't you? Well, you just put your trust in Ben Gunn—Ben Gunn's the man to do it. Would you think it likely, now, that your squire would prove a liberal-minded one in case of help—him being in a clove hitch, as you remark?"

I told him the squire was the most liberal of men.

"Aye, but you see," returned Ben Gunn, "I didn't mean giving me a gate to keep, and a suit of livery clothes, and such; that's not my mark, Jim. What I mean is, would he be likely to come down to the toon of, say one thousand pounds out of money that's as good as a man's own already?"

"I am sure he would," said I. "As it was, all hands were to share."

"*And* a passage home?" he added with a look of great shrewdness.

"Why," I cried, "the squire's a gentleman. And besides, if we got rid of the others, we should want you to help work the vessel home."

"Ah," said he, "so you would." And he seemed very much relieved.

"Now, I'll tell you what," he went on. "So much I'll tell you, and no more. I were in Flint's ship when he buried the treasure; he and six along—six strong seamen. They was ashore nigh on a week, and us standing off and on in the old *Walrus*. One fine day up went the signal, and here come Flint by himself in a little boat, and his head done up in a blue scarf. The sun was getting up, and mortal white he looked about the cutwater. But, there he was, you mind, and the six all dead—dead and buried. How he done it, not a man aboard us could make out. It was battle, murder, and sudden death, leastways—him against six. Billy Bones was the mate; Long John, he was quartermaster; and they asked him where the treasure was. 'Ah,' says he, 'you can go ashore, if you like, and stay,' he says; 'but as for the ship, she'll beat up for more, by thunder!' That's what he said.

"Well, I was in another ship three years back, and we sighted this island. 'Boys,' said I, 'here's Flint's treasure; let's land and find it.' The cap'n was displeased at that, but my messmates were all of a mind and landed. Twelve days they looked for it, and every day they had the worse word for me, until one fine morning all hands went aboard. 'As for you, Benjamin Gunn,' says they, 'here's a musket,' they says, 'and a spade, and pick-axe. You can stay here and find Flint's money for yourself,' they says.

"Well, Jim, three years have I been here, and not a bite of Christian diet from that day to this. But now, you look here; look at me. Do I look like a man before the mast? No, says you. Nor I weren't, neither, I says."

And with that he winked and pinched me hard.

"Just you mention them words to your squire, Jim," he went on. "Nor he weren't, neither—that's the words. Three years he were the man of this island, light and dark, fair and rain; and sometimes he would maybe think upon a prayer (says you), and sometimes he would maybe think of his old mother, so be as she's alive (you'll say); but the most part of Gunn's time (this is what you'll say)—the most part of his time was took up with another matter. And then you'll give him a nip, like I do."

And he pinched me again in the most confidential manner.

"Then," he continued, "then you'll up, and you'll say this: Gunn is a good man (you'll say), and he puts a precious sight more confidence—a precious sight, mind that—in a gen'leman born than in these gen'leman of fortune, having been one hisself."

"Well," I said, "I don't understand one word that you've been saying. But that's neither here nor there; for how am I to get on board?"

"Ah," said he, "that's the hitch, for sure. Well, there's my boat, that I made with my two hands. I keep her under the white rock. If the worst come to the worst, we might try that after dark. Hi!" he broke out. "What's that?"

For just then, although the sun had still an hour or two to run, all the echoes of the island awoke and bellowed to the thunder of a cannon.

"They have begun to fight!" I cried. "Follow me."

And I began to run towards the anchorage, my terrors all forgotten, while close at my side the marooned man in his goatskins trotted easily and lightly.

"Left, left," says he; "keep to your left hand, mate Jim! Under the trees with you! Theer's where I killed my first goat. They don't come down here now; they're all mastheaded on them mountings for the fear of Benjamin Gunn. Ah! And there's the cetemery"—cemetery, he must have meant. "You see the mounds? I come here and prayed, nows and thens, when I thought maybe a Sunday would be about doo. It weren't quite a chapel, but it seemed more solemn like; and then, says you, Ben Gunn was short-handed—no chapling, nor so much as a Bible and a flag, you says."

So he kept talking as I ran, neither expecting nor receiving any answer.

The cannon-shot was followed after a considerable interval by a volley of small arms.

Another pause, and then, not a quarter of a mile in front of me, I beheld the Union Jack flutter in the air above a wood.

# IV

# THE STOCKADE

## I

# NARRATIVE CONTINUED BY THE DOCTOR: HOW THE SHIP WAS ABANDONED

It was about half past one—three bells in the sea phrase—that the two boats went ashore from the *Hispaniola*. The captain, the squire, and I were talking matters over in the cabin. Had there been a breath of wind, we should have fallen on the six mutineers who were left aboard with us, slipped our cable, and away to sea. But the wind was wanting; and to complete our helplessness, down came Hunter with the news that Jim Hawkins had slipped into a boat and was gone ashore with the rest.

It never occurred to us to doubt Jim Hawkins, but we were alarmed for his safety. With the men in the temper they were in, it seemed an even chance if we should see the lad again. We ran on deck. The pitch was bubbling in the seams; the nasty stench of the place turned me sick; if ever a man smelt fever and dysentery, it was in that abominable anchorage. The six scoundrels were sitting grumbling under a sail in the forecastle; ashore we could see the gigs made fast and a man sitting in each, hard by where the river runs in. One of them was whistling "Lillibullero."

Waiting was a strain, and it was decided that Hunter and I should go ashore with the jolly-boat in quest of information.

The gigs had leaned to their right, but Hunter and I pulled straight in, in the direction of the stockade upon the chart. The two who were left guarding their boats seemed in a bustle at our appearance; "Lillibullero" stopped off, and I could see the pair discussing what they ought to do. Had they gone and told Silver, all might have turned out differently; but they had their orders, I suppose, and decided to sit quietly where they were and hark back again to "Lillibullero."

There was a slight bend in the coast, and I steered so as to put it between us; even before we landed we had thus lost sight of the gigs. I jumped out and came as near running as I durst, with a big silk handkerchief under my hat for coolness' sake and a brace of pistols ready primed for safety.

I had not gone a hundred yards when I reached the stockade.

This was how it was: a spring of clear water rose almost at the top of a knoll. Well, on the knoll, and enclosing the spring, they had clapped a stout loghouse fit to hold two score of people on a pinch and loopholed for musketry on either side. All round this they had cleared a wide space, and then the thing was completed by a paling six feet high, without door or opening, too strong to pull down without time and labour and too open to shelter the besiegers. The people in the log-house had them in every way; they stood quiet in shelter and shot the others like partridges. All they wanted was a good watch and food; for, short of a complete surprise, they might have held the place against a regiment.

What particularly took my fancy was the spring. For though we had a good enough place of it in the cabin of the *Hispaniola,* with plenty of arms and ammunition, and things to eat, and excellent wines, there had been one thing overlooked—we had no water. I was thinking this over when there came ringing over the island the cry of a man at the point of death. I was not new to violent death—I have served his Royal Highness the Duke of Cumberland, and got a wound myself at Fontenoy—but I know my pulse went dot and carry one. "Jim Hawkins is gone," was my first thought.

It is something to have been an old soldier, but more still to have been a doctor. There is no time to dilly-dally in our work. And so now I made up my mind instantly, and with no time lost returned to the shore and jumped on board the jolly-boat.

By good fortune Hunter pulled a good oar. We made the water fly, and the boat was soon alongside and I aboard the schooner.

I found them all shaken, as was natural. The squire was sitting down, as white as a sheet, thinking of the harm he had led us to, the good soul! And one of the six forecastle hands was little better.

"There's a man," says Captain Smollett, nodding towards him, "new to this work. He came nigh-hand fainting, doctor, when he heard the cry. Another touch of the rudder and that man would join us."

I told my plan to the captain, and between us we settled on the details of its accomplishment.

We put old Redruth in the gallery between the cabin and the forecastle, with three or four loaded muskets and a mattress for protection. Hunter brought the boat round under the stern-port, and Joyce and I set to work loading her with powder tins, muskets, bags of biscuits, kegs of pork, a cask of cognac, and my invaluable medicine chest.

In the meantime, the squire and the captain stayed on deck, and the latter hailed the coxswain, who was the principal man aboard.

"Mr. Hands," he said, "here are two of us with a brace of pistols each. If any one of you six make a signal of any description, that man's dead."

They were a good deal taken aback, and after a little consultation one and all tumbled down the fore companion, thinking no doubt to take us on the rear. But when they saw Redruth waiting for them in the sparred galley, they went about ship at once, and a head popped out again on deck.

"Down, dog!" cries the captain.

And the head popped back again; and we heard no more, for the time, of these six very faint-hearted seamen.

By this time, tumbling things in as they came, we had the jolly-boat loaded as much as we dared. Joyce and I got out through the stern-port, and we made for shore again as fast as oars could take us.

This second trip fairly aroused the watchers along shore. "Lillibullero" was dropped again; and just before we lost sight of them behind the little point, one of them whipped ashore and disappeared. I had half a mind to change my plan and destroy their boats, but I feared that Silver and the others might be close at hand, and all might very well be lost by trying for too much.

We had soon touched land in the same place as before and set to provision the block house. All three made the first journey, heavily laden, and tossed our stores over the palisade. Then, leaving Joyce to guard them—one man, to be sure, but with half a dozen muskets—Hunter and I returned to the jolly-boat and loaded ourselves once more. So we proceeded without pausing to take breath, till the whole cargo was bestowed, when the two servants took up their position in the block house, and I, with all my power, sculled back to the *Hispaniola*.

That we should have risked a second boat load seems more daring than it really was. They had the advantage of numbers, of course, but we had the advantage of arms. Not one of the men ashore had a musket, and before they could get within range for pistol shooting, we flattered ourselves we should be able to give a good account of a half-dozen at least.

The squire was waiting for me at the stern window, all his faintness gone from him. He caught the painter and made it fast, and we fell to loading the boat for our very lives. Pork, powder, and biscuit was the cargo, with only a musket and a cutlass apiece for the squire and me and Redruth and the captain. The rest of the arms and powder we dropped overboard in two fathoms and a half of water, so that we could see the bright steel shining far below us in the sun, on the clean, sandy bottom.

By this time the tide was beginning to ebb, and the ship was swinging round to her anchor. Voices were heard faintly halloaing in the direction of the two gigs; and though this reassured us for Joyce and Hunter, who were well to the eastward, it warned our party to be off.

Redruth retreated from his place in the gallery and dropped into the boat, which we then brought round to the ship's counter, to be handier for Captain Smollett.

"Now, men," said he, "do you hear me?"

There was no answer from the forecastle.

"It's to you, Abraham Gray—it's to you I am speaking."

Still no reply.

"Gray," resumed Mr. Smollett, a little louder, "I am leaving this ship, and I order you to follow your captain. I know you are a good man at bottom, and I dare say not one of the lot of you's as bad as he makes out. I have my watch here in my hand; I give you thirty seconds to join me in."

There was a pause.

"Come, my fine fellow," continued the captain; "don't hang so long in stays. I'm risking my life and the lives of these good gentlemen every second."

There was a sudden scuffle, a sound of blows, and out burst Abraham Gray with a knife cut on the side of the cheek, and came running to the captain like a dog to the whistle.

"I'm with you, sir," said he.

And the next moment he and the captain had dropped aboard of us, and we had shoved off and given way.

We were clear out of the ship, but not yet ashore in our stockade.

## 2

# NARRATIVE CONTINUED BY THE DOCTOR: THE JOLLY-BOAT'S LAST TRIP

This fifth trip was quite different from any of the others. In the first place, the little gallipot of a boat that we were in was gravely overloaded. Five grown men, and three of them—Trelawney, Redruth, and the captain—over six feet high, was already more than she was meant to carry. Add to that the powder, pork, and bread-bags. The gunwale was lipping astern. Several times we shipped a little water, and my breeches and the tails of my coat were all soaking wet before we had gone a hundred yards.

The captain made us trim the boat, and we got her to lie a little more evenly. All the same, we were afraid to breathe.

In the second place, the ebb was now making—a strong rippling current running westward through the basin, and then south'ard and seaward down the straits by which we had entered in the morning. Even the ripples were a danger to our overloaded craft, but the worst of it was that we were swept out of our true course and away from our proper landing-place behind the point. If we let the current have its way we should come ashore beside the gigs, where the pirates might appear at any moment.

"I cannot keep her head for the stockade, sir," said I to the captain. I was steering, while he and Redruth, two fresh men, were at the oars. "The tide keeps washing her down. Could you pull a little stronger?"

"Not without swamping the boat," said he. "You must bear up, sir, if you please—bear up until you see you're gaining."

I tried and found by experiment that the tide kept sweeping us westward until I had laid her head due east, or just about right angles to the way we ought to go.

"We'll never get ashore at this rate," said I.

"If it's the only course that we can lie, sir, we must even lie it," returned the captain. "We must keep upstream. You see, sir," he went on, "if once we dropped to leeward of the landing-place, it's hard to say where we should get ashore, besides the chance of being boarded by the gigs; whereas, the way we go the current must slacken, and then we can dodge back along the shore."

"The current's less a'ready, sir," said the man Gray, who was sitting in the fore-sheets; "you can ease her off a bit."

"Thank you, my man," said I, quite as if nothing had happened, for we had all quietly made up our minds to treat him like one of ourselves.

Suddenly the captain spoke up again, and I thought his voice was a little changed.

"The gun!" said he.

"I have thought of that," said I, for I made sure he was thinking of a bombardment of the fort. "They could never get the gun ashore, and if they did, they could never haul it through the woods."

"Look astern, doctor," replied the captain.

We had entirely forgotten the long nine; and there, to our horror, were the five rogues busy about her, getting off her jacket, as they called the stout tarpaulin cover under which she sailed. Not only that, but it flashed into my mind at the same moment that the round-shot and the powder for the gun had been left behind, and a stroke with an axe would put it all into the possession of the evil ones abroad.

"Israel was Flint's gunner," said Gray hoarsely.

At any risk, we put the boat's head direct for the landing-place. By this time we had got so far out of the run of the current that we kept steerage way even at our necessarily gentle rate of rowing, and I could keep her steady for the goal. But the worst of it was that with the course I now held we turned our broadside instead of our stern to the *Hispaniola*and offered a target like a barn door.

I could hear as well as see that brandy-faced rascal Israel Hands plumping down a round-shot on the deck.

"Who's the best shot?" asked the captain.

"Mr. Trelawney, out and away," said I.

"Mr. Trelawney, will you please pick me off one of these men, sir? Hands, if possible," said the captain.

Trelawney was as cool as steel. He looked to the priming of his gun.

"Now," cried the captain, "easy with that gun, sir, or you'll swamp the boat. All hands stand by to trim her when he aims."

The squire raised his gun, the rowing ceased, and we leaned over to the other side to keep the balance, and all was so nicely contrived that we did not ship a drop.

They had the gun, by this time, slewed round upon the swivel, and Hands, who was at the muzzle with the rammer, was in consequence the most exposed. However, we had no luck, for just as Trelawney fired, down he stooped, the ball whistled over him, and it was one of the other four who fell.

The cry he gave was echoed not only by his companions on board but by a great number of voices from the shore, and looking in that direction I saw the other pirates trooping out from among the trees and tumbling into their places in the boats.

"Here come the gigs, sir," said I.

"Give way, then," cried the captain. "We mustn't mind if we swamp her now. If we can't get ashore, all's up."

"Only one of the gigs is being manned, sir," I added; "the crew of the other most likely going round by shore to cut us off."

"They'll have a hot run, sir," returned the captain. "Jack ashore, you know. It's not them I mind; it's the round-shot. Carpet bowls! My lady's maid couldn't miss. Tell us, squire, when you see the match, and we'll hold water."

In the meanwhile we had been making headway at a good pace for a boat so overloaded, and we had shipped but little water in the process. We were now close in; thirty or forty strokes and we should beach her, for the ebb had already disclosed a narrow belt of sand below the clustering trees. The gig was no longer to be feared; the little point had already concealed it from our eyes. The ebb-tide, which had so cruelly delayed us, was now making reparation and delaying our assailants. The one source of danger was the gun.

"If I durst," said the captain, "I'd stop and pick off another man."

But it was plain that they meant nothing should delay their shot. They had never so much as looked at their fallen comrade, though he was not dead, and I could see him trying to crawl away.

"Ready!" cried the squire.

"Hold!" cried the captain, quick as an echo.

And he and Redruth backed with a great heave that sent her stern bodily under water. The report fell in at the same instant of time. This was the first that Jim heard, the sound of the squire's shot not having reached him. Where the ball passed, not one of us precisely knew, but I fancy it must have been over our heads and that the wind of it may have contributed to our disaster.

At any rate, the boat sank by the stern, quite gently, in three feet of water, leaving the captain and myself, facing each other, on our feet. The other three took complete headers, and came up again drenched and bubbling.

So far there was no great harm. No lives were lost, and we could wade ashore in safety. But there were all our stores at the bottom, and to make things worse, only two guns out of five remained in a state for service. Mine I had snatched from my knees and held over my head, by a sort of instinct. As for the captain, he had carried his over his shoulder by a bandoleer, and like a wise man, lock uppermost. The other three had gone down with the boat.

To add to our concern, we heard voices already drawing near us in the woods along shore, and we had not only the danger of being cut off from the stockade in our half-crippled state but the fear before us whether, if Hunter and Joyce were attacked by half a dozen, they would have the sense and conduct to stand firm. Hunter was steady, that we knew; Joyce was a doubtful case—a pleasant, polite man for a valet and to brush one's clothes, but not entirely fitted for a man of war.

With all this in our minds, we waded ashore as fast as we could, leaving behind us the poor jolly-boat and a good half of all our powder and provisions.

## 3

# NARRATIVE CONTINUED BY THE DOCTOR: END OF THE FIRST DAY'S FIGHTING

We made our best speed across the strip of wood that now divided us from the stockade, and at every step we took the voices of the buccaneers rang nearer. Soon we could hear their footfalls as they ran and the cracking of the branches as they breasted across a bit of thicket.

I began to see we should have a brush for it in earnest and looked to my priming.

"Captain," said I, "Trelawney is the dead shot. Give him your gun; his own is useless."

They exchanged guns, and Trelawney, silent and cool as he had been since the beginning of the bustle, hung a moment on his heel to see that all was fit for service. At the same time, observing Gray to be unarmed, I handed him my cutlass. It did all our hearts good to see him spit in his hand, knit his brows, and make the blade sing through the air. It was plain from every line of his body that our new hand was worth his salt.

Forty paces farther we came to the edge of the wood and saw the stockade in front of us. We struck the enclosure about the middle of the south side, and almost at the same time, seven mutineers—Job Anderson, the boatswain, at their head—appeared in full cry at the southwestern corner.

They paused as if taken aback, and before they recovered, not only the squire and I, but Hunter and Joyce from the block house, had time to fire. The four shots came in rather a scattering volley, but they did the business: one of the enemy actually fell, and the rest, without hesitation, turned and plunged into the trees.

After reloading, we walked down the outside of the palisade to see to the fallen enemy. He was stone dead—shot through the heart.

We began to rejoice over our good success when just at that moment a pistol cracked in the bush, a ball whistled close past my ear, and poor Tom Redruth stumbled and fell his length on the ground. Both the squire and I returned the shot, but as we had nothing to aim at, it is probable we only wasted powder. Then we reloaded and turned our attention to poor Tom.

The captain and Gray were already examining him, and I saw with half an eye that all was over.

I believe the readiness of our return volley had scattered the mutineers once more, for we were suffered without further molestation to get the poor old gamekeeper hoisted over the stockade and carried, groaning and bleeding, into the log-house.

Poor old fellow, he had not uttered one word of surprise, complaint, fear, or even acquiescence from the very beginning of our troubles till now, when we had laid him down in the log-house to die. He had lain like a Trojan behind his mattress in the gallery; he had followed every order silently, doggedly, and well; he was the oldest of our party by a score of years; and now, sullen, old, serviceable servant, it was he that was to die.

The squire dropped down beside him on his knees and kissed his hand, crying like a child.

"Be I going, doctor?" he asked.

"Tom, my man," said I, "you're going home."

"I wish I had had a lick at them with the gun first," he replied.

"Tom," said the squire, "say you forgive me, won't you?"

"Would that be respectful like, from me to you, squire?" was the answer. "Howsoever, so be it, amen!"

After a little while of silence, he said he thought somebody might read a prayer. "It's the custom, sir," he added apologetically. And not long after, without another word, he passed away.

In the meantime the captain, whom I had observed to be wonderfully swollen about the chest and pockets, had turned out a great many various stores—the British colours, a Bible, a coil of stoutish rope, pen, ink, the log-book, and pounds of tobacco. He had found a longish fir-tree lying felled and trimmed in the enclosure, and with the help of Hunter he had set it up at the corner of the log-house where the trunks crossed and made an angle. Then, climbing on the roof, he had with his own hand bent and run up the colours.

This seemed mightily to relieve him. He re-entered the log-house and set about counting up the stores as if nothing else existed. But he had an eye on Tom's passage for all that, and as soon as all was over, came forward with another flag and reverently spread it on the body.

"Don't you take on, sir," he said, shaking the squire's hand. "All's well with him; no fear for a hand that's been shot down in his duty to captain and owner. It mayn't be good divinity, but it's a fact."

Then he pulled me aside.

"Dr. Livesey," he said, "in how many weeks do you and squire expect the consort?"

I told him it was a question not of weeks but of months, that if we were not back by the end of August Blandly was to send to find us, but neither sooner nor later. "You can calculate for yourself," I said.

"Why, yes," returned the captain, scratching his head; "and making a large allowance, sir, for all the gifts of Providence, I should say we were pretty close hauled."

"How do you mean?" I asked.

"It's a pity, sir, we lost that second load. That's what I mean," replied the captain. "As for powder and shot, we'll do. But the rations are short, very short—so short, Dr. Livesey, that we're perhaps as well without that extra mouth."

And he pointed to the dead body under the flag.

Just then, with a roar and a whistle, a round-shot passed high above the roof of the log-house and plumped far beyond us in the wood.

"Oho!" said the captain. "Blaze away! You've little enough powder already, my lads."

At the second trial, the aim was better, and the ball descended inside the stockade, scattering a cloud of sand but doing no further damage.

"Captain," said the squire, "the house is quite invisible from the ship. It must be the flag they are aiming at. Would it not be wiser to take it in?"

"Strike my colours!" cried the captain. "No, sir, not I"; and as soon as he had said the words, I think we all agreed with him. For it was not only a piece of stout, seamanly, good feeling; it was good policy besides and showed our enemies that we despised their cannonade.

All through the evening they kept thundering away. Ball after ball flew over or fell short or kicked up the sand in the enclosure, but they had to fire so high that the shot fell dead and buried itself in the soft sand. We had no ricochet to fear, and though one popped in through the roof of the log-house and out again through the floor, we soon got used to that sort of horse-play and minded it no more than cricket.

"There is one good thing about all this," observed the captain; "the wood in front of us is likely clear. The ebb has made a good while; our stores should be uncovered. Volunteers to go and bring in pork."

Gray and Hunter were the first to come forward. Well armed, they stole out of the stockade, but it proved a useless mission. The mutineers were bolder than we fancied or they put more trust in Israel's gunnery. For four or five of them were busy carrying off our stores and wading out with them to one of the gigs that lay close by, pulling an oar or so to hold her steady against the current. Silver was in the stern-sheets in command; and every man of them was now provided with a musket from some secret magazine of their own.

The captain sat down to his log, and here is the beginning of the entry:

*Alexander Smollett, master; David Livesey, ship's doctor; Abraham Gray, carpenter's mate; John Trelawney, owner; John Hunter and Richard Joyce, owner's servants, landsmen—being all that is left faithful of the ship's company—with stores for ten days at short rations, came ashore this day and flew British colours on the log-house in Treasure Island. Thomas Redruth, owner's servant, landsman, shot by the mutineers; James Hawkins, cabin-boy—*

And at the same time, I was wondering over poor Jim Hawkins' fate.

A hail on the land side.

"Somebody hailing us," said Hunter, who was on guard.

"Doctor! Squire! Captain! Hullo, Hunter, is that you?" came the cries.

And I ran to the door in time to see Jim Hawkins, safe and sound, come climbing over the stockade.

## 4

# NARRATIVE RESUMED BY JIM HAWKINS: THE GARRISON IN THE STOCKADE

As soon as Ben Gunn saw the colours he came to a halt, stopped me by the arm, and sat down.

"Now," said he, "there's your friends, sure enough."

"Far more likely it's the mutineers," I answered.

"That!" he cried. "Why, in a place like this, where nobody puts in but gen'lemen of fortune, Silver would fly the Jolly Roger, you don't make no doubt of that. No, that's your friends. There's been blows too, and I reckon your friends has had the best of it; and here they are ashore in the old stockade, as was made years and years ago by Flint. Ah, he was the man to have a headpiece, was Flint! Barring rum, his match were never seen. He were afraid of none, not he; on'y Silver—Silver was that genteel."

"Well," said I, "that may be so, and so be it; all the more reason that I should hurry on and join my friends."

"Nay, mate," returned Ben, "not you. You're a good boy, or I'm mistook; but you're on'y a boy, all told. Now, Ben Gunn is fly. Rum wouldn't bring me there, where you're going—not rum wouldn't, till I see your born gen'leman and gets it on his word of honour. And you won't forget my words; 'A precious sight (that's what you'll say), a precious sight more confidence'—and then nips him."

And he pinched me the third time with the same air of cleverness.

"And when Ben Gunn is wanted, you know where to find him, Jim. Just wheer you found him today. And him that comes is to have a white thing in his hand, and he's to come alone. Oh! And you'll say this: 'Ben Gunn,' says you, 'has reasons of his own.'"

"Well," said I, "I believe I understand. You have something to propose, and you wish to see the squire or the doctor, and you're to be found where I found you. Is that all?"

"And when? says you," he added. "Why, from about noon observation to about six bells."

"Good," said I, "and now may I go?"

"You won't forget?" he inquired anxiously. "Precious sight, and reasons of his own, says you. Reasons of his own; that's the mainstay; as between man and man. Well, then"—still holding me—"I reckon you can go, Jim. And, Jim, if you was to see Silver, you wouldn't go for to sell Ben Gunn? Wild horses wouldn't draw it from you? No, says you. And if them pirates camp ashore, Jim, what would you say but there'd be widders in the morning?"

Here he was interrupted by a loud report, and a cannonball came tearing through the trees and pitched in the sand not a hundred yards from where we two were talking. The next moment each of us had taken to his heels in a different direction.

For a good hour to come frequent reports shook the island, and balls kept crashing through the woods. I moved from hiding-place to hiding-place, always pursued, or so it seemed to me, by these terrifying missiles. But towards the end of the bombardment, though still I durst not venture in the direction of the stockade, where the balls fell oftenest, I had begun, in a manner, to pluck up my heart again, and after a long detour to the east, crept down among the shore-side trees.

The sun had just set, the sea breeze was rustling and tumbling in the woods and ruffling the grey surface of the anchorage; the tide, too, was far out, and great tracts of sand lay uncovered; the air, after the heat of the day, chilled me through my jacket.

The *Hispaniola* still lay where she had anchored; but, sure enough, there was the Jolly Roger—the black flag of piracy—flying from her peak. Even as I looked, there came another red flash and another report that sent the echoes clattering, and one more round-shot whistled through the air. It was the last of the cannonade.

I lay for some time watching the bustle which succeeded the attack. Men were demolishing something with axes on the beach near the stockade—the poor jolly-boat, I afterwards discovered. Away, near the mouth of the river, a great fire was glowing among the trees, and between that point and the ship one of the gigs kept coming and going, the men, whom I had seen so gloomy, shouting at the oars like children. But there was a sound in their voices which suggested rum.

At length I thought I might return towards the stockade. I was pretty far down on the low, sandy spit that encloses the anchorage to the east, and is joined at half-water to Skeleton Island; and now, as I rose to my feet, I saw, some distance further down the spit and rising from among low bushes, an isolated rock, pretty high, and peculiarly white in colour. It occurred to me that this might be the white rock of which Ben Gunn had spoken and that some day or other a boat might be wanted and I should know where to look for one.

Then I skirted among the woods until I had regained the rear, or shoreward side, of the stockade, and was soon warmly welcomed by the faithful party.

I had soon told my story and began to look about me. The log-house was made of unsquared trunks of pine—roof, walls, and floor. The latter stood in several places as much as a foot or a foot and a half above the surface of the sand. There was a porch at the door, and under this porch the little spring welled up into an artificial basin of a rather odd kind—no other than a great ship's kettle of iron, with the bottom knocked out, and sunk "to her bearings," as the captain said, among the sand.

Little had been left besides the framework of the house, but in one corner there was a stone slab laid down by way of hearth and an old rusty iron basket to contain the fire.

The slopes of the knoll and all the inside of the stockade had been cleared of timber to build the house, and we could see by the stumps what a fine and lofty grove had been destroyed. Most of the soil had been washed away or buried in drift after the removal of the trees; only where the streamlet ran down from the kettle a thick bed of moss and some ferns and little creeping bushes were still green among the sand. Very close around the stockade—too close for defence, they said—the wood still flourished high and dense, all of fir on the land side, but towards the sea with a large admixture of live-oaks.

The cold evening breeze, of which I have spoken, whistled through every chink of the rude building and sprinkled the floor with a continual rain of fine sand. There was sand in our eyes, sand in our teeth, sand in our suppers, sand dancing in the spring at the bottom of the kettle, for all the world like porridge beginning to boil. Our chimney was a square hole in the roof; it was but a little part of the smoke that found its way out, and the rest eddied about the house and kept us coughing and piping the eye.

Add to this that Gray, the new man, had his face tied up in a bandage for a cut he had got in breaking away from the mutineers and that poor old Tom Redruth, still unburied, lay along the wall, stiff and stark, under the Union Jack.

If we had been allowed to sit idle, we should all have fallen in the blues, but Captain Smollett was never the man for that. All hands were called up before him, and he divided us into watches. The doctor and Gray and I for one; the squire, Hunter, and Joyce upon the other. Tired though we all were, two were sent out for firewood; two more were set to dig a grave for Redruth; the doctor was named cook; I was put sentry at the door; and the captain himself went from one to another, keeping up our spirits and lending a hand wherever it was wanted.

From time to time the doctor came to the door for a little air and to rest his eyes, which were almost smoked out of his head, and whenever he did so, he had a word for me.

"That man Smollett," he said once, "is a better man than I am. And when I say that it means a deal, Jim."

Another time he came and was silent for a while. Then he put his head on one side, and looked at me.

"Is this Ben Gunn a man?" he asked.

"I do not know, sir," said I. "I am not very sure whether he's sane."

"If there's any doubt about the matter, he is," returned the doctor. "A man who has been three years biting his nails on a desert island, Jim, can't expect to appear as sane as you or me. It doesn't lie in human nature. Was it cheese you said he had a fancy for?"

"Yes, sir, cheese," I answered.

"Well, Jim," says he, "just see the good that comes of being dainty in your food. You've seen my snuff-box, haven't you? And you never saw me take snuff, the reason being that in my snuff-box I carry a piece of Parmesan cheese—a cheese made in Italy, very nutritious. Well, that's for Ben Gunn!"

Before supper was eaten we buried old Tom in the sand and stood round him for a while bare-headed in the breeze. A good deal of firewood had been got in, but not enough for the captain's fancy, and he shook his head over it and told us we "must get back to this tomorrow rather livelier." Then, when we had eaten our pork and each had a good stiff glass of brandy grog, the three chiefs got together in a corner to discuss our prospects.

It appears they were at their wits' end what to do, the stores being so low that we must have been starved into surrender long before help came. But our best hope, it was decided, was to kill off the buccaneers until they either hauled down their flag or ran away with the *Hispaniola.* From nineteen they were already reduced to fifteen, two others were wounded, and one at least—the man shot beside the gun—severely wounded, if he were not dead. Every time we had a crack at them, we were to take it, saving our own lives, with the extremest care. And besides that, we had two able allies—rum and the climate.

As for the first, though we were about half a mile away, we could hear them roaring and singing late into the night; and as for the second, the doctor staked his wig that, camped where they were in the marsh and unprovided with remedies, the half of them would be on their backs before a week.

"So," he added, "if we are not all shot down first they'll be glad to be packing in the schooner. It's always a ship, and they can get to buccaneering again, I suppose."

"First ship that ever I lost," said Captain Smollett.

I was dead tired, as you may fancy; and when I got to sleep, which was not till after a great deal of tossing, I slept like a log of wood.

The rest had long been up and had already breakfasted and increased the pile of firewood by about half as much again when I was wakened by a bustle and the sound of voices.

"Flag of truce!" I heard someone say; and then, immediately after, with a cry of surprise, "Silver himself!"

And at that, up I jumped, and rubbing my eyes, ran to a loophole in the wall.

# 5
## SILVER'S EMBASSY

Sure enough, there were two men just outside the stockade, one of them waving a white cloth, the other, no less a person than Silver himself, standing placidly by.

It was still quite early, and the coldest morning that I think I ever was abroad in—a chill that pierced into the marrow. The sky was bright and cloudless overhead, and the tops of the trees shone rosily in the sun. But where Silver stood with his lieutenant, all was still in shadow, and they waded knee-deep in a low white vapour that had crawled during the night out of the morass. The chill and the vapour taken together told a poor tale of the island. It was plainly a damp, feverish, unhealthy spot.

"Keep indoors, men," said the captain. "Ten to one this is a trick."

Then he hailed the buccaneer.

"Who goes? Stand, or we fire."

"Flag of truce," cried Silver.

The captain was in the porch, keeping himself carefully out of the way of a treacherous shot, should any be intended. He turned and spoke to us, "Doctor's watch on the lookout. Dr. Livesey take the north side, if you please; Jim, the east; Gray, west. The watch below, all hands to load muskets. Lively, men, and careful."

And then he turned again to the mutineers.

"And what do you want with your flag of truce?" he cried.

This time it was the other man who replied.

"Cap'n Silver, sir, to come on board and make terms," he shouted.

"Cap'n Silver! Don't know him. Who's he?" cried the captain. And we could hear him adding to himself, "Cap'n, is it? My heart, and here's promotion!"

Long John answered for himself. "Me, sir. These poor lads have chosen me cap'n, after your desertion, sir"—laying a particular emphasis upon the word "desertion." "We're willing to submit, if we can come to terms, and no bones about it. All I ask is your word, Cap'n Smollett, to let me safe and sound out of this here stockade, and one minute to get out o' shot before a gun is fired."

"My man," said Captain Smollett, "I have not the slightest desire to talk to you. If you wish to talk to me, you can come, that's all. If there's any treachery, it'll be on your side, and the Lord help you."

"That's enough, cap'n," shouted Long John cheerily. "A word from you's enough. I know a gentleman, and you may lay to that."

We could see the man who carried the flag of truce attempting to hold Silver back. Nor was that wonderful, seeing how cavalier had been the captain's answer. But Silver laughed at him aloud and slapped him on the back as if the idea of alarm had been absurd. Then he advanced to the stockade, threw over his crutch, got a leg up, and with great vigour and skill succeeded in surmounting the fence and dropping safely to the other side.

I will confess that I was far too much taken up with what was going on to be of the slightest use as sentry; indeed, I had already deserted my eastern loophole and crept up behind the captain, who had now seated himself on the threshold, with his elbows on his knees, his head in his hands, and his eyes fixed on the water as it bubbled out of the old iron kettle in the sand. He was whistling "Come, Lasses and Lads."

Silver had terrible hard work getting up the knoll. What with the steepness of the incline, the thick tree stumps, and the soft sand, he and his crutch were as helpless as a ship in stays. But he stuck to it like a man in silence, and at last arrived before the captain, whom he saluted in the handsomest style. He was tricked out in his best; an immense blue coat, thick with brass buttons, hung as low as to his knees, and a fine laced hat was set on the back of his head.

"Here you are, my man," said the captain, raising his head. "You had better sit down."

"You ain't a-going to let me inside, cap'n?" complained Long John. "It's a main cold morning, to be sure, sir, to sit outside upon the sand."

"Why, Silver," said the captain, "if you had pleased to be an honest man, you might have been sitting in your galley. It's your own doing. You're either my ship's cook—and then you were treated handsome—or Cap'n Silver, a common mutineer and pirate, and then you can go hang!"

"Well, well, cap'n," returned the sea-cook, sitting down as he was bidden on the sand, "you'll have to give me a hand up again, that's all. A sweet pretty place you have of it here. Ah, there's Jim! The top of the morning to you, Jim. Doctor, here's my service. Why, there you all are together like a happy family, in a manner of speaking."

"If you have anything to say, my man, better say it," said the captain.

"Right you were, Cap'n Smollett," replied Silver. "Dooty is dooty, to be sure. Well now, you look here, that was a good lay of yours last night. I don't deny it was a good lay. Some of you pretty handy with a handspike-end. And I'll not deny neither but what some of my people was shook—maybe all was shook; maybe I was shook myself; maybe that's why I'm here for terms. But you mark me, cap'n, it won't do twice, by thunder! We'll have to do sentry-go and ease off a point or so on the rum. Maybe you think we were all a sheet in the wind's eye. But I'll tell you I was sober; I was on'y dog tired; and if I'd awoke a second sooner, I'd 'a caught you at the act, I would. He wasn't dead when I got round to him, not he."

"Well?" says Captain Smollett as cool as can be.

All that Silver said was a riddle to him, but you would never have guessed it from his tone. As for me, I began to have an inkling. Ben Gunn's last words came back to my mind. I began to suppose that he had paid the buccaneers a visit while they all lay drunk together round their fire, and I reckoned up with glee that we had only fourteen enemies to deal with.

"Well, here it is," said Silver. "We want that treasure, and we'll have it—that's our point!

You would just as soon save your lives, I reckon; and that's yours. You have a chart, haven't you?"

"That's as may be," replied the captain.

"Oh, well, you have, I know that," returned Long John. "You needn't be so husky with a man; there ain't a particle of service in that, and you may lay to it. What I mean is, we want your chart. Now, I never meant you no harm, myself."

"That won't do with me, my man," interrupted the captain. "We know exactly what you meant to do, and we don't care, for now, you see, you can't do it."

And the captain looked at him calmly and proceeded to fill a pipe.

"If Abe Gray—" Silver broke out.

"Avast there!" cried Mr. Smollett. "Gray told me nothing, and I asked him nothing; and what's more, I would see you and him and this whole island blown clean out of the water into blazes first. So there's my mind for you, my man, on that."

This little whiff of temper seemed to cool Silver down. He had been growing nettled before, but now he pulled himself together.

"Like enough," said he. "I would set no limits to what gentlemen might consider shipshape, or might not, as the case were. And seein' as how you are about to take a pipe, cap'n, I'll make so free as do likewise."

And he filled a pipe and lighted it; and the two men sat silently smoking for quite a while, now looking each other in the face, now stopping their tobacco, now leaning forward to spit. It was as good as the play to see them.

"Now," resumed Silver, "here it is. You give us the chart to get the treasure by, and drop shooting poor seamen and stoving of their heads in while asleep. You do that, and we'll offer you a choice. Either you come aboard along of us, once the treasure shipped, and then I'll give you my affy-davy, upon my word of honour, to clap you somewhere safe ashore. Or if that ain't to your fancy, some of my hands being rough and having old scores on account of hazing, then you can stay here, you can. We'll divide stores with you, man for man; and I'll give my affy-davy, as before to speak the first ship I sight, and send 'em here to pick you up. Now, you'll own that's talking. Handsomer you couldn't look to get, now you. And I hope"—raising his voice—"that all hands in this here block house will overhaul my words, for what is spoke to one is spoke to all."

Captain Smollett rose from his seat and knocked out the ashes of his pipe in the palm of his left hand.

"Is that all?" he asked.

"Every last word, by thunder!" answered John. "Refuse that, and you've seen the last of me but musket-balls."

"Very good," said the captain. "Now you'll hear me. If you'll come up one by one, unarmed, I'll engage to clap you all in irons and take you home to a fair trial in England. If you won't, my name is Alexander Smollett, I've flown my sovereign's colours, and I'll see you all to Davy Jones. You can't find the treasure. You can't sail the ship—there's not a man among you fit to sail the ship. You can't fight us—Gray, there, got away from five of you. Your ship's in irons, Master Silver; you're on a lee shore, and so you'll find. I stand here and tell you so; and they're the last good words you'll get from me, for in the name of heaven, I'll put a bullet in your back when next I meet you. Tramp, my lad. Bundle out of this, please, hand over hand, and double quick."

Silver's face was a picture; his eyes started in his head with wrath. He shook the fire out of his pipe.

"Give me a hand up!" he cried.

"Not I," returned the captain.

"Who'll give me a hand up?" he roared.

Not a man among us moved. Growling the foulest imprecations, he crawled along the sand till he got hold of the porch and could hoist himself again upon his crutch. Then he spat into the spring.

"There!" he cried. "That's what I think of ye. Before an hour's out, I'll stove in your old block house like a rum puncheon. Laugh, by thunder, laugh! Before an hour's out, ye'll laugh upon the other side. Them that die'll be the lucky ones."

And with a dreadful oath he stumbled off, ploughed down the sand, was helped across the stockade, after four or five failures, by the man with the flag of truce, and disappeared in an instant afterwards among the trees.

## 6

# THE ATTACK

As soon as Silver disappeared, the captain, who had been closely watching him, turned towards the interior of the house and found not a man of us at his post but Gray. It was the first time we had ever seen him angry.

"Quarters!" he roared. And then, as we all slunk back to our places, "Gray," he said, "I'll put your name in the log; you've stood by your duty like a seaman. Mr. Trelawney, I'm surprised at you, sir. Doctor, I thought you had worn the king's coat! If that was how you served at Fontenoy, sir, you'd have been better in your berth."

The doctor's watch were all back at their loopholes, the rest were busy loading the spare muskets, and everyone with a red face, you may be certain, and a flea in his ear, as the saying is.

The captain looked on for a while in silence. Then he spoke.

"My lads," said he, "I've given Silver a broadside. I pitched it in red-hot on purpose; and before the hour's out, as he said, we shall be boarded. We're outnumbered, I needn't tell you that, but we fight in shelter; and a minute ago I should have said we fought with discipline. I've no manner of doubt that we can drub them, if you choose."

Then he went the rounds and saw, as he said, that all was clear.

On the two short sides of the house, east and west, there were only two loopholes; on the south side where the porch was, two again; and on the north side, five. There was a round score of muskets for the seven of us; the firewood had been built into four piles—tables, you might say—one about the middle of each side, and on each of these tables some ammunition and four loaded muskets were laid ready to the hand of the defenders. In the middle, the cutlasses lay ranged.

"Toss out the fire," said the captain; "the chill is past, and we mustn't have smoke in our eyes."

The iron fire-basket was carried bodily out by Mr. Trelawney, and the embers smothered among sand.

"Hawkins hasn't had his breakfast. Hawkins, help yourself, and back to your post to eat it," continued Captain Smollett. "Lively, now, my lad; you'll want it before you've done. Hunter, serve out a round of brandy to all hands."

And while this was going on, the captain completed, in his own mind, the plan of the defence.

"Doctor, you will take the door," he resumed. "See, and don't expose yourself; keep within, and fire through the porch. Hunter, take the east side, there. Joyce, you stand by the west, my man. Mr. Trelawney, you are the best shot—you and Gray will take this long north side, with the five loopholes; it's there the danger is. If they can get up to it and fire in upon us through our own ports, things would begin to look dirty. Hawkins, neither you nor I are much account at the shooting; we'll stand by to load and bear a hand."

As the captain had said, the chill was past. As soon as the sun had climbed above our girdle of trees, it fell with all its force upon the clearing and drank up the vapours at a draught. Soon the sand was baking and the resin melting in the logs of the block house. Jackets and coats were flung aside, shirts thrown open at the neck and rolled up to the shoulders; and we stood there, each at his post, in a fever of heat and anxiety.

An hour passed away.

"Hang them!" said the captain. "This is as dull as the doldrums. Gray, whistle for a wind."

And just at that moment came the first news of the attack.

"If you please, sir," said Joyce, "if I see anyone, am I to fire?"

"I told you so!" cried the captain.

"Thank you, sir," returned Joyce with the same quiet civility.

Nothing followed for a time, but the remark had set us all on the alert, straining ears and eyes—the musketeers with their pieces balanced in their hands, the captain out in the middle of the block house with his mouth very tight and a frown on his face.

So some seconds passed, till suddenly Joyce whipped up his musket and fired. The report had scarcely died away ere it was repeated and repeated from without in a scattering volley, shot behind shot, like a string of geese, from every side of the enclosure. Several bullets struck the log-house, but not one entered; and as the smoke cleared away and vanished, the stockade and the woods around it looked as quiet and empty as before. Not a bough waved, not the gleam of a musket-barrel betrayed the presence of our foes.

"Did you hit your man?" asked the captain.

"No, sir," replied Joyce. "I believe not, sir."

"Next best thing to tell the truth," muttered Captain Smollett. "Load his gun, Hawkins. How many should say there were on your side, doctor?"

"I know precisely," said Dr. Livesey. "Three shots were fired on this side. I saw the three flashes—two close together—one farther to the west."

"Three!" repeated the captain. "And how many on yours, Mr. Trelawney?"

But this was not so easily answered. There had come many from the north—seven by the squire's computation, eight or nine according to Gray. From the east and west only a single shot had been fired. It was plain, therefore, that the attack would be developed from the north and that on the other three sides we were only to be annoyed by a show of hostilities. But Captain Smollett made no change in his arrangements. If the mutineers succeeded in crossing the stockade, he argued, they would take possession of any unprotected loophole and shoot us down like rats in our own stronghold.

Nor had we much time left to us for thought. Suddenly, with a loud huzza, a little cloud of pirates leaped from the woods on the north side and ran straight on the stockade. At the same moment, the fire was once more opened from the woods, and a rifle ball sang through the doorway and knocked the doctor's musket into bits.

The boarders swarmed over the fence like monkeys. Squire and Gray fired again and yet again; three men fell, one forwards into the enclosure, two back on the outside. But of these, one was evidently more frightened than hurt, for he was on his feet again in a crack and instantly disappeared among the trees.

Two had bit the dust, one had fled, four had made good their footing inside our defences, while from the shelter of the woods seven or eight men, each evidently supplied with several muskets, kept up a hot though useless fire on the log-house.

The four who had boarded made straight before them for the building, shouting as they ran, and the men among the trees shouted back to encourage them. Several shots were fired, but such was the hurry of the marksmen that not one appears to have taken effect. In a moment, the four pirates had swarmed up the mound and were upon us.

The head of Job Anderson, the boatswain, appeared at the middle loophole.

"At 'em, all hands—all hands!" he roared in a voice of thunder.

At the same moment, another pirate grasped Hunter's musket by the muzzle, wrenched it from his hands, plucked it through the loophole, and with one stunning blow, laid the poor fellow senseless on the floor. Meanwhile a third, running unharmed all around the house, appeared suddenly in the doorway and fell with his cutlass on the doctor.

Our position was utterly reversed. A moment since we were firing, under cover, at an exposed enemy; now it was we who lay uncovered and could not return a blow.

The log-house was full of smoke, to which we owed our comparative safety. Cries and confusion, the flashes and reports of pistol-shots, and one loud groan rang in my ears.

"Out, lads, out, and fight 'em in the open! Cutlasses!" cried the captain.

I snatched a cutlass from the pile, and someone, at the same time snatching another, gave me a cut across the knuckles which I hardly felt. I dashed out of the door into the clear sunlight. Someone was close behind, I knew not whom. Right in front, the doctor was pursuing his assailant down the hill, and just as my eyes fell upon him, beat down his guard and sent him sprawling on his back with a great slash across the face.

"Round the house, lads! Round the house!" cried the captain; and even in the hurly-burly, I perceived a change in his voice.

Mechanically, I obeyed, turned eastwards, and with my cutlass raised, ran round the corner of the house. Next moment I was face to face with Anderson. He roared aloud, and his hanger went up above his head, flashing in the sunlight. I had not time to be afraid, but as the blow still hung impending, leaped in a trice upon one side, and missing my foot in the soft sand, rolled headlong down the slope.

When I had first sallied from the door, the other mutineers had been already swarming up the palisade to make an end of us. One man, in a red night-cap, with his cutlass in his mouth, had even got upon the top and thrown a leg across. Well, so short had been the interval that when I found my feet again all was in the same posture, the fellow with the red night-cap still half-way over, another still just showing his head above the top of the stockade. And yet, in this breath of time, the fight was over and the victory was ours.

Gray, following close behind me, had cut down the big boatswain ere he had time to recover from his last blow. Another had been shot at a loophole in the very act of firing into the house and now lay in agony, the pistol still smoking in his hand. A third, as I had seen, the doctor had disposed of at a blow. Of the four who had scaled the palisade, one only remained unaccounted for, and he, having left his cutlass on the field, was now clambering out again with the fear of death upon him.

"Fire—fire from the house!" cried the doctor. "And you, lads, back into cover."

But his words were unheeded, no shot was fired, and the last boarder made good his escape and disappeared with the rest into the wood. In three seconds nothing remained of the attacking party but the five who had fallen, four on the inside and one on the outside of the palisade.

The doctor and Gray and I ran full speed for shelter. The survivors would soon be back where they had left their muskets, and at any moment the fire might recommence.

The house was by this time somewhat cleared of smoke, and we saw at a glance the price we had paid for victory. Hunter lay beside his loophole, stunned; Joyce by his, shot through the head, never to move again; while right in the centre, the squire was supporting the captain, one as pale as the other.

"The captain's wounded," said Mr. Trelawney.

"Have they run?" asked Mr. Smollett.

"All that could, you may be bound," returned the doctor; "but there's five of them will never run again."

"Five!" cried the captain. "Come, that's better. Five against three leaves us four to nine. That's better odds than we had at starting. We were seven to nineteen then, or thought we were, and that's as bad to bear." *

*The mutineers were soon only eight in number, for the man shot by Mr. Trelawney on board the schooner died that same evening of his wound. But this was, of course, not known till after by the faithful party.

# V

# MY SEA ADVENTURE

## I

# HOW MY SEA ADVENTURE BEGAN

There was no return of the mutineers—not so much as another shot out of the woods. They had "got their rations for that day," as the captain put it, and we had the place to ourselves and a quiet time to overhaul the wounded and get dinner. Squire and I cooked outside in spite of the danger, and even outside we could hardly tell what we were at, for horror of the loud groans that reached us from the doctor's patients.

Out of the eight men who had fallen in the action, only three still breathed—that one of the pirates who had been shot at the loophole, Hunter, and Captain Smollett; and of these, the first two were as good as dead; the mutineer indeed died under the doctor's knife, and Hunter, do what we could, never recovered consciousness in this world. He lingered all day, breathing loudly like the old buccaneer at home in his apoplectic fit, but the bones of his chest had been crushed by the blow and his skull fractured in falling, and some time in the following night, without sign or sound, he went to his Maker.

As for the captain, his wounds were grievous indeed, but not dangerous. No organ was fatally injured. Anderson's ball—for it was Job that shot him first—had broken his shoulder-blade and touched the lung, not badly; the second had only torn and displaced some muscles in the calf. He was sure to recover, the doctor said, but in the meantime, and for weeks to come, he must not walk nor move his arm, nor so much as speak when he could help it.

My own accidental cut across the knuckles was a flea-bite. Doctor Livesey patched it up with plaster and pulled my ears for me into the bargain.

After dinner the squire and the doctor sat by the captain's side awhile in consultation; and when they had talked to their hearts' content, it being then a little past noon, the doctor took up his hat and pistols, girt on a cutlass, put the chart in his pocket, and with a musket over his shoulder crossed the palisade on the north side and set off briskly through the trees.

Gray and I were sitting together at the far end of the block house, to be out of earshot of our officers consulting; and Gray took his pipe out of his mouth and fairly forgot to put it back again, so thunder-struck he was at this occurrence.

"Why, in the name of Davy Jones," said he, "is Dr. Livesey mad?"

"Why no," says I. "He's about the last of this crew for that, I take it."

"Well, shipmate," said Gray, "mad he may not be; but if *he's* not, you mark my words, *I* am."

"I take it," replied I, "the doctor has his idea; and if I am right, he's going now to see Ben Gunn."

I was right, as appeared later; but in the meantime, the house being stifling hot and the little patch of sand inside the palisade ablaze with midday sun, I began to get another thought into my head, which was not by any means so right. What I began to do was to envy the doctor walking in the cool shadow of the woods with the birds about him and the pleasant smell of the pines, while I sat grilling, with my clothes stuck to the hot resin, and so much blood about me and so many poor dead bodies lying all around that I took a disgust of the place that was almost as strong as fear.

All the time I was washing out the block house, and then washing up the things from dinner, this disgust and envy kept growing stronger and stronger, till at last, being near a bread-bag, and no one then observing me, I took the first step towards my escapade and filled both pockets of my coat with biscuit.

I was a fool, if you like, and certainly I was going to do a foolish, over-bold act; but I was determined to do it with all the precautions in my power. These biscuits, should anything befall me, would keep me, at least, from starving till far on in the next day.

The next thing I laid hold of was a brace of pistols, and as I already had a powder-horn and bullets, I felt myself well supplied with arms.

As for the scheme I had in my head, it was not a bad one in itself. I was to go down the sandy spit that divides the anchorage on the east from the open sea, find the white rock I had observed last evening, and ascertain whether it was there or not that Ben Gunn had hidden his boat, a thing quite worth doing, as I still believe. But as I was certain I should not be allowed to leave the enclosure, my only plan was to take French leave and slip out when nobody was watching, and that was so bad a way of doing it as made the thing itself wrong. But I was only a boy, and I had made my mind up.

Well, as things at last fell out, I found an admirable opportunity. The squire and Gray were busy helping the captain with his bandages, the coast was clear, I made a bolt for it over the stockade and into the thickest of the trees, and before my absence was observed I was out of cry of my companions.

This was my second folly, far worse than the first, as I left but two sound men to guard the house; but like the first, it was a help towards saving all of us.

I took my way straight for the east coast of the island, for I was determined to go down the sea side of the spit to avoid all chance of observation from the anchorage. It was already late in the afternoon, although still warm and sunny. As I continued to thread the tall woods, I could hear from far before me not only the continuous thunder of the surf, but a certain tossing of foliage and grinding of boughs which showed me the sea breeze had set in higher than usual. Soon cool draughts of air began to reach me, and a few steps farther I came forth into the open borders of the grove, and saw the sea lying blue and sunny to the horizon and the surf tumbling and tossing its foam along the beach.

I have never seen the sea quiet round Treasure Island. The sun might blaze overhead, the air be without a breath, the surface smooth and blue, but still these great rollers would be running along all the external coast, thundering and thundering by day and night; and I scarce believe there is one spot in the island where a man would be out of earshot of their noise.

I walked along beside the surf with great enjoyment, till, thinking I was now got far enough to the south, I took the cover of some thick bushes and crept warily up to the ridge of the spit.

Behind me was the sea, in front the anchorage. The sea breeze, as though it had the sooner blown itself out by its unusual violence, was already at an end; it had been succeeded by light, variable airs from the south and south-east, carrying great banks of fog; and the anchorage, under lee of Skeleton Island, lay still and leaden as when first we entered it. The *Hispaniola,* in that unbroken mirror, was exactly portrayed from the truck to the waterline, the Jolly Roger hanging from her peak.

Alongside lay one of the gigs, Silver in the stern-sheets—him I could always recognize—while a couple of men were leaning over the stern bulwarks, one of them with a red cap—the very rogue that I had seen some hours before stride-legs upon the palisade. Apparently they were talking and laughing, though at that distance—upwards of a mile—I could, of course, hear no word of what was said. All at once there began the most horrid, unearthly screaming, which at first startled me badly, though I had soon remembered the voice of Captain Flint and even thought I could make out the bird by her bright plumage as she sat perched upon her master's wrist.

Soon after, the jolly-boat shoved off and pulled for shore, and the man with the red cap and his comrade went below by the cabin companion.

Just about the same time, the sun had gone down behind the Spy-glass, and as the fog was collecting rapidly, it began to grow dark in earnest. I saw I must lose no time if I were to find the boat that evening.

The white rock, visible enough above the brush, was still some eighth of a mile further down the spit, and it took me a goodish while to get up with it, crawling, often on all fours, among the scrub. Night had almost come when I laid my hand on its rough sides. Right below it there was an exceedingly small hollow of green turf, hidden by banks and a thick underwood about knee-deep, that grew there very plentifully; and in the centre of the dell, sure enough, a little tent of goat-skins, like what the gipsies carry about with them in England.

I dropped into the hollow, lifted the side of the tent, and there was Ben Gunn's boat—home-made if ever anything was home-made; a rude, lop-sided framework of tough wood, and stretched upon that a covering of goat-skin, with the hair inside. The thing was extremely small, even for me, and I can hardly imagine that it could have floated with a full-sized man. There was one thwart set as low as possible, a kind of stretcher in the bows, and a double paddle for propulsion.

I had not then seen a coracle, such as the ancient Britons made, but I have seen one since, and I can give you no fairer idea of Ben Gunn's boat than by saying it was like the first and the worst coracle ever made by man. But the great advantage of the coracle it certainly possessed, for it was exceedingly light and portable.

Well, now that I had found the boat, you would have thought I had had enough of truantry for once, but in the meantime I had taken another notion and become so obstinately fond of it that I would have carried it out, I believe, in the teeth of Captain Smollett himself. This was to slip out under cover of the night, cut the *Hispaniola* adrift, and let her go ashore where she fancied. I had quite made up my mind that the mutineers, after their repulse of the morning, had nothing nearer their hearts than to up anchor and away to sea; this, I thought, it would be a fine thing to prevent, and now that I had seen how they left their watchmen unprovided with a boat, I thought it might be done with little risk.

Down I sat to wait for darkness, and made a hearty meal of biscuit. It was a night out of ten thousand for my purpose. The fog had now buried all heaven. As the last rays of daylight dwindled and disappeared, absolute blackness settled down on Treasure Island. And when, at last, I shouldered the coracle and groped my way stumblingly out of the hollow where I had supped, there were but two points visible on the whole anchorage.

One was the great fire on shore, by which the defeated pirates lay carousing in the swamp. The other, a mere blur of light upon the darkness, indicated the position of the anchored ship. She had swung round to the ebb—her bow was now towards me—the only lights on board were in the cabin, and what I saw was merely a reflection on the fog of the strong rays that flowed from the stern window.

The ebb had already run some time, and I had to wade through a long belt of swampy sand, where I sank several times above the ankle, before I came to the edge of the retreating water, and wading a little way in, with some strength and dexterity, set my coracle, keel downwards, on the surface.

## 2

# THE EBB-TIDE RUNS

The coracle—as I had ample reason to know before I was done with her—was a very safe boat for a person of my height and weight, both buoyant and clever in a seaway; but she was the most cross-grained, lop-sided craft to manage. Do as you pleased, she always made more leeway than anything else, and turning round and round was the manoeuvre she was best at. Even Ben Gunn himself has admitted that she was "queer to handle till you knew her way."

Certainly I did not know her way. She turned in every direction but the one I was bound to go; the most part of the time we were broadside on, and I am very sure I never should have made the ship at all but for the tide. By good fortune, paddle as I pleased, the tide was still sweeping me down; and there lay the *Hispaniola* right in the fairway, hardly to be missed.

First she loomed before me like a blot of something yet blacker than darkness, then her spars and hull began to take shape, and the next moment, as it seemed (for, the farther I went, the brisker grew the current of the ebb), I was alongside of her hawser and had laid hold.

The hawser was as taut as a bowstring, and the current so strong she pulled upon her anchor. All round the hull, in the blackness, the rippling current bubbled and chattered like a little mountain stream. One cut with my sea-gully and the *Hispaniola* would go humming down the tide.

So far so good, but it next occurred to my recollection that a taut hawser, suddenly cut, is a thing as dangerous as a kicking horse. Ten to one, if I were so foolhardy as to cut the *Hispaniola* from her anchor, I and the coracle would be knocked clean out of the water.

This brought me to a full stop, and if fortune had not again particularly favoured me, I should have had to abandon my design. But the light airs which had begun blowing from the south-east and south had hauled round after nightfall into the south-west. Just while I was meditating, a puff came, caught the *Hispaniola*, and forced her up into the current; and to my great joy, I felt the hawser slacken in my grasp, and the hand by which I held it dip for a second under water.

With that I made my mind up, took out my gully, opened it with my teeth, and cut one strand after another, till the vessel swung only by two. Then I lay quiet, waiting to sever these last when the strain should be once more lightened by a breath of wind.

All this time I had heard the sound of loud voices from the cabin, but to say truth, my mind had been so entirely taken up with other thoughts that I had scarcely given ear. Now, however, when I had nothing else to do, I began to pay more heed.

One I recognized for the coxswain's, Israel Hands, that had been Flint's gunner in former days. The other was, of course, my friend of the red night-cap. Both men were plainly the worse of drink, and they were still drinking, for even while I was listening, one of them, with a drunken cry, opened the stern window and threw out something, which I divined to be an empty bottle. But they were not only tipsy; it was plain that they were furiously angry. Oaths flew like hailstones, and every now and then there came forth such an explosion as I thought was sure to end in blows. But each time the quarrel passed off and the voices grumbled lower for a while, until the next crisis came and in its turn passed away without result.

On shore, I could see the glow of the great camp-fire burning warmly through the shore-side trees. Someone was singing, a dull, old, droning sailor's song, with a droop and a quaver at the end of every verse, and seemingly no end to it at all but the patience of the singer. I had heard it on the voyage more than once and remembered these words:

"But one man of her crew alive,
What put to sea with seventy-five."

And I thought it was a ditty rather too dolefully appropriate for a company that had met such cruel losses in the morning. But, indeed, from what I saw, all these buccaneers were as callous as the sea they sailed on.

At last the breeze came; the schooner sidled and drew nearer in the dark; I felt the hawser slacken once more, and with a good, tough effort, cut the last fibres through.

The breeze had but little action on the coracle, and I was almost instantly swept against the bows of the *Hispaniola.* At the same time, the schooner began to turn upon her heel, spinning slowly, end for end, across the current.

I wrought like a fiend, for I expected every moment to be swamped; and since I found I could not push the coracle directly off, I now shoved straight astern. At length I was clear of my dangerous neighbour, and just as I gave the last impulsion, my hands came across a light cord that was trailing overboard across the stern bulwarks. Instantly I grasped it.

Why I should have done so I can hardly say. It was at first mere instinct, but once I had it in my hands and found it fast, curiosity began to get the upper hand, and I determined I should have one look through the cabin window.

I pulled in hand over hand on the cord, and when I judged myself near enough, rose at infinite risk to about half my height and thus commanded the roof and a slice of the interior of the cabin.

By this time the schooner and her little consort were gliding pretty swiftly through the water; indeed, we had already fetched up level with the camp-fire. The ship was talking, as sailors say, loudly, treading the innumerable ripples with an incessant weltering splash; and until I got my eye above the window-sill I could not comprehend why the watchmen had taken no alarm. One glance, however, was sufficient; and it was only one glance that I durst take from that unsteady skiff. It showed me Hands and his companion locked together in deadly wrestle, each with a hand upon the other's throat.

I dropped upon the thwart again, none too soon, for I was near overboard. I could see nothing for the moment but these two furious, encrimsoned faces swaying together under the smoky lamp, and I shut my eyes to let them grow once more familiar with the darkness.

The endless ballad had come to an end at last, and the whole diminished company about the camp-fire had broken into the chorus I had heard so often:

"Fifteen men on the dead man's chest—
Yo-ho-ho, and a bottle of rum!
Drink and the devil had done for the rest—
Yo-ho-ho, and a bottle of rum!"

I was just thinking how busy drink and the devil were at that very moment in the cabin of the *Hispaniola,* when I was surprised by a sudden lurch of the coracle. At the same moment, she yawed sharply and seemed to change her course. The speed in the meantime had strangely increased.

I opened my eyes at once. All round me were little ripples, combing over with a sharp, bristling sound and slightly phosphorescent. The *Hispaniola* herself, a few yards in whose wake I was still being whirled along, seemed to stagger in her course, and I saw her spars toss a little against the blackness of the night; nay, as I looked longer, I made sure she also was wheeling to the southward.

I glanced over my shoulder, and my heart jumped against my ribs. There, right behind me, was the glow of the camp-fire. The current had turned at right angles, sweeping round along with it the tall schooner and the little dancing coracle; ever quickening, ever bubbling higher, ever muttering louder, it went spinning through the narrows for the open sea.

Suddenly the schooner in front of me gave a violent yaw, turning, perhaps, through twenty degrees; and almost at the same moment one shout followed another from on board; I could hear feet pounding on the companion ladder and I knew that the two drunkards had at last been interrupted in their quarrel and awakened to a sense of their disaster.

I lay down flat in the bottom of that wretched skiff and devoutly recommended my spirit to its Maker. At the end of the straits, I made sure we must fall into some bar of raging breakers, where all my troubles would be ended speedily; and though I could, perhaps, bear to die, I could not bear to look upon my fate as it approached.

So I must have lain for hours, continually beaten to and fro upon the billows, now and again wetted with flying sprays, and never ceasing to expect death at the next plunge. Gradually weariness grew upon me; a numbness, an occasional stupor, fell upon my mind even in the midst of my terrors, until sleep at last supervened and in my sea-tossed coracle I lay and dreamed of home and the old Admiral Benbow.

## ⁂ 3 ⁂

# THE CRUISE OF THE CORACLE

It was broad day when I awoke and found myself tossing at the south-west end of Treasure Island. The sun was up but was still hid from me behind the great bulk of the Spy-glass, which on this side descended almost to the sea in formidable cliffs.

Haulbowline Head and Mizzen-mast Hill were at my elbow, the hill bare and dark, the head bound with cliffs forty or fifty feet high and fringed with great masses of fallen rock. I was scarce a quarter of a mile to seaward, and it was my first thought to paddle in and land.

That notion was soon given over. Among the fallen rocks the breakers spouted and bellowed; loud reverberations, heavy sprays flying and falling, succeeded one another from second to second; and I saw myself, if I ventured nearer, dashed to death upon the rough shore or spending my strength in vain to scale the beetling crags.

Nor was that all, for crawling together on flat tables of rock or letting themselves drop into the sea with loud reports I beheld huge slimy monsters—soft snails, as it were, of incredible bigness—two or three score of them together, making the rocks to echo with their barkings.

I have understood since that they were sea lions, and entirely harmless. But the look of them, added to the difficulty of the shore and the high running of the surf, was more than enough to disgust me of that landing-place. I felt willing rather to starve at sea than to confront such perils.

In the meantime I had a better chance, as I supposed, before me. North of Haulbowline Head, the land runs in a long way, leaving at low tide a long stretch of yellow sand. To the north of that, again, there comes another cape—Cape of the Woods, as it was marked upon the chart—buried in tall green pines, which descended to the margin of the sea.

I remembered what Silver had said about the current that sets northward along the whole west coast of Treasure Island, and seeing from my position that I was already under its influence, I preferred to leave Haulbowline Head behind me and reserve my strength for an attempt to land upon the kindlier-looking Cape of the Woods.

There was a great, smooth swell upon the sea. The wind blowing steady and gentle from the south, there was no contrariety between that and the current, and the billows rose and fell unbroken.

Had it been otherwise, I must long ago have perished; but as it was, it is surprising how easily and securely my little and light boat could ride. Often, as I still lay at the bottom and kept no more than an eye above the gunwale, I would see a big blue summit heaving close above me; yet the coracle would but bounce a little, dance as if on springs, and subside on the other side into the trough as lightly as a bird.

I began after a little to grow very bold and sat up to try my skill at paddling. But even a small change in the disposition of the weight will produce violent changes in the behaviour of a coracle. And I had hardly moved before the boat, giving up at once her gentle dancing movement, ran straight down a slope of water so steep that it made me giddy, and struck her nose, with a spout of spray, deep into the side of the next wave.

I was drenched and terrified, and fell instantly back into my old position, whereupon the coracle seemed to find her head again and led me as softly as before among the billows. It was plain she was not to be interfered with, and at that rate, since I could in no way influence her course, what hope had I left of reaching land?

I began to be horribly frightened, but I kept my head, for all that. First, moving with all care, I gradually baled out the coracle with my sea-cap; then, getting my eye once more above the gunwale, I set myself to study how it was she managed to slip so quietly through the rollers.

I found each wave, instead of the big, smooth glossy mountain it looks from shore or from a vessel's deck, was for all the world like any range of hills on dry land, full of peaks and smooth places and valleys. The coracle, left to herself, turning from side to side, threaded, so to speak, her way through these lower parts and avoided the steep slopes and higher, toppling summits of the wave.

"Well, now," thought I to myself, "it is plain I must lie where I am and not disturb the balance; but it is plain also that I can put the paddle over the side and from time to time, in smooth places, give her a shove or two towards land." No sooner thought upon than done. There I lay on my elbows in the most trying attitude, and every now and again gave a weak stroke or two to turn her head to shore.

It was very tiring and slow work, yet I did visibly gain ground; and as we drew near the Cape of the Woods, though I saw I must infallibly miss that point, I had still made some hundred yards of easting. I was, indeed, close in. I could see the cool green tree-tops swaying together in the breeze, and I felt sure I should make the next promontory without fail.

It was high time, for I now began to be tortured with thirst. The glow of the sun from above, its thousandfold reflection from the waves, the sea-water that fell and dried upon me, caking my very lips with salt, combined to make my throat burn and my brain ache. The sight of the trees so near at hand had almost made me sick with longing, but the current had soon carried me past the point, and as the next reach of sea opened out, I beheld a sight that changed the nature of my thoughts.

Right in front of me, not half a mile away, I beheld the *Hispaniola* under sail. I made sure, of course, that I should be taken; but I was so distressed for want of water that I scarce knew whether to be glad or sorry at the thought, and long before I had come to a conclusion, surprise had taken entire possession of my mind and I could do nothing but stare and wonder.

The *Hispaniola* was under her main-sail and two jibs, and the beautiful white canvas shone in the sun like snow or silver. When I first sighted her, all her sails were drawing; she was lying a course about north-west, and I presumed the men on board were going round the island on their way back to the anchorage. Presently she began to fetch more and more to the westward, so that I thought they had sighted me and were going about in chase. At last, however, she fell right into the wind's eye, was taken dead aback, and stood there awhile helpless, with her sails shivering.

"Clumsy fellows," said I; "they must still be drunk as owls." And I thought how Captain Smollett would have set them skipping.

Meanwhile the schooner gradually fell off and filled again upon another tack, sailed swiftly for a minute or so, and brought up once more dead in the wind's eye. Again and again was this repeated. To and fro, up and down, north, south, east, and west, the *Hispaniola* sailed by swoops and dashes, and at each repetition ended as she had begun, with idly flapping canvas. It became plain to me that nobody was steering. And if so, where were the men? Either they were dead drunk or had deserted her, I thought, and perhaps if I could get on board I might return the vessel to her captain.

The current was bearing coracle and schooner southward at an equal rate. As for the latter's sailing, it was so wild and intermittent, and she hung each time so long in irons, that she certainly gained nothing, if she did not even lose. If only I dared to sit up and paddle, I made sure that I could overhaul her. The scheme had an air of adventure that inspired me, and the thought of the water breaker beside the fore companion doubled my growing courage.

Up I got, was welcomed almost instantly by another cloud of spray, but this time stuck to my purpose and set myself, with all my strength and caution, to paddle after the unsteered *Hispaniola.* Once I shipped a sea so heavy that I had to stop and bail, with my heart fluttering like a bird, but gradually I got into the way of the thing and guided my coracle among the waves, with only now and then a blow upon her bows and a dash of foam in my face.

I was now gaining rapidly on the schooner; I could see the brass glisten on the tiller as it banged about, and still no soul appeared upon her decks. I could not choose but suppose she was deserted. If not, the men were lying drunk below, where I might batten them down, perhaps, and do what I chose with the ship.

For some time she had been doing the worse thing possible for me—standing still. She headed nearly due south, yawing, of course, all the time. Each time she fell off, her sails partly filled, and these brought her in a moment right to the wind again. I have said this was the worst thing possible for me, for helpless as she looked in this situation, with the canvas cracking like cannon and the blocks trundling and banging on the deck, she still continued to run away from me, not only with the speed of the current, but by the whole amount of her leeway, which was naturally great.

But now, at last, I had my chance. The breeze fell for some seconds, very low, and the current gradually turning her, the *Hispaniola* revolved slowly round her centre and at last presented me her stern, with the cabin window still gaping open and the lamp over the table still burning on into the day. The main-sail hung drooped like a banner. She was stock-still but for the current.

For the last little while I had even lost, but now redoubling my efforts, I began once more to overhaul the chase.

I was not a hundred yards from her when the wind came again in a clap; she filled on the port tack and was off again, stooping and skimming like a swallow.

My first impulse was one of despair, but my second was towards joy. Round she came, till she was broadside on to me—round still till she had covered a half and then two thirds and then three quarters of the distance that separated us. I could see the waves boiling white under her forefoot. Immensely tall she looked to me from my low station in the coracle.

And then, of a sudden, I began to comprehend. I had scarce time to think—scarce time to act and save myself. I was on the summit of one swell when the schooner came stooping over the next. The bowsprit was over my head. I sprang to my feet and leaped, stamping the coracle under water. With one hand I caught the jib-boom, while my foot was lodged between the stay and the brace; and as I still clung there panting, a dull blow told me that the schooner had charged down upon and struck the coracle and that I was left without retreat on the *Hispaniola*.

## 4

# I STRIKE THE JOLLY ROGER

I had scarce gained a position on the bowsprit when the flying jib flapped and filled upon the other tack, with a report like a gun. The schooner trembled to her keel under the reverse, but next moment, the other sails still drawing, the jib flapped back again and hung idle.

This had nearly tossed me off into the sea; and now I lost no time, crawled back along the bowsprit, and tumbled head foremost on the deck.

I was on the lee side of the forecastle, and the mainsail, which was still drawing, concealed from me a certain portion of the after-deck. Not a soul was to be seen. The planks, which had not been swabbed since the mutiny, bore the print of many feet, and an empty bottle, broken by the neck, tumbled to and fro like a live thing in the scuppers.

Suddenly the *Hispaniola* came right into the wind. The jibs behind me cracked aloud, the rudder slammed to, the whole ship gave a sickening heave and shudder, and at the same moment the main-boom swung inboard, the sheet groaning in the blocks, and showed me the lee after-deck.

There were the two watchmen, sure enough: red-cap on his back, as stiff as a handspike, with his arms stretched out like those of a crucifix and his teeth showing through his open lips; Israel Hands propped against the bulwarks, his chin on his chest, his hands lying open before him on the deck, his face as white, under its tan, as a tallow candle.

For a while the ship kept bucking and sidling like a vicious horse, the sails filling, now on one tack, now on another, and the boom swinging to and fro till the mast groaned aloud under the strain. Now and again too there would come a cloud of light sprays over the bulwark and a heavy blow of the ship's bows against the swell; so much heavier weather was made of it by this great rigged ship than by my home-made, lop-sided coracle, now gone to the bottom of the sea.

At every jump of the schooner, red-cap slipped to and fro, but—what was ghastly to behold—neither his attitude nor his fixed teeth-disclosing grin was anyway disturbed by this rough usage. At every jump too, Hands appeared still more to sink into himself and settle down upon the deck, his feet sliding ever the farther out, and the whole body canting towards the stern, so that his face became, little by little, hid from me; and at last I could see nothing beyond his ear and the frayed ringlet of one whisker.

At the same time, I observed, around both of them, splashes of dark blood upon the planks and began to feel sure that they had killed each other in their drunken wrath.

While I was thus looking and wondering, in a calm moment, when the ship was still, Israel Hands turned partly round and with a low moan writhed himself back to the position in which I had seen him first. The moan, which told of pain and deadly weakness, and the way in which his jaw hung open went right to my heart. But when I remembered the talk I had overheard from the apple barrel, all pity left me.

I walked aft until I reached the main-mast.

"Come aboard, Mr. Hands," I said ironically.

He rolled his eyes round heavily, but he was too far gone to express surprise. All he could do was to utter one word, "Brandy."

It occurred to me there was no time to lose, and dodging the boom as it once more lurched across the deck, I slipped aft and down the companion stairs into the cabin.

It was such a scene of confusion as you can hardly fancy. All the lockfast places had been broken open in quest of the chart. The floor was thick with mud where ruffians had sat down to drink or consult after wading in the marshes round their camp. The bulkheads, all painted in clear white and beaded round with gilt, bore a pattern of dirty hands. Dozens of empty bottles clinked together in corners to the rolling of the ship. One of the doctor's medical books lay open on the table, half of the leaves gutted out, I suppose, for pipelights. In the midst of all this the lamp still cast a smoky glow, obscure and brown as umber.

I went into the cellar; all the barrels were gone, and of the bottles a most surprising number had been drunk out and thrown away. Certainly, since the mutiny began, not a man of them could ever have been sober.

Foraging about, I found a bottle with some brandy left, for Hands; and for myself I routed out some biscuit, some pickled fruits, a great bunch of raisins, and a piece of cheese. With these I came on deck, put down my own stock behind the rudder head and well out of the coxswain's reach, went forward to the water-breaker, and had a good deep drink of water, and then, and not till then, gave Hands the brandy.

He must have drunk a gill before he took the bottle from his mouth.

"Aye," said he, "by thunder, but I wanted some o' that!"

I had sat down already in my own corner and begun to eat.

"Much hurt?" I asked him.

He grunted, or rather, I might say, he barked.

"If that doctor was aboard," he said, "I'd be right enough in a couple of turns, but I don't have no manner of luck, you see, and that's what's the matter with me. As for that swab, he's good and dead, he is," he added, indicating the man with the red cap. "He warn't no seaman anyhow. And where mought you have come from?"

"Well," said I, "I've come aboard to take possession of this ship, Mr. Hands; and you'll please regard me as your captain until further notice."

He looked at me sourly enough but said nothing. Some of the colour had come back into his cheeks, though he still looked very sick and still continued to slip out and settle down as the ship banged about.

"By the by," I continued, "I can't have these colours, Mr. Hands; and by your leave, I'll strike 'em. Better none than these."

And again dodging the boom, I ran to the colour lines, handed down their cursed black flag, and chucked it overboard.

"God save the king!" said I, waving my cap. "And there's an end to Captain Silver!"

He watched me keenly and slyly, his chin all the while on his breast.

"I reckon," he said at last, "I reckon, Cap'n Hawkins, you'll kind of want to get ashore now. S'pose we talks."

"Why, yes," says I, "with all my heart, Mr. Hands. Say on." And I went back to my meal with a good appetite.

"This man," he began, nodding feebly at the corpse "—O'Brien were his name, a rank Irelander—this man and me got the canvas on her, meaning for to sail her back. Well, *he's*dead now, he is—as dead as bilge; and who's to sail this ship, I don't see. Without I gives you a hint, you ain't that man, as far's I can tell. Now, look here, you gives me food and drink and a old scarf or ankecher to tie my wound up, you do, and I'll tell you how to sail her, and that's about square all round, I take it."

"I'll tell you one thing," says I: "I'm not going back to Captain Kidd's anchorage. I mean to get into North Inlet and beach her quietly there."

"To be sure you did," he cried. "Why, I ain't sich an infernal lubber after all. I can see, can't I? I've tried my fling, I have, and I've lost, and it's you has the wind of me. North Inlet? Why, I haven't no ch'ice, not I! I'd help you sail her up to Execution Dock, by thunder! So I would."

Well, as it seemed to me, there was some sense in this. We struck our bargain on the spot. In three minutes I had the *Hispaniola* sailing easily before the wind along the coast of Treasure Island, with good hopes of turning the northern point ere noon and beating down again as far as North Inlet before high water, when we might beach her safely and wait till the subsiding tide permitted us to land.

Then I lashed the tiller and went below to my own chest, where I got a soft silk handkerchief of my mother's. With this, and with my aid, Hands bound up the great bleeding stab he had received in the thigh, and after he had eaten a little and had a swallow or two more of the brandy, he began to pick up visibly, sat straighter up, spoke louder and clearer, and looked in every way another man.

The breeze served us admirably. We skimmed before it like a bird, the coast of the island flashing by and the view changing every minute. Soon we were past the high lands and bowling beside low, sandy country, sparsely dotted with dwarf pines, and soon we were beyond that again and had turned the corner of the rocky hill that ends the island on the north.

I was greatly elated with my new command, and pleased with the bright, sunshiny weather and these different prospects of the coast. I had now plenty of water and good things to eat, and my conscience, which had smitten me hard for my desertion, was quieted by the great conquest I had made. I should, I think, have had nothing left me to desire but for the eyes of the coxswain as they followed me derisively about the deck and the odd smile that appeared continually on his face. It was a smile that had in it something both of pain and weakness—a haggard old man's smile; but there was, besides that, a grain of derision, a shadow of treachery, in his expression as he craftily watched, and watched, and watched me at my work.

# 5
# ISRAEL HANDS

The wind, serving us to a desire, now hauled into the west. We could run so much the easier from the north-east corner of the island to the mouth of the North Inlet. Only, as we had no power to anchor and dared not beach her till the tide had flowed a good deal farther, time hung on our hands. The coxswain told me how to lay the ship to; after a good many trials I succeeded, and we both sat in silence over another meal.

"Cap'n," said he at length with that same uncomfortable smile, "here's my old shipmate, O'Brien; s'pose you was to heave him overboard. I ain't partic'lar as a rule, and I don't take no blame for settling his hash, but I don't reckon him ornamental now, do you?"

"I'm not strong enough, and I don't like the job; and there he lies, for me," said I.

"This here's an unlucky ship, this *Hispaniola*, Jim," he went on, blinking. "There's a power of men been killed in this *Hispaniola*—a sight o' poor seamen dead and gone since you and me took ship to Bristol. I never seen sich dirty luck, not I. There was this here O'Brien now—he's dead, ain't he? Well now, I'm no scholar, and you're a lad as can read and figure, and to put it straight, do you take it as a dead man is dead for good, or do he come alive again?"

"You can kill the body, Mr. Hands, but not the spirit; you must know that already," I replied. "O'Brien there is in another world, and may be watching us."

"Ah!" says he. "Well, that's unfort'nate—appears as if killing parties was a waste of time. Howsomever, sperrits don't reckon for much, by what I've seen. I'll chance it with the sperrits, Jim. And now, you've spoke up free, and I'll take it kind if you'd step down into that there cabin and get me a—well, a—shiver my timbers! I can't hit the name on 't; well, you get me a bottle of wine, Jim—this here brandy's too strong for my head."

Now, the coxswain's hesitation seemed to be unnatural, and as for the notion of his preferring wine to brandy, I entirely disbelieved it. The whole story was a pretext. He wanted me to leave the deck—so much was plain; but with what purpose I could in no way imagine. His eyes never met mine; they kept wandering to and fro, up and down, now with a look to the sky, now with a flitting glance upon the dead O'Brien. All the time he kept smiling and putting his tongue out in the most guilty, embarrassed manner, so that a child could have told that he was bent on some deception. I was prompt with my answer, however, for I saw where my advantage lay and that with a fellow so densely stupid I could easily conceal my suspicions to the end.

"Some wine?" I said. "Far better. Will you have white or red?"

"Well, I reckon it's about the blessed same to me, shipmate," he replied; "so it's strong, and plenty of it, what's the odds?"

"All right," I answered. "I'll bring you port, Mr. Hands. But I'll have to dig for it."

With that I scuttled down the companion with all the noise I could, slipped off my shoes, ran quietly along the sparred gallery, mounted the forecastle ladder, and popped my head out of the fore companion. I knew he would not expect to see me there, yet I took every precaution possible, and certainly the worst of my suspicions proved too true.

He had risen from his position to his hands and knees, and though his leg obviously hurt him pretty sharply when he moved—for I could hear him stifle a groan—yet it was at a good, rattling rate that he trailed himself across the deck. In half a minute he had reached the port scuppers and picked, out of a coil of rope, a long knife, or rather a short dirk, discoloured to the hilt with blood. He looked upon it for a moment, thrusting forth his under jaw, tried the point upon his hand, and then, hastily concealing it in the bosom of his jacket, trundled back again into his old place against the bulwark.

This was all that I required to know. Israel could move about, he was now armed, and if he had been at so much trouble to get rid of me, it was plain that I was meant to be the victim. What he would do afterwards—whether he would try to crawl right across the island from North Inlet to the camp among the swamps or whether he would fire Long Tom, trusting that his own comrades might come first to help him—was, of course, more than I could say.

Yet I felt sure that I could trust him in one point, since in that our interests jumped together, and that was in the disposition of the schooner. We both desired to have her stranded safe enough, in a sheltered place, and so that, when the time came, she could be got off again with as little labour and danger as might be; and until that was done I considered that my life would certainly be spared.

While I was thus turning the business over in my mind, I had not been idle with my body. I had stolen back to the cabin, slipped once more into my shoes, and laid my hand at random on a bottle of wine, and now, with this for an excuse, I made my reappearance on the deck.

Hands lay as I had left him, all fallen together in a bundle and with his eyelids lowered as though he were too weak to bear the light. He looked up, however, at my coming, knocked the neck off the bottle like a man who had done the same thing often, and took a good swig, with his favourite toast of "Here's luck!" Then he lay quiet for a little, and then, pulling out a stick of tobacco, begged me to cut him a quid.

"Cut me a junk o' that," says he, "for I haven't no knife and hardly strength enough, so be as I had. Ah, Jim, Jim, I reckon I've missed stays! Cut me a quid, as'll likely be the last, lad, for I'm for my long home, and no mistake."

"Well," said I, "I'll cut you some tobacco, but if I was you and thought myself so badly, I would go to my prayers like a Christian man."

"Why?" said he. "Now, you tell me why."

"Why?" I cried. "You were asking me just now about the dead. You've broken your trust; you've lived in sin and lies and blood; there's a man you killed lying at your feet this moment, and you ask me why! For God's mercy, Mr. Hands, that's why."

I spoke with a little heat, thinking of the bloody dirk he had hidden in his pocket and designed, in his ill thoughts, to end me with. He, for his part, took a great draught of the wine and spoke with the most unusual solemnity.

"For thirty years," he said, "I've sailed the seas and seen good and bad, better and worse, fair weather and foul, provisions running out, knives going, and what not. Well, now I tell you, I never seen good come o' goodness yet. Him as strikes first is my fancy; dead men don't bite; them's my views—amen, so be it. And now, you look here," he added, suddenly changing his tone, "we've had about enough of this foolery. The tide's made good enough by now. You just take my orders, Cap'n Hawkins, and we'll sail slap in and be done with it."

All told, we had scarce two miles to run; but the navigation was delicate, the entrance to this northern anchorage was not only narrow and shoal, but lay east and west, so that the schooner must be nicely handled to be got in. I think I was a good, prompt subaltern, and I am very sure that Hands was an excellent pilot, for we went about and about and dodged in, shaving the banks, with a certainty and a neatness that were a pleasure to behold.

Scarcely had we passed the heads before the land closed around us. The shores of North Inlet were as thickly wooded as those of the southern anchorage, but the space was longer and narrower and more like, what in truth it was, the estuary of a river. Right before us, at the southern end, we saw the wreck of a ship in the last stages of dilapidation. It had been a great vessel of three masts but had lain so long exposed to the injuries of the weather that it was hung about with great webs of dripping seaweed, and on the deck of it shore bushes had taken root and now flourished thick with flowers. It was a sad sight, but it showed us that the anchorage was calm.

"Now," said Hands, "look there; there's a pet bit for to beach a ship in. Fine flat sand, never a cat's paw, trees all around of it, and flowers a-blowing like a garding on that old ship."

"And once beached," I inquired, "how shall we get her off again?"

"Why, so," he replied: "you take a line ashore there on the other side at low water, take a turn about one of them big pines; bring it back, take a turn around the capstan, and lie to for the tide. Come high water, all hands take a pull upon the line, and off she comes as sweet as natur'. And now, boy, you stand by. We're near the bit now, and she's too much way on her. Starboard a little—so—steady—starboard—larboard a little—steady—steady!"

So he issued his commands, which I breathlessly obeyed, till, all of a sudden, he cried, "Now, my hearty, luff!" And I put the helm hard up, and the *Hispaniola* swung round rapidly and ran stem on for the low, wooded shore.

The excitement of these last manoeuvres had somewhat interfered with the watch I had kept hitherto, sharply enough, upon the coxswain. Even then I was still so much interested, waiting for the ship to touch, that I had quite forgot the peril that hung over my head and stood craning over the starboard bulwarks and watching the ripples spreading wide before the bows. I might have fallen without a struggle for my life had not a sudden disquietude seized upon me and made me turn my head. Perhaps I had heard a creak or seen his shadow moving with the tail of my eye; perhaps it was an instinct like a cat's; but, sure enough, when I looked round, there was Hands, already half-way towards me, with the dirk in his right hand.

We must both have cried out aloud when our eyes met, but while mine was the shrill cry of terror, his was a roar of fury like a charging bully's. At the same instant, he threw himself forward and I leapt sideways towards the bows. As I did so, I let go of the tiller, which sprang sharp to leeward, and I think this saved my life, for it struck Hands across the chest and stopped him, for the moment, dead.

Before he could recover, I was safe out of the corner where he had me trapped, with all the deck to dodge about. Just forward of the main-mast I stopped, drew a pistol from my pocket, took a cool aim, though he had already turned and was once more coming directly after me, and drew the trigger. The hammer fell, but there followed neither flash nor sound; the priming was useless with sea-water. I cursed myself for my neglect. Why had not I, long before, reprimed and reloaded my only weapons? Then I should not have been as now, a mere fleeing sheep before this butcher.

Wounded as he was, it was wonderful how fast he could move, his grizzled hair tumbling over his face, and his face itself as red as a red ensign with his haste and fury. I had no time to try my other pistol, nor indeed much inclination, for I was sure it would be useless. One thing I saw plainly: I must not simply retreat before him, or he would speedily hold me boxed into the bows, as a moment since he had so nearly boxed me in the stern. Once so caught, and nine or ten inches of the blood-stained dirk would be my last experience on this side of eternity. I placed my palms against the main-mast, which was of a goodish bigness, and waited, every nerve upon the stretch.

Seeing that I meant to dodge, he also paused; and a moment or two passed in feints on his part and corresponding movements upon mine. It was such a game as I had often played at home about the rocks of Black Hill Cove, but never before, you may be sure, with such a wildly beating heart as now. Still, as I say, it was a boy's game, and I thought I could hold my own at it against an elderly seaman with a wounded thigh. Indeed my courage had begun to rise so high that I allowed myself a few darting thoughts on what would be the end of the affair, and while I saw certainly that I could spin it out for long, I saw no hope of any ultimate escape.

Well, while things stood thus, suddenly the *Hispaniola* struck, staggered, ground for an instant in the sand, and then, swift as a blow, canted over to the port side till the deck stood at an angle of forty-five degrees and about a puncheon of water splashed into the scupper holes and lay, in a pool, between the deck and bulwark.

We were both of us capsized in a second, and both of us rolled, almost together, into the scuppers, the dead red-cap, with his arms still spread out, tumbling stiffly after us. So near were we, indeed, that my head came against the coxswain's foot with a crack that made my teeth rattle. Blow and all, I was the first afoot again, for Hands had got involved with the dead body. The sudden canting of the ship had made the deck no place for running on; I had to find some new way of escape, and that upon the instant, for my foe was almost touching me. Quick as thought, I sprang into the mizzen shrouds, rattled up hand over hand, and did not draw a breath till I was seated on the cross-trees.

I had been saved by being prompt; the dirk had struck not half a foot below me as I pursued my upward flight; and there stood Israel Hands with his mouth open and his face upturned to mine, a perfect statue of surprise and disappointment.

Now that I had a moment to myself, I lost no time in changing the priming of my pistol, and then, having one ready for service, and to make assurance doubly sure, I proceeded to draw the load of the other and recharge it afresh from the beginning.

My new employment struck Hands all of a heap; he began to see the dice going against him, and after an obvious hesitation, he also hauled himself heavily into the shrouds, and with the dirk in his teeth, began slowly and painfully to mount. It cost him no end of time and groans to haul his wounded leg behind him, and I had quietly finished my arrangements before he was much more than a third of the way up. Then, with a pistol in either hand, I addressed him.

"One more step, Mr. Hands," said I, "and I'll blow your brains out! Dead men don't bite, you know," I added with a chuckle.

He stopped instantly. I could see by the working of his face that he was trying to think, and the process was so slow and laborious that, in my new-found security, I laughed aloud.

At last, with a swallow or two, he spoke, his face still wearing the same expression of extreme perplexity. In order to speak he had to take the dagger from his mouth, but in all else he remained unmoved.

"Jim," says he, "I reckon we're fouled, you and me, and we'll have to sign articles. I'd have had you but for that there lurch, but I don't have no luck, not I; and I reckon I'll have to strike, which comes hard, you see, for a master mariner to a ship's younker like you, Jim."

I was drinking in his words and smiling away, as conceited as a cock upon a wall, when, all in a breath, back went his right hand over his shoulder. Something sang like an arrow through the air; I felt a blow and then a sharp pang, and there I was pinned by the shoulder to the mast. In the horrid pain and surprise of the moment—I scarce can say it was by my own volition, and I am sure it was without a conscious aim—both my pistols went off, and both escaped out of my hands. They did not fall alone; with a choked cry, the coxswain loosed his grasp upon the shrouds and plunged head first into the water.

## 6

# "PIECES OF EIGHT"

Owing to the cant of the vessel, the masts hung far out over the water, and from my perch on the cross-trees I had nothing below me but the surface of the bay. Hands, who was not so far up, was in consequence nearer to the ship and fell between me and the bulwarks. He rose once to the surface in a lather of foam and blood and then sank again for good. As the water settled, I could see him lying huddled together on the clean, bright sand in the shadow of the vessel's sides. A fish or two whipped past his body. Sometimes, by the quivering of the water, he appeared to move a little, as if he were trying to rise. But he was dead enough, for all that, being both shot and drowned, and was food for fish in the very place where he had designed my slaughter.

I was no sooner certain of this than I began to feel sick, faint, and terrified. The hot blood was running over my back and chest. The dirk, where it had pinned my shoulder to the mast, seemed to burn like a hot iron; yet it was not so much these real sufferings that distressed me, for these, it seemed to me, I could bear without a murmur; it was the horror I had upon my mind of falling from the cross-trees into that still green water, beside the body of the coxswain.

I clung with both hands till my nails ached, and I shut my eyes as if to cover up the peril. Gradually my mind came back again, my pulses quieted down to a more natural time, and I was once more in possession of myself.

It was my first thought to pluck forth the dirk, but either it stuck too hard or my nerve failed me, and I desisted with a violent shudder. Oddly enough, that very shudder did the business. The knife, in fact, had come the nearest in the world to missing me altogether; it held me by a mere pinch of skin, and this the shudder tore away. The blood ran down the faster, to be sure, but I was my own master again and only tacked to the mast by my coat and shirt.

These last I broke through with a sudden jerk, and then regained the deck by the starboard shrouds. For nothing in the world would I have again ventured, shaken as I was, upon the overhanging port shrouds from which Israel had so lately fallen.

I went below and did what I could for my wound; it pained me a good deal and still bled freely, but it was neither deep nor dangerous, nor did it greatly gall me when I used my arm. Then I looked around me, and as the ship was now, in a sense, my own, I began to think of clearing it from its last passenger—the dead man, O'Brien.

He had pitched, as I have said, against the bulwarks, where he lay like some horrible, ungainly sort of puppet, life-size, indeed, but how different from life's colour or life's comeliness! In that position I could easily have my way with him, and as the habit of tragical adventures had worn off almost all my terror for the dead, I took him by the waist as if he had been a sack of bran and with one good heave, tumbled him overboard. He went in with a sounding plunge; the red cap came off and remained floating on the surface; and as soon as the splash subsided, I could see him and Israel lying side by side, both wavering with the tremulous movement of the water. O'Brien, though still quite a young man, was very bald. There he lay, with that bald head across the knees of the man who had killed him and the quick fishes steering to and fro over both.

I was now alone upon the ship; the tide had just turned. The sun was within so few degrees of setting that already the shadow of the pines upon the western shore began to reach right across the anchorage and fall in patterns on the deck. The evening breeze had sprung up, and though it was well warded off by the hill with the two peaks upon the east, the cordage had begun to sing a little softly to itself and the idle sails to rattle to and fro.

I began to see a danger to the ship. The jibs I speedily doused and brought tumbling to the deck, but the main-sail was a harder matter. Of course, when the schooner canted over, the boom had swung out-board, and the cap of it and a foot or two of sail hung even under water. I thought this made it still more dangerous; yet the strain was so heavy that I half feared to meddle. At last I got my knife and cut the halyards. The peak dropped instantly, a great belly of loose canvas floated broad upon the water, and since, pull as I liked, I could not budge the downhall, that was the extent of what I could accomplish. For the rest, the *Hispaniola* must trust to luck, like myself.

By this time the whole anchorage had fallen into shadow—the last rays, I remember, falling through a glade of the wood and shining bright as jewels on the flowery mantle of the wreck. It began to be chill; the tide was rapidly fleeting seaward, the schooner settling more and more on her beam-ends.

I scrambled forward and looked over. It seemed shallow enough, and holding the cut hawser in both hands for a last security, I let myself drop softly overboard. The water scarcely reached my waist; the sand was firm and covered with ripple marks, and I waded ashore in great spirits, leaving the *Hispaniola* on her side, with her main-sail trailing wide upon the surface of the bay. About the same time, the sun went fairly down and the breeze whistled low in the dusk among the tossing pines.

At least, and at last, I was off the sea, nor had I returned thence empty-handed. There lay the schooner, clear at last from buccaneers and ready for our own men to board and get to sea again. I had nothing nearer my fancy than to get home to the stockade and boast of my achievements. Possibly I might be blamed a bit for my truantry, but the recapture of the *Hispaniola* was a clenching answer, and I hoped that even Captain Smollett would confess I had not lost my time.

So thinking, and in famous spirits, I began to set my face homeward for the block house and my companions. I remembered that the most easterly of the rivers which drain into Captain Kidd's anchorage ran from the two-peaked hill upon my left, and I bent my course in that direction that I might pass the stream while it was small. The wood was pretty open, and keeping along the lower spurs, I had soon turned the corner of that hill, and not long after waded to the mid-calf across the watercourse.

This brought me near to where I had encountered Ben Gunn, the maroon; and I walked more circumspectly, keeping an eye on every side. The dusk had come nigh hand completely, and as I opened out the cleft between the two peaks, I became aware of a wavering glow against the sky, where, as I judged, the man of the island was cooking his supper before a roaring fire. And yet I wondered, in my heart, that he should show himself so careless. For if I could see this radiance, might it not reach the eyes of Silver himself where he camped upon the shore among the marshes?

Gradually the night fell blacker; it was all I could do to guide myself even roughly towards my destination; the double hill behind me and the Spy-glass on my right hand loomed faint and fainter; the stars were few and pale; and in the low ground where I wandered I kept tripping among bushes and rolling into sandy pits.

Suddenly a kind of brightness fell about me. I looked up; a pale glimmer of moonbeams had alighted on the summit of the Spy-glass, and soon after I saw something broad and silvery moving low down behind the trees, and knew the moon had risen.

With this to help me, I passed rapidly over what remained to me of my journey, and sometimes walking, sometimes running, impatiently drew near to the stockade. Yet, as I began to thread the grove that lies before it, I was not so thoughtless but that I slacked my pace and went a trifle warily. It would have been a poor end of my adventures to get shot down by my own party in mistake.

The moon was climbing higher and higher, its light began to fall here and there in masses through the more open districts of the wood, and right in front of me a glow of a different colour appeared among the trees. It was red and hot, and now and again it was a little darkened—as it were, the embers of a bonfire smouldering.

For the life of me I could not think what it might be.

At last I came right down upon the borders of the clearing. The western end was already steeped in moonshine; the rest, and the block house itself, still lay in a black shadow chequered with long silvery streaks of light. On the other side of the house an immense fire had burned itself into clear embers and shed a steady, red reverberation, contrasted strongly with the mellow paleness of the moon. There was not a soul stirring nor a sound beside the noises of the breeze.

I stopped, with much wonder in my heart, and perhaps a little terror also. It had not been our way to build great fires; we were, indeed, by the captain's orders, somewhat niggardly of firewood, and I began to fear that something had gone wrong while I was absent.

I stole round by the eastern end, keeping close in shadow, and at a convenient place, where the darkness was thickest, crossed the palisade.

To make assurance surer, I got upon my hands and knees and crawled, without a sound, towards the corner of the house. As I drew nearer, my heart was suddenly and greatly lightened. It is not a pleasant noise in itself, and I have often complained of it at other times, but just then it was like music to hear my friends snoring together so loud and peaceful in their sleep. The sea-cry of the watch, that beautiful "All's well," never fell more reassuringly on my ear.

In the meantime, there was no doubt of one thing; they kept an infamous bad watch. If it had been Silver and his lads that were now creeping in on them, not a soul would have seen daybreak. That was what it was, thought I, to have the captain wounded; and again I blamed myself sharply for leaving them in that danger with so few to mount guard.

By this time I had got to the door and stood up. All was dark within, so that I could distinguish nothing by the eye. As for sounds, there was the steady drone of the snorers and a small occasional noise, a flickering or pecking that I could in no way account for.

With my arms before me I walked steadily in. I should lie down in my own place (I thought with a silent chuckle) and enjoy their faces when they found me in the morning.

My foot struck something yielding—it was a sleeper's leg; and he turned and groaned, but without awaking.

And then, all of a sudden, a shrill voice broke forth out of the darkness:

"Pieces of eight! Pieces of eight! Pieces of eight! Pieces of eight! Pieces of eight!" and so forth, without pause or change, like the clacking of a tiny mill.

Silver's green parrot, Captain Flint! It was she whom I had heard pecking at a piece of bark; it was she, keeping better watch than any human being, who thus announced my arrival with her wearisome refrain.

I had no time left me to recover. At the sharp, clipping tone of the parrot, the sleepers awoke and sprang up; and with a mighty oath, the voice of Silver cried, "Who goes?"

I turned to run, struck violently against one person, recoiled, and ran full into the arms of a second, who for his part closed upon and held me tight.

"Bring a torch, Dick," said Silver when my capture was thus assured.

And one of the men left the log-house and presently returned with a lighted brand.

# VI
# CAPTAIN SILVER

# I

# IN THE ENEMY'S CAMP

The red glare of the torch, lighting up the interior of the block house, showed me the worst of my apprehensions realized. The pirates were in possession of the house and stores: there was the cask of cognac, there were the pork and bread, as before, and what tenfold increased my horror, not a sign of any prisoner. I could only judge that all had perished, and my heart smote me sorely that I had not been there to perish with them.

There were six of the buccaneers, all told; not another man was left alive. Five of them were on their feet, flushed and swollen, suddenly called out of the first sleep of drunkenness. The sixth had only risen upon his elbow; he was deadly pale, and the blood-stained bandage round his head told that he had recently been wounded, and still more recently dressed. I remembered the man who had been shot and had run back among the woods in the great attack, and doubted not that this was he.

The parrot sat, preening her plumage, on Long John's shoulder. He himself, I thought, looked somewhat paler and more stern than I was used to. He still wore the fine broadcloth suit in which he had fulfilled his mission, but it was bitterly the worse for wear, daubed with clay and torn with the sharp briers of the wood.

"So," said he, "here's Jim Hawkins, shiver my timbers! Dropped in, like, eh? Well, come, I take that friendly."

And thereupon he sat down across the brandy cask and began to fill a pipe.

"Give me a loan of the link, Dick," said he; and then, when he had a good light, "That'll do, lad," he added; "stick the glim in the wood heap; and you, gentlemen, bring yourselves to! You needn't stand up for Mr. Hawkins; *he'll* excuse you, you may lay to that. And so, Jim"—stopping the tobacco—"here you were, and quite a pleasant surprise for poor old John. I see you were smart when first I set my eyes on you, but this here gets away from me clean, it do."

To all this, as may be well supposed, I made no answer. They had set me with my back against the wall, and I stood there, looking Silver in the face, pluckily enough, I hope, to all outward appearance, but with black despair in my heart.

Silver took a whiff or two of his pipe with great composure and then ran on again.

"Now, you see, Jim, so be as you *are* here," says he, "I'll give you a piece of my mind. I've always liked you, I have, for a lad of spirit, and the picter of my own self when I was young and handsome. I always wanted you to jine and take your share, and die a gentleman, and now, my cock, you've got to. Cap'n Smollett's a fine seaman, as I'll own up to any day, but stiff on discipline. 'Dooty is dooty,' says he, and right he is. Just you keep clear of the cap'n. The doctor himself is gone dead again you—'ungrateful scamp' was what he said; and the short and the long of the whole story is about here: you can't go back to your own lot, for they won't have you; and without you start a third ship's company all by yourself, which might be lonely, you'll have to jine with Cap'n Silver."

So far so good. My friends, then, were still alive, and though I partly believed the truth of Silver's statement, that the cabin party were incensed at me for my desertion, I was more relieved than distressed by what I heard.

"I don't say nothing as to your being in our hands," continued Silver, "though there you are, and you may lay to it. I'm all for argyment; I never seen good come out o' threatening. If you like the service, well, you'll jine; and if you don't, Jim, why, you're free to answer no—free and welcome, shipmate; and if fairer can be said by mortal seaman, shiver my sides!"

"Am I to answer, then?" I asked with a very tremulous voice. Through all this sneering talk, I was made to feel the threat of death that overhung me, and my cheeks burned and my heart beat painfully in my breast.

"Lad," said Silver, "no one's a-pressing of you. Take your bearings. None of us won't hurry you, mate; time goes so pleasant in your company, you see."

"Well," says I, growing a bit bolder, "if I'm to choose, I declare I have a right to know what's what, and why you're here, and where my friends are."

"Wot's wot?" repeated one of the buccaneers in a deep growl. "Ah, he'd be a lucky one as knowed that!"

"You'll perhaps batten down your hatches till you're spoke to, my friend," cried Silver truculently to this speaker. And then, in his first gracious tones, he replied to me, "Yesterday morning, Mr. Hawkins," said he, "in the dog-watch, down came Doctor Livesey with a flag of truce. Says he, 'Cap'n Silver, you're sold out. Ship's gone.' Well, maybe we'd been taking a glass, and a song to help it round. I won't say no. Leastways, none of us had looked out. We looked out, and by thunder, the old ship was gone! I never seen a pack o' fools look fishier; and you may lay to that, if I tells you that looked the fishiest. 'Well,' says the doctor, 'let's bargain.' We bargained, him and I, and here we are: stores, brandy, block house, the firewood you was thoughtful enough to cut, and in a manner of speaking, the whole blessed boat, from cross-trees to kelson. As for them, they've tramped; I don't know where's they are."

He drew again quietly at his pipe.

"And lest you should take it into that head of yours," he went on, "that you was included in the treaty, here's the last word that was said: 'How many are you,' says I, 'to leave?' 'Four,' says he; 'four, and one of us wounded. As for that boy, I don't know where he is, confound him,' says he, 'nor I don't much care. We're about sick of him.' These was his words.

"Is that all?" I asked.

"Well, it's all that you're to hear, my son," returned Silver.

"And now I am to choose?"

"And now you are to choose, and you may lay to that," said Silver.

"Well," said I, "I am not such a fool but I know pretty well what I have to look for. Let the worst come to the worst, it's little I care. I've seen too many die since I fell in with you. But there's a thing or two I have to tell you," I said, and by this time I was quite excited; "and the first is this: here you are, in a bad way—ship lost, treasure lost, men lost, your whole business gone to wreck; and if you want to know who did it—it was I! I was in the apple barrel the night we sighted land, and I heard you, John, and you, Dick Johnson, and Hands, who is now at the bottom of the sea, and told every word you said before the hour was out. And as for the schooner, it was I who cut her cable, and it was I that killed the men you had aboard of her, and it was I who brought her where you'll never see her more, not one of you. The laugh's on my side; I've had the top of this business from the first; I no more fear you than I fear a fly. Kill me, if you please, or spare me. But one thing I'll say, and no more; if you spare me, bygones are bygones, and when you fellows are in court for piracy, I'll save you all I can. It is for you to choose. Kill another and do yourselves no good, or spare me and keep a witness to save you from the gallows."

I stopped, for, I tell you, I was out of breath, and to my wonder, not a man of them moved, but all sat staring at me like as many sheep. And while they were still staring, I broke out again, "And now, Mr. Silver," I said, "I believe you're the best man here, and if things go to the worst, I'll take it kind of you to let the doctor know the way I took it."

"I'll bear it in mind," said Silver with an accent so curious that I could not, for the life of me, decide whether he were laughing at my request or had been favourably affected by my courage.

"I'll put one to that," cried the old mahogany-faced seaman—Morgan by name—whom I had seen in Long John's public-house upon the quays of Bristol. "It was him that knowed Black Dog."

"Well, and see here," added the sea-cook. "I'll put another again to that, by thunder! For it was this same boy that faked the chart from Billy Bones. First and last, we've split upon Jim Hawkins!"

"Then here goes!" said Morgan with an oath.

And he sprang up, drawing his knife as if he had been twenty.

"Avast, there!" cried Silver. "Who are you, Tom Morgan? Maybe you thought you was cap'n here, perhaps. By the powers, but I'll teach you better! Cross me, and you'll go where many a good man's gone before you, first and last, these thirty year back—some to the yard-arm, shiver my timbers, and some by the board, and all to feed the fishes. There's never a man looked me between the eyes and seen a good day a'terwards, Tom Morgan, you may lay to that."

Morgan paused, but a hoarse murmur rose from the others.

"Tom's right," said one.

"I stood hazing long enough from one," added another. "I'll be hanged if I'll be hazed by you, John Silver."

"Did any of you gentlemen want to have it out with *me*?" roared Silver, bending far forward from his position on the keg, with his pipe still glowing in his right hand. "Put a name on what you're at; you ain't dumb, I reckon. Him that wants shall get it. Have I lived this many years, and a son of a rum puncheon cock his hat athwart my hawse at the latter end of it? You know the way; you're all gentlemen o' fortune, by your account. Well, I'm ready. Take a cutlass, him that dares, and I'll see the colour of his inside, crutch and all, before that pipe's empty."

Not a man stirred; not a man answered.

"That's your sort, is it?" he added, returning his pipe to his mouth. "Well, you're a gay lot to look at, anyway. Not much worth to fight, you ain't. P'r'aps you can understand King George's English. I'm cap'n here by 'lection. I'm cap'n here because I'm the best man by a long sea-mile. You won't fight, as gentlemen o' fortune should; then, by thunder, you'll obey, and you may lay to it! I like that boy, now; I never seen a better boy than that. He's more a man than any pair of rats of you in this here house, and what I say is this: let me see him that'll lay a hand on him—that's what I say, and you may lay to it."

There was a long pause after this. I stood straight up against the wall, my heart still going like a sledge-hammer, but with a ray of hope now shining in my bosom. Silver leant back against the wall, his arms crossed, his pipe in the corner of his mouth, as calm as though he had been in church; yet his eye kept wandering furtively, and he kept the tail of it on his unruly followers. They, on their part, drew gradually together towards the far end of the block house, and the low hiss of their whispering sounded in my ear continuously, like a stream. One after another, they would look up, and the red light of the torch would fall for a second on their nervous faces; but it was not towards me, it was towards Silver that they turned their eyes.

"You seem to have a lot to say," remarked Silver, spitting far into the air. "Pipe up and let me hear it, or lay to."

"Ax your pardon, sir," returned one of the men; "you're pretty free with some of the rules; maybe you'll kindly keep an eye upon the rest. This crew's dissatisfied; this crew don't vally bullying a marlin-spike; this crew has its rights like other crews, I'll make so free as that; and by your own rules, I take it we can talk together. I ax your pardon, sir, acknowledging you for to be captaing at this present; but I claim my right, and steps outside for a council."

And with an elaborate sea-salute, this fellow, a long, ill-looking, yellow-eyed man of five and thirty, stepped coolly towards the door and disappeared out of the house. One after another the rest followed his example, each making a salute as he passed, each adding some apology. "According to rules," said one. "Forecastle council," said Morgan. And so with one remark or another all marched out and left Silver and me alone with the torch.

The sea-cook instantly removed his pipe.

"Now, look you here, Jim Hawkins," he said in a steady whisper that was no more than audible, "you're within half a plank of death, and what's a long sight worse, of torture. They're going to throw me off. But, you mark, I stand by you through thick and thin. I didn't mean to; no, not till you spoke up. I was about desperate to lose that much blunt, and be hanged into the bargain. But I see you was the right sort. I says to myself, you stand by Hawkins, John, and Hawkins'll stand by you. You're his last card, and by the living thunder, John, he's yours! Back to back, says I. You save your witness, and he'll save your neck!"

I began dimly to understand.

"You mean all's lost?" I asked.

"Aye, by gum, I do!" he answered. "Ship gone, neck gone—that's the size of it. Once I looked into that bay, Jim Hawkins, and seen no schooner—well, I'm tough, but I gave out. As for that lot and their council, mark me, they're outright fools and cowards. I'll save your life —if so be as I can—from them. But, see here, Jim—tit for tat—you save Long John from swinging."

I was bewildered; it seemed a thing so hopeless he was asking—he, the old buccaneer, the ringleader throughout.

"What I can do, that I'll do," I said.

"It's a bargain!" cried Long John. "You speak up plucky, and by thunder, I've a chance!"

He hobbled to the torch, where it stood propped among the firewood, and took a fresh light to his pipe.

"Understand me, Jim," he said, returning. "I've a head on my shoulders, I have. I'm on squire's side now. I know you've got that ship safe somewheres. How you done it, I don't know, but safe it is. I guess Hands and O'Brien turned soft. I never much believed in neither of *them*. Now you mark me. I ask no questions, nor I won't let others. I know when a game's up, I do; and I know a lad that's staunch. Ah, you that's young—you and me might have done a power of good together!"

He drew some cognac from the cask into a tin cannikin.

"Will you taste, messmate?" he asked; and when I had refused: "Well, I'll take a dram myself, Jim," said he. "I need a caulker, for there's trouble on hand. And talking o' trouble, why did that doctor give me the chart, Jim?"

My face expressed a wonder so unaffected that he saw the needlessness of further questions.

"Ah, well, he did, though," said he. "And there's something under that, no doubt—something, surely, under that, Jim—bad or good."

And he took another swallow of the brandy, shaking his great fair head like a man who looks forward to the worst.

## 2

# THE BLACK SPOT AGAIN

The council of buccaneers had lasted some time, when one of them re-entered the house, and with a repetition of the same salute, which had in my eyes an ironical air, begged for a moment's loan of the torch. Silver briefly agreed, and this emissary retired again, leaving us together in the dark.

"There's a breeze coming, Jim," said Silver, who had by this time adopted quite a friendly and familiar tone.

I turned to the loophole nearest me and looked out. The embers of the great fire had so far burned themselves out and now glowed so low and duskily that I understood why these conspirators desired a torch. About half-way down the slope to the stockade, they were collected in a group; one held the light, another was on his knees in their midst, and I saw the blade of an open knife shine in his hand with varying colours in the moon and torchlight. The rest were all somewhat stooping, as though watching the manoeuvres of this last. I could just make out that he had a book as well as a knife in his hand, and was still wondering how anything so incongruous had come in their possession when the kneeling figure rose once more to his feet and the whole party began to move together towards the house.

"Here they come," said I; and I returned to my former position, for it seemed beneath my dignity that they should find me watching them.

"Well, let 'em come, lad—let 'em come," said Silver cheerily. "I've still a shot in my locker."

The door opened, and the five men, standing huddled together just inside, pushed one of their number forward. In any other circumstances it would have been comical to see his slow advance, hesitating as he set down each foot, but holding his closed right hand in front of him.

"Step up, lad," cried Silver. "I won't eat you. Hand it over, lubber. I know the rules, I do; I won't hurt a depytation."

Thus encouraged, the buccaneer stepped forth more briskly, and having passed something to Silver, from hand to hand, slipped yet more smartly back again to his companions.

The sea-cook looked at what had been given him.

"The black spot! I thought so," he observed. "Where might you have got the paper? Why, hillo! Look here, now; this ain't lucky! You've gone and cut this out of a Bible. What fool's cut a Bible?"

"Ah, there!" said Morgan. "There! Wot did I say? No good'll come o' that, I said."

"Well, you've about fixed it now, among you," continued Silver. "You'll all swing now, I reckon. What soft-headed lubber had a Bible?"

"It was Dick," said one.

"Dick, was it? Then Dick can get to prayers," said Silver. "He's seen his slice of luck, has Dick, and you may lay to that."

But here the long man with the yellow eyes struck in.

"Belay that talk, John Silver," he said. "This crew has tipped you the black spot in full council, as in dooty bound; just you turn it over, as in dooty bound, and see what's wrote there. Then you can talk."

"Thanky, George," replied the sea-cook. "You always was brisk for business, and has the rules by heart, George, as I'm pleased to see. Well, what is it, anyway? Ah! 'Deposed'—that's it, is it? Very pretty wrote, to be sure; like print, I swear. Your hand o' write, George? Why, you was gettin' quite a leadin' man in this here crew. You'll be cap'n next, I shouldn't wonder. Just oblige me with that torch again, will you? This pipe don't draw."

"Come, now," said George, "you don't fool this crew no more. You're a funny man, by your account; but you're over now, and you'll maybe step down off that barrel and help vote."

"I thought you said you knowed the rules," returned Silver contemptuously. "Leastways, if you don't, I do; and I wait here—and I'm still your cap'n, mind—till you outs with your grievances and I reply; in the meantime, your black spot ain't worth a biscuit. After that, we'll see."

"Oh," replied George, "you don't be under no kind of apprehension; *we're* all square, we are. First, you've made a hash of this cruise—you'll be a bold man to say no to that. Second, you let the enemy out o' this here trap for nothing. Why did they want out? I dunno, but it's pretty plain they wanted it. Third, you wouldn't let us go at them upon the march. Oh, we see through you, John Silver; you want to play booty, that's what's wrong with you. And then, fourth, there's this here boy."

"Is that all?" asked Silver quietly.

"Enough, too," retorted George. "We'll all swing and sun-dry for your bungling."

"Well now, look here, I'll answer these four p'ints; one after another I'll answer 'em. I made a hash o' this cruise, did I? Well now, you all know what I wanted, and you all know if that had been done that we'd 'a been aboard the *Hispaniola* this night as ever was, every man of us alive, and fit, and full of good plum-duff, and the treasure in the hold of her, by thunder! Well, who crossed me? Who forced my hand, as was the lawful cap'n? Who tipped me the black spot the day we landed and began this dance? Ah, it's a fine dance—I'm with you there—and looks mighty like a hornpipe in a rope's end at Execution Dock by London town, it does. But who done it? Why, it was Anderson, and Hands, and you, George Merry! And you're the last above board of that same meddling crew; and you have the Davy Jones's insolence to up and stand for cap'n over me—you, that sank the lot of us! By the powers! But this tops the stiffest yarn to nothing."

Silver paused, and I could see by the faces of George and his late comrades that these words had not been said in vain.

"That's for number one," cried the accused, wiping the sweat from his brow, for he had been talking with a vehemence that shook the house. "Why, I give you my word, I'm sick to speak to you. You've neither sense nor memory, and I leave it to fancy where your mothers was that let you come to sea. Sea! Gentlemen o' fortune! I reckon tailors is your trade."

"Go on, John," said Morgan. "Speak up to the others."

"Ah, the others!" returned John. "They're a nice lot, ain't they? You say this cruise is bungled. Ah! By gum, if you could understand how bad it's bungled, you would see! We're that near the gibbet that my neck's stiff with thinking on it. You've seen 'em, maybe, hanged in chains, birds about 'em, seamen p'inting 'em out as they go down with the tide. 'Who's that?' says one. 'That! Why, that's John Silver. I knowed him well,' says another. And you can hear the chains a-jangle as you go about and reach for the other buoy. Now, that's about where we are, every mother's son of us, thanks to him, and Hands, and Anderson, and other ruination fools of you. And if you want to know about number four, and that boy, why, shiver my timbers, isn't he a hostage? Are we a-going to waste a hostage? No, not us; he might be our last chance, and I shouldn't wonder. Kill that boy? Not me, mates! And number three? Ah, well, there's a deal to say to number three. Maybe you don't count it nothing to have a real college doctor to see you every day—you, John, with your head broke—or you, George Merry, that had the ague shakes upon you not six hours agone, and has your eyes the colour of lemon peel to this same moment on the clock? And maybe, perhaps, you didn't know there was a consort coming either? But there is, and not so long till then; and we'll see who'll be glad to have a hostage when it comes to that. And as for number two, and why I made a bargain—well, you came crawling on your knees to me to make it—on your knees you came, you was that downhearted—and you'd have starved too if I hadn't—but that's a trifle! You look there—that's why!"

And he cast down upon the floor a paper that I instantly recognized—none other than the chart on yellow paper, with the three red crosses, that I had found in the oilcloth at the bottom of the captain's chest. Why the doctor had given it to him was more than I could fancy.

But if it were inexplicable to me, the appearance of the chart was incredible to the surviving mutineers. They leaped upon it like cats upon a mouse. It went from hand to hand, one tearing it from another; and by the oaths and the cries and the childish laughter with which they accompanied their examination, you would have thought, not only they were fingering the very gold, but were at sea with it, besides, in safety.

"Yes," said one, "that's Flint, sure enough. J. F., and a score below, with a clove hitch to it; so he done ever."

"Mighty pretty," said George. "But how are we to get away with it, and us no ship."

Silver suddenly sprang up, and supporting himself with a hand against the wall: "Now I give you warning, George," he cried. "One more word of your sauce, and I'll call you down and fight you. How? Why, how do I know? You had ought to tell me that—you and the rest, that lost me my schooner, with your interference, burn you! But not you, you can't; you hain't got the invention of a cockroach. But civil you can speak, and shall, George Merry, you may lay to that."

"That's fair enow," said the old man Morgan.

"Fair! I reckon so," said the sea-cook. "You lost the ship; I found the treasure. Who's the better man at that? And now I resign, by thunder! Elect whom you please to be your cap'n now; I'm done with it."

"Silver!" they cried. "Barbecue forever! Barbecue for cap'n!"

"So that's the toon, is it?" cried the cook. "George, I reckon you'll have to wait another turn, friend; and lucky for you as I'm not a revengeful man. But that was never my way. And now, shipmates, this black spot? 'Tain't much good now, is it? Dick's crossed his luck and spoiled his Bible, and that's about all."

"It'll do to kiss the book on still, won't it?" growled Dick, who was evidently uneasy at the curse he had brought upon himself.

"A Bible with a bit cut out!" returned Silver derisively. "Not it. It don't bind no more'n a ballad-book."

"Don't it, though?" cried Dick with a sort of joy. "Well, I reckon that's worth having too."

"Here, Jim—here's a cur'osity for you," said Silver, and he tossed me the paper.

It was around about the size of a crown piece. One side was blank, for it had been the last leaf; the other contained a verse or two of Revelation—these words among the rest, which struck sharply home upon my mind: "Without are dogs and murderers." The printed side had been blackened with wood ash, which already began to come off and soil my fingers; on the blank side had been written with the same material the one word "Depposed." I have that curiosity beside me at this moment, but not a trace of writing now remains beyond a single scratch, such as a man might make with his thumb-nail.

That was the end of the night's business. Soon after, with a drink all round, we lay down to sleep, and the outside of Silver's vengeance was to put George Merry up for sentinel and threaten him with death if he should prove unfaithful.

It was long ere I could close an eye, and heaven knows I had matter enough for thought in the man whom I had slain that afternoon, in my own most perilous position, and above all, in the remarkable game that I saw Silver now engaged upon—keeping the mutineers together with one hand and grasping with the other after every means, possible and impossible, to make his peace and save his miserable life. He himself slept peacefully and snored aloud, yet my heart was sore for him, wicked as he was, to think on the dark perils that environed and the shameful gibbet that awaited him.

## 3

# ON PAROLE

I was wakened—indeed, we were all wakened, for I could see even the sentinel shake himself together from where he had fallen against the door-post—by a clear, hearty voice hailing us from the margin of the wood:

"Block house, ahoy!" it cried. "Here's the doctor."

And the doctor it was. Although I was glad to hear the sound, yet my gladness was not without admixture. I remembered with confusion my insubordinate and stealthy conduct, and when I saw where it had brought me—among what companions and surrounded by what dangers—I felt ashamed to look him in the face.

He must have risen in the dark, for the day had hardly come; and when I ran to a loophole and looked out, I saw him standing, like Silver once before, up to the mid-leg in creeping vapour.

"You, doctor! Top o' the morning to you, sir!" cried Silver, broad awake and beaming with good nature in a moment. "Bright and early, to be sure; and it's the early bird, as the saying goes, that gets the rations. George, shake up your timbers, son, and help Dr. Livesey over the ship's side. All a-doin' well, your patients was—all well and merry."

So he pattered on, standing on the hilltop with his crutch under his elbow and one hand upon the side of the log-house—quite the old John in voice, manner, and expression.

"We've quite a surprise for you too, sir," he continued. "We've a little stranger here—he! he! A noo boarder and lodger, sir, and looking fit and taut as a fiddle; slep' like a supercargo, he did, right alongside of John—stem to stem we was, all night."

Dr. Livesey was by this time across the stockade and pretty near the cook, and I could hear the alteration in his voice as he said, "Not Jim?"

"The very same Jim as ever was," says Silver.

The doctor stopped outright, although he did not speak, and it was some seconds before he seemed able to move on.

"Well, well," he said at last, "duty first and pleasure afterwards, as you might have said yourself, Silver. Let us overhaul these patients of yours."

A moment afterwards he had entered the block house and with one grim nod to me proceeded with his work among the sick. He seemed under no apprehension, though he must have known that his life, among these treacherous demons, depended on a hair; and he rattled on to his patients as if he were paying an ordinary professional visit in a quiet English family. His manner, I suppose, reacted on the men, for they behaved to him as if nothing had occurred, as if he were still ship's doctor and they still faithful hands before the mast.

"You're doing well, my friend," he said to the fellow with the bandaged head, "and if ever any person had a close shave, it was you; your head must be as hard as iron. Well, George, how goes it? You're a pretty colour, certainly; why, your liver, man, is upside down. Did you take that medicine? Did he take that medicine, men?"

"Aye, aye, sir, he took it, sure enough," returned Morgan.

"Because, you see, since I am mutineers' doctor, or prison doctor as I prefer to call it," says Doctor Livesey in his pleasantest way, "I make it a point of honour not to lose a man for King George (God bless him!) and the gallows."

The rogues looked at each other but swallowed the home-thrust in silence.

"Dick don't feel well, sir," said one.

"Don't he?" replied the doctor. "Well, step up here, Dick, and let me see your tongue. No, I should be surprised if he did! The man's tongue is fit to frighten the French. Another fever."

"Ah, there," said Morgan, "that comed of sp'iling Bibles."

"That comes—as you call it—of being arrant asses," retorted the doctor, "and not having sense enough to know honest air from poison, and the dry land from a vile, pestiferous slough. I think it most probable—though of course it's only an opinion—that you'll all have the deuce to pay before you get that malaria out of your systems. Camp in a bog, would you? Silver, I'm surprised at you. You're less of a fool than many, take you all round; but you don't appear to me to have the rudiments of a notion of the rules of health.

"Well," he added after he had dosed them round and they had taken his prescriptions, with really laughable humility, more like charity schoolchildren than blood-guilty mutineers and pirates—"well, that's done for today. And now I should wish to have a talk with that boy, please."

And he nodded his head in my direction carelessly.

George Merry was at the door, spitting and spluttering over some bad-tasted medicine; but at the first word of the doctor's proposal he swung round with a deep flush and cried "No!" and swore.

Silver struck the barrel with his open hand.

"Si-lence!" he roared and looked about him positively like a lion. "Doctor," he went on in his usual tones, "I was a-thinking of that, knowing as how you had a fancy for the boy. We're all humbly grateful for your kindness, and as you see, puts faith in you and takes the drugs down like that much grog. And I take it I've found a way as'll suit all. Hawkins, will you give me your word of honour as a young gentleman—for a young gentleman you are, although poor born—your word of honour not to slip your cable?"

I readily gave the pledge required.

"Then, doctor," said Silver, "you just step outside o' that stockade, and once you're there I'll bring the boy down on the inside, and I reckon you can yarn through the spars. Good day to you, sir, and all our dooties to the squire and Cap'n Smollett."

The explosion of disapproval, which nothing but Silver's black looks had restrained, broke out immediately the doctor had left the house. Silver was roundly accused of playing double—of trying to make a separate peace for himself, of sacrificing the interests of his accomplices and victims, and, in one word, of the identical, exact thing that he was doing. It seemed to me so obvious, in this case, that I could not imagine how he was to turn their anger. But he was twice the man the rest were, and his last night's victory had given him a huge preponderance on their minds. He called them all the fools and dolts you can imagine, said it was necessary I should talk to the doctor, fluttered the chart in their faces, asked them if they could afford to break the treaty the very day they were bound a-treasure-hunting.

"No, by thunder!" he cried. "It's us must break the treaty when the time comes; and till then I'll gammon that doctor, if I have to ile his boots with brandy."

And then he bade them get the fire lit, and stalked out upon his crutch, with his hand on my shoulder, leaving them in a disarray, and silenced by his volubility rather than convinced.

"Slow, lad, slow," he said. "They might round upon us in a twinkle of an eye if we was seen to hurry."

Very deliberately, then, did we advance across the sand to where the doctor awaited us on the other side of the stockade, and as soon as we were within easy speaking distance Silver stopped.

"You'll make a note of this here also, doctor," says he, "and the boy'll tell you how I saved his life, and were deposed for it too, and you may lay to that. Doctor, when a man's steering as near the wind as me—playing chuck-farthing with the last breath in his body, like—you wouldn't think it too much, mayhap, to give him one good word? You'll please bear in mind it's not my life only now—it's that boy's into the bargain; and you'll speak me fair, doctor, and give me a bit o' hope to go on, for the sake of mercy."

Silver was a changed man once he was out there and had his back to his friends and the block house; his cheeks seemed to have fallen in, his voice trembled; never was a soul more dead in earnest.

"Why, John, you're not afraid?" asked Dr. Livesey.

"Doctor, I'm no coward; no, not I—not *so* much!" and he snapped his fingers. "If I was I wouldn't say it. But I'll own up fairly, I've the shakes upon me for the gallows. You're a good man and a true; I never seen a better man! And you'll not forget what I done good, not any more than you'll forget the bad, I know. And I step aside—see here—and leave you and Jim alone. And you'll put that down for me too, for it's a long stretch, is that!"

So saying, he stepped back a little way, till he was out of earshot, and there sat down upon a tree-stump and began to whistle, spinning round now and again upon his seat so as to command a sight, sometimes of me and the doctor and sometimes of his unruly ruffians as they went to and fro in the sand between the fire—which they were busy rekindling—and the house, from which they brought forth pork and bread to make the breakfast.

"So, Jim," said the doctor sadly, "here you are. As you have brewed, so shall you drink, my boy. Heaven knows, I cannot find it in my heart to blame you, but this much I will say, be it kind or unkind: when Captain Smollett was well, you dared not have gone off; and when he was ill and couldn't help it, by George, it was downright cowardly!"

I will own that I here began to weep. "Doctor," I said, "you might spare me. I have blamed myself enough; my life's forfeit anyway, and I should have been dead by now if Silver hadn't stood for me; and doctor, believe this, I can die—and I dare say I deserve it—but what I fear is torture. If they come to torture me—"

"Jim," the doctor interrupted, and his voice was quite changed, "Jim, I can't have this. Whip over, and we'll run for it."

"Doctor," said I, "I passed my word."

"I know, I know," he cried. "We can't help that, Jim, now. I'll take it on my shoulders, holus bolus, blame and shame, my boy; but stay here, I cannot let you. Jump! One jump, and you're out, and we'll run for it like antelopes."

"No," I replied; "you know right well you wouldn't do the thing yourself—neither you nor squire nor captain; and no more will I. Silver trusted me; I passed my word, and back I go. But, doctor, you did not let me finish. If they come to torture me, I might let slip a word of where the ship is, for I got the ship, part by luck and part by risking, and she lies in North Inlet, on the southern beach, and just below high water. At half tide she must be high and dry."

"The ship!" exclaimed the doctor.

Rapidly I described to him my adventures, and he heard me out in silence.

"There is a kind of fate in this," he observed when I had done. "Every step, it's you that saves our lives; and do you suppose by any chance that we are going to let you lose yours? That would be a poor return, my boy. You found out the plot; you found Ben Gunn—the best deed that ever you did, or will do, though you live to ninety. Oh, by Jupiter, and talking of Ben Gunn! Why, this is the mischief in person. Silver!" he cried. "Silver! I'll give you a piece of advice," he continued as the cook drew near again; "don't you be in any great hurry after that treasure."

"Why, sir, I do my possible, which that ain't," said Silver. "I can only, asking your pardon, save my life and the boy's by seeking for that treasure; and you may lay to that."

"Well, Silver," replied the doctor, "if that is so, I'll go one step further: look out for squalls when you find it."

"Sir," said Silver, "as between man and man, that's too much and too little. What you're after, why you left the block house, why you given me that there chart, I don't know, now, do I? And yet I done your bidding with my eyes shut and never a word of hope! But no, this here's too much. If you won't tell me what you mean plain out, just say so and I'll leave the helm."

"No," said the doctor musingly; "I've no right to say more; it's not my secret, you see, Silver, or, I give you my word, I'd tell it you. But I'll go as far with you as I dare go, and a step beyond, for I'll have my wig sorted by the captain or I'm mistaken! And first, I'll give you a bit of hope; Silver, if we both get alive out of this wolf-trap, I'll do my best to save you, short of perjury."

Silver's face was radiant. "You couldn't say more, I'm sure, sir, not if you was my mother," he cried.

"Well, that's my first concession," added the doctor. "My second is a piece of advice: keep the boy close beside you, and when you need help, halloo. I'm off to seek it for you, and that itself will show you if I speak at random. Good-bye, Jim."

And Dr. Livesey shook hands with me through the stockade, nodded to Silver, and set off at a brisk pace into the wood.

## 4

# THE TREASURE-HUNT—FLINT'S POINTER

"Jim," said Silver when we were alone, "if I saved your life, you saved mine; and I'll not forget it. I seen the doctor waving you to run for it—with the tail of my eye, I did; and I seen you say no, as plain as hearing. Jim, that's one to you. This is the first glint of hope I had since the attack failed, and I owe it you. And now, Jim, we're to go in for this here treasure-hunting, with sealed orders too, and I don't like it; and you and me must stick close, back to back like, and we'll save our necks in spite o' fate and fortune."

Just then a man hailed us from the fire that breakfast was ready, and we were soon seated here and there about the sand over biscuit and fried junk. They had lit a fire fit to roast an ox, and it was now grown so hot that they could only approach it from the windward, and even there not without precaution. In the same wasteful spirit, they had cooked, I suppose, three times more than we could eat; and one of them, with an empty laugh, threw what was left into the fire, which blazed and roared again over this unusual fuel. I never in my life saw men so careless of the morrow; hand to mouth is the only word that can describe their way of doing; and what with wasted food and sleeping sentries, though they were bold enough for a brush and be done with it, I could see their entire unfitness for anything like a prolonged campaign.

Even Silver, eating away, with Captain Flint upon his shoulder, had not a word of blame for their recklessness. And this the more surprised me, for I thought he had never shown himself so cunning as he did then.

"Aye, mates," said he, "it's lucky you have Barbecue to think for you with this here head. I got what I wanted, I did. Sure enough, they have the ship. Where they have it, I don't know yet; but once we hit the treasure, we'll have to jump about and find out. And then, mates, us that has the boats, I reckon, has the upper hand."

Thus he kept running on, with his mouth full of the hot bacon; thus he restored their hope and confidence, and, I more than suspect, repaired his own at the same time.

"As for hostage," he continued, "that's his last talk, I guess, with them he loves so dear. I've got my piece o' news, and thanky to him for that; but it's over and done. I'll take him in a line when we go treasure-hunting, for we'll keep him like so much gold, in case of accidents, you mark, and in the meantime. Once we got the ship and treasure both and off to sea like jolly companions, why then we'll talk Mr. Hawkins over, we will, and we'll give him his share, to be sure, for all his kindness."

It was no wonder the men were in a good humour now. For my part, I was horribly cast down. Should the scheme he had now sketched prove feasible, Silver, already doubly a traitor, would not hesitate to adopt it. He had still a foot in either camp, and there was no doubt he would prefer wealth and freedom with the pirates to a bare escape from hanging, which was the best he had to hope on our side.

Nay, and even if things so fell out that he was forced to keep his faith with Dr. Livesey, even then what danger lay before us! What a moment that would be when the suspicions of his followers turned to certainty and he and I should have to fight for dear life—he a cripple and I a boy—against five strong and active seamen!

Add to this double apprehension the mystery that still hung over the behaviour of my friends, their unexplained desertion of the stockade, their inexplicable cession of the chart, or harder still to understand, the doctor's last warning to Silver, "Look out for squalls when you find it," and you will readily believe how little taste I found in my breakfast and with how uneasy a heart I set forth behind my captors on the quest for treasure.

We made a curious figure, had anyone been there to see us—all in soiled sailor clothes and all but me armed to the teeth. Silver had two guns slung about him—one before and one behind—besides the great cutlass at his waist and a pistol in each pocket of his square-tailed coat. To complete his strange appearance, Captain Flint sat perched upon his shoulder and gabbling odds and ends of purposeless sea-talk. I had a line about my waist and followed obediently after the sea-cook, who held the loose end of the rope, now in his free hand, now between his powerful teeth. For all the world, I was led like a dancing bear.

The other men were variously burthened, some carrying picks and shovels—for that had been the very first necessary they brought ashore from the *Hispaniola*—others laden with pork, bread, and brandy for the midday meal. All the stores, I observed, came from our stock, and I could see the truth of Silver's words the night before. Had he not struck a bargain with the doctor, he and his mutineers, deserted by the ship, must have been driven to subsist on clear water and the proceeds of their hunting. Water would have been little to their taste; a sailor is not usually a good shot; and besides all that, when they were so short of eatables, it was not likely they would be very flush of powder.

Well, thus equipped, we all set out—even the fellow with the broken head, who should certainly have kept in shadow—and straggled, one after another, to the beach, where the two gigs awaited us. Even these bore trace of the drunken folly of the pirates, one in a broken thwart, and both in their muddy and unbailed condition. Both were to be carried along with us for the sake of safety; and so, with our numbers divided between them, we set forth upon the bosom of the anchorage.

As we pulled over, there was some discussion on the chart. The red cross was, of course, far too large to be a guide; and the terms of the note on the back, as you will hear, admitted of some ambiguity. They ran, the reader may remember, thus:

*Tall tree, Spy-glass shoulder, bearing a point to the N. of N.N.E.*
*Skeleton Island E.S.E. and by E.*
*Ten feet.*

A tall tree was thus the principal mark. Now, right before us the anchorage was bounded by a plateau from two to three hundred feet high, adjoining on the north the sloping southern shoulder of the Spy-glass and rising again towards the south into the rough, cliffy eminence called the Mizzen-mast Hill. The top of the plateau was dotted thickly with pine-trees of varying height. Every here and there, one of a different species rose forty or fifty feet clear above its neighbours, and which of these was the particular "tall tree" of Captain Flint could only be decided on the spot, and by the readings of the compass.

Yet, although that was the case, every man on board the boats had picked a favourite of his own ere we were half-way over, Long John alone shrugging his shoulders and bidding them wait till they were there.

We pulled easily, by Silver's directions, not to weary the hands prematurely, and after quite a long passage, landed at the mouth of the second river—that which runs down a woody cleft of the Spy-glass. Thence, bending to our left, we began to ascend the slope towards the plateau.

At the first outset, heavy, miry ground and a matted, marish vegetation greatly delayed our progress; but by little and little the hill began to steepen and become stony under foot, and the wood to change its character and to grow in a more open order. It was, indeed, a most pleasant portion of the island that we were now approaching. A heavy-scented broom and many flowering shrubs had almost taken the place of grass. Thickets of green nutmeg-trees were dotted here and there with the red columns and the broad shadow of the pines; and the first mingled their spice with the aroma of the others. The air, besides, was fresh and stirring, and this, under the sheer sunbeams, was a wonderful refreshment to our senses.

The party spread itself abroad, in a fan shape, shouting and leaping to and fro. About the centre, and a good way behind the rest, Silver and I followed—I tethered by my rope, he ploughing, with deep pants, among the sliding gravel. From time to time, indeed, I had to lend him a hand, or he must have missed his footing and fallen backward down the hill.

We had thus proceeded for about half a mile and were approaching the brow of the plateau when the man upon the farthest left began to cry aloud, as if in terror. Shout after shout came from him, and the others began to run in his direction.

"He can't 'a found the treasure," said old Morgan, hurrying past us from the right, "for that's clean a-top."

Indeed, as we found when we also reached the spot, it was something very different. At the foot of a pretty big pine and involved in a green creeper, which had even partly lifted some of the smaller bones, a human skeleton lay, with a few shreds of clothing, on the ground. I believe a chill struck for a moment to every heart.

"He was a seaman," said George Merry, who, bolder than the rest, had gone up close and was examining the rags of clothing. "Leastways, this is good sea-cloth."

"Aye, aye," said Silver; "like enough; you wouldn't look to find a bishop here, I reckon. But what sort of a way is that for bones to lie? 'Tain't in natur'."

Indeed, on a second glance, it seemed impossible to fancy that the body was in a natural position. But for some disarray (the work, perhaps, of the birds that had fed upon him or of the slow-growing creeper that had gradually enveloped his remains) the man lay perfectly straight—his feet pointing in one direction, his hands, raised above his head like a diver's, pointing directly in the opposite.

"I've taken a notion into my old numbskull," observed Silver. "Here's the compass; there's the tip-top p'int o' Skeleton Island, stickin' out like a tooth. Just take a bearing, will you, along the line of them bones."

It was done. The body pointed straight in the direction of the island, and the compass read duly E.S.E. and by E.

"I thought so," cried the cook; "this here is a p'inter. Right up there is our line for the Pole

Star and the jolly dollars. But, by thunder! If it don't make me cold inside to think of Flint. This is one of *his* jokes, and no mistake. Him and these six was alone here; he killed 'em, every man; and this one he hauled here and laid down by compass, shiver my timbers! They're long bones, and the hair's been yellow. Aye, that would be Allardyce. You mind Allardyce, Tom Morgan?"

"Aye, aye," returned Morgan; "I mind him; he owed me money, he did, and took my knife ashore with him."

"Speaking of knives," said another, "why don't we find his'n lying round? Flint warn't the man to pick a seaman's pocket; and the birds, I guess, would leave it be."

"By the powers, and that's true!" cried Silver.

"There ain't a thing left here," said Merry, still feeling round among the bones; "not a copper doit nor a baccy box. It don't look nat'ral to me."

"No, by gum, it don't," agreed Silver; "not nat'ral, nor not nice, says you. Great guns! Messmates, but if Flint was living, this would be a hot spot for you and me. Six they were, and six are we; and bones is what they are now."

"I saw him dead with these here deadlights," said Morgan. "Billy took me in. There he laid, with penny-pieces on his eyes."

"Dead—aye, sure enough he's dead and gone below," said the fellow with the bandage; "but if ever sperrit walked, it would be Flint's. Dear heart, but he died bad, did Flint!"

"Aye, that he did," observed another; "now he raged, and now he hollered for the rum, and now he sang. 'Fifteen Men' were his only song, mates; and I tell you true, I never rightly liked to hear it since. It was main hot, and the windy was open, and I hear that old song comin' out as clear as clear—and the death-haul on the man already."

"Come, come," said Silver; "stow this talk. He's dead, and he don't walk, that I know; leastways, he won't walk by day, and you may lay to that. Care killed a cat. Fetch ahead for the doubloons."

We started, certainly; but in spite of the hot sun and the staring daylight, the pirates no longer ran separate and shouting through the wood, but kept side by side and spoke with bated breath. The terror of the dead buccaneer had fallen on their spirits.

5

# THE TREASURE-HUNT—THE VOICE AMONG THE TREES

Partly from the damping influence of this alarm, partly to rest Silver and the sick folk, the whole party sat down as soon as they had gained the brow of the ascent.

The plateau being somewhat tilted towards the west, this spot on which we had paused commanded a wide prospect on either hand. Before us, over the tree-tops, we beheld the Cape of the Woods fringed with surf; behind, we not only looked down upon the anchorage and Skeleton Island, but saw—clear across the spit and the eastern lowlands—a great field of open sea upon the east. Sheer above us rose the Spyglass, here dotted with single pines, there black with precipices. There was no sound but that of the distant breakers, mounting from all round, and the chirp of countless insects in the brush. Not a man, not a sail, upon the sea; the very largeness of the view increased the sense of solitude.

Silver, as he sat, took certain bearings with his compass.

"There are three 'tall trees'" said he, "about in the right line from Skeleton Island. 'Spyglass shoulder,' I take it, means that lower p'int there. It's child's play to find the stuff now. I've half a mind to dine first."

"I don't feel sharp," growled Morgan. "Thinkin' o' Flint—I think it were—as done me."

"Ah, well, my son, you praise your stars he's dead," said Silver.

"He were an ugly devil," cried a third pirate with a shudder; "that blue in the face too!"

"That was how the rum took him," added Merry. "Blue! Well, I reckon he was blue. That's a true word."

Ever since they had found the skeleton and got upon this train of thought, they had spoken lower and lower, and they had almost got to whispering by now, so that the sound of their talk hardly interrupted the silence of the wood. All of a sudden, out of the middle of the trees in front of us, a thin, high, trembling voice struck up the well-known air and words:

"Fifteen men on the dead man's chest—
Yo-ho-ho, and a bottle of rum!"

I never have seen men more dreadfully affected than the pirates. The colour went from their six faces like enchantment; some leaped to their feet, some clawed hold of others; Morgan grovelled on the ground.

"It's Flint, by ——!" cried Merry.

The song had stopped as suddenly as it began—broken off, you would have said, in the middle of a note, as though someone had laid his hand upon the singer's mouth. Coming through the clear, sunny atmosphere among the green tree-tops, I thought it had sounded airily and sweetly; and the effect on my companions was the stranger.

"Come," said Silver, struggling with his ashen lips to get the word out; "this won't do. Stand by to go about. This is a rum start, and I can't name the voice, but it's someone skylarking—someone that's flesh and blood, and you may lay to that."

His courage had come back as he spoke, and some of the colour to his face along with it. Already the others had begun to lend an ear to this encouragement and were coming a little to themselves, when the same voice broke out again—not this time singing, but in a faint distant hail that echoed yet fainter among the clefts of the Spy-glass.

"Darby M'Graw," it wailed—for that is the word that best describes the sound—"Darby M'Graw! Darby M'Graw!" again and again and again; and then rising a little higher, and with an oath that I leave out: "Fetch aft the rum, Darby!"

The buccaneers remained rooted to the ground, their eyes starting from their heads. Long after the voice had died away they still stared in silence, dreadfully, before them.

"That fixes it!" gasped one. "Let's go."

"They was his last words," moaned Morgan, "his last words above board."

Dick had his Bible out and was praying volubly. He had been well brought up, had Dick, before he came to sea and fell among bad companions.

Still Silver was unconquered. I could hear his teeth rattle in his head, but he had not yet surrendered.

"Nobody in this here island ever heard of Darby," he muttered; "not one but us that's here." And then, making a great effort: "Shipmates," he cried, "I'm here to get that stuff, and I'll not be beat by man or devil. I never was feared of Flint in his life, and, by the powers, I'll face him dead. There's seven hundred thousand pound not a quarter of a mile from here. When did ever a gentleman o' fortune show his stern to that much dollars for a boozy old seaman with a blue mug—and him dead too?"

But there was no sign of reawakening courage in his followers, rather, indeed, of growing terror at the irreverence of his words.

"Belay there, John!" said Merry. "Don't you cross a sperrit."

And the rest were all too terrified to reply. They would have run away severally had they dared; but fear kept them together, and kept them close by John, as if his daring helped them. He, on his part, had pretty well fought his weakness down.

"Sperrit? Well, maybe," he said. "But there's one thing not clear to me. There was an echo. Now, no man ever seen a sperrit with a shadow; well then, what's he doing with an echo to him, I should like to know? That ain't in natur', surely?"

This argument seemed weak enough to me. But you can never tell what will affect the superstitious, and to my wonder, George Merry was greatly relieved.

"Well, that's so," he said. "You've a head upon your shoulders, John, and no mistake. 'Bout ship, mates! This here crew is on a wrong tack, I do believe. And come to think on it, it was like Flint's voice, I grant you, but not just so clear-away like it, after all. It was liker somebody else's voice now—it was liker—"

"By the powers, Ben Gunn!" roared Silver.

"Aye, and so it were," cried Morgan, springing on his knees. "Ben Gunn it were!"

"It don't make much odds, do it, now?" asked Dick. "Ben Gunn's not here in the body any more'n Flint."

But the older hands greeted this remark with scorn.

"Why, nobody minds Ben Gunn," cried Merry; "dead or alive, nobody minds him."

It was extraordinary how their spirits had returned and how the natural colour had revived in their faces. Soon they were chatting together, with intervals of listening; and not long after, hearing no further sound, they shouldered the tools and set forth again, Merry walking first with Silver's compass to keep them on the right line with Skeleton Island. He had said the truth: dead or alive, nobody minded Ben Gunn.

Dick alone still held his Bible, and looked around him as he went, with fearful glances; but he found no sympathy, and Silver even joked him on his precautions.

"I told you," said he—"I told you you had sp'iled your Bible. If it ain't no good to swear by, what do you suppose a sperrit would give for it? Not that!" and he snapped his big fingers, halting a moment on his crutch.

But Dick was not to be comforted; indeed, it was soon plain to me that the lad was falling sick; hastened by heat, exhaustion, and the shock of his alarm, the fever, predicted by Dr. Livesey, was evidently growing swiftly higher.

It was fine open walking here, upon the summit; our way lay a little downhill, for, as I have said, the plateau tilted towards the west. The pines, great and small, grew wide apart; and even between the clumps of nutmeg and azalea, wide open spaces baked in the hot sunshine. Striking, as we did, pretty near north-west across the island, we drew, on the one hand, ever nearer under the shoulders of the Spy-glass, and on the other, looked ever wider over that western bay where I had once tossed and trembled in the coracle.

The first of the tall trees was reached, and by the bearings proved the wrong one. So with the second. The third rose nearly two hundred feet into the air above a clump of underwood—a giant of a vegetable, with a red column as big as a cottage, and a wide shadow around in which a company could have manoeuvred. It was conspicuous far to sea both on the east and west and might have been entered as a sailing mark upon the chart.

But it was not its size that now impressed my companions; it was the knowledge that seven hundred thousand pounds in gold lay somewhere buried below its spreading shadow. The thought of the money, as they drew nearer, swallowed up their previous terrors. Their eyes burned in their heads; their feet grew speedier and lighter; their whole soul was bound up in that fortune, that whole lifetime of extravagance and pleasure, that lay waiting there for each of them.

Silver hobbled, grunting, on his crutch; his nostrils stood out and quivered; he cursed like a madman when the flies settled on his hot and shiny countenance; he plucked furiously at the line that held me to him and from time to time turned his eyes upon me with a deadly look. Certainly he took no pains to hide his thoughts, and certainly I read them like print. In the immediate nearness of the gold, all else had been forgotten: his promise and the doctor's warning were both things of the past, and I could not doubt that he hoped to seize upon the treasure, find and board the *Hispaniola* under cover of night, cut every honest throat about that island, and sail away as he had at first intended, laden with crimes and riches.

Shaken as I was with these alarms, it was hard for me to keep up with the rapid pace of the treasure-hunters. Now and again I stumbled, and it was then that Silver plucked so roughly at the rope and launched at me his murderous glances. Dick, who had dropped behind us and now brought up the rear, was babbling to himself both prayers and curses as his fever kept rising. This also added to my wretchedness, and to crown all, I was haunted by the thought of the tragedy that had once been acted on that plateau, when that ungodly buccaneer with the blue face—he who died at Savannah, singing and shouting for drink—had there, with his own hand, cut down his six accomplices. This grove that was now so peaceful must then have rung with cries, I thought; and even with the thought I could believe I heard it ringing still.

We were now at the margin of the thicket.

"Huzza, mates, all together!" shouted Merry; and the foremost broke into a run.

And suddenly, not ten yards further, we beheld them stop. A low cry arose. Silver doubled his pace, digging away with the foot of his crutch like one possessed; and next moment he and I had come also to a dead halt.

Before us was a great excavation, not very recent, for the sides had fallen in and grass had sprouted on the bottom. In this were the shaft of a pick broken in two and the boards of several packing-cases strewn around. On one of these boards I saw, branded with a hot iron, the name *Walrus*—the name of Flint's ship.

All was clear to probation. The *cache* had been found and rifled; the seven hundred thousand pounds were gone!

## 6

# THE FALL OF A CHIEFTAIN

There never was such an overturn in this world. Each of these six men was as though he had been struck. But with Silver the blow passed almost instantly. Every thought of his soul had been set full-stretch, like a racer, on that money; well, he was brought up, in a single second, dead; and he kept his head, found his temper, and changed his plan before the others had had time to realize the disappointment.

"Jim," he whispered, "take that, and stand by for trouble."

And he passed me a double-barrelled pistol.

At the same time, he began quietly moving northward, and in a few steps had put the hollow between us two and the other five. Then he looked at me and nodded, as much as to say, "Here is a narrow corner," as, indeed, I thought it was. His looks were not quite friendly, and I was so revolted at these constant changes that I could not forbear whispering, "So you've changed sides again."

There was no time left for him to answer in. The buccaneers, with oaths and cries, began to leap, one after another, into the pit and to dig with their fingers, throwing the boards aside as they did so. Morgan found a piece of gold. He held it up with a perfect spout of oaths. It was a two-guinea piece, and it went from hand to hand among them for a quarter of a minute.

"Two guineas!" roared Merry, shaking it at Silver. "That's your seven hundred thousand pounds, is it? You're the man for bargains, ain't you? You're him that never bungled nothing, you wooden-headed lubber!"

"Dig away, boys," said Silver with the coolest insolence; "you'll find some pig-nuts and I shouldn't wonder."

"Pig-nuts!" repeated Merry, in a scream. "Mates, do you hear that? I tell you now, that man there knew it all along. Look in the face of him and you'll see it wrote there."

"Ah, Merry," remarked Silver, "standing for cap'n again? You're a pushing lad, to be sure."

But this time everyone was entirely in Merry's favour. They began to scramble out of the excavation, darting furious glances behind them. One thing I observed, which looked well for us: they all got out upon the opposite side from Silver.

Well, there we stood, two on one side, five on the other, the pit between us, and nobody screwed up high enough to offer the first blow. Silver never moved; he watched them, very upright on his crutch, and looked as cool as ever I saw him. He was brave, and no mistake.

At last Merry seemed to think a speech might help matters.

"Mates," says he, "there's two of them alone there; one's the old cripple that brought us all here and blundered us down to this; the other's that cub that I mean to have the heart of. Now, mates—"

He was raising his arm and his voice, and plainly meant to lead a charge. But just then—crack! crack! crack!—three musket-shots flashed out of the thicket. Merry tumbled head foremost into the excavation; the man with the bandage spun round like a teetotum and fell all his length upon his side, where he lay dead, but still twitching; and the other three turned and ran for it with all their might.

Before you could wink, Long John had fired two barrels of a pistol into the struggling Merry, and as the man rolled up his eyes at him in the last agony, "George," said he, "I reckon I settled you."

At the same moment, the doctor, Gray, and Ben Gunn joined us, with smoking muskets, from among the nutmeg-trees.

"Forward!" cried the doctor. "Double quick, my lads. We must head 'em off the boats."

And we set off at a great pace, sometimes plunging through the bushes to the chest.

I tell you, but Silver was anxious to keep up with us. The work that man went through, leaping on his crutch till the muscles of his chest were fit to burst, was work no sound man ever equalled; and so thinks the doctor. As it was, he was already thirty yards behind us and on the verge of strangling when we reached the brow of the slope.

"Doctor," he hailed, "see there! No hurry!"

Sure enough there was no hurry. In a more open part of the plateau, we could see the three survivors still running in the same direction as they had started, right for Mizzenmast Hill. We were already between them and the boats; and so we four sat down to breathe, while Long John, mopping his face, came slowly up with us.

"Thank ye kindly, doctor," says he. "You came in in about the nick, I guess, for me and Hawkins. And so it's you, Ben Gunn!" he added. "Well, you're a nice one, to be sure."

"I'm Ben Gunn, I am," replied the maroon, wriggling like an eel in his embarrassment. "And," he added, after a long pause, "how do, Mr. Silver? Pretty well, I thank ye, says you."

"Ben, Ben," murmured Silver, "to think as you've done me!"

The doctor sent back Gray for one of the pick-axes deserted, in their flight, by the mutineers, and then as we proceeded leisurely downhill to where the boats were lying, related in a few words what had taken place. It was a story that profoundly interested Silver; and Ben Gunn, the half-idiot maroon, was the hero from beginning to end.

Ben, in his long, lonely wanderings about the island, had found the skeleton—it was he that had rifled it; he had found the treasure; he had dug it up (it was the haft of his pick-axe that lay broken in the excavation); he had carried it on his back, in many weary journeys, from the foot of the tall pine to a cave he had on the two-pointed hill at the north-east angle of the island, and there it had lain stored in safety since two months before the arrival of the *Hispaniola*.

When the doctor had wormed this secret from him on the afternoon of the attack, and when next morning he saw the anchorage deserted, he had gone to Silver, given him the chart, which was now useless—given him the stores, for Ben Gunn's cave was well supplied with goats' meat salted by himself—given anything and everything to get a chance of moving in safety from the stockade to the two-pointed hill, there to be clear of malaria and keep a guard upon the money.

"As for you, Jim," he said, "it went against my heart, but I did what I thought best for those who had stood by their duty; and if you were not one of these, whose fault was it?"

That morning, finding that I was to be involved in the horrid disappointment he had prepared for the mutineers, he had run all the way to the cave, and leaving the squire to guard the captain, had taken Gray and the maroon and started, making the diagonal across the island to be at hand beside the pine. Soon, however, he saw that our party had the start of him; and Ben Gunn, being fleet of foot, had been dispatched in front to do his best alone. Then it had occurred to him to work upon the superstitions of his former shipmates, and he was so far successful that Gray and the doctor had come up and were already ambushed before the arrival of the treasure-hunters.

"Ah," said Silver, "it were fortunate for me that I had Hawkins here. You would have let old John be cut to bits, and never given it a thought, doctor."

"Not a thought," replied Dr. Livesey cheerily.

And by this time we had reached the gigs. The doctor, with the pick-axe, demolished one of them, and then we all got aboard the other and set out to go round by sea for North Inlet.

This was a run of eight or nine miles. Silver, though he was almost killed already with fatigue, was set to an oar, like the rest of us, and we were soon skimming swiftly over a smooth sea. Soon we passed out of the straits and doubled the south-east corner of the island, round which, four days ago, we had towed the *Hispaniola*.

As we passed the two-pointed hill, we could see the black mouth of Ben Gunn's cave and a figure standing by it, leaning on a musket. It was the squire, and we waved a handkerchief and gave him three cheers, in which the voice of Silver joined as heartily as any.

Three miles farther, just inside the mouth of North Inlet, what should we meet but the *Hispaniola*, cruising by herself? The last flood had lifted her, and had there been much wind or a strong tide current, as in the southern anchorage, we should never have found her more, or found her stranded beyond help. As it was, there was little amiss beyond the wreck of the main-sail. Another anchor was got ready and dropped in a fathom and a half of water. We all pulled round again to Rum Cove, the nearest point for Ben Gunn's treasure-house; and then Gray, single-handed, returned with the gig to the *Hispaniola*, where he was to pass the night on guard.

A gentle slope ran up from the beach to the entrance of the cave. At the top, the squire met us. To me he was cordial and kind, saying nothing of my escapade either in the way of blame or praise. At Silver's polite salute he somewhat flushed.

"John Silver," he said, "you're a prodigious villain and imposter—a monstrous imposter, sir. I am told I am not to prosecute you. Well, then, I will not. But the dead men, sir, hang about your neck like mill-stones."

"Thank you kindly, sir," replied Long John, again saluting.

"I dare you to thank me!" cried the squire. "It is a gross dereliction of my duty. Stand back."

And thereupon we all entered the cave. It was a large, airy place, with a little spring and a pool of clear water, overhung with ferns. The floor was sand. Before a big fire lay Captain Smollett; and in a far corner, only duskily flickered over by the blaze, I beheld great heaps of coin and quadrilaterals built of bars of gold. That was Flint's treasure that we had come so far to seek and that had cost already the lives of seventeen men from the *Hispaniola*. How many it had cost in the amassing, what blood and sorrow, what good ships scuttled on the deep, what brave men walking the plank blindfold, what shot of cannon, what shame and lies and cruelty, perhaps no man alive could tell. Yet there were still three upon that island—Silver, and old Morgan, and Ben Gunn—who had each taken his share in these crimes, as each had hoped in vain to share in the reward.

"Come in, Jim," said the captain. "You're a good boy in your line, Jim, but I don't think you and me'll go to sea again. You're too much of the born favourite for me. Is that you, John Silver? What brings you here, man?"

"Come back to my dooty, sir," returned Silver.

"Ah!" said the captain, and that was all he said.

What a supper I had of it that night, with all my friends around me; and what a meal it was, with Ben Gunn's salted goat and some delicacies and a bottle of old wine from the *Hispaniola*. Never, I am sure, were people gayer or happier. And there was Silver, sitting back almost out of the firelight, but eating heartily, prompt to spring forward when anything was wanted, even joining quietly in our laughter—the same bland, polite, obsequious seaman of the voyage out.

## 7
# AND LAST

The next morning we fell early to work, for the transportation of this great mass of gold near a mile by land to the beach, and thence three miles by boat to the *Hispaniola,* was a considerable task for so small a number of workmen. The three fellows still abroad upon the island did not greatly trouble us; a single sentry on the shoulder of the hill was sufficient to ensure us against any sudden onslaught, and we thought, besides, they had had more than enough of fighting.

Therefore the work was pushed on briskly. Gray and Ben Gunn came and went with the boat, while the rest during their absences piled treasure on the beach. Two of the bars, slung in a rope's end, made a good load for a grown man—one that he was glad to walk slowly with. For my part, as I was not much use at carrying, I was kept busy all day in the cave packing the minted money into bread-bags.

It was a strange collection, like Billy Bones's hoard for the diversity of coinage, but so much larger and so much more varied that I think I never had more pleasure than in sorting them. English, French, Spanish, Portuguese, Georges, and Louises, doubloons and double guineas and moidores and sequins, the pictures of all the kings of Europe for the last hundred years, strange Oriental pieces stamped with what looked like wisps of string or bits of spider's web, round pieces and square pieces, and pieces bored through the middle, as if to wear them round your neck—nearly every variety of money in the world must, I think, have found a place in that collection; and for number, I am sure they were like autumn leaves, so that my back ached with stooping and my fingers with sorting them out.

Day after day this work went on; by every evening a fortune had been stowed aboard, but there was another fortune waiting for the morrow; and all this time we heard nothing of the three surviving mutineers.

At last—I think it was on the third night—the doctor and I were strolling on the shoulder of the hill where it overlooks the lowlands of the isle, when, from out the thick darkness below, the wind brought us a noise between shrieking and singing. It was only a snatch that reached our ears, followed by the former silence.

"Heaven forgive them," said the doctor; "'tis the mutineers!"

"All drunk, sir," struck in the voice of Silver from behind us.

Silver, I should say, was allowed his entire liberty, and in spite of daily rebuffs, seemed to regard himself once more as quite a privileged and friendly dependent. Indeed, it was remarkable how well he bore these slights and with what unwearying politeness he kept on trying to ingratiate himself with all. Yet, I think, none treated him better than a dog, unless it was Ben Gunn, who was still terribly afraid of his old quartermaster, or myself, who had really something to thank him for; although for that matter, I suppose, I had reason to think even worse of him than anybody else, for I had seen him meditating a fresh treachery upon the plateau. Accordingly, it was pretty gruffly that the doctor answered him.

"Drunk or raving," said he.

"Right you were, sir," replied Silver; "and precious little odds which, to you and me."

"I suppose you would hardly ask me to call you a humane man," returned the doctor with a sneer, "and so my feelings may surprise you, Master Silver. But if I were sure they were raving—as I am morally certain one, at least, of them is down with fever—I should leave this camp, and at whatever risk to my own carcass, take them the assistance of my skill."

"Ask your pardon, sir, you would be very wrong," quoth Silver. "You would lose your precious life, and you may lay to that. I'm on your side now, hand and glove; and I shouldn't wish for to see the party weakened, let alone yourself, seeing as I know what I owes you. But these men down there, they couldn't keep their word—no, not supposing they wished to; and what's more, they couldn't believe as you could."

"No," said the doctor. "You're the man to keep your word, we know that."

Well, that was about the last news we had of the three pirates. Only once we heard a gunshot a great way off and supposed them to be hunting. A council was held, and it was decided that we must desert them on the island—to the huge glee, I must say, of Ben Gunn, and with the strong approval of Gray. We left a good stock of powder and shot, the bulk of the salt goat, a few medicines, and some other necessaries, tools, clothing, a spare sail, a fathom or two of rope, and by the particular desire of the doctor, a handsome present of tobacco.

That was about our last doing on the island. Before that, we had got the treasure stowed and had shipped enough water and the remainder of the goat meat in case of any distress; and at last, one fine morning, we weighed anchor, which was about all that we could manage, and stood out of North Inlet, the same colours flying that the captain had flown and fought under at the palisade.

The three fellows must have been watching us closer than we thought for, as we soon had proved. For coming through the narrows, we had to lie very near the southern point, and there we saw all three of them kneeling together on a spit of sand, with their arms raised in supplication. It went to all our hearts, I think, to leave them in that wretched state; but we could not risk another mutiny; and to take them home for the gibbet would have been a cruel sort of kindness. The doctor hailed them and told them of the stores we had left, and where they were to find them. But they continued to call us by name and appeal to us, for God's sake, to be merciful and not leave them to die in such a place.

At last, seeing the ship still bore on her course and was now swiftly drawing out of earshot, one of them—I know not which it was—leapt to his feet with a hoarse cry, whipped his musket to his shoulder, and sent a shot whistling over Silver's head and through the main-sail.

After that, we kept under cover of the bulwarks, and when next I looked out they had disappeared from the spit, and the spit itself had almost melted out of sight in the growing distance. That was, at least, the end of that; and before noon, to my inexpressible joy, the highest rock of Treasure Island had sunk into the blue round of sea.

We were so short of men that everyone on board had to bear a hand—only the captain lying on a mattress in the stern and giving his orders, for though greatly recovered he was still in want of quiet. We laid her head for the nearest port in Spanish America, for we could not risk the voyage home without fresh hands; and as it was, what with baffling winds and a couple of fresh gales, we were all worn out before we reached it.

It was just at sundown when we cast anchor in a most beautiful land-locked gulf, and were immediately surrounded by shore boats full of Negroes and Mexican Indians and half-bloods selling fruits and vegetables and offering to dive for bits of money. The sight of so many good-humoured faces (especially the blacks), the taste of the tropical fruits, and above all the lights that began to shine in the town made a most charming contrast to our dark and bloody sojourn on the island; and the doctor and the squire, taking me along with them, went ashore to pass the early part of the night. Here they met the captain of an English man-of-war, fell in talk with him, went on board his ship, and, in short, had so agreeable a time that day was breaking when we came alongside the *Hispaniola*.

Ben Gunn was on deck alone, and as soon as we came on board he began, with wonderful contortions, to make us a confession. Silver was gone. The maroon had connived at his escape in a shore boat some hours ago, and he now assured us he had only done so to preserve our lives, which would certainly have been forfeit if "that man with the one leg had stayed aboard." But this was not all. The sea-cook had not gone empty-handed. He had cut through a bulkhead unobserved and had removed one of the sacks of coin, worth perhaps three or four hundred guineas, to help him on his further wanderings.

I think we were all pleased to be so cheaply quit of him.

Well, to make a long story short, we got a few hands on board, made a good cruise home, and the *Hispaniola* reached Bristol just as Mr. Blandly was beginning to think of fitting out her consort. Five men only of those who had sailed returned with her. "Drink and the devil had done for the rest," with a vengeance, although, to be sure, we were not quite in so bad a case as that other ship they sang about:

With one man of her crew alive,
What put to sea with seventy-five.

All of us had an ample share of the treasure and used it wisely or foolishly, according to our natures. Captain Smollett is now retired from the sea. Gray not only saved his money, but being suddenly smit with the desire to rise, also studied his profession, and he is now mate and part owner of a fine full-rigged ship, married besides, and the father of a family. As for Ben Gunn, he got a thousand pounds, which he spent or lost in three weeks, or to be more exact, in nineteen days, for he was back begging on the twentieth. Then he was given a lodge to keep, exactly as he had feared upon the island; and he still lives, a great favourite, though something of a butt, with the country boys, and a notable singer in church on Sundays and saints' days.

Of Silver we have heard no more. That formidable seafaring man with one leg has at last gone clean out of my life; but I dare say he met his old Negress, and perhaps still lives in comfort with her and Captain Flint. It is to be hoped so, I suppose, for his chances of comfort in another world are very small.

The bar silver and the arms still lie, for all that I know, where Flint buried them; and certainly they shall lie there for me. Oxen and wain-ropes would not bring me back again to that accursed island; and the worst dreams that ever I have are when I hear the surf booming about its coasts or start upright in bed with the sharp voice of Captain Flint still ringing in my ears: "Pieces of eight! Pieces of eight!"

# PETER AND WENDY

J. M. BARRIE

# I

# PETER BREAKS THROUGH

All children, except one, grow up. They soon know that they will grow up, and the way Wendy knew was this. One day when she was two years old she was playing in a garden, and she plucked another flower and ran with it to her mother. I suppose she must have looked rather delightful, for Mrs. Darling put her hand to her heart and cried, 'Oh, why can't you remain like this for ever!' This was all that passed between them on the subject, but henceforth Wendy knew that she must grow up. You always know after you are two. Two is the beginning of the end.

Of course they lived at 14, and until Wendy came her mother was the chief one. She was a lovely lady, with a romantic mind and such a sweet mocking mouth. Her romantic mind was like the tiny boxes, one within the other, that come from the puzzling East, however many you discover there is always one more; and her sweet mocking mouth had one kiss on it that Wendy could never get, though there it was, perfectly conspicuous in the right-hand corner.

The way Mr. Darling won her was this: the many gentlemen who had been boys when she was a girl discovered simultaneously that they loved her, and they all ran to her house to propose to her except Mr. Darling, who took a cab and nipped in first, and so he got her. He got all of her, except the innermost box and the kiss. He never knew about the box, and in time he gave up trying for the kiss. Wendy thought Napoleon could have got it, but I can picture him trying, and then going off in a passion, slamming the door.

Mr. Darling used to boast to Wendy that her mother not only loved him but respected him. He was one of those deep ones who know about stocks and shares. Of course no one really knows, but he quite seemed to know, and he often said stocks were up and shares were down in a way that would have made any woman respect him.

Mrs. Darling was married in white, and at first she kept the books perfectly, almost gleefully, as if it were a game, not so much as a brussels sprout was missing; but by and by whole cauliflowers dropped out, and instead of them there were pictures of babies without faces. She drew them when she should have been totting up. They were Mrs. Darling's guesses.

Wendy came first, then John, then Michael.

For a week or two after Wendy came it was doubtful whether they would be able to keep her, as she was another mouth to feed. Mr. Darling was frightfully proud of her, but he was very honourable, and he sat on the edge of Mrs. Darling's bed, holding her hand and calculating expenses, while she looked at him imploringly. She wanted to risk it, come what might, but that was not his way; his way was with a pencil and a piece of paper, and if she confused him with suggestions he had to begin at the beginning again.

'Now don't interrupt,' he would beg of her. 'I have one pound seventeen here, and two and six at the office; I can cut off my coffee at the office, say ten shillings, making two nine and six, with your eighteen and three makes three nine seven, with five naught naught in my cheque-book makes eight nine seven,—who is that moving?—eight nine seven, dot and carry seven—don't speak, my own—and the pound you lent to that man who came to the door—quiet, child—dot and carry child—there, you've done it!—did I say nine nine seven? yes, I said nine nine seven; the question is, can we try it for a year on nine nine seven?'

'Of course we can, George,' she cried. But she was prejudiced in Wendy's favour, and he was really the grander character of the two.

'Remember mumps,' he warned her almost threateningly, and off he went again. 'Mumps one pound, that is what I have put down, but I daresay it will be more like thirty shillings—don't speak—measles one five, German measles half a guinea, makes two fifteen six—don't waggle your finger—whooping-cough, say fifteen shillings'—and so on it went, and it added up differently each time; but at last Wendy just got through, with mumps reduced to twelve six, and the two kinds of measles treated as one.

There was the same excitement over John, and Michael had even a narrower squeak; but both were kept, and soon you might have seen the three of them going in a row to Miss Fulsom's Kindergarten school, accompanied by their nurse.

Mrs. Darling loved to have everything just so, and Mr. Darling had a passion for being exactly like his neighbours; so, of course, they had a nurse. As they were poor, owing to the amount of milk the children drank, this nurse was a prim Newfoundland dog, called Nana, who had belonged to no one in particular until the Darlings engaged her. She had always thought children important, however, and the Darlings had become acquainted with her in Kensington Gardens, where she spent most of her spare time peeping into perambulators, and was much hated by careless nursemaids, whom she followed to their homes and complained of to their mistresses. She proved to be quite a treasure of a nurse. How thorough she was at bath-time; and up at any moment of the night if one of her charges made the slightest cry. Of course her kennel was in the nursery. She had a genius for knowing when a cough is a thing to have no patience with and when it needs stocking round your throat. She believed to her last day in old-fashioned remedies like rhubarb leaf, and made sounds of contempt over all this new-fangled talk about germs, and so on. It was a lesson in propriety to see her escorting the children to school, walking sedately by their side when they were well behaved, and butting them back into line if they strayed. On John's footer days she never once forgot his sweater, and she usually carried an umbrella in her mouth in case of rain. There is a room in the basement of Miss Fulsom's school where the nurses wait. They sat on forms, while Nana lay on the floor, but that was the only difference. They affected to ignore her as of an inferior social status to themselves, and she despised their light talk. She resented visits to the nursery from Mrs. Darling's friends, but if they did come she first whipped off Michael's pinafore and put him into the one with blue braiding, and smoothed out Wendy and made a dash at John's hair.

No nursery could possibly have been conducted more correctly, and Mr. Darling knew it, yet he sometimes wondered uneasily whether the neighbours talked.

He had his position in the city to consider.

Nana also troubled him in another way. He had sometimes a feeling that she did not admire him. 'I know she admires you tremendously, George,' Mrs. Darling would assure him, and then she would sign to the children to be specially nice to father. Lovely dances followed, in which the only other servant, Liza, was sometimes allowed to join. Such a midget she looked in her long skirt and maid's cap, though she had sworn, when engaged, that she would never see ten again. The gaiety of those romps! And gayest of all was Mrs. Darling, who would pirouette so wildly that all you could see of her was the kiss, and then if you had dashed at her you might have got it. There never was a simpler happier family until the coming of Peter Pan.

Mrs. Darling first heard of Peter when she was tidying up her children's minds. It is the nightly custom of every good mother after her children are asleep to rummage in their minds and put things straight for next morning, repacking into their proper places the many articles that have wandered during the day. If you could keep awake (but of course you can't) you would see your own mother doing this, and you would find it very interesting to watch her. It is quite like tidying up drawers. You would see her on her knees, I expect, lingering humorously over some of your contents, wondering where on earth you had picked this thing up, making discoveries sweet and not so sweet, pressing this to her cheek as if it were as nice as a kitten, and hurriedly stowing that out of sight. When you wake in the morning, the naughtinesses and evil passions with which you went to bed have been folded up small and placed at the bottom of your mind; and on the top, beautifully aired, are spread out your prettier thoughts, ready for you to put on.

I don't know whether you have ever seen a map of a person's mind. Doctors sometimes draw maps of other parts of you, and your own map can become intensely interesting, but catch them trying to draw a map of a child's mind, which is not only confused, but keeps going round all the time. There are zigzag lines on it, just like your temperature on a card, and these are probably roads in the island; for the Neverland is always more or less an island, with astonishing splashes of colour here and there, and coral reefs and rakish-looking craft in the offing, and savages and lonely lairs, and gnomes who are mostly tailors, and caves through which a river runs, and princes with six elder brothers, and a hut fast going to decay, and one very small old lady with a hooked nose. It would be an easy map if that were all; but there is also first day at school, religion, fathers, the round pond, needlework, murders, hangings, verbs that take the dative, chocolate pudding day, getting into braces, say ninety-nine, three-pence for pulling out your tooth yourself, and so on; and either these are part of the island or they are another map showing through, and it is all rather confusing, especially as nothing will stand still.

Of course the Neverlands vary a good deal. John's, for instance, had a lagoon with flamingoes flying over it at which John was shooting, while Michael, who was very small, had a flamingo with lagoons flying over it. John lived in a boat turned upside down on the sands, Michael in a wigwam, Wendy in a house of leaves deftly sewn together. John had no friends, Michael had friends at night, Wendy had a pet wolf forsaken by its parents; but on the whole the Neverlands have a family resemblance, and if they stood still in a row you could say of them that they have each other's nose, and so forth. On these magic shores children at play are for ever beaching their coracles. We too have been there; we can still hear the sound of the surf, though we shall land no more.

Of all delectable islands the Neverland is the snuggest and most compact; not large and sprawly, you know, with tedious distances between one adventure and another, but nicely crammed. When you play at it by day with the chairs and table-cloth, it is not in the least alarming, but in the two minutes before you go to sleep it becomes very nearly real. That is why there are night-lights.

Occasionally in her travels through her children's minds Mrs. Darling found things she could not understand, and of these quite the most perplexing was the word Peter. She knew of no Peter, and yet he was here and there in John and Michael's minds, while Wendy's began to be scrawled all over with him. The name stood out in bolder letters than any of the other words, and as Mrs. Darling gazed she felt that it had an oddly cocky appearance.

'Yes, he is rather cocky,' Wendy admitted with regret. Her mother had been questioning her.

'But who is he, my pet?'

'He is Peter Pan, you know, mother.'

At first Mrs. Darling did not know, but after thinking back into her childhood she just remembered a Peter Pan who was said to live with the fairies. There were odd stories about him; as that when children died he went part of the way with them, so that they should not be frightened. She had believed in him at the time, but now that she was married and full of sense she quite doubted whether there was any such person.

'Besides,' she said to Wendy, 'he would be grown up by this time.'

'Oh no, he isn't grown up,' Wendy assured her confidently, 'and he is just my size.' She meant that he was her size in both mind and body; she didn't know how she knew it, she just knew it.

Mrs. Darling consulted Mr. Darling, but he smiled pooh-pooh. 'Mark my words,' he said, 'it is some nonsense Nana has been putting into their heads; just the sort of idea a dog would have. Leave it alone, and it will blow over.'

But it would not blow over; and soon the troublesome boy gave Mrs. Darling quite a shock.

Children have the strangest adventures without being troubled by them. For instance, they may remember to mention, a week after the event happened, that when they were in the wood they met their dead father and had a game with him. It was in this casual way that Wendy one morning made a disquieting revelation. Some leaves of a tree had been found on the nursery floor, which certainly were not there when the children went to bed, and Mrs. Darling was puzzling over them when Wendy said with a tolerant smile:

'I do believe it is that Peter again!'

'Whatever do you mean, Wendy?'

'It is so naughty of him not to wipe,' Wendy said, sighing. She was a tidy child.

She explained in quite a matter-of-fact way that she thought Peter sometimes came to the nursery in the night and sat on the foot of her bed and played on his pipes to her. Unfortunately she never woke, so she didn't know how she knew, she just knew.

'What nonsense you talk, precious. No one can get into the house without knocking.'

'I think he comes in by the window,' she said.

'My love, it is three floors up.'

'Were not the leaves at the foot of the window, mother?'

It was quite true; the leaves had been found very near the window.

Mrs. Darling did not know what to think, for it all seemed so natural to Wendy that you could not dismiss it by saying she had been dreaming.

'My child,' the mother cried, 'why did you not tell me of this before?'

'I forgot,' said Wendy lightly. She was in a hurry to get her breakfast.

Oh, surely she must have been dreaming.

But, on the other hand, there were the leaves. Mrs. Darling examined them carefully; they were skeleton leaves, but she was sure they did not come from any tree that grew in England. She crawled about the floor, peering at it with a candle for marks of a strange foot. She rattled the poker up the chimney and tapped the walls. She let down a tape from the window to the pavement, and it was a sheer drop of thirty feet, without so much as a spout to climb up by.

Certainly Wendy had been dreaming.

But Wendy had not been dreaming, as the very next night showed, the night on which the extraordinary adventures of these children may be said to have begun.

On the night we speak of all the children were once more in bed. It happened to be Nana's evening off, and Mrs. Darling had bathed them and sung to them till one by one they had let go her hand and slid away into the land of sleep.

All were looking so safe and cosy that she smiled at her fears now and sat down tranquilly by the fire to sew.

It was something for Michael, who on his birthday was getting into shirts. The fire was warm, however, and the nursery dimly lit by three night-lights, and presently the sewing lay on Mrs. Darling's lap. Then her head nodded, oh, so gracefully. She was asleep. Look at the four of them, Wendy and Michael over there, John here, and Mrs. Darling by the fire. There should have been a fourth night-light.

While she slept she had a dream. She dreamt that the Neverland had come too near and that a strange boy had broken through from it. He did not alarm her, for she thought she had seen him before in the faces of many women who have no children. Perhaps he is to be found in the faces of some mothers also. But in her dream he had rent the film that obscures the Neverland, and she saw Wendy and John and Michael peeping through the gap.

The dream by itself would have been a trifle, but while she was dreaming the window of the nursery blew open, and a boy did drop on the floor. He was accompanied by a strange light, no bigger than your fist, which darted about the room like a living thing; and I think it must have been this light that wakened Mrs. Darling.

She started up with a cry, and saw the boy, and somehow she knew at once that he was Peter Pan. If you or I or Wendy had been there we should have seen that he was very like Mrs. Darling's kiss. He was a lovely boy, clad in skeleton leaves and the juices that ooze out of trees; but the most entrancing thing about him was that he had all his first teeth. When he saw she was a grown-up, he gnashed the little pearls at her.

## 2

# THE SHADOW

Mrs. Darling screamed, and, as if in answer to a bell, the door opened, and Nana entered, returned from her evening out. She growled and sprang at the boy, who leapt lightly through the window. Again Mrs. Darling screamed, this time in distress for him, for she thought he was killed, and she ran down into the street to look for his little body, but it was not there; and she looked up, and in the black night she could see nothing but what she thought was a shooting star.

She returned to the nursery, and found Nana with something in her mouth, which proved to be the boy's shadow. As he leapt at the window Nana had closed it quickly, too late to catch him, but his shadow had not had time to get out; slam went the window and snapped it off.

You may be sure Mrs. Darling examined the shadow carefully, but it was quite the ordinary kind.

Nana had no doubt of what was the best thing to do with this shadow. She hung it out at the window, meaning 'He is sure to come back for it; let us put it where he can get it easily without disturbing the children.'

But unfortunately Mrs. Darling could not leave it hanging out at the window; it looked so like the washing and lowered the whole tone of the house. She thought of showing it to Mr. Darling, but he was totting up winter greatcoats for John and Michael, with a wet towel round his head to keep his brain clear, and it seemed a shame to trouble him; besides, she knew exactly what he would say: 'It all comes of having a dog for a nurse.'

She decided to roll the shadow up and put it away carefully in a drawer, until a fitting opportunity came for telling her husband. Ah me!

The opportunity came a week later, on that never-to-be-forgotten Friday. Of course it was a Friday.

'I ought to have been specially careful on a Friday,' she used to say afterwards to her husband, while perhaps Nana was on the other side of her, holding her hand.

'No, no,' Mr. Darling always said, 'I am responsible for it all. I, George Darling, did it. *Mea culpa, mea culpa.*' He had had a classical education.

They sat thus night after night recalling that fatal Friday, till every detail of it was stamped on their brains and came through on the other side like the faces on a bad coinage.

'If only I had not accepted that invitation to dine at 27,' Mrs. Darling said.

'If only I had not poured my medicine into Nana's bowl,' said Mr. Darling.

'If only I had pretended to like the medicine,' was what Nana's wet eyes said.

'My liking for parties, George.'

'My fatal gift of humour, dearest.'

'My touchiness about trifles, dear master and mistress.'

Then one or more of them would break down altogether; Nana at the thought, 'It's true, it's true, they ought not to have had a dog for a nurse.' Many a time it was Mr. Darling who put the handkerchief to Nana's eyes.

'That fiend!' Mr. Darling would cry, and Nana's bark was the echo of it, but Mrs. Darling never upbraided Peter; there was something in the right-hand corner of her mouth that wanted her not to call Peter names.

They would sit there in the empty nursery, recalling fondly every smallest detail of that dreadful evening. It had begun so uneventfully, so precisely like a hundred other evenings, with Nana putting on the water for Michael's bath and carrying him to it on her back.

'I won't go to bed,' he had shouted, like one who still believed that he had the last word on the subject, 'I won't, I won't. Nana, it isn't six o'clock yet. Oh dear, oh dear, I shan't love you any more, Nana. I tell you I won't be bathed, I won't, I won't!'

Then Mrs. Darling had come in, wearing her white evening-gown. She had dressed early because Wendy so loved to see her in her evening-gown, with the necklace George had given her. She was wearing Wendy's bracelet on her arm; she had asked for the loan of it. Wendy so loved to lend her bracelet to her mother.

She had found her two older children playing at being herself and father on the occasion of Wendy's birth, and John was saying:

'I am happy to inform you, Mrs. Darling, that you are now a mother,' in just such a tone as Mr. Darling himself may have used on the real occasion.

Wendy had danced with joy, just as the real Mrs. Darling must have done.

Then John was born, with the extra pomp that he conceived due to the birth of a male, and Michael came from his bath to ask to be born also, but John said brutally that they did not want any more.

Michael had nearly cried. 'Nobody wants me,' he said, and of course the lady in evening-dress could not stand that.

'I do,' she said, 'I so want a third child.'

'Boy or girl?' asked Michael, not too hopefully.

'Boy.'

Then he had leapt into her arms. Such a little thing for Mr. and Mrs. Darling and Nana to recall now, but not so little if that was to be Michael's last night in the nursery.

They go on with their recollections.

'It was then that I rushed in like a tornado, wasn't it?' Mr. Darling would say, scorning himself; and indeed he had been like a tornado.

Perhaps there was some excuse for him. He, too, had been dressing for the party, and all had gone well with him until he came to his tie. It is an astounding thing to have to tell, but this man, though he knew about stocks and shares, had no real mastery of his tie. Sometimes the thing yielded to him without a contest, but there were occasions when it would have been better for the house if he had swallowed his pride and used a made-up tie.

This was such an occasion. He came rushing into the nursery with the crumpled little brute of a tie in his hand.

'Why, what is the matter, father dear?'

'Matter!' he yelled; he really yelled. 'This tie, it will not tie.' He became dangerously sarcastic. 'Not round my neck! Round the bed-post! Oh yes, twenty times have I made it up round the bed-post, but round my neck, no! Oh dear no! begs to be excused!'

He thought Mrs. Darling was not sufficiently impressed, and he went on sternly, 'I warn you of this, mother, that unless this tie is round my neck we don't go out to dinner to-night, and if I don't go out to dinner to-night, I never go to the office again, and if I don't go to the office again, you and I starve, and our children will be flung into the streets.'

Even then Mrs. Darling was placid. 'Let me try, dear,' she said, and indeed that was what he had come to ask her to do; and with her nice cool hands she tied his tie for him, while the children stood around to see their fate decided. Some men would have resented her being able to do it so easily, but Mr. Darling was far too fine a nature for that; he thanked her carelessly, at once forgot his rage, and in another moment was dancing round the room with Michael on his back.

'How wildly we romped!' says Mrs. Darling now, recalling it.

'Our last romp!' Mr. Darling groaned.

'O George, do you remember Michael suddenly said to me, "How did you get to know me, mother?"'

'I remember!'

'They were rather sweet, don't you think, George?'

'And they were ours, ours, and now they are gone.'

The romp had ended with the appearance of Nana, and most unluckily Mr. Darling collided against her, covering his trousers with hairs. They were not only new trousers, but they were the first he had ever had with braid on them, and he had to bite his lip to prevent the tears coming. Of course Mrs. Darling brushed him, but he began to talk again about its being a mistake to have a dog for a nurse.

'George, Nana is a treasure.'

'No doubt, but I have an uneasy feeling at times that she looks upon the children as puppies.'

'Oh no, dear one, I feel sure she knows they have souls.'

'I wonder,' Mr. Darling said thoughtfully, 'I wonder.' It was an opportunity, his wife felt, for telling him about the boy. At first he pooh-poohed the story, but he became thoughtful when she showed him the shadow.

'It is nobody I know,' he said, examining it carefully, 'but he does look a scoundrel.'

'We were still discussing it, you remember,' says Mr. Darling, 'when Nana came in with Michael's medicine. You will never carry the bottle in your mouth again, Nana, and it is all my fault.

Strong man though he was, there is no doubt that he had behaved rather foolishly over the medicine. If he had a weakness, it was for thinking that all his life he had taken medicine boldly; and so now, when Michael dodged the spoon in Nana's mouth, he had said reprovingly, 'Be a man, Michael.'

'Won't; won't,' Michael cried naughtily. Mrs. Darling left the room to get a chocolate for him, and Mr. Darling thought this showed want of firmness.

'Mother, don't pamper him,' he called after her. 'Michael, when I was your age I took medicine without a murmur. I said "Thank you, kind parents, for giving me bottles to make me well."'

He really thought this was true, and Wendy, who was now in her night-gown, believed it also, and she said, to encourage Michael, 'That medicine you sometimes take, father, is much nastier, isn't it?'

'Ever so much nastier,' Mr. Darling said bravely, 'and I would take it now as an example to you, Michael, if I hadn't lost the bottle.'

He had not exactly lost it; he had climbed in the dead of night to the top of the wardrobe and hidden it there. What he did not know was that the faithful Liza had found it, and put it back on his wash-stand.

'I know where it is, father,' Wendy cried, always glad to be of service. 'I'll bring it,' and she was off before he could stop her. Immediately his spirits sank in the strangest way.

'John,' he said, shuddering, 'it's most beastly stuff. It's that nasty, sticky, sweet kind.'

'It will soon be over, father,' John said cheerily, and then in rushed Wendy with the medicine in a glass.

'I have been as quick as I could,' she panted.

'You have been wonderfully quick,' her father retorted, with a vindictive politeness that was quite thrown away upon her. 'Michael first,' he said doggedly.

'Father first,' said Michael, who was of a suspicious nature.

'I shall be sick, you know,' Mr. Darling said threateningly.

'Come on, father,' said John.

'Hold your tongue, John,' his father rapped out.

Wendy was quite puzzled. 'I thought you took it quite easily, father.'

'That is not the point,' he retorted. 'The point is, that there is more in my glass than in Michael's spoon.' His proud heart was nearly bursting. 'And it isn't fair; I would say it though it were with my last breath; it isn't fair.'

'Father, I am waiting,' said Michael coldly.

'It's all very well to say you are waiting; so am I waiting.'

'Father's a cowardy custard.'

'So are you a cowardy custard.'

'I'm not frightened.'

'Neither am I frightened.'

'Well, then, take it.'

'Well, then, you take it.'

Wendy had a splendid idea. 'Why not both take it at the same time?'

'Certainly,' said Mr. Darling. 'Are you ready, Michael?'

Wendy gave the words, one, two, three, and Michael took his medicine, but Mr. Darling slipped his behind his back.

There was a yell of rage from Michael, and 'O father!' Wendy exclaimed.

'What do you mean by "O father"?' Mr. Darling demanded. 'Stop that row, Michael. I meant to take mine, but I—I missed it.'

It was dreadful the way all the three were looking at him, just as if they did not admire him. 'Look here, all of you,' he said entreatingly, as soon as Nana had gone into the bathroom, 'I have just thought of a splendid joke. I shall pour my medicine into Nana's bowl, and she will drink it, thinking it is milk!'

It was the colour of milk; but the children did not have their father's sense of humour, and they looked at him reproachfully as he poured the medicine into Nana's bowl. 'What fun,' he said doubtfully, and they did not dare expose him when Mrs. Darling and Nana returned.

'Nana, good dog,' he said, patting her, 'I have put a little milk into your bowl, Nana.'

Nana wagged her tail, ran to the medicine, and began lapping it. Then she gave Mr. Darling such a look, not an angry look: she showed him the great red tear that makes us so sorry for noble dogs, and crept into her kennel.

Mr. Darling was frightfully ashamed of himself, but he would not give in. In a horrid silence Mrs. Darling smelt the bowl. 'O George,' she said, 'it's your medicine!'

'It was only a joke,' he roared, while she comforted her boys, and Wendy hugged Nana. 'Much good,' he said bitterly, 'my wearing myself to the bone trying to be funny in this house.'

And still Wendy hugged Nana. 'That's right,' he shouted. 'Coddle her! Nobody coddles me. Oh dear no! I am only the breadwinner, why should I be coddled, why, why, why!'

'George,' Mrs. Darling entreated him, 'not so loud; the servants will hear you.' Somehow they had got into the way of calling Liza the servants.

'Let them,' he answered recklessly. 'Bring in the whole world. But I refuse to allow that dog to lord it in my nursery for an hour longer.'

The children wept, and Nana ran to him beseechingly, but he waved her back. He felt he was a strong man again. 'In vain, in vain,' he cried; 'the proper place for you is the yard, and there you go to be tied up this instant.'

'George, George,' Mrs. Darling whispered, 'remember what I told you about that boy.'

Alas, he would not listen. He was determined to show who was master in that house, and when commands would not draw Nana from the kennel, he lured her out of it with honeyed words, and seizing her roughly, dragged her from the nursery. He was ashamed of himself, and yet he did it. It was all owing to his too affectionate nature, which craved for admiration. When he had tied her up in the back-yard, the wretched father went and sat in the passage, with his knuckles to his eyes.

In the meantime Mrs. Darling had put the children to bed in unwonted silence and lit their night-lights. They could hear Nana barking, and John whimpered, 'It is because he is chaining her up in the yard,' but Wendy was wiser.

'That is not Nana's unhappy bark,' she said, little guessing what was about to happen; 'that is her bark when she smells danger.'

Danger!

'Are you sure, Wendy?'

'Oh yes.'

Mrs. Darling quivered and went to the window. It was securely fastened. She looked out, and the night was peppered with stars. They were crowding round the house, as if curious to see what was to take place there, but she did not notice this, nor that one or two of the smaller ones winked at her. Yet a nameless fear clutched at her heart and made her cry, 'Oh, how I wish that I wasn't going to a party to-night!'

Even Michael, already half asleep, knew that she was perturbed, and he asked, 'Can anything harm us, mother, after the night-lights are lit?'

'Nothing, precious,' she said; 'they are the eyes a mother leaves behind her to guard her children.'

She went from bed to bed singing enchantments over them, and little Michael flung his arms round her. 'Mother,' he cried, 'I'm glad of you.' They were the last words she was to hear from him for a long time.

No. 27 was only a few yards distant, but there had been a slight fall of snow, and Father and Mother Darling picked their way over it deftly not to soil their shoes. They were already the only persons in the street, and all the stars were watching them. Stars are beautiful, but they may not take an active part in anything, they must just look on for ever. It is a punishment put on them for something they did so long ago that no star now knows what it was. So the older ones have become glassy-eyed and seldom speak (winking is the star language), but the little ones still wonder. They are not really friendly to Peter, who has a mischievous way of stealing up behind them and trying to blow them out; but they are so fond of fun that they were on his side to-night, and anxious to get the grown-ups out of the way. So as soon as the door of 27 closed on Mr. and Mrs. Darling there was a commotion in the firmament, and the smallest of all the stars in the Milky Way screamed out:

'Now, Peter!'

## ❧ 3 ❧

# COME AWAY, COME AWAY!

For a moment after Mr. and Mrs. Darling left the house the night-lights by the beds of the three children continued to burn clearly. They were awfully nice little night-lights, and one cannot help wishing that they could have kept awake to see Peter; but Wendy's light blinked and gave such a yawn that the other two yawned also, and before they could close their mouths all the three went out.

There was another light in the room now, a thousand times brighter than the night-lights, and in the time we have taken to say this, it has been in all the drawers in the nursery, looking for Peter's shadow, rummaged the wardrobe and turned every pocket inside out. It was not really a light; it made this light by flashing about so quickly, but when it came to rest for a second you saw it was a fairy, no longer than your hand, but still growing. It was a girl called Tinker Bell exquisitely gowned in a skeleton leaf, cut low and square, through which her figure could be seen to the best advantage. She was slightly inclined to *embonpoint*.

A moment after the fairy's entrance the window was blown open by the breathing of the little stars, and Peter dropped in. He had carried Tinker Bell part of the way, and his hand was still messy with the fairy dust.

'Tinker Bell,' he called softly, after making sure that the children were asleep, 'Tink, where are you?' She was in a jug for the moment, and liking it extremely; she had never been in a jug before.

'Oh, do come out of that jug, and tell me, do you know where they put my shadow?'

The loveliest tinkle as of golden bells answered him. It is the fairy language. You ordinary children can never hear it, but if you were to hear it you would know that you had heard it once before.

Tink said that the shadow was in the big box. She meant the chest of drawers, and Peter jumped at the drawers, scattering their contents to the floor with both hands, as kings toss ha'pence to the crowd. In a moment he had recovered his shadow, and in his delight he forgot that he had shut Tinker Bell up in the drawer.

If he thought at all, but I don't believe he ever thought, it was that he and his shadow, when brought near each other, would join like drops of water; and when they did not he was appalled. He tried to stick it on with soap from the bathroom, but that also failed. A shudder passed through Peter, and he sat on the floor and cried.

His sobs woke Wendy, and she sat up in bed. She was not alarmed to see a stranger crying on the nursery floor; she was only pleasantly interested.

'Boy,' she said courteously, 'why are you crying?'

Peter could be exceedingly polite also, having learned the grand manner at fairy ceremonies, and he rose and bowed to her beautifully. She was much pleased, and bowed beautifully to him from the bed.

'What's your name?' he asked.

'Wendy Moira Angela Darling,' she replied with some satisfaction. 'What is your name?'

'Peter Pan.'

She was already sure that he must be Peter, but it did seem a comparatively short name.

'Is that all?'

'Yes,' he said rather sharply. He felt for the first time that it was a shortish name.

'I'm so sorry,' said Wendy Moira Angela.

'It doesn't matter,' Peter gulped.

She asked where he lived.

'Second to the right,' said Peter, 'and then straight on till morning.'

'What a funny address!'

Peter had a sinking. For the first time he felt that perhaps it was a funny address.

'No, it isn't,' he said.

'I mean,' Wendy said nicely, remembering that she was hostess, 'is that what they put on the letters?'

He wished she had not mentioned letters.

'Don't get any letters,' he said contemptuously.

'But your mother gets letters?'

'Don't have a mother,' he said. Not only had he no mother, but he had not the slightest desire to have one. He thought them very overrated persons. Wendy, however, felt at once that she was in the presence of a tragedy.

'O Peter, no wonder you were crying,' she said, and got out of bed and ran to him.

'I wasn't crying about mothers,' he said rather indignantly. 'I was crying because I can't get my shadow to stick on. Besides, I wasn't crying.'

'It has come off?'

'Yes.'

Then Wendy saw the shadow on the floor, looking so draggled, and she was frightfully sorry for Peter. 'How awful!' she said, but she could not help smiling when she saw that he had been trying to stick it on with soap. How exactly like a boy!

Fortunately she knew at once what to do 'It must be sewn on,' she said, just a little patronisingly.

'What's sewn?' he asked.

'You're dreadfully ignorant.'

'No, I'm not.'

But she was exulting in his ignorance. 'I shall sew it on for you, my little man,' she said, though he was as tall as herself; and she got out her housewife, and sewed the shadow on to Peter's foot.

'I daresay it will hurt a little,' she warned him.

'Oh, I shan't cry,' said Peter, who was already of opinion that he had never cried in his life. And he clenched his teeth and did not cry; and soon his shadow was behaving properly, though still a little creased.

'Perhaps I should have ironed it,' Wendy said thoughtfully; but Peter, boylike, was indifferent to appearances, and he was now jumping about in the wildest glee. Alas, he had already forgotten that he owed his bliss to Wendy. He thought he had attached the shadow himself. 'How clever I am,' he crowed rapturously, 'oh, the cleverness of me!'

It is humiliating to have to confess that this conceit of Peter was one of his most fascinating qualities. To put it with brutal frankness, there never was a cockier boy.

But for the moment Wendy was shocked. 'You conceit,' she exclaimed, with frightful sarcasm; 'of course I did nothing!'

'You did a little,' Peter said carelessly, and continued to dance.

'A little!' she replied with hauteur; 'if I am no use I can at least withdraw'; and she sprang in the most dignified way into bed and covered her face with the blankets.

To induce her to look up he pretended to be going away, and when this failed he sat on the end of the bed and tapped her gently with his foot. 'Wendy,' he said, 'don't withdraw. I can't help crowing, Wendy, when I'm pleased with myself.' Still she would not look up, though she was listening eagerly. 'Wendy,' he continued, in a voice that no woman has ever yet been able to resist, 'Wendy, one girl is more use than twenty boys.'

Now Wendy was every inch a woman, though there were not very many inches, and she peeped out of the bedclothes.

'Do you really think so, Peter?'

'Yes, I do.'

'I think it's perfectly sweet of you,' she declared, 'and I'll get up again'; and she sat with him on the side of the bed. She also said she would give him a kiss if he liked, but Peter did not know what she meant, and he held out his hand expectantly.

'Surely you know what a kiss is?' she asked, aghast.

'I shall know when you give it to me,' he replied stiffly; and not to hurt his feelings she gave him a thimble.

'Now,' said he, 'shall I give you a kiss?' and she replied with a slight primness, 'If you please.' She made herself rather cheap by inclining her face toward him, but he merely dropped an acorn button into her hand; so she slowly returned her face to where it had been before, and said nicely that she would wear his kiss on the chain round her neck. It was lucky that she did put it on that chain, for it was afterwards to save her life.

When people in our set are introduced, it is customary for them to ask each other's age, and so Wendy, who always liked to do the correct thing, asked Peter how old he was. It was not really a happy question to ask him; it was like an examination paper that asks grammar, when what you want to be asked is Kings of England.

'I don't know,' he replied uneasily, 'but I am quite young.' He really knew nothing about it; he had merely suspicions, but he said at a venture, 'Wendy, I ran away the day I was born.'

Wendy was quite surprised, but interested; and she indicated in the charming drawing-room manner, by a touch on her night-gown, that he could sit nearer her.

'It was because I heard father and mother,' he explained in a low voice, 'talking about what I was to be when I became a man.' He was extraordinarily agitated now. 'I don't want ever to be a man,' he said with passion. 'I want always to be a little boy and to have fun. So I ran away to Kensington Gardens and lived a long long time among the fairies.'

She gave him a look of the most intense admiration, and he thought it was because he had run away, but it was really because he knew fairies. Wendy had lived such a home life that to know fairies struck her as quite delightful. She poured out questions about them, to his surprise, for they were rather a nuisance to him, getting in his way and so on, and indeed he sometimes had to give them a hiding. Still, he liked them on the whole, and he told her about the beginning of fairies.

'You see, Wendy, when the first baby laughed for the first time, its laugh broke into a thousand pieces, and they all went skipping about, and that was the beginning of fairies.'

Tedious talk this, but being a stay-at-home she liked it.

'And so,' he went on good-naturedly, 'there ought to be one fairy for every boy and girl.'

'Ought to be? Isn't there?'

'No. You see children know such a lot now, they soon don't believe in fairies, and every time a child says, 'I don't believe in fairies,' there is a fairy somewhere that falls down dead.

Really, he thought they had now talked enough about fairies, and it struck him that Tinker Bell was keeping very quiet. 'I can't think where she has gone to,' he said, rising, and he called Tink by name. Wendy's heart went flutter with a sudden thrill.

'Peter,' she cried, clutching him, 'you don't mean to tell me that there is a fairy in this room!'

'She was here just now,' he said a little impatiently. 'You don't hear her, do you?' and they both listened.

'The only sound I hear,' said Wendy, 'is like a tinkle of bells.'

'Well, that's Tink, that's the fairy language. I think I hear her too.'

The sound came from the chest of drawers, and Peter made a merry face. No one could ever look quite so merry as Peter, and the loveliest of gurgles was his laugh. He had his first laugh still.

'Wendy,' he whispered gleefully, 'I do believe I shut her up in the drawer!'

He let poor Tink out of the drawer, and she flew about the nursery screaming with fury. 'You shouldn't say such things,' Peter retorted. 'Of course I'm very sorry, but how could I know you were in the drawer?'

Wendy was not listening to him. 'O Peter,' she cried, 'if she would only stand still and let me see her!'

'They hardly ever stand still,' he said, but for one moment Wendy saw the romantic figure come to rest on the cuckoo clock. 'O the lovely!' she cried, though Tink's face was still distorted with passion.

'Tink,' said Peter amiably, 'this lady says she wishes you were her fairy.'

Tinker Bell answered insolently.

'What does she say, Peter?'

He had to translate. 'She is not very polite. She says you are a great ugly girl, and that she is my fairy.'

He tried to argue with Tink. 'You know you can't be my fairy, Tink, because I am a gentleman and you are a lady.'

To this Tink replied in these words, 'You silly ass,' and disappeared into the bathroom. 'She is quite a common fairy,' Peter explained apologetically; 'she is called Tinker Bell because she mends the pots and kettles.'

They were together in the armchair by this time, and Wendy plied him with more questions.

'If you don't live in Kensington Gardens now——'

'Sometimes I do still.'

'But where do you live mostly now?'

'With the lost boys.'

'Who are they?'

'They are the children who fall out of their perambulators when the nurse is looking the other way. If they are not claimed in seven days they are sent far away to the Neverland to defray expenses. I'm captain.'

'What fun it must be!'

'Yes,' said cunning Peter, 'but we are rather lonely. You see we have no female companionship.'

'Are none of the others girls?'

'Oh no; girls, you know, are much too clever to fall out of their prams.'

This flattered Wendy immensely. 'I think,' she said, 'it is perfectly lovely the way you talk about girls; John there just despises us.'

For reply Peter rose and kicked John out of bed, blankets and all; one kick. This seemed to Wendy rather forward for a first meeting, and she told him with spirit that he was not captain in her house. However, John continued to sleep so placidly on the floor that she allowed him to remain there. 'And I know you meant to be kind,' she said, relenting, 'so you may give me a kiss.'

For the moment she had forgotten his ignorance about kisses. 'I thought you would want it back,' he said a little bitterly, and offered to return her the thimble.

'Oh dear,' said the nice Wendy, 'I don't mean a kiss, I mean a thimble.'

'What's that?'

'It's like this.' She kissed him.

'Funny!' said Peter gravely. 'Now shall I give you a thimble?'

'If you wish to,' said Wendy, keeping her head erect this time.

Peter thimbled her, and almost immediately she screeched. 'What is it, Wendy?'

'It was exactly as if some one were pulling my hair.'

'That must have been Tink. I never knew her so naughty before.'

And indeed Tink was darting about again, using offensive language.

'She says she will do that to you, Wendy, every time I give you a thimble.'

'But why?'

'Why, Tink?'

Again Tink replied, 'You silly ass.' Peter could not understand why, but Wendy understood; and she was just slightly disappointed when he admitted that he came to the nursery window not to see her but to listen to stories.

'You see I don't know any stories. None of the lost boys know any stories.'

'How perfectly awful,' Wendy said.

'Do you know,' Peter asked, 'why swallows build in the eaves of houses? It is to listen to the stories. O Wendy, your mother was telling you such a lovely story.'

'Which story was it?'

'About the prince who couldn't find the lady who wore the glass slipper.'

'Peter,' said Wendy excitedly, 'that was Cinderella, and he found her, and they lived happy ever after.'

Peter was so glad that he rose from the floor, where they had been sitting, and hurried to the window. 'Where are you going?' she cried with misgiving.

'To tell the other boys.'

'Don't go, Peter,' she entreated, 'I know such lots of stories.'

Those were her precise words, so there can be no denying that it was she who first tempted him.

He came back, and there was a greedy look in his eyes now which ought to have alarmed her, but did not.

'Oh, the stories I could tell to the boys!' she cried, and then Peter gripped her and began to draw her toward the window.

'Let me go!' she ordered him.

'Wendy, do come with me and tell the other boys.'

Of course she was very pleased to be asked, but she said, 'Oh dear, I can't. Think of mummy! Besides, I can't fly.'

'I'll teach you.'

'Oh, how lovely to fly.'

'I'll teach you how to jump on the wind's back, and then away we go.'

'Oo!' she exclaimed rapturously.

'Wendy, Wendy, when you are sleeping in your silly bed you might be flying about with me saying funny things to the stars.'

'Oo!'

'And, Wendy, there are mermaids.'

'Mermaids! With tails?'

'Such long tails.'

'Oh,' cried Wendy, 'to see a mermaid!'

He had become frightfully cunning. 'Wendy,' he said, 'how we should all respect you.'

She was wriggling her body in distress. It was quite as if she were trying to remain on the nursery floor.

But he had no pity for her.

'Wendy,' he said, the sly one, 'you could tuck us in at night.'

'Oo!'

'None of us has ever been tucked in at night.'

'Oo,' and her arms went out to him.

'And you could darn our clothes, and make pockets for us. None of us has any pockets.'

How could she resist. 'Of course it's awfully fascinating!' she cried. 'Peter, would you teach John and Michael to fly too?'

'If you like,' he said indifferently; and she ran to John and Michael and shook them. 'Wake up,' she cried, 'Peter Pan has come and he is to teach us to fly.'

John rubbed his eyes. 'Then I shall get up,' he said. Of course he was on the floor already. 'Hallo,' he said, 'I am up!'

Michael was up by this time also, looking as sharp as a knife with six blades and a saw, but Peter suddenly signed silence. Their faces assumed the awful craftiness of children listening for sounds from the grown-up world. All was as still as salt. Then everything was right. No, stop! Everything was wrong. Nana, who had been barking distressfully all the evening, was quiet now. It was her silence they had heard.

'Out with the light! Hide! Quick!' cried John, taking command for the only time throughout the whole adventure. And thus when Liza entered, holding Nana, the nursery seemed quite its old self, very dark; and you could have sworn you heard its three wicked inmates breathing angelically as they slept. They were really doing it artfully from behind the window curtains.

Liza was in a bad temper, for she was mixing the Christmas puddings in the kitchen, and had been drawn away from them, with a raisin still on her cheek, by Nana's absurd suspicions. She thought the best way of getting a little quiet was to take Nana to the nursery for a moment, but in custody of course.

'There, you suspicious brute,' she said, not sorry that Nana was in disgrace, 'they are perfectly safe, aren't they? Every one of the little angels sound asleep in bed. Listen to their gentle breathing.'

Here Michael, encouraged by his success, breathed so loudly that they were nearly detected. Nana knew that kind of breathing, and she tried to drag herself out of Liza's clutches.

But Liza was dense. 'No more of it, Nana,' she said sternly, pulling her out of the room. 'I warn you if you bark again I shall go straight for master and missus and bring them home from the party, and then, oh, won't master whip you, just.'

She tied the unhappy dog up again, but do you think Nana ceased to bark? Bring master and missus home from the party! Why, that was just what she wanted. Do you think she cared whether she was whipped so long as her charges were safe? Unfortunately Liza returned to her puddings, and Nana, seeing that no help would come from her, strained and strained at the chain until at last she broke it. In another moment she had burst into the dining-room of 27 and flung up her paws to heaven, her most expressive way of making a communication. Mr. and Mrs. Darling knew at once that something terrible was happening in their nursery, and without a good-bye to their hostess they rushed into the street.

But it was now ten minutes since three scoundrels had been breathing behind the curtains; and Peter Pan can do a great deal in ten minutes.

We now return to the nursery.

'It's all right,' John announced, emerging from his hiding-place. 'I say, Peter, can you really fly?'

Instead of troubling to answer him Peter flew round the room, taking the mantelpiece on the way.

'How topping!' said John and Michael.

'How sweet!' cried Wendy.

'Yes, I'm sweet, oh, I am sweet!' said Peter, forgetting his manners again.

It looked delightfully easy, and they tried it first from the floor and then from the beds, but they always went down instead of up.

'I say, how do you do it?' asked John, rubbing his knee. He was quite a practical boy.

'You just think lovely wonderful thoughts,' Peter explained, 'and they lift you up in the air.'

He showed them again.

'You're so nippy at it,' John said; 'couldn't you do it very slowly once?'

Peter did it both slowly and quickly. 'I've got it now, Wendy!' cried John, but soon he found he had not. Not one of them could fly an inch, though even Michael was in words of two syllables, and Peter did not know A from Z.

Of course Peter had been trifling with them, for no one can fly unless the fairy dust has been blown on him. Fortunately, as we have mentioned, one of his hands was messy with it, and he blew some on each of them, with the most superb results.

'Now just wriggle your shoulders this way,' he said, 'and let go.'

They were all on their beds, and gallant Michael let go first. He did not quite mean to let go, but he did it, and immediately he was borne across the room.

'I flewed!' he screamed while still in mid-air.

John let go and met Wendy near the bathroom.

'Oh, lovely!'

'Oh, ripping!'

'Look at me!'

'Look at me!'

'Look at me!'

They were not nearly so elegant as Peter, they could not help kicking a little, but their heads were bobbing against the ceiling, and there is almost nothing so delicious as that. Peter gave Wendy a hand at first, but had to desist, Tink was so indignant.

Up and down they went, and round and round. Heavenly was Wendy's word.

'I say,' cried John, 'why shouldn't we all go out!'

Of course it was to this that Peter had been luring them.

Michael was ready: he wanted to see how long it took him to do a billion miles. But Wendy hesitated.

'Mermaids!' said Peter again.

'Oo!'

'And there are pirates.'

'Pirates,' cried John, seizing his Sunday hat, 'let us go at once.'

It was just at this moment that Mr. and Mrs. Darling hurried with Nana out of 27. They ran into the middle of the street to look up at the nursery window; and, yes, it was still shut, but the room was ablaze with light, and most heart-gripping sight of all, they could see in shadow on the curtain three little figures in night attire circling round and round, not on the floor but in the air.

Not three figures, four!

In a tremble they opened the street door. Mr. Darling would have rushed upstairs, but Mrs. Darling signed to him to go softly. She even tried to make her heart go softly.

Will they reach the nursery in time? If so, how delightful for them, and we shall all breathe a sigh of relief, but there will be no story. On the other hand, if they are not in time, I solemnly promise that it will all come right in the end.

They would have reached the nursery in time had it not been that the little stars were watching them. Once again the stars blew the window open, and that smallest star of all called out:

'Cave, Peter!'

Then Peter knew that there was not a moment to lose. 'Come,' he cried imperiously, and soared out at once into the night, followed by John and Michael and Wendy.

Mr. and Mrs. Darling and Nana rushed into the nursery too late. The birds were flown.

## 4
# THE FLIGHT

'Second to the right, and straight on till morning.'

That, Peter had told Wendy, was the way to the Neverland; but even birds, carrying maps and consulting them at windy corners, could not have sighted it with these instructions. Peter, you see, just said anything that came into his head.

At first his companions trusted him implicitly, and so great were the delights of flying that they wasted time circling round church spires or any other tall objects on the way that took their fancy.

John and Michael raced, Michael getting a start.

They recalled with contempt that not so long ago they had thought themselves fine fellows for being able to fly round a room.

Not so long ago. But how long ago? They were flying over the sea before this thought began to disturb Wendy seriously. John thought it was their second sea and their third night.

Sometimes it was dark and sometimes light, and now they were very cold and again too warm. Did they really feel hungry at times, or were they merely pretending, because Peter had such a jolly new way of feeding them? His way was to pursue birds who had food in their mouths suitable for humans and snatch it from them; then the birds would follow and snatch it back; and they would all go chasing each other gaily for miles, parting at last with mutual expressions of good-will. But Wendy noticed with gentle concern that Peter did not seem to know that this was rather an odd way of getting your bread and butter, nor even that there are other ways.

Certainly they did not pretend to be sleepy, they were sleepy; and that was a danger, for the moment they popped off, down they fell. The awful thing was that Peter thought this funny.

'There he goes again!' he would cry gleefully, as Michael suddenly dropped like a stone.

'Save him, save him!' cried Wendy, looking with horror at the cruel sea far below. Eventually Peter would dive through the air, and catch Michael just before he could strike the sea, and it was lovely the way he did it; but he always waited till the last moment, and you felt it was his cleverness that interested him and not the saving of human life. Also he was fond of variety, and the sport that engrossed him one moment would suddenly cease to engage him, so there was always the possibility that the next time you fell he would let you go.

He could sleep in the air without falling, by merely lying on his back and floating, but this was, partly at least, because he was so light that if you got behind him and blew he went faster.

'Do be more polite to him,' Wendy whispered to John, when they were playing 'Follow my Leader.'

'Then tell him to stop showing off,' said John.

When playing Follow my Leader, Peter would fly close to the water and touch each shark's tail in passing, just as in the street you may run your finger along an iron railing. They could not follow him in this with much success, so perhaps it was rather like showing off, especially as he kept looking behind to see how many tails they missed.

'You must be nice to him,' Wendy impressed on her brothers. 'What could we do if he were to leave us?'

'We could go back,' Michael said.

'How could we ever find our way back without him?'

'Well, then, we could go on,' said John.

'That is the awful thing, John. We should have to go on, for we don't know how to stop.'

This was true; Peter had forgotten to show them how to stop.

John said that if the worst came to the worst, all they had to do was to go straight on, for the world was round, and so in time they must come back to their own window.

'And who is to get food for us, John?'

'I nipped a bit out of that eagle's mouth pretty neatly, Wendy.'

'After the twentieth try,' Wendy reminded him. 'And even though we became good at picking up food, see how we bump against clouds and things if he is not near to give us a hand.'

Indeed they were constantly bumping. They could now fly strongly, though they still kicked far too much; but if they saw a cloud in front of them, the more they tried to avoid it, the more certainly did they bump into it. If Nana had been with them, she would have had a bandage round Michael's forehead by this time.

Peter was not with them for the moment, and they felt rather lonely up there by themselves. He could go so much faster than they that he would suddenly shoot out of sight, to have some adventure in which they had no share. He would come down laughing over something fearfully funny he had been saying to a star, but he had already forgotten what it was, or he would come up with mermaid scales still sticking to him, and yet not be able to say for certain what had been happening. It was really rather irritating to children who had never seen a mermaid.

'And if he forgets them, so quickly,' Wendy argued, 'how can we expect that he will go on remembering us?'

Indeed, sometimes when he returned he did not remember them, at least not well. Wendy was sure of it. She saw recognition come into his eyes as he was about to pass them the time of day and go on; once even she had to tell him her name.

'I'm Wendy,' she said agitatedly.

He was very sorry. 'I say, Wendy,' he whispered to her, 'always if you see me forgetting you, just keep on saying "I'm Wendy," and then I'll remember.'

Of course this was rather unsatisfactory. However, to make amends he showed them how to lie out flat on a strong wind that was going their way, and this was such a pleasant change that they tried it several times and found they could sleep thus with security. Indeed they would have slept longer, but Peter tired quickly of sleeping, and soon he would cry in his captain voice, 'We get off here.' So with occasional tiffs, but on the whole rollicking, they drew near the Neverland; for after many moons they did reach it, and, what is more, they had been going pretty straight all the time, not perhaps so much owing to the guidance of Peter or Tink as because the island was out looking for them. It is only thus that any one may sight those magic shores.

'There it is,' said Peter calmly.

'Where, where?'

'Where all the arrows are pointing.'

Indeed a million golden arrows were pointing out the island to the children, all directed by their friend the sun, who wanted them to be sure of their way before leaving them for the night.

Wendy and John and Michael stood on tiptoe in the air to get their first sight of the island. Strange to say, they all recognised it at once, and until fear fell upon them they hailed it, not as something long dreamt of and seen at last, but as a familiar friend to whom they were returning home for the holidays.

'John, there's the lagoon.'

'Wendy, look at the turtles burying their eggs in the sand.'

'I say, John, I see your flamingo with the broken leg.'

'Look, Michael, there's your cave.'

'John, what's that in the brushwood?'

'It's a wolf with her whelps. Wendy, I do believe that's your little whelp.'

'There's my boat, John, with her sides stove in.'

'No, it isn't. Why, we burned your boat.'

'That's her, at any rate. I say, John, I see the smoke of the redskin camp.'

'Where? Show me, and I'll tell you by the way the smoke curls whether they are on the war-path.'

'There, just across the Mysterious River.'

'I see now. Yes, they are on the war-path right enough.'

Peter was a little annoyed with them for knowing so much; but if he wanted to lord it over them his triumph was at hand, for have I not told you that anon fear fell upon them?

It came as the arrows went, leaving the island in gloom.

In the old days at home the Neverland had always begun to look a little dark and threatening by bedtime. Then unexplored patches arose in it and spread; black shadows moved about in them; the roar of the beasts of prey was quite different now, and above all, you lost the certainty that you would win. You were quite glad that the night-lights were in. You even liked Nana to say that this was just the mantelpiece over here, and that the Neverland was all make-believe.

Of course the Neverland had been make-believe in those days; but it was real now, and there were no night-lights, and it was getting darker every moment, and where was Nana?

They had been flying apart, but they huddled close to Peter now. His careless manner had gone at last, his eyes were sparkling, and a tingle went through them every time they touched his body. They were now over the fearsome island, flying so low that sometimes a tree grazed their feet. Nothing horrid was visible in the air, yet their progress had become slow and laboured, exactly as if they were pushing their way through hostile forces. Sometimes they hung in the air until Peter had beaten on it with his fists.

'They don't want us to land,' he explained.

'Who are they?' Wendy whispered, shuddering.

But he could not or would not say. Tinker Bell had been asleep on his shoulder, but now he wakened her and sent her on in front.

Sometimes he poised himself in the air, listening intently with his hand to his ear, and again he would stare down with eyes so bright that they seemed to bore two holes to earth. Having done these things, he went on again.

His courage was almost appalling. 'Do you want an adventure now,' he said casually to John, 'or would you like to have your tea first?'

Wendy said 'tea first' quickly, and Michael pressed her hand in gratitude, but the braver John hesitated.

'What kind of adventure?' he asked cautiously.

'There's a pirate asleep in the pampas just beneath us,' Peter told him. 'If you like, we'll go down and kill him.'

'I don't see him,' John said after a long pause.

'I do.'

'Suppose,' John said a little huskily, 'he were to wake up.'

Peter spoke indignantly. 'You don't think I would kill him while he was sleeping! I would wake him first, and then kill him. That's the way I always do.'

'I say! Do you kill many?'

'Tons.'

John said 'how ripping,' but decided to have tea first. He asked if there were many pirates on the island just now, and Peter said he had never known so many.

'Who is captain now?'

'Hook,' answered Peter; and his face became very stern as he said that hated word.

'Jas. Hook?'

'Ay.'

Then indeed Michael began to cry, and even John could speak in gulps only, for they knew Hook's reputation.

'He was Blackbeard's bo'sun,' John whispered huskily. 'He is the worst of them all. He is the only man of whom Barbecue was afraid.'

'That's him,' said Peter.

'What is he like? Is he big?'

'He is not so big as he was.'

'How do you mean?'

'I cut off a bit of him.'

'You!'

'Yes, me,' said Peter sharply.

'I wasn't meaning to be disrespectful.'

'Oh, all right'

'But, I say, what bit?'

'His right hand.'

'Then he can't fight now?'

'Oh, can't he just!'

'Left-hander?'

'He has an iron hook instead of a right hand, and he claws with it.'

'Claws!'

'I say, John,' said Peter.

'Yes.'

'Say, "Ay, ay, sir."'

'Ay, ay, sir.'

'There is one thing,' Peter continued, 'that every boy who serves under me has to promise, and so must you.'

John paled.

'It is this, if we meet Hook in open fight, you must leave him to me.'

'I promise,' John said loyally.

For the moment they were feeling less eerie, because Tink was flying with them, and in her light they could distinguish each other. Unfortunately she could not fly so slowly as they, and so she had to go round and round them in a circle in which they moved as in a halo. Wendy quite liked it, until Peter pointed out the drawback.

'She tells me,' he said, 'that the pirates sighted us before the darkness came, and got Long Tom out.'

'The big gun?'

'Yes. And of course they must see her light, and if they guess we are near it they are sure to let fly.'

'Wendy!'

'John!'

'Michael!'

'Tell her to go away at once, Peter,' the three cried simultaneously, but he refused.

'She thinks we have lost the way,' he replied stiffly, 'and she is rather frightened. You don't think I would send her away all by herself when she is frightened!'

For a moment the circle of light was broken, and something gave Peter a loving little pinch.

'Then tell her,' Wendy begged, 'to put out her light.'

'She can't put it out. That is about the only thing fairies can't do. It just goes out of itself when she falls asleep, same as the stars.'

'Then tell her to sleep at once,' John almost ordered.

'She can't sleep except when she's sleepy. It is the only other thing fairies can't do.'

'Seems to me,' growled John, 'these are the only two things worth doing.'

Here he got a pinch, but not a loving one.

'If only one of us had a pocket,' Peter said, 'we could carry her in it.' However, they had set off in such a hurry that there was not a pocket between the four of them.

He had a happy idea. John's hat!

Tink agreed to travel by hat if it was carried in the hand. John carried it, though she had hoped to be carried by Peter. Presently Wendy took the hat, because John said it struck against his knee as he flew; and this, as we shall see, led to mischief, for Tinker Bell hated to be under an obligation to Wendy.

In the black topper the light was completely hidden, and they flew on in silence. It was the stillest silence they had ever known, broken once by a distant lapping, which Peter explained was the wild beasts drinking at the ford, and again by a rasping sound that might have been the branches of trees rubbing together, but he said it was the redskins sharpening their knives.

Even these noises ceased. To Michael the loneliness was dreadful. 'If only something would make a sound!' he cried.

As if in answer to his request, the air was rent by the most tremendous crash he had ever heard. The pirates had fired Long Tom at them.

The roar of it echoed through the mountains, and the echoes seemed to cry savagely, 'Where are they, where are they, where are they?'

Thus sharply did the terrified three learn the difference between an island of make-believe and the same island come true.

When at last the heavens were steady again, John and Michael found themselves alone in the darkness. John was treading the air mechanically, and Michael without knowing how to float was floating.

'Are you shot?' John whispered tremulously.

'I haven't tried yet,' Michael whispered back.

We know now that no one had been hit. Peter, however, had been carried by the wind of the shot far out to sea, while Wendy was blown upwards with no companion but Tinker Bell.

It would have been well for Wendy if at that moment she had dropped the hat.

I don't know whether the idea came suddenly to Tink, or whether she had planned it on the way, but she at once popped out of the hat and began to lure Wendy to her destruction.

Tink was not all bad: or, rather, she was all bad just now, but, on the other hand, sometimes she was all good. Fairies have to be one thing or the other, because being so small they unfortunately have room for one feeling only at a time. They are, however, allowed to change, only it must be a complete change. At present she was full of jealousy of Wendy. What she said in her lovely tinkle Wendy could not of course understand, and I believe some of it was bad words, but it sounded kind, and she flew back and forward, plainly meaning 'Follow me, and all will be well.'

What else could poor Wendy do? She called to Peter and John and Michael, and got only mocking echoes in reply. She did not yet know that Tink hated her with the fierce hatred of a very woman. And so, bewildered, and now staggering in her flight, she followed Tink to her doom.

## 5

# THE ISLAND COME TRUE

Feeling that Peter was on his way back, the Neverland had again woke into life. We ought to use the pluperfect and say wakened, but woke is better and was always used by Peter.

In his absence things are usually quiet on the island. The fairies take an hour longer in the morning, the beasts attend to their young, the redskins feed heavily for six days and nights, and when pirates and lost boys meet they merely bite their thumbs at each other. But with the coming of Peter, who hates lethargy, they are all under way again: if you put your ear to the ground now, you would hear the whole island seething with life.

On this evening the chief forces of the island were disposed as follows. The lost boys were out looking for Peter, the pirates were out looking for the lost boys, the redskins were out looking for the pirates, and the beasts were out looking for the redskins. They were going round and round the island, but they did not meet because all were going at the same rate.

All wanted blood except the boys, who liked it as a rule, but to-night were out to greet their captain. The boys on the island vary, of course, in numbers, according as they get killed and so on; and when they seem to be growing up, which is against the rules, Peter thins them out; but at this time there were six of them, counting the twins as two. Let us pretend to lie here among the sugar-cane and watch them as they steal by in single file, each with his hand on his dagger.

They are forbidden by Peter to look in the least like him, and they wear the skins of bears slain by themselves, in which they are so round and furry that when they fall they roll. They have therefore become very sure-footed.

The first to pass is Tootles, not the least brave but the most unfortunate of all that gallant band. He had been in fewer adventures than any of them, because the big things constantly happened just when he had stepped round the corner; all would be quiet, he would take the opportunity of going off to gather a few sticks for firewood, and then when he returned the others would be sweeping up the blood. This ill-luck had given a gentle melancholy to his countenance, but instead of souring his nature had sweetened it, so that he was quite the humblest of the boys. Poor kind Tootles, there is danger in the air for you to-night. Take care lest an adventure is now offered you, which, if accepted, will plunge you in deepest woe.

Tootles, the fairy Tink who is bent on mischief this night is looking for a tool, and she thinks you the most easily tricked of the boys. 'Ware Tinker Bell.

Would that he could hear us, but we are not really on the island, and he passes by, biting his knuckles.

Next comes Nibs, the gay and debonair, followed by Slightly, who cuts whistles out of the trees and dances ecstatically to his own tunes. Slightly is the most conceited of the boys. He thinks he remembers the days before he was lost, with their manners and customs, and this has given his nose an offensive tilt. Curly is fourth; he is a pickle, and so often has he had to deliver up his person when Peter said sternly, 'Stand forth the one who did this thing,' that now at the command he stands forth automatically whether he has done it or not. Last come the Twins, who cannot be described because we should be sure to be describing the wrong one. Peter never quite knew what twins were, and his band were not allowed to know anything he did not know, so these two were always vague about themselves, and did their best to give satisfaction by keeping close together in an apologetic sort of way.

The boys vanish in the gloom, and after a pause, but not a long pause, for things go briskly on the island, come the pirates on their track. We hear them before they are seen, and it is always the same dreadful song:

'Avast belay, yo ho, heave to,
A-pirating we go,
And if we're parted by a shot
We're sure to meet below!'

A more villainous-looking lot never hung in a row on Execution dock. Here, a little in advance, ever and again with his head to the ground listening, his great arms bare, pieces of eight in his ears as ornaments, is the handsome Italian Cecco, who cut his name in letters of blood on the back of the governor of the prison at Gao. That gigantic black behind him has had many names since he dropped the one with which dusky mothers still terrify their children on the banks of the Guadjo-mo. Here is Bill Jukes, every inch of him tattooed, the same Bill Jukes who got six dozen on the *Walrus* from Flint before he would drop the bag of moidores; and Cookson, said to be Black Murphy's brother (but this was never proved); and Gentleman Starkey, once an usher in a public school and still dainty in his ways of killing; and Skylights (Morgan's Skylights); and the Irish bo'sun Smee, an oddly genial man who stabbed, so to speak, without offence, and was the only Nonconformist in Hook's crew; and Noodler, whose hands were fixed on backwards; and Robt. Mullins and Alf Mason and many another ruffian long known and feared on the Spanish Main.

In the midst of them, the blackest and largest jewel in that dark setting, reclined James Hook, or as he wrote himself, Jas. Hook, of whom it is said he was the only man that the Sea-Cook feared. He lay at his ease in a rough chariot drawn and propelled by his men, and instead of a right hand he had the iron hook with which ever and anon he encouraged them to increase their pace. As dogs this terrible man treated and addressed them, and as dogs they obeyed him. In person he was cadaverous and blackavized, and his hair was dressed in long curls, which at a little distance looked like black candles, and gave a singularly threatening expression to his handsome countenance. His eyes were of the blue of the forget-me-not, and of a profound melancholy, save when he was plunging his hook into you, at which time two red spots appeared in them and lit them up horribly. In manner, something of the grand seigneur still clung to him, so that he even ripped you up with an air, and I have been told that he was a *raconteur* of repute. He was never more sinister than when he was most polite, which is probably the truest test of breeding; and the elegance of his diction, even when he was swearing, no less than the distinction of his demeanour, showed him one of a different caste from his crew. A man of indomitable courage, it was said of him that the only thing he shied at was the sight of his own blood, which was thick and of an unusual colour. In dress he somewhat aped the attire associated with the name of Charles II., having heard it said in some earlier period of his career that he bore a strange resemblance to the ill-fated Stuarts; and in his mouth he had a holder of his own contrivance which enabled him to smoke two cigars at once. But undoubtedly the grimmest part of him was his iron claw.

Let us now kill a pirate, to show Hook's method. Skylights will do. As they pass, Skylights lurches clumsily against him, ruffling his lace collar; the hook shoots forth, there is a tearing sound and one screech, then the body is kicked aside, and the pirates pass on. He has not even taken the cigars from his mouth.

Such is the terrible man against whom Peter Pan is pitted. Which will win?

On the trail of the pirates, stealing noiselessly down the war-path, which is not visible to inexperienced eyes, come the redskins, every one of them with his eyes peeled. They carry tomahawks and knives, and their naked bodies gleam with paint and oil. Strung around them are scalps, of boys as well as of pirates, for these are the Piccaninny tribe, and not to be confused with the softer-hearted Delawares or the Hurons. In the van, on all fours, is Great Big Little Panther, a brave of so many scalps that in his present position they somewhat impede his progress. Bringing up the rear, the place of greatest danger, comes Tiger Lily, proudly erect, a princess in her own right. She is the most beautiful of dusky Dianas and the belle of the Piccaninnies, coquettish, cold and amorous by turns; there is not a brave who would not have the wayward thing to wife, but she staves off the altar with a hatchet. Observe how they pass over fallen twigs without making the slightest noise. The only sound to be heard is their somewhat heavy breathing. The fact is that they are all a little fat just now after the heavy gorging, but in time they will work this off. For the moment, however, it constitutes their chief danger.

The redskins disappear as they have come like shadows, and soon their place is taken by the beasts, a great and motley procession: lions, tigers, bears, and the innumerable smaller savage things that flee from them, for every kind of beast, and, more particularly; all the man-eaters, live cheek by jowl on the favoured island. Their tongues are hanging out, they are hungry to-night.

When they have passed, comes the last figure of all, a gigantic crocodile. We shall see for whom she is looking presently.

The crocodile passes, but soon the boys appear again, for the procession must continue indefinitely until one of the parties stops or changes its pace. Then quickly they will be on top of each other.

All are keeping a sharp look-out in front, but none suspects that the danger may be creeping up from behind. This shows how real the island was.

The first to fall out of the moving circle was the boys. They flung themselves down on the sward, close to their underground home.

'I do wish Peter would come back,' every one of them said nervously, though in height and still more in breadth they were all larger than their captain.

'I am the only one who is not afraid of the pirates,' Slightly said, in the tone that prevented his being a general favourite; but perhaps some distant sound disturbed him, for he added hastily, 'but I wish he would come back, and tell us whether he has heard anything more about Cinderella.'

They talked of Cinderella, and Tootles was confident that his mother must have been very like her.

It was only in Peter's absence that they could speak of mothers, the subject being forbidden by him as silly.

'All I remember about my mother,' Nibs told them, 'is that she often said to father, "Oh, how I wish I had a cheque-book of my own." I don't know what a cheque-book is, but I should just love to give my mother one.'

While they talked they heard a distant sound. You or I, not being wild things of the woods, would have heard nothing, but they heard it, and it was the grim song:

'Yo ho, yo ho, the pirate life,
The flag o' skull and bones,
A merry hour, a hempen rope,
And hey for Davy Jones.'

At once the lost boys—but where are they? They are no longer there. Rabbits could not have disappeared more quickly.

I will tell you where they are. With the exception of Nibs, who has darted away to reconnoitre, they are already in their home under the ground, a very delightful residence of which we shall see a good deal presently. But how have they reached it? for there is no entrance to be seen, not so much as a pile of brushwood, which if removed would disclose the mouth of a cave. Look closely, however, and you may note that there are here seven large trees, each having in its hollow trunk a hole as large as a boy. These are the seven entrances to the home under the ground, for which Hook has been searching in vain these many moons. Will he find it to-night?

As the pirates advanced, the quick eye of Starkey sighted Nibs disappearing through the wood, and at once his pistol flashed out. But an iron claw gripped his shoulder.

'Captain, let go,' he cried, writhing.

Now for the first time we hear the voice of Hook. It was a black voice. 'Put back that pistol first,' it said threateningly.

'It was one of those boys you hate. I could have shot him dead.'

'Ay, and the sound would have brought Tiger Lily's redskins upon us. Do you want to lose your scalp?'

'Shall I after him, captain,' asked pathetic Smee, 'and tickle him with Johnny Corkscrew?' Smee had pleasant names for everything, and his cutlass was Johnny Corkscrew, because he wriggled it in the wound. One could mention many lovable traits in Smee. For instance, after killing, it was his spectacles he wiped instead of his weapon.

'Johnny's a silent fellow,' he reminded Hook.

'Not now, Smee,' Hook said darkly. 'He is only one, and I want to mischief all the seven. Scatter and look for them.'

The pirates disappeared among the trees, and in a moment their captain and Smee were alone. Hook heaved a heavy sigh; and I know not why it was, perhaps it was because of the soft beauty of the evening, but there came over him a desire to confide to his faithful bo'sun the story of his life. He spoke long and earnestly, but what it was all about Smee, who was rather stupid, did not know in the least.

Anon he caught the word Peter.

'Most of all,' Hook was saying passionately, 'I want their captain, Peter Pan. 'Twas he cut off my arm.' He brandished the hook threateningly. 'I've waited long to shake his hand with this. Oh, I'll tear him.'

'And yet,' said Smee, 'I have often heard you say that hook was worth a score of hands, for combing the hair and other homely uses.'

'Ay,' the captain answered, 'if I was a mother I would pray to have my children born with this instead of that,' and he cast a look of pride upon his iron hand and one of scorn upon the other. Then again he frowned.

'Peter flung my arm,' he said, wincing, 'to a crocodile that happened to be passing by.'

'I have often,' said Smee, 'noticed your strange dread of crocodiles.'

'Not of crocodiles,' Hook corrected him, 'but of that one crocodile.' He lowered his voice. 'It liked my arm so much, Smee, that it has followed me ever since, from sea to sea and from land to land, licking its lips for the rest of me.'

'In a way,' said Smee, 'it's a sort of compliment.'

'I want no such compliments,' Hook barked petulantly. 'I want Peter Pan, who first gave the brute its taste for me.'

He sat down on a large mushroom, and now there was a quiver in his voice. 'Smee,' he said huskily, 'that crocodile would have had me before this, but by a lucky chance it swallowed a clock which goes tick tick inside it, and so before it can reach me I hear the tick and bolt.' He laughed, but in a hollow way.

'Some day,' said Smee, 'the clock will run down, and then he'll get you.'

Hook wetted his dry lips. 'Ay,' he said, 'that's the fear that haunts me.'

Since sitting down he had felt curiously warm. 'Smee,' he said, 'this seat is hot.' He jumped up. 'Odds bobs, hammer and tongs I'm burning.'

They examined the mushroom, which was of a size and solidity unknown on the mainland; they tried to pull it up, and it came away at once in their hands, for it had no root. Stranger still, smoke began at once to ascend. The pirates looked at each other. 'A chimney!' they both exclaimed.

They had indeed discovered the chimney of the home under the ground. It was the custom of the boys to stop it with a mushroom when enemies were in the neighbourhood.

Not only smoke came out of it. There came also children's voices, for so safe did the boys feel in their hiding-place that they were gaily chattering. The pirates listened grimly, and then replaced the mushroom. They looked around them and noted the holes in the seven trees.

'Did you hear them say Peter Pan's from home?' Smee whispered, fidgeting with Johnny Corkscrew.

Hook nodded. He stood for a long time lost in thought, and at last a curdling smile lit up his swarthy face. Smee had been waiting for it. 'Unrip your plan, captain,' he cried eagerly.

'To return to the ship,' Hook replied slowly through his teeth, 'and cook a large rich cake of a jolly thickness with green sugar on it. There can be but one room below, for there is but one chimney. The silly moles had not the sense to see that they did not need a door apiece. That shows they have no mother. We will leave the cake on the shore of the mermaids' lagoon. These boys are always swimming about there, playing with the mermaids. They will find the cake and they will gobble it up, because, having no mother, they don't know how dangerous 'tis to eat rich damp cake.' He burst into laughter, not hollow laughter now, but honest laughter. 'Aha, they will die.'

Smee had listened with growing admiration.

'It's the wickedest, prettiest policy ever I heard of,' he cried, and in their exultation they danced and sang:

'Avast, belay, when I appear,

By fear they're overtook;
Nought's left upon your bones when you
Have shaken claws with Cook.'

They began the verse, but they never finished it, for another sound broke in and stilled them. It was at first such a tiny sound that a leaf might have fallen on it and smothered it, but as it came nearer it was more distinct.

Tick tick tick tick.

Hook stood shuddering, one foot in the air.

'The crocodile,' he gasped, and bounded away, followed by his bo'sun.

It was indeed the crocodile. It had passed the redskins, who were now on the trail of the other pirates. It oozed on after Hook.

Once more the boys emerged into the open; but the dangers of the night were not yet over, for presently Nibs rushed breathless into their midst, pursued by a pack of wolves. The tongues of the pursuers were hanging out; the baying of them was horrible.

'Save me, save me!' cried Nibs, falling on the ground.

'But what can we do, what can we do?'

It was a high compliment to Peter that at that dire moment their thoughts turned to him.

'What would Peter do?' they cried simultaneously.

Almost in the same breath they added, 'Peter would look at them through his legs.'

And then, 'Let us do what Peter would do.'

It is quite the most successful way of defying wolves, and as one boy they bent and looked through their legs. The next moment is the long one; but victory came quickly, for as the boys advanced upon them in this terrible attitude, the wolves dropped their tails and fled.

Now Nibs rose from the ground, and the others thought that his staring eyes still saw the wolves. But it was not wolves he saw.

'I have seen a wonderfuller thing,' he cried, as they gathered round him eagerly. 'A great white bird. It is flying this way.'

'What kind of a bird, do you think?'

'I don't know,' Nibs said, awestruck, 'but it looks so weary, and as it flies it moans, "Poor Wendy."'

'Poor Wendy?'

'I remember,' said Slightly instantly, 'there are birds called Wendies.'

'See, it comes,' cried Curly, pointing to Wendy in the heavens.

Wendy was now almost overhead, and they could hear her plaintive cry. But more distinct came the shrill voice of Tinker Bell. The jealous fairy had now cast off all disguise of friendship, and was darting at her victim from every direction, pinching savagely each time she touched.

'Hullo, Tink,' cried the wondering boys.

Tink's reply rang out: 'Peter wants you to shoot the Wendy.'

It was not in their nature to question when Peter ordered. 'Let us do what Peter wishes,' cried the simple boys. 'Quick, bows and arrows.'

All but Tootles popped down their trees. He had a bow and arrow with him, and Tink noted it, and rubbed her little hands.

'Quick, Tootles, quick,' she screamed. 'Peter will be so pleased.'

Tootles excitedly fitted the arrow to his bow. 'Out of the way, Tink,' he shouted; and then he fired, and Wendy fluttered to the ground with an arrow in her breast.

# 6
# THE LITTLE HOUSE

Foolish Tootles was standing like a conqueror over Wendy's body when the other boys sprang, armed, from their trees.

'You are too late,' he cried proudly, 'I have shot the Wendy. Peter will be so pleased with me.'

Overhead Tinker Bell shouted 'Silly ass!' and darted into hiding. The others did not hear her. They had crowded round Wendy, and as they looked a terrible silence fell upon the wood. If Wendy's heart had been beating they would all have heard it.

Slightly was the first to speak. 'This is no bird,' he said in a scared voice. 'I think it must be a lady.'

'A lady?' said Tootles, and fell a-trembling.

'And we have killed her,' Nibs said hoarsely.

They all whipped off their caps.

'Now I see,' Curly said; 'Peter was bringing her to us.' He threw himself sorrowfully on the ground.

'A lady to take care of us at last,' said one of the twins, 'and you have killed her.'

They were sorry for him, but sorrier for themselves, and when he took a step nearer them they turned from him.

Tootles' face was very white, but there was a dignity about him now that had never been there before.

'I did it,' he said, reflecting. 'When ladies used to come to me in dreams, I said, "Pretty mother, pretty mother." But when at last she really came, I shot her.'

He moved slowly away.

'Don't go,' they called in pity.

'I must,' he answered, shaking; 'I am so afraid of Peter.'

It was at this tragic moment that they heard a sound which made the heart of every one of them rise to his mouth. They heard Peter crow.

'Peter!' they cried, for it was always thus that he signalled his return.

'Hide her,' they whispered, and gathered hastily around Wendy. But Tootles stood aloof.

Again came that ringing crow, and Peter dropped in front of them. 'Greeting, boys,' he cried, and mechanically they saluted, and then again was silence.

He frowned.

'I am back,' he said hotly, 'why do you not cheer?'

They opened their mouths, but the cheers would not come. He overlooked it in his haste to tell the glorious tidings.

'Great news, boys,' he cried, 'I have brought at last a mother for you all.'

Still no sound, except a little thud from Tootles as he dropped on his knees.

'Have you not seen her?' asked Peter, becoming troubled. 'She flew this way.'

'Ah me,' one voice said, and another said, 'Oh, mournful day.'

Tootles rose. 'Peter,' he said quietly, 'I will show her to you'; and when the others would still have hidden her he said, 'Back, twins, let Peter see.'

So they all stood back, and let him see, and after he had looked for a little time he did not know what to do next.

'She is dead,' he said uncomfortably. 'Perhaps she is frightened at being dead.'

He thought of hopping off in a comic sort of way till he was out of sight of her, and then never going near the spot any more. They would all have been glad to follow if he had done this.

But there was the arrow. He took it from her heart and faced his band.

'Whose arrow?' he demanded sternly.

'Mine, Peter,' said Tootles on his knees.

'Oh, dastard hand,' Peter said, and he raised the arrow to use it as a dagger.

Tootles did not flinch. He bared his breast.

'Strike, Peter,' he said firmly, 'strike true.'

Twice did Peter raise the arrow, and twice did his hand fall. 'I cannot strike,' he said with awe, 'there is something stays my hand.'

All looked at him in wonder, save Nibs, who fortunately looked at Wendy.

'It is she,' he cried, 'the Wendy lady; see, her arm.'

Wonderful to relate, Wendy had raised her arm. Nibs bent over her and listened reverently. 'I think she said "Poor Tootles,"' he whispered.

'She lives,' Peter said briefly.

Slightly cried instantly, 'The Wendy lady lives.'

Then Peter knelt beside her and found his button. You remember she had put it on a chain that she wore round her neck.

'See,' he said, 'the arrow struck against this. It is the kiss I gave her. It has saved her life.'

'I remember kisses,' Slightly interposed quickly, 'let me see it. Ay, that's a kiss.'

Peter did not hear him. He was begging Wendy to get better quickly, so that he could show her the mermaids. Of course she could not answer yet, being still in a frightful faint; but from overhead came a wailing note.

'Listen to Tink,' said Curly, 'she is crying because the Wendy lives.'

Then they had to tell Peter of Tink's crime, and almost never had they seen him look so stern.

'Listen, Tinker Bell,' he cried; 'I am your friend no more. Begone from me for ever.'

She flew on to his shoulder and pleaded, but he brushed her off. Not until Wendy again raised her arm did he relent sufficiently to say, 'Well, not for ever, but for a whole week.'

Do you think Tinker Bell was grateful to Wendy for raising her arm? Oh dear no, never wanted to pinch her so much. Fairies indeed are strange, and Peter, who understood them best, often cuffed them.

But what to do with Wendy in her present delicate state of health?

'Let us carry her down into the house,' Curly suggested.

'Ay,' said Slightly, 'that is what one does with ladies.'

'No, no,' Peter said, 'you must not touch her. It would not be sufficiently respectful.'

'That,' said Slightly, 'is what I was thinking.'

'But if she lies there,' Tootles said, 'she will die.'

'Ay, she will die,' Slightly admitted, 'but there is no way out.'

'Yes, there is,' cried Peter. 'Let us build a little house round her.'

They were all delighted. 'Quick,' he ordered them, 'bring me each of you the best of what we have. Gut our house. Be sharp.'

In a moment they were as busy as tailors the night before a wedding. They skurried this way and that, down for bedding, up for firewood, and while they were at it, who should appear but John and Michael. As they dragged along the ground they fell asleep standing, stopped, woke up, moved another step and slept again.

'John, John,' Michael would cry, 'wake up. Where is Nana, John, and mother?'

And then John would rub his eyes and mutter, 'It is true, we did fly.'

You may be sure they were very relieved to find Peter.

'Hullo, Peter,' they said.

'Hullo,' replied Peter amicably, though he had quite forgotten them. He was very busy at the moment measuring Wendy with his feet to see how large a house she would need. Of course he meant to leave room for chairs and a table. John and Michael watched him.

'Is Wendy asleep?' they asked.

'Yes.'

'John,' Michael proposed, 'let us wake her and get her to make supper for us'; but as he said it some of the other boys rushed on carrying branches for the building of the house.

'Look at them!' he cried.

'Curly,' said Peter in his most captainy voice, 'see that these boys help in the building of the house.'

'Ay, ay, sir.'

'Build a house?' exclaimed John.

'For the Wendy,' said Curly.

'For Wendy?' John said, aghast. 'Why, she is only a girl.'

'That,' explained Curly, 'is why we are her servants.'

'You? Wendy's servants!'

'Yes,' said Peter, 'and you also. Away with them.'

The astounded brothers were dragged away to hack and hew and carry. 'Chairs and a fender first,' Peter ordered. 'Then we shall build the house round them.'

'Ay,' said Slightly, 'that is how a house is built; it all comes back to me.'

Peter thought of everything. 'Slightly,' he ordered, 'fetch a doctor.'

'Ay, ay,' said Slightly at once, and disappeared, scratching his head. But he knew Peter must be obeyed, and he returned in a moment, wearing John's hat and looking solemn.

'Please, sir,' said Peter, going to him, 'are you a doctor?'

The difference between him and the other boys at such a time was that they knew it was make-believe, while to him make-believe and true were exactly the same thing. This sometimes troubled them, as when they had to make-believe that they had had their dinners.

If they broke down in their make-believe he rapped them on the knuckles.

'Yes, my little man,' anxiously replied Slightly, who had chapped knuckles.

'Please, sir,' Peter explained, 'a lady lies very ill.'

She was lying at their feet, but Slightly had the sense not to see her.

'Tut, tut, tut,' he said, 'where does she lie?'

'In yonder glade.'

'I will put a glass thing in her mouth,' said Slightly; and he made-believe to do it, while Peter waited. It was an anxious moment when the glass thing was withdrawn.

'How is she?' inquired Peter.

'Tut, tut, tut,' said Slightly, 'this has cured her.'

'I am glad,' Peter cried.

'I will call again in the evening,' Slightly said; 'give her beef tea out of a cup with a spout to it'; but after he had returned the hat to John he blew big breaths, which was his habit on escaping from a difficulty.

In the meantime the wood had been alive with the sound of axes; almost everything needed for a cosy dwelling already lay at Wendy's feet.

'If only we knew,' said one, 'the kind of house she likes best.'

'Peter,' shouted another, 'she is moving in her sleep.'

'Her mouth opens,' cried a third, looking respectfully into it. 'Oh, lovely!'

'Perhaps she is going to sing in her sleep,' said Peter. 'Wendy, sing the kind of house you would like to have.'

Immediately, without opening her eyes, Wendy began to sing:

'I wish I had a pretty house,
The littlest ever seen,
With funny little red walls
And roof of mossy green.'

They gurgled with joy at this, for by the greatest good luck the branches they had brought were sticky with red sap, and all the ground was carpeted with moss. As they rattled up the little house they broke into song themselves:

'We've built the little walls and roof
And made a lovely door,
So tell us, mother Wendy,
What are you wanting more?'

To this she answered rather greedily:

'Oh, really next I think I'll have
Gay windows all about,
With roses peeping in, you know,
And babies peeping out.'

With a blow of their fists they made windows, and large yellow leaves were the blinds. But roses——?

'Roses,' cried Peter sternly.

Quickly they made-believe to grow the loveliest roses up the walls.

Babies?

To prevent Peter ordering babies they hurried into song again:

'We've made the roses peeping out,
The babes are at the door,
We cannot make ourselves, you know,
'Cos we've been made before.'

Peter, seeing this to be a good idea, at once pretended that it was his own. The house was quite beautiful, and no doubt Wendy was very cosy within, though, of course, they could no longer see her. Peter strode up and down, ordering finishing touches. Nothing escaped his eagle eye. Just when it seemed absolutely finished,

'There's no knocker on the door,' he said.

They were very ashamed, but Tootles gave the sole of his shoe, and it made an excellent knocker.

Absolutely finished now, they thought.

Not a bit of it. 'There's no chimney,' Peter said; 'we must have a chimney.'

'It certainly does need a chimney,' said John importantly. This gave Peter an idea. He snatched the hat off John's head, knocked out the bottom, and put the hat on the roof. The little house was so pleased to have such a capital chimney that, as if to say thank you, smoke immediately began to come out of the hat.

Now really and truly it was finished. Nothing remained to do but to knock.

'All look your best,' Peter warned them; 'first impressions are awfully important.'

He was glad no one asked him what first impressions are; they were all too busy looking their best.

He knocked politely; and now the wood was as still as the children, not a sound to be heard except from Tinker Bell, who was watching from a branch and openly sneering.

What the boys were wondering was, would any one answer the knock? If a lady, what would she be like?

The door opened and a lady came out. It was Wendy. They all whipped off their hats.

She looked properly surprised, and this was just how they had hoped she would look.

'Where am I?' she said.

Of course Slightly was the first to get his word in. 'Wendy lady,' he said rapidly, 'for you we built this house.'

'Oh, say you're pleased,' cried Nibs.

'Lovely, darling house,' Wendy said, and they were the very words they had hoped she would say.

'And we are your children,' cried the twins.

Then all went on their knees, and holding out their arms cried, 'O Wendy lady, be our mother.'

'Ought I?' Wendy said, all shining. 'Of course it's frightfully fascinating, but you see I am only a little girl. I have no real experience.'

'That doesn't matter,' said Peter, as if he were the only person present who knew all about it, though he was really the one who knew least. 'What we need is just a nice motherly person.'

'Oh dear!' Wendy said, 'you see I feel that is exactly what I am.'

'It is, it is,' they all cried; 'we saw it at once.'

'Very well,' she said, 'I will do my best. Come inside at once, you naughty children; I am sure your feet are damp. And before I put you to bed I have just time to finish the story of Cinderella.'

In they went; I don't know how there was room for them, but you can squeeze very tight in the Neverland. And that was the first of the many joyous evenings they had with Wendy. By and by she tucked them up in the great bed in the home under the trees, but she herself slept that night in the little house, and Peter kept watch outside with drawn sword, for the pirates could be heard carousing far away and the wolves were on the prowl. The little house looked so cosy and safe in the darkness, with a bright light showing through its blinds, and the chimney smoking beautifully, and Peter standing on guard. After a time he fell asleep, and some unsteady fairies had to climb over him on their way home from an orgy. Any of the other boys obstructing the fairy path at night they would have mischiefed, but they just tweaked Peter's nose and passed on.

## 7

# THE HOME UNDER THE GROUND

One of the first things Peter did next day was to measure Wendy and John and Michael for hollow trees. Hook, you remember, had sneered at the boys for thinking they needed a tree apiece, but this was ignorance, for unless your tree fitted you it was difficult to go up and down, and no two of the boys were quite the same size. Once you fitted, you drew in your breath at the top, and down you went at exactly the right speed, while to ascend you drew in and let out alternately, and so wriggled up. Of course, when you have mastered the action you are able to do these things without thinking of them, and then nothing can be more graceful.

But you simply must fit, and Peter measures you for your tree as carefully as for a suit of clothes: the only difference being that the clothes are made to fit you, while you have to be made to fit the tree. Usually it is done quite easily, as by your wearing too many garments or too few; but if you are bumpy in awkward places or the only available tree is an odd shape, Peter does some things to you, and after that you fit. Once you fit, great care must be taken to go on fitting, and this, as Wendy was to discover to her delight, keeps a whole family in perfect condition.

Wendy and Michael fitted their trees at the first try, but John had to be altered a little.

After a few days' practice they could go up and down as gaily as buckets in a well. And how ardently they grew to love their home under the ground; especially Wendy. It consisted of one large room, as all houses should do, with a floor in which you could dig if you wanted to go fishing, and in this floor grew stout mushrooms of a charming colour, which were used as stools. A Never tree tried hard to grow in the centre of the room, but every morning they sawed the trunk through, level with the floor. By tea-time it was always about two feet high, and then they put a door on top of it, the whole thus becoming a table; as soon as they cleared away, they sawed off the trunk again, and thus there was more room to play. There was an enormous fireplace which was in almost any part of the room where you cared to light it, and across this Wendy stretched strings, made of fibre, from which she suspended her washing. The bed was tilted against the wall by day, and let down at 6.30, when it filled nearly half the room; and all the boys except Michael slept in it, lying like sardines in a tin.

There was a strict rule against turning round until one gave the signal, when all turned at once. Michael should have used it also; but Wendy would have a baby, and he was the littlest, and you know what women are, and the short and the long of it is that he was hung up in a basket.

It was rough and simple, and not unlike what baby bears would have made of an underground house in the same circumstances. But there was one recess in the wall, no larger than a bird-cage, which was the private apartment of Tinker Bell. It could be shut off from the rest of the home by a tiny curtain, which Tink, who was most fastidious, always kept drawn when dressing or undressing. No woman, however large, could have had a more exquisite boudoir and bedchamber combined. The couch, as she always called it, was a genuine Queen Mab, with club legs; and she varied the bedspreads according to what fruit-blossom was in season. Her mirror was a Puss-in-boots, of which there are now only three, unchipped, known to the fairy dealers; the wash-stand was Pie-crust and reversible, the chest of drawers an authentic Charming the Sixth, and the carpet and rugs of the best (the early) period of Margery and Robin. There was a chandelier from Tiddly winks for the look of the thing, but of course she lit the residence herself. Tink was very contemptuous of the rest of the house, as indeed was perhaps inevitable; and her chamber, though beautiful, looked rather conceited, having the appearance of a nose permanently turned up.

I suppose it was all especially entrancing to Wendy, because those rampagious boys of hers gave her so much to do. Really there were whole weeks when, except perhaps with a stocking in the evening, she was never above ground. The cooking, I can tell you, kept her nose to the pot. Their chief food was roasted breadfruit, yams, cocoa-nuts, baked pig, mammee-apples, tappa rolls and bananas, washed down with calabashes of poe-poe; but you never exactly knew whether there would be a real meal or just a make-believe, it all depended upon Peter's whim. He could eat, really eat, if it was part of a game, but he could not stodge just to feel stodgy, which is what most children like better than anything else; the next best thing being to talk about it. Make-believe was so real to him that during a meal of it you could see him getting rounder. Of course it was trying, but you simply had to follow his lead, and if you could prove to him that you were getting loose for your tree he let you stodge.

Wendy's favourite time for sewing and darning was after they had all gone to bed. Then, as she expressed it, she had a breathing time for herself; and she occupied it in making new things for them, and putting double pieces on the knees, for they were all most frightfully hard on their knees.

When she sat down to a basketful of their stockings, every heel with a hole in it, she would fling up her arms and exclaim, 'Oh dear, I am sure I sometimes think spinsters are to be envied.'

Her face beamed when she exclaimed this.

You remember about her pet wolf. Well, it very soon discovered that she had come to the island and it found her out, and they just ran into each other's arms. After that it followed her about everywhere.

As time wore on did she think much about the beloved parents she had left behind her? This is a difficult question, because it is quite impossible to say how time does wear on in the Neverland, where it is calculated by moons and suns, and there are ever so many more of them than on the mainland. But I am afraid that Wendy did not really worry about her father and mother; she was absolutely confident that they would always keep the window open for her to fly back by, and this gave her complete ease of mind. What did disturb her at times was that John remembered his parents vaguely only, as people he had once known, while

Michael was quite willing to believe that she was really his mother. These things scared her a little, and nobly anxious to do her duty, she tried to fix the old life in their minds by setting them examination papers on it, as like as possible to the ones she used to do at school. The other boys thought this awfully interesting, and insisted on joining, and they made slates for themselves, and sat round the table, writing and thinking hard about the questions she had written on another slate and passed round. They were the most ordinary questions—'What was the colour of Mother's eyes? Which was taller, Father or Mother? Was Mother blonde or brunette? Answer all three questions if possible.' '(A) Write an essay of not less than 40 words on How I spent my last Holidays, or The Caracters of Father and Mother compared. Only one of these to be attempted.' Or '(1) Describe Mother's laugh; (2) Describe Father's laugh; (3) Describe Mother's Party Dress; (4) Describe the Kennel and its Inmate.'

They were just everyday questions like these, and when you could not answer them you were told to make a cross; and it was really dreadful what a number of crosses even John made. Of course the only boy who replied to every question was Slightly, and no one could have been more hopeful of coming out first, but his answers were perfectly ridiculous, and he really came out last: a melancholy thing.

Peter did not compete. For one thing he despised all mothers except Wendy, and for another he was the only boy on the island who could neither write nor spell; not the smallest word. He was above all that sort of thing.

By the way, the questions were all written in the past tense. What was the colour of Mother's eyes, and so on. Wendy, you see, had been forgetting too.

Adventures, of course, as we shall see, were of daily occurrence; but about this time Peter invented, with Wendy's help, a new game that fascinated him enormously, until he suddenly had no more interest in it, which, as you have been told, was what always happened with his games. It consisted in pretending not to have adventures, in doing the sort of thing John and Michael had been doing all their lives: sitting on stools flinging balls in the air, pushing each other, going out for walks and coming back without having killed so much as a grizzly. To see Peter doing nothing on a stool was a great sight; he could not help looking solemn at such times, to sit still seemed to him such a comic thing to do. He boasted that he had gone a walk for the good of his health. For several suns these were the most novel of all adventures to him; and John and Michael had to pretend to be delighted also; otherwise he would have treated them severely.

He often went out alone, and when he came back you were never absolutely certain whether he had had an adventure or not. He might have forgotten it so completely that he said nothing about it; and then when you went out you found the body; and, on the other hand, he might say a great deal about it, and yet you could not find the body. Sometimes he came home with his head bandaged, and then Wendy cooed over him and bathed it in lukewarm water, while he told a dazzling tale. But she was never quite sure, you know. There were, however, many adventures which she knew to be true because she was in them herself, and there were still more that were at least partly true, for the other boys were in them and said they were wholly true. To describe them all would require a book as large as an English-Latin, Latin-English Dictionary, and the most we can do is to give one as a specimen of an average hour on the island. The difficulty is which one to choose. Should we take the brush with the redskins at Slightly Gulch? It was a sanguinary affair, and especially interesting as showing one of Peter's peculiarities, which was that in the middle of a fight he would suddenly change sides. At the Gulch, when victory was still in the balance, sometimes leaning this way and sometimes that, he called out, 'I'm redskin to-day; what are you, Tootles?' And Tootles answered, 'Redskin; what are you, Nibs?' and Nibs said,'Redskin; what are you, Twin?' and so on; and they were all redskin; and of course this would have ended the fight had not the real redskins, fascinated by Peter's methods, agreed to be lost boys for that once, and so at it they all went again, more fiercely than ever.

The extraordinary upshot of this adventure was—but we have not decided yet that this is the adventure we are to narrate. Perhaps a better one would be the night attack by the redskins on the house under the ground, when several of them stuck in the hollow trees and had to be pulled out like corks. Or we might tell how Peter saved Tiger Lily's life in the Mermaids' Lagoon, and so made her his ally.

Or we could tell of that cake the pirates cooked so that the boys might eat it and perish; and how they placed it in one cunning spot after another; but always Wendy snatched it from the hands of her children, so that in time it lost its succulence, and became as hard as a stone, and was used as a missile, and Hook fell over it in the dark.

Or suppose we tell of the birds that were Peter's friends, particularly of the Never bird that built in a tree overhanging the lagoon, and how the nest fell into the water, and still the bird sat on her eggs, and Peter gave orders that she was not to be disturbed. That is a pretty story, and the end shows how grateful a bird can be; but if we tell it we must also tell the whole adventure of the lagoon, which would of course be telling two adventures rather than just one. A shorter adventure, and quite as exciting, was Tinker Bell's attempt, with the help of some street fairies, to have the sleeping Wendy conveyed on a great floating leaf to the mainland. Fortunately the leaf gave way and Wendy woke, thinking it was bath-time, and swam back. Or again, we might choose Peter's defiance of the lions, when he drew a circle round him on the ground with an arrow and defied them to cross it; and though he waited for hours, with the other boys and Wendy looking on breathlessly from trees, not one of them dared to accept his challenge.

Which of these adventures shall we choose? The best way will be to toss for it.

I have tossed, and the lagoon has won. This almost makes one wish that the gulch or the cake or Tink's leaf had won. Of course I could do it again, and make it best out of three; however, perhaps fairest to stick to the lagoon.

# 8

# THE MERMAIDS' LAGOON

If you shut your eyes and are a lucky one, you may see at times a shapeless pool of lovely pale colours suspended in the darkness; then if you squeeze your eyes tighter, the pool begins to take shape, and the colours become so vivid that with another squeeze they must go on fire. But just before they go on fire you see the lagoon. This is the nearest you ever get to it on the mainland, just one heavenly moment; if there could be two moments you might see the surf and hear the mermaids singing.

The children often spent long summer days on this lagoon, swimming or floating most of the time, playing the mermaid games in the water, and so forth. You must not think from this that the mermaids were on friendly terms with them; on the contrary, it was among Wendy's lasting regrets that all the time she was on the island she never had a civil word from one of them. When she stole softly to the edge of the lagoon she might see them by the score, especially on Marooners' Rock, where they loved to bask, combing out their hair in a lazy way that quite irritated her; or she might even swim, on tiptoe as it were, to within a yard of them, but then they saw her and dived, probably splashing her with their tails, not by accident, but intentionally.

They treated all the boys in the same way, except of course Peter, who chatted with them on Marooners' Rock by the hour, and sat on their tails when they got cheeky. He gave Wendy one of their combs.

The most haunting time at which to see them is at the turn of the moon, when they utter strange wailing cries; but the lagoon is dangerous for mortals then, and until the evening of which we have now to tell, Wendy had never seen the lagoon by moonlight, less from fear, for of course Peter would have accompanied her, than because she had strict rules about every one being in bed by seven. She was often at the lagoon, however, on sunny days after rain, when the mermaids come up in extraordinary numbers to play with their bubbles. The bubbles of many colours made in rainbow water they treat as balls, hitting them gaily from one to another with their tails, and trying to keep them in the rainbow till they burst. The goals are at each end of the rainbow, and the keepers only are allowed to use their hands.

Sometimes hundreds of mermaids will be playing in the lagoon at a time, and it is quite a pretty sight.

But the moment the children tried to join in they had to play by themselves, for the mermaids immediately disappeared. Nevertheless we have proof that they secretly watched the interlopers, and were not above taking an idea from them; for John introduced a new way of hitting the bubble, with the head instead of the hand, and the mermaid goal-keepers adopted it. This is the one mark that John has left on the Neverland.

It must also have been rather pretty to see the children resting on a rock for half an hour after their midday meal. Wendy insisted on their doing this, and it had to be a real rest even though the meal was make-believe. So they lay there in the sun, and their bodies glistened in it, while she sat beside them and looked important.

It was one such day, and they were all on Marooners' Rock. The rock was not much larger than their great bed, but of course they all knew how not to take up much room, and they were dozing, or at least lying with their eyes shut, and pinching occasionally when they thought Wendy was not looking. She was very busy, stitching.

While she stitched a change came to the lagoon. Little shivers ran over it, and the sun went away and shadows stole across the water, turning it cold. Wendy could no longer see to thread her needle, and when she looked up, the lagoon that had always hitherto been such a laughing place seemed formidable and unfriendly.

It was not, she knew, that night had come, but something as dark as night had come. No, worse than that. It had not come, but it had sent that shiver through the sea to say that it was coming. What was it?

There crowded upon her all the stories she had been told of Marooners' Rock, so called because evil captains put sailors on it and leave them there to drown. They drown when the tide rises, for then it is submerged.

Of course she should have roused the children at once; not merely because of the unknown that was stalking toward them, but because it was no longer good for them to sleep on a rock grown chilly. But she was a young mother and she did not know this; she thought you simply must stick to your rule about half an hour after the midday meal. So, though fear was upon her, and she longed to hear male voices, she would not waken them. Even when she heard the sound of muffled oars, though her heart was in her mouth, she did not waken them. She stood over them to let them have their sleep out. Was it not brave of Wendy?

It was well for those boys then that there was one among them who could sniff danger even in his sleep. Peter sprang erect, as wide awake at once as a dog, and with one warning cry he roused the others.

He stood motionless, one hand to his ear.

'Pirates!' he cried. The others came closer to him. A strange smile was playing about his face, and Wendy saw it and shuddered. While that smile was on his face no one dared address him; all they could do was to stand ready to obey. The order came sharp and incisive.

'Dive!'

There was a gleam of legs, and instantly the lagoon seemed deserted. Marooners' Rock stood alone in the forbidding waters, as if it were itself marooned.

The boat drew nearer. It was the pirate dinghy, with three figures in her, Smee and Starkey, and the third a captive, no other than Tiger Lily. Her hands and ankles were tied, and she knew what was to be her fate. She was to be left on the rock to perish, an end to one of her race more terrible than death by fire or torture, for is it not written in the book of the tribe that there is no path through water to the happy hunting-ground? Yet her face was impassive; she was the daughter of a chief, she must die as a chief's daughter, it is enough.

They had caught her boarding the pirate ship with a knife in her mouth. No watch was kept on the ship, it being Hook's boast that the wind of his name guarded the ship for a mile around. Now her fate would help to guard it also. One more wail would go the round in that wind by night.

In the gloom that they brought with them the two pirates did not see the rock till they crashed into it.

'Luff, you lubber,' cried an Irish voice that was Smee's; 'here's the rock. Now, then, what we have to do is to hoist the redskin on to it and leave her there to drown.'

It was the work of one brutal moment to land the beautiful girl on the rock; she was too proud to offer a vain resistance.

Quite near the rock, but out of sight, two heads were bobbing up and down, Peter's and Wendy's. Wendy was crying, for it was the first tragedy she had seen. Peter had seen many tragedies, but he had forgotten them all. He was less sorry than Wendy for Tiger Lily: it was two against one that angered him, and he meant to save her. An easy way would have been to wait until the pirates had gone, but he was never one to choose the easy way.

There was almost nothing he could not do, and he now imitated the voice of Hook.

'Ahoy there, you lubbers,' he called. It was a marvellous imitation.

'The captain,' said the pirates, staring at each other in surprise.

'He must be swimming out to us,' Starkey said, when they had looked for him in vain.

'We are putting the redskin on the rock,' Smee called out.

'Set her free,' came the astonishing answer.

'Free!'

'Yes, cut her bonds and let her go.'

'But, captain——'

'At once, d'ye hear,' cried Peter, 'or I'll plunge my hook in you.'

'This is queer,' Smee gasped.

'Better do what the captain orders,' said Starkey nervously.

'Ay, ay,' Smee said, and he cut Tiger Lily's cords. At once like an eel she slid between Starkey's legs into the water.

Of course Wendy was very elated over Peter's cleverness; but she knew that he would be elated also and very likely crow and thus betray himself, so at once her hand went out to cover his mouth. But it was stayed even in the act, for 'Boat ahoy!' rang over the lagoon in Hook's voice, and this time it was not Peter who had spoken.

Peter may have been about to crow, but his face puckered in a whistle of surprise instead.

'Boat ahoy!' again came the cry.

Now Wendy understood. The real Hook was also in the water.

He was swimming to the boat, and as his men showed a light to guide him he had soon reached them. In the light of the lantern Wendy saw his hook grip the boat's side; she saw his evil swarthy face as he rose dripping from the water, and, quaking, she would have liked to swim away, but Peter would not budge. He was tingling with life and also top-heavy with conceit. 'Am I not a wonder, oh, I am a wonder!' he whispered to her; and though she thought so also, she was really glad for the sake of his reputation that no one heard him except herself.

He signed to her to listen.

The two pirates were very curious to know what had brought their captain to them, but he sat with his head on his hook in a position of profound melancholy.

'Captain, is all well?' they asked timidly, but he answered with a hollow moan.

'He sighs,' said Smee.

'He sighs again,' said Starkey.

'And yet a third time he sighs,' said Smee.

'What's up, captain?'

Then at last he spoke passionately.

'The game's up,' he cried, 'those boys have found a mother.'

Affrighted though she was, Wendy swelled with pride.

'O evil day,' cried Starkey.

'What's a mother?' asked the ignorant Smee.

Wendy was so shocked that she exclaimed, 'He doesn't know!' and always after this she felt that if you could have a pet pirate Smee would be her one.

Peter pulled her beneath the water, for Hook had started up, crying, 'What was that?'

'I heard nothing,' said Starkey, raising the lantern over the waters, and as the pirates looked they saw a strange sight. It was the nest I have told you of, floating on the lagoon, and the Never bird was sitting on it.

'See,' said Hook in answer to Smee's question, 'that is a mother. What a lesson. The nest must have fallen into the water, but would the mother desert her eggs? No.'

There was a break in his voice, as if for a moment he recalled innocent days when—but he brushed away this weakness with his hook.

Smee, much impressed, gazed at the bird as the nest was borne past, but the more suspicious Starkey said, 'If she is a mother, perhaps she is hanging about here to help Peter.'

Hook winced. 'Ay,' he said, 'that is the fear that haunts me.'

He was roused from this dejection by Smee's eager voice.

'Captain,' said Smee, 'could we not kidnap these boys' mother and make her our mother?'

'It is a princely scheme,' cried Hook, and at once it took practical shape in his great brain. 'We will seize the children and carry them to the boat: the boys we will make walk the plank, and Wendy shall be our mother.'

Again Wendy forgot herself.

'Never!' she cried, and bobbed.

'What was that?'

But they could see nothing. They thought it must have been but a leaf in the wind. 'Do you agree, my bullies?' asked Hook.

'There is my hand on it,' they both said.

'And there is my hook. Swear.'

'They all swore. By this time they were on the rock, and suddenly Hook remembered Tiger Lily.

'Where is the redskin?' he demanded abruptly.

He had a playful humour at moments, and they thought this was one of the moments.

'That is all right, captain,' Smee answered complacently; 'we let her go.'

'Let her go!' cried Hook.

''Twas your own orders,' the bo'sun faltered.

'You called over the water to us to let her go,' said Starkey.

'Brimstone and gall,' thundered Hook, 'what cozening is here?' His face had gone black with rage, but he saw that they believed their words, and he was startled. 'Lads,' he said, shaking a little, 'I gave no such order.'

'It is passing queer,' Smee said, and they all fidgeted uncomfortably. Hook raised his voice, but there was a quiver in it.

'Spirit that haunts this dark lagoon to-night,' he cried, 'dost hear me?'

Of course Peter should have kept quiet, but of course he did not. He immediately answered in Hook's voice:

'Odds, bobs, hammer and tongs, I hear you.'

In that supreme moment Hook did not blanch, even at the gills, but Smee and Starkey clung to each other in terror.

'Who are you, stranger, speak?' Hook demanded.

'I am James Hook,' replied the voice, 'captain of the *Jolly Roger*.'

'You are not; you are not,' Hook cried hoarsely.

'Brimstone and gall,' the voice retorted, 'say that again, and I'll cast anchor in you.'

Hook tried a more ingratiating manner. 'If you are Hook,' he said almost humbly, 'come tell me, who am I?'

'A codfish,' replied the voice, 'only a codfish.'

'A codfish!' Hook echoed blankly; and it was then, but not till then, that his proud spirit broke. He saw his men draw back from him.

'Have we been captained all this time by a codfish!' they muttered. 'It is lowering to our pride.'

They were his dogs snapping at him, but, tragic figure though he had become, he scarcely heeded them. Against such fearful evidence it was not their belief in him that he needed, it was his own. He felt his ego slipping from him. 'Don't desert me, bully,' he whispered hoarsely to it.

In his dark nature there was a touch of the feminine, as in all the great pirates, and it sometimes gave him intuitions. Suddenly he tried the guessing game.

'Hook,' he called, 'have you another voice?'

Now Peter could never resist a game, and he answered blithely in his own voice, 'I have.'

'And another name?'

'Ay, ay.'

'Vegetable?' asked Hook.

'No.'

'Mineral?'

'No.'

'Animal?'

'Yes.'

'Man?'

'No!' This answer rang out scornfully.

'Boy?'

'Yes.'

'Ordinary boy?'

'No!'

'Wonderful boy?'

To Wendy's pain the answer that rang out this time was 'Yes.'

'Are you in England?'

'No.'

'Are you here?'

'Yes.'

Hook was completely puzzled. 'You ask him some questions,' he said to the others, wiping his damp brow.

Smee reflected. 'I can't think of a thing,' he said regretfully.

'Can't guess, can't guess,' crowed Peter. 'Do you give it up?'

Of course in his pride he was carrying the game too far, and the miscreants saw their chance.

'Yes, yes,' they answered eagerly.

'Well, then,' he cried, 'I am Peter Pan.'

Pan!

In a moment Hook was himself again, and Smee and Starkey were his faithful henchmen.

'Now we have him,' Hook shouted. 'Into the water, Smee. Starkey, mind the boat. Take him dead or alive.'

He leaped as he spoke, and simultaneously came the gay voice of Peter.

'Are you ready, boys?'

'Ay, ay,' from various parts of the lagoon.

'Then lam into the pirates.'

The fight was short and sharp. First to draw blood was John, who gallantly climbed into the boat and held Starkey. There was a fierce struggle, in which the cutlass was torn from the pirate's grasp. He wriggled overboard and John leapt after him. The dinghy drifted away.

Here and there a head bobbed up in the water, and there was a flash of steel followed by a cry or a whoop. In the confusion some struck at their own side. The corkscrew of Smee got Tootles in the fourth rib, but he was himself pinked in turn by Curly. Farther from the rock Starkey was pressing Slightly and the twins hard.

Where all this time was Peter? He was seeking bigger game.

The others were all brave boys, and they must not be blamed for backing from the pirate captain. His iron claw made a circle of dead water round him, from which they fled like affrighted fishes.

But there was one who did not fear him: there was one prepared to enter that circle.

Strangely, it was not in the water that they met. Hook rose to the rock to breathe, and at the same moment Peter scaled it on the opposite side. The rock was slippery as a ball, and they had to crawl rather than climb. Neither knew that the other was coming. Each feeling for a grip met the other's arm: in surprise they raised their heads; their faces were almost touching; so they met.

Some of the greatest heroes have confessed that just before they fell to they had a sinking. Had it been so with Peter at that moment I would admit it. After all, this was the only man that the Sea-Cook had feared. But Peter had no sinking, he had one feeling only, gladness; and he gnashed his pretty teeth with joy. Quick as thought he snatched a knife from Hook's belt and was about to drive it home, when he saw that he was higher up the rock than his foe. It would not have been fighting fair. He gave the pirate a hand to help him up.

It was then that Hook bit him.

Not the pain of this but its unfairness was what dazed Peter. It made him quite helpless. He could only stare, horrified. Every child is affected thus the first time he is treated unfairly. All he thinks he has a right to when he comes to you to be yours is fairness. After you have been unfair to him he will love you again, but he will never afterwards be quite the same boy. No one ever gets over the first unfairness; no one except Peter. He often met it, but he always forgot it. I suppose that was the real difference between him and all the rest.

So when he met it now it was like the first time; and he could just stare, helpless. Twice the iron hand clawed him.

A few minutes afterwards the other boys saw Hook in the water striking wildly for the ship; no elation on his pestilent face now, only white fear, for the crocodile was in dogged pursuit of him. On ordinary occasions the boys would have swum alongside cheering; but now they were uneasy, for they had lost both Peter and Wendy, and were scouring the lagoon for them, calling them by name. They found the dinghy and went home in it, shouting 'Peter, Wendy' as they went, but no answer came save mocking laughter from the mermaids. 'They must be swimming back or flying,' the boys concluded. They were not very anxious, they had such faith in Peter. They chuckled, boylike, because they would be late for bed; and it was all mother Wendy's fault!

When their voices died away there came cold silence over the lagoon, and then a feeble cry.

'Help, help!'

Two small figures were beating against the rock; the girl had fainted and lay on the boy's arm. With a last effort Peter pulled her up the rock and then lay down beside her. Even as he also fainted he saw that the water was rising. He knew that they would soon be drowned, but he could do no more.

As they lay side by side a mermaid caught Wendy by the feet, and began pulling her softly into the water. Peter, feeling her slip from him, woke with a start, and was just in time to draw her back. But he had to tell her the truth.

'We are on the rock, Wendy,' he said, 'but it is growing smaller. Soon the water will be over it.'

She did not understand even now.

'We must go,' she said, almost brightly.

'Yes,' he answered faintly.

'Shall we swim or fly, Peter?'

He had to tell her.

'Do you think you could swim or fly as far as the island, Wendy, without my help?'

She had to admit that she was too tired.

He moaned.

'What is it?' she asked, anxious about him at once.

'I can't help you, Wendy. Hook wounded me. I can neither fly nor swim.'

'Do you mean we shall both be drowned?'

'Look how the water is rising.'

They put their hands over their eyes to shut out the sight. They thought they would soon be no more. As they sat thus something brushed against Peter as light as a kiss, and stayed there, as if saying timidly, 'Can I be of any use?'

It was the tail of a kite, which Michael had made some days before. It had torn itself out of his hand and floated away.

'Michael's kite,' Peter said without interest, but next moment he had seized the tail, and was pulling the kite toward him.

'It lifted Michael off the ground,' he cried; 'why should it not carry you?'

'Both of us!'

'It can't lift two; Michael and Curly tried.'

'Let us draw lots,' Wendy said bravely.

'And you a lady; never.' Already he had tied the tail round her. She clung to him; she refused to go without him; but with a 'Good-bye, Wendy,' he pushed her from the rock; and in a few minutes she was borne out of his sight. Peter was alone on the lagoon.

The rock was very small now; soon it would be submerged. Pale rays of light tiptoed across the waters; and by and by there was to be heard a sound at once the most musical and the most melancholy in the world: the mermaids calling to the moon.

Peter was not quite like other boys; but he was afraid at last. A tremor ran through him, like a shudder passing over the sea; but on the sea one shudder follows another till there are hundreds of them, and Peter felt just the one. Next moment he was standing erect on the rock again, with that smile on his face and a drum beating within him. It was saying, 'To die will be an awfully big adventure.'

# 9
# THE NEVER BIRD

The last sounds Peter heard before he was quite alone were the mermaids retiring one by one to their bedchambers under the sea. He was too far away to hear their doors shut; but every door in the coral caves where they live rings a tiny bell when it opens or closes (as in all the nicest houses on the mainland), and he heard the bells.

Steadily the waters rose till they were nibbling at his feet; and to pass the time until they made their final gulp, he watched the only thing moving on the lagoon. He thought it was a piece of floating paper, perhaps part of the kite, and wondered idly how long it would take to drift ashore.

Presently he noticed as an odd thing that it was undoubtedly out upon the lagoon with some definite purpose, for it was fighting the tide, and sometimes winning; and when it won, Peter, always sympathetic to the weaker side, could not help clapping; it was such a gallant piece of paper.

It was not really a piece of paper; it was the Never bird, making desperate efforts to reach Peter on her nest. By working her wings, in a way she had learned since the nest fell into the water, she was able to some extent to guide her strange craft, but by the time Peter recognised her she was very exhausted. She had come to save him, to give him her nest, though there were eggs in it. I rather wonder at the bird, for though he had been nice to her, he had also sometimes tormented her. I can suppose only that, like Mrs. Darling and the rest of them, she was melted because he had all his first teeth.

She called out to him what she had come for, and he called out to her what was she doing there; but of course neither of them understood the other's language. In fanciful stories people can talk to the birds freely, and I wish for the moment I could pretend that this was such a story, and say that Peter replied intelligently to the Never bird; but truth is best, and I want to tell only what really happened. Well, not only could they not understand each other, but they forgot their manners.

'I—want—you—to—get—into—the—nest,' the bird called, speaking as slowly and distinctly as possible, 'and—then—you—can—drift—ashore, but—I—am—too—tired—to—bring—it—any—nearer—so—you—must—try—to—swim—to—it.'

'What are you quacking about?' Peter answered. 'Why don't you let the nest drift as usual?'

'I—want—you—' the bird said, and repeated it all over.

Then Peter tried slow and distinct.

'What—are—you—quacking—about?' and so on.

The Never bird became irritated; they have very short tempers.

'You dunderheaded little jay,' she screamed, 'why don't you do as I tell you?'

Peter felt that she was calling him names, and at a venture he retorted hotly:

'So are you!'

Then rather curiously they both snapped out the same remark:

'Shut up!'

'Shut up!'

Nevertheless the bird was determined to save him if she could, and by one last mighty effort she propelled the nest against the rock. Then up she flew; deserting her eggs, so as to make her meaning clear.

Then at last he understood, and clutched the nest and waved his thanks to the bird as she fluttered overhead. It was not to receive his thanks, however, that she hung there in the sky; it was not even to watch him get into the nest; it was to see what he did with her eggs.

There were two large white eggs, and Peter lifted them up and reflected. The bird covered her face with her wings, so as not to see the last of her eggs; but she could not help peeping between the feathers.

I forget whether I have told you that there was a stave on the rock, driven into it by some buccaneers of long ago to mark the site of buried treasure. The children had discovered the glittering hoard, and when in mischievous mood used to fling showers of moidores, diamonds, pearls and pieces of eight to the gulls, who pounced upon them for food, and then flew away, raging at the scurvy trick that had been played upon them. The stave was still there, and on it Starkey had hung his hat, a deep tarpaulin, watertight, with a broad brim. Peter put the eggs into this hat and set it on the lagoon. It floated beautifully.

The Never bird saw at once what he was up to, and screamed her admiration of him; and, alas, Peter crowed his agreement with her. Then he got into the nest, reared the stave in it as a mast, and hung up his shirt for a sail. At the same moment the bird fluttered down upon the hat and once more sat snugly on her eggs. She drifted in one direction, and he was borne off in another, both cheering.

Of course when Peter landed he beached his barque in a place where the bird would easily find it; but the hat was such a great success that she abandoned the nest. It drifted about till it went to pieces, and often Starkey came to the shore of the lagoon, and with many bitter feelings watched the bird sitting on his hat. As we shall not see her again, it may be worth mentioning here that all Never birds now build in that shape of nest, with a broad brim on which the youngsters take an airing.

Great were the rejoicings when Peter reached the home under the ground almost as soon as Wendy, who had been carried hither and thither by the kite. Every boy had adventures to tell; but perhaps the biggest adventure of all was that they were several hours late for bed. This so inflated them that they did various dodgy things to get staying up still longer, such as demanding bandages; but Wendy, though glorying in having them all home again safe and sound, was scandalised by the lateness of the hour, and cried, 'To bed, to bed,' in a voice that had to be obeyed. Next day, however, she was awfully tender, and gave out bandages to every one; and they played till bed-time at limping about and carrying their arms in slings.

## 10

# THE HAPPY HOME

One important result of the brush on the lagoon was that it made the redskins their friends. Peter had saved Tiger Lily from a dreadful fate, and now there was nothing she and her braves would not do for him. All night they sat above, keeping watch over the home under the ground and awaiting the big attack by the pirates which obviously could not be much longer delayed. Even by day they hung about, smoking the pipe of peace, and looking almost as if they wanted tit-bits to eat.

They called Peter the Great White Father, prostrating themselves before him; and he liked this tremendously, so that it was not really good for him.

'The great white father,' he would say to them in a very lordly manner, as they grovelled at his feet, 'is glad to see the Piccaninny warriors protecting his wigwam from the pirates.'

'Me Tiger Lily,' that lovely creature would reply. 'Peter Pan save me, me his velly nice friend. Me no let pirates hurt him.'

She was far too pretty to cringe in this way, but Peter thought it his due, and he would answer condescendingly, 'It is good. Peter Pan has spoken.'

Always when he said, 'Peter Pan has spoken,' it meant that they must now shut up, and they accepted it humbly in that spirit; but they were by no means so respectful to the other boys, whom they looked upon as just ordinary braves. They said 'How-do?' to them, and things like that; and what annoyed the boys was that Peter seemed to think this all right.

Secretly Wendy sympathised with them a little, but she was far too loyal a housewife to listen to any complaints against father. 'Father knows best,' she always said, whatever her private opinion must be. Her private opinion was that the redskins should not call her a squaw.

We have now reached the evening that was to be known among them as the Night of Nights, because of its adventures and their upshot. The day, as if quietly gathering its forces, had been almost uneventful, and now the redskins in their blankets were at their posts above, while, below, the children were having their evening meal; all except Peter, who had gone out to get the time. The way you got the time on the island was to find the crocodile, and then stay near him till the clock struck.

This meal happened to be a make-believe tea, and they sat round the board, guzzling in their greed; and really, what with their chatter and recriminations, the noise, as Wendy said, was positively deafening. To be sure, she did not mind noise, but she simply would not have them grabbing things, and then excusing themselves by saying that Tootles had pushed their elbow. There was a fixed rule that they must never hit back at meals, but should refer the matter of dispute to Wendy by raising the right arm politely and saying, 'I complain of so-and-so'; but what usually happened was that they forgot to do this or did it too much.

'Silence,' cried Wendy when for the twentieth time she had told them that they were not all to speak at once. 'Is your calabash empty, Slightly darling?'

'Not quite empty, mummy,' Slightly said, after looking into an imaginary mug.

'He hasn't even begun to drink his milk,' Nibs interposed.

This was telling, and Slightly seized his chance.

'I complain of Nibs,' he cried promptly.

John, however, had held up his hand first.

'Well, John?'

'May I sit in Peter's chair, as he is not here?'

'Sit in father's chair, John!' Wendy was scandalised. 'Certainly not.'

'He is not really our father,' John answered. 'He didn't even know how a father does till I showed him.'

This was grumbling. 'We complain of John,' cried the twins.

Tootles held up his hand. He was so much the humblest of them, indeed he was the only humble one, that Wendy was specially gentle with him.

'I don't suppose,' Tootles said diffidently, 'that I could be father.'

'No, Tootles.'

Once Tootles began, which was not very often, he had a silly way of going on.

'As I can't be father,' he said heavily, 'I don't suppose, Michael, you would let me be baby?'

'No, I won't,' Michael rapped out. He was already in his basket.

'As I can't be baby,' Tootles said, getting heavier and heavier, 'do you think I could be a twin?'

'No, indeed,' replied the twins; 'it's awfully difficult to be a twin.'

'As I can't be anything important,' said Tootles, 'would any of you like to see me do a trick?'

'No,' they all replied.

Then at last he stopped. 'I hadn't really any hope,' he said.

The hateful telling broke out again.

'Slightly is coughing on the table.'

'The twins began with mammee-apples.'

'Curly is taking both tappa rolls and yams.'

'Nibs is speaking with his mouth full.'

'I complain of the twins.'

'I complain of Curly.'

'I complain of Nibs.'

'Oh dear, oh dear,' cried Wendy, 'I'm sure I sometimes think that children are more trouble than they are worth.'

She told them to clear away, and sat down to her work-basket: a heavy load of stockings and every knee with a hole in it as usual.

'Wendy,' remonstrated Michael, 'I'm too big for a cradle.'

'I must have somebody in a cradle,' she said almost tartly, 'and you are the littlest. A cradle is such a nice homely thing to have about a house.'

While she sewed they played around her; such a group of happy faces and dancing limbs lit up by that romantic fire. It had become a very familiar scene this in the home under the ground, but we are looking on it for the last time.

There was a step above, and Wendy, you may be sure, was the first to recognise it.

'Children, I hear your father's step. He likes you to meet him at the door.'

Above, the redskins crouched before Peter.

'Watch well, braves. I have spoken.'

And then, as so often before, the gay children dragged him from his tree. As so often before, but never again.

He had brought nuts for the boys as well as the correct time for Wendy.

'Peter, you just spoil them, you know,' Wendy simpered.

'Ah, old lady,' said Peter, hanging up his gun.

'It was me told him mothers are called old lady,' Michael whispered to Curly.

'I complain of Michael,' said Curly instantly.

The first twin came to Peter. 'Father, we want to dance.'

'Dance away, my little man,' said Peter, who was in high good humour.

'But we want you to dance.'

Peter was really the best dancer among them, but he pretended to be scandalised.

'Me! My old bones would rattle.'

'And mummy too.'

'What,' cried Wendy, 'the mother of such an armful, dance!'

'But on a Saturday night,' Slightly insinuated.

It was not really Saturday night, at least it may have been, for they had long lost count of the days; but always if they wanted to do anything special they said this was Saturday night, and then they did it.

'Of course it is Saturday night, Peter,' Wendy said, relenting.

'People of our figure, Wendy.'

'But it is only among our own progeny.'

'True, true.'

So they were told they could dance, but they must put on their nighties first.

'Ah, old lady,' Peter said aside to Wendy, warming himself by the fire and looking down at her as she sat turning a heel, 'there is nothing more pleasant, of an evening for you and me when the day's toil is over than to rest by the fire with the little ones near by.'

'It is sweet, Peter, isn't it?' Wendy said, frightfully gratified. 'Peter, I think Curly has your nose.'

'Michael takes after you.'

She went to him and put her hand on his shoulder.

'Dear Peter,' she said, 'with such a large family, of course, I have now passed my best, but you don't want to change me, do you?'

'No, Wendy.'

Certainly he did not want a change, but he looked at her uncomfortably; blinking, you know, like one not sure whether he was awake or asleep.

'Peter, what is it?'

'I was just thinking,' he said, a little scared. 'It is only make-believe, isn't it, that I am their father?'

'Oh yes,' Wendy said primly.

'You see,' he continued apologetically, 'it would make me seem so old to be their real father.'

'But they are ours, Peter, yours and mine.'

'But not really, Wendy?' he asked anxiously.

'Not if you don't wish it,' she replied; and she distinctly heard his sigh of relief. 'Peter,' she asked, trying to speak firmly, 'what are your exact feelings for me?'

'Those of a devoted son, Wendy.'

'I thought so,' she said, and went and sat by herself at the extreme end of the room.

'You are so queer,' he said, frankly puzzled, 'and Tiger Lily is just the same. There is something she wants to be to me, but she says it is not my mother.'

'No, indeed, it is not,' Wendy replied with frightful emphasis. Now we know why she was prejudiced against the redskins.

'Then what is it?'

'It isn't for a lady to tell.'

'Oh, very well,' Peter said, a little nettled. 'Perhaps Tinker Bell will tell me.'

'Oh yes, Tinker Bell will tell you,' Wendy retorted scornfully. 'She is an abandoned little creature.'

Here Tink, who was in her boudoir, eavesdropping, squeaked out something impudent.

'She says she glories in being abandoned,' Peter interpreted.

He had a sudden idea. 'Perhaps Tink wants to be my mother?'

'You silly ass!' cried Tinker Bell in a passion.

She had said it so often that Wendy needed no translation.

'I almost agree with her,' Wendy snapped. Fancy Wendy snapping. But she had been much tried, and she little knew what was to happen before the night was out. If she had known she would not have snapped.

None of them knew. Perhaps it was best not to know. Their ignorance gave them one more glad hour; and as it was to be their last hour on the island, let us rejoice that there were sixty glad minutes in it. They sang and danced in their night-gowns. Such a deliciously creepy song it was, in which they pretended to be frightened at their own shadows; little witting that so soon shadows would close in upon them, from whom they would shrink in real fear. So uproariously gay was the dance, and how they buffeted each other on the bed and out of it! It was a pillow fight rather than a dance, and when it was finished, the pillows insisted on one bout more, like partners who know that they may never meet again. The stories they told, before it was time for Wendy's good-night story! Even Slightly tried to tell a story that night, but the beginning was so fearfully dull that it appalled even himself, and he said gloomily:

'Yes, it is a dull beginning. I say, let us pretend that it is the end.'

And then at last they all got into bed for Wendy's story, the story they loved best, the story Peter hated. Usually when she began to tell this story he left the room or put his hands over his ears; and possibly if he had done either of those things this time they might all still be on the island. But to-night he remained on his stool; and we shall see what happened.

# II

# WENDY'S STORY

'Listen, then,' said Wendy, settling down to her story, with Michael at her feet and seven boys in the bed. 'There was once a gentleman——'

'I had rather he had been a lady,' Curly said.

'I wish he had been a white rat,' said Nibs.

'Quiet,' their mother admonished them. 'There was a lady also, and——'

'O mummy,' cried the first twin, 'you mean that there is a lady also, don't you? She is not dead, is she?'

'Oh no.'

'I am awfully glad she isn't dead,' said Tootles. 'Are you glad, John?'

'Of course I am.'

'Are you glad, Nibs?'

'Rather.'

'Are you glad, Twins?'

'We are just glad.'

'Oh dear,' sighed Wendy.

'Little less noise there,' Peter called out, determined that she should have fair play, however beastly a story it might be in his opinion.

'The gentleman's name,' Wendy continued, 'was Mr. Darling, and her name was Mrs. Darling.'

'I knew them,' John said, to annoy the others.

'I think I knew them,' said Michael rather doubtfully.

'They were married, you know,' explained Wendy, 'and what do you think they had?'

'White rats,' cried Nibs, inspired.

'No.'

'It's awfully puzzling,' said Tootles, who knew the story by heart.

'Quiet, Tootles. They had three descendants.'

'What is descendants?'

'Well, you are one, Twin.

'Do you hear that, John? I am a descendant.'

'Descendants are only children,' said John.

'Oh dear, oh dear,' sighed Wendy. 'Now these three children had a faithful nurse called Nana; but Mr. Darling was angry with her and chained her up in the yard; and so all the children flew away.'

'It's an awfully good story,' said Nibs.

'They flew away,' Wendy continued, 'to the Neverland, where the lost children are.'

'I just thought they did,' Curly broke in excitedly. 'I don't know how it is, but I just thought they did.'

'O Wendy,' cried Tootles, 'was one of the lost children called Tootles?'

'Yes, he was.'

'I am in a story. Hurrah, I am in a story, Nibs.'

'Hush. Now I want you to consider the feelings of the unhappy parents with all their children flown away.'

'Oo!' they all moaned, though they were not really considering the feelings of the unhappy parents one jot.

'Think of the empty beds!'

'Oo!'

'It's awfully sad,' the first twin said cheerfully.

'I don't see how it can have a happy ending,' said the second twin. 'Do you, Nibs?'

'I'm frightfully anxious.'

'If you knew how great is a mother's love,' Wendy told them triumphantly, 'you would have no fear.' She had now come to the part that Peter hated.

'I do like a mother's love,' said Tootles, hitting Nibs with a pillow. 'Do you like a mother's love, Nibs?'

'I do just,' said Nibs, hitting back.

'You see,' Wendy said complacently, 'our heroine knew that the mother would always leave the window open for her children to fly back by; so they stayed away for years and had a lovely time.'

'Did they ever go back?'

'Let us now,' said Wendy, bracing herself for her finest effort, 'take a peep into the future'; and they all gave themselves the twist that makes peeps into the future easier. 'Years have rolled by; and who is this elegant lady of uncertain age alighting at London Station?'

'O Wendy, who is she?' cried Nibs, every bit as excited as if he didn't know.

'Can it be—yes—no—it is—the fair Wendy!'

'Oh!'

'And who are the two noble portly figures accompanying her, now grown to man's estate? Can they be John and Michael? They are!'

'Oh!'

'"See, dear brothers," says Wendy, pointing upwards, '"there is the window still standing open. Ah, now we are rewarded for our sublime faith in a mother's love." So up they flew to their mummy and daddy; and pen cannot describe the happy scene, over which we draw a veil.'

That was the story, and they were as pleased with it as the fair narrator herself. Everything just as it should be, you see. Off we skip like the most heartless things in the world, which is what children are, but so attractive; and we have an entirely selfish time; and then when we have need of special attention we nobly return for it, confident that we shall be embraced instead of smacked.

So great indeed was their faith in a mother's love that they felt they could afford to be callous for a bit longer.

But there was one there who knew better; and when Wendy finished he uttered a hollow groan.

'What is it, Peter?' she cried, running to him, thinking he was ill. She felt him solicitously, lower down than his chest. 'Where is it, Peter?'

'It isn't that kind of pain,' Peter replied darkly.

'Then what kind is it?'

'Wendy, you are wrong about mothers.'

They all gathered round him in affright, so alarming was his agitation; and with a fine candour he told them what he had hitherto concealed.

'Long ago,' he said, 'I thought like you that my mother would always keep the window open for me; so I stayed away for moons and moons and moons, and then flew back; but the window was barred, for mother had forgotten all about me, and there was another little boy sleeping in my bed.'

I am not sure that this was true, but Peter thought it was true; and it scared them.

'Are you sure mothers are like that?'

'Yes.'

So this was the truth about mothers. The toads!

Still it is best to be careful; and no one knows so quickly as a child when he should give in. 'Wendy, let us go home,' cried John and Michael together.

'Yes,' she said, clutching them.

'Not to-night?' asked the lost boys bewildered. They knew in what they called their hearts that one can get on quite well without a mother, and that it is only the mothers who think you can't.

'At once,' Wendy replied resolutely, for the horrible thought had come to her: 'Perhaps mother is in half mourning by this time.'

This dread made her forgetful of what must be Peter's feelings, and she said to him rather sharply, 'Peter, will you make the necessary arrangements?'

'If you wish it,', he replied, as coolly as if she had asked him to pass the nuts.

Not so much as a sorry-to-lose-you between them! If she did not mind the parting, he was going to show her, was Peter, that neither did he.

But of course he cared very much; and he was so full of wrath against grown-ups, who, as usual, were spoiling everything, that as soon as he got inside his tree he breathed intentionally quick short breaths at the rate of about five to a second. He did this because there is a saying in the Neverland that, every time you breathe, a grown-up dies; and Peter was killing them off vindictively as fast as possible.

Then having given the necessary instructions to the redskins he returned to the home, where an unworthy scene had been enacted in his absence. Panic-stricken at the thought of losing Wendy the lost boys had advanced upon her threateningly.

'It will be worse than before she came,' they cried.

'We shan't let her go.'

'Let's keep her prisoner.'

'Ay, chain her up.'

In her extremity an instinct told her to which of them to turn.

'Tootles,' she cried, 'I appeal to you.'

Was it not strange? she appealed to Tootles, quite the silliest one.

Grandly, however, did Tootles respond. For that one moment he dropped his silliness and spoke with dignity.

'I am just Tootles,' he said, 'and nobody minds me. But the first who does not behave to Wendy like an English gentleman I will blood him severely.'

He drew his hanger; and for that instant his sun was at noon. The others held back uneasily. Then Peter returned, and they saw at once that they would get no support from him. He would keep no girl in the Neverland against her will.

'Wendy,' he said, striding up and down, 'I have asked the redskins to guide you through the wood, as flying tires you so.'

'Thank you, Peter.'

'Then,' he continued, in the short sharp voice of one accustomed to be obeyed, 'Tinker Bell will take you across the sea. Wake her, Nibs.'

Nibs had to knock twice before he got an answer, though Tink had really been sitting up in bed listening for some time.

'Who are you? How dare you? Go away,' she cried.

'You are to get up, Tink,' Nibs called, 'and take Wendy on a journey.'

Of course Tink had been delighted to hear that Wendy was going; but she was jolly well determined not to be her courier, and she said so in still more offensive language. Then she pretended to be asleep again.

'She says she won't,' Nibs exclaimed, aghast at such insubordination, whereupon Peter went sternly toward the young lady's chamber.

'Tink,' he rapped out, 'if you don't get up and dress at once I will open the curtains, and then we shall all see you in your *négligée*.'

This made her leap to the floor. 'Who said I wasn't getting up?' she cried.

In the meantime the boys were gazing very forlornly at Wendy, now equipped with John and Michael for the journey. By this time they were dejected, not merely because they were about to lose her, but also because they felt that she was going off to something nice to which they had not been invited. Novelty was beckoning to them as usual.

Crediting them with a nobler feeling Wendy melted.

'Dear ones,' she said, 'if you will all come with me I feel almost sure I can get my father and mother to adopt you.'

The invitation was meant specially for Peter; but each of the boys was thinking exclusively of himself, and at once they jumped with joy.

'But won't they think us rather a handful?' Nibs asked in the middle of his jump.

'Oh no,' said Wendy, rapidly thinking it out, 'it will only mean having a few beds in the drawing-room; they can be hidden behind screens on first Thursdays.'

'Peter, can we go?' they all cried imploringly. They took it for granted that if they went he would go also, but really they scarcely cared. Thus children are ever ready, when novelty knocks, to desert their dearest ones.

'All right,' Peter replied with a bitter smile; and immediately they rushed to get their things.

'And now, Peter,' Wendy said, thinking she had put everything right, 'I am going to give you your medicine before you go.' She loved to give them medicine, and undoubtedly gave them too much. Of course it was only water, but it was out of a calabash, and she always shook the calabash and counted the drops, which gave it a certain medicinal quality. On this occasion, however, she did not give Peter his draught, for just as she had prepared it, she saw a look on his face that made her heart sink.

'Get your things, Peter,' she cried, shaking.

'No,' he answered, pretending indifference, 'I am not going with you, Wendy.'

'Yes, Peter.'

'No.'

To show that her departure would leave him unmoved, he skipped up and down the room, playing gaily on his heartless pipes. She had to run about after him, though it was rather undignified.

'To find your mother,' she coaxed.

Now, if Peter had ever quite had a mother, he no longer missed her. He could do very well without one. He had thought them out, and remembered only their bad points.

'No, no,' he told Wendy decisively; 'perhaps she would say I was old, and I just want always to be a little boy and to have fun.'

'But, Peter——'

'No.'

And so the others had to be told.

'Peter isn't coming.'

Peter not coming! They gazed blankly at him, their sticks over their backs, and on each stick a bundle. Their first thought was that if Peter was not going he had probably changed his mind about letting them go.

But he was far too proud for that. 'If you find your mothers,' he said darkly, 'I hope you will like them.'

The awful cynicism of this made an uncomfortable impression, and most of them began to look rather doubtful. After all, their faces said, were they not noodles to want to go?

'Now then,' cried Peter, 'no fuss, no blubbering; good-bye, Wendy'; and he held out his hand cheerily, quite as if they must really go now, for he had something important to do.

She had to take his hand, as there was no indication that he would prefer a thimble.

'You will remember about changing your flannels, Peter?' she said, lingering over him. She was always so particular about their flannels.

'Yes.'

'And you will take your medicine?'

'Yes.'

That seemed to be everything; and an awkward pause followed. Peter, however, was not the kind that breaks down before people. 'Are you ready, Tinker Bell?' he called out.

'Ay, ay.'

'Then lead the way.'

Tink darted up the nearest tree; but no one followed her, for it was at this moment that the pirates made their dreadful attack upon the redskins. Above, where all had been so still, the air was rent with shrieks and the clash of steel. Below, there was dead silence. Mouths opened and remained open. Wendy fell on her knees, but her arms were extended toward Peter. All arms were extended to him, as if suddenly blown in his direction; they were beseeching him mutely not to desert them. As for Peter, he seized his sword, the same he thought he had slain Barbecue with; and the lust of battle was in his eye.

# 12

# THE CHILDREN ARE CARRIED OFF

The pirate attack had been a complete surprise: a sure proof that the unscrupulous Hook had conducted it improperly, for to surprise redskins fairly is beyond the wit of the white man.

By all the unwritten laws of savage warfare it is always the redskin who attacks, and with the wiliness of his race he does it just before the dawn, at which time he knows the courage of the whites to be at its lowest ebb. The white men have in the meantime made a rude stockade on the summit of yonder undulating ground, at the foot of which a stream runs; for it is destruction to be too far from water. There they await the onslaught, the inexperienced ones clutching their revolvers and treading on twigs, but the old hands sleeping tranquilly until just before the dawn. Through the long black night the savage scouts wriggle, snake-like, among the grass without stirring a blade. The brushwood closes behind them as silently as sand into which a mole has dived. Not a sound is to be heard, save when they give vent to a wonderful imitation of the lonely call of the coyote. The cry is answered by other braves; and some of them do it even better than the coyotes, who are not very good at it. So the chill hours wear on, and the long suspense is horribly trying to the paleface who has to live through it for the first time; but to the trained hand those ghastly calls and still ghastlier silences are but an intimation of how the night is marching.

That this was the usual procedure was so well known to Hook that in disregarding it he cannot be excused on the plea of ignorance.

The Piccaninnies, on their part, trusted implicitly to his honour, and their whole action of the night stands out in marked contrast to his. They left nothing undone that was consistent with the reputation of their tribe. With that alertness of the senses which is at once the marvel and despair of civilised peoples, they knew that the pirates were on the island from the moment one of them trod on a dry stick; and in an incredibly short space of time the coyote cries began. Every foot of ground between the spot where Hook had landed his forces and the home under the trees was stealthily examined by braves wearing their mocassins with the heels in front. They found only one hillock with a stream at its base, so that Hook had no choice; here he must establish himself and wait for just before the dawn. Everything being thus mapped out with almost diabolical cunning, the main body of the redskins folded their blankets around them, and in the phlegmatic manner that is to them the pearl of manhood squatted above the children's home, awaiting the cold moment when they should deal pale death.

Here dreaming, though wide-awake, of the exquisite tortures to which they were to put him at break of day, those confiding savages were found by the treacherous Hook. From the accounts afterwards supplied by such of the scouts as escaped the carnage, he does not seem even to have paused at the rising ground, though it is certain that in that grey light he must have seen it: no thought of waiting to be attacked appears from first to last to have visited his subtle mind; he would not even hold off till the night was nearly spent; on he pounded with no policy but to fall to. What could the bewildered scouts do, masters as they were of every warlike artifice save this one, but trot helplessly after him, exposing themselves fatally to view, the while they gave pathetic utterance to the coyote cry.

Around the brave Tiger Lily were a dozen of her stoutest warriors, and they suddenly saw the perfidious pirates bearing down upon them. Fell from their eyes then the film through which they had looked at victory. No more would they torture at the stake. For them the happy hunting-grounds now. They knew it; but as their fathers' sons they acquitted themselves. Even then they had time to gather in a phalanx that would have been hard to break had they risen quickly, but this they were forbidden to do by the traditions of their race. It is written that the noble savage must never express surprise in the presence of the white. Thus terrible as the sudden appearance of the pirates must have been to them, they remained stationary for a moment, not a muscle moving; as if the foe had come by invitation. Then, indeed, the tradition gallantly upheld, they seized their weapons, and the air was torn with the warcry; but it was now too late.

It is no part of ours to describe what was a massacre rather than a fight. Thus perished many of the flower of the Piccaninny tribe. Not all unavenged did they die, for with Lean Wolf fell Alf Mason, to disturb the Spanish Main no more; and among others who bit the dust were Geo. Scourie, Chas. Turley, and the Alsatian Foggerty. Turley fell to the tomahawk of the terrible Panther, who ultimately cut a way through the pirates with Tiger Lily and a small remnant of the tribe.

To what extent Hook is to blame for his tactics on this occasion is for the historian to decide. Had he waited on the rising ground till the proper hour he and his men would probably have been butchered; and in judging him it is only fair to take this into account. What he should perhaps have done was to acquaint his opponents that he proposed to follow a new method. On the other hand this, as destroying the element of surprise, would have made his strategy of no avail, so that the whole question is beset with difficulties. One cannot at least withhold a reluctant admiration for the wit that had conceived so bold a scheme, and the fell genius with which it was carried out.

What were his own feelings about himself at that triumphant moment? Fain would his dogs have known, as breathing heavily and wiping their cutlasses, they gathered at a discreet distance from his hook, and squinted through their ferret eyes at this extraordinary man. Elation must have been in his heart, but his face did not reflect it: ever a dark and solitary enigma, he stood aloof from his followers in spirit as in substance.

The night's work was not yet over, for it was not the redskins he had come out to destroy; they were but the bees to be smoked, so that he should get at the honey. It was Pan he wanted, Pan and Wendy and their band, but chiefly Pan.

Peter was such a small boy that one tends to wonder at the man's hatred of him. True he had flung Hook's arm to the crocodile; but even this and the increased insecurity of life to which it led, owing to the crocodile's pertinacity, hardly account for a vindictiveness so relentless and malignant. The truth is that there was a something about Peter which goaded the pirate captain to frenzy. It was not his courage, it was not his engaging appearance, it was not—. There is no beating about the bush, for we know quite well what it was, and have got to tell. It was Peter's cockiness.

This had got on Hook's nerves; it made his iron claw twitch, and at night it disturbed him like an insect. While Peter lived, the tortured man felt that he was a lion in a cage into which a sparrow had come.

The question now was how to get down the trees, or how to get his dogs down? He ran his greedy eyes over them, searching for the thinnest ones. They wriggled uncomfortably, for they knew he would not scruple to ram them down with poles.

In the meantime, what of the boys? We have seen them at the first clang of weapons, turned as it were into stone figures, open-mouthed, all appealing with outstretched arms to Peter; and we return to them as their mouths close, and their arms fall to their sides. The pandemonium above has ceased almost as suddenly as it arose, passed like a fierce gust of wind; but they know that in the passing it has determined their fate.

Which side had won?

The pirates, listening avidly at the mouths of the trees, heard the question put by every boy, and alas, they also heard Peter's answer.

'If the redskins have won,' he said, 'they will beat the tom-tom; it is always their sign of victory.'

Now Smee had found the tom-tom, and was at that moment sitting on it. 'You will never hear the tom-tom again,' he muttered, but inaudibly of course, for strict silence had been enjoined. To his amazement Hook signed to him to beat the tom-tom; and slowly there came to Smee an understanding of the dreadful wickedness of the order. Never, probably, had this simple man admired Hook so much.

Twice Smee beat upon the instrument, and then stopped to listen gleefully.

'The tom-tom,' the miscreants heard Peter cry; 'an Indian victory!'

The doomed children answered with a cheer that was music to the black hearts above, and almost immediately they repeated their goodbyes to Peter. This puzzled the pirates, but all their other feelings were swallowed by a base delight that the enemy were about to come up the trees. They smirked at each other and rubbed their hands. Rapidly and silently Hook gave his orders: one man to each tree, and the others to arrange themselves in a line two yards apart.

# 13

# DO YOU BELIEVE IN FAIRIES?

The more quickly this horror is disposed of the better. The first to emerge from his tree was Curly. He rose out of it into the arms of Cecco, who flung him to Smee, who flung him to Starkey, who flung him to Bill Jukes, who flung him to Noodler, and so he was tossed from one to another till he fell at the feet of the black pirate. All the boys were plucked from their trees in this ruthless manner; and several of them were in the air at a time, like bales of goods flung from hand to hand.

A different treatment was accorded to Wendy, who came last. With ironical politeness Hook raised his hat to her, and, offering her his arm, escorted her to the spot where the others were being gagged. He did it with such an air, he was so frightfully *distingué*, that she was too fascinated to cry out. She was only a little girl.

Perhaps it is tell-tale to divulge that for a moment Hook entranced her, and we tell on her only because her slip led to strange results. Had she haughtily unhanded him (and we should have loved to write it of her), she would have been hurled through the air like the others, and then Hook would probably not have been present at the tying of the children; and had he not been at the tying he would not have discovered Slightly's secret, and without the secret he could not presently have made his foul attempt on Peter's life.

They were tied to prevent their flying away, doubled up with their knees close to their ears; and for the trussing of them the black pirate had cut a rope into nine equal pieces. All went well until Slightly's turn came, when he was found to be like those irritating parcels that use up all the string in going round and leave no tags with which to tie a knot. The pirates kicked him in their rage, just as you kick the parcel (though in fairness you should kick the string); and strange to say it was Hook who told them to belay their violence. His lip was curled with malicious triumph. While his dogs were merely sweating because every time they tried to pack the unhappy lad tight in one part he bulged out in another, Hook's master mind had gone far beneath Slightly's surface, probing not for effects but for causes; and his exultation showed that he had found them. Slightly, white to the gills, knew that Hook had surprised his secret, which was this, that no boy so blown out could use a tree wherein an average man need stick. Poor Slightly, most wretched of all the children now, for he was in a panic about Peter, bitterly regretted what he had done. Madly addicted to the drinking of water when he was hot, he had swelled in consequence to his present girth, and instead of reducing himself to fit his tree he had, unknown to the others, whittled his tree to make it fit him.

Sufficient of this Hook guessed to persuade him that Peter at last lay at his mercy; but no word of the dark design that now formed in the subterranean caverns of his mind crossed his lips; he merely signed that the captives were to be conveyed to the ship, and that he would be alone.

How to convey them? Hunched up in their ropes they might indeed be rolled down hill like barrels, but most of the way lay through a morass. Again Hook's genius surmounted difficulties. He indicated that the little house must be used as a conveyance. The children were flung into it, four stout pirates raised it on their shoulders, the others fell in behind, and singing the hateful pirate chorus the strange procession set off through the wood. I don't know whether any of the children were crying; if so, the singing drowned the sound; but as the little house disappeared in the forest, a brave though tiny jet of smoke issued from its chimney as if defying Hook.

Hook saw it, and it did Peter a bad service. It dried up any trickle of pity for him that may have remained in the pirate's infuriated breast.

The first thing he did on finding himself alone in the fast falling night was to tiptoe to Slightly's tree, and make sure that it provided him with a passage. Then for long he remained brooding; his hat of ill omen on the sward, so that a gentle breeze which had arisen might play refreshingly through his hair. Dark as were his thoughts his blue eyes were as soft as the periwinkle. Intently he listened for any sound from the nether world, but all was as silent below as above; the house under the ground seemed to be but one more empty tenement in the void. Was that boy asleep, or did he stand waiting at the foot of Slightly's tree, with his dagger in his hand?

There was no way of knowing, save by going down. Hook let his cloak slip softly to the ground, and then biting his lips till a lewd blood stood on them, he stepped into the tree. He was a brave man; but for a moment he had to stop there and wipe his brow, which was dripping like a candle. Then silently he let himself go into the unknown.

He arrived unmolested at the foot of the shaft, and stood still again, biting at his breath, which had almost left him. As his eyes became accustomed to the dim light various objects in the home under the trees took shape; but the only one on which his greedy gaze rested, long sought for and found at last, was the great bed. On the bed lay Peter fast asleep.

Unaware of the tragedy being enacted above, Peter had continued, for a little time after the children left, to play gaily on his pipes: no doubt rather a forlorn attempt to prove to himself that he did not care. Then he decided not to take his medicine, so as to grieve Wendy. Then he lay down on the bed outside the coverlet, to vex her still more; for she had always tucked them inside it, because you never know that you may not grow chilly at the turn of the night. Then he nearly cried; but it struck him how indignant she would be if he laughed instead; so he laughed a haughty laugh and fell asleep in the middle of it.

Sometimes, though not often, he had dreams, and they were more painful than the dreams of other boys. For hours he could not be separated from these dreams, though he wailed piteously in them. They had to do, I think, with the riddle of his existence. At such times it had been Wendy's custom to take him out of bed and sit with him on her lap, soothing him in dear ways of her own invention, and when he grew calmer to put him back to bed before he quite woke up, so that he should not know of the indignity to which she had subjected him. But on this occasion he had fallen at once into a dreamless sleep. One arm dropped over the edge of the bed, one leg was arched, and the unfinished part of his laugh was stranded on his mouth, which was open, showing the little pearls.

Thus defenceless Hook found him. He stood silent at the foot of the tree looking across the chamber at his enemy. Did no feeling of compassion disturb his sombre breast? The man was not wholly evil; he loved flowers (I have been told) and sweet music (he was himself no mean performer on the harpsichord); and, let it be frankly admitted, the idyllic nature of the scene stirred him profoundly. Mastered by his better self he would have returned reluctantly up the tree, but for one thing.

What stayed him was Peter's impertinent appearance as he slept. The open mouth, the drooping arm, the arched knee: they were such a personification of cockiness as, taken together, will never again one may hope be presented to eyes so sensitive to their offensiveness. They steeled Hook's heart. If his rage had broken him into a hundred pieces every one of them would have disregarded the incident, and leapt at the sleeper.

Though a light from the one lamp shone dimly on the bed Hook stood in darkness himself, and at the first stealthy step forward he discovered an obstacle, the door of Slightly's tree. It did not entirely fill the aperture, and he had been looking over it. Feeling for the catch, he found to his fury that it was low down, beyond his reach. To his disordered brain it seemed then that the irritating quality in Peter's face and figure visibly increased, and he rattled the door and flung himself against it. Was his enemy to escape him after all.

But what was that? The red in his eye had caught sight of Peter's medicine standing on a ledge within easy reach. He fathomed what it was straightway, and immediately he knew that the sleeper was in his power.

Lest he should be taken alive, Hook always carried about his person a dreadful drug, blended by himself of all the death-dealing rings that had come into his possession. These he had boiled down into a yellow liquid quite unknown to science, which was probably the most virulent poison in existence.

Five drops of this he now added to Peter's cup. His hand shook, but it was in exultation rather than in shame. As he did it he avoided glancing at the sleeper, but not lest pity should unnerve him; merely to avoid spilling. Then one long gloating look he cast upon his victim, and turning, wormed his way with difficulty up the tree. As he emerged at the top he looked the very spirit of evil breaking from its hole. Donning his hat at its most rakish angle, he wound his cloak around him, holding one end in front as if to conceal his person from the night, of which it was the blackest part, and muttering strangely to himself stole away through the trees.

Peter slept on. The light guttered and went out, leaving the tenement in darkness; but still he slept. It must have been not less than ten o'clock by the crocodile, when he suddenly sat up in his bed, wakened by he knew not what. It was a soft cautious tapping on the door of his tree.

Soft and cautious, but in that stillness it was sinister. Peter felt for his dagger till his hand gripped it. Then he spoke.

'Who is that?'

For long there was no answer: then again the knock.

'Who are you?'

No answer.

He was thrilled, and he loved being thrilled. In two strides he reached his door. Unlike Slightly's door it filled the aperture, so that he could not see beyond it, nor could the one knocking see him.

'I won't open unless you speak,' Peter cried.

Then at last the visitor spoke, in a lovely bell-like voice.

'Let me in, Peter.'

It was Tink, and quickly he unbarred to her. She flew in excitedly, her face flushed and her dress stained with mud.

'What is it?'

'Oh, you could never guess,' she cried, and offered him three guesses. 'Out with it!' he shouted; and in one ungrammatical sentence, as long as the ribbons conjurers pull from their mouths, she told of the capture of Wendy and the boys.

Peter's heart bobbed up and down as he listened. Wendy bound, and on the pirate ship; she who loved everything to be just so!

'I'll rescue her,' he cried, leaping at his weapons. As he leapt he thought of something he could do to please her. He could take his medicine.

His hand closed on the fatal draught.

'No!' shrieked Tinker Bell, who had heard Hook muttering about his deed as he sped through the forest.

'Why not?'

'It is poisoned.'

'Poisoned? Who could have poisoned it?'

'Hook.'

'Don't be silly. How could Hook have got down here?'

Alas, Tinker Bell could not explain this, for even she did not know the dark secret of Slightly's tree. Nevertheless Hook's words had left no room for doubt. The cup was poisoned.

'Besides,' said Peter, quite believing himself, 'I never fell asleep.'

He raised the cup. No time for words now; time for deeds; and with one of her lightning movements Tink got between his lips and the draught, and drained it to the dregs.

'Why, Tink, how dare you drink my medicine?'

But she did not answer. Already she was reeling in the air.

'What is the matter with you?' cried Peter, suddenly afraid.

'It was poisoned, Peter,' she told him softly; 'and now I am going to be dead.'

'O Tink, did you drink it to save me?'

'Yes.'

'But why, Tink?'

Her wings would scarcely carry her now, but in reply she alighted on his shoulder and gave his chin a loving bite. She whispered in his ear 'You silly ass'; and then, tottering to her chamber, lay down on the bed.

His head almost filled the fourth wall of her little room as he knelt near her in distress. Every moment her light was growing fainter; and he knew that if it went out she would be no more. She liked his tears so much that she put out her beautiful finger and let them run over it.

Her voice was so low that at first he could not make out what she said. Then he made it out. She was saying that she thought she could get well again if children believed in fairies.

Peter flung out his arms. There were no children there, and it was night-time; but he addressed all who might be dreaming of the Neverland, and who were therefore nearer to him than you think: boys and girls in their nighties, and naked papooses in their baskets hung from trees.

'Do you believe?' he cried.

Tink sat up in bed almost briskly to listen to her fate.

She fancied she heard answers in the affirmative, and then again she wasn't sure.

'What do you think?' she asked Peter.

'If you believe,' he shouted to them, 'clap your hands; don't let Tink die.'

Many clapped.

Some didn't.

A few little beasts hissed.

The clapping stopped suddenly; as if countless mothers had rushed to their nurseries to see what on earth was happening; but already Tink was saved. First her voice grew strong; then she popped out of bed; then she was flashing through the room more merry and impudent than ever. She never thought of thanking those who believed, but she would have liked to get at the ones who had hissed.

'And now to rescue Wendy.'

The moon was riding in a cloudy heaven when Peter rose from his tree, begirt with weapons and wearing little else, to set out upon his perilous quest. It was not such a night as he would have chosen. He had hoped to fly, keeping not far from the ground so that nothing unwonted should escape his eyes; but in that fitful light to have flown low would have meant trailing his shadow through the trees, thus disturbing the birds and acquainting a watchful foe that he was astir.

He regretted now that he had given the birds of the island such strange names that they are very wild and difficult of approach.

There was no other course but to press forward in redskin fashion, at which happily he was an adept. But in what direction, for he could not be sure that the children had been taken to the ship? A slight fall of snow had obliterated all footmarks; and a deathly silence pervaded the island, as if for a space Nature stood still in horror of the recent carnage. He had taught the children something of the forest lore that he had himself learned from Tiger Lily and Tinker Bell, and knew that in their dire hour they were not likely to forget it. Slightly, if he had an opportunity, would blaze the trees, for instance, Curly would drop seeds, and Wendy would leave her handkerchief at some important place. But morning was needed to search for such guidance, and he could not wait. The upper world had called him, but would give no help.

The crocodile passed him, but not another living thing, not a sound, not a movement; and yet he knew well that sudden death might be at the next tree, or stalking him from behind.

He swore this terrible oath: 'Hook or me this time.'

Now he crawled forward like a snake; and again, erect, he darted across a space on which the moonlight played: one finger on his lip and his dagger at the ready. He was frightfully happy.

# 14
# THE PIRATE SHIP

One green light squinting over Kidd's Creek, which is near the mouth of the pirate river, marked where the brig, the *Jolly Roger*, lay, low in the water; a rakish-looking craft foul to the hull, every beam in her detestable like ground strewn with mangled feathers. She was the cannibal of the seas, and scarce needed that watchful eye, for she floated immune in the horror of her name.

She was wrapped in the blanket of night, through which no sound from her could have reached the shore. There was little sound, and none agreeable save the whir of the ship's sewing machine at which Smee sat, ever industrious and obliging, the essence of the commonplace, pathetic Smee. I know not why he was so infinitely pathetic, unless it were because he was so pathetically unaware of it; but even strong men had to turn hastily from looking at him, and more than once on summer evenings he had touched the fount of Hook's tears and made it flow. Of this, as of almost everything else, Smee was quite unconscious.

A few of the pirates leant over the bulwarks drinking in the miasma of the night; others sprawled by barrels over games of dice and cards; and the exhausted four who had carried the little house lay prone on the deck, where even in their sleep they rolled skilfully to this side or that out of Hook's reach, lest he should claw them mechanically in passing.

Hook trod the deck in thought. O man unfathomable. It was his hour of triumph. Peter had been removed for ever from his path, and all the other boys were on the brig, about to walk the plank. It was his grimmest deed since the days when he had brought Barbecue to heel; and knowing as we do how vain a tabernacle is man, could we be surprised had he now paced the deck unsteadily, bellied out by the winds of his success?

But there was no elation in his gait, which kept pace with the action of his sombre mind. Hook was profoundly dejected.

He was often thus when communing with himself on board ship in the quietude of the night. It was because he was so terribly alone. This inscrutable man never felt more alone than when surrounded by his dogs. They were socially so inferior to him.

Hook was not his true name. To reveal who he really was would even at this date set the country in a blaze; but as those who read between the lines must already have guessed, he had been at a famous public school; and its traditions still clung to him like garments, with which indeed they are largely concerned. Thus it was offensive to him even now to board a ship in the same dress in which he grappled her; and he still adhered in his walk to the school's distinguished slouch. But above all he retained the passion for good form.

Good form! However much he may have degenerated, he still knew that this is all that really matters.

From far within him he heard a creaking as of rusty portals, and through them came a stern tap-tap-tap, like hammering in the night when one cannot sleep. 'Have you been good form to-day?' was their eternal question.

'Fame, fame, that glittering bauble, it is mine,' he cried.

'Is it quite good form to be distinguished at anything?' the tap-tap from his school replied.

'I am the only man whom Barbecue feared,' he urged; 'and Flint himself feared Barbecue.'

'Barbecue, Flint—what house?' came the cutting retort.

Most disquieting reflection of all, was it not bad form to think about good form?

His vitals were tortured by this problem. It was a claw within him sharper than the iron one; and as it tore him, the perspiration dripped down his tallow countenance and streaked his doublet. Ofttimes he drew his sleeve across his face, but there was no damming that trickle.

Ah, envy not Hook.

There came to him a presentiment of his early dissolution. It was as if Peter's terrible oath had boarded the ship. Hook felt a gloomy desire to make his dying speech, lest presently there should be no time for it.

'Better for Hook,' he cried, 'if he had had less ambition.' It was in his darkest hours only that he referred to himself in the third person.

'No little children love me.'

Strange that he should think of this, which had never troubled him before; perhaps the sewing machine brought it to his mind. For long he muttered to himself, staring at Smee, who was hemming placidly, under the conviction that all children feared him.

Feared him! Feared Smee! There was not a child on board the brig that night who did not already love him. He had said horrid things to them and hit them with the palm of his hand, because he could not hit with his fist; but they had only clung to him the more. Michael had tried on his spectacles.

To tell poor Smee that they thought him lovable! Hook itched to do it, but it seemed too brutal. Instead, he revolved this mystery in his mind: why do they find Smee lovable? He pursued the problem like the sleuth-hound that he was. If Smee was lovable, what was it that made him so? A terrible answer suddenly presented itself: 'Good form?'

Had the bo'sun good form without knowing it, which is the best form of all?

He remembered that you have to prove you don't know you have it before you are eligible for Pop.

With a cry of rage he raised his iron hand over Smee's head; but he did not tear. What arrested him was this reflection:

'To claw a man because he is good form, what would that be?'

'Bad form!'

The unhappy Hook was as impotent as he was damp, and he fell forward like a cut flower.

His dogs thinking him out of the way for a time, discipline instantly relaxed; and they broke into a bacchanalian dance, which brought him to his feet at once; all traces of human weakness gone, as if a bucket of water had passed over him.

'Quiet, you scugs,' he cried, 'or I'll cast anchor in you'; and at once the din was hushed. 'Are all the children chained, so that they cannot fly away?'

'Ay, ay.'

'Then hoist them up.'

The wretched prisoners were dragged from the hold, all except Wendy, and ranged in line in front of him. For a time he seemed unconscious of their presence. He lolled at his ease, humming, not unmelodiously, snatches of a rude song, and fingering a pack of cards. Ever and anon the light from his cigar gave a touch of colour to his face.

'Now then, bullies,' he said briskly, 'six of you walk the plank to-night, but I have room for two cabin boys. Which of you is it to be?'

'Don't irritate him unnecessarily,' had been Wendy's instructions in the hold; so Tootles stepped forward politely. Tootles hated the idea of signing under such a man, but an instinct told him that it would be prudent to lay the responsibility on an absent person; and though a somewhat silly boy, he knew that mothers alone are always willing to be the buffer. All children know this about mothers, and despise them for it, but make constant use of it.

So Tootles explained prudently, 'You see, sir, I don't think my mother would like me to be a pirate. Would your mother like you to be a pirate, Slightly?'

He winked at Slightly, who said mournfully, 'I don't think so,' as if he wished things had been otherwise. 'Would your mother like you to be a pirate, Twin?'

'I don't think so,' said the first twin, as clever as the others. 'Nibs, would——'

'Stow this gab,' roared Hook, and the spokesmen were dragged back. 'You, boy,' he said, addressing John, 'you look as if you had a little pluck in you. Didst never want to be a pirate, my hearty?'

Now John had sometimes experienced this hankering at maths. prep.; and he was struck by Hook's picking him out.

'I once thought of calling myself Red-handed Jack,' he said diffidently.

'And a good name too. We'll call you that here, bully, if you join.'

'What do you think, Michael?' asked John.

'What would you call me if I join?' Michael demanded.

'Blackbeard Joe.'

Michael was naturally impressed. 'What do you think, John?' He wanted John to decide, and John wanted him to decide.

'Shall we still be respectful subjects of the King?' John inquired.

Through Hook's teeth came the answer: 'You would have to swear, "Down with the King."'

Perhaps John had not behaved very well so far, but he shone out now.

'Then I refuse,' he cried, banging the barrel in front of Hook.

'And I refuse,' cried Michael.

'Rule Britannia!' squeaked Curly.

The infuriated pirates buffeted them in the mouth; and Hook roared out, 'That seals your doom. Bring up their mother. Get the plank ready.'

They were only boys, and they went white as they saw Jukes and Cecco preparing the fatal plank. But they tried to look brave when Wendy was brought up.

No words of mine can tell you how Wendy despised those pirates. To the boys there was at least some glamour in the pirate calling; but all that she saw was that the ship had not been scrubbed for years. There was not a porthole, on the grimy glass of which you might not have written with your finger 'Dirty pig'; and she had already written it on several. But as the boys gathered round her she had no thought, of course, save for them.

'So, my beauty,' said Hook, as if he spoke in syrup, 'you are to see your children walk the plank.'

Fine gentleman though he was, the intensity of his communings had soiled his ruff, and suddenly he knew that she was gazing at it. With a hasty gesture he tried to hide it, but he was too late.

'Are they to die?' asked Wendy, with a look of such frightful contempt that he nearly fainted.

'They are,' he snarled. 'Silence all,' he called gloatingly, 'for a mother's last words to her children.'

At this moment Wendy was grand. 'These are my last words, dear boys,' she said firmly. 'I feel that I have a message to you from your real mothers, and it is this: "We hope our sons will die like English gentlemen."'

Even the pirates were awed; and Tootles cried out hysterically, 'I am going to do what my mother hopes. What are you to do, Nibs?'

'What my mother hopes. What are you to do, Twin?'

'What my mother hopes. John, what are——'

But Hook had found his voice again.

'Tie her up,' he shouted.

It was Smee who tied her to the mast. 'See here, honey,' he whispered, 'I'll save you if you promise to be my mother.'

But not even for Smee would she make such a promise. 'I would almost rather have no children at all,' she said disdainfully.

It is sad to know that not a boy was looking at her as Smee tied her to the mast; the eyes of all were on the plank: that last little walk they were about to take. They were no longer able to hope that they would walk it manfully, for the capacity to think had gone from them; they could stare and shiver only.

Hook smiled on them with his teeth closed, and took a step toward Wendy. His intention was to turn her face so that she should see the boys walking the plank one by one. But he never reached her, he never heard the cry of anguish he hoped to wring from her. He heard something else instead.

It was the terrible tick-tick of the crocodile.

They all heard it—pirates, boys, Wendy; and immediately every head was blown in one direction; not to the water whence the sound proceeded, but toward Hook. All knew that what was about to happen concerned him alone, and that from being actors they were suddenly become spectators.

Very frightful was it to see the change that came over him. It was as if he had been clipped at every joint. He fell in a little heap.

The sound came steadily nearer; and in advance of it came this ghastly thought, 'The crocodile is about to board the ship.'

Even the iron claw hung inactive; as if knowing that it was no intrinsic part of what the attacking force wanted. Left so fearfully alone, any other man would have lain with his eyes shut where he fell: but the gigantic brain of Hook was still working, and under its guidance he crawled on his knees along the deck as far from the sound as he could go. The pirates respectfully cleared a passage for him, and it was only when he brought up against the bulwarks that he spoke.

'Hide me,' he cried hoarsely.

They gathered round him; all eyes averted from the thing that was coming aboard. They had no thought of fighting it. It was Fate.

Only when Hook was hidden from them did curiosity loosen the limbs of the boys so that they could rush to the ship's side to see the crocodile climbing it. Then they got the strangest surprise of this Night of Nights; for it was no crocodile that was coming to their aid. It was Peter.

He signed to them not to give vent to any cry of admiration that might rouse suspicion. Then he went on ticking.

# 15

## 'HOOK OR ME THIS TIME'

Odd things happen to all of us on our way through life without our noticing for a time that they have happened. Thus, to take an instance, we suddenly discover that we have been deaf in one ear for we don't know how long, but, say, half an hour. Now such an experience had come that night to Peter. When last we saw him he was stealing across the island with one finger to his lips and his dagger at the ready. He had seen the crocodile pass by without noticing anything peculiar about it, but by and by he remembered that it had not been ticking. At first he thought this eerie, but soon he concluded rightly that the clock had run down.

Without giving a thought to what might be the feelings of a fellow-creature thus abruptly deprived of its closest companion, Peter at once considered how he could turn the catastrophe to his own use; and he decided to tick, so that wild beasts should believe he was the crocodile and let him pass unmolested. He ticked superbly, but with one unforeseen result. The crocodile was among those who heard the sound, and it followed him, though whether with the purpose of regaining what it had lost, or merely as a friend under the belief that it was again ticking itself, will never be certainly known, for, like all slaves to a fixed idea, it was a stupid beast.

Peter reached the shore without mishap, and went straight on; his legs encountering the water as if quite unaware that they had entered a new element. Thus many animals pass from land to water, but no other human of whom I know. As he swam he had but one thought: 'Hook or me this time.' He had ticked so long that he now went on ticking without knowing that he was doing it. Had he known he would have stopped, for to board the brig by the help of the tick, though an ingenious idea, had not occurred to him.

On the contrary, he thought he had scaled her side as noiseless as a mouse; and he was amazed to see the pirates cowering from him, with Hook in their midst as abject as if he had heard the crocodile.

The crocodile! No sooner did Peter remember it than he heard the ticking. At first he thought the sound did come from the crocodile, and he looked behind him swiftly. Then he realised that he was doing it himself, and in a flash he understood the situation. 'How clever of me,' he thought at once, and signed to the boys not to burst into applause.

It was at this moment that Ed Teynte the quartermaster emerged from the forecastle and came along the deck. Now, reader, time what happened by your watch. Peter struck true and deep. John clapped his hands on the ill-fated pirate's mouth to stifle the dying groan. He fell forward. Four boys caught him to prevent the thud. Peter gave the signal, and the carrion was cast overboard. There was a splash, and then silence. How long has it taken?

'One!' (Slightly had begun to count.)

None too soon, Peter, every inch of him on tiptoe, vanished into the cabin; for more than one pirate was screwing up his courage to look round. They could hear each other's distressed breathing now, which showed them that the more terrible sound had passed.

'It's gone, captain,' Smee said, wiping his spectacles. 'All's still again.'

Slowly Hook let his head emerge from his ruff, and listened so intently that he could have caught the echo of the tick. There was not a sound, and he drew himself up firmly to his full height.

'Then here's to Johnny Plank,' he cried brazenly, hating the boys more than ever because they had seen him unbend. He broke into the villainous ditty:

'Yo ho, yo ho, the frisky plank,
You walks along it so,
Till it goes down and you goes down
To Davy Jones below!'

To terrorise the prisoners the more, though with a certain loss of dignity, he danced along an imaginary plank, grimacing at them as he sang; and when he finished he cried, 'Do you want a touch of the cat before you walk the plank?'

At that they fell on their knees. 'No, no,' they cried so piteously that every pirate smiled.

'Fetch the cat, Jukes,' said Hook; 'it's in the cabin.'

The cabin! Peter was in the cabin! The children gazed at each other.

'Ay, ay,' said Jukes blithely, and he strode into the cabin. They followed him with their eyes; they scarce knew that Hook had resumed his song, his dogs joining in with him:

'Yo ho, yo ho, the scratching cat,
Its tails are nine, you know,
And when they're writ upon your back—

What was the last line will never be known, for of a sudden the song was stayed by a dreadful screech from the cabin. It wailed through the ship, and died away. Then was heard a crowing sound which was well understood by the boys, but to the pirates was almost more eerie than the screech.

'What was that?' cried Hook.

'Two,' said Slightly solemnly.

The Italian Cecco hesitated for a moment and then swung into the cabin. He tottered out, haggard.

'What's the matter with Bill Jukes, you dog?' hissed Hook, towering over him.

'The matter wi' him is he's dead, stabbed,' replied Cecco in a hollow Voice.

'Bill Jukes dead!' cried the startled pirates.

'The cabin's as black as a pit,' Cecco said, almost gibbering, 'but there is something terrible in there: the thing you heard crowing.'

The exultation of the boys, the lowering looks of the pirates, both were seen by Hook.

'Cecco,' he said in his most steely voice, 'go back and fetch me out that doodle-doo.'

Cecco, bravest of the brave, cowered before his captain, crying 'No, no'; but Hook was purring to his claw.

'Did you say you would go, Cecco?' he said musingly.

Cecco went, first flinging up his arms despairingly. There was no more singing, all listened now; and again came a death-screech and again a crow.

No one spoke except Slightly. 'Three,' he said.

Hook rallied his dogs with a gesture. ''Sdeath and odds fish,' he thundered, 'who is to bring me that doodle-doo?'

'Wait till Cecco comes out,' growled Starkey, and the others took up the cry.

'I think I heard you volunteer, Starkey,' said Hook, purring again.

'No, by thunder!' Starkey cried.

'My hook thinks you did,' said Hook, crossing to him. 'I wonder if it would not be advisable, Starkey, to humour the hook?'

'I'll swing before I go in there,' replied Starkey doggedly, and again he had the support of the crew.

'Is it mutiny?' asked Hook more pleasantly than ever. 'Starkey's ringleader.'

'Captain, mercy,' Starkey whimpered, all of a tremble now.

'Shake hands, Starkey,' said Hook, proffering his claw.

Starkey looked round for help, but all deserted him. As he backed Hook advanced, and now the red spark was in his eye. With a despairing scream the pirate leapt upon Long Tom and precipitated himself into the sea.

'Four,' said Slightly.

'And now,' Hook asked courteously, 'did any other gentleman say mutiny?' Seizing a lantern and raising his claw with a menacing gesture, 'I'll bring out that doodle-doo myself,' he said, and sped into the cabin.

'Five.' How Slightly longed to say it. He wetted his lips to be ready, but Hook came staggering out, without his lantern.

'Something blew out the light,' he said a little unsteadily.

'Something!' echoed Mullins.

'What of Cecco?' demanded Noodler.

'He's as dead as Jukes,' said Hook shortly.

His reluctance to return to the cabin impressed them all unfavourably, and the mutinous sounds again broke forth. All pirates are superstitious; and Cookson cried, 'They do say the surest sign a ship's accurst is when there's one on board more than can be accounted for.'

'I've heard,' muttered Mullins, 'he always boards the pirate craft at last. Had he a tail, captain?'

'They say,' said another, looking viciously at Hook, 'that when he comes it's in the likeness of the wickedest man aboard.'

'Had he a hook, captain?' asked Cookson insolently; and one after another took up the cry, 'The ship's doomed.' At this the children could not resist raising a cheer. Hook had well-nigh forgotten his prisoners, but as he swung round on them now his face lit up again.

'Lads,' he cried to his crew, 'here's a notion. Open the cabin door and drive them in. Let them fight the doodle-doo for their lives. If they kill him, we're so much the better; if he kills them, we're none the worse.'

For the last time his dogs admired Hook, and devotedly they did his bidding. The boys, pretending to struggle, were pushed into the cabin and the door was closed on them.

'Now, listen,' cried Hook, and all listened. But not one dared to face the door. Yes, one, Wendy, who all this time had been bound to the mast. It was for neither a scream nor a crow that she was watching; it was for the reappearance of Peter.

She had not long to wait. In the cabin he had found the thing for which he had gone in search: the key that would free the children of their manacles; and now they all stole forth, armed with such weapons as they could find. First signing to them to hide, Peter cut Wendy's bonds, and then nothing could have been easier than for them all to fly off together; but one thing barred the way, an oath, 'Hook or me this time.' So when he had freed Wendy, he whispered to her to conceal herself with the others, and himself took her place by the mast, her cloak around him so that he should pass for her. Then he took a great breath and crowed.

To the pirates it was a voice crying that all the boys lay slain in the cabin; and they were panic-stricken. Hook tried to hearten them; but like the dogs he had made them they showed him their fangs, and he knew that if he took his eyes off them now they would leap at him.

'Lads,' he said, ready to cajole or strike as need be, but never quailing for an instant, 'I've thought it out. There's a Jonah abroad.'

'Ay,' they snarled, 'a man wi' a hook.'

'No, lads, no, it's the girl. Never was luck on a pirate ship wi' a woman on board. We'll right the ship when she's gone.'

Some of them remembered that this had been a saying of Flint's. 'It's worth trying,' they said doubtfully.

'Fling the girl overboard,' cried Hook; and they made a rush at the figure in the cloak.

'There's none can save you now, missy,' Mullins hissed jeeringly.

'There's one,' replied the figure.

'Who's that?'

'Peter Pan the avenger!' came the terrible answer; and as he spoke Peter flung off his cloak. Then they all knew who 'twas that had been undoing them in the cabin, and twice Hook essayed to speak and twice he failed. In that frightful moment I think his fierce heart broke.

At last he cried, 'Cleave him to the brisket,' but without conviction.

'Down, boys, and at them,' Peter's voice rang out; and in another moment the clash of arms was resounding through the ship. Had the pirates kept together it is certain that they would have won; but the onset came when they were all unstrung, and they ran hither and thither, striking wildly, each thinking himself the last survivor of the crew. Man to man they were the stronger; but they fought on the defensive only, which enabled the boys to hunt in pairs and choose their quarry. Some of the miscreants leapt into the sea; others hid in dark recesses, where they were found by Slightly, who did not fight, but ran about with a lantern which he flashed in their faces, so that they were half blinded and fell an easy prey to the reeking swords of the other boys. There was little sound to be heard but the clang of weapons, an occasional screech or splash, and Slightly monotonously counting—five—six—seven—eight—nine—ten—eleven.

I think all were gone when a group of savage boys surrounded Hook, who seemed to have a charmed life, as he kept them at bay in that circle of fire. They had done for his dogs, but this man alone seemed to be a match for them all. Again and again they closed upon him, and again and again he hewed a clear space. He had lifted up one boy with his hook, and was using him as a buckler, when another, who had just passed his sword through Mullins, sprang into the fray.

'Put up your swords, boys,' cried the newcomer, 'this man is mine.'

Thus suddenly Hook found himself face to face with Peter. The others drew back and formed a ring round them.

For long the two enemies looked at one another; Hook shuddering slightly, and Peter with the strange smile upon his face.

'So, Pan,' said Hook at last, 'this is all your doing.'

'Ay, James Hook,' came the stern answer, 'it is all my doing.'

'Proud and insolent youth,' said Hook, 'prepare to meet thy doom.'

'Dark and sinister man,' Peter answered, 'have at thee.'

Without more words they fell to, and for a space there was no advantage to either blade. Peter was a superb swordsman, and parried with dazzling rapidity; ever and anon he followed up a feint with a lunge that got past his foe's defence, but his shorter reach stood him in ill stead, and he could not drive the steel home. Hook, scarcely his inferior in brilliancy, but not quite so nimble in wrist play, forced him back by the weight of his onset, hoping suddenly to end all with a favourite thrust, taught him long ago by Barbecue at Rio; but to his astonishment he found this thrust turned aside again and again. Then he sought to close and give the quietus with his iron hook, which all this time had been pawing the air; but Peter doubled under it and, lunging fiercely, pierced him in the ribs. At sight of his own blood, whose peculiar colour, you remember, was offensive to him, the sword fell from Hook's hand, and he was at Peter's mercy.

'Now!' cried all the boys; but with a magnificent gesture Peter invited his opponent to pick up his sword. Hook did so instantly, but with a tragic feeling that Peter was showing good form.

Hitherto he had thought it was some fiend fighting him, but darker suspicions assailed him now.

'Pan, who and what art thou?' he cried huskily.

'I'm youth, I'm joy,' Peter answered at a venture, 'I'm a little bird that has broken out of the egg.'

This, of course, was nonsense; but it was proof to the unhappy Hook that Peter did not know in the least who or what he was, which is the very pinnacle of good form.

'To 't again,' he cried despairingly.

He fought now like a human flail, and every sweep of that terrible sword would have severed in twain any man or boy who obstructed it; but Peter fluttered round him as if the very wind it made blew him out of the danger zone. And again and again he darted in and pricked.

Hook was fighting now without hope. That passionate breast no longer asked for life; but for one boon it craved: to see Peter bad form before it was cold for ever.

Abandoning the fight he rushed into the powder magazine and fired it.

'In two minutes,' he cried, 'the ship will be blown to pieces.'

Now, now, he thought, true form will show.

But Peter issued from the powder magazine with the shell in his hands, and calmly flung it overboard.

What sort of form was Hook himself showing? Misguided man though he was, we may be glad, without sympathising with him, that in the end he was true to the traditions of his race. The other boys were flying around him now, flouting, scornful; and as he staggered about the deck striking up at them impotently, his mind was no longer with them; it was slouching in the playing fields of long ago, or being sent up for good, or watching the wall-game from a famous wall. And his shoes were right, and his waistcoat was right, and his tie was right, and his socks were right.

James Hook, thou not wholly unheroic figure, farewell.

For we have come to his last moment.

Seeing Peter slowly advancing upon him through the air with dagger poised, he sprang upon the bulwarks to cast himself into the sea. He did not know that the crocodile was waiting for him; for we purposely stopped the clock that this knowledge might be spared him: a little mark of respect from us at the end.

He had one last triumph, which I think we need not grudge him. As he stood on the bulwark looking over his shoulder at Peter gliding through the air, he invited him with a gesture to use his foot. It made Peter kick instead of stab.

At last Hook had got the boon for which he craved.

'Bad form,' he cried jeeringly, and went content to the crocodile.

Thus perished James Hook.

'Seventeen,' Slightly sang out; but he was not quite correct in his figures. Fifteen paid the penalty for their crimes that night; but two reached the shore: Starkey to be captured by the redskins, who made him nurse for all their papooses, a melancholy come-down for a pirate; and Smee, who henceforth wandered about the world in his spectacles, making a precarious living by saying he was the only man that Jas. Hook had feared.

Wendy, of course, had stood by taking no part in the fight, though watching Peter with glistening eyes; but now that all was over she became prominent again. She praised them equally, and shuddered delightfully when Michael showed her the place where he had killed one; and then she took them into Hook's cabin and pointed to his watch which was hanging on a nail. It said 'half-past one'!

The lateness of the hour was almost the biggest thing of all. She got them to bed in the pirates' bunks pretty quickly, you may be sure; all but Peter, who strutted up and down on deck, until at last he fell asleep by the side of Long Tom. He had one of his dreams that night, and cried in his sleep for a long time, and Wendy held him tight.

# 16

# THE RETURN HOME

By two bells that morning they were all stirring their stumps; for there was a big sea running; and Tootles, the bo'sun, was among them, with a rope's end in his hand and chewing tobacco. They all donned pirate clothes cut off at the knee, shaved smartly, and tumbled up, with the true nautical roll and hitching their trousers.

It need not be said who was the captain. Nibs and John were first and second mate. There was a woman aboard. The rest were tars before the mast, and lived in the fo'c'sle. Peter had already lashed himself to the wheel; but he piped all hands and delivered a short address to them; said he hoped they would do their duty like gallant hearties, but that he knew they were the scum of Rio and the Gold Coast, and if they snapped at him he would tear them. His bluff strident words struck the note sailors understand, and they cheered him lustily. Then a few sharp orders were given, and they turned the ship round, and nosed her for the mainland.

Captain Pan calculated, after consulting the ship's chart, that if this weather lasted they should strike the Azores about the 21st of June, after which it would save time to fly.

Some of them wanted it to be an honest ship and others were in favour of keeping it a pirate; but the captain treated them as dogs, and they dared not express their wishes to him even in a round robin. Instant obedience was the only safe thing. Slightly got a dozen for looking perplexed when told to take soundings. The general feeling was that Peter was honest just now to lull Wendy's suspicions, but that there might be a change when the new suit was ready, which, against her will, she was making for him out of some of Hook's wickedest garments. It was afterwards whispered among them that on the first night he wore this suit he sat long in the cabin with Hook's cigar-holder in his mouth and one hand clenched, all but the forefinger, which he bent and held threateningly aloft like a hook.

Instead of watching the ship, however, we must now return to that desolate home from which three of our characters had taken heartless flight so long ago. It seems a shame to have neglected No. 14 all this time; and yet we may be sure that Mrs. Darling does not blame us. If we had returned sooner to look with sorrowful sympathy at her, she would probably have cried, 'Don't be silly; what do I matter? Do go back and keep an eye on the children.' So long as mothers are like this their children will take advantage of them; and they may lay to that.

Even now we venture into that familiar nursery only because its lawful occupants are on their way home; we are merely hurrying on in advance of them to see that their beds are properly aired and that Mr. and Mrs. Darling do not go out for the evening. We are no more than servants. Why on earth should their beds be properly aired, seeing that they left them in such a thankless hurry? Would it not serve them jolly well right if they came back and found that their parents were spending the week-end in the country? It would be the moral lesson they have been in need of ever since we met them; but if we contrived things in this way Mrs. Darling would never forgive us.

One thing I should like to do immensely, and that is to tell her, in the way authors have, that the children are coming back, that indeed they will be here on Thursday week. This would spoil so completely the surprise to which Wendy and John and Michael are looking forward. They have been planning it out on the ship: mother's rapture, father's shout of joy, Nana's leap through the air to embrace them first, when what they ought to be preparing for is a good hiding. How delicious to spoil it all by breaking the news in advance; so that when they enter grandly Mrs. Darling may not even offer Wendy her mouth, and Mr. Darling may exclaim pettishly, 'Dash it all, here are those boys again.' However, we should get no thanks even for this. We are beginning to know Mrs. Darling by this time, and may be sure that she would upbraid us for depriving the children of their little pleasure.

'But, my dear madam, it is ten days till Thursday week; so that by telling you what's what, we can save you ten days of unhappiness.'

'Yes, but at what a cost! By depriving the children of ten minutes of delight.'

'Oh, if you look at it in that way.'

'What other way is there in which to look at it?'

You see, the woman had no proper spirit. I had meant to say extraordinarily nice things about her; but I despise her, and not one of them will I say now. She does not really need to be told to have things ready, for they are ready. All the beds are aired, and she never leaves the house, and observe, the window is open. For all the use we are to her, we might go back to the ship. However, as we are here we may as well stay and look on. That is all we are, lookers-on. Nobody really wants us. So let us watch and say jaggy things, in the hope that some of them will hurt.

The only change to be seen in the night-nursery is that between nine and six the kennel is no longer there. When the children flew away, Mr. Darling felt in his bones that all the blame was his for having chained Nana up, and that from first to last she had been wiser than he. Of course, as we have seen, he was quite a simple man; indeed he might have passed for a boy again if he had been able to take his baldness off; but he had also a noble sense of justice and a lion courage to do what seemed right to him; and having thought the matter out with anxious care after the flight of the children, he went down on all fours and crawled into the kennel. To all Mrs. Darling's dear invitations to him to come out he replied sadly but firmly:

'No, my own one, this is the place for me.'

In the bitterness of his remorse he swore that he would never leave the kennel until his children came back. Of course this was a pity; but whatever Mr. Darling did he had to do in excess; otherwise he soon gave up doing it. And there never was a more humble man than the once proud George Darling, as he sat in the kennel of an evening talking with his wife of their children and all their pretty ways.

Very touching was his deference to Nana. He would not let her come into the kennel, but on all other matters he followed her wishes implicitly.

Every morning the kennel was carried with Mr. Darling in it to a cab, which conveyed him to his office, and he returned home in the same way at six. Something of the strength of character of the man will be seen if we remember how sensitive he was to the opinion of neighbours: this man whose every movement now attracted surprised attention. Inwardly he must have suffered torture; but he preserved a calm exterior even when the young criticised his little home, and he always lifted his hat courteously to any lady who looked inside.

It may have been quixotic, but it was magnificent. Soon the inward meaning of it leaked out, and the great heart of the public was touched. Crowds followed the cab, cheering it lustily; charming girls scaled it to get his autograph; interviews appeared in the better class of papers, and society invited him to dinner and added, 'Do come in the kennel.'

On that eventful Thursday week Mrs. Darling was in the night-nursery awaiting George's return home: a very sad-eyed woman. Now that we look at her closely and remember the gaiety of her in the old days, all gone now just because she has lost her babes, I find I won't be able to say nasty things about her after all. If she was too fond of her rubbishy children she couldn't help it. Look at her in her chair, where she has fallen asleep. The corner of her mouth, where one looks first, is almost withered up. Her hand moves restlessly on her breast as if she had a pain there. Some like Peter best and some like Wendy best, but I like her best. Suppose, to make her happy, we whisper to her in her sleep that the brats are coming back. They are really within two miles of the window now, and flying strong, but all we need whisper is that they are on the way. Let's.

It is a pity we did it, for she has started up, calling their names; and there is no one in the room but Nana.

'O Nana, I dreamt my dear ones had come back.'

Nana had filmy eyes, but all she could do was to put her paw gently on her mistress's lap; and they were sitting together thus when the kennel was brought back. As Mr. Darling puts his head out at it to kiss his wife, we see that his face is more worn than of yore, but has a softer expression.

He gave his hat to Liza, who took it scornfully; for she had no imagination, and was quite incapable of understanding the motives of such a man. Outside, the crowd who had accompanied the cab home were still cheering, and he was naturally not unmoved.

'Listen to them,' he said; 'it is very gratifying.'

'Lot of little boys,' sneered Liza.

'There were several adults to-day,' he assured her with a faint flush; but when she tossed her head he had not a word of reproof for her. Social success had not spoilt him; it had made him sweeter. For some time he sat half out of the kennel, talking with Mrs. Darling of this success, and pressing her hand reassuringly when she said she hoped his head would not be turned by it.

'But if I had been a weak man,' he said. 'Good heavens, if I had been a weak man!'

'And, George,' she said timidly, 'you are as full of remorse as ever, aren't you?'

'Full of remorse as ever, dearest! See my punishment: living in a kennel.'

'But it is punishment, isn't it, George? You are sure you are not enjoying it?'

'My love!'

You may be sure she begged his pardon; and then, feeling drowsy, he curled round in the kennel.

'Won't you play me to sleep,' he asked, 'on the nursery piano?' and as she was crossing to the day nursery he added thoughtlessly, 'And shut that window. I feel a draught.'

'O George, never ask me to do that. The window must always be left open for them, always, always.'

Now it was his turn to beg her pardon; and she went into the day nursery and played, and soon he was asleep; and while he slept, Wendy and John and Michael flew into the room.

Oh no. We have written it so, because that was the charming arrangement planned by them before we left the ship; but something must have happened since then, for it is not they who have flown in, it is Peter and Tinker Bell.

Peter's first words tell all.

'Quick, Tink,' he whispered, 'close the window; bar it. That's right. Now you and I must get away by the door; and when Wendy comes she will think her mother has barred her out; and she will have to go back with me.'

Now I understand what had hitherto puzzled me, why when Peter had exterminated the pirates he did not return to the island and leave Tink to escort the children to the mainland. This trick had been in his head all the time.

Instead of feeling that he was behaving badly he danced with glee; then he peeped into the day-nursery to see who was playing. He whispered to Tink, 'It's Wendy's mother. She is a pretty lady, but not so pretty as my mother. Her mouth is full of thimbles, but not so full as my mother's was.'

Of course he knew nothing whatever about his mother; but he sometimes bragged about her.

He did not know the tune, which was 'Home, Sweet Home,' but he knew it was saying, 'Come back, Wendy, Wendy, Wendy'; and he cried exultantly, 'You will never see Wendy again, lady, for the window is barred.'

He peeped in again to see why the music had stopped; and now he saw that Mrs. Darling had laid her head on the box, and that two tears were sitting on her eyes.

'She wants me to unbar the window,' thought Peter, 'but I won't, not I.'

He peeped again, and the tears were still there, or another two had taken their place.

'She's awfully fond of Wendy,' he said to himself. He was angry with her now for not seeing why she could not have Wendy.

The reason was so simple: 'I'm fond of her too. We can't both have her, lady.'

But the lady would not make the best of it, and he was unhappy. He ceased to look at her, but even then she would not let go of him. He skipped about and made funny faces, but when he stopped it was just as if she were inside him, knocking.

'Oh, all right,' he said at last, and gulped. Then he unbarred the window. 'Come on, Tink,' he cried, with a frightful sneer at the laws of nature; 'we don't want any silly mothers'; and he flew away.

Thus Wendy and John and Michael found the window open for them after all, which of course was more than they deserved. They alighted on the floor, quite unashamed of themselves; and the youngest one had already forgotten his home.

'John,' he said, looking around him doubtfully, 'I think I have been here before.'

'Of course you have, you silly. There is your old bed.'

'So it is,' Michael said, but not with much conviction.

'I say,' cried John, 'the kennel!' and he dashed across to look into it.

'Perhaps Nana is inside it,' Wendy said.

But John whistled. 'Hullo,' he said, 'there's a man inside it.'

'It's father!' exclaimed Wendy.

'Let me see father,' Michael begged eagerly, and he took a good look. 'He is not so big as the pirate I killed,' he said with such frank disappointment that I am glad Mr. Darling was asleep; it would have been sad if those had been the first words he heard his little Michael say.

Wendy and John had been taken aback somewhat at finding their father in the kennel.

'Surely,' said John, like one who had lost faith in his memory, 'he used not to sleep in the kennel?'

'John,' Wendy said falteringly, 'perhaps we don't remember the old life as well as we thought we did.'

A chill fell upon them; and serve them right.

'It is very careless of mother,' said that young scoundrel John, 'not to be here when we come back.'

It was then that Mrs. Darling began playing again.

'It's mother!' cried Wendy, peeping.

'So it is!' said John.

'Then are you not really our mother, Wendy?' asked Michael, who was surely sleepy.

'Oh dear!' exclaimed Wendy, with her first real twinge of remorse, 'it was quite time we came back.'

'Let us creep in,' John suggested, 'and put our hands over her eyes.'

But Wendy, who saw that they must break the joyous news more gently, had a better plan.

'Let us all slip into our beds, and be there when she comes in, just as if we had never been away.'

And so when Mrs. Darling went back to the night-nursery to see if her husband was asleep, all the beds were occupied. The children waited for her cry of joy, but it did not come. She saw them, but she did not believe they were there. You see, she saw them in their beds so often in her dreams that she thought this was just the dream hanging around her still.

She sat down in the chair by the fire, where in the old days she had nursed them.

They could not understand this, and a cold fear fell upon all the three of them.

'Mother!' Wendy cried.

'That's Wendy,' she said, but still she was sure it was the dream.

'Mother!'

'That's John,' she said.

'Mother!' cried Michael. He knew her now.

'That's Michael,' she said, and she stretched out her arms for the three little selfish children they would never envelop again. Yes, they did, they went round Wendy and John and Michael, who had slipped out of bed and run to her.

'George, George,' she cried when she could speak; and Mr. Darling woke to share her bliss, and Nana came rushing in. There could not have been a lovelier sight; but there was none to see it except a strange boy who was staring in at the window. He had ecstasies innumerable that other children can never know; but he was looking through the window at the one joy from which he must be for ever barred.

## 17

# WHEN WENDY GREW UP

I hope you want to know what became of the other boys. They were waiting below to give Wendy time to explain about them; and when they had counted five hundred they went up. They went up by the stair, because they thought this would make a better impression. They stood in a row in front of Mrs. Darling, with their hats off, and wishing they were not wearing their pirate clothes. They said nothing, but their eyes asked her to have them. They ought to have looked at Mr. Darling also, but they forgot about him.

Of course Mrs. Darling said at once that she would have them; but Mr. Darling was curiously depressed, and they saw that he considered six a rather large number.

'I must say,' he said to Wendy, 'that you don't do things by halves,' a grudging remark which the twins thought was pointed at them.

The first twin was the proud one, and he asked, flushing, 'Do you think we should be too much of a handful, sir? Because if so we can go away.'

'Father!' Wendy cried, shocked; but still the cloud was on him. He knew he was behaving unworthily, but he could not help it.

'We could lie doubled up,' said Nibs.

'I always cut their hair myself,' said Wendy.

'George!' Mrs. Darling exclaimed, pained to see her dear one showing himself in such an unfavourable light.

Then he burst into tears, and the truth came out. He was as glad to have them as she was, he said, but he thought they should have asked his consent as well as hers, instead of treating him as a cypher in his own house.

'I don't think he is a cypher,' Tootles cried instantly. 'Do you think he is a cypher, Curly?'

'No, I don't. Do you think he is a cypher, Slightly?'

'Rather not. Twin, what do you think?'

It turned out that not one of them thought him a cypher; and he was absurdly gratified, and said he would find space for them all in the drawing-room if they fitted in.

'We'll fit in, sir,' they assured him.

'Then follow the leader,' he cried gaily. 'Mind you, I am not sure that we have a drawing-room, but we pretend we have, and it's all the same. Hoop la!'

He went off dancing through the house, and they all cried 'Hoop la!' and danced after him, searching for the drawing-room; and I forget whether they found it, but at any rate they found corners, and they all fitted in.

As for Peter, he saw Wendy once again before he flew away. He did not exactly come to the window, but he brushed against it in passing, so that she could open it if she liked and call to him. That was what she did.

'Hullo, Wendy, good-bye,' he said.

'Oh dear, are you going away?'

'Yes.'

'You don't feel, Peter,' she said falteringly, 'that you would like to say anything to my parents about a very sweet subject?'

'No.'

'About me, Peter?'

'No.'

Mrs. Darling came to the window, for at present she was keeping a sharp eye on Wendy. She told Peter that she had adopted all the other boys, and would like to adopt him also.

'Would you send me to school?' he inquired craftily.

'Yes.'

'And then to an office?'

'I suppose so.'

'Soon I should be a man?'

'Very soon.'

'I don't want to go to school and learn solemn things,' he told her passionately. 'I don't want to be a man. O Wendy's mother, if I was to wake up and feel there was a beard!'

'Peter,' said Wendy the comforter, 'I should love you in a beard'; and Mrs. Darling stretched out her arms to him, but he repulsed her.

'Keep back, lady, no one is going to catch me and make me a man.'

'But where are you going to live?'

'With Tink in the house we built for Wendy. The fairies are to put it high up among the tree tops where they sleep at nights.'

'How lovely,' cried Wendy so longingly that Mrs. Darling tightened her grip.

'I thought all the fairies were dead,' Mrs. Darling said.

'There are always a lot of young ones,' explained Wendy, who was now quite an authority, 'because you see when a new baby laughs for the first time a new fairy is born, and as there are always new babies there are always new fairies. They live in nests on the tops of trees; and the mauve ones are boys and the white ones are girls, and the blue ones are just little sillies who are not sure what they are.'

'I shall have such fun,' said Peter, with one eye on Wendy.

'It will be rather lonely in the evening,' she said, 'sitting by the fire.'

'I shall have Tink.'

'Tink can't go a twentieth part of the way round,' she reminded him a little tartly.

'Sneaky tell-tale!' Tink called out from somewhere round the corner.

'It doesn't matter,' Peter said.

'O Peter, you know it matters.'

'Well, then, come with me to the little house.'

'May I, mummy?'

'Certainly not. I have got you home again, and I mean to keep you.'

'But he does so need a mother.'

'So do you, my love.'

'Oh, all right,' Peter said, as if he had asked her from politeness merely; but Mrs. Darling saw his mouth twitch, and she made this handsome offer: to let Wendy go to him for a week every year to do his spring cleaning. Wendy would have preferred a more permanent arrangement; and it seemed to her that spring would be long in coming; but this promise sent Peter away quite gay again. He had no sense of time, and was so full of adventures that all I have told you about him is only a halfpenny-worth of them. I suppose it was because Wendy knew this that her last words to him were these rather plaintive ones:

'You won't forget me, Peter, will you, before spring-cleaning time comes?'

Of course Peter promised; and then he flew away. He took Mrs. Darling's kiss with him. The kiss that had been for no one else Peter took quite easily. Funny. But she seemed satisfied.

Of course all the boys went to school; and most of them got into Class III., but Slightly was put first into Class IV. and then into Class V. Class I. is the top class. Before they had attended school a week they saw what goats they had been not to remain on the island; but it was too late now, and soon they settled down to being as ordinary as you or me or Jenkins minor. It is sad to have to say that the power to fly gradually left them. At first Nana tied their feet to the bed-posts so that they should not fly away in the night; and one of their diversions by day was to pretend to fall off 'buses; but by and by they ceased to tug at their bonds in bed, and found that they hurt themselves when they let go of the 'bus. In time they could not even fly after their hats. Want of practice, they called it; but what it really meant was that they no longer believed.

Michael believed longer than the other boys, though they jeered at him; so he was with Wendy when Peter came for her at the end of the first year. She flew away with Peter in the frock she had woven from leaves and berries in the Neverland, and her one fear was that he might notice how short it had become; but he never noticed, he had so much to say about himself.

She had looked forward to thrilling talks with him about old times, but new adventures had crowded the old ones from his mind.

'Who is Captain Hook?' he asked with interest when she spoke of the arch enemy.

'Don't you remember,' she asked, amazed, 'how you killed him and saved all our lives?'

'I forget them after I kill them,' he replied carelessly.

When she expressed a doubtful hope that Tinker Bell would be glad to see her he said, 'Who is Tinker Bell?'

'O Peter,' she said, shocked; but even when she explained he could not remember.

'There are such a lot of them,' he said. 'I expect she is no more.'

I expect he was right, for fairies don't live long, but they are so little that a short time seems a good while to them.

Wendy was pained too to find that the past year was but as yesterday to Peter; it had seemed such a long year of waiting to her. But he was exactly as fascinating as ever, and they had a lovely spring cleaning in the little house on the tree tops.

Next year he did not come for her. She waited in a new frock because the old one simply would not meet; but he never came.

'Perhaps he is ill,' Michael said.

'You know he is never ill.'

Michael came close to her and whispered, with a shiver, 'Perhaps there is no such person, Wendy!' and then Wendy would have cried if Michael had not been crying.

Peter came next spring cleaning; and the strange thing was that he never knew he had missed a year.

That was the last time the girl Wendy ever saw him. For a little longer she tried for his sake not to have growing pains; and she felt she was untrue to him when she got a prize for general knowledge. But the years came and went without bringing the careless boy; and when they met again Wendy was a married woman, and Peter was no more to her than a little dust in the box in which she had kept her toys. Wendy was grown up. You need not be sorry for her. She was one of the kind that likes to grow up. In the end she grew up of her own free will a day quicker than other girls.

All the boys were grown up and done for by this time; so it is scarcely worth while saying anything more about them. You may see the twins and Nibs and Curly any day going to an office, each carrying a little bag and an umbrella. Michael is an engine-driver. Slightly married a lady of title, and so he became a lord. You see that judge in a wig coming out at the iron door? That used to be Tootles. The bearded man who doesn't know any story to tell his children was once John.

Wendy was married in white with a pink sash. It is strange to think that Peter did not alight in the church and forbid the banns.

Years rolled on again, and Wendy had a daughter. This ought not to be written in ink but in a golden splash.

She was called Jane, and always had an odd inquiring look, as if from the moment she arrived on the mainland she wanted to ask questions. When she was old enough to ask them they were mostly about Peter Pan. She loved to hear of Peter, and Wendy told her all she could remember in the very nursery from which the famous flight had taken place. It was Jane's nursery now, for her father had bought it at the three per cents. from Wendy's father, who was no longer fond of stairs. Mrs. Darling was now dead and forgotten.

There were only two beds in the nursery now, Jane's and her nurse's; and there was no kennel, for Nana also had passed away. She died of old age, and at the end she had been rather difficult to get on with; being very firmly convinced that no one knew how to look after children except herself.

Once a week Jane's nurse had her evening off; and then it was Wendy's part to put Jane to bed. That was the time for stories. It was Jane's invention to raise the sheet over her mother's head and her own, thus making a tent, and in the awful darkness to whisper:

'What do we see now?'

'I don't think I see anything to-night,' says Wendy, with a feeling that if Nana were here she would object to further conversation.

'Yes, you do,' says Jane, 'you see when you were a little girl.'

'That is a long time ago, sweetheart,' says Wendy. 'Ah me, how time flies!'

'Does it fly,' asks the artful child, 'the way you flew when you were a little girl?'

'The way I flew! Do you know, Jane, I sometimes wonder whether I ever did really fly.'

'Yes, you did.'

'The dear old days when I could fly!'

'Why can't you fly now, mother?'

'Because I am grown up, dearest. When people grow up they forget the way.'

'Why do they forget the way?'

'Because they are no longer gay and innocent and heartless. It is only the gay and innocent and heartless who can fly.'

'What is gay and innocent and heartless? I do wish I was gay and innocent and heartless.'

Or perhaps Wendy admits that she does see something. 'I do believe,' she says, 'that it is this nursery.'

'I do believe it is,' says Jane. 'Go on.'

They are now embarked on the great adventure of the night when Peter flew in looking for his shadow.

'The foolish fellow,' says Wendy, 'tried to stick it on with soap, and when he could not he cried, and that woke me, and I sewed it on for him.'

'You have missed a bit,' interrupts Jane, who now knows the story better than her mother. 'When you saw him sitting on the floor crying what did you say?'

'I sat up in bed and I said, "Boy, why are you crying?"'

'Yes, that was it,' says Jane, with a big breath.

'And then he flew us all away to the Neverland and the fairies and the pirates and the redskins and the mermaids' lagoon, and the home under the ground, and the little house.'

'Yes! which did you like best of all?'

'I think I liked the home under the ground best of all.'

'Yes, so do I. What was the last thing Peter ever said to you?'

'The last thing he ever said to me was, "Just always be waiting for me, and then some night you will hear me crowing."'

'Yes.'

'But, alas, he forgot all about me.' Wendy said it with a smile. She was as grown up as that.

'What did his crow sound like?' Jane asked one evening.

'It was like this,' Wendy said, trying to imitate Peter's crow.

'No, it wasn't,' Jane said gravely, 'it was like this'; and she did it ever so much better than her mother.

Wendy was a little startled. 'My darling, how can you know?'

'I often hear it when I am sleeping,' Jane said.

'Ah yes, many girls hear it when they are sleeping, but I was the only one who heard it awake.'

'Lucky you,' said Jane.

And then one night came the tragedy. It was the spring of the year, and the story had been told for the night, and Jane was now asleep in her bed. Wendy was sitting on the floor, very close to the fire, so as to see to darn, for there was no other light in the nursery; and while she sat darning she heard a crow. Then the window blew open as of old, and Peter dropped on the floor.

He was exactly the same as ever, and Wendy saw at once that he still had all his first teeth.

He was a little boy, and she was grown up. She huddled by the fire not daring to move, helpless and guilty, a big woman.

'Hullo, Wendy,' he said, not noticing any difference, for he was thinking chiefly of himself; and in the dim light her white dress might have been the night-gown in which he had seen her first.

'Hullo, Peter,' she replied faintly, squeezing herself as small as possible. Something inside her was crying 'Woman, woman, let go of me.'

'Hullo, where is John?' he asked, suddenly missing the third bed.

'John is not here now,' she gasped.

'Is Michael asleep?' he asked, with a careless glance at Jane.

'Yes,' she answered; and now she felt that she was untrue to Jane as well as to Peter.

'That is not Michael,' she said quickly, lest a judgment should fall on her.

Peter looked. 'Hullo, is it a new one?'

'Yes.'

'Boy or girl?'

'Girl.'

Now surely he would understand; but not a bit of it.

'Peter,' she said, faltering, 'are you expecting me to fly away with you?'

'Of course that is why I have come.' He added a little sternly, 'Have you forgotten that this is spring-cleaning time?'

She knew it was useless to say that he had let many spring-cleaning times pass.

'I can't come,' she said apologetically, 'I have forgotten how to fly.'

'I'll soon teach you again.'

'O Peter, don't waste the fairy dust on me.'

She had risen; and now at last a fear assailed him. 'What is it?' he cried, shrinking.

'I will turn up the light,' she said, 'and then you can see for yourself.'

For almost the only time in his life that I know of, Peter was afraid. 'Don't turn up the light,' he cried.

She let her hands play in the hair of the tragic boy. She was not a little girl heart-broken about him; she was a grown woman smiling at it all, but they were wet smiles.

Then she turned up the light, and Peter saw. He gave a cry of pain; and when the tall beautiful creature stooped to lift him in her arms he drew back sharply.

'What is it?' he cried again.

She had to tell him.

'I am old, Peter. I am ever so much more than twenty. I grew up long ago.'

'You promised not to!'

'I couldn't help it. I am a married woman, Peter.'

'No, you're not.'

'Yes, and the little girl in the bed is my baby.'

'No, she's not.'

But he supposed she was; and he took a step towards the sleeping child with his dagger upraised. Of course he did not strike. He sat down on the floor instead and sobbed; and Wendy did not know how to comfort him, though she could have done it so easily once. She was only a woman now, and she ran out of the room to try to think.

Peter continued to cry, and soon his sobs woke Jane. She sat up in bed, and was interested at once.

'Boy,' she said, 'why are you crying?'

Peter rose and bowed to her, and she bowed to him from the bed.

'Hullo,' he said.

'Hullo,' said Jane.

'My name is Peter Pan,' he told her.

'Yes, I know.'

'I came back for my mother,' he explained; 'to take her to the Neverland.'

'Yes, I know,' Jane said, 'I been waiting for you.'

When Wendy returned diffidently she found Peter sitting on the bed-post crowing gloriously, while Jane in her nighty was flying round the room in solemn ecstasy.

'She is my mother,' Peter explained; and Jane descended and stood by his side, with the look on her face that he liked to see on ladies when they gazed at him.

'He does so need a mother,' Jane said.

'Yes, I know,' Wendy admitted rather forlornly; 'no one knows it so well as I.'

'Good-bye,' said Peter to Wendy; and he rose in the air, and the shameless Jane rose with him; it was already her easiest way of moving about.

Wendy rushed to the window.

'No, no,' she cried.

'It is just for spring-cleaning time,' Jane said; 'he wants me always to do his spring cleaning.'

'If only I could go with you,' Wendy sighed.

'You see you can't fly,' said Jane.

Of course in the end Wendy let them fly away together. Our last glimpse of her shows her at the window, watching them receding into the sky until they were as small as stars.

As you look at Wendy you may see her hair becoming white, and her figure little again, for all this happened long ago. Jane is now a common grown-up, with a daughter called Margaret; and every spring-cleaning time, except when he forgets, Peter comes for Margaret and takes her to the Neverland, where she tells him stories about himself, to which he listens eagerly. When Margaret grows up she will have a daughter, who is to be Peter's mother in turn; and thus it will go on, so long as children are gay and innocent and heartless.

# CAPTAIN BOLDHEART AND THE LATIN-GRAMMAR MASTER

A Holiday Romance from the Pen of Lieut-Col. Robin Redforth, Aged. 9

CHARLES DICKENS

# CAPTAIN BOLDHEART AND THE LATIN-GRAMMAR MASTER

The subject of our present narrative would appear to have devoted himself to the Pirate profession at a comparatively early age. We find him in command of a splendid schooner of one hundred guns, loaded to the muzzle, 'ere yet he had had a party in honour of his tenth birthday.

It seems that our hero, considering himself spited by a Latin-Grammar-Master, demanded the satisfaction due from one man of honour to another. Not getting it, he privately withdrew his haughty spirit from such low company, bought a second-hand pocket-pistol, folded up some sandwiches in a paper bag, made a bottle of Spanish liquorice-water, and entered on a career of valour.

It were tedious to follow Boldheart (for such was his name) through the commencing stages of his history. Suffice it that we find him bearing the rank of Captain Boldheart, reclining in full uniform on a crimson hearth-rug spread out upon the quarter-deck of his schooner the Beauty, in the China Seas. It was a lovely evening, and as his crew lay grouped about him, he favoured them with the following melody:

O landsmen are folly!
O Pirates are jolly!
O Diddleum Dolly,
Di!
(*Chorus*) Heave yo.

The soothing effect of these animated sounds floating over the waters, as the common sailors united their rough voices to take up the rich tones of Boldheart, may be more easily conceived than described.

It was under these circumstances that the lookout at the masthead gave the word, "Whales!"

All was now activity.

"Where away?" cried Captain Boldheart, starting up.

"On the larboard bow, sir," replied the fellow at the masthead, touching his hat. For such was the height of discipline on board of the Beauty, that even at that height he was obliged to mind it or be shot through the head.

"This adventure belongs to me," said Boldheart. "Boy, my harpoon. Let no man follow;" and leaping alone into his boat, the captain rowed with admirable dexterity in the direction of the monster.

All was now excitement.

"He nears him!" said an elderly seaman, following the captain through his spy-glass.

"He strikes him!" said another seaman, a mere stripling, but also with a spy-glass.

"He tows him towards us!" said another seaman, a man in the full vigour of life, but also with a spy-glass.

In fact the captain was seen approaching, with the huge bulk following. We will not dwell on the deafening cries of "Boldheart! Boldheart!" with which he was received, when, carelessly leaping on the quarter-deck, he presented his prize to his men. They afterwards made two thousand four hundred and seventeen pound ten and sixpence by it.

Ordering the sails to be braced up, the captain now stood W.N.W. The Beauty flew rather than floated over the dark blue waters. Nothing particular occurred for a fortnight, except taking, with considerable slaughter, four Spanish galleons, and a Snow from South America, all richly laden. Inaction began to tell upon the spirits of the men. Captain Boldheart called all hands aft, and said:

"My lads, I hear there are discontented ones among ye. Let any such stand forth."

After some murmuring, in which the expressions, "Aye, aye, sir!" "Union Jack!" "Avast," "Starboard," "Port," "Bowsprit," and similar indications of a mutinous undercurrent, though subdued, were audible, Bill Boozey, captain of the foretop, came out from the rest. His form was that of a giant, but he quailed under the captain's eye.

"What are your wrongs?" said the captain.

"Why, d'ye see, Captain Boldheart," replied the towering mariner, "I've sailed man and boy for many a year, but I never yet know'd the milk served out for the ship's company's teas to be so sour as 'tis aboard this craft."

At this moment the thrilling cry, "Man overboard!" announced to the astonished crew that Boozey, in stepping back, as the captain (in mere thoughtfulness) laid his hand upon the faithful pocket-pistol which he wore in his belt, had lost his balance, and was struggling with the foaming tide.

All was now stupefaction.

But, with Captain Boldheart, to throw off his uniform coat regardless of the various rich orders with which it was decorated, and to plunge into the sea after the drowning giant, was the work of a moment. Maddening was the excitement when boats were lowered; intense the joy when the captain was seen holding up the drowning man with his teeth; deafening the cheering when both were restored to the main deck of the Beauty. And from the instant of his changing his wet clothes for dry ones, Captain Boldheart had no such devoted though humble friend as William Boozey.

Boldheart now pointed to the horizon, and called the attention of his crew to the taper spars of a ship lying snug in harbour under the guns of a fort.

"She shall be ours at sunrise," said he. "Serve out a double allowance of grog, and prepare for action."

All was now preparation.

When morning dawned after a sleepless night, it was seen that the stranger was crowding on all sail to come out of the harbour and offer battle. As the two ships came nearer to each other, the stranger fired a gun and hoisted Roman colours. Boldheart then perceived her to be the Latin-Grammar-Master's bark. Such indeed she was, and had been tacking about the world in unavailing pursuit, from the time of his first taking to a roving life.

Boldheart now addressed his men, promising to blow them up if he should feel convinced that their reputation required it, and giving orders that the Latin-Grammar-Master should be taken alive. He then dismissed them to their quarters, and the fight began with a broadside from The Beauty. She then veered round, and poured in another. The Scorpion (so was the bark of the Latin-Grammar-Master appropriately called) was not slow to return her fire, and a terrific cannonading ensued, in which the guns of The Beauty did tremendous execution.

The Latin-Grammar-Master was seen upon the poop, in the midst of the smoke and fire, encouraging his men. To do him justice, he was no Craven, though his white hat, his short grey trousers, and his long snuff-coloured surtout reaching to his heels—the self-same coat in which he had spited Boldheart—contrasted most unfavourably with the brilliant uniform of the latter. At this moment Boldheart, seizing a pike and putting himself at the head of his men, gave the word to board.

A desperate conflict ensued in the hammock nettings—or somewhere in about that direction—until the Latin-Grammar-Master, having all his masts gone, his hull and rigging shot through and through, and seeing Boldheart slashing a path towards him, hauled down his flag himself, gave up his sword to Boldheart, and asked for quarter. Scarce had he been put into the captain's boat, 'ere The Scorpion went down with all on board.

On Captain Boldheart's now assembling his men, a circumstance occurred. He found it necessary with one blow of his cutlass to kill the Cook, who, having lost his brother in the late action, was making at the Latin-Grammar-Master in an infuriated state, intent on his destruction with a carving-knife.

Captain Boldheart then turned to the Latin-Grammar-Master, severely reproaching him with his perfidy, and put it to his crew what they considered that a master who spited a boy deserved?

They answered with one voice, "Death."

"It may be so," said the Captain; "but it shall never be said that Boldheart stained his hour of triumph with the blood of his enemy. Prepare the cutter."

The cutter was immediately prepared.

"Without taking your life," said the Captain, "I must yet for ever deprive you of the power of spiting other boys. I shall turn you adrift in this boat. You will find in her two oars, a compass, a bottle of rum, a small cask of water, a piece of pork, a bag of biscuit, and my Latin grammar. Go! and spite the natives, if you can find any."

Deeply conscious of this bitter sarcasm, the unhappy wretch was put into the cutter, and was soon left far behind. He made no effort to row, but was seen lying on his back with his legs up, when last made out by the ship's telescopes.

A stiff breeze now beginning to blow, Captain Boldheart gave orders to keep her S.S.W., easing her a little during the night by falling off a point or two W. by W., or even by W.S., if she complained much. He then retired for the night, having in truth much need of repose. In addition to the fatigues he had undergone, this brave officer had received sixteen wounds in the engagement, but had not mentioned it.

In the morning a white squall came on, and was succeeded by other squalls of various colours. It thundered and lightened heavily for six weeks. Hurricanes then set in for two months. Waterspouts and tornadoes followed. The oldest sailor on board—and he was a very old one—had never seen such weather. The Beauty lost all idea where she was, and the carpenter reported six feet two of water in the hold. Everybody fell senseless at the pumps every day.

Provisions now ran very low. Our hero put the crew on short allowance, and put himself on shorter allowance than any man in the ship. But his spirit kept him fat. In this extremity, the gratitude of Boozey, the captain of the foretop whom our readers may remember, was truly affecting. The loving though lowly William repeatedly requested to be killed, and preserved for the captain's table.

We now approach a change in affairs.

One day during a gleam of sunshine and when the weather had moderated, the man at the masthead—too weak now to touch his hat, besides its having been blown away—called out,

"Savages!"

All was now expectation.

Presently fifteen hundred canoes, each paddled by twenty savages, were seen advancing in excellent order. They were a light green colour (the Savages were), and sang, with great energy, the following strain:

Choo a choo a choo tooth.
Muntch, muntch. Nycey!
Choo a choo a choo tooth.
Muntch, muntch. Nyce!

As the shades of night were by this time closing in, these expressions were supposed to embody this simple people's views of the Evening Hymn. But it too soon appeared that the song was a translation of "For what we are going to receive," &c.

The chief, imposingly decorated with feathers of lively colours, and having the majestic appearance of a fighting Parrot, no sooner understood (he understood English perfectly) that the ship was The Beauty, Captain Boldheart, than he fell upon his face on the deck, and could not be persuaded to rise until the captain had lifted him up, & told him he wouldn't hurt him. All the rest of the savages also fell on their faces with marks of terror, and had also to be lifted up one by one. Thus the fame of the great Boldheart had gone before him, even among these children of Nature.

Turtles and oysters were now produced in astonishing numbers, and on these and yams the people made a hearty meal. After dinner the Chief told Captain Boldheart that there was better feeding up at the village, and that he would be glad to take him and his officers there. Apprehensive of treachery, Boldheart ordered his boat's crew to attend him completely armed. And well were it for other commanders if their precautions—but let us not anticipate.

When the canoes arrived at the beach, the darkness of the night was illumined by the light of an immense fire. Ordering his boat's crew (with the intrepid though illiterate William at their head) to keep close and be upon their guard, Boldheart bravely went on, arm-in-arm with the Chief.

But how to depict the captain's surprise when he found a ring of Savages singing in chorus that barbarous translation of "For what we are going to receive, &c.," which has been given above, and dancing hand-in-hand round the Latin-Grammar-Master, in a hamper with his head shaved, while two savages floured him, before putting him to the fire to be cooked!

Boldheart now took counsel with his officers on the course to be adopted. In the mean time, the miserable captive never ceased begging pardon and imploring to be delivered. On the generous Boldheart's proposal, it was at length resolved that he should not be cooked, but should be allowed to remain raw, on two conditions. Namely,

1. That he should never under any circumstances presume to teach any boy any thing any more.
2. That, if taken back to England, he should pass his life in travelling to find out boys who wanted their exercises done, and should do their exercises for those boys for nothing, and never say a word about it.

Drawing his sword from its sheath, Boldheart swore him to these conditions on its shining blade. The prisoner wept bitterly, and appeared acutely to feel the errors of his past career.

The captain then ordered his boat's crew to make ready for a volley, and after firing to re-load quickly. "And expect a score or two on ye to go head over heels," murmured William Boozey; "for I'm a looking at ye." With those words the derisive though deadly William took a good aim.

"Fire!"

The ringing voice of Boldheart was lost in the report of the guns and the screeching of the savages. Volley after volley awakened the numerous echoes. Hundreds of savages were killed, hundreds wounded, and thousands ran howling into the woods. The Latin-Grammar-Master had a spare night-cap lent him, and a longtail coat which he wore hind side before. He presented a ludicrous though pitiable appearance, and serve him right.

We now find Captain Boldheart, with this rescued wretch on board, standing off for other islands. At one of these, not a cannibal island, but a pork and vegetable one, he married (only in fun on his part) the King's daughter. Here he rested some time, receiving from the natives great quantities of precious stones, gold dust, elephants' teeth, and sandal wood, and getting very rich. This, too, though he almost every day made presents of enormous value to his men.

The ship being at length as full as she could hold of all sorts of valuable things, Boldheart gave orders to weigh the anchor, and turn the Beauty's head towards England. These orders were obeyed with three cheers, and ere the sun went down full many a hornpipe had been danced on deck by the uncouth though agile William.

We next find Captain Boldheart about three leagues off Madeira, surveying through his spy-glass a stranger of suspicious appearance making sail towards him. On his firing a gun ahead of her to bring her to, she ran up a flag, which he instantly recognized as the flag from the mast in the back-garden at home.

Inferring from this, that his father had put to sea to seek his long-lost son, the captain sent his own boat on board the stranger, to inquire if this was so, and if so, whether his father's intentions were strictly honourable. The boat came back with a present of greens and fresh meat, and reported that the stranger was The Family of twelve hundred tons, and had not only the captain's father on board, but also his mother, with the majority of his aunts and uncles, and all his cousins. It was further reported to Boldheart that the whole of these relations had expressed themselves in a becoming manner, and were anxious to embrace him and thank him for the glorious credit he had done them. Boldheart at once invited them to breakfast next morning on board the Beauty, and gave orders for a brilliant ball that should last all day.

It was in the course of the night that the captain discovered the hopelessness of reclaiming the Latin-Grammar-Master. That thankless traitor was found out, as the two ships lay near each other, communicating with The Family by signals, and offering to give up

Boldheart. He was hanged at the yard-arm the first thing in the morning, after having it impressively pointed out to him by Boldheart that this was what spiters came to.

The meeting between the captain and his parents was attended with tears. His uncles and aunts would have attended their meeting with tears too, but he wasn't going to stand that. His cousins were very much astonished by the size of his ship and the discipline of his men, and were greatly overcome by the splendour of his uniform. He kindly conducted them round the vessel, and pointed out every thing worthy of notice. He also fired his hundred guns, and found it amusing to witness their alarm.

The entertainment surpassed everything ever seen on board ship, and lasted from ten in the morning until seven the next morning. Only one disagreeable incident occurred. Captain Boldheart found himself obliged to put his cousin Tom in irons, for being disrespectful. On the boy's promising amendment, however, he was humanely released after a few hours' close confinement.

Boldheart now took his mother down into the great cabin, and asked after the young lady with whom, it was well known to the world, he was in love. His mother replied that the object of his affections was then at school at Margate, for the benefit of sea-bathing (it was the month of September), but that she feared the young lady's friends were still opposed to the union. Boldheart at once resolved, if necessary, to bombard the town.

Taking the command of his ship with this intention, and putting all but fighting men on board The Family, with orders to that vessel to keep in company, Boldheart soon anchored in Margate Roads. Here he went ashore well-armed, and attended by his boat's crew (at their head the faithful though ferocious William), and demanded to see the Mayor, who came out of his office.

"Dost know the name of yon ship, Mayor?" asked Boldheart fiercely.

"No," said the Mayor, rubbing his eyes, which he could scarce believe when he saw the goodly vessel riding at anchor.

"She is named the Beauty," said the captain.

"Hah!" exclaimed the Mayor, with a start. "And you, then, are Captain Boldheart?"

"The same."

A pause ensued. The Mayor trembled.

"Now, Mayor," said the captain, "choose. Help me to my Bride, or be bombarded."

The Mayor begged for two hours' grace, in which to make inquiries respecting the young lady. Boldheart accorded him but one; and during that one placed William Boozey sentry over him, with a drawn sword and instructions to accompany him wherever he went, and to run him through the body if he showed a sign of playing false.

At the end of the hour, the Mayor re-appeared more dead than alive, closely waited on by Boozey more alive than dead.

"Captain," said the Mayor, "I have ascertained that the young lady is going to bathe. Even now she waits her turn for a machine. The tide is low, though rising. I, in one of our town-boats, shall not be suspected. When she comes forth in her bathing-dress into the shallow water from behind the hood of the machine, my boat shall intercept her and prevent her return. Do you the rest."

"Mayor," returned Capt. Boldheart, "thou hast saved thy town."

The captain then signalled his boat to take him off, and steering her himself ordered her crew to row towards the bathing-ground, and there to rest upon their oars. All happened as had been arranged. His lovely bride came forth, the Mayor glided in behind her, she became confused and had floated out of her depth, when, with one skilful touch of the rudder and one quivering stroke from the boat's crew, her adoring Boldheart held her in his strong arms. There her shrieks of terror were changed to cries of joy.

Before the Beauty could get under weigh, the hoisting of all the flags in the town and harbour, and the ringing of all the bells, announced to the brave Boldheart that he had nothing to fear. He therefore determined to be married on the spot, and signalled for a clergyman and clerk, who came off promptly in a sailing-boat named the Skylark. Another great entertainment was then given on board the Beauty, in the midst of which the Mayor was called out by a messenger. He returned with the news that Government had sent down to know whether Captain Boldheart, in acknowledgment of the great services he had done his country by being a Pirate, would consent to be made a Lieutenant-Colonel. For himself he would have spurned the worthless boon, but his Bride wished it and he consented.

Only one thing further happened before the good ship Family was dismissed, with rich presents to all on board. It is painful to record (but such is human nature in some cousins) that Captain Boldheart's unmannerly cousin Tom was actually tied up to receive three dozen with a rope's end "for cheekyness and making games," when Captain Boldheart's lady begged for him and he was spared. The Beauty then refitted, and the Captain and his Bride departed for the Indian Ocean to enjoy themselves for evermore.

# TALES OF THE FISH PATROL

JACK LONDON

❧ I ❧

# WHITE AND YELLOW

San Francisco Bay is so large that often its storms are more disastrous to ocean-going craft than is the ocean itself in its violent moments. The waters of the bay contain all manner of fish, wherefore its surface is ploughed by the keels of all manner of fishing boats manned by all manner of fishermen. To protect the fish from this motley floating population many wise laws have been passed, and there is a fish patrol to see that these laws are enforced. Exciting times are the lot of the fish patrol: in its history more than one dead patrolman has marked defeat, and more often dead fishermen across their illegal nets have marked success.

Wildest among the fisher-folk may be accounted the Chinese shrimp-catchers. It is the habit of the shrimp to crawl along the bottom in vast armies till it reaches fresh water, when it turns about and crawls back again to the salt. And where the tide ebbs and flows, the Chinese sink great bag-nets to the bottom, with gaping mouths, into which the shrimp crawls and from which it is transferred to the boiling-pot. This in itself would not be bad, were it not for the small mesh of the nets, so small that the tiniest fishes, little new-hatched things not a quarter of an inch long, cannot pass through. The beautiful beaches of Points Pedro and Pablo, where are the shrimp-catchers' villages, are made fearful by the stench from myriads of decaying fish, and against this wasteful destruction it has ever been the duty of the fish patrol to act.

When I was a youngster of sixteen, a good sloop-sailor and all-round bay-waterman, my sloop, the *Reindeer*, was chartered by the Fish Commission, and I became for the time being a deputy patrolman. After a deal of work among the Greek fishermen of the Upper Bay and rivers, where knives flashed at the beginning of trouble and men permitted themselves to be made prisoners only after a revolver was thrust in their faces, we hailed with delight an expedition to the Lower Bay against the Chinese shrimp-catchers.

There were six of us, in two boats, and to avoid suspicion we ran down after dark and dropped anchor under a projecting bluff of land known as Point Pinole. As the east paled with the first light of dawn we got under way again, and hauled close on the land breeze as we slanted across the bay toward Point Pedro. The morning mists curled and clung to the water so that we could see nothing, but we busied ourselves driving the chill from our bodies with hot coffee. Also we had to devote ourselves to the miserable task of bailing, for in some incomprehensible way the *Reindeer* had sprung a generous leak. Half the night had been spent in overhauling the ballast and exploring the seams, but the labor had been without avail. The water still poured in, and perforce we doubled up in the cockpit and tossed it out again.

After coffee, three of the men withdrew to the other boat, a Columbia River salmon boat, leaving three of us in the *Reindeer*. Then the two craft proceeded in company till the sun showed over the eastern sky-line. Its fiery rays dispelled the clinging vapors, and there, before our eyes, like a picture, lay the shrimp fleet, spread out in a great half-moon, the tips of the crescent fully three miles apart, and each junk moored fast to the buoy of a shrimp-net. But there was no stir, no sign of life.

The situation dawned upon us. While waiting for slack water, in which to lift their heavy nets from the bed of the bay, the Chinese had all gone to sleep below. We were elated, and our plan of battle was swiftly formed.

"Throw each of your two men on to a junk," whispered Le Grant to me from the salmon boat. "And you make fast to a third yourself. We'll do the same, and there's no reason in the world why we shouldn't capture six junks at the least."

Then we separated. I put the *Reindeer* about on the other tack, ran up under the lee of a junk, shivered the mainsail into the wind and lost headway, and forged past the stern of the junk so slowly and so near that one of the patrolmen stepped lightly aboard. Then I kept off, filled the mainsail, and bore away for a second junk.

Up to this time there had been no noise, but from the first junk captured by the salmon boat an uproar now broke forth. There was shrill Oriental yelling, a pistol shot, and more yelling.

"It's all up. They're warning the others," said George, the remaining patrolman, as he stood beside me in the cockpit.

By this time we were in the thick of the fleet, and the alarm was spreading with incredible swiftness. The decks were beginning to swarm with half-awakened and half-naked Chinese. Cries and yells of warning and anger were flying over the quiet water, and somewhere a conch shell was being blown with great success. To the right of us I saw the captain of a junk chop away his mooring line with an axe and spring to help his crew at the hoisting of the huge, outlandish lug-sail. But to the left the first heads were popping up from below on another junk, and I rounded up the *Reindeer* alongside long enough for George to spring aboard.

The whole fleet was now under way. In addition to the sails they had gotten out long sweeps, and the bay was being ploughed in every direction by the fleeing junks. I was now alone in the *Reindeer*, seeking feverishly to capture a third prize. The first junk I took after was a clean miss, for it trimmed its sheets and shot away surprisingly into the wind. By fully half a point it outpointed the *Reindeer*, and I began to feel respect for the clumsy craft. Realizing the hopelessness of the pursuit, I filled away, threw out the main-sheet, and drove down before the wind upon the junks to leeward, where I had them at a disadvantage.

The one I had selected wavered indecisively before me, and, as I swung wide to make the boarding gentle, filled suddenly and darted away, the smart Mongols shouting a wild rhythm as they bent to the sweeps. But I had been ready for this. I luffed suddenly. Putting the tiller hard down, and holding it down with my body, I brought the main-sheet in, hand over hand, on the run, so as to retain all possible striking force. The two starboard sweeps of the junk were crumpled up, and then the two boats came together with a crash. The

*Reindeer's* bowsprit, like a monstrous hand, reached over and ripped out the junk's chunky mast and towering sail.

This was met by a curdling yell of rage. A big Chinaman, remarkably evil-looking, with his head swathed in a yellow silk handkerchief and face badly pock-marked, planted a pike-pole on the *Reindeer's* bow and began to shove the entangled boats apart. Pausing long enough to let go the jib halyards, and just as the *Reindeer* cleared and began to drift astern, I leaped aboard the junk with a line and made fast. He of the yellow handkerchief and pock-marked face came toward me threateningly, but I put my hand into my hip pocket, and he hesitated. I was unarmed, but the Chinese have learned to be fastidiously careful of American hip pockets, and it was upon this that I depended to keep him and his savage crew at a distance.

I ordered him to drop the anchor at the junk's bow, to which he replied, "No sabbe." The crew responded in like fashion, and though I made my meaning plain by signs, they refused to understand. Realizing the inexpediency of discussing the matter, I went forward myself, overran the line, and let the anchor go.

"Now get aboard, four of you," I said in a loud voice, indicating with my fingers that four of them were to go with me and the fifth was to remain by the junk. The Yellow Handkerchief hesitated; but I repeated the order fiercely (much more fiercely than I felt), at the same time sending my hand to my hip. Again the Yellow Handkerchief was overawed, and with surly looks he led three of his men aboard the *Reindeer*. I cast off at once, and, leaving the jib down, steered a course for George's junk. Here it was easier, for there were two of us, and George had a pistol to fall back on if it came to the worst. And here, as with my junk, four Chinese were transferred to the sloop and one left behind to take care of things.

Four more were added to our passenger list from the third junk. By this time the salmon boat had collected its twelve prisoners and came alongside, badly overloaded. To make matters worse, as it was a small boat, the patrolmen were so jammed in with their prisoners that they would have little chance in case of trouble.

"You'll have to help us out," said Le Grant.

I looked over my prisoners, who had crowded into the cabin and on top of it. "I can take three," I answered.

"Make it four," he suggested, "and I'll take Bill with me." (Bill was the third patrolman.) "We haven't elbow room here, and in case of a scuffle one white to every two of them will be just about the right proportion."

The exchange was made, and the salmon boat got up its spritsail and headed down the bay toward the marshes off San Rafael. I ran up the jib and followed with the *Reindeer*. San Rafael, where we were to turn our catch over to the authorities, communicated with the bay by way of a long and tortuous slough, or marshland creek, which could be navigated only when the tide was in. Slack water had come, and, as the ebb was commencing, there was need for hurry if we cared to escape waiting half a day for the next tide.

But the land breeze had begun to die away with the rising sun, and now came only in failing puffs. The salmon boat got out its oars and soon left us far astern. Some of the Chinese stood in the forward part of the cockpit, near the cabin doors, and once, as I leaned over the cockpit rail to flatten down the jib-sheet a bit, I felt some one brush against my hip pocket. I made no sign, but out of the corner of my eye I saw that the Yellow Handkerchief had discovered the emptiness of the pocket which had hitherto overawed him.

To make matters serious, during all the excitement of boarding the junks the *Reindeer* had not been bailed, and the water was beginning to slush over the cockpit floor. The shrimp-catchers pointed at it and looked to me questioningly.

"Yes," I said. "Bime by, allee same dlown, velly quick, you no bail now. Sabbe?"

No, they did not "sabbe," or at least they shook their heads to that effect, though they chattered most comprehendingly to one another in their own lingo. I pulled up three or four of the bottom boards, got a couple of buckets from a locker, and by unmistakable sign-language invited them to fall to. But they laughed, and some crowded into the cabin and some climbed up on top.

Their laughter was not good laughter. There was a hint of menace in it, a maliciousness which their black looks verified. The Yellow Handkerchief, since his discovery of my empty pocket, had become most insolent in his bearing, and he wormed about among the other prisoners, talking to them with great earnestness.

Swallowing my chagrin, I stepped down into the cockpit and began throwing out the water. But hardly had I begun, when the boom swung overhead, the mainsail filled with a jerk, and the *Reindeer* heeled over. The day wind was springing up. George was the veriest of landlubbers, so I was forced to give over bailing and take the tiller. The wind was blowing directly off Point Pedro and the high mountains behind, and because of this was squally and uncertain, half the time bellying the canvas out and the other half flapping it idly.

George was about the most all-round helpless man I had ever met. Among his other disabilities, he was a consumptive, and I knew that if he attempted to bail, it might bring on a hemorrhage. Yet the rising water warned me that something must be done. Again I ordered the shrimp-catchers to lend a hand with the buckets. They laughed defiantly, and those inside the cabin, the water up to their ankles, shouted back and forth with those on top.

"You'd better get out your gun and make them bail," I said to George.

But he shook his head and showed all too plainly that he was afraid. The Chinese could see the funk he was in as well as I could, and their insolence became insufferable. Those in the cabin broke into the food lockers, and those above scrambled down and joined them in a feast on our crackers and canned goods.

"What do we care?" George said weakly.

I was fuming with helpless anger. "If they get out of hand, it will be too late to care. The best thing you can do is to get them in check right now."

The water was rising higher and higher, and the gusts, forerunners of a steady breeze, were growing stiffer and stiffer. And between the gusts, the prisoners, having gotten away with a week's grub, took to crowding first to one side and then to the other till the *Reindeer* rocked like a cockle-shell. Yellow Handkerchief approached me, and, pointing out his village on the Point Pedro beach, gave me to understand that if I turned the *Reindeer* in that direction and put them ashore, they, in turn, would go to bailing. By now the water in the cabin was up to the bunks, and the bed-clothes were sopping. It was a foot deep on the cockpit floor. Nevertheless I refused, and I could see by George's face that he was disappointed.

"If you don't show some nerve, they'll rush us and throw us overboard," I said to him. "Better give me your revolver, if you want to be safe."

"The safest thing to do," he chattered cravenly, "is to put them ashore. I, for one, don't want to be drowned for the sake of a handful of dirty Chinamen."

"And I, for another, don't care to give in to a handful of dirty Chinamen to escape drowning," I answered hotly.

"You'll sink the *Reindeer* under us all at this rate," he whined. "And what good that'll do I can't see."

"Every man to his taste," I retorted.

He made no reply, but I could see he was trembling pitifully. Between the threatening Chinese and the rising water he was beside himself with fright; and, more than the Chinese and the water, I feared him and what his fright might impel him to do. I could see him casting longing glances at the small skiff towing astern, so in the next calm I hauled the skiff alongside. As I did so his eyes brightened with hope; but before he could guess my intention, I stove the frail bottom through with a hand-axe, and the skiff filled to its gunwales.

"It's sink or float together," I said. "And if you'll give me your revolver, I'll have the *Reindeer* bailed out in a jiffy."

"They're too many for us," he whimpered. "We can't fight them all."

I turned my back on him in disgust. The salmon boat had long since passed from sight behind a little archipelago known as the Marin Islands, so no help could be looked for from that quarter. Yellow Handkerchief came up to me in a familiar manner, the water in the cockpit slushing against his legs. I did not like his looks. I felt that beneath the pleasant smile he was trying to put on his face there was an ill purpose. I ordered him back, and so sharply that he obeyed.

"Now keep your distance," I commanded, "and don't you come closer!"

"Wha' fo'?" he demanded indignantly. "I t'ink-um talkee talkee heap good."

"Talkee talkee," I answered bitterly, for I knew now that he had understood all that passed between George and me. "What for talkee talkee? You no sabbe talkee talkee."

He grinned in a sickly fashion. "Yep, I sabbe velly much. I honest Chinaman."

"All right," I answered. "You sabbe talkee talkee, then you bail water plenty plenty. After that we talkee talkee."

He shook his head, at the same time pointing over his shoulder to his comrades. "No can do. Velly bad Chinamen, heap velly bad. I t'ink-um—"

"Stand back!" I shouted, for I had noticed his hand disappear beneath his blouse and his body prepare for a spring.

Disconcerted, he went back into the cabin, to hold a council, apparently, from the way the jabbering broke forth. The *Reindeer* was very deep in the water, and her movements had grown quite loggy. In a rough sea she would have inevitably swamped; but the wind, when it did blow, was off the land, and scarcely a ripple disturbed the surface of the bay.

"I think you'd better head for the beach," George said abruptly, in a manner that told me his fear had forced him to make up his mind to some course of action.

"I think not," I answered shortly.

"I command you," he said in a bullying tone.

"I was commanded to bring these prisoners into San Rafael," was my reply.

Our voices were raised, and the sound of the altercation brought the Chinese out of the cabin.

"Now will you head for the beach?"

This from George, and I found myself looking into the muzzle of his revolver—of the revolver he dared to use on me, but was too cowardly to use on the prisoners.

My brain seemed smitten with a dazzling brightness. The whole situation, in all its bearings, was focussed sharply before me—the shame of losing the prisoners, the worthlessness and cowardice of George, the meeting with Le Grant and the other patrol men and the lame explanation; and then there was the fight I had fought so hard, victory wrenched from me just as I thought I had it within my grasp. And out of the tail of my eye I could see the Chinese crowding together by the cabin doors and leering triumphantly. It would never do.

I threw my hand up and my head down. The first act elevated the muzzle, and the second removed my head from the path of the bullet which went whistling past. One hand closed on George's wrist, the other on the revolver. Yellow Handkerchief and his gang sprang toward me. It was now or never. Putting all my strength into a sudden effort, I swung George's body forward to meet them. Then I pulled back with equal suddenness, ripping the revolver out of his fingers and jerking him off his feet. He fell against Yellow Handkerchief's knees, who stumbled over him, and the pair wallowed in the bailing hole where the cockpit floor was torn open. The next instant I was covering them with my revolver, and the wild shrimp-catchers were cowering and cringing away.

But I swiftly discovered that there was all the difference in the world between shooting men who are attacking and men who are doing nothing more than simply refusing to obey. For obey they would not when I ordered them into the bailing hole. I threatened them with the revolver, but they sat stolidly in the flooded cabin and on the roof and would not move.

Fifteen minutes passed, the *Reindeer* sinking deeper and deeper, her mainsail flapping in the calm. But from off the Point Pedro shore I saw a dark line form on the water and travel toward us. It was the steady breeze I had been expecting so long. I called to the Chinese and pointed it out. They hailed it with exclamations. Then I pointed to the sail and to the water in the *Reindeer*, and indicated by signs that when the wind reached the sail, what of the water aboard we would capsize. But they jeered defiantly, for they knew it was in my power to luff the helm and let go the main-sheet, so as to spill the wind and escape damage.

But my mind was made up. I hauled in the main-sheet a foot or two, took a turn with it, and bracing my feet, put my back against the tiller. This left me one hand for the sheet and one for the revolver. The dark line drew nearer, and I could see them looking from me to it and back again with an apprehension they could not successfully conceal. My brain and will and endurance were pitted against theirs, and the problem was which could stand the strain of imminent death the longer and not give in.

Then the wind struck us. The main-sheet tautened with a brisk rattling of the blocks, the boom uplifted, the sail bellied out, and the *Reindeer* heeled over—over, and over, till the lee-rail went under, the cabin windows went under, and the bay began to pour in over the cockpit rail. So violently had she heeled over, that the men in the cabin had been thrown on top of one another into the lee bunk, where they squirmed and twisted and were washed about, those underneath being perilously near to drowning.

The wind freshened a bit, and the *Reindeer* went over farther than ever. For the moment I thought she was gone, and I knew that another puff like that and she surely would go. While I pressed her under and debated whether I should give up or not, the Chinese cried for mercy. I think it was the sweetest sound I have ever heard. And then, and not until then, did I luff up and ease out the main-sheet. The *Reindeer* righted very slowly, and when she was on an even keel was so much awash that I doubted if she could be saved.

But the Chinese scrambled madly into the cockpit and fell to bailing with buckets, pots, pans, and everything they could lay hands on. It was a beautiful sight to see that water flying over the side! And when the *Reindeer* was high and proud on the water once more, we dashed away with the breeze on our quarter, and at the last possible moment crossed the mud flats and entered the slough.

The spirit of the Chinese was broken, and so docile did they become that ere we made San Rafael they were out with the tow-rope, Yellow Handkerchief at the head of the line. As for George, it was his last trip with the fish patrol. He did not care for that sort of thing, he explained, and he thought a clerkship ashore was good enough for him. And we thought so too.

## 2

# THE KING OF THE GREEKS

Big Alec had never been captured by the fish patrol. It was his boast that no man could take him alive, and it was his history that of the many men who had tried to take him dead none had succeeded. It was also history that at least two patrolmen who had tried to take him dead had died themselves. Further, no man violated the fish laws more systematically and deliberately than Big Alec.

He was called "Big Alec" because of his gigantic stature. His height was six feet three inches, and he was correspondingly broad-shouldered and deep-chested. He was splendidly muscled and hard as steel, and there were innumerable stories in circulation among the fisher-folk concerning his prodigious strength. He was as bold and dominant of spirit as he was strong of body, and because of this he was widely known by another name, that of "The King of the Greeks." The fishing population was largely composed of Greeks, and they looked up to him and obeyed him as their chief. And as their chief, he fought their fights for them, saw that they were protected, saved them from the law when they fell into its clutches, and made them stand by one another and himself in time of trouble.

In the old days, the fish patrol had attempted his capture many disastrous times and had finally given it over, so that when the word was out that he was coming to Benicia, I was most anxious to see him. But I did not have to hunt him up. In his usual bold way, the first thing he did on arriving was to hunt us up. Charley Le Grant and I at the time were under a patrolman named Carmintel, and the three of us were on the *Reindeer*, preparing for a trip, when Big Alec stepped aboard. Carmintel evidently knew him, for they shook hands in recognition. Big Alec took no notice of Charley or me.

"I've come down to fish sturgeon a couple of months," he said to Carmintel.

His eyes flashed with challenge as he spoke, and we noticed the patrolman's eyes drop before him.

"That's all right, Alec," Carmintel said in a low voice. "I'll not bother you. Come on into the cabin, and we'll talk things over," he added.

When they had gone inside and shut the doors after them, Charley winked with slow deliberation at me. But I was only a youngster, and new to men and the ways of some men, so I did not understand. Nor did Charley explain, though I felt there was something wrong about the business.

Leaving them to their conference, at Charley's suggestion we boarded our skiff and pulled over to the Old Steamboat Wharf, where Big Alec's ark was lying. An ark is a house-boat of small though comfortable dimensions, and is as necessary to the Upper Bay fisherman as are nets and boats. We were both curious to see Big Alec's ark, for history said that it had been the scene of more than one pitched battle, and that it was riddled with bullet-holes.

We found the holes (stopped with wooden plugs and painted over), but there were not so many as I had expected. Charley noted my look of disappointment, and laughed; and then to comfort me he gave an authentic account of one expedition which had descended upon Big Alec's floating home to capture him, alive preferably, dead if necessary. At the end of half a day's fighting, the patrolmen had drawn off in wrecked boats, with one of their number killed and three wounded. And when they returned next morning with reinforcements they found only the mooring-stakes of Big Alec's ark; the ark itself remained hidden for months in the fastnesses of the Suisun tules.

"But why was he not hanged for murder?" I demanded. "Surely the United States is powerful enough to bring such a man to justice."

"He gave himself up and stood trial," Charley answered. "It cost him fifty thousand dollars to win the case, which he did on technicalities and with the aid of the best lawyers in the state. Every Greek fisherman on the river contributed to the sum. Big Alec levied and collected the tax, for all the world like a king. The United States may be all-powerful, my lad, but the fact remains that Big Alec is a king inside the United States, with a country and subjects all his own."

"But what are you going to do about his fishing for sturgeon? He's bound to fish with a 'Chinese line.'"

Charley shrugged his shoulders. "We'll see what we will see," he said enigmatically.

Now a "Chinese line" is a cunning device invented by the people whose name it bears. By a simple system of floats, weights, and anchors, thousands of hooks, each on a separate leader, are suspended at a distance of from six inches to a foot above the bottom. The remarkable thing about such a line is the hook. It is barbless, and in place of the barb, the hook is filed long and tapering to a point as sharp as that of a needle. These hoods are only a few inches apart, and when several thousand of them are suspended just above the bottom, like a fringe, for a couple of hundred fathoms, they present a formidable obstacle to the fish that travel along the bottom.

Such a fish is the sturgeon, which goes rooting along like a pig, and indeed is often called "pig-fish." Pricked by the first hook it touches, the sturgeon gives a startled leap and comes into contact with half a dozen more hooks. Then it threshes about wildly, until it receives hook after hook in its soft flesh; and the hooks, straining from many different angles, hold the luckless fish fast until it is drowned. Because no sturgeon can pass through a Chinese line, the device is called a trap in the fish laws; and because it bids fair to exterminate the sturgeon, it is branded by the fish laws as illegal. And such a line, we were confident, Big Alec intended setting, in open and flagrant violation of the law.

Several days passed after the visit of Big Alec, during which Charley and I kept a sharp watch on him. He towed his ark around the Solano Wharf and into the big bight at Turner's Shipyard. The bight we knew to be good ground for sturgeon, and there we felt sure the King of the Greeks intended to begin operations. The tide circled like a mill-race in and out of this bight, and made it possible to raise, lower, or set a Chinese line only at slack water. So between the tides Charley and I made it a point for one or the other of us to keep a lookout from the Solano Wharf.

On the fourth day I was lying in the sun behind the stringer-piece of the wharf, when I saw a skiff leave the distant shore and pull out into the bight. In an instant the glasses were at my eyes and I was following every movement of the skiff. There were two men in it, and though it was a good mile away, I made out one of them to be Big Alec; and ere the skiff returned to shore I made out enough more to know that the Greek had set his line.

"Big Alec has a Chinese line out in the bight off Turner's Shipyard," Charley Le Grant said that afternoon to Carmintel.

A fleeting expression of annoyance passed over the patrolman's face, and then he said, "Yes?" in an absent way, and that was all.

Charley bit his lip with suppressed anger and turned on his heel.

"Are you game, my lad?" he said to me later on in the evening, just as we finished washing down the *Reindeer's* decks and were preparing to turn in.

A lump came up in my throat, and I could only nod my head.

"Well, then," and Charley's eyes glittered in a determined way, "we've got to capture Big Alec between us, you and I, and we've got to do it in spite of Carmintel. Will you lend a hand?"

"It's a hard proposition, but we can do it," he added after a pause.

"Of course we can," I supplemented enthusiastically.

And then he said, "Of course we can," and we shook hands on it and went to bed.

But it was no easy task we had set ourselves. In order to convict a man of illegal fishing, it was necessary to catch him in the act with all the evidence of the crime about him—the hooks, the lines, the fish, and the man himself. This meant that we must take Big Alec on the open water, where he could see us coming and prepare for us one of the warm receptions for which he was noted.

"There's no getting around it," Charley said one morning. "If we can only get alongside it's an even toss, and there's nothing left for us but to try and get alongside. Come on, lad."

We were in the Columbia River salmon boat, the one we had used against the Chinese shrimp-catchers. Slack water had come, and as we dropped around the end of the Solano Wharf we saw Big Alec at work, running his line and removing the fish.

"Change places," Charley commanded, "and steer just astern of him as though you're going into the shipyard."

I took the tiller, and Charley sat down on a thwart amidships, placing his revolver handily beside him.

"If he begins to shoot," he cautioned, "get down in the bottom and steer from there, so that nothing more than your hand will be exposed."

I nodded, and we kept silent after that, the boat slipping gently through the water and Big Alec growing nearer and nearer. We could see him quite plainly, gaffing the sturgeon and throwing them into the boat while his companion ran the line and cleared the hooks as he dropped them back into the water. Nevertheless, we were five hundred yards away when the big fisherman hailed us.

"Here! You! What do you want?" he shouted.

"Keep going," Charley whispered, "just as though you didn't hear him."

The next few moments were very anxious ones. The fisherman was studying us sharply, while we were gliding up on him every second.

"You keep off if you know what's good for you!" he called out suddenly, as though he had made up his mind as to who and what we were. "If you don't, I'll fix you!"

He brought a rifle to his shoulder and trained it on me.

"Now will you keep off?" he demanded.

I could hear Charley groan with disappointment. "Keep off," he whispered; "it's all up for this time."

I put up the tiller and eased the sheet, and the salmon boat ran off five or six points. Big Alec watched us till we were out of range, when he returned to his work.

"You'd better leave Big Alec alone," Carmintel said, rather sourly, to Charley that night.

"So he's been complaining to you, has he?" Charley said significantly.

Carmintel flushed painfully. "You'd better leave him alone, I tell you," he repeated. "He's a dangerous man, and it won't pay to fool with him."

"Yes," Charley answered softly; "I've heard that it pays better to leave him alone."

This was a direct thrust at Carmintel, and we could see by the expression of his face that it sank home. For it was common knowledge that Big Alec was as willing to bribe as to fight, and that of late years more than one patrolman had handled the fisherman's money.

"Do you mean to say—" Carmintel began, in a bullying tone.

But Charley cut him off shortly. "I mean to say nothing," he said. "You heard what I said, and if the cap fits, why—"

He shrugged his shoulders, and Carmintel glowered at him, speechless.

"What we want is imagination," Charley said to me one day, when we had attempted to creep upon Big Alec in the gray of dawn and had been shot at for our trouble.

And thereafter, and for many days, I cudgelled my brains trying to imagine some possible way by which two men, on an open stretch of water, could capture another who knew how to use a rifle and was never to be found without one. Regularly, every slack water, without slyness, boldly and openly in the broad day, Big Alec was to be seen running his line. And what made it particularly exasperating was the fact that every fisherman, from Benicia to Vallejo knew that he was successfully defying us. Carmintel also bothered us, for he kept us busy among the shad-fishers of San Pablo, so that we had little time to spare on the King of the Greeks. But Charley's wife and children lived at Benicia, and we had made the place our headquarters, so that we always returned to it.

"I'll tell you what we can do," I said, after several fruitless weeks had passed; "we can wait some slack water till Big Alec has run his line and gone ashore with the fish, and then we can go out and capture the line. It will put him to time and expense to make another, and then we'll figure to capture that too. If we can't capture him, we can discourage him, you see."

Charley saw, and said it wasn't a bad idea. We watched our chance, and the next low-water slack, after Big Alec had removed the fish from the line and returned ashore, we went out in the salmon boat. We had the bearings of the line from shore marks, and we knew we would have no difficulty in locating it. The first of the flood tide was setting in, when we ran below where we thought the line was stretched and dropped over a fishing-boat anchor. Keeping a short rope to the anchor, so that it barely touched the bottom, we dragged it slowly along until it stuck and the boat fetched up hard and fast.

"We've got it," Charley cried. "Come on and lend a hand to get it in."

Together we hove up the rope till the anchor I came in sight with the sturgeon line caught across one of the flukes. Scores of the murderous-looking hooks flashed into sight as we cleared the anchor, and we had just started to run along the line to the end where we could begin to lift it, when a sharp thud in the boat startled us. We looked about, but saw nothing and returned to our work. An instant later there was a similar sharp thud and the gunwale splintered between Charley's body and mine.

"That's remarkably like a bullet, lad," he said reflectively. "And it's a long shot Big Alec's making."

"And he's using smokeless powder," he concluded, after an examination of the mile-distant shore. "That's why we can't hear the report."

I looked at the shore, but could see no sign of Big Alec, who was undoubtedly hidden in some rocky nook with us at his mercy. A third bullet struck the water, glanced, passed singing over our heads, and struck the water again beyond.

"I guess we'd better get out of this," Charley remarked coolly. "What do you think, lad?"

I thought so, too, and said we didn't want the line anyway. Whereupon we cast off and hoisted the spritsail. The bullets ceased at once, and we sailed away, unpleasantly confident that Big Alec was laughing at our discomfiture.

And more than that, the next day on the fishing wharf, where we were inspecting nets, he saw fit to laugh and sneer at us, and this before all the fishermen. Charley's face went black with anger; but beyond promising Big Alec that in the end he would surely land him behind the bars, he controlled himself and said nothing. The King of the Greeks made his boast that no fish patrol had ever taken him or ever could take him, and the fishermen cheered him and said it was true. They grew excited, and it looked like trouble for a while; but Big Alec asserted his kingship and quelled them.

Carmintel also laughed at Charley, and dropped sarcastic remarks, and made it hard for him. But Charley refused to be angered, though he told me in confidence that he intended to capture Big Alec if it took all the rest of his life to accomplish it.

"I don't know how I'll do it," he said, "but do it I will, as sure as I am Charley Le Grant. The idea will come to me at the right and proper time, never fear."

And at the right time it came, and most unexpectedly. Fully a month had passed, and we were constantly up and down the river, and down and up the bay, with no spare moments to devote to the particular fisherman who ran a Chinese line in the bight of Turner's Shipyard. We had called in at Selby's Smelter one afternoon, while on patrol work, when all unknown to us our opportunity happened along. It appeared in the guise of a helpless yacht loaded with seasick people, so we could hardly be expected to recognize it as the opportunity. It was a large sloop-yacht, and it was helpless inasmuch as the trade-wind was blowing half a gale and there were no capable sailors aboard.

From the wharf at Selby's we watched with careless interest the lubberly manœuvre performed of bringing the yacht to anchor, and the equally lubberly manœuvre of sending the small boat ashore. A very miserable-looking man in draggled ducks, after nearly swamping the boat in the heavy seas, passed us the painter and climbed out. He staggered about as though the wharf were rolling, and told us his troubles, which were the troubles of the yacht. The only rough-weather sailor aboard, the man on whom they all depended, had been called back to San Francisco by a telegram, and they had attempted to continue the cruise alone. The high wind and big seas of San Pablo Bay had been too much for them; all hands were sick, nobody knew anything or could do anything; and so they had run in to the smelter either to desert the yacht or to get somebody to bring it to Benicia. In short, did we know of any sailors who would bring the yacht into Benicia?

Charley looked at me. The *Reindeer* was lying in a snug place. We had nothing on hand in the way of patrol work till midnight. With the wind then blowing, we could sail the yacht into Benicia in a couple of hours, have several more hours ashore, and come back to the smelter on the evening train.

"All right, captain," Charley said to the disconsolate yachtsman, who smiled in sickly fashion at the title.

"I'm only the owner," he explained.

We rowed him aboard in much better style than he had come ashore, and saw for ourselves the helplessness of the passengers. There were a dozen men and women, and all of them too sick even to appear grateful at our coming. The yacht was rolling savagely, broad on, and no sooner had the owner's feet touched the deck than he collapsed and joined, the others. Not one was able to bear a hand, so Charley and I between us cleared the badly tangled running gear, got up sail, and hoisted anchor.

It was a rough trip, though a swift one. The Carquinez Straits were a welter of foam and smother, and we came through them wildly before the wind, the big mainsail alternately dipping and flinging its boom skyward as we tore along. But the people did not mind. They did not mind anything. Two or three, including the owner, sprawled in the cockpit, shuddering when the yacht lifted and raced and sank dizzily into the trough, and between-whiles regarding the shore with yearning eyes. The rest were huddled on the cabin floor among the cushions. Now and again some one groaned, but for the most part they were as limp as so many dead persons.

As the bight at Turner's Shipyard opened out, Charley edged into it to get the smoother water. Benicia was in view, and we were bowling along over comparatively easy water, when a speck of a boat danced up ahead of us, directly in our course. It was low-water slack. Charley and I looked at each other. No word was spoken, but at once the yacht began a most astonishing performance, veering and yawing as though the greenest of amateurs was at the wheel. It was a sight for sailormen to see. To all appearances, a runaway yacht was careering madly over the bight, and now and again yielding a little bit to control in a desperate effort to make Benicia.

The owner forgot his seasickness long enough to look anxious. The speck of a boat grew larger and larger, till we could see Big Alec and his partner, with a turn of the sturgeon line around a cleat, resting from their labor to laugh at us. Charley pulled his sou'wester over his eyes, and I followed his example, though I could not guess the idea he evidently had in mind and intended to carry into execution.

We came foaming down abreast of the skiff, so close that we could hear above the wind the voices of Big Alec and his mate as they shouted at us with all the scorn that professional watermen feel for amateurs, especially when amateurs are making fools of themselves.

We thundered on past the fishermen, and nothing had happened. Charley grinned at the disappointment he saw in my face, and then shouted:

"Stand by the main-sheet to jibe!"

He put the wheel hard over, and the yacht whirled around obediently. The main-sheet slacked and dipped, then shot over our heads after the boom and tautened with a crash on the traveller. The yacht heeled over almost on her beam ends, and a great wail went up from the seasick passengers as they swept across the cabin floor in a tangled mass and piled into a heap in the starboard bunks.

But we had no time for them. The yacht, completing the manœuvre, headed into the wind with slatting canvas, and righted to an even keel. We were still plunging ahead, and directly in our path was the skiff. I saw Big Alec dive overboard and his mate leap for our bowsprit. Then came the crash as we struck the boat, and a series of grinding bumps as it passed under our bottom.

"That fixes his rifle," I heard Charley mutter, as he sprang upon the deck to look for Big Alec somewhere astern.

The wind and sea quickly stopped our forward movement, and we began to drift backward over the spot where the skiff had been. Big Alec's black head and swarthy face popped up within arm's reach; and all unsuspecting and very angry with what he took to be the clumsiness of amateur sailors, he was hauled aboard. Also he was out of breath, for he had dived deep and stayed down long to escape our keel.

The next instant, to the perplexity and consternation of the owner, Charley was on top of Big Alec in the cockpit, and I was helping bind him with gaskets. The owner was dancing excitedly about and demanding an explanation, but by that time Big Alec's partner had crawled aft from the bowsprit and was peering apprehensively over the rail into the cockpit. Charley's arm shot around his neck and the man landed on his back beside Big Alec.

"More gaskets!" Charley shouted, and I made haste to supply them.

The wrecked skiff was rolling sluggishly a short distance to windward, and I trimmed the sheets while Charley took the wheel and steered for it.

"These two men are old offenders," he explained to the angry owner; "and they are most persistent violators of the fish and game laws. You have seen them caught in the act, and you may expect to be subpœnaed as witness for the state when the trial comes off."

As he spoke he rounded alongside the skiff. It had been torn from the line, a section of which was dragging to it. He hauled in forty or fifty feet with a young sturgeon still fast in a tangle of barbless hooks, slashed that much of the line free with his knife, and tossed it into the cockpit beside the prisoners.

"And there's the evidence, Exhibit A, for the people," Charley continued. "Look it over carefully so that you may identify it in the court-room with the time and place of capture."

And then, in triumph, with no more veering and yawing, we sailed into Benicia, the King of the Greeks bound hard and fast in the cockpit, and for the first time in his life a prisoner of the fish patrol.

❧ 3 ❧

# A RAID ON THE OYSTER PIRATES

Of the fish patrolmen under whom we served at various times, Charley Le Grant and I were agreed, I think, that Neil Partington was the best. He was neither dishonest nor cowardly; and while he demanded strict obedience when we were under his orders, at the same time our relations were those of easy comradeship, and he permitted us a freedom to which we were ordinarily unaccustomed, as the present story will show.

Neil's family lived in Oakland, which is on the Lower Bay, not more than six miles across the water from San Francisco. One day, while scouting among the Chinese shrimp-catchers of Point Pedro, he received word that his wife was very ill; and within the hour the *Reindeer* was bowling along for Oakland, with a stiff northwest breeze astern. We ran up the Oakland Estuary and came to anchor, and in the days that followed, while Neil was ashore, we tightened up the *Reindeer's* rigging, overhauled the ballast, scraped down, and put the sloop into thorough shape.

This done, time hung heavy on our hands. Neil's wife was dangerously ill, and the outlook was a week's lie-over, awaiting the crisis. Charley and I roamed the docks, wondering what we should do, and so came upon the oyster fleet lying at the Oakland City Wharf. In the main they were trim, natty boats, made for speed and bad weather, and we sat down on the stringer-piece of the dock to study them.

"A good catch, I guess," Charley said, pointing to the heaps of oysters, assorted in three sizes, which lay upon their decks.

Pedlers were backing their wagons to the edge of the wharf, and from the bargaining and chaffering that went on, I managed to learn the selling price of the oysters.

"That boat must have at least two hundred dollars' worth aboard," I calculated. "I wonder how long it took to get the load?"

"Three or four days," Charley answered. "Not bad wages for two men—twenty-five dollars a day apiece."

The boat we were discussing, the *Ghost*, lay directly beneath us. Two men composed its crew. One was a squat, broad-shouldered fellow with remarkably long and gorilla-like arms, while the other was tall and well proportioned, with clear blue eyes and a mat of straight black hair. So unusual and striking was this combination of hair and eyes that Charley and I remained somewhat longer than we intended.

And it was well that we did. A stout, elderly man, with the dress and carriage of a successful merchant, came up and stood beside us, looking down upon the deck of the *Ghost*. He appeared angry, and the longer he looked the angrier he grew.

"Those are my oysters," he said at last. "I know they are my oysters. You raided my beds last night and robbed me of them."

The tall man and the short man on the *Ghost* looked up.

"Hello, Taft," the short man said, with insolent familiarity. (Among the bayfarers he had gained the nickname of "The Centipede" on account of his long arms.) "Hello, Taft," he repeated, with the same touch of insolence. "Wot 'r you growling about now?"

"Those are my oysters—that's what I said. You've stolen them from my beds."

"Yer mighty wise, ain't ye?" was the Centipede's sneering reply. "S'pose you can tell your oysters wherever you see 'em?"

"Now, in my experience," broke in the tall man, "oysters is oysters wherever you find 'em, an' they're pretty much alike all the Bay over, and the world over, too, for that matter. We're not wantin' to quarrel with you, Mr. Taft, but we jes' wish you wouldn't insinuate that them oysters is yours an' that we're thieves an' robbers till you can prove the goods."

"I know they're mine; I'd stake my life on it!" Mr. Taft snorted.

"Prove it," challenged the tall man, who we afterward learned was known as "The Porpoise" because of his wonderful swimming abilities.

Mr. Taft shrugged his shoulders helplessly. Of course he could not prove the oysters to be his, no matter how certain he might be.

"I'd give a thousand dollars to have you men behind the bars!" he cried. "I'll give fifty dollars a head for your arrest and conviction, all of you!"

A roar of laughter went up from the different boats, for the rest of the pirates had been listening to the discussion.

"There's more money in oysters," the Porpoise remarked dryly.

Mr. Taft turned impatiently on his heel and walked away. From out of the corner of his eye, Charley noted the way he went. Several minutes later, when he had disappeared around a corner, Charley rose lazily to his feet. I followed him, and we sauntered off in the opposite direction to that taken by Mr. Taft.

"Come on! Lively!" Charley whispered, when we passed from the view of the oyster fleet.

Our course was changed at once, and we dodged around corners and raced up and down side-streets till Mr. Taft's generous form loomed up ahead of us.

"I'm going to interview him about that reward," Charley explained, as we rapidly overhauled the oyster-bed owner. "Neil will be delayed here for a week, and you and I might as well be doing something in the meantime. What do you say?"

"Of course, of course," Mr. Taft said, when Charley had introduced himself and explained his errand. "Those thieves are robbing me of thousands of dollars every year, and I shall be glad to break them up at any price,—yes, sir, at any price. As I said, I'll give fifty dollars a head, and call it cheap at that. They've robbed my beds, torn down my signs, terrorized my watchmen, and last year killed one of them. Couldn't prove it. All done in the blackness of night. All I had was a dead watchman and no evidence. The detectives could do nothing. Nobody has been able to do anything with those men. We have never succeeded in arresting one of them. So I say, Mr.—What did you say your name was?"

"Le Grant," Charley answered.

"So I say, Mr. Le Grant, I am deeply obliged to you for the assistance you offer. And I shall be glad, most glad, sir, to co-operate with you in every way. My watchmen and boats are at your disposal. Come and see me at the San Francisco offices any time, or telephone at my expense. And don't be afraid of spending money. I'll foot your expenses, whatever they are, so long as they are within reason. The situation is growing desperate, and something must be done to determine whether I or that band of ruffians own those oyster beds."

"Now we'll see Neil," Charley said, when he had seen Mr. Taft upon his train to San Francisco.

Not only did Neil Partington interpose no obstacle to our adventure, but he proved to be of the greatest assistance. Charley and I knew nothing of the oyster industry, while his head was an encyclopædia of facts concerning it. Also, within an hour or so, he was able to bring to us a Greek boy of seventeen or eighteen who knew thoroughly well the ins and outs of oyster piracy.

At this point I may as well explain that we of the fish patrol were free lances in a way. While Neil Partington, who was a patrolman proper, received a regular salary, Charley and I, being merely deputies, received only what we earned—that is to say, a certain percentage of the fines imposed on convicted violators of the fish laws. Also, any rewards that chanced our way were ours. We offered to share with Partington whatever we should get from Mr. Taft, but the patrolman would not hear of it. He was only too happy, he said, to do a good turn for us, who had done so many for him.

We held a long council of war, and mapped out the following line of action. Our faces were unfamiliar on the Lower Bay, but as the *Reindeer* was well known as a fish-patrol sloop, the Greek boy, whose name was Nicholas, and I were to sail some innocent-looking craft down to Asparagus Island and join the oyster pirates' fleet. Here, according to Nicholas's description of the beds and the manner of raiding, it was possible for us to catch the pirates in the act of stealing oysters, and at the same time to get them in our power. Charley was to be on the shore, with Mr. Taft's watchmen and a posse of constables, to help us at the right time.

"I know just the boat," Neil said, at the conclusion of the discussion, "a crazy old sloop that's lying over at Tiburon. You and Nicholas can go over by the ferry, charter it for a song, and sail direct for the beds."

"Good luck be with you, boys," he said at parting, two days later. "Remember, they are dangerous men, so be careful."

Nicholas and I succeeded in chartering the sloop very cheaply; and between laughs, while getting up sail, we agreed that she was even crazier and older than she had been described. She was a big, flat-bottomed, square-sterned craft, sloop-rigged, with a sprung mast, slack rigging, dilapidated sails, and rotten running-gear, clumsy to handle and uncertain in bringing about, and she smelled vilely of coal tar, with which strange stuff she had been smeared from stem to stern and from cabin-roof to centreboard. And to cap it all, *Coal Tar Maggie* was printed in great white letters the whole length of either side.

It was an uneventful though laughable run from Tiburon to Asparagus Island, where we arrived in the afternoon of the following day. The oyster pirates, a fleet of a dozen sloops, were lying at anchor on what was known as the "Deserted Beds." The *Coal Tar Maggie* came sloshing into their midst with a light breeze astern, and they crowded on deck to see us. Nicholas and I had caught the spirit of the crazy craft, and we handled her in most lubberly fashion.

"Wot is it?" some one called.

"Name it 'n' ye kin have it!" called another.

"I swan naow, ef it ain't the old Ark itself!" mimicked the Centipede from the deck of the *Ghost*.

"Hey! Ahoy there, clipper ship!" another wag shouted. "Wot's yer port?"

We took no notice of the joking, but acted, after the manner of greenhorns, as though the *Coal Tar Maggie* required our undivided attention. I rounded her well to windward of the *Ghost*, and Nicholas ran for'ard to drop the anchor. To all appearances it was a bungle, the way the chain tangled and kept the anchor from reaching the bottom. And to all appearances Nicholas and I were terribly excited as we strove to clear it. At any rate, we quite deceived the pirates, who took huge delight in our predicament.

But the chain remained tangled, and amid all kinds of mocking advice we drifted down upon and fouled the *Ghost*, whose bowsprit poked square through our mainsail and ripped a hole in it as big as a barn door. The Centipede and the Porpoise doubled up on the cabin in paroxysms of laughter, and left us to get clear as best we could. This, with much unseamanlike performance, we succeeded in doing, and likewise in clearing the anchor-chain, of which we let out about three hundred feet. With only ten feet of water under us, this would permit the *Coal Tar Maggie* to swing in a circle six hundred feet in diameter, in which circle she would be able to foul at least half the fleet.

The oyster pirates lay snugly together at short hawsers, the weather being fine, and they protested loudly at our ignorance in putting out such an unwarranted length of anchor-chain. And not only did they protest, for they made us heave it in again, all but thirty feet.

Having sufficiently impressed them with our general lubberliness, Nicholas and I went below to congratulate ourselves and to cook supper. Hardly had we finished the meal and washed the dishes, when a skiff ground against the *Coal Tar Maggie's* side, and heavy feet trampled on deck. Then the Centipede's brutal face appeared in the companionway, and he descended into the cabin, followed by the Porpoise. Before they could seat themselves on a bunk, another skiff came alongside, and another, and another, till the whole fleet was represented by the gathering in the cabin.

"Where'd you swipe the old tub?" asked a squat and hairy man, with cruel eyes and Mexican features.

"Didn't swipe it," Nicholas answered, meeting them on their own ground and encouraging the idea that we had stolen the *Coal Tar Maggie*. "And if we did, what of it?"

"Well, I don't admire your taste, that's all," sneered he of the Mexican features. "I'd rot on the beach first before I'd take a tub that couldn't get out of its own way."

"How were we to know till we tried her?" Nicholas asked, so innocently as to cause a laugh. "And how do you get the oysters?" he hurried on. "We want a load of them; that's what we came for, a load of oysters."

"What d'ye want 'em for?" demanded the Porpoise.

"Oh, to give away to our friends, of course," Nicholas retorted. "That's what you do with yours, I suppose."

This started another laugh, and as our visitors grew more genial we could see that they had not the slightest suspicion of our identity or purpose.

"Didn't I see you on the dock in Oakland the other day?" the Centipede asked suddenly of me.

"Yep," I answered boldly, taking the bull by the horns. "I was watching you fellows and figuring out whether we'd go oystering or not. It's a pretty good business, I calculate, and so we're going in for it. That is," I hastened to add, "if you fellows don't mind."

"I'll tell you one thing, which ain't two things," he replied, "and that is you'll have to hump yerself an' get a better boat. We won't stand to be disgraced by any such box as this. Understand?"

"Sure," I said. "Soon as we sell some oysters we'll outfit in style."

"And if you show yerself square an' the right sort," he went on, "why, you kin run with us. But if you don't" (here his voice became stern and menacing), "why, it'll be the sickest day of yer life. Understand?"

"Sure," I said.

After that and more warning and advice of similar nature, the conversation became general, and we learned that the beds were to be raided that very night. As they got into their boats, after an hour's stay, we were invited to join them in the raid with the assurance of "the more the merrier."

"Did you notice that short, Mexican-looking chap?" Nicholas asked, when they had departed to their various sloops. "He's Barchi, of the Sporting Life Gang, and the fellow that came with him is Skilling. They're both out now on five thousand dollars' bail."

I had heard of the Sporting Life Gang before, a crowd of hoodlums and criminals that terrorized the lower quarters of Oakland, and two-thirds of which were usually to be found in state's prison for crimes that ranged from perjury and ballot-box stuffing to murder.

"They are not regular oyster pirates," Nicholas continued. "They've just come down for the lark and to make a few dollars. But we'll have to watch out for them."

We sat in the cockpit and discussed the details of our plan till eleven o'clock had passed, when we heard the rattle of an oar in a boat from the direction of the *Ghost*. We hauled up our own skiff, tossed in a few sacks, and rowed over. There we found all the skiffs assembling, it being the intention to raid the beds in a body.

To my surprise, I found barely a foot of water where we had dropped anchor in ten feet. It was the big June run-out of the full moon, and as the ebb had yet an hour and a half to run, I knew that our anchorage would be dry ground before slack water.

Mr. Taft's beds were three miles away, and for a long time we rowed silently in the wake of the other boats, once in a while grounding and our oar blades constantly striking bottom. At last we came upon soft mud covered with not more than two inches of water—not enough to float the boats. But the pirates at once were over the side, and by pushing and pulling on the flat-bottomed skiffs, we moved steadily along.

The full moon was partly obscured by high-flying clouds, but the pirates went their way with the familiarity born of long practice. After half a mile of the mud, we came upon a deep channel, up which we rowed, with dead oyster shoals looming high and dry on either side. At last we reached the picking grounds. Two men, on one of the shoals, hailed us and warned us off. But the Centipede, the Porpoise, Barchi, and Skilling took the lead, and followed by the rest of us, at least thirty men in half as many boats, rowed right up to the watchmen.

"You'd better slide outa this here," Barchi said threateningly, "or we'll fill you so full of holes you wouldn't float in molasses."

The watchmen wisely retreated before so overwhelming a force, and rowed their boat along the channel toward where the shore should be. Besides, it was in the plan for them to retreat.

We hauled the noses of the boats up on the shore side of a big shoal, and all hands, with sacks, spread out and began picking. Every now and again the clouds thinned before the face of the moon, and we could see the big oysters quite distinctly. In almost no time sacks were filled and carried back to the boats, where fresh ones were obtained. Nicholas and I returned often and anxiously to the boats with our little loads, but always found some one of the pirates coming or going.

"Never mind," he said; "no hurry. As they pick farther and farther away, it will take too long to carry to the boats. Then they'll stand the full sacks on end and pick them up when the tide comes in and the skiffs will float to them."

Fully half an hour went by, and the tide had begun to flood, when this came to pass. Leaving the pirates at their work, we stole back to the boats. One by one, and noiselessly, we shoved them off and made them fast in an awkward flotilla. Just as we were shoving off the last skiff, our own, one of the men came upon us. It was Barchi. His quick eye took in the situation at a glance, and he sprang for us; but we went clear with a mighty shove, and he was left floundering in the water over his head. As soon as he got back to the shoal he raised his voice and gave the alarm.

We rowed with all our strength, but it was slow going with so many boats in tow. A pistol cracked from the shoal, a second, and a third; then a regular fusillade began. The bullets spat and spat all about us; but thick clouds had covered the moon, and in the dim darkness it was no more than random firing. It was only by chance that we could be hit.

"Wish we had a little steam launch," I panted.

"I'd just as soon the moon stayed hidden," Nicholas panted back.

It was slow work, but every stroke carried us farther away from the shoal and nearer the shore, till at last the shooting died down, and when the moon did come out we were too far away to be in danger. Not long afterward we answered a shoreward hail, and two Whitehall boats, each pulled by three pairs of oars, darted up to us. Charley's welcome face bent over to us, and he gripped us by the hands while he cried, "Oh, you joys! You joys! Both of you!"

When the flotilla had been landed, Nicholas and I and a watchman rowed out in one of the Whitehalls, with Charley in the stern-sheets. Two other Whitehalls followed us, and as the moon now shone brightly, we easily made out the oyster pirates on their lonely shoal. As we drew closer, they fired a rattling volley from their revolvers, and we promptly retreated beyond range.

"Lot of time," Charley said. "The flood is setting in fast, and by the time it's up to their necks there won't be any fight left in them."

So we lay on our oars and waited for the tide to do its work. This was the predicament of the pirates: because of the big run-out, the tide was now rushing back like a mill-race, and it was impossible for the strongest swimmer in the world to make against it the three miles to the sloops. Between the pirates and the shore were we, precluding escape in that direction. On the other hand, the water was rising rapidly over the shoals, and it was only a question of a few hours when it would be over their heads.

It was beautifully calm, and in the brilliant white moonlight we watched them through our night glasses and told Charley of the voyage of the *Coal Tar Maggie*. One o'clock came, and two o'clock, and the pirates were clustering on the highest shoal, waist-deep in water.

"Now this illustrates the value of imagination," Charley was saying. "Taft has been trying for years to get them, but he went at it with bull strength and failed. Now we used our heads . . ."

Just then I heard a scarcely audible gurgle of water, and holding up my hand for silence, I turned and pointed to a ripple slowly widening out in a growing circle. It was not more than fifty feet from us. We kept perfectly quiet and waited. After a minute the water broke six feet away, and a black head and white shoulder showed in the moonlight. With a snort of surprise and of suddenly expelled breath, the head and shoulder went down.

We pulled ahead several strokes and drifted with the current. Four pairs of eyes searched the surface of the water, but never another ripple showed, and never another glimpse did we catch of the black head and white shoulder.

"It's the Porpoise," Nicholas said. "It would take broad daylight for us to catch him."

At a quarter to three the pirates gave their first sign of weakening. We heard cries for help, in the unmistakable voice of the Centipede, and this time, on rowing closer, we were not fired upon. The Centipede was in a truly perilous plight. Only the heads and shoulders of his fellow-marauders showed above the water as they braced themselves against the current, while his feet were off the bottom and they were supporting him.

"Now, lads," Charley said briskly, "we have got you, and you can't get away. If you cut up rough, we'll have to leave you alone and the water will finish you. But if you're good we'll take you aboard, one man at a time, and you'll all be saved. What do you say?"

"Ay," they chorused hoarsely between their chattering teeth.

"Then one man at a time, and the short men first."

The Centipede was the first to be pulled aboard, and he came willingly, though he objected when the constable put the handcuffs on him. Barchi was next hauled in, quite meek and resigned from his soaking. When we had ten in, our boat we drew back, and the second Whitehall was loaded. The third Whitehall received nine prisoners only—a catch of twenty-nine in all.

"You didn't get the Porpoise," the Centipede said exultantly, as though his escape materially diminished our success.

Charley laughed. "But we saw him just the same, a-snorting for shore like a puffing pig."

It was a mild and shivering band of pirates that we marched up the beach to the oyster house. In answer to Charley's knock, the door was flung open, and a pleasant wave of warm air rushed out upon us.

"You can dry your clothes here, lads, and get some hot coffee," Charley announced, as they filed in.

And there, sitting ruefully by the fire, with a steaming mug in his hand, was the Porpoise. With one accord Nicholas and I looked at Charley. He laughed gleefully.

"That comes of imagination," he said. "When you see a thing, you've got to see it all around, or what's the good of seeing it at all? I saw the beach, so I left a couple of constables behind to keep an eye on it. That's all."

## 4

# THE SIEGE OF THE "LANCASHIRE QUEEN"

Possibly our most exasperating experience on the fish patrol was when Charley Le Grant and I laid a two weeks' siege to a big four-masted English ship. Before we had finished with the affair, it became a pretty mathematical problem, and it was by the merest chance that we came into possession of the instrument that brought it to a successful termination.

After our raid on the oyster pirates we had returned to Oakland, where two more weeks passed before Neil Partington's wife was out of danger and on the highroad to recovery. So it was after an absence of a month, all told, that we turned the *Reindeer's* nose toward Benicia. When the cat's away the mice will play, and in these four weeks the fishermen had become very bold in violating the law. When we passed Point Pedro we noticed many signs of activity among the shrimp-catchers, and, well into San Pablo Bay, we observed a widely scattered fleet of Upper Bay fishing-boats hastily pulling in their nets and getting up sail.

This was suspicious enough to warrant investigation, and the first and only boat we succeeded in boarding proved to have an illegal net. The law permitted no smaller mesh for catching shad than one that measured seven and one-half inches inside the knots, while the mesh of this particular net measured only three inches. It was a flagrant breach of the rules, and the two fishermen were forthwith put under arrest. Neil Partington took one of them with him to help manage the *Reindeer*, while Charley and I went on ahead with the other in the captured boat.

But the shad fleet had headed over toward the Petaluma shore in wild flight, and for the rest of the run through San Pablo Bay we saw no more fishermen at all. Our prisoner, a bronzed and bearded Greek, sat sullenly on his net while we sailed his craft. It was a new Columbia River salmon boat, evidently on its first trip, and it handled splendidly. Even when Charley praised it, our prisoner refused to speak or to notice us, and we soon gave him up as a most unsociable fellow.

We ran up the Carquinez Straits and edged into the bight at Turner's Shipyard for smoother water. Here were lying several English steel sailing ships, waiting for the wheat harvest; and here, most unexpectedly, in the precise place where we had captured Big Alec, we came upon two Italians in a skiff that was loaded with a complete "Chinese" sturgeon line. The surprise was mutual, and we were on top of them before either they or we were aware. Charley had barely time to luff into the wind and run up to them. I ran forward and tossed them a line with orders to make it fast. One of the Italians took a turn with it over a cleat, while I hastened to lower our big spritsail. This accomplished, the salmon boat dropped astern, dragging heavily on the skiff.

Charley came forward to board the prize, but when I proceeded to haul alongside by means of the line, the Italians cast it off. We at once began drifting to leeward, while they got out two pairs of oars and rowed their light craft directly into the wind. This manœuvre for the moment disconcerted us, for in our large and heavily loaded boat we could not hope to catch them with the oars. But our prisoner came unexpectedly to our aid. His black eyes were flashing eagerly, and his face was flushed with suppressed excitement, as he dropped the centre-board, sprang forward with a single leap, and put up the sail.

"I've always heard that Greeks don't like Italians," Charley laughed, as he ran aft to the tiller.

And never in my experience have I seen a man so anxious for the capture of another as was our prisoner in the chase that followed. His eyes fairly snapped, and his nostrils quivered and dilated in a most extraordinary way. Charley steered while he tended the sheet; and though Charley was as quick and alert as a cat, the Greek could hardly control his impatience.

The Italians were cut off from the shore, which was fully a mile away at its nearest point. Did they attempt to make it, we could haul after them with the wind abeam, and overtake them before they had covered an eighth of the distance. But they were too wise to attempt it, contenting themselves with rowing lustily to windward along the starboard side of a big ship, the *Lancashire Queen*. But beyond the ship lay an open stretch of fully two miles to the shore in that direction. This, also, they dared not attempt, for we were bound to catch them before they could cover it. So, when they reached the bow of the *Lancashire Queen*, nothing remained but to pass around and row down her port side toward the stern, which meant rowing to leeward and giving us the advantage.

We in the salmon boat, sailing close on the wind, tacked about and crossed the ship's bow. Then Charley put up the tiller and headed down the port side of the ship, the Greek letting out the sheet and grinning with delight. The Italians were already half-way down the ship's length; but the stiff breeze at our back drove us after them far faster than they could row. Closer and closer we came, and I, lying down forward, was just reaching out to grasp the skiff, when it ducked under the great stern of the *Lancashire Queen*.

The chase was virtually where it had begun. The Italians were rowing up the starboard side of the ship, and we were hauled close on the wind and slowly edging out from the ship as we worked to windward. Then they darted around her bow and began the row down her port side, and we tacked about, crossed her bow, and went plunging down the wind hot after them. And again, just as I was reaching for the skiff, it ducked under the ship's stern and out of danger. And so it went, around and around, the skiff each time just barely ducking into safety.

By this time the ship's crew had become aware of what was taking place, and we could see their heads in a long row as they looked at us over the bulwarks. Each time we missed the skiff at the stern, they set up a wild cheer and dashed across to the other side of the *Lancashire Queen* to see the chase to windward. They showered us and the Italians with jokes and advice, and made our Greek so angry that at least once on each circuit he raised his fist and shook it at them in a rage. They came to look for this, and at each display greeted it with uproarious mirth.

"Wot a circus!" cried one.

"Tork about yer marine hippodromes,—if this ain't one, I'd like to know!" affirmed another.

"Six-days-go-as-yer-please," announced a third. "Who says the dagoes won't win?"

On the next tack to windward the Greek offered to change places with Charley.

"Let-a me sail-a de boat," he demanded. "I fix-a them, I catch-a them, sure."

This was a stroke at Charley's professional pride, for pride himself he did upon his boat-sailing abilities; but he yielded the tiller to the prisoner and took his place at the sheet. Three times again we made the circuit, and the Greek found that he could get no more speed out of the salmon boat than Charley had.

"Better give it up," one of the sailors advised from above.

The Greek scowled ferociously and shook his fist in his customary fashion. In the meanwhile my mind had not been idle, and I had finally evolved an idea.

"Keep going, Charley, one time more," I said.

And as we laid out on the next tack to windward, I bent a piece of line to a small grappling hook I had seen lying in the bail-hole. The end of the line I made fast to the ring-bolt in the bow, and with the hook out of sight I waited for the next opportunity to use it. Once more they made their leeward pull down the port side of the *Lancashire Queen*, and once more we churned down after them before the wind. Nearer and nearer we drew, and I was making believe to reach for them as before. The stern of the skiff was not six feet away, and they were laughing at me derisively as they ducked under the ship's stern. At that instant I suddenly arose and threw the grappling iron. It caught fairly and squarely on the rail of the skiff, which was jerked backward out of safety as the rope tautened and the salmon boat ploughed on.

A groan went up from the row of sailors above, which quickly changed to a cheer as one of the Italians whipped out a long sheath-knife and cut the rope. But we had drawn them out of safety, and Charley, from his place in the stern-sheets, reached over and clutched the stern of the skiff. The whole thing happened in a second of time, for the first Italian was cutting the rope and Charley was clutching the skiff when the second Italian dealt him a rap over the head with an oar, Charley released his hold and collapsed, stunned, into the bottom of the salmon boat, and the Italians bent to their oars and escaped back under the ship's stern.

The Greek took both tiller and sheet and continued the chase around the *Lancashire Queen*, while I attended to Charley, on whose head a nasty lump was rapidly rising. Our sailor audience was wild with delight, and to a man encouraged the fleeing Italians. Charley sat up, with one hand on his head, and gazed about him sheepishly.

"It will never do to let them escape now," he said, at the same time drawing his revolver.

On our next circuit, he threatened the Italians with the weapon; but they rowed on stolidly, keeping splendid stroke and utterly disregarding him.

"If you don't stop, I'll shoot," Charley said menacingly.

But this had no effect, nor were they to be frightened into surrendering even when he fired several shots dangerously close to them. It was too much to expect him to shoot unarmed men, and this they knew as well as we did; so they continued to pull doggedly round and round the ship.

"We'll run them down, then!" Charley exclaimed. "We'll wear them out and wind them!"

So the chase continued. Twenty times more we ran them around the *Lancashire Queen*, and at last we could see that even their iron muscles were giving out. They were nearly exhausted, and it was only a matter of a few more circuits, when the game took on a new feature. On the row to windward they always gained on us, so that they were half-way down the ship's side on the row to leeward when we were passing the bow. But this last time, as we passed the bow, we saw them escaping up the ship's gangway, which had been suddenly lowered. It was an organized move on the part of the sailors, evidently countenanced by the captain; for by the time we arrived where the gangway had been, it was being hoisted up, and the skiff, slung in the ship's davits, was likewise flying aloft out of reach.

The parley that followed with the captain was short and snappy. He absolutely forbade us to board the *Lancashire Queen*, and as absolutely refused to give up the two men. By this time Charley was as enraged as the Greek. Not only had he been foiled in a long and ridiculous chase, but he had been knocked senseless into the bottom of his boat by the men who had escaped him.

"Knock off my head with little apples," he declared emphatically, striking the fist of one hand into the palm of the other, "if those two men ever escape me! I'll stay here to get them if it takes the rest of my natural life, and if I don't get them, then I promise you I'll live unnaturally long or until I do get them, or my name's not Charley Le Grant!"

And then began the siege of the *Lancashire Queen*, a siege memorable in the annals of both fishermen and fish patrol. When the *Reindeer* came along, after a fruitless pursuit of the shad fleet, Charley instructed Neil Partington to send out his own salmon boat, with blankets, provisions, and a fisherman's charcoal stove. By sunset this exchange of boats was made, and we said good-by to our Greek, who perforce had to go into Benicia and be locked up for his own violation of the law. After supper, Charley and I kept alternate four-hour watches till daylight. The fishermen made no attempt to escape that night, though the ship sent out a boat for scouting purposes to find if the coast were clear.

By the next day we saw that a steady siege was in order, and we perfected our plans with an eye to our own comfort. A dock, known as the Solano Wharf, which ran out from the Benicia shore, helped us in this. It happened that the *Lancashire Queen*, the shore at Turner's Shipyard, and the Solano Wharf were the corners of a big equilateral triangle. From ship to shore, the side of the triangle along which the Italians had to escape, was a distance equal to that from the Solano Wharf to the shore, the side of the triangle along which we had to travel to get to the shore before the Italians. But as we could sail much faster than they could row, we could permit them to travel about half their side of the triangle before we darted out along our side. If we allowed them to get more than half-way, they were certain to beat us to shore; while if we started before they were half-way, they were equally certain to beat us back to the ship.

We found that an imaginary line, drawn from the end of the wharf to a windmill farther along the shore, cut precisely in half the line of the triangle along which the Italians must escape to reach the land. This line made it easy for us to determine how far to let them run away before we bestirred ourselves in pursuit. Day after day we would watch them through our glasses as they rowed leisurely along toward the half-way point; and as they drew close into line with the windmill, we would leap into the boat and get up sail. At sight of our preparation, they would turn and row slowly back to the *Lancashire Queen*, secure in the knowledge that we could not overtake them.

To guard against calms—when our salmon boat would be useless—we also had in readiness a light rowing skiff equipped with spoon-oars. But at such times, when the wind failed us, we were forced to row out from the wharf as soon as they rowed from the ship. In the night-time, on the other hand, we were compelled to patrol the immediate vicinity of the ship; which we did, Charley and I standing four-hour watches turn and turn about. The Italians, however, preferred the daytime in which to escape, and so our long night vigils were without result.

"What makes me mad," said Charley, "is our being kept from our honest beds while those rascally lawbreakers are sleeping soundly every night. But much good may it do them," he threatened. "I'll keep them on that ship till the captain charges them board, as sure as a sturgeon's not a catfish!"

It was a tantalizing problem that confronted us. As long as we were vigilant, they could not escape; and as long as they were careful, we would be unable to catch them. Charley cudgelled his brains continually, but for once his imagination failed him. It was a problem apparently without other solution than that of patience. It was a waiting game, and whichever waited the longer was bound to win. To add to our irritation, friends of the Italians established a code of signals with them from the shore, so that we never dared relax the siege for a moment. And besides this, there were always one or two suspicious-looking fishermen hanging around the Solano Wharf and keeping watch on our actions. We could do nothing but "grin and bear it," as Charley said, while it took up all our time and prevented us from doing other work.

The days went by, and there was no change in the situation. Not that no attempts were made to change it. One night friends from the shore came out in a skiff and attempted to confuse us while the two Italians escaped. That they did not succeed was due to the lack of a little oil on the ship's davits. For we were drawn back from the pursuit of the strange boat by the creaking of the davits, and arrived at the *Lancashire Queen* just as the Italians were lowering their skiff. Another night, fully half a dozen skiffs rowed around us in the darkness, but we held on like a leech to the side of the ship and frustrated their plan till they grew angry and showered us with abuse. Charley laughed to himself in the bottom of the boat.

"It's a good sign, lad," he said to me. "When men begin to abuse, make sure they're losing patience; and shortly after they lose patience, they lose their heads. Mark my words, if we only hold out, they'll get careless some fine day, and then we'll get them."

But they did not grow careless, and Charley confessed that this was one of the times when all signs failed. Their patience seemed equal to ours, and the second week of the siege dragged monotonously along. Then Charley's lagging imagination quickened sufficiently to suggest a ruse. Peter Boyelen, a new patrolman and one unknown to the fisher-folk, happened to arrive in Benicia and we took him into our plan. We were as secret as possible about it, but in some unfathomable way the friends ashore got word to the beleaguered Italians to keep their eyes open.

On the night we were to put our ruse into effect, Charley and I took up our usual station in our rowing skiff alongside the *Lancashire Queen*. After it was thoroughly dark, Peter Boyelen came out in a crazy duck boat, the kind you can pick up and carry away under one arm. When we heard him coming along, paddling noisily, we slipped away a short distance into the darkness, and rested on our oars. Opposite the gangway, having jovially hailed the anchor-watch of the *Lancashire Queen* and asked the direction of the *Scottish Chiefs*, another wheat ship, he awkwardly capsized himself. The man who was standing the anchor-watch ran down the gangway and hauled him out of the water. This was what he wanted, to get aboard the ship; and the next thing he expected was to be taken on deck and then below to warm up and dry out. But the captain inhospitably kept him perched on the lowest gangway step, shivering miserably and with his feet dangling in the water, till we, out of very pity, rowed in from the darkness and took him off. The jokes and gibes of the awakened crew sounded anything but sweet in our ears, and even the two Italians climbed up on the rail and laughed down at us long and maliciously.

"That's all right," Charley said in a low voice, which I only could hear. "I'm mighty glad it's not us that's laughing first. We'll save our laugh to the end, eh, lad?"

He clapped a hand on my shoulder as he finished, but it seemed to me that there was more determination than hope in his voice.

It would have been possible for us to secure the aid of United States marshals and board the English ship, backed by Government authority. But the instructions of the Fish Commission were to the effect that the patrolmen should avoid complications, and this one, did we call on the higher powers, might well end in a pretty international tangle.

The second week of the siege drew to its close, and there was no sign of change in the situation. On the morning of the fourteenth day the change came, and it came in a guise as unexpected and startling to us as it was to the men we were striving to capture.

Charley and I, after our customary night vigil by the side of the *Lancashire Queen*, rowed into the Solana Wharf.

"Hello!" cried Charley, in surprise. "In the name of reason and common sense, what is that? Of all unmannerly craft did you ever see the like?"

Well might he exclaim, for there, tied up to the dock, lay the strangest looking launch I had ever seen. Not that it could be called a launch, either, but it seemed to resemble a launch more than any other kind of boat. It was seventy feet long, but so narrow was it, and so bare of superstructure, that it appeared much smaller than it really was. It was built wholly of steel, and was painted black. Three smokestacks, a good distance apart and raking well aft, arose in single file amidships; while the bow, long and lean and sharp as a knife, plainly advertised that the boat was made for speed. Passing under the stern, we read *Streak*, painted in small white letters.

Charley and I were consumed with curiosity. In a few minutes we were on board and talking with an engineer who was watching the sunrise from the deck. He was quite willing to satisfy our curiosity, and in a few minutes we learned that the *Streak* had come in after dark from San Francisco; that this was what might be called the trial trip; and that she was the property of Silas Tate, a young mining millionaire of California, whose fad was high-speed yachts. There was some talk about turbine engines, direct application of steam, and the absence of pistons, rods, and cranks,—all of which was beyond me, for I was familiar only with sailing craft; but I did understand the last words of the engineer.

"Four thousand horse-power and forty-five miles an hour, though you wouldn't think it," he concluded proudly.

"Say it again, man! Say it again!" Charley exclaimed in an excited voice.

"Four thousand horse-power and forty-five miles an hour," the engineer repeated, grinning good-naturedly.

"Where's the owner?" was Charley's next question. "Is there any way I can speak to him?"

The engineer shook his head. "No, I'm afraid not. He's asleep, you see."

At that moment a young man in blue uniform came on deck farther aft and stood regarding the sunrise.

"There he is, that's him, that's Mr. Tate," said the engineer.

Charley walked aft and spoke to him, and while he talked earnestly the young man listened with an amused expression on his face. He must have inquired about the depth of water close in to the shore at Turner's Shipyard, for I could see Charley making gestures and explaining. A few minutes later he came back in high glee.

"Come on lad," he said. "On to the dock with you. We've got them!"

It was our good fortune to leave the *Streak* when we did, for a little later one of the spy fishermen appeared. Charley and I took up our accustomed places, on the stringer-piece, a little ahead of the *Streak* and over our own boat, where we could comfortably watch the

*Lancashire Queen*. Nothing occurred till about nine o'clock, when we saw the two Italians leave the ship and pull along their side of the triangle toward the shore. Charley looked as unconcerned as could be, but before they had covered a quarter of the distance, he whispered to me:

"Forty-five miles an hour . . . nothing can save them . . . they are ours!"

Slowly the two men rowed along till they were nearly in line with the windmill. This was the point where we always jumped into our salmon boat and got up the sail, and the two men, evidently expecting it, seemed surprised when we gave no sign.

When they were directly in line with the windmill, as near to the shore as to the ship, and nearer the shore than we had ever allowed them before, they grew suspicious. We followed them through the glasses, and saw them standing up in the skiff and trying to find out what we were doing. The spy fisherman, sitting beside us on the stringer-piece was likewise puzzled. He could not understand our inactivity. The men in the skiff rowed nearer the shore, but stood up again and scanned it, as if they thought we might be in hiding there. But a man came out on the beach and waved a handkerchief to indicate that the coast was clear. That settled them. They bent to the oars to make a dash for it. Still Charley waited. Not until they had covered three-quarters of the distance from the *Lancashire Queen*, which left them hardly more than a quarter of a mile to gain the shore, did Charley slap me on the shoulder and cry:

"They're ours! They're ours!"

We ran the few steps to the side of the *Streak* and jumped aboard. Stern and bow lines were cast off in a jiffy. The *Streak* shot ahead and away from the wharf. The spy fisherman we had left behind on the stringer-piece pulled out a revolver and fired five shots into the air in rapid succession. The men in the skiff gave instant heed to the warning, for we could see them pulling away like mad.

But if they pulled like mad, I wonder how our progress can be described? We fairly flew. So frightful was the speed with which we displaced the water, that a wave rose up on either side our bow and foamed aft in a series of three stiff, up-standing waves, while astern a great crested billow pursued us hungrily, as though at each moment it would fall aboard and destroy us. The *Streak* was pulsing and vibrating and roaring like a thing alive. The wind of our progress was like a gale—a forty-five-mile gale. We could not face it and draw breath without choking and strangling. It blew the smoke straight back from the mouths of the smoke-stacks at a direct right angle to the perpendicular. In fact, we were travelling as fast as an express train. "We just *streaked* it," was the way Charley told it afterward, and I think his description comes nearer than any I can give.

As for the Italians in the skiff—hardly had we started, it seemed to me, when we were on top of them. Naturally, we had to slow down long before we got to them; but even then we shot past like a whirlwind and were compelled to circle back between them and the shore. They had rowed steadily, rising from the thwarts at every stroke, up to the moment we passed them, when they recognized Charley and me. That took the last bit of fight out of them. They hauled in their oars, and sullenly submitted to arrest.

"Well, Charley," Neil Partington said, as we discussed it on the wharf afterward, "I fail to see where your boasted imagination came into play this time."

But Charley was true to his hobby. "Imagination?" he demanded, pointing to the *Streak*. "Look at that! just look at it! If the invention of that isn't imagination, I should like to know what is."

"Of course," he added, "it's the other fellow's imagination, but it did the work all the same."

## 5

# CHARLEY'S COUP

Perhaps our most laughable exploit on the fish patrol, and at the same time our most dangerous one, was when we rounded in, at a single haul, an even score of wrathful fishermen. Charley called it a "coop," having heard Neil Partington use the term; but I think he misunderstood the word, and thought it meant "coop," to catch, to trap. The fishermen, however, coup or coop, must have called it a Waterloo, for it was the severest stroke ever dealt them by the fish patrol, while they had invited it by open and impudent defiance of the law.

During what is called the "open season" the fishermen might catch as many salmon as their luck allowed and their boats could hold. But there was one important restriction. From sun-down Saturday night to sun-up Monday morning, they were not permitted to set a net. This was a wise provision on the part of the Fish Commission, for it was necessary to give the spawning salmon some opportunity to ascend the river and lay their eggs. And this law, with only an occasional violation, had been obediently observed by the Greek fishermen who caught salmon for the canneries and the market.

One Sunday morning, Charley received a telephone call from a friend in Collinsville, who told him that the full force of fishermen was out with its nets. Charley and I jumped into our salmon boat and started for the scene of the trouble. With a light favoring wind at our back we went through the Carquinez Straits, crossed Suisun Bay, passed the Ship Island Light, and came upon the whole fleet at work.

But first let me describe the method by which they worked. The net used is what is known as a gill-net. It has a simple diamond-shaped mesh which measures at least seven and one-half inches between the knots. From five to seven and even eight hundred feet in length, these nets are only a few feet wide. They are not stationary, but float with the current, the upper edge supported on the surface by floats, the lower edge sunk by means of leaden weights.

This arrangement keeps the net upright in the current and effectually prevents all but the smaller fish from ascending the river. The salmon, swimming near the surface, as is their custom, run their heads through these meshes, and are prevented from going on through by their larger girth of body, and from going back because of their gills, which catch in the mesh. It requires two fishermen to set such a net,—one to row the boat, while the other, standing in the stern, carefully pays out the net. When it is all out, stretching directly across the stream, the men make their boat fast to one end of the net and drift along with it.

As we came upon the fleet of law-breaking fishermen, each boat two or three hundred yards from its neighbors, and boats and nets dotting the river as far as we could see, Charley said:

"I've only one regret, lad, and that is that I have'nt a thousand arms so as to be able to catch them all. As it is, we'll only be able to catch one boat, for while we are tackling that one it will be up nets and away with the rest."

As we drew closer, we observed none of the usual flurry and excitement which our appearance invariably produced. Instead, each boat lay quietly by its net, while the fishermen favored us with not the slightest attention.

"It's curious," Charley muttered. "Can it be they don't recognize us?"

I said that it was impossible, and Charley agreed; yet there was a whole fleet, manned by men who knew us only too well, and who took no more notice of us than if we were a hay scow or a pleasure yacht.

This did not continue to be the case, however, for as we bore down upon the nearest net, the men to whom it belonged detached their boat and rowed slowly toward the shore. The rest of the boats showed no, sign of uneasiness.

"That's funny," was Charley's remark. "But we can confiscate the net, at any rate."

We lowered sail, picked up one end of the net, and began to heave it into the boat. But at the first heave we heard a bullet zip-zipping past us on the water, followed by the faint report of a rifle. The men who had rowed ashore were shooting at us. At the next heave a second bullet went zipping past, perilously near. Charley took a turn around a pin and sat down. There were no more shots. But as soon as he began to heave in, the shooting recommenced.

"That settles it," he said, flinging the end of the net overboard. "You fellows want it worse than we do, and you can have it."

We rowed over toward the next net, for Charley was intent on finding out whether or not we were face to face with an organized defiance. As we approached, the two fishermen proceeded to cast off from their net and row ashore, while the first two rowed back and made fast to the net we had abandoned. And at the second net we were greeted by rifle shots till we desisted and went on to the third, where the manœuvre was again repeated.

Then we gave it up, completely routed, and hoisted sail and started on the long windward beat back to Benicia. A number of Sundays went by, on each of which the law was persistently violated. Yet, short of an armed force of soldiers, we could do nothing. The fishermen had hit upon a new idea and were using it for all it was worth, while there seemed no way by which we could get the better of them.

About this time Neil Partington happened along from the Lower Bay, where he had been for a number of weeks. With him was Nicholas, the Greek boy who had helped us in our raid on the oyster pirates, and the pair of them took a hand. We made our arrangements carefully. It was planned that while Charley and I tackled the nets, they were to be hidden ashore so as to ambush the fishermen who landed to shoot at us.

It was a pretty plan. Even Charley said it was. But we reckoned not half so well as the Greeks. They forestalled us by ambushing Neil and Nicholas and taking them prisoners, while, as of old, bullets whistled about our ears when Charley and I attempted to take possession of the nets. When we were again beaten off, Neil Partington and Nicholas were released. They were rather shamefaced when they put in an appearance, and Charley chaffed them unmercifully. But Neil chaffed back, demanding to know why Charley's imagination had not long since overcome the difficulty.

"Just you wait; the idea'll come all right," Charley promised.

"Most probably," Neil agreed. "But I'm afraid the salmon will be exterminated first, and then there will be no need for it when it does come."

Neil Partington, highly disgusted with his adventure, departed for the Lower Bay, taking Nicholas with him, and Charley and I were left to our own resources. This meant that the Sunday fishing would be left to itself, too, until such time as Charley's idea happened along. I puzzled my head a good deal to find out some way of checkmating the Greeks, as also did Charley, and we broached a thousand expedients which on discussion proved worthless.

The fishermen, on the other hand, were in high feather, and their boasts went up and down the river to add to our discomfiture. Among all classes of them we became aware of a growing insubordination. We were beaten, and they were losing respect for us. With the loss of respect, contempt began to arise. Charley began to be spoken of as the "olda woman," and I received my rating as the "pee-wee kid." The situation was fast becoming unbearable, and we knew that we should have to deliver a stunning stroke at the Greeks in order to regain the old-time respect in which we had stood.

Then one morning the idea came. We were down on Steamboat Wharf, where the river steamers made their landings, and where we found a group of amused long-shoremen and loafers listening to the hard-luck tale of a sleepy-eyed young fellow in long sea-boots. He was a sort of amateur fisherman, he said, fishing for the local market of Berkeley. Now Berkeley was on the Lower Bay, thirty miles away. On the previous night, he said, he had set his net and dozed off to sleep in the bottom of the boat.

The next he knew it was morning, and he opened his eyes to find his boat rubbing softly against the piles of Steamboat Wharf at Benicia. Also he saw the river steamer *Apache* lying ahead of him, and a couple of deck-hands disentangling the shreds of his net from the paddle-wheel. In short, after he had gone to sleep, his fisherman's riding light had gone out, and the *Apache* had run over his net. Though torn pretty well to pieces, the net in some way still remained foul, and he had had a thirty-mile tow out of his course.

Charley nudged me with his elbow. I grasped his thought on the instant, but objected:

"We can't charter a steamboat."

"Don't intend to," he rejoined. "But let's run over to Turner's Shipyard. I've something in my mind there that may be of use to us."

And over we went to the shipyard, where Charley led the way to the *Mary Rebecca,* lying hauled out on the ways, where she was being cleaned and overhauled. She was a scow-schooner we both knew well, carrying a cargo of one hundred and forty tons and a spread of canvas greater than other schooner on the bay.

"How d'ye do, Ole," Charley greeted a big blue-shirted Swede who was greasing the jaws of the main gaff with a piece of pork rind.

Ole grunted, puffed away at his pipe, and went on greasing. The captain of a bay schooner is supposed to work with his hands just as well as the men.

Ole Ericsen verified Charley's conjecture that the *Mary Rebecca,* as soon as launched, would run up the San Joaquin River nearly to Stockton for a load of wheat. Then Charley made his proposition, and Ole Ericsen shook his head.

"Just a hook, one good-sized hook," Charley pleaded.

"No, Ay tank not," said Ole Ericsen. "Der *Mary Rebecca* yust hang up on efery mud-bank with that hook. Ay don't want to lose der *Mary Rebecca*. She's all Ay got."

"No, no," Charley hurried to explain. "We can put the end of the hook through the bottom from the outside, and fasten it on the inside with a nut. After it's done its work, why, all we have to do is to go down into the hold, unscrew the nut, and out drops the hook. Then drive a wooden peg into the hole, and the *Mary Rebecca* will be all right again."

Ole Ericsen was obstinate for a long time; but in the end, after we had had dinner with him, he was brought round to consent.

"Ay do it, by Yupiter!" he said, striking one huge fist into the palm of the other hand. "But yust hurry you up wid der hook. Der *Mary Rebecca* slides into der water to-night."

It was Saturday, and Charley had need to hurry. We headed for the shipyard blacksmith shop, where, under Charley's directions, a most generously curved book of heavy steel was made. Back we hastened to the *Mary Rebecca*. Aft of the great centre-board case, through what was properly her keel, a hole was bored. The end of the hook was inserted from the outside, and Charley, on the inside, screwed the nut on tightly. As it stood complete, the hook projected over a foot beneath the bottom of the schooner. Its curve was something like the curve of a sickle, but deeper.

In the late afternoon the *Mary Rebecca* was launched, and preparations were finished for the start up-river next morning. Charley and Ole intently studied the evening sky for signs of wind, for without a good breeze our project was doomed to failure. They agreed that there were all the signs of a stiff westerly wind—not the ordinary afternoon sea-breeze, but a half-gale, which even then was springing up.

Next morning found their predictions verified. The sun was shining brightly, but something more than a half-gale was shrieking up the Carquinez Straits, and the *Mary Rebecca* got under way with two reefs in her mainsail and one in her foresail. We found it quite rough in the Straits and in Suisun Bay; but as the water grew more land-locked it became calm, though without let-up in the wind.

Off Ship Island Light the reefs were shaken out, and at Charley's suggestion a big fisherman's staysail was made all ready for hoisting, and the maintopsail, bunched into a cap at the masthead, was overhauled so that it could be set on an instant's notice.

We were tearing along, wing-and-wing, before the wind, foresail to starboard and mainsail to port, as we came upon the salmon fleet. There they were, boats and nets, as on that first Sunday when they had bested us, strung out evenly over the river as far as we could see. A narrow space on the right-hand side of the channel was left clear for steamboats, but the rest of the river was covered with the wide-stretching nets. The narrow space was our logical course, but Charley, at the wheel, steered the *Mary Rebecca* straight for the nets. This did not cause any alarm among the fishermen, because up-river sailing craft are always provided with "shoes" on the ends of their keels, which permit them to slip over the nets without fouling them.

"Now she takes it!" Charley cried, as we dashed across the middle of a line of floats which marked a net. At one end of this line was a small barrel buoy, at the other the two fishermen in their boat. Buoy and boat at once began to draw together, and the fishermen to cry out, as they were jerked after us. A couple of minutes later we hooked a second net, and then a third, and in this fashion we tore straight up through the centre of the fleet.

The consternation we spread among the fishermen was tremendous. As fast as we hooked a net the two ends of it, buoy and boat, came together as they dragged out astern; and so many buoys and boats, coming together at such breakneck speed, kept the fishermen on the jump to avoid smashing into one another. Also, they shouted at us like mad to heave to into the wind, for they took it as some drunken prank on the part of scow-sailors, little dreaming that we were the fish patrol.

The drag of a single net is very heavy, and Charley and Ole Ericsen decided that even in such a wind ten nets were all the *Mary Rebecca* could take along with her. So when we had hooked ten nets, with ten boats containing twenty men streaming along behind us, we veered to the left out of the fleet and headed toward Collinsville.

We were all jubilant. Charley was handling the wheel as though he were steering the winning yacht home in a race. The two sailors who made up the crew of the *Mary Rebecca,* were grinning and joking. Ole Ericsen was rubbing his huge hands in child-like glee.

"Ay tank you fish patrol fallers never ban so lucky as when you sail with Ole Ericsen," he was saying, when a rifle cracked sharply astern, and a bullet gouged along the newly painted cabin, glanced on a nail, and sang shrilly onward into space.

This was too much for Ole Ericsen. At sight of his beloved paintwork thus defaced, he jumped up and shook his fist at the fishermen; but a second bullet smashed into the cabin not six inches from his head, and he dropped down to the deck under cover of the rail.

All the fishermen had rifles, and they now opened a general fusillade. We were all driven to cover—even Charley, who was compelled to desert the wheel. Had it not been for the heavy drag of the nets, we would inevitably have broached to at the mercy of the enraged fishermen. But the nets, fastened to the bottom of the *Mary Rebecca* well aft, held her stern into the wind, and she continued to plough on, though somewhat erratically.

Charley, lying on the deck, could just manage to reach the lower spokes of the wheel; but while he could steer after a fashion, it was very awkward. Ole Ericsen bethought himself of a large piece of sheet steel in the empty hold.

It was in fact a plate from the side of the *New Jersey*, a steamer which had recently been wrecked outside the Golden Gate, and in the salving of which the *Mary Rebecca* had taken part.

Crawling carefully along the deck, the two sailors, Ole, and myself got the heavy plate on deck and aft, where we reared it as a shield between the wheel and the fishermen. The bullets whanged and banged against it till it rang like a bull's-eye, but Charley grinned in its shelter, and coolly went on steering.

So we raced along, behind us a howling, screaming bedlam of wrathful Greeks, Collinsville ahead, and bullets spat-spatting all around us.

"Ole," Charley said in a faint voice, "I don't know what we're going to do."

Ole Ericsen, lying on his back close to the rail and grinning upward at the sky, turned over on his side and looked at him. "Ay tank we go into Collinsville yust der same," he said.

"But we can't stop," Charley groaned. "I never thought of it, but we can't stop."

A look of consternation slowly overspread Ole Ericsen's broad face. It was only too true. We had a hornet's nest on our hands, and to stop at Collinsville would be to have it about our ears.

"Every man Jack of them has a gun," one of the sailors remarked cheerfully.

"Yes, and a knife, too," the other sailor added.

It was Ole Ericsen's turn to groan. "What for a Svaidish faller like me monkey with none of my biziness, I don't know," he soliloquized.

A bullet glanced on the stern and sang off to starboard like a spiteful bee. "There's nothing to do but plump the *Mary Rebecca* ashore and run for it," was the verdict of the first cheerful sailor.

"And leaf der *Mary Rebecca*?" Ole demanded, with unspeakable horror in his voice.

"Not unless you want to," was the response. "But I don't want to be within a thousand miles of her when those fellers come aboard"—indicating the bedlam of excited Greeks towing behind.

We were right in at Collinsville then, and went foaming by within biscuit-toss of the wharf.

"I only hope the wind holds out," Charley said, stealing a glance at our prisoners.

"What of der wind?" Ole demanded disconsolately. "Der river will not hold out, and then . . . and then . . ."

"It's head for tall timber, and the Greeks take the hindermost," adjudged the cheerful sailor, while Ole was stuttering over what would happen when we came to the end of the river.

We had now reached a dividing of the ways. To the left was the mouth of the Sacramento River, to the right the mouth of the San Joaquin. The cheerful sailor crept forward and jibed over the foresail as Charley put the helm to starboard and we swerved to the right into the San Joaquin. The wind, from which we had been running away on an even keel, now caught us on our beam, and the *Mary Rebecca* was pressed down on her port side as if she were about to capsize.

Still we dashed on, and still the fishermen dashed on behind. The value of their nets was greater than the fines they would have to pay for violating the fish laws; so to cast off from their nets and escape, which they could easily do, would profit them nothing. Further, they remained by their nets instinctively, as a sailor remains by his ship. And still further, the desire for vengeance was roused, and we could depend upon it that they would follow us to the ends of the earth, if we undertook to tow them that far.

The rifle-firing had ceased, and we looked astern to see what our prisoners were doing. The boats were strung along at unequal distances apart, and we saw the four nearest ones bunching together. This was done by the boat ahead trailing a small rope astern to the one behind. When this was caught, they would cast off from their net and heave in on the line till they were brought up to the boat in front. So great was the speed at which we were travelling, however, that this was very slow work. Sometimes the men would strain to their utmost and fail to get in an inch of the rope; at other times they came ahead more rapidly.

When the four boats were near enough together for a man to pass from one to another, one Greek from each of three got into the nearest boat to us, taking his rifle with him. This made five in the foremost boat, and it was plain that their intention was to board us. This they undertook to do, by main strength and sweat, running hand over hand the float-line of a net. And though it was slow, and they stopped frequently to rest, they gradually drew nearer.

Charley smiled at their efforts, and said, "Give her the topsail, Ole."

The cap at the mainmast head was broken out, and sheet and downhaul pulled flat, amid a scattering rifle fire from the boats; and the *Mary Rebecca* lay over and sprang ahead faster than ever.

But the Greeks were undaunted. Unable, at the increased speed, to draw themselves nearer by means of their hands, they rigged from the blocks of their boat sail what sailors call a "watch-tackle." One of them, held by the legs by his mates, would lean far over the bow and make the tackle fast to the float-line. Then they would heave in on the tackle till the blocks were together, when the manœuvre would be repeated.

"Have to give her the staysail," Charley said.

Ole Ericsen looked at the straining *Mary Rebecca* and shook his head. "It will take der masts out of her," he said.

"And we'll be taken out of her if you don't," Charley replied.

Ole shot an anxious glance at his masts, another at the boat load of armed Greeks, and consented.

The five men were in the bow of the boat—a bad place when a craft is towing. I was watching the behavior of their boat as the great fisherman's staysail, far, far larger than the topsail and used only in light breezes, was broken out. As the *Mary Rebecca* lurched forward with a tremendous jerk, the nose of the boat ducked down into the water, and the men tumbled over one another in a wild rush into the stern to save the boat from being dragged sheer under water.

"That settles them!" Charley remarked, though he was anxiously studying the behavior of the *Mary Rebecca*, which was being driven under far more canvas than she was rightly able to carry.

"Next stop is Antioch!" announced the cheerful sailor, after the manner of a railway conductor. "And next comes Merryweather!"

"Come here, quick," Charley said to me.

I crawled across the deck and stood upright beside him in the shelter of the sheet steel.

"Feel in my inside pocket," he commanded, "and get my notebook. That's right. Tear out a blank page and write what I tell you."

And this is what I wrote:

> Telephone to Merryweather, to the sheriff, the constable, or the judge. Tell them we are coming and to turn out the town. Arm everybody. Have them down on the wharf to meet us or we are gone gooses.

"Now make it good and fast to that marlin-spike, and stand by to toss it ashore."

I did as he directed. By then we were close to Antioch. The wind was shouting through our rigging, the *Mary Rebecca* was half over on her side and rushing ahead like an ocean greyhound. The seafaring folk of Antioch had seen us breaking out topsail and staysail, a most reckless performance in such weather, and had hurried to the wharf-ends in little groups to find out what was the matter.

Straight down the water front we boomed, Charley edging in till a man could almost leap ashore. When he gave the signal I tossed the marlinspike. It struck the planking of the wharf a resounding smash, bounced along fifteen or twenty feet, and was pounced upon by the amazed onlookers.

It all happened in a flash, for the next minute Antioch was behind and we were heeling it up the San Joaquin toward Merryweather, six miles away. The river straightened out here into its general easterly course, and we squared away before the wind, wing-and-wing once more, the foresail bellying out to starboard.

Ole Ericsen seemed sunk into a state of stolid despair. Charley and the two sailors were looking hopeful, as they had good reason to be. Merryweather was a coal-mining town, and, it being Sunday, it was reasonable to expect the men to be in town. Further, the coal-miners had never lost any love for the Greek fishermen, and were pretty certain to render us hearty assistance.

We strained our eyes for a glimpse of the town, and the first sight we caught of it gave us immense relief. The wharves were black with men. As we came closer, we could see them still arriving, stringing down the main street, guns in their hands and on the run. Charley glanced astern at the fishermen with a look of ownership in his eye which till then had been missing. The Greeks were plainly overawed by the display of armed strength and were putting their own rifles away.

We took in topsail and staysail, dropped the main peak, and as we got abreast of the principal wharf jibed the mainsail. The *Mary Rebecca* shot around into the wind, the captive fishermen describing a great arc behind her, and forged ahead till she lost way, when lines we're flung ashore and she was made fast. This was accomplished under a hurricane of cheers from the delighted miners.

Ole Ericsen heaved a great sigh. "Ay never tank Ay see my wife never again," he confessed.

"Why, we were never in any danger," said Charley.

Ole looked at him incredulously.

"Sure, I mean it," Charley went on. "All we had to do, any time, was to let go our end—as I am going to do now, so that those Greeks can untangle their nets."

He went below with a monkey-wrench, unscrewed the nut, and let the hook drop off. When the Greeks had hauled their nets into their boats and made everything shipshape, a posse of citizens took them off our hands and led them away to jail.

"Ay tank Ay ban a great big fool," said Ole Ericsen. But he changed his mind when the admiring townspeople crowded aboard to shake hands with him, and a couple of enterprising newspaper men took photographs of the *Mary Rebecca* and her captain.

# 6

# DEMETRIOS CONTOS

It must not be thought, from what I have told of the Greek fishermen, that they were altogether bad. Far from it. But they were rough men, gathered together in isolated communities and fighting with the elements for a livelihood. They lived far away from the law and its workings, did not understand it, and thought it tyranny. Especially did the fish laws seem tyrannical. And because of this, they looked upon the men of the fish patrol as their natural enemies.

We menaced their lives, or their living, which is the same thing, in many ways. We confiscated illegal traps and nets, the materials of which had cost them considerable sums and the making of which required weeks of labor. We prevented them from catching fish at many times and seasons, which was equivalent to preventing them from making as good a living as they might have made had we not been in existence. And when we captured them, they were brought into the courts of law, where heavy cash fines were collected from them. As a result, they hated us vindictively. As the dog is the natural enemy of the cat, the snake of man, so were we of the fish patrol the natural enemies of the fishermen.

But it is to show that they could act generously as well as hate bitterly that this story of Demetrios Contos is told. Demetrios Contos lived in Vallejo. Next to Big Alec, he was the largest, bravest, and most influential man among the Greeks. He had given us no trouble, and I doubt if he would ever have clashed with us had he not invested in a new salmon boat. This boat was the cause of all the trouble. He had had it built upon his own model, in which the lines of the general salmon boat were somewhat modified.

To his high elation he found his new boat very fast—in fact, faster than any other boat on the bay or rivers. Forthwith he grew proud and boastful: and, our raid with the *Mary Rebecca* on the Sunday salmon fishers having wrought fear in their hearts, he sent a challenge up to Benicia. One of the local fishermen conveyed it to us; it was to the effect that Demetrios Contos would sail up from Vallejo on the following Sunday, and in the plain sight of Benicia set his net and catch salmon, and that Charley Le Grant, patrolman, might come and get him if he could. Of course Charley and I had heard nothing of the new boat. Our own boat was pretty fast, and we were not afraid to have a brush with any other that happened along.

Sunday came. The challenge had been bruited abroad, and the fishermen and seafaring folk of Benicia turned out to a man, crowding Steamboat Wharf till it looked like the grand stand at a football match. Charley and I had been sceptical, but the fact of the crowd convinced us that there was something in Demetrios Contos's dare.

In the afternoon, when the sea-breeze had picked up in strength, his sail hove into view as he bowled along before the wind. He tacked a score of feet from the wharf, waved his hand theatrically, like a knight about to enter the lists, received a hearty cheer in return, and stood away into the Straits for a couple of hundred yards. Then he lowered sail, and, drifting the boat sidewise by means of the wind, proceeded to set his net. He did not set much of it, possibly fifty feet; yet Charley and I were thunderstruck at the man's effrontery. We did not know at the time, but we learned afterward, that the net he used was old and worthless. It *could* catch fish, true; but a catch of any size would have torn it to pieces.

Charley shook his head and said:

"I confess, it puzzles me. What if he has out only fifty feet? He could never get it in if we once started for him. And why does he come here anyway, flaunting his law-breaking in our faces? Right in our home town, too."

Charley's voice took on an aggrieved tone, and he continued for some minutes to inveigh against the brazenness of Demetrios Contos.

In the meantime, the man in question was lolling in the stern of his boat and watching the net floats. When a large fish is meshed in a gill-net, the floats by their agitation advertise the fact. And they evidently advertised it to Demetrios, for he pulled in about a dozen feet of net, and held aloft for a moment, before he flung it into the bottom of the boat, a big, glistening salmon. It was greeted by the audience on the wharf with round after round of cheers. This was more than Charley could stand.

"Come on, lad," he called to me; and we lost no time jumping into our salmon boat and getting up sail.

The crowd shouted warning to Demetrios, and as we darted out from the wharf we saw him slash his worthless net clear with a long knife. His sail was all ready to go up, and a moment later it fluttered in the sunshine. He ran aft, drew in the sheet, and filled on the long tack toward the Contra Costa Hills.

By this time we were not more than thirty feet astern. Charley was jubilant. He knew our boat was fast, and he knew, further, that in fine sailing few men were his equals. He was confident that we should surely catch Demetrios, and I shared his confidence. But somehow we did not seem to gain.

It was a pretty sailing breeze. We were gliding sleekly through the water, but Demetrios was slowly sliding away from us. And not only was he going faster, but he was eating into the wind a fraction of a point closer than we. This was sharply impressed upon us when he went about under the Contra Costa Hills and passed us on the other tack fully one hundred feet dead to windward.

"Whew!" Charley exclaimed. "Either that boat is a daisy, or we've got a five-gallon coal-oil can fast to our keel!"

It certainly looked it one way or the other. And by the time Demetrios made the Sonoma Hills, on the other side of the Straits, we were so hopelessly outdistanced that Charley told me to slack off the sheet, and we squared away for Benicia. The fishermen on Steamboat Wharf showered us with ridicule when we returned and tied up. Charley and I got out and walked away, feeling rather sheepish, for it is a sore stroke to one's pride when he thinks he has a good boat and knows how to sail it, and another man comes along and beats him.

Charley mooned over it for a couple of days; then word was brought to us, as before, that on the next Sunday Demetrios Contos would repeat his performance. Charley roused himself. He had our boat out of the water, cleaned and repainted its bottom, made a trifling alteration about the centre-board, overhauled the running gear, and sat up nearly all of Saturday night sewing on a new and much larger sail. So large did he make it, in fact, that additional ballast was imperative, and we stowed away nearly five hundred extra pounds of old railroad iron in the bottom of the boat.

Sunday came, and with it came Demetrios Contos, to break the law defiantly in open day. Again we had the afternoon sea-breeze, and again Demetrios cut loose some forty or more feet of his rotten net, and got up sail and under way under our very noses. But he had anticipated Charley's move, and his own sail peaked higher than ever, while a whole extra cloth had been added to the after leech.

It was nip and tuck across to the Contra Costa Hills, neither of us seeming to gain or to lose. But by the time we had made the return tack to the Sonoma Hills, we could see that, while we footed it at about equal speed, Demetrios had eaten into the wind the least bit more than we. Yet Charley was sailing our boat as finely and delicately as it was possible to sail it, and getting more out of it than he ever had before.

Of course, he could have drawn his revolver and fired at Demetrios; but we had long since found it contrary to our natures to shoot at a fleeing man guilty of only a petty offence. Also a sort of tacit agreement seemed to have been reached between the patrolmen and the fishermen. If we did not shoot while they ran away, they, in turn, did not fight if we once laid hands on them. Thus Demetrios Contos ran away from us, and we did no more than try our best to overtake him; and, in turn, if our boat proved faster than his, or was sailed better, he would, we knew, make no resistance when we caught up with him.

With our large sails and the healthy breeze romping up the Carquinez Straits, we found that our sailing was what is called "ticklish." We had to be constantly on the alert to avoid a capsize, and while Charley steered I held the main-sheet in my hand with but a single turn round a pin, ready to let go at any moment. Demetrios, we could see, sailing his boat alone, had his hands full.

But it was a vain undertaking for us to attempt to catch him. Out of his inner consciousness he had evolved a boat that was better than ours. And though Charley sailed fully as well, if not the least bit better, the boat he sailed was not so good as the Greek's.

"Slack away the sheet," Charley commanded; and as our boat fell off before the wind, Demetrios's mocking laugh floated down to us.

Charley shook his head, saying, "It's no use. Demetrios has the better boat. If he tries his performance again, we must meet it with some new scheme."

This time it was my imagination that came to the rescue.

"What's the matter," I suggested, on the Wednesday following, "with my chasing Demetrios in the boat next Sunday, while you wait for him on the wharf at Vallejo when he arrives?"

Charley considered it a moment and slapped his knee.

"A good idea! You're beginning to use that head of yours. A credit to your teacher, I must say."

"But you mustn't chase him too far," he went on, the next moment, "or he'll head out into San Pablo Bay instead of running home to Vallejo, and there I'll be, standing lonely on the wharf and waiting in vain for him to arrive."

On Thursday Charley registered an objection to my plan.

"Everybody'll know I've gone to Vallejo, and you can depend upon it that Demetrios will know, too. I'm afraid we'll have to give up the idea."

This objection was only too valid, and for the rest of the day I struggled under my disappointment. But that night a new way seemed to open to me, and in my eagerness I awoke Charley from a sound sleep.

"Well," he grunted, "what's the matter? House afire?"

"No," I replied, "but my head is. Listen to this. On Sunday you and I will be around Benicia up to the very moment Demetrios's sail heaves into sight. This will lull everybody's suspicions. Then, when Demetrios's sail does heave in sight, do you stroll leisurely away and up-town. All the fishermen will think you're beaten and that you know you're beaten."

"So far, so good," Charley commented, while I paused to catch breath.

"And very good indeed," I continued proudly. "You stroll carelessly up-town, but when you're once out of sight you leg it for all you're worth for Dan Maloney's. Take the little mare of his, and strike out on the country road for Vallejo. The road's in fine condition, and you can make it in quicker time than Demetrios can beat all the way down against the wind."

"And I'll arrange right away for the mare, first thing in the morning," Charley said, accepting the modified plan without hesitation.

"But, I say," he said, a little later, this time waking *me* out of a sound sleep.

I could hear him chuckling in the dark.

"I say, lad, isn't it rather a novelty for the fish patrol to be taking to horseback?"

"Imagination," I answered. "It's what you're always preaching—'keep thinking one thought ahead of the other fellow, and you're bound to win out.'"

"He! he!" he chuckled. "And if one thought ahead, including a mare, doesn't take the other fellow's breath away this time, I'm not your humble servant, Charley Le Grant."

"But can you manage the boat alone?" he asked, on Friday. "Remember, we've a ripping big sail on her."

I argued my proficiency so well that he did not refer to the matter again till Saturday, when he suggested removing one whole cloth from the after leech. I guess it was the disappointment written on my face that made him desist; for I, also, had a pride in my boat-sailing abilities, and I was almost wild to get out alone with the big sail and go tearing down the Carquinez Straits in the wake of the flying Greek.

As usual, Sunday and Demetrios Contos arrived together. It had become the regular thing for the fishermen to assemble on Steamboat Wharf to greet his arrival and to laugh at our discomfiture. He lowered sail a couple of hundred yards out and set his customary fifty feet of rotten net.

"I suppose this nonsense will keep up as long as his old net holds out," Charley grumbled, with intention, in the hearing of several of the Greeks.

"Den I give-a heem my old-a net-a," one of them spoke up, promptly and maliciously.

"I don't care," Charley answered. "I've got some old net myself he can have—if he'll come around and ask for it."

They all laughed at this, for they could afford to be sweet-tempered with a man so badly outwitted as Charley was.

"Well, so long, lad," Charley called to me a moment later. "I think I'll go up-town to Maloney's."

"Let me take the boat out?" I asked.

"If you want to," was his answer, as he turned on his heel and walked slowly away.

Demetrios pulled two large salmon out of his net, and I jumped into the boat. The fishermen crowded around in a spirit of fun, and when I started to get up sail overwhelmed me with all sorts of jocular advice. They even offered extravagant bets to one another that I would surely catch Demetrios, and two of them, styling themselves the committee of judges, gravely asked permission to come along with me to see how I did it.

But I was in no hurry. I waited to give Charley all the time I could, and I pretended dissatisfaction with the stretch of the sail and slightly shifted the small tackle by which the huge sprit forces up the peak. It was not until I was sure that Charley had reached Dan Maloney's and was on the little mare's back, that I cast off from the wharf and gave the big sail to the wind. A stout puff filled it and suddenly pressed the lee gunwale down till a couple of buckets of water came inboard. A little thing like this will happen to the best small-boat sailors, and yet, though I instantly let go the sheet and righted, I was cheered sarcastically, as though I had been guilty of a very awkward blunder.

When Demetrios saw only one person in the fish patrol boat, and that one a boy, he proceeded to play with me. Making a short tack out, with me not thirty feet behind, he returned, with his sheet a little free, to Steamboat Wharf. And there he made short tacks, and turned and twisted and ducked around, to the great delight of his sympathetic audience. I was right behind him all the time, and I dared to do whatever he did, even when he squared away before the wind and jibed his big sail over—a most dangerous trick with such a sail in such a wind.

He depended upon the brisk sea breeze and the strong ebb-tide, which together kicked up a nasty sea, to bring me to grief. But I was on my mettle, and never in all my life did I sail a boat better than on that day. I was keyed up to concert pitch, my brain was working smoothly and quickly, my hands never fumbled once, and it seemed that I almost divined the thousand little things which a small-boat sailor must be taking into consideration every second.

It was Demetrios who came to grief instead. Something went wrong with his centre-board, so that it jammed in the case and would not go all the way down. In a moment's breathing space, which he had gained from me by a clever trick, I saw him working impatiently with the centre-board, trying to force it down. I gave him little time, and he was compelled quickly to return to the tiller and sheet.

The centre-board made him anxious. He gave over playing with me, and started on the long beat to Vallejo. To my joy, on the first long tack across, I found that I could eat into the wind just a little bit closer than he. Here was where another man in the boat would have been of value to him; for, with me but a few feet astern, he did not dare let go the tiller and run amidships to try to force down the centre-board.

Unable to hang on as close in the eye of the wind as formerly, he proceeded to slack his sheet a trifle and to ease off a bit, in order to outfoot me. This I permitted him to do till I had worked to windward, when I bore down upon him. As I drew close, he feinted at coming about. This led me to shoot into the wind to forestall him. But it was only a feint, cleverly executed, and he held back to his course while I hurried to make up lost ground.

He was undeniably smarter than I when it came to manœuvring. Time after time I all but had him, and each time he tricked me and escaped. Besides, the wind was freshening, constantly, and each of us had his hands full to avoid capsizing. As for my boat, it could not have been kept afloat but for the extra ballast. I sat cocked over the weather gunwale, tiller in one hand and sheet in the other; and the sheet, with a single turn around a pin, I was very often forced to let go in the severer puffs. This allowed the sail to spill the wind, which was equivalent to taking off so much driving power, and of course I lost ground. My consolation was that Demetrios was as often compelled to do the same thing.

The strong ebb-tide, racing down the Straits in the teeth of the wind, caused an unusually heavy and spiteful sea, which dashed aboard continually. I was dripping wet, and even the sail was wet half-way up the after leech. Once I did succeed in outmanœuvring Demetrios, so that my bow bumped into him amidships. Here was where I should have had another man. Before I could run forward and leap aboard, he shoved the boats apart with an oar, laughing mockingly in my face as he did so.

We were now at the mouth of the Straits, in a bad stretch of water. Here the Vallejo Straits and the Carquinez Straits rushed directly at each other. Through the first flowed all the water of Napa River and the great tide-lands; through the second flowed all the water of Suisun Bay and the Sacramento and San Joaquin rivers. And where such immense bodies of water, flowing swiftly, clashed together, a terrible tide-rip was produced. To make it worse, the wind howled up San Pablo Bay for fifteen miles and drove in a tremendous sea upon the tide-rip.

Conflicting currents tore about in all directions, colliding, forming whirlpools, sucks, and boils, and shooting up spitefully into hollow waves which fell aboard as often from leeward as from windward. And through it all, confused, driven into a madness of motion, thundered the great smoking seas from San Pablo Bay.

I was as wildly excited as the water. The boat was behaving splendidly, leaping and lurching through the welter like a race-horse. I could hardly contain myself with the joy of it. The huge sail, the howling wind, the driving seas, the plunging boat—I, a pygmy, a mere speck in the midst of it, was mastering the elemental strife, flying through it and over it, triumphant and victorious.

And just then, as I roared along like a conquering hero, the boat received a frightful smash and came instantly to a dead stop. I was flung forward and into the bottom. As I sprang up I caught a fleeting glimpse of a greenish, barnacle-covered object, and knew it at once for what it was, that terror of navigation, a sunken pile. No man may guard against such a thing. Water-logged and floating just beneath the surface, it was impossible to sight it in the troubled water in time to escape.

The whole bow of the boat must have been crushed in, for in a few seconds the boat was half full. Then a couple of seas filled it, and it sank straight down, dragged to bottom by the heavy ballast. So quickly did it all happen that I was entangled in the sail and drawn under. When I fought my way to the surface, suffocating, my lungs almost bursting, I could see nothing of the oars. They must have been swept away by the chaotic currents. I saw Demetrios Contos looking back from his boat, and heard the vindictive and mocking tones of his voice as he shouted exultantly. He held steadily on his course, leaving me to perish.

There was nothing to do but to swim for it, which, in that wild confusion, was at the best a matter of but a few moments. Holding my breath and working with my hands, I managed to get off my heavy sea-boots and my jacket. Yet there was very little breath I could catch to hold, and I swiftly discovered that it was not so much a matter of swimming as of breathing.

I was beaten and buffeted, smashed under by the great San Pablo whitecaps, and strangled by the hollow tide-rip waves which flung themselves into my eyes, nose, and mouth. Then the strange sucks would grip my legs and drag me under, to spout me up in some fierce boiling, where, even as I tried to catch my breath, a great whitecap would crash down upon my head.

It was impossible to survive any length of time. I was breathing more water than air, and drowning all the time. My senses began to leave me, my head to whirl around. I struggled on, spasmodically, instinctively, and was barely half conscious when I felt myself caught by the shoulders and hauled over the gunwale of a boat.

For some time I lay across a seat where I had been flung, face downward, and with the water running out of my mouth. After a while, still weak and faint, I turned around to see who was my rescuer. And there, in the stern, sheet in one hand and tiller in the other, grinning and nodding good-naturedly, sat Demetrios Contos. He had intended to leave me to drown,—he said so afterward,—but his better self had fought the battle, conquered, and sent him back to me.

"You all-a right?" he asked.

I managed to shape a "yes" on my lips, though I could not yet speak.

"You sail-a de boat verr-a good-a," he said. "So good-a as a man."

A compliment from Demetrios Contos was a compliment indeed, and I keenly appreciated it, though I could only nod my head in acknowledgment.

We held no more conversation, for I was busy recovering and he was busy with the boat. He ran in to the wharf at Vallejo, made the boat fast, and helped me out. Then it was, as we both stood on the wharf, that Charley stepped out from behind a net-rack and put his hand on Demetrios Contos's arm.

"He saved my life, Charley," I protested; "and I don't think he ought to be arrested."

A puzzled expression came into Charley's face, which cleared immediately after, in a way it had when he made up his mind.

"I can't help it, lad," he said kindly. "I can't go back on my duty, and it's plain duty to arrest him. To-day is Sunday; there are two salmon in his boat which he caught to-day. What else can I do?"

"But he saved my life," I persisted, unable to make any other argument.

Demetrios Contos's face went black with rage when he learned Charley's judgment. He had a sense of being unfairly treated. The better part of his nature had triumphed, he had performed a generous act and saved a helpless enemy, and in return the enemy was taking him to jail.

Charley and I were out of sorts with each other when we went back to Benicia. I stood for the spirit of the law and not the letter; but by the letter Charley made his stand. As far as he could see, there was nothing else for him to do. The law said distinctly that no salmon should be caught on Sunday. He was a patrolman, and it was his duty to enforce that law. That was all there was to it. He had done his duty, and his conscience was clear. Nevertheless, the whole thing seemed unjust to me, and I felt very sorry for Demetrios Contos.

Two days later we went down to Vallejo to the trial. I had to go along as a witness, and it was the most hateful task that I ever performed in my life when I testified on the witness stand to seeing Demetrios catch the two salmon Charley had captured him with.

Demetrios had engaged a lawyer, but his case was hopeless. The jury was out only fifteen minutes, and returned a verdict of guilty. The judge sentenced Demetrios to pay a fine of one hundred dollars or go to jail for fifty days.

Charley stepped up to the clerk of the court. "I want to pay that fine," he said, at the same time placing five twenty-dollar gold pieces on the desk. "It—it was the only way out of it, lad," he stammered, turning to me.

The moisture rushed into my eyes as I seized his hand. "I want to pay—" I began.

"To pay your half?" he interrupted. "I certainly shall expect you to pay it."

In the meantime Demetrios had been informed by his lawyer that his fee likewise had been paid by Charley.

Demetrios came over to shake Charley's hand, and all his warm Southern blood flamed in his face. Then, not to be outdone in generosity, he insisted on paying his fine and lawyer's fee himself, and flew half-way into a passion because Charley refused to let him.

More than anything else we ever did, I think, this action of Charley's impressed upon the fishermen the deeper significance of the law. Also Charley was raised high in their esteem, while I came in for a little share of praise as a boy who knew how to sail a boat. Demetrios Contos not only never broke the law again, but he became a very good friend of ours, and on more than one occasion he ran up to Benicia to have a gossip with us.

## 7

# YELLOW HANDKERCHIEF

"I'm not wanting to dictate to you, lad," Charley said; "but I'm very much against your making a last raid. You've gone safely through rough times with rough men, and it would be a shame to have something happen to you at the very end."

"But how can I get out of making a last raid?" I demanded, with the cocksureness of youth. "There always has to be a last, you know, to anything."

Charley crossed his legs, leaned back, and considered the problem. "Very true. But why not call the capture of Demetrios Contos the last? You're back from it safe and sound and hearty, for all your good wetting, and—and—" His voice broke and he could not speak for a moment. "And I could never forgive myself if anything happened to you now."

I laughed at Charley's fears while I gave in to the claims of his affection, and agreed to consider the last raid already performed. We had been together for two years, and now I was leaving the fish patrol in order to go back and finish my education. I had earned and saved money to put me through three years at the high school, and though the beginning of the term was several months away, I intended doing a lot of studying for the entrance examinations.

My belongings were packed snugly in a sea-chest, and I was all ready to buy my ticket and ride down on the train to Oakland, when Neil Partington arrived in Benicia. The *Reindeer* was needed immediately for work far down on the Lower Bay, and Neil said he intended to run straight for Oakland. As that was his home and as I was to live with his family while going to school, he saw no reason, he said, why I should not put my chest aboard and come along.

So the chest went aboard, and in the middle of the afternoon we hoisted the *Reindeer's* big mainsail and cast off. It was tantalizing fall weather. The sea-breeze, which had blown steadily all summer, was gone, and in its place were capricious winds and murky skies which made the time of arriving anywhere extremely problematical. We started on the first of the ebb, and as we slipped down the Carquinez Straits, I looked my last for some time upon Benicia and the bight at Turner's Shipyard, where we had besieged the *Lancashire Queen*, and had captured Big Alec, the King of the Greeks. And at the mouth of the Straits I looked with not a little interest upon the spot where a few days before I should have drowned but for the good that was in the nature of Demetrios Contos.

A great wall of fog advanced across San Pablo Bay to meet us, and in a few minutes the *Reindeer* was running blindly through the damp obscurity. Charley, who was steering, seemed to have an instinct for that kind of work. How he did it, he himself confessed that he did not know; but he had a way of calculating winds, currents, distance, time, drift, and sailing speed that was truly marvellous.

"It looks as though it were lifting," Neil Partington said, a couple of hours after we had entered the fog. "Where do you say we are, Charley?"

Charley looked at his watch, "Six o'clock, and three hours more of ebb," he remarked casually.

"But where do you say we are?" Neil insisted.

Charley pondered a moment, and then answered, "The tide has edged us over a bit out of our course, but if the fog lifts right now, as it is going to lift, you'll find we're not more than a thousand miles off McNear's Landing."

"You might be a little more definite by a few miles, anyway," Neil grumbled, showing by his tone that he disagreed.

"All right, then," Charley said, conclusively, "not less than a quarter of a mile, not more than a half."

The wind freshened with a couple of little puffs, and the fog thinned perceptibly.

"McNear's is right off there," Charley said, pointing directly into the fog on our weather beam.

The three of us were peering intently in that direction, when the *Reindeer* struck with a dull crash and came to a standstill. We ran forward, and found her bowsprit entangled in the tanned rigging of a short, chunky mast. She had collided, head on, with a Chinese junk lying at anchor.

At the moment we arrived forward, five Chinese, like so many bees, came swarming out of the little 'tween-decks cabin, the sleep still in their eyes.

Leading them came a big, muscular man, conspicuous for his pock-marked face and the yellow silk handkerchief swathed about his head. It was Yellow Handkerchief, the Chinaman whom we had arrested for illegal shrimp-fishing the year before, and who, at that time, had nearly sunk the *Reindeer*, as he had nearly sunk it now by violating the rules of navigation.

"What d'ye mean, you yellow-faced heathen, lying here in a fairway without a horn a-going?" Charley cried hotly.

"Mean?" Neil calmly answered. "Just take a look—that's what he means."

Our eyes followed the direction indicated by Neil's finger, and we saw the open amidships of the junk, half filled, as we found on closer examination, with fresh-caught shrimps. Mingled with the shrimps were myriads of small fish, from a quarter of an inch upward in size.

Yellow Handkerchief had lifted the trap-net at high-water slack, and, taking advantage of the concealment offered by the fog, had boldly been lying by, waiting to lift the net again at low-water slack.

"Well," Neil hummed and hawed, "in all my varied and extensive experience as a fish patrolman, I must say this is the easiest capture I ever made. What'll we do with them, Charley?"

"Tow the junk into San Rafael, of course," came the answer. Charley turned to me. "You stand by the junk, lad, and I'll pass you a towing line. If the wind doesn't fail us, we'll make the creek before the tide gets too low, sleep at San Rafael, and arrive in Oakland to-morrow by midday."

So saying, Charley and Neil returned to the *Reindeer* and got under way, the junk towing astern. I went aft and took charge of the prize, steering by means of an antiquated tiller and a rudder with large, diamond-shaped holes, through which the water rushed back and forth.

By now the last of the fog had vanished, and Charley's estimate of our position was confirmed by the sight of McNear's Landing a short half-mile away. Following along the west shore, we rounded Point Pedro in plain view of the Chinese shrimp villages, and a great to-do was raised when they saw one of their junks towing behind the familiar fish patrol sloop.

The wind, coming off the land, was rather puffy and uncertain, and it would have been more to our advantage had it been stronger. San Rafael Creek, up which we had to go to reach the town and turn over our prisoners to the authorities, ran through wide-stretching marshes, and was difficult to navigate on a falling tide, while at low tide it was impossible to navigate at all. So, with the tide already half-ebbed, it was necessary for us to make time. This the heavy junk prevented, lumbering along behind and holding the *Reindeer* back by just so much dead weight.

"Tell those coolies to get up that sail," Charley finally called to me. "We don't want to hang up on the mud flats for the rest of the night."

I repeated the order to Yellow Handkerchief, who mumbled it huskily to his men. He was suffering from a bad cold, which doubled him up in convulsive coughing spells and made his eyes heavy and bloodshot. This made him more evil-looking than ever, and when he glared viciously at me I remembered with a shiver the close shave I had had with him at the time of his previous arrest.

His crew sullenly tailed on to the halyards, and the strange, outlandish sail, lateen in rig and dyed a warm brown, rose in the air. We were sailing on the wind, and when Yellow Handkerchief flattened down the sheet the junk forged ahead and the tow-line went slack. Fast as the *Reindeer* could sail, the junk outsailed her; and to avoid running her down I hauled a little closer on the wind. But the junk likewise outpointed, and in a couple of minutes I was abreast of the *Reindeer* and to windward. The tow-line had now tautened, at right angles to the two boats, and the predicament was laughable.

"Cast off!" I shouted.

Charley hesitated.

"It's all right," I added. "Nothing can happen. We'll make the creek on this tack, and you'll be right behind me all the way up to San Rafael."

At this Charley cast off, and Yellow Handkerchief sent one of his men forward to haul in the line. In the gathering darkness I could just make out the mouth of San Rafael Creek, and by the time we entered it I could barely see its banks. The *Reindeer* was fully five minutes astern, and we continued to leave her astern as we beat up the narrow, winding channel. With Charley behind us, it seemed I had little to fear from my five prisoners; but the darkness prevented my keeping a sharp eye on them, so I transferred my revolver from my trousers pocket to the side pocket of my coat, where I could more quickly put my hand on it.

Yellow Handkerchief was the one I feared, and that he knew it and made use of it, subsequent events will show. He was sitting a few feet away from me, on what then happened to be the weather side of the junk. I could scarcely see the outlines of his form, but I soon became convinced that he was slowly, very slowly, edging closer to me. I watched him carefully. Steering with my left hand, I slipped my right into my pocket and got hold of the revolver.

I saw him shift along for a couple of inches, and I was just about to order him back—the words were trembling on the tip of my tongue—when I was struck with great force by a heavy figure that had leaped through the air upon me from the lee side. It was one of the crew. He pinioned my right arm so that I could not withdraw my hand from my pocket, and at the same time clapped his other hand over my mouth. Of course, I could have struggled away from him and freed my hand or gotten my mouth clear so that I might cry an alarm, but in a trice Yellow Handkerchief was on top of me.

I struggled around to no purpose in the bottom of the junk, while my legs and arms were tied and my mouth securely bound in what I afterward found to be a cotton shirt. Then I was left lying in the bottom. Yellow Handkerchief took the tiller, issuing his orders in whispers; and from our position at the time, and from the alteration of the sail, which I could dimly make out above me as a blot against the stars, I knew the junk was being headed into the mouth of a small slough which emptied at that point into San Rafael Creek.

In a couple of minutes we ran softly alongside the bank, and the sail was silently lowered. The Chinese kept very quiet. Yellow Handkerchief sat down in the bottom alongside of me, and I could feel him straining to repress his raspy, hacking cough. Possibly seven or eight minutes later I heard Charley's voice as the *Reindeer* went past the mouth of the slough.

"I can't tell you how relieved I am," I could plainly hear him saying to Neil, "that the lad has finished with the fish patrol without accident."

Here Neil said something which I could not catch, and then Charley's voice went on:

"The youngster takes naturally to the water, and if, when he finishes high school, he takes a course in navigation and goes deep sea, I see no reason why he shouldn't rise to be master of the finest and biggest ship afloat."

It was all very flattering to me, but lying there, bound and gagged by my own prisoners, with the voices growing faint and fainter as the *Reindeer* slipped on through the darkness toward San Rafael, I must say I was not in quite the proper situation to enjoy my smiling future. With the *Reindeer* went my last hope. What was to happen next I could not imagine, for the Chinese were a different race from mine, and from what I knew I was confident that fair play was no part of their make-up.

After waiting a few minutes longer, the crew hoisted the lateen sail, and Yellow Handkerchief steered down toward the mouth of San Rafael Creek. The tide was getting lower, and he had difficulty in escaping the mud-banks. I was hoping he would run aground, but he succeeded in making the Bay without accident.

As we passed out of the creek a noisy discussion arose, which I knew related to me. Yellow Handkerchief was vehement, but the other four as vehemently opposed him. It was very evident that he advocated doing away with me and that they were afraid of the consequences. I was familiar enough with the Chinese character to know that fear alone restrained them. But what plan they offered in place of Yellow Handkerchief's murderous one, I could not make out.

My feelings, as my fate hung in the balance, may be guessed. The discussion developed into a quarrel, in the midst of which Yellow Handkerchief unshipped the heavy tiller and sprang toward me. But his four companions threw themselves between, and a clumsy struggle took place for possession of the tiller. In the end Yellow Handkerchief was overcome, and sullenly returned to the steering, while they soundly berated him for his rashness.

Not long after, the sail was run down and the junk slowly urged forward by means of the sweeps. I felt it ground gently on the soft mud. Three of the Chinese—they all wore long sea-boots—got over the side, and the other two passed me across the rail. With Yellow

Handkerchief at my legs and his two companions at my shoulders, they began to flounder along through the mud. After some time their feet struck firmer footing, and I knew they were carrying me up some beach. The location of this beach was not doubtful in my mind. It could be none other than one of the Marin Islands, a group of rocky islets which lay off the Marin County shore.

When they reached the firm sand that marked high tide, I was dropped, and none too gently. Yellow Handkerchief kicked me spitefully in the ribs, and then the trio floundered back through the mud to the junk. A moment later I heard the sail go up and slat in the wind as they drew in the sheet. Then silence fell, and I was left to my own devices for getting free.

I remembered having seen tricksters writhe and squirm out of ropes with which they were bound, but though I writhed and squirmed like a good fellow, the knots remained as hard as ever, and there was no appreciable slack. In the course of my squirming, however, I rolled over upon a heap of clam-shells—the remains, evidently, of some yachting party's clam-bake. This gave me an idea. My hands were tied behind my back; and, clutching a shell in them, I rolled over and over, up the beach, till I came to the rocks I knew to be there.

Rolling around and searching, I finally discovered a narrow crevice, into which I shoved the shell. The edge of it was sharp, and across the sharp edge I proceeded to saw the rope that bound my wrists. The edge of the shell was also brittle, and I broke it by bearing too heavily upon it. Then I rolled back to the heap and returned with as many shells as I could carry in both hands. I broke many shells, cut my hands a number of times, and got cramps in my legs from my strained position and my exertions.

While I was suffering from the cramps, and resting, I heard a familiar halloo drift across the water. It was Charley, searching for me. The gag in my mouth prevented me from replying, and I could only lie there, helplessly fuming, while he rowed past the island and his voice slowly lost itself in the distance.

I returned to the sawing process, and at the end of half an hour succeeded in severing the rope. The rest was easy. My hands once free, it was a matter of minutes to loosen my legs and to take the gag out of my mouth. I ran around the island to make sure it *was* an island and not by any chance a portion of the mainland. An island it certainly was, one of the Marin group, fringed with a sandy beach and surrounded by a sea of mud. Nothing remained but to wait till daylight and to keep warm; for it was a cold, raw night for California, with just enough wind to pierce the skin and cause one to shiver.

To keep up the circulation, I ran around the island a dozen times or so, and clambered across its rocky backbone as many times more—all of which was of greater service to me, as I afterward discovered, than merely to warm me up. In the midst of this exercise I wondered if I had lost anything out of my pockets while rolling over and over in the sand. A search showed the absence of my revolver and pocket-knife. The first Yellow Handkerchief had taken; but the knife had been lost in the sand.

I was hunting for it when the sound of rowlocks came to my ears. At first, of course, I thought of Charley; but on second thought I knew Charley would be calling out as he rowed along. A sudden premonition of danger seized me. The Marin Islands are lonely places; chance visitors in the dead of night are hardly to be expected. What if it were Yellow Handkerchief? The sound made by the rowlocks grew more distinct. I crouched in the sand and listened intently. The boat, which I judged a small skiff from the quick stroke of the oars, was landing in the mud about fifty yards up the beach. I heard a raspy, hacking cough, and my heart stood still. It was Yellow Handkerchief. Not to be robbed of his revenge by his more cautious companions, he had stolen away from the village and come back alone.

I did some swift thinking. I was unarmed and helpless on a tiny islet, and a yellow barbarian, whom I had reason to fear, was coming after me. Any place was safer than the island, and I turned instinctively to the water, or rather to the mud. As he began to flounder ashore through the mud, I started to flounder out into it, going over the same course which the Chinese had taken in landing me and in returning to the junk.

Yellow Handkerchief, believing me to be lying tightly bound, exercised no care, but came ashore noisily. This helped me, for, under the shield of his noise and making no more myself than necessary, I managed to cover fifty feet by the time he had made the beach. Here I lay down in the mud. It was cold and clammy, and made me shiver, but I did not care to stand up and run the risk of being discovered by his sharp eyes.

He walked down the beach straight to where he had left me lying, and I had a fleeting feeling of regret at not being able to see his surprise when he did not find me. But it was a very fleeting regret, for my teeth were chattering with the cold.

What his movements were after that I had largely to deduce from the facts of the situation, for I could scarcely see him in the dim starlight. But I was sure that the first thing he did was to make the circuit of the beach to learn if landings had been made by other boats. This he would have known at once by the tracks through the mud.

Convinced that no boat had removed me from the island, he next started to find out what had become of me. Beginning at the pile of clam-shells, he lighted matches to trace my tracks in the sand. At such times I could see his villanous face plainly, and, when the sulphur from the matches irritated his lungs, between the raspy cough that followed and the clammy mud in which I was lying, I confess I shivered harder than ever.

The multiplicity of my footprints puzzled him. Then the idea that I might be out in the mud must have struck him, for he waded out a few yards in my direction, and, stooping, with his eyes searched the dim surface long and carefully. He could not have been more than fifteen feet from me, and had he lighted a match he would surely have discovered me.

He returned to the beach and clambered about, over the rocky backbone, again hunting for me with lighted matches, The closeness of the shave impelled me to further flight. Not daring to wade upright, on account of the noise made by floundering and by the suck of the mud, I remained lying down in the mud and propelled myself over its surface by means of my hands. Still keeping the trail made by the Chinese in going from and to the junk, I held on until I reached the water. Into this I waded to a depth of three feet, and then I turned off to the side on a line parallel with the beach.

The thought came to me of going toward Yellow Handkerchief's skiff and escaping in it, but at that very moment he returned to the beach, and, as though fearing the very thing I had in mind, he slushed out through the mud to assure himself that the skiff was safe. This turned me in the opposite direction. Half swimming, half wading, with my head just out of water and avoiding splashing, I succeeded in putting about a hundred feet between myself and the spot where the Chinese had begun to wade ashore from the junk. I drew myself out on the mud and remained lying flat.

Again Yellow Handkerchief returned to the beach and made a search of the island, and again he returned to the heap of clam-shells. I knew what was running in his mind as well as he did himself. No one could leave or land without making tracks in the mud. The only tracks to be seen were those leading from his skiff and from where the junk had been. I was not on the island. I must have left it by one or the other of those two tracks. He had just been over the one to his skiff, and was certain I had not left that way. Therefore I could have left the island only by going over the tracks of the junk landing. This he proceeded to verify by wading out over them himself, lighting matches as he came along.

When he arrived at the point where I had first lain, I knew, by the matches he burned and the time he took, that he had discovered the marks left by my body. These he followed straight to the water and into it, but in three feet of water he could no longer see them. On the other hand, as the tide was still falling, he could easily make out the impression made by the junk's bow, and could have likewise made out the impression of any other boat if it had landed at that particular spot. But there was no such mark; and I knew that he was absolutely convinced that I was hiding somewhere in the mud.

But to hunt on a dark night for a boy in a sea of mud would be like hunting for a needle in a haystack, and he did not attempt it. Instead he went back to the beach and prowled around for some time. I was hoping he would give me up and go, for by this time I was suffering severely from the cold. At last he waded out to his skiff and rowed away. What if this departure of Yellow Handkerchief's were a sham? What if he had done it merely to entice me ashore?

The more I thought of it the more certain I became that he had made a little too much noise with his oars as he rowed away. So I remained, lying in the mud and shivering. I shivered till the muscles of the small of my back ached and pained me as badly as the cold, and I had need of all my self-control to force myself to remain in my miserable situation.

It was well that I did, however, for, possibly an hour later, I thought I could make out something moving on the beach. I watched intently, but my ears were rewarded first, by a raspy cough I knew only too well. Yellow Handkerchief had sneaked back, landed on the other side of the island, and crept around to surprise me if I had returned.

After that, though hours passed without sign of him, I was afraid to return to the island at all. On the other hand, I was almost equally afraid that I should die of the exposure I was undergoing. I had never dreamed one could suffer so. I grew so cold and numb, finally, that I ceased to shiver. But my muscles and bones began to ache in a way that was agony. The tide had long since begun to rise, and, foot by foot, it drove me in toward the beach. High water came at three o'clock, and at three o'clock I drew myself up on the beach, more dead than alive, and too helpless to have offered any resistance had Yellow Handkerchief swooped down upon me.

But no Yellow Handkerchief appeared. He had given me up and gone back to Point Pedro. Nevertheless, I was in a deplorable, not to say dangerous, condition. I could not stand upon my feet, much less walk. My clammy, muddy garments clung to me like sheets of ice. I thought I should never get them off. So numb and lifeless were my fingers, and so weak was I, that it seemed to take an hour to get off my shoes. I had not the strength to break the porpoise-hide laces, and the knots defied me. I repeatedly beat my hands upon the rocks to get some sort of life into them. Sometimes I felt sure I was going to die.

But in the end,—after several centuries, it seemed to me,—I got off the last of my clothes. The water was now close at hand, and I crawled painfully into it and washed the mud from my naked body. Still, I could not get on my feet and walk and I was afraid to lie still. Nothing remained but to crawl weakly, like a snail, and at the cost of constant pain, up and down the sand. I kept this up as long as possible, but as the east paled with the coming of dawn I began to succumb. The sky grew rosy-red, and the golden rim of the sun, showing above the horizon, found me lying helpless and motionless among the clam-shells.

As in a dream, I saw the familiar mainsail of the *Reindeer* as she slipped out of San Rafael Creek on a light puff of morning air. This dream was very much broken. There are intervals I can never recollect on looking back over it. Three things, however, I distinctly remember: the first sight of the *Reindeer's* mainsail; her lying at anchor a few hundred feet away and a small boat leaving her side; and the cabin stove roaring red-hot, myself swathed all over with blankets, except on the chest and shoulders, which Charley was pounding and mauling unmercifully, and my mouth and throat burning with the coffee which Neil Partington was pouring down a trifle too hot.

But burn or no burn, I tell you it felt good. By the time we arrived in Oakland I was as limber and strong as ever,—though Charlie and Neil Partington were afraid I was going to have pneumonia, and Mrs. Partington, for my first six months of school, kept an anxious eye upon me to discover the first symptoms of consumption.

Time flies. It seems but yesterday that I was a lad of sixteen on the fish patrol. Yet I know that I arrived this very morning from China, with a quick passage to my credit, and master of the barkentine *Harvester*. And I know that to-morrow morning I shall run over to Oakland to see Neil Partington and his wife and family, and later on up to Benicia to see Charley Le Grant and talk over old times. No; I shall not go to Benicia, now that I think about it. I expect to be a highly interested party to a wedding, shortly to take place. Her name is Alice Partington, and, since Charley has promised to be best man, he will have to come down to Oakland instead.

# KIDD THE PIRATE & THE MONEY DIGGERS

WASHINGTON IRVING

# THE MONEY DIGGERS

## (FOUND AMONG THE PAPERS OF THE LATE DIEDRICH KNICKERBOCKER)

Now I remember those old women's words
  Who in my youth would tell me winter's tales;
  And speak of spirits and ghosts that glide by night
  About the place where treasure had been hid.

— MARLOW'S JEW OF MALTA.

### HELL GATE

About six miles from the renowned city of the Manhattoes, and in that Sound, or arm of the sea, which passes between the main land and Nassau or Long Island, there is a narrow strait, where the current is violently compressed between shouldering promontories, and horribly irritated and perplexed by rocks and shoals. Being at the best of times a very violent, hasty current, its takes these impediments in mighty dudgeon; boiling in whirlpools; brawling and fretting in ripples and breakers; and, in short, indulging in all kinds of wrong-headed paroxysms. At such times, woe to any unlucky vessel that ventures within its clutches.

This termagant humor is said to prevail only at half tides. At low water it is as pacific as any other stream. As the tide rises, it begins to fret; at half tide it rages and roars as if bellowing for more water; but when the tide is full it relapses again into quiet, and for a time seems almost to sleep as soundly as an alderman after dinner. It may be compared to an inveterate hard drinker, who is a peaceable fellow enough when he has no liquor at all, or when he has a skin full, but when half seas over plays the very devil.

This mighty, blustering, bullying little strait was a place of great Difficulty and danger to the Dutch navigators of ancient days; hectoring their tub-built barks in a most unruly style; whirling them about, in a manner to make any but a Dutchman giddy, and not unfrequently stranding them upon rocks and reefs. Whereupon out of sheer spleen they denominated it Hellegat (literally Hell Gut) and solemnly gave it over to the devil. This appellation has since been aptly rendered into English by the name of Hell Gate; and into nonsense by the name of

Hurl Gate, according to certain foreign intruders who neither understood Dutch nor English. May St. Nicholas confound them!

From this strait to the city of the Manhattoes the borders of the Sound are greatly diversified; in one part, on the eastern shore of the island of Manhata and opposite Blackwell's Island, being very much broken and indented by rocky nooks, overhung with trees which give them a wild and romantic look.

The flux and reflux of the tide through this part of the Sound is extremely rapid, and the navigation troublesome, by reason of the whirling eddies and counter currents. I speak this from experience, having been much of a navigator of these small seas in my boyhood, and having more than once run the risk of shipwreck and drowning in the course of divers holiday voyages, to which in common with the Dutch urchins I was rather prone.

In the midst of this perilous strait, and hard by a group of rocks called "the Hen and Chickens," there lay in my boyish days the wreck of a vessel which had been entangled in the whirlpools and stranded during a storm. There was some wild story about this being the wreck of a pirate, and of some bloody murder, connected with it, which I cannot now recollect. Indeed, the desolate look of this forlorn hulk, and the fearful place where it lay rotting, were sufficient to awaken strange notions concerning it. A row of timber heads, blackened by time, peered above the surface at high water; but at low tide a considerable part of the hull was bare, and its great ribs or timbers, partly stripped of their planks, looked like the skeleton of some sea monster. There was also the stump of a mast, with a few ropes and blocks swinging about and whistling in the wind, while the sea gull wheeled and screamed around this melancholy carcass.

The stories connected with this wreck made it an object of great awe to my boyish fancy; but in truth the whole neighborhood was full of fable and romance for me, abounding with traditions about pirates, hobgoblins, and buried money. As I grew to more mature years I made many researches after the truth of these strange traditions; for I have always been a curious investigator of the valuable, but obscure branches of the history of my native province. I found infinite difficulty, however, in arriving at any precise information. In seeking to dig up one fact it is incredible the number of fables which I unearthed; for the whole course of the Sound seemed in my younger days to be like the straits of Pylorus of yore, the very region of fiction. I will say nothing of the Devil's Stepping Stones, by which that arch fiend made his retreat from Connecticut to Long Island, seeing that the subject is likely to be learnedly treated by a worthy friend and contemporary historian[1] whom I have furnished with particulars thereof. Neither will I say anything of the black man in a three-cornered hat, seated in the stern of a jolly boat who used to be seen about Hell Gate in stormy weather; and who went by the name of the Pirate's Spuke, or Pirate's Ghost, because I never could meet with any person of stanch credibility who professed to have seen this spectrum; unless it were the widow of Manus Conklin, the blacksmith of Frog's Neck, but then, poor woman, she was a little purblind, and might have been mistaken; though they said she saw farther than other folks in the dark. All this, however, was but little satisfactory in regard to the tales of buried money about which I was most curious; and the following was all that I could for a long time collect that had anything like an air of authenticity.

## KIDD THE PIRATE

In old times, just after the territory of the New Netherlands had been wrested from the hands of their High Mightinesses, the Lords States General of Holland, by Charles the Second, and while it was as yet in an unquiet state, the province was a favorite resort of adventurers of all kinds, and particularly of buccaneers. These were piratical rovers of the deep, who made sad work in times of peace among the Spanish settlements and Spanish merchant ships. They took advantage of the easy access to the harbor of the Manhattoes, and of the laxity of its scarcely-organized government, to make it a kind of rendezvous, where they might dispose of their ill-gotten spoils, and concert new depredations. Crews of these desperadoes, the runagates of every country and clime, might be seen swaggering, in open day, about the streets of the little burgh; elbowing its quiet Mynheers; trafficking away their rich outlandish plunder, at half price, to the wary merchant, and then squandering their gains in taverns; drinking, gambling, singing, swearing, shouting, and astounding the neighborhood with sudden brawl and ruffian revelry.

At length the indignation of government was aroused, and it was determined to ferret out this vermin brood from, the colonies. Great consternation took place among the pirates on finding justice in pursuit of them, and their old haunts turned to places of peril. They secreted their money and jewels in lonely out-of-the-way places; buried them about the wild shores of the rivers and sea-coast, and dispersed themselves over the face of the country.

Among the agents employed to hunt them by sea was the renowned Captain Kidd. He had long been a hardy adventurer, a kind of equivocal borderer, half trader, half smuggler, with a tolerable dash of the pickaroon. He had traded for some time among the pirates, lurking about the seas in a little rakish, musquito-built vessel, prying into all kinds of odd places, as busy as a Mother Carey's chicken in a gale of wind.

This nondescript personage was pitched upon by government as the very man to command a vessel fitted out to cruise against the pirates, since he knew all their haunts and lurking-places: acting upon the shrewd old maxim of "setting a rogue to catch a rogue." Kidd accordingly sailed from New York in the Adventure galley, gallantly armed and duly commissioned, and steered his course to the Madeiras, to Bonavista, to Madagascar, and cruised at the entrance of the Red Sea. Instead, however, of making war upon the pirates, he turned pirate himself: captured friend or foe; enriched himself with the spoils of a wealthy Indiaman, manned by Moors, though commanded by an Englishman, and having disposed of his prize, had the hardihood to return to Boston, laden with wealth, with a crew of his comrades at his heels.

His fame had preceded him. The alarm was given of the reappearance of this cut-purse of the ocean. Measures were taken for his arrest; but he had time, it is said, to bury the greater part of his treasures. He even attempted to draw his sword and defend himself when arrested; but was secured and thrown into prison, with several of his followers. They were carried to England in a frigate, where they were tried, condemned, and hanged at Execution Dock. Kidd died hard, for the rope with which he was first tied up broke with his weight, and he tumbled to the ground; he was tied up a second time, and effectually; from whence arose the story of his having been twice hanged.

Such is the main outline of Kidd's history; but it has given birth to an innumerable progeny of traditions. The circumstance of his having buried great treasures of gold and jewels after returning from his cruising set the brains of all the good people along the coast in a ferment. There were rumors on rumors of great sums found here and there; sometimes in one part of the country, sometimes in another; of trees and rocks bearing mysterious marks; doubtless indicating the spots where treasure lay hidden; of coins found with Moorish characters, the plunder of Kidd's eastern prize, but which the common people took for diabolical or magic inscriptions.

Some reported the spoils to have been buried in solitary unsettled places about Plymouth and Cape Cod; many other parts of the Eastern coast, also, and various places in Long Island

Sound, have been gilded by these rumors, and have been ransacked by adventurous money-diggers.

In all the stories of these enterprises the devil played a conspicuous part. Either he was conciliated by ceremonies and invocations, or some bargain or compact was made with him. Still he was sure to play the money-diggers some slippery trick. Some had succeeded so far as to touch the iron chest which contained the treasure, when some baffling circumstance was sure to take place. Either the earth would fall in and fill up the pit or some direful noise or apparition would throw the party into a panic and frighten them from the place; and sometimes the devil himself would appear and bear off the prize from their very grasp; and if they visited the place on the next day, not a trace would be seen of their labors of the preceding night.

Such were the vague rumors which for a long time tantalized without gratifying my curiosity on the interesting subject of these pirate traditions. There is nothing in this world so hard to get at as truth. I sought among my favorite sources of authentic information, the oldest inhabitants, and particularly the old Dutch wives of the province; but though I flatter myself I am better versed than most men in the curious history of my native province, yet for a long time my inquiries were unattended with any substantial result.

At length it happened, one calm day in the latter part of summer, that I was relaxing myself from the toils of severe study by a day's amusement in fishing in those waters which had been the favorite resort of my boyhood. I was in company with several worthy burghers of my native city. Our sport was indifferent; the fish did not bite freely; and we had frequently changed our fishing ground without bettering our luck. We at length anchored close under a ledge of rocky coast, on the eastern side of the island of Manhata. It was a still, warm day. The stream whirled and dimpled by us without a wave or even a ripple, and every thing was so calm and quiet that it was almost startling when the kingfisher would pitch himself from the branch of some dry tree, and after suspending himself for a moment in the air to take his aim, would souse into the smooth water after his prey. While we were lolling in our boat, half drowsy with the warm stillness of the day and the dullness of our sport, one of our party, a worthy alderman, was overtaken by a slumber, and, as he dozed, suffered the sinker of his drop-line to lie upon the bottom of the river. On waking, he found he had caught something of importance, from the weight; on drawing it to the surface, we were much surprised to find a long pistol of very curious and outlandish fashion, which, from its rusted condition, and its stock being worm-eaten and covered with barnacles, appeared to have been a long time under water. The unexpected appearance of this document of warfare occasioned much speculation among my pacific companions. One supposed it to have fallen there during the revolutionary war. Another, from the peculiarity of its fashion, attributed it to the voyagers in the earliest days of the settlement; perchance to the renowned Adrian Block, who explored the Sound and discovered Block Island, since so noted for its cheese. But a third, after regarding it for some time, pronounced it to be of veritable Spanish workmanship.

"I'll warrant," said he, "if this pistol could talk it would tell strange stories of hard fights among the Spanish Dons. I've not a doubt but it's a relique of the buccaneers of old times."

"Like enough," said another of the party. "There was Bradish the pirate, who at the time Lord Bellamont made such a stir after the buccaneers, buried money and jewels somewhere in these parts or on Long-Island; and then there was Captain Kidd—"

"Ah, that Kidd was a daring dog," said an iron-faced Cape Cod whaler. "There's a fine old song about him, all to the tune of:

'My name is Robert Kidd,
As I sailed, as I sailed.'

And it tells how he gained the devil's good graces by burying the Bible:

'I had the Bible in my hand,
  As I sailed, as I sailed,
And I buried it in the sand,
  As I sailed.'

Egad, if this pistol had belonged to him I should set some store by it out of sheer curiosity. Ah, well, there's an odd story I have heard about one Tom Walker, who, they say, dug up some of Kidd's buried money; and as the fish don't seem to bite at present, I'll tell it to you to pass away time."

## THE DEVIL AND TOM WALKER

A few miles from Boston, in Massachusetts, there is a deep inlet winding several miles into the interior of the country from Charles Bay, and terminating in a thickly-wooded swamp, or morass. On one side of this inlet is a beautiful dark grove; on the opposite side the land rises abruptly from the water's edge, into a high ridge on which grow a few scattered oaks of great age and immense size. It was under one of these gigantic trees, according to old stories, that Kidd the pirate buried his treasure. The inlet allowed a facility to bring the money in a boat secretly and at night to the very foot of the hill. The elevation of the place permitted a good look-out to be kept that no one was at hand, while the remarkable trees formed good landmarks by which the place might easily be found again. The old stories add, moreover, that the devil presided at the hiding of the money, and took it under his guardianship; but this, it is well-known, he always does with buried treasure, particularly when it has been ill gotten. Be that as it may, Kidd never returned to recover his wealth; being shortly after seized at Boston, sent out to England, and there hanged for a pirate.

About the year 1727, just at the time when earthquakes were prevalent in New England, and shook many tall sinners down upon their knees, there lived near this place a meagre miserly fellow of the name of Tom Walker. He had a wife as miserly as himself; they were so miserly that they even conspired to cheat each other. Whatever the woman could lay hands on she hid away; a hen could not cackle but she was on the alert to secure the new-laid egg. Her husband was continually prying about to detect her secret hoards, and many and fierce were the conflicts that took place about what ought to have been common property. They lived in a forlorn-looking house, that stood alone and had an air of starvation. A few straggling savin trees, emblems of sterility, grew near it; no smoke ever curled from its chimney; no traveller stopped at its door. A miserable horse, whose ribs were as articulate as the bars of a gridiron, stalked about a field where a thin carpet of moss, scarcely covering the ragged beds of pudding-stone, tantalized and balked his hunger; and sometimes he would lean his head over the fence, looked piteously at the passer-by, and seem to petition deliverance from this land of famine.

The house and its inmates had altogether a bad name. Tom's wife was a tall termagant, fierce of temper, loud of tongue, and strong of arm. Her voice was often heard in wordy warfare with her husband; and his face sometimes showed signs that their conflicts were not confined to words. No one ventured, however, to interfere between them; the lonely wayfarer shrunk within himself at the horrid clamor and clapper-clawing; eyed the den of discord askance, and hurried on his way, rejoicing, if a bachelor, in his celibacy.

One day that Tom Walker had been to a distant part of the neighborhood, he took what he considered a short cut homewards through the swamp. Like most short cuts, it was an ill-chosen route. The swamp was thickly grown with great gloomy pines and hemlocks, some of them ninety feet high; which made it dark at noon-day, and a retreat for all the owls of the neighborhood. It was full of pits and quagmires, partly covered with weeds and mosses; where the green surface often betrayed the traveller into a gulf of black smothering mud; there were also dark and stagnant pools, the abodes of the tadpole, the bull-frog, and the water-snake, and where trunks of pines and hemlocks lay half drowned, half rotting, looking like alligators, sleeping in the mire.

Tom had long been picking his way cautiously through this treacherous forest; stepping from tuft to tuft of rushes and roots which afforded precarious footholds among deep sloughs; or pacing carefully, like a cat, among the prostrate trunks of trees; startled now and then by the sudden screaming of the bittern, or the quacking of a wild duck, rising on the wing from some solitary pool. At length he arrived at a piece of firm ground, which ran out like a peninsula into the deep bosom of the swamp. It had been one of the strongholds of the Indians during their wars with the first colonists. Here they had thrown up a kind of fort which they had looked upon as almost impregnable, and had used as a place of refuge for their squaws and children. Nothing remained of the Indian fort but a few embankments gradually sinking to the level of the surrounding earth, and already overgrown in part by oaks and other forest trees, the foliage of which formed a contrast to the dark pines and hemlocks of the swamp.

It was late in the dusk of evening that Tom Walker reached the old fort, and he paused there for a while to rest himself. Any one but he would have felt unwilling to linger in this lonely, melancholy place, for the common people had a bad opinion of it from the stories handed down from the time of the Indian wars; when it was asserted that the savages held incantations here and made sacrifices to the evil spirit. Tom Walker, however, was not a man to be troubled with any fears of the kind.

He reposed himself for some time on the trunk of a fallen hemlock, listening to the boding cry of the tree-toad, and delving with his walking-staff into a mound of black mould at his feet. As he turned up the soil unconsciously, his staff struck against something hard. He raked it out of the vegetable mould, and lo! a cloven skull with an Indian tomahawk buried deep in it, lay before him. The rust on the weapon showed the time that had elapsed since this death blow had been given. It was a dreary memento of the fierce struggle that had taken place in this last foothold of the Indian warriors.

"Humph!" said Tom Walker, as he gave the skull a kick to shake the dirt from it.

"Let that skull alone!" said a gruff voice.

Tom lifted up his eyes and beheld a great black man, seated directly Opposite him on the stump of a tree. He was exceedingly surprised, having neither seen nor heard any one approach, and he was still more perplexed on observing, as well as the gathering gloom would permit, that the stranger was neither negro nor Indian. It is true, he was dressed in a rude, half Indian garb, and had a red belt or sash swathed round his body, but his face was neither black nor copper color, but swarthy and dingy and begrimed with soot, as if he had been accustomed to toil among fires and forges. He had a shock of coarse black hair, that stood out from his head in all directions; and bore an axe on his shoulder.

He scowled for a moment at Tom with a pair of great red eyes.

"What are you doing in my grounds?" said the black man, with a hoarse growling voice.

"Your grounds?" said Tom, with a sneer; "no more your grounds than mine: they belong to Deacon Peabody."

"Deacon Peabody be d——d," said the stranger, "as I flatter myself he will be, if he does not look more to his own sins and less to his neighbor's. Look yonder, and see how Deacon Peabody is faring."

Tom looked in the direction that the stranger pointed, and beheld one of the great trees, fair and flourishing without, but rotten at the core, and saw that it had been nearly hewn through, so that the first high wind was likely to blow it down. On the bark of the tree was scored the name of Deacon Peabody. He now looked round and found most of the tall trees marked with the names of some great men of the colony, and all more or less scored by the axe. The one on which he had been seated, and which had evidently just been hewn down, bore the name of Crowninshield; and he recollected a mighty rich man of that name, who made a vulgar display of wealth, which it was whispered he had acquired by buccaneering.

"He's just ready for burning!" said the black man, with a growl of triumph. "You see I am likely to have a good stock of firewood for winter."

"But what right have you," said Tom, "to cut down Deacon Peabody's timber?"

"The right of prior claim," said the other. "This woodland belonged to me long before one of your white-faced race put foot upon the soil."

"And pray, who are you, if I may be so bold?" said Tom.

"Oh, I go by various names. I am the Wild Huntsman in some countries; the Black Miner in others. In this neighborhood I am known by the name of the Black Woodsman. I am he to whom the red men devoted this spot, and now and then roasted a white man by way of sweet-smelling sacrifice. Since the red men have been exterminated by you white savages, I amuse myself by presiding at the persecutions of quakers and anabaptists; I am the great patron and prompter of slave dealers, and the grand master of the Salem witches."

"The upshot of all which is, that, if I mistake not," said Tom, sturdily, "you are he commonly called Old Scratch."

"The same at your service!" replied the black man, with a half civil nod.

Such was the opening of this interview, according to the old story, though it has almost too familiar an air to be credited. One would think that to meet with such a singular personage in this wild, lonely place, would have shaken any man's nerves; but Tom was a hard-minded fellow, not easily daunted, and he had lived so long with a termagant wife, that he did not even fear the devil.

It is said that after this commencement they had a long and earnest Conversation together, as Tom returned homewards. The black man told him of great sums of money which had been buried by Kidd the pirate, under the oak trees on the high ridge not far from the morass. All these were under his command and protected by his power, so that none could find them but such as propitiated his favor. These he offered to place within Tom Walker's reach, having conceived an especial kindness for him: but they were to be had only on certain conditions. What these conditions were, may easily be surmised, though Tom never disclosed them publicly. They must have been very hard, for he required time to think of them, and he was not a man to stick at trifles where money was in view. When they had reached the edge of the swamp the stranger paused.

"What proof have I that all you have been telling me is true?" said Tom.

"There is my signature," said the black man, pressing his finger on Tom's forehead. So saying, he turned off among the thickets of the swamp, and seemed, as Tom said, to go down, down, down, into the earth, until nothing but his head and shoulders could be seen, and so on until he totally disappeared.

When Tom reached home he found the black print of a finger burnt, as it were, into his forehead, which nothing could obliterate.

The first news his wife had to tell him was the sudden death of Absalom Crowninshield, the rich buccaneer. It was announced in the papers with the usual flourish, that "a great man had fallen in Israel."

Tom recollected the tree which his black friend had just hewn down, and which was ready for burning. "Let the freebooter roast," said Tom, "who cares!" He now felt convinced that all he had heard and seen was no illusion.

He was not prone to let his wife into his confidence; but as this was an uneasy secret, he willingly shared it with her. All her avarice was awakened at the mention of hidden gold, and she urged her husband to comply with the black man's terms and secure what would make them wealthy for life. However Tom might have felt disposed to sell himself to the devil, he was determined not to do so to oblige his wife; so he flatly refused out of the mere spirit of contradiction. Many and bitter were the quarrels they had on the subject, but the more she talked the more resolute was Tom not to be damned to please her. At length she determined to drive the bargain on her own account, and if she succeeded, to keep all the gain to herself.

Being of the same fearless temper as her husband, she sat off for the old Indian fort towards the close of a summer's day. She was many hour's absent. When she came back she was reserved and sullen in her replies. She spoke something of a black man whom she had met about twilight, hewing at the root of a tall tree. He was sulky, however, and would not come to terms; she was to go again with a propitiatory offering, but what it was she forebore to say.

The next evening she sat off again for the swamp, with her apron heavily laden. Tom waited and waited for her, but in vain: midnight came, but she did not make her appearance; morning, noon, night returned, but still she did not come. Tom now grew uneasy for her safety; especially as he found she had carried off in her apron the silver tea pot and spoons and every portable article of value. Another night elapsed, another morning came; but no wife. In a word, she was ever heard of more.

What was her real fate nobody knows, in consequence of so many pretending to know. It is one of those facts that have become confounded by a variety of historians. Some asserted that she lost her way among the tangled mazes of the swamp and sunk into some pit or slough; others, more uncharitable, hinted that she had eloped with the household booty, and made off to some other province; while others assert that the tempter had decoyed her into a dismal quagmire, on top of which her hat was found lying. In confirmation of this, it was said a great black man with an axe on his shoulder was seen late that very evening coming out of the swamp, carrying a bundle tied in a check apron, with an air of surly triumph.

The most current and probable story, however, observes that Tom Walker grew so anxious about the fate of his wife and his property that he sat out at length to seek them both at the Indian fort. During a long summer's afternoon he searched about the gloomy place, but no wife was to be seen. He called her name repeatedly, but she was no where to be heard. The bittern alone responded to his voice, as he flew screaming by; or the bull-frog croaked dolefully from a neighboring pool. At length, it is said, just in the brown hour of twilight, when the owls began to hoot and the bats to flit about, his attention was attracted by the clamor of carrion crows that were hovering about a cypress tree. He looked and beheld a bundle tied in a check apron and hanging in the branches of a tree; with a great vulture perched hard by, as if keeping watch upon it. He leaped with joy, for he recognized his wife's apron, and supposed it to contain the household valuables.

"Let us get hold of the property," said he consolingly to himself, "and we will endeavor to do without the woman."

As he scrambled up the tree the vulture spread its wide wings, and sailed off screaming into the deep shadows of the forest. Tom seized the check apron, but, woful sight! found nothing but a heart and liver tied up in it.

Such, according to the most authentic old story, was all that was to be found of Tom's wife. She had probably attempted to deal with the black man as she had been accustomed to deal with her husband; but though a female scold is generally considered a match for the devil, yet in this instance she appears to have had the worst of it. She must have died game, however: from the part that remained unconquered. Indeed, it is said Tom noticed many prints of cloven feet deeply stamped about the tree, and several handfuls of hair that looked as if they had been plucked from the coarse black shock of the woodsman. Tom knew his wife's prowess by experience. He shrugged his shoulders as he looked at the signs of a fierce clapper-clawing. "Egad," said he to himself, "Old Scratch must have had a tough time of it!"

Tom consoled himself for the loss of his property by the loss of his wife; for he was a little of a philosopher. He even felt something like gratitude towards the black woodsman, who he considered had done him a kindness. He sought, therefore, to cultivate a farther acquaintance with him, but for some time without success; the old black legs played shy, for whatever people may think, he is not always to be had for calling for; he knows how to play his cards when pretty sure of his game.

At length, it is said, when delay had whetted Tom's eagerness to the quick, and prepared him to agree to any thing rather than not gain the promised treasure, he met the black man one evening in his usual woodman dress, with his axe on his shoulder, sauntering along the edge of the swamp, and humming a tune. He affected to receive Tom's advance with great indifference, made brief replies, and went on humming his tune.

By degrees, however, Tom brought him to business, and they began to haggle about the terms on which the former was to have the pirate's treasure. There was one condition which need not be mentioned, being generally understood in all cases where the devil grants favors; but there were others about which, though of less importance, he was inflexibly obstinate. He insisted that the money found through his means should be employed in his service. He proposed, therefore, that Tom should employ it in the black traffic; that is to say, that he should fit out a slave ship. This, however, Tom resolutely refused; he was bad enough, in all conscience; but the devil himself could not tempt him to turn slave dealer.

Finding Tom so squeamish on this point, he did not insist upon it, but proposed instead that he should turn usurer; the devil being extremely anxious for the increase of usurers, looking upon them as his peculiar people.

To this no objections were made, for it was just to Tom's taste.

"You shall open a broker's shop in Boston next month," said the black man.

"I'll do it to-morrow, if you wish," said Tom Walker.

"You shall lend money at two per cent a month."

"Egad, I'll charge four!" replied Tom Walker.

"You shall extort bonds, foreclose mortgages, drive the merchant to bankruptcy—"

"I'll drive him to the d—l," cried Tom Walker, eagerly.

"You are the usurer for my money!" said the black legs, with delight. "When will you want the rhino?"

"This very night."

"Done!" said the devil.

"Done!" said Tom Walker.—So they shook hands and struck a bargain.

A few days' time saw Tom Walker seated behind his desk in a counting house in Boston. His reputation for a ready-moneyed man, who would lend money out for a good consideration, soon spread abroad. Every body remembers the days of Governor Belcher, when money was particularly scarce. It was a time of paper credit. The country had been deluged with government bills; the famous Land Bank had been established; there had been a rage for speculating; the people had run mad with schemes for new settlements; for building cities in the wilderness; land jobbers went about with maps of grants, and townships, and Eldorados, lying nobody knew where, but which every body was ready to purchase. In a word, the great speculating fever which breaks out every now and then in the country, had raged to an alarming degree, and body was dreaming of making sudden fortunes from nothing. As usual, the fever had subsided; the dream had gone off, and the imaginary fortunes with it; the patients were left in doleful plight, and the whole country resounded with the consequent cry of "hard times."

At this propitious time of public distress did Tom Walker set up as a usurer in Boston. His door was soon thronged by customers. The needy and the adventurous; the gambling speculator; the dreaming land jobber; the thriftless tradesman; the merchant with cracked credit; in short, every one driven to raise money by desperate means and desperate sacrifices, hurried to Tom Walker.

Thus Tom was the universal friend of the needy, and he acted like a "friend in need;" that is to say, he always exacted good pay and good security. In proportion to the distress of the applicant was the hardness of his terms. He accumulated bonds and mortgages; gradually squeezed his customers closer and closer; and sent them, at length, dry as a sponge from his door.

In this way he made money hand over hand; became a rich and mighty man, and exalted his cocked hat upon 'change. He built himself, as usual, a vast house, out of ostentation; but left the greater part of it unfinished and unfurnished out of parsimony. He even set up a carriage in the fullness of his vain-glory, though he nearly starved the horses which drew it; and as the ungreased wheels groaned and screeched on the axle trees, you would have thought you heard the souls of the poor debtors he was squeezing.

As Tom waxed old, however, he grew thoughtful. Having secured the good things of this world, he began to feel anxious about those of the next. He thought with regret on the bargain he had made with his black friend, and set his wits to work to cheat him out of the conditions. He became, therefore, all of a sudden, a violent church-goer. He prayed loudly and strenuously as if heaven were to be taken by force of lungs. Indeed, one might always tell when he had sinned most during the week, by the clamor of his Sunday devotion. The quiet Christians who had been modestly and steadfastly travelling Zion-ward, were struck with self-reproach at seeing themselves so suddenly outstripped in their career by this new-made convert. Tom was as rigid in religious, as in money matters; he was a stern supervisor and censurer of his neighbors, and seemed to think every sin entered up to their account became a credit on his own side of the page. He even talked of the expediency of reviving the persecution of quakers and anabaptists. In a word, Tom's zeal became as notorious as his riches.

Still, in spite of all this strenuous attention to forms, Tom had a Lurking dread that the devil, after all, would have his due. That he might not be taken unawares, therefore, it is said he always carried a small Bible in his coat pocket. He had also a great folio Bible on his counting-house desk, and would frequently be found reading it when people called on business; on such occasions he would lay his green spectacles on the book, to mark the place, while he turned round to drive some usurious bargain.

Some say that Tom grew a little crack-brained in his old days, and that fancying his end approaching, he had his horse new shod, saddled and bridled, and buried with his feet uppermost; because he supposed that at the last day the world would be turned upside down; in which case he should find his horse standing ready for mounting, and he was determined at the worst to give his old friend a run for it. This, however, is probably a mere old wives' fable. If he really did take such a precaution it was totally superfluous; at least so says the authentic old legend, which closes his story in the following manner:

On one hot afternoon in the dog days, just as a terrible black thunder-gust was coming up, Tom sat in his counting-house in his white linen cap and India silk morning-gown. He was on the point of foreclosing a mortgage, by which he would complete the ruin of an unlucky land speculator for whom he had professed the greatest friendship. The poor land jobber begged him to grant a few months' indulgence. Tom had grown testy and irritated and refused another day.

"My family will be ruined and brought upon the parish," said the land jobber.

"Charity begins at home," replied Tom, "I must take care of myself in these hard times."

"You have made so much money out of me," said the speculator.

Tom lost his patience and his piety—"The devil take me," said he, "if I have made a farthing!"

Just then there were three loud knocks at the street door. He stepped out to see who was there. A black man was holding a black horse which neighed and stamped with impatience.

"Tom, you're come for!" said the black fellow, gruffly. Tom shrunk back, but too late. He had left his little Bible at the bottom of his coat pocket, and his big Bible on the desk buried under the mortgage he was about to foreclose: never was sinner taken more unawares. The black man whisked him like a child astride the horse and away he galloped in the midst of a thunder-storm. The clerks stuck their pens behind their ears and stared after him from the windows. Away went Tom Walker, dashing down the street; his white cap bobbing up and down; his morning-gown fluttering in the wind, and his steed striking fire out of the pavement at every bound. When the clerks turned to look for the black man he had disappeared.

Tom Walker never returned to foreclose the mortgage. A countryman who lived on the borders of the swamp, reported that in the height of the thunder-gust he had heard a great clattering of hoofs and a howling along the road, and that when he ran to the window he just caught sight of a figure, such as I have described, on a horse that galloped like mad across the fields, over the hills and down into the black hemlock swamp towards the old Indian fort; and that shortly after a thunder-bolt fell in that direction which seemed to set the whole forest in a blaze.

The good people of Boston shook their heads and shrugged their shoulders, but had been so much accustomed to witches and goblins and tricks of the devil in all kinds of shapes from the first settlement of the colony, that they were not so much horror-struck as might have been expected. Trustees were appointed to take charge of Tom's effects. There was nothing, however, to administer upon. On searching his coffers all his bonds and mortgages were found reduced to cinders. In place of gold and silver, his iron chest was filled with chips and shavings; two skeletons lay in his stable instead of his half-starved horses, and the very next day his great house took fire and was burnt to the ground.

Such was the end of Tom Walker and his ill-gotten wealth. Let all griping money-brokers lay this story to heart. The truth of it is not to be doubted. The very hole under the oak trees, from whence he dug Kidd's money, is to be seen to this day; and the neighboring swamp and old Indian fort is often haunted in stormy nights by a figure on horseback, in a morning-gown and white cap, which is doubtless the troubled spirit of the usurer. In fact, the story has resolved itself into a proverb, and is the origin of that popular saying prevalent throughout New-England, of "The Devil and Tom Walker."

Such, as nearly as I can recollect, was the tenor of the tale told by the Cape Cod whaler. There were divers trivial particulars which I have omitted, and which wiled away the morning very pleasantly, until the time of tide favorable for fishing being passed, it was proposed that we should go to land, and refresh ourselves under the trees, until the noontide heat should have abated.

We accordingly landed on a delectable part of the island of Mannahatta, in that shady and embowered tract formerly under dominion of the ancient family of the Hardenbrooks. It was a spot well known to me in the course of the aquatic expeditions of my boyhood. Not far from where we landed, was an old Dutch family vault, in the side of a bank, which had been an object of great awe and fable among my schoolboy associates. There were several mouldering coffins within; but what gave it a fearful interest with us, was its being connected in our minds with the pirate wreck which lay among the rocks of Hell Gate. There were also stories of smuggling connected with it, particularly during a time that this retired spot was owned by a noted burgher called Ready Money Prevost; a man of whom it was whispered that he had many and mysterious dealings with parts beyond seas. All these things, however, had been jumbled together in our minds in that vague way in which such things are mingled up in the tales of boyhood.

While I was musing upon these matters my companions had spread a repast, from the contents of our well-stored pannier, and we solaced ourselves during the warm sunny hours of mid-day under the shade of a broad chestnut, on the cool grassy carpet that swept down to the water's edge. While lolling on the grass I summoned up the dusky recollections of my boyhood respecting this place, and repeated them like the imperfectly remembered traces of a dream, for the entertainment of my companions. When I had finished, a worthy old burgher, John Josse Vandermoere, the same who once related to me the adventures of Dolph Heyliger, broke silence and observed, that he recollected a story about money-digging which occurred in this very neighborhood. As we knew him to be one of the most authentic narrators of the province we begged him to let us have the particulars, and accordingly, while we refreshed ourselves with a clean long pipe of Blase Moore's tobacco, the authentic John Josse Vandermoere related the following tale.

## WOLFERT WEBBER; OR, GOLDEN DREAMS

In the year of grace one thousand seven hundred and—blank—for I do not remember the precise date; however, it was somewhere in the early part of the last century, there lived in the ancient city of the Manhattoes a worthy burgher, Wolfert Webber by name. He was descended from old Cobus Webber of the Brille in Holland, one of the original settlers, famous for introducing the cultivation of cabbages, and who came over to the province during the protectorship of Oloffe Van Kortlandt, otherwise called the Dreamer. The field in which Cobus Webber first planted himself and his cabbages had remained ever since in the family, who continued in the same line of husbandry, with that praiseworthy perseverance for which our Dutch burghers are noted. The whole family genius, during several generations was devoted to the study and development of this one noble vegetable; and to this concentration of intellect may doubtless be ascribed the prodigious size and renown to which the Webber cabbages attained.

The Webber dynasty continued in uninterrupted succession; and never did a line give more unquestionable proofs of legitimacy. The eldest son succeeded to the looks, as well as the territory of his sire; and had the portraits of this line of tranquil potentates been taken, they would have presented a row of heads marvellously resembling in shape and magnitude the vegetables over which they reigned.

The seat of government continued unchanged in the family mansion:—a Dutch-built house, with a front, or rather gable-end of yellow brick, tapering to a point, with the customary iron weathercock at the top. Every thing about the building bore the air of long-settled ease and security. Flights of martins peopled the little coops nailed against the walls, and swallows built their nests under the eaves; and every one knows that these house-loving birds bring good luck to the dwelling where they take up their abode. In a bright sunny morning in early summer, it was delectable to hear their cheerful notes, as they sported about in the pure, sweet air, chirping forth, as it were, the greatness and prosperity of the Webbers.

Thus quietly and comfortably did this excellent family vegetate under the shade of a mighty button-wood tree, which by little and little grew so great as entirely to overshadow their palace. The city gradually spread its suburbs round their domain. Houses sprung up to interrupt their prospects. The rural lanes in the vicinity began to grow into the bustle and populousness of streets; in short, with all the habits of rustic life they began to find themselves the inhabitants of a city.

Still, however, they maintained their hereditary character, and Hereditary possessions, with all the tenacity of petty German princes in the midst of the Empire. Wolfert was the last of the line, and succeeded to the patriarchal bench at the door, under the family tree, and swayed the sceptre of his fathers, a kind of rural potentate in the midst of a metropolis.

To share the cares and sweets of sovereignty, he had taken unto himself a help-mate, one of that excellent kind called stirring women; that is to say, she was one of those notable little housewives who are always busy when there is nothing to do. Her activity however, took one particular direction; her whole life seemed devoted to intense knitting; whether at home or abroad; walking or sitting, her needles were continually in motion, and it is even affirmed that by her unwearied industry she very nearly supplied her household with stockings throughout the year. This worthy couple were blessed with one daughter, who was brought up with great tenderness and care; uncommon pains had been taken with her education, so that she could stitch in every variety of way; make all kinds of pickles and preserves, and mark her own name on a sampler. The influence of her taste was seen also in the family garden, where the ornamental began to mingle with the useful; whole rows of fiery marigolds and splendid hollyhocks bordered the cabbage-beds; and gigantic sunflowers lolled their broad, jolly faces over the fences, seeming to ogle most affectionately the passers-by.

Thus reigned and vegetated Wolfert Webber over his paternal acres, peaceably and contentedly. Not but that, like all other sovereigns, he had his occasional cares and vexations. The growth of his native city sometimes caused him annoyance. His little territory gradually became hemmed in by streets and houses, which intercepted air and sunshine. He was now and then subject to the irruptions of the border population, that infest the streets of a metropolis, who would sometimes make midnight forays into his dominions, and carry off captive whole platoons of his noblest subjects. Vagrant swine would make a descent, too, now and then, when the gate was left open, and lay all waste before them; and mischievous urchins would often decapitate the illustrious sunflowers, the glory of the garden, as they lolled their heads so fondly over the walls. Still all these were petty grievances, which might now and then ruffle the surface of his mind, as a summer breeze will ruffle the surface of a mill-pond; but they could not disturb the deep-seated quiet of his soul. He would seize a trusty staff, that stood behind the door, issue suddenly out, and anoint the back of the aggressor, whether pig or urchin, and then return within doors, marvellously refreshed and tranquillized.

The chief cause of anxiety to honest Wolfert, however, was the growing prosperity of the city. The expenses of living doubled and trebled; but he could not double and treble the magnitude of his cabbages; and the number of competitors prevented the increase of price; thus, therefore, while every one around him grew richer, Wolfert grew poorer, and he could not, for the life of him, perceive how the evil was to be remedied.

This growing care which increased from day to day, had its gradual effect upon our worthy burgher; insomuch, that it at length implanted two or three wrinkles on his brow; things unknown before in the family of the Webbers; and it seemed to pinch up the corners of his cocked hat into an expression of anxiety, totally opposite to the tranquil, broad-brimmed, low-crowned beavers of his illustrious progenitors.

Perhaps even this would not have materially disturbed the serenity of his mind had he had only himself and his wife to care for; but there was his daughter gradually growing to maturity; and all the world knows when daughters begin to ripen no fruit or flower requires so much looking after. I have no talent at describing female charms, else fain would I depict the progress of this little Dutch beauty. How her blue eyes grew deeper and deeper, and her cherry lips redder and redder; and how she ripened and ripened, and rounded and rounded in the opening breath of sixteen summers, until, in her seventeenth spring, she seemed ready to burst out of her bodice like a half-blown rose-bud.

Ah, well-a-day! could I but show her as she was then, tricked out on a Sunday morning in the hereditary finery of the old Dutch clothes-press, of which her mother had confided to her the key. The wedding dress of her grandmother, modernized for use, with sundry ornaments, handed down as heirlooms in the family. Her pale brown hair smoothed with buttermilk in flat waving lines on each side of her fair forehead. The chain of yellow virgin gold, that encircled her neck; the little cross, that just rested at the entrance of a soft valley of happiness, as if it would sanctify the place. The—but pooh!—it is not for an old man like me to be prosing about female beauty: suffice it to say, Amy had attained her seventeenth year. Long since had her sampler exhibited hearts in couples desperately transfixed with arrows, and true lovers' knots worked in deep blue silk; and it was evident she began to languish for some more interesting occupation than the rearing of sunflowers or pickling of cucumbers.

At this critical period of female existence, when the heart within a damsel's bosom, like its emblem, the miniature which hangs without, is apt to be engrossed by a single image, a new visitor began to make his appearance under the roof of Wolfert Webber. This was Dirk Waldron, the only son of a poor widow, but who could boast of more fathers than any lad in the province; for his mother had had four husbands, and this only child, so that though born in her last wedlock, he might fairly claim to be the tardy fruit of a long course of cultivation. This son of four fathers united the merits and the vigor of his sires. If he had not a great family before him, he seemed likely to have a great one after him; for you had only to look at the fresh gamesome youth, to see that he was formed to be the founder of a mighty race.

This youngster gradually became an intimate visitor of the family. He talked little, but he sat long. He filled the father's pipe when it was empty, gathered up the mother's knitting-needle, or ball of worsted when it fell to the ground; stroked the sleek coat of the tortoise-shell cat, and replenished the teapot for the daughter from the bright copper kettle that sung before the fire. All these quiet little offices may seem of trifling import, but when true love is translated into Low Dutch, it is in this way that it eloquently expresses itself. They were not lost upon the Webber family. The winning youngster found marvellous favor in the eyes of the mother; the tortoise-shell cat, albeit the most staid and demure of her kind, gave indubitable signs of approbation of his visits, the tea-kettle seemed to sing out a cheering note of welcome at his approach, and if the sly glances of the daughter might be rightly read, as she sat bridling and dimpling, and sewing by her mother's side, she was not a wit behind Dame Webber, or grimalkin, or the tea-kettle in good-will.

Wolfert alone saw nothing of what was going on. Profoundly wrapt up in meditation on the growth of the city and his cabbages, he sat looking in the fire, and puffing his pipe in silence. One night, however, as the gentle Amy, according to custom, lighted her lover to the outer door, and he, according to custom, took his parting salute, the smack resounded so vigorously through the long, silent entry as to startle even the dull ear of Wolfert. He was slowly roused to a new source of anxiety. It had never entered into his head, that this mere child, who, as it seemed but the other day, had been climbing about his knees, and playing with dolls and baby-houses, could all at once be thinking of love and matrimony. He rubbed his eyes, examined into the fact, and really found that while he had been dreaming of other matters, she had actually grown into a woman, and what was more, had fallen in love. Here were new cares for poor Wolfert. He was a kind father, but he was a prudent man. The young man was a very stirring lad; but then he had neither money or land. Wolfert's ideas all ran in one channel, and he saw no alternative in case of a marriage, but to portion off the young couple with a corner of his cabbage garden, the whole of which was barely sufficient for the support of his family.

Like a prudent father, therefore, he determined to nip this passion in the bud, and forbade the youngster the house, though sorely did it go against his fatherly heart, and many a silent tear did it cause in the bright eye of his daughter. She showed herself, however, a pattern of filial piety and obedience. She never pouted and sulked; she never flew in the face of parental authority; she never fell into a passion, or fell into hysterics, as many romantic novel-read young ladies would do. Not she, indeed! She was none such heroical rebellious trumpery, I warrant ye. On the contrary, she acquiesced like an obedient daughter; shut the street-door in her lover's face, and if ever she did grant him an interview, it was either out of the kitchen window, or over the garden fence.

Wolfert was deeply cogitating these things in his mind, and his brow wrinkled with unusual care, as he wended his way one Saturday afternoon to a rural inn, about two miles from the city. It was a favorite resort of the Dutch part of the community from being always held by a Dutch line of landlords, and retaining an air and relish of the good old times. It was a Dutch-built house, that had probably been a country seat of some opulent burgher in the early time of the settlement. It stood near a point of land, called Corlears Hook, which stretches out into the Sound, and against which the tide, at its flux and reflux, sets with extraordinary rapidity. The venerable and somewhat crazy mansion was distinguished from afar, by a grove of elms and sycamores that seemed to wave a hospitable invitation, while a few weeping willows with their dank, drooping foliage, resembling falling waters, gave an idea of coolness, that rendered it an attractive spot during the heats of summer.

Here, therefore, as I said, resorted many of the old inhabitants of the Manhattoes, where, while some played at the shuffle-board and quoits and ninepins, others smoked a deliberate pipe, and talked over public affairs.

It was on a blustering autumnal afternoon that Wolfert made his visit to the inn. The grove of elms and willows was stripped of its leaves, which whirled in rustling eddies about the fields.

The ninepin alley was deserted, for the premature chilliness of the day had driven the company within doors. As it was Saturday afternoon, the habitual club was in session, composed principally of regular Dutch burghers, though mingled occasionally with persons of various, character and country, as is natural in a place of such motley population.

Beside the fire-place, and in a huge leather-bottomed armchair, sat the dictator of this little world, the venerable Rem, or, as it was pronounced, Ramm Rapelye.

He was a man of Walloon race, and illustrious for the antiquity of his line, his great grandmother having been the first white child born in the province. But he was still more illustrious for his wealth and dignity: he had long filled the noble office of alderman, and was a man to whom the governor himself took off his hat. He had maintained possession of the leathern-bottomed chair from time immemorial; and had gradually waxed in bulk as he sat in his seat of government, until in the course of years he filled its whole magnitude. His word was decisive with his subjects; for he was so rich a man, that he was never expected to support any opinion by argument. The landlord waited on him with peculiar officiousness; not that he paid better than his neighbors, but then the coin of a rich man seems always to be so much more acceptable. The landlord had always a pleasant word and a joke, to insinuate in the ear of the august Ramm. It is true, Ramm never laughed, and, indeed, maintained a mastiff-like gravity, and even surliness of aspect, yet he now and then rewarded mine host with a token of approbation; which, though nothing more nor less than a kind of grunt, yet delighted the landlord more than a broad laugh from a poorer man.

"This will be a rough night for the money-diggers," said mine host, as a gust of wind howled round the house, and rattled at the windows.

"What, are they at their works again?" said an English half-pay captain, with one eye, who was a frequent attendant at the inn.

"Aye, are they," said the landlord, "and well may they be. They've had luck of late. They say a great pot of money has been dug up in the field, just behind Stuyvesant's orchard. Folks think it must have been buried there in old times by Peter Stuyvesant, the Dutch Governor."

"Fudge!" said the one-eyed man of war, as he added a small portion of water to a bottom of brandy.

"Well, you may believe, or not, as you please," said mine host, somewhat nettled; "but every body knows that the old governor buried a great deal of his money at the time of the Dutch troubles, when the English red-coats seized on the province. They say, too, the old gentleman walks; aye, and in the very Same dress that he wears in the picture which hangs up in the family house."

"Fudge!" said the half-pay officer.

"Fudge, if you please!—But didn't Corney Van Zandt see him at midnight, stalking about in the meadow with his wooden leg, and a drawn sword in his hand, that flashed like fire? And what can he be walking for, but because people have been troubling the place where he buried his money in old times?"

Here the landlord was interrupted by several guttural sounds from Ramm Rapelye, betokening that he was laboring with the unusual production of an idea. As he was too great a man to be slighted by a prudent publican, mine host respectfully paused until he should deliver himself. The corpulent frame of this mighty burgher now gave all the symptoms of a volcanic mountain on the point of an eruption. First, there was a certain heaving of the abdomen, not unlike an earthquake; then was emitted a cloud of tobacco smoke from that crater, his mouth; then there was a kind of rattle in the throat, as if the idea were working its way up through a region of phlegm; then there were several disjointed members of a sentence thrown out, ending in a cough; at length his voice forced its way in the slow, but absolute tone of a man who feels the weight of his purse, if not of his ideas; every portion of his speech being marked by a testy puff of tobacco smoke.

"Who talks of old Peter Stuyvesant's walking?—puff—Have people no respect for persons?—puff—puff—Peter Stuyvesant knew better what to do with his money than to bury it—puff—I know the Stuyvesant family—puff—every one of them—puff—not a more respectable family in the province—puff—old standers—puff—warm householders—puff—none of your upstarts—puff—puff—puff.—Don't talk to me of Peter Stuyvesant's walking—puff—puff—puff—puff."

Here the redoubtable Ramm contracted his brow, clasped up his mouth, till it wrinkled at each corner, and redoubled his smoking with such vehemence, that the cloudly volumes soon wreathed round his head, as the smoke envelopes the awful summit of Mount Etna.

A general silence followed the sudden rebuke of this very rich man. The subject, however, was too interesting to be readily abandoned. The conversation soon broke forth again from the lips of Peechy Prauw Van Hook, the chronicler of the club, one of those narrative old men who seem to grow incontinent of words, as they grow old, until their talk flows from them almost involuntarily.

Peechy, who could at any time tell as many stories in an evening as his hearers could digest in a month, now resumed the conversation, by affirming that, to his knowledge, money had at different times been dug up in various parts of the island. The lucky persons who had discovered them had always dreamt of them three times beforehand, and what was worthy of remark, these treasures had never been found but by some descendant of the good old Dutch families, which clearly proved that they had been buried by Dutchmen in the olden time.

"Fiddle-stick with your Dutchmen!" cried the half-pay officer. "The Dutch had nothing to do with them. They were all buried by Kidd, the pirate, and his crew."

Here a key-note was touched that roused the whole company. The name of Captain Kidd was like a talisman in those times, and was associated with a thousand marvellous stories.

The half-pay officer was a man of great weight among the peaceable members of the club, by reason of his military character, and of the gunpowder scenes which, by his own account, he had witnessed.

The golden stories of Kidd, however, were resolutely rivalled by the tales of Peechy Prauw, who, rather than suffer his Dutch progenitors to be eclipsed by a foreign freebooter, enriched every spot in the neighborhood with the hidden wealth of Peter Stuyvesant and his contemporaries.

Not a word of this conversation was lost upon Wolfert Webber. He returned pensively home, full of magnificent ideas of buried riches. The soil of his native island seemed to be turned into gold-dust; and every field teemed with treasure. His head almost reeled at the thought how often he must have heedlessly rambled over places where countless sums lay, scarcely covered by the turf beneath his feet. His mind was in a vertigo with this whirl of new ideas. As he came in sight of the venerable mansion of his forefathers, and the little realm where the Webbers had so long and so contentedly flourished, his gorge rose at the narrowness of his destiny.

"Unlucky Wolfert!" exclaimed he, "others can go to bed and dream themselves into whole mines of wealth; they have but to seize a spade in the morning, and turn up doubloons like potatoes; but thou must dream of hardship, and rise to poverty—must dig thy field from year's end to year's end, and—and yet raise nothing but cabbages!"

Wolfert Webber went to bed with a heavy heart; and it was long before the golden visions that disturbed his brain, permitted him to sink into repose. The same visions, however, extended into his sleeping thoughts, and assumed a more definite form. He dreamt that he had discovered an immense treasure in the centre of his garden. At every stroke of the spade he laid bare a golden ingot; diamond crosses sparkled out of the dust; bags of money turned up their bellies, corpulent with pieces of eight, or venerable doubloons; and chests, wedged close with moidores, ducats, and pistareens, yawned before his ravished eyes, and vomited forth their glittering contents.

Wolfert awoke a poorer man than ever. He had no heart to go about his daily concerns, which appeared so paltry and profitless; but sat all day long in the chimney-corner, picturing to himself ingots and heaps of gold in the fire. The next night his dream was repeated. He was again in his garden, digging, and laying open stores of hidden wealth. There was something very singular in this repetition. He passed another day of reverie, and though it was cleaning-day, and the house, as usual in Dutch households, completely topsy-turvy, yet he sat unmoved amidst the general uproar.

The third night he went to bed with a palpitating heart. He put on his red nightcap, wrong side outwards for good luck. It was deep midnight before his anxious mind could settle itself into sleep. Again the golden dream was repeated, and again he saw his garden teeming with ingots and money-bags.

Wolfert rose the next morning in complete bewilderment. A dream three times repeated was never known to lie; and if so, his fortune was made.

In his agitation he put on his waistcoat with the hind part before, and this was a corroboration of good luck. He no longer doubted that a huge store of money lay buried somewhere in his cabbage-field, coyly waiting to be sought for, and he half repined at having so long been scratching about the surface of the soil, instead of digging to the centre.

He took his seat at the breakfast-table full of these speculations; asked his daughter to put a lump of gold in to his tea, and on handing his wife a plate of slap-jacks, begging her to help herself to a doubloon.

His grand care now was how to secure this immense treasure without it being known. Instead of working regularly in his grounds in the day-time, he now stole from his bed at night, and with spade and pickaxe, went to work to rip up and dig about his paternal acres, from one end to the other. In a little time the whole garden, which had presented such a goodly and regular appearance, with its phalanx of cabbages, like a vegetable army in battle array, was reduced to a scene of devastation, while the relentless Wolfert, with nightcap on head, and lantern and spade in hand, stalked through the slaughtered ranks, the destroying angel of his own vegetable world.

Every morning bore testimony to the ravages of the preceding night in cabbages of all ages and conditions, from the tender sprout to the full-grown head, piteously rooted from their quiet beds like worthless weeds, and left to wither in the sunshine. It was in vain Wolfert's wife remonstrated; it was in vain his darling daughter wept over the destruction of some favorite marygold. "Thou shalt have gold of another guess-sort," he would cry, chucking her under the chin; "thou shalt have a string of crooked ducats for thy wedding-necklace, my child." His family began really to fear that the poor man's wits were diseased. He muttered in his sleep at night of mines of wealth, of pearls and diamonds and bars of gold. In the day-time he was moody and abstracted, and walked about as if in a trance. Dame Webber held frequent councils with all the old women of the neighborhood, not omitting the parish dominie; scarce an hour in the day but a knot of them might be seen wagging their white caps together round her door, while the poor woman made some piteous recital. The daughter, too, was fain to seek for more frequent consolation from the stolen interviews of her favored swain, Dirk Waldron. The delectable little Dutch songs with which she used to dulcify the house grew less and less frequent, and she would forget her sewing and look wistfully in her father's face as he sat pondering by the fireside.

Wolfert caught her eye one day fixed on him thus anxiously, and for a moment was roused from his golden reveries—"Cheer up, my girl," said he, exultingly, "why dost thou droop?—thou shalt hold up thy head one day with the—and the Schenaerhorns, the Van Hornes, and the Van Dams—the patroon himself shall be glad to get thee for his son!"

Amy shook her head at this vain-glorious boast, and was more than ever in doubt of the soundness of the good man's intellect.

In the meantime Wolfert went on digging, but the field was extensive, and as his dream had indicated no precise spot, he had to dig at random. The winter set in before one-tenth of the scene of promise had been explored. The ground became too frozen and the nights too cold for the labors of the spade. No sooner, however, did the returning warmth of spring loosen the soil, and the small frogs begin to pipe in the meadows, but Wolfert resumed his labors with renovated zeal. Still, however, the hours of industry were reversed. Instead of working cheerily all day, planting and setting out his vegetables, he remained thoughtfully idle, until the shades of night summoned him to his secret labors. In this way he continued to dig from night to night, and week to week, and month to month, but not a stiver did he find. On the contrary, the more he digged the poorer he grew. The rich soil of his garden was digged away, and the sand and gravel from beneath were thrown to the surface, until the whole field presented an aspect of sandy barrenness.

In the meantime the seasons gradually rolled on. The little frogs that had piped in the meadows in early spring, croaked as bull-frogs in the brooks during the summer heats, and then sunk into silence. The peach tree budded, blossomed, and bore its fruit. The swallows and martins came, twittered about the roof, built their nests, reared their young, held their congress along the eaves, and then winged their flight in search of another spring. The caterpillar spun its winding-sheet, dangled in it from the great buttonwood tree that shaded the house, turned into a moth, fluttered with the last sunshine of summer, and disappeared; and finally the leaves of the buttonwood tree turned yellow, then brown, then rustled one by one to the ground, and whirling about in little eddies of wind and dust, whispered that winter was at hand.

Wolfert gradually awoke from his dream of wealth as the year declined. He had reared no crop to supply the wants of his household during the sterility of winter. The season was long and severe, and for the first time the family was really straightened in its comforts. By degrees a revulsion of thought took place in Wolfert's mind, common to those whose golden dreams have been disturbed by pinching realities. The idea gradually stole upon him that he should come to want. He already considered himself one of the most unfortunate men in the province, having lost such an incalculable amount of undiscovered treasure, and now, when thousands of pounds had eluded his search, to be perplexed for shillings and pence was cruel in the extreme.

Haggard care gathered about his brow; he went about with a money-seeking air, his eyes bent downwards into the dust, and carrying his hands in his pockets, as men are apt to do when they have nothing else to put into them. He could not even pass the city almshouse without giving it a rueful glance, as if destined to be his future abode.

The strangeness of his conduct and of his looks occasioned much speculation and remark. For a long time he was suspected of being crazy, and then every body pitied him; at length it began to be suspected that he was poor, and then every body avoided him.

The rich old burghers of his acquaintance met him, outside of the door when he called, entertained him hospitably on the threshold, pressed him warmly by the hand on parting, shook their heads as he walked away, with the kind-hearted expression of "poor Wolfert," and turned a corner nimbly, if by chance they saw him approaching as they walked the streets. Even the barber and cobbler of the neighborhood, and a tattered tailor in an alley hard by, three of the poorest and merriest rogues in the world, eyed him with that abundant sympathy which usually attends a lack of means, and there is not a doubt but their pockets would have been at his command, only that they happened to be empty.

Thus every body deserted the Webber mansion, as if poverty were contagious, like the plague; every body but honest Dirk Waldron, who still kept up his stolen visits to the daughter, and indeed seemed to wax more affectionate as the fortunes of his mistress were on the wane.

Many months had elapsed since Wolfert had frequented his old resort, the rural inn. He was taking a long lonely walk one Saturday afternoon, musing over his wants and disappointments, when his feet took instinctively their wonted direction, and on awaking out of a reverie, he found himself before the door of the inn. For some moments he hesitated whether to enter, but his heart yearned for companionship; and where can a ruined man find better companionship than at a tavern, where there is neither sober example nor sober advice to put him out of countenance?

Wolfert found several of the old frequenters of the tavern at their usual posts, and seated in their usual places; but one was missing, the great Ramm Rapelye, who for many years had filled the chair of state. His place was supplied by a stranger, who seemed, however, completely at home in the chair and the tavern. He was rather under-size, but deep-chested, square, and muscular. His broad shoulders, double joints, and bow-knees, gave tokens of prodigious strength. His face was dark and weather-beaten; a deep scar, as if from the slash of a cutlass, had almost divided his nose, and made a gash in his upper lip, through which his teeth shone like a bull-dog's. A mass of iron gray hair gave a grizzly finish to his hard-favored visage. His dress was of an amphibious character. He wore an old hat edged with tarnished lace, and cocked in martial style, on one side of his head; a rusty blue military coat with brass buttons, and a wide pair of short petticoat trousers, or rather breeches, for they were gathered up at the knees. He ordered every body about him with an authoritative air; talked in a brattling voice, that sounded like the crackling of thorns under a pot; damned the landlord and servants with perfect impunity, and was waited upon with greater obsequiousness than had ever been shown to the mighty Ramm himself.

Wolfert's curiosity was awakened to know who and what was this stranger who had thus usurped absolute sway in this ancient domain. He could get nothing, however, but vague information. Peechy Prauw took him aside, into a remote corner of the hall, and there in an under-voice, and with great caution, imparted to him all that he knew on the subject. The inn had been aroused several months before, on a dark stormy night, by repeated long shouts, that seemed like the howlings of a wolf. They came from the water-side; and at length were distinguished to be hailing the house in the seafaring manner. "House-a-hoy!" The landlord turned out with his head-waiter, tapster, hostler, and errand boy—that is to say with his old negro Cuff. On approaching the place from whence the voice proceeded, they found this amphibious-looking personage at the water's edge, quite alone, and seated on a great oaken sea-chest. How he came there, whether he had been set on shore from some boat, or had floated to land on his chest, nobody could tell, for he did not seem disposed to answer questions, and there was something in his looks and manners that put a stop to all questioning. Suffice it to say, he took possession of a corner room of the inn, to which his chest was removed with great difficulty. Here he had remained ever since, keeping about the inn and its vicinity. Sometimes, it is true, he disappeared for one, two, or three days at a time, going and returning without giving any notice or account of his movements. He always appeared to have plenty of money, though often of very strange, outlandish coinage; and he regularly paid his bill every evening before turning in.

He had fitted up his room to his own fancy, having slung a hammock from the ceiling instead of a bed, and decorated the walls with rusty pistols and cutlasses of foreign workmanship. A great part of his time was passed in this room, seated by the window, which commanded a wide view of the Sound, a short old-fashioned pipe in his mouth, a glass of rum toddy at his elbow, and a pocket telescope in his hand, with which he reconnoitred every boat that moved upon the water. Large square-rigged vessels seemed to excite but little attention; but the moment he descried any thing with a shoulder-of-mutton sail, or that a barge, or yawl, or jolly boat hove in sight, up went the telescope, and he examined it with the most scrupulous attention.

All this might have passed without much notice, for in those times the province was so much the resort of adventurers of all characters and climes that any oddity in dress or behavior attracted but little attention. But in a little while this strange sea monster, thus strangely cast up on dry land, began to encroach upon the long-established customs and customers of the place; to interfere in a dictatorial manner in the affairs of the ninepin alley and the bar-room, until in the end he usurped an absolute command over the little inn. It was in vain to attempt to withstand his authority. He was not exactly quarrelsome, but boisterous and peremptory, like one accustomed to tyrannize on a quarter deck; and there was a dare-devil air about every thing he said and did, that inspired a wariness in all bystanders. Even the half-pay officer, so long the hero of the club, was soon silenced by him; and the quiet burghers stared with wonder at seeing their inflammable man of war so readily and quietly extinguished.

And then the tales that he would tell were enough to make a peaceable man's hair stand on end. There was not a sea fight, or marauding or free-booting adventure that had happened within the last twenty years but he seemed perfectly versed in it. He delighted to talk of the exploits of the buccaneers in the West-Indies and on the Spanish Main. How his eyes would glisten as he described the waylaying of treasure ships, the desperate fights, yard arm and yard arm—broadside and broad side—the boarding and capturing of large Spanish galleons! with what chuckling relish would he describe the descent upon some rich Spanish colony; the rifling of a church; the sacking of a convent! You would have thought you heard some gormandizer dilating upon the roasting a savory goose at Michaelmas as he described the roasting of some Spanish Don to make him discover his treasure—a detail given with a minuteness that made every rich old burgher present turn uncomfortably in his chair. All this would be told with infinite glee, as if he considered it an excellent joke; and then he would give such a tyrannical leer in the face of his next neighbor, that the poor man would be fain to laugh out of sheer faint-heartedness. If any one, however, pretended to contradict him in any of his stories he was on fire in an instant. His very cocked hat assumed a momentary fierceness, and seemed to resent the contradiction.—"How the devil should you know as well as I! I tell you it was as I say!" and he would at the same time let slip a broadside of thundering oaths and tremendous sea phrases, such as had never been heard before within those peaceful walls.

Indeed, the worthy burghers began to surmise that he knew more of these stories than mere hearsay. Day after day their conjectures concerning him grew more and more wild and fearful. The strangeness of his manners, the mystery that surrounded him, all made him something incomprehensible in their eyes. He was a kind of monster of the deep to them—he was a merman—he was behemoth—he was leviathan—in short, they knew not what he was.

The domineering spirit of this boisterous sea urchin at length grew quite intolerable. He was no respecter of persons; he contradicted the richest burghers without hesitation; he took possession of the sacred elbow chair, which time out of mind had been the seat of sovereignty of the illustrious Ramm Rapelye. Nay, he even went so far in one of his rough jocular moods, as to slap that mighty burgher on the back, drink his toddy and wink in his face, a thing scarcely to be believed. From this time Ramm Rapelye appeared no more at the inn; his example was followed by several of the most eminent customers, who were too rich to tolerate being bullied out of their opinions, or being obliged to laugh at another man's jokes. The landlord was almost in despair, but he knew not how to get rid of this sea monster and his sea-chest, which seemed to have grown like fixtures, or excrescences on his establishment.

Such was the account whispered cautiously in Wolfert's ear, by the narrator, Peechy Prauw, as he held him by the button in a corner of the hall, casting a wary glance now and then towards the door of the bar-room, lest he should be overheard by the terrible hero of his tale.

Wolfert took his seat in a remote part of the room in silence; impressed with profound awe of this unknown, so versed in freebooting history. It was to him a wonderful instance of the revolutions of mighty empires, to find the venerable Ramm Rapelye thus ousted from the throne; a rugged tarpaulin dictating from his elbow chair, hectoring the patriarchs, and filling this tranquil little realm with brawl and bravado.

The stranger was on this evening in a more than usually communicative mood, and was narrating a number of astounding stories of plunderings and burnings upon the high seas. He dwelt upon them with peculiar relish, heightening the frightful particulars in proportion to their effect on his peaceful auditors. He gave a long swaggering detail of the capture of a Spanish merchantman. She was laying becalmed during a long summer's day, just off from an island which was one of the lurking places of the pirates. They had reconnoitred her with their spy-glasses from the shore, and ascertained her character and force. At night a picked crew of daring fellows set off for her in a whale boat. They approached with muffled oars, as she lay rocking idly with the undulations of the sea and her sails flapping against the masts. They were close under her stern before the guard on deck was aware of their approach. The alarm was given; the pirates threw hand grenades on deck and sprang up the main chains sword in hand.

The crew flew to arms, but in great confusion some were shot down, others took refuge in the tops; others were driven overboard and drowned, while others fought hand to hand from the main deck to the quarter deck, disputing gallantly every inch of ground. There were three Spanish gentlemen on board with their ladies, who made the most desperate resistance; they defended the companion-way, cut down several of their assailants, and fought like very devils, for they were maddened by the shrieks of the ladies from the cabin. One of the Dons was old and soon despatched. The other two kept their ground vigorously, even though the captain of the pirates was among their assailants. Just then there was a shout of victory from the main deck. "The ship is ours!" cried the pirates.

One of the Dons immediately dropped his sword and surrendered; the other, who was a hot-headed youngster, and just married, gave the captain a slash in the face that laid all open. The captain just made out to articulate the words "no quarter."

"And what did they do with their prisoners?" said Peechy Prauw, eagerly.

"Threw them all overboard!" said the merman.

A dead pause followed this reply. Peechy Prauw shrunk quietly back like a man who had unwarily stolen upon the lair of a sleeping lion. The honest burghers cast fearful glances at the deep scar slashed across the visage of the stranger, and moved their chairs a little farther off. The seaman, however, smoked on without moving a muscle, as though he either did not perceive or did not regard the unfavorable effect he had produced upon his hearers.

The half-pay officer was the first to break the silence; for he was Continually tempted to make ineffectual head against this tyrant of the seas, and to regain his lost consequence in the eyes of his ancient companions. He now tried to match the gunpowder tales of the stranger by others equally tremendous. Kidd, as usual, was his hero, concerning whom he had picked up many of the floating traditions of the province. The seaman had always evinced a settled pique against the red-faced warrior. On this occasion he listened with peculiar impatience. He sat with one arm a-kimbo, the other elbow on a table, the hand holding on to the small pipe he was pettishly puffing; his legs crossed, drumming with one foot on the ground and casting every now and then the side glance of a basilisk at the prosing captain. At length the latter spoke of Kidd's having ascended the Hudson with some of his crew, to land his plunder in secrecy.

"Kidd up the Hudson!" burst forth the seaman, with a tremendous oath; "Kidd never was up the Hudson!"

"I tell you he was," said the other. "Aye, and they say he buried a quantity of treasure on the little flat that runs out into the river, called the Devil's Dans Kammer."

"The Devil's Dans Kammer in your teeth!" cried the seaman. "I tell you Kidd never was up the Hudson—what the plague do you know of Kidd and his haunts?"

"What do I know?" echoed the half-pay officer; "why, I was in London at the time of his trial, aye, and I had the pleasure of seeing him hanged at Execution Dock."

"Then, sir, let me tell you that you saw as pretty a fellow hanged as ever trod shoe leather. Aye!" putting his face nearer to that of the officer, "and there was many a coward looked on, that might much better have swung in his stead."

The half-pay officer was silenced; but the indignation thus pent up in his bosom glowed with intense vehemence in his single eye, which kindled like a coal.

Peechy Prauw, who never could remain silent, now took up the word, and in a pacifying tone observed that the gentleman certainly was in the right. Kidd never did bury money up the Hudson, nor indeed in any of those parts, though many affirm the fact. It was Bradish and others of the buccaneers who had buried money, some said in Turtle Bay, others on Long-Island, others in the neighborhood of Hell Gate. Indeed, added he, I recollect an adventure of Mud Sam, the negro fisherman, many years ago, which some think had something to do with the buccaneers. As we are all friends here, and as it will go no farther, I'll tell it to you.

"Upon a dark night many years ago, as Sam was returning from fishing in Hell Gate—"

Here the story was nipped in the bud by a sudden movement from the unknown, who, laying his iron fist on the table, knuckles downward, with a quiet force that indented the very boards, and looking grimly over his shoulder, with the grin of an angry bear. "Heark'ee, neighbor," said he, with significant nodding of the head, "you'd better let the buccaneers and their money alone—they're not for old men and old women to meddle with. They fought hard for their money, they gave body and soul for it, and wherever it lies buried, depend upon it he must have a tug with the devil who gets it."

This sudden explosion was succeeded by a blank silence throughout the room. Peechy Prauw shrunk within himself, and even the red-faced officer turned pale. Wolfert, who, from a dark corner of the room, had listened with intense eagerness to all this talk about buried treasure, looked with mingled awe and reverence on this bold buccaneer, for such he really suspected him to be. There was a chinking of gold and a sparkling of jewels in all his stories about the Spanish Main that gave a value to every period, and Wolfert would have given any thing for the rummaging of the ponderous sea-chest, which his imagination crammed full of golden chalices and crucifixes and jolly round bags of doubloons.

The dead stillness that had fallen upon the company was at length interrupted by the stranger, who pulled out a prodigious watch of curious and ancient workmanship, and which in Wolferts' eyes had a decidedly Spanish look. On touching a spring it struck ten o'clock; upon which the sailor called for his reckoning, and having paid it out of a handful of outlandish coin, he drank off the remainder of his beverage, and without taking leave of any one, rolled out of the room, muttering to himself as he stamped up-stairs to his chamber.

It was some time before the company could recover from the silence into which they had been thrown. The very footsteps of the stranger, which were heard now and then as he traversed his chamber, inspired awe.

Still the conversation in which they had been engaged was too interesting not to be resumed. A heavy thunder-gust had gathered up unnoticed while they were lost in talk, and the torrents of rain that fell forbade all thoughts of setting off for home until the storm should subside. They drew nearer together, therefore, and entreated the worthy Peechy Prauw to continue the tale which had been so discourteously interrupted. He readily complied, whispering, however, in a tone scarcely above his breath, and drowned occasionally by the rolling of the thunder, and he would pause every now and then, and listen with evident awe, as he heard the heavy footsteps of the stranger pacing overhead.

The following is the purport of his story.

## THE ADVENTURE OF SAM, THE BLACK FISHERMAN COMMONLY DENOMINATED MUD SAM

Every body knows Mud Sam, the old negro fisherman who has fished about the Sound for the last twenty or thirty years. Well, it is now many years since that Sam, who was then a young fellow, and worked on the farm of Killian Suydam on Long Island, having finished his work early, was fishing, one still summer evening, just about the neighborhood of Hell Gate. He was in a light skiff, and being well acquainted with the currents and eddies, he had been able to shift his station with the shifting of the tide, from the Hen and Chickens to the Hog's back, and from the Hog's back to the Pot, and from the Pot to the Frying-pan; but in the eagerness of his sport Sam did not see that the tide was rapidly ebbing; until the roaring of the whirlpools and rapids warned him of his danger, and he had some difficulty in shooting his skiff from among the rocks and breakers, and getting to the point of Blackwell's Island. Here he cast anchor for some time, waiting the turn of the tide to enable him to return homewards.

As the night set in it grew blustering and gusty. Dark clouds came bundling up in the west; and now and then a growl of thunder or a flash of lightning told that a summer storm was at hand. Sam pulled over, therefore, under the lee of Manhattan Island, and coasting along came to a snug nook, just under a steep beetling rock, where he fastened his skiff to the root of a tree that shot out from a cleft and spread its broad branches like a canopy over the water. The gust came scouring along; the wind threw up the river in white surges; the rain rattled among the leaves, the thunder bellowed worse than that which is now bellowing, the lightning seemed to lick up the surges of the stream; but Sam, snugly sheltered under rock and tree, lay crouched in his skiff, rocking upon the billows, until he fell asleep. When he awoke all was quiet. The gust had passed away, and only now and then a faint gleam of lightning in the east showed which way it had gone. The night was dark and moonless; and from the state of the tide Sam concluded it was near midnight. He was on the point of making loose his skiff to return homewards, when he saw a light gleaming along the water from a distance, which seemed rapidly approaching. As it drew near he perceived that it came from a lanthorn in the bow of a boat which was gliding along under shadow of the land. It pulled up in a small cove, close to where he was. A man jumped on shore, and searching about with the lanthorn exclaimed, "This is the place—here's the Iron ring." The boat was then made fast, and the man returning on board, assisted his comrades in conveying something heavy on shore. As the light gleamed among them, Sam saw that they were five stout, desperate-looking fellows, in red woollen caps, with a leader in a three-cornered hat, and that some of them were armed with dirks, or long knives, and pistols. They talked low to one another, and occasionally in some outlandish tongue which he could not understand.

On landing they made their way among the bushes, taking turns to relieve each other in lugging their burthen up the rocky bank. Sam's curiosity was now fully aroused, so leaving his skiff he clambered silently up the ridge that overlooked their path. They had stopped to rest for a moment, and the leader was looking about among the bushes with his lanthorn. "Have you brought the spades?" said one. "They are here," replied another, who had them on his shoulder. "We must dig deep, where there will be no risk of discovery," said a third.

A cold chill ran through Sam's veins. He fancied he saw before him a gang of murderers, about to bury their victim. His knees smote together. In his agitation he shook the branch of a tree with which he was supporting himself as he looked over the edge of the cliff.

"What's that?" cried one of the gang. "Some one stirs among the bushes!"

The lanthorn was held up in the direction of the noise. One of the red-caps cocked a pistol, and pointed it towards the very lace where Sam was standing. He stood motionless—breathless; expecting the next moment to be his last. Fortunately, his dingy complexion was in his favor, and made no glare among the leaves.

"'Tis no one," said the man with the lanthorn. "What a plague! you would not fire off your pistol and alarm the country."

The pistol was uncocked; the burthen was resumed, and the party slowly toiled up the bank. Sam watched them as they went; the light sending back fitful gleams through the dripping bushes, and it was not till they were fairly out of sight that he ventured to draw breath freely. He now thought of getting back to his boat, and making his escape out of the reach of such dangerous neighbors; but curiosity was all-powerful with poor Sam. He hesitated and lingered and listened. By and bye he heard the strokes of spades.

"They are digging the grave!" said he to himself; the cold sweat started upon his forehead. Every stroke of a spade, as it sounded through the silent groves, went to his heart; it was evident there was as little noise made as possible; every thing had an air of mystery and secrecy. Sam had a great relish for the horrible—a tale of murder was a treat for him; and he was a constant attendant at executions. He could not, therefore, resist an impulse, in spite of every danger, to steal nearer, and overlook the villains at their work. He crawled along cautiously, therefore, inch by inch; stepping with the utmost care among the dry leaves, lest their rustling should betray him. He came at length to where a steep rock intervened between him and the gang; he saw the light of their lanthorn shining up against the branches of the trees on the other side. Sam slowly and silently clambered up the surface of the rock, and raising his head above its naked edge, beheld the villains immediately below him, and so near that though he dreaded discovery, he dared not withdraw lest the least movement should be heard. In this way he remained, with his round black face peering over the edge of the rock, like the sun just emerging above the edge of the horizon, or the round-cheeked moon on the dial of a clock.

The red-caps had nearly finished their work; the grave was filled up, and they were carefully replacing the turf. This done, they scattered dry leaves over the place. "And now," said the leader, "I defy the devil himself to find it out."

"The murderers!" exclaimed Sam involuntarily.

The whole gang started, and looking up, beheld the round black head of Sam just above them. His white eyes strained half out of their orbits; his white teeth chattering, and his whole visage shining with cold perspiration.

"We're discovered!" cried one.

"Down with him!" cried another.

Sam heard the cocking of a pistol, but did not pause for the report. He scrambled over rock and stone, through bush and briar; rolled down banks like a hedgehog; scrambled up others like a catamount. In every direction he heard some one or other of the gang hemming him in. At length he reached the rocky ridge along the river; one of the red-caps was hard behind him. A steep rock like a wall rose directly in his way; it seemed to cut off all retreat, when he espied the strong cord-like branch of a grape-vine reaching half way down it. He sprang at it with the force of a desperate man, seized it with both hands, and being young and agile, succeeded in swinging himself to the summit of the cliff. Here he stood in full relief against the sky, when the red-cap cocked his pistol and fired. The ball whistled by Sam's head. With the lucky thought of a man in an emergency, he uttered a yell, fell to the ground, and detached at the same time a fragment of the rock, which tumbled with a loud splash into the river.

"I've done his business," said the red-cap, to one or two of his comrades as they arrived panting. "He'll tell no tales, except to the fishes in the river."

His pursuers now turned off to meet their companions. Sam sliding silently down the surface of the rock, let himself quietly into his skiff, cast loose the fastening, and abandoned himself to the rapid current, which in that place runs like a mill-stream, and soon swept him off from the neighborhood. It was not, however, until he had drifted a great distance that he ventured to ply his oars; when he made his skiff dart like an arrow through the strait of Hell Gate, never heeding the danger of Pot, Frying-pan, or Hog's-back itself; nor did he feel himself thoroughly secure until safely nestled in bed in the cockloft of the ancient farm-house of the Suydams.

Here the worthy Peechy paused to take breath and to take a sip of the gossip tankard that stood at his elbow. His auditors remained with open mouths and outstretched necks, gaping like a nest of swallows for an additional mouthful.

"And is that all?" exclaimed the half-pay officer.

"That's all that belongs to the story," said Peechy Prauw.

"And did Sam never find out what was buried by the redcaps?" said Wolfert, eagerly; whose mind was haunted by nothing but ingots and doubloons.

"Not that I know of; he had no time to spare from his work; and to tell the truth, he did not like to run the risk of another race among the rocks. Besides, how should he recollect the spot where the grave had been digged? every thing would look different by daylight. And then, where was the use of looking for a dead body, when there was no chance of hanging the murderers?"

"Aye, but are you sure it was a dead body they buried?" said Wolfert.

"To be sure," cried Peechy Prauw, exultingly. "Does it not haunt in the neighborhood to this very day?"

"Haunts!" exclaimed several of the party, opening their eyes still wider and edging their chairs still closer.

"Aye, haunts," repeated Peechy; "has none of you heard of father red-cap that haunts the old burnt farm-house in the woods, on the border of the Sound, near Hell Gate?"

"Oh, to be sure, I've heard tell of something of the kind, but then I took it for some old wives' fable."

"Old wives' fable or not," said Peechy Prauw, "that farmhouse stands hard by the very spot. It's been unoccupied time out of mind, and stands in a wild, lonely part of the coast; but those who fish in the neighborhood have often heard strange noises there; and lights have been seen about the wood at night; and an old fellow in a red cap has been seen at the windows more than once, which people take to be the ghost of the body that was buried there. Once upon a time three soldiers took shelter in the building for the night, and rummaged it from top to bottom, when they found old father red-cap astride of a cider-barrel in the cellar, with a jug in one hand and a goblet in the other. He offered them a drink out of his goblet, but just as one of the soldiers was putting it to his mouth-Whew! a flash of fire blazed through the cellar, blinded every mother's son of them for several minutes, and when they recovered their eye-sight, jug, goblet, and red-cap had vanished, and nothing but the empty cider-barrel remained."

Here the half-pay officer, who was growing very muzzy and sleepy, and nodding over his liquor, with half-extinguished eye, suddenly gleamed up like an expiring rushlight.

"That's all humbug!" said he, as Peechy finished his last story.

"Well, I don't vouch for the truth of it myself," said Peechy Prauw, "though all the world knows that there's something strange about the house and grounds; but as to the story of Mud Sam, I believe it just as well as if it had happened to myself."

The deep interest taken in this conversation by the company, had made them unconscious of the uproar that prevailed abroad, among the elements, when suddenly they were all electrified by a tremendous clap of thunder. A lumbering crash followed instantaneously that made the building shake to its foundation. All started from their seats, imagining it the shock of an earthquake, or that old father red-cap was coming among them in all his terrors. They listened for a moment, but only heard the rain pelting against the windows, and the wind howling among the trees. The explosion was soon explained by the apparition of an old negro's bald head thrust in at the door, his white goggle eyes contrasting with his jetty poll, which was wet with rain and shone like a bottle. In a jargon but half intelligible he announced that the kitchen chimney had been struck with lightning.

A sullen pause of the storm, which now rose and sunk in gusts, produced a momentary stillness. In this interval the report of a musket was heard, and a long shout, almost like a yell, resounded from the shore. Every one crowded to the window; another musket shot was heard, and another long shout, that mingled wildly with a rising blast of wind. It seemed as if the cry came up from the bosom of the waters; for though incessant flashes of lightning spread a light about the shore, no one was to be seen.

Suddenly the window of the room overhead was opened, and a loud halloo uttered by the mysterious stranger. Several hailings passed from one party to the other, but in a language which none of the company in the bar-room could understand; and presently they heard the window closed, and a great noise overhead as if all the furniture were pulled and hauled about the room. The negro servant was summoned, and shortly after was seen assisting the veteran to lug the ponderous sea-chest down stairs.

The landlord was in amazement. "What, you are not going on the water in such a storm?"

"Storm!" said the other, scornfully, "do you call such a sputter of weather a storm?"

"You'll get drenched to the skin—You'll catch your death!" said Peechy Prauw, affectionately.

"Thunder and lightning!" exclaimed the merman, "don't preach about weather to a man that has cruised in whirlwinds and tornadoes."

The obsequious Peechy was again struck dumb. The voice from the water was again heard in a tone of impatience; the bystanders stared with redoubled awe at this man of storms, which seemed to have come up out of the deep and to be called back to it again. As, with the assistance of the negro, he slowly bore his ponderous sea-chest towards the shore, they eyed it with a superstitious feeling; half doubting whether he were not really about to embark upon it, and launch forth upon the wild waves. They followed him at a distance with a lanthorn.

"Douse the light!" roared the hoarse voice from the water. "No one wants light here!"

"Thunder and lightning!" exclaimed the veteran; "back to the house with you!"

Wolfert and his companions shrunk back is dismay. Still their curiosity would not allow them entirely to withdraw. A long sheet of lightning now flickered across the waves, and discovered a boat, filled with men, just under a rocky point, rising and sinking with the heavy surges, and swashing the water at every heave. It was with difficulty held to the rocks by a boat hook, for the current rushed furiously round the point. The veteran hoisted one end of the lumbering sea-chest on the gunwale of the boat; he seized the handle at the other end to lift it in, when the motion propelled the boat from the shore; the chest slipped off from the gunwale, sunk into the waves, and pulled the veteran headlong after it. A loud shriek was uttered by all on shore, and a volley of execrations by those on board; but boat and man were hurried away by the rushing swiftness of the tide. A pitchy darkness succeeded; Wolfert Webber indeed fancied that He distinguished a cry for help, and that he beheld the drowning man beckoning for assistance; but when the lightning again gleamed along the water all was drear and void. Neither man nor boat was to be seen; nothing but the dashing and weltering of the waves as they hurried past.

The company returned to the tavern, for they could not leave it before the storm should subside. They resumed their seats and gazed on each other with dismay. The whole transaction had not occupied five minutes and not a dozen words had been spoken. When they looked at the oaken chair they could scarcely realize the fact that the strange being who had so lately tenanted it, full of life and Herculean vigor, should already be a corpse. There was the very glass he had just drunk from; there lay the ashes from the pipe which he had smoked as it were with his last breath. As the worthy burghers pondered on these things, they felt a terrible conviction of the uncertainty of human existence, and each felt as if the ground on which he stood was rendered less stable by this awful example.

As, however, the most of the company were possessed of that valuable philosophy which enables a man to bear up with fortitude against the misfortunes of his neighbors, they soon managed to console themselves for the tragic end of the veteran. The landlord was happy that the poor dear man had paid his reckoning before he went.

"He came in a storm, and he went in a storm; he came in the night, and he went in the night; he came nobody knows from whence, and he has gone nobody knows where. For aught I know he has gone to sea once more on his chest and may land to bother some people on the other side of the world! Though it's a thousand pities," added the landlord, "if he has gone to Davy Jones that he had not left his sea-chest behind him."

"The sea-chest! St. Nicholas preserve us!" said Peechy Prauw. "I'd not have had that sea-chest in the house for any money; I'll warrant he'd come racketing after it at nights, and making a haunted house of the inn. And as to his going to sea on his chest, I recollect what happened to Skipper Onderdonk's ship on his voyage from Amsterdam.

"The boatswain died during a storm, so they wrapped him up in a sheet, and put him in his own sea-chest, and threw him overboard; but they neglected in their hurry-skurry to say prayers over him—and the storm raged and roared louder than ever, and they saw the dead man seated in his chest, with his shroud for a sail, coming hard after the ship; and the sea breaking before him in great sprays like fire, and there they kept scudding day after day and night after night, expecting every moment to go to wreck; and every night they saw the dead boatswain in his sea-chest trying to get up with them, and they heard his whistle above the blasts of wind, and he seemed to send great seas mountain high after them, that would have swamped the ship if they had not put up the dead lights. And so it went on till they lost sight of him in the fogs of Newfoundland, and supposed he had veered ship and stood for Dead Man's Isle. So much for burying a man at sea without saying prayers over him."

The thunder-gust which had hitherto detained the company was now at an end. The cuckoo clock in the hall struck midnight; every one pressed to depart, for seldom was such a late hour trespassed on by these quiet burghers. As they sallied forth they found the heavens once more serene. The storm which had lately obscured them had rolled aways and lay piled up in fleecy masses on the horizon, lighted up by the bright crescent of the moon, which looked like a silver lamp hung up in a palace of clouds.

The dismal occurrence of the night, and the dismal narrations they had made, had left a superstitious feeling in every mind. They cast a fearful glance at the spot where the buccaneer had disappeared, almost expecting to see him sailing on his chest in the cool moonshine. The trembling rays glittered along the waters, but all was placid; and the current dimpled over the spot where he had gone down. The party huddled together in a little crowd as they repaired homewards; particularly when they passed a lonely field where a man had been murdered; and he who had farthest to go and had to complete his journey alone, though a veteran sexton, and accustomed, one would think to ghosts and goblins, yet went a long way round, rather than pass by his own church-yard.

Wolfert Webber had now carried home a fresh stock of stories and notions to ruminate upon. His mind was all of a whirl with these freebooting tales; and then these accounts of pots of money and Spanish treasures, buried here and there and every where about the rocks and bays of this wild shore, made him almost dizzy.

"Blessed St. Nicholas!" ejaculated he, half aloud, "is it not possible to come upon one of these golden hoards, and so make one's self rich in a twinkling. How hard that I must go on, delving and delving, day in and day out, merely to make a morsel of bread, when one lucky stroke of a spade might enable me to ride in my carriage for the rest of my life!"

As he turned over in his thoughts all that he had been told of the singular adventure of the black fisherman, his imagination gave a totally different complexion to the tale. He saw in the gang of redcaps nothing but a crew of pirates burying their spoils, and his cupidity was once more awakened by the possibility of at length getting on the traces of some of this lurking wealth. Indeed, his infected fancy tinged every thing with gold. He felt like the greedy inhabitant of Bagdad, when his eye had been greased with the magic ointment of the dervise, that gave him to see all the treasures of the earth. Caskets of buried jewels, chests of ingots, bags of outlandish coins, seemed to court him from their concealments, and supplicate him to relieve them from their untimely graves.

On making private inquiries about the grounds said to be haunted by father red-cap, he was more and more confirmed in his surmise. He learned that the place had several times been visited by experienced money-diggers, who had heard Mud Sam's story, though none of them had met with success. On the contrary, they had always been dogged with ill luck of some kind or other, in consequence, as Wolfert concluded, of their not going to work at the proper time, and with the proper ceremonials. The last attempt had been made by Cobus

Quackenbos, who dug for a whole night and met with incredible difficulty, for as fast as he threw one shovel full of earth out of the hole, two were thrown in by invisible hands. He succeeded so far, however, as to uncover an iron chest, when there was a terrible roaring, and ramping, and raging of uncouth figures about the hole, and at length a shower of blows, dealt by invisible cudgels, that fairly belabored him off the forbidden ground. This Cobus Quackenbos had declared on his death-bed, so that there could not be any doubt of it. He was a man that had devoted many years of his life to money-digging, and it was thought would have ultimately succeeded, had he not died suddenly of a brain fever in the alms-house.

Wolfert Webber was now in a worry of trepidation and impatience; fearful lest some rival adventurer should get a scent of the buried gold. He determined privately to seek out the negro fisherman and get him to serve as guide to the place where he had witnessed the mysterious scene of interment. Sam was easily found; for he was one of those old habitual beings that live about a neighborhood until they wear themselves a place in the public mind, and become, in a manner, public characters. There was not an unlucky urchin about the town that did not know Mud Sam the fisherman, and think that he had a right to play his tricks upon the old negro. Sam was an amphibious kind of animal, something more of a fish than a man; he had led the life of an otter for more than half a century, about the shores of the bay, and the fishing grounds of the Sound. He passed the greater part of his time on and in the water, particularly about Hell Gate; and might have been taken, in bad weather, for one of the hobgoblins that used to haunt that strait. There would he be seen, at all times, and in all weathers; sometimes in his skiff, anchored among the eddies, or prowling, like a shark about some wreck, where the fish are supposed to be most abundant. Sometimes seated on a rock from hour to hour, looming through mist and drizzle, like a solitary heron watching for its prey. He was well acquainted with every hole and corner of the Sound; from the Wallabout to Hell Gate, and from Hell Gate even unto the Devil's Stepping Stones; and it was even affirmed that he knew all the fish in the river by their Christian names.

Wolfert found him at his cabin, which was not much larger than a tolerable dog-house. It was rudely constructed of fragments of wrecks and drift-wood, and built on the rocky shore, at the foot of the old fort, just about what at present forms the point of the Battery. A "most ancient and fish-like smell" pervaded the place. Oars, paddles, and fishing-rods were leaning against the wall of the fort; a net was spread on the sands to dry; a skiff was drawn up on the beach, and at the door of his cabin lay Mud Sam himself, indulging in a true negro's luxury—sleeping in the sunshine.

Many years had passed away since the time of Sam's youthful adventure, and the snows of many a winter had grizzled the knotty wool upon his head. He perfectly recollected the circumstances, however, for he had often been called upon to relate them, though in his version of the story he differed in many points from Peechy Prauw; as is not unfrequently the case with authentic historians. As to the subsequent researches of money-diggers, Sam knew nothing about them; they were matters quite out of his line; neither did the cautious Wolfert care to disturb his thoughts on that point. His only wish was to secure the old fisherman as a pilot to the spot, and this was readily effected. The long time that had intervened since his nocturnal adventure had effaced all Sam's awe of the place, and the promise of a trifling reward roused him at once from his sleep and his sunshine.

The tide was adverse to making the expedition by water, and Wolfert was too impatient to get to the land of promise, to wait for its turning; they set off, therefore, by land. A walk of four or five miles brought them to the edge of a wood, which at that time covered the greater part of the eastern side of the island. It was just beyond the pleasant region of Bloomen-dael.

Here they struck into a long lane, straggling among trees and bushes, very much overgrown with weeds and mullein stalks as if but seldom used, and so completely overshadowed as to enjoy but a kind of twilight. Wild vines entangled the trees and flaunted in their faces; brambles and briars caught their clothes as they passed; the garter-snake glided across their path; the spotted toad hopped and waddled before them, and the restless cat-bird mewed at them from every thicket. Had Wolfert Webber been deeply read in romantic legend he might have fancied himself entering upon forbidden, enchanted ground; or that these were some of the guardians set to keep a watch upon buried treasure. As it was, the loneliness of the place, and the wild stories connected with it, had their effect upon his mind.

On reaching the lower end of the lane they found themselves near the shore of the Sound, in a kind of amphitheatre, surrounded by forest tree. The area had once been a grass-plot, but was now shagged with briars and rank weeds. At one end, and just on the river bank, was a ruined building, little better than a heap of rubbish, with a stack of chimneys rising like a solitary tower out of the centre. The current of the Sound rushed along just below it, with wildly-grown trees drooping their branches into its waves.

Wolfert had not a doubt that this was the haunted house of father red-cap, and called to mind the story of Peechy Prauw. The evening was approaching, and the light falling dubiously among these places, gave a melancholy tone to the scene, well calculated to foster any lurking feeling of awe or superstition. The night-hawk, wheeling about in the highest regions of the air, emitted his peevish, boding cry. The woodpecker gave a lonely tap now and then on some hollow tree, and the firebird,[2] as he streamed by them with his deep-red plumage, seemed like some genius flitting about this region of mystery.

They now came to an enclosure that had once been a garden. It extended along the foot of a rocky ridge, but was little better than a wilderness of weeds, with here and there a matted rose-bush, or a peach or plum tree grown wild and ragged, and covered with moss. At the lower end of the garden they passed a kind of vault in the side of the bank, facing the water. It had the look of a root-house. The door, though decayed, was still strong, and appeared to have been recently patched up. Wolfert pushed it open. It gave a harsh grating upon its hinges, and striking against something like a box, a rattling sound ensued, and a skull rolled on the floor. Wolfert drew back shuddering, but was reassured on being informed by Sam that this was a family vault belonging to one of the old Dutch families that owned this estate; an assertion which was corroborated by the sight of coffins of various sizes piled within. Sam had been familiar with all these scenes when a boy, and now knew that he could not be far from the place of which they were in quest.

They now made their way to the water's edge, scrambling along ledges of rocks, and having often to hold by shrubs and grape-vines to avoid slipping into the deep and hurried stream. At length they came to a small cove, or rather indent of the shore. It was protected by steep rocks and overshadowed by a thick copse of oaks and chestnuts, so as to be sheltered and almost concealed. The beach sloped gradually within the cove, but the current swept deep and black and rapid along its jutting points. Sam paused; raised his remnant of a hat, and scratched his grizzled poll for a moment, as he regarded this nook: then suddenly clapping his hands, he stepped exultingly forward, and pointing to a large iron ring, stapled firmly in the rock, just where a broad shelve of stone furnished a commodious landing-place. It was the very spot where the red-caps had landed. Years had changed the more perishable features of the scene; but rock and iron yield slowly to the influence of time. On looking more narrowly, Wolfert remarked three crosses cut in the rock just above the ring, which had no doubt some mysterious signification. Old Sam now readily recognized the overhanging rock under which his skiff had been sheltered during the thunder-gust. To follow up the course which the midnight gang had taken, however, was a harder task. His mind had been so much taken up on that eventful occasion by the persons of the drama, as to pay but little attention to the scenes; and places looked different by night and day. After wandering about for some time, however, they came to an opening among the trees which Sam thought resembled the place. There was a ledge of rock of moderate height like a wall on one side, which Sam thought might be the very ridge from which he overlooked the diggers. Wolfert examined it narrowly, and at length described three crosses similar to those above the iron ring, cut deeply into the face of the rock, but nearly obliterated by the moss that had grown on them. His heart leaped with joy, for he doubted not but they were the private marks of the buccaneers, to denote the places where their treasure lay buried. All now that remained was to ascertain the precise spot; for otherwise he might dig at random without coming upon the spoil, and he has already had enough of such profitless labor. Here, however, Sam was perfectly at a loss, and, indeed, perplexed him by a variety of opinions; for his recollections were all confused. Sometimes he declared it must have been at the foot of a mulberry tree hard by; then it was just beside a great white stone; then it must have been under a small green knoll, a short distance from the ledge of rock: until at length Wolfert became as bewildered as himself.

The shadows of evening were now spreading themselves over the woods, and rock and tree began to mingle together. It was evidently too late to attempt anything farther at present; and, indeed, Wolfert had come unprepared with implements to prosecute his researches. Satisfied, therefore, with having ascertained the place, he took note of all its landmarks, that he might recognize it again, and set out on his return homeward, resolved to prosecute this golden enterprise without delay.

The leading anxiety which had hitherto absorbed every feeling being now in some measure appeased, fancy began to wander, and to conjure up a thousand shapes and chimeras as he returned through this haunted region. Pirates hanging in chains seemed to swing on every tree, and he almost expected to see some Spanish Don, with his throat cut from ear to ear, rising slowly out of the ground, and shaking the ghost of a money-bag.

Their way back lay through the desolate garden, and Wolfert's nerves had arrived at so sensitive a state that the flitting of a bird, the rustling of a leaf, or the falling of a nut was enough to startle him. As they entered the confines of the garden, they caught sight of a figure at a distance advancing slowly up one of the walks and bending under the weight of a burthen. They paused and regarded him attentively. He wore what appeared to be a woollen cap, and still more alarming, of a most sanguinary red. The figure moved slowly on, ascended the bank, and stopped at the very door of the sepulchral vault. Just before entering he looked around. What was the horror of Wolfert when he recognized the grizzly visage of the drowned buccaneer. He uttered an ejaculation of horror. The figure slowly raised his iron fist and shook it with a terrible menace. Wolfert did not pause to see more, but hurried off as fast as his legs could carry him, nor was Sam slow in following at his heels, having all his ancient terrors revived. Away, then, did they scramble, through bush and brake, horribly frightened at every bramble that tagged at their skirts, nor did they pause to breathe, until they had blundered their way through this perilous wood and had fairly reached the high-road to the city.

Several days elapsed before Wolfert could summon courage enough to prosecute the enterprise, so much had he been dismayed by the apparition, whether living dead, of the grizzly buccaneer. In the meantime, what a conflict of mind did he suffer! He neglected all his concerns, was moody and restless all day, lost his appetite; wandered in his thoughts and words, and committed a thousand blunders. His rest was broken; and when he fell asleep, the nightmare, in shape of a huge money-bag, sat squatted upon his breast. He babbled about incalculable sums; fancied himself engaged in money digging; threw the bed-clothes right and left, in the idea that he was shovelling among the dirt, groped under the bed in quest of the treasure, and lugged forth, as he supposed, an inestimable pot of gold.

Dame Webber and her daughter were in despair at what they conceived a returning touch of insanity. There are two family oracles, one or other of which Dutch housewives consult in all cases of great doubt and perplexity: the dominie and the doctor. In the present instance they repaired to the doctor. There was at that time a little, dark, mouldy man of medicine famous among the old wives of the Manhattoes for his skill not only in the healing art, but in all matters of strange and mysterious nature. His name was Dr. Knipperhausen, but he was more commonly known by the appellation of the High German doctor.[3] To him did the poor women repair for counsel and assistance touching the mental vagaries of Wolfert Webber.

They found the doctor seated in his little study, clad in his dark camblet robe of knowledge, with his black velvet cap, after the manner of Boorhaave, Van Helmont, and other medical sages: a pair of green spectacles set in black horn upon his clubbed nose, and poring over a German folio that seemed to reflect back the darkness of his physiognomy. The doctor listened to their statement of the symptoms of Wolfert's malady with profound attention; but when they came to mention his raving about buried money, the little man pricked up his ears. Alas, poor women! they little knew the aid they had called in.

Dr. Knipperhausen had been half his life engaged in seeking the short cuts to fortune, in quest of which so many a long lifetime is wasted. He had passed some years of his youth in the Harz mountains of Germany, and had derived much valuable instruction from the miners, touching the mode of seeking treasure buried in the earth. He had prosecuted his studies also under a travelling sage who united all the mysteries of medicine with magic and legerdemain. His mind, therefore, had become stored with all kinds of mystic lore: he had dabbled a little in astrology, alchemy, and divination; knew how to detect stolen money, and to tell where springs of water lay hidden; in a word, by the dark nature of his knowledge he had acquired the name of the High German doctor, which is pretty nearly equivalent to that of necromancer. The doctor had often heard rumors of treasure being buried in various parts of the island, and' had long been anxious to get on the traces of it. No sooner were Wolfert's waking and sleeping vagaries confided to him, than he beheld in them the confirmed symptoms of a case of money-digging, and lost no time in probing it to the bottom. Wolfert had long been sorely depressed in mind by the golden secret, and as a family physician is a kind of father confessor, he was glad of the opportunity of unburthening himself. So far from curing, the doctor caught the malady from his patient. The circumstances unfolded to him awakened all his cupidity; he had not a doubt of money being buried somewhere in the neighborhood of the mysterious crosses, and offered to join Wolfert in the search. He informed him that much secrecy and caution must be observed in enterprises of the kind; that money is only to be digged for at night; with certain forms and ceremonies; the burning of drugs; the repeating of mystic words, and above all, that the seekers must be provided with a divining rod, which had the wonderful property of pointing to the very spot on the surface of the earth under which treasure lay hidden. As the doctor had given much of his mind to these matters, he charged himself with all the necessary preparations, and, as the quarter of the moon was propitious, he undertook to have the divining rod ready by a certain night.[4]

Wolfert's heart leaped with joy at having met with so learned and able a coadjutor. Every thing went on secretly, but swimmingly. The doctor had many consultations with his patient, and the good women of the household lauded the comforting effect of his visits. In the meantime, the wonderful divining rod, that great key to nature's secrets, was duly prepared. The doctor had thumbed over all his books of knowledge for the occasion; and Mud Sam was engaged to take them in his skiff to the scene of enterprise; to work with spade and pick-axe in unearthing the treasure; and to freight his bark with the weighty spoils they were certain of finding.

At length the appointed night arrived for this perilous undertaking. Before Wolfert left his home he counselled his wife and daughter to go to bed, and feel no alarm if he should not return during the night. Like reasonable women, on being told not to feel alarm, they fell immediately into a panic. They saw at once by his manner that something unusual was in agitation; all their fears about the unsettled state of his mind were roused with tenfold force: they hung about him entreating him not to expose himself to the night air, but all in vain. When Wolfert was once mounted on his hobby, it was no easy matter to get him out of the saddle. It was a clear starlight night, when he issued out of the portal of the Webber palace. He wore a large napped hat tied under the chin with a handkerchief of his daughter's, to secure him from the night damp, while Dame Webber threw her long red cloak about his shoulders, and fastened it round his neck.

The doctor had been no less carefully armed and accoutred by his housekeeper, the vigilant Frau Ilsy, and sallied forth in his camblet robe by way of surtout; his black velvet cap under his cocked hat, a thick clasped book under his arm, a basket of drugs and dried herbs in one hand, and in the other the miraculous rod of divination.

The great church clock struck ten as Wolfert and the doctor passed by the church-yard, and the watchman bawled in hoarse voice a long and doleful "All's well!" A deep sleep had already fallen upon this primitive little burgh; nothing disturbed this awful silence, excepting now and then the bark of some profligate night-walking dog, or the serenade of some romantic cat. It is true, Wolfert fancied more than once that he heard the sound of a stealthy footfall at a distance behind them; but it might have been merely the echo of their own steps echoing along the quiet streets. He thought also at one time that he saw a tall figure skulking after them—stopping when they stopped, and moving on as they proceeded; but the dim and uncertain lamp light threw such vague gleams and shadows, that this might all have been mere fancy.

They found the negro fisherman waiting for them, smoking his pipe in the stern of his skiff, which was moored just in front of his little cabin. A pick-axe and spade were lying in the bottom of the boat, with a dark lanthorn, and a stone jug of good Dutch courage, in which honest Sam no doubt, put even more faith than Dr. Knipperhausen in his drugs.

Thus then did these three worthies embark in their cockleshell of a skiff upon this nocturnal expedition, with a wisdom and valor equalled only by the three wise men of Gotham, who went to sea in a bowl. The tide was rising and running rapidly up the Sound. The current bore them along, almost without the aid of an oar. The profile of the town lay all in shadow. Here and there a light feebly glimmered from some sick chamber, or from the cabin window of some vessel at anchor in the stream. Not a cloud obscured the deep starry firmament, the lights of which wavered on the surface of the placid river; and a shooting meteor, streaking its pale course in the very direction they were taking, was interpreted by the doctor into a most propitious omen.

In a little while they glided by the point of Corlears Hook with the rural inn which had been the scene of such night adventures. The family had retired to rest, and the house was dark and still. Wolfert felt a chill pass over him as they passed the point where the buccaneer had disappeared. He pointed it out to Dr. Knipperhausen. While regarding it, they thought they saw a boat actually lurking at the very place; but the shore cast such a shadow over the border of the water that they could discern nothing distinctly. They had not proceeded far when they heard the low sounds of distant oars, as if cautiously pulled. Sam plied his oars with redoubled vigor, and knowing all the eddies and currents of the stream, soon left their followers, if such they were, far astern. In a little while they stretched across Turtle bay and Kip's bay, then shrouded themselves in the deep shadows of the Manhattan shore, and glided swiftly along, secure from observation. At length Sam shot his skiff into a little cove, darkly embowered by trees, and made it fast to the well known iron ring. They now landed, and lighting the lanthorn, gathered their various implements and proceeded slowly through the bushes. Every sound startled them, even that of their footsteps among the dry leaves; and the hooting of a screech owl, from the shattered chimney of father red-cap's ruin, made their blood run cold.

In spite of all Wolfert's caution in taking note of the landmarks, it was some time before they could find the open place among the trees, where the treasure was supposed to be buried. At length they came to the ledge of rock; and on examining its surface by the aid of the lanthorn, Wolfert recognized the three mystic crosses. Their hearts beat quick, for the momentous trial was at hand that was to determine their hopes.

The lanthorn was now held by Wolfert Webber, while the doctor produced the divining rod. It was a forked twig, one end of which was grasped firmly in each hand, while the centre, forming the stem, pointed perpendicularly upwards. The doctor moved this wand about, within a certain distance of the earth, from place to place, but for some time without any effect, while Wolfert kept the light of the lanthorn turned full upon it, and watched it with the most breathless interest. At length the rod began slowly to turn. The doctor grasped it with greater earnestness, his hand trembling with the agitation of his mind. The wand continued slowly to turn, until at length the stem had reversed its position, and pointed perpendicularly downward; and remained pointing to one spot as fixedly as the needle to the pole.

"This is the spot!" said the doctor in an almost inaudible tone.

Wolfert's heart was in his throat.

"Shall I dig?" said Sam, grasping the spade.

"*Pots tousends*, no!" replied the little doctor, hastily. He now ordered his companions to keep close by him and to maintain the most inflexible silence. That certain precautions must be taken, and ceremonies used to prevent the evil spirits which keep about buried treasure from doing them any harm. The doctor then drew a circle round the place, enough to include the whole party. He next gathered dry twigs and leaves, and made a fire, upon which he threw certain drugs and dried herbs which he had brought in his basket. A thick smoke rose, diffusing a potent odor, savoring marvellously of brimstone and assafoetida, which, however grateful it might be to the olfactory nerves of spirits, nearly strangled poor Wolfert, and produced a fit of coughing and wheezing that made the whole grove resound. Doctor Knipperhausen then unclasped the volume which he had brought under his arm, which was printed in red and black characters in German text. While Wolfert held the lanthorn, the doctor, by the aid of his spectacles, read off several forms of conjuration in Latin and German. He then ordered Sam to seize the pick-axe and proceed to work. The close-bound soil gave obstinate signs of not having been disturbed for many a year. After having picked his way through the surface, Sam came to a bed of sand and gravel, which he threw briskly to right and left with the spade.

"Hark!" said Wolfert, who fancied he heard a trampling among the dry leaves, and a rustling through the bushes. Sam paused for a moment, and they listened. No footstep was near. The bat flitted about them in silence; a bird roused from its nest by the light which glared up among the trees, flew circling about the flame. In the profound stillness of the woodland they could distinguish the current rippling along the rocky shore, and the distant murmuring and roaring of Hell Gate.

Sam continued his labors, and had already digged a considerable hole. The doctor stood on the edge, reading formulae every now and then from the black letter volume, or throwing more drugs and herbs upon the fire; while Wolfert bent anxiously over the pit, watching every stroke of the spade. Any one witnessing the scene thus strangely lighted up by fire, lanthorn, and the reflection of Wolfert's red mantle, might have mistaken the little doctor for some foul magician, busied in his incantations, and the grizzled-headed Sam as some swart goblin, obedient to his commands.

At length the spade of the fisherman struck upon something that sounded hollow. The sound vibrated to Wolfert's heart. He struck his spade again.

"'Tis a chest," said Sam.

"Full of gold, I'll warrant it!" cried Wolfert, clasping his hands with rapture.

Scarcely had he uttered the words when a sound from overhead caught his ear. He cast up his eyes, and lo! by the expiring light of the fire he beheld, just over the disk of the rock, what appeared to be the grim visage of the drowned buccaneer, grinning hideously down upon him.

Wolfert gave a loud cry and let fall the lanthorn. His panic communicated itself to his companions. The negro leaped out of the hole, the doctor dropped his book and basket and began to pray in German. All was horror and confusion. The fire was scattered about, the lanthorn extinguished. In their hurry-skurry they ran against and confounded one another. They fancied a legion of hobgoblins let loose upon them, and that they saw by the fitful gleams of the scattered embers, strange figures in red caps gibbering and ramping around them. The doctor ran one way, Mud Sam another, and Wolfert made for the water side. As he plunged struggling onwards through bush and brake, he heard the tread of some one in pursuit.

He scrambled frantically forward. The footsteps gained upon him. He felt himself grasped by his cloak, when suddenly his pursuer was attacked in turn: a fierce fight and struggle ensued—a pistol was discharged that lit up rock and bush for a period, and showed two figures grappling together—all was then darker than ever. The contest continued—the combatants clenched each other, and panted and groaned, and rolled among the rocks. There was snarling and growling as of a cur, mingled with curses in which Wolfert fancied he could recognize the voice of the buccaneer. He would fain have fled, but he was on the brink of a precipice and could go no farther.

Again the parties were on their feet; again there was a tugging and struggling, as if strength alone could decide the combat, until one was precipitated from the brow of the cliff and sent headlong into the deep stream that whirled below. Wolfert heard the plunge, and a kind of strangling bubbling murmur, but the darkness of the night hid every thing from view, and the swiftness of the current swept every thing instantly out of hearing. One of the combatants was disposed of, but whether friend or foe Wolfert could not tell, nor whether they might not both be foes. He heard the survivor approach and his terror revived. He saw, where the profile of the rocks rose against the horizon, a human form advancing. He could not be mistaken: it must be the buccaneer. Whither should he fly! a precipice was on one side; a murderer on the other. The enemy approached: he was close at hand. Wolfert attempted to let himself down the face of the cliff. His cloak caught in a thorn that grew on the edge. He was jerked from off his feet and held dangling in the air, half choaked by the string with which his careful wife had fastened the garment round his neck. Wolfert thought his last moment had arrived; already had he committed his soul to St. Nicholas, when the string broke and he tumbled down the bank, bumping from rock to rock and bush to bush, and leaving the red cloak fluttering like a bloody banner in the air.

It was a long while before Wolfert came to himself. When he opened his eyes the ruddy streaks of the morning were already shooting up the sky. He found himself lying in the bottom of a boat, grievously battered. He attempted to sit up but was too sore and stiff to move. A voice requested him in friendly accents to lie still. He turned his eyes toward the speaker: it was Dirk Waldron. He had dogged the party, at the earnest request of Dame Webber and her daughter, who, with the laudable curiosity of their sex, had pried into the secret consultations of Wolfert and the doctor. Dirk had been completely distanced in following the light skiff of the fisherman, and had just come in time to rescue the poor money-digger from his pursuer.

Thus ended this perilous enterprise. The doctor and Mud Sam severally found their way back to the Manhattoes, each having some dreadful tale of peril to relate. As to poor Wolfert, instead of returning in triumph, laden with bags of gold, he was borne home on a shutter, followed by a rabble route of curious urchins. His wife and daughter saw the dismal pageant from a distance, and alarmed the neighborhood with their cries: they thought the poor man had suddenly settled the great debt of nature in one of his wayward moods. Finding him, however, still living, they had him conveyed speedily to bed, and a jury of old matrons of the neighborhood assembled to determine how he should be doctored. The whole town was in a buzz with the story of the money-diggers. Many repaired to the scene of the previous night's adventures: but though they found the very place of the digging, they discovered nothing that compensated for their trouble. Some say they found the fragments of an oaken chest and an iron pot lid, which savored strongly of hidden money; and that in the old family vault there were traces of holes and boxes, but this is all very dubious.

In fact, the secret of all this story has never to this day been discovered: whether any treasure was ever actually buried at that place, whether, if so, it was carried off at night by those who had buried it; or whether it still remains there under the guardianship of gnomes and spirits until it shall be properly sought for, is all matter of conjecture. For my part I incline to the latter opinion; and make no doubt that great sums lie buried, both there and in many other parts of this island and its neighborhood, ever since the times of the buccaneers and the Dutch colonists; and I would earnestly recommend the search after them to such of my fellow citizens as are not engaged in any other speculations.

There were many conjectures formed, also, as to who and what was the strange man of the seas who had domineered over the little fraternity at Corlears Hook for a time; disappeared so strangely, and reappeared so fearfully. Some supposed him a smuggler stationed at that place to assist his comrades in landing their goods among the rocky coves of the island. Others that he was a buccaneer; one of the ancient comrades either of Kidd or Bradish, returned to convey away treasures formerly hidden in the vicinity. The only circumstance that throws any thing like a vague light over this mysterious matter is a report that prevailed of a strange foreign-built shallop, with the look of a piccaroon, having been seen hovering about the Sound for several days without landing or reporting herself, though boats were seen going to and from her at night: and that she was seen standing out of the mouth of the harbor, in the gray of the dawn after the catastrophe of the money-diggers.

I must not omit to mention another report, also, which I confess is rather apocryphal, of the buccaneer, who was supposed to have been drowned, being seen before daybreak, with a lanthorn in his hand, seated astride his great sea-chest and sailing through Hell Gate, which just then began to roar and bellow with redoubled fury.

While all the gossip world was thus filled with talk and rumor, poor Wolfert lay sick and sorrowful in his bed, bruised in body and sorely beaten down in mind. His wife and daughter did all they could to bind up his wounds both corporal and spiritual. The good old dame never stirred from his bedside, where she sat knitting from morning till night; while his daughter busied herself about him with the fondest care. Nor did they lack assistance from abroad. Whatever may be said of the desertions of friends in distress, they had no complaint of the kind to make. Not an old wife of the neighborhood but abandoned her work to crowd to the mansion of Wolfert Webber, inquire after his health and the particulars of his story. Not one came, moreover, without her little pipkin of pennyroyal, sage, balm, or other herb-tea, delighted at an opportunity of signalizing her kindness and her doctorship. What drenchings did not the poor Wolfert undergo, and all in vain. It was a moving sight to behold him wasting away day by day; growing thinner and thinner and ghastlier and ghastlier, and staring with rueful visage from under an old patchwork counterpane upon the jury of matrons kindly assembled to sigh and groan and look unhappy around him.

Dirk Waldron was the only being that seemed to shed a ray of sunshine into this house of mourning. He came in with cheery look and manly spirit, and tried to reanimate the expiring heart of the poor money-digger, but it was all in vain. Wolfert was completely done over. If any thing was wanting to complete his despair, it was a notice served upon him in the midst of his distress, that the corporation were about to run a new street through the very centre of his cabbage garden. He saw nothing before him but poverty and ruin; his last reliance, the garden of his forefathers, was to be laid waste, and what then was to become of his poor wife and child?

His eyes filled with tears as they followed the dutiful Amy out of the room one morning. Dirk Waldron was seated beside him; Wolfert grasped his hand, pointed after his daughter, and for the first time since his illness broke the silence he had maintained.

"I am going!" said he, shaking his head feebly, "and when I am gone—my poordaughter—"

"Leave her to me, father!" said Dirk, manfully—"I'll take care of her!"

Wolfert looked up in the face of the cheery, strapping youngster, and saw there was none better able to take care of a woman.

"Enough," said he, "she is yours!—and now fetch me a lawyer—let me make my will and die."

The lawyer was brought—a dapper, bustling, round-headed little man, Roorback (or Rollebuck, as it was pronounced) by name. At the sight of him the women broke into loud lamentations, for they looked upon the signing of a will as the signing of a death-warrant. Wolfert made a feeble motion for them to be silent. Poor Amy buried her face and her grief in the bed-curtain. Dame Webber resumed her knitting to hide her distress, which betrayed itself, however, in a pellucid tear, that trickled silently down and hung at the end of her peaked nose; while the cat, the only unconcerned member of the family, played with the good dame's ball of worsted, as it rolled about the floor.

Wolfert lay on his back, his nightcap drawn over his forehead; his eyes closed; his whole visage the picture of death. He begged the lawyer to be brief, for he felt his end approaching, and that he had no time to lose. The lawyer nibbed his pen, spread out his paper, and prepared to write.

"I give and bequeath," said Wolfert, faintly, "my small farm—"

"What—all!" exclaimed the lawyer.

Wolfert half opened his eyes and looked upon the lawyer.

"Yes—all" said he.

"What! all that great patch of land with cabbages and sunflowers, which the corporation is just going to run a main street through?"

"The same," said Wolfert, with a heavy sigh and sinking back upon his pillow.

"I wish him joy that inherits it!" said the little lawyer, chuckling and rubbing his hands involuntarily.

"What do you mean?" said Wolfert, again opening his eyes.

"That he'll be one of the richest men in the place!" cried little Rollebuck.

The expiring Wolfert seemed to step back from the threshold of existence: his eyes again lighted up; he raised himself in his bed, shoved back his red worsted nightcap, and stared broadly at the lawyer.

"You don't say so!" exclaimed he.

"Faith, but I do!" rejoined the other. "Why, when that great field and that piece of meadow come to be laid out in streets, and cut up into snug building lots—why, whoever owns them need not pull off his hat to the patroon!"

"Say you so?" cried Wolfert, half thrusting one leg out of bed, "why, then I think I'll not make my will yet!"

To the surprise of everybody the dying man actually recovered. The vital spark which had glimmered faintly in the socket, received fresh fuel from the oil of gladness, which the little lawyer poured into his soul. It once more burnt up into a flame.

Give physic to the heart, ye who would revive the body of a spirit-broken man! In a few days Wolfert left his room; in a few days more his table was covered with deeds, plans of streets and building lots. Little Rollebuck was constantly with him, his right-hand man and adviser, and instead of making his will, assisted in the more agreeable task of making his fortune. In fact, Wolfert Webber was one of those worthy Dutch burghers of the Manhattoes whose fortunes have been made, in a manner, in spite of themselves; who have tenaciously held on to their hereditary acres, raising turnips and cabbages about the skirts of the city, hardly able to make both ends meet, until the corporation has cruelly driven streets through their abodes, and they have suddenly awakened out of a lethargy, and, to their astonishment, found themselves rich men.

Before many months had elapsed a great bustling street passed through the very centre of the Webber garden, just where Wolfert had dreamed of finding a treasure. His golden dream was accomplished; he did indeed find an unlooked-for source of wealth; for, when his paternal lands were distributed into building lots, and rented out to safe tenants, instead of producing a paltry crop of cabbages, they returned him an abundant crop of rents; insomuch that on quarter day, it was a goodly sight to see his tenants rapping at his door, from morning to night, each with a little round-bellied bag of money, the golden produce of the soil.

The ancient mansion of his forefathers was still kept up, but instead of being a little yellow-fronted Dutch house in a garden, it now stood boldly in the midst of a street, the grand house of the neighborhood; for Wolfert enlarged it with a wing on each side, and a cupola or tea room on top, where he might climb up and smoke his pipe in hot weather; and in the course of time the whole mansion was overrun by the chubby-faced progeny of Amy Webber and Dirk Waldron.

As Wolfert waxed old and rich and corpulent, he also set up a great gingerbread-colored carriage drawn by a pair of black Flanders mares with tails that swept the ground; and to commemorate the origin of his greatness he had for a crest a fullblown cabbage painted on the pannels, with the pithy motto *Alles Kopf* that is to say, ALL HEAD; meaning thereby that he had risen by sheer head-work.

To fill the measure of his greatness, in the fullness of time the renowned Ramm Rapelye slept with his fathers, and Wolfert Webber succeeded to the leathern-bottomed arm-chair in the inn parlor at Corlears Hook; where he long reigned greatly honored and respected, insomuch that he was never known to tell a story without its being believed, nor to utter a joke without its being laughed at.

---

1. For a very interesting account of the Devil and his Stepping Stones, see the learned memoir read before the New York Historical Society since the death of Mr. Knickerbocker, by his friend, an eminent jurist of the place.
2. Orchard Oreole.
3. The same, no doubt, of whom mention is made in the history of Dolph Heyliger.
4. The following note was found appended to this paper in the handwriting of Mr. Knickerbocker. "There has been much written against the divining rod by those light minds who are ever ready to scoff at the mysteries of nature, but I fully join with Dr. Knipperhausen in giving it my faith. I shall not insist upon its efficacy in discovering the concealment of stolen goods, the boundary-stones of fields, the traces of robbers and murderers, or even the existence of subterraneous springs and streams of water; albeit, I think these properties not easily to be discredited; but of its potency in discovering vein of precious metal, and hidden sums of money and jewels, I have not the least doubt. Some said that the rod turned only in the hands of persons who had been born in particular months of the year; hence astrologers had recourse to planetary influence when they would procure a talisman. Others declared that the properties of the rod were either an effect of chance, or the fraud of the holder, or the work of the devil. Thus sayeth the reverend Father Gaspard Schott in his Treatise on Magic. 'Propter haec et similia argumenta audacter ego pronuncio vim conversivam virgulae befurcatae nequaquam naturalem esse, sed vel casa vel fraude virgulam tractantis vel ope diaboli,' etc.

   "Georgius Agricula also was of opinion that it was a mere delusion of the devil to inveigle the avaricious and unwary into his clutches, and in his treatise 'de re Metallica,' lays particular stress on the mysterious words pronounced by those persons who employed the divining rod during his time. But I make not a doubt that the divining rod is one of those secrets of natural magic, the mystery of which is to be explained by the sympathies existing between physical things operated upon by the planets, and rendered efficacious by the strong faith of the individual. Let the divining rod be properly gathered at the proper time of the moon, cut into the proper form, used with the necessary ceremonies, and with a perfect faith in its efficacy, and I can confidently recommend it to my fellow-citizens as an infallible means of discovering the various places on the island of the Manhattoes where treasure hath been buried in the olden time. D.K."]

# THE DEALINGS OF CAPTAIN SHARKEY & OTHER STORIES OF PIRATES

ARTHUR CONAN DOYLE

# TALES OF PIRATES

## I

# CAPTAIN SHARKEY: HOW THE GOVERNOR OF SAINT KITT'S CAME HOME

When the great wars of the Spanish Succession had been brought to an end by the Treaty of Utrecht, the vast number of privateers which had been fitted out by the contending parties found their occupation gone. Some took to the more peaceful but less lucrative ways of ordinary commerce, others were absorbed into the fishing-fleets, and a few of the more reckless hoisted the Jolly Rodger at the mizzen and the bloody flag at the main, declaring a private war upon their own account against the whole human race.

With mixed crews, recruited from every nation they scoured the seas, disappearing occasionally to careen in some lonely inlet, or putting in for a debauch at some outlaying port, where they dazzled the inhabitants by their lavishness and horrified them by their brutalities.

On the Coromandel Coast, at Madagascar, in the African waters, and above all in the West Indian and American seas, the pirates were a constant menace. With an insolent luxury they would regulate their depredations by the comfort of the seasons, harrying New England in the summer and dropping south again to the tropical islands in the winter.

They were the more to be dreaded because they had none of that discipline and restraint which made their predecessors, the Buccaneers, both formidable and respectable. These Ishmaels of the sea rendered an account to no man, and treated their prisoners according to the drunken whim of the moment. Flashes of grotesque generosity alternated with longer stretches of inconceivable ferocity, and the skipper who fell into their hands might find himself dismissed with his cargo, after serving as boon companion in some hideous debauch, or might sit at his cabin table with his own nose and his lips served up with pepper and salt in front of him. It took a stout seaman in those days to ply his calling in the Caribbean Gulf.

Such a man was Captain John Scarrow, of the ship *Morning Star*, and yet he breathed a long sigh of relief when he heard the splash of the falling anchor and swung at his moorings within a hundred yards of the guns of the citadel of Basseterre. St. Kitt's was his final port of call, and early next morning his bowsprit would be pointed for Old England. He had had enough of those robber-haunted seas. Ever since he had left Maracaibo upon the Main, with his full lading of sugar and red pepper, he had winced at every topsail which glimmered over the violet edge of the tropical sea. He had coasted up the Windward Islands, touching here and there, and assailed continually by stories of villainy and outrage.

Captain Sharkey, of the 20-gun pirate barque, *Happy Delivery*, had passed down the coast, and had littered it with gutted vessels and with murdered men. Dreadful anecdotes were current of his grim pleasantries and of his inflexible ferocity. From the Bahamas to the Main his coal-black barque, with the ambiguous name, had been freighted with death and many things which are worse than death. So nervous was Captain Scarrow, with his new full-rigged ship and her full and valuable lading, that he struck out to the west as far as Bird's Island to be out of the usual track of commerce. And yet even in those solitary waters he had been unable to shake off sinister traces of Captain Sharkey.

One morning they had raised a single skiff adrift upon the face of the ocean. Its only occupant was a delirious seaman, who yelled hoarsely as they hoisted him aboard, and showed a dried-up tongue like a black and wrinkled fungus at the back of his mouth. Water and nursing soon transformed him into the strongest and smartest sailor on the ship. He was from Marblehead, in New England, it seemed, and was the sole survivor of a schooner which had been scuttled by the dreadful Sharkey.

For a week Hiram Evanson, for that was his name, had been adrift beneath a tropical sun. Sharkey had ordered the mangled remains of his late captain to be thrown into the boat, "as provisions for the voyage," but the seaman had at once committed them to the deep, lest the temptation should be more than he could bear. He had lived upon his own huge frame, until, at the last moment, the *Morning Star* had found him in that madness which is the precursor of such a death. It was no bad fior Captain Scarrow, for, with a short-handed crew, such a seaman as this big New Englander was a prize worth having. He vowed that he was the only man whom Captain Sharkey had ever placed under an obligation.

Now that they lay under the guns of Basseterre, all danger from the pirate was at an end, and yet the thought of him lay heavily upon the seaman's mind as he watched the agent's boat shooting out from the custom-house quay.

"I'll lay you a wager, Morgan," said he to the first mate, "that the agent will speak of Sharkey in the first hundred words that pass his lips."

"Well, captain, I'll have you a silver dollar, and chance it," said the rough old Bristol man beside him.

The negro rowers shot the boat alongside, and the linen-clad steersman sprang up the ladder.

"Welcome, Captain Scarrow!" he cried. "Have you heard about Sharkey?"

The captain grinned at the mate.

"What devilry has he been up to now?" he asked.

"Devilry! You've not heard, then! Why, we've got him safe under lock and key here at Basseterre. He was tried last Wednesday, and he is to be hanged to-morrow morning."

Captain and mate gave a shout of joy, which an instant later was taken up by the crew. Discipline was forgotten as they scrambled up through the break of the poop to hear the news. The New Englander was in the front of them with a radiant face turned up to heaven, for he came of the Puritan stock.

"Sharkey to be hanged!" he cried. "You don't know, Master Agent, if they lack a hangman, do you?"

"Stand back!" cried the mate, whose outraged sense of discipline was even stronger than his interest at the news. "I'll pay that dollar, Captain Scarrow, with the lightest heart that ever I paid a wager yet. How came the villain to be taken?"

"Why, as to that, he became more than his own comrades could abide, and they took such a horror of him that they would not have him on the ship. So they marooned him upon the Little Mangles to the south of the Mysteriosa Bank, and there he was found by a Portobello trader, who brought him in. There was talk of sending him to Jamaica to be tried, but our good little governor, Sir Charles Ewan, would not hear of it. 'He's my meat,' said he, 'and I claim the cooking of it.' If you can stay till to-morrow morning at ten, you'll see the joint swinging."

"I wish I could," said the captain, wistfully, "but I am sadly behind time now. I should start with the evening tide."

"That you can't do," said the agent with decision. "The Governor is going back with you."

"The Governor!"

"Yes. He's had a dispatch from Government to return without delay. The fly-boat that brought it has gone on to Virginia. So Sir Charles has been waiting for you, as I told him you were due before the rains."

"Well, well!" cried the captain, in some perplexity, "I'm a plain seaman, and I don't know much of governors and baronets and their ways. I don't remember that I ever so much as spoke to one. But if it's in King George's service, and he asks a cast in the *Morning Star* as far as London, I'll do what I can for him. There's my own cabin he can have and welcome. As to the cooking, it's lobscouse and salmagundy six days in the week; but he can bring his own cook aboard with him if he thinks our galley too rough for his taste."

"You need not trouble your mind, Captain Scarrow," said the agent. "Sir Charles is in weak health just now, only clear of a quartan ague, and it is likely he will keep his cabin most of the voyage. Dr. Larousse said that he would have sunk had the hanging of Sharkey not put fresh life into him. He has a great spirit in him, though, and you must not blame him if he is somewhat short in his speech."

"He may say what he likes and do what he likes so long as he does not come athwart my hawse when I am working the ship," said the captain. "He is Governor of St. Kitt's, but I am Governor of the *Morning Star*. And, by his leave, I must weigh with the first tide, for I owe a duty to my employer, just as he does to King George."

"He can scarce be ready to-night, for he has many things to set in order before he leaves."

"The early morning tide, then."

"Very good. I shall send his things aboard to-night, and he will follow them to-morrow early if I can prevail upon him to leave St. Kitt's without seeing Sharkey do the rogue's hornpipe. His own orders were instant, so it may be that he will come at once. It is likely that Dr. Larousse may attend him upon the journey."

Left to themselves, the captain and mate made the best preparations which they could for their illustrious passenger. The largest cabin was turned out and adorned in his honour, and orders were given by which barrels of fruit and some cases of wine should be brought off to vary the plain food of an ocean-going trader. In the evening the Governor's baggage began to arrive—great ironbound ant-proof trunks, and official tin packing-cases, with other strange-shaped packages, which suggested the cocked hat or the sword within. And then there came a note, with a heraldic device upon the big red seal, to say that Sir Charles Ewan made his compliments to Captain Scarrow, and that he hoped to be with him in the morning as early as his duties and his infirmities would permit.

He was as good as his word, for the first grey of dawn had hardly begun to deepen into pink when he was brought alongside, and climbed with some difficulty up the ladder. The captain had heard that the Governor was an eccentric, but he was hardly prepared for the curious figure who came limping feebly down his quarter-deck, his steps supported by a thick bamboo cane. He wore a Ramillies wig, all twisted into little tails like a poodle's coat, and cut so low across the brow that the large green glasses which covered his eyes looked as if they were hung from it. A fierce beak of a nose, very long and very thin, cut the air in front of him. His ague had caused him to swathe his throat and chin with a broad linen cravat, and he wore a loose damask powdering-gown secured by a cord round the waist. As he advanced he carried his masterful nose high in the air, but his head turned slowly from side to side in the helpless manner of the purblind, and he called in a high, querulous voice for the captain.

"You have my things?" he asked.

"Yes, Sir Charles."

"Have you wine aboard?"

"I have ordered five cases, sir."

"And tobacco?"

"There is a keg of Trinidad."

"You play a hand at piquet?"

"Passably well, sir."

"Then up anchor, and to sea!"

There was a fresh westerly wind, so by the time the sun was fairly through the morning haze, the ship was hull down from the islands. The decrepit Governor still limped the deck, with one guiding hand upon the quarter-rail.

"You are on Government service now, Captain," said he. "They are counting the days till I come to Westminster, I promise you. Have you all that she will carry?"

"Every inch, Sir Charles."

"Keep her so if you blow the sails out of her. I fear, Captain Scarrow, that you will find a blind and broken man a poor companion for your voyage."

"I am honoured in enjoying your Excellency's society," said the Captain. "But I am sorry that your eyes should be so afflicted."

"Yes, indeed. It is the cursed glare of the sun on the white streets of Basseterre which has gone far to burn them out."

"I had heard also that you had been plagued by a quartan ague."

"Yes; I have had a pyrexy, which has reduced me much."

"We had set aside a cabin for your surgeon."

"Ah, the rascal! There was no budging him, for he has a snug business amongst the merchants. But hark!"

He raised his ring-covered hand in the air. From far astern there came the low deep thunder of cannon.

"It is from the island!" cried the captain in astonishment. "Can it be a signal for us to put back?"

The Governor laughed.

"You have heard that Sharkey, the pirate, is to be hanged this morning. I ordered the batteries to salute when the rascal was kicking his last, so that I might know of it out at sea. There's an end of Sharkey!"

"There's an end of Sharkey!" cried the captain; and the crew took up the cry as they gathered in little knots upon the deck and stared back at the low, purple line of the vanishing land.

It was a cheering omen for their start across the Western Ocean, and the invalid Governor found himself a popular man on board, for it was generally understood that but for his insistence upon an immediate trial and sentence, the villain might have played upon some more venal judge and so escaped. At dinner that day Sir Charles gave many anecdotes of the deceased pirate; and so affable was he, and so skilful in adapting his conversation to men of lower degree, that captain, mate, and Governor smoked their long pipes and drank their claret as three good comrades should.

"And what figure did Sharkey cut in the dock?" asked the captain.

"He is a man of some presence," said the Governor.

"I had always understood that he was an ugly, sneering devil," remarked the mate.

"Well, I dare say he could look ugly upon occasions," said the Governor.

"I have heard a New Bedford whaleman say that he could not forget his eyes," said Captain Scarrow. "They were of the lightest filmy blue, with red-rimmed lids. Was that not so, Sir Charles?"

"Alas, my own eyes will not permit me to know much of those of others! But I remember now that the Adjutant-General said that he had such an eye as you describe, and added that the jury were so foolish as to be visibly discomposed when it was turned upon them. It is well for them that he is dead, for he was a man who would never forget an injury, and if he had laid hands upon any one of them he would have stuffed him with straw and hung him for a figure-head."

The idea seemed to amuse the Governor, for he broke suddenly into a high, neighing laugh, and the two seamen laughed also, but not so heartily, for they remembered that Sharkey was not the last pirate who sailed the western seas, and that as grotesque a fate might come to be their own. Another bottle was broached to drink to a pleasant voyage, and the Governor would drink just one other on the top of it, so that the seamen were glad at last to stagger off—the one to his watch and the other to his bunk. But when after his four hours' spell the mate came down again, he was amazed to see the Governor in his Ramillies wig, his glasses, and his powdering-gown still seated sedately at the lonely table with his reeking pipe and six black bottles by his side.

"I have drunk with the Governor of St. Kitt's when he was sick," said he, "and God forbid that I should ever try to keep pace with him when he is well."

The voyage of the *Morning Star* was a successful one, and in about three weeks she was at the mouth of the British Channel. From the first day the infirm Governor had begun to recover his strength, and before they were half-way across the Atlantic he was, save only for his eyes, as well as any man upon the ship. Those who uphold the nourishing qualities of wine might point to him in triumph, for never a night passed that he did not repeat the performance of his first one. And yet he would be out upon deck in the early morning as fresh and brisk as the best of them, peering about with his weak eyes, and asking questions about the sails and the rigging, for he was anxious to learn the ways of the sea. And he made up for the deficiency of his eyes by obtaining leave from the captain that the New England seaman—he who had been cast away in the boat—should lead him about, and above all that he should sit beside him when he played cards and count the number of the pips, for unaided he could not tell the king from the knave.

It was natural that this Evanson should do the Governor willing service, since the one was the victim of the vile Sharkey, and the other was his avenger. One could see that it was a pleasure to the big American to lend his arm to the invalid, and at night he would stand with all respect behind his chair in the cabin and lay his great stub-nailed forefinger upon the card which he should play. Between them there was little in the pockets either of Captain Scarrow or of Morgan, the first mate, by the time they sighted the Lizard.

And it was not long before they found that all they had heard of the high temper of Sir Charles Ewan fell short of the mark. At a sign of opposition or a word of argument his chin would shoot out from his cravat, his masterful nose would be cocked at a higher and more insolent angle, and his bamboo cane would whistle up over his shoulder. He cracked it once over the head of the carpenter when the man had accidentally jostled him upon the deck. Once, too, when there was some grumbling and talk of a mutiny over the state of the provisions, he was of opinion that they should not wait for the dogs to rise, but that they should march forward and set upon them until they had trounced the devilment out of them. "Give me a knife and a bucket!" he cried with an oath, and could hardly be withheld from setting forth alone to deal with the spokesman of the seamen.

Captain Scarrow had to remind him that though he might be only answerable to himself at St. Kitt's, killing became murder upon the high seas. In politics he was, as became his official position, a stout prop of the House of Hanover, and he swore in his cups that he had never met a Jacobite without pistolling him where he stood. Yet for all his vapouring and his violence he was so good a companion, with such a stream of strange anecdote and reminiscence, that Scarrow and Morgan had never known a voyage pass so pleasantly.

And then at length came the last day, when, after passing the island, they had struck land again at the high white cliffs at Beachy Head. As evening fell the ship lay rolling in an oily calm, a league off from Winchelsea, with the long dark snout of Dungeness jutting out in front of her. Next morning they would pick up their pilot at the Foreland, and Sir Charles might meet the king's ministers at Westminster before the evening. The boatswain had the watch, and the three friends were met for a last turn of cards in the cabin, the faithful American still serving as eyes to the Governor. There was a good stake upon the table, for the sailors had tried on this last night to win their losses back from their passenger. Suddenly he threw his cards down, and swept all the money into the pocket of his long-flapped silken waistcoat.

"The game's mine!" said he.

"Heh, Sir Charles, not so fast!" cried Captain Scarrow; "you have not played out the hand, and we are not the losers."

"Sink you for a liar!" said the Governor. "I tell you that I *have* played out the hand, and that you *are* a loser." He whipped off his wig and his glasses as he spoke, and there was a high, bald forehead, and a pair of shifty blue eyes with the red rims of a bull terrier.

"Good God!" cried the mate. "It's Sharkey!"

The two sailors sprang from their seats, but the big American castaway had put his huge back against the cabin door, and he held a pistol in each of his hands. The passenger had also laid a pistol upon the scattered cards in front of him, and he burst into his high, neighing laugh.

"Captain Sharkey is the name, gentlemen," said he, "and this is Roaring Ned Galloway, the quartermaster of the *Happy Delivery*. We made it hot, and so they marooned us: me on a dry Tortuga cay, and him in an oarless boat. You dogs—you poor, fond, water-hearted dogs —we hold you at the end of our pistols!"

"You may shoot, or you may not!" cried Scarrow, striking his hand upon the breast of his frieze jacket. "If it's my last breath, Sharkey, I tell you that you are a bloody rogue and miscreant, with a halter and hell-fire in store for you!"

"There's a man of spirit, and one of my own kidney, and he's going to make a very pretty death of it!" cried Sharkey. "There's no one aft save the man at the wheel, so you may keep your breath, for you'll need it soon. Is the dinghy astern, Ned?"

"Ay, ay, captain!"

"And the other boats scuttled?"

"I bored them all in three places."

"Then we shall have to leave you, Captain Scarrow. You look as if you hadn't quite got your bearings yet. Is there anything you'd like to ask me?"

"I believe you're the devil himself!" cried the captain. "Where is the Governor of St. Kitt's?"

"When last I saw him his Excellency was in bed with his throat cut. When I broke prison I learnt from my friends—for Captain Sharkey has those who love him in every port—that the Governor was starting for Europe under a master who had never seen him. I climbed his verandah and I paid him the little debt that I owed him. Then I came aboard you with such of his things as I had need of, and a pair of glasses to hide these tell-tale eyes of mine, and I have ruffled it as a governor should. Now, Ned, you can get to work upon them."

"Help! Help! Watch ahoy!" yelled the mate; but the butt of the pirate's pistol crashed down on to his head, and he dropped like a pithed ox. Scarrow rushed for the door, but the sentinel clapped his hand over his mouth, and threw his other arm round his waist.

"No use, Master Scarrow," said Sharkey. "Let us see you go down on your knees and beg for your life."

"I'll see you——" cried Scarrow, shaking his mouth clear.

"Twist his arm round, Ned. Now will you?"

"No; not if you twist it off."

"Put an inch of your knife into him."

"You may put six inches, and then I won't."

"Sink me, but I like his spirit!" cried Sharkey. "Put your knife in your pocket, Ned. You've saved your skin, Scarrow, and it's a pity so stout a man should not take to the only trade where a pretty fellow can pick up a living. You must be born for no common death, Scarrow, since you have lain at my mercy and lived to tell the story. Tie him up, Ned."

"To the stove, captain?"

"Tut, tut! there's a fire in the stove. None of your rover tricks, Ned Galloway, unless they are called for, or I'll let you know which of us two is captain and which is quartermaster. Make him fast to the table.

"Nay, I thought you meant to roast him!" said the quartermaster. "You surely do not mean to let him go?"

"If you and I were marooned on a Bahama cay, Ned Galloway, it is still for me to command and for you to obey. Sink you for a villain, do you dare to question my orders?"

"Nay, nay, Captain Sharkey, not so hot, sir!" said the quartermaster, and, lifting Scarrow like a child, he laid him on the table. With the quick dexterity of a seaman, he tied his spreadeagled hands and feet with a rope which was passed underneath, and gagged him securely with the long cravat which used to adorn the chin of the Governor of St. Kitt's.

"Now, Captain Scarrow, we must take our leave of you," said the pirate. "If I had half a dozen of my brisk boys at my heels I should have had your cargo and your ship, but Roaring Ned could not find a foremast hand with the spirit of a mouse. I see there are some small craft about, and we shall get one of them. When Captain Sharkey has a boat he can get a smack, when he has a smack he can get a brig, when he has a brig he can get a barque, and when he has a barque he'll soon have a full-rigged ship of his own—so make haste into London town, or I may be coming back, after all, for the *Morning Star*."

Captain Scarrow heard the key turn in the lock as they left the cabin. Then, as he strained at his bonds, he heard their foot-steps pass up the companion and along the quarter-deck to where the dinghy hung in the stern. Then, still struggling and writhing, he heard the creak of the falls and the splash of the boat in the water. In a mad fury he tore and dragged at his ropes, until at last, with flayed wrists and ankles, he rolled from the table, sprang over the dead mate, kicked his way through the closed door, and rushed hatless on to the deck.

"Ahoy! Peterson, Armitage, Wilson!" he screamed. "Cutlasses and pistols! Clear away the long-boat! Clear away the gig! Sharkey, the pirate, is in yonder dinghy. Whistle up the larboard watch, bo'sun, and tumble into the boats all hands."

Down splashed the long-boat and down splashed the gig, but in an instant the coxswains and crews were swarming up the falls on to the deck once more.

"The boats are scuttled!" they cried. "They are leaking like a sieve."

The captain gave a bitter curse. He had been beaten and outwitted at every point. Above was a cloudless, starlit sky, with neither wind nor the promise of it. The sails flapped idly in the moonlight. Far away lay a fishing-smack, with the men clustering over their net.

Close to them was the little dinghy, dipping and lifting over the shining swell.

"They are dead men!" cried the captain. "A shout all together, boys, to warn them of their danger."

But it was too late.

At that very moment the dinghy shot into the shadow of the fishing-boat. There were two rapid pistol-shots, a scream, and then another pistol-shot, followed by silence. The clustering fishermen had disappeared. And then, suddenly, as the first puffs of a land-breeze came out from the Sussex shore, the boom swung out, the mainsail filled, and the little craft crept out with her nose to the Atlantic.

## 2

# THE DEALINGS OF CAPTAIN SHARKEY WITH STEPHEN CRADDOCK

Careening was a very necessary operation for the old pirate. On his superior speed he depended both for overhauling the trader and escaping the man-of-war. But it was impossible to retain his sailing qualities unless he periodically—once a year, at the least—cleared his vessel's bottom from the long, trailing plants and crusting barnacles which gather so rapidly in the tropical seas.

For this purpose he lightened his vessel, thrust her into some narrow inlet where she would be left high and dry at low water, fastened blocks and tackles to her masts to pull her over on to her bilge, and then scraped her thoroughly from rudder-post to cutwater.

During the weeks which were thus occupied the ship was, of course, defenceless; but, on the other hand, she was unapproachable by anything heavier than an empty hull, and the place for careening was chosen with an eye to secrecy, so that there was no great danger.

So secure did the captains feel, that it was not uncommon for them, at such times, to leave their ships under a sufficient guard and to start off in the long-boat, either upon a sporting expedition or, more frequently, upon a visit to some outlying town, where they turned the heads of the women by their swaggering gallantry, or broached pipes of wine in the market square, with a threat to pistol all who would not drink with them.

Sometimes they would even appear in cities of the size of Charleston, and walk the streets with their clattering sidearms—an open scandal to the whole law-abiding colony. Such visits were not always paid with impunity. It was one of them, for example, which provoked Lieutenant Maynard to hack off Blackbeard's head, and to spear it upon the end of his bowsprit. But, as a rule, the pirate ruffled and bullied and drabbed without let or hindrance, until it was time for him to go back to his ship once more.

There was one pirate, however, who never crossed even the skirts of civilisation, and that was the sinister Sharkey, of the barque *Happy Delivery*. It may have been from his morose and solitary temper, or, as is more probable, that he knew that his name upon the coast was such that outraged humanity would, against all odds, have thrown themselves upon him, but never once did he show his face in a settlement.

When his ship was laid up he would leave her under the charge of Ned Galloway—her

New England quartermaster—and would take long voyages in his boat, sometimes, it was said, for the purpose of burying his share of the plunder, and sometimes to shoot the wild oxen of Hispaniola, which, when dressed and barbecued, provided provisions for his next voyage. In the latter case the barque would come round to some pre-arranged spot to pick him up and take on board what he had shot.

There had always been a hope in the islands that Sharkey might be taken on one of these occasions; and at last there came news to Kingston which seemed to justify an attempt upon him. It was brought by an elderly logwood-cutter who had fallen into the pirate's hands, and in some freak of drunken benevolence had been allowed to get away with nothing worse than a slit nose and a drubbing. His account was recent and definite. The *Happy Delivery* was careening at Torbec on the south-west of Hispaniola. Sharkey, with four men, was buccaneering on the outlying island of La Vache. The blood of a hundred murdered crews was calling out for vengeance, and now at last it seemed as if it might not call in vain.

Sir Edward Compton, the high-nosed, red-faced Governor, sitting in solemn conclave with the commandant and the head of the council, was sorely puzzled in his mind as to how he should use his chance. There was no man-of-war nearer than Jamestown, and she was a clumsy old fly-boat, which could neither overhaul the pirate on the seas, nor reach her in a shallow inlet. There were forts and artillerymen both at Kingston and Port Royal, but no soldiers available for an expedition.

A private venture might be fitted out—and there were many who had a blood-feud with Sharkey—but what could a private venture do? The pirates were numerous and desperate. As to taking Sharkey and his four companions, that, of course, would be easy if they could get at them; but how were they to get at them on a large well-wooded island like La Vache, full of wild hills and impenetrable jungles? A reward was offered to whoever could find a solution, and that brought a man to the front who had a singular plan, and was himself prepared to carry it out.

Stephen Craddock had been that most formidable person, the Puritan gone wrong. Sprung from a decent Salem family, his ill-doing seemed to be a recoil from the austerity of their religion, and he brought to vice all the physical strength and energy with which the virtues of his ancestors had endowed him. He was ingenious, fearless, and exceedingly tenacious of purpose, so that when he was still young his name became notorious upon the American coast.

He was the same Craddock who was tried for his life in Virginia for the slaying of the Seminole Chief, and, though he escaped, it was well known that he had corrupted the witnesses and bribed the judge.

Afterwards, as a slaver, and even, as it was hinted, as a pirate, he had left an evil name behind him in the Bight of Benin. Finally he had returned to Jamaica with a considerable fortune, and had settled down to a life of sombre dissipation. This was the man, gaunt, austere, and dangerous, who now waited upon the Governor with a plan for the extirpation of Sharkey.

Sir Edward received him with little enthusiasm, for in spite of some rumours of conversion and reformation, he had always regarded him as an infected sheep who might taint the whole of his little flock. Craddock saw the Governor's mistrust under his thin veil of formal and restrained courtesy.

"You've no call to fear me, sir," said he; "I'm a changed man from what you've known. I've seen the light again, of late, after losing sight of it for many a black year. It was through the ministration of the Rev. John Simons, of our own people. Sir, if your spirit should be in need of quickening, you would find a very sweet savour in his discourse."

The Governor cocked his Episcopalian nose at him.

"You came here to speak of Sharkey, Master Craddock," said he.

"The man Sharkey is a vessel of wrath," said Craddock. "His wicked horn has been exalted over long, and it is borne in upon me that if I can cut him off and utterly destroy him, it will be a goodly deed, and one which may atone for many backslidings in the past. A plan has been given to me whereby I may encompass his destruction."

The Governor was keenly interested, for there was a grim and practical air about the man's freckled face which showed that he was in earnest. After all, he was a seaman and a fighter, and, if it were true that he was eager to atone for his past, no better man could be chosen for the business.

"This will be a dangerous task, Master Craddock," said he.

"If I meet my death at it, it may be that it will cleanse the memory of an ill-spent life. I have much to atone for."

The Governor did not see his way to contradict him.

"What was your plan?" he asked.

"You have heard that Sharkey's barque, the *Happy Delivery*, came from this very port of Kingston?"

"It belonged to Mr. Codrington, and it was taken by Sharkey, who scuttled his own sloop and moved into her because she was faster," said Sir Edward.

"Yes; but it may be that you have never heard that Mr. Codrington has a sister ship, the *White Rose*, which lies even now in the harbour, and which is so like the pirate, that, if it were not for a white paint line, none could tell them apart."

"Ah! and what of that?" asked the Governor keenly, with the air of one who is just on the edge of an idea.

"By the help of it this man shall be delivered into our hands."

"And how?"

"I will paint out the streak upon the *White Rose*, and make it in all things like the *Happy Delivery*. Then I will set sail for the Island of La Vache, where this man is slaying the wild oxen. When he sees me he will surely mistake me for his own vessel which he is awaiting, and he will come on board to his own undoing."

It was a simple plan, and yet it seemed to the Governor that it might be effective. Without hesitation he gave Craddock permission to carry it out, and to take any steps he liked in order to further the object which he had in view. Sir Edward was not very sanguine, for many attempts had been made upon Sharkey, and their results had shown, that he was as cunning as he was ruthless. But this gaunt Puritan with the evil record was cunning and ruthless also.

The contest of wits between two such men as Sharkey and Craddock appealed to the Governor's acute sense of sport, and though he was inwardly convinced that the chances were against him, he backed his man with the same loyalty which he would have shown to his horse or his cock.

Haste was, above all things, necessary, for upon any day the careening might be finished, and the pirates out at sea once more. But there was not very much to do, and there were many willing hands to do it, so the second day saw the *White Rose* beating out for the open sea. There were many seamen in the port who knew the lines and rig of the pirate barque, and not one of them could see the slightest difference in this counterfeit. Her white side line had been painted out, her masts and yards were smoked, to give them the dingy appearance of the weather-beaten rover, and a large diamond shaped patch was let into her fore-topsail.

Her crew were volunteers, many of them being men who had sailed with Stephen

Craddock before—the mate, Joshua Hird, an old slaver, had been his accomplice in many voyages, and came now at the bidding of his chief.

The avenging barque sped across the Caribbean Sea, and, at the sight of that patched topsail, the little craft which they met flew left and right like frightened trout in a pool. On the fourth evening Point Abacou bore five miles to the north and east of them.

On the fifth they were at anchor in the Bay of Tortoises at the Island of La Vache, where Sharkey and his four men had been hunting. It was a well-wooded place, with the palms and underwood growing down to the thin crescent of silver sand which skirted the shore. They had hoisted the black flag and the red pennant, but no answer came from the shore. Craddock strained his eyes, hoping every instant to see a boat shoot out to them with Sharkey seated in the sheets. But the night passed away, and a day and yet another night, without any sign of the men whom they were endeavouring to trap. It looked as if they were already gone.

On the second morning Craddock went ashore in search of some proof whether Sharkey and his men were still upon the island. What he found reassured him greatly. Close to the shore was a boucan of green wood, such as was used for preserving the meat, and a great store of barbecued strips of ox-flesh was hung upon lines all round it. The pirate ship had not taken off her provisions, and therefore the hunters were still upon the island.

Why had they not shown themselves? Was it that they had detected that this was not their own ship? Or was it that they were hunting in the interior of the island, and were not on the lookout for a ship yet? Craddock was still hesitating between the two alternatives, when a Carib Indian came down with information. The pirates were in the island, he said, and their camp was a day's march from the sea. They had stolen his wife, and the marks of their stripes were still pink upon his brown back. Their enemies were his friends, and he would lead them to where they lay.

Craddock could not have asked for anything better; so early next morning, with a small party armed to the teeth, he set off under the guidance of the Carib. All day they struggled through brushwood and clambered over rocks, pushing their way further and further into the desolate heart of the island. Here and there they found traces of the hunters, the bones of a slain ox, or the marks of feet in a morass, and once, towards evening, it seemed to some of them that they heard the distant rattle of guns.

That night they spent under the trees, and pushed on again with the earliest light. About noon they came to the huts of bark, which, the Carib told them, were the camp of the hunters, but they were silent and deserted. No doubt their occupants were away at the hunt and would return in the evening, so Craddock and his men lay in ambush in the brushwood around them. But no one came, and another night was spent in the forest. Nothing more could be done, and it seemed to Craddock that after the two days' absence it was time that he returned to his ship once more.

The return journey was less difficult, as they had already blazed a path for themselves. Before evening they found themselves once more at the Bay of Palms, and saw their ship riding at anchor where they had left her. Their boat and oars had been hauled up among the bushes, so they launched it and pulled out to the barque.

"No luck, then!" cried Joshua Hird, the mate, looking down with a pale face from the poop.

"His camp was empty, but he may come down to us yet," said Craddock, with his hand on the ladder.

Somebody upon deck began to laugh. "I think," said the mate, "that these men had better stay in the boat."

"Why so?"

"If you will come aboard, sir, you will understand it." He spoke in a curious hesitating fashion.

The blood flushed to Craddock's gaunt face.

"How is this, Master Hird?" he cried, springing up the side. "What mean you by giving orders to my boat's crew?"

But as he passed over the bulwarks, with one foot upon the deck and one knee upon the rail, a tow-bearded man, whom he had never before observed aboard his vessel, grabbed suddenly at his pistol. Craddock clutched at the fellow's wrist, but at the same instant his mate snatched the cutlass from his side.

"What roguery is this?" shouted Craddock looking furiously around him. But the crew stood in little knots about the deck, laughing and whispering amongst themselves without showing any desire to go to his assistance. Even in that hurried glance Craddock noticed that they were dressed in the most singular manner, with long riding-coats, full-skirted velvet gowns and coloured ribands at their knees, more like men of fashion than seamen.

As he looked at their grotesque figures he struck his brow with his clenched fist to be sure that he was awake. The deck seemed to be much dirtier than when he had left it, and there were strange, sun-blackened faces turned upon him from every side. Not one of them did he know save only Joshua Hird. Had the ship been captured in his absence? Were these Sharkey's men who were around him? At the thought he broke furiously away and tried to climb over to his boat, but a dozen hands were on him in an instant, and he was pushed aft through the open door of his own cabin.

And it was all different from the cabin which he had left. The floor was different, the ceiling was different, the furniture was different. His had been plain and austere. This was sumptuous and yet dirty, hung with rare velvet curtains splashed with wine-stains, and panelled with costly woods which were pocked with pistol-marks.

On the table was a great chart of the Caribbean Sea, and beside it, with compasses in his hand, sat a clean-shaven, pale-faced man with a fur cap and a claret-coloured coat of damask. Craddock turned white under his freckles as he looked upon the long, thin, high-nostrilled nose and the red-rimmed eyes which were turned upon him with the fixed, humorous gaze of the master player who has left his opponent without a move.

"Sharkey?" cried Craddock.

Sharkey's thin lips opened and he broke into his high, sniggering laugh.

"You fool!" he cried, and, leaning over, he stabbed Craddock's shoulder again and again with his compasses. "You poor, dull-witted fool, would you match yourself against me?"

It was not the pain of the wounds, but it was the contempt in Sharkey's voice which turned Craddock into a savage madman. He flew at the pirate, roaring with rage, striking, kicking, writhing, and foaming. It took six men to drag him down on to the floor amidst the splintered remains of the table—and not one of the six who did not bear the prisoner's mark upon him. But Sharkey still surveyed him with the same contemptuous eye. From outside there came the crash of breaking wood and the clamour of startled voices.

"What is that?" asked Sharkey.

"They have stove the boat with cold shot, and the men are in the water."

"Let them stay there," said the pirate. "Now, Craddock, you know where you are. You are aboard my ship the *Happy Delivery*, and you lie at my mercy. I knew you for a stout seaman, you rogue, before you took to this long-shore canting. Your hands then were no cleaner than my own. Will you sign articles, as your mate has done, and join us, or shall I heave you over to follow your ship's company?"

"Where is my ship?" asked Craddock.

"Scuttled in the bay."

"And the hands?"

"In the bay, too."

"Hock him and heave him over," said Sharkey.

Many rough hands had dragged Craddock out upon deck, and Galloway, the quartermaster, had already drawn his hangar to cripple him, when Sharkey came hurrying from his cabin with an eager face.

"We can do better with the hound!" he cried. "Sink me if it is not a rare plan. Throw him into the sail-room with the irons on, and do you come here, quartermaster, that I may tell you what I have in my mind."

So Craddock, bruised and wounded in soul and body, was thrown into the dark sail-room, so fettered that he could not stir hand or foot, but his Northern blood was running strong in his veins, and his grim spirit aspired only to make such an ending as might go some way towards atoning for the evil of his life. All night he lay in the curve of the bilge listening to the rush of the water and the straining of the timbers which told him that the ship was at sea, and driving fast. In the early morning some one came crawling to him in the darkness over the heaps of sails.

"Here's rum and biscuits," said the voice of his late mate. "It's at the risk of my life, Master Craddock, that I bring them to you."

"It was you who trapped me and caught me as in a snare!" cried Craddock. "How shall you answer for what you have done?"

"What I did I did with the point of a knife betwixt my blade-bones."

"God forgive you for a coward, Joshua Hird. How came you into their hands?"

"Why, Master Craddock, the pirate ship came back from its careening upon the very day that you left us. They laid us aboard, and, short-handed as we were, with the best of the men ashore with you, we could offer but a poor defence. Some were cut down, and they were the happiest. The others were killed afterwards. As to me, I saved my life by signing on with them."

"And they scuttled my ship?"

"They scuttled her, and then Sharkey and his men, who had been watching us from the brushwood, came off to the ship. His main-yard had been cracked and fished last voyage, so he had suspicions of us, seeing that ours was whole. Then he thought of laying the same trap for you which you had set for him."

Craddock groaned.

"How came I not to see that fished main-yard?" he muttered. "But whither are we bound?"

"We are running north and west."

"North and west! Then we are heading back towards Jamaica."

"With an eight-knot wind."

"Have you heard what they mean to do with me?"

"I have not heard. If you would but sign the articles——"

"Enough, Joshua Hird! I have risked my soul too often."

"As you wish! I have done what I could. Farewell!"

All that night and the next day the *Happy Delivery* ran before the easterly trades, and Stephen Craddock lay in the dark of the sail-room working patiently at his wrist-irons. One he had slipped off at the cost of a row of broken and bleeding knuckles, but, do what he would, he could not free the other, and his ankles were securely fastened.

From hour to hour he heard the swish of the water, and knew that the barque must be driving with all set, in front of the trade wind. In that case they must be nearly back again to Jamaica by now. What plan could Sharkey have in his head, and what use did he hope to make of him? Craddock set his teeth, and vowed that if he had once been a villain from choice he would, at least, never be one by compulsion.

On the second morning Craddock became aware that sail had been reduced in the vessel, and that she was tacking slowly, with a light breeze on her beam. The varying slope of the sail-room and the sounds from the deck told his practised senses exactly what she was doing. The short reaches showed him that she was maneuvering near shore, and making for some definite point. If so, she must have reached Jamaica. But what could she be doing there?

And then suddenly there was a burst of hearty cheering from the deck, and then the crash of a gun above his head, and then the answering booming of guns from far over the water. Craddock sat up and strained his ears. Was the ship in action? Only the one gun had been fired, and though many had answered there were none of the crashings which told of a shot coming home.

Then, if it was not an action, it must be a salute. But who would salute Sharkey, the pirate? It could only be another pirate ship which would do so. So Craddock lay back again with a groan, and continued to work at the manacle which still held his right wrist.

But suddenly there came the shuffling of steps outside, and he had hardly time to wrap the loose links round his free hand, when the door was unbolted and two pirates came in.

"Got your hammer, carpenter?" asked one, whom Craddock recognised as the big quartermaster. "Knock off his leg shackles, then. Better leave the bracelets—he's safer with them on."

With hammer and chisel the carpenter loosened the irons.

"What are you going to do with me?" asked Craddock.

"Come on deck and you'll see."

The sailor seized him by the arm and dragged him roughly to the foot of the companion. Above him was a square of blue sky cut across by the mizzen gaff with the colours flying at the peak. But it was the sight of those colours which struck the breath from Stephen Craddock's lips. For there were two of them, and the British ensign was flying above the Jolly Rodger—the honest flag above that of the rogue.

For an instant Craddock stopped in amazement, but a brutal push from the pirates behind drove him up the companion ladder. As he stepped out upon deck, his eyes turned up to the main, and there again were the British colours flying above the red pennant, and all the shrouds and rigging were garlanded with streamers.

Had the ship been taken, then? But that was impossible, for there were the pirates clustering in swarms along the port bulwarks, and waving their hats joyously in the air. Most prominent of all was the renegade mate, standing on the foc'sle head, and gesticulating wildly. Craddock looked over the side to see what they were cheering at, and then in a flash he saw how critical was the moment.

On the port bow, and about a mile off, lay the white houses and forts of Port Royal, with flags breaking out everywhere over their roofs. Right ahead was the opening of the palisades leading to the town of Kingston. Not more than a quarter of a mile off was a small sloop working out against the very slight wind. The British ensign was at her peak, and her rigging was all decorated. On her deck could be seen a dense crowd of people cheering and waving their hats, and the gleam of scarlet told that there were officers of the garrison among them.

In an instant, with the quick perception of a man of action, Craddock saw through it all. Sharkey, with that diabolical cunning and audacity which were among his main characteristics, was simulating the part which Craddock would himself have played, had he come back victorious. It was in *his* honour that the salutes were firing and the flags flying. It was to welcome *him* that this ship with the Governor, the commandant, and the chiefs of the island was approaching. In another ten minutes they would all be under the guns of the *Happy Delivery*, and Sharkey would have won the greatest stake that ever a pirate played for yet.

"Bring him forward," cried the pirate captain, as Craddock appeared between the carpenter and the quartermaster. "Keep the ports closed, but clear away the port guns, and stand by for a broadside. Another two cable lengths and we have them."

"They are edging away," said the boatswain. "I think they smell us."

"That's soon set right," said Sharkey, turning his filmy eyes upon Craddock. "Stand there, you—right there, where they can recognise you, with your hand on the guy, and wave your hat to them. Quick, or your brains will be over your coat. Put an inch of your knife into him, Ned. Now, will you wave your hat? Try him again, then. Hey, shoot him! stop him!"

But it was too late. Relying upon the manacles, the quartermaster had taken his hands for a moment off Craddock's arm. In that instant he had flung off the carpenter and, amid a spatter of pistol bullets, had sprung the bulwarks and was swimming for his life. He had been hit and hit again, but it takes many pistols to kill a resolute and powerful man who has his mind set upon doing something before he dies. He was a strong swimmer, and, in spite of the red trail which he left in the water behind him, he was rapidly increasing his distance from the pirate.

"Give me a musket!" cried Sharkey, with a savage oath.

He was a famous shot, and his iron nerves never failed him in an emergency. The dark head appearing on the crest of a roller, and then swooping down on the other side, was already half-way to the sloop. Sharkey dwelt long upon his aim before he fired. With the crack of the gun the swimmer reared himself up in the water, waved his hands in a gesture of warning, and roared out in a voice which rang over the bay. Then, as the sloop swung round her head-sails, and the pirate fired an impotent broadside, Stephen Craddock, smiling grimly in his death agony, sank slowly down to that golden couch which glimmered far beneath him.

## 3

# THE BLIGHTING OF SHARKEY

Sharkey, the abominable Sharkey, was out again. After two years of the Coromandel coast, his black barque of death, the *Happy Delivery*, was prowling off the Spanish Main, while trader and fisher flew for dear life at the menace of that patched fore-topsail, rising slowly over the violet rim of the tropical sea.

As the birds cower when the shadow of the hawk falls athwart the field, or as the jungle folk crouch and shiver when the coughing cry of the tiger is heard in the night-time, so through all the busy world of ships, from the whalers of Nantucket to the tobacco ships of Charleston, and from the Spanish supply ships of Cadiz to the sugar merchants of the Main, there spread the rumour of the black curse of the ocean.

Some hugged the shore, ready to make for the nearest port, while others struck far out beyond the known lines of commerce, but none were so stout-hearted that they did not breathe more freely when their passengers and cargoes were safe under the guns of some mothering fort.

Through all the islands there ran tales of charred derelicts at sea, of sudden glares seen afar in the night-time, and of withered bodies stretched upon the sand of waterless Bahama Keys. All the old signs were there to show that Sharkey was at his bloody game once more.

These fair waters and yellow-rimmed palm-nodding islands are the traditional home of the sea rover. First it was the gentleman adventurer, the man of family and honour, who fought as a patriot, though he was ready to take his payment in Spanish plunder.

Then, within a century, his debonair figure had passed to make room for the buccaneers, robbers pure and simple, yet with some organised code of their own, commanded by notable chieftains, and taking in hand great concerted enterprises.

They, too, passed with their fleets and their sacking of cities, to make room for the worst of all, the lonely, outcast pirate, the bloody Ishmael of the seas, at war with the whole human race. This was the vile brood which the early eighteenth century had spawned forth, and of them all there was none who could compare in audacity, wickedness, and evil repute with the unutterable Sharkey.

It was early in May, in the year 1720, that the *Happy Delivery* lay with her fore-yard aback some five leagues west of the Windward Passage, waiting to see what rich, helpless craft the trade-wind might bring down to her.

Three days she had lain there, a sinister black speck, in the centre of the great sapphire circle of the ocean. Far to the south-east the low blue hills of Hispaniola showed up on the skyline.

Hour by hour as he waited without avail, Sharkey's savage temper had risen, for his arrogant spirit chafed against any contradiction, even from Fate itself. To his quartermaster, Ned Galloway, he had said that night, with his odious neighing laugh, that the crew of the next captured vessel should answer to him for having kept him waiting so long.

The cabin of the pirate barque was a good-sized room, hung with much tarnished finery, and presenting a strange medley of luxury and disorder. The panelling of carved and polished sandal-wood was blotched with foul smudges and chipped with bullet-marks fired in some drunken revelry.

Rich velvets and laces were heaped upon the brocaded settees, while metal-work and pictures of great price filled every niche and corner, for anything which caught the pirate's fancy in the sack of a hundred vessels was thrown haphazard into his chamber. A rich, soft carpet covered the floor, but it was mottled with wine-stains and charred with burned tobacco.

Above, a great brass hanging-lamp threw a brilliant yellow light upon this singular apartment, and upon the two men who sat in their shirt-sleeves with the wine between them, and the cards in their hands, deep in a game of piquet. Both were smoking long pipes, and the thin blue reek filled the cabin and floated through the skylight above them, which, half opened, disclosed a slip of deep violet sky spangled with great silver stars.

Ned Galloway, the quartermaster, was a huge New England wastrel, the one rotten branch upon a goodly Puritan family tree. His robust limbs and giant frame were the heritage of a long line of God-fearing ancestors, while his black savage heart was all his own. Bearded to the temples, with fierce blue eyes, a tangled lion's mane of coarse, dark hair, and huge gold rings in his ears, he was the idol of the women in every waterside hell from the Tortugas to Maracaibo on the Main. A red cap, a blue silken shirt, brown velvet breeches with gaudy knee-ribbons, and high sea-boots made up the costume of the rover Hercules.

A very different figure was Captain John Sharkey. His thin, drawn, clean-shaven face was corpse-like in its pallor, and all the suns of the Indies could but turn it to a more deathly parchment tint. He was part bald, with a few lank locks of tow-like hair, and a steep, narrow forehead. His thin nose jutted sharply forth, and near-set on either side of it were those filmy blue eyes, red-rimmed like those of a white bull-terrier, from which strong men winced away in fear and loathing. His bony hands, with long, thin fingers which quivered ceaselessly like the antennae of an insect, were toying constantly with the cards and the heap of gold moidores which lay before him. His dress was of some sober drab material, but, indeed, the men who looked upon that fearsome face had little thought for the costume of its owner.

The game was brought to a sudden interruption, for the cabin door was swung rudely open, and two rough fellows—Israel Martin, the boatswain, and Red Foley, the gunner—rushed into the cabin. In an instant Sharkey was on his feet with a pistol in either hand and murder in his eyes.

"Sink you for villains!" he cried. "I see well that if I do not shoot one of you from time to time you will forget the man I am. What mean you by entering my cabin as though it were a Wapping alehouse?"

"Nay, Captain Sharkey," said Martin, with a sullen frown upon his brick-red face, "it is even such talk as this which has set us by the ears. We have had enough of it."

"And more than enough," said Red Foley, the gunner. "There be no mates aboard a pirate craft, and so the boatswain, the gunner, and the quartermaster are the officers."

"Did I gainsay it?" asked Sharkey with an oath.

"You have miscalled us and mishandled us before the men, and we scarce know at this moment why we should risk our lives in fighting for the cabin and against the foc'sle."

Sharkey saw that something serious was in the wind. He laid down his pistols and leaned back in his chair with a flash of his yellow fangs.

"Nay, this is sad talk," said he, "that two stout fellows who have emptied many a bottle and cut many a throat with me, should now fall out over nothing. I know you to be roaring boys who would go with me against the devil himself if I bid you. Let the steward bring cups and drown all unkindness between us."

"It is no time for drinking, Captain Sharkey," said Martin. "The men are holding council round the mainmast, and may be aft at any minute. They mean mischief, Captain Sharkey, and we have come to warn you."

Sharkey sprang for the brass-handled sword which hung from the wall.

"Sink them for rascals!" he cried. "When I have gutted one or two of them they may hear reason."

But the others barred his frantic way to the door.

"There are forty of them under the lead of Sweetlocks, the master," said Martin, "and on the open deck they would surely cut you to pieces. Here within the cabin it may be that we can hold them off at the points of our pistols." He had hardly spoken when there came the tread of many heavy feet upon the deck. Then there was a pause with no sound but the gentle lapping of the water against the sides of the pirate vessel. Finally, a crashing blow as from a pistol-butt fell upon the door, and an instant afterwards Sweetlocks himself, a tall, dark man, with a deep red birth-mark blazing upon his cheek, strode into the cabin. His swaggering air sank somewhat as he looked into those pale and filmy eyes.

"Captain Sharkey," said he, "I come as spokesman of the crew."

"So I have heard, Sweetlocks," said the captain, softly. "I may live to rip you the length of your vest for this night's work."

"That is as it may be, Captain Sharkey," the master answered, "but if you will look up you will see that I have those at my back who will not see me mishandled."

"Cursed if we do!" growled a deep voice from above, and glancing upwards the officers in the cabin were aware of a line of fierce, bearded, sun-blackened faces looking down at them through the open skylight.

"Well, what would you have?" asked Sharkey. "Put it in words, man, and let us have an end of it."

"The men think," said Sweetlocks, "that you are the devil himself, and that there will be no luck for them whilst they sail the sea in such company. Time was when we did our two or three craft a day, and every man had women and dollars to his liking, but now for a long week we have not raised a sail, and save for three beggarly sloops, have taken never a vessel since we passed the Bahama Bank. Also, they know that you killed Jack Bartholomew, the carpenter, by beating his head in with a bucket, so that each of us goes in fear of his life. Also, the rum has given out, and we are hard put to it for liquor. Also, you sit in your cabin whilst it is in the articles that you should drink and roar with the crew. For all these reasons it has been this day in general meeting decreed——"

Sharkey had stealthily cocked a pistol under the table, so it may have been as well for the mutinous master that he never reached the end of his discourse, for even as he came to it there was a swift patter of feet upon the deck, and a ship lad, wild with his tidings, rushed into the room.

"A craft!" he yelled. "A great craft, and close aboard us!"

In a flash the quarrel was forgotten, and the pirates were rushing to quarters. Sure enough, surging slowly down before the gentle trade-wind, a great full-rigged ship, with all sail set, was close beside them.

It was clear that she had come from afar and knew nothing of the ways of the Caribbean Sea, for she made no effort to avoid the low, dark craft which lay so close upon her bow, but blundered on as if her mere size would avail her.

So daring was she, that for an instant the Rovers, as they flew to loose the tackles of their guns, and hoisted their battle-lanterns, believed that a man-of-war had caught them napping.

But at the sight of her bulging, portless sides and merchant rig a shout of exultation broke from amongst them, and in an instant they had swung round their fore-yard, and darting alongside they had grappled with her and flung a spray of shrieking, cursing ruffians upon her deck.

Half a dozen seamen of the night-watch were cut down where they stood, the mate was felled by Sharkey and tossed overboard by Ned Galloway, and before the sleepers had time to sit up in their berths, the vessel was in the hands of the pirates.

The prize proved to be the full-rigged ship *Portobello*—Captain Hardy, master—bound from London to Kingston in Jamaica, with a cargo of cotton goods and hoop-iron.

Having secured their prisoners, all huddled together in a dazed, distracted group, the pirates spread over the vessel in search of plunder, handing all that was found to the giant quartermaster, who in turn passed it over the side of the *Happy Delivery* and laid it under guard at the foot of her mainmast.

The cargo was useless, but there were a thousand guineas in the ship's strong-box, and there were some eight or ten passengers, three of them wealthy Jamaica merchants, all bringing home well-filled boxes from their London visit.

When all the plunder was gathered, the passengers and crew were dragged to the waist, and under the cold smile of Sharkey each in turn was thrown over the side—Sweetlocks standing by the rail and hamstringing them with his cutlass as they passed over, lest some strong swimmer should rise in judgment against them. A portly, grey-haired woman, the wife of one of the planters, was among the captives, but she also was thrust screaming and clutching over the side.

"Mercy, you hussy!" neighed Sharkey, "you are surely a good twenty years too old for that."

The captain of the *Portobello*, a hale, blue-eyed grey-beard, was the last upon the deck. He stood, a thick-set resolute figure, in the glare of the lanterns, while Sharkey bowed and smirked before him.

"One skipper should show courtesy to another," said he, "and sink me if Captain Sharkey would be behind in good manners! I have held you to the last, as you see, where a brave man should be; so now, my bully, you have seen the end of them, and may step over with an easy mind."

"So I shall, Captain Sharkey," said the old seaman, "for I have done my duty so far as my power lay. But before I go over I would say a word in your ear."

"If it be to soften me, you may save your breath. You have kept us waiting here for three days, and curse me if one of you shall live!"

"Nay, it is to tell you what you should know. You have not yet found what is the true treasure aboard of this ship."

"Not found it? Sink me, but I will slice your liver, Captain Hardy, if you do not make good your words! Where is this treasure you speak of?"

"It is not a treasure of gold, but it is a fair maid, which may be no less welcome."

"Where is she, then? And why was she not with the others?"

"I will tell you why she was not with the others. She is the only daughter of the Count and Countess Ramirez, who are amongst those whom you have murdered. Her name is Inez Ramirez, and she is of the best blood of Spain, her father being Governor of Chagre, to which he was now bound. It chanced that she was found to have formed an attachment, as maids will, to one far beneath her in rank aboard this ship; so her parents, being people of great power, whose word is not to be gainsaid, constrained me to confine her close in a special cabin aft of my own. Here she was held straitly, all food being carried to her, and she allowed to see no one. This I tell you as a last gift, though why I should make it to you I do not know, for indeed you are a most bloody rascal, and it comforts me in dying to think that you will surely be gallow's-meat in this world, and hell's-meat in the next."

At the words he ran to the rail, and vaulted over into the darkness, praying as he sank into the depths of the sea, that the betrayal of this maid might not be counted too heavily against his soul.

The body of Captain Hardy had not yet settled upon the sand forty fathoms deep before the pirates had rushed along the cabin gangway. There, sure enough, at the further end, was a barred door, overlooked in their previous search. There was no key, but they beat it in with their gunstocks, whilst shriek after shriek came from within. In the light of their outstretched, lanterns they saw a young woman, in the very prime and fullness of her youth, crouching in a corner, her unkempt hair hanging to the ground, her dark eyes glaring with fear, her lovely form straining away in horror from this inrush of savage blood-stained men. Rough hands seized her, she was jerked to her feet, and dragged with scream on scream to where John Sharkey awaited her. He held the light long and fondly to her face, then, laughing loudly, he bent forward and left his red hand-print upon her cheek.

"'Tis the rovers' brand, lass, that he marks his ewes. Take her to the cabin and use her well. Now, hearties, get her under water, and out to our luck once more."

Within an hour the good ship *Portobello* had settled down to her doom, till she lay beside her murdered passengers upon the Caribbean sand, while the pirate barque, her deck littered with plunder, was heading northward in search of another victim.

There was a carouse that night in the cabin of the *Happy Delivery*, at which three men drank deep. They were the captain, the quartermaster, and Baldy Stable, the surgeon, a man who had held the first practice in Charleston, until, misusing a patient, he fled from justice, and took his skill over to the pirates. A bloated fat man he was, with a creased neck and a great shining scalp, which gave him his name. Sharkey had put for the moment all thought of mutiny out of his head, knowing that no animal is fierce when it is over-fed, and that whilst the plunder of the great ship was new to them he need fear no trouble from his crew. He gave himself up, therefore, to the wine and the riot, shouting and roaring with his boon companions. All three were flushed and mad, ripe for any devilment, when the thought of the woman crossed the pirate's evil mind. He yelled to the negro steward that he should bring her on the instant.

Inez Ramirez had now realised it all—the death of her father and mother, and her own position in the hands of their murderers. Yet calmness had come with the knowledge, and there was no sign of terror in her proud, dark face as she was led into the cabin, but rather a strange, firm set of the mouth and an exultant gleam of the eyes, like one who sees great hopes in the future. She smiled at the pirate captain as he rose and seized her by the waist.

"'Fore God! this is a lass of spirit," cried Sharkey; passing his arm round her. "She was born to be a Rover's bride. Come, my bird, and drink to our better friendship."

"Article Six!" hiccoughed the doctor. "All *bona robas* in common."

"Aye! we hold you to that, Captain Sharkey," said Galloway. "It is so writ in Article Six."

"I will cut the man into ounces who comes betwixt us!" cried Sharkey, as he turned his fish-like eyes from one to the other. "Nay, lass, the man is not born that will take you from John Sharkey. Sit here upon my knee, and place your arm round me so. Sink me, if she has not learned to love me at sight! Tell me, my pretty, why you were so mishandled and laid in the bilboes aboard yonder craft?"

The woman shook her head and smiled. "No Inglese—no Inglese," she lisped. She had drunk off the bumper of wine which Sharkey held to her, and her dark eyes gleamed more brightly than before. Sitting on Sharkey's knee, her arm encircled his neck, and her hand toyed with his hair, his ear, his cheek. Even the strange quartermaster and the hardened surgeon felt a horror as they watched her, but Sharkey laughed in his joy. "Curse me, if she is not a lass of metal!" he cried, as he pressed her to him and kissed her unresisting lips.

But a strange intent look of interest had come into the surgeon's eyes as he watched her, and his face set rigidly, as if a fearsome thought had entered his mind. There stole a grey pallor over his bull face, mottling all the red of the tropics and the flush of the wine.

"Look at her hand, Captain Sharkey!" he cried. "For the Lord's sake, look at her hand!"

Sharkey stared down at the hand which had fondled him. It was of a strange dead pallor, with a yellow shiny web betwixt the fingers. All over it was a white fluffy dust, like the flour of a new-baked loaf. It lay thick on Sharkey's neck and cheek. With a cry he flung the woman from his lap; but in an instant, with a wild-cat bound, and a scream of triumphant malice, she had sprung at the surgeon, who vanished yelling under the table. One of her clawing hands grasped Galloway by the beard, but he tore himself away, and snatching a pike, held her off from him as she gibbered and mowed with the blazing eyes of a maniac.

The black steward had run in on the sudden turmoil, and among them they forced the mad creature back into the cabin and turned the key upon her. Then the three sank panting into their chairs and looked with eyes of horror upon each other. The same word was in the mind of each, but Galloway was the first to speak it.

"A leper!" he cried. "She has us all, curse her!"

"Not me," said the surgeon; "she never laid her finger on me."

"For that matter," cried Galloway, "it was but my beard that she touched. I will have every hair of it off before morning."

"Dolts that we are!" the surgeon shouted, beating his head with-his hand. "Tainted or no, we shall never know a moment's peace till the year is up and the time of danger past. 'Fore God, that merchant skipper has left his mark on us, and pretty fools we were to think that such a maid would be quarantined for the cause he gave. It is easy to see now that her corruption broke forth in the journey, and that save throwing her over they had no choice but to board her up until they should come to some port with a lazarette."

Sharkey had sat leaning back in his chair with a ghastly face while he listened to the surgeon's words. He mopped himself with his red handkerchief, and wiped away the fatal dust with which he was smeared.

"What of me?" he croaked. "What say you, Baldy Stable? Is there a chance for me? Curse you for a villain! speak out, or I will drub you within an inch of your life, and that inch also! Is there a chance for me, I say!"

But the surgeon shook his head. "Captain Sharkey," said he, "it would be an ill deed to speak you false. The taint is on you. No man on whom the leper scales have rested is ever clean again."

Sharkey's head fell forward on his chest, and he sat motionless, stricken by this great and sudden horror, looking with his smouldering eyes into his fearsome future. Softly the mate and the surgeon rose from their places, and stealing out from the poisoned air of the cabin, came forth into the freshness of the early dawn, with the soft, scent-laden breeze in their faces and the first red feathers of cloud catching the earliest gleam of the rising sun as it shot its golden rays over the palm-clad ridges of distant Hispaniola.

That morning a second council of the Rovers was held at the base of the mainmast, and a deputation chosen to see the captain. They were approaching the after-cabins when Sharkey came forth, the old devil in his eyes, and his bandolier with a pair of pistols over his shoulder.

"Sink you all for villains!" he cried. "Would you dare cross my hawse? Stand out, Sweetlocks, and I will lay you open! Here, Galloway, Martin, Foley, stand by me and lash the dogs to their kennel!"

But his officers had deserted him, and there was none to come to his aid. There was a rush of the pirates. One was shot through the body, but an instant afterwards Sharkey had been seized and was triced to his own mainmast. His filmy eyes looked round from face to face, and there was none who felt the happier for having met them.

"Captain Sharkey," said Sweetlocks, "you have mishandled many of us, and you have now pistolled John Masters, besides killing Bartholomew, the carpenter, by braining him with a bucket. All this might have been forgiven you, in that you have been our leader for years, and that we have signed articles to serve under you while the voyage lasts. But now we have heard of this *bona roba* on board, and we know that you are poisoned to the marrow, and that while you rot there will be no safety for any of us, but that we shall all be turned into filth and corruption. Therefore, John Sharkey, we Rovers of the *Happy Delivery*, in council assembled, have decreed that while there be yet time, before the plague spreads, you shall be set adrift in a boat to find such a fate as Fortune may be pleased to send you."

John Sharkey said nothing, but slowly circling his head, he cursed them all with his baleful gaze. The ship's dinghy had been lowered, and he, with his hands still tied, was dropped into it on the bight of a rope.

"Cast her off!" cried Sweetlocks.

"Nay, hold hard a moment, Master Sweetlocks!" shouted one of the crew. "What of the wench? Is she to bide aboard and poison us all?"

"Send her off with her mate!" cried another, and the Rovers roared their approval. Driven forth at the end of pikes, the girl was pushed towards the boat. With all the spirit of Spain in her rotting body she flashed triumphant glances on her captors.

"Perros! Perros Ingleses! Lepero, Lepero!" she cried in exultation, as they thrust her over into the boat.

"Good luck, captain! God speed you on your honeymoon!" cried a chorus of mocking voices, as the painter was unloosed, and the *Happy Delivery*, running full before the trade-wind, left the little boat astern, a tiny dot upon the vast expanse of the lonely sea.

❧

Extract from the log of H.M. fifty-gun ship *Hecate* in her cruise off the American Main.

"*Jan. 26, 1721.*—This day, the junk having become unfit for food, and five of the crew down with scurvy, I ordered that we send two boats ashore at the nor'-western point of Hispaniola, to seek for fresh fruit, and perchance shoot some of the wild oxen with which the island abounds.

"7 *p.m.*—The boats have returned with good store of green stuff and two bullocks. Mr. Woodruff, the master, reports that near the landing-place at the edge of the forest was found the skeleton of a woman, clad in European dress, of such sort as to show that she may have been a person of quality. Her head had been crushed by a great stone which lay beside her. Hard by was a grass hut, and signs that a man had dwelt therein for some time, as was shown by charred wood, bones and other traces. There is a rumour upon the coast that Sharkey, the bloody pirate, was marooned in these parts last year, but whether he has made his way into the interior, or whether he has been picked up by some craft, there is no means of knowing. If he be once again afloat, then I pray that God send him under our guns."

## 4

# HOW COPLEY BANKS SLEW CAPTAIN SHARKEY

The Buccaneers were something higher than a mere band of marauders. They were a floating republic, with laws, usages, and discipline of their own. In their endless and remorseless quarrel with the Spaniards they had some semblance of right upon their side. Their bloody harryings of the cities of the Main were not more barbarous than the inroads of Spain upon the Netherlands—or upon the Caribs in these same American lands.

The chief of the Buccaneers, were he English or French, a Morgan or a Granmont, was still a responsible person, whose country might countenance him, or even praise him, so long as he refrained from any deed which might shock the leathery seventeenth-century conscience too outrageously. Some of them were touched with religion, and it is still remembered how Sawkins threw the dice overboard upon the Sabbath, and Daniel pistolled a man before the altar for irreverence.

But there came a day when the fleets of the Buccaneers no longer mustered at the Tortugas, and the solitary and outlawed pirate took their place. Yet even with him the tradition of restraint and of discipline still lingered; and among the early pirates, the Avorys, the Englands, and the Robertses, there remained some respect for human sentiment. They were more dangerous to the merchant than to the seaman.

But they in turn were replaced by more savage and desperate men, who frankly recognised that they would get no quarter in their war with the human race, and who swore that they would give as little as they got. Of their histories we know little that is trustworthy. They wrote no memoirs and left no trace, save an occasional blackened and blood-stained derelict adrift upon the face of the Atlantic. Their deeds could only be surmised from the long roll of ships which never made their port.

Searching the records of history, it is only here and there in an old-world trial that the veil that shrouds them seems for an instant to be lifted, and we catch a glimpse of some amazing and grotesque brutality behind. Such was the breed of Ned Low, of Gow the Scotchman, and of the infamous Sharkey, whose coal-black barque, the *Happy Delivery*, was known from the Newfoundland Banks to the mouths of the Orinoco as the dark forerunner of misery and of death.

There were many men, both among the islands and on the main, who had a blood feud with Sharkey, but not one who had suffered more bitterly than Copley Banks, of Kingston. Banks had been one of the leading sugar merchants of the West Indies. He was a man of position, a member of the Council, the husband of a Percival, and the cousin of the Governor of Virginia. His two sons had been sent to London to be educated, and their mother had gone over to bring them back. On their return voyage the ship, the *Duchess of Cornwall*, fell into the hands of Sharkey, and the whole family met with an infamous death.

Copley Banks said little when he heard the news, but he sank into a morose and enduring melancholy. He neglected his business, avoided his friends, and spent much of his time in the low taverns of the fishermen and seamen. There, amidst riot and devilry, he sat silently puffing at his pipe, with a set face and a smouldering eye. It was generally supposed that his misfortunes had shaken his wits, and his old friends looked at him askance, for the company which he kept was enough to bar him from honest men.

From time to time there came rumours of Sharkey over the sea. Sometimes it was from some schooner which had seen a great flame upon the horizon, and approaching to offer help to the burning ship, had fled away at the sight of the sleek, black barque, lurking like a wolf near a mangled sheep. Sometimes it was a frightened trader, which had come tearing in with her canvas curved like a lady's bodice, because she had seen a patched fore-topsail rising slowly above the violet water-line. Sometimes it was from a Coaster, which had found a waterless Bahama Cay littered with sun-dried bodies.

Once there came a man who had been mate of a Guineaman, and who had escaped from the pirate's hands. He could not speak—for reasons which Sharkey could best supply—but he could write, and he did write, to the very great interest of Copley Banks. For hours they sat together over the map, and the dumb man pointed here and there to outlying reefs and tortuous inlets, while his companion sat smoking in silence, with his unvarying face and his fiery eyes.

One morning, some two years after his misfortune, Mr. Copley Banks strode into his own office with his old air of energy and alertness. The manager stared at him in surprise, for it was months since he had shown any interest in business.

"Good morning, Mr. Banks!" said he.

"Good morning, Freeman. I see that *Ruffling Harry* is in the Bay."

"Yes, sir; she clears for the Windward Islands on Wednesday."

"I have other plans for her, Freeman. I have determined upon a slaving venture to Whydah."

"But her cargo is ready, sir."

"Then it must come out again, Freeman. My mind is made up, and the *Ruffling Harry* must go slaving to Whydah."

All argument and persuasion were vain, so the manager had dolefully to clear the ship once more.

And then Copley Banks began to make preparations for his African voyage. It appeared that he relied upon force rather than barter for the filling of his hold, for he carried none of those showy trinkets which savages love, but the brig was fitted with eight nine-pounder guns and racks full of muskets and cutlasses. The after sail-room next the cabin was transformed into a powder magazine, and she carried as many round shot as a well-found privateer. Water and provisions were shipped for a long voyage.

But the preparation of his ship's company was most surprising. It made Freeman, the manager, realise that there was truth in the rumour that his master had taken leave of his senses. For, under one pretext or another, he began to dismiss the old and tried hands, who had served the firm for years, and in their place he embarked the scum of the port—men whose reputations were so vile that the lowest crimp would have been ashamed to furnish them.

There was Birthmark Sweetlocks, who was known to have been present at the killing of the log-wood cutters, so that his hideous scarlet disfigurement was put down by the fanciful as being a red afterglow from that great crime. He was first mate, and under him was Israel Martin, a little sun-wilted fellow who had served with Howell Davies at the taking of Cape Coast Castle.

The crew were chosen from amongst those whom Banks had met and known in their own infamous haunts, and his own table-steward was a haggard-faced man, who gobbled at you when he tried to talk. His beard had been shaved, and it was impossible to recognise him as the same man whom Sharkey had placed under the knife, and who had escaped to tell his experiences to Copley Banks.

These doings were not unnoticed, nor yet uncommented upon in the town of Kingston. The Commandant of the troops—Major Harvey, of the Artillery—made serious representations to the Governor.

"She is not a trader, but a small warship," said he. "I think it would be as well to arrest Copley Banks and to seize the vessel."

"What do you suspect?" asked the Governor, who was a slow-witted man, broken down with fevers and port wine.

"I suspect," said the soldier, "that it is Stede Bonnet over again."

Now, Stede Bonnet was a planter of high reputation and religious character, who, from some sudden and overpowering freshet of wildness in his blood, had given up everything in order to start off pirating in the Caribbean Sea. The example was a recent one, and it had caused the utmost consternation in the islands. Governors had before now been accused of being in league with pirates, and of receiving commissions upon their plunder, so that any want of vigilance was open to a sinister construction.

"Well, Major Harvey," said he, "I am vastly sorry to do anything which may offend my friend Copley Banks, for many a time have my knees been under his mahogany, but in face of what you say there is no choice for me but to order you to board the vessel and to satisfy yourself as to her character and destination."

So at one in the morning Major Harvey, with a launchful of his soldiers, paid a surprise visit to the *Ruffling Harry*, with the result that they picked up nothing more solid than a hempen cable floating at the moorings. It had been slipped by the brig, whose owner had scented danger. She had already passed the Palisades, and was beating out against the north-east trades on a course for the Windward Passage.

When upon the next morning the brig had left Morant Point a mere haze upon the Southern horizon, the men were called aft, and Copley Banks revealed his plans to them. He had chosen them, he said, as brisk boys and lads of spirit, who would rather run some risk upon the sea than starve for a living upon the shore. King's ships were few and weak, and they could master any trader who might come their way. Others had done well at the business, and with a handy, well-found vessel, there was no reason why they should not turn their tarry jackets into velvet coats. If they were prepared to sail under the black flag, he was ready to command them; but if any wished to withdraw, they might have the gig and row back to Jamaica.

Four men out of six-and-forty asked for their discharge, went over the ship's side into the boat, and rowed away amidst the jeers and howlings of the crew. The rest assembled aft, and drew up the articles of their association. A square of black tarpaulin had the white skull painted upon it, and was hoisted amidst cheering at the main.

Officers were elected, and the limits of their authority fixed. Copley Banks was chosen Captain, but, as there are no mates upon a pirate craft, Birthmark Sweetlocks became quartermaster, and Israel Martin the boatswain. There was no difficulty in knowing what was the custom of the brotherhood, for half the men at least had served upon pirates before. Food should be the same for all, and no man should interfere with another man's drink! The Captain should have a cabin, but all hands should be welcome to enter it when they chose.

All should share and share alike, save only the captain, quartermaster, boatswain, carpenter, and master-gunner, who had from a quarter to a whole share extra. He who saw a prize first should have the best weapon taken out of her. He who boarded her first should have the richest suit of clothes aboard of her. Every man might treat his own prisoner, be it man or woman, after his own fashion. If a man flinched from his gun, the quartermaster should pistol him. These were some of the rules which the crew of the *Ruffling Harry* subscribed by putting forty-two crosses at the foot of the paper upon which they had been drawn.

So a new rover was afloat upon the seas, and her name before a year was over became as well known as that of the *Happy Delivery*. From the Bahamas to the Leewards, and from the Leewards to the Windwards, Copley Banks became the rival of Sharkey and the terror of traders. For a long time the barque and the brig never met, which was the more singular, as the *Ruffling Harry* was for ever looking in at Sharkey's resorts; but at last one day, when she was passing down the inlet of Coxon's Hole, at the east end of Cuba, with the intention of careening, there was the *Happy Delivery*, with her blocks and tackle-falls already rigged for the same purpose.

Copley Banks fired a shotted salute and hoisted the green trumpeter ensign, as the custom was among gentlemen of the sea. Then he dropped his boat and went aboard.

Captain Sharkey was not a man of a genial mood, nor had he any kindly sympathy for those who were of the same trade as himself. Copley Banks found him seated astride upon one of the after guns, with his New England quartermaster, Ned Galloway, and a crowd of roaring ruffians standing about him. Yet none of them roared with quite such assurance when Sharkey's pale face and filmy blue eyes were turned upon him.

He was in his shirt-sleeves, with his cambric frills breaking through his open red satin long-flapped vest. The scorching sun seemed to have no power upon his fleshless frame, for he wore a low fur cap, as though it had been winter. A many-coloured band of silk passed across his body and supported a short murderous sword, while his broad, brass-buckled belt was stuffed with pistols.

"Sink you for a poacher!" he cried, as Copley Banks passed over the bulwarks. "I will drub you within an inch of your life, and that inch also! What mean you by fishing in my waters?"

Copley Banks looked at him, and his eyes were like those of a traveller who sees his home at last.

"I am glad that we are of one mind," said he, "for I am myself of opinion that the seas are not large enough for the two of us. But if you will take your sword and pistols and come upon a sand-bank with me, then the world will be rid of a damned villain whichever way it goes."

"Now, this is talking!" cried Sharkey, jumping off the gun and holding out his hand. "I have not met many who could look John Sharkey in the eyes and speak with a full breath.

May the devil seize me if I do not choose you as a consort! But if you play me false, then I will come aboard of you and gut you upon your own poop."

"And I pledge you the same!" said Copley Banks, and so the two pirates became sworn comrades to each other.

That summer they went north as far as the Newfoundland Banks, and harried the New York traders and the whale-ships from New England. It was Copley Banks who captured the Liverpool ship, *House of Hanover*, but it was Sharkey who fastened her master to the windlass and pelted him to death with empty claret-bottles.

Together they engaged the King's ship *Royal Fortune*, which had been sent in search of them, and beat her off after a night action of five hours, the drunken, raving crews fighting naked in the light of the battle-lanterns, with a bucket of rum and a pannikin laid by the tackles of every gun. They ran to Topsail Inlet in North Carolina to refit, and then in the spring they were at the Grand Caicos, ready for a long cruise down the West Indies.

By this time Sharkey and Copley Banks had become very excellent friends, for Sharkey loved a wholehearted villain, and he loved a man of metal, and it seemed to him that the two met in the captain of the *Ruffling Harry*. It was long before he gave his confidence to him, for cold suspicion lay deep in his character. Never once would he trust himself outside his own ship and away from his own men.

But Copley Banks came often on board the *Happy Delivery*, and joined Sharkey in many of his morose debauches, so that at last any lingering misgivings of the latter were set at rest. He knew nothing of the evil that he had done to his new boon companion, for of his many victims how could he remember the woman and the two boys whom he had slain with such levity so long ago! When, therefore, he received a challenge to himself and to his quartermaster for a carouse upon the last evening of their stay at the Caicos Bank, he saw no reason to refuse.

A well-found passenger ship had been rifled the week before, so their fare was of the best, and after supper five of them drank deeply together. There were the two captains, Birthmark Sweetlocks, Ned Galloway, and Israel Martin, the old buccaneersman. To wait upon them was the dumb steward, whose head Sharkey split with his glass, because he had been too slow in the filling of it.

The quartermaster had slipped Sharkey's pistols away from him, for it was an old joke with him to fire them cross-handed under the table, and see who was the luckiest man. It was a pleasantry which had cost his boatswain his leg, so now, when the table was cleared, they would coax Sharkey's weapons away from him on the excuse of the heat, and lay them out of his reach.

The Captain's cabin of the *Ruffling Harry* was in a deck-house upon the poop, and a sternchaser gun was mounted at the back of it. Round shot were racked round the wall, and three great hogsheads of powder made a stand for dishes and for bottles. In this grim room the five pirates sang and roared and drank, while the silent steward still filled up their glasses, and passed the box and the candle round for their tobacco-pipes. Hour after hour the talk became fouler, the voices hoarser, the curses and shoutings more incoherent, until three of the five had closed their blood-shot eyes, and dropped their swimming heads upon the table.

Copley Banks and Sharkey were left face to face, the one because he had drunk the least, the other because no amount of liquor would ever shake his iron nerve or warm his sluggish blood. Behind him stood the watchful steward, for ever filling up his waning glass. From without came the low lapping of the tide, and from over the water a sailor's chanty from the barque.

In the windless tropical night the words came clearly to their ears:

"A trader sailed from Stepney Town,
Wake her up! Shake her up! Try her with the mainsail!
A trader sailed from Stepney Town
With a keg full of gold and a velvet gown.
Ho, the bully Rover Jack,
Waiting with his yard aback
Out upon the Lowland Sea."

The two boon companions sat listening in silence. Then Copley Banks glanced at the steward, and the man took a coil of rope from the shot-rack behind him.

"Captain Sharkey," said Copley Banks, "do you remember the *Duchess of Cornwall*, hailing from London, which you took and sank three years ago off the Statira Shoal?"

"Curse me if I can bear their names in mind," said Sharkey. "We did as many as ten ships a week about that time."

"There were a mother and two sons among the passengers. Maybe that will bring it back to your mind."

Captain Sharkey leant back in thought, with his huge thin beak of a nose jutting upwards. Then he burst suddenly into a high treble, neighing laugh. He remembered it, he said, and he added details to prove it.

"But burn me if it had not slipped from my mind!" he cried. "How came you to think of it?"

"It was of interest to me," said Copley Banks, "for the woman was my wife and the lads were my only sons."

Sharkey stared across at his companion, and saw that the smouldering fire which lurked always in his eyes had burned up into a lurid flame. He read their menace, and he clapped his hands to his empty belt. Then he turned to seize a weapon, but the bight of a rope was cast round him, and in an instant his arms were bound to his side. He fought like a wild cat and screamed for help.

"Ned!" he yelled. "Ned! Wake up! Here's damned villainy! Help, Ned, help!"

But the three men were far too deeply sunk in their swinish sleep for any voice to wake them. Round and round went the rope, until Sharkey was swathed like a mummy from ankle to neck. They propped him stiff and helpless against a powder barrel, and they gagged him with a handkerchief, but his filmy, red-rimmed eyes still looked curses at them. The dumb man chattered in his exultation, and Sharkey winced for the first time when he saw the empty mouth before him. He understood that vengeance, slow and patient, had dogged him long, and clutched him at last.

The two captors had their plans all arranged, and they were somewhat elaborate.

First of all they stove the heads of two of the great powder barrels, and they heaped the contents out upon the table and floor. They piled it round and under the three drunken men, until each sprawled in a heap of it. Then they carried Sharkey to the gun and they triced him sitting over the port-hole, with his body about a foot from the muzzle. Wriggle as he would he could not move an inch either to right or left, and the dumb man trussed him up with a sailor's cunning, so that there was no chance that he should work free.

"Now, you bloody devil," said Copley Banks, softly, "you must listen to what I have to say to you, for they are the last words that you will hear. You are my man now, and I have bought you at a price, for I have given all that a man can give here below, and I have given my soul as well.

"To reach you I have had to sink to your level. For two years I strove against it, hoping that some other way might come, but I learnt that there was no other way. I've robbed and I have murdered—worse still, I have laughed and lived with you—and all for the one end. And now my time has come, and you will die as I would have you die, seeing the shadow creeping slowly upon you and the devil waiting for you in the shadow."

Sharkey could hear the hoarse voices of his rovers singing their chanty over the water.

"Where is the trader of Stepney Town?
Wake her up! Shake her up! Every stick a-bending!
Where is the trader of Stepney Town?
His gold's on the capstan, his blood's on his gown.
All for bully rover Jack,
Reaching on the weather tack
Right across the Lowland Sea."

The words came clear to his ear, and just outside he could hear two men pacing backwards and forwards upon the deck. And yet he was helpless, staring down the mouth of the nine-pounder, unable to move an inch or to utter so much as a groan. Again there came the burst of voices from the deck of the barque.

"So it's up and it's over to Stornoway Bay,
Pack it on! Crack it on! Try her with the stun-sails!
It's off on a bowline to Stornoway Bay,
Where the liquor is good and the lasses are gay,
Waiting for their bully Jack,
Watching for him sailing back,
Right across the Lowland Sea."

To the dying pirate the jovial words and rollicking tune made his own fate seem the harsher, but there was no softening in his venomous blue eyes. Copley Banks had brushed away the priming of the gun, and had sprinkled fresh powder over the touch-hole. Then he had taken up the candle and cut it to the length of about an inch. This he placed upon the loose powder at the breach of the gun. Then he scattered powder thickly over the floor beneath, so that when the candle fell at the recoil it must explode the huge pile in which the three drunkards were wallowing.

"You've made others look death in the face, Sharkey," said he; "now it has come to be your own turn. You and these swine here shall go together!" He lit the candle-end as he spoke, and blew out the other lights upon the table. Then he passed out with the dumb man, and locked the cabin door upon the outer side. But before he closed it he took an exultant look backwards and received one last curse from those unconquerable eyes. In the single dim circle of light that ivory-white face, with the gleam of moisture upon the high, bald forehead, was the last that was ever seen of Sharkey.

There was a skiff alongside, and in it Copley Banks and the dumb steward made their way to the beach, and looked back upon the brig riding in the moonlight just outside the shadow of the palm trees. They waited and waited, watching that dim light which shone through the stern port. And then at last there came the dull thud of a gun, and an instant later the shattering crash of the explosion. The long, sleek, black barque, the sweep of white sand, and the fringe of nodding, feathery palm trees sprang into dazzling light and back into darkness again. Voices screamed and called upon the bay.

Then Copley Banks, his heart singing within him touched his companion upon the shoulder, and they plunged together into the lonely jungle of the Caicos.

## 5

# THE "SLAPPING SAL"

It was in the days when France's power was already broken upon the seas, and when more of her three-deckers lay rotting in the Medway than were to be found in Brest harbour. But her frigates and corvettes still scoured the ocean, closely followed ever by those of her rival. At the uttermost ends of the earth these dainty vessels, with sweet names of girls or of flowers, mangled and shattered each other for the honour of the four yards of bunting which flapped from the end of their gaffs.

It had blown hard in the night, but the wind had dropped with the dawning, and now the rising sun tinted the fringe of the storm-wrack as it dwindled into the west and glinted on the endless crests of the long, green waves. To north and south and west lay a skyline which was unbroken save by the spout of foam when two of the great Atlantic seas dashed each other into spray. To the east was a rocky island, jutting out into craggy points, with a few scattered clumps of palm trees and a pennant of mist streaming out from the bare, conical hill which capped it. A heavy surf beat upon the shore, and, at a safe distance from it, the British 32-gun frigate *Leda*, Captain A. P. Johnson, raised her black, glistening side upon the crest of a wave, or swooped down into an emerald valley, dipping away to the nor'ard under easy sail. On her snow-white quarter-deck stood a stiff little brown-faced man, who swept the horizon with his glass.

"Mr. Wharton!" he cried, with a voice like a rusty hinge.

A thin, knock-kneed officer shambled across the poop to him.

"Yes, sir."

"I've opened the sealed orders, Mr. Wharton."

A glimmer of curiosity shone upon the meagre features of the first lieutenant. The *Leda* had sailed with her consort, the *Dido*, from Antigua the week before, and the admiral's orders had been contained in a sealed envelope.

"We were to open them on reaching the deserted island of Sombriero, lying in north latitude eighteen, thirty-six, west longitude sixty-three, twenty-eight. Sombriero bore four miles to the north-east from our port-bow when the gale cleared, Mr. Wharton."

The lieutenant bowed stiffly. He and the captain had been bosom friends from childhood.

They had gone to school together, joined the navy together, fought again and again together, and married into each other's families, but so long as their feet were on the poop the iron discipline of the service struck all that was human out of them and left only the superior and the subordinate. Captain Johnson took from his pocket a blue paper, which crackled as he unfolded it.

> "The 32-gun frigates *Leda* and *Dido* (Captains A. P. Johnson and James Munro) are to cruise from the point at which these instructions are read to the mouth of the Caribbean sea, in the hope of encountering the French frigate *La Gloire* (48), which has recently harassed our merchant ships in that quarter. H.M. frigates are also directed to hunt down the piratical craft known sometimes as the *Slapping Sal* and sometimes as the *Hairy Hudson*, which has plundered the British ships as per margin, inflicting barbarities upon their crews. She is a small brig, carrying ten light guns, with one twenty-four pound carronade forward. She was last seen upon the 23rd. ult. to the north-east of the island of Sombriero.
>
> "(Signed) James Montgomery"(*Rear-Admiral*).
>
> "H.M.S. *Colossus*, Antigua."

"We appear to have lost our consort," said Captain Johnson, folding up his instructions and again sweeping the horizon with his glass. "She drew away after we reefed down. It would be a pity if we met this heavy Frenchman without the *Dido*, Mr. Wharton. Eh?"

The lieutenant twinkled and smiled.

"She has eighteen-pounders on the main and twelves on the poop, sir," said the captain. "She carries four hundred to our two hundred and thirty-one. Captain de Milon is the smartest man in the French service. Oh, Bobby boy, I'd give my hopes of my flag to rub my side up against her!" He turned on his heel, ashamed of his momentary lapse. "Mr. Wharton," said he, looking back sternly over his shoulder, "get those square sails shaken out and bear away a point more to the west."

"A brig on the port-bow," came a voice from the forecastle.

"A brig on the port-bow," said the lieutenant.

The captain sprang upon the bulwarks and held on by the mizzen-shrouds, a strange little figure with flying skirts and puckered eyes. The lean lieutenant craned his neck and whispered to Smeaton, the second, while officers and men came popping up from below and clustered along the weather-rail, shading their eyes with their hands—for the tropical sun was already clear of the palm trees. The strange brig lay at anchor in the throat of a curving estuary, and it was already obvious that she could not get out without passing under the guns of the frigate. A long, rocky point to the north of her held her in.

"Keep her as she goes, Mr. Wharton," said the captain. "Hardly worth while our clearing for action, Mr. Smeaton, but the men can stand by the guns in case she tries to pass us. Cast loose the bow-chasers and send the small-arm men to the forecastle."

A British crew went to its quarters in those days with the quiet serenity of men on their daily routine. In a few minutes, without fuss or sound, the sailors were knotted round their guns, the marines were drawn up and leaning on their muskets, and the frigate's bowsprit pointed straight for her little victim.

"Is it the *Slapping Sal*, sir?"

"I have no doubt of it, Mr. Wharton."

"They don't seem to like the look of us, sir. They've cut their cable and are clapping on sail."

It was evident that the brig meant struggling for her freedom. One little patch of canvas fluttered out above another, and her people could be seen working like madmen in the rigging. She made no attempt to pass her antagonist, but headed up the estuary. The captain rubbed his hands.

"She's making for shoal water, Mr. Wharton, and we shall have to cut her out, sir. She's a footy little brig, but I should have thought a fore-and-after would have been more handy."

"It was a mutiny, sir."

"Ah, indeed!"

"Yes, sir, I heard of it at Manilla: a bad business, sir. Captain and two mates murdered. This Hudson, or Hairy Hudson as they call him, led the mutiny. He's a Londoner, sir, and a cruel villain as ever walked."

"His next walk will be to Execution Dock, Mr. Wharton. She seems heavily manned. I wish I could take twenty topmen out of her, but they would be enough to corrupt the crew of the ark, Mr. Wharton."

Both officers were looking through their glasses at the brig. Suddenly the lieutenant showed his teeth in a grin, while the captain flushed a deeper red.

"That's Hairy Hudson on the after-rail, sir."

"The low, impertinent blackguard! He'll play some other antics before we are done with him. Could you reach him with the long eighteen, Mr. Smeaton?"

"Another cable length will do it, sir."

The brig yawed as they spoke, and as she came round a spurt of smoke whiffed out from her quarter. It was a pure piece of bravado, for the gun could scarce carry half-way. Then with a jaunty swing the little ship came into the wind again, and shot round a fresh curve in the winding channel.

"The water's shoaling rapidly, sir," repeated the second lieutenant.

"There's six fathoms by the chart."

"Four by the lead, sir."

"When we clear this point we shall see how we lie. Ha! I thought as much! Lay her to, Mr. Wharton. Now we have got her at our mercy!"

The frigate was quite out of sight of the sea now at the head of this river-like estuary. As she came round the curve the two shores were seen to converge at a point about a mile distant. In the angle, as near shore as she could get, the brig was lying with her broadside towards her pursuer and a wisp of black cloth streaming from her mizzen. The lean lieutenant, who had reappeared upon deck with a cutlass strapped to his side and two pistols rammed into his belt, peered curiously at the ensign.

"Is it the Jolly Rodger, sir?" he asked.

But the captain was furious.

"He may hang where his breeches are hanging before I have done with him!" said he. "What boats will you want, Mr. Wharton?"

"We should do it with the launch and the jolly-boat."

"Take four and make a clean job of it. Pipe away the crews at once, and I'll work her in and help you with the long eighteens."

With a rattle of ropes and a creaking of blocks the four boats splashed into the water. Their crews clustered thickly into them: bare-footed sailors, stolid marines, laughing middies, and in the sheets of each the senior officers with their stern schoolmaster faces. The captain, his elbows on the binnacle, still watched the distant brig. Her crew were tricing up the boarding-netting, dragging round the starboard guns, knocking new portholes for them, and making every preparation for a desperate resistance. In the thick of it all a huge man, bearded to the eyes, with a red nightcap upon his head, was straining and stooping and hauling. The captain watched him with a sour smile, and then snapping up his glass he turned upon his heel. For an instant he stood staring.

"Call back the boats!" he cried in his thin, creaking voice. "Clear away for action there! Cast loose those main-deck guns. Brace back the yards, Mr. Smeaton, and stand by to go about when she has weigh enough."

Round the curve of the estuary was coming a huge vessel. Her great yellow bowsprit and white-winged figure-head were jutting out from the cluster of palm trees, while high above them towered three immense masts with the tricolour flag floating superbly from the mizzen. Round she came, the deep-blue water creaming under her fore foot, until her long, curving, black side, her line of shining copper beneath and of snow-white hammocks above, and the thick clusters of men who peered over her bulwarks were all in full view. Her lower yards were slung, her ports triced up, and her guns run out all ready for action. Lying behind one of the promontories of the island, the lookout men of the *Gloire* upon the shore had seen the *cul de sac* into which the British frigate was headed, so that Captain de Milon had served the *Leda* as Captain Johnson had the *Slapping Sal*.

But the splendid discipline of the British service was at its best in such a crisis. The boats flew back; their crews clustered aboard, they were swung up at the davits and the fall-ropes made fast. Hammocks were brought up and stowed, bulkheads sent down, ports and magazines opened, the fires put out in the galley, and the drums beat to quarters. Swarms of men set the head-sails and brought the frigate round, while the gun-crews threw off their jackets and shirts, tightened their belts, and ran out their eighteen-pounders, peering through the open portholes at the stately Frenchman. The wind was very light. Hardly a ripple showed itself upon the clear blue water, but the sails blew gently out as the breeze came over the wooded banks. The Frenchman had gone about also, and both ships were now heading slowly for the sea under fore-and-aft canvas, the *Gloire* a hundred yards in advance. She luffed up to cross the *Leda's* bows, but the British ship came round also, and the two rippled slowly on in such a silence that the ringing of ramrods as the French marines drove home their charges clanged quite loudly upon the ear.

"Not much sea-room, Mr. Wharton," remarked the captain.

"I have fought actions in less, sir."

"We must keep our distance and trust to our gunnery. She is very heavily manned, and if she got alongside we might find ourselves in trouble."

"I see the shakos of soldiers aboard of her."

"Two companies of light infantry from Martinique. Now we have her! Hard-a-port, and let her have it as we cross her stern!"

The keen eye of the little commander had seen the surface ripple, which told of a passing breeze. He had used it to dart across the big Frenchman and to rake her with every gun as he passed. But, once past her, the *Leda* had to come back into the wind to keep out of shoal water. The maneuver brought her on to the starboard side of the Frenchman, and the trim little frigate seemed to heel right over under the crashing broadside which burst from the gaping ports. A moment later her topmen were swarming aloft to set her topsails and royals, and she strove to cross the *Gloire's* bows and rake her again. The French captain, however, brought his frigate's head round, and the two rode side by side within easy pistol-shot, pouring broadsides into each other in one of those murderous duels which, could they all be recorded, would mottle our charts with blood.

In that heavy tropical air, with so faint a breeze, the smoke formed a thick bank round the two vessels, from which the topmasts only protruded. Neither could see anything of its enemy save the throbs of fire in the darkness, and the guns were sponged and trained and fired into a dense wall of vapour. On the poop and forecastle the marines, in two little red lines, were pouring in their volleys, but neither they nor the sea-men-gunners could see what effect their fire was having. Nor, indeed, could they tell how far they were suffering themselves, for, standing at a gun, one could but hazily see that upon the right and the left. But above the roar of the cannon came the sharper sound of the piping shot, the crashing of riven planks, and the occasional heavy thud as spar or block came hurtling on to the deck. The lieutenants paced up and down the line of guns, while Captain Johnson fanned the smoke away with his cocked-hat and peered eagerly out.

"This is rare, Bobby!" said he, as the lieutenant joined him. Then, suddenly restraining himself, "What have we lost, Mr. Wharton?"

"Our maintopsail yard and our gaff, sir."

"Where's the flag?"

"Gone overboard, sir."

"They'll think we've struck! Lash a boat's ensign on the starboard arm of the mizzen cross-jackyard."

"Yes, sir."

A round-shot dashed the binnacle to pieces between them. A second knocked two marines into a bloody, palpitating mash. For a moment the smoke rose, and the English captain saw that his adversary's heavier metal was producing a horrible effect. The *Leda* was a shattered wreck. Her deck was strewed with corpses. Several of her portholes were knocked into one, and one of her eighteen-pounder guns had been thrown right back on to her breech, and pointed straight up to the sky. The thin line of marines still loaded and fired, but half the guns were silent, and their crews were piled thickly round them.

"Stand by to repel boarders!" yelled the captain.

"Cutlasses, lads, cutlasses!" roared Wharton.

"Hold your volley till they touch!" cried the captain of marines.

The huge loom of the Frenchman was seen bursting through the smoke. Thick clusters of boarders hung upon her sides and shrouds. A final broadside leapt from her ports, and the mainmast of the *Leda*, snapping short off a few feet above the deck, spun into the air and crashed down upon the port guns, killing ten men and putting the whole battery out of action. An instant later the two ships scraped together, and the starboard bower anchor of the *Gloire* caught the mizzen-chains of the *Leda* upon the port side. With a yell the black swarm of boarders steadied themselves for a spring.

But their feet were never to reach that blood-stained deck. From somewhere there came a well-aimed whiff of grape, and another, and another. The English marines and seamen, waiting with cutlass and musket behind the silent guns, saw with amazement the dark masses thinning and shredding away. At the same time the port broadside of the Frenchman burst into a roar.

"Clear away the wreck!" roared the captain. "What the devil are they firing at?"

"Get the guns clear!" panted the lieutenant. "We'll do them yet, boys!"

The wreckage was torn and hacked and splintered until first one gun and then another roared into action again. The Frenchman's anchor had been cut away, and the *Leda* had worked herself free from that fatal hug. But now, suddenly, there was a scurry up the shrouds of the *Gloire*, and a hundred Englishmen were shouting themselves hoarse: "They're running! They're running! They're running!"

And it was true. The Frenchman had ceased to fire, and was intent only upon clapping on every sail that he could carry. But that shouting hundred could not claim it all as their own. As the smoke cleared it was not difficult to see the reason. The ships had gained the mouth of the estuary during the fight, and there, about four miles out to sea, was the *Leda's* consort bearing down under full sail to the sound of the guns. Captain de Milon had done his part for one day, and presently the *Gloire* was drawing off swiftly to the north, while the *Dido* was bowling along at her skirts, rattling away with her bow-chasers, until a headland hid them both from view.

But the *Leda* lay sorely stricken, with her mainmast gone, her bulwarks shattered, her mizzen-topmast and gaff shot away, her sails like a beggar's rags, and a hundred of her crew dead and wounded. Close beside her a mass of wreckage floated upon the waves. It was the stern-post of a mangled vessel, and across it, in white letters on a black ground, was painted, *"The Slapping Sal."*

"By the Lord! it was the brig that saved us!" cried Mr. Wharton. "Hudson brought her into action with the Frenchman, and was blown out of the water by a broadside!"

The little captain turned on his heel and paced up and down the deck. Already his crew were plugging the shot-holes, knotting and splicing and mending. When he came back, the lieutenant saw a softening of the stern lines about his eyes and mouth.

"Are they all gone?"

"Every man. They must have sunk with the wreck."

The two officers looked down at the sinister name, and at the stump of wreckage which floated in the discoloured water. Something black washed to and fro beside a splintered gaff and a tangle of halliards. It was the outrageous ensign, and near it a scarlet cap was floating.

"He was a villain, but he was a Briton!" said the captain, at last. "He lived like a dog, but, by God, he died like a man!"

# 6

# A PIRATE OF THE LAND

## ONE CROWDED HOUR

The place was the Eastbourne-Tunbridge road, not very far from the Cross in Hand—a lonely stretch, with a heath running upon either side. The time was half-past eleven upon a Sunday night in the late summer. A motor was passing slowly down the road.

It was a long, lean Rolls-Royce, running smoothly with a gentle purring of the engine. Through the two vivid circles cast by the electric head-lights the waving grass fringes and clumps of heather streamed swiftly like some golden cinematograph, leaving a blacker darkness behind and around them. One ruby-red spot shone upon the road, but no number-plate was visible within the dim ruddy halo of the tail-lamp which cast it. The car was open and of a tourist type, but even in that obscure light, for the night was moonless, an observer could hardly fail to have noticed a curious indefiniteness in its lines. As it slid into and across the broad stream of light from an open cottage door the reason could be seen. The body was hung with a singular loose arrangement of brown holland. Even the long black bonnet was banded with some close-drawn drapery.

The solitary man who drove this curious car was broad and burly. He sat hunched up over his steering-wheel, with the brim of a Tyrolean hat drawn down over his eyes. The red end of a cigarette smouldered under the black shadow thrown by the headgear. A dark ulster of some frieze-like material was turned up in the collar until it covered his ears. His neck was pushed forward from his rounded shoulders, and he seemed, as the car now slid noiselessly down the long sloping road, with the clutch disengaged and the engine running free, to be peering ahead of him through the darkness in search of some eagerly-expected object.

The distant toot of a motor-horn came faintly from some point far to the south of him. On such a night, at such a place, all traffic must be from south to north when the current of London week-enders sweeps back from the watering-place to the capital—from pleasure to duty. The man sat straight and listened intently. Yes, there it was again, and certainly to the south of him. His face was over the wheel and his eyes strained through the darkness. Then suddenly he spat out his cigarette and gave a sharp intake of the breath. Far away down the road two little yellow points had rounded a curve. They vanished into a dip, shot upwards once more, and then vanished again. The inert man in the draped car woke suddenly into intense life. From his pocket he pulled a mask of dark cloth, which he fastened securely across his face, adjusting it carefully that his sight might be unimpeded. For an instant he uncovered an acetylene hand-lantern, took a hasty glance at his own preparations, and laid it beside a Mauser pistol upon the seat alongside him. Then, twitching his hat down lower than ever, he released his clutch and slid downward his gear-lever. With a chuckle and shudder the long, black machine sprang forward, and shot with a soft sigh from her powerful engines down the sloping gradient. The driver stooped and switched off his electric head-lights. Only a dim grey swathe cut through the black heath indicated the line of his road. From in front there came presently a confused puffing and rattling and clanging as the oncoming car breasted the slope. It coughed and spluttered on a powerful, old-fashioned low gear, while its engine throbbed like a weary heart. The yellow, glaring lights dipped for the last time into a switchback curve. When they reappeared over the crest the two cars were within thirty yards of each other. The dark one darted across the road and barred the other's passage, while a warning acetylene lamp was waved in the air. With a jarring of brakes the noisy newcomer was brought to a halt.

"I say," cried an aggrieved voice, "'pon my soul, you know, we might have had an accident. Why the devil don't you keep your head-lights on? I never saw you till I nearly burst my radiators on you!"

The acetylene lamp, held forward, discovered a very angry young man, blue-eyed, yellow-moustached, and florid, sitting alone at the wheel of an antiquated twelve-horse Wolseley. Suddenly the aggrieved look upon his flushed face changed to one of absolute bewilderment. The driver in the dark car had sprung out of the seat, a black, long-barrelled, wicked-looking pistol was poked in the traveller's face, and behind the further sights of it was a circle of black cloth with two deadly eyes looking from as many slits.

"Hands up!" said a quick, stern voice. "Hands up! or, by the Lord——"

The young man was as brave as his neighbours, but the hands went up all the same.

"Get down!" said his assailant, curtly.

The young man stepped forth into the road, followed closely by the covering lantern and pistol. Once he made as if he would drop his hands, but a short, stern word jerked them up again.

"I say, look here, this is rather out o' date, ain't it?" said the traveller. "I expect you're joking—what?"

"Your watch," said the man behind the Mauser pistol.

"You can't really mean it!"

"Your watch, I say!"

"Well, take it, if you must. It's only plated, anyhow. You're two centuries out in time, or a few thousand miles longitude. The bush is your mark—or America. You don't seem in the picture on a Sussex road."

"Purse," said the man. There was something very compelling in his voice and methods. The purse was handed over.

"Any rings?"

"Don't wear 'em."

"Stand there! Don't move!"

The highwayman passed his victim and threw open the bonnet of the Wolseley. His hand, with a pair of steel pliers, was thrust deep into the works. There was the snap of a parting wire.

"Hang it all, don't crock my car!" cried the traveller.

He turned, but quick as a flash the pistol was at his head once more. And yet even in that flash, whilst the robber whisked round from the broken circuit, something had caught the young man's eye which made him gasp and start. He opened his mouth as if about to shout some words. Then with an evident effort he restrained himself.

"Get in," said the highwayman.

The traveller climbed back to his seat.

"What is your name?"

"Ronald Barker. What's yours?"

The masked man ignored the impertinence.

"Where do you live?" he asked.

"My cards are in my purse. Take one."

The highwayman sprang into his car, the engine of which had hissed and whispered in gentle accompaniment to the interview. With a clash he threw back his side-brake, flung in his gears, twirled the wheel hard round, and cleared the motionless Wolseley. A minute later he was gliding swiftly, with all his lights gleaming, some half-mile southward on the road, while Mr. Ronald Barker, a side-lamp in his hand, was rummaging furiously among the odds and ends of his repair-box for a strand of wire which would connect up his electricity and set him on his way once more.

When he had placed a safe distance between himself and his victim, the adventurer eased up, took his booty from his pocket, replaced the watch, opened the purse, and counted out the money. Seven shillings constituted the miserable spoil. The poor result of his efforts seemed to amuse rather than annoy him, for he chuckled as he held the two half-crowns and the florin in the glare of his lantern. Then suddenly his manner changed. He thrust the thin purse back into his pocket, released his brake, and shot onwards with the same tense bearing with which he had started upon his adventure. The lights of another car were coming down the road.

On this occasion the methods of the highwayman were less furtive. Experience had clearly given him confidence. With lights still blazing he ran towards the new-comers, and, halting in the middle of the road, summoned them to stop. From the point of view of the astonished travellers the result was sufficiently impressive. They saw in the glare of their own head-lights two glowing discs on either side of the long, black-muzzled snout of a high-power car, and above the masked face and menacing figure of its solitary driver. In the golden circle thrown by the Rover there stood an elegant, open-topped, twenty-horse Humber, with an undersized and very astonished chauffeur blinking from under his peaked cap. From behind the wind-screen the veil-bound hats and wondering faces of two very pretty young women protruded, one upon either side, and a little crescendo of frightened squeaks announced the acute emotion of one of them. The other was cooler and more critical.

"Don't give it away, Hilda," she whispered. "Do shut up, and don't be such a silly. It's Bertie or one of the boys playing it on us."

"No, no! It's the real thing, Flossie. It's a robber, sure enough. Oh, my goodness, whatever shall we do?"

"What an 'ad.'!" cried the other. "Oh, what a glorious 'ad.'! Too late now for the mornings, but they'll have it in every evening paper, sure."

"What's it going to cost?" groaned the other. "Oh, Flossie, Flossie, I'm sure I'm going to faint! Don't you think if we both screamed together we could do some good? Isn't he too awful with that black thing over his face? Oh, dear, oh, dear! He's killing poor little Alf!"

The proceedings of the robber were indeed somewhat alarming. Springing down from his car, he had pulled the chauffeur out of his seat by the scruff of his neck. The sight of the Mauser had cut short all remonstrance, and under its compulsion the little man had pulled open the bonnet and extracted the sparking plugs. Having thus secured the immobility of his capture, the masked man walked forward, lantern in hand, to the side of the car. He had laid aside the gruff sternness with which he had treated Mr. Ronald Barker, and his voice and manner were gentle, though determined. He even raised his hat as a prelude to his address.

"I am sorry to inconvenience you, ladies," said he, and his voice had gone up several notes since the previous interview. "May I ask who you are?"

Miss Hilda was beyond coherent speech, but Miss Flossie was of a sterner mould.

"This is a pretty business," said she. "What right have you to stop us on the public road, I should like to know?"

"My time is short," said the robber, in a sterner voice. "I must ask you to answer my question."

"Tell him, Flossie! For goodness' sake be nice to him!" cried Hilda.

"Well, we're from the Gaiety Theatre, London, if you want to know," said the young lady. "Perhaps you've heard of Miss Flossie Thornton and Miss Hilda Mannering? We've been playing a week at the Royal at Eastbourne, and took a Sunday off to ourselves. So now you know!"

"I must ask you for your purses and for your jewellery."

Both ladies set up shrill expostulations, but they found, as Mr. Ronald Barker had done, that there was something quietly compelling in this man's methods. In a very few minutes they had handed over their purses, and a pile of glittering rings, bangles, brooches and chains was lying upon the front seat of the car. The diamonds glowed and shimmered like little electric points in the light of the lantern. He picked up the glittering tangle and weighed it in his hand.

"Anything you particularly value?" he asked the ladies; but Miss Flossie was in no humour for concessions.

"Don't come the Claude Duval over us," said she. "Take the lot or leave the lot. We don't want bits of our own given back to us."

"Except just Billy's necklace!" cried Hilda, and snatched at a little rope of pearls. The robber bowed, and released his hold of it.

"Anything else?"

The valiant Flossie began suddenly to cry. Hilda did the same. The effect upon the robber was surprising. He threw the whole heap of jewellery into the nearest lap.

"There! there! Take it!" he said. "It's trumpery stuff, anyhow. It's worth something to you, and nothing to me."

Tears changed in a moment to smiles.

"You're welcome to the purses. The 'ad.' is worth ten times the money. But what a funny way of getting a living nowadays! Aren't you afraid of being caught? It's all so wonderful, like a scene from a comedy."

"It may be a tragedy," said the robber.

"Oh, I hope not—I'm sure I hope not!" cried the two ladies of the drama.

But the robber was in no mood for further conversation. Far away down the road tiny points of light had appeared. Fresh business was coming to him, and he must not mix his cases. Disengaging his machine, he raised his hat, and slipped off to meet this new arrival, while Miss Flossie and Miss Hilda leaned out of their derelict car, still palpitating from their adventure, and watched the red gleam of the tail-light until it merged into the darkness.

This time there was every sign of a rich prize. Behind its four grand lamps set in a broad frame of glittering brasswork the magnificent sixty-horse Daimler breasted the slope with the low, deep, even snore which proclaimed its enormous latent strength. Like some rich-laden, high-pooped Spanish galleon, she kept her course until the prowling craft ahead of her swept across her bows and brought her to a sudden halt. An angry face, red, blotched, and evil, shot out of the open window of the closed limousine. The robber was aware of a high, bald forehead, gross pendulous cheeks, and two little crafty eyes which gleamed between creases of fat.

"Out of my way, sir! Out of my way this instant!" cried a rasping voice. "Drive over him, Hearn! Get down and pull him off the seat. The fellow's drunk—he's drunk, I say!"

Up to this point the proceedings of the modern highwayman might have passed as gentle. Now they turned in an instant to savagery. The chauffeur, a burly, capable fellow, incited by that raucous voice behind him, sprang from the car and seized the advancing robber by the throat. The latter hit out with the butt-end of his pistol, and the man dropped groaning on the road. Stepping over his prostrate body the adventurer pulled open the door, seized the stout occupant savagely by the ear, and dragged him bellowing on the highway. Then, very deliberately, he struck him twice across the face with his open hand. The blows rang out like pistol-shots in the silence of the night. The fat traveller turned a ghastly colour and fell back half senseless against the side of the limousine. The robber dragged open his coat, wrenched away the heavy gold watch-chain with all that it held, plucked out the great diamond pin that sparkled in the black satin tie, dragged off four rings—not one of which could have cost less than three figures—and finally tore from his inner pocket a bulky leather notebook. All this property he transferred to his own black overcoat, and added to it the man's pearl cuff-links, and even the golden stud which held his collar. Having made sure that there was nothing else to take, the robber flashed his lantern upon the prostrate chauffeur, and satisfied himself that he was stunned and not dead. Then, returning to the master, he proceeded very deliberately to tear all his clothes from his body with a ferocious energy which set his victim whimpering and writhing in imminent expectation of murder.

Whatever the tormentor's intention may have been, it was very effectually frustrated. A sound made him turn his head, and there, no very great distance off, were the lights of a car coming swiftly from the north. Such a car must have already passed the wreckage which this pirate had left behind him. It was following his track with a deliberate purpose, and might be crammed with every county constable of the district.

The adventurer had no time to lose. He darted from his bedraggled victim, sprang into his own seat, and with his foot on the accelerator shot swiftly off down the road. Some way down there was a narrow side lane, and into this the fugitive turned, cracking on his high speed and leaving a good five miles between him and any pursuer before he ventured to stop. Then, in a quiet corner, he counted over his booty of the evening—the paltry plunder of Mr. Ronald Barker, the rather better-furnished purses of the actresses, which contained four pounds between them, and, finally, the gorgeous jewellery and well-filled notebook of the plutocrat upon the Daimler. Five notes of fifty pounds, four of ten, fifteen sovereigns, and a number of valuable papers made up a most noble haul. It was clearly enough for one night's work. The adventurer replaced all his ill-gotten gains in his pocket, and, lighting a cigarette, set forth upon his way with the air of a man who has no further care upon his mind.

It was on the Monday morning following upon this eventful evening that Sir Henry Hailworthy, of Walcot Old Place, having finished his breakfast in a leisurely fashion, strolled down to his study with the intention of writing a few letters before setting forth to take his place upon the county bench. Sir Henry was a Deputy-Lieutenant of the county; he was a baronet of ancient blood; he was a magistrate of ten years' standing; and he was famous above all as the breeder of many a good horse and the most desperate rider in all the Weald country. A tall, upstanding man, with a strong clean-shaven face, heavy black eyebrows, and a square, resolute jaw, he was one whom it was better to call friend than foe. Though nearly fifty years of age, he bore no sign of having passed his youth, save that Nature, in one of her freakish moods, had planted one little feather of white hair above his right ear, making the rest of his thick black curls the darker by contrast. He was in thoughtful mood this morning, for having lit his pipe he sat at his desk with his blank note-paper in front of him, lost in a deep reverie.

Suddenly his thoughts were brought back to the present. From behind the laurels of the curving drive there came a low, clanking sound, which swelled into the clatter and jingle of an ancient car. Then from round the corner there swung an old-fashioned Wolseley, with a fresh-complexioned, yellow-moustached young man at the wheel. Sir Henry sprang to his feet at the sight, and then sat down once more. He rose again as a minute later the footman announced Mr. Ronald Barker. It was an early visit, but Barker was Sir Henry's intimate friend. As each was a fine shot, horseman, and billiard-player, there was much in common between the two men, and the younger (and poorer) was in the habit of spending at least two evenings a week at Walcot Old Place. Therefore, Sir Henry advanced cordially with outstretched hand to welcome him.

"You're an early bird this morning," said he. "What's up? If you are going over to Lewes we could motor together."

But the younger man's demeanour was peculiar and ungracious. He disregarded the hand which was held out to him, and he stood pulling at his own long moustache and staring with troubled, questioning eyes at the county magistrate.

"Well, what's the matter?" asked the latter.

Still the young man did not speak. He was clearly on the edge of an interview which he found it most difficult to open. His host grew impatient.

"You don't seem yourself this morning. What on earth is the matter? Anything upset you?"

"Yes," said Ronald Barker, with emphasis.

"What has?"

"*You* have."

Sir Henry smiled. "Sit down, my dear fellow. If you have any grievance against me, let me hear it."

Barker sat down. He seemed to be gathering himself for a reproach. When it did come it was like a bullet from a gun.

"Why did you rob me last night?"

The magistrate was a man of iron nerve. He showed neither surprise nor resentment. Not a muscle twitched upon his calm, set face.

"Why do you say that I robbed you last night?"

"A big, tall fellow in a motor-car stopped me on the Mayfield road. He poked a pistol in my face and took my purse and my watch. Sir Henry, that man was you."

The magistrate smiled.

"Am I the only big, tall man in the district? Am I the only man with a motor-car?"

"Do you think I couldn't tell a Rolls-Royce when I see it—I, who spend half my life on a car and the other half under it? Who has a Rolls-Royce about here except you?"

"My dear Barker, don't you think that such a modern highwayman as you describe would be more likely to operate outside his own district? How many hundred Rolls-Royces are there in the South of England?"

"No, it won't do, Sir Henry—it won't do! Even your voice, though you sunk it a few notes, was familiar enough to me. But hang it, man! What did you do it *for*? That's what gets over me. That you should stick up me, one of your closest friends, a man that worked himself to the bone when you stood for the division—and all for the sake of a Brummagem watch and a few shillings—is simply incredible."

"Simply incredible," repeated the magistrate, with a smile.

"And then those actresses, poor little devils, who have to earn all they get. I followed you down the road, you see. That was a dirty trick, if ever I heard one. The City shark was different. If a chap must go a-robbing, that sort of fellow is fair game. But your friend, and then the girls—well, I say again, I couldn't have believed it."

"Then why believe it?"

"Because it *is* so."

"Well, you seem to have persuaded yourself to that effect. You don't seem to have much evidence to lay before any one else."

"I could swear to you in a police-court. What put the lid on it was that when you were cutting my wire—and an infernal liberty it was!—I saw that white tuft of yours sticking out from behind your mask."

For the first time an acute observer might have seen some slight sign of emotion upon the face of the baronet.

"You seem to have a fairly vivid imagination," said he.

His visitor flushed with anger.

"See here, Hailworthy," said he, opening his hand and showing a small, jagged triangle of black cloth. "Do you see that? It was on the ground near the car of the young women. You must have ripped it off as you jumped out from your seat. Now send for that heavy black driving-coat of yours. If you don't ring the bell I'll ring it myself, and we shall have it in. I'm going to see this thing through, and don't you make any mistake about that."

The baronet's answer was a surprising one. He rose, passed Barker's chair, and, walking over to the door, he locked it and placed the key in his pocket.

"You *are* going to see it through," said he. "I'll lock you in until you do. Now we must have a straight talk, Barker, as man to man, and whether it ends in tragedy or not depends on you."

He had half-opened one of the drawers in his desk as he spoke. His visitor frowned in anger.

"You won't make matters any better by threatening me, Hailworthy. I am going to do my duty, and you won't bluff me out of it."

"I have no wish to bluff you. When I spoke of a tragedy I did not mean to you. What I meant was that there are some turns which this affair cannot be allowed to take. I have neither kith nor kin, but there is the family honour, and some things are impossible."

"It is late to talk like that."

"Well, perhaps it is, but not too late. And now I have a good deal to say to you. First of all, you are quite right, and it was I who held you up last night on the Mayfield road."

"But why on earth——"

"All right. Let me tell it my own way. First I want you to look at these." He unlocked a drawer and he took out two small packages. "These were to be posted in London to-night. This one is addressed to you, and I may as well hand it over to you at once. It contains your watch and your purse. So, you see bar your cut wire you would have been none the worse for your adventure. This other packet is addressed to the young ladies of the Gaiety Theatre, and their properties are enclosed. I hope I have convinced you that I had intended full reparation in each case before you came to accuse me?"

"Well?" asked Barker.

"Well, we will now deal with Sir George Wilde, who is, as you may not know, the senior partner of Wilde and Guggendorf, the founders of the Ludgate Bank of infamous memory. His chauffeur is a case apart. You may take it from me, upon my word of honour, that I had plans for the chauffeur. But it is the master that I want to speak of. You know that I am not a rich man myself. I expect all the county knows that. When Black Tulip lost the Derby I was hard hit. And other things as well. Then I had a legacy of a thousand. This infernal bank was paying 7 per cent. on deposits. I knew Wilde. I saw him. I asked him if it was safe. He said it was. I paid it in, and within forty-eight hours the whole thing went to bits. It came out before the Official Receiver that Wilde had known for three months that nothing could save him. And yet he took all my cargo aboard his sinking vessel. He was all right—confound him! He had plenty besides. But I had lost all my money and no law could help me. Yet he had robbed me as clearly as one man could rob another. I saw him and he laughed in my face. Told me to stick to Consols, and that the lesson was cheap at the price. So I just swore that, by hook or by crook, I would get level with him. I knew his habits, for I had made it my business to do so. I knew that he came back from Eastbourse on Sunday nights. I knew that he carried a good sum with him in his pocket-book. Well it's *my* pocket-book now. Do you mean to tell me that I'm not morally justified in what I have done? By the Lord, I'd have left the devil as bare as he left many a widow and orphan if I'd had the time!"

"That's all very well. But what about me? What about the girls?"

"Have some common sense, Barker. Do you suppose that I could go and stick up this one personal enemy of mine and escape detection? It was impossible. I was bound to make myself out to be just a common robber who had run up against him by accident. So I turned myself loose on the high road and took my chance. As the devil would have it, the first man I met was yourself. I was a fool not to recognise that old ironmonger's store of yours by the row it made coming up the hill. When I saw you I could hardly speak for laughing. But I was bound to carry it through. The same with the actresses. I'm afraid I gave myself away, for I couldn't take their little fallals, but I had to keep up a show. Then came my man himself. There was no bluff about that. I was out to skin him, and I did. Now, Barker, what do you think of it all? I had a pistol at your head last night, and, by George! whether you believe it or not, you have one at mine this morning!"

The young man rose slowly, and with a broad smile he wrung the magistrate by the hand.

"Don't do it again. It's too risky," said he. "The swine would score heavily if you were taken."

"You're a good chap, Barker," said the magistrate. "No, I won't do it again. Who's the fellow who talks of 'one crowded hour of glorious life'? By George! it's too fascinating. I had the time of my life! Talk of fox-hunting! No, I'll never touch it again, for it might get a grip of me."

A telephone rang sharply upon the table, and the baronet put the receiver to his ear. As he listened, he smiled at his companion.

"I'm rather late this morning," said he, "and they are awaiting for me to try some petty larcenies on the county bench."

# TALES OF BLUE WATER

## ❧ I ❧

# THE STRIPED CHEST

"What do you make of her, Allardyce?" I asked.

My second mate was standing beside me upon the poop, with his short, thick legs astretch, for the gale had left a considerable swell behind it, and our two quarter-boats nearly touched the water with every roll. He steadied his glass against the mizzen-shrouds, and he looked long and hard at this disconsolate stranger every time she came reeling up on to the crest of a roller and hung balanced for a few seconds before swooping down upon the other side. She lay so low in the water that I could only catch an occasional glimpse of a pea-green line of bulwark.

She was a brig, but her mainmast had been snapped short off some ten feet above the deck, and no effort seemed to have been made to cut away the wreckage, which floated, sails and yards, like the broken wing of a wounded gull, upon the water beside her. The foremast was still standing, but the fore-topsail was flying loose, and the head-sails were streaming out in long white pennons in front of her. Never have I seen a vessel which appeared to have gone through rougher handling.

But we could not be surprised at that, for there had been times during the last three days when it was a question whether our own barque would ever see land again. For thirty-six hours we had kept her nose to it, and if the *Mary Sinclair* had not been as good a seaboat as ever left the Clyde, we could not have gone through. And yet here we were at the end of it with the loss only of our gig and of part of the starboard bulwark. It did not astonish us, however, when the smother had cleared away, to find that others had been less lucky, and that this mutilated brig, staggering about upon a blue sea, and under a cloudless sky, had been left, like a blinded man after a lightning flash, to tell of the terror which is past.

Allardyce, who was a slow and methodical Scotchman, stared long and hard at the little craft, while our seamen lined the bulwark or clustered upon the fore shrouds to have a view of the stranger. In latitude 20° and longitude 10°, which were about our bearings, one becomes a little curious as to whom one meets, for one has left the main lines of Atlantic commerce to the north. For ten days we had been sailing over a solitary sea.

"She's derelict, I'm thinking," said the second mate.

I had come to the same conclusion, for I could see no sign of life upon her deck, and there was no answer to the friendly wavings from our seamen. The crew had probably deserted her under the impression that she was about to founder.

"She can't last long," continued Allardyce, in his measured way. "She may put her nose down and her tail up any minute. The water's lipping up to the edge of her rail."

"What's her flag?" I asked.

"I'm trying to make out. It's got all twisted and tangled with the halyards. Yes, I've got it now, clear enough. It's the Brazilian flag, but it's wrong side up."

She had hoisted a signal of distress, then, before her people abandoned her. Perhaps they had only just gone. I took the mate's glass and looked round over the tumultuous face of the deep blue Atlantic, still veined and starred with white lines and spoutings of foam. But nowhere could I see anything human beyond ourselves.

"There may be living men aboard," said I.

"There may be salvage," muttered the second mate.

"Then we will run down upon her lee side, and lie to."

We were not more than a hundred yards from her when we swung our fore-yard aback, and there we were, the barque and the brig, ducking and bowing like two clowns in a dance.

"Drop one of the quarter-boats," said I. "Take four men, Mr. Allardyce, and see what you can learn of her."

But just at that moment my first officer, Mr. Armstrong, came on deck, for seven bells had struck, and it was but a few minutes off his watch. It would interest me to go myself to this abandoned vessel and to see what there might be aboard of her. So, with a word to Armstrong, I swung myself over the side, slipped down the falls, and took my place in the sheets of the boat.

It was but a little distance, but it took some time to traverse, and so heavy was the roll, that often, when we were in the trough of the sea, we could not see either the barque which we had left or the brig which we were approaching. The sinking sun did not penetrate down there, and it was cold and dark in the hollows of the waves, but each passing billow heaved us up into the warmth and the sunshine once more. At each of these moments, as we hung upon a white-capped ridge between the two dark valleys, I caught a glimpse of the long, pea-green line, and the nodding foremast of the brig, and I steered so as to come round by her stern, so that we might determine which was the best way of boarding her. As we passed her we saw the name *Nossa Sehnora da Vittoria* painted across her dripping counter.

"The weather side, sir," said the second mate. "Stand by with the boat-hook, carpenter!" An instant later we had jumped over the bulwarks, which were hardly higher than our boat, and found ourselves upon the deck of the abandoned vessel.

Our first thought was to provide for our own safety in case—as seemed very probable—the vessel should settle down beneath our feet. With this object two of our men held on to the painter of the boat, and fended her off from the vessel's side, so that she might be ready in case we had to make a hurried retreat. The carpenter was sent to find out how much water there was, and whether it was still gaining, while the other seaman, Allardyce, and myself, made a rapid inspection of the vessel and her cargo.

The deck was littered with wreckage and with hen-coops, in which the dead birds were washing about. The boats were gone, with the exception of one, the bottom of which had been stove, and it was certain that the crew had abandoned the vessel. The cabin was in a deck house, one side of which had been beaten in by a heavy sea. Allardyce and I entered it, and found the captain's table as he had left it, his books and papers—all Spanish or Portuguese—scattered over it, with piles of cigarette ash everywhere. I looked about for the log, but could not find it.

"As likely as not he never kept one," said Allardyce. "Things are pretty slack aboard a South American trader, and they don't do more than they can help. If there was one it must have been taken away with him in the boat."

"I should like to take all these books and papers," said I. "Ask the carpenter how much time we have."

His report was reassuring. The vessel was full of water, but some of the cargo was buoyant, and there was no immediate danger of her sinking. Probably she would never sink, but would drift about as one of those terrible, unmarked reefs which have sent so many stout vessels to the bottom.

"In that case there is no danger in your going below, Mr. Allardyce," said I. "See what you can make of her, and find out how much of her cargo may be saved. I'll look through these papers while you are gone."

The bills of lading, and some notes and letters which lay upon the desk, sufficed to inform me that the Brazilian brig *Nossa Sehnora da Vittoria* had cleared from Bahia a month before. The name of the captain was Texeira, but there was no record as to the number of the crew. She was bound for London, and a glance at the bills of lading was sufficient to show me that we were not likely to profit much in the way of salvage. Her cargo consisted of nuts, ginger, and wood, the latter in the shape of great logs of valuable tropical growths. It was these, no doubt, which had prevented the ill-fated vessel from going to the bottom, but they were of such a size as to make it impossible for us to extract them. Besides these, there were a few fancy goods, such as a number of ornamental birds for millinery purposes, and a hundred cases of preserved fruits. And then, as I turned over the papers, I came upon a short note in English, which arrested my attention.

"It is requested," said the note, "that the various old Spanish and Indian curiosities, which came out of the Santarem collection, and which are consigned to Prontfoot and Neuman, of Oxford Street, London, should be put in some place where there may be no danger of these very valuable and unique articles being injured or tampered with. This applies most particularly to the treasure-chest of Don Ramirez di Leyra, which must on no account be placed where any one can get at it."

The treasure-chest of Don Ramirez! Unique and valuable articles! Here was a chance of salvage after all! I had risen to my feet with the paper in my hand, when my Scotch mate appeared in the doorway.

"I'm thinking all isn't quite as it should be aboard of this ship, sir," said he. He was a hard-faced man, and yet I could see that he had been startled.

"What's the matter?"

"Murder's the matter, sir. There's a man Here with his brains beaten out."

"Killed in the storm?" said I.

"May be so, sir. But I'll be surprised if you think so after you have seen him."

"Where is he, then?"

"This way, sir; here in the main-deck house."

There appeared to have been no accommodation below in the brig, for there was the afterhouse for the captain, another by the main hatchway with the cook's galley attached to it, and a third in the forecastle for the men. It was to this middle one that the mate led me. As you entered the galley, with its litter of tumbled pots and dishes, was upon the right, and upon the left was a small room with two bunks for the officers. Then beyond there was a place about twelve feet square, which was littered with flags and spare canvas. All round the walls were a number of packets done up in coarse cloth and carefully lashed to the woodwork. At the other end was a great box, striped red and white, though the red was so faded and the white so dirty that it was only where the light fell directly upon it that one could see the colouring. The box was, by subsequent measurement, four feet three inches in length, three feet two inches in height, and three feet across—considerably larger than a seaman's chest.

But it was not to the box that my eyes or my thoughts were turned as I entered the store-room. On the floor, lying across the litter of bunting, there was stretched a small, dark man with a short, curling beard. He lay as far as it was possible from the box, with his feet towards it and his head away. A crimson patch was printed upon the white canvas on which his head was resting, and little red ribbons wreathed themselves round his swarthy neck and trailed away on to the floor, but there was no sign of a wound that I could see, and his face was as placid as that of a sleeping child.

It was only when I stooped that I could perceive his injury, and then I turned away with an exclamation of horror. He had been pole-axed; apparently by some person standing behind him. A frightful blow had smashed in the top of his head and penetrated deeply into his brain. His face might well be placid, for death must have been absolutely instantaneous, and the position of the wound showed that he could never have seen the person who had inflicted it.

"Is that foul play or accident, Captain Barclay?" asked my second mate, demurely.

"You are quite right, Mr. Allardyce. The man has been murdered, struck down from above by a sharp and heavy weapon. But who was he, and why did they murder him?"

"He was a common seaman, sir," said the mate. "You can see that if you look at his fingers." He turned out his pockets as he spoke and brought to light a pack of cards, some tarred string, and a bundle of Brazilian tobacco.

"Hullo, look at this!" said he.

It was a large, open knife with a stiff spring blade which he had picked up from the floor. The steel was shining and bright, so that we could not associate it with the crime, and yet the dead man had apparently held it in his hand when he was struck down, for it still lay within his grasp.

"It looks to me, sir, as if he knew he was in danger, and kept his knife handy," said the mate. "However, we can't help the poor beggar now. I can't make out these things that are lashed to the wall. They seem to be idols and weapons and curios of all sorts done up in old sacking."

"That's right," said I. "They are the only things of value that we are likely to get from the cargo. Hail the barque and tell them to send the other quarter-boat to help us to get the stuff aboard."

While he was away I examined this curious plunder which had come into our possession. The curiosities were so wrapped up that I could only form a general idea as to their nature, but the striped box stood in a good light where I could thoroughly examine it. On the lid, which was clamped and cornered with metal-work, there was engraved a complex coat of arms, and beneath it was a line of Spanish which I was able to decipher as meaning, "The treasure-chest of Don Ramirez di Leyra, Knight of the Order of Saint James, Governor and Captain-General of Terra Firma and of the Province of Veraquas." In one corner was the date 1606, and on the other a large white label, upon which was written in English, "You are earnestly requested, upon no account, to open this box." The same warning was repeated underneath in Spanish. As to the lock, it was a very complex and heavy one of engraved steel, with a Latin motto, which was above a seaman's comprehension.

By the time I had finished this examination of the peculiar box, the other quarter-boat with Mr. Armstrong, the first officer, had come alongside, and we began to carry out and place in her the various curiosities which appeared to be the only objects worth moving from the derelict ship. When she was full I sent her back to the barque, and then Allardyce and I, with a carpenter and one seaman, shifted the striped box, which was the only thing left, to our boat, and lowered it over, balancing it upon the two middle thwarts, for it was so heavy that it would have given the boat a dangerous tilt had we placed it at either end. As to the dead man, we left him where we had found him.

The mate had a theory that at the moment of the desertion of the ship, this fellow had started plundering, and that the captain in an attempt to preserve discipline, had struck him down with a hatchet or some other heavy weapon. It seemed more probable than any other explanation, and yet it did not entirely satisfy me either. But the ocean is full of mysteries, and we were content to leave the fate of the dead seaman of the Brazilian brig to be added to that long list which every sailor can recall.

The heavy box was slung up by ropes on to the deck of the *Mary Sinclair*, and was carried by four seamen into the cabin, where, between the table and the after-lockers, there was just space for it to stand. There it remained during supper, and after that meal the mates remained with me, and discussed over a glass of grog the event of the day. Mr. Armstrong was a long, thin, vulture-like man, an excellent seaman, but famous for his nearness and cupidity. Our treasure-trove had excited him greatly, and already he had begun with glistening eyes to reckon up how much it might be worth to each of us when the shares of the salvage came to be divided.

"If the paper said that they were unique, Mr. Barclay, then they may be worth anything that you like to name. You wouldn't believe the sums that the rich collectors give. A thousand pounds is nothing to them. We'll have something to show for our voyage, or I am mistaken."

"I don't think that," said I. "As far as I can see they are not very different from any other South American curios."

"Well, sir, I've traded there for fourteen voyages, and I have never seen anything like that chest before. That's worth a pile of money, just as it stands. But it's so heavy, that surely there must be something valuable inside it. Don't you think we ought to open it and see?"

"If you break it open you will spoil it, as likely as not," said the second mate.

Armstrong squatted down in front of it, with his head on one side, and his long, thin nose within a few inches of the lock.

"The wood is oak," said he, "and it has shrunk a little with age. If I had a chisel or a strong-bladed knife I could force the lock back without doing any damage at all."

The mention of a strong-bladed knife made me think of the dead seaman upon the brig.

"I wonder if he could have been on the job when some one came to interfere with him," said I.

"I don't know about that, sir, but I am perfectly certain that I could open the box. There's a screwdriver here in the locker. Just hold the lamp, Allardyce, and I'll have it done in a brace of shakes."

"Wait a bit," said I, for already, with eyes which gleamed with curiosity and with avarice, he was stooping over the lid. "I don't see that there is any hurry over this matter. You've read that card which warns us not to open it. It may mean anything or it may mean nothing, but somehow I feel inclined to obey it. After all, whatever is in it will keep, and if it is valuable it will be worth as much if it is opened in the owner's offices as in the cabin of the *Mary Sinclair*."

The first officer seemed bitterly disappointed at my decision.

"Surely, sir, you are not superstitious about it," said he, with a slight sneer upon his thin lips. "If it gets out of our own hands, and we don't see for ourselves what is inside it, we may be done out of our rights; besides——"

"That's enough, Mr. Armstrong," said I, abruptly. "You may have every confidence that you will get your rights, but I will not have that box opened to-night."

"Why, the label itself shows that the box has been examined by Europeans," Allardyce added. "Because a box is a treasure-box is no reason that it has treasures inside it now. A good many folk have had a peep into it since the days of the old Governor of Terra Firma."

Armstrong threw the screwdriver down upon the table and shrugged his shoulders.

"Just as you like," said he; but for the rest of the evening, although we spoke upon many subjects, I noticed that his eyes were continually coming round, with the same expression of curiosity and greed, to the old striped box.

And now I come to that portion of my story which fills me even now with a shuddering horror when I think of it. The main cabin had the rooms of the officers round it, but mine was the farthest away from it at the end of the little passage which led to the companion. No regular watch was kept by me, except in cases of emergency, and the three mates divided the watches among them. Armstrong had the middle watch, which ends at four in the morning, and he was relieved by Allardyce. For my part I have always been one of the soundest of sleepers, and it is rare for anything less than a hand upon my shoulder to arouse me.

And yet I was aroused that night, or rather in the early grey of the morning. It was just half-past four by my chronometer when something caused me to sit up in my berth wide awake and with every nerve tingling. It was a sound of some sort, a crash with a human cry at the end of it, which still jarred upon my ears. I sat listening, but all was now silent. And yet it could not have been imagination, that hideous cry, for the echo of it still rang in my head, and it seemed to have come from some place quite close to me. I sprang from my bunk, and, pulling on some clothes, I made my way into the cabin.

At first I saw nothing unusual there. In the cold, grey light I made out the red-clothed table, the six rotating chairs, the walnut lockers, the swinging barometer, and there, at the end, the big striped chest. I was turning away with the intention of going upon deck and asking the second mate if he had heard anything, when my eyes fell suddenly upon something which projected from under the table. It was the leg of a man—a leg with a long sea-boot upon it. I stooped, and there was a figure sprawling upon his face, his arms thrown forward and his body twisted. One glance told me that it was Armstrong, the first officer, and a second that he was a dead man. For a few moments I stood gasping. Then I rushed on to the deck, called Allardyce to my assistance, and came back with him into the cabin.

Together we pulled the unfortunate fellow from under the table, and as we looked at his dripping head, we exchanged glances, and I do not know which was the paler of the two.

"The same as the Spanish sailor," said I.

"The very same. God preserve us! It's that infernal chest! Look at Armstrong's hand!"

He held up the mate's right hand, and there was the screwdriver which he had wished to use the night before.

"He's been at the chest, sir. He knew that I was on deck and you asleep. He knelt down in front of it, and he pushed the lock back with that tool. Then something happened to him, and he cried out so that you heard him."

"Allardyce," I whispered, "what *could* have happened to him?"

The second mate put his hand upon my sleeve and drew me into his cabin.

"We can talk here, sir, and we don't know who may be listening to us in there. What do you suppose is in that box, Captain Barclay?"

"I give you my word, Allardyce, that I have no idea."

"Well, I can only find one theory which will fit all the facts. Look at the size of the box. Look at all the carving and metal-work which may conceal any number of holes. Look at the weight of it; it took four men to carry it. On the top of that, remember that two men have tried to open it, and both have come to their end through it. Now, sir, what can it mean except one thing?"

"You mean there is a man in it?"

"Of course there is a man in it. You know how it is in these South American States, sir. A man may be President one week and hunted like a dog the next. They are for ever flying for their lives. My idea is that there is some fellow in hiding there, who is armed and desperate, and who will fight to the death before he is taken."

"But his food and drink?"

"It's a roomy chest, sir, and he may have some provisions stowed away. As to his drink, he had a friend among the crew upon the brig who saw that he had what he needed."

"You think, then, that the label asking people not to open the box was simply written in his interest?"

"Yes, sir, that is my idea. Have you any other way of explaining the facts?"

I had to confess that I had not.

"The question is what are we to do?" I asked.

"The man's a dangerous ruffian who sticks at nothing. I'm thinking it wouldn't be a bad thing to put a rope round the chest and tow it alongside for half an hour; then we could open it at our ease. Or if we just tied the box up and kept him from getting any water maybe that would do as well. Or the carpenter could put a coat of varnish over it and stop all the blowholes."

"Come, Allardyce," said I, angrily. "You don't seriously mean to say that a whole ship's company are going to be terrorised by a single man in a box. If he's there I'll engage to fetch him out!" I went to my room and came back with my revolver in my hand. "Now, Allardyce," said I. "Do you open the lock, and I'll stand on guard."

"For God's sake, think what you are doing, sir," cried the mate. "Two men have lost their lives over it, and the blood of one not yet dry upon the carpet."

"The more reason why we should revenge him."

"Well, sir, at least let me call the carpenter. Three are better than two, and he is a good stout man."

He went off in search of him, and I was left alone with the striped chest in the cabin. I don't think that I'm a nervous man, but I kept the table between me and this solid old relic of the Spanish Main. In the growing light of morning the red and white striping was beginning to appear, and the curious scrolls and wreaths of metal and carving which showed the loving pains which cunning craftsmen had expended upon it. Presently the carpenter and the mate came back together, the former with a hammer in his hand.

"It's a bad business, this, sir," said he, shaking his head, as he looked at the body of the mate. "And you think there's someone hiding in the box?"

"There's no doubt about it," said Allardyce, picking up the screwdriver and setting his jaw like a man who needs to brace his courage. "I'll drive the lock back if you will both stand by. If he rises let him have it on the head with your hammer, carpenter! Shoot at once, sir, if he raises his hand. Now!"

He had knelt down in front of the striped chest, and passed the blade of the tool under the lid. With a sharp snick the lock flew back. "Stand by!" yelled the mate, and with a heave he threw open the massive top of the box. As it swung up, we all three sprang back, I with my pistol levelled, and the carpenter with the hammer above his head. Then, as nothing happened, we each took a step forward and peeped in. The box was empty.

Not quite empty either, for in one corner was lying an old yellow candlestick, elaborately engraved, which appeared to be as old as the box itself. Its rich yellow tone and artistic shape suggested that it was an object of value. For the rest there was nothing more weighty or valuable than dust in the old striped treasure-chest.

"Well, I'm blessed!" cried Allardyce, staring blankly into it. "Where does the weight come in, then?"

"Look at the thickness of the sides and look at the lid. Why, it's five inches through. And see that great metal spring across it."

"That's for holding the lid up," said the mate. "You see, it won't lean back. What's that German printing on the inside?"

"It means that it was made by Johann Rothstein of Augsburg, in 1606."

"And a solid bit of work, too. But it doesn't throw much light on what has passed, does it, Captain Barclay? That candlestick looks like gold. We shall have something for our trouble after all."

He leant forward to grasp it, and from that moment I have never doubted as to the reality of inspiration, for on the instant I caught him by the collar and pulled him straight again. It may have been some story of the Middle Ages which had come back to my mind, or it may have been that my eye had caught some red which was not that of rust upon the upper part of the lock, but to him and to me it will always seem an inspiration, so prompt and sudden was my action.

"There's devilry here," said I. "Give me the crooked stick from the corner."

It was an ordinary walking-cane with a hooked top. I passed it over the candlestick and gave it a pull. With a flash a row of polished steel fangs shot out from below the upper lip, and the great striped chest snapped at us like a wild animal. Clang came the huge lid into its place, and the glasses on the swinging rack sang and tinkled with the shock. The mate sat down on the edge of the table, and shivered like a frightened horse.

"You've saved my life, Captain Barclay!" said he.

So this was the secret of the striped treasure-chest of old Don Ramirez di Leyra, and this was how he preserved his ill-gotten gains from the Terra Firma and the Province of Veraquas. Be the thief ever so cunning he could not tell that golden candlestick from the other articles of value, and the instant that he laid hand upon it the terrible spring was unloosed and the murderous steel spikes were driven into his brain, while the shock of the blow sent the victim backwards and enabled the chest to automatically close itself. How many, I wondered, had fallen victims to the ingenuity of the Mechanic of Augsburg. And as I thought of the possible history of that grim striped chest my resolution was very quickly taken.

"Carpenter, bring three men and carry this on deck."

"Going to throw it overboard, sir?"

"Yes, Mr. Allardyce. I'm not superstitious as a rule, but there are some things which are more than a sailor can be called upon to stand."

"No wonder that brig made heavy weather, Captain Barclay, with such a thing on board. The glass is dropping fast, sir, and we are only just in time."

So we did not even wait for the three sailors, but we carried it out, the mate, the carpenter, and I, and we pushed it with our own hands over the bulwarks. There was a white spout of water, and it was gone. There it lies, the striped chest, a thousand fathoms deep, and if, as they say, the sea will some day be dry land, I grieve for the man who finds that old box and tries to penetrate into its secret.

2

# THE CAPTAIN OF THE "POLESTAR"

## (BEING AN EXTRACT FROM THE SINGULAR JOURNAL OF JOHN M'ALISTER RAY, STUDENT OF MEDICINE.)

*September 11th.*—Lat. 81° 40′ N.; long. 2° E. Still lying-to amid enormous ice fields. The one which stretches away to the north of us, and to which our ice-anchor is attached, cannot be smaller than an English county. To the right and left unbroken sheets extend to the horizon. This morning the mate reported that there were signs of pack ice to the southward. Should this form of sufficient thickness to bar our return, we shall be in a position of danger, as the food, I hear, is already running somewhat short. It is late in the season, and the nights are beginning to reappear. This morning I saw a star twinkling just over the fore-yard, the first since the beginning of May. There is considerable discontent among the crew, many of whom are anxious to get back home to be in time for the herring season, when labour always commands a high price upon the Scotch coast. As yet their displeasure is only signified by sullen countenances and black looks, but I heard from the second mate this afternoon that they contemplated sending a deputation to the Captain to explain their grievance. I much doubt how he will receive it, as he is a man of fierce temper, and very sensitive about anything approaching to an infringement of his rights. I shall venture after dinner to say a few words to him upon the subject. I have always found that he will tolerate from me what he would resent from any other member of the crew. Amsterdam Island, at the north-west corner of Spitzbergen, is visible upon our starboard quarter—a rugged line of volcanic rocks, intersected by white seams, which represent glaciers. It is curious to think that at the present moment there is probably no human being nearer to us than the Danish settlements in the south of Greenland—a good nine hundred miles as the crow flies. A captain takes a great responsibility upon himself when he risks his vessel under such circumstances. No whaler has ever remained in these latitudes till so advanced a period of the year.

9 P.M.—I have spoken to Captain Craigie, and though the result has been hardly satisfactory, I am bound to say that he listened to what I had to say very quietly and even deferentially. When I had finished he put on that air of iron determination which I have frequently observed upon his face, and paced rapidly backwards and forwards across the narrow cabin for some minutes. At first I feared that I had seriously offended him, but he dispelled the idea by sitting down again, and putting his hand upon my arm with a gesture

which almost amounted to a caress. There was a depth of tenderness too in his wild dark eyes which surprised me considerably. "Look here, Doctor," he said, "I'm sorry I ever took you—I am indeed—and I would give fifty pounds this minute to see you standing safe upon the Dundee quay. It's hit or miss with me this time. There are fish to the north of us. How dare you shake your head, sir, when I tell you I saw them blowing from the mast-head?"—this in a sudden burst of fury, though I was not conscious of having shown any signs of doubt. "Two-and-twenty fish in as many minutes as I am a living man, and not one under ten foot. Now, doctor, do you think I can leave the country when there is only one infernal strip of ice between me and my fortune? If it came on to blow from the north to-morrow we could fill the ship and be away before the frost could catch us. If it came on to blow from the south —well, I suppose the men are paid for risking their lives, and as for myself it matters but little to me, for I have more to bind me to the other world than to this one. I confess that I am sorry for *you*, though. I wish I had old Angus Tait who was with me last voyage, for he was a man that would never be missed, and you—you said once that you were engaged, did you not?"

"Yes," I answered, snapping the spring of the locket which hung from my watch-chain, and holding up the little vignette of Flora.

"Curse you!" he yelled, springing out of his seat, with his very beard bristling with passion. "What is your happiness to me? What have I to do with her that you must dangle her photograph before my eyes?" I almost thought that he was about to strike me in the frenzy of his rage, but with another imprecation he dashed open the door of the cabin and rushed out upon deck, leaving me considerably astonished at his extraordinary violence. It is the first time that he has ever shown me anything but courtesy and kindness. I can hear him pacing excitedly up and down overhead as I write these lines.

I should like to give a sketch of the character of this man, but it seems presumptuous to attempt such a thing upon paper, when the idea in my own mind is at best a vague and uncertain one. Several times I have thought that I grasped the clue which might explain it, but only to be disappointed by his presenting himself in some new light which would upset all my conclusions. It may be that no human eye but my own shall ever rest upon these lines, yet as a psychological study I shall attempt to leave some record of Captain Nicholas Craigie.

A man's outer case generally gives some indication of the soul within. The Captain is tall and well-formed, with dark, handsome face, and a curious way of twitching his limbs, which may arise from nervousness, or be simply an outcome of his excessive energy. His jaw and whole cast of countenance is manly and resolute, but the eyes are the distinctive feature of his face. They are of the very darkest hazel, bright and eager, with a singular mixture of recklessness in their expression, and of something else which I have sometimes thought was more allied with horror than any other emotion. Generally the former predominated, but on occasions, and more particularly when he was thoughtfully inclined, the look of fear would spread and deepen until it imparted a new character to his whole countenance. It is at these times that he is most subject to tempestuous fits of anger, and he seems to be aware of it, for I have known him lock himself up so that no one might approach him until his dark hour was passed. He sleeps badly, and I have heard him shouting during the night, but his cabin is some little distance from mine, and I could never distinguish the words which he said.

This is one phase of his character, and the most disagreeable one. It is only through my close association with him, thrown together as we are day after day, that I have observed it. Otherwise he is an agreeable companion, well-read and entertaining, and as gallant a seaman as ever trod a deck. I shall not easily forget the way in which he handled the ship when we were caught by a gale among the loose ice at the beginning of April. I have never seen him so cheerful, and even hilarious, as he was that night, as he paced backwards and forwards upon the bridge amid the flashing of the lightning and the howling of the wind. He has told me several times that the thought of death was a pleasant one to him, which is a sad thing for a young man to say; he cannot be much more than thirty, though his hair and moustache are already slightly grizzled. Some great sorrow must have overtaken him and blighted his whole life. Perhaps I should be the same if I lost my Flora—God knows! I think if it were not for her that I should care very little whether the wind blew from the north or the south to-morrow. There, I hear him come down the companion, and he has locked himself up in his room, which shows that he is still in an unamiable mood. And so to bed, as old Pepys would say, for the candle is burning down (we have to use them now since the nights are closing in), and the steward has turned in, so there are no hopes of another one.

*September 12th.*—Calm, clear day, and still lying in the same position. What wind there is comes from the south-east, but it is very slight. Captain is in a better humour, and apologised to me at breakfast for his rudeness. He still looks somewhat distrait, however, and retains that wild look in his eyes which in a Highlander would mean that he was "fey"—at least so our chief engineer remarked to me, and he has some reputation among the Celtic portion of our crew as a seer and expounder of omens.

It is strange that superstition should have obtained such mastery over this hard-headed and practical race. I could not have believed to what an extent it is carried had I not observed it for myself. We have had a perfect epidemic of it this voyage, until I have felt inclined to serve out rations of sedatives and nerve-tonics with the Saturday allowance of grog. The first symptom of it was that shortly after leaving Shetland the men at the wheel used to complain that they heard plaintive cries and screams in the wake of the ship, as if something were following it and were unable to overtake it. This fiction has been kept up during the whole voyage, and on dark nights at the beginning of the seal-fishing it was only with great difficulty that men could be induced to do their spell. No doubt what they heard was either the creaking of the rudder-chains, or the cry of some passing sea-bird. I have been fetched out of bed several times to listen to it, but I need hardly say that I was never able to distinguish anything unnatural. The men, however, are so absurdly positive upon the subject that it is hopeless to argue with them. I mentioned the matter to the Captain once, but to my surprise he took it very gravely, and indeed appeared to be considerably disturbed by what I told him. I should have thought that he at least would have been above such vulgar delusions.

All this disquisition upon superstition leads me up to the fact that Mr. Manson, our second mate, saw a ghost last night—or, at least, says that he did, which of course is the same thing. It is quite refreshing to have some new topic of conversation after the eternal routine of bears and whales which has served us for so many months. Manson swears the ship is haunted, and that he would not stay in her a day if he had any other place to go to. Indeed the fellow is honestly frightened, and I had to give him some chloral and bromide of potassium this morning to steady him down. He seemed quite indignant when I suggested that he had been having an extra glass the night before, and I was obliged to pacify him by keeping as grave a countenance as possible during his story, which he certainly narrated in a very straightforward and matter-of-fact way.

"I was on the bridge," he said, "about four bells in the middle watch, just when the night was at its darkest. There was a bit of a moon, but the clouds were blowing across it so that you couldn't see far from the ship. John M'Leod, the harpooner, came aft from the fo'c'sle-head and reported a strange noise on the starboard bow. I went forrard and we both heard it, sometimes like a bairn crying and sometimes like a wench in pain. I've been seventeen years to the country and I never heard seal, old or young, make a sound like that. As we were standing there on the fo'c'sle-head the moon came out from behind a cloud, and we both saw a sort of white figure moving across the ice field in the same direction that we had heard the cries. We lost sight of it for a while, but it came back on the port bow, and we could just make it out like a shadow on the ice. I sent a hand aft for the rifles, and M'Leod and I went down on to the pack, thinking that maybe it might be a bear. When we got on the ice I lost sight of M'Leod, but I pushed on in the direction where I could still hear the cries. I followed them for a mile or maybe more, and then running round a hummock I came right on to the top of it standing and waiting for me seemingly. I don't know what it was. It wasn't a bear, anyway. It was tall and white and straight, and if it wasn't a man nor a woman, I'll stake my davy it was something worse. I made for the ship as hard as I could run, and precious glad I was to find myself aboard. I signed articles to do my duty by the ship, and on the ship I'll stay, but you don't catch me on the ice again after sundown."

That is his story, given as far as I can in his own words. I fancy what he saw must, in spite of his denial, have been a young bear erect upon its hind legs, an attitude which they often assume when alarmed. In the uncertain light this would bear a resemblance to a human figure, especially to a man whose nerves were already somewhat shaken. Whatever it may have been, the occurrence is unfortunate, for it has produced a most unpleasant effect upon the crew. Their looks are more sullen than before, and their discontent more open. The double grievance of being debarred from the herring fishing and of being detained in what they choose to call a haunted vessel, may lead them to do something rash. Even the harpooners, who are the oldest and steadiest among them, are joining in the general agitation.

Apart from this absurd outbreak of superstition, things are looking rather more cheerful. The pack which was forming to the south of us has partly cleared away, and the water is so warm as to lead me to believe that we are lying in one of those branches of the gulf-stream which run up between Greenland and Spitzbergen. There are numerous small Medusæ and sealemons about the ship, with abundance of shrimps, so that there is every possibility of "fish" being sighted. Indeed one was seen blowing about dinner-time, but in such a position that it was impossible for the boats to follow it.

*September 13th.*—Had an interesting conversation with the chief mate, Mr. Milne, upon the bridge. It seems that our captain is as great an enigma to the seamen, and even to the owners of the vessel, as he has been to me. Mr. Milne tells me that when the ship is paid off, upon returning from a voyage, Captain Craigie disappears, and is not seen again until the approach of another season, when he walks quietly into the office of the company, and asks whether his services will be required. He has no friend in Dundee, nor does any one pretend to be acquainted with his early history. His position depends entirely upon his skill as a seaman, and the name for courage and coolness which he had earned in the capacity of mate, before being entrusted with a separate command. The unanimous opinion seems to be that he is not a Scotchman, and that his name is an assumed one. Mr. Milne thinks that he has devoted himself to whaling simply for the reason that it is the most dangerous occupation which he could select, and that he courts death in every possible manner. He mentioned several instances of this, one of which is rather curious, if true. It seems that on one occasion he did not put in an appearance at the office, and a substitute had to be selected in his place. That was at the time of the last Russian and Turkish War. When he turned up again next spring he had a puckered wound in the side of his neck which he used to endeavor to conceal with his cravat. Whether the mate's inference that he had been engaged in the war is true or not I cannot say. It was certainly a strange coincidence.

The wind is veering round in an easterly direction, but is still very slight. I think the ice is lying closer than it did yesterday. As far as the eye can reach on every side there is one wide expanse of spotless white, only broken by an occasional rift or the dark shadow of a hummock. To the south there is the narrow lane of blue water which is our sole means of escape, and which is closing up every day. The Captain is taking a heavy responsibility upon himself. I hear that the tank of potatoes has been finished, and even the biscuits are running short, but he preserves the same impassable countenance, and spends the greater part of the day at the crow's nest, sweeping the horizon with his glass. His manner is very variable, and he seems to avoid my society, but there has been no repetition of the violence which he showed the other night.

7.30 P.M.—My deliberate opinion is that we are commanded by a madman. Nothing else can account for the extraordinary vagaries of Captain Craigie. It is fortunate that I have kept this journal of our voyage, as it will serve to justify us in case we have to put him under any sort of restraint, a step which I should only consent to as a last resource. Curiously enough it was he himself who suggested lunacy and not mere eccentricity as the secret of his strange conduct. He was standing upon the bridge about an hour ago, peering as usual through his glass, while I was walking up and down the quarter-deck. The majority of the men were below at their tea, for the watches have not been regularly kept of late. Tired of walking, I leaned against the bulwarks, and admired the mellow glow cast by the sinking sun upon the great ice fields which surround us. I was suddenly aroused from the reverie into which I had fallen by a hoarse voice at my elbow, and starting round I found that the Captain had descended and was standing by my side. He was staring out over the ice with an expression in which horror, surprise, and something approaching to joy were contending for the mastery. In spite of the cold, great drops of perspiration were coursing down his forehead, and he was evidently fearfully excited. His limbs twitched like those of a man upon the verge of an epileptic fit, and the lines about his mouth were drawn and hard.

"Look!" he gasped, seizing me by the wrist, but still keeping his eyes upon the distant ice, and moving his head slowly in a horizontal direction, as if following some object which was moving across the field of vision. "Look! There, man, there! Between the hummocks! Now coming out from behind the far one! You see her—you *must* see her! There still! Flying from me, by God, flying from me—and gone!"

He uttered the last two words in a whisper of concentrated agony which shall never fade from my remembrance. Clinging to the ratlines he endeavoured to climb up upon the top of the bulwarks as if in the hope of obtaining a last glance at the departing object. His strength was not equal to the attempt, however, and he staggered back against the saloon skylights, where he leaned panting and exhausted. His face was so livid that I expected him to become unconscious, so lost no time in leading him down the companion, and stretching him upon one of the sofas in the cabin. I then poured him out some brandy, which I held to his lips, and which had a wonderful effect upon him, bringing the blood back into his white face and steadying his poor shaking limbs. He raised himself up upon his elbow, and looking round to see that we were alone, he beckoned to me to come and sit beside him.

"You saw it, didn't you?" he asked, still in the same subdued awesome tone so foreign to the nature of the man.

"No, I saw nothing."

His head sank back again upon the cushions. "No, he wouldn't without the glass," he murmured. "He couldn't. It was the glass that showed her to me, and then the eyes of love—the eyes of love. I say, Doc, don't let the steward in! He'll think I'm mad. Just bolt the door, will you!"

I rose and did what he commanded.

He lay quiet for a while, lost in thought apparently, and then raised himself up upon his elbow again, and asked for some more brandy.

"You don't think I am, do you Doc?" he asked, as I was putting the bottle back into the after-locker. "Tell me now, as man to man, do you think that I am mad?"

"I think you have something on your mind," I answered, "which is exciting you and doing you a good deal of harm."

"Right there, lad!" he cried, his eyes sparkling from the effects of the brandy. "Plenty on my mind—plenty! But I can work out the latitude and the longitude, and I can handle my sextant and manage my logarithms. You couldn't prove me mad in a court of law, could you, now?" It was curious to hear the man lying back and coolly arguing out the question of his own sanity.

"Perhaps not," I said; "but still I think you would be wise to get home as soon as you can, and settle down to a quiet life for a while."

"Get home, eh?" he muttered, with a sneer upon his face. "One word for me and two for yourself, lad. Settle down with Flora—pretty little Flora. Are bad dreams signs of madness?"

"Sometimes," I answered.

"What else? What would be the first symptoms?"

"Pains in the head, noises in the ears, flashes before the eyes, delusions——"

"Ah! what about them?" he interrupted. "What would you call a delusion?"

"Seeing a thing which is not there is a delusion."

"But she *was* there!" he groaned to himself. "She *was* there!" and rising, he unbolted the door and walked with slow and uncertain steps to his own cabin, where I have no doubt that he will remain until to-morrow morning. His system seems to have received a terrible shock, whatever it may have been that he imagined himself to have seen. The man becomes a greater mystery every day, though I fear that the solution which he has himself suggested is the correct one, and that his reason is affected. I do not think that a guilty conscience has anything to do with his behaviour. The idea is a popular one among the officers, and, I believe, the crew; but I have seen nothing to support it. He has not the air of a guilty man, but of one who has had terrible usage at the hands of fortune, and who should be regarded as a martyr rather than a criminal.

The wind is veering round to the south to-night. God help us if it blocks that narrow pass which is our only road to safety! Situated as we are on the edge of the main Arctic pack, or the "barrier" as it is called by the whalers, any wind from the north has the effect of shredding out the ice around us and allowing our escape, while a wind from the south blows up all the loose ice behind us and hems us in between two packs. God help us, I say again!

*September 14th.*—Sunday, and a day of rest. My fears have been confirmed, and the thin strip of blue water has disappeared from the southward. Nothing but the great motionless ice fields around us, with their weird hummocks and fantastic pinnacles. There is a deathly silence over their wide expanse which is horrible. No lapping of the waves now, no cries of seagulls or straining of sails, but one deep universal silence in which the murmurs of the seamen, and the creak of their boots upon the white shining deck, seem discordant and out of place. Our only visitor was an Arctic fox, a rare animal upon the pack, though common enough upon the land. He did not come near the ship, however, but after surveying us from a distance fled rapidly across the ice. This was curious conduct, as they generally know nothing of man, and being of an inquisitive nature, become so familiar that they are easily captured. Incredible as it may seem, even this little incident produced a bad effect upon the crew. "Yon puir beastie kens mair, ay, an' sees mair nor you nor me!" was the comment of one of the leading harpooners, and the others nodded their acquiescence. It is vain to attempt to argue against such puerile superstition. They have made up their minds that there is a curse upon the ship, and nothing will ever persuade them to the contrary.

The Captain remained in seclusion all day except for about half an hour in the afternoon, when he came out upon the quarter-deck. I observed that he kept his eye fixed upon the spot where the vision of yesterday had appeared, and was quite prepared for another outburst, but none such came. He did not seem to see me although I was standing close beside him. Divine service was read as usual by the chief engineer. It is a curious thing that in whaling vessels the Church of England Prayer-book is always employed, although there is never a member of that Church among either officers or crew. Our men are all Roman Catholics or Presbyterians, the former predominating. Since a ritual is used which is foreign to both, neither can complain that the other is preferred to them, and they listen with all attention and devotion, so that the system has something to recommend it.

A glorious sunset, which made the great fields of ice look like a lake of blood. I have never seen a finer and at the same time more weird effect. Wind is veering round. If it will blow twenty-four hours from the north all will yet be well.

*September 15th.*—To-day is Flora's birthday. Dear lass! it is well that she cannot see her boy, as she used to call me, shut up among the ice fields with a crazy captain and a few weeks' provisions. No doubt she scans the shipping list in the *Scotsman* every morning to see if we are reported from Shetland. I have to set an example to the men and look cheery and unconcerned; but God knows, my heart is very heavy at times.

The thermometer is at nineteen Fahrenheit to-day. There is but little wind, and what there is comes from an unfavourable quarter. Captain is in an excellent humour; I think he imagines he has seen some other omen or vision, poor fellow, during the night, for he came into my room early in the morning, and stooping down over my bunk, whispered, "It wasn't a delusion, Doc; it's all right!" After breakfast he asked me to find out how much food was left, which the second mate and I proceeded to do. It is even less than we had expected. Forward they have half a tank full of biscuits, three barrels of salt meat, and a very limited supply of coffee beans and sugar. In the after-hold and lockers there are a good many luxuries, such as tinned salmon, soups, haricot mutton, etc., but they will go a very short way among a crew of fifty men. There are two barrels of flour in the store-room, and an unlimited supply of tobacco. Altogether there is about enough to keep the men on half rations for eighteen or twenty days—certainly not more. When we reported the state of things to the Captain, he ordered all hands to be piped, and addressed them from the quarter-deck. I never saw him to better advantage. With his tall, well-knit figure, and dark animated face, he seemed a man born to command, and he discussed the situation in a cool sailor-like way which showed that while appreciating the danger he had an eye for every loophole of escape.

"My lads," he said, "no doubt you think I brought you into this fix, if it is a fix, and maybe some of you feel bitter against me on account of it. But you must remember that for many a season no ship that comes to the country has brought in as much oil-money as the old *Polestar*, and every one of you has had his share of it. You can leave your wives behind you in comfort, while other poor fellows come back to find their lasses on the parish. If you have to thank me for the one you have to thank me for the other, and we may call it quits. We've tried a bold venture before this and succeeded, so now that we've tried one and failed we've no cause to cry out about it. If the worst comes to the worst, we can make the land across the ice, and lay in a stock of seals which will keep us alive until the spring. It won't come to that, though, for you'll see the Scotch coast again before three weeks are out. At present every man must go on half rations, share and share alike, and no favour to any. Keep up your hearts and you'll pull through this as you've pulled through many a danger before." These few simple words of his had a wonderful effect upon the crew. His former unpopularity was forgotten, and the old harpooner whom I have already mentioned for his superstition, led off three cheers, which were heartily joined in by all hands.

*September 16th.*—The wind has veered round to the north during the night, and the ice shows some symptoms of opening out. The men are in good humour in spite of the short allowance upon which they have been placed. Steam is kept up in the engine-room, that there may be no delay should an opportunity for escape present itself. The Captain is in exuberant spirits, though he still retains that wild "fey" expression which I have already remarked upon. This burst of cheerfulness puzzles me more than his former gloom. I cannot understand it. I think I mentioned in an early part of this journal that one of his oddities is that he never permits any person to enter his cabin, but insists upon making his own bed, such as it is, and performing every other office for himself. To my surprise he handed me the key to-day and requested me to go down there and take the time by his chronometer while he measured the altitude of the sun at noon. It is a bare little room, containing a washing-stand and a few books, but little else in the way of luxury, except some pictures upon the walls. The majority of these are small cheap oleographs, but there was one water-coloured sketch of the head of a young lady which arrested my attention. It was evidently a portrait, and not one of those fancy types of female beauty which sailors particularly affect. No artist could have evolved from his own mind such a curious mixture of character and weakness. The languid, dreamy eyes, with their drooping lashes, and the broad, low brow, unruffled by thought or care, were in strong contrast with the clean-cut, prominent jaw, and the resolute set of the lower lip. Underneath it in one of the corners was written, "M. B., æt. 19." That any one in the short space of nineteen years of existence could develop such strength of will as was stamped upon her face seemed to me at the time to be well-nigh incredible. She must have been an extraordinary woman. Her features have thrown such a glamour over me that, though I had but a fleeting glance at them, I could, were I a draughtsman, reproduce them line for line upon this page of the journal. I wonder what part she has played in our Captain's life. He has hung her picture at the end of his berth, so that his eyes continually rest upon it. Were he a less reserved man I should make some remark upon the subject. Of the other things in his cabin there was nothing worthy of mention—uniform coats, a camp-stool, small looking-glass, tobacco-box, and numerous pipes, including an oriental hookah—which, by the by, gives some colour to Mr. Milne's story about his participation in the war, though the connection may seem rather a distant one.

11.20 P.M.—Captain just gone to bed after a long and interesting conversation on general topics. When he chooses he can be a most fascinating companion, being remarkably well-read, and having the power of expressing his opinion forcibly without appearing to be dogmatic. I hate to have my intellectual toes trod upon. He spoke about the nature of the soul, and sketched out the views of Aristotle and Plato upon the subject in a masterly manner. He seems to have a leaning for metempsychosis and the doctrines of Pythagoras. In discussing them we touched upon modern spiritualism, and I made some joking allusion to the impostures of Slade, upon which, to my surprise, he warned me most impressively against confusing the innocent with the guilty, and argued that it would be as logical to brand Christianity as an error because Judas, who professed that religion, was a villain. He shortly afterwards bade me good-night and retired to his room.

The wind is freshening up, and blows steadily from the north. The nights are as dark now as they are in England. I hope to-morrow may set us free from our frozen fetters.

*September 17th.*—The Bogie again. Thank Heaven that I have strong nerves! The superstition of these poor fellows, and the circumstantial accounts which they give, with the utmost earnestness and self-conviction, would horrify any man not accustomed to their ways. There are many versions of the matter, but the sum-total of them all is that something uncanny has been flitting round the ship all night, and that Sandie M'Donald of Peterhead and "lang" Peter Williamson of Shetland saw it, as also did Mr. Milne on the bridge—so, having three witnesses, they can make a better case of it than the second mate did. I spoke to Milne after breakfast, and told him that he should be above such nonsense, and that as an officer he ought to set the men a better example. He shook his weather-beaten head ominously, but answered with characteristic caution, "Mebbe, aye, mebbe na, Doctor," he said, "I didna ca' it a ghaist. I canna' say I preen my faith in sea-bogles an' the like, though there's a mony as claims to ha' seen a' that and waur. I'm no easy feared, but maybe your ain bluid would run a bit cauld, mun, if instead o' speerin' aboot it in daylicht ye were wi' me last night, an' seed an awfu' like shape, white an' gruesome, whiles here, whiles there, an' it greetin' an' ca'ing in the darkness like a bit lambie that hae lost its mither. Ye would na' be sae ready to put it a' doon to auld wives' clavers then, I'm thinkin'." I saw it was hopeless to reason with him, so contented myself with begging him as a personal favour to call me up the next time the spectre appeared—a request to which he acceded with many ejaculations expressive of his hopes that such an opportunity might never arise.

As I had hoped, the white desert behind us has become broken by many thin streaks of water which intersect it in all directions. Our latitude to-day was 80° 52′ N., which shows that there is a strong southerly drift upon the pack. Should the wind continue favourable it will break up as rapidly as it formed. At present we can do nothing but smoke and wait and hope for the best. I am rapidly becoming a fatalist. When dealing with such uncertain factors as wind and ice a man can be nothing else. Perhaps it was the wind and sand of the Arabian deserts which gave the minds of the original followers of Mahomet their tendency to bow to kismet.

These spectral alarms have a very bad effect upon the Captain. I feared that it might excite his sensitive mind, and endeavoured to conceal the absurd story from him, but unfortunately he overheard one of the men making an allusion to it, and insisted upon being informed about it. As I had expected, it brought out all his latent lunacy in an exaggerated form. I can hardly believe that this is the same man who discoursed philosophy last night with the most critical acumen and coolest judgment. He is pacing backwards and forwards upon the quarter-deck like a caged tiger, stopping now and again to throw out his hands with a yearning gesture, and stare impatiently out over the ice. He keeps up a continual mutter to himself, and once he called out, "But a little time, love—but a little time!" Poor fellow, it is sad to see a gallant seaman and accomplished gentleman reduced to such a pass, and to think that imagination and delusion can cow a mind to which real danger was but the salt of life. Was ever a man in such a position as I, between a demented captain and a ghost-seeing mate? I sometimes think I am the only really sane man aboard the vessel—except perhaps the second engineer, who is a kind of ruminant, and would care nothing for all the fiends in the Red Sea so long as they would leave him alone and not disarrange his tools.

The ice is still opening rapidly, and there is every probability of our being able to make a start to-morrow morning. They will think I am inventing when I tell them at home all the strange things that have befallen me.

12 P.M.—I have been a good deal startled, though I feel steadier now, thanks to a stiff glass of brandy. I am hardly myself yet, however, as this handwriting will testify. The fact is, that I have gone through a very strange experience, and am beginning to doubt whether I was justified in branding every one on board as madmen because they professed to have

seen things which did not seem reasonable to my understanding. Pshaw! I am a fool to let such a trifle unnerve me; and yet, coming as it does after all these alarms, it has an additional significance, for I cannot doubt either Mr. Manson's story or that of the mate, now that I have experienced that which I used formerly to scoff at.

After all it was nothing very alarming—a mere sound, and that was all. I cannot expect that any one reading this, if any one should read it, will sympathise with my feelings, or realise the effect which it produced upon me at the time. Supper was over, and I had gone on deck to have a quiet pipe before turning in. The night was very dark—so dark that, standing under the quarter-boat, I was unable to see the officer upon the bridge. I think I have already mentioned the extraordinary silence which prevails in these frozen seas. In other parts of the world, be they ever so barren, there is some slight vibration of the air—some faint hum, be it from the distant haunts of men, or from the leaves of the trees, of the wings of the birds, or even the faint rustle of the grass that covers the ground. One may not actively perceive the sound, and yet if it were withdrawn it would be missed. It is only here in these Arctic seas that stark, unfathomable stillness obtrudes itself upon you in all its gruesome reality. You find your tympanum straining to catch some little murmur, and dwelling eagerly upon every accidental sound within the vessel. In this state I was leaning against the bulwarks when there arose from the ice almost directly underneath me a cry, sharp and shrill, upon the silent air of the night, beginning, as it seemed to me, at a note such as prima donna never reached, and mounting from that ever higher and higher until it culminated in a long wail of agony, which might have been the last cry of a lost soul. The ghastly scream is still ringing in my ears. Grief, unutterable grief, seemed to be expressed in it, and a great longing, and yet through it all there was an occasional wild note of exultation. It shrilled out from close beside me, and yet as I glared into the darkness I could discern nothing. I waited some little time, but without hearing any repetition of the sound, so I came below, more shaken than I have ever been in my life before. As I came down the companion I met Mr. Milne coming up to relieve the watch. "Weel, Doctor," he said, "maybe that's auld wives' clavers tae? Did ye no hear it skirling? Maybe that's a supersteetion? What d'ye think o't noo?" I was obliged to apologise to the honest fellow, and acknowledge that I was as puzzled by it as he was. Perhaps to-morrow things may look different. At present I dare hardly write all that I think. Reading it again in days to come, when I have shaken off all these associations, I should despise myself for having been so weak.

*September 18th.*—Passed a restless and uneasy night, still haunted by that strange sound. The Captain does not look as if he had had much repose either, for his face is haggard and his eyes blood-shot. I have not told him of my adventure of last night, nor shall I. He is already restless and excited, standing up, sitting down, and apparently utterly unable to keep still.

A fine lead appeared in the pack this morning, as I had expected, and we were able to cast off our ice-anchor, and steam about twelve miles in a west-sou'-westerly direction. We were then brought to a halt by a great floe as massive as any which we have left behind us. It bars our progress completely, so we can do nothing but anchor again and wait until it breaks up, which it will probably do within twenty-four hours, if the wind holds. Several bladder-nosed seals were seen swimming in the water, and one was shot, an immense creature more than eleven feet long. They are fierce, pugnacious animals, and are said to be more than a match for a bear. Fortunately they are slow and clumsy in their movements, so that there is little danger in attacking them upon the ice.

The Captain evidently does not think we have seen the last of our troubles, though why he should take a gloomy view of the situation is more than I can fathom, since every one else on board considers that we have had a miraculous escape, and are sure now to reach the open sea.

"I suppose you think it's all right now, Doctor?" he said, as we sat together after dinner.

"I hope so," I answered.

"We mustn't be too sure—and yet no doubt you are right. We'll all be in the arms of our own true loves before long, lad, won't we? But we mustn't be too sure—we mustn't be too sure."

He sat silent a little, swinging his leg thoughtfully backward and forwards. "Look here," he continued; "it's a dangerous place this, even at its best—a treacherous, dangerous place. I have known men cut off very suddenly in a land like this. A slip would do it sometimes—a single slip, and down you go through a crack, and only a bubble on the green water to show where it was that you sank. It's a queer thing," he continued with a nervous laugh, "but all the years I've been in this country I never once thought of making a will—not that I have anything to leave in particular, but still when a man is exposed to danger he should have everything arranged and ready—don't you think so?"

"Certainly," I answered, wondering what on earth he was driving at.

"He feels better for knowing it's all settled," he went on. "Now if anything should ever befall me, I hope that you will look after things for me. There is very little in the cabin, but such as it is I should like it to be sold, and the money divided in the same proportion as the oil-money among the crew. The chronometer I wish you to keep yourself as some slight remembrance of our voyage. Of course all this is a mere precaution, but I thought I would take the opportunity of speaking to you about it. I suppose I might rely upon you if there were any necessity?"

"Most assuredly," I answered; "and since you are taking this step, I may as well——"

"You! you!" he interrupted. "*You're* all right. What the devil is the matter with *you*? There, I didn't mean to be peppery, but I don't like to hear a young fellow, that has hardly begun life, speculating about death. Go up on deck and get some fresh air into your lungs instead of talking nonsense in the cabin, and encouraging me to do the same."

The more I think of this conversation of ours the less do I like it. Why should the man be settling his affairs at the very time when we seem to be emerging from all danger? There must be some method in his madness. Can it be that he contemplates suicide? I remember that upon one occasion he spoke in a deeply reverent manner of the heinousness of the crime of self-destruction. I shall keep my eye upon him, however, and though I cannot obtrude upon the privacy of his cabin, I shall at least make a point of remaining on deck as long as he stays up.

Mr. Milne pooh-poohs my fears, and says it is only the "skipper's little way." He himself takes a very rosy view of the situation. According to him we shall be out of the ice by the day after to-morrow, pass Jan Meyen two days after that, and sight Shetland in little more than a week. I hope he may not be too sanguine. His opinion may be fairly balanced against the gloomy precautions of the Captain, for he is an old and experienced seaman, and weighs his words well before uttering them.

The long-impending catastrophe has come at last. I hardly know what to write about it. The Captain is gone. He may come back to us again alive, but I fear me—I fear me. It is now seven o'clock of the morning of the 19th of September. I have spent the whole night traversing the great ice-floe in front of us with a party of seamen in the hope of coming upon some trace of him, but in vain. I shall try to give some account of the circumstances which attended upon his disappearance. Should any one ever chance to read the words which I put down, I trust they will remember that I do not write from conjecture or from hearsay, but that I, a sane and educated man, am describing accurately what actually occurred before my very eyes. My inferences are my own, but I shall be answerable for the facts.

The Captain remained in excellent spirits after the conversation which I have recorded. He appeared to be nervous and impatient, however, frequently changing his position, and moving his limbs in an aimless choreic way which is characteristic of him at times. In a quarter of an hour he went upon deck seven times, only to descend after a few hurried paces. I followed him each time, for there was something about his face which confirmed my resolution of not letting him out of my sight. He seemed to observe the effect which his movements had produced, for he endeavoured by an over-done hilarity, laughing boisterously at the very smallest of jokes, to quiet my apprehensions.

After supper he went on to the poop once more, and I with him. The night was dark and very still, save for the melancholy soughing of the wind among the spars. A thick cloud was coming up from the north-west, and the ragged tentacles which it threw out in front of it were drifting across the face of the moon, which only shone now and again through a rift in the wrack. The Captain paced rapidly backwards and forwards, and then seeing me still dogging him, he came across and hinted that he thought I should be better below—which, I need hardly say, had the effect of strengthening my resolution to remain on deck.

I think he forgot about my presence after this, for he stood silently leaning over the taffrail and peering out across the great desert of snow, part of which lay in shadow, while part glittered mistily in the moonlight. Several times I could see by his movements that he was referring to his watch, and once he muttered a short sentence, of which I could only catch the one word "ready." I confess to having felt an eerie feeling creeping over me as I watched the loom of his tall figure through the darkness, and noted how completely he fulfilled the idea of a man who is keeping a tryst. A tryst with whom? Some vague perception began to dawn upon me as I pieced one fact with another, but I was utterly unprepared for the sequel.

By the sudden intensity of his attitude I felt that he saw something. I crept up behind him. He was staring with an eager questioning gaze at what seemed to be a wreath of mist, blown swiftly in a line with the ship. It was a dim nebulous body, devoid of shape, sometimes more, sometimes less apparent, as the light fell on it. The moon was dimmed in its brilliancy at the moment by a canopy of thinnest cloud, like the coating of an anemone.

"Coming, lass, coming," cried the skipper, in a voice of unfathomable tenderness and compassion, like one who soothes a beloved one by some favour long looked for, and as pleasant to bestow as to receive.

What followed happened in an instant. I had no power to interfere. He gave one spring to the top of the bulwarks, and another which took him on to the ice, almost to the feet of the pale misty figure. He held out his hands as if to clasp it, and so ran into the darkness with outstretched arms and loving words. I still stood rigid and motionless, straining my eyes after his retreating form, until his voice died away in the distance. I never thought to see him again, but at that moment the moon shone out brilliantly through a chink in the cloudy heaven, and illuminated the great field of ice. Then I saw his dark figure already a very long way off, running with prodigious speed across the frozen plain. That was the last glimpse which we caught of him—perhaps the last we ever shall. A party was organised to follow him, and I accompanied them, but the men's hearts were not in the work, and nothing was found. Another will be formed within a few hours. I can hardly believe I have not been dreaming, or suffering from some hideous nightmare, as I write these things down.

7.30 P.M.—Just returned dead beat and utterly tired out from a second unsuccessful search for the Captain. The floe is of enormous extent, for though we have traversed at least twenty miles of its surface, there has been no sign of its coming to an end. The frost has been so severe of late that the overlying snow is frozen as hard as granite, otherwise we might have had the foot-steps to guide us. The crew are anxious that we should cast off and steam round the floe and so to the southward, for the ice has opened up during the night, and the sea is visible upon the horizon. They argue that Captain Craigie is certainly dead, and that we are all risking our lives to no purpose by remaining when we have an opportunity of escape. Mr. Milne and I have had the greatest difficulty in persuading them to wait until to-morrow night, and have been compelled to promise that we will not under any circumstances delay our departure longer than that. We propose therefore to take a few hours' sleep, and then to start upon a final search.

*September 20th, evening.*—I crossed the ice this morning with a party of men exploring the southern part of the floe, while Mr. Milne went off in a northerly direction. We pushed on for ten or twelve miles without seeing a trace of any living thing except a single bird, which fluttered a great way over our heads, and which by its flight I should judge to have been a falcon. The southern extremity of the ice field tapered away into a long narrow spit which projected out into the sea. When we came to the base of this promontory, the men halted, but I begged them to continue to the extreme end of it, that we might have the satisfaction of knowing that no possible chance had been neglected.

We had hardly gone a hundred yards before M'Donald of Peterhead cried out that he saw something in front of us, and began to run. We all got a glimpse of it and ran too. At first it was only a vague darkness against the white ice, but as we raced along together it took the shape of a man, and eventually of the man of whom we were in search. He was lying face downwards upon a frozen bank. Many little crystals of ice and feathers of snow had drifted on to him as he lay, and sparkled upon his dark seaman's jacket. As we came up some wandering puff of wind caught these tiny flakes in its vortex, and they whirled up into the air, partially descended again, and then, caught once more in the current, sped rapidly away in the direction of the sea. To my eyes it seemed but a snow-drift, but many of my companions averred that it started up in the shape of a woman, stooped over the corpse and kissed it, and then hurried away across the floe. I have learned never to ridicule any man's opinion, however strange it may seem. Sure it is that Captain Nicholas Craigie had met with no painful end, for there was a bright smile upon his blue pinched features, and his hands were still outstretched as though grasping at the strange visitor which had summoned him away into the dim world that lies beyond the grave.

We buried him the same afternoon with the ship's ensign around him, and a thirty-two pound shot at his feet. I read the burial service, while the rough sailors wept like children, for there were many who owed much to his kind heart, and who showed now the affection which his strange ways had repelled during his lifetime. He went off the grating with a dull, sullen splash, and as I looked into the green water I saw him go down, down, down until he was but a little flickering patch of white hanging upon the outskirts of eternal darkness. Then even that faded away, and he was gone. There he shall lie, with his secret and his sorrows and his mystery all still buried in his breast, until that great day when the sea shall give up its dead, and Nicholas Craigie come out from among the ice with the smile upon his face, and his stiffened arms outstretched in greeting. I pray that his lot may be a happier one in that life than it has been in this.

I shall not continue my journal. Our road to home lies plain and clear before us, and the great ice field will soon be but a remembrance of the past. It will be some time before I get over the shock produced by recent events. When I began this record of our voyage I little thought of how I should be compelled to finish it. I am writing these final words in the lonely cabin, still starting at times and fancying I hear the quick nervous step of the dead man upon the deck above me. I entered his cabin to-night, as was my duty, to make a list of his effects in order that they might be entered in the official log. All was as it had been upon my previous visit, save that the picture which I have described as having hung at the end of his bed had been cut out of its frame, as with a knife, and was gone. With this last link in a strange chain of evidence I close my diary of the voyage of the *Polestar*.

Note by Dr. John M'Alister Ray, senior.—I have read over the strange events connected with the death of the Captain of the *Polestar*, as narrated in the journal of my son. That everything occurred exactly as he describes it I have the fullest confidence, and, indeed, the most positive certainty, for I know him to be a strong-nerved and unimaginative man, with the strictest regard for veracity. Still, the story is, on the face of it, so vague and so improbable, that I was long opposed to its publication. Within the last few days, however, I have had independent testimony upon the subject which throws a new light upon it. I had run down to Edinburgh to attend a meeting of the British Medical Association, when I chanced to come across Dr. P.——, an old college chum of mine, now practising at Saltash, in Devonshire. Upon my telling him of this experience of my son's, he declared to me that he was familiar with the man, and proceeded, to my no small surprise, to give me a description of him, which tallied remarkably well with that given in the journal, except that he depicted him as a younger man. According to his account, he had been engaged to a young lady of singular beauty residing upon the Cornish coast. During his absence at sea his betrothed had died under circumstances of peculiar horror.

## ❧ 3 ❧

# THE FIEND OF THE COOPERAGE

It was no easy matter to bring the *Gamecock* up to the island, for the river had swept down so much silt that the banks extended for many miles out into the Atlantic. The coast was hardly to be seen when the first white curl of the breakers warned us of our danger, and from there onwards we made our way very carefully under mainsail and jib, keeping the broken water well to the left, as is indicated on the chart. More than once her bottom touched the sand (we were drawing something under six feet at the time), but we had always way enough and luck enough to carry us through. Finally, the water shoaled, very rapidly, but they had sent a canoe from the factory, and the Krooboy pilot brought us within two hundred yards of the island. Here we dropped our anchor, for the gestures of the negro indicated that we could not hope to get any farther. The blue of the sea had changed to the brown of the river, and, even under the shelter of the island, the current was singing and swirling round our bows. The stream appeared to be in spate, for it was over the roots of the palm trees, and everywhere upon its muddy, greasy surface we could see logs of wood and debris of all sorts which had been carried down by the flood.

When I had assured myself that we swung securely at our moorings, I thought it best to begin watering at once, for the place looked as if it reeked with fever. The heavy river, the muddy, shining banks, the bright poisonous green of the jungle, the moist steam in the air, they were all so many danger signals to one who could read them. I sent the long-boat off, therefore, with two large hogsheads, which should be sufficient to last us until we made St. Paul de Loanda. For my own part I took the dinghy and rowed for the island, for I could see the Union Jack fluttering above the palms to mark the position of Armitage and Wilson's trading station.

When I had cleared the grove, I could see the place, a long, low, whitewashed building, with a deep verandah in front, and an immense pile of palm oil barrels heaped upon either flank of it. A row of surf boats and canoes lay along the beach, and a single small jetty projected into the river. Two men in white suits with red cummerbunds round their waists were waiting upon the end of it to receive me. One was a large portly fellow with a greyish beard. The other was slender and tall, with a pale pinched face, which was half concealed by a great mushroom-shaped hat.

"Very glad to see you," said the latter, cordially. "I am Walker, the agent of Armitage and Wilson. Let me introduce Dr. Severall of the same company. It is not often we see a private yacht in these parts."

"She's the *Gamecock*," I explained. "I'm owner and captain—Meldrum is the name."

"Exploring?" he asked.

"I'm a lepidopterist—a butterfly-catcher. I've been doing the west coast from Senegal downwards."

"Good sport?" asked the Doctor, turning a slow yellow-shot eye upon me.

"I have forty cases full. We came in here to water, and also to see what you have in my line."

These introductions and explanations had filled up the time whilst my two Krooboys were making the dinghy fast. Then I walked down the jetty with one of my new acquaintances upon either side, each plying me with questions, for they had seen no white man for months.

"What do we do?" said the Doctor, when I had begun asking questions in my turn. "Our business keeps us pretty busy, and in our leisure time we talk politics."

"Yes, by the special mercy of Providence Severall is a rank Radical, and I am a good stiff Unionist, and we talk Home Rule for two solid hours every evening."

"And drink quinine cocktails," said the Doctor. "We're both pretty well salted now, but our normal temperature was about 103 last year. I shouldn't, as an impartial adviser, recommend you to stay here very long unless you are collecting bacilli as well as butterflies. The mouth of the Ogowai River will never develop into a health resort."

There is nothing finer than the way in which these outlying pickets of civilisation distil a grim humour out of their desolate situation, and turn not only a bold, but a laughing face upon the chances which their lives may bring. Everywhere from Sierra Leone downwards I had found the same reeking swamps, the same isolated fever-racked communities and the same bad jokes. There is something approaching to the divine in that power of man to rise above his conditions and to use his mind for the purpose of mocking at the miseries of his body.

"Dinner will be ready in about half an hour, Captain Meldrum," said the Doctor. "Walker has gone in to see about it; he's the housekeeper this week. Meanwhile, if you like, we'll stroll round and I'll show you the sights of the island."

The sun had already sunk beneath the line of palm trees, and the great arch of the heaven above our head was like the inside of a huge shell, shimmering with dainty pinks and delicate iridescence. No one who has not lived in a land where the weight and heat of a napkin become intolerable upon the knees can imagine the blessed relief which the coolness of evening brings along with it. In this sweeter and purer air the Doctor and I walked round the little island, he pointing out the stores, and explaining the routine of his work.

"There's a certain romance about the place," said he, in answer to some remark of mine about the dullness of their lives. "We are living here just upon the edge of the great unknown. Up there," he continued, pointing to the north-east, "Du Chaillu penetrated, and found the home of the gorilla. That is the Gaboon country—the land of the great apes. In this direction," pointing to the south-east, "no one has been very far. The land which is drained by this river is practically unknown to Europeans. Every log which is carried past us by the current has come from an undiscovered country. I've often wished that I was a better botanist when I have seen the singular orchids and curious-looking plants which have been cast up on the eastern end of the island."

The place which the Doctor indicated was a sloping brown beach, freely littered with the flotsam of the stream. At each end was a curved point, like a little natural breakwater, so that a small shallow bay was left between. This was full of floating vegetation, with a single huge splintered tree lying stranded in the middle of it, the current rippling against its high black side.

"These are all from up country," said the Doctor. "They get caught in our little bay, and then when some extra freshet comes they are washed out again and carried out to sea."

"What is the tree?" I asked.

"Oh, some kind of teak, I should imagine, but pretty rotten by the look of it. We get all sorts of big hardwood trees floating past here, to say nothing of the palms. Just come in here, will you?"

He led the way into a long building with an immense quantity of barrel staves and iron hoops littered about in it.

"This is our cooperage," said he. "We have the staves sent out in bundles, and we put them together ourselves. Now, you don't see anything particularly sinister about this building, do you?"

I looked round at the high corrugated iron roof, the white wooden walls, and the earthen floor. In one corner lay a mattress and a blanket.

"I see nothing very alarming," said I.

"And yet there's something out of the common, too," he remarked. "You see that bed? Well, I intend to sleep there to-night. I don't want to buck, but I think it's a bit of a test for nerve."

"Why?"

"Oh, there have been some funny goings on. You were talking about the monotony of our lives, but I assure you that they are sometimes quite as exciting as we wish them to be. You'd better come back to the house now, for after sundown we begin to get the fever-fog up from the marshes. There, you can see it coming across the river."

I looked and saw long tentacles of white vapour writhing out from among the thick green underwood and crawling at us over the broad swirling surface of the brown river. At the same time the air turned suddenly dank and cold.

"There's the dinner gong," said the Doctor. "If this matter interests you I'll tell you about it afterwards."

It did interest me very much, for there was something earnest and subdued in his manner as he stood in the empty cooperage, which appealed very forcibly to my imagination. He was a big, bluff, hearty man, this Doctor, and yet I had detected a curious expression in his eyes as he glanced about him—an expression which I would not describe as one of fear, but rather of a man who is alert and on his guard.

"By the way," said I, as we returned to the house, "you have shown me the huts of a good many of your native assistants, but I have not seen any of the natives themselves."

"They sleep in the hulk over yonder," the Doctor answered, pointing over to one of the banks.

"Indeed. I should not have thought in that case that they would need the huts."

"Oh, they used the huts until quite recently. We've put them on the hulk until they recover their confidence a little. They were all half mad with fright, so we let them go, and nobody sleeps on the island except Walker and myself."

"What frightened them?" I asked.

"Well, that brings us back to the same story. I suppose Walker has no objection to your hearing all about it. I don't know why we should make any secret about it, though it is certainly a pretty bad business."

He made no further allusion to it during the excellent dinner which had been prepared in my honour. It appeared that no sooner had the little white topsail of the *Gamecock* shown round Cape Lopez than these kind fellows had begun to prepare their famous pepper-pot—which is the pungent stew peculiar to the West Coast—and to boil their yams and sweet potatoes. We sat down to as good a native dinner as one could wish, served by a smart Sierra Leone waiting boy. I was just remarking to myself that he at least had not shared in the general fright when, having laid the dessert and wine upon the table, he raised his hand to his turban.

"Anyting else I do, Massa Walker?" he asked.

"No, I think that is all right, Moussa," my host answered. "I am not feeling very well to-night, though, and I should much prefer if you would stay on the island."

I saw a struggle between his fears and his duty upon the swarthy face of the African. His skin had turned of that livid purplish tint which stands for pallor in a negro, and his eyes looked furtively about him.

"No, no, Massa Walker," he cried, at last, "you better come to the hulk with me, sah. Look after you much better in the hulk, sah!"

"That won't do, Moussa. White men don't run away from the posts where they are placed."

Again I saw the passionate struggle in the negro's face, and again his fears prevailed.

"No use, Massa Walker, sah!" he cried. "S'elp me, I can't do it. If it was yesterday or if it was to-morrow, but this is the third night, sah, an' it's more than I can face."

Walker shrugged his shoulders.

"Off with you then!" said he. "When the mail-boat comes you can get back to Sierra Leone, for I'll have no servant who deserts me when I need him most. I suppose this is all mystery to you, or has the Doctor told you, Captain Meldrum?"

"I showed Captain Meldrum the cooperage, but I did not tell him anything," said Dr. Severall. "You're looking bad, Walker," he added, glancing at his companion. "You have a strong touch coming on you."

"Yes, I've had the shivers all day, and now my head is like a cannon-ball. I took ten grains of quinine, and my ears are singing like a kettle. But I want to sleep with you in the cooperage to-night."

"No, no, my dear chap. I won't hear of such a thing. You must get to bed at once, and I am sure Meldrum will excuse you. I shall sleep in the cooperage, and I promise you that I'll be round with your medicine before breakfast."

It was evident that Walker had been struck by one of those sudden and violent attacks of remittent fever which are the curse of the West Coast. His sallow cheeks were flushed and his eyes shining with fever, and suddenly as he sat there he began to croon out a song in the high-pitched voice of delirium.

"Come, come, we must get you to bed, old chap," said the Doctor, and with my aid he led his friend into his bedroom. There we undressed him and presently, after taking a strong sedative, he settled down into a deep slumber.

"He's right for the night," said the Doctor, as we sat down and filled our glasses once more. "Sometimes it is my turn and sometimes his, but, fortunately, we have never been down together. I should have been sorry to be out of it to-night, for I have a little mystery to unravel. I told you that I intended to sleep in the cooperage."

"Yes, you said so."

"When I said sleep I meant watch, for there will be no sleep for me. We've had such a scare here that no native will stay after sundown, and I mean to find out to-night what the cause of it all may be. It has always been the custom for a native watchman to sleep in the cooperage, to prevent the barrel hoops being stolen. Well, six days ago the fellow who slept there disappeared, and we have never seen a trace of him since. It was certainly singular, for no canoe had been taken, and these waters are too full of crocodiles for any man to swim to shore. What became of the fellow, or how he could have left the island is a complete mystery. Walker and I were merely surprised, but the blacks were badly scared and queer Voodoo tales began to get about amongst them. But the real stampede broke out three nights ago, when the new watchman in the cooperage also disappeared."

"What became of him?" I asked.

"Well, we not only don't know, but we can't even give a guess which would fit the facts. The niggers swear there is a fiend in the cooperage who claims a man every third night. They wouldn't stay in the island—nothing could persuade them. Even Moussa, who is a faithful boy enough, would, as you have seen, leave his master in a fever rather than remain for the night. If we are to continue to run this place we must reassure our niggers, and I don't know any better way of doing it than by putting in a night there myself. This is the third night, you see, so I suppose the thing is due, whatever it may be."

"Have you no clue?" I asked. "Was there no mark of violence, no blood-stain, no foot-prints, nothing to give you a hint as to what kind of danger you may have to meet?"

"Absolutely nothing. The man was gone and that was all. Last time it was old Ali, who has been wharf-tender here since the place was started. He was always as steady as a rock, and nothing but foul play would take him from his work."

"Well," said I, "I really don't think that this is a one-man job. Your friend is full of laudanum, and come what might he can be of no assistance to you. You must let me stay and put in a night with you at the cooperage."

"Well, now, that's very good of you, Meldrum," said he heartily, shaking my hand across the table. "It's not a thing that I should have ventured to propose, for it is asking a good deal of a casual visitor, but if you really mean it——"

"Certainly I mean it. If you will excuse me a moment, I will hail the *Gamecock* and let them know that they need not expect me."

As we came back from the other end of the little jetty we were both struck by the appearance of the night. A huge blue-black pile of clouds had built itself up upon the landward side, and the wind came from it in little hot pants, which beat upon our faces like the draught from a blast furnace. Under the jetty the river was swirling and hissing, tossing little white spurts of spray over the planking.

"Confound it!" said Doctor Severall. "We are likely to have a flood on the top of all our troubles. That rise in the river means heavy rain up-country, and when it once begins you never know how far it will go. We've had the island nearly covered before now. Well, we'll just go and see that Walker is comfortable, and then if you like we'll settle down in our quarters."

The sick man was sunk in a profound slumber, and we left him with some crushed limes in a glass beside him in case he should awake with the thirst of fever upon him. Then we made our way through the unnatural gloom thrown by that menacing cloud. The river had risen so high that the little bay which I have described at the end of the island had become almost obliterated through the submerging of its flanking peninsula. The great raft of driftwood, with the huge black tree in the middle, was swaying up and down in the swollen current.

"That's one good thing a flood will do for us," said the Doctor. "It carries away all the vegetable stuff which is brought down on to the east end of the island. It came down with the freshet the other day, and here it will stay until a flood sweeps it out into the main stream. Well, here's our room, and here are some books and here is my tobacco pouch, and we must try and put in the night as best we may."

By the light of our single lantern the great lonely room looked very gaunt and dreary. Save for the piles of staves and heaps of hoops there was absolutely nothing in it, with the exception of the mattress for the Doctor, which had been laid in the corner. We made a couple of seats and a table out of the staves, and settled down together for a long vigil. Severall had brought a revolver for me and was himself armed with a double-barrelled shot-gun. We loaded our weapons and laid them cocked within reach of our hands. The little circle of light and the black shadows arching over us were so melancholy that he went off to the house, and returned with two candles. One side of the cooperage was pierced, however, by several open windows, and it was only by screening our lights behind staves that we could prevent them from being extinguished.

The Doctor, who appeared to be a man of iron nerves, had settled down to a book, but I observed that every now and then he laid it upon his knee, and took an earnest look all round him. For my part, although I tried once or twice to read, I found it impossible to concentrate my thoughts upon the book. They would always wander back to this great empty silent room, and to the sinister mystery which overshadowed it. I racked my brains for some possible theory which would explain the disappearance of these two men. There was the black fact that they were gone, and not the least tittle of evidence as to why or whither. And here we were waiting in the same place—waiting without an idea as to what we were waiting for. I was right in saying that it was not a one-man job. It was trying enough as it was, but no force upon earth would have kept me there without a comrade.

What an endless, tedious night it was! Outside we heard the lapping and gurgling of the great river, and the soughing of the rising wind. Within, save for our breathing, the turning of the Doctor's pages, and the high, shrill ping of an occasional mosquito, there was a heavy silence. Once my heart sprang into my mouth as Severall's book suddenly fell to the ground and he sprang to his feet with his eyes on one of the windows.

"Did you see anything, Meldrum?"

"No. Did you?"

"Well, I had a vague sense of movement outside that window." He caught up his gun and approached it. "No, there's nothing to be seen, and yet I could have sworn that something passed slowly across it."

"A palm leaf, perhaps," said I, for the wind was growing stronger every instant.

"Very likely," said he, and settled down to his book again, but his eyes were for ever darting little suspicious glances up at the window. I watched it also, but all was quiet outside.

And then suddenly our thoughts were turned into a new direction by the bursting of the storm. A blinding flash was followed by a clap which shook the building. Again and again came the vivid white glare with thunder at the same instant, like the flash and roar of a monstrous piece of artillery. And then down came the tropical rain, crashing and rattling on the corrugated iron roofing of the cooperage. The big hollow room boomed like a drum. From the darkness arose a strange mixture of noises, a gurgling, splashing, tinkling, bubbling, washing, dripping—every liquid sound that nature can produce from the thrashing and swishing of the rain to the deep steady boom of the river. Hour after hour the uproar grew louder and more sustained.

"My word," said Severall, "we are going to have the father of all the floods this time. Well, here's the dawn coming at last and that is a blessing. We've about exploded the third night superstition anyhow."

A grey light was stealing through the room, and there was the day upon us in an instant. The rain had eased off, but the coffee-coloured river was roaring past like a waterfall. Its power made me fear for the anchor of the *Gamecock*.

"I must get aboard," said I. "If she drags she'll never be able to beat up the river again."

"The island is as good as a breakwater," the Doctor answered. "I can give you a cup of coffee if you will come up to the house."

I was chilled and miserable, so the suggestion was a welcome one. We left the ill-omened cooperage with its mystery still unsolved, and we splashed our way up to the house.

"There's the spirit lamp," said Severall. "If you would just put a light to it, I will see how Walker feels this morning."

He left me, but was back in an instant with a dreadful face.

"He's gone!" he cried hoarsely.

The words sent a thrill of horror through me. I stood with the lamp in my hand, glaring at him.

"Yes, he's gone!" he repeated. "Come and look!"

I followed him without a word, and the first thing that I saw as I entered the bedroom was Walker himself lying huddled on his bed in the grey flannel sleeping suit in which I had helped to dress him on the night before.

"Not dead, surely!" I gasped.

The Doctor was terribly agitated. His hands were shaking like leaves in the wind.

"He's been dead some hours."

"Was it fever?"

"Fever! Look at his foot!"

I glanced down and a cry of horror burst from my lips. One foot was not merely dislocated, but was turned completely round in a most grotesque contortion.

"Good God!" I cried. "What can have done this?"

Severall had laid his hand upon the dead man's chest.

"Feel here," he whispered.

I placed my hand at the same spot. There was no resistance. The body was absolutely soft and limp. It was like pressing a sawdust doll.

"The breast-bone is gone," said Severall in the same awed whisper. "He's broken to bits. Thank God that he had the laudanum. You can see by his face that he died in his sleep."

"But who can have done this?"

"I've had about as much as I can stand," said the Doctor, wiping his forehead. "I don't know that I'm a greater coward than my neighbors, but this gets beyond me. If you're going out to the *Gamecock*——"

"Come on!" said I, and off we started. If we did not run it was because each of us wished to keep up the last shadow of his self-respect before the other. It was dangerous in a light canoe on that swollen river, but we never paused to give the matter a thought. He bailing and I paddling we kept her above water, and gained the deck of the yacht. There, with two hundred yards of water between us and this cursed island we felt that we were our own men once more.

"We'll go back in an hour or so," said he. "But we need a little time to steady ourselves. I wouldn't have had the niggers see me as I was just now for a year's salary."

"I've told the steward to prepare breakfast. Then we shall go back," said I. "But in God's name, Doctor Severall, what do you make of it all?"

"It beats me—beats me clean. I've heard of Voodoo deviltry, and I've laughed at it with the others. But that poor old Walker, a decent, God-fearing, nineteenth-century, Primrose-League Englishman should go under like this without a whole bone in his body—it's given me a shake, I won't deny it. But look there, Meldrum, is that hand of yours mad or drunk, or what is it?"

Old Patterson, the oldest man of my crew, and as steady as the Pyramids, had been stationed in the bows with a boat-hook to fend off the drifting logs which came sweeping down with the current. Now he stood with crooked knees, glaring out in front of him, and one forefinger stabbing furiously at the air.

"Look at it!" he yelled. "Look at it!"

And at the same instant we saw it.

A huge black trunk was coming down the river, its broad glistening back just lapped by the water. And in front of it—about three feet in front—arching upwards like the figure-head of a ship, there hung a dreadful face, swaying slowly from side to side. It was flattened, malignant, as large as a small beer-barrel, of a faded fungoid colour, but the neck which supported it was mottled with a dull yellow and black As it flew past the *Gamecock* in the swirl of the waters I saw two immense coils roll up out of some great hollow in the tree, and the villainous head rose suddenly to the height of eight or ten feet, looking with dull, skin-covered eyes at the yacht. An instant later the tree had shot past us and was plunging with its horrible passenger towards the Atlantic.

"What was it?" I cried.

"It is our fiend of the cooperage," said Dr. Severall, and he had become in an instant the same bluff, self-confident man that he had been before. "Yes, that is the devil who has been haunting our island. It is the great python of the Gaboon."

I thought of the stories which I had heard all down the coast of the monstrous constrictors of the interior, of their periodical appetite, and of the murderous effects of their deadly squeeze. Then it all took shape in my mind. There had been a freshet the week before. It had brought down this huge hollow tree with its hideous occupant. Who knows from what far distant tropical forest it may have come! It had been stranded on the little east bay of the island. The cooperage had been the nearest house. Twice with the return of its appetite it had carried off the watchman. Last night it had doubtless come again, when Severall had thought he saw something move at the window, but our lights had driven it away. It had writhed onwards and had slain poor Walker in his sleep.

"Why did it not carry him off?" I asked.

"The thunder and lightning must have scared the brute away. There's your steward, Meldrum. The sooner we have breakfast and get back to the island the better, or some of those niggers might think that we had been frightened."

# 4
# JELLAND'S VOYAGE

"Well," said our Anglo-Jap as we all drew up our chairs round the smoking-room fire, "it's an old tale out yonder, and may have spilt over into print for all I know. I don't want to turn this club-room into a chestnut stall, but it is a long way to the Yellow Sea, and it is just as likely that none of you have ever heard of the yawl *Matilda*, and of what happened to Henry Jelland and Willy McEvoy aboard of her.

"The middle of the sixties was a stirring time out in Japan. That was just after the Simonosaki bombardment, and before the Daimio affair. There was a Tory party and there was a Liberal party among the natives, and the question that they were wrangling over was whether the throats of the foreigners should be cut or not. I tell you all, politics have been tame to me since then. If you lived in a treaty port, you were bound to wake up and take an interest in them. And to make it better, the outsider had no way of knowing how the game was going. If the opposition won it would not be a newspaper paragraph that would tell him of it, but a good old Tory in a suit of chain mail, with a sword in each hand, would drop in and let him know all about it in a single upper cut.

"Of course it makes men reckless when they are living on the edge of a volcano like that. Just at first they are very jumpy, and then there comes a time when they learn to enjoy life while they have it. I tell you there's nothing makes life so beautiful as when the shadow of death begins to fall across it. Time is too precious to be dawdled away then, and a man lives every minute of it. That was the way with us in Yokohama. There were many European places of business which had to go on running, and the men who worked them made the place lively for seven nights in the week.

"One of the heads of the European colony was Randolph Moore, the big export merchant. His offices were in Yokohama, but he spent a good deal of his time at his house up in Jeddo, which had only just been opened to the trade. In his absence he used to leave his affairs in the hands of his head clerk, Jelland, whom he knew to be a man of great energy and resolution. But energy and resolution are two-edged things, you know, and when they are used against you you don't appreciate them so much.

"It was gambling that set Jelland wrong. He was a little dark-eyed fellow with black curly hair—more than three-quarters Celt, I should imagine. Every night in the week you would see him in the same place, on the left-hand side of the croupier at Matheson's *rouge et noir* table. For a long time he won, and lived in better style than his employer. And then came a turn of luck, and he began to lose so that at the end of a single week his partner and he were stone broke, without a dollar to their names.

"This partner was a clerk in the employ of the same firm—a tall, straw-haired young Englishman called McEvoy. He was a good boy enough at the start, but he was clay in the hands of Jelland, who fashioned him into a kind of weak model of himself. They were for ever on the prowl together, but it was Jelland who led and McEvoy who followed. Lynch and I and one or two others tried to show the youngster that he could come to no good along that line, and when we were talking to him we could win him round easily enough, but five minutes of Jelland would swing him back again. It may have been animal magnetism or what you like, but the little man could pull the big one along like a sixty-foot tug in front of a full-rigged ship. Even when they had lost all their money they would still take their places at the table and look on with shining eyes when any one else was raking in the stamps.

"But one evening they could keep out of it no longer. Red had turned up sixteen times running, and it was more than Jelland could bear. He whispered to McEvoy, and then said a word to the croupier.

"'Certainly, Mr. Jelland; your cheque is as good as notes,' said he.

"Jelland scribbled a cheque and threw it on the black. The card was the king of hearts, and the croupier raked in the little bit of paper. Jelland grew angry, and McEvoy white. Another and a heavier cheque was written and thrown on the table. The card was the nine of diamonds. McEvoy leaned his head upon his hands and looked as if he would faint. 'By God!' growled Jelland, 'I won't be beat,' and he threw on a cheque that covered the other two. The card was the deuce of hearts. A few minutes later they were walking down the Bund, with the cool night-air playing upon their fevered faces.

"'Of course you know what this means,' said Jelland, lighting a cheroot; 'we'll have to transfer some of the office money to our current account. There's no occasion to make a fuss over it. Old Moore won't look over the books before Easter. If we have any luck, we can easily replace it before then.'

"'But if we have no luck?' faltered McEvoy.

"'Tut, man, we must take things as they come. You stick to me, and I'll stick to you, and we'll pull through together. You shall sign the cheques to-morrow night, and we shall see if your luck is better than mine.'

"But if anything it was worse. When the pair rose from the table on the following evening, they had spent over £5,000 of their employer's money. But the resolute Jelland was as sanguine as ever.

"'We have a good nine weeks before us before the books will be examined,' said he. 'We must play the game out, and it will all come straight.'

"McEvoy returned to his rooms that night in an agony of shame and remorse. When he was with Jelland he borrowed strength from him; but alone he recognised the full danger of his position, and the vision of his old white-capped mother in England, who had been so proud when he had received his appointment, rose up before him to fill him with loathing and madness. He was still tossing upon his sleepless couch when his Japanese servant entered the bedroom. For an instant McEvoy thought that the long-expected outbreak had come, and plunged for his revolver. Then, with his heart in his mouth, he listened to the message which the servant had brought.

"Jelland was downstairs, and wanted to see him.

"What on earth could he want at that hour of night? McEvoy dressed hurriedly and rushed downstairs. His companion, with a set smile upon his lips, which was belied by the ghastly pallor of his face, was sitting in the dim light of a solitary candle, with a slip of paper in his hands.

"'Sorry to knock you up, Willy,' said he. 'No eavesdroppers, I suppose?'

"McEvoy shook his head. He could not trust himself to speak.

"'Well, then, our little game is played out. This note was waiting for me at home. It is from Moore, and says that he will be down on Monday morning for an examination of the books. It leaves us in a tight place.'

"'Monday!' gasped McEvoy; 'to-day is Friday.'

"'Saturday, my son, and 3 A.M. We have not much time to turn round in.'

"'We are lost!' screamed McEvoy.

"'We soon will be, if you make such an infernal row,' said Jelland harshly. 'Now do what I tell you, Willy, and we'll pull through yet.'

"'I will do anything—anything.'

"'That's better. Where's your whisky? It's a beastly time of the day to have to get your back stiff, but there must be no softness with us, or we are gone. First of all, I think there is something due to our relations, don't you?'

"McEvoy stared.

"'We must stand or fall together, you know. Now I, for one, don't intend to set my foot inside a felon's dock under any circumstances. D'ye see? I'm ready to swear to that. Are you?'

"'What d'you mean?' asked McEvoy, shrinking back.

"'Why, man, we all have to die, and it's only the pressing of a trigger. I swear that I shall never be taken alive. Will you? If you don't, I leave you to your fate.'

"'All right. I'll do whatever you think best.'

"'You swear it?'

"'Yes.'

"'Well, mind, you must be as good as your word. Now we have two clear days to get off in. The yawl *Matilda* is on sale, and she has all her fixings and plenty of tinned stuff aboard. We'll buy the lot to-morrow morning, and whatever we want, and get away in her. But, first, we'll clear all that is left in the office. There are 5,000 sovereigns in the safe. After dark we'll get them aboard the yawl, and take our chance of reaching California. There's no use hesitating, my son, for we have no ghost of a look-in in any other direction. It's that or nothing.'

"'I'll do what you advise.'

"'All right; and mind you get a bright face on you to-morrow, for if Moore gets the tip and comes before Monday, then——' He tapped the side-pocket of his coat and looked across at his partner with eyes that were full of a sinister meaning.

"All went well with their plans next day. The *Matilda* was bought without difficulty; and, though she was a tiny craft for so long a voyage, had she been larger two men could not have hoped to manage her. She was stocked with water during the day, and after dark the two clerks brought down the money from the office and stowed it in the hold. Before midnight they had collected all their own possessions without exciting suspicion, and at two in the morning they left their moorings and stole quietly out from among the shipping. They were seen, of course, and were set down as keen yachtsmen who were on for a good long Sunday cruise; but there was no one who dreamed that that cruise would only end either on the American coast or at the bottom of the North Pacific Ocean. Straining and hauling, they got their mainsail up and set their foresail and jib. There was a slight breeze from the south-east, and the little craft went dipping along upon her way. Seven miles from land, however, the wind fell away and they lay becalmed, rising and falling on the long swell of a glassy sea. All Sunday they did not make a mile, and in the evening Yokohama still lay along the horizon.

"On Monday morning down came Randolph Moore from Jeddo, and made straight for the offices. He had had the tip from some one that his clerks had been spreading themselves a bit, and that had made him come down out of his usual routine; but when he reached his place and found the three juniors waiting in the street with their hands in their pockets he knew that the matter was serious.

"'What's this?' he asked. He was a man of action, and a nasty chap to deal with when he had his topmasts lowered.

"'We can't get in,' said the clerks.

"Where is Mr. Jelland?'

"'He has not come to-day.'

"'And Mr. McEvoy?'

"'He has not come either.'

"Randolph Moore looked serious. 'We must have the door down,' said he.

"They don't build houses very solid in that land of earthquakes, and in a brace of shakes they were all in the office. Of course, the thing told its own story. The safe was open, the money gone, and the clerks fled. Their employer lost no time in talk.

"'Where were they seen last?'

"'On Saturday they bought the *Matilda* and started for a cruise.'

"Saturday! The matter seemed hopeless if they had got two days' start. But there was still the shadow of a chance. He rushed to the beach and swept the ocean with his glasses.

"'My God!' he cried. 'There's the *Matilda* out yonder. I know her by the rake of her mast. I have my hand upon the villains after all!'

"But there was a hitch even then. No boat had steam up, and the eager merchant had not patience to wait. Clouds were banking up along the haunch of the hills, and there was every sign of an approaching change of weather. A police boat was ready with ten armed men in her, and Randolph Moore himself took the tiller as she shot out in pursuit of the becalmed yawl.

"Jelland and McEvoy, waiting wearily for the breeze which never came, saw the dark speck which sprang out from the shadow of the land and grew larger with every swish of the oars. As she drew nearer, they could see also that she was packed with men, and the gleam of weapons told what manner of men they were. Jelland stood leaning against the tiller, and he looked at the threatening sky, the limp sails, and the approaching boat.

"'It's a case with us, Willy,' said he. 'By the Lord, we are two most unlucky devils, for there's wind in that sky, and another hour would have brought it to us.'

"McEvoy groaned.

"'There's no good softening over it, my lad,' said Jelland. 'It's the police boat right enough, and there's old Moore driving them to row like hell. It'll be a ten-dollar job for every man of them.'

"Willy McEvoy crouched against the side with his knees on the deck. 'My mother! my poor old mother!' he sobbed.

"'She'll never hear that you have been in the dock anyway,' said Jelland. 'My people never did much for me, but I will do that much for them. It's no good, Mac. We can chuck our hands. God bless you, old man! Here's the pistol!'

"He cocked the revolver, and held the butt towards the youngster. But the other shrunk away from it with little gasps and cries. Jelland glanced at the approaching boat. It was not more than a few hundred yards away.

"'There's no time for nonsense,' said he. 'Damn it! man, what's the use of flinching? You swore it!'

"'No, no, Jelland!'

"'Well, anyhow, I swore that neither of us should be taken. Will you do it?'

"'I can't! I can't!'

"'Then I will for you.'

"The rowers in the boat saw him lean forwards, they heard two pistol shots, they saw him double himself across the tiller, and then, before the smoke had lifted, they found that they had something else to think of.

"For at that instant the storm broke—one of those short sudden squalls which are common in these seas. The *Matilda* heeled over, her sails bellied out, she plunged her lee-rail into a wave, and was off like a frightened deer. Jelland's body had jammed the helm, and she kept a course right before the wind, and fluttered away over the rising sea like a blown piece of paper. The rowers worked frantically, but the yawl still drew a head, and in five minutes it had plunged into the storm wrack never to be seen again by mortal eye. The boat put back, and reached Yokohama with the water washing half-way up to the thwarts.

"And that was how it came that the yawl *Matilda,* with a cargo of five thousand pounds and a crew of two dead young men, set sail across the Pacific Ocean. What the end of Jelland's voyage may have been no man knows. He may have foundered in that gale, or he may have been picked up by some canny merchant-man, who stuck to the bullion and kept his mouth shut, or he may still be cruising in that vast waste of waters, blown north to the Behring Sea, or south to the Malay Islands. It's better to leave it unfinished than to spoil a true story by inventing a tag to it."

⁂ 5 ⁂

# J. HABAKUK JEPHSON'S STATEMENT

In the month of December in the year 1873, the British ship *Dei Gratia* steered into Gibraltar, having in tow the derelict brigantine *Marie Celeste*, which had been picked up in latitude 38° 40′, longitude 17° 15′ W. There were several circumstances in connection with the condition and appearance of this abandoned vessel which excited considerable comment at the time, and aroused a curiosity which has never been satisfied. What these circumstances were was summed up in an able article which appeared in the *Gibraltar Gazette*. The curious can find it in the issue for January 4, 1874, unless my memory deceives me. For the benefit of those, however, who may be unable to refer to the paper in question, I shall subjoin a few extracts which touch upon the leading features of the case.

"We have ourselves," says the anonymous writer in the *Gazette*, "been over the derelict *Marie Celeste*, and have closely questioned the officers of the *Dei Gratia* on every point which might throw light on the affair. They are of opinion that she had been abandoned several days, or perhaps weeks, before being picked up. The official log, which was found in the cabin, states that the vessel sailed from Boston to Lisbon, starting upon October 16. It is, however, most imperfectly kept, and affords little information. There is no reference to rough weather, and, indeed, the state of the vessel's paint and rigging excludes the idea that she was abandoned for any such reason. She is perfectly watertight. No signs of a struggle or of violence are to be detected, and there is absolutely nothing to account for the disappearance of the crew. There are several indications that a lady was present on board, a sewing-machine being found in the cabin and some articles of female attire. These probably belonged to the captain's wife, who is mentioned in the log as having accompanied her husband. As an instance of the mildness of the weather, it may be remarked that a bobbin of silk was found standing upon the sewing-machine, though the least roll of the vessel would have precipitated it to the floor. The boats were intact and slung upon the davits; and the cargo, consisting of tallow and American clocks, was untouched. An old-fashioned sword of curious workmanship was discovered among some lumber in the forecastle, and this weapon is said to exhibit a longitudinal striation on the steel, as if it had been recently wiped. It has been placed in the hands of the police, and submitted to Dr. Monaghan, the analyst, for inspection. The result of his examination has not yet been published. We may remark, in conclusion, that Captain Dalton, of the *Dei Gratia*, an able and intelligent seaman, is of opinion that the *Marie Celeste* may have been abandoned a considerable distance from the spot at which she was picked up, since a powerful current runs up in that latitude from the African coast. He confesses his inability, however, to advance any hypothesis which can reconcile all the facts of the case. In the utter absence of a clue or grain of evidence, it is to be feared that the fate of the crew of the *Marie Celeste* will be added to those numerous mysteries of the deep which will never be solved until the great day when the sea shall give up its dead. If crime has been committed, as is much to be suspected, there is little hope of bringing the perpetrators to justice."

I shall supplement this extract from the *Gibraltar Gazette* by quoting a telegram from Boston, which went the round of the English papers, and represented the total amount of information which had been collected about the *Marie Celeste*. "She was," it said, "a brigantine of 170 tons burden, and belonged to White, Russell & White, wine importers, of this city. Captain J. W. Tibbs was an old servant of the firm, and was a man of known ability and tried probity. He was accompanied by his wife, aged thirty-one, and their youngest child, five years old. The crew consisted of seven hands, including two coloured seamen, and a boy. There were three passengers, one of whom was the well-known Brooklyn specialist on consumption, Dr. Habakuk Jephson, who was a distinguished advocate for Abolition in the early days of the movement, and whose pamphlet, entitled, 'Where is thy Brother?' exercised a strong influence on public opinion before the war. The other passengers were Mr. J. Harton, a writer in the employ of the firm, and Mr. Septimius Goring, a half-caste gentleman, from New Orleans. All investigations have failed to throw any light upon the fate of these fourteen human beings. The loss of Dr. Jephson will be felt both in political and scientific circles."

I have here epitomised, for the benefit of the public, all that has been hitherto known concerning the *Marie Celeste* and her crew, for the past ten years have not in any way helped to elucidate the mystery. I have now taken up my pen with the intention of telling all that I know of the ill-fated voyage. I consider that it is a duty which I owe to society, for symptoms which I am familiar with in others lead me to believe that before many months my tongue and hand may be alike incapable of conveying information. Let me remark, as a preface to my narrative, that I am Joseph Habakuk Jephson, Doctor of Medicine of the University of Harvard, and ex-Consulting Physician of the Samaritan Hospital of Brooklyn.

Many will doubtless wonder why I have not proclaimed myself before, and why I have suffered so many conjectures and surmises to pass unchallenged. Could the ends of justice have been served in any way by my revealing the facts in my possession I should unhesitatingly have done so. It seemed to me, however, that there was no possibility of such a result; and when I attempted after the occurrence, to state my case to an English official, I was met with such offensive incredulity that I determined never again to expose myself to the chance of such an indignity. I can excuse the discourtesy of the Liverpool magistrate, however, when I reflect upon the treatment which I received at the hands of my own relatives, who, though they knew my unimpeachable character, listened to my statement with an indulgent smile as if humouring the delusion of a monomaniac. This slur upon my veracity led to a quarrel between myself and John Vanburger, the brother of my wife, and confirmed me in my resolution to let the matter sink into oblivion—a determination which I have only altered through my son's solicitations. In order to make my narrative intelligible, I must run lightly over one or two incidents in my former life which throw light upon subsequent events.

My father, William K. Jephson, was a preacher of the sect called Plymouth Brethren, and was one of the most respected citizens of Lowell. Like most of the other Puritans of New England, he was a determined opponent of slavery, and it was from his lips that I received those lessons which tinged every action of my life. While I was studying medicine at Harvard University, I had already made a mark as an advanced Abolitionist; and when, after taking my degree, I bought a third share of the practice of Dr. Willis, of Brooklyn, I managed, in spite of my professional duties, to devote a considerable time to the cause which I had at heart, my pamphlet, "Where is thy Brother?" (Swarburgh, Lister & Co., 1849) attracting considerable attention.

When the war broke out I left Brooklyn and accompanied the 113th New York Regiment through the campaign. I was present at the second battle of Bull's Run and at the battle of Gettysburg. Finally, I was severely wounded at Antietam, and would probably have perished on the field had it not been for the kindness of a gentleman named Murray, who had me carried to his house and provided me with every comfort. Thanks to his charity, and to the nursing which I received from his black domestics, I was soon able to get about the plantation with the help of a stick. It was during this period of convalescence that an incident occurred which is closely connected with my story.

Among the most assiduous of the negresses who had watched my couch during my illness there was one old crone who appeared to exert considerable authority over the others. She was exceedingly attentive to me, and I gathered from the few words that passed between us that she had heard of me, and that she was grateful to me for championing her oppressed race.

One day as I was sitting alone in the verandah, basking in the sun, and debating whether I should rejoin Grant's army, I was surprised to see this old creature hobbling towards me. After looking cautiously around to see that we were alone, she fumbled in the front of her dress and produced a small chamois leather bag which was hung round her neck by a white cord.

"Massa," she said, bending down and croaking the words into my ear, "me die soon. Me very old woman. Not stay long on Massa Murray's plantation."

"You may live a long time yet, Martha," I answered. "You know I am a doctor. If you feel ill let me know about it, and I will try to cure you."

"No wish to live—wish to die. I'm gwine to join the heavenly host." Here she relapsed into one of those half-heathenish rhapsodies in which negroes indulge. "But, massa, me have one thing must leave behind me when I go. No able to take it with me across the Jordan. That one thing very precious, more precious and more holy than all thing else in the world. Me, a poor old black woman, have this because my people, very great people, 'spose they was back in the old country. But you cannot understand this same as black folk could. My fader give it me, and his fader give it him, but now who shall I give it to? Poor Martha hab no child, no relation, nobody. All round I see black man very bad man. Black woman very stupid woman. Nobody worthy of the stone. And so I say, Here is Massa Jephson who write books and fight for coloured folk—he must be a good man, and he shall have it though he is white man, and nebber can know what it mean or where it came from." Here the old woman fumbled in the chamois leather bag and pulled out a flattish black stone with a hole through the middle of it. "Here, take it," she said, pressing it into my hand; "take it. No harm nebber come from anything good. Keep it safe—nebber lose it!" and with a warning gesture the old crone hobbled away in the same cautious way as she had come, looking from side to side to see if we had been observed.

I was more amused than impressed by the old woman's earnestness, and was only prevented from laughing during her oration by the fear of hurting her feelings. When she was gone I took a good look at the stone which she had given me. It was intensely black, of extreme hardness, and oval in shape—just such a flat stone as one would pick up on the seashore if one wished to throw a long way. It was about three inches long, and an inch and a half broad at the middle, but rounded off at the extremities. The most curious part about it was several well-marked ridges which ran in semicircles over its surface, and gave it exactly the appearance of a human ear. Altogether I was rather interested in my new possession, and determined to submit it, as a geological specimen, to my friend Professor Shroeder of the New York Institute, upon the earliest opportunity. In the meantime I thrust it into my pocket, and rising from my chair started off for a short stroll in the shrubbery, dismissing the incident from my mind.

As my wound had nearly healed by this time, I took my leave of Mr. Murray shortly afterwards. The Union armies were everywhere victorious and converging on Richmond, so that my assistance seemed unnecessary, and I returned to Brooklyn. There I resumed my practice, and married the second daughter of Josiah Vanburger, the well-known wood engraver. In the course of a few years I built up a good connection and acquired considerable reputation in the treatment of pulmonary complaints. I still kept the old black stone in my pocket, and frequently told the story of the dramatic way in which I had become possessed of it. I also kept my resolution of showing it to Professor Shroeder, who was much interested both by the anecdote and the specimen. He pronounced it to be a piece of meteoric stone, and drew my attention to the fact that its resemblance to an ear was not accidental, but that it was most carefully worked into that shape. A dozen little anatomical points showed that the worker had been as accurate as he was skilful. "I should not wonder," said the Professor, "if it were broken off from some larger statue, though how such hard material could be so perfectly worked is more than I can understand. If there is a statue to correspond I should like to see it!" So I thought at the time, but I have changed my opinion since.

The next seven or eight years of my life were quiet and uneventful. Summer followed spring, and spring followed winter, without any variation in my duties. As the practice increased I admitted J. S. Jackson as partner, he to have one-fourth of the profits. The continued strain had told upon my constitution, however, and I became at last so unwell that my wife insisted upon my consulting Dr. Kavanagh Smith, who was my colleague at the Samaritan Hospital. That gentleman examined me, and pronounced the apex of my left lung to be in a state of consolidation, recommending me at the same time to go through a course of medical treatment and to take a long sea-voyage.

My own disposition, which is naturally restless, predisposed me strongly in favour of the latter piece of advice, and the matter was clinched by my meeting young Russell, of the firm of White, Russell & White, who offered me a passage in one of his father's ships, the *Marie Celeste*, which was just starting from Boston. "She is a snug little ship," he said, "and Tibbs, the captain, is an excellent fellow. There is nothing like a sailing ship for an invalid." I was very much of the same opinion myself, so I closed with the offer on the spot.

My original plan was that my wife should accompany me on my travels. She has always been a very poor sailor, however, and there were strong family reasons against her exposing herself to any risk at the time, so we determined that she should remain at home. I am not a religious or an effusive man; but oh, thank God for that! As to leaving my practice, I was easily reconciled to it, as Jackson, my partner, was a reliable and hard-working man.

I arrived in Boston on October 12, 1873, and proceeded immediately to the office of the firm in order to thank them for their courtesy. As I was sitting in the counting-house waiting until they should be at liberty to see me, the words *Marie Celeste* suddenly attracted my attention. I looked round and saw a very tall, gaunt man, who was leaning across the polished mahogany counter asking some questions of the clerk at the other side. His face was turned half towards me, and I could see that he had a strong dash of negro blood in him, being probably a quadroon or even nearer akin to the black. His curved aquiline nose and straight lank hair showed the white strain; but the dark, restless eye, sensuous mouth, and gleaming teeth all told of his African origin. His complexion was of a sickly unhealthy yellow, and as his face was deeply pitted with small-pox, the general impression was so unfavourable as to be almost revolting. When he spoke, however, it was in a soft, melodious voice, and in well-chosen words, and he was evidently a man of some education.

"I wished to ask a few questions about the *Marie Celeste,*" he repeated, leaning across to the clerk. "She sails the day after to-morrow, does she not?"

"Yes, sir," said the young clerk, awed into unusual politeness by the glimmer of a large diamond in the stranger's shirt front.

"Where is she bound for?"

"Lisbon."

"How many of a crew?"

"Seven, sir."

"Passengers?"

"Yes, two. One of our young gentlemen, and a doctor from New York."

"No gentleman from the South?" asked the stranger eagerly.

"No, none, sir."

"Is there room for another passenger?"

"Accommodation for three more," answered the clerk.

"I'll go," said the quadroon decisively; "I'll go, I'll engage my passage at once. Put it down, will you—Mr. Septimius Goring, of New Orleans."

The clerk filled up a form and handed it over to the stranger, pointing to a blank space at the bottom. As Mr. Goring stooped over to sign it I was horrified to observe that the fingers of his right hand had been lopped off, and that he was holding the pen between his thumb and the palm. I have seen thousands slain in battle, and assisted at every conceivable surgical operation, but I cannot recall any sight which gave me such a thrill of disgust as that great brown sponge-like hand with the single member protruding from it. He used it skilfully enough, however, for dashing off his signature, he nodded to the clerk and strolled out of the office just as Mr. White sent out word that he was ready to receive me.

I went down to the *Marie Celeste* that evening, and looked over my berth, which was extremely comfortable considering the small size of the vessel. Mr. Goring, whom I had seen in the morning, was to have the one next mine. Opposite was the captain's cabin and a small berth for Mr. John Harton, a gentleman who was going out in the interests of the firm. These little rooms were arranged on each side of the passage which led from the main-deck to the saloon. The latter was a comfortable room, the panelling tastefully done in oak and mahogany, with a rich Brussels carpet and luxurious settees. I was very much pleased with the accommodation, and also with Tibbs the captain, a bluff, sailor-like fellow, with a loud voice and hearty manner, who welcomed me to the ship with effusion, and insisted upon our splitting a bottle of wine in his cabin. He told me that he intended to take his wife and youngest child with him on the voyage, and that he hoped with good luck to make Lisbon in three weeks. We had a pleasant chat and parted the best of friends, he warning me to make the last of my preparations next morning, as he intended to make a start by the midday tide, having now shipped all his cargo. I went back to my hotel, where I found a letter from my wife awaiting me, and, after a refreshing night's sleep, returned to the boat in the morning. From this point I am able to quote from the journal which I kept in order to vary the monotony of the long sea-voyage. If it is somewhat bald in places I can at least rely upon its accuracy in details, as it was written conscientiously from day to day.

*October 16th.*—Cast off our warps at half-past two and were towed out into the bay, where the tug left us, and with all sail set we bowled along at about nine knots an hour. I stood upon the poop watching the low land of America sinking gradually upon the horizon until the evening haze hid it from my sight. A single red light, however, continued to blaze balefully behind us, throwing a long track like a trail of blood upon the water, and it is still visible as I write, though reduced to a mere speck. The Captain is in a bad humour, for two of his hands disappointed him at the last moment, and he was compelled to ship a couple of negroes who happened to be on the quay. The missing men were steady, reliable fellows, who had been with him several voyages, and their non-appearance puzzled as well as irritated him. Where a crew of seven men have to work a fair-sized ship the loss of two experienced seamen is a serious one, for though the negroes may take a spell at the wheel or swab the decks, they are of little or no use in rough weather. Our cook is also a black man, and Mr. Septimius Goring has a little darkie servant, so that we are rather a piebald community. The accountant, John Harton, promises to be an acquisition, for he is a cheery, amusing young fellow. Strange how little wealth has to do with happiness! He has all the world before him and is seeking his fortune in a far land, yet he is as transparently happy as a man can be. Goring is rich, if I am not mistaken, and so am I; but I know that I have a lung, and Goring has some deeper trouble still, to judge by his features. How poorly do we both contrast with the careless, penniless clerk!

*October 17th.*—Mrs. Tibbs appeared upon the deck for the first time this morning—a cheerful, energetic woman, with a dear little child just able to walk and prattle. Young Harton pounced on it at once, and carried it away to his cabin, where no doubt he will lay the seeds of future dyspepsia in the child's stomach. Thus medicine doth make cynics of us all! The weather is still all that could be desired, with a fine fresh breeze from the west-sou'-west. The vessel goes so steadily that you would hardly know that she was moving were it not for the creaking of the cordage, the bellying of the sails, and the long white furrow in our wake. Walked the quarter-deck all morning with the Captain, and I think the keen fresh air has already done my breathing good, for the exercise did not fatigue me in any way. Tibbs is a remarkably intelligent man, and we had an interesting argument about Maury's observations on ocean currents, which we terminated by going down into his cabin to consult the original work. There we found Goring, rather to the Captain's surprise, as it is not usual for passengers to enter that sanctum unless specially invited. He apologised for his intrusion, however, pleading his ignorance of the usages of ship life; and the good-natured sailor simply laughed at the incident, begging him to remain and favour us with his company. Goring pointed to the chronometers, the case of which he had opened, and remarked that he had been admiring them. He has evidently some practical knowledge of mathematical instruments, as he told at a glance which was the most trustworthy of the three, and also named their price within a few dollars. He had a discussion with the Captain too upon the variation of the compass, and when we came back to the ocean currents he showed a thorough grasp of the subject. Altogether he rather improves upon acquaintance, and is a man of decided culture and refinement. His voice harmonises with his conversation, and both are the very antithesis of his face and figure.

The noonday observation shows that we have run two hundred and twenty miles. Towards evening the breeze freshened up, and the first mate ordered reefs to be taken in the topsails and top-gallant sails in expectation of a windy night. I observe that the barometer has fallen to twenty-nine. I trust our voyage will not be a rough one, as I am a poor sailor, and my health would probably derive more harm than good from a stormy trip, though I have the greatest confidence in the Captain's seamanship and in the soundness of the vessel. Played cribbage with Mrs. Tibbs after supper, and Harton gave us a couple of tunes on the violin.

*October 18th.*—The gloomy prognostications of last night were not fulfilled, as the wind died away again, and we are lying now in a long greasy swell, ruffled here and there by a fleeting catspaw which is insufficient to fill the sails. The air is colder than it was yesterday, and I have put on one of the thick woollen jerseys which my wife knitted for me. Harton came into my cabin in the morning, and we had a cigar together. He says that he remembers having seen Goring in Cleveland, Ohio, in '69. He was, it appears, a mystery then as now, wandering about without any visible employment, and extremely reticent on his own affairs. The man interests me as a psychological study. At breakfast this morning I suddenly had that vague feeling of uneasiness which comes over some people when closely stared at, and, looking quickly up, I met his eyes bent upon me with an intensity which amounted to ferocity, though their expression instantly softened as he made some conventional remark upon the weather. Curiously enough, Harton says that he had a very similar experience yesterday upon deck. I observe that Goring frequently talks to the coloured seamen as he strolls about—a trait which I rather admire, as it is common to find half-breeds ignore their dark strain and treat their black kinsfolk with greater intolerance than a white man would do. His little page is devoted to him, apparently, which speaks well for his treatment of him. Altogether, the man is a curious mixture of incongruous qualities, and unless I am deceived in him will give me food for observation during the voyage.

The Captain is grumbling about his chronometers, which do not register exactly the same time. He says it is the first time that they have ever disagreed. We were unable to get a noonday observation on account of the haze. By dead reckoning, we have done about a hundred and seventy miles in the twenty-four hours. The dark seamen have proved, as the skipper prophesied, to be very inferior hands, but as they can both manage the wheel well they are kept steering, and so leave the more experienced men to work the ship. These details are trivial enough, but a small thing serves as food for gossip aboard ship. The appearance of a whale in the evening caused quite a flutter among us. From its sharp back and forked tail, I should pronounce it to have been a rorqual, or "finner," as they are called by the fishermen.

*October 19th.*—Wind was cold, so I prudently remained in my cabin all day, only creeping out for dinner. Lying in my bunk I can, without moving, reach my books, pipes, or anything else I may want, which is one advantage of a small apartment. My old wound began to ache a little to-day, probably from the cold. Read *Montaigne's Essays* and nursed myself. Harton came in in the afternoon with Doddy, the Captain's child, and the skipper himself followed, so that I held quite a reception.

*October 20th and 21st.*—Still cold, with a continual drizzle of rain, and I have not been able to leave the cabin. This confinement makes me feel weak and depressed. Goring came in to see me, but his company did not tend to cheer me up much, as he hardly uttered a word, but contented himself with staring at me in a peculiar and rather irritating manner. He then got up and stole out of the cabin without saying anything. I am beginning to suspect that the man is a lunatic. I think I mentioned that his cabin is next to mine. The two are simply divided by a thin wooden partition which is cracked in many places, some of the cracks being so large that I can hardly avoid, as I lie in my bunk, observing his motions in the adjoining room. Without any wish to play the spy, I see him continually stooping over what appears to be a chart and working with a pencil and compasses. I have remarked the interest he displays in matters connected with navigation, but I am surprised that he should take the trouble to work out the course of the ship. However, it is a harmless amusement enough, and no doubt he verifies his results by those of the Captain.

I wish the man did not run in my thoughts so much. I had a nightmare on the night of the 20th, in which I thought my bunk was a coffin, that I was laid out in it, and that Goring was endeavouring to nail up the lid, which I was frantically pushing away. Even when I woke up, I could hardly persuade myself that I was not in a coffin. As a medical man, I know that a nightmare is simply a vascular derangement of the cerebral hemispheres, and yet in my weak state I cannot shake off the morbid impression which it produces.

*October 22nd.*—A fine day, with hardly a cloud in the sky, and a fresh breeze from the sou'-west which wafts us gaily on our way. There has evidently been some heavy weather near us, as there is a tremendous swell on, and the ship lurches until the end of the fore-yard nearly touches the water. Had a refreshing walk up and down the quarter-deck, though I have hardly found my sea-legs yet. Several small birds—chaffinches, I think—perched in the rigging.

4.40 P.M.—While I was on deck this morning I heard a sudden explosion from the direction of my cabin, and, hurrying down, found that I had very nearly met with a serious accident. Goring was cleaning a revolver, it seems, in his cabin, when one of the barrels which he thought was unloaded went off. The ball passed through the side partition and imbedded itself in the bulwarks in the exact place where my head usually rests. I have been under fire too often to magnify trifles, but there is no doubt that if I had been in the bunk it must have killed me. Goring, poor fellow, did not know that I had gone on deck that day, and must therefore have felt terribly frightened. I never saw such emotion in a man's face as when, on rushing out of his cabin with the smoking pistol in his hand, he met me face to face as I came down from deck. Of course, he was profuse in his apologies, though I simply laughed at the incident.

11 P.M.—A misfortune has occurred so unexpected and so horrible that my little escape of the morning dwindles into insignificance. Mrs. Tibbs and her child have disappeared—utterly and entirely disappeared. I can hardly compose myself to write the sad details. About half-past eight Tibbs rushed into my cabin with a very white face and asked me if I had seen his wife. I answered that I had not. He then ran wildly into the saloon and began groping about for any trace of her, while I followed him, endeavouring vainly to persuade him that his fears were ridiculous. We hunted over the ship for an hour and a half without coming on any sign of the missing woman or child. Poor Tibbs lost his voice completely from calling her name. Even the sailors, who are generally stolid enough, were deeply affected by the sight of him as he roamed bareheaded and dishevelled about the deck, searching with feverish anxiety the most impossible places, and returning to them again and again with a piteous pertinacity. The last time she was seen was about seven o'clock, when she took Doddy on to the poop to give him a breath of fresh air before putting him to bed. There was no one there at the time except the black seaman at the wheel, who denies having seen her at all. The whole affair is wrapped in mystery. My own theory is that while Mrs. Tibbs was holding the child and standing near the bulwarks it gave a spring and fell overboard, and that in her convulsive attempt to catch or save it, she followed it. I cannot account for the double disappearance in any other way. It is quite feasible that such a tragedy should be enacted without the knowledge of the man at the wheel, since it was dark at the time, and the peaked skylights of the saloon screen the greater part of the quarter-deck. Whatever the truth may be it is a terrible catastrophe, and has cast the darkest gloom upon our voyage. The mate has put the ship about, but of course there is not the slightest hope of picking them up. The Captain is lying in a state of stupor in his cabin. I gave him a

powerful dose of opium in his coffee that for a few hours at least his anguish may be deadened.

*October 23rd.*—Woke with a vague feeling of heaviness and misfortune, but it was not until a few moments' reflection that I was able to recall our loss of the night before. When I came on deck I saw the poor skipper standing gazing back at the waste of waters behind us which contains everything dear to him upon earth. I attempted to speak to him, but he turned brusquely away, and began pacing the deck with his head sunk upon his breast. Even now, when the truth is so clear, he cannot pass a boat or an unbent sail without peering under it. He looks ten years older than he did yesterday morning. Harton is terribly cut up, for he was fond of little Doddy, and Goring seems sorry too. At least he has shut himself up in his cabin all day, and when I got a casual glance at him his head was resting on his two hands as if in a melancholy reverie. I fear we are about as dismal a crew as ever sailed. How shocked my wife will be to hear of our disaster! The swell has gone down now, and we are doing about eight knots with all sail set and a nice little breeze. Hyson is practically in command of the ship, as Tibbs, though he does his best to bear up and keep a brave front, is incapable of applying himself to serious work.

*October 24th.*—Is the ship accursed? Was there ever a voyage which began so fairly and which changed so disastrously? Tibbs shot himself through the head during the night. I was awakened about three o'clock in the morning by an explosion, and immediately sprang out of bed and rushed into the Captain's cabin to find out the cause, though with a terrible presentiment in my heart. Quickly as I went, Goring went more quickly still, for he was already in the cabin stooping over the dead body of the Captain. It was a hideous sight, for the whole front of his face was blown in, and the little room was swimming in blood. The pistol was lying beside him on the floor, just as it had dropped from his hand. He had evidently put it to his mouth before pulling the trigger. Goring and I picked him reverently up and laid him on his bed. The crew had all clustered into his cabin, and the six white men were deeply grieved, for they were old hands who had sailed with him many years. There were dark looks and murmurs among them too, and one of them openly declared that the ship was haunted. Harton helped to lay the poor skipper out, and we did him up in canvas between us. At twelve o'clock the fore-yard was hauled aback, and we committed his body to the deep, Goring reading the Church of England burial service. The breeze has freshened up, and we have done ten knots all day and sometimes twelve. The sooner we reach Lisbon and get away from this accursed ship the better pleased shall I be. I feel as though we were in a floating coffin. Little wonder that the poor sailors are superstitious when I, an educated man, feel it so strongly.

*October 25th.*—Made a good run all day. Feel listless and depressed.

*October 26th.*—Goring, Harton, and I had a chat together on deck in the morning. Harton tried to draw Goring out as to his profession, and his object in going to Europe, but the quadroon parried all his questions and gave us no information. Indeed, he seemed to be slightly offended by Harton's pertinacity, and went down into his cabin. I wonder why we should both take such an interest in this man! I suppose it is his striking appearance, coupled with his apparent wealth, which piques our curiosity. Harton has a theory that he is really a detective, that he is after some criminal who has got away to Portugal, and that he chooses this peculiar way of travelling that he may arrive unnoticed and pounce upon his quarry unawares. I think the supposition is rather a farfetched one, but Harton bases it upon a book which Goring left on deck, and which he picked up and glanced over. It was a sort of scrap-book, it seems, and contained a large number of newspaper cuttings. All these cuttings related to murders which had been committed at various times in the States during the last twenty years or so. The curious thing which Harton observed about them, however, was that they were invariably murders the authors of which had never been brought to justice. They varied in every detail, he says, as to the manner of execution and the social status of the victim, but they uniformly wound up with the same formula that the murderer was still at large, though, of course, the police had every reason to expect his speedy capture. Certainly the incident seems to support Harton's theory, though it may be a mere whim of Goring's, or, as I suggested to Harton, he may be collecting materials for a book which shall outvie De Quincey. In any case it is no business of ours.

*October 27th, 28th.*—Wind still fair, and we are making good progress. Strange how easily a human unit may drop out of its place and be forgotten! Tibbs is hardly ever mentioned now; Hyson has taken possession of his cabin, and all goes on as before. Were it not for Mrs. Tibbs's sewing-machine upon a side-table we might forget that the unfortunate family had ever existed. Another accident occurred on board to-day, though fortunately not a very serious one. One of our white hands had gone down the after-hold to fetch up a spare coil of rope, when one of the hatches which he had removed came crashing down on the top of him. He saved his life by springing out of the way, but one of his feet was terribly crushed, and he will be of little use for the remainder of the voyage. He attributes the accident to the carelessness of his negro companion, who had helped him to shift the hatches. The latter, however, puts it down to the roll of the ship. Whatever be the cause, it reduces our short-handed crew still further. This run of ill-luck seems to be depressing Harton, for he has lost his usual good spirits and joviality. Goring is the only one who preserves his cheerfulness. I see him still working at his chart in his own cabin. His nautical knowledge would be useful should anything happen to Hyson—which God forbid!

*October 29th, 30th.*—Still bowling along with a fresh breeze. All quiet and nothing of note to chronicle.

*October 31st.*—My weak lungs, combined with the exciting episodes of the voyage, have shaken my nervous system so much that the most trivial incident affects me. I can hardly believe that I am the same man who tied the external iliac artery, an operation requiring the nicest precision, under a heavy rifle fire at Antietam. I am as nervous as a child. I was lying half dozing last night about four bells in the middle watch trying in vain to drop into a refreshing sleep. There was no light inside my cabin, but a single ray of moonlight streamed in through the port-hole, throwing a silvery flickering circle upon the door. As I lay I kept my drowsy eyes upon this circle, and was conscious that it was gradually becoming less well-defined as my senses left me, when I was suddenly recalled to full wakefulness by the appearance of a small dark object in the very centre of the luminous disc. I lay quietly and breathlessly watching it. Gradually it grew larger and plainer, and then I perceived that it was a human hand which had been cautiously inserted through the chink of the half-closed door—a hand which, as I observed with a thrill of horror, was not provided with fingers. The door swung cautiously backwards, and Goring's head followed his hand. It appeared in the centre of the moonlight, and was framed as it were in a ghastly uncertain halo, against which his features showed out plainly. It seemed to me that I had never seen such an utterly fiendish and merciless expression upon a human face. His eyes were dilated and glaring, his lips drawn back so as to show his white fangs, and his straight black hair appeared to bristle over his low forehead like the hood of a cobra. The sudden and noiseless apparition had such an effect upon me that I sprang up in bed trembling in every limb, and held out my hand towards my revolver. I was heartily ashamed of my hastiness when he explained the object of his intrusion, as he immediately did in the most courteous language. He had been suffering from toothache, poor fellow! and had come in to beg some laudanum, knowing that I possessed a medicine chest. As to a sinister expression he is never a beauty, and what with my state of nervous tension and the effect of the shifting moonlight it was easy to conjure up something horrible. I gave him twenty drops, and he went off again with many expressions of gratitude. I can hardly say how much this trivial incident affected me. I have felt unstrung all day.

A week's record of our voyage is here omitted, as nothing eventful occurred during the time, and my log consists merely of a few pages of unimportant gossip.

*November 7th.*—Harton and I sat on the poop all the morning, for the weather is becoming very warm as we come into southern latitudes. We reckon that we have done two-thirds of our voyage. How glad we shall be to see the green banks of the Tagus, and leave this unlucky ship for ever! I was endeavouring to amuse Harton to-day and to while away the time by telling him some of the experiences of my past life. Among others I related to him how I came into the possession of my black stone, and as a finale I rummaged in the side pocket of my old shooting coat and produced the identical object in question. He and I were bending over it together, I pointing out to him the curious ridges upon its surface, when we were conscious of a shadow falling between us and the sun, and looking round saw Goring standing behind us glaring over our shoulders at the stone. For some reason or other he appeared to be powerfully excited, though he was evidently trying to control himself and to conceal his emotion. He pointed once or twice at my relic with his stubby thumb before he could recover himself sufficiently to ask what it was and how I obtained it—a question put in such a brusque manner that I should have been offended had I not known the man to be an eccentric. I told him the story very much as I had told it to Harton. He listened with the deepest interest and then asked me if I had any idea what the stone was. I said I had not, beyond that it was meteoric. He asked me if I had ever tried its effect upon a negro. I said I had not. "Come," said he, "we'll see what our black friend at the wheel thinks of it." He took the stone in his hand and went across to the sailor, and the two examined it carefully. I could see the man gesticulating and nodding his head excitedly as if making some assertion, while his face betrayed the utmost astonishment, mixed, I think, with some reverence. Goring came across the deck to as presently, still holding the stone in his hand. "He says it is a worthless, useless thing," he said, "and fit only to be chucked overboard," with which he raised his hand and would most certainly have made an end of my relic, had the black sailor behind him not rushed forward and seized him by the wrist. Finding himself secured Goring dropped the stone and turned away with a very bad grace to avoid my angry remonstrances at his breach of faith. The black picked up the stone and handed it to me with a low bow and every sign of profound respect. The whole affair is inexplicable. I am rapidly coming to the conclusion that Goring is a maniac or something very near one. When I compare the effect produced by the stone upon the sailor, however, with the respect shown to Martha on the plantation, and the surprise of Goring on its first production, I cannot but come to the conclusion that I have really got hold of some powerful talisman which appeals to the whole dark race. I must not trust it in Goring's hands again.

*November 8th, 9th.*—What splendid weather we are having! Beyond one little blow, we have had nothing but fresh breezes the whole voyage. These two days we have made better runs than any hitherto. It is a pretty thing to watch the spray fly up from our prow as it cuts through the waves. The sun shines through it and breaks it up into a number of miniature rainbows—"sun-dogs," the sailors call them. I stood on the fo'c'sle-head for several hours to-day watching the effect, and surrounded by a halo of prismatic colours. The steersman has evidently told the other blacks about my wonderful stone, for I am treated by them all with the greatest respect. Talking about optical phenomena, we had a curious one yesterday evening which was pointed out to me by Hyson. This was the appearance of a triangular well-defined object high up in the heavens to the north of us. He explained that it was exactly like the Peak of Teneriffe as seen from a great distance—the peak was, however, at that moment at least five hundred miles to the south. It may have been a cloud, or it may have been one of those strange reflections of which one reads. The weather is very warm. The mate says that he never knew it so warm in these latitudes. Played chess with Harton in the evening.

*November 10th.*—It is getting warmer and warmer. Some land birds came and perched in the rigging to-day, though we are still a considerable way from our destination. The heat is so great that we are too lazy to do anything but lounge about the decks and smoke. Goring came over to me to-day and asked me some more questions about my stone; but I answered him rather shortly, for I have not quite forgiven him yet for the cool way in which he attempted to deprive me of it.

*November 11th, 12th.*—Still making good progress. I had no idea Portugal was ever as hot as this, but no doubt it is cooler on land. Hyson himself seemed surprised at it, and so do the men.

*November 13th.*—A most extraordinary event has happened, so extraordinary as to be almost inexplicable. Either Hyson has blundered wonderfully, or some magnetic influence has disturbed our instruments. Just about daybreak the watch on the fo'c'sle-head shouted out that he heard the sound of surf ahead, and Hyson thought he saw the loom of land. The ship was put about, and, though no lights were seen, none of us doubted that we had struck the Portuguese coast a little sooner than we had expected. What was our surprise to see the scene which was revealed to us at break of day! As far as we could look on either side was one long line of surf, great, green billows rolling in and breaking into a cloud of foam. But behind the surf what was there! Not the green banks nor the high cliffs of the shores of Portugal, but a great sandy waste which stretched away and away until it blended with the skyline. To right and left, look where you would, there was nothing but yellow sand, heaped in some places into fantastic mounds, some of them several hundred feet high, while in other parts were long stretches as level apparently as a billiard board. Harton and I, who had come on deck together, looked at each other in astonishment, and Harton burst out laughing. Hyson is exceedingly mortified at the occurrence, and protests that the instruments have been tampered with. There is no doubt that this is the mainland of Africa, and that it was really the Peak of Teneriffe which we saw some days ago upon the northern horizon. At the time when we saw the land birds we must have been passing some of the Canary Islands. If we continued on the same course, we are now to the north of Cape Blanco, near the unexplored country which skirts the great Sahara. All we can do is to rectify our instruments as far as possible and start afresh for our destination.

8.30 P.M.—Have been lying in a calm all day. The coast is now about a mile and a half from us. Hyson has examined the instruments, but cannot find any reason for their extraordinary deviation.

This is the end of my private journal, and I must make the remainder of my statement from memory. There is little chance of my being mistaken about facts, which have seared themselves into my recollection. That very night the storm which had been brewing so long burst over us, and I came to learn whither all those little incidents were tending which I had recorded so aimlessly. Blind fool that I was not to have seen it sooner! I shall tell what occurred as precisely as I can.

I had gone into my cabin about half-past eleven, and was preparing to go to bed, when a tap came at my door. On opening it I saw Goring's little black page, who told me that his master would like to have a word with me on deck. I was rather surprised that he should want me at such a late hour, but I went up without hesitation. I had hardly put my foot on the quarter-deck before I was seized from behind, dragged down upon my back, and a handkerchief slipped round my mouth. I struggled as hard as I could, but a coil of rope was rapidly and firmly wound round me, and I found myself lashed to the davit of one of the boats, utterly powerless to do or say anything, while the point of a knife pressed to my throat warned me to cease my struggles. The night was so dark that I had been unable hitherto to recognise my assailants, but as my eyes became accustomed to the gloom, and the moon broke out through the clouds that obscured it, I made out that I was surrounded by the two negro sailors, the black cook, and my fellow-passenger, Goring. Another man was crouching on the deck at my feet, but he was in the shadow and I could not recognise him.

All this occurred so rapidly that a minute could hardly have elapsed from the time I mounted the companion until I found myself gagged and powerless. It was so sudden that I could scarce bring myself to realise it, or to comprehend what it all meant. I heard the gang round me speaking in short, fierce whispers to each other, and some instinct told me that my life was the question at issue. Goring spoke authoritatively and angrily—the others doggedly and all together, as if disputing his commands. Then they moved away in a body to the opposite side of the deck, where I could still hear them whispering, though they were concealed from my view by the saloon skylights.

All this time the voices of the watch on deck chatting and laughing at the other end of the ship were distinctly audible, and I could see them gathered in a group, little dreaming of the dark doings which were going on within thirty yards of them. Oh! That I could have given them one word of warning, even though I had lost my life in doing it! but it was impossible. The moon was shining fitfully through the scattered clouds, and I could see the silvery gleam of the surge, and beyond it the vast weird desert with its fantastic sand-hills. Glancing down, I saw that the man who had been crouching on the deck was still lying there, and as I gazed at him a flickering ray of moonlight fell full upon his upturned face. Great heaven! even now, when more than twelve years have elapsed, my hand trembles as I write that, in spite of distorted features and projecting eyes, I recognised the face of Harton, the cheery young clerk who had been my companion during the voyage. It needed no medical eye to see that he was quite dead, while the twisted handkerchief round the neck, and the gag in his mouth, showed the silent way in which the hell-hounds had done their work. The clue which explained every event of our voyage came upon me like a flash of light as I gazed on poor Harton's corpse. Much was dark and unexplained, but I felt a great dim perception of the truth.

I heard the striking of a match at the other side of the skylights, and then I saw the tall, gaunt figure of Goring standing up on the bulwarks and holding in his hands what appeared to be a dark lantern. He lowered this for a moment over the side of the ship, and, to my inexpressible astonishment, I saw it answered instantaneously by a flash among the sand-hills on shore, which came and went so rapidly, that unless I had been following the direction of Goring's gaze, I should never have detected it. Again he lowered the lantern, and again it was answered from the shore. He then stepped down from the bulwarks, and in doing so slipped, making such a noise, that for a moment my heart bounded with the thought that the attention of the watch would be directed to his proceedings. It was a vain hope. The night was calm and the ship motionless, so that no idea of duty kept them vigilant. Hyson, who after the death of Tibbs was in command of both watches, had gone below to snatch a few hours' sleep, and the boatswain, who was left in charge, was standing with the other two men at the foot of the foremast. Powerless, speechless, with the cords cutting into my flesh and the murdered man at my feet, I awaited the next act in the tragedy.

The four ruffians were standing up now at the other side of the deck. The cook was armed with some sort of a cleaver, the others had knives, and Goring had a revolver. They were all leaning against the rail and looking out over the water as if watching for something. I saw one of them grasp another's arm and point as if at some object, and following the direction I made out the loom of a large moving mass making towards the ship. As it emerged from the gloom I saw that it was a great canoe crammed with men and propelled by at least a score of paddles. As it shot under our stern the watch caught sight of it also, and raising a cry hurried aft. They were too late, however. A swarm of gigantic negroes clambered over the quarter, and led by Goring swept down the deck in an irresistible torrent. All opposition was overpowered in a moment, the unarmed watch were knocked over and bound, and the sleepers dragged out of their bunks and secured in the same manner. Hyson made an attempt to defend the narrow passage leading to his cabin, and I heard a scuffle, and his voice shouting for assistance. There was none to assist, however, and he was brought on to the poop with the blood streaming from a deep cut in his forehead. He was gagged like the others, and a council was held upon our fate by the negroes. I saw our black seamen pointing towards me and making some statement, which was received with murmurs of astonishment and incredulity by the savages. One of them then came over to me, and plunging his hand into my pocket took out my black stone and held it up. He then handed it to a man who appeared to be a chief, who examined it as minutely as the light would permit, and muttering a few words passed it on to the warrior beside him, who also scrutinised it and passed it on until it had gone from hand to hand round the whole circle. The chief then said a few words to Goring in the native tongue, on which the quadroon addressed me in English. At this moment I seem to see the scene. The tall masts of the ship with the moonlight streaming down, silvering the yards and bringing the network of cordage into hard relief; the group of dusky warriors leaning on their spears; the dead man at my feet; the line of white-faced prisoners, and in front of me the loathsome half-breed, looking in his white linen and elegant clothes a strange contrast to his associates.

"You will bear me witness," he said in his softest accents, "that I am no party to sparing your life. If it rested with me you would die as these other men are about to do. I have no personal grudge against either you or them, but I have devoted my life to the destruction of the white race, and you are the first that has ever been in my power and has escaped me. You may thank that stone of yours for your life. These poor fellows reverence it, and indeed if it really be what they think it is they have cause. Should it prove when we get ashore that they are mistaken, and this its shape and material is a mere chance, nothing can save your life. In the meantime we wish to treat you well, so if there are any of your possessions which you would like to take with you, you are at liberty to get them." As he finished he gave a sign, and a couple of the negroes unbound me, though without removing the gag. I was led down into the cabin, where I put a few valuables into my pockets, together with a pocket-compass and my journal of the voyage. They then pushed me over the side into a small canoe, which was lying beside the large one, and my guards followed me, and shoving off began paddling for the shore. We had got about a hundred yards or so from the ship when our steersman held up his hand, and the paddlers paused for a moment and listened. Then on the silence of the night I heard a sort of dull, moaning sound, followed by a succession of splashes in the water. That is all I know of the fate of my poor shipmates. Almost immediately afterwards the large canoe followed us, and the deserted ship was left drifting about—a dreary spectre-like hulk. Nothing was taken from her by the savages. The whole fiendish transaction was carried through as decorously and temperately as though it were a religious rite.

The first grey of daylight was visible in the east as we passed through the surge and reached the shore. Leaving half-a-dozen men with the canoes, the rest of the negroes set off through the sand-hills, leading me with them, but treating me very gently and respectfully. It was difficult walking, as we sank over our ankles into the loose, shifting sand at every step, and I was nearly dead beat by the time we reached the native village, or town rather, for it was a place of considerable dimensions. The houses were conical structures not unlike bee-hives, and were made of compressed seaweed cemented over with a rude form of mortar, there being neither stick nor stone upon the coast nor anywhere within many hundreds of miles. As we entered the town an enormous crowd of both sexes came swarming out to meet us, beating tom-toms and howling and screaming. On seeing me they redoubled their yells and assumed a threatening attitude, which was instantly quelled by a few words shouted by my escort. A buzz of wonder succeeded the war-cries and yells of the moment before, and the whole dense mass proceeded down the broad central street of the town, having my escort and myself in the centre.

My statement hitherto may seem so strange as to excite doubt in the minds of those who do not know me, but it was the fact which I am now about to relate which caused my own brother-in-law to insult me by disbelief. I can but relate the occurrence in the simplest words, and trust to chance and time to prove their truth. In the centre of this main street there was a large building, formed in the same primitive way as the others, but towering high above them; a stockade of beautifully polished ebony rails was planted all round it, the framework of the door was formed by two magnificent elephant's tusks sunk in the ground on each side and meeting at the top, and the aperture was closed by a screen of native cloth richly embroidered with gold. We made our way to this imposing-looking structure, but on reaching the opening in the stockade, the multitude stopped and squatted down upon their hams, while I was led through into the enclosure by a few of the chiefs and elders of the tribe, Goring accompanying us, and in fact directing the proceedings. On reaching the screen which closed the temple—for such it evidently was—my hat and my shoes were removed, and I was then led in, a venerable old negro leading the way carrying in his hand my stone, which had been taken from my pocket. The building was only lit up by a few long slits in the roof through which the tropical sun poured, throwing broad golden bars upon the clay floor, alternating with intervals of darkness.

The interior was even larger than one would have imagined from the outside appearance. The walls were hung with native mats, shells, and other ornaments, but the remainder of the great space was quite empty, with the exception of a single object in the centre. This was the figure of a colossal negro, which I at first thought to be some real king or high priest of titanic size, but as I approached it I saw by the way in which the light was reflected from it that it was a statue admirably cut in jet-black stone. I was led up to this idol, for such it seemed to be, and looking at it closer I saw that though it was perfect in every other respect, one of its ears had been broken short off.

The grey-haired negro who held my relic mounted upon a small stool, and stretching up his arm fitted Martha's black stone on to the jagged surface on the side of the statue's head. There could not be a doubt that the one had been broken off from the other. The parts dovetailed together so accurately that when the old man removed his hand the ear stuck in its place for a few seconds before dropping into his open palm. The group round me prostrated themselves upon the ground at the sight with a cry of reverence, while the crowd outside, to whom the result was communicated, set up a wild whooping and cheering.

In a moment I found myself converted from a prisoner into a demi-god. I was escorted back through the town in triumph, the people pressing forward to touch my clothing and to gather up the dust on which my foot had trod. One of the largest huts was put at my disposal, and a banquet of every native delicacy was served me. I still felt, however, that I was not a free man, as several spearmen were placed as a guard at the entrance of my hut. All day my mind was occupied with plans of escape, but none seemed in any way feasible. On the one side was the great arid desert stretching away to Timbuctoo, on the other was a sea untraversed by vessels. The more I pondered over the problem the more hopeless did it seem. I little dreamed how near I was to its solution.

Night had fallen, and the clamour of the negroes had died gradually away. I was stretched on the couch of skins which had been provided for me, and was still meditating over my future, when Goring walked stealthily into the hut. My first idea was that he had come to complete his murderous holocaust by making away with me, the last survivor, and I sprang up upon my feet, determined to defend myself to the last. He smiled when he saw the action, and motioned me down again while he seated himself upon the other end of the couch.

"What do you think of me?" was the astonishing question with which he commenced our conversation.

"Think of you!" I almost yelled. "I think you the vilest, most unnatural renegade that ever polluted the earth. If we were away from these black devils of yours I would strangle you with my hands!"

"Don't speak so loud," he said, without the slightest appearance of irritation. "I don't want our chat to be cut short. So you would strangle me, would you!" he went on, with an amused smile. "I suppose I am returning good for evil, for I have come to help you to escape."

"You!" I gasped incredulously.

"Yes, I," he continued. "Oh, there is no credit to me in the matter. I am quite consistent. There is no reason why I should not be perfectly candid with you. I wish to be king over these fellows—not a very high ambition, certainly, but you know what Cæsar said about being first in a village in Gaul. Well, this unlucky stone of yours has not only saved your life, but has turned all their heads, so that they think you are come down from heaven, and my influence will be gone until you are out of the way. That is why I am going to help you to escape, since I cannot kill you"—this in the most natural and dulcet voice, as if the desire to do so were a matter of course.

"You would give the world to ask me a few questions," he went on, after a pause; "but you are too proud to do it. Never mind, I'll tell you one or two things, because I want your fellow white men to know them when you go back—if you are lucky enough to get back. About that cursed stone of yours, for instance. These negroes, or at least so the legend goes, were Mahometans originally. While Mahomet himself was still alive, there was a schism among his followers, and the smaller party moved away from Arabia, and eventually crossed Africa. They took away with them, in their exile, a valuable relic of their old faith in the shape of a large piece of the black stone of Mecca. The stone was a meteoric one, as you may have heard, and in its fall upon the earth it broke into two pieces. One of these pieces is still at Mecca. The larger piece was carried away to Barbary, where a skilful worker modelled it into the fashion which you saw to-day. These men are the descendents of the original seceders from Mahomet, and they have brought their relic safely through all their wanderings until they settled in this strange place, where the desert protects them from their enemies."

"And the ear?" I asked, almost involuntarily.

"Oh, that was the same story over again. Some of the tribe wandered away to the south a few hundred years ago, and one of them, wishing to have good luck for the enterprise, got into the temple at night and carried off one of the ears. There has been a tradition among the negroes ever since that the ear would come back some day. The fellow who carried it was caught by some slaver, no doubt, and that was how it got into America, and so into your hands—and you have had the honour of fulfilling the prophecy."

He paused for a few minutes, resting his head upon his hands, waiting apparently for me to speak. When he looked up again, the whole expression of his face had changed. His features were firm and set, and he changed the air of half-levity with which he had spoken before for one of sternness and almost ferocity.

"I wish you to carry a message back," he said, "to the white race, the great dominating race whom I hate and defy. Tell them that I have battened on their blood for twenty years, that I have slain them until even I became tired of what had once been a joy, that I did this unnoticed and unsuspected in the face of every precaution which their civilisation could suggest. There is no satisfaction in revenge when your enemy does not know who has struck him. I am not sorry, therefore, to have you as a messenger. There is no need why I should tell you how this great hate became born in me. See this," and he held up his mutilated hand; "that was done by a white man's knife. My father was white, my mother was a slave. When he died she was sold again, and I, a child then, saw her lashed to death to break her of some of the little airs and graces which her late master had encouraged in her. My young wife, too, oh, my young wife!" a shudder ran through his whole frame. "No matter! I swore my oath, and I kept it. From Maine to Florida, and from Boston to San Francisco, you could track my steps by sudden deaths which baffled the police. I warred against the whole white race as they for centuries had warred against the black one. At last, as I tell you, I sickened of blood. Still, the sight of a white face was abhorrent to me, and I determined to find some bold free black people and to throw in my lot with them, to cultivate their latent powers and to form a nucleus for a great coloured nation. This idea possessed me, and I travelled over the world for two years seeking for what I desired. At last I almost despaired of finding it. There was no hope of regeneration in the slave-dealing Soudanese, the debased Fantee, or the Americanised negroes of Liberia. I was returning from my quest when chance brought me in contact with this magnificent tribe of dwellers in the desert, and I threw in my lot with them. Before doing so, however, my old instinct of revenge prompted me to make one last visit to the United States, and I returned from it in the *Marie Celeste*.

"As to the voyage itself, your intelligence will have told you by this time that, thanks to my manipulation, both compasses and chronometers were entirely untrustworthy. I alone worked out the course with correct instruments of my own, while the steering was done by my black friends under my guidance. I pushed Tibb's wife overboard. What! You look surprised and shrink away. Surely you had guessed that by this time. I would have shot you that day through the partition, but unfortunately you were not there. I tried again afterwards, but you were awake. I shot Tibbs. I think the idea of suicide was carried out rather neatly. Of course when once we got on the coast the rest was simple. I had bargained that all on board should die; but that stone of yours upset my plans. I also bargained that there should be no plunder. No one can say we are pirates. We have acted from principle, not from any sordid motive."

I listened in amazement to the summary of his crimes which this strange man gave me, all in the quietest and most composed of voices, as though detailing incidents of every-day occurrence. I still seem to see him sitting like a hideous nightmare at the end of my couch, with the single rude lamp flickering over his cadaverous features.

"And now," he continued, "there is no difficulty about your escape. These stupid adopted children of mine will say that you have gone back to heaven from whence you came. The wind blows off the land. I have a boat all ready for you, well stored with provisions and water. I am anxious to be rid of you, so you may rely that nothing is neglected. Rise up and follow me."

I did what he commanded, and he led me through the door of the hut. The guards had either been withdrawn, or Goring had arranged matters with them. We passed unchallenged through the town and across the sandy plain. Once more I heard the roar of the sea, and saw the long white line of the surge. Two figures were standing upon the shore arranging the gear of a small boat. They were the two sailors who had been with us on the voyage.

"See him safely through the surf," said Goring. The two men sprang in and pushed off, pulling me in after them. With mainsail and jib we ran out from the land and passed safely over the bar. Then my two companions without a word of farewell sprang overboard, and I saw their heads like black dots on the white foam as they made their way back to the shore, while I scudded away into the blackness of the night. Looking back I caught my last glimpse of Goring. He was standing upon the summit of a sand-hill, and the rising moon behind him threw his gaunt angular figure into hard relief. He was waving his arms frantically to and fro; it may have been to encourage me on my way, but the gestures seemed to me at the time to be threatening ones, and I have often thought that it was more likely that his old savage instinct had returned when he realised that I was out of his power. Be that as it may, it was the last that I ever saw or ever shall see of Septimius Goring.

There is no need for me to dwell upon my solitary voyage. I steered as well as I could for the Canaries, but was picked up upon the fifth day by the British and African Steam Navigation Company's boat *Monrovia*. Let me take this opportunity of tendering my sincerest thanks to Captain Stornoway and his officers for the great kindness which they showed me from that time till they landed me in Liverpool, where I was enabled to take one of the Guion boats to New York.

From the day on which I found myself once more in the bosom of my family I have said little of what I have undergone. The subject is still an intensely painful one to me, and the little which I have dropped has been discredited. I now put the facts before the public as they occurred, careless how far they may be believed, and simply writing them down because my lung is growing weaker, and I feel the responsibility of holding my peace longer. I make no vague statement. Turn to your map of Africa. There above Cape Blanco, where the land trends away north and south from the westernmost point of the continent, there it is that Septimius Goring still reigns over his dark subjects, unless retribution has overtaken him; and there, where the long green ridges run swiftly in to roar and hiss upon the hot yellow sand, it is there that Harton lies with Hyson and the other poor fellows who were done to death in the *Marie Celeste*.

## 6

# THAT LITTLE SQUARE BOX

"All aboard?" said the captain.

"All aboard, sir!" said the mate.

"Then stand by to let her go."

It was nine o'clock on a Wednesday morning. The good ship *Spartan* was lying off Boston Quay with her cargo under hatches, her passengers shipped, and everything prepared for a start. The warning whistle had been sounded twice; the final bell had been rung. Her bowsprit was turned towards England, and the hiss of escaping steam showed that all was ready for her run of three thousand miles. She strained at the warps that held her like a greyhound at its leash.

I have the misfortune to be a very nervous man. A sedentary literary life has helped to increase the morbid love of solitude which, even in my boyhood, was one of my distinguishing characteristics. As I stood upon the quarter-deck of the Transatlantic steamer, I bitterly cursed the necessity which drove me back to the land of my forefathers. The shouts of the sailors, the rattle of the cordage, the farewells of my fellow-passengers, and the cheers of the mob, each and all jarred upon my sensitive nature. I felt sad too. An indescribable feeling, as of some impending calamity, seemed to haunt me. The sea was calm, and the breeze light. There was nothing to disturb the equanimity of the most confirmed of landsmen, yet I felt as if I stood upon the verge of a great though indefinable danger. I have noticed that such presentiments occur often in men of my peculiar temperament, and that they are not uncommonly fulfilled. There is a theory that it arises from a species of second-sight, a subtle spiritual communication with the future. I well remember that Herr Raumer, the eminent spiritualist, remarked on one occasion that I was the most sensitive subject as regards supernatural phenomena that he had ever encountered in the whole of his wide experience. Be that as it may, I certainly felt far from happy as I threaded my way among the weeping, cheering groups which dotted the white decks of the good ship *Spartan*. Had I known the experience which awaited me in the course of the next twelve hours I should even then at the last moment have sprung upon the shore, and made my escape from the accursed vessel.

"Time's up!" said the captain, closing his chronometer with a snap, and replacing it in his pocket. "Time's up!" said the mate. There was a last wail from the whistle, a rush of friends and relatives upon the land. One warp was loosened, the gangway was being pushed away, when there was a shout from the bridge, and two men appeared, running rapidly down the quay. They were waving their hands and making frantic gestures, apparently with the intention of stopping the ship. "Look sharp!" shouted the crowd. "Hold hard!" cried the captain. "Ease her! stop her! Up with the gangway!" and the two men sprang aboard just as the second warp parted, and a convulsive throb of the engine shot us clear of the shore. There was a cheer from the deck, another from the quay, a mighty fluttering of handkerchiefs, and the great vessel ploughed its way out of the harbour, and steamed grandly away across the placid bay.

We were fairly started upon our fortnight's voyage. There was a general dive among the passengers in quest of berths and luggage, while a popping of corks in the saloon proved that more than one bereaved traveller was adopting artificial means for drowning the pangs of separation. I glanced round the deck and took a running inventory of my *compagnons de voyage*. They presented the usual types met with upon these occasions. There was no striking face among them. I speak as a connoisseur, for faces are a speciality of mine. I pounce upon a characteristic feature as a botanist does on a flower, and bear it away with me to analyse at my leisure, and classify and label it in my little anthropological museum. There was nothing worthy of me here. Twenty types of young America going to "Yurrup," a few respectable middle-aged couples as an antidote, a sprinkling of clergymen and professional men, young ladies, bagmen, British exclusives, and all the *olla podrida* of an ocean-going steamer. I turned away from them and gazed back at the receding shores of America, and, as a cloud of remembrances rose before me, my heart warmed towards the land of my adoption. A pile of portmanteaus and luggage chanced to be lying on one side of the deck, awaiting their turn to be taken below. With my usual love for solitude I walked behind these, and sitting on a coil of rope between them and the vessel's side, I indulged in a melancholy reverie.

I was aroused from this by a whisper behind me. "Here's a quiet place," said the voice. "Sit down, and we can talk it over in safety."

Glancing through a chink between two colossal chests, I saw that the passengers who had joined us at the last moment were standing at the other side of the pile. They had evidently failed to see me as I crouched in the shadow of the boxes. The one who had spoken was a tall and very thin man with a blue-black beard and a colourless face. His manner was nervous and excited. His companion was a short plethoric little fellow, with a brisk and resolute air. He had a cigar in his mouth, and a large ulster slung over his left arm. They both glanced round uneasily, as if to ascertain whether they were alone. "This is just the place," I heard the other say. They sat down on a bale of goods with their backs turned towards me, and I found myself, much against my will, playing the unpleasant part of eavesdropper to their conversation.

"Well, Muller," said the taller of the two, "we've got it aboard right enough."

"Yes," assented the man whom he had addressed as Muller, "it's safe aboard."

"It was rather a near go."

"It was that, Flannigan."

"It wouldn't have done to have missed the ship."

"No, it would have put our plans out."

"Ruined them entirely," said the little man, and puffed furiously at his cigar for some minutes.

"I've got it here," he said at last.

"Let me see it."

"Is no one looking?"

"No, they are nearly all below."

"We can't be too careful where so much is at stake," said Muller, as he uncoiled the ulster which hung over his arm, and disclosed a dark object which he laid upon the deck. One glance at it was enough to cause me to spring to my feet with an exclamation of horror. Luckily they were so engrossed in the matter on hand that neither of them observed me. Had they turned their heads they would infallibly have seen my pale face glaring at them over the pile of boxes.

From the first moment of their conversation a horrible misgiving had come over me. It seemed more than confirmed as I gazed at what lay before me. It was a little square box made of some dark wood, and ribbed with brass. I suppose it was about the size of a cubic foot. It reminded me of a pistol-case, only it was decidedly higher. There was an appendage to it, however, on which my eyes were riveted, and which suggested the pistol itself rather than its receptacle. This was a trigger-like arrangement upon the lid, to which a coil of string was attached. Beside this trigger there was a small square aperture through the wood. The tall man, Flannigan, as his companion called him, applied his eye to this, and peered in for several minutes with an expression of intense anxiety upon his face.

"It seems right enough," he said at last.

"I tried not to shake it," said his companion.

"Such delicate things need delicate treatment. Put in some of the needful, Muller."

The shorter man fumbled in his pocket for some time, and then produced a small paper packet. He opened this, and took out of it half a handful of whitish granules, which he poured down through the hole. A curious clicking noise followed from the inside of the box, and both men smiled in a satisfied way.

"Nothing much wrong there," said Flannigan.

"Right as a trivet," answered his companion.

"Look out! here's some one coming. Take it down to our berth. It wouldn't do to have any one suspecting what our game is, or, worse still, have them fumbling with it, and letting it off by mistake."

"Well, it would come to the same, whoever let it off," said Muller.

"They'd be rather astonished if they pulled the trigger," said the taller, with a sinister laugh. "Ha, ha! fancy their faces! It's not a bad bit of workmanship, I flatter myself."

"No," said Muller. "I hear it is your own design, every bit of it, isn't it?"

"Yes, the spring and the sliding shutter are my own."

"We should take out a patent."

And the two men laughed again with a cold harsh laugh, as they took up the little brass-bound package, and concealed it in Muller's voluminous overcoat.

"Come down, and we'll stow it in our berth," said Flannigan. "We won't need it until to-night, and it will be safe there."

His companion assented, and the two went arm-in-arm along the deck and disappeared down the hatchway, bearing the mysterious little box away with them. The last words I heard were a muttered injunction from Flannigan to carry it carefully, and avoid knocking it against the bulwarks.

How long I remained sitting on that coil of rope I shall never know. The horror of the conversation I had just overheard was aggravated by the first sinking qualms of sea-sickness. The long roll of the Atlantic was beginning to assert itself over both ship and passengers. I felt prostrated in mind and in body, and fell into a state of collapse, from which I was finally aroused by the hearty voice of our worthy quartermaster.

"Do you mind moving out of that, sir?" he said. "We want to get this lumber cleared off the deck."

His bluff manner and ruddy healthy face seemed to be a positive insult to me in my present condition. Had I been a courageous or a muscular man I could have struck him. As it was, I treated the honest sailor to a melodramatic scowl which seemed to cause him no small astonishment, and strode past him to the other side of the deck. Solitude was what I wanted —solitude in which I could brood over the frightful crime which was being hatched before my very eyes. One of the quarter-boats was hanging rather low down upon the davits. An idea struck me, and climbing on the bulwarks, I stepped into the empty boat and lay down in the bottom of it. Stretched on my back, with nothing but the blue sky above me, and an occasional view of the mizzen as the vessel rolled, I was at last alone with my sickness and my thoughts.

I tried to recall the words which had been spoken in the terrible dialogue I had overheard. Would they admit of any construction but the one which stared me in the face? My reason forced me to confess that they would not. I endeavoured to array the various facts which formed the chain of circumstantial evidence, and to find a flaw in it; but no, not a link was missing. There was the strange way in which our passengers had come aboard, enabling them to evade any examination of their luggage. The very name of "Flannigan" smacked of Fenianism, while "Muller" suggested nothing but socialism and murder. Then their mysterious manner; their remark that their plans would have been ruined had they missed the ship; their fear of being observed; last, but not least, the clenching evidence in the production of the little square box with the trigger, and their grim joke about the face of the man who should let it off by mistake—could these facts lead to any conclusion other than that they were the desperate emissaries of somebody, political or otherwise, who intended to sacrifice themselves, their fellow-passengers, and the ship, in one great holocaust? The whitish granules which I had seen one of them pour into the box formed no doubt a fuse or train for exploding it. I had myself heard a sound come from it which might have emanated from some delicate piece of machinery. But what did they mean by their allusion to to-night? Could it be that they contemplated putting their horrible design into execution on the very first evening of our voyage? The mere thought of it sent a cold shudder over me, and made me for a moment superior even to the agonies of sea-sickness.

I have remarked that I am a physical coward. I am a moral one also. It is seldom that the two defects are united to such a degree in the one character. I have known many men who were most sensitive to bodily danger, and yet were distinguished for the independence and strength of their minds. In my own case, however, I regret to say that my quiet and retiring habits had fostered a nervous dread of doing anything remarkable or making myself conspicuous, which exceeded, if possible, my fear of personal peril. An ordinary mortal placed under the circumstances in which I now found myself would have gone at once to the Captain, confessed his fears, and put the matter into his hands. To me, however, constituted as I am, the idea was most repugnant. The thought of becoming the observed of all observers, cross-questioned by a stranger, and confronted with two desperate conspirators in the character of a denouncer, was hateful to me. Might it not by some remote possibility prove that I was mistaken? What would be my feelings if there should turn out to be no grounds for my accusation? No, I would procrastinate; I would keep my eye on the two desperadoes and dog them at every turn. Anything was better than the possibility of being wrong.

Then it struck me that even at that moment some new phase of the conspiracy might be developing itself. The nervous excitement seemed to have driven away my incipient attack of sickness, for I was able to stand up and lower myself from the boat without experiencing any return of it. I staggered along the deck with the intention of descending into the cabin and finding how my acquaintances of the morning were occupying themselves. Just as I had my hand on the companion-rail, I was astonished by receiving a hearty slap on the back, which nearly shot me down the steps with more haste than dignity.

"Is that you, Hammond?" said a voice which I seemed to recognise.

"God bless me," I said, as I turned round, "it can't be Dick Merton! Why, how are you, old man?"

This was an unexpected piece of luck in the midst of my perplexities. Dick was just the man I wanted; kindly and shrewd in his nature, and prompt in his actions, I should have no difficulty in telling him my suspicions, and could rely upon his sound sense to point out the best course to pursue. Since I was a little lad in the second form at Harrow, Dick had been my adviser and protector. He saw at a glance that something had gone wrong with me.

"Hullo!" he said, in his kindly way, "what's put you about, Hammond? You look as white as a sheet. *Mal de mer*, eh?"

"No, not that altogether," said I. "Walk up and down with me, Dick; I want to speak to you. Give me your arm."

Supporting myself on Dick's stalwart frame, I tottered along by his side; but it was some time before I could muster resolution to speak.

"Have a cigar?" said he, breaking the silence.

"No, thanks," said I. "Dick, we shall be all corpses to-night."

"That's no reason against your having a cigar now," said Dick, in his cool way, but looking hard at me from under his shaggy eyebrows as he spoke. He evidently thought that my intellect was a little gone.

"No," I continued, "it's no laughing matter; and I speak in sober earnest, I assure you. I have discovered an infamous conspiracy, Dick, to destroy this ship and every soul that is in her;" and I then proceeded systematically, and in order, to lay before him the chain of evidence which I had collected. "There, Dick," I said, as I concluded, "what do you think of that and, above all, what am I to do?"

To my astonishment he burst into a hearty fit of laughter.

"I'd be frightened," he said, "if any fellow but you had told me as much. You always had a way, Hammond, of discovering mares' nests. I like to see the old traits breaking out again. Do you remember at school how you swore there was a ghost in the long room, and how it turned out to be your own reflection in the mirror? Why, man," he continued, "what object would any one have in destroying this ship? We have no great political guns aboard. On the contrary, the majority of the passengers are Americans. Besides, in this sober nineteenth century, the most wholesale murderers stop at including themselves among their victims. Depend upon it, you have misunderstood them, and have mistaken a photographic camera, or something equally innocent, for an infernal machine."

"Nothing of the sort, sir," said I, rather touchily. "You will learn to your cost, I fear, that I have neither exaggerated nor misinterpreted a word. As to the box, I have certainly never before seen one like it. It contained delicate machinery; of that I am convinced, from the way in which the men handled it and spoke of it."

"You'd make out every packet of perishable goods to be a torpedo," said Dick, "if that is to be your only test."

"The man's name was Flannigan," I continued.

"I don't think that would go very far in a court of law," said Dick; "but come, I have finished my cigar. Suppose we go down together and split a bottle of claret. You can point out these two Orsinis to me if they are still in the cabin."

"All right," I answered; "I am determined not to lose sight of them all day. Don't look hard at them, though, for I don't want them to think that they are being watched."

"Trust me," said Dick; "I'll look as unconscious and guileless as a lamb;" and with that we passed down the companion and into the saloon.

A good many passengers were scattered about the great central table, some wrestling with refractory carpet-bags and rug-straps, some having their luncheon, and a few reading and otherwise amusing themselves. The objects of our quest were not there. We passed down the room and peered into every berth, but there was no sign of them. "Heavens!" thought I, "perhaps at this very moment they are beneath our feet, in the hold or engine-room, preparing their diabolical contrivance!" It was better to know the worst than to remain in such suspense.

"Steward," said Dick, "are there any other gentlemen about?"

"There's two in the smoking room, sir," answered the steward.

The smoking-room was a little snuggery, luxuriously fitted up, and adjoining the pantry. We pushed the door opened and entered. A sigh of relief escaped from my bosom. The very first object on which my eye rested was the cadaverous face of Flannigan, with its hard-set mouth and unwinking eye. His companion sat opposite to him. They were both drinking, and a pile of cards lay upon the table. They were engaged in playing as we entered. I nudged Dick to show him that we had found our quarry, and we sat down beside them with as unconcerned an air as possible. The two conspirators seemed to take little notice of our presence. I watched them both narrowly. The game at which they were playing was "Napoleon." Both were adepts at it, and I could not help admiring the consummate nerve of men who, with such a secret at their hearts, could devote their minds to the manipulation of a long suit or the finessing of a queen. Money changed hands rapidly; but the run of luck seemed to be all against the taller of the two players. At last he threw down his cards on the table with an oath, and refused to go on.

"No, I'm hanged if I do," he said; "I haven't had more than two of a suit for five hands."

"Never mind," said his comrade, as he gathered up his winnings; "a few dollars one way or the other won't go very far after to-night's work."

I was astonished at the rascal's audacity, but took care to keep my eyes fixed abstractedly upon the ceiling, and drank my wine in as unconscious a manner as possible. I felt that Flannigan was looking towards me with his wolfish eyes to see if I had noticed the allusion. He whispered something to his companion which I failed to catch. It was a caution, I suppose, for the other answered rather angrily—

"Nonsense! Why shouldn't I say what I like? Over-caution is just what would ruin us."

"I believe you want it not to come off," said Flannigan.

"You believe nothing of the sort," said the other, speaking rapidly and loudly. "You know as well as I do that when I play for a stake I like to win it. But I won't have my words criticised and cut short by you or any other man. I have as much interest in our success as you have—more, I hope."

He was quite hot about it, and puffed furiously at his cigar for some minutes. The eyes of the other ruffian wandered alternately from Dick Merton to myself. I knew that I was in the presence of a desperate man, that a quiver of my lip might be the signal for him to plunge a weapon into my heart, but I betrayed more self-command than I should have given myself credit for under such trying circumstances. As to Dick, he was as immovable and apparently as unconscious as the Egyptian Sphinx.

There was silence for some time in the smoking-room, broken only by the crisp rattle of the cards, as the man Muller shuffled them up before replacing them in his pocket. He still seemed to be somewhat flushed and irritable. Throwing the end of his cigar into the spittoon, he glanced defiantly at his companion and turned towards me.

"Can you tell me, sir," he said, "when this ship will be heard of again?"

They were both looking at me; but though my face may have turned a trifle paler, my voice was as steady as ever as I answered—

"I presume, sir, that it will be heard of first when it enters Queenstown Harbour."

"Ha, ha!" laughed the angry little man, "I knew you would say that. Don't you kick me under the table, Flannigan, I won't stand it. I know what I am doing. You are wrong, sir," he continued, turning to me, "utterly wrong."

"Some passing ship, perhaps," suggested Dick.

"No, nor that either."

"The weather is fine," I said; "why should we not be heard of at our destination?"

"I didn't say we shouldn't be heard of at our destination. Possibly we may not, and in any case that is not where we shall be heard of first."

"Where, then?" asked Dick.

"That you shall never know. Suffice it that a rapid and mysterious agency will signal our whereabouts, and that before the day is out. Ha, ha!" and he chuckled once again.

"Come on deck!" growled his comrade; "you have drunk too much of that confounded brandy-and-water. It has loosened your tongue. Come away!" and taking him by the arm he half led him, half forced him out of the smoking-room, and we heard them stumbling up the companion together, and on to the deck.

"Well, what do you think now?" I gasped, as I turned towards Dick. He was as imperturbable as ever.

"Think!" he said; "why, I think what his companion thinks, that we have been listening to the ravings of a half-drunken man. The fellow stunk of brandy."

"Nonsense, Dick! you saw how the other tried to stop his tongue."

"Of course he did. He didn't want his friend to make a fool of himself before strangers. Maybe the short one is a lunatic, and the other his private keeper. It's quite possible."

"O, Dick, Dick," I cried, "how can you be so blind! Don't you see that every word confirmed our previous suspicion?"

"Humbug, man!" said Dick; "you're working yourself into a state of nervous excitement. Why, what the devil do *you* make of all that nonsense about a mysterious agent which would signal our whereabouts?"

"I'll tell you what he meant, Dick," I said, bending forward and grasping my friend's arm. "He meant a sudden glare and a flash seen far out at sea by some lonely fisherman off the American coast. That's what he meant."

"I didn't think you were such a fool, Hammond," said Dick Merton testily. "If you try to fix a literal meaning on the twaddle that every drunken man talks, you will come to some queer conclusions. Let us follow their example, and go on deck. You need fresh air, I think. Depend upon it, your liver is out of order. A sea-voyage will do you a world of good."

"If ever I see the end of this one," I groaned, "I'll promise never to venture on another. They are laying the cloth, so it's hardly worth while my going up. I'll stay below and unpack my things."

"I hope dinner will find you in a more pleasant state of mind," said Dick; and he went out, leaving me to my thoughts until the clang of the great gong summoned us to the saloon.

My appetite, I need hardly say, had not been improved by the incidents which had occurred during the day. I sat down, however, mechanically at the table, and listened to the talk which was going on around me. There were nearly a hundred first-class passengers, and as the wine began to circulate, their voices combined with the clash of the dishes to form a perfect Babel. I found myself seated between a very stout and nervous old lady and a prim little clergyman; and as neither made any advances I retired into my shell, and spent my time in observing the appearance of my fellow-voyagers. I could see Dick in the dim distance dividing his attentions between a jointless fowl in front of him and a self-possessed young lady at his side. Captain Dowie was doing the honours at my end, while the surgeon of the vessel was seated at the other. I was glad to notice that Flannigan was placed almost opposite to me. As long as I had him before my eyes I knew that, for the time at least, we were safe. He was sitting with what was meant to be a sociable smile on his grim face. It did not escape me that he drank largely of wine—so largely that even before the dessert appeared his voice had become decidedly husky. His friend Muller was seated a few places lower down. He ate little, and appeared to be nervous and restless.

"Now, ladies," said our genial Captain, "I trust that you will consider yourselves at home aboard my vessel. I have no fears for the gentlemen. A bottle of champagne, steward. Here's to a fresh breeze and a quick passage! I trust our friends in America will hear of our safe arrival in eight days, or in nine at the very latest."

I looked up. Quick as was the glance which passed between Flannigan and his confederate, I was able to intercept it. There was an evil smile upon the former's thin lips.

The conversation rippled on. Politics, the sea, amusements, religion, each was in turn discussed. I remained a silent though an interested listener. It struck me that no harm could be done by introducing the subject which was ever in my mind. It could be managed in an off-hand way, and would at least have the effect of turning the Captain's thoughts in that direction. I could watch, too, what effect it would have upon the faces of the conspirators.

There was a sudden lull in the conversation. The ordinary subjects of interest appeared to be exhausted. The opportunity was a favourable one.

"May I ask, Captain," I said, bending forward and speaking very distinctly, "what you think of Fenian manifestos?"

The Captain's ruddy face became a shade darker from honest indignation.

"They are poor cowardly things," he said, "as silly as they are wicked."

"The impotent threats of a set of anonymous scoundrels," said a pompous-looking old gentleman beside him.

"O Captain!" said the fat lady at my side, "you don't really think they would blow up a ship?"

"I have no doubt they would if they could. But I am very sure they shall never blow up mine."

"May I ask what precautions are taken against them?" asked an elderly man at the end of the table.

"All goods sent aboard the ship are strictly examined," said Captain Dowie.

"But suppose a man brought explosives aboard with him?" I suggested.

"They are too cowardly to risk their own lives in that way."

During this conversation Flannigan had not betrayed the slightest interest in what was going on. He raised his head now and looked at the Captain.

"Don't you think you are rather underrating them?" he said. "Every secret society has produced desperate men—why shouldn't the Fenians have them too? Many men think it a privilege to die in the service of a cause which seems right in their eyes, though others may think it wrong."

"Indiscriminate murder cannot be fight in anybody's eyes," said the little clergyman.

"The bombardment of Paris was nothing else," said Flannigan; "yet the whole civilised world agreed to look on with folded arms, and change the ugly word 'murder' into the more euphonious one of 'war.' It seemed right enough to German eyes; why shouldn't dynamite seem so to the Fenian?"

"At any rate their empty vapourings have led to nothing as yet," said the Captain.

"Excuse me," returned Flannigan, "but is there not some room for doubt yet as to the fate of the *Dotterel*? I have met men in America who asserted from their own personal knowledge that there was a coal torpedo aboard that vessel."

"Then they lied," said the Captain. "It was proved conclusively at the court-martial to have arisen from an explosion of coal-gas—but we had better change the subject, or we may cause the ladies to have a restless night;" and the conversation once more drifted back into its original channel.

During this little discussion Flannigan had argued his point with a gentlemanly deference and a quiet power for which I had not given him credit. I could not help admiring a man who, on the eve of a desperate enterprise, could courteously argue upon a point which must touch him so nearly. He had, as I have already mentioned, partaken of a considerable quantity of wine; but though there was a slight flush upon his pale cheek, his manner was as reserved as ever. He did not join in the conversation again, but seemed to be lost in thought.

A whirl of conflicting ideas was battling in my own mind. What was I to do? Should I stand up now and denounce them before both passengers and Captain? Should I demand a few minutes' conversation with the latter in his own cabin, and reveal it all? For an instant I was half resolved to do it, but then the old constitutional timidity came back with redoubled force. After all there might be some mistake. Dick had heard the evidence and had refused to believe in it. I determined to let things go on their course. A strange reckless feeling came over me. Why should I help men who were blind to their own danger? Surely it was the duty of the officers to protect us, not ours to give warning to them. I drank off a couple of glasses of wine, and staggered up on deck with the determination of keeping my secret locked in my own bosom.

It was a glorious evening. Even in my excited state of mind I could not help leaning against the bulwarks and enjoying the refreshing breeze. Away to the westward a solitary sail stood out as a dark speck against the great sheet of flame left by the setting sun. I shuddered as I looked at it. It was grand but appalling. A single star was twinkling faintly above our mainmast, but a thousand seemed to gleam in the water below with every stroke of our propeller. The only blot in the fair scene was the great trail of smoke which stretched away behind us like a black slash upon a crimson curtain. It was hard to believe that the great peace which hung over all Nature could be marred by a poor miserable mortal.

"After all," I thought, as I gazed into the blue depths beneath me, "if the worst comes to the worst, it is better to die here than to linger in agony upon a sickbed on land." A man's life seems a very paltry thing amid the great forces of Nature. All my philosophy could not prevent my shuddering, however, when I turned my head and saw two shadowy figures at the other side of the deck, which I had no difficulty in recognising. They seemed to be conversing earnestly, but I had no opportunity of overhearing what was said; so I contented myself with pacing up and down, and keeping a vigilant watch upon their movements.

It was a relief to me when Dick came on deck. Even an incredulous confidant is better than none at all.

"Well, old man," he said, giving me a facetious dig in the ribs, "we've not been blown up yet."

"No, not yet," said I; "but that's no proof that we are not going to be."

"Nonsense, man!" said Dick; "I can't conceive what has put this extraordinary idea into your head. I have been talking to one of your supposed assassins, and he seems a pleasant fellow enough; quite a sporting character, I should think, from the way he speaks."

"Dick," I said, "I am as certain that those men have an infernal machine, and that we are on the verge of eternity, as if I saw them putting the match to the fuse."

"Well, if you really think so," said Dick, half awed for the moment by the earnestness of my manner, "it is your duty to let the Captain know of your suspicions."

"You are right," I said; "I will. My absurd timidity has prevented my doing so sooner. I believe our lives can only be saved by laying the whole matter before him."

"Well, go and do it now," said Dick; "but for goodness' sake don't mix me up in the matter."

"I'll speak to him when he comes off the bridge," I answered; "and in the meantime I don't mean to lose sight of them."

"Let me know of the result," said my companion; and with a nod he strolled away in search, I fancy, of his partner at the dinner-table.

Left to myself, I bethought me of my retreat of the morning, and climbing on the bulwark I mounted into the quarter-boat, and lay down there. In it I could reconsider my course of action, and by raising my head I was able at any time to get a view of my disagreeable neighbours.

An hour passed, and the Captain was still on the bridge. He was talking to one of the passengers, a retired naval officer, and the two were deep in debate concerning some abstruse point of navigation. I could see the red tips of their cigars from where I lay. It was dark now, so dark that I could hardly make out the figures of Flannigan and his accomplice. They were still standing in the position which they had taken up after dinner. A few of the passengers were scattered about the deck, but many had gone below. A strange stillness seemed to pervade the air. The voices of the watch and the rattle of the wheel were the only sounds which broke the silence.

Another half-hour passed. The Captain was still upon the bridge. It seemed as if he would never come down. My nerves were in a state of unnatural tension, so much so that the sound of two steps upon the deck made me start up in a quiver of excitement. I peered over the edge of the boat, and saw that our suspicious passengers had crossed from the other side, and were standing almost directly beneath me. The light of a binnacle fell full upon the ghastly face of the ruffian Flannigan. Even in that short glance I saw that Muller had the ulster, whose use I knew so well, slung loosely over his arm. I sank back with a groan. It seemed that my fatal procrastination had sacrificed two hundred innocent lives.

I had read of the fiendish vengeance which awaited a spy. I knew that men with their lives in their hands would stick at nothing. All I could do was to cower at the bottom of the boat and listen silently to their whispered talk below.

"This place will do," said a voice.

"Yes, the leeward side is best."

"I wonder if the trigger will act?"

"I am sure it will."

"We were to let it off at ten, were we not?"

"Yes, at ten sharp. We have eight minutes yet." There was a pause. Then the voice began again—

"They'll hear the drop of the trigger, won't they?"

"It doesn't matter. It will be too late for any one to prevent its going off."

"That's true. There will be some excitement among those we have left behind, won't there?"

"Rather. How long do you reckon it will be before they hear of us?"

"The first news will get in at about midnight at earliest."

"That will be my doing."

"No, mine."

"Ha, ha! we'll settle that."

There was a pause here. Then I heard Muller's voice in a ghastly whisper, "There's only five minutes more."

How slowly the moments seemed to pass! I could count them by the throbbing of my heart.

"It'll make a sensation on land," said a voice.

"Yes, it will make a noise in the newspapers."

I raised my head and peered over the side of the boat. There seemed no hope, no help. Death stared me in the face, whether I did or did not give the alarm. The Captain had at last left the bridge. The deck was deserted, save for those two dark figures crouching in the shadow of the boat.

Flannigan had a watch lying open in his hand.

"Three minutes more," he said. "Put it down upon the deck."

"No, put it here on the bulwarks."

It was the little square box. I knew by the sound that they had placed it near the davit, and almost exactly under my head.

I looked over again. Flannigan was pouring something out of a paper into his hand. It was white and granular—the same that I had seen him use in the morning. It was meant as a fuse, no doubt, for he shovelled it into the little box, and I heard the strange noise which had previously arrested my attention.

"A minute and a half more," he said. "Shall you or I pull the string?"

"I will pull it," said Muller.

He was kneeling down and holding the end in his hand. Flannigan stood behind with his arms folded, and an air of grim resolution upon his face.

I could stand it no longer. My nervous system seemed to give way in a moment.

"Stop!" I screamed, springing to my feet. "Stop, misguided and unprincipled men!"

They both staggered backwards. I fancy they thought I was a spirit, with the moonlight streaming down upon my pale face.

I was brave enough now. I had gone too far to retreat.

"Cain was damned," I cried, "and he slew but one; would you have the blood of two hundred upon your souls?"

"He's mad!" said Flannigan. "Time's up. Let it off, Muller."

I sprang down upon the deck.

"You shan't do it!" I said.

"By what right do you prevent us?"

"By every right, human and divine."

"It's no business of yours. Clear out of this."

"Never!" said I.

"Confound the fellow! There's too much at stake to stand on ceremony. I'll hold him, Muller, while you pull the trigger."

Next moment I was struggling in the herculean grasp of the Irishman. Resistance was useless; I was a child in his hands.

He pinned me up against the side of the vessel, and held me there.

"Now," he said, "look sharp. He can't prevent us."

I felt that I was standing on the verge of eternity. Half-strangled in the arms of the taller ruffian, I saw the other approach the fatal box. He stooped over it and seized the string. I breathed one prayer when I saw his grasp tighten upon it. Then came a sharp snap, a strange rasping noise. The trigger had fallen, the side of the box flew out, and let off—*two grey carrier pigeons*!

Little more need be said. It is not a subject on which I care to dwell. The whole thing is too utterly disgusting and absurd. Perhaps the best thing I can do is to retire gracefully from the scene, and let the sporting correspondent of the *New York Herald* fill my unworthy place. Here is an extract clipped from its columns shortly after our departure from America:

"*Pigeon-flying Extraordinary.*—A novel match has been brought off last week between the birds of John H. Flannigan, of Boston, and Jeremiah Muller, a well-known citizen of Lowell. Both men have devoted much time and attention to an improved breed of bird, and the challenge is an old-standing one. The pigeons were backed to a large amount, and there was considerable local interest in the result. The start was from the deck of the Transatlantic steamship *Spartan*, at ten o'clock on the evening of the day of starting, the vessel being then reckoned to be about a hundred miles from the land. The bird which reached home first was to be declared the winner. Considerable caution had, we believe, to be observed, as some captains have a prejudice against the bringing off of sporting events aboard their vessels. In spite of some little difficulty at the last moment, the trap was sprung almost exactly at ten o'clock. Muller's bird arrived in Lowell in an extreme state of exhaustion on the following morning, while Flannigan's has not been heard of. The backers of the latter have the satisfaction of knowing, however, that the whole affair has been characterised by extreme fairness. The pigeons were confined in a specially invented trap, which could only be opened by the spring. It was thus possible to feed them through an aperture in the top, but any tampering with their wings was quite out of the question. A few such matches would go far towards popularising pigeon-flying in America, and form an agreeable variety to the morbid exhibitions of human endurance which have assumed such proportions during the last few years."

# THE GOLD-BUG

EDGAR ALLAN POE

# THE GOLD-BUG

What ho! what ho! this fellow is dancing mad!
He hath been bitten by the Tarantula.

—ALL IN THE WRONG

Many years ago, I contracted an intimacy with a Mr. William Legrand. He was of an ancient Huguenot family, and had once been wealthy; but a series of misfortunes had reduced him to want. To avoid the mortification consequent upon his disasters, he left New Orleans, the city of his forefathers, and took up his residence at Sullivan's Island, near Charleston, South Carolina. This Island is a very singular one. It consists of little else than the sea sand, and is about three miles long. Its breadth at no point exceeds a quarter of a mile. It is separated from the main land by a scarcely perceptible creek, oozing its way through a wilderness of reeds and slime, a favorite resort of the marsh hen. The vegetation, as might be supposed, is scant, or at least dwarfish. No trees of any magnitude are to be seen. Near the western extremity, where Fort Moultrie stands, and where are some miserable frame buildings, tenanted, during summer, by the fugitives from Charleston dust and fever, may be found, indeed, the bristly palmetto; but the whole island, with the exception of this western point, and a line of hard, white beach on the seacoast, is covered with a dense undergrowth of the sweet myrtle, so much prized by the horticulturists of England. The shrub here often attains the height of fifteen or twenty feet, and forms an almost impenetrable coppice, burthening the air with its fragrance.

In the inmost recesses of this coppice, not far from the eastern or more remote end of the island, Legrand had built himself a small hut, which he occupied when I first, by mere accident, made his acquaintance. This soon ripened into friendship—for there was much in the recluse to excite interest and esteem. I found him well educated, with unusual powers of mind, but infected with misanthropy, and subject to perverse moods of alternate enthusiasm and melancholy. He had with him many books, but rarely employed them. His chief amusements were gunning and fishing, or sauntering along the beach and through the myrtles, in quest of shells or entomological specimens;—his collection of the latter might have been envied by a Swammerdamm. In these excursions he was usually accompanied by an old negro, called Jupiter, who had been manumitted before the reverses of the family, but who could be induced, neither by threats nor by promises, to abandon what he considered his right of attendance upon the footsteps of his young "Massa Will." It is not improbable that the relatives of Legrand, conceiving him to be somewhat unsettled in intellect, had contrived to instil this obstinacy into Jupiter, with a view to the supervision and guardianship of the wanderer.

The winters in the latitude of Sullivan's Island are seldom very severe, and in the fall of the year it is a rare event indeed when a fire is considered necessary. About the middle of October, 18-, there occurred, however, a day of remarkable chilliness. Just before sunset I scrambled my way through the evergreens to the hut of my friend, whom I had not visited for several weeks—my residence being, at that time, in Charleston, a distance of nine miles from the Island, while the facilities of passage and re-passage were very far behind those of the present day. Upon reaching the hut I rapped, as was my custom, and getting no reply, sought for the key where I knew it was secreted, unlocked the door and went in. A fine fire was blazing upon the hearth. It was a novelty, and by no means an ungrateful one. I threw off an overcoat, took an arm-chair by the crackling logs, and awaited patiently the arrival of my hosts.

Soon after dark they arrived, and gave me a most cordial welcome. Jupiter, grinning from ear to ear, bustled about to prepare some marsh-hens for supper. Legrand was in one of his fits—how else shall I term them?—of enthusiasm. He had found an unknown bivalve, forming a new genus, and, more than this, he had hunted down and secured, with Jupiter's assistance, a scarab?us which he believed to be totally new, but in respect to which he wished to have my opinion on the morrow.

"And why not to-night?" I asked, rubbing my hands over the blaze, and wishing the whole tribe of scarab?i at the devil.

"Ah, if I had only known you were here!" said Legrand, "but it's so long since I saw you; and how could I foresee that you would pay me a visit this very night of all others? As I was coming home I met Lieutenant G—, from the fort, and, very foolishly, I lent him the bug; so it will be impossible for you to see it until the morning. Stay here to-night, and I will send Jup down for it at sunrise. It is the loveliest thing in creation!"

"What?—sunrise?"

"Nonsense! no!—the bug. It is of a brilliant gold color—about the size of a large hickory-nut—with two jet black spots near one extremity of the back, and another, somewhat longer, at the other. The antennæ are—"

"Dey aint no tin in him, Massa Will, I keep a tellin on you," here interrupted Jupiter; "de bug is a goole bug, solid, ebery bit of him, inside and all, sep him wing—neber feel half so hebby a bug in my life."

"Well, suppose it is, Jup," replied Legrand, somewhat more earnestly, it seemed to me, than the case demanded, "is that any reason for your letting the birds burn? The color"—here he turned to me—"is really almost enough to warrant Jupiter's idea. You never saw a more brilliant metallic lustre than the scales emit—but of this you cannot judge till tomorrow. In the mean time I can give you some idea of the shape." Saying this, he seated himself at a small table, on which were a pen and ink, but no paper. He looked for some in a drawer, but found none.

"Never mind," said he at length, "this will answer;" and he drew from his waistcoat pocket a scrap of what I took to be very dirty foolscap, and made upon it a rough drawing with the pen. While he did this, I retained my seat by the fire, for I was still chilly. When the design was complete, he handed it to me without rising. As I received it, a loud growl was heard, succeeded by a scratching at the door. Jupiter opened it, and a large Newfoundland, belonging to Legrand, rushed in, leaped upon my shoulders, and loaded me with caresses; for I had shown him much attention during previous visits. When his gambols were over, I looked at the paper, and, to speak the truth, found myself not a little puzzled at what my friend had depicted.

"Well!" I said, after contemplating it for some minutes, "this is a strange scarab?us, I must confess: new to me: never saw anything like it before—unless it was a skull, or a death's-head—which it more nearly resembles than anything else that has come under my observation."

"A death's-head!" echoed Legrand—"Oh—yes—well, it has something of that appearance upon paper, no doubt. The two upper black spots look like eyes, eh? and the longer one at the bottom like a mouth—and then the shape of the whole is oval."

"Perhaps so," said I; "but, Legrand, I fear you are no artist. I must wait until I see the beetle itself, if I am to form any idea of its personal appearance."

"Well, I don't know," said he, a little nettled, "I draw tolerably—should do it at least—have had good masters, and flatter myself that I am not quite a blockhead."

"But, my dear fellow, you are joking then," said I, "this is a very passable skull—indeed, I may say that it is a very excellent skull, according to the vulgar notions about such specimens of physiology—and your scarab?us must be the queerest scarab?us in the world if it resembles it. Why, we may get up a very thrilling bit of superstition upon this hint. I presume you will call the bug scarabæus caput hominis, or something of that kind—there are many similar titles in the Natural Histories. But where are the antennæ you spoke of?"

"The antennæ!" said Legrand, who seemed to be getting unaccountably warm upon the subject; "I am sure you must see the antennæ. I made them as distinct as they are in the original insect, and I presume that is sufficient."

"Well, well," I said, "perhaps you have—still I don't see them;" and I handed him the paper without additional remark, not wishing to ruffle his temper; but I was much surprised at the turn affairs had taken; his ill humor puzzled me—and, as for the drawing of the beetle, there were positively no antennæ visible, and the whole did bear a very close resemblance to the ordinary cuts of a death's-head.

He received the paper very peevishly, and was about to crumple it, apparently to throw it in the fire, when a casual glance at the design seemed suddenly to rivet his attention. In an instant his face grew violently red—in another as excessively pale. For some minutes he continued to scrutinize the drawing minutely where he sat. At length he arose, took a candle from the table, and proceeded to seat himself upon a sea-chest in the farthest corner of the room. Here again he made an anxious examination of the paper; turning it in all directions. He said nothing, however, and his conduct greatly astonished me; yet I thought it prudent not to exacerbate the growing moodiness of his temper by any comment. Presently he took from his coat pocket a wallet, placed the paper carefully in it, and deposited both in a writing-desk, which he locked. He now grew more composed in his demeanor; but his original air of enthusiasm had quite disappeared. Yet he seemed not so much sulky as abstracted. As the evening wore away he became more and more absorbed in reverie, from which no sallies of mine could arouse him. It had been my intention to pass the night at the hut, as I had frequently done before, but, seeing my host in this mood, I deemed it proper to take leave. He did not press me to remain, but, as I departed, he shook my hand with even more than his usual cordiality.

It was about a month after this (and during the interval I had seen nothing of Legrand) when I received a visit, at Charleston, from his man, Jupiter. I had never seen the good old negro look so dispirited, and I feared that some serious disaster had befallen my friend.

"Well, Jup," said I, "what is the matter now?—how is your master?"

"Why, to speak de troof, massa, him not so berry well as mought be."

"Not well! I am truly sorry to hear it. What does he complain of?"

"Dar! dat's it!—him neber plain of notin—but him berry sick for all dat."

"Very sick, Jupiter!—why didn't you say so at once? Is he confined to bed?"

"No, dat he aint!—he aint find nowhar—dat's just whar de shoe pinch—my mind is got to be berry hebby bout poor Massa Will."

"Jupiter, I should like to understand what it is you are talking about. You say your master is sick. Hasn't he told you what ails him?"

"Why, massa, taint worf while for to git mad about de matter—Massa Will say noffin at all aint de matter wid him—but den what make him go about looking dis here way, wid he head down and he soldiers up, and as white as a gose? And den he keep a syphon all de time—"

"Keeps a what, Jupiter?"

"Keeps a syphon wid de figgurs on de slate—de queerest figgurs I ebber did see. Ise gittin to be skeered, I tell you. Hab for to keep mighty tight eye pon him noovers. Todder day he gib me slip fore de sun up and was gone de whole ob de blessed day. I had a big stick ready cut for to gib him deuced good beating when he did come—but Ise sich a fool dat I hadn't de heart arter all—he look so berry poorly."

"Eh?—what?—ah yes!—upon the whole I think you had better not be too severe with the poor fellow—don't flog him, Jupiter—he can't very well stand it—but can you form no idea of what has occasioned this illness, or rather this change of conduct? Has anything unpleasant happened since I saw you?"

"No, massa, dey aint bin noffin unpleasant since den—'twas fore den I'm feared—'twas de berry day you was dare."

"How? what do you mean?"

"Why, massa, I mean de bug—dare now."

"The what?"

"De bug,—I'm berry sartain dat Massa Will bin bit somewhere bout de head by dat goole-bug."

"And what cause have you, Jupiter, for such a supposition?"

"Claws enuff, massa, and mouth too. I nebber did see sick a deuced bug—he kick and he bite ebery ting what cum near him. Massa Will cotch him fuss, but had for to let him go gin mighty quick, I tell you—den was de time he must ha got de bite. I did n't like de look oh de bug mouff, myself, no how, so I would n't take hold ob him wid my finger, but I cotch him wid a piece ob paper dat I found. I rap him up in de paper and stuff piece ob it in he mouff—dat was de way."

"And you think, then, that your master was really bitten by the beetle, and that the bite made him sick?"

"I do n't tink noffin about it—I nose it. What make him dream bout de goole so much, if taint cause he bit by de goole-bug? Ise heerd bout dem goole-bugs fore dis."

"But how do you know he dreams about gold?"

"How I know? why cause he talk about it in he sleep—dat's how I nose."

"Well, Jup, perhaps you are right; but to what fortunate circumstance am I to attribute the honor of a visit from you to-day?"

"What de matter, massa?"

"Did you bring any message from Mr. Legrand?"

"No, massa, I bring dis here pissel;" and here Jupiter handed me a note which ran thus:

*MY DEAR — —*

Why have I not seen you for so long a time? I hope you have not been so foolish as to take offence at any little *brusquerie* of mine; but no, that is improbable. Since I saw you I have had great cause for anxiety. I have something to tell you, yet scarcely know how to tell it, or whether I should tell it at all.

I have not been quite well for some days past, and poor old Jup annoys me, almost beyond endurance, by his well-meant attentions Would you believe it?—he had prepared a huge stick, the other day, with which to chastise me for giving him the slip, and spending the day, *solus*, among the hills on the main land. I verily believe that my ill looks alone saved me a flogging.

I have made no addition to my cabinet since we met.

If you can, in any way, make it convenient, come over with Jupiter. *Do* come, I wish to see you to-*night*, upon business of importance. I assure you that it is of the *highest* importance.

*Ever yours, WILLIAM LEGRAND.*

There was something in the tone of this note which gave me great uneasiness. Its whole style differed materially from that of Legrand. What could he be dreaming of? What new crotchet possessed his excitable brain? What "business of the highest importance" could he possibly have to transact? Jupiter's account of him boded no good. I dreaded lest the continued pressure of misfortune had, at length, fairly unsettled the reason of my friend. Without a moment's hesitation, therefore, I prepared to accompany the negro.

Upon reaching the wharf, I noticed a scythe and three spades, all apparently new, lying in the bottom of the boat in which we were to embark.

"What is the meaning of all this, Jup?" I inquired.

"Him syfe, massa, and spade."

"Very true; but what are they doing here?"

"Him de syfe and de spade what Massa Will sis pon my buying for him in de town, and de debbils own lot of money I had to gib for em."

"But what, in the name of all that is mysterious, is your 'Massa Will' going to do with scythes and spades?"

"Dat's more dan I know, and debbil take me if I don't blieve 'tis more dan he know, too. But it's all cum ob do bug."

Finding that no satisfaction was to be obtained of Jupiter, whose whole intellect seemed to be absorbed by "de bug," I now stepped into the boat and made sail. With a fair and strong breeze we soon ran into the little cove to the northward of Fort Moultrie, and a walk of some two miles brought us to the hut. It was about three in the afternoon when we arrived. Legrand had been awaiting us in eager expectation. He grasped my hand with a nervous empressement which alarmed me and strengthened the suspicions already entertained. His countenance was pale even to ghastliness, and his deep-set eyes glared with unnatural lustre. After some inquiries respecting his health, I asked him, not knowing what better to say, if he had yet obtained the scarabæus from Lieutenant G ——.

"Oh, yes," he replied, coloring violently, "I got it from him the next morning. Nothing should tempt me to part with that scarabæus. Do you know that Jupiter is quite right about it?"

"In what way?" I asked, with a sad foreboding at heart.

"In supposing it to be a bug of real gold." He said this with an air of profound seriousness, and I felt inexpressibly shocked.

"This bug is to make my fortune," he continued, with a triumphant smile, "to reinstate me in my family possessions. Is it any wonder, then, that I prize it? Since Fortune has thought fit to bestow it upon me, I have only to use it properly and I shall arrive at the gold of which it is the index. Jupiter; bring me that scarabæus!"

"What! de bug, massa? I'd rudder not go fer trubble dat bug—you mus git him for your own self." Hereupon Legrand arose, with a grave and stately air, and brought me the beetle from a glass case in which it was enclosed. It was a beautiful scarabæus, and, at that time, unknown to naturalists—of course a great prize in a scientific point of view. There were two round, black spots near one extremity of the back, and a long one near the other. The scales were exceedingly hard and glossy, with all the appearance of burnished gold. The weight of the insect was very remarkable, and, taking all things into consideration, I could hardly blame Jupiter for his opinion respecting it; but what to make of Legrand's concordance with that opinion, I could not, for the life of me, tell.

"I sent for you," said he, in a grandiloquent tone, when I had completed my examination of the beetle, "I sent for you, that I might have your counsel and assistance in furthering the views of Fate and of the bug"—

"My dear Legrand," I cried, interrupting him, "you are certainly unwell, and had better use some little precautions. You shall go to bed, and I will remain with you a few days, until you get over this. You are feverish and"—

"Feel my pulse," said he.

I felt it, and, to say the truth, found not the slightest indication of fever.

"But you may be ill and yet have no fever. Allow me this once to prescribe for you. In the first place, go to bed. In the next"—

"You are mistaken," he interposed, "I am as well as I can expect to be under the excitement which I suffer. If you really wish me well, you will relieve this excitement."

"And how is this to be done?"

"Very easily. Jupiter and myself are going upon an expedition into the hills, upon the main land, and, in this expedition we shall need the aid of some person in whom we can confide. You are the only one we can trust. Whether we succeed or fail, the excitement which you now perceive in me will be equally allayed."

"I am anxious to oblige you in any way," I replied; "but do you mean to say that this infernal beetle has any connection with your expedition into the hills?"

"It has."

"Then, Legrand, I can become a party to no such absurd proceeding."

"I am sorry—very sorry—for we shall have to try it by ourselves."

"Try it by yourselves! The man is surely mad!—but stay!—how long do you propose to be absent?"

"Probably all night. We shall start immediately, and be back, at all events, by sunrise."

"And will you promise me, upon your honor, that when this freak of yours is over, and the bug business (good God!) settled to your satisfaction, you will then return home and follow my advice implicitly, as that of your physician?"

"Yes; I promise; and now let us be off, for we have no time to lose."

With a heavy heart I accompanied my friend. We started about four o'clock—Legrand, Jupiter, the dog, and myself. Jupiter had with him the scythe and spades—the whole of which he insisted upon carrying—more through fear, it seemed to me, of trusting either of the implements within reach of his master, than from any excess of industry or complaisance.

His demeanor was dogged in the extreme, and "dat deuced bug" were the sole words which escaped his lips during the journey. For my own part, I had charge of a couple of dark lanterns, while Legrand contented himself with the scarabæus, which he carried attached to the end of a bit of whip-cord; twirling it to and fro, with the air of a conjuror, as he went. When I observed this last, plain evidence of my friend's aberration of mind, I could scarcely refrain from tears. I thought it best, however, to humor his fancy, at least for the present, or until I could adopt some more energetic measures with a chance of success. In the mean time I endeavored, but all in vain, to sound him in regard to the object of the expedition. Having succeeded in inducing me to accompany him, he seemed unwilling to hold conversation upon any topic of minor importance, and to all my questions vouchsafed no other reply than "we shall see!"

We crossed the creek at the head of the island by means of a skiff; and, ascending the high grounds on the shore of the main land, proceeded in a northwesterly direction, through a tract of country excessively wild and desolate, where no trace of a human footstep was to be seen. Legrand led the way with decision; pausing only for an instant, here and there, to consult what appeared to be certain landmarks of his own contrivance upon a former occasion.

In this manner we journeyed for about two hours, and the sun was just setting when we entered a region infinitely more dreary than any yet seen. It was a species of table land, near the summit of an almost inaccessible hill, densely wooded from base to pinnacle, and interspersed with huge crags that appeared to lie loosely upon the soil, and in many cases were prevented from precipitating themselves into the valleys below, merely by the support of the trees against which they reclined. Deep ravines, in various directions, gave an air of still sterner solemnity to the scene.

The natural platform to which we had clambered was thickly overgrown with brambles, through which we soon discovered that it would have been impossible to force our way but for the scythe; and Jupiter, by direction of his master, proceeded to clear for us a path to the foot of an enormously tall tulip-tree, which stood, with some eight or ten oaks, upon the level, and far surpassed them all, and all other trees which I had then ever seen, in the beauty of its foliage and form, in the wide spread of its branches, and in the general majesty of its appearance. When we reached this tree, Legrand turned to Jupiter, and asked him if he thought he could climb it. The old man seemed a little staggered by the question, and for some moments made no reply. At length he approached the huge trunk, walked slowly around it, and examined it with minute attention. When he had completed his scrutiny, he merely said,

"Yes, massa, Jup climb any tree he ebber see in he life."

"Then up with you as soon as possible, for it will soon be too dark to see what we are about."

"How far mus go up, massa?" inquired Jupiter.

"Get up the main trunk first, and then I will tell you which way to go—and here—stop! take this beetle with you."

"De bug, Massa Will!—de goole bug!" cried the negro, drawing back in dismay—"what for mus tote de bug way up de tree?—d-n if I do!"

"If you are afraid, Jup, a great big negro like you, to take hold of a harmless little dead beetle, why you can carry it up by this string—but, if you do not take it up with you in some way, I shall be under the necessity of breaking your head with this shovel."

"What de matter now, massa?" said Jup, evidently shamed into compliance; "always want for to raise fuss wid old nigger. Was only funnin any how. Me feered de bug! what I keer for de bug?" Here he took cautiously hold of the extreme end of the string, and, maintaining the insect as far from his person as circumstances would permit, prepared to ascend the tree.

In youth, the tulip-tree, or Liriodendron Tulipferum, the most magnificent of American foresters, has a trunk peculiarly smooth, and often rises to a great height without lateral branches; but, in its riper age, the bark becomes gnarled and uneven, while many short limbs make their appearance on the stem. Thus the difficulty of ascension, in the present case, lay more in semblance than in reality. Embracing the huge cylinder, as closely as possible, with his arms and knees, seizing with his hands some projections, and resting his naked toes upon others, Jupiter, after one or two narrow escapes from falling, at length wriggled himself into the first great fork, and seemed to consider the whole business as virtually accomplished. The risk of the achievement was, in fact, now over, although the climber was some sixty or seventy feet from the ground.

"Which way mus go now, Massa Will?" he asked.

"Keep up the largest branch—the one on this side," said Legrand. The negro obeyed him promptly, and apparently with but little trouble; ascending higher and higher, until no glimpse of his squat figure could be obtained through the dense foliage which enveloped it. Presently his voice was heard in a sort of halloo.

"How much fudder is got for go?"

"How high up are you?" asked Legrand.

"Ebber so fur," replied the negro; "can see de sky fru de top ob de tree."

"Never mind the sky, but attend to what I say. Look down the trunk and count the limbs below you on this side. How many limbs have you passed?"

"One, two, tree, four, fibe—I done pass fibe big limb, massa, pon dis side."

"Then go one limb higher."

In a few minutes the voice was heard again, announcing that the seventh limb was attained.

"Now, Jup," cried Legrand, evidently much excited, "I want you to work your way out upon that limb as far as you can. If you see anything strange, let me know." By this time what little doubt I might have entertained of my poor friend's insanity, was put finally at rest. I had no alternative but to conclude him stricken with lunacy, and I became seriously anxious about getting him home. While I was pondering upon what was best to be done, Jupiter's voice was again heard.

"Mos feerd for to ventur pon dis limb berry far—tis dead limb putty much all de way."

"Did you say it was a dead limb, Jupiter?" cried Legrand in a quavering voice.

"Yes, massa, him dead as de door-nail—done up for sartain—done departed dis here life."

"What in the name heaven shall I do?" asked Legrand, seemingly in the greatest distress. "Do!" said I, glad of an opportunity to interpose a word, "why come home and go to bed. Come now!—that's a fine fellow. It's getting late, and, besides, you remember your promise."

"Jupiter," cried he, without heeding me in the least, "do you hear me?"

"Yes, Massa Will, hear you ebber so plain."

"Try the wood well, then, with your knife, and see if you think it very rotten."

"Him rotten, massa, sure nuff," replied the negro in a few moments, "but not so berry rotten as mought be. Mought ventur out leetle way pon de limb by myself, dat's true."

"By yourself!—what do you mean?"

"Why I mean de bug. 'Tis berry hebby bug. Spose I drop him down fuss, and den de limb won't break wid just de weight ob one nigger."

"You infernal scoundrel!" cried Legrand, apparently much relieved, "what do you mean by telling me such nonsense as that? As sure as you drop that beetle I'll break your neck. Look here, Jupiter, do you hear me?"

"Yes, massa, needn't hollo at poor nigger dat style."

"Well! now listen!—if you will venture out on the limb as far as you think safe, and not let go the beetle, I'll make you a present of a silver dollar as soon as you get down."

"I'm gwine, Massa Will—deed I is," replied the negro very promptly—"mos out to the eend now."

"Out to the end!" here fairly screamed Legrand, "do you say you are out to the end of that limb?"

"Soon be to de eend, massa,—o-o-o-o-oh! Lor-gol-a-marcy! what is dis here pon de tree?"

"Well!" cried Legrand, highly delighted, "what is it?"

"Why taint noffin but a skull—somebody bin lef him head up de tree, and de crows done gobble ebery bit ob de meat off."

"A skull, you say!—very well!—how is it fastened to the limb?—what holds it on?"

"Sure nuff, massa; mus look. Why dis berry curous sarcumstance, pon my word—dare's a great big nail in de skull, what fastens ob it on to de tree."

"Well now, Jupiter, do exactly as I tell you—do you hear?"

"Yes, massa."

"Pay attention, then!—find the left eye of the skull."

"Hum! hoo! dat's good! why dare aint no eye lef at all."

"Curse your stupidity! do you know your right hand from your left?"

"Yes, I nose dat—nose all bout dat—tis my lef hand what I chops de wood wid."

"To be sure! you are left-handed; and your left eye is on the same side as your left hand. Now, I suppose, you can find the left eye of the skull, or the place where the left eye has been. Have you found it?"

Here was a long pause. At length the negro asked,

"Is de lef eye of de skull pon de same side as de lef hand of de skull, too?—cause de skull aint got not a bit ob a hand at all—nebber mind! I got de lef eye now—here de lef eye! what mus do wid it?"

"Let the beetle drop through it, as far as the string will reach—but be careful and not let go your hold of the string."

"All dat done, Massa Will; mighty easy ting for to put de bug fru de hole—look out for him dare below!"

During this colloquy no portion of Jupiter's person could be seen; but the beetle, which he had suffered to descend, was now visible at the end of the string, and glistened, like a globe of burnished gold, in the last rays of the setting sun, some of which still faintly illumined the eminence upon which we stood. The scarabæus hung quite clear of any branches, and, if allowed to fall, would have fallen at our feet. Legrand immediately took the scythe, and cleared with it a circular space, three or four yards in diameter, just beneath the insect, and, having accomplished this, ordered Jupiter to let go the string and come down from the tree.

Driving a peg, with great nicety, into the ground, at the precise spot where the beetle fell, my friend now produced from his pocket a tape measure. Fastening one end of this at that point of the trunk, of the tree which was nearest the peg, he unrolled it till it reached the peg, and thence farther unrolled it, in the direction already established by the two points of the tree and the peg, for the distance of fifty feet—Jupiter clearing away the brambles with the scythe. At the spot thus attained a second peg was driven, and about this, as a centre, a rude circle, about four feet in diameter, described. Taking now a spade himself, and giving one to Jupiter and one to me, Legrand begged us to set about digging as quickly as possible.

To speak the truth, I had no especial relish for such amusement at any time, and, at that particular moment, would most willingly have declined it; for the night was coming on, and I felt much fatigued with the exercise already taken; but I saw no mode of escape, and was fearful of disturbing my poor friend's equanimity by a refusal. Could I have depended, indeed, upon Jupiter's aid, I would have had no hesitation in attempting to get the lunatic home by force; but I was too well assured of the old negro's disposition, to hope that he would assist me, under any circumstances, in a personal contest with his master. I made no doubt that the latter had been infected with some of the innumerable Southern superstitions about money buried, and that his phantasy had received confirmation by the finding of the scarabæus, or, perhaps, by Jupiter's obstinacy in maintaining it to be "a bug of real gold." A mind disposed to lunacy would readily be led away by such suggestions—especially if chiming in with favorite preconceived ideas—and then I called to mind the poor fellow's speech about the beetle's being "the index of his fortune." Upon the whole, I was sadly vexed and puzzled, but, at length, I concluded to make a virtue of necessity—to dig with a good will, and thus the sooner to convince the visionary, by ocular demonstration, of the fallacy of the opinions he entertained.

The lanterns having been lit, we all fell to work with a zeal worthy a more rational cause; and, as the glare fell upon our persons and implements, I could not help thinking how picturesque a group we composed, and how strange and suspicious our labors must have appeared to any interloper who, by chance, might have stumbled upon our whereabouts.

We dug very steadily for two hours. Little was said; and our chief embarrassment lay in the yelpings of the dog, who took exceeding interest in our proceedings. He, at length, became so obstreperous that we grew fearful of his giving the alarm to some stragglers in the vicinity;—or, rather, this was the apprehension of Legrand;—for myself, I should have rejoiced at any interruption which might have enabled me to get the wanderer home. The noise was, at length, very effectually silenced by Jupiter, who, getting out of the hole with a dogged air of deliberation, tied the brute's mouth up with one of his suspenders, and then returned, with a grave chuckle, to his task.

When the time mentioned had expired, we had reached a depth of five feet, and yet no signs of any treasure became manifest. A general pause ensued, and I began to hope that the farce was at an end. Legrand, however, although evidently much disconcerted, wiped his brow thoughtfully and recommenced. We had excavated the entire circle of four feet diameter, and now we slightly enlarged the limit, and went to the farther depth of two feet. Still nothing appeared. The gold-seeker, whom I sincerely pitied, at length clambered from the pit, with the bitterest disappointment imprinted upon every feature, and proceeded, slowly and reluctantly, to put on his coat, which he had thrown off at the beginning of his labor. In the mean time I made no remark. Jupiter, at a signal from his master, began to gather up his tools. This done, and the dog having been unmuzzled, we turned in profound silence towards home.

We had taken, perhaps, a dozen steps in this direction, when, with a loud oath, Legrand strode up to Jupiter, and seized him by the collar. The astonished negro opened his eyes and mouth to the fullest extent, let fall the spades, and fell upon his knees.

"You scoundrel," said Legrand, hissing out the syllables from between his clenched teeth —"you infernal black villain!—speak, I tell you!—answer me this instant, without prevarication!—which—which is your left eye?"

"Oh, my golly, Massa Will! aint dis here my lef eye for sartain?" roared the terrified

Jupiter, placing his hand upon his right organ of vision, and holding it there with a desperate pertinacity, as if in immediate dread of his master's attempt at a gouge.

"I thought so!—I knew it! hurrah!" vociferated Legrand, letting the negro go, and executing a series of curvets and caracols, much to the astonishment of his valet, who, arising from his knees, looked, mutely, from his master to myself, and then from myself to his master.

"Come! we must go back," said the latter, "the game's not up yet;" and he again led the way to the tulip-tree.

"Jupiter," said he, when we reached its foot, "come here! was the skull nailed to the limb with the face outwards, or with the face to the limb?"

"De face was out, massa, so dat de crows could get at de eyes good, widout any trouble."

"Well, then, was it this eye or that through which you dropped the beetle?"—here Legrand touched each of Jupiter's eyes.

"Twas dis eye, massa—de lef eye—jis as you tell me," and here it was his right eye that the negro indicated.

"That will do—must try it again."

Here my friend, about whose madness I now saw, or fancied that I saw, certain indications of method, removed the peg which marked the spot where the beetle fell, to a spot about three inches to the westward of its former position. Taking, now, the tape measure from the nearest point of the trunk to the peg, as before, and continuing the extension in a straight line to the distance of fifty feet, a spot was indicated, removed, by several yards, from the point at which we had been digging.

Around the new position a circle, somewhat larger than in the former instance, was now described, and we again set to work with the spades. I was dreadfully weary, but, scarcely understanding what had occasioned the change in my thoughts, I felt no longer any great aversion from the labor imposed. I had become most unaccountably interested—nay, even excited. Perhaps there was something, amid all the extravagant demeanor of Legrand—some air of forethought, or of deliberation, which impressed me. I dug eagerly, and now and then caught myself actually looking, with something that very much resembled expectation, for the fancied treasure, the vision of which had demented my unfortunate companion. At a period when such vagaries of thought most fully possessed me, and when we had been at work perhaps an hour and a half, we were again interrupted by the violent howlings of the dog. His uneasiness, in the first instance, had been, evidently, but the result of playfulness or caprice, but he now assumed a bitter and serious tone. Upon Jupiter's again attempting to muzzle him, he made furious resistance, and, leaping into the hole, tore up the mould frantically with his claws. In a few seconds he had uncovered a mass of human bones, forming two complete skeletons, intermingled with several buttons of metal, and what appeared to be the dust of decayed woollen. One or two strokes of a spade upturned the blade of a large Spanish knife, and, as we dug farther, three or four loose pieces of gold and silver coin came to light.

At sight of these the joy of Jupiter could scarcely be restrained, but the countenance of his master wore an air of extreme disappointment He urged us, however, to continue our exertions, and the words were hardly uttered when I stumbled and fell forward, having caught the toe of my boot in a large ring of iron that lay half buried in the loose earth.

We now worked in earnest, and never did I pass ten minutes of more intense excitement. During this interval we had fairly unearthed an oblong chest of wood, which, from its perfect preservation and wonderful hardness, had plainly been subjected to some mineralizing process—perhaps that of the Bi-chloride of Mercury. This box was three feet and a half long, three feet broad, and two and a half feet deep. It was firmly secured by bands of wrought iron, riveted, and forming a kind of open trelliswork over the whole. On each side of the chest, near the top, were three rings of iron—six in all—by means of which a firm hold could be obtained by six persons. Our utmost united endeavors served only to disturb the coffer very slightly in its bed. We at once saw the impossibility of removing so great a weight. Luckily, the sole fastenings of the lid consisted of two sliding bolts. These we drew back—trembling and panting with anxiety. In an instant, a treasure of incalculable value lay gleaming before us. As the rays of the lanterns fell within the pit, there flashed upwards a glow and a glare, from a confused heap of gold and of jewels, that absolutely dazzled our eyes.

I shall not pretend to describe the feelings with which I gazed. Amazement was, of course, predominant. Legrand appeared exhausted with excitement, and spoke very few words. Jupiter's countenance wore, for some minutes, as deadly a pallor as it is possible, in nature of things, for any negro's visage to assume. He seemed stupified—thunderstricken. Presently he fell upon his knees in the pit, and, burying his naked arms up to the elbows in gold, let them there remain, as if enjoying the luxury of a bath. At length, with a deep sigh, he exclaimed, as if in a soliloquy,

"And dis all cum ob de goole-bug! de putty goole bug! de poor little goole-bug, what I boosed in dat sabage kind ob style! Aint you shamed ob yourself, nigger?—answer me dat!"

It became necessary, at last, that I should arouse both master and valet to the expediency of removing the treasure. It was growing late, and it behooved us to make exertion, that we might get every thing housed before daylight. It was difficult to say what should be done, and much time was spent in deliberation—so confused were the ideas of all. We, finally, lightened the box by removing two thirds of its contents, when we were enabled, with some trouble, to raise it from the hole. The articles taken out were deposited among the brambles, and the dog left to guard them, with strict orders from Jupiter neither, upon any pretence, to stir from the spot, nor to open his mouth until our return. We then hurriedly made for home with the chest; reaching the hut in safety, but after excessive toil, at one o'clock in the morning. Worn out as we were, it was not in human nature to do more immediately. We rested until two, and had supper; starting for the hills immediately afterwards, armed with three stout sacks, which, by good luck, were upon the premises. A little before four we arrived at the pit, divided the remainder of the booty, as equally as might be, among us, and, leaving the holes unfilled, again set out for the hut, at which, for the second time, we deposited our golden burthens, just as the first faint streaks of the dawn gleamed from over the tree-tops in the East.

We were now thoroughly broken down; but the intense excitement of the time denied us repose. After an unquiet slumber of some three or four hours' duration, we arose, as if by preconcert, to make examination of our treasure.

The chest had been full to the brim, and we spent the whole day, and the greater part of the next night, in a scrutiny of its contents. There had been nothing like order or arrangement. Every thing had been heaped in promiscuously. Having assorted all with care, we found ourselves possessed of even vaster wealth than we had at first supposed. In coin there was rather more than four hundred and fifty thousand dollars—estimating the value of the pieces, as accurately as we could, by the tables of the period. There was not a particle of silver. All was gold of antique date and of great variety—French, Spanish, and German money, with a few English guineas, and some counters, of which we had never seen specimens before. There were several very large and heavy coins, so worn that we could make nothing of their inscriptions. There was no American money. The value of the jewels we found more difficulty in estimating. There were diamonds—some of them exceedingly large and fine—a hundred and ten in all, and not one of them small; eighteen rubies of remarkable brilliancy;—three hundred and ten emeralds, all very beautiful; and twenty-one sapphires, with an opal. These stones had all been broken from their settings and thrown loose in the chest. The settings themselves, which we picked out from among the other gold, appeared to have been beaten up with hammers, as if to prevent identification. Besides all this, there was a vast quantity of solid gold ornaments;—nearly two hundred massive finger and earrings;—rich chains—thirty of these, if I remember;—eighty-three very large and heavy crucifixes;—five gold censers of great value;—a prodigious golden punch bowl, ornamented with richly chased vine-leaves and Bacchanalian figures; with two sword-handles exquisitely embossed, and many other smaller articles which I cannot recollect. The weight of these valuables exceeded three hundred and fifty pounds avoirdupois; and in this estimate I have not included one hundred and ninety-seven superb gold watches; three of the number being worth each five hundred dollars, if one. Many of them were very old, and as time keepers valueless; the works having suffered, more or less, from corrosion—but all were richly jewelled and in cases of great worth. We estimated the entire contents of the chest, that night, at a million and a half of dollars; and upon the subsequent disposal of the trinkets and jewels (a few being retained for our own use), it was found that we had greatly undervalued the treasure. When, at length, we had concluded our examination, and the intense excitement of the time had, in some measure, subsided, Legrand, who saw that I was dying with impatience for a solution of this most extraordinary riddle, entered into a full detail of all the circumstances connected with it.

"You remember;" said he, "the night when I handed you the rough sketch I had made of the scarabæus. You recollect also, that I became quite vexed at you for insisting that my drawing resembled a death's-head. When you first made this assertion I thought you were jesting; but afterwards I called to mind the peculiar spots on the back of the insect, and admitted to myself that your remark had some little foundation in fact. Still, the sneer at my graphic powers irritated me—for I am considered a good artist—and, therefore, when you handed me the scrap of parchment, I was about to crumple it up and throw it angrily into the fire."

"The scrap of paper, you mean," said I.

"No; it had much of the appearance of paper, and at first I supposed it to be such, but when I came to draw upon it, I discovered it, at once, to be a piece of very thin parchment. It was quite dirty, you remember. Well, as I was in the very act of crumpling it up, my glance fell upon the sketch at which you had been looking, and you may imagine my astonishment when I perceived, in fact, the figure of a death's-head just where, it seemed to me, I had made the drawing of the beetle. For a moment I was too much amazed to think with accuracy. I knew that my design was very different in detail from this—although there was a certain similarity in general outline. Presently I took a candle, and seating myself at the other end of the room, proceeded to scrutinize the parchment more closely. Upon turning it over, I saw my own sketch upon the reverse, just as I had made it. My first idea, now, was mere surprise at the really remarkable similarity of outline—at the singular coincidence involved in the fact, that unknown to me, there should have been a skull upon the other side of the parchment, immediately beneath my figure of the scarabæus, and that this skull, not only in outline, but in size, should so closely resemble my drawing. I say the singularity of this coincidence absolutely stupified me for a time. This is the usual effect of such coincidences. The mind struggles to establish a connexion—a sequence of cause and effect—and, being unable to do so, suffers a species of temporary paralysis. But, when I recovered from this stupor, there dawned upon me gradually a conviction which startled me even far more than the coincidence. I began distinctly, positively, to remember that there had been no drawing upon the parchment when I made my sketch of the scarab?us. I became perfectly certain of this; for I recollected turning up first one side and then the other, in search of the cleanest spot. Had the skull been then there, of course I could not have failed to notice it. Here was indeed a mystery which I felt it impossible to explain; but, even at that early moment, there seemed to glimmer, faintly, within the most remote and secret chambers of my intellect, a glow-worm-like conception of that truth which last night's adventure brought to so magnificent a demonstration. I arose at once, and putting the parchment securely away, dismissed all farther reflection until I should be alone.

"When you had gone, and when Jupiter was fast asleep, I betook myself to a more methodical investigation of the affair. In the first place I considered the manner in which the parchment had come into my possession. The spot where we discovered the scarabaeus was on the coast of the main land, about a mile eastward of the island, and but a short distance above high water mark. Upon my taking hold of it, it gave me a sharp bite, which caused me to let it drop. Jupiter, with his accustomed caution, before seizing the insect, which had flown towards him, looked about him for a leaf, or something of that nature, by which to take hold of it. It was at this moment that his eyes, and mine also, fell upon the scrap of parchment, which I then supposed to be paper. It was lying half buried in the sand, a corner sticking up. Near the spot where we found it, I observed the remnants of the hull of what appeared to have been a ship's long boat. The wreck seemed to have been there for a very great while; for the resemblance to boat timbers could scarcely be traced.

"Well, Jupiter picked up the parchment, wrapped the beetle in it, and gave it to me. Soon afterwards we turned to go home, and on the way met Lieutenant G-. I showed him the insect, and he begged me to let him take it to the fort. Upon my consenting, he thrust it forthwith into his waistcoat pocket, without the parchment in which it had been wrapped, and which I had continued to hold in my hand during his inspection. Perhaps he dreaded my changing my mind, and thought it best to make sure of the prize at once—you know how enthusiastic he is on all subjects connected with Natural History. At the same time, without being conscious of it, I must have deposited the parchment in my own pocket.

"You remember that when I went to the table, for the purpose of making a sketch of the beetle, I found no paper where it was usually kept. I looked in the drawer, and found none there. I searched my pockets, hoping to find an old letter, when my hand fell upon the parchment. I thus detail the precise mode in which it came into my possession; for the circumstances impressed me with peculiar force.

"No doubt you will think me fanciful—but I had already established a kind of connexion. I had put together two 2147links of a great chain. There was a boat lying upon a sea-coast, and not far from the boat was a parchment—not a paper—with a skull depicted upon it. You will, of course, ask 'where is the connexion?' I reply that the skull, or death's-head, is the well-known emblem of the pirate. The flag of the death's head is hoisted in all engagements.

"I have said that the scrap was parchment, and not paper. Parchment is durable—almost imperishable. Matters of little moment are rarely consigned to parchment; since, for the mere ordinary purposes of drawing or writing, it is not nearly so well adapted as paper. This reflection suggested some meaning—some relevancy—in the death's-head. I did not fail to observe, also, the form of the parchment. Although one of its corners had been, by some accident, destroyed, it could be seen that the original form was oblong. It was just such a slip, indeed, as might have been chosen for a memorandum—for a record of something to be long remembered and carefully preserved."

"But," I interposed, "you say that the skull was not upon the parchment when you made the drawing of the beetle. How then do you trace any connexion between the boat and the skull—since this latter, according to your own admission, must have been designed (God only knows how or by whom) at some period subsequent to your sketching the scarabæus?"

"Ah, hereupon turns the whole mystery; although the secret, at this point, I had comparatively little difficulty in solving. My steps were sure, and could afford but a single result. I reasoned, for example, thus: When I drew the scarabæus, there was no skull apparent upon the parchment. When I had completed the drawing I gave it to you, and observed you narrowly until you returned it. You, therefore, did not design the skull, and no one else was present to do it. Then it was not done by human agency. And nevertheless it was done.

"At this stage of my reflections I endeavored to remember, and did remember, with entire distinctness, every incident which occurred about the period in question. The weather was chilly (oh rare and happy accident!), and a fire was blazing upon the hearth. I was heated with exercise and sat near the table. You, however, had drawn a chair close to the chimney. Just as I placed the parchment in your hand, and as you were in the act of inspecting it, Wolf, the Newfoundland, entered, and leaped upon your shoulders. With your left hand you caressed him and kept him off, while your right, holding the parchment, was permitted to fall listlessly between your knees, and in close proximity to the fire. At one moment I thought the blaze had caught it, and was about to caution you, but, before I could speak, you had withdrawn it, and were engaged in its examination. When I considered all these particulars, I doubted not for a moment that heat had been the agent in bringing to light, upon the parchment, the skull which I saw designed upon it. You are well aware that chemical preparations exist, and have existed time out of mind, by means of which it is possible to write upon either paper or vellum, so that the characters shall become visible only when subjected to the action of fire. Zaffre, digested in aqua regia, and diluted with four times its weight of water, is sometimes employed; a green tint results. The regulus of cobalt, dissolved in spirit of nitre, gives a red. These colors disappear at longer or shorter intervals after the material written upon cools, but again become apparent upon the re-application of heat.

"I now scrutinized the death's-head with care. Its outer edges—the edges of the drawing nearest the edge of the vellum—were far more distinct than the others. It was clear that the action of the caloric had been imperfect or unequal. I immediately kindled a fire, and subjected every portion of the parchment to a glowing heat. At first, the only effect was the strengthening of the faint lines in the skull; but, upon persevering in the experiment, there became visible, at the corner of the slip, diagonally opposite to the spot in which the death's-head was delineated, the figure of what I at first supposed to be a goat. A closer scrutiny, however, satisfied me that it was intended for a kid."

"Ha! ha!" said I, "to be sure I have no right to laugh at you—a million and a half of money is too serious a matter for mirth—but you are not about to establish a third 2147link in your chain—you will not find any especial connexion between your pirates and a goat—pirates, you know, have nothing to do with goats; they appertain to the farming interest."

"But I have just said that the figure was not that of a goat."

"Well, a kid then—pretty much the same thing."

"Pretty much, but not altogether," said Legrand. "You may have heard of one Captain Kidd. I at once looked upon the figure of the animal as a kind of punning or hieroglyphical signature. I say signature; because its position upon the vellum suggested this idea. The death's-head at the corner diagonally opposite, had, in the same manner, the air of a stamp, or seal. But I was sorely put out by the absence of all else—of the body to my imagined instrument—of the text for my context."

"I presume you expected to find a letter between the stamp and the signature."

"Something of that kind. The fact is, I felt irresistibly impressed with a presentiment of some vast good fortune impending. I can scarcely say why. Perhaps, after all, it was rather a desire than an actual belief;—but do you know that Jupiter's silly words, about the bug being of solid gold, had a remarkable effect upon my fancy? And then the series of accidents and coincidences—these were so very extraordinary. Do you observe how mere an accident it was that these events should have occurred upon the sole day of all the year in which it has been, or may be, sufficiently cool for fire, and that without the fire, or without the intervention of the dog at the precise moment in which he appeared, I should never have become aware of the death's-head, and so never the possessor of the treasure?"

"But proceed—I am all impatience."

"Well; you have heard, of course, the many stories current—the thousand vague rumors afloat about money buried, somewhere upon the Atlantic coast, by Kidd and his associates. These rumors must have had some foundation in fact. And that the rumors have existed so long and so continuous, could have resulted, it appeared to me, only from the circumstance of the buried treasure still remaining entombed. Had Kidd concealed his plunder for a time, and afterwards reclaimed it, the rumors would scarcely have reached us in their present unvarying form. You will observe that the stories told are all about money-seekers, not about money-finders. Had the pirate recovered his money, there the affair would have dropped. It seemed to me that some accident—say the loss of a memorandum indicating its locality—had deprived him of the means of recovering it, and that this accident had become known to his followers, who otherwise might never have heard that treasure had been concealed at all, and who, busying themselves in vain, because unguided attempts, to regain it, had given first birth, and then universal currency, to the reports which are now so common. Have you ever heard of any important treasure being unearthed along the coast?"

"Never."

"But that Kidd's accumulations were immense, is well known. I took it for granted, therefore, that the earth still held them; and you will scarcely be surprised when I tell you that I felt a hope, nearly amounting to certainty, that the parchment so strangely found, involved a lost record of the place of deposit."

"But how did you proceed?"

"I held the vellum again to the fire, after increasing the heat; but nothing appeared. I now thought it possible that the coating of dirt might have something to do with the failure; so I carefully rinsed the parchment by pouring warm water over it, and, having done this, I placed it in a tin pan, with the skull downwards, and put the pan upon a furnace of lighted charcoal. In a few minutes, the pan having become thoroughly heated, I removed the slip, and, to my inexpressible joy, found it spotted, in several places, with what appeared to be figures arranged in lines. Again I placed it in the pan, and suffered it to remain another minute. Upon taking it off, the whole was just as you see it now." Here Legrand, having re-heated the parchment, submitted it to my inspection. The following characters were rudely traced, in a red tint, between the death's-head and the goat:

53‡‡†305))6*;4826)4‡.)4‡);80
6*;48†8¶60))85;1‡(;:‡*8†83(88)
5*†;46(;88*96*?;8)*‡(;485);5*†
2:*‡(;4956*2(5*-4)8¶8*;40692

85);)6†8)4‡‡;1(‡9;48081;8:8‡1
;48†85;4)485†528806*81(‡9;48
;(88;4(‡?34;48)4‡;161;:188;‡?;

"But," said I, returning him the slip, "I am as much in the dark as ever. Were all the jewels of Golconda awaiting me upon my solution of this enigma, I am quite sure that I should be unable to earn them."

"And yet," said Legrand, "the solution is by no means so difficult as you might be lead to imagine from the first hasty inspection of the characters. These characters, as any one might readily guess, form a cipher—that is to say, they convey a meaning; but then, from what is known of Kidd, I could not suppose him capable of constructing any of the more abstruse cryptographs. I made up my mind, at once, that this was of a simple species—such, however, as would appear, to the crude intellect of the sailor, absolutely insoluble without the key."

"And you really solved it?"

"Readily; I have solved others of an abstruseness ten thousand times greater. Circumstances, and a certain bias of mind, have led me to take interest in such riddles, and it may well be doubted whether human ingenuity can construct an enigma of the kind which human ingenuity may not, by proper application, resolve. In fact, having once established connected and legible characters, I scarcely gave a thought to the mere difficulty of developing their import.

"In the present case—indeed in all cases of secret writing—the first question regards the language of the cipher; for the principles of solution, so far, especially, as the more simple ciphers are concerned, depend upon, and are varied by, the genius of the particular idiom. In general, there is no alternative but experiment (directed by probabilities) of every tongue known to him who attempts the solution, until the true one be attained. But, with the cipher now before us, all difficulty was removed by the signature. The pun upon the word 'Kidd' is appreciable in no other language than the English. But for this consideration I should have begun my attempts with the Spanish and French, as the tongues in which a secret of this kind would most naturally have been written by a pirate of the Spanish main. As it was, I assumed the cryptograph to be English.

"You observe there are no divisions between the words. Had there been divisions, the task would have been comparatively easy. In such case I should have commenced with a collation and analysis of the shorter words, and, had a word of a single letter occurred, as is most likely, (a or I, for example,) I should have considered the solution as assured. But, there being no division, my first step was to ascertain the predominant letters, as well as the least frequent. Counting all, I constructed a table, thus:

Of the character 8 there are 33.
of ; there are 26.
of 4 there are 19.
of ‡ ) there are 16.
of * there are 13.
of 5 there are 12.
of 6 there are 11.
of † 1 there are 8.
of 0 there are 6.
of 92 there are 5.
of : 3 there are 4.
of ? there are 3.

of ¶ there are 2.
of —. there are 1.

"Now, in English, the letter which most frequently occurs is e. Afterwards, succession runs thus: *a o i d h n r s t u y c f g l m w b k p q x z*. *E* predominates so remarkably that an individual sentence of any length is rarely seen, in which it is not the prevailing character.

"Here, then, we leave, in the very beginning, the groundwork for something more than a mere guess. The general use which may be made of the table is obvious—but, in this particular cipher, we shall only very partially require its aid. As our predominant character is 8, we will commence by assuming it as the *e* of the natural alphabet. To verify the supposition, let us observe if the 8 be seen often in couples—for *e* is doubled with great frequency in English—in such words, for example, as 'meet,' '.fleet,' 'speed,' 'seen,' been,' 'agree,' &c. In the present instance we see it doubled no less than five times, although the cryptograph is brief.

"Let us assume 8, then, as *e*. Now, of all *words* in the language, 'the' is most usual; let us see, therefore, whether there are not repetitions of any three characters, in the same order of collocation, the last of them being 8. If we discover repetitions of such letters, so arranged, they will most probably represent the word 'the.' Upon inspection, we find no less than seven such arrangements, the characters being ;48. We may, therefore, assume that ; represents *t*, 4 represents *h*, and 8 represents *e*—the last being now well confirmed. Thus a great step has been taken.

"But, having established a single word, we are enabled to establish a vastly important point; that is to say, several commencements and terminations of other words. Let us refer, for example, to the last instance but one, in which the combination ;48 occurs—not far from the end of the cipher. We know that the; immediately ensuing is the commencement of a word, and, of the six characters succeeding this 'the,' we are cognizant of no less than five. Let us set these characters down, thus, by the letters we know them to represent, leaving a space for the unknown—

t eeth.

"Here we are enabled, at once, to discard the 'th,' as forming no portion of the word commencing with the first t; since, by experiment of the entire alphabet for a letter adapted to the vacancy, we perceive that no word can be formed of which this *th* can be a part. We are thus narrowed into

t ee

and, going through the alphabet, if necessary, as before, we arrive at the word 'tree,' as the sole possible reading. We thus gain another letter, *r*, represented by (, with the words 'the tree' in juxtaposition.

"Looking beyond these words, for a short distance, we again see the combination;48, and employ it by way of *termination* to what immediately precedes. We have thus this arrangement:

the tree ;4(‡?34 the,

or, substituting the natural letters, where known, it reads thus:

the tree thr‡?3h the.

"Now, if, in place of the unknown characters, we leave blank spaces, or substitute dots, we read thus:

the tree thr...h the,

when the word '*through*' makes itself evident at once. But this discovery gives us three new letters, *o*, *u* and *g*, represented by ‡, ? and 3.

"Looking now, narrowly, through the cipher for combinations of known characters, we find, not very far from the beginning, this arrangement,

83(88, or egree,

which, plainly, is the conclusion of the word 'degree,' and gives us another letter, *d*, represented by †.

"Four letters beyond the word 'degree,' we perceive the combination

;46(;88*

"Translating the known characters, and representing the unknown by dots, as before, we read thus:

th.rtee.,

an arrangement immediately suggestive of the word 'thirteen,' and again furnishing us with two new characters, *i* and *n*, represented by 6 and *.

"Referring, now, to the beginning of the cryptograph, we find the combination,

53‡‡†.

"Translating, as before, we obtain

.good,
8

which assures us that the first letter is *A*, and that the first two words are 'A good.'

"It is now time that we arrange our key, as far as discovered, in a tabular form, to avoid confusion. It will stand thus:

*5 represents a*
*† " d*
*8 " e*
*3 " g*
*4 " h*
*6 " i*
** " n*
*‡ " o*

( " *r*
; " *t*

"We have, therefore, no less than ten of the most important letters represented, and it will be unnecessary to proceed with the details of the solution. I have said enough to convince you that ciphers of this nature are readily soluble, and to give you some insight into the rationale of their development. But be assured that the specimen before us appertains to the very simplest species of cryptograph. It now only remains to give you the full translation of the characters upon the parchment, as unriddled. Here it is:

*"'A good glass in the bishop's hostel in the devil's seat forty-one degrees and thirteen minutes northeast and by north main branch seventh limb east side shoot from the left eye of the death's-head a bee line from the tree through the shot fifty feet out.'"*

"But," said I, "the enigma seems still in as bad a condition as ever. How is it possible to extort a meaning from all this jargon about 'devil's seats,' 'death's heads,' and 'bishop's hotels?'"

"I confess," replied Legrand, "that the matter still wears a serious aspect, when regarded with a casual glance. My first endeavor was to divide the sentence into the natural division intended by the cryptographist."

"You mean, to punctuate it?"

"Something of that kind."

"But how was it possible to effect this?"

"I reflected that it had been a point with the writer to run his words together without division, so as to increase the difficulty of solution. Now, a not over-acute man, in pursuing such an object would be nearly certain to overdo the matter. When, in the course of his composition, he arrived at a break in his subject which would naturally require a pause, or a point, he would be exceedingly apt to run his characters, at this place, more than usually close together. If you will observe the MS., in the present instance, you will easily detect five such cases of unusual crowding. Acting upon this hint, I made the division thus: 'A good glass in the Bishop's hostel in the Devil's seat—forty-one degrees and thirteen minutes—northeast and by north—main branch seventh limb east side—shoot from the left eye of the death's-head—a bee-line from the tree through the shot fifty feet out.'"

"Even this division," said I, "leaves me still in the dark."

"It left me also in the dark," replied Legrand, "for a few days; during which I made diligent inquiry, in the neighborhood of Sullivan's Island, for any building which went by the name of the 'Bishop's Hotel;' for, of course, I dropped the obsolete word 'hostel.' Gaining no information on the subject, I was on the point of extending my sphere of search, and proceeding in a more systematic manner, when, one morning, it entered into my head, quite suddenly, that this 'Bishop's Hostel' might have some reference to an old family, of the name of Bessop, which, time out of mind, had held possession of an ancient manor-house, about four miles to the northward of the Island. I accordingly went over to the plantation, and re-instituted my inquiries among the older negroes of the place. At length one of the most aged of the women said that she had heard of such a place as Bessop's Castle, and thought that she could guide me to it, but that it was not a castle nor a tavern, but a high rock.

"I offered to pay her well for her trouble, and, after some demur, she consented to accompany me to the spot. We found it without much difficulty, when, dismissing her, I proceeded to examine the place. The 'castle' consisted of an irregular assemblage of cliffs and rocks—one of the latter being quite remarkable for its height as well as for its insulated and artificial appearance I clambered to its apex, and then felt much at a loss as to what should be next done.

"While I was busied in reflection, my eyes fell upon a narrow ledge in the eastern face of the rock, perhaps a yard below the summit upon which I stood. This ledge projected about eighteen inches, and was not more than a foot wide, while a niche in the cliff just above it, gave it a rude resemblance to one of the hollow-backed chairs used by our ancestors. I made no doubt that here was the 'devil's seat' alluded to in the MS., and now I seemed to grasp the full secret of the riddle.

"The 'good glass,' I knew, could have reference to nothing but a telescope; for the word 'glass' is rarely employed in any other sense by seamen. Now here, I at once saw, was a telescope to be used, and a definite point of view, admitting no variation, from which to use it. Nor did I hesitate to believe that the phrases, "forty-one degrees and thirteen minutes,' and 'northeast and by north,' were intended as directions for the levelling of the glass. Greatly excited by these discoveries, I hurried home, procured a telescope, and returned to the rock.

"I let myself down to the ledge, and found that it was impossible to retain a seat upon it except in one particular position. This fact confirmed my preconceived idea. I proceeded to use the glass. Of course, the 'forty-one degrees and thirteen minutes' could allude to nothing but elevation above the visible horizon, since the horizontal direction was clearly indicated by the words, 'northeast and by north.' This latter direction I at once established by means of a pocket-compass; then, pointing the glass as nearly at an angle of forty-one degrees of elevation as I could do it by guess, I moved it cautiously up or down, until my attention was arrested by a circular rift or opening in the foliage of a large tree that overtopped its fellows in the distance. In the centre of this rift I perceived a white spot, but could not, at first, distinguish what it was. Adjusting the focus of the telescope, I again looked, and now made it out to be a human skull.

"Upon this discovery I was so sanguine as to consider the enigma solved; for the phrase 'main branch, seventh limb, east side,' could refer only to the position of the skull upon the tree, while 'shoot from the left eye of the death's head' admitted, also, of but one interpretation, in regard to a search for buried treasure. I perceived that the design was to drop a bullet from the left eye of the skull, and that a bee-line, or, in other words, a straight line, drawn from the nearest point of the trunk through 'the shot,' (or the spot where the bullet fell,) and thence extended to a distance of fifty feet, would indicate a definite point—and beneath this point I thought it at least possible that a deposit of value lay concealed."

"All this," I said, "is exceedingly clear, and, although ingenious, still simple and explicit. When you left the Bishop's Hotel, what then?"

"Why, having carefully taken the bearings of the tree, I turned homewards. The instant that I left 'the devil's seat,' however, the circular rift vanished; nor could I get a glimpse of it afterwards, turn as I would. What seems to me the chief ingenuity in this whole business, is the fact (for repeated experiment has convinced me it is a fact) that the circular opening in question is visible from no other attainable point of view than that afforded by the narrow ledge upon the face of the rock.

"In this expedition to the 'Bishop's Hotel' I had been attended by Jupiter, who had, no doubt, observed, for some weeks past, the abstraction of my demeanor, and took especial care not to leave me alone. But, on the next day, getting up very early, I contrived to give him the slip, and went into the hills in search of the tree. After much toil I found it. When I came home at night my valet proposed to give me a flogging. With the rest of the adventure I believe you are as well acquainted as myself."

"I suppose," said I, "you missed the spot, in the first attempt at digging, through Jupiter's stupidity in letting the bug fall through the right instead of through the left eye of the skull."

"Precisely. This mistake made a difference of about two inches and a half in the 'shot'—that is to say, in the position of the peg nearest the tree; and had the treasure been beneath the 'shot,' the error would have been of little moment; but 'the shot,' together with the nearest point of the tree, were merely two points for the establishment of a line of direction; of course the error, however trivial in the beginning, increased as we proceeded with the line, and by the time we had gone fifty feet, threw us quite off the scent. But for my deep-seated impressions that treasure was here somewhere actually buried, we might have had all our labor in vain."

"But your grandiloquence, and your conduct in swinging the beetle—how excessively odd! I was sure you were mad. And why did you insist upon letting fall the bug, instead of a bullet, from the skull?"

"Why, to be frank, I felt somewhat annoyed by your evident suspicions touching my sanity, and so resolved to punish you quietly, in my own way, by a little bit of sober mystification. For this reason I swung the beetle, and for this reason I let it fall it from the tree. An observation of yours about its great weight suggested the latter idea."

"Yes, I perceive; and now there is only one point which puzzles me. What are we to make of the skeletons found in the hole?"

"That is a question I am no more able to answer than yourself. There seems, however, only one plausible way of accounting for them—and yet it is dreadful to believe in such atrocity as my suggestion would imply. It is clear that Kidd—if Kidd indeed secreted this treasure, which I doubt not—it is clear that he must have had assistance in the labor. But this labor concluded, he may have thought it expedient to remove all participants in his secret. Perhaps a couple of blows with a mattock were sufficient, while his coadjutors were busy in the pit; perhaps it required a dozen—who shall tell?"

# THE QUEEN OF THE PIRATE ISLE

BRET HARTE

# THE QUEEN OF THE PIRATE ISLE

I first knew her as the Queen of the Pirate Isle. To the best of my recollection she had no reasonable right to that title. She was only nine years old, inclined to plumpness and good humor, deprecated violence, and had never been to sea. Need it be added that she did NOT live in an island and that her name was Polly?

Perhaps I ought to explain that she had already known other experiences of a purely imaginative character. Part of her existence had been passed as a Beggar Child,—solely indicated by a shawl tightly folded round her shoulders, and chills; as a Schoolmistress, unnecessarily severe; as a Preacher, singularly personal in his remarks, and once, after reading one of Cooper's novels, as an Indian Maiden. This was, I believe, the only instance when she had borrowed from another's fiction. Most of the characters that she assumed for days and sometimes weeks at a time were purely original in conception; some so much so as to be vague to the general understanding. I remember that her personation of a certain Mrs. Smith, whose individuality was supposed to be sufficiently represented by a sunbonnet worn wrong side before and a weekly addition to her family, was never perfectly appreciated by her own circle although she lived the character for a month. Another creation known as "The Proud Lady"—a being whose excessive and unreasonable haughtiness was so pronounced as to give her features the expression of extreme nausea—caused her mother so much alarm that it had to be abandoned. This was easily effected. The Proud Lady was understood to have died. Indeed, most of Polly's impersonations were got rid of in this way, although it by no means prevented their subsequent reappearance. "I thought Mrs. Smith was dead," remonstrated her mother at the posthumous appearance of that lady with a new infant. "She was buried alive and kem to!" said Polly with a melancholy air. Fortunately, the representation of a resuscitated person required such extraordinary acting, and was, through some uncertainty of conception, so closely allied in facial expression to the Proud Lady, that Mrs. Smith was resuscitated only for a day.

The origin of the title of the Queen of the Pirate Isle may be briefly stated as follows:—

An hour after luncheon, one day, Polly, Hickory Hunt, her cousin, and Wan Lee, a Chinese page, were crossing the nursery floor in a Chinese junk. The sea was calm and the sky cloudless. Any change in the weather was as unexpected as it is in books. Suddenly a West Indian Hurricane, purely local in character and unfelt anywhere else, struck Master Hickory and threw him overboard, whence, wildly swimming for his life and carrying Polly on his back, he eventually reached a Desert Island in the closet. Here the rescued party put up a tent made of a table-cloth providentially snatched from the raging billows, and, from two o'clock until four, passed six weeks on the island, supported only by a piece of candle, a box of matches, and two peppermint lozenges. It was at this time that it became necessary to account for Polly's existence among them, and this was only effected by an alarming sacrifice of their morality; Hickory and Wan Lee instantly became PIRATES, and at once elected Polly as their Queen. The royal duties, which seemed to be purely maternal, consisted in putting the Pirates to bed after a day of rapine and bloodshed, and in feeding them with licorice water through a quill in a small bottle. Limited as her functions were, Polly performed them with inimitable gravity and unquestioned sincerity. Even when her companions sometimes hesitated from actual hunger or fatigue and forgot their guilty part, she never faltered. It was her real existence; her other life of being washed, dressed, and put to bed at certain hours by her mother was the ILLUSION.

Doubt and skepticism came at last,—and came from Wan Lee! Wan Lee of all creatures! Wan Lee, whose silent, stolid, mechanical performance of a pirate's duties—a perfect imitation like all his household work—had been their one delight and fascination!

It was just after the exciting capture of a merchantman, with the indiscriminate slaughter of all on board,—a spectacle on which the round blue eyes of the plump Polly had gazed with royal and maternal tolerance,—and they were burying the booty, two tablespoons and a thimble, in the corner of the closet, when Wan Lee stolidly rose.

"Melican boy pleenty foolee! Melican boy no Pilat!" said the little Chinaman, substituting "l's" for "r's" after his usual fashion.

"Wotcher say?" said Hickory, reddening with sudden confusion.

"Melican boy's papa heap lickee him—s'pose him leal Pilat," continued Wan Lee doggedly. "Melican boy Pilat INSIDE housee. Chinee boy Pilat OUTSIDE housee. First chop Pilat."

Staggered by this humiliating statement, Hickory recovered himself in character. "Ah! Ho!" he shrieked, dancing wildly on one leg, "Mutiny and Splordinashun! 'Way with him to the yard-arm."

"Yald-alm—heap foolee! Alee same clothes-horse for washee washee."

It was here necessary for the Pirate Queen to assert her authority, which, as I have before stated, was somewhat confusingly maternal.

"Go to bed instantly without your supper," she said seriously. "Really, I never saw such bad pirates. Say your prayers, and see that you're up early to church tomorrow."

It should be explained that in deference to Polly's proficiency as a preacher, and probably as a relief to their uneasy consciences, Divine Service had always been held on the Island. But Wan Lee continued:—

"Me no shabbee Pilat INSIDE housee; me shabbee Pilat OUTSIDE housee. S'pose you lun away longside Chinee boy—Chinee boy make you Pilat."

Hickory softly scratched his leg; while a broad, bashful smile almost closed his small eyes. "Wot?" he asked.

"Mebbe you too flightened to lun away. Melican boy's papa heap lickee."

This last infamous suggestion fired the corsair's blood. "Dy'ar think we daresen't?" said Hickory desperately, but with an uneasy glance at Polly. "I'll show yer to-morrow."

The entrance of Polly's mother at this moment put an end to Polly's authority and dispersed the pirate band, but left Wan Lee's proposal and Hickory's rash acceptance ringing in the ears of the Pirate Queen. That evening she was unusually silent. She would have taken Bridget, her nurse, into her confidence, but this would have involved a long explanation of her own feelings, from which, like all imaginative children, she shrank. She, however, made preparation for the proposed flight by settling in her mind which of her two dolls she would take. A wooden creature with easy-going knees and movable hair seemed to be more fit for hard service and any indiscriminate scalping that might turn up hereafter. At supper, she timidly asked a question of Bridget. "Did ye ever hear the loikes uv that, ma'am?" said the Irish handmaid with affectionate pride. "Shure the darlint's head is filled noight and day with ancient history. She's after asking me now if Queens ever run away!" To Polly's remorseful confusion here her good father, equally proud of her precocious interest and his own knowledge, at once interfered with an unintelligible account of the abdication of various queens in history until Polly's head ached again. Well meant as it was, it only settled in the child's mind that she must keep the awful secret to herself and that no one could understand her.

The eventful day dawned without any unusual sign of importance. It was one of the cloudless summer days of the Californian foothills, bright, dry, and, as the morning advanced, hot in the white sunshine. The actual, prosaic house in which the Pirates apparently lived was a mile from a mining settlement on a beautiful ridge of pine woods sloping gently towards a valley on the one side, and on the other falling abruptly into a dark deep olive gulf of pine-trees, rocks, and patches of red soil. Beautiful as the slope was, looking over to the distant snow peaks which seemed to be in another world than theirs, the children found a greater attraction in the fascinating depths of a mysterious gulf, or canyon, as it was called, whose very name filled their ears with a weird music. To creep to the edge of the cliff, to sit upon the brown branches of some fallen pine, and, putting aside the dried tassels, to look down upon the backs of wheeling hawks that seemed to hang in mid-air was a never-failing delight. Here Polly would try to trace the winding red ribbon of road that was continually losing itself among the dense pines of the opposite mountains; here she would listen to the far-off strokes of a woodman's axe, or the rattle of some heavy wagon, miles away, crossing the pebbles of a dried-up watercourse. Here, too, the prevailing colors of the mountains, red and white and green, most showed themselves. There were no frowning rocks to depress the children's fancy, but everywhere along the ridge pure white quartz bared itself through the red earth like smiling teeth; the very pebbles they played with were streaked with shining mica like bits of looking-glass. The distance was always green and summer-like, but the color they most loved, and which was most familiar to them, was the dark red of the ground beneath their feet everywhere. It showed itself in the roadside bushes; its red dust pervaded the leaves of the overhanging laurel; it colored their shoes and pinafores; I am afraid it was often seen in Indian-like patches on their faces and hands. That it may have often given a sanguinary tone to their fancies I have every reason to believe.

It was on this ridge that the three children gathered at ten o'clock that morning. An earlier flight had been impossible on account of Wan Lee being obliged to perform his regular duty of blacking the shoes of Polly and Hickory before breakfast,—a menial act which in the pure republic of childhood was never thought inconsistent with the loftiest piratical ambition. On the ridge they met one "Patsey," the son of a neighbor, sun-burned, broad-brimmed hatted, red-handed, like themselves. As there were afterwards some doubts expressed whether he joined the Pirates of his own free will, or was captured by them, I endeavor to give the colloquy exactly as it occurred:—

Patsey: "Hallo, fellers."

The Pirates: "Hello!"

Patsey: "Goin' to hunt bars? Dad seed a lot o' tracks at sun-up."

The Pirates (hesitating): "No—o—"

Patsey: "I am; know where I kin get a six-shooter?"

The Pirates (almost ready to abandon piracy for bear-hunting, but preserving their dignity): "Can't! We've runn'd away for real pirates."

Patsey: "Not for good!"

The Queen (interposing with sad dignity and real tears in her round blue eyes): "Yes!" (slowly and shaking her head). "Can't go back again. Never! Never! Never! The—the—eye is cast!"

Patsey (bursting with excitement): "No-o! Sho'o! Wanter know."

The Pirates (a little frightened themselves, but tremulous with gratified vanity): "The Perleese is on our track!"

Patsey: "Lemme go with yer!"

Hickory: "Wot'll yer giv?"

Patsey: "Pistol and er bananer."

Hickory (with judicious prudence): "Let's see 'em."

Patsey was off like a shot; his bare little red feet trembling under him. In a few minutes he returned with an old-fashioned revolver known as one of "Allen's pepper-boxes" and a large banana. He was at once enrolled, and the banana eaten.

As yet they had resolved on no definite nefarious plan. Hickory, looking down at Patsey's bare feet, instantly took off his own shoes. This bold act sent a thrill through his companions. Wan Lee took off his cloth leggings, Polly removed her shoes and stockings, but, with royal foresight, tied them up in her handkerchief. The last link between them and civilization was broken.

"Let's go to the Slumgullion."

"Slumgullion" was the name given by the miners to a certain soft, half-liquid mud, formed of the water and finely powdered earth that was carried off by the sluice-boxes during gold-washing, and eventually collected in a broad pool or lagoon before the outlet. There was a pool of this kind a quarter of a mile away, where there were "diggings" worked by Patsey's father, and thither they proceeded along the ridge in single file. When it was reached they solemnly began to wade in its viscid paint-like shallows. Possibly its unctuousness was pleasant to the touch; possibly there was a fascination in the fact that their parents had forbidden them to go near it, but probably the principal object of this performance was to produce a thick coating of mud on the feet and ankles, which, when dried in the sun, was supposed to harden the skin and render their shoes superfluous. It was also felt to be the first real step towards independence; they looked down at their ensanguined extremities and recognized the impossibility of their ever again crossing (unwashed) the family threshold.

Then they again hesitated. There was a manifest need of some well-defined piratical purpose. The last act was reckless and irretrievable, but it was vague. They gazed at each other. There was a stolid look of resigned and superior tolerance in Wan Lee's eyes.

Polly's glance wandered down the side of the slope to the distant little tunnels or openings made by the miners who were at work in the bowels of the mountain. "I'd like to go into one of them funny holes," she said to herself, half aloud.

Wan Lee suddenly began to blink his eyes with unwonted excitement. "Catchee tunnel—heap gold," he said quickly. "When manee come outside to catchee dinner—Pilats go inside catchee tunnel! Shabbee! Pilats catchee gold allee samee Melican man!"

"And take perseshiun," said Hickory.

"And hoist the Pirate flag," said Patsey.

"And build a fire, and cook, and have a family," said Polly.

The idea was fascinating to the point of being irresistible. The eyes of the four children became rounder and rounder. They seized each other's hands and swung them backwards and forwards, occasionally lifting their legs in a solemn rhythmic movement known only to childhood.

"It's orful far off!" said Patsey with a sudden look of dark importance. "Pap says it's free miles on the road. Take all day ter get there."

The bright faces were overcast.

"Less go down er slide!" said Hickory boldly.

They approached the edge of the cliff. The "slide" was simply a sharp incline zigzagging down the side of the mountain used for sliding goods and provisions from the summit to the tunnel-men at the different openings below. The continual traffic had gradually worn a shallow gully half filled with earth and gravel into the face of the mountain which checked the momentum of the goods in their downward passage, but afforded no foothold for a pedestrian. No one had ever been known to descend a slide. That feat was evidently reserved for the Pirate band. They approached the edge of the slide, hand in hand, hesitated, and the next moment disappeared.

Five minutes later the tunnel-men of the Excelsior mine, a mile below, taking their luncheon on the rude platform of debris before their tunnel, were suddenly driven to shelter in the tunnel from an apparent rain of stones, and rocks, and pebbles, from the cliffs above. Looking up, they were startled at seeing four round objects revolving and bounding in the dust of the slide, which eventually resolved themselves into three boys and a girl. For a moment the good men held their breath in helpless terror. Twice one of the children had struck the outer edge of the bank, and displaced stones that shot a thousand feet down into the dizzy depths of the valley; and now one of them, the girl, had actually rolled out of the slide and was hanging over the chasm supported only by a clump of chamisal to which she clung!

"Hang on by your eyelids, sis! but don't stir, for Heaven's sake!" shouted one of the men, as two others started on a hopeless ascent of the cliff above them.

But a light childish laugh from the clinging little figure seemed to mock them! Then two small heads appeared at the edge of the slide; then a diminutive figure, whose feet were apparently held by some invisible companion, was shoved over the brink and stretched its tiny arms towards the girl. But in vain, the distance was too great. Another laugh of intense youthful enjoyment followed the failure, and a new insecurity was added to the situation by the unsteady hands and shoulders of the relieving party, who were apparently shaking with laughter. Then the extended figure was seen to detach what looked like a small black rope from its shoulders and throw it to the girl. There was another little giggle. The faces of the men below paled in terror. Then Polly,—for it was she,—hanging to the long pigtail of Wan Lee, was drawn with fits of laughter back in safety to the slide. Their childish treble of appreciation was answered by a ringing cheer from below.

"Darned ef I ever want to cut off a Chinaman's pigtail again, boys," said one of the tunnel-men as he went back to dinner.

Meantime the children had reached the goal and stood before the opening of one of the tunnels. Then these four heroes who had looked with cheerful levity on the deadly peril of their descent became suddenly frightened at the mysterious darkness of the cavern and turned pale at its threshold.

"Mebbee a wicked Joss backside holee, he catchee Pilats," said Wan Lee gravely.

Hickory began to whimper, Patsey drew back, Polly alone stood her ground, albeit with a trembling lip.

"Let's say our prayers and frighten it away," she said stoutly.

"No! no!" said Wan Lee, with a sudden alarm. "No frighten Spillits! You waitee! Chinee boy he talkee Spillit not to frighten you." *

* *The Chinese pray devoutly to the Evil Spirits NOT to injure them.*

Tucking his hands under his blue blouse, Wan Lee suddenly produced from some mysterious recess of his clothing a quantity of red paper slips which he scattered at the entrance of the cavern. Then drawing from the same inexhaustible receptacle certain squibs or fireworks, he let them off and threw them into the opening. There they went off with a slight fizz and splutter, a momentary glittering of small points in the darkness, and a strong smell of gunpowder. Polly gazed at the spectacle with undisguised awe and fascination. Hickory and Patsey breathed hard with satisfaction: it was beyond their wildest dreams of mystery and romance. Even Wan Lee appeared transfigured into a superior being by the potency of his own spells. But an unaccountable disturbance of some kind in the dim interior of the tunnel quickly drew the blood from their blanched cheeks again. It was a sound like coughing, followed by something like an oath.

"He's made the Evil Spirit orful sick," said Hickory in a loud whisper.

A slight laugh, that to the children seemed demoniacal, followed.

"See!" said Wan Lee. "Evil Spillet he likee Chinee; try talkee him."

The Pirates looked at Wan Lee, not without a certain envy of this manifest favoritism. A fearful desire to continue their awful experiments, instead of pursuing their piratical avocations, was taking possession of them; but Polly, with one of the swift transitions of childhood, immediately began to extemporize a house for the party at the mouth of the tunnel, and, with parental foresight, gathered the fragments of the squibs to build a fire for supper. That frugal meal, consisting of half a ginger biscuit divided into five small portions, each served on a chip of wood, and having a deliciously mysterious flavor of gunpowder and smoke, was soon over. It was necessary after this that the pirates should at once seek repose after a day of adventure, which they did for the space of forty seconds in singularly impossible attitudes and far too aggressive snoring. Indeed, Master Hickory's almost upright pose, with tightly folded arms and darkly frowning brows, was felt to be dramatic, but impossible for a longer period. The brief interval enabled Polly to collect herself and to look around her in her usual motherly fashion. Suddenly she started and uttered a cry. In the excitement of the descent she had quite overlooked her doll, and was now regarding it with round-eyed horror.

"Lady Mary's hair's gone!" she cried, convulsively grasping the Pirate Hickory's legs.

Hickory at once recognized the battered doll under the aristocratic title which Polly had long ago bestowed upon it. He stared at the bald and battered head.

"Ha! ha!" he said hoarsely; "skelped by Injins!"

For an instant the delicious suggestion soothed the imaginative Polly. But it was quickly dispelled by Wan Lee.

"Lady Maley's pigtail hangee top side hillee. Catchee on big quartz stone allee same Polly; me go fetchee."

"No!" quickly shrieked the others. The prospect of being left in the proximity of Wan Lee's evil spirit, without Wan Lee's exorcising power, was anything but reassuring. "No, don't go!" Even Polly (dropping a maternal tear on the bald head of Lady Mary) protested against this breaking up of the little circle. "Go to bed!" she said authoritatively, "and sleep till morning."

Thus admonished, the Pirates again retired. This time effectively; for, worn by actual fatigue or soothed by the delicious coolness of the cave, they gradually, one by one, succumbed to real slumber. Polly, withheld from joining them by official and maternal responsibility, sat and blinked at them affectionately.

Gradually she, too, felt herself yielding to the fascination and mystery of the place and the solitude that encompassed her. Beyond the pleasant shadows where she sat, she saw the great world of mountain and valley through a dreamy haze that seemed to rise from the depths below and occasionally hang before the cavern like a veil. Long waves of spicy heat rolling up the mountain from the valley brought her the smell of pine-trees and bay, and made the landscape swim before her eyes. She could hear the far-off cry of teamsters on some unseen road; she could see the far-off cloud of dust following the mountain stagecoach, whose rattling wheels she could not hear. She felt very lonely, but was not quite afraid; she felt very melancholy, but was not entirely sad; and she could have easily awakened her sleeping companions if she wished.

No; she was a lone widow with nine children, six of whom were already in the lone churchyard on the hill, and the others lying ill with measles and scarlet fever beside her. She had just walked many weary miles that day, and had often begged from door to door for a slice of bread for the starving little ones. It was of no use now—they would die! They would never see their dear mother again. This was a favorite imaginative situation of Polly's, but only indulged when her companions were asleep, partly because she could not trust confederates with her more serious fancies, and partly because they were at such times passive in her hands. She glanced timidly around. Satisfied that no one could observe her, she softly visited the bedside of each of her companions, and administered from a purely fictitious bottle spoonfuls of invisible medicine. Physical correction in the form of slight taps, which they always required, and in which Polly was strong, was only withheld now from a sense of their weak condition. But in vain; they succumbed to the fell disease,—they always died at this juncture,—and Polly was left alone. She thought of the little church where she had once seen a funeral, and remembered the nice smell of the flowers; she dwelt with melancholy satisfaction of the nine little tombstones in the graveyard, each with an inscription, and looked forward with gentle anticipation to the long summer days when, with Lady Mary in her lap, she would sit on those graves clad in the deepest mourning. The fact that the unhappy victims at times moved as it were uneasily in their graves, or snored, did not affect Polly's imaginative contemplation, nor withhold the tears that gathered in her round eyes.

Presently, the lids of the round eyes began to droop, the landscape beyond began to be more confused, and sometimes to disappear entirely and reappear again with startling distinctness. Then a sound of rippling water from the little stream that flowed from the mouth of the tunnel soothed her and seemed to carry her away with it, and then everything was dark.

The next thing that she remembered was that she was apparently being carried along on some gliding object to the sound of rippling water. She was not alone, for her three companions were lying beside her, rather tightly packed and squeezed in the same mysterious vehicle. Even in the profound darkness that surrounded her, Polly could feel and hear that they were accompanied, and once or twice a faint streak of light from the side of the tunnel showed her gigantic shadows walking slowly on either side of the gliding car. She felt the little hands of her associates seeking hers, and knew they were awake and conscious, and she returned to each a reassuring pressure from the large protecting instinct of her maternal little heart. Presently the car glided into an open space of bright light, and stopped. The transition from the darkness of the tunnel at first dazzled their eyes. It was like a dream.

They were in a circular cavern from which three other tunnels, like the one they had passed through, diverged. The walls, lit up by fifty or sixty candles stuck at irregular intervals in crevices of the rock, were of glittering quartz and mica. But more remarkable than all were the inmates of the cavern, who were ranged round the walls,—men who, like their attendants, seemed to be of extra stature; who had blackened faces, wore red bandana handkerchiefs round their heads and their waists, and carried enormous knives and pistols stuck in their belts. On a raised platform made of a packing-box on which was rudely painted a skull and cross-bones, sat the chief or leader of the band covered with a buffalo robe; on either side of him were two small barrels marked "Grog" and "Gunpowder." The children stared and clung closer to Polly. Yet, in spite of these desperate and warlike accessories, the strangers bore a singular resemblance to "Christy Minstrels" in their blackened faces and attitudes that somehow made them seem less awful. In particular, Polly was impressed with the fact that even the most ferocious had a certain kindliness of eye, and showed their teeth almost idiotically.

"Welcome!" said the leader,—"welcome to the Pirates' Cave! The Red Rover of the North Fork of the Stanislaus River salutes the Queen of the Pirate Isle!" He rose up and made an extraordinary bow. It was repeated by the others with more or less exaggeration, to the point of one humorist losing his balance!

"Oh, thank you very much," said Polly timidly, but drawing her little flock closer to her with a small protecting arm; "but could you—would you—please—tell us—what time it is?"

"We are approaching the middle of Next Week," said the leader gravely; "but what of that? Time is made for slaves! The Red Rover seeks it not! Why should the Queen?"

"I think we must be going," hesitated Polly, yet by no means displeased with the recognition of her rank.

"Not until we have paid homage to Your Majesty," returned the leader. "What ho! there! Let Brother Step-and-Fetch-It pass the Queen around that we may do her honor." Observing that Polly shrank slightly back, he added: "Fear nothing; the man who hurts a hair of Her Majesty's head dies by this hand. Ah! ha!"

The others all said ha! ha! and danced alternately on one leg and then on the other, but always with the same dark resemblance to Christy Minstrels. Brother Step-and-Fetch-It, whose very long beard had a confusing suggestion of being a part of the leader's buffalo robe, lifted her gently in his arms and carried her to the Red Rovers in turn. Each one bestowed a kiss upon her cheek or forehead, and would have taken her in his arms, or on his knees, or otherwise lingered over his salute, but they were sternly restrained by their leader. When the solemn rite was concluded, Step-and-Fetch-It paid his own courtesy with an extra squeeze of the curly head, and deposited her again in the truck, a little frightened, a little astonished, but with a considerable accession to her dignity. Hickory and Patsey looked on with stupefied amazement. Wan Lee alone remained stolid and unimpressed, regarding the scene with calm and triangular eyes.

"Will Your Majesty see the Red Rovers dance?"

"No, if you please," said Polly, with gentle seriousness.

"Will Your Majesty fire this barrel of gunpowder, or tap this breaker of grog?"

"No, I thank you."

"Is there no command Your Majesty would lay upon us?"

"No, please," said Polly, in a failing voice.

"Is there anything Your Majesty has lost? Think again! Will Your Majesty deign to cast your royal eyes on this?"

He drew from under his buffalo robe what seemed like a long tress of blond hair, and held it aloft. Polly instantly recognized the missing scalp of her hapless doll.

"If you please, sir, it's Lady Mary's. She's lost it."

"And lost it—Your Majesty—only to find something more precious. Would Your Majesty hear the story?"

A little alarmed, a little curious, a little self-anxious, and a little induced by the nudges and pinches of her companions, the Queen blushingly signified her royal assent.

"Enough. Bring refreshments. Will Your Majesty prefer wintergreen, peppermint, rose, or acidulated drops? Red or white? Or perhaps Your Majesty will let me recommend these bull's-eyes," said the leader, as a collection of sweets in a hat were suddenly produced from the barrel labeled "Gunpowder" and handed to the children.

"Listen," he continued, in a silence broken only by the gentle sucking of bull's-eyes. "Many years ago the old Red Rovers of these parts locked up all their treasures in a secret cavern in this mountain. They used spells and magic to keep it from being entered or found by anybody, for there was a certain mark upon it made by a peculiar rock that stuck out of it, which signified what there was below. Long afterwards, other Red Rovers who had heard of it came here and spent days and days trying to discover it, digging holes and blasting tunnels like this, but of no use! Sometimes they thought they discovered the magic marks in the peculiar rock that stuck out of it, but when they dug there they found no treasure. And why? Because there was a magic spell upon it. And what was that magic spell? Why, this! It could only be discovered by a person who could not possibly know that he or she had discovered it; who never could or would be able to enjoy it; who could never see it, never feel it, never, in fact, know anything at all about it! It wasn't a dead man, it wasn't an animal, it wasn't a baby!"

"Why," said Polly, jumping up and clapping her hands, "it was a Dolly."

"Your Majesty's head is level! Your Majesty has guessed it!" said the leader, gravely. "It was Your Majesty's own dolly, Lady Mary, who broke the spell! When Your Majesty came down the slide, the doll fell from your gracious hand when your foot slipped. Your Majesty recovered Lady Mary, but did not observe that her hair had caught in a peculiar rock, called the 'Outcrop,' and remained behind! When, later on, while sitting with your attendants at the mouth of the tunnel, Your Majesty discovered that Lady Mary's hair was gone, I overheard Your Majesty, and dispatched the trusty Step-and-Fetch-It to seek it at the mountain side. He did so, and found it clinging to the rock, and beneath it—the entrance to the Secret Cave!"

Patsey and Hickory, who, failing to understand a word of this explanation, had given themselves up to the unconstrained enjoyment of the sweets, began now to apprehend that some change was impending, and prepared for the worst by hastily swallowing what they had in their mouths, thus defying enchantment, and getting ready for speech. Polly, who had closely followed the story, albeit with the embellishments of her own imagination, made her eyes rounder than ever. A bland smile broke on Wan Lee's face, as to the children's amazement, he quietly disengaged himself from the group and stepped before the leader.

"Melican man plenty foolee Melican chillern. No foolee China boy! China boy knowee you. YOU no Led Lofer. YOU no Pilat—you allee same tunnel-man—you Bob Johnson! Me shabbee you! You dressee up allee same as Led Lofer—but you Bob Johnson—allee same. My fader washee washee for you. You no payee him. You owee him folty dolla! Me blingee you billee. You no payee billee! You say, 'Chalkee up, John.' You say, 'Bimeby, John.' But me no catchee folty dolla!"

A roar of laughter followed, in which even the leader apparently forgot himself enough to join. But the next moment springing to his feet he shouted, "Ho! ho! A traitor! Away with him to the deepest dungeon beneath the castle moat!"

Hickory and Patsey began to whimper, but Polly, albeit with a tremulous lip, stepped to the side of her little Pagan friend. "Don't you dare touch him," she said with a shake of unexpected determination in her little curly head; "if you do, I'll tell my father, and he will slay you! All of you—there!"

"Your father! Then you are NOT the Queen!"

It was a sore struggle to Polly to abdicate her royal position; it was harder to do it with befitting dignity. To evade the direct question she was obliged to abandon her defiant attitude. "If you please, sir," she said hurriedly, with an increasing color and no stops, "we're not always Pirates, you know, and Wan Lee is only our boy what brushes my shoes in the morning, and runs of errands, and he doesn't mean anything bad, sir, and we'd like to take him back home with us."

"Enough," said the leader, changing his entire manner with the most sudden and shameless inconsistency. "You shall go back together, and woe betide the miscreant who would prevent it! What say you, brothers? What shall be his fate who dares to separate our noble Queen from her faithful Chinese henchman?"

"He shall die!" roared the others, with beaming cheerfulness.

"And what say you—shall we see them home?"

"We will!" roared the others.

Before the children could fairly comprehend what had passed, they were again lifted into the truck and began to glide back into the tunnel they had just quitted. But not again in darkness and silence; the entire band of Red rovers accompanied them, illuminating the dark passage with the candles they had snatched from the walls. In a few moments they were at the entrance again. The great world lay beyond them once more with rocks and valleys suffused by the rosy light of the setting sun. The past seemed like a dream.

But were they really awake now? They could not tell. They accepted everything with the confidence and credulity of all children who have no experience to compare with their first impressions and to whom the future contains nothing impossible. It was without surprise, therefore, that they felt themselves lifted on the shoulders of the men who were making quite a procession along the steep trail towards the settlement again. Polly noticed that at the mouth of the other tunnels they were greeted by men as if they were carrying tidings of great joy; that they stopped to rejoice together, and that in some mysterious manner their conductors had got their faces washed, and had become more like beings of the outer world. When they neared the settlement the excitement seemed to have become greater; people rushed out to shake hands with the men who were carrying them, and overpowered even the children with questions they could not understand. Only one sentence Polly could clearly remember as being the burden of all congratulations. "Struck the old lead at last!" With a faint consciousness that she knew something about it, she tried to assume a dignified attitude on the leader's shoulders, even while she was beginning to be heavy with sleep.

And then she remembered a crowd near her father's house, out of which her father came smiling pleasantly on her, but not interfering with her triumphal progress until the leader finally deposited her in her mother's lap in their own sitting-room. And then she remembered being "cross," and declining to answer any questions, and shortly afterwards found herself comfortably in bed. Then she heard her mother say to her father:—

"It really seems too ridiculous for anything, John; the idea of those grown men dressing themselves up to play with children."

"Ridiculous or not," said her father, "these grown men of the Excelsior mine have just struck the famous old lode of Red Mountain, which is as good as a fortune to everybody on the Ridge, and were as wild as boys! And they say it never would have been found if Polly hadn't tumbled over the slide directly on top of the outcrop, and left the absurd wig of that wretched doll of hers to mark its site."

"And that," murmured Polly sleepily to her doll as she drew it closer to her breast, "is all that they know of it."

# THE CORAL ISLAND

R.M. BALLANTYNE

# I

## BEGINNING—MY EARLY LIFE AND CHARACTER—I THIRST FOR ADVENTURE IN FOREIGN LANDS, AND GO TO SEA.

Roving has always been, and still is, my ruling passion, the joy of my heart, the very sunshine of my existence. In childhood, in boyhood, and in man's estate I have been a rover; not a mere rambler among the woody glens and upon the hill-tops of my own native land, but an enthusiastic rover throughout the length and breadth of the wide, wide world.

It was a wild, black night of howling storm, the night on which I was born on the foaming bosom of the broad Atlantic Ocean. My father was a sea-captain; my grandfather was a sea-captain; my great-grandfather had been a marine. Nobody could tell positively what occupation *his* father had followed; but my dear mother used to assert that he had been a midshipman, whose grandfather, on the mother's side, had been an admiral in the Royal Navy. At any rate, we knew that as far back as our family could be traced, it had been intimately connected with the great watery waste. Indeed, this was the case on both sides of the house; for my mother always went to sea with my father on his long voyages, and so spent the greater part of her life upon the water.

Thus it was, I suppose, that I came to inherit a roving disposition. Soon after I was born, my father, being old, retired from a seafaring life, purchased a small cottage in a fishing village on the west coast of England, and settled down to spend the evening of his life on the shores of that sea which had for so many years been his home. It was not long after this that I began to show the roving spirit that dwelt within me. For some time past my infant legs had been gaining strength, so that I came to be dissatisfied with rubbing the skin off my chubby knees by walking on them, and made many attempts to stand up and walk like a man—all of which attempts, however, resulted in my sitting down violently and in sudden surprise. One day I took advantage of my dear mother's absence to make another effort; and, to my joy, I actually succeeded in reaching the doorstep, over which I tumbled into a pool of muddy water that lay before my father's cottage door. Ah, how vividly I remember the horror of my poor mother when she found me sweltering in the mud amongst a group of cackling ducks, and the tenderness with which she stripped off my dripping clothes and washed my dirty little body! From this time forth my rambles became more frequent and, as I grew older, more distant, until at last I had wandered far and near on the shore and in the woods around our humble dwelling, and did not rest content until my father bound me apprentice to a coasting-vessel and let me go to sea.

For some years I was happy in visiting the seaports, and in coasting along the shores, of my native land. My Christian name was Ralph; and my comrades added to this the name of Rover, in consequence of the passion which I always evinced for travelling. Rover was not my real name; but as I never received any other, I came at last to answer to it as naturally as to my proper name. And as it is not a bad one, I see no good reason why I should not introduce myself to the reader as Ralph Rover. My shipmates were kind, good-natured fellows, and they and I got on very well together. They did, indeed, very frequently make game of and banter me, but not unkindly; and I overheard them sometimes saying that Ralph Rover was a "queer, old-fashioned fellow." This, I must confess, surprised me much; and I pondered the saying long, but could come at no satisfactory conclusion as to that wherein my old-fashionedness lay. It is true I was a quiet lad, and seldom spoke except when spoken to. Moreover, I never could understand the jokes of my companions even when they were explained to me, which dulness in apprehension occasioned me much grief. However, I tried to make up for it by smiling and looking pleased when I observed that they were laughing at some witticism which I had failed to detect. I was also very fond of inquiring into the nature of things and their causes, and often fell into fits of abstraction while thus engaged in my mind. But in all this I saw nothing that did not seem to be exceedingly natural, and could by no means understand why my comrades should call me "an old-fashioned fellow."

Now, while engaged in the coasting trade I fell in with many seamen who had travelled to almost every quarter of the globe; and I freely confess that my heart glowed ardently within me as they recounted their wild adventures in foreign lands—the dreadful storms they had weathered, the appalling dangers they had escaped, the wonderful creatures they had seen both on the land and in the sea, and the interesting lands and strange people they had visited. But of all the places of which they told me, none captivated and charmed my imagination so much as the Coral Islands of the Southern Seas. They told me of thousands of beautiful, fertile islands that had been formed by a small creature called the coral insect, where summer reigned nearly all the year round, where the trees were laden with a constant harvest of luxuriant fruit, where the climate was almost perpetually delightful; yet where, strange to say, men were wild, bloodthirsty savages, excepting in those favoured isles to which the Gospel of our Saviour had been conveyed. These exciting accounts had so great an effect upon my mind that, when I reached the age of fifteen, I resolved to make a voyage to the South Seas.

I had no little difficulty, at first, in prevailing on my dear parents to let me go; but when I urged on my father that he would never have become a great captain had he remained in the coasting trade, he saw the truth of what I said and gave his consent. My dear mother, seeing that my father had made up his mind, no longer offered opposition to my wishes. "But, oh Ralph!" she said on the day I bade her adieu, "come back soon to us, my dear boy; for we are getting old now, Ralph, and may not have many years to live."

I will not take up my readers' time with a minute account of all that occurred before I took my final leave of my dear parents. Suffice it to say that my father placed me under the charge of an old messmate of his own, a merchant captain, who was on the point of sailing to the South Seas in his own ship, the *Arrow*. My mother gave me her blessing and a small Bible; and her last request was that I would never forget to read a chapter every day and say my prayers, which I promised, with tears in my eyes, that I would certainly do.

Soon afterwards I went on board the *Arrow*, which was a fine, large ship, and set sail for the islands of the Pacific Ocean.

## ❧ 2 ❧

## THE DEPARTURE—THE SEA—MY COMPANIONS—SOME ACCOUNT OF THE WONDERFUL SIGHTS WE SAW ON THE GREAT DEEP—A DREADFUL STORM AND A FRIGHTFUL WRECK.

It was a bright, beautiful, warm day when our ship spread her canvas to the breeze and sailed for the regions of the south. Oh, how my heart bounded with delight as I listened to the merry chorus of the sailors while they hauled at the ropes and got in the anchor! The captain shouted; the men ran to obey; the noble ship bent over to the breeze, and the shore gradually faded from my view; while I stood looking on, with a kind of feeling that the whole was a delightful dream.

The first thing that struck me as being different from anything I had yet seen during my short career on the sea, was the hoisting of the anchor on deck and lashing it firmly down with ropes, as if we had now bid adieu to the land for ever and would require its services no more.

"There, lass!" cried a broad-shouldered jack-tar, giving the fluke of the anchor a hearty slap with his hand after the housing was completed—"there, lass, take a good nap now, for we sha'n't ask you to kiss the mud again for many a long day to come!"

And so it was. That anchor did not "kiss the mud" for many long days afterwards; and when at last it did, it was for the last time!

There were a number of boys in the ship, but two of them were my special favourites. Jack Martin was a tall, strapping, broad-shouldered youth of eighteen, with a handsome, good-humoured, firm face. He had had a good education, was clever and hearty and lion-like in his actions, but mild and quiet in disposition. Jack was a general favourite, and had a peculiar fondness for me. My other companion was Peterkin Gay. He was little, quick, funny, decidedly mischievous, and about fourteen years old. But Peterkin's mischief was almost always harmless, else he could not have been so much beloved as he was.

"Hallo, youngster!" cried Jack Martin, giving me a slap on the shoulder the day I joined the ship, "come below and I'll show you your berth. You and I are to be messmates; and I think we shall be good friends, for I like the look o' you."

Jack was right. He and I, and Peterkin afterwards, became the best and staunchest friends that ever tossed together on the stormy waves.

I shall say little about the first part of our voyage. We had the usual amount of rough weather and calm; also we saw many strange fish rolling in the sea, and I was greatly delighted one day by seeing a shoal of flying-fish dart out of the water and skim through the air about a foot above the surface. They were pursued by dolphins, which feed on them; and one flying-fish, in its terror, flew over the ship, struck on the rigging, and fell upon the deck. Its wings were just fins elongated; and we found that they could never fly far at a time, and never mounted into the air like birds, but skimmed along the surface of the sea. Jack and I had it for dinner, and found it remarkably good.

When we approached Cape Horn, at the southern extremity of America, the weather became very cold and stormy, and the sailors began to tell stories about the furious gales and the dangers of that terrible cape.

"Cape Horn," said one, "is the most horrible headland I ever doubled. I've sailed round it twice already, and both times the ship was a'most blow'd out o' the water."

"I've been round it once," said another; "an' that time the sails were split, and the ropes frozen in the blocks so that they wouldn't work, and we wos all but lost."

"An' I've been round it five times," cried a third; "an' every time wos wuss than another, the gales wos so tree-mendous!"

"And I've been round it, no times at all," cried Peterkin with an impudent wink in his eye, "an' that time I wos blow'd inside out!"

Nevertheless we passed the dreaded cape without much rough weather, and in the course of a few weeks afterwards were sailing gently, before a warm tropical breeze, over the Pacific Ocean. Thus we proceeded on our voyage—sometimes bounding merrily before a fair breeze; at other times floating calmly on the glassy wave and fishing for the curious inhabitants of the deep, all of which, although the sailors thought little of them, were strange, and interesting, and very wonderful to me.

At last we came among the Coral Islands of the Pacific; and I shall never forget the delight with which I gazed—when we chanced to pass one—at the pure white, dazzling shores, and the verdant palm-trees, which looked bright and beautiful in the sunshine. And often did we three long to be landed on one, imagining that we should certainly find perfect happiness there! Our wish was granted sooner than we expected.

One night, soon after we entered the tropics, an awful storm burst upon our ship. The first squall of wind carried away two of our masts, and left only the foremast standing. Even this, however, was more than enough, for we did not dare to hoist a rag of sail on it. For five days the tempest raged in all its fury. Everything was swept off the decks, except one small boat. The steersman was lashed to the wheel lest he should be washed away, and we all gave ourselves up for lost. The captain said that he had no idea where we were, as we had been blown far out of our course; and we feared much that we might get among the dangerous coral reefs which are so numerous in the Pacific. At daybreak on the sixth morning of the gale we saw land ahead; it was an island encircled by a reef of coral, on which the waves broke in fury. There was calm water within this reef, but we could see only one narrow opening into it. For this opening we steered; but ere we reached it a tremendous wave broke on our stern, tore the rudder completely off, and left us at the mercy of the winds and waves.

"It's all over with us now, lads!" said the captain to the men. "Get the boat ready to launch; we shall be on the rocks in less than half-an-hour."

The men obeyed in gloomy silence, for they felt that there was little hope of so small a boat living in such a sea.

"Come, boys," said Jack Martin, in a grave tone, to me and Peterkin, as we stood on the quarter-deck awaiting our fate—"come, boys; we three shall stick together. You see it is impossible that the little boat can reach the shore, crowded with men. It will be sure to upset, so I mean rather to trust myself to a large oar. I see through the telescope that the ship will strike at the tail of the reef, where the waves break into the quiet water inside; so if we manage to cling to the oar till it is driven over the breakers, we may perhaps gain the shore. What say you? Will you join me?"

We gladly agreed to follow Jack, for he inspired us with confidence—although I could perceive, by the sad tone of his voice, that he had little hope; and indeed, when I looked at the white waves that lashed the reef and boiled against the rocks as if in fury, I felt that there was but a step between us and death. My heart sank within me; but at that moment my thoughts turned to my beloved mother, and I remembered those words, which were among the last that she said to me: "Ralph, my dearest child, always remember, in the hour of danger, to look to your Lord and Saviour Jesus Christ. He alone is both able and willing to save your body and your soul." So I felt much comforted when I thought thereon.

The ship was now very near the rocks. The men were ready with the boat, and the captain beside them giving orders, when a tremendous wave came towards us. We three ran towards the bow to lay hold of our oar, and had barely reached it when the wave fell on the deck with a crash like thunder. At the same moment the ship struck; the foremast broke off close to the deck and went over the side, carrying the boat and men along with it. Our oar got entangled with the wreck, and Jack seized an axe to cut it free; but owing to the motion of the ship, he missed the cordage and struck the axe deep into the oar. Another wave, however, washed it clear of the wreck. We all seized hold of it, and the next instant we were struggling in the wild sea. The last thing I saw was the boat whirling in the surf, and all the sailors tossed into the foaming waves. Then I became insensible.

On recovering from my swoon I found myself lying on a bank of soft grass, under shelter of an overhanging rock, with Peterkin on his knees by my side, tenderly bathing my temples with water, and endeavouring to stop the blood that flowed from a wound in my forehead.

## 3

## THE CORAL ISLAND—OUR FIRST COGITATIONS AFTER LANDING AND THE RESULT OF THEM—WE CONCLUDE THAT THE ISLAND IS UNINHABITED.

There is a strange and peculiar sensation experienced in recovering from a state of insensibility which is almost indescribable: a sort of dreamy, confused consciousness; a half-waking, half-sleeping condition, accompanied with a feeling of weariness, which, however, is by no means disagreeable. As I slowly recovered, and heard the voice of Peterkin inquiring whether I felt better, I thought that I must have overslept myself, and should be sent to the masthead for being lazy; but before I could leap up in haste, the thought seemed to vanish suddenly away, and I fancied that I must have been ill. Then a balmy breeze fanned my cheek; and I thought of home, and the garden at the back of my father's cottage with its luxuriant flowers, and the sweet-scented honeysuckle that my dear mother trained so carefully upon the trellised porch. But the roaring of the surf put these delightful thoughts to flight, and I was back again at sea, watching the dolphins and the flying-fish, and reefing topsails off the wild and stormy Cape Horn. Gradually the roar of the surf became louder and more distinct. I thought of being wrecked far, far away from my native land, and slowly opened my eyes to meet those of my companion Jack, who, with a look of intense anxiety, was gazing into my face.

"Speak to us, my dear Ralph!" whispered Jack tenderly. "Are you better now?"

I smiled and looked up, saying, "Better! Why, what do you mean, Jack? I'm quite well."

"Then what are you shamming for, and frightening us in this way?" said Peterkin, smiling through his tears; for the poor boy had been really under the impression that I was dying.

I now raised myself on my elbow, and putting my hand to my forehead, found that it had been cut pretty severely, and that I had lost a good deal of blood.

"Come, come, Ralph," said Jack, pressing me gently backward, "lie down, my boy; you're not right yet. Wet your lips with this water; it's cool and clear as crystal. I got it from a spring close at hand. There, now, don't say a word—hold your tongue," he said, seeing me about to speak. "I'll tell you all about it, but you must not utter a syllable till you have rested well."

"Oh, don't stop him from speaking, Jack!" said Peterkin, who, now that his fears for my safety were removed, busied himself in erecting a shelter of broken branches in order to protect me from the wind—which, however, was almost unnecessary, for the rock beside which I had been laid completely broke the force of the gale. "Let him speak, Jack; it's a comfort to hear that he's alive after lying there stiff and white and sulky for a whole hour, just like an Egyptian mummy.—Never saw such a fellow as you are, Ralph—always up to mischief. You've almost knocked out all my teeth and more than half-choked me, and now you go shamming dead! It's very wicked of you, indeed it is."

While Peterkin ran on in this style my faculties became quite clear again, and I began to understand my position. "What do you mean by saying I half-choked you, Peterkin?" said I.

"What do I mean? Is English not your mother-tongue? or do you want me to repeat it in French by way of making it clearer? Don't you remember?"

"I remember nothing," said I, interrupting him, "after we were thrown into the sea."

"Hush, Peterkin!" said Jack; "you're exciting Ralph with your nonsense.—I'll explain it to you. You recollect that, after the ship struck, we three sprang over the bow into the sea? Well, I noticed that the oar struck your head and gave you that cut on the brow which nearly stunned you, so that you grasped Peterkin round the neck without knowing apparently what you were about. In doing so, you pushed the telescope—which you clung to as if it had been your life—against Peterkin's mouth—"

"Pushed it against his mouth!" interrupted Peterkin; "say crammed it down his throat! Why, there's a distinct mark of the brass rim on the back of my gullet at this moment!"

"Well, well, be that as it may," continued Jack, "you clung to him, Ralph, till I feared you really would choke him. But I saw that he had a good hold of the oar; so I exerted myself to the utmost to push you towards the shore, which we luckily reached without much trouble, for the water inside the reef is quite calm."

"But the captain and crew, what of them?" I inquired anxiously.

Jack shook his head.

"Are they lost?"

"No, they are not lost, I hope; but, I fear, there is not much chance of their being saved. The ship struck at the very tail of the island on which we are cast. When the boat was tossed into the sea it fortunately did not upset, although it shipped a good deal of water, and all the men managed to scramble into it; but before they could get the oars out, the gale carried them past the point and away to leeward of the island. After we landed I saw them endeavouring to pull towards us; but as they had only one pair of oars out of the eight that belonged to the boat, and as the wind was blowing right in their teeth, they gradually lost ground. Then I saw them put about and hoist some sort of sail—a blanket, I fancy, for it was too small for the boat—and in half-an-hour they were out of sight."

"Poor fellows!" I murmured sorrowfully.

"But the more I think about it I've better hope of them," continued Jack in a more cheerful tone. "You see, Ralph, I've read a great deal about these South Sea Islands, and I know that in many places they are scattered about in thousands over the sea, so they're almost sure to fall in with one of them before long."

"I'm sure I hope so," said Peterkin earnestly. "But what has become of the wreck, Jack? I saw you clambering up the rocks there while I was watching Ralph. Did you say she had gone to pieces?"

"No, she has not gone to pieces; but she has gone to the bottom," replied Jack. "As I said before, she struck on the tail of the island and stove in her bow; but the next breaker swung her clear, and she floated away to leeward. The poor fellows in the boat made a hard struggle to reach her, but long before they came near her she filled and went down. It was after she had foundered that I saw them trying to pull to the island."

There was a long silence after Jack had ceased speaking, and I have no doubt that each was revolving in his mind our extraordinary position. For my part, I cannot say that my reflections were very agreeable. I knew that we were on an island, for Jack had said so; but whether it was inhabited or not, I did not know. If it should be inhabited, I felt certain, from all I had heard of South Sea Islanders, that we should be roasted alive and eaten. If it should turn out to be uninhabited, I fancied that we should be starved to death. "Oh," thought I, "if the ship had only struck on the rocks we might have done pretty well, for we could have obtained provisions from her, and tools to enable us to build a shelter; but now—alas! alas! we are lost!" These last words I uttered aloud in my distress.

"Lost, Ralph!" exclaimed Jack, while a smile overspread his hearty countenance. "Saved, you should have said. Your cogitations seem to have taken a wrong road, and led you to a wrong conclusion."

"Do you know what conclusion I have come to?" said Peterkin. "I have made up my mind that it's capital—first-rate—the best thing that ever happened to us, and the most splendid prospect that ever lay before three jolly young tars. We've got an island all to ourselves. We'll take possession in the name of the king. We'll go and enter the service of its black inhabitants. Of course we'll rise, naturally, to the top of affairs: white men always do in savage countries. You shall be king, Jack; Ralph, prime minister; and I shall be—"

"The court-jester," interrupted Jack.

"No," retorted Peterkin; "I'll have no title at all. I shall merely accept a highly responsible situation under government; for you see, Jack, I'm fond of having an enormous salary and nothing to do."

"But suppose there are no natives?"

"Then we'll build a charming villa, and plant a lovely garden round it, stuck all full of the most splendiferous tropical flowers; and we'll farm the land, plant, sow, reap, eat, sleep, and be merry."

"But to be serious," said Jack, assuming a grave expression of countenance—which, I observed, always had the effect of checking Peterkin's disposition to make fun of everything—"we are really in rather an uncomfortable position. If this is a desert island, we shall have to live very much like the wild beasts; for we have not a tool of any kind—not even a knife."

"Yes, we have *that*," said Peterkin, fumbling in his trousers pocket, from which he drew forth a small penknife with only one blade, and that was broken.

"Well, that's better than nothing.—But come," said Jack, rising; "we are wasting our time in *talking* instead of *doing*.—You seem well enough to walk now, Ralph.—Let us see what we have got in our pockets; and then let us climb some hill and ascertain what sort of island we have been cast upon, for, whether good or bad, it seems likely to be our home for some time to come."

# 4

## WE EXAMINE INTO OUR PERSONAL PROPERTY, AND MAKE A HAPPY DISCOVERY—OUR ISLAND DESCRIBED—JACK PROVES HIMSELF TO BE LEARNED AND SAGACIOUS ABOVE HIS FELLOWS—CURIOUS DISCOVERIES—NATURAL LEMONADE!

We now seated ourselves upon a rock, and began to examine into our personal property. When we reached the shore after being wrecked, my companions had taken off part of their clothes and spread them out in the sun to dry; for although the gale was raging fiercely, there was not a single cloud in the bright sky. They had also stripped off most part of my wet clothes and spread them also on the rocks. Having resumed our garments, we now searched all our pockets with the utmost care, and laid their contents out on a flat stone before us; and now that our minds were fully alive to our condition, it was with no little anxiety that we turned our several pockets inside out in order that nothing might escape us. When all was collected together, we found that our worldly goods consisted of the following articles:

First, a small penknife with a single blade, broken off about the middle and very rusty, besides having two or three notches on its edge. (Peterkin said of this, with his usual pleasantry, that it would do for a saw as well as a knife, which was a great advantage.) Second, an old German-silver pencil-case without any lead in it. Third, a piece of whip-cord about six yards long. Fourth, a sailmaker's needle of a small size. Fifth, a ship's telescope, which I happened to have in my hand at the time the ship struck, and which I had clung to firmly all the time I was in the water; indeed, it was with difficulty that Jack got it out of my grasp when I was lying insensible on the shore. I cannot understand why I kept such a firm hold of this telescope. They say that a drowning man will clutch at a straw. Perhaps it may have been some such feeling in me, for I did not know that it was in my hand at the time we were wrecked. However, we felt some pleasure in having it with us now—although we did not see that it could be of much use to us, as the glass at the small end was broken to pieces. Our sixth article was a brass ring which Jack always wore on his little finger. I never understood why he wore it; for Jack was not vain of his appearance, and did not seem to care for ornaments of any kind. Peterkin said, "it was in memory of the girl he left behind him!" But as he never spoke of this girl to either of us, I am inclined to think that Peterkin was either jesting or mistaken. In addition to these articles, we had a little bit of tinder and the clothes on our backs. These last were as follows:

Each of us had on a pair of stout canvas trousers and a pair of sailors' thick shoes. Jack wore a red flannel shirt, a blue jacket, and a red Kilmarnock bonnet or nightcap, besides a pair of worsted socks, and a cotton pocket-handkerchief with sixteen portraits of Lord Nelson printed on it and a union-jack in the middle. Peterkin had on a striped flannel shirt—which he wore outside his trousers and belted round his waist, after the manner of a tunic—and a round black straw hat. He had no jacket, having thrown it off just before we were cast into the sea; but this was not of much consequence, as the climate of the island proved to be extremely mild—so much so, indeed, that Jack and I often preferred to go about without our jackets. Peterkin had also a pair of white cotton socks and a blue handkerchief with white spots all over it. My own costume consisted of a blue flannel shirt, a blue jacket, a black cap, and a pair of worsted socks, besides the shoes and canvas trousers already mentioned. This was all we had, and besides these things we had nothing else; but when we thought of the danger from which we had escaped, and how much worse off we might have been had the ship struck on the reef during the night, we felt very thankful that we were possessed of so much, although, I must confess, we sometimes wished that we had had a little more.

While we were examining these things and talking about them, Jack suddenly started and exclaimed:

"The oar! We have forgotten the oar!"

"What good will that do us?" said Peterkin. "There's wood enough on the island to make a thousand oars."

"Ay, lad," replied Jack; "but there's a bit of hoop-iron at the end of it, and that may be of much use to us."

"Very true," said I; "let us go fetch it." And with that we all three rose and hastened down to the beach. I still felt a little weak from loss of blood, so that my companions soon began to leave me behind; but Jack perceived this, and, with his usual considerate good-nature, turned back to help me. This was now the first time that I had looked well about me since landing, as the spot where I had been laid was covered with thick bushes, which almost hid the country from our view. As we now emerged from among these and walked down the sandy beach together, I cast my eyes about, and truly my heart glowed within me and my spirits rose at the beautiful prospect which I beheld on every side. The gale had suddenly died away, just as if it had blown furiously till it dashed our ship upon the rocks, and had nothing more to do after accomplishing that. The island on which we stood was hilly, and covered almost everywhere with the most beautiful and richly coloured trees, bushes, and shrubs, none of which I knew the names of at that time—except, indeed, the cocoa-nut palms, which I recognised at once from the many pictures that I had seen of them before I left home. A sandy beach of dazzling whiteness lined this bright-green shore, and upon it there fell a gentle ripple of the sea. This last astonished me much, for I recollected that at home the sea used to fall in huge billows on the shore long after a storm had subsided. But on casting my glance out to sea the cause became apparent. About a mile distant from the shore I saw the great billows of the ocean rolling like a green wall, and falling with a long, loud roar upon a low coral reef, where they were dashed into white foam and flung up in clouds of spray. This spray sometimes flew exceedingly high, and every here and there a beautiful rainbow was formed for a moment among the falling drops. We afterwards found that this coral reef extended quite round the island, and formed a natural breakwater to it. Beyond this, the sea rose and tossed violently from the effects of the storm; but between the reef and the shore it was as calm and as smooth as a pond.

My heart was filled with more delight than I can express at sight of so many glorious objects, and my thoughts turned suddenly to the contemplation of the Creator of them all. I mention this the more gladly, because at that time, I am ashamed to say, I very seldom thought of my Creator, although I was constantly surrounded by the most beautiful and wonderful of His works. I observed, from the expression of my companion's countenance, that he too derived much joy from the splendid scenery, which was all the more agreeable to us after our long voyage on the salt sea. There the breeze was fresh and cold; but here it was delightfully mild, and when a puff blew off the land it came laden with the most exquisite perfume that can be imagined. While we thus gazed we were startled by a loud "Huzza!" from Peterkin, and on looking towards the edge of the sea we saw him capering and jumping about like a monkey, and ever and anon tugging with all his might at something that lay upon the shore.

"What an odd fellow he is, to be sure!" said Jack, taking me by the arm and hurrying forward. "Come, let us hasten to see what it is."

"Here it is, boys—hurrah! Come along! Just what we want!" cried Peterkin as we drew near, still tugging with all his power. "First-rate; just the very ticket!"

I need scarcely say to my readers that my companion Peterkin was in the habit of using very remarkable and peculiar phrases. And I am free to confess that I did not well understand the meaning of some of them—such, for instance, as "the very ticket;" but I think it my duty to recount everything relating to my adventures with a strict regard to truthfulness in as far as my memory serves me, so I write, as nearly as possible, the exact words that my companions spoke. I often asked Peterkin to explain what he meant by "ticket," but he always answered me by going into fits of laughter. However, by observing the occasions on which he used it, I came to understand that it meant to show that something was remarkably good or fortunate.

On coming up we found that Peterkin was vainly endeavouring to pull the axe out of the oar into which, it will be remembered, Jack struck it while endeavouring to cut away the cordage among which it had become entangled at the bow of the ship. Fortunately for us, the axe had remained fast in the oar, and even now all Peterkin's strength could not draw it out of the cut.

"Ah, that is capital indeed!" cried Jack, at the same time giving the axe a wrench that plucked it out of the tough wood. "How fortunate this is! It will be of more value to us than a hundred knives, and the edge is quite new and sharp."

"I'll answer for the toughness of the handle, at any rate!" cried Peterkin; "my arms are nearly pulled out of the sockets. But see here, our luck is great. There is iron on the blade." He pointed to a piece of hoop-iron as he spoke, which had been nailed round the blade of the oar to prevent it from splitting.

This also was a fortunate discovery. Jack went down on his knees, and with the edge of the axe began carefully to force out the nails. But as they were firmly fixed in, and the operation blunted our axe, we carried the oar up with us to the place where we had left the rest of our things, intending to burn the wood away from the iron at a more convenient time.

"Now, lads," said Jack after we had laid it on the stone which contained our little all, "I propose that we should go to the tail of the island, where the ship struck, which is only a quarter of a mile off; and see if anything else has been thrown ashore. I don't expect anything, but it is well to see. When we get back here it will be time to have our supper and prepare our beds."

"Agreed!" cried Peterkin and I together, as, indeed, we would have agreed to any proposal that Jack made; for, besides his being older and much stronger and taller than either of us, he was a very clever fellow, and, I think, would have induced people much older than himself to choose him for their leader, especially if they required to be led on a bold enterprise.

Now as we hastened along the white beach, which shone so brightly in the rays of the setting sun that our eyes were quite dazzled by its glare, it suddenly came into Peterkin's head that we had nothing to eat except the wild berries which grew in profusion at our feet.

"What shall we do, Jack?" said he with a rueful look. "Perhaps they may be poisonous!"

"No fear," replied Jack confidently. "I have observed that a few of them are not unlike some of the berries that grow wild on our own native hills. Besides, I saw one or two strange birds eating them just a few minutes ago, and what won't kill the birds won't kill us. But look up there, Peterkin," continued Jack, pointing to the branched head of a cocoa-nut palm. "There are nuts for us in all stages."

"So there are!" cried Peterkin, who, being of a very unobservant nature, had been too much taken up with other things to notice anything so high above his head as the fruit of a palm-tree. But whatever faults my young comrade had, he could not be blamed for want of activity or animal spirits. Indeed, the nuts had scarcely been pointed out to him when he bounded up the tall stem of the tree like a squirrel, and in a few minutes returned with three nuts, each as large as a man's fist.

"You had better keep them till we return," said Jack. "Let us finish our work before eating."

"So be it, captain; go ahead!" cried Peterkin, thrusting the nuts into his trousers pocket. "In fact, I don't want to eat just now; but I would give a good deal for a drink. Oh, that I could find a spring! but I don't see the smallest sign of one hereabouts. I say, Jack, how does it happen that you seem to be up to everything? You have told us the names of half-a-dozen trees already, and yet you say that you were never in the South Seas before."

"I'm not up to everything, Peterkin, as you'll find out ere long," replied Jack with a smile; "but I have been a great reader of books of travel and adventure all my life, and that has put me up to a good many things that you are, perhaps, not acquainted with."

"Oh, Jack, that's all humbug! If you begin to lay everything to the credit of books, I'll quite lose my opinion of you," cried Peterkin with a look of contempt. "I've seen a lot o' fellows that were *always* poring over books, and when they came to try to *do* anything, they were no better than baboons!"

"You are quite right," retorted Jack; "and I have seen a lot of fellows, who never looked into books at all, who knew nothing about anything except the things they had actually seen, and very little they knew even about these. Indeed, some were so ignorant that they did not know that cocoa-nuts grew on cocoa-nut trees!"

I could not refrain from laughing at this rebuke, for there was much truth in it as to Peterkin's ignorance.

"Humph! maybe you're right," answered Peterkin; "but I would not give *tuppence* for a man of books if he had nothing else in him."

"Neither would I," said Jack; "but that's no reason why you should run books down, or think less of me for having read them. Suppose, now, Peterkin, that you wanted to build a ship, and I were to give you a long and particular account of the way to do it, would not that be very useful?"

"No doubt of it," said Peterkin, laughing.

"And suppose I were to write the account in a letter instead of telling you in words, would that be less useful?"

"Well—no, perhaps not."

"Well, suppose I were to print it and send it to you in the form of a book, would it not be as good and useful as ever?"

"Oh, bother! Jack, you're a philosopher, and that's worse than anything!" cried Peterkin with a look of pretended horror.

"Very well, Peterkin, we shall see," returned Jack, halting under the shade of a cocoa-nut tree. "You said you were thirsty just a minute ago. Now jump up that tree and bring down a nut—not a ripe one; bring a green, unripe one."

Peterkin looked surprised, but seeing that Jack was in earnest, he obeyed.

"Now cut a hole in it with your penknife and clap it to your mouth, old fellow," said Jack.

Peterkin did as he was directed, and we both burst into uncontrollable laughter at the changes that instantly passed over his expressive countenance. No sooner had he put the nut to his mouth, and thrown back his head in order to catch what came out of it, than his eyes opened to twice their ordinary size with astonishment, while his throat moved vigorously in the act of swallowing. Then a smile and a look of intense delight overspread his face, except, indeed, the mouth, which, being firmly fixed to the hole in the nut, could not take part in the expression; but he endeavoured to make up for this by winking at us excessively with his right eye. At length he stopped, and drawing a long breath, exclaimed:

"Nectar! perfect nectar!—I say, Jack, you're a Briton—the best fellow I ever met in my life—Only taste that!" said he, turning to me and holding the nut to my mouth. I immediately drank, and certainly I was much surprised at the delightful liquid that flowed copiously down my throat. It was extremely cool, and had a sweet taste, mingled with acid; in fact, it was the likest thing to lemonade I ever tasted, and was most grateful and refreshing. I handed the nut to Jack, who, after tasting it, said, "Now, Peterkin, you unbeliever! I never saw or tasted a cocoa-nut in my life before, except those sold in shops at home; but I once read that the green nuts contain that stuff; and you see it is true."

"And, pray," asked Peterkin, "what sort of 'stuff' does the ripe nut contain?"

"A hollow kernel," answered Jack, "with a liquid like milk in it; but it does not satisfy thirst so well as hunger. It is very wholesome food, I believe."

"Meat and drink on the same tree!" cried Peterkin; "washing in the sea, lodging on the ground—and all for nothing! My dear boys, we're set up for life! It must be the ancient Paradise—hurrah!" and Peterkin tossed his straw hat in the air and ran along the beach, hallooing like a madman with delight.

We afterwards found, however, that these lovely islands were very unlike Paradise in many things. But more of this in its proper place.

We had now come to the point of rocks on which the ship had struck, but did not find a single article, although we searched carefully among the coral rocks, which at this place jutted out so far as nearly to join the reef that encircled the island. Just as we were about to return, however, we saw something black floating in a little cove that had escaped our observation. Running forward, we drew it from the water, and found it to be a long, thick, leather boot, such as fishermen at home wear; and a few paces farther on, we picked up its fellow. We at once recognised these as having belonged to our captain, for he had worn them during the whole of the storm in order to guard his legs from the waves and spray that constantly washed over our decks. My first thought on seeing them was that our dear captain had been drowned; but Jack soon put my mind more at rest on that point by saying that if the captain had been drowned with the boots on, he would certainly have been washed ashore along with them, and that he had no doubt whatever he had kicked them off while in the sea that he might swim more easily.

Peterkin immediately put them on; but they were so large that, as Jack said, they would have done for boots, trousers, and vest too. I also tried them; but although I was long enough in the legs for them, they were much too large in the feet for me. So we handed them to Jack, who was anxious to make me keep them; but as they fitted his large limbs and feet as if they had been made for him, I would not hear of it, so he consented at last to use them. I may remark, however, that Jack did not use them often, as they were extremely heavy.

It was beginning to grow dark when we returned to our encampment; so we put off our visit to the top of a hill till next day, and employed the light that yet remained to us in cutting down a quantity of boughs and the broad leaves of a tree of which none of us knew the name. With these we erected a sort of rustic bower, in which we meant to pass the night. There was no absolute necessity for this, because the air of our island was so genial and balmy that we could have slept quite well without any shelter; but we were so little used to sleeping in the open air that we did not quite relish the idea of lying down without any covering over us. Besides, our bower would shelter us from the night-dews or rain, if any should happen to fall. Having strewed the floor with leaves and dry grass, we bethought ourselves of supper.

But it now occurred to us, for the first time, that we had no means of making a fire.

"Now, there's a fix! What shall we do?" said Peterkin, while we both turned our eyes to Jack, to whom we always looked in our difficulties. Jack seemed not a little perplexed.

"There are flints enough, no doubt, on the beach," said he; "but they are of no use at all without a steel. However, we must try." So saying, he went to the beach, and soon returned with two flints. On one of these he placed the tinder, and endeavoured to ignite it; but it was with great difficulty that a very small spark was struck out of the flints, and the tinder, being a bad, hard piece, would not catch. He then tried the bit of hoop-iron, which would not strike fire at all; and after that the back of the axe, with no better success. During all these trials Peterkin sat with his hands in his pockets, gazing with a most melancholy visage at our comrade, his face growing longer and more miserable at each successive failure.

"Oh dear!" he sighed; "I would not care a button for the cooking of our victuals—perhaps they don't need it—but it's so dismal to eat one's supper in the dark, and we have had such a capital day that it's a pity to finish off in this glum style. Oh, I have it!" he cried, starting up: "the spy-glass—the big glass at the end is a burning-glass!"

"You forget that we have no sun," said I.

Peterkin was silent. In his sudden recollection of the telescope he had quite overlooked the absence of the sun.

"Ah, boys, I've got it now!" exclaimed Jack, rising and cutting a branch from a neighbouring bush, which he stripped of its leaves. "I recollect seeing this done once at home. Hand me the bit of whip-cord." With the cord and branch Jack soon formed a bow. Then he cut a piece about three inches long off the end of a dead branch, which he pointed at the two ends. Round this he passed the cord of the bow, and placed one end against his chest, which was protected from its point by a chip of wood; the other point he placed against the bit of tinder, and then began to saw vigorously with the bow, just as a blacksmith does with his drill while boring a hole in a piece of iron. In a few seconds the tinder began to smoke; in less than a minute it caught fire; and in less than a quarter of an hour we were drinking our lemonade and eating cocoa-nuts round a fire that would have roasted an entire sheep, while the smoke, flames, and sparks flew up among the broad leaves of the overhanging palm-trees, and cast a warm glow upon our leafy bower.

That night the starry sky looked down through the gently rustling trees upon our slumbers, and the distant roaring of the surf upon the coral reef was our lullaby.

## 5

## MORNING, AND COGITATIONS CONNECTED THEREWITH—WE LUXURIATE IN THE SEA, TRY OUR DIVING POWERS, AND MAKE ENCHANTING EXCURSIONS AMONG THE CORAL GROVES AT THE BOTTOM OF THE OCEAN—THE WONDERS OF THE DEEP ENLARGED UPON.

What a joyful thing it is to awaken on a fresh, glorious morning, and find the rising sun staring into your face with dazzling brilliancy! to hear the birds twittering in the bushes, and to hear the murmuring of a rill, or the soft, hissing ripples as they fall upon the seashore! At any time, and in any place, such sights and sounds are most charming; but more especially are they so when one awakens to them, for the first time, in a novel and romantic situation, with the soft, sweet air of a tropical climate mingling with the fresh smell of the sea, and stirring the strange leaves that flutter overhead and around one, or ruffling the plumage of the stranger birds that fly inquiringly around as if to demand what business we have to intrude uninvited on their domains. When I awoke on the morning after the shipwreck, I found myself in this most delightful condition; and as I lay on my back upon my bed of leaves, gazing up through the branches of the cocoa-nut trees into the clear blue sky, and watched the few fleecy clouds that passed slowly across it, my heart expanded more and more with an exulting gladness, the like of which I had never felt before. While I meditated, my thoughts again turned to the great and kind Creator of this beautiful world, as they had done on the previous day when I first beheld the sea and the coral reef, with the mighty waves dashing over it into the calm waters of the lagoon.

While thus meditating, I naturally bethought me of my Bible, for I had faithfully kept the promise which I gave at parting to my beloved mother—that I would read it every morning; and it was with a feeling of dismay that I remembered I had left it in the ship. I was much troubled about this. However, I consoled myself with reflecting that I could keep the second part of my promise to her—namely, that I should never omit to say my prayers. So I rose quietly lest I should disturb my companions, who were still asleep, and stepped aside into the bushes for this purpose.

On my return I found them still slumbering, so I again lay down to think over our situation. Just at that moment I was attracted by the sight of a very small parrot, which Jack afterwards told me was called a paroquet. It was seated on a twig that overhung Peterkin's head, and I was speedily lost in admiration of its bright-green plumage, which was mingled with other gay colours. While I looked I observed that the bird turned its head slowly from side to side and looked downwards, first with the one eye and then with the other. On glancing downwards I observed that Peterkin's mouth was wide open, and that this remarkable bird was looking into it. Peterkin used to say that I had not an atom of fun in my composition, and that I never could understand a joke. In regard to the latter, perhaps he was right; yet I think that, when they were explained to me, I understood jokes as well as most people. But in regard to the former, he must certainly have been wrong, for this bird seemed to me to be extremely funny; and I could not help thinking that if it should happen to faint, or slip its foot, and fall off the twig into Peterkin's mouth, he would perhaps think it funny too! Suddenly the paroquet bent down its head and uttered a loud scream in his face. This awoke him, and with a cry of surprise, he started up, while the foolish bird flew precipitately away.

"Oh, you monster!" cried Peterkin, shaking his fist at the bird. Then he yawned, and rubbed his eyes, and asked what o'clock it was.

I smiled at this question, and answered that, as our watches were at the bottom of the sea, I could not tell, but it was a little past sunrise.

Peterkin now began to remember where we were. As he looked up into the bright sky, and snuffed the scented air, his eyes glistened with delight, and he uttered a faint "Hurrah!" and yawned again. Then he gazed slowly round, till, observing the calm sea through an opening in the bushes, he started suddenly up as if he had received an electric shock, uttered a vehement shout, flung off his garments, and rushing over the white sands, plunged into the water. The cry awoke Jack, who rose on his elbow with a look of grave surprise; but this was followed by a quiet smile of intelligence on seeing Peterkin in the water. With an energy that he only gave way to in moments of excitement, Jack bounded to his feet, threw off his clothes, shook back his hair, and with a lion-like spring, dashed over the sands and plunged into the sea with such force as quite to envelop Peterkin in a shower of spray. Jack was a remarkably good swimmer and diver, so that after his plunge we saw no sign of him for nearly a minute, after which he suddenly emerged, with a cry of joy, a good many yards out from the shore. My spirits were so much raised by seeing all this that I, too, hastily threw off my garments and endeavoured to imitate Jack's vigorous bound; but I was so awkward that my foot caught on a stump, and I fell to the ground. Then I slipped on a stone while running over the sand and nearly fell again, much to the amusement of Peterkin, who laughed heartily and called me a "slow coach;" while Jack cried out, "Come along, Ralph, and I'll help you!" However, when I got into the water I managed very well; for I was really a good swimmer and diver too. I could not, indeed, equal Jack, who was superior to any Englishman I ever saw; but I infinitely surpassed Peterkin, who could only swim a little, and could not dive at all.

While Peterkin enjoyed himself in the shallow water and in running along the beach, Jack and I swam out into the deep water and occasionally dived for stones. I shall never forget my surprise and delight on first beholding the bottom of the sea. As I have before stated, the water within the reef was as calm as a pond; and as there was no wind, it was quite clear from the surface to the bottom, so that we could see down easily even at a depth of twenty or thirty yards. When Jack and I dived into shallower water we expected to have found sand and stones, instead of which we found ourselves in what appeared really to be an enchanted garden. The whole of the bottom of the lagoon, as we called the calm water within the reef, was covered with coral of every shape, size, and hue. Some portions were formed like large mushrooms; others appeared like the brain of a man, having stalks or necks attached to them; but the most common kind was a species of branching coral, and some portions were of a lovely pale-pink colour, others were pure white. Among this there grew large quantities of seaweed of the richest hues imaginable, and of the most graceful forms; while innumerable fishes—blue, red, yellow, green, and striped—sported in and out amongst the flower-beds of this submarine garden, and did not appear to be at all afraid of our approaching them.

On darting to the surface for breath after our first dive, Jack and I rose close to each other.

"Did you ever in your life, Ralph, see anything so lovely?" said Jack as he flung the spray from his hair.

"Never," I replied. "It appears to me like fairy realms. I can scarcely believe that we are not dreaming."

"Dreaming!" cried Jack. "Do you know, Ralph, I'm half-tempted to think that we really are dreaming! But if so, I am resolved to make the most of it and dream another dive; so here goes—down again, my boy!"

We took the second dive together, and kept beside each other while under water; and I was greatly surprised to find that we could keep down much longer than I ever recollect having done in our own seas at home. I believe that this was owing to the heat of the water, which was so warm that we afterwards found we could remain in it for two and three hours at a time without feeling any unpleasant effects such as we used to experience in the sea at home. When Jack reached the bottom, he grasped the coral stems and crept along on his hands and knees, peeping under the seaweed and among the rocks. I observed him, also, pick up one or two large oysters and retain them in his grasp, as if he meant to take them up with him; so I also gathered a few. Suddenly he made a grasp at a fish with blue and yellow stripes on its back, and actually touched its tail, but did not catch it. At this he turned towards me and attempted to smile; but no sooner had he done so than he sprang like an arrow to the surface, where, on following him, I found him gasping and coughing and spitting water from his mouth. In a few minutes he recovered, and we both turned to swim ashore.

"I declare, Ralph," said he, "that I actually tried to laugh under water!"

"So I saw," I replied; "and I observed that you very nearly caught that fish by the tail. It would have done capitally for breakfast, if you had."

"Breakfast enough here," said he, holding up the oysters as we landed and ran up the beach.—"Hallo, Peterkin! Here you are, boy! split open these fellows while Ralph and I put on our clothes. They'll agree with the cocoa-nuts excellently, I have no doubt."

Peterkin, who was already dressed, took the oysters and opened them with the edge of our axe, exclaiming, "Now, that's capital! There's nothing I'm so fond of."

"Ah! that's lucky," remarked Jack. "I'll be able to keep you in good order now, Master Peterkin. You know you can't dive any better than a cat. So, sir, whenever you behave ill you shall have no oysters for breakfast."

"I'm very glad that our prospect of breakfast is so good," said I, "for I'm very hungry."

"Here, then, stop your mouth with that, Ralph," said Peterkin, holding a large oyster to my lips. I opened my mouth and swallowed it in silence, and really it was remarkably good.

We now set ourselves earnestly about our preparations for spending the day. We had no difficulty with the fire this morning as our burning-glass was an admirable one; and while we roasted a few oysters and ate our cocoa-nuts, we held a long, animated conversation about our plans for the future. What those plans were, and how we carried them into effect, the reader shall see hereafter.

# 6

## AN EXCURSION INTO THE INTERIOR IN WHICH WE MAKE MANY VALUABLE AND INTERESTING DISCOVERIES—WE GET A DREADFUL FRIGHT—THE BREAD-FRUIT TREE—WONDERFUL PECULIARITY OF SOME OF THE FRUIT-TREES—SIGNS OF FORMER INHABITANTS.

Our first care, after breakfast, was to place the few articles we possessed in the crevice of a rock at the farther end of a small cave which we discovered near our encampment. This cave, we hoped, might be useful to us afterwards as a storehouse. Then we cut two large clubs off a species of very hard tree which grew near at hand. One of these was given to Peterkin, the other to me, and Jack armed himself with the axe. We took these precautions because we purposed to make an excursion to the top of the mountains of the interior, in order to obtain a better view of our island. Of course we knew not what dangers might befall us by the way, so thought it best to be prepared.

Having completed our arrangements and carefully extinguished our fire, we sallied forth and walked a short distance along the sea-beach till we came to the entrance of a valley, through which flowed the rivulet before mentioned. Here we turned our backs on the sea and struck into the interior.

The prospect that burst upon our view on entering the valley was truly splendid. On either side of us there was a gentle rise in the land, which thus formed two ridges, about a mile apart, on each side of the valley. These ridges—which, as well as the low grounds between them, were covered with trees and shrubs of the most luxuriant kind—continued to recede inland for about two miles, when they joined the foot of a small mountain. This hill rose rather abruptly from the head of the valley, and was likewise entirely covered, even to the top, with trees—except on one particular spot near the left shoulder, where was a bare and rocky place of a broken and savage character. Beyond this hill we could not see, and we therefore directed our course up the banks of the rivulet towards the foot of it, intending to climb to the top, should that be possible—as, indeed, we had no doubt it was.

Jack, being the wisest and boldest among us, took the lead, carrying the axe on his shoulder. Peterkin, with his enormous club, came second, as he said he should like to be in a position to defend me if any danger should threaten. I brought up the rear; but having been more taken up with the wonderful and curious things I saw at starting than with thoughts of possible danger, I had very foolishly left my club behind me. Although, as I have said, the trees and bushes were very luxuriant, they were not so thickly crowded together as to hinder our progress among them. We were able to wind in and out, and to follow the banks of the stream quite easily, although, it is true, the height and thickness of the foliage prevented us from seeing far ahead. But sometimes a jutting-out rock on the hillsides afforded us a position whence we could enjoy the romantic view and mark our progress towards the foot of the hill. I was particularly struck, during the walk, with the richness of the undergrowth in most places, and recognised many berries and plants that resembled those of my native land, especially a tall, elegantly formed fern, which emitted an agreeable perfume. There were several kinds of flowers, too; but I did not see so many of these as I should have expected in such a climate. We also saw a great variety of small birds of bright plumage, and many paroquets similar to the one, that awoke Peterkin so rudely in the morning.

Thus we advanced to the foot of the hill without encountering anything to alarm us, except, indeed, once, when we were passing close under a part of the hill which was hidden from our view by the broad leaves of the banana-trees, which grew in great luxuriance in that part. Jack was just preparing to force his way through this thicket when we were startled and arrested by a strange pattering or rumbling sound, which appeared to us quite different from any of the sounds we had heard during the previous part of our walk.

"Hallo!" cried Peterkin, stopping short, and grasping his club with both hands; "what's that?"

Neither of us replied; but Jack seized his axe in his right hand, while with the other he pushed aside the broad leaves and endeavoured to peer amongst them.

"I can see nothing," he said after a short pause. "I think it—"

Again the rumbling sound came, louder than before, and we all sprang back and stood on the defensive. For myself, having forgotten my club, and not having taken the precaution to cut another, I buttoned my jacket, doubled my fists, and threw myself into a boxing attitude. I must say, however, that I felt somewhat uneasy; and my companions afterwards confessed that their thoughts at this moment had been instantly filled with all they had ever heard or read of wild beasts and savages, torturings at the stake, roastings alive, and such-like horrible things. Suddenly the pattering noise increased with tenfold violence. It was followed by a fearful crash among the bushes, which was rapidly repeated, as if some gigantic animal were bounding towards us. In another moment an enormous rock came crashing through the shrubbery, followed by a cloud of dust and small stones, and flew close past the spot where we stood, carrying bushes and young trees along with it.

"Pooh! is that all?" exclaimed Peterkin, wiping the perspiration off his forehead. "Why, I thought it was all the wild men and beasts in the South Sea Islands, galloping on in one grand charge to sweep us off the face of the earth, instead of a mere stone tumbling down the mountain-side!"

"Nevertheless," remarked Jack, "if that same stone had hit any of us it would have rendered the charge you speak of quite unnecessary, Peterkin."

This was true, and I felt very thankful for our escape. On examining the spot more narrowly, we found that it lay close to the foot of a very rugged precipice, from which stones of various sizes were always tumbling at intervals. Indeed, the numerous fragments lying scattered all round might have suggested the cause of the sound had we not been too suddenly alarmed to think of anything.

We now resumed our journey, resolving that, in our future excursions into the interior, we would be careful to avoid this dangerous precipice.

Soon afterwards we arrived at the foot of the hill, and prepared to ascend it. Here Jack made a discovery which caused us all very great joy. This was a tree of a remarkably beautiful appearance, which Jack confidently declared to be the celebrated bread-fruit tree.

"Is it celebrated?" inquired Peterkin with a look of great simplicity.

"It is," replied Jack.

"That's odd, now," rejoined Peterkin; "I never heard of it before."

"Then it's not so celebrated as I thought it was," returned Jack, quietly squeezing Peterkin's hat over his eyes; "but listen, you ignorant boobie! and hear of it now."

Peterkin readjusted his hat, and was soon listening with as much interest as myself while Jack told us that this tree is one of the most valuable in the islands of the south; that it bears two, sometimes three, crops of fruit in the year; that the fruit is very like wheaten bread in appearance, and that it constitutes the principal food of many of the islanders.

"So," said Peterkin, "we seem to have everything ready prepared to our hands in this wonderful island—lemonade ready bottled in nuts, and loaf-bread growing on the trees!"

Peterkin, as usual, was jesting; nevertheless, it is a curious fact that he spoke almost the literal truth.

"Moreover," continued Jack, "the bread-fruit tree affords a capital gum, which serves the natives for pitching their canoes; the bark of the young branches is made by them into cloth; and of the wood, which is durable and of a good colour, they build their houses. So you see, lads, that we have no lack of material here to make us comfortable, if we are only clever enough to use it."

"But are you sure that that's it?" asked Peterkin.

"Quite sure," replied Jack; "for I was particularly interested in the account I once read of it, and I remember the description well. I am sorry, however that I have forgotten the descriptions of many other trees which I am sure we have seen to-day, if we could but recognise them. So you see, Peterkin, I'm not up to everything yet."

"Never mind, Jack," said Peterkin with a grave, patronising expression of countenance, patting his tall companion on the shoulder—"never mind, Jack; you know a good deal for your age. You're a clever boy, sir—a promising young man; and if you only go on as you have begun, sir, you will—"

The end of this speech was suddenly cut short by Jack tripping up Peterkin's heels and tumbling him into a mass of thick shrubs, where, finding himself comfortable, he lay still, basking in the sunshine, while Jack and I examined the bread-fruit tree.

We were much struck with the deep, rich green colour of its broad leaves, which were twelve or eighteen inches long, deeply indented, and of a glossy smoothness, like the laurel. The fruit, with which it was loaded, was nearly round, and appeared to be about six inches in diameter, with a rough rind, marked with lozenge-shaped divisions. It was of various colours, from light pea-green to brown and rich yellow. Jack said that the yellow was the ripe fruit. We afterwards found that most of the fruit-trees on the island were evergreens, and that we might, when we wished, pluck the blossom and the ripe fruit from the same tree. Such a wonderful difference from the trees of our own country surprised us not a little. The bark of the tree was rough and light-coloured; the trunk was about two feet in diameter, and it appeared to be twenty feet high, being quite destitute of branches up to that height, where it branched off into a beautiful and umbrageous head. We noticed that the fruit hung in clusters of twos and threes on the branches; but as we were anxious to get to the top of the hill, we refrained from attempting to pluck any at that time.

Our hearts were now very much cheered by our good fortune, and it was with light and active steps that we clambered up the steep sides of the hill. On reaching the summit a new, and if possible a grander, prospect met our gaze. We found that this was not the highest part of the island, but that another hill lay beyond, with a wide valley between it and the one on which we stood. This valley, like the first, was also full of rich trees—some dark and some light green, some heavy and thick in foliage, and others light, feathery, and graceful, while the beautiful blossoms on many of them threw a sort of rainbow tint over all, and gave to the valley the appearance of a garden of flowers. Among these we recognised many of the bread-fruit trees, laden with yellow fruit, and also a great many cocoa-nut palms. After gazing our fill we pushed down the hillside, crossed the valley, and soon began to ascend the second mountain. It was clothed with trees nearly to the top; but the summit was bare, and in some places broken.

While on our way up we came to an object which filled us with much interest. This was the stump of a tree that had evidently been cut down with an axe! So, then, we were not the first who had viewed this beautiful isle. The hand of man had been at work there before us. It now began to recur to us again that perhaps the island was inhabited, although we had not seen any traces of man until now. But a second glance at the stump convinced us that we had not more reason to think so now than formerly; for the surface of the wood was quite decayed and partly covered with fungus and green matter, so that it must have been cut many years ago.

"Perhaps," said Peterkin, "some ship or other has touched here long ago for wood, and only taken one tree."

We did not think this likely, however, because, in such circumstances, the crew of a ship would cut wood of small size and near the shore; whereas this was a large tree, and stood near the top of the mountain. In fact, it was the highest large tree on the mountain, all above it being wood of very recent growth.

"I can't understand it," said Jack, scratching the surface of the stump with his axe. "I can only suppose that the savages have been here and cut it for some purpose known only to themselves. But, hallo! what have we here?"

As he spoke Jack began carefully to scrape away the moss and fungus from the stump, and soon laid bare three distinct traces of marks, as if some inscription or initials had been cut thereon. But although the traces were distinct, beyond all doubt, the exact form of the letters could not be made out. Jack thought they looked like JS, but we could not be certain. They had apparently been carelessly cut, and long exposure to the weather had so broken them up that we could not make out what they were. We were exceedingly perplexed at this discovery, and stayed a long time at the place conjecturing what these marks could have been, but without avail; so, as the day was advancing, we left it, and quickly reached the top of the mountain.

We found this to be the highest point of the island, and from it we saw our kingdom lying, as it were, like a map around us. As I have always thought it impossible to get a thing properly into one's understanding without comprehending it, I shall beg the reader's patience for a little while I describe our island, thus, shortly:

It consisted of two mountains: the one we guessed at five hundred feet; the other, on which we stood, at one thousand. Between these lay a rich, beautiful valley, as already said. This valley crossed the island from one end to the other, being high in the middle and sloping on each side towards the sea. The large mountain sloped, on the side farthest from where we had been wrecked, gradually towards the sea; but although, when viewed at a glance, it had thus a regular sloping appearance, a more careful observation showed that it was broken up into a multitude of very small vales—or, rather, dells and glens—intermingled with little rugged spots and small but abrupt precipices here and there, with rivulets tumbling over their edges and wandering down the slopes in little white streams, sometimes glistening among the broad leaves of the bread-fruit and cocoa-nut trees, or hiding altogether beneath the rich underwood. At the base of this mountain lay a narrow bright-green plain or meadow, which terminated abruptly at the shore. On the other side of the island, whence we had come, stood the smaller hill, at the foot of which diverged three valleys—one being that which we had ascended, with a smaller vale on each side of it, and separated from it by the two ridges before mentioned. In these smaller valleys there were no streams, but they were clothed with the same luxuriant vegetation.

The diameter of the island seemed to be about ten miles, and as it was almost circular in form, its circumference must have been thirty miles—perhaps a little more, if allowance be made for the numerous bays and indentations of the shore. The entire island was belted by a beach of pure white sand, on which laved the gentle ripples of the lagoon. We now also observed that the coral reef completely encircled the island; but it varied its distance from it here and there—in some places being a mile from the beach, in others a few hundred yards, but the average distance was half-a-mile. The reef lay very low, and the spray of the surf broke quite over it in many places. This surf never ceased its roar; for, however calm the weather might be, there is always a gentle swaying motion in the great Pacific, which, although scarce noticeable out at sea, reaches the shore at last in a huge billow. The water within the lagoon, as before said, was perfectly still. There were three narrow openings in the reef: one opposite each end of the valley which I have described as crossing the island; the other opposite our own valley, which we afterwards named the Valley of the Wreck. At each of these openings the reef rose into two small green islets, covered with bushes, and having one or two cocoa-nut palms on each. These islets were very singular, and appeared as if planted expressly for the purpose of marking the channel into the lagoon. Our captain was making for one of these openings the day we were wrecked—and would have reached it, too, I doubt not, had not the rudder been torn away. Within the lagoon were several pretty, low coral islands, just opposite our encampment; and immediately beyond these, out at sea, lay about a dozen other islands, at various distances, from half-a-mile to ten miles—all of them, as far as we could discern, smaller than ours and apparently uninhabited. They seemed to be low coral islands, raised but little above the sea, yet covered with cocoa-nut trees.

All this we noted, and a great deal more, while we sat on the top of the mountain. After we had satisfied ourselves we prepared to return; but here, again, we discovered traces of the presence of man. These were a pole or staff, and one or two pieces of wood which had been squared with an axe. All of these were, however, very much decayed, and they had evidently not been touched for many years.

Full of these discoveries, we returned to our encampment. On the way we fell in with the traces of some four-footed animal, but whether old or of recent date none of us were able to guess. This also tended to raise our hopes of obtaining some animal food on the island; so we reached home in good spirits, quite prepared for supper, and highly satisfied with our excursion.

After much discussion, in which Peterkin took the lead, we came to the conclusion that the island was uninhabited, and went to bed.

# 7

## JACK'S INGENUITY—WE GET INTO DIFFICULTIES ABOUT FISHING, AND GET OUT OF THEM BY A METHOD WHICH GIVES US A COLD BATH—HORRIBLE ENCOUNTER WITH A SHARK.

For several days after the excursion related in the last chapter we did not wander far from our encampment, but gave ourselves up to forming plans for the future and making our present abode comfortable.

There were various causes that induced this state of comparative inaction. In the first place, although everything around us was so delightful, and we could without difficulty obtain all that we required for our bodily comfort, we did not quite like the idea of settling down here for the rest of our lives, far away from our friends and our native land. To set energetically about preparations for a permanent residence seemed so like making up our minds to saying adieu to home and friends for ever that we tacitly shrank from it, and put off our preparations, for one reason and another, as long as we could. Then there was a little uncertainty still as to there being natives on the island, and we entertained a kind of faint hope that a ship might come and take us off. But as day after day passed, and neither savages nor ships appeared, we gave up all hope of an early deliverance, and set diligently to work at our homestead.

During this time, however, we had not been altogether idle. We made several experiments in cooking the cocoa-nut, most of which did not improve it. Then we removed our goods and took up our abode in the cave, but found the change so bad that we returned gladly to the bower. Besides this, we bathed very frequently, and talked a great deal—at least Jack and Peterkin did; I listened. Among other useful things, Jack, who was ever the most active and diligent, converted about three inches of the hoop-iron into an excellent knife. First, he beat it quite flat with the axe; then he made a rude handle, and tied the hoop-iron to it with our piece of whip-cord, and ground it to an edge on a piece of sandstone. When it was finished he used it to shape a better handle, to which he fixed it with a strip of his cotton handkerchief—in which operation he had, as Peterkin pointed out, torn off one of Lord Nelson's noses. However, the whip-cord, thus set free, was used by Peterkin as a fishing-line. He merely tied a piece of oyster to the end of it. This the fish were allowed to swallow, and then they were pulled quickly ashore. But as the line was very short and we had no boat, the fish we caught were exceedingly small.

One day Peterkin came up from the beach, where he had been angling, and said in a very cross tone, "I'll tell you what, Jack, I'm not going to be humbugged with catching such contemptible things any longer. I want you to swim out with me on your back, and let me fish in deep water!"

"Dear me, Peterkin!" replied Jack; "I had no idea you were taking the thing so much to heart, else I would have got you out of that difficulty long ago. Let me see;" and Jack looked down at a piece of timber, on which he had been labouring, with a peculiar gaze of abstraction which he always assumed when trying to invent or discover anything.

"What say you to building a boat?" he inquired, looking up hastily.

"Take far too long," was the reply; "can't be bothered waiting. I want to begin at once!"

Again Jack considered. "I have it!" he cried. "We'll fell a large tree and launch the trunk of it in the water, so that when you want to fish you've nothing to do but to swim out to it."

"Would not a small raft do better?" said I.

"Much better; but we have no ropes to bind it together with. Perhaps we may find something hereafter that will do as well, but in the meantime let us try the tree."

This was agreed on; so we started off to a spot, not far distant, where we knew of a tree that would suit us which grew near the water's edge. As soon as we reached it Jack threw off his coat, and wielding the axe with his sturdy arms, hacked and hewed at it for a quarter of an hour without stopping. Then he paused, and while he sat down to rest I continued the work. Then Peterkin made a vigorous attack on it; so that when Jack renewed his powerful blows, a few minutes' cutting brought it down with a terrible crash.

"Hurrah! Now for it!" cried Jack. "Let us off with its head!"

So saying, he began to cut through the stem again at about six yards from the thick end. This done, he cut three strong, short poles or levers from the stout branches, with which to roll the log down the beach into the sea; for, as it was nearly two feet thick at the large end, we could not move it without such helps. With the levers, however, we rolled it slowly into the sea.

Having been thus successful in launching our vessel, we next shaped the levers into rude oars or paddles, and then attempted to embark. This was easy enough to do; but after seating ourselves astride the log, it was with the utmost difficulty we kept it from rolling round and plunging us into the water. Not that we minded that much; but we preferred, if possible, to fish in dry clothes. To be sure, our trousers were necessarily wet, as our legs were dangling in the water on each side of the log; but as they could be easily dried, we did not care. After half-an-hour's practice, we became expert enough to keep our balance pretty steadily. Then Peterkin laid down his paddle, and having baited his line with a whole oyster, dropped it into deep water.

"Now, then, Jack," said he, "be cautious; steer clear o' that seaweed. There! that's it; gently, now—gently. I see a fellow at least a foot long down there coming to — Ha! that's it! Oh bother! he's off!"

"Did he bite?" said Jack, urging the log onwards a little with his paddle.

"Bite? Ay! he took it into his mouth, but the moment I began to haul he opened his jaws and let it out again."

"Let him swallow it next time," said Jack, laughing at the melancholy expression of Peterkin's visage.

"There he's again!" cried Peterkin, his eyes flashing with excitement. "Look out! Now, then! No! Yes! No! Why, the brute *won't* swallow it!"

"Try to haul him up by the mouth, then!" cried Jack. "Do it gently."

A heavy sigh and a look of blank despair showed that poor Peterkin had tried and failed again.

"Never mind, lad," said Jack in a voice of sympathy; "we'll move on and offer it to some other fish." So saying, Jack plied his paddle; but scarcely had he moved from the spot when a fish with an enormous head and a little body darted from under a rock and swallowed the bait at once.

"Got him this time—that's a fact!" cried Peterkin, hauling in the line. "He's swallowed the bait right down to his tail, I declare! Oh, what a thumper!"

As the fish came struggling to the surface we leaned forward to see it, and overbalanced the log. Peterkin threw his arms round the fish's neck, and in another instant we were all floundering in the water!

A shout of laughter burst from us as we rose to the surface, like three drowned rats, and seized hold of the log. We soon recovered our position, and sat more warily; while Peterkin secured the fish, which had well-nigh escaped in the midst of our struggles. It was little worth having, however. But, as Peterkin remarked, it was better than the smouts he had been catching for the last two or three days; so we laid it on the log before us, and having re-baited the line, dropped it in again for another.

Now, while we were thus intent upon our sport, our attention was suddenly attracted by a ripple on the sea, just a few yards away from us. Peterkin shouted to us to paddle in that direction, as he thought it was a big fish and we might have a chance of catching it. But Jack, instead of complying, said, in a deep, earnest tone of voice, which I never before heard him use, "Haul up your line, Peterkin; seize your paddle. Quick—it's a shark!"

The horror with which we heard this may well be imagined; for it must be remembered that our legs were hanging down in the water, and we could not venture to pull them up without upsetting the log. Peterkin instantly hauled up the line, and grasping his paddle, exerted himself to the utmost, while we also did our best to make for shore. But we were a good way off, and the log being, as I have before said, very heavy, moved but slowly through the water. We now saw the shark quite distinctly swimming round and round us, its sharp fin every now and then protruding above the water. From its active and unsteady motions, Jack knew it was making up its mind to attack us; so he urged us vehemently to paddle for our lives, while he himself set us the example. Suddenly he shouted, "Look out! there he comes!" and in a second we saw the monstrous fish dive close under us and turn half-over on his side. But we all made a great commotion with our paddles, which, no doubt, frightened it away for that time, as we saw it immediately after circling round us as before.

"Throw the fish to him!" cried Jack in a quick, suppressed voice; "we'll make the shore in time yet if we can keep him off for a few minutes."

Peterkin stopped one instant to obey the command, and then plied his paddle again with all his might. No sooner had the fish fallen on the water than we observed the shark to sink. In another second we saw its white breast rising; for sharks always turn over on their sides when about to seize their prey, their mouths being not at the point of their heads like those of other fish, but, as it were, under their chins. In another moment his snout rose above the water; his wide jaws, armed with a terrific double row of teeth, appeared; the dead fish was engulfed, and the shark sank out of sight. But Jack was mistaken in supposing that it would be satisfied. In a very few minutes it returned to us, and its quick motions led us to fear that it would attack us at once.

"Stop paddling!" cried Jack suddenly. "I see it coming up behind us. Now, obey my orders *quickly*. Our lives may depend on it. Ralph—Peterkin—do your best to *balance the log*. Don't look out for the shark. Don't glance behind you. Do nothing but balance the log."

Peterkin and I instantly did as we were ordered, being only too glad to do anything that afforded us a chance or a hope of escape, for we had implicit confidence in Jack's courage and wisdom. For a few seconds, that seemed long minutes to my mind, we sat thus silently; but I could not resist glancing backward, despite the orders to the contrary. On doing so, I saw Jack sitting rigid like a statue, with his paddle raised, his lips compressed, and his eyebrows bent over his eyes, which glared savagely from beneath them down into the water.

I also saw the shark, to my horror, quite close under the log, in the act of darting towards Jack's foot. I could scarce suppress a cry on beholding this. In another moment the shark rose. Jack drew his leg suddenly from the water and threw it over the log. The monster's snout rubbed against the log as it passed, and revealed its hideous jaws, into which Jack instantly plunged the paddle and thrust it down its throat. So violent was this act that Jack rose to his feet in performing it; the log was thereby rolled completely over, and we were once more plunged into the water. We all rose, spluttering and gasping, in a moment.

"Now, then, strike out for shore!" cried Jack.—"Here, Peterkin, catch hold of my collar, and kick out with a will!"

Peterkin did as he was desired, and Jack struck out with such force that he cut through the water like a boat; while I, being free from all encumbrance, succeeded in keeping up with him. As we had by this time drawn pretty near to the shore, a few minutes more sufficed to carry us into shallow water; and finally, we landed in safety, though very much exhausted, and not a little frightened, by our terrible adventure.

# 8

## THE BEAUTIES OF THE BOTTOM OF THE SEA TEMPT PETERKIN TO DIVE—HOW HE DID IT—MORE DIFFICULTIES OVERCOME—THE WATER GARDEN—CURIOUS CREATURES OF THE SEA—THE TANK—CANDLES MISSED VERY MUCH, AND THE CANDLE-NUT TREE DISCOVERED—WONDERFUL ACCOUNT OF PETERKIN'S FIRST VOYAGE—CLOTH FOUND GROWING ON A TREE—A PLAN PROJECTED, AND ARMS PREPARED FOR OFFENCE AND DEFENCE—A DREADFUL CRY.

Our encounter with the shark was the first great danger that had befallen us since landing on this island; and we felt very seriously affected by it, especially when we considered that we had so often unwittingly incurred the same danger before while bathing. We were now forced to take to fishing again in the shallow water until we should succeed in constructing a raft. What troubled us most, however, was that we were compelled to forego our morning swimming-excursions. We did, indeed, continue to enjoy our bathe in the shallow water; but Jack and I found that one great source of our enjoyment was gone when we could no longer dive down among the beautiful coral groves at the bottom of the lagoon. We had come to be so fond of this exercise, and to take such an interest in watching the formations of coral and the gambols of the many beautiful fish amongst the forest of red and green seaweeds, that we had become quite familiar with the appearance of the fish and the localities that they chiefly haunted. We had also become expert divers. But we made it a rule never to stay long under water at a time. Jack told me that to do so often was bad for the lungs, and instead of affording us enjoyment, would ere long do us a serious injury. So we never stayed at the bottom as long as we might have done, but came up frequently to the top for fresh air, and dived down again immediately. Sometimes, when Jack happened to be in a humorous frame, he would seat himself at the bottom of the sea on one of the brain-corals, as if he were seated on a large paddock-stool, and then make faces at me in order, if possible, to make me laugh under water. At first, when he took me unawares, he nearly succeeded, and I had to shoot to the surface in order to laugh; but afterwards I became aware of his intentions, and being naturally of a grave disposition, I had no difficulty in restraining myself. I used often to wonder how poor Peterkin would have liked to be with us; and he sometimes expressed much regret at being unable to join us. I used to do my best to gratify him, poor fellow, by relating all the wonders that we saw; but this, instead of satisfying, seemed only to whet his curiosity the more, so one day we prevailed on him to try to go down with us. But although a brave boy in every other way, Peterkin was very nervous in the water; and it was with difficulty we got him to consent to be taken down, for he could never have managed to push himself down to the bottom without assistance. But no sooner had we pulled him down a yard or so into the deep, clear water than he began to struggle and kick violently; so we were forced to let him go, when he rose out of the water like a cork, gave a loud gasp and a frightful roar, and struck out for the land with the utmost possible haste.

Now all this pleasure we were to forego, and when we thought thereon, Jack and I felt very much depressed in our spirits. I could see, also, that Peterkin grieved and sympathised with us; for, when talking about this matter, he refrained from jesting and bantering us upon it.

As, however, a man's difficulties usually set him upon devising methods to overcome them, whereby he often discovers better things than those he may have lost, so this our difficulty induced us to think of searching for a large pool among the rocks, where the water should be deep enough for diving, yet so surrounded by rocks as to prevent sharks from getting at us. And such a pool we afterwards found, which proved to be very much better than our most sanguine hopes anticipated. It was situated not more than ten minutes' walk from our camp, and was in the form of a small, deep bay or basin, the entrance to which, besides being narrow, was so shallow that no fish so large as a shark could get in—at least, not unless he should be a remarkably thin one.

Inside of this basin, which we called our Water Garden, the coral formations were much more wonderful, and the seaweed plants far more lovely and vividly coloured, than in the lagoon itself. And the water was so clear and still that, although very deep, you could see the minutest object at the bottom. Besides this, there was a ledge of rock which overhung the basin at its deepest part, from which we could dive pleasantly, and whereon Peterkin could sit and see not only all the wonders I had described to him, but also see Jack and me creeping amongst the marine shrubbery at the bottom, like—as he expressed it—"two great white sea-monsters." During these excursions of ours to the bottom of the sea we began to get an insight into the manners and customs of its inhabitants, and to make discoveries of wonderful things, the like of which we never before conceived. Among other things, we were deeply interested with the operations of the little coral insect, which, I was informed by Jack, is supposed to have entirely constructed many of the numerous islands in the Pacific Ocean. And certainly, when we considered the great reef which these insects had formed round the island on which we were cast, and observed their ceaseless activity in building their myriad cells, it did at first seem as if this might be true; but then, again, when I looked at the mountains of the island, and reflected that there were thousands of such (many of them much higher) in the South Seas, I doubted that there must be some mistake here. But more of this hereafter.

I also became much taken up with the manners and appearance of the anemones, and starfish, and crabs, and sea-urchins, and such-like creatures; and was not content with watching those I saw during my dives in the Water Garden, but I must needs scoop out a hole in the coral rock close to it, which I filled with salt water, and stocked with sundry specimens of anemones and shell-fish, in order to watch more closely how they were in the habit of passing their time. Our burning-glass, also, now became a great treasure to me, as it enabled me to magnify, and so to perceive more clearly, the forms and actions of these curious creatures of the deep.

Having now got ourselves into a very comfortable condition, we began to talk of a project which we had long had in contemplation—namely, to travel entirely round the island, in order, first, to ascertain whether it contained any other productions which might be useful to us; and, second, to see whether there might be any place more convenient and suitable for our permanent residence than that on which we were now encamped. Not that we were in any degree dissatisfied with it. On the contrary, we entertained quite a home-feeling to our bower and its neighbourhood; but if a better place did exist, there was no reason why we should not make use of it. At any rate, it would be well to know of its existence.

We had much earnest talk over this matter. But Jack proposed that, before undertaking such an excursion, we should supply ourselves with good defensive arms; for, as we intended not only to go round all the shore, but to descend most of the valleys, before returning home, we should be likely to meet in with—he would not say *dangers*—but at least with everything that existed on the island, whatever that might be.

"Besides," said Jack, "it won't do for us to live on cocoa-nuts and oysters always. No doubt they are very excellent in their way, but I think a little animal food now and then would be agreeable as well as good for us; and as there are many small birds among the trees, some of which are probably very good to eat, I think it would be a capital plan to make bows and arrows, with which we could easily knock them over."

"First-rate!" cried Peterkin. "You will make the bows, Jack, and I'll try my hand at the arrows. The fact is, I'm quite tired of throwing stones at the birds. I began the very day we landed, I think, and have persevered up to the present time, but I've never hit anything yet."

"You forget," said I, "you hit me one day on the shin."

"Ah, true!" replied Peterkin; "and a precious shindy you kicked up in consequence. But you were at least four yards away from the impudent paroquet I aimed at, so you see what a horribly bad shot I am."

"But, Jack," said I, "you cannot make three bows and arrows before to-morrow; and would it not be a pity to waste time, now that we have made up our minds to go on this expedition?—Suppose that you make one bow and arrow for yourself, and we can take our clubs?"

"That's true, Ralph. The day is pretty far advanced, and I doubt if I can make even one bow before dark. To be sure, I might work by firelight after the sun goes down."

We had, up to this time, been in the habit of going to bed with the sun, as we had no pressing call to work o' nights; and, indeed, our work during the day was usually hard enough—what between fishing, and improving our bower, and diving in the Water Garden, and rambling in the woods—so that when night came we were usually very glad to retire to our beds. But now that we had a desire to work at night, we felt a wish for candles.

"Won't a good blazing fire give you light enough?" inquired Peterkin.

"Yes," replied Jack, "quite enough; but then it will give us a great deal more than enough of heat in this warm climate of ours."

"True," said Peterkin; "I forgot that. It would roast us."

"Well, as you're always doing that at any rate," remarked Jack, "we could scarcely call it a change. But the fact is, I've been thinking over this subject before. There is a certain nut growing in these islands which is called the candle-nut, because the natives use it instead of candles; and I know all about it, and how to prepare it for burning—"

"Then why don't you do it?" interrupted Peterkin. "Why have you kept us in the dark so long, you vile philosopher?"

"Because," said Jack, "I have not seen the tree yet, and I'm not sure that I should know either the tree or the nuts if I did see them. You see, I forget the description."

"Ah! that's just the way with me," said Peterkin with a deep sigh. "I never could keep in my mind for half-an-hour the few descriptions I ever attempted to remember. The very first voyage I ever made was caused by my mistaking a description—or forgetting it, which is the same thing. And a horrible voyage it was. I had to fight with the captain the whole way out, and made the homeward voyage by swimming!"

"Come, Peterkin," said I, "you can't get even *me* to believe that."

"Perhaps not, but it's true notwithstanding," returned Peterkin, pretending to be hurt at my doubting his word.

"Let us hear how it happened," said Jack, while a good-natured smile overspread his face.

"Well, you must know," began Peterkin, "that the very day before I went to sea I was greatly taken up with a game at hockey, which I was playing with my old school-fellows for the last time before leaving them.—You see I was young then, Ralph." Peterkin gazed, in an abstracted and melancholy manner, out to sea.—"Well, in the midst of the game, my uncle, who had taken all the bother and trouble of getting me bound 'prentice and rigged out, came and took me aside, and told me that he was called suddenly away from home, and would not be able to see me aboard, as he had intended. 'However,' said he, 'the captain knows you are coming, so that's not of much consequence; but as you'll have to find the ship yourself, you must remember her name and description. D'ye hear, boy?' I certainly did hear, but I'm afraid I did not understand; for my mind was so taken up with the game, which I saw my side was losing, that I began to grow impatient, and the moment my uncle finished his description of the ship and bade me good-bye I bolted back to my game, with only a confused idea of three masts, and a green-painted taffrail, and a gilt figurehead of Hercules with his club at the bow. Next day I was so much cast down with everybody saying good-bye, and a lot o' my female friends cryin' horribly over me, that I did not start for the harbour, where the ship was lying among a thousand others, till it was almost too late. So I had to run the whole way. When I reached the pier, there were so many masts, and so much confusion, that I felt quite humble-bumbled in my faculties. 'Now,' said I to myself, 'Peterkin, you're in a fix.' Then I fancied I saw a gilt figurehead and three masts belonging to a ship just about to start; so I darted on board, but speedily jumped on shore again when I found that two of the masts belonged to another vessel and the figurehead to a third! At last I caught sight of what I made sure was it—a fine large vessel just casting off her moorings. The taffrail was green. Three masts—yes, that must be it—and the gilt figurehead of Hercules. To be sure, it had a three-pronged pitchfork in its hand instead of a club; but that might be my uncle's mistake, or perhaps Hercules sometimes varied his weapons. 'Cast off!' roared a voice from the quarter-deck. 'Hold on!' cried I, rushing frantically through the crowd. 'Hold on! hold on!' repeated some of the bystanders, while the men at the ropes delayed for a minute. This threw the captain into a frightful rage; for some of his friends had come down to see him off, and having his orders contradicted so flatly was too much for him. However, the delay was sufficient. I took a race and a good leap; the ropes were cast off; the steam-tug gave a puff, and we started. Suddenly the captain walks up to me: 'Where did you come from, you scamp, and what do you want here?'

"'Please, sir,' said I, touching my cap, 'I'm your new 'prentice come aboard.'

"'New 'prentice!' said he, stamping; 'I've got no new 'prentice. My boys are all aboard already. This is a trick, you young blackguard! You've run away, you have!' And the captain stamped about the deck and swore dreadfully; for, you see, the thought of having to stop the ship and lower a boat and lose half-an-hour, all for the sake of sending a small boy ashore, seemed to make him very angry. Besides, it was blowin' fresh outside the harbour, so that to have let the steamer alongside to put me into it was no easy job. Just as we were passing the pier-head, where several boats were rowing into the harbour, the captain came up to me.

"'You've run away, you blackguard!' he said, giving me a box on the ear.

"'No, I haven't!' said I angrily, for the box was by no means a light one.

"'Hark'ee, boy, can you swim?'

"'Yes,' said I.

"'Then do it!' and seizing me by my trousers and the nape of my neck, he tossed me over the side into the sea. The fellows in the boats at the end of the pier backed their oars on seeing this; but observing that I could swim, they allowed me to make the best of my way to the pier-head.—So you see, Ralph, that I really did swim my first homeward voyage."

Jack laughed, and patted Peterkin on the shoulder.

"But tell us about the candle-nut tree," said I. "You were talking about it."

"Very true," said Jack; "but I fear I can remember little about it. I believe the nut is about the size of a walnut; and I think that the leaves are white, but I am not sure."

"Eh! ha! hum!" exclaimed Peterkin; "I saw a tree answering to that description this very day."

"Did you?" cried Jack. "Is it far from this?"

"No, not half-a-mile."

"Then lead me to it," said Jack, seizing his axe.

In a few minutes we were all three pushing through the underwood of the forest, headed by Peterkin.

We soon came to the tree in question, which, after Jack had closely examined it, we concluded must be the candle-nut tree. Its leaves were of a beautiful silvery white, and formed a fine contrast to the dark-green foliage of the surrounding trees. We immediately filled our pockets with the nuts, after which Jack said:

"Now, Peterkin, climb that cocoa-nut tree and cut me one of the long branches."

This was soon done; but it cost some trouble, for the stem was very high, and as Peterkin usually pulled nuts from the younger trees, he was not much accustomed to climbing the high ones. The leaf or branch was a very large one, and we were surprised at its size and strength. Viewed from a little distance, the cocoa-nut tree seems to be a tall, straight stem, without a single branch except at the top, where there is a tuft of feathery-looking leaves that seem to wave like soft plumes in the wind. But when we saw one of these leaves or branches at our feet, we found it to be a strong stalk, about fifteen feet long, with a number of narrow, pointed leaflets ranged alternately on each side. But what seemed to us the most wonderful thing about it was a curious substance resembling cloth, which was wrapped round the thick end of the stalk where it had been cut from the tree. Peterkin told us that he had the greatest difficulty in separating the branch from the stem on account of this substance, as it was wrapped quite round the tree, and, he observed, round all the other branches, thus forming a strong support to the large leaves while exposed to high winds. When I call this substance cloth I do not exaggerate. Indeed, with regard to all the things I saw during my eventful career in the South Seas, I have been exceedingly careful not to exaggerate, or in any way to mislead or deceive my readers. This cloth, I say, was remarkably like to coarse brown cotton cloth. It had a seam or fibre down the centre of it, from which diverged other fibres, about the size of a bristle. There were two layers of these fibres, very long and tough, the one layer crossing the other obliquely, and the whole was cemented together with a still finer fibrous and adhesive substance. When we regarded it attentively, we could with difficulty believe that it had not been woven by human hands. This remarkable piece of cloth we stripped carefully off, and found it to be above two feet long by a foot broad, and we carried it home with us as a great prize.

Jack now took one of the leaflets, and cutting out the central spine or stalk, hurried back with it to our camp. Having made a small fire, he baked the nuts slightly and then peeled off the husks. After this he wished to bore a hole in them, which, not having anything better at hand at the time, he did with the point of our useless pencil-case. Then he strung them on the cocoa-nut spine, and on putting a light to the topmost nut we found, to our joy, that it burned with a clear, beautiful flame, upon seeing which Peterkin sprang up and danced round the fire for at least five minutes in the excess of his satisfaction.

"Now, lads," said Jack, extinguishing our candle, "the sun will set in an hour, so we have no time to lose. I shall go and cut a young tree to make my bow out of, and you had better each of you go and select good strong sticks for clubs, and we'll set to work at them after dark."

So saying, he shouldered his axe and went off; followed by Peterkin; while I took up the piece of newly discovered cloth, and fell to examining its structure. So engrossed was I in this that I was still sitting in the same attitude and occupation when my companions returned.

"I told you so!" cried Peterkin with a loud laugh.—"Oh Ralph, you're incorrigible! See, there's a club for you. I was sure, when we left you looking at that bit of stuff, that we would find you poring over it when we came back, so I just cut a club for you as well as for myself."

"Thank you, Peterkin," said I. "It was kind of you to do that instead of scolding me for a lazy fellow, as I confess I deserve."

"Oh, as to that," returned Peterkin, "I'll blow you up yet if you wish it; only it would be of no use if I did, for you're a perfect mule!"

As it was now getting dark we lighted our candle, and placing it in a holder made of two crossing branches inside of our bower, we seated ourselves on our leafy beds and began to work.

"I intend to appropriate the bow for my own use," said Jack, chipping the piece of wood he had brought with his axe. "I used to be a pretty fair shot once.—But what's that you're doing?" he added, looking at Peterkin, who had drawn the end of a long pole into the tent, and was endeavouring to fit a small piece of the hoop-iron to the end of it.

"I'm going to enlist into the Lancers," answered Peterkin. "You see, Jack, I find the club rather an unwieldy instrument for my delicately formed muscles, and I flatter myself I shall do more execution with a spear."

"Well, if length constitutes power," said Jack, "you'll certainly be invincible."

The pole which Peterkin had cut was full twelve feet long, being a very strong but light and tough young tree, which merely required thinning at the butt to be a serviceable weapon.

"That's a very good idea," said I.

"Which—this?" inquired Peterkin, pointing to the spear.

"Yes," I replied.

"Humph!" said he; "you'd find it a pretty tough and matter-of-fact idea if you had it stuck through your gizzard, old boy!"

"I mean the idea of making it is a good one," said I, laughing. "And, now I think of it, I'll change my plan too. I don't think much of a club, so I'll make me a sling out of this piece of cloth. I used to be very fond of slinging, ever since I read of David slaying Goliath the Philistine, and I was once thought to be expert at it."

So I set to work to manufacture a sling. For a long time we all worked very busily without speaking. At length Peterkin looked up. "I say, Jack, I'm sorry to say I must apply to you for another strip of your handkerchief to tie on this rascally head with. It's pretty well torn at any rate, so you won't miss it."

Jack proceeded to comply with this request, when Peterkin suddenly laid his hand on his arm and arrested him.

"Hist, man!" said he; "be tender! You should never be needlessly cruel if you can help it. Do try to shave past Lord Nelson's mouth without tearing it, if possible! Thanks. There are plenty more handkerchiefs on the cocoa-nut trees."

Poor Peterkin! with what pleasant feelings I recall and record his jests and humorous sayings now!

While we were thus engaged we were startled by a distant, but most strange and horrible, cry. It seemed to come from the sea, but was so far away that we could not clearly distinguish its precise direction. Rushing out of our bower, we hastened down to the beach and stayed to listen. Again it came, quite loud and distinct on the night air—a prolonged, hideous cry, something like the braying of an ass. The moon had risen, and we could see the islands in and beyond the lagoon quite plainly; but there was no object visible to account for such a cry. A strong gust of wind was blowing from the point whence the sound came, but this died away while we were gazing out to sea.

"What can it be?" said Peterkin in a low whisper, while we all involuntarily crept closer to each other.

"Do you know," said Jack, "I have heard that mysterious sound twice before, but never so loud as to-night. Indeed, it was so faint that I thought I must have merely fancied it; so, as I did not wish to alarm you, I said nothing about it."

We listened for a long time for the sound again; but as it did not come, we returned to the bower and resumed our work.

"Very strange!" said Peterkin quite gravely.—"Do you believe in ghosts, Ralph?"

"No," I answered, "I do not. Nevertheless, I must confess that strange, unaccountable sounds, such as we have just heard, make me feel a little uneasy."

"What say you to it, Jack?"

"I neither believe in ghosts nor feel uneasy," he replied. "I never saw a ghost myself, and I never met with any one who had; and I have generally found that strange and unaccountable things have almost always been accounted for, and found to be quite simple, on close examination. I certainly can't imagine what *that* sound is; but I'm quite sure I shall find out before long, and if it's a ghost I'll—I'll—"

"Eat it!" cried Peterkin.

"Yes, I'll eat it!—Now, then, my bow and two arrows are finished; so, if you're ready, we had better turn in."

By this time Peterkin had thinned down his spear, and tied an iron point very cleverly to the end of it; I had formed a sling, the lines of which were composed of thin strips of the cocoa-nut cloth, plaited; and Jack had made a stout bow, nearly five feet long, with two arrows, feathered with two or three large plumes which some bird had dropped. They had no barbs; but Jack said that if arrows were well feathered they did not require iron points, but would fly quite well if merely sharpened at the point, which I did not know before.

"A feathered arrow without a barb," said he, "is a good weapon, but a barbed arrow without feathers is utterly useless."

The string of the bow was formed of our piece of whip-cord, part of which, as he did not like to cut it, was rolled round the bow.

Although thus prepared for a start on the morrow we thought it wise to exercise ourselves a little in the use of our weapons before starting, so we spent the whole of the next day in practising. And it was well we did so, for we found that our arms were very imperfect, and that we were far from perfect in the use of them. First, Jack found that the bow was much too strong, and he had to thin it. Also the spear was much too heavy, and so had to be reduced in thickness, although nothing would induce Peterkin to have it shortened. My sling answered very well; but I had fallen so much out of practice that my first stone knocked off Peterkin's hat, and narrowly missed making a second Goliath of him. However, after having spent the whole day in diligent practice, we began to find some of our former expertness returning, at least Jack and I did. As for Peterkin, being naturally a neat-handed boy, he soon handled his spear well, and could run full tilt at a cocoa-nut, and hit it with great precision once out of every five times.

But I feel satisfied that we owed much of our rapid success to the unflagging energy of Jack, who insisted that since we had made him captain, we should obey him; and he kept us at work from morning till night, perseveringly, at the same thing. Peterkin wished very much to run about and stick his spear into everything he passed; but Jack put up a cocoa-nut, and would not let him leave off running at that for a moment except when he wanted to rest. We laughed at Jack for this, but we were both convinced that it did us much good.

That night we examined and repaired our arms ere we lay down to rest, although we were much fatigued, in order that we might be in readiness to set out on our expedition at daylight on the following morning.

# 9

## PREPARE FOR A JOURNEY ROUND THE ISLAND—SAGACIOUS REFLECTIONS—MYSTERIOUS APPEARANCES AND STARTLING OCCURRENCES.

Scarcely had the sun shot its first ray across the bosom of the broad Pacific when Jack sprang to his feet, and hallooing in Peterkin's ear to awaken him, ran down the beach to take his customary dip in the sea. We did not, as was our wont, bathe that morning in our Water Garden, but in order to save time, refreshed ourselves in the shallow water just opposite the bower. Our breakfast was also despatched without loss of time, and in less than an hour afterwards all our preparations for the journey were completed.

In addition to his ordinary dress, Jack tied a belt of cocoa-nut cloth round his waist, into which he thrust the axe. I was also advised to put on a belt and carry a short cudgel or bludgeon in it, for, as Jack truly remarked, the sling would be of little use if we should chance to come to close quarters with any wild animal. As for Peterkin, notwithstanding that he carried such a long and, I must add, frightful-looking spear over his shoulder, we could not prevail on him to leave his club behind; "for," said he, "a spear at close quarters is not worth a button." I must say that it seemed to me that the club was, to use his own style of language, not worth a button-hole; for it was all knotted over at the head, something like the club which I remember to have observed in picture-books of Jack the Giant-killer, besides being so heavy that he required to grasp it with both hands in order to wield it at all. However, he took it with him, and in this manner we set out upon our travels.

We did not consider it necessary to carry any food with us, as we knew that wherever we went we should be certain to fall in with cocoa-nut trees—having which we were amply supplied, as Peterkin said, with meat and drink and pocket-handkerchiefs! I took the precaution, however, to put the burning-glass into my pocket lest we should want fire.

The morning was exceedingly lovely. It was one of that very still and peaceful sort which made the few noises that we heard seem to be quiet noises (I know no other way of expressing this idea)—noises which, so far from interrupting the universal tranquillity of earth, sea, and sky, rather tended to reveal to us how quiet the world round us really was. Such sounds as I refer to were the peculiar, melancholy—yet, it seemed to me, cheerful—plaint of sea-birds floating on the glassy waters or sailing in the sky; also the subdued twittering of little birds among the bushes, the faint ripples on the beach, and the solemn boom of the surf upon the distant coral reef. We felt very glad in our hearts as we walked along the sands, side by side. For my part, I felt so deeply overjoyed that I was surprised at my own sensations, and fell into a reverie upon the causes of happiness. I came to the conclusion that a state of profound peace and repose, both in regard to outward objects and within the soul, is the happiest condition in which man can be placed; for although I had many a time been most joyful and happy when engaged in bustling, energetic, active pursuits or amusements, I never found that such joy or satisfaction was so deep or so pleasant to reflect upon as that which I now experienced. And I was the more confirmed in this opinion when I observed—and, indeed, as told by himself—that Peterkin's happiness was also very great; yet he did not express this by dancing, as was his wont, nor did he give so much as a single shout, but walked quietly between us with his eye sparkling and a joyful smile upon his countenance. My reader must not suppose that I thought all this in the clear and methodical manner in which I have set it down here. These thoughts did indeed pass through my mind; but they did so in a very confused and indefinite manner, for I was young at that time and not much given to deep reflections. Neither did I consider that the peace whereof I write is not to be found in this world—at least in its perfection—although I have since learned that, by religion, a man may attain to a very great degree of it.

I have said that Peterkin walked along the sands between us. We had two ways of walking together about our island. When we travelled through the woods we always did so in single file, as by this method we advanced with greater facility, the one treading in the other's footsteps. In such cases Jack always took the lead, Peterkin followed, and I brought up the rear. But when we travelled along the sands, which extended almost in an unbroken line of glistening white round the island, we marched abreast, as we found this method more sociable and every way more pleasant. Jack, being the tallest, walked next the sea, and Peterkin marched between us, as by this arrangement either of us could talk to him or he to us, while if Jack and I happened to wish to converse together we could conveniently do so over Peterkin's head. Peterkin used to say, in reference to this arrangement, that had he been as tall as either of us, our order of march might have been the same; for, as Jack often used to scold him for letting everything we said to him pass in at one ear and out at the other, his head could, of course, form no interruption to our discourse.

We were now fairly started. Half-a-mile's walk conveyed us round a bend in the land which shut out our bower from view, and for some time we advanced at a brisk pace without speaking, though our eyes were not idle, but noted everything—in the woods, on the shore, or in the sea—that was interesting. After passing the ridge of land that formed one side of our valley—the Valley of the Wreck—we beheld another small vale lying before us in all the luxuriant loveliness of tropical vegetation. We had indeed seen it before from the mountain-top, but we had no idea that it would turn out to be so much more lovely when we were close to it. We were about to commence the exploration of this valley when Peterkin stopped us, and directed our attention to a very remarkable appearance in advance along the shore.

"What's yon, think you?" said he, levelling his spear as if he expected an immediate attack from the object in question, though it was full half-a-mile distant.

As he spoke, there appeared a white column above the rocks, as if of steam or spray. It rose upwards to a height of several feet, and then disappeared. Had this been near the sea, we would not have been so greatly surprised, as it might in that case have been the surf, for at this part of the coast the coral reef approached so near to the island that in some parts it almost joined it. There was, therefore, no lagoon between, and the heavy surf of the ocean beat almost up to the rocks. But this white column appeared about fifty yards inland. The rocks at the place were rugged, and they stretched across the sandy beach into the sea. Scarce had we ceased expressing our surprise at this sight when another column flew upwards for a few seconds, not far from the spot where the first had been seen, and disappeared; and so, at long, irregular intervals, these strange sights recurred. We were now quite sure that the columns were watery, or composed of spray; but what caused them we could not guess, so we determined to go and see.

In a few minutes we gained the spot, which was very rugged and precipitous, and, moreover, quite damp with the falling of the spray. We had much ado to pass over dry-shod. The ground, also, was full of holes here and there. Now, while we stood anxiously waiting for the reappearance of these waterspouts, we heard a low, rumbling sound near us, which quickly increased to a gurgling and hissing noise, and a moment afterwards a thick spout of water burst upwards from a hole in the rock and spouted into the air with much violence, and so close to where Jack and I were standing that it nearly touched us. We sprang aside, but not before a cloud of spray descended and drenched us both to the skin.

Peterkin, who was standing farther off; escaped with a few drops, and burst into an uncontrollable fit of laughter on beholding our miserable plight.

"Mind your eye!" he shouted eagerly; "there goes another!" The words were scarcely out of his mouth when there came up a spout from another hole, which served us exactly in the same manner as before.

Peterkin now shrieked with laughter; but his merriment was abruptly put a stop to by the gurgling noise occurring close to where he stood.

"Where'll it spout this time, I wonder?" he said, looking about with some anxiety and preparing to run. Suddenly there came a loud hiss or snort; a fierce spout of water burst up between Peterkin's legs, blew him off his feet, enveloped him in its spray, and hurled him to the ground. He fell with so much violence that we feared he must have broken some of his bones, and ran anxiously to his assistance; but fortunately he had fallen on a clump of tangled herbage, in which he lay sprawling in a most deplorable condition.

It was now our turn to laugh; but as we were not yet quite sure that he was unhurt, and as we knew not when or where the next spout might arise, we assisted him hastily to jump up and hurry from the spot.

I may here add that, although I am quite certain that the spout of water was very strong, and that it blew Peterkin completely off his legs, I am not quite certain of the exact height to which it lifted him, being somewhat startled by the event, and blinded partially by the spray, so that my power of observation was somewhat impaired for the moment.

"What's to be done now?" asked Peterkin ruefully.

"Make a fire, lad, and dry ourselves," replied Jack.

"And here is material ready to our hand," said I, picking up a dried branch of a tree as we hurried up to the woods.

In about an hour after this mishap our clothes were again dried. While they were hanging up before the fire we walked down to the beach, and soon observed that these curious spouts took place immediately after the fall of a huge wave, never before it; and, moreover, that the spouts did not take place excepting when the billow was an extremely large one. From this we concluded that there must be a subterraneous channel in the rock into which the water was driven by the larger waves, and finding no way of escape except through these small holes, was thus forced up violently through them. At any rate, we could not conceive any other reason for these strange waterspouts, and as this seemed a very simple and probable one, we forthwith adopted it.

"I say, Ralph, what's that in the water? Is it a shark?" said Jack just as we were about to quit the place.

I immediately ran to the overhanging ledge of rock, from which he was looking down into the sea, and bent over it. There I saw a very faint, pale object of a greenish colour, which seemed to move slightly while I looked at it.

"It's like a fish of some sort," said I.

"Hallo, Peterkin!" cried Jack. "Fetch your spear; here's work for it!"

But when we tried to reach the object, the spear proved to be too short.

"There, now," said Peterkin with a sneer; "you were always telling me it was too long."

Jack now drove the spear forcibly towards the object, and let go his hold. But although it seemed to be well aimed, he must have missed, for the handle soon rose again; and when the spear was drawn up, there was the pale-green object in exactly the same spot, slowly moving its tail.

"Very odd!" said Jack.

But although it was undoubtedly very odd, and although Jack and all of us plunged the spear at it repeatedly, we could neither hit it nor drive it away, so we were compelled to continue our journey without discovering what it was. I was very much perplexed at this strange appearance in the water, and could not get it out of my mind for a long time afterwards. However, I quieted myself by resolving that I would pay a visit to it again at some more convenient season.

## 10

## MAKE DISCOVERY OF MANY EXCELLENT ROOTS AND FRUITS—THE RESOURCES OF THE CORAL ISLAND GRADUALLY UNFOLDED—THE BANYAN TREE—ANOTHER TREE WHICH IS SUPPORTED BY NATURAL PLANKS—WATER-FOWL FOUND—A VERY REMARKABLE DISCOVERY, AND A VERY PECULIAR MURDER—WE LUXURIATE ON THE FAT OF THE LAND.

Our examination of the little valley proved to be altogether most satisfactory. We found in it not only similar trees to those we had already seen in our own valley, but also one or two others of a different species. We had also the satisfaction of discovering a peculiar vegetable, which, Jack concluded, must certainly be that of which he had read as being very common among the South Sea Islanders, and which was named taro. Also we found a large supply of yams, and another root like a potato in appearance. As these were all quite new to us, we regarded our lot as a most fortunate one, in being thus cast on an island which was so prolific and so well stored with all the necessaries of life. Long afterwards we found out that this island of ours was no better in these respects than thousands of other islands in those seas. Indeed, many of them were much richer and more productive; but that did not render us the less grateful for our present good fortune. We each put one of these roots in our pocket, intending to use them for our supper—of which more hereafter. We also saw many beautiful birds here, and traces of some four-footed animal again. Meanwhile the sun began to descend; so we returned to the shore and pushed on, round the spouting rocks, into the next valley. This was that valley of which I have spoken as running across the entire island. It was by far the largest and most beautiful that we had yet looked upon. Here were trees of every shape and size and hue which it is possible to conceive of, many of which we had not seen in the other valleys; for, the stream in this valley being larger, and the mould much richer than in the Valley of the Wreck, it was clothed with a more luxuriant growth of trees and plants. Some trees were dark, glossy green; others of a rich and warm hue, contrasting well with those of a pale, light green, which were everywhere abundant. Among these we recognised the broad, dark heads of the bread-fruit, with its golden fruit; the pure, silvery foliage of the candle-nut, and several species which bore a strong resemblance to the pine; while here and there, in groups and in single trees, rose the tall forms of the cocoa-nut palms, spreading abroad, and waving their graceful plumes high above all the rest, as if they were a superior race of stately giants keeping guard over these luxuriant forests. Oh, it was a most enchanting scene! and I thanked God for having created such delightful spots for the use of man.

Now, while we were gazing around us in silent admiration, Jack uttered an exclamation of surprise, and pointing to an object a little to one side of us, said:

"That's a banyan tree."

"And what's a banyan tree?" inquired Peterkin as we walked towards it.

"A very curious one, as you shall see presently," replied Jack. "It is called the *aoa* here, if I recollect rightly, and has a wonderful peculiarity about it. What an enormous one it is, to be sure!"

"*It*!" repeated Peterkin. "Why, there are dozens of banyans here! What do you mean by talking bad grammar? Is your philosophy deserting you, Jack?"

"There is but one tree here of this kind," returned Jack, "as you will perceive if you will examine it." And, sure enough, we did find that what we had supposed was a forest of trees was in reality only one. Its bark was of a light colour, and had a shining appearance, the leaves being lance-shaped, small, and of a beautiful pea-green. But the wonderful thing about it was that the branches, which grew out from the stem horizontally, sent down long shoots or fibres to the ground, which, taking root, had themselves become trees, and were covered with bark like the tree itself. Many of these fibres had descended from the branches at various distances, and thus supported them on natural pillars, some of which were so large and strong that it was not easy at first to distinguish the offspring from the parent stem. The fibres were of all sizes and in all states of advancement, from the pillars we have just mentioned to small cords which hung down and were about to take root, and thin brown threads still far from the ground, which swayed about with every motion of wind. In short, it seemed to us that, if there were only space afforded to it, this single tree would at length cover the whole island.

Shortly after this we came upon another remarkable tree, which, as its peculiar formation afterwards proved extremely useful to us, merits description. It was a splendid chestnut, but its proper name Jack did not know. However, there were quantities of fine nuts upon it, some of which we put in our pockets. But its stem was the most wonderful part of it. It rose to about twelve feet without a branch, and was not of great thickness; on the contrary, it was remarkably slender for the size of the tree. But to make up for this, there were four or five wonderful projections in this stem, which I cannot better describe than by asking the reader to suppose that five planks of two inches thick and three feet broad had been placed round the trunk of the tree, with their *edges* closely fixed to it, from the ground up to the branches, and that these planks had been covered over with the bark of the tree and incorporated with it. In short, they were just natural buttresses, without which the stem could not have supported its heavy and umbrageous top. We found these chestnuts to be very numerous. They grew chiefly on the banks of the stream, and were of all sizes.

While we were examining a small tree of this kind Jack chipped a piece off a buttress with his axe, and found the wood to be firm and easily cut. He then struck the axe into it with all his force, and very soon split it off close to the tree—first, however, having cut it across transversely above and below. By this means he satisfied himself that we could now obtain short planks, as it were all ready sawn, of any size and thickness that we desired, which was a very great discovery indeed—perhaps the most important we had yet made.

We now wended our way back to the coast, intending to encamp near the beach, as we found that the mosquitoes were troublesome in the forest. On our way we could not help admiring the birds which flew and chirped around us. Among them we observed a pretty kind of paroquet, with a green body, a blue head, and a red breast; also a few beautiful turtle-doves, and several flocks of wood-pigeons. The hues of many of these birds were extremely vivid—bright green, blue, and scarlet being the prevailing tints. We made several attempts throughout the day to bring down one of these, both with the bow and the sling—not for mere sport, but to ascertain whether they were good for food. But we invariably missed, although once or twice we were very near hitting. As evening drew on however, a flock of pigeons flew past. I slung a stone into the midst of them at a venture, and had the good fortune to kill one. We were startled soon after by a loud whistling noise above our heads, and on looking up, saw a flock of wild ducks making for the coast. We watched these, and observing where they alighted, followed them up until we came upon a most lovely blue lake, not more than two hundred yards long, embosomed in verdant trees. Its placid surface, which reflected every leaf and stem as if in a mirror, was covered with various species of wild ducks, feeding among the sedges and broad-leaved water-plants which floated on it, while numerous birds like water-hens ran to and fro most busily on its margin. These all, with one accord, flew tumultuously away the instant we made our appearance. While walking along the margin we observed fish in the water, but of what sort we could not tell.

Now, as we neared the shore, Jack and I said we would go a little out of our way to see if we could procure one of those ducks; so, directing Peterkin to go straight to the shore and kindle a fire, we separated, promising to rejoin him speedily. But we did not find the ducks, although we made a diligent search for half-an-hour. We were about to retrace our steps when we were arrested by one of the strangest sights that we had yet beheld.

Just in front of us, at the distance of about ten yards, grew a superb tree, which certainly was the largest we had yet seen on the island. Its trunk was at least five feet in diameter, with a smooth, grey bark; above this the spreading branches were clothed with light-green leaves, amid which were clusters of bright-yellow fruit, so numerous as to weigh down the boughs with their great weight. This fruit seemed to be of the plum species, of an oblong form, and a good deal larger than the magnum bonum plum. The ground at the foot of this tree was thickly strewn with the fallen fruit, in the midst of which lay sleeping, in every possible attitude, at least twenty hogs of all ages and sizes, apparently quite surfeited with a recent banquet.

Jack and I could scarce restrain our laughter as we gazed at these coarse, fat, ill-looking animals while they lay groaning and snoring heavily amid the remains of their supper.

"Now, Ralph," said Jack in a low whisper, "put a stone in your sling—a good big one—and let fly at that fat fellow with his back toward you. I'll try to put an arrow into yon little pig."

"Don't you think we had better put them up first?" I whispered. "It seems cruel to kill them while asleep."

"If I wanted *sport*, Ralph, I would certainly set them up; but as we only want *pork*, we'll let them lie. Besides, we're not sure of killing them; so, fire away."

Thus admonished, I slung my stone with so good aim that it went bang against the hog's flank as if against the head of a drum; but it had no other effect than that of causing the animal to start to its feet, with a frightful yell of surprise, and scamper away. At the same instant Jack's bow twanged, and the arrow pinned the little pig to the ground by the ear.

"I've missed, after all!" cried Jack, darting forward with uplifted axe; while the little pig uttered a loud squeal, tore the arrow from the ground, and ran away with it, along with the whole drove, into the bushes and disappeared, though we heard them screaming long afterwards in the distance.

"That's very provoking, now," said Jack, rubbing the point of his nose.

"Very," I replied, stroking my chin.

"Well, we must make haste and rejoin Peterkin," said Jack; "it's getting late." And without further remark, we threaded our way quickly through the woods towards the shore.

When we reached it we found wood laid out, the fire lighted and beginning to kindle up, with other signs of preparation for our encampment; but Peterkin was nowhere to be found. We wondered very much at this; but Jack suggested that he might have gone to fetch water, so he gave a shout to let him know that we had arrived, and sat down upon a rock, while I threw off my jacket and seized the axe, intending to split up one or two billets of wood. But I had scarce moved from the spot when, in the distance, we heard a most appalling shriek, which was followed up by a chorus of yells from the hogs, and a loud hurrah.

"I do believe," said I, "that Peterkin has met with the hogs."

"When Greek meets Greek," said Jack, soliloquising, "then comes the tug of—"

"Hurrah!" shouted Peterkin in the distance.

We turned hastily towards the direction whence the sound came, and soon descried Peterkin walking along the beach towards us with a little pig transfixed on the end of his long spear!

"Well done, my boy!" exclaimed Jack, slapping him on the shoulder when he came up. "You're the best shot amongst us."

"Look here, Jack!" cried Peterkin as he disengaged the animal from his spear. "Do you recognise that hole?" said he, pointing to the pig's ear; "and are you familiar with this arrow, eh?"

"Well, I declare!" said Jack.

"Of course you do," interrupted Peterkin; "but, pray, restrain your declarations at this time, and let's have supper—for I'm uncommonly hungry, I can tell you. And it's no joke to charge a whole herd of swine with their great-grandmother bristling like a giant porcupine, at the head of them!"

We now set about preparing supper; and, truly, a good display of viands we made when all was laid out on a flat rock in the light of the blazing fire. There was, first of all, the little pig; then there were the taro-root, and the yam, and the potato, and six plums; and lastly, the wood-pigeon. To these Peterkin added a bit of sugar-cane, which he had cut from a little patch of that plant which he had found not long after separating from us; "and," said he, "the patch was somewhat in a square form, which convinces me it must have been planted by man."

"Very likely," replied Jack. "From all we have seen, I'm inclined to think that some of the savages must have dwelt here long ago."

We found no small difficulty in making up our minds how we were to cook the pig. None of us had ever cut up one before, and we did not know exactly how to begin; besides, we had nothing but the axe to do it with, our knife having been forgotten. At last Jack started up and said:

"Don't let us waste more time talking about it, boys.—Hold it up, Peterkin. There, lay the hind leg on this block of wood—so;" and he cut it off; with a large portion of the haunch, at a single blow of the axe. "Now the other—that's it." And having thus cut off the two hind legs, he made several deep gashes in them, thrust a sharp-pointed stick through each, and stuck them up before the blaze to roast. The wood-pigeon was then split open, quite flat, washed clean in salt water, and treated in a similar manner. While these were cooking we scraped a hole in the sand and ashes under the fire, into which we put our vegetables and covered them up.

The taro-root was of an oval shape, about ten inches long and four or five thick. It was of a mottled-grey colour, and had a thick rind. We found it somewhat like an Irish potato, and exceedingly good. The yam was roundish, and had a rough brown skin. It was very sweet and well flavoured. The potato, we were surprised to find, was quite sweet and exceedingly palatable, as also were the plums—and, indeed, the pork and pigeon too—when we came to taste them. Altogether, this was decidedly the most luxurious supper we had enjoyed for many a day. Jack said it was out-of-sight better than we ever got on board ship; and Peterkin said he feared that if we should remain long on the island he would infallibly become a glutton or an epicure, whereat Jack remarked that he need not fear that, for he was both already! And so, having eaten our fill, not forgetting to finish off with a plum, we laid ourselves comfortably down to sleep, upon a couch of branches, under the overhanging ledge of a coral rock.

## II

## EFFECTS OF OVEREATING, AND REFLECTIONS THEREON—HUMBLE ADVICE REGARDING COLD WATER—THE "HORRIBLE CRY" ACCOUNTED FOR—THE CURIOUS BIRDS CALLED PENGUINS—PECULIARITY OF THE COCOA-NUT PALM—QUESTIONS ON THE FORMATION OF CORAL ISLANDS—MYSTERIOUS FOOTSTEPS—STRANGE DISCOVERIES AND SAD SIGHTS.

When we awoke on the following morning we found that the sun was already a good way above the horizon, so I came to the conclusion that a heavy supper is not conducive to early rising. Never-the-less, we felt remarkably strong and well, and much disposed to have our breakfast. First, however, we had our customary morning bathe, which refreshed us greatly.

I have often wondered very much in after years that the inhabitants of my own dear land did not make more frequent use of this most charming element, water—I mean in the way of cold bathing. Of course, I have perceived that it is not convenient for them to go into the sea or the rivers in winter, as we used to do on the Coral Island; but then I knew from experience that a large washing-tub and a sponge do form a most pleasant substitute. The feelings of freshness, of cleanliness, of vigour, and extreme hilarity that always followed my bathes in the sea—and even, when in England, my ablutions in the wash-tub—were so delightful that I would sooner have gone without my breakfast than without my bathe in cold water. My readers will forgive me for asking whether they are in the habit of bathing thus every morning; and if they answer "No", they will pardon me for recommending them to begin at once. Of late years, since retiring from the stirring life of adventure which I have led so long in foreign climes, I have heard of a system called the cold-water cure. Now, I do not know much about that system; so I do not mean to uphold it, neither do I intend to run it down. Perhaps, in reference to it, I may just hint that there may be too much of a good thing—I know not. But of this I am quite certain, that there may also be too little of a good thing; and the great delight I have had in cold bathing during the course of my adventurous career inclines me to think that it is better to risk taking too much than to content one's self with too little. Such is my opinion, derived from much experience; but I put it before my readers with the utmost diffidence and with profound modesty, knowing that it may possibly jar with their feelings of confidence in their own ability to know and judge as to what is best and fittest in reference to their own affairs. But to return from this digression, for which I humbly crave forgiveness.

We had not advanced on our journey much above a mile or so, and were just beginning to feel the pleasant glow that usually accompanies vigorous exercise, when, on turning a point that revealed to us a new and beautiful cluster of islands, we were suddenly arrested by the appalling cry which had so alarmed us a few nights before. But this time we were by no means so much alarmed as on the previous occasion, because, whereas at that time it was night, now it was day; and I have always found, though I am unable to account for it, that daylight banishes many of the fears that are apt to assail us in the dark.

On hearing the sound, Peterkin instantly threw forward his spear.

"Now, what can it be?" said he, looking round at Jack. "I tell you what it is: if we are to go on being pulled up in a constant state of horror and astonishment, as we have been for the last week, the sooner we're out o' this island the better, notwithstanding the yams and lemonade, and pork and plums!"

Peterkin's remark was followed by a repetition of the cry, louder than before.

"It comes from one of these islands," said Jack.

"It must be the ghost of a jackass, then," said Peterkin, "for I never heard anything so like."

We all turned our eyes towards the cluster of islands, where, on the largest, we observed curious objects moving on the shore.

"Soldiers they are—that's flat!" cried Peterkin, gazing at them in the utmost amazement.

And, in truth, Peterkin's remark seemed to me to be correct; for at the distance from which we saw them, they appeared to be an army of soldiers. There they stood, rank and file, in lines and in squares, marching and counter-marching, with blue coats and white trousers. While we were looking at them the dreadful cry came again over the water, and Peterkin suggested that it must be a regiment sent out to massacre the natives in cold blood. At this remark Jack laughed and said:

"Why, Peterkin, they are penguins!"

"Penguins?" repeated Peterkin.

"Ay, penguins, Peterkin, penguins—nothing more or less than big sea-birds, as you shall see one of these days when we pay them a visit in our boat, which I mean to set about building the moment we return to our bower."

"So, then, our dreadful yelling ghosts and our murdering army of soldiers," remarked Peterkin, "have dwindled down to penguins—big sea-birds! Very good. Then I propose that we continue our journey as fast as possible, lest our island should be converted into a dream before we get completely round it."

Now, as we continued on our way, I pondered much over this new discovery and the singular appearance of these birds, of which Jack could only give us a very slight and vague account; and I began to long to commence our boat, in order that we might go and inspect them more narrowly. But by degrees these thoughts left me, and I began to be much taken up again with the interesting peculiarities of the country which we were passing through.

The second night we passed in a manner somewhat similar to the first—at about two-thirds of the way round the island, as we calculated—and we hoped to sleep on the night following at our bower. I will not here note so particularly all that we said and saw during the course of this second day, as we did not make any further discoveries of great importance. The shore along which we travelled, and the various parts of the woods through which we passed, were similar to those which have been already treated of. There were one or two observations that we made, however, and these were as follows:

We saw that, while many of the large fruit-bearing trees grew only in the valleys, and some of them only near the banks of the streams, where the soil was peculiarly rich, the cocoa-nut palm grew in every place whatsoever—not only on the hillsides, but also on the seashore, and even, as has been already stated, on the coral reef itself, where the soil, if we may use the name, was nothing better than loose sand mingled with broken shells and coral rock. So near to the sea, too, did this useful tree grow, that in many places its roots were washed by the spray from the breakers. Yet we found the trees growing thus on the sands to be quite as luxuriant as those growing in the valleys, and the fruit as good and refreshing also. Besides this, I noticed that on the summit of the high mountain, which we once more ascended at a different point from our first ascent, were found abundance of shells and broken coral formations, which, Jack and I agreed, proved either that this island must have once been under the sea, or that the sea must once have been above the island: in other words, that as shells and coral could not possibly climb to the mountain-top, they must have been washed upon it while the mountain-top was on a level with the sea. We pondered this very much; and we put to ourselves the question, "What raised the island to its present height above the sea?" But to this we could by no means give to ourselves a satisfactory reply. Jack thought it might have been blown up by a volcano; and Peterkin said he thought it must have jumped up of its own accord! We also noticed, what had escaped us before, that the solid rocks of which the island was formed were quite different from the live coral rocks on the shore, where, the wonderful little insects were continually working. They seemed, indeed, to be of the same material—a substance like limestone; but while the coral rocks were quite full of minute cells in which the insects lived, the other rocks inland were hard and solid, without the appearance of cells at all. Our thoughts and conversations on this subject were sometimes so profound that Peterkin said we should certainly get drowned in them at last, even although we were such good divers! Nevertheless, we did not allow his pleasantry on this and similar points to deter us from making our notes and observations as we went along.

We found several more droves of hogs in the woods, but abstained from killing any of them, having more than sufficient for our present necessities. We saw, also, many of their footprints in this neighbourhood. Among these we also observed the footprints of a smaller animal, which we examined with much care, but could form no certain opinion as to them. Peterkin thought they were those of a little dog, but Jack and I thought differently. We became very curious on this matter, the more so that we observed these footprints to lie scattered about in one locality, as if the animal which had made them was wandering round about in a very irregular manner and without any object in view. Early in the forenoon of our third day we observed these footprints to be much more numerous than ever, and in one particular spot they diverged off into the woods in a regular beaten track, which was, however, so closely beset with bushes that we pushed through it with difficulty. We had now become so anxious to find out what animal this was, and where it went to, that we determined to follow the track and, if possible, clear up the mystery. Peterkin said, in a bantering tone, that he was sure it would be cleared up, as usual, in some frightfully simple way, and prove to be no mystery at all!

The beaten track seemed much too large to have been formed by the animal itself, and we concluded that some larger animal had made it, and that the smaller one made use of it. But everywhere the creeping plants and tangled bushes crossed our path, so that we forced our way along with some difficulty. Suddenly, as we came upon an open space, we heard a faint cry, and observed a black animal standing in the track before us.

"A wild cat!" cried Jack, fitting an arrow to his bow, and discharging it so hastily that he missed the animal, and hit the earth about half-a-foot to one side of it. To our surprise, the wild cat did not fly, but walked slowly towards the arrow and snuffed at it.

"That's the most comical wild cat I ever saw!" cried Jack.

"It's a tame wild cat, I think," said Peterkin, levelling his spear to make a charge.

"Stop!" cried I, laying my hand on his shoulder. "I do believe the poor beast is blind. See, it strikes against the branches as it walks along. It must be a very old one;" and I hastened towards it.

"Only think," said Peterkin with a suppressed laugh, "of a superannuated wild cat!"

We now found that the poor cat was not only blind, or nearly so, but extremely deaf, as it did not hear our footsteps until we were quite close behind it. Then it sprang round, and, putting up its back and tail, while the black hair stood all on end, uttered a hoarse mew and a fuff.

Poor thing said Peterkin, gently extending his hand and endeavouring to pat the cat's head. "Poor pussy! chee, chee, chee! puss, puss, puss! cheetie pussy!"

No sooner did the cat hear these sounds than all signs of anger fled, and advancing eagerly to Peterkin, it allowed itself to be stroked, and rubbed itself against his legs, purring loudly all the time, and showing every symptom of the most extreme delight.

"It's no more a wild cat than I am!" cried Peterkin, taking it in his arms; "it's quite tame. —Poor pussy! cheetie pussy!"

We now crowded around Peterkin, and were not a little surprised—and, to say truth, a good deal affected—by the sight of the poor animal's excessive joy. It rubbed its head against Peterkin's cheek, licked his chin, and thrust its head almost violently into his neck, while it purred more loudly than I ever heard a cat purr before, and appeared to be so much overpowered by its feelings that it occasionally mewed and purred almost in the same breath. Such demonstrations of joy and affection led us at once to conclude that this poor cat must have known man before, and we conjectured that it had been left either accidentally or by design on the island many years ago, and was now evincing its extreme joy at meeting once more with human beings. While we were fondling the cat and talking about it, Jack glanced round the open space in the midst of which we stood.

"Hallo!" exclaimed he; "this looks something like a clearing. The axe has been at work here. Just look at these tree-stumps."

We now turned to examine these, and without doubt we found trees that had been cut down here and there, also stumps and broken branches—all of which, however, were completely covered over with moss, and bore evidence of having been in this condition for some years. No human footprints were to be seen either on the track or among the bushes, but those of the cat were found everywhere. We now determined to follow up the track as far as it went, and Peterkin put the cat down; but it seemed to be so weak, and mewed so very pitifully, that he took it up again and carried it in his arms, where in a few minutes it fell sound asleep.

About ten yards farther on, the felled trees became more numerous, and the track, diverging to the right, followed for a short space the banks of a stream. Suddenly we came to a spot where once must have been a rude bridge, the stones of which were scattered in the stream, and those on each bank entirely covered over with moss. In silent surprise and expectancy we continued to advance, and a few yards farther on, beheld, under the shelter of some bread-fruit trees, a small hut or cottage. I cannot hope to convey to my readers a very correct idea of the feelings that affected us on witnessing this unexpected sight. We stood for a long time in silent wonder, for there was a deep and most melancholy stillness about the place that quite overpowered us; and when we did at length speak, it was in subdued whispers, as if we were surrounded by some awful or supernatural influence. Even Peterkin's voice, usually so quick and lively on all occasions, was hushed now; for there was a dreariness about this silent, lonely, uninhabited cottage—so strange in its appearance, so far away from the usual dwellings of man, so old, decayed, and deserted in its aspect that fell upon our spirits like a thick cloud, and blotted out as with a pall the cheerful sunshine that had filled us since the commencement of our tour round the island.

The hut or cottage was rude and simple in its construction. It was not more than twelve feet long by ten feet broad, and about seven or eight feet high. It had one window, or rather a small frame in which a window might perhaps once have been, but which was now empty. The door was exceedingly low, and formed of rough boards, and the roof was covered with broad cocoa-nut and plantain leaves. But every part of it was in a state of the utmost decay. Moss and green matter grew in spots all over it. The woodwork was quite perforated with holes; the roof had nearly fallen in, and appeared to be prevented from doing so altogether by the thick matting of creeping plants and the interlaced branches which years of neglect had allowed to cover it almost entirely; while the thick, luxuriant branches of the bread-fruit and other trees spread above it, and flung a deep, sombre shadow over the spot, as if to guard it from the heat and the light of day. We conversed long and in whispers about this strange habitation ere we ventured to approach it; and when at length we did so, it was, at least on my part, with feelings of awe.

At first Jack endeavoured to peep in at the window; but from the deep shadow of the trees already mentioned, and the gloom within, he could not clearly discern objects, so we lifted the latch and pushed open the door. We observed that the latch was made of iron, and almost eaten away with rust. In the like condition were also the hinges, which creaked as the door swung back. On entering, we stood still and gazed around us, while we were much impressed with the dreary stillness of the room. But what we saw there surprised and shocked us not a little. There was no furniture in the apartment save a little wooden stool and an iron pot, the latter almost eaten through with rust. In the corner farthest from the door was a low bedstead, on which lay two skeletons, embedded in a little heap of dry dust. With beating hearts we went forward to examine them. One was the skeleton of a man; the other that of a dog, which was extended close beside that of the man, with its head resting on his bosom.

Now we were very much concerned about this discovery, and could scarce refrain from tears on beholding these sad remains. After some time we began to talk about what we had seen, and to examine in and around the hut, in order to discover some clue to the name or history of this poor man, who had thus died in solitude, with none to mourn his loss save his cat and his faithful dog. But we found nothing—neither a book nor a scrap of paper. We found, however, the decayed remnants of what appeared to have been clothing, and an old axe. But none of these things bore marks of any kind, and indeed they were so much decayed as to convince us that they had lain in the condition in which we found them for many years.

This discovery now accounted to us for the tree-stump at the top of the mountain with the initials cut on it; also for the patch of sugar-cane and other traces of man which we had met with in the course of our rambles over the island. And we were much saddened by the reflection that the lot of this poor wanderer might possibly be our own, after many years' residence on the island, unless we should be rescued by the visit of some vessel or the arrival of natives. Having no clue whatever to account for the presence of this poor human being in such a lonely spot, we fell to conjecturing what could have brought him there. I was inclined to think that he must have been a shipwrecked sailor, whose vessel had been lost here, and all the crew been drowned except himself and his dog and cat. But Jack thought it more likely that he had run away from his vessel, and had taken the dog and cat to keep him company. We were also much occupied in our minds with the wonderful difference between the cat and the dog. For here we saw that while the one perished like a loving friend by its master's side, with its head resting on his bosom, the other had sought to sustain itself by prowling abroad in the forest, and had lived in solitude to a good old age. However, we did not conclude from this that the cat was destitute of affection, for we could not forget its emotions on first meeting with us; but we saw from this that the dog had a great deal more of generous love in its nature than the cat, because it not only found it impossible to live after the death of its master, but it must needs, when it came to die, crawl to his side and rest its head upon his lifeless breast.

While we were thinking on these things, and examining into everything about the room, we were attracted by an exclamation from Peterkin.

"I say, Jack," said he, "here is something that will be of use to us."

"What is it?" said Jack, hastening across the room.

"An old pistol," replied Peterkin, holding up the weapon, which he had just pulled from under a heap of broken wood and rubbish that lay in a corner.

"That, indeed, might have been useful," said Jack, examining it, "if we had any powder; but I suspect the bow and the sling will prove more serviceable."

"True, I forgot that," said Peterkin; "but we may as well take it with us, for the flint will serve to strike fire with when the sun does not shine."

After having spent more than an hour at this place without discovering anything of further interest, Peterkin took up the old cat, which had lain very contentedly asleep on the stool whereon he had placed it, and we prepared to take our departure. In leaving the hut, Jack stumbled heavily against the door-post, which was so much decayed as to break across, and the whole fabric of the hut seemed ready to tumble about our ears. This put it into our heads that we might as well pull it down, and so form a mound over the skeleton. Jack, therefore, with his axe, cut down the other door-post, which, when it was done, brought the whole hut in ruins to the ground, and thus formed a grave to the bones of the poor recluse and his dog. Then we left the spot, having brought away the iron pot, the pistol, and the old axe, as they might be of much use to us hereafter.

During the rest of this day we pursued our journey, and examined the other end of the large valley, which we found to be so much alike to the parts already described that I shall not recount the particulars of what we saw in this place. I may, however, remark that we did not quite recover our former cheerful spirits until we arrived at our bower, which we did late in the evening, and found everything just in the same condition as we had left it three days before.

## ☙ 12 ❧

## SOMETHING WRONG WITH THE TANK—JACK'S WISDOM AND PETERKIN'S IMPERTINENCE—WONDERFUL BEHAVIOUR OF A CRAB—GOOD WISHES FOR THOSE WHO DWELL FAR FROM THE SEA—JACK COMMENCES TO BUILD A LITTLE BOAT.

Rest is sweet, as well for the body as for the mind. During my long experience, amid the vicissitudes of a chequered life, I have found that periods of profound rest at certain intervals, in addition to the ordinary hours of repose, are necessary to the well-being of man. And the nature, as well as the period, of this rest varies according to the different temperaments of individuals and the peculiar circumstances in which they may chance to be placed. To those who work with their minds, bodily labour is rest; to those who labour with the body, deep sleep is rest; to the downcast, the weary, and the sorrowful, joy and peace are rest. Nay, further, I think that to the gay, the frivolous, the reckless, when sated with pleasures that cannot last, even sorrow proves to be rest of a kind, although, perchance, it were better that I should call it relief than rest. There is, indeed, but one class of men to whom rest is denied—there is no rest to the wicked. At this I do but hint, however, as I treat not of that rest which is spiritual, but more particularly of that which applies to the mind and to the body.

Of this rest we stood much in need on our return home, and we found it exceedingly sweet when we indulged in it after completing the journey just related. It had not, indeed, been a very long journey; nevertheless, we had pursued it so diligently that our frames were not a little prostrated. Our minds were also very much exhausted in consequence of the many surprises, frequent alarms, and much profound thought to which they had been subjected; so that when we lay down, on the night of our return, under the shelter of the bower, we fell immediately into very deep repose. I can state this with much certainty; for Jack afterwards admitted the fact, and Peterkin, although he stoutly denied it, I heard snoring loudly at least two minutes after lying down. In this condition we remained all night and the whole of the following day without awaking once, or so much as moving our positions. When we did awake it was near sunset, and we were all in such a state of lassitude that we merely rose to swallow a mouthful of food. As Peterkin remarked, in the midst of a yawn, we took breakfast at tea-time, and then went to bed again, where we lay till the following forenoon.

After this we arose very greatly refreshed, but much alarmed lest we had lost count of a day. I say we were much alarmed on this head; for we had carefully kept count of the days, since we were cast upon our island, in order that we might remember the Sabbath-day, which day we had hitherto, with one accord, kept as a day of rest, and refrained from all work whatsoever. However, on considering the subject, we all three entertained the same opinion as to how long we had slept, and so our minds were put at ease.

We now hastened to our Water Garden to enjoy a bathe, and to see how did the animals which I had placed in the tank. We found the garden more charming, pellucid, and inviting than ever; and Jack and I plunged into its depths and gambolled among its radiant coral groves, while Peterkin wallowed at the surface, and tried occasionally to kick us as we passed below. Having dressed, I then hastened to the tank; but what was my surprise and grief to find nearly all the animals dead, and the water in a putrid condition! I was greatly distressed at this, and wondered what could be the cause of it.

"Why, you precious humbug!" said Peterkin, coming up to me, "how could you expect it to be otherwise? When fishes are accustomed to live in the Pacific Ocean, how can you expect them to exist in a hole like that?"

"Indeed, Peterkin," I replied, "there seems to be truth in what you say. Nevertheless, now I think of it, there must be some error in your reasoning; for if I put in but a few very small animals, they will bear the same proportion to this pond that the millions of fish bear to the ocean."

"I say, Jack!" cried Peterkin, waving his hand; "come here, like a good fellow. Ralph is actually talking philosophy. Do come to our assistance, for he's out o' sight beyond me already!"

"What's the matter?" inquired Jack, coming up, while he endeavoured to scrub his long hair dry with a towel of cocoa-nut cloth.

I repeated my thoughts to Jack, who, I was happy to find, quite agreed with me. "The best plan," he said, "will be to put very few animals at first into your tank, and add more as you find it will bear them. And look here," he added, pointing to the sides of the tank, which, for the space of two inches above the water-level, were encrusted with salt, "you must carry your philosophy a little further, Ralph. That water has evaporated so much that it is too salt for anything to live in. You will require to add *fresh* water now and then, in order to keep it at the same degree of saltness as the sea."

"Very true, Jack; that never struck me before," said I.

"And, now I think of it," continued Jack, "it seems to me that the surest way of arranging your tank so as to get it to keep pure and in good condition will be to *imitate* the ocean in it; in fact, make it a miniature Pacific. I don't see how you can hope to succeed unless you do that."

"Most true," said I, pondering what my companion said. "But I fear that that will be very difficult."

"Not at all," cried Jack, rolling his towel up into a ball and throwing it into the face of Peterkin, who had been grinning and winking at him during the last five minutes—"not at all. Look here. There is water of a certain saltness in the sea; well, fill your tank with sea-water, and keep it at that saltness by marking the height at which the water stands on the sides. When it evaporates a little, pour in *fresh* water from the brook till it comes up to the mark, and then it will be right, for the salt does not evaporate with the water. Then there's lots of seaweed in the sea; well, go and get one or two bits of seaweed and put them into your tank. Of course the weed must be alive, and growing to little stones; or you can chip a bit off the rocks with the weed sticking to it. Then, if you like, you can throw a little sand and gravel into your tank, and the thing's complete."

"Nay, not quite," said Peterkin, who had been gravely attentive to this off-hand advice —"not quite. You must first make three little men to dive in it before it can be said to be perfect; and that would be rather difficult, I fear, for two of them would require to be philosophers. But hallo! what's this?—I say, Ralph, look here! There's one o' your crabs up to something uncommon. It's performing the most remarkable operation for a crab I ever saw—taking off its coat, I do believe, before going to bed!"

We hastily stooped over the tank, and certainly were not a little amused at the conduct of one of the crabs which still survived its companions. It was one of the common small crabs, like to those that are found running about everywhere on the coast of England. While we gazed at it we observed its back to split away from the lower part of its body, and out of the gap thus formed came a soft lump which moved and writhed unceasingly. This lump continued to increase in size until it appeared like a bunch of crab's legs; and, indeed, such it proved in a very few minutes to be, for the points of the toes were at length extricated from the hole in its back, the legs spread out, the body followed, and the crab walked away quite entire, even to the points of its nipper-claws, leaving a perfectly entire shell behind it, so that, when we looked, it seemed as though there were two complete crabs instead of one.

"Well," exclaimed Peterkin, drawing a long breath, "I've *heard* of a man jumping out of his skin and sitting down in his skeleton in order to cool himself, but I never expected to *see* a crab do it!"

We were, in truth, much amazed at this spectacle, and the more so when we observed that the new crab was larger than the crab that it came out of. It was also quite soft, but by next morning its skin had hardened into a good shell. We came thus to know that crabs grow in this way, and not by the growing of their shells, as we had always thought before we saw this wonderful operation.

Now I considered well the advice which Jack had given me about preparing my tank, and the more I thought of it the more I came to regard it as very sound and worthy of being acted on. So I forthwith put his plan in execution, and found it to answer excellently well—indeed, much beyond my expectation; for I found that after a little experience had taught me the proper proportion of seaweed and animals to put into a certain amount of water, the tank needed no further attendance. And, moreover, I did not require ever afterwards to renew or change the sea-water, but only to add a very little fresh water from the brook, now and then, as the other evaporated. I therefore concluded that if I had been suddenly conveyed, along with my tank, into some region where there was no salt sea at all, my little sea and my sea-fish would have continued to thrive and to prosper notwithstanding. This made me greatly to desire that those people in the world who live far inland might know of my wonderful tank, and by having materials like to those of which it was made conveyed to them, thus be enabled to watch the habits of those most mysterious animals that reside in the sea, and examine with their own eyes the wonders of the great deep.

For many days after this, while Peterkin and Jack were busily employed in building a little boat out of the curious natural planks of the chestnut-tree, I spent much of my time in examining with the burning-glass the marvellous operations that were constantly going on in my tank. Here I saw those anemones which cling, like little red, yellow, and green blobs of jelly, to the rocks, put forth, as it were, a multitude of arms and wait till little fish or other small animalcules unwarily touched them, when they would instantly seize them, fold arm after arm round their victims, and so engulf them in their stomachs. Here I saw the ceaseless working of those little coral insects whose efforts have encrusted the islands of the Pacific with vast rocks, and surrounded them with enormous reefs; and I observed that many of these insects, though extremely minute, were very beautiful, coming out of their holes in a circle of fine threads, and having the form of a shuttlecock. Here I saw curious little barnacles opening a hole in their backs and constantly putting out a thin, feathery hand, with which, I doubt not, they dragged their food into their mouths. Here, also, I saw those crabs which have shells only on the front of their bodies, but no shell whatever on their remarkably tender tails, so that, in order to find a protection to them, they thrust them into the empty shells of whelks, or some such fish, and when they grow too big for one, change into another. But, most curious of all, I saw an animal which had the wonderful power, when it became ill, of casting its stomach and its teeth away from it, and getting an entirely new set in the course of a few months! All this I saw, and a great deal more, by means of my tank and my burning-glass; but I refrain from setting down more particulars here, as I have still much to tell of the adventures that befell us while we remained on this island.

## 13

## NOTABLE DISCOVERY AT THE SPOUTING CLIFFS—THE MYSTERIOUS GREEN MONSTER EXPLAINED—WE ARE THROWN INTO UNUTTERABLE TERROR BY THE IDEA THAT JACK IS DROWNED—THE DIAMOND CAVE.

"Come, Jack," cried Peterkin one morning about three weeks after our return from our long excursion, "let's be jolly to-day, and do something vigorous. I'm quite tired of hammering and bammering, hewing and screwing, cutting and butting at that little boat of ours, that seems as hard to build as Noah's ark. Let us go on an excursion to the mountain-top, or have a hunt after the wild ducks, or make a dash at the pigs. I'm quite flat—flat as bad ginger-beer—flat as a pancake; in fact, I want something to rouse me—to toss me up, as it were. Eh! what do you say to it?"

"Well," answered Jack, throwing down the axe with which he was just about to proceed towards the boat, "if that's what you want, I would recommend you to make an excursion to the waterspouts. The last one we had to do with tossed you up a considerable height; perhaps the next will send you higher—who knows?—if you're at all reasonable or moderate in your expectations!"

"Jack, my dear boy," said Peterkin gravely, "you are really becoming too fond of jesting. It's a thing I don't at all approve of; and if you don't give it up, I fear that, for our mutual good, we shall have to part."

"Well, then, Peterkin," replied Jack with a smile, "what would you have?"

"Have?" said Peterkin. "I would *have* nothing. I didn't say I wanted to *have*; I said that I wanted to *do*."

"By the bye," said I, interrupting their conversation, "I am reminded by this that we have not yet discovered the nature of yon curious appearance that we saw near the waterspouts on our journey round the island. Perhaps it would be well to go for that purpose."

"Humph!" ejaculated Peterkin, "I know the nature of it well enough."

"What was it?" said I.

"It was of a *mysterious* nature, to be sure!" said he with a wave of his hand, while he rose from the log on which he had been sitting and buckled on his belt, into which he thrust his enormous club.

"Well, then, let us away to the waterspouts," cried Jack, going up to the bower for his bow and arrows.—"And bring your spear, Peterkin; it may be useful."

We now, having made up our minds to examine into this matter, sallied forth eagerly in the direction of the waterspout rocks, which, as I have before mentioned, were not far from our present place of abode. On arriving there we hastened down to the edge of the rocks and gazed over into the sea, where we observed the pale-green object still distinctly visible, moving its tail slowly to and fro in the water.

"Most remarkable!" said Jack.

"Exceedingly curious!" said I.

"Beats everything!" said Peterkin.—"Now, Jack," he added, "you made such a poor figure in your last attempt to stick that object that I would advise you to let me try it. If it has got a heart at all, I'll engage to send my spear right through the core of it; if it hasn't got a heart, I'll send it through the spot where its heart ought to be."

"Fire away, then, my boy," replied Jack with a laugh.

Peterkin immediately took the spear, poised it for a second or two above his head, then darted it like an arrow into the sea. Down it went straight into the centre of the green object, passed quite through it, and came up immediately afterwards, pure and unsullied, while the mysterious tail moved quietly as before!

"Now," said Peterkin gravely, "that brute is a heartless monster; I'll have nothing more to do with it."

"I'm pretty sure now," said Jack, "that it is merely a phosphoric light; but I must say I'm puzzled at its staying always in that exact spot."

I also was much puzzled, and inclined to think with Jack that it must be phosphoric light, of which luminous appearance we had seen much while on our voyage to these seas. "But," said I, "there is nothing to hinder us from diving down to it, now that we are sure it is not a shark."

"True," returned Jack, stripping off his clothes. "I'll go down, Ralph, as I'm better at diving than you are.—Now, then, Peterkin, out o' the road!" Jack stepped forward, joined his hands above his head, bent over the rocks, and plunged into the sea. For a second or two the spray caused by his dive hid him from view; then the water became still, and we saw him swimming far down in the midst of the green object. Suddenly he sank below it, and vanished altogether from our sight! We gazed anxiously down at the spot where he had disappeared for nearly a minute, expecting every moment to see him rise again for breath; but fully a minute passed and still he did not reappear. Two minutes passed! and then a flood of alarm rushed in upon my soul when I considered that, during all my acquaintance with him, Jack had never stayed under water more than a minute at a time—indeed, seldom so long.

"Oh Peterkin!" I said in a voice that trembled with increasing anxiety, "something has happened. It is more than three minutes now." But Peterkin did not answer; and I observed that he was gazing down into the water with a look of intense fear mingled with anxiety, while his face was overspread with a deadly paleness. Suddenly he sprang to his feet and rushed about in a frantic state, wringing his hands, and exclaiming, "Oh Jack! Jack! He is gone! It must have been a shark, and he is gone for ever!"

For the next five minutes I know not what I did; the intensity of my feelings almost bereft me of my senses. But I was recalled to myself by Peterkin seizing me by the shoulders and staring wildly into my face, while he exclaimed, "Ralph! Ralph! perhaps he has only fainted! Dive for him, Ralph!"

It seemed strange that this did not occur to me sooner. In a moment I rushed to the edge of the rocks, and without waiting to throw off my garments, was on the point to spring into the waves when I observed something black rising up through the green object.

In another moment Jack's head rose to the surface, and he gave a wild shout, flinging back the spray from his locks, as was his wont after a dive. Now we were almost as much amazed at seeing him reappear, well and strong, as we had been at first at his non-appearance; for, to the best of our judgment, he had been nearly ten minutes under water—perhaps longer—and it required no exertion of our reason to convince us that this was utterly impossible for mortal man to do and retain his strength and faculties. It was, therefore, with a feeling akin to superstitious awe that I held down my hand and assisted him to clamber up the steep rocks. But no such feeling affected Peterkin. No sooner did Jack gain the rocks and seat himself on one, panting for breath, than he threw his arms round his neck and burst into a flood of tears. "Oh Jack! Jack!" said he, "where were you? What kept you so long?"

After a few moments Peterkin became composed enough to sit still and listen to Jack's explanation, although he could not restrain himself from attempting to wink every two minutes at me in order to express his joy at Jack's safety. I say he attempted to wink, but I am bound to add that he did not succeed; for his eyes were so much swollen with weeping that his frequent attempts only resulted in a series of violent and altogether idiotical contortions of the face, that were very far from expressing what he intended. However, I knew what the poor fellow meant by it; so I smiled to him in return, and endeavoured to make believe that he was winking.

"Now, lads," said Jack when we were composed enough to listen to him, "yon green object is not a shark; it is a stream of light issuing from a cave in the rocks. Just after I made my dive, I observed that this light came from the side of the rock above which we are now sitting; so I struck out for it, and saw an opening into some place or other that appeared to be luminous within. For one instant I paused to think whether I ought to venture. Then I made up my mind and dashed into it; for you see, Peterkin, although I take some time to tell this, it happened in the space of a few seconds, so that I knew I had wind enough in me to serve to bring me out o' the hole and up to the surface again. Well, I was just on the point of turning—for I began to feel a little uncomfortable in such a place—when it seemed to me as if there was a faint light right above me. I darted upwards, and found my head out of water. This relieved me greatly, for I now felt that I could take in air enough to enable me to return the way I came. Then it all at once occurred to me that I might not be able to find the way out again; but on glancing downwards, my mind was put quite at rest by seeing the green light below me streaming into the cave, just like the light that we had seen streaming out of it, only what I now saw was much brighter.

"At first I could scarcely see anything as I gazed around me, it was so dark; but gradually my eyes became accustomed to it, and I found that I was in a huge cave, part of the walls of which I observed on each side of me. The ceiling just above me was also visible, and I fancied that I could perceive beautiful, glittering objects there; but the farther end of the cave was shrouded in darkness. While I was looking around me in great wonder, it came into my head that you two would think I was drowned; so I plunged down through the passage again in a great hurry, rose to the surface, and—here I am!"

When Jack concluded his recital of what he had seen in this remarkable cave, I could not rest satisfied till I had dived down to see it; which I did, but found it so dark, as Jack had said, that I could scarcely see anything. When I returned we had a long conversation about, it, during which I observed that Peterkin had a most lugubrious expression on his countenance.

"What's the matter, Peterkin?" said I.

"The matter?" he replied. "It's all very well for you two to be talking away like mermaids about the wonders of this cave; but you know I must be content to hear about it, while you are enjoying yourselves down there like mad dolphins. It's really too bad!"

"I'm very sorry for you, Peterkin—indeed I am," said Jack; "but we cannot help you. If you would only learn to dive—"

"Learn to fly, you might as well say!" retorted Peterkin in a very sulky tone.

"If you would only consent to keep still," said I, "we would take you down with us in ten seconds."

"Hum!" returned Peterkin; "suppose a salamander was to propose to you 'only to keep still' and he would carry you through a blazing fire in a few seconds, what would you say?"

We both laughed and shook our heads, for it was evident that nothing was to be made of Peterkin in the water. But we could not rest satisfied till we had seen more of this cave; so, after further consultation, Jack and I determined to try if we could take down a torch with us, and set fire to it in the cavern. This we found to be an undertaking of no small difficulty, but we accomplished it at last by the following means: First, we made a torch of a very inflammable nature out of the bark of a certain tree, which we cut into strips, and after twisting, cemented together with a kind of resin or gum, which we also obtained from another tree; neither of which trees, however, was known by name to Jack. This, when prepared, we wrapped up in a great number of plies of cocoa-nut cloth, so that we were confident it could not get wet during the short time it should be under water. Then we took a small piece of the tinder, which we had carefully treasured up lest we should require it, as before said, when the sun should fail us; also, we rolled up some dry grass and a few chips, which, with a little bow and drill, like those described before, we made into another bundle and wrapped it up in cocoa-nut cloth. When all was ready we laid aside our garments, with the exception of our trousers, which, as we did not know what rough scraping against the rocks we might be subjected to, we kept on.

Then we advanced to the edge of the rocks—Jack carrying one bundle, with the torch; I the other, with the things for producing fire.

"Now don't weary for us, Peterkin, should we be gone some time," said Jack. "We'll be sure to return in half-an-hour at the very latest, however interesting the cave should be, that we may relieve your mind."

"Farewell!" said Peterkin, coming up to us with a look of deep but pretended solemnity, while he shook hands and kissed each of us on the cheek—"farewell! And while you are gone I shall repose my weary limbs under the shelter of this bush, and meditate on the changefulness of all things earthly, with special reference to the forsaken condition of a poor shipwrecked sailor-boy!" So saying, Peterkin waved his hand, turned from us, and cast himself upon the ground with a look of melancholy resignation, which was so well feigned that I would have thought it genuine had he not accompanied it with a gentle wink. We both laughed, and springing from the rocks together, plunged head first into the sea.

We gained the interior of the submarine cave without difficulty, and on emerging from the waves, supported ourselves for some time by treading water, while we held the two bundles above our heads. This we did in order to let our eyes become accustomed to the obscurity. Then, when we could see sufficiently, we swam to a shelving rock, and landed in safety. Having wrung the water from our trousers, and dried ourselves as well as we could under the circumstances, we proceeded to ignite the torch. This we accomplished without difficulty in a few minutes; and no sooner did it flare up than we were struck dumb with the wonderful objects that were revealed to our gaze. The roof of the cavern just above us seemed to be about ten feet high, but grew higher as it receded into the distance until it was lost in darkness. It seemed to be made of coral, and was supported by massive columns of the same material. Immense icicles (as they appeared to us) hung from it in various places. These, however, were formed, not of ice, but of a species of limestone, which seemed to flow in a liquid form towards the point of each, where it became solid. A good many drops fell, however, to the rock below, and these formed little cones, which rose to meet the points above. Some of them had already met, and thus we saw how the pillars were formed, which at first seemed to us as if they had been placed there by some human architect to support the roof. As we advanced farther in we saw that the floor was composed of the same material as the pillars, and it presented the curious appearance of ripples such as are formed on water when gently ruffled by the wind. There were several openings on either hand in the walls that seemed to lead into other caverns, but these we did not explore at this time. We also observed that the ceiling was curiously marked in many places, as if it were the fretwork of a noble cathedral; and the walls, as well as the roof, sparkled in the light of our torch, and threw back gleams and flashes as if they were covered with precious stones. Although we proceeded far into this cavern, we did not come to the end of it; and we were obliged to return more speedily than we would otherwise have done, as our torch was nearly expended. We did not observe any openings in the roof, or any indications of places whereby light might enter; but near the entrance to the cavern stood an immense mass of pure-white coral rock, which caught and threw back the little light that found an entrance through the cave's mouth, and thus produced, we conjectured, the pale-green object which had first attracted our attention. We concluded, also, that the reflecting power of this rock was that which gave forth the dim light that faintly illumined the first part of the cave.

Before diving through the passage again we extinguished the small piece of our torch that remained, and left it in a dry spot—conceiving that we might possibly stand in need of it if, at any future time, we should chance to wet our torch while diving into the cavern. As we stood for a few minutes after it was out, waiting till our eyes became accustomed to the gloom, we could not help remarking the deep, intense stillness and the unutterable gloom of all around us; and as I thought of the stupendous dome above, and the countless gems that had sparkled in the torchlight a few minutes before, it came into my mind to consider how strange it is that God should make such wonderful and exquisitely beautiful works never to be seen at all—except, indeed, by chance visitors such as ourselves.

I afterwards found that there were many such caverns among the islands of the South Seas, some of them larger and more beautiful than the one I have just described.

"Now, Ralph, are you ready?" said Jack in a low voice, that seemed to echo up into the dome above.

"Quite ready."

"Come along, then," said he; and plunging off the ledge of the rock into the water, we dived through the narrow entrance. In a few seconds we were panting on the rocks above, and receiving the congratulations of our friend Peterkin.

# 14

## STRANGE PECULIARITY OF THE TIDES—ALSO OF THE TWILIGHT—PETERKIN'S REMARKABLE CONDUCT IN EMBRACING A LITTLE PIG AND KILLING A BIG SOW—SAGE REMARKS ON JESTING—ALSO ON LOVE.

It was quite a relief to us to breathe the pure air and to enjoy the glad sunshine after our long ramble in the Diamond Cave, as we named it; for although we did not stay more than half-an-hour away, it seemed to us much longer. While we were dressing, and during our walk home, we did our best to satisfy the curiosity of poor Peterkin, who seemed to regret, with lively sincerity, his inability to dive.

There was no help for it, however, so we condoled with him as we best could. Had there been any great rise or fall in the tide of these seas, we might perhaps have found it possible to take him down with us at low water; but as the tide never rose or fell more than eighteen inches or two feet, this was impossible.

This peculiarity of the tide—its slight rise and fall—had not attracted our observation till some time after our residence on the island. Neither had we observed another curious circumstance until we had been some time there. This was the fact that the tide rose and fell with constant regularity, instead of being affected by the changes of the moon as in our own country, and as it is in most other parts of the world—at least, in all those parts with which I am acquainted. Every day and every night, at twelve o'clock precisely, the tide is at the full; and at six o'clock, every morning and evening, it is ebb. I can speak with much confidence on this singular circumstance, as we took particular note of it, and never found it to alter. Of course I must admit we had to guess the hour of twelve midnight, and I think we could do this pretty correctly; but in regard to twelve noon we are quite positive, because we easily found the highest point that the sun reached in the sky by placing ourselves at a certain spot whence we observed the sharp summit of a cliff resting against the sky, just where the sun passed.

Jack and I were surprised that we had not noticed this the first few days of our residence here, and could only account for it by our being so much taken up with the more obvious wonders of our novel situation. I have since learned, however, that this want of observation is a sad and very common infirmity of human nature, there being hundreds of persons before whose eyes the most wonderful things are passing every day who nevertheless, are totally ignorant of them. I therefore have to record my sympathy with such persons, and to recommend to them a course of conduct which I have now for a long time myself adopted—namely, the habit of forcing my attention upon all things that go on around me, and of taking some degree of interest in them whether I feel it naturally or not. I suggest this the more earnestly, though humbly, because I have very frequently come to know that my indifference to a thing has generally been caused by my ignorance in regard to it.

We had much serious conversation on this subject of the tides; and Jack told us, in his own quiet, philosophical way, that these tides did great good to the world in many ways, particularly in the way of cleansing the shores of the land, and carrying off the filth that was constantly poured into the sea therefrom—which, Peterkin suggested, was remarkably tidy of it to do. Poor Peterkin could never let slip an opportunity to joke, however inopportune it might be, which at first we found rather a disagreeable propensity, as it often interrupted the flow of very agreeable conversation—and, indeed, I cannot too strongly record my disapprobation of this tendency in general; but we became so used to it at last that we found it no interruption whatever. Indeed, strange to say, we came to feel that it was a necessary part of our enjoyment (such is the force of habit), and found the sudden outbursts of mirth, resulting from his humorous disposition, quite natural and refreshing to us in the midst of our more serious conversations. But I must not misrepresent Peterkin. We often found, to our surprise, that he knew many things which we did not; and I also observed that those things which he learned from experience were never forgotten. From all these things I came at length to understand that things very opposite and dissimilar in themselves, when united, do make an agreeable whole; as, for example, we three on this our island, although most unlike in many things, when united, made a trio so harmonious that I question if there ever met before such an agreeable triumvirate. There was, indeed, no note of discord whatever in the symphony we played together on that sweet Coral Island; and I am now persuaded that this was owing to our having been all tuned to the same key—namely, that of *love*! Yes, we loved one another with much fervency while we lived on that island; and, for the matter of that, we love each other still.

And while I am on this subject, or rather the subject that just preceded it—namely, the tides—I may here remark on another curious natural phenomenon. We found that there was little or no twilight in this island. We had a distinct remembrance of the charming long twilight at home, which some people think the most delightful part of the day—though, for my part, I have always preferred sunrise; and when we first landed, we used to sit down on some rocky point or eminence, at the close of our day's work, to enjoy the evening breeze, but no sooner had the sun sunk below the horizon than all became suddenly dark. This rendered it necessary that we should watch the sun when we happened to be out hunting; for to be suddenly left in the dark while in the woods was very perplexing, as, although the stars shone with great beauty and brilliancy, they could not pierce through the thick umbrageous boughs that interlaced above our heads.

But to return. After having told all we could to Peterkin about the Diamond Cave under Spouting Cliff, as we named the locality, we were wending our way rapidly homewards when a grunt and a squeal were borne down by the land breeze to our ears.

"That's the ticket!" was Peterkin's remarkable exclamation as he started convulsively and levelled his spear.

"Hist!" cried Jack; "these are your friends, Peterkin. They must have come over expressly to pay you a friendly visit, for it is the first time we have seen them on this side of the island."

"Come along!" cried Peterkin, hurrying towards the wood; while Jack and I followed, smiling at his impatience.

Another grunt and half-a-dozen squeals, much louder than before, came down the valley. At this time we were just opposite the small vale which lay between the Valley of the Wreck and Spouting Cliff.

"I say, Peterkin!" cried Jack in a hoarse whisper.

"Well, what is't?"

"Stay a bit, man! These grunters are just up there on the hillside. If you go and stand with Ralph in the lee of yon cliff I'll cut round behind and drive them through the gorge, so that you'll have a better chance of picking out a good one. Now, mind you pitch into a fat young pig, Peterkin!" added Jack as he sprang into the bushes.

"Won't I, just!" said Peterkin, licking his lips, as we took our station beside the cliff. "I feel quite a tender affection for young pigs in my heart. Perhaps it would be more correct to say in my tum—"

"There they come!" cried I as a terrific yell from Jack sent the whole herd screaming down the hill. Now Peterkin, being unable to hold back, crept a short way up a very steep grassy mound in order to get a better view of the hogs before they came up; and just as he raised his head above its summit, two little pigs, which had outrun their companions, rushed over the top with the utmost precipitation. One of these brushed close past Peterkin's ear; the other, unable to arrest its headlong flight, went, as Peterkin himself afterwards expressed it, 'bash' into his arms with a sudden squeal, which was caused more by the force of the blow than the will of the animal, and both of them rolled violently down to the foot of the mound. No sooner was this reached than the little pig recovered its feet, tossed up its tail, and fled shrieking from the spot. But I slung a large stone after it, which, being fortunately well aimed, hit it behind the ear and felled it to the earth.

"Capital, Ralph! that's your sort!" cried Peterkin, who, to my surprise and great relief, had risen to his feet apparently unhurt, though much dishevelled. He rushed frantically towards the gorge, which the yells of the hogs told us they were now approaching. I had made up my mind that I would abstain from killing another, as, if Peterkin should be successful, two were more than sufficient for our wants at the present time. Suddenly they all burst forth—two or three little round ones in advance, and an enormous old sow with a drove of hogs at her heels.

"Now, Peterkin," said I, "there's a nice little fat one; just spear it."

But Peterkin did not move; he allowed it to pass unharmed. I looked at him in surprise, and saw that his lips were compressed and his eyebrows knitted, as if he were about to fight with some awful enemy.

"What is it?" I inquired with some trepidation.

Suddenly he levelled his spear, darted forward, and with a yell that nearly froze the blood in my veins, stabbed the old sow to the heart. Nay, so vigorously was it done that the spear went in at one side and came out at the other!

"Oh Peterkin!" said I, going up to him, "what have you done?"

"Done? I've killed their great-great-grandmother, that's all," said he, looking with a somewhat awestruck expression at the transfixed animal.

"Hallo! what's this?" said Jack as he came up. "Why, Peterkin, you must be fond of a tough chop. If you mean to eat this old hog, she'll try your jaws, I warrant. What possessed you to stick *her*, Peterkin?"

"Why, the fact is, I want a pair of shoes."

"What have your shoes to do with the old hog?" said I, smiling.

"My present shoes have certainly nothing to do with her," replied Peterkin; "nevertheless, she will have a good deal to do with my future shoes. The fact is, when I saw you floor that pig so neatly, Ralph, it struck me that there was little use in killing another. Then I remembered all at once that I had long wanted some leather or tough substance to make shoes of, and this old grandmother seemed so tough that I just made up my mind to stick her —and you see I've done it!"

"That you certainly have, Peterkin," said Jack as he was examining the transfixed animal.

We now considered how we were to carry our game home, for, although the distance was short, the hog was very heavy. At length we hit on the plan of tying its four feet together, and passing the spear-handle between them. Jack took one end on his shoulder, I took the other on mine, and Peterkin carried the small pig.

Thus we returned in triumph to our bower, laden, as Peterkin remarked, with the glorious spoils of a noble hunt. As he afterwards spoke in similarly glowing terms in reference to the supper that followed, there is every reason to believe that we retired that night to our leafy beds in a high state of satisfaction.

## 15

## BOAT-BUILDING EXTRAORDINARY—PETERKIN TRIES HIS HAND AT COOKERY, AND FAILS MOST SIGNALLY—THE BOAT FINISHED—CURIOUS CONVERSATION WITH THE CAT, AND OTHER MATTERS.

For many days after this, Jack applied himself with unremitting assiduity to the construction of our boat, which at length began to look something like one. But those only who have had the thing to do can entertain a right idea of the difficulty involved in such an undertaking, with no other implements than an axe, a bit of hoop-iron, a sail-needle, and a broken penknife. But Jack did it. He was of that disposition which *will* not be conquered. When he believed himself to be acting rightly, he overcame all obstacles. I have seen Jack, when doubtful whether what he was about to do were right or wrong, as timid and vacillating as a little girl; and I honour him for it!

As this boat was a curiosity in its way, a few words here relative to the manner of its construction may not be amiss.

I have already mentioned the chestnut-tree with its wonderful buttresses or planks. This tree, then, furnished us with the chief part of our material. First of all, Jack sought out a limb of a tree of such a form and size as, while it should form the keel, a bend at either end should form the stem and stern-posts. Such a piece, however, was not easy to obtain; but at last he procured it by rooting up a small tree which had a branch growing at the proper angle about ten feet up its stem, with two strong roots growing in such a form as enabled him to make a flat-sterned boat. This placed, he procured three branching roots of suitable size, which he fitted to the keel at equal distances, thus forming three strong ribs. Now the squaring and shaping of these, and the cutting of the grooves in the keel, was an easy enough matter, as it was all work for the axe, in the use of which Jack was become wonderfully expert; but it was quite a different affair when he came to nailing the ribs to the keel, for we had no instrument capable of boring a large hole, and no nails to fasten them with. We were, indeed, much perplexed here; but Jack at length devised an instrument that served very well. He took the remainder of our hoop-iron and beat it into the form of a pipe or cylinder, about as thick as a man's finger. This he did by means of our axe and the old rusty axe we had found at the house of the poor man at the other side of the island. This, when made red hot, bored slowly through the timbers; and the better to retain the heat, Jack shut up one end of it and filled it with sand. True, the work was very slowly done; but it mattered not—we had little else to do. Two holes were bored in each timber, about an inch and a half apart, and also down into the keel, but not quite through. Into these were placed stout pegs made of a tree called iron-wood, and when they were hammered well home, the timbers were as firmly fixed as if they had been nailed with iron. The gunwales, which were very stout, were fixed in a similar manner. But besides the wooden nails, they were firmly lashed to the stem and stern-posts and ribs by means of a species of cordage which we had contrived to make out of the fibrous husk of the cocoa-nut. This husk was very tough, and when a number of the threads were joined together they formed excellent cordage. At first we tied the different lengths together; but this was such a clumsy and awkward complication of knots that we contrived, by careful interlacing of the ends together before twisting, to make good cordage of any size or length we chose. Of course it cost us much time and infinite labour; but Jack kept up our spirits when we grew weary, and so all that we required was at last constructed.

Planks were now cut off the chestnut-trees of about an inch thick. These were dressed with the axe—but clumsily, for an axe is ill-adapted for such work. Five of these planks on each side were sufficient; and we formed the boat in a very rounded, barrel-like shape, in order to have as little twisting of the planks as possible, for although we could easily bend them, we could not easily twist them. Having no nails to rivet the planks with, we threw aside the ordinary fashion of boat-building and adopted one of our own. The planks were therefore placed on each other's edges, and sewed together with the tough cordage already mentioned; they were also thus sewed to the stem, the stern, and the keel. Each stitch or tie was six inches apart, and was formed thus: Three holes were bored in the upper plank and three in the lower, the holes being above each other—that is, in a vertical line. Through these holes the cord was passed, and when tied, formed a powerful stitch of three-ply. Besides this, we placed between the edges of the planks layers of cocoa-nut fibre, which, as it swelled when wetted, would, we hoped, make our little vessel water-tight. But in order further to secure this end, we collected a large quantity of pitch from the bread-fruit tree, with which, when boiled in our old iron pot, we paid the whole of the inside of the boat, and while it was yet hot, placed large pieces of cocoa-nut cloth on it, and then gave it another coat above that. Thus the interior was covered with a tough, water-tight material; while the exterior, being uncovered, and so exposed to the swelling action of the water, was, we hoped, likely to keep the boat quite dry. I may add that our hopes were not disappointed.

While Jack was thus engaged, Peterkin and I sometimes assisted him; but as our assistance was not much required, we more frequently went a-hunting on the extensive mud-flats at the entrance of the long valley which lay nearest to our bower. Here we found large flocks of ducks of various kinds, some of them bearing so much resemblance to the wild ducks of our own country that I think they must have been the same. On these occasions we took the bow and the sling, with both of which we were often successful, though I must confess that I was the least so. Our suppers were thus pleasantly varied, and sometimes we had such a profusion spread out before us that we frequently knew not with which of the dainties to begin.

I must also add that the poor old cat which we had brought home had always a liberal share of our good things; and so well was it looked after, especially by Peterkin, that it recovered much of its former strength, and seemed to improve in sight as well as hearing.

The large flat stone, or rock of coral, which stood just in front of the entrance to our bower, was our table. On this rock we had spread out the few articles we possessed the day we were shipwrecked; and on the same rock, during many a day afterwards, we spread out the bountiful supply with which we had been blessed on our Coral Island. Sometimes we sat down at this table to a feast consisting of hot rolls—as Peterkin called the newly baked bread-fruit—a roast pig, roast duck, boiled and roasted yams, cocoa-nuts, taro, and sweet potatoes; which we followed up with a dessert of plums, apples, and plantains—the last being a large-sized and delightful fruit, which grew on a large shrub or tree not more than twelve feet high, with light-green leaves of enormous length and breadth. These luxurious feasts were usually washed down with cocoa-nut lemonade.

Occasionally Peterkin tried to devise some new dish—"a conglomerate," as he used to say; but these generally turned out such atrocious compounds that he was ultimately induced to give up his attempts in extreme disgust—not forgetting, however, to point out to Jack that his failure was a direct contradiction to the proverb which he (Jack) was constantly thrusting down his throat—namely, that "where there's a will there's a way." For he had a great will to become a cook, but could by no means find a way to accomplish that end.

One day, while Peterkin and I were seated beside our table, on which dinner was spread, Jack came up from the beach, and flinging down his axe, exclaimed:

"There, lads, the boat's finished at last! So we've nothing to do now but shape two pair of oars, and then we may put to sea as soon as we like."

This piece of news threw us into a state of great joy; for although we were aware that the boat had been gradually getting near its completion, it had taken so long that we did not expect it to be quite ready for at least two or three weeks. But Jack had wrought hard and said nothing, in order to surprise us.

"My dear fellow," cried Peterkin, "you're a perfect trump! But why did you not tell us it was so nearly ready? Won't we have a jolly sail to-morrow, eh?"

"Don't talk so much, Peterkin," said Jack; "and, pray, hand me a bit of that pig."

"Certainly, my dear," cried Peterkin, seizing the axe. "What part will you have? A leg, or a wing, or a piece of the breast—which?"

"A hind leg, if you please," answered Jack; "and, pray, be so good as to include the tail."

"With all my heart," said Peterkin, exchanging the axe for his hoop-iron knife, with which he cut off the desired portion. "I'm only too glad, my dear boy, to see that your appetite is so wholesale, and there's no chance whatever of its dwindling down into re-tail again—at least, in so far as this pig is concerned.—Ralph, lad, why don't you laugh, eh?" he added, turning suddenly to me with a severe look of inquiry.

"Laugh!" said I. "What at, Peterkin? Why should I laugh?"

Both Jack and Peterkin answered this inquiry by themselves laughing so immoderately that I was induced to believe I had missed noticing some good joke, so I begged that it might be explained to me; but as this only produced repeated roars of laughter, I smiled and helped myself to another slice of plantain.

"Well, but," continued Peterkin, "I was talking of a sail to-morrow. Can't we have one, Jack?"

"No," replied Jack, "we can't have a sail; but I hope we shall have a row, as I intend to work hard at the oars this afternoon, and if we can't get them finished by sunset, we'll light our candle-nuts, and turn them out of hands before we turn into bed."

"Very good," said Peterkin, tossing a lump of pork to the cat, who received it with a mew of satisfaction. "I'll help you, if I can."

"Afterwards," continued Jack, "we will make a sail out of the cocoa-nut cloth, and rig up a mast; and then we shall be able to sail to some of the other islands, and visit our old friends the penguins."

The prospect of being so soon in a position to extend our observations to the other islands, and enjoy a sail over the beautiful sea, afforded us much delight, and after dinner we set about making the oars in good earnest. Jack went into the woods and blocked them roughly out with the axe, and I smoothed them down with the knife, while Peterkin remained in the bower spinning, or rather twisting, some strong, thick cordage with which to fasten them to the boat.

We worked hard and rapidly, so that when the sun went down Jack and I returned to the bower with four stout oars, which required little to be done to them save a slight degree of polishing with the knife. As we drew near we were suddenly arrested by the sound of a voice. We were not a little surprised at this—indeed, I may almost say alarmed; for although Peterkin was undoubtedly fond of talking, we had never, up to this time, found him talking to himself. We listened intently, and still heard the sound of a voice as if in conversation. Jack motioned me to be silent, and advancing to the bower on tiptoe, we peeped in.

The sight that met our gaze was certainly not a little amusing. On the top of a log which we sometimes used as a table sat the black cat with a very demure expression on its countenance, and in front of it, sitting on the ground with his legs extended on either side of the log, was Peterkin. At the moment we saw him he was gazing intently into the cat's face, with his nose about four inches from it, his hands being thrust into his breeches pockets.

"Cat," said Peterkin, turning his head a little on one side, "I love you!"

There was a pause, as if Peterkin awaited a reply to this affectionate declaration. But the cat said nothing.

"Do you hear me?" cried Peterkin sharply. "I love you—I do! Don't you love me?"

To this touching appeal the cat said "mew" faintly.

"Ah, that's right! You're a jolly old rascal! Why did you not speak at once, eh?" and Peterkin put forward his mouth and kissed the cat on the nose!

"Yes," continued Peterkin after a pause, "I love you. D'you think I'd say so if I didn't, you black villain? I love you because I've got to take care of you, and to look after you, and to think about you, and to see that you don't die—"

"Mew, me-a-w!" said the cat.

"Very good," continued Peterkin; "quite true, I have no doubt. But you've no right to interrupt me, sir. Hold your tongue till I have done speaking. Moreover, cat, I love you because you came to me the first time you ever saw me, and didn't seem to be afraid, and appeared to be fond of me, though you didn't know that I wasn't going to kill you. Now that was brave, that was bold, and very jolly, old boy, and I love you for it—I do!"

Again there was a pause of a few minutes, during which the cat looked placid, and Peterkin dropped his eyes upon its toes as if in contemplation. Suddenly he looked up.

"Well, cat, what are you thinking about now? Won't speak, eh? Now tell me: don't you think it's a monstrous shame that those two scoundrels, Jack and Ralph, should keep us waiting for our supper so long?"

Here the cat arose, put up its back and stretched itself, yawned slightly, and licked the point of Peterkin's nose!

"Just so, old boy; you're a clever fellow.—I really do believe the brute understands me!" said Peterkin, while a broad grin overspread his face as he drew back and surveyed the cat.

At this point Jack burst into a loud fit of laughter. The cat uttered an angry fuff and fled, while Peterkin sprang up and exclaimed:

"Bad luck to you, Jack! You've nearly made the heart jump out of my body, you have!"

"Perhaps I have," replied Jack, laughing, as we entered the bower; "but as I don't intend to keep you or the cat any longer from your supper, I hope that you'll both forgive me."

Peterkin endeavoured to turn this affair off with a laugh. But I observed that he blushed very deeply at the time we discovered ourselves, and he did not seem to relish any allusion to the subject afterwards; so we refrained from remarking on it ever after, though it tickled us not a little at the time.

After supper we retired to rest, and to dream of wonderful adventures in our little boat and distant voyages upon the sea.

## 16

### THE BOAT LAUNCHED—WE VISIT THE CORAL REEF —THE GREAT BREAKER THAT NEVER GOES DOWN— CORAL INSECTS—THE WAY IN WHICH CORAL ISLANDS ARE MADE—THE BOATS SAIL—WE TAX OUR INGENUITY TO FORM FISH-HOOKS—SOME OF THE FISH WE SAW—AND A MONSTROUS WHALE— WONDERFUL SHOWER OF LITTLE FISH— WATERSPOUTS.

It was a bright, clear, beautiful morning when we first launched our little boat and rowed out upon the placid waters of the lagoon. Not a breath of wind ruffled the surface of the deep. Not a cloud spotted the deep-blue sky. Not a sound that was discordant broke the stillness of the morning, although there were many sounds—sweet, tiny, and melodious—that mingled in the universal harmony of nature. The sun was just rising from the Pacific's ample bosom, and tipping the mountain-tops with a red glow. The sea was shining like a sheet of glass, yet heaving with the long, deep swell that, all the world round, indicates the life of Ocean; and the bright seaweeds and the brilliant corals shone in the depths of that pellucid water, as we rowed over it, like rare and precious gems. Oh, it was a sight fitted to stir the soul of man to its profoundest depths! and if he owned a heart at all, to lift that heart in adoration and gratitude to the great Creator of this magnificent and glorious universe!

At first, in the strength of our delight, we rowed hither and thither without aim or object. But after the effervescence of our spirits was abated, we began to look about us and to consider what we should do.

"I vote that we row to the reef," cried Peterkin.

"And I vote that we visit the islands within the lagoon," said I.

"And I vote we do both," cried Jack; "so pull away, boys!"

As I have already said, we had made four oars; but our boat was so small that only two were necessary. The extra pair were reserved in case any accident should happen to the others. It was therefore only needful that two of us should row, while the third steered by means of an oar—and relieved the rowers occasionally.

First we landed on one of the small islands and ran all over it, but saw nothing worthy of particular notice. Then we landed on a larger island, on which were growing a few cocoa-nut trees. Not having eaten anything that morning, we gathered a few of the nuts and breakfasted. After this we pulled straight out to sea, and landed on the coral reef.

This was indeed a novel and interesting sight to us. We had now been so long on shore that we had almost forgotten the appearance of breakers, for there were none within the lagoon. But now, as we stood beside the foam-crested billow of the open sea, all the enthusiasm of the sailor was awakened in our breasts; and as we gazed on the widespread ruin of that single magnificent breaker that burst in thunder at our feet, we forgot the Coral Island behind us, we forgot our bower and the calm repose of the scented woods, we forgot all that had passed during the last few months, and remembered nothing but the storms, the calms, the fresh breezes, and the surging billows of the open sea.

This huge, ceaseless breaker, to which I have so often alluded, was a much larger and more sublime object than we had at all imagined it to be. It rose many yards above the level of the sea, and could be seen approaching at some distance from the reef. Slowly and majestically it came on, acquiring greater volume and velocity as it advanced, until it assumed the form of a clear watery arch, which sparkled in the bright sun. On it came with resistless and solemn majesty, the upper edge lipped gently over, and it fell with a roar that seemed as though the heart of Ocean were broken in the crash of tumultuous water, while the foam-clad coral reef appeared to tremble beneath the mighty shock!

We gazed long and wonderingly at this great sight, and it was with difficulty we could tear ourselves away from it. As I have once before mentioned, this wave broke in many places over the reef and scattered some of its spray into the lagoon; but in most places the reef was sufficiently broad and elevated to receive and check its entire force. In many places the coral rocks were covered with vegetation—the beginning, as it appeared to us, of future islands. Thus, on this reef, we came to perceive how most of the small islands of those seas are formed. On one part we saw the spray of the breaker washing over the rocks, and millions of little, active, busy creatures continuing the work of building up this living rampart. At another place, which was just a little too high for the waves to wash over it, the coral insects were all dead; for we found that they never did their work above water. They had faithfully completed the mighty work which their Creator had given them to do, and they were now all dead. Again, in other spots the ceaseless lashing of the sea had broken the dead coral in pieces, and cast it up in the form of sand. Here sea-birds had alighted, little pieces of seaweed and stray bits of wood had been washed up, seeds of plants had been carried by the wind, and a few lovely blades of bright green had already sprung up, which, when they died, would increase the size and fertility of these emeralds of Ocean. At other places these islets had grown apace, and were shaded by one or two cocoa-nut trees, which grew literally in the sand, and were constantly washed by the ocean spray—yet, as I have before remarked, their fruit was most refreshing and sweet to our taste.

Again, at this time Jack and I pondered the formation of the large coral islands. We could now understand how the low ones were formed; but the larger islands cost us much consideration, yet we could arrive at no certain conclusion on the subject.

Having satisfied our curiosity, and enjoyed ourselves during the whole day in our little boat, we returned, somewhat wearied, and withal rather hungry, to our bower.

"Now," said Jack, "as our boat answers so well we will get a mast and sail made immediately."

"So we will!" cried Peterkin as we all assisted to drag the boat above high-water mark. "We'll light our candle and set about it this very night. Hurrah, my boys, pull away!"

As we dragged our boat, we observed that she grated heavily on her keel; and as the sands were in this place mingled with broken coral rocks, we saw portions of the wood being scraped off.

"Hallo!" cried Jack on seeing this, "that won't do. Our keel will be worn off in no time at this rate."

"So it will," said I, pondering deeply as to how this might be prevented. But I am not of a mechanical turn naturally, so I could conceive no remedy save that of putting a plate of iron on the keel; but as we had no iron, I knew not what was to be done. "It seems to me, Jack," I added, "that it is impossible to prevent the keel being worn off thus."

"Impossible?" cried Peterkin. "My dear Ralph, you are mistaken; there is nothing so easy."

"How?" I inquired in some surprise.

"Why, by not using the boat at all!" replied Peterkin.

"Hold your impudent tongue, Peterkin!" said Jack as he shouldered the oars. "Come along with me, and I'll give you work to do. In the first place, you will go and collect coca-nut fibre, and set to work to make sewing-twine with it—"

"Please, captain," interrupted Peterkin, "I've got lots of it made already—more than enough, as a little friend of mine used to be in the habit of saying every day after dinner."

"Very well," continued Jack; "then you'll help Ralph to collect cocoa-nut cloth and cut it into shape, after which we'll make a sail of it. I'll see to getting the mast and the gearing; so let's to work."

And to work we went right busily, so that in three days from that time we had set up a mast and sail, with the necessary rigging, in our little boat. The sail was not, indeed, very handsome to look at, as it was formed of a number of oblong patches of cloth; but we had sewed it well by means of our sail-needle, so that it was strong, which was the chief point.—Jack had also overcome the difficulty about the keel by pinning to it a *false* keel. This was a piece of tough wood, of the same length and width as the real keel, and about five inches deep. He made it of this depth because the boat would be thereby rendered not only much more safe, but more able to beat against the wind—which, in a sea where the trade-winds blow so long and so steadily in one direction, was a matter of great importance. This piece of wood was pegged very firmly to the keel; and we now launched our boat with the satisfaction of knowing that when the false keel should be scraped off we could easily put on another,—whereas, should the real keel have been scraped away, we could not have renewed it without taking our boat to pieces, which Peterkin said made his "marrow quake to think upon."

The mast and sail answered excellently; and we now sailed about in the lagoon with great delight, and examined with much interest the appearance of our island from a distance. Also, we gazed into the depths of the water, and watched for hours the gambols of the curious and bright-coloured fish among the corals and seaweed. Peterkin also made a fishing-line; and Jack constructed a number of hooks, some of which were very good, others remarkably bad. Some of these hooks were made of iron-wood—which did pretty well, the wood being extremely hard—and Jack made them very thick and large. Fish there are not particular. Some of the crooked bones in fish-heads also answered for this purpose pretty well. But that which formed our best and most serviceable hook was the brass finger-ring belonging to Jack. It gave him not a little trouble to manufacture it. First he cut it with the axe, then twisted it into the form of a hook. The barb took him several hours to cut. He did it by means of constant sawing with the broken penknife. As for the point, an hour's rubbing on a piece of sandstone made an excellent one.

It would be a matter of much time and labour to describe the appearance of the multitudes of fish that were day after day drawn into our boat by means of the brass hook. Peterkin always caught them—for we observed that he derived much pleasure from fishing—while Jack and I found ample amusement in looking on, also in gazing down at the coral groves, and in baiting the hook. Among the fish that we saw, but did not catch, were porpoises and swordfish, whales and sharks. The porpoises came frequently into our lagoon in shoals, and amused us not a little by their bold leaps into the air and their playful gambols in the sea. The swordfish were wonderful creatures—some of them apparently ten feet in length, with an ivory spear six or eight feet long projecting from their noses. We often saw them darting after other fish, and no doubt they sometimes killed them with their ivory swords. Jack remembered having heard once of a swordfish attacking a ship, which seemed strange indeed; but as they are often in the habit of attacking whales, perhaps it mistook the ship for one. This swordfish ran against the vessel with such force that it drove its sword quite through the thick planks; and when the ship arrived in harbour, long afterwards, the sword was found still sticking in it!

Sharks did not often appear; but we took care never again to bathe in deep water without leaving one of our number in the boat, to give us warning if he should see a shark approaching. As for the whales, they never came into our lagoon; but we frequently saw them spouting in the deep water beyond the reef. I shall never forget my surprise the first day I saw one of these huge monsters close to me. We had been rambling about on the reef during the morning, and were about to re-embark in our little boat to return home, when a loud blowing sound caused us to wheel rapidly round. We were just in time to see a shower of spray falling, and the flukes or tail of some monstrous fish disappear in the sea a few hundred yards off. We waited some time to see if he would rise again. As we stood, the sea seemed to open up at our very feet; an immense spout of water was sent with a snort high into the air, and the huge, blunt head of a sperm-whale rose before us. It was so large that it could easily have taken our little boat, along with ourselves, into its mouth! It plunged slowly back into the sea, like a large ship foundering, and struck the water with its tail so forcibly as to cause a sound like a cannon-shot.

We also saw a great number of flying-fish, although we caught none; and we noticed that they never flew out of the water except when followed by their bitter foe the dolphin, from whom they thus endeavoured to escape. But of all the fish that we saw, none surprised us so much as those that we used to find in shallow pools after a shower of rain; and this not on account of their appearance, for they were ordinary-looking and very small, but on account of their having descended in a shower of rain! We could account for them in no other way, because the pools in which we found these fish were quite dry before the shower, and at some distance above high-water mark. Jack, however, suggested a cause which seemed to me very probable. We used often to see waterspouts in the sea. A waterspout is a whirling body of water, which rises from the sea like a sharp-pointed pillar. After rising a good way, it is met by a long tongue, which comes down from the clouds; and when the two have joined, they look something like an hour-glass. The waterspout is then carried by the wind—sometimes gently, sometimes with violence—over the sea, sometimes up into the clouds; and then, bursting asunder, it descends in a deluge. This often happens over the land as well as over the sea; and it sometimes does much damage, but frequently it passes gently away. Now, Jack thought that the little fish might perhaps have been carried up in a waterspout, and so sent down again in a shower of rain. But we could not be certain as to this point, yet we thought it likely.

During these delightful fishing and boating excursions we caught a good many eels, which we found to be very good to eat. We also found turtles among the coral rocks, and made excellent soup in our iron kettle. Moreover, we discovered many shrimps and prawns, so that we had no lack of variety in our food; and, indeed, we never passed a week without making some new and interesting discovery of some sort or other, either on the land or in the sea.

## 17

## A MONSTER WAVE AND ITS CONSEQUENCES—THE BOAT LOST AND FOUND—PETERKIN'S TERRIBLE ACCIDENT—SUPPLIES OF FOOD FOR A VOYAGE IN THE BOAT—WE VISIT PENGUIN ISLAND, AND ARE AMAZED BEYOND MEASURE—ACCOUNT OF THE PENGUINS.

One day, not long after our little boat was finished, we were sitting on the rocks at Spouting Cliff, and talking of an excursion which we intended to make to Penguin Island the next day.

"You see," said Peterkin, "it might be all very well for a stupid fellow like me to remain here and leave the penguins alone; but it would be quite inconsistent with your characters as philosophers to remain any longer in ignorance of the habits and customs of these birds, so the sooner we go the better."

"Very true," said I. "There is nothing I desire so much as to have a closer inspection of them."

"And I think," said Jack, "that you had better remain at home, Peterkin, to take care of the cat; for I'm sure the hogs will be at it in your absence, out of revenge for your killing their great-grandmother so recklessly."

"Stay at home!" cried Peterkin. "My dear fellow, you would certainly lose your way, or get upset, if I were not there to take care of you."

"Ah, true!" said Jack gravely; "that did not occur to me. No doubt you must go. Our boat does require a good deal of ballast; and all that you say, Peterkin, carries so much weight with it that we won't need stones if you go."

Now, while my companions were talking, a notable event occurred, which, as it is not generally known, I shall be particular in recording here.

While we were talking, as I have said, we noticed a dark line, like a low cloud or fog-bank, on the seaward horizon. The day was a fine one, though cloudy, and a gentle breeze was blowing; but the sea was not rougher, or the breaker on the reef higher, than usual. At first we thought that this looked like a thundercloud, and as we had had a good deal of broken weather of late, accompanied by occasional peals of thunder, we supposed that a storm must be approaching. Gradually, however, this line seemed to draw nearer without spreading up over the sky, as would certainly have been the case if it had been a storm-cloud. Still nearer it came, and soon we saw that it was moving swiftly towards the island; but there was no sound till it reached the islands out at sea. As it passed these islands we observed, with no little anxiety, that a cloud of white foam encircled them, and burst in spray into the air; it was accompanied by a loud roar. This led us to conjecture that the approaching object was an enormous wave of the sea; but we had no idea how large it was till it came near to ourselves. When it approached the outer reef, however, we were awestruck with its unusual magnitude; and we sprang to our feet, and clambered hastily up to the highest point of the precipice, under an indefinable feeling of fear.

I have said before that the reef opposite Spouting Cliff was very near to the shore, while just in front of the bower it was at a considerable distance out to sea. Owing to this formation, the wave reached the reef at the latter point before it struck at the foot of Spouting Cliff. The instant it touched the reef we became aware, for the first time, of its awful magnitude. It burst completely over the reef at all points with a roar that seemed louder to me than thunder, and this roar continued for some seconds while the wave rolled gradually along towards the cliff on which we stood. As its crest reared before us we felt that we were in great danger, and turned to flee; but we were too late. With a crash that seemed to shake the solid rock, the gigantic billow fell, and instantly the spouting-holes sent up a gush of waterspouts with such force that they shrieked on issuing from their narrow vents. It seemed to us as if the earth had been blown up with water. We were stunned and confused by the shock, and so drenched and blinded with spray that we knew not for a few moments whither to flee for shelter. At length we all three gained an eminence beyond the reach of the water. But what a scene of devastation met our gaze as we looked along the shore! This enormous wave not only burst over the reef, but continued its way across the lagoon, and fell on the sandy beach of the island with such force that it passed completely over it and dashed into the woods, levelling the smaller trees and bushes in its headlong course.

On seeing this, Jack said he feared our bower must have been swept away, and that the boat, which was on the beach, must have been utterly destroyed. Our hearts sank within us as we thought of this, and we hastened round through the woods towards our home. On reaching it we found, to our great relief of mind, that the force of the wave had been expended just before reaching the bower; but the entrance to it was almost blocked up by the torn-up bushes and tangled heaps of seaweed. Having satisfied ourselves as to the bower, we hurried to the spot where the boat had been left; but no boat was there. The spot on which it had stood was vacant, and no sign of it could we see on looking around us.

"It may have been washed up into the woods," said Jack, hurrying up the beach as he spoke. Still no boat was to be seen, and we were about to give ourselves over to despair when Peterkin called to Jack and said:

"Jack, my friend, you were once so exceedingly sagacious and wise as to make me acquainted with the fact that cocoa-nuts grow upon trees. Will you now be so good as to inform me what sort of fruit that is growing on the top of yonder bush? for I confess to being ignorant, or at least doubtful, on the point."

We looked towards the bush indicated, and there, to our surprise, beheld our little boat snugly nestled among the leaves. We were very much overjoyed at this, for we would have suffered any loss rather than the loss of our boat. We found that the wave had actually borne the boat on its crest from the beach into the woods, and there launched it into the heart of this bush, which was extremely fortunate; for had it been tossed against a rock or a tree, it would have been dashed to pieces, whereas it had not received the smallest injury. It was no easy matter, however, to get it out of the bush and down to the sea again. This cost us two days of hard labour to accomplish.

We had also much ado to clear away the rubbish from before the bower, and spent nearly a week in constant labour ere we got the neighbourhood to look as clean and orderly as before; for the uprooted bushes and seaweed that lay on the beach formed a more dreadfully confused-looking mass than one who had not seen the place after the inundation could conceive.

Before leaving the subject I may mention, for the sake of those who interest themselves in the curious natural phenomena of our world, that this gigantic wave occurs regularly on some of the islands of the Pacific once, and sometimes twice, in the year. I heard this stated by the missionaries during my career in those seas. They could not tell me whether it visited all of the islands, but I was certainly assured that it occurred periodically in some of them.

After we had got our home put to rights, and cleared of the débris of the inundation, we again turned our thoughts to paying the penguins a visit. The boat was therefore overhauled and a few repairs done. Then we prepared a supply of provisions, for we intended to be absent at least a night or two—perhaps longer. This took us some time to do; for, while Jack was busy with the boat, Peterkin was sent into the woods to spear a hog or two, and had to search long, sometimes, ere he found them. Peterkin was usually sent on this errand when we wanted a pork chop (which was not seldom), because he was so active and could run so wonderfully fast that he found no difficulty in overtaking the hogs; but being dreadfully reckless, he almost invariably tumbled over stumps and stones in the course of his wild chase, and seldom returned home without having knocked the skin off his shins. Once, indeed, a more serious accident happened to him. He had been out all the morning alone, and did not return at the usual time to dinner. We wondered at this, for Peterkin was always very punctual at the dinner-hour. As supper-time drew near we began to be anxious about him, and at length sallied forth to search the woods. For a long time we sought in vain; but a little before dark we came upon the tracks of the hogs, which we followed up until we came to the brow of a rather steep bank or precipice. Looking over this, we beheld Peterkin lying in a state of insensibility at the foot, with his cheek resting on the snout of a little pig, which was pinned to the earth by the spear. We were dreadfully alarmed, but hastened to bathe his forehead with water, and had soon the satisfaction of seeing him revive. After we had carried him home, he related to us how the thing had happened.

"You must know," said he, "I walked about all the forenoon, till I was as tired as an old donkey, without seeing a single grunter—not so much as a track of one; but as I was determined not to return empty-handed, I resolved to go without my dinner, and—"

"What!" exclaimed Jack, "did you *really* resolve to do that?"

"Now, Jack, hold your tongue," returned Peterkin. "I say that I resolved to forego my dinner and to push to the head of the small valley, where I felt pretty sure of discovering the hogs. I soon found that I was on the right scent, for I had scarcely walked half-a-mile in the direction of the small plum-tree we found there the other day when a squeak fell on my ear. 'Ho, ho,' said I, 'there you go, my boys;' and I hurried up the glen. I soon started them, and singling out a fat pig, ran tilt at him. In a few seconds I was up with him, and stuck my spear right through his dumpy body. Just as I did so, I saw that we were on the edge of a precipice —whether high or low, I knew not; but I had been running at such a pace that I could not stop, so the pig and I gave a howl in concert and went plunging over together. I remembered nothing more after that till I came to my senses, and found you bathing my temples, and Ralph wringing his hands over me."

But although Peterkin was often unfortunate in the way of getting tumbles, he was successful on the present occasion in hunting, and returned before evening with three very nice little hogs. I also was successful in my visit to the mud-flats, where I killed several ducks. So that when we launched and loaded our boat at sunrise the following morning, we found our store of provisions to be more than sufficient. Part had been cooked the night before, and on taking note of the different items, we found the account to stand thus:

10 Bread-fruits (two baked, eight unbaked).
20 Yams (six roasted, the rest raw).
6 Taro-roots.
50 Fine large plums.
6 Cocoa-nuts, ripe.
6 Ditto, green (for drinking).
4 Large ducks and two small ones, raw.
3 Cold roast pigs, with stuffing.

I may here remark that the stuffing had been devised by Peterkin specially for the occasion. He kept the manner of its compounding a profound secret, so I cannot tell what it was; but I can say, with much confidence, that we found it to be atrociously bad, and after the first tasting, scraped it carefully out and threw it overboard. We calculated that this supply would last us for several days; but we afterwards found that it was much more than we required, especially in regard to the cocoa-nuts, of which we found large supplies wherever we went. However, as Peterkin remarked, it was better to have too much than too little, as we knew not to what straits we might be put during our voyage.

It was a very calm, sunny morning when we launched forth and rowed over the lagoon towards the outlet in the reef, and passed between the two green islets that guarded the entrance. We experienced some difficulty and no little danger in passing the surf of the breaker, and shipped a good deal of water in the attempt; but once past the billow, we found ourselves floating placidly on the long, oily swell that rose and fell slowly as it rolled over the wide ocean.

Penguin Island lay on the other side of our own island, at about a mile beyond the outer reef, and we calculated that it must be at least twenty miles distant by the way we should have to go. We might, indeed, have shortened the way by coasting round our island inside of the lagoon, and going out at the passage in the reef nearly opposite to Penguin Island; but we preferred to go by the open sea—first, because it was more adventurous, and secondly, because we should have the pleasure of again feeling the motion of the deep, which we all loved very much, not being liable to sea-sickness.

"I wish we had a breeze," said Jack.

"So do I," cried Peterkin, resting on his oar and wiping his heated brow; "pulling is hard work. Oh dear, if we could only catch a hundred or two of these gulls, tie them to the boat with long strings, and make them fly as we want them, how capital it would be!"

"Or bore a hole through a shark's tail and reeve a rope through it, eh?" remarked Jack. "But, I say, it seems that my wish is going to be granted, for here comes a breeze. Ship your oar, Peterkin.—Up with the mast, Ralph; I'll see to the sail. Mind your helm; look out for squalls!"

This last speech was caused by the sudden appearance of a dark-blue line on the horizon, which, in an incredibly short space of time, swept down on us, lashing up the sea in white foam as it went. We presented the stern of the boat to its first violence, and in a few seconds it moderated into a steady breeze, to which we spread our sail and flew merrily over the waves. Although the breeze died away soon afterwards, it had been so stiff while it lasted that we were carried over the greater part of our way before it fell calm again; so that when the flapping of the sail against the mast told us that it was time to resume the oars, we were not much more than a mile from Penguin Island.

"There go the soldiers!" cried Peterkin as we came in sight of it. "How spruce their white trousers look this morning! I wonder if they will receive us kindly?—D'you think they are hospitable, Jack?"

"Don't talk, Peterkin, but pull away, and you shall see shortly."

As we drew near to the island, we were much amused by the manoeuvres and appearance of these strange birds. They seemed to be of different species: for some had crests on their heads, while others had none; and while some were about the size of a goose, others appeared nearly as large as a swan. We also saw a huge albatross soaring above the heads of the penguins. It was followed and surrounded by numerous flocks of sea-gulls. Having approached to within a few yards of the island, which was a low rock, with no other vegetation on it than a few bushes, we lay on our oars and gazed at the birds with surprise and pleasure, they returning our gaze with interest. We now saw that their soldierlike appearance was owing to the stiff erect manner in which they sat on their short legs—"bolt-upright," as Peterkin expressed it. They had black heads, long, sharp beaks, white breasts, and bluish backs. Their wings were so short that they looked more like the fins of a fish, and indeed we soon saw that they used them for the purpose of swimming under water. There were no quills on these wings, but a sort of scaly feathers, which also thickly covered their bodies. Their legs were short, and placed so far back that the birds, while on land, were obliged to stand quite upright in order to keep their balance; but in the water they floated like other water-fowl. At first we were so stunned with the clamour which they and other sea-birds kept up around us that we knew not which way to look, for they covered the rocks in thousands; but as we continued to gaze, we observed several quadrupeds (as we thought) walking in the midst of the penguins.

"Pull in a bit," cried Peterkin, "and let's see what these are. They must be fond of noisy company to consort with such creatures."

To our surprise, we found that these were no other than penguins which had gone down on all fours, and were crawling among the bushes on their feet and wings, just like quadrupeds. Suddenly one big old bird, that had been sitting on a point very near to us, gazing in mute astonishment, became alarmed, and scuttling down the rocks, plumped or fell, rather than ran, into the sea. It dived in a moment, and, a few seconds afterwards, came out of the water far ahead with such a spring, and such a dive back into the sea again, that we could scarcely believe it was not a fish that had leaped in sport.

"That beats everything!" said Peterkin, rubbing his nose, and screwing up his face with an expression of exasperated amazement. "I've heard of a thing being neither fish, flesh, nor fowl; but I never did expect to live to see a brute that was all three together—at once—in one! But look there!" he continued, pointing with a look of resignation to the shore—"look there! there's no end to it. What has that brute got under its tail?"

We turned to look in the direction pointed out, and there saw a penguin walking slowly and very sedately along the shore with an egg under its tail. There were several others, we observed, burdened in the same way; and we found afterwards that these were a species of penguin that always carried their eggs so. Indeed, they had a most convenient cavity for the purpose, just between the tail and the legs. We were very much impressed with the regularity and order of this colony. The island seemed to be apportioned out into squares, of which each penguin possessed one, and sat in stiff solemnity in the middle of it, or took a slow march up and down the spaces between. Some were hatching their eggs, but others were feeding their young ones in a manner that caused us to laugh not a little. The mother stood on a mound or raised rock, while the young one stood patiently below her on the ground. Suddenly the mother raised her head and uttered a series of the most discordant cackling sounds.

"She's going to choke," cried Peterkin.

But this was not the case, although, I confess, she looked like it. In a few seconds she put down her head and opened her mouth, into which the young one thrust its beak and seemed to suck something from her throat. Then the cackling was renewed, the sucking continued, and so the operation of feeding was carried on till the young one was satisfied; but what she fed her little one with we could not tell.

"Now, just look yonder!" said Peterkin in an excited tone. "If that isn't the most abominable piece of maternal deception I ever saw! That rascally old lady penguin has just pitched her young one into the sea, and there's another about to follow her example."

This indeed seemed to be the case, for on the top of a steep rock close to the edge of the sea we observed an old penguin endeavouring to entice her young one into the water; but the young one seemed very unwilling to go, and notwithstanding the enticements of its mother, moved very slowly towards her. At last she went gently behind the young bird and pushed it a little towards the water, but with great tenderness, as much as to say, "Don't be afraid, darling; I won't hurt you, my pet!" But no sooner did she get it to the edge of the rock, where it stood looking pensively down at the sea, than she gave it a sudden and violent push, sending it headlong down the slope into the water, where its mother left it to scramble ashore as it best could. We observed many of them employed in doing this, and we came to the conclusion that this is the way in which old penguins teach their children to swim.

Scarcely had we finished making our remarks on this, when we were startled by about a dozen of the old birds hopping in the most clumsy and ludicrous manner towards the sea. The beach here was a sloping rock, and when they came to it some of them succeeded in hopping down in safety, but others lost their balance and rolled and scrambled down the slope in the most helpless manner. The instant they reached the water, however, they seemed to be in their proper element. They dived, and bounded out of it and into it again with the utmost agility; and so, diving and bounding and sputtering—for they could not fly—they went rapidly out to sea.

On seeing this, Peterkin turned with a grave face to us and said, "It's my opinion that these birds are all stark, staring mad, and that this is an enchanted island. I therefore propose that we should either put about ship and fly in terror from the spot, or land valorously on the island and sell our lives as dearly as we can."

"I vote for landing; so pull in, lads!" said Jack, giving a stroke with his oar that made the boat spin. In a few seconds we ran the boat into a little creek, where we made her fast to a projecting piece of coral, and running up the beach, entered the ranks of the penguins, armed with our cudgels and our spear. We were greatly surprised to find that instead of attacking us, or showing signs of fear at our approach, these curious birds did not move from their places until we laid hands on them, and merely turned their eyes on us in solemn, stupid wonder as we passed. There was one old penguin, however, that began to walk slowly towards the sea; and Peterkin took it into his head that he would try to interrupt its progress, so he ran between it and the sea and brandished his cudgel in its face. But this proved to be a resolute old bird. It would not retreat; nay, more, it would not cease to advance, but battled with Peterkin bravely, and drove him before it until it reached the sea. Had Peterkin used his club he could easily have felled it, no doubt; but as he had no wish to do so cruel an act merely out of sport, he let the bird escape.

We spent fully three hours on this island in watching the habit of these curious birds; but when we finally left them, we all three concluded, after much consultation, that they were the most wonderful creatures we had ever seen, and further, we thought it probable that they were the most wonderful creatures in the world!

# 18

## AN AWFUL STORM AND ITS CONSEQUENCES— NARROW ESCAPE—A ROCK PROVES A SURE FOUNDATION—A FEARFUL NIGHT AND A BRIGHT MORNING—DELIVERANCE FROM DANGER.

It was evening before we left the island of the penguins. As we had made up our minds to encamp for the night on a small island whereon grew a few cocoa-nut trees, which was about two miles off, we lay-to our oars with some energy. But a danger was in store for us which we had not anticipated. The wind, which had carried us so quickly to Penguin Island, freshened as evening drew on to a stiff breeze, and before we had made half the distance to the small island, it became a regular gale. Although it was not so directly against us as to prevent our rowing in the course we wished to go, yet it checked us very much; and although the force of the sea was somewhat broken by the island, the waves soon began to rise and to roll their broken crests against our small craft, so that she began to take in water, and we had much ado to keep ourselves afloat. At last the wind and sea together became so violent that we found it impossible to make the island; so Jack suddenly put the head of the boat round, and ordered Peterkin and me to hoist a corner of the sail, intending to run back to Penguin Island.

"We shall at least have the shelter of the bushes," he said as the boat flew before the wind, "and the penguins will keep us company."

As Jack spoke, the wind suddenly shifted and blew so much against us that we were forced to hoist more of the sail in order to beat up for the island, being by this change thrown much to leeward of it. What made matters worse was that the gale came in squalls, so that we were more than once nearly upset.

"Stand by, both of you!" cried Jack in a quick, earnest tone. "Be ready to deuce the sail. I very much fear we won't make the island after all."

Peterkin and I were so much in the habit of trusting everything to Jack that we had fallen into the way of not considering things, especially such things as were under Jack's care. We had, therefore, never doubted for a moment that all was going well, so that it was with no little anxiety that we heard him make the above remark. However, we had no time for question or surmise, for at the moment he spoke a heavy squall was bearing down upon us, and as we were then flying with our lee gunwale dipping occasionally under the waves, it was evident that we should have to lower our sail altogether. In a few seconds the squall struck the boat; but Peterkin and I had the sail down in a moment, so that it did not upset us. But when it was past we were more than half-full of water. This I soon bailed out, while Peterkin again hoisted a corner of the sail. But the evil which Jack had feared came upon us. We found it quite impossible to make Penguin Island. The gale carried us quickly past it towards the open sea, and the terrible truth flashed upon us that we should be swept out and left to perish miserably in a small boat in the midst of the wide ocean.

This idea was forced very strongly upon us, because we saw nothing in the direction whither the wind was blowing us save the raging billows of the sea; and indeed we trembled as we gazed around us, for we were now beyond the shelter of the islands, and it seemed as though any of the huge billows, which curled over in masses of foam, might swallow us up in a moment. The water also began to wash in over our sides, and I had to keep constantly bailing; for Jack could not quit the helm, nor Peterkin the sail, for an instant, without endangering our lives. In the midst of this distress Jack uttered an exclamation of hope, and pointed towards a low island or rock which lay directly ahead. It had been hitherto unobserved, owing to the dark clouds that obscured the sky and the blinding spray that seemed to fill the whole atmosphere.

As we neared this rock we observed that it was quite destitute of trees and verdure, and so low that the sea broke completely over it. In fact, it was nothing more than the summit of one of the coral formations, which rose only a few feet above the level of the water, and was, in stormy weather, all but invisible. Over this island the waves were breaking in the utmost fury, and our hearts sank within us as we saw that there was not a spot where we could thrust our little boat without its being dashed to pieces.

"Show a little bit more sail!" cried Jack as we swept past the weather side of the rock with fearful speed.

"Ay, ay!" answered Peterkin, hoisting about a foot more of our sail.

Little though the addition was, it caused the boat to lie over and creak so loudly, as we cleft the foaming waves, that I expected to be upset every instant; and I blamed Jack in my heart for his rashness. But I did him injustice; for although during two seconds the water rushed inboard in a torrent, he succeeded in steering us sharply round to the leeward side of the rock, where the water was comparatively calm and the force of the breeze broken.

"Out your oars now, lads! That's well done! Give way!" We obeyed instantly. The oars splashed into the waves together. One good, hearty pull, and we were floating in a comparatively calm creek that was so narrow as to be barely able to admit our boat. Here we were in perfect safety, and as we leaped on shore and fastened our cable to the rocks, I thanked God in my heart for our deliverance from so great danger. But although I have said we were now in safety, I suspect that few of my readers would have envied our position. It is true we had no lack of food; but we were drenched to the skin; the sea was foaming round us, and the spray flying over our heads, so that we were completely enveloped, as it were, in water; the spot on which we had landed was not more than twelve yards in diameter, and from this spot we could not move without the risk of being swept away by the storm. At the upper end of the creek was a small hollow or cave in the rock, which sheltered us from the fury of the winds and waves; and as the rock extended in a sort of ledge over our heads, it prevented the spray from falling upon us.

"Why," said Peterkin, beginning to feel cheery again, "it seems to me that we have got into a mermaid's cave, for there is nothing but water all round us; and as for earth and sky, they are things of the past."

Peterkin's idea was not inappropriate, for what with the sea roaring in white foam up to our very feet, and the spray flying in white sheets continually over our heads, and the water dripping heavily from the ledge above like a curtain in front of our cave, it did seem to us very much more like being below than above water.

"Now, boys," cried Jack, "bestir yourselves, and let's make ourselves comfortable.—Toss out our provisions, Peterkin; and here, Ralph, lend a hand to haul up the boat. Look sharp!"

"Ay, ay, captain!" we cried as we hastened to obey, much cheered by the hearty manner of our comrade.

Fortunately the cave, although not very deep, was quite dry, so that we succeeded in making ourselves much more comfortable than could have been expected. We landed our provisions, wrung the water out of our garments, spread our sail below us for a carpet, and after having eaten a hearty meal, began to feel quite cheerful. But as night drew on our spirits sank again, for with the daylight all evidence of our security vanished away. We could no longer see the firm rock on which we lay, while we were stunned with the violence of the tempest that raged around us. The night grew pitchy dark as it advanced, so that we could not see our hands when we held them up before our eyes, and were obliged to feel each other occasionally to make sure that we were safe, for the storm at last became so terrible that it was difficult to make our voices audible. A slight variation of the wind, as we supposed, caused a few drops of spray ever and anon to blow into our faces; and the eddy of the sea, in its mad boiling, washed up into our little creek until it reached our feet and threatened to tear away our boat. In order to prevent this latter calamity, we hauled the boat farther up and held the cable in our hands. Occasional flashes of lightning shone with a ghastly glare through the watery curtains around us, and lent additional horror to the scene. Yet we longed for those dismal flashes, for they were less appalling than the thick blackness that succeeded them. Crashing peals of thunder seemed to tear the skies in twain, and fell upon our ears through the wild yelling of the hurricane as if it had been but a gentle summer breeze; while the billows burst upon the weather side of the island until we fancied that the solid rock was giving way, and in our agony we clung to the bare ground, expecting every moment to be whirled away and whelmed in the black, howling sea. Oh, it was a night of terrible anxiety! and no one can conceive the feelings of intense gratitude and relief with which we at last saw the dawn of day break through the vapoury mists around us.

For three days and three nights we remained on this rock, while the storm continued to rage with unabated fury. On the morning of the fourth day it suddenly ceased, and the wind fell altogether; but the waves still ran so high that we did not dare to put off in our boat. During the greater part of this period we scarcely slept above a few minutes at a time; but on the third night we slept soundly, and awoke early on the fourth morning to find the sea very much down, and the sun shining brightly again in the clear blue sky.

It was with light hearts that we launched forth once more in our little boat and steered away for our island home, which, we were overjoyed to find, was quite visible on the horizon, for we had feared that we had been blown out of sight of it altogether. As it was a dead calm, we had to row during the greater part of the day; but towards the afternoon a fair breeze sprang up, which enabled us to hoist our sail. We soon passed Penguin Island and the other island which we had failed to reach on the day the storm commenced; but as we had still enough of provisions, and were anxious to get home, we did not land—to the great disappointment of Peterkin, who seemed to entertain quite an affection for the penguins.

Although the breeze was pretty fresh for several hours, we did not reach the outer reef of our island till nightfall; and before we had sailed more than a hundred yards into the lagoon, the wind died away altogether, so that we had to take to our oars again. It was late, and the moon and stars were shining brightly when we arrived opposite the bower and leaped upon the strand. So glad were we to be safe back again on our beloved island that we scarcely took time to drag the boat a short way up the beach, and then ran up to see that all was right at the bower. I must confess, however, that my joy was mingled with a vague sort of fear lest our home had been visited and destroyed during our absence; but on reaching it we found everything just as it had been left, and the poor black cat curled up, sound asleep, on the coral table in front of our humble dwelling.

## 19

## SHOEMAKING—THE EVEN TENOR OF OUR WAY SUDDENLY INTERRUPTED—AN UNEXPECTED VISIT AND AN APPALLING BATTLE—WE ALL BECOME WARRIORS, AND JACK PROVES HIMSELF TO BE A HERO.

For many months after this we continued to live on our island in uninterrupted harmony and happiness. Sometimes we went out a-fishing in the lagoon, and sometimes went a-hunting in the woods, or ascended to the mountain-top by way of variety, although Peterkin always asserted that we went for the purpose of hailing any ship that might chance to heave in sight. But I am certain that none of us wished to be delivered from our captivity, for we were extremely happy; and Peterkin used to say that as we were very young, we should not feel the loss of a year or two. Peterkin, as I have said before, was thirteen years of age, Jack eighteen, and I fifteen. But Jack was very tall, strong, and manly for his age, and might easily have been mistaken for twenty.

The climate was so beautiful that it seemed to be a perpetual summer, and as many of the fruit-trees continued to bear fruit and blossom all the year round, we never wanted for a plentiful supply of food. The hogs, too, seemed rather to increase than diminish, although Peterkin was very frequent in his attacks on them with his spear. If at any time we failed in finding a drove, we had only to pay a visit to the plum-tree before mentioned, where we always found a large family of them asleep under its branches.

We employed ourselves very busily during this time in making various garments of cocoa-nut cloth, as those with which we had landed were beginning to be very ragged. Peterkin also succeeded in making excellent shoes out of the skin of the old hog in the following manner: He first cut a piece of the hide, of an oblong form, a few inches longer than his foot. This he soaked in water, and while it was wet he sewed up one end of it so as to form a rough imitation of that part of the heel of a shoe where the seam is. This done, he bored a row of holes all round the edge of the piece of skin, through which a tough line was passed. Into the sewed-up part of this shoe he thrust his heel; then, drawing the string tight, the edges rose up and overlapped his foot all round. It is true there were a great many ill-looking puckers in these shoes; but we found them very serviceable notwithstanding, and Jack came at last to prefer them to his long boots. We also made various other useful articles, which added to our comfort, and once or twice spoke of building us a house; but we had so great an affection for the bower, and withal found it so serviceable, that we determined not to leave it, nor to attempt the building of a house, which in such a climate might turn out to be rather disagreeable than useful.

We often examined the pistol that we had found in the house on the other side of the island, and Peterkin wished much that we had powder and shot, as it would render pig-killing much easier; but, after all, we had become so expert in the use of our sling and bow and spear that we were independent of more deadly weapons.

Diving in the Water Garden also continued to afford us as much pleasure as ever, and Peterkin began to be a little more expert in the water from constant practice. As for Jack and me, we began to feel as if water were our native element, and revelled in it with so much confidence and comfort that Peterkin said he feared we would turn into fish some day and swim off and leave him, adding that he had been for a long time observing that Jack was becoming more and more like a shark every day. Whereupon Jack remarked that if he (Peterkin) were changed into a fish, he would certainly turn into nothing better or bigger than a shrimp. Poor Peterkin did not envy us our delightful excursions under water—except, indeed, when Jack would dive down to the bottom of the Water Garden, sit down on a rock, and look up and make faces at him. Peterkin did feel envious then, and often said he would give anything to be able to do that. I was much amused when Peterkin said this; for if he could only have seen his own face when he happened to take a short dive, he would have seen that Jack's was far surpassed by it—the great difference being, however, that Jack made faces on purpose, Peterkin couldn't help it!

Now, while we were engaged with these occupations and amusements, an event occurred one day which was as unexpected as it was exceedingly alarming and very horrible.

Jack and I were sitting, as we were often wont to do, on the rocks at Spouting Cliff, and Peterkin was wringing the water from his garments, having recently fallen by accident into the sea—a thing he was constantly doing—when our attention was suddenly arrested by two objects which appeared on the horizon.

"What are yon, think you?" I said, addressing Jack.

"I can't imagine," answered he. "I've noticed them for some time, and fancied they were black sea-gulls; but the more I look at them, the more I feel convinced they are much larger than gulls."

"They seem to be coming towards us," said I.

"Hallo! what's wrong?" inquired Peterkin, coming up.

"Look there," said Jack.

"Whales!" cried Peterkin, shading his eyes with his hand. "No—eh—can they be boats, Jack?"

Our hearts beat with excitement at the very thought of seeing human faces again.

"I think you are about right, Peterkin. But they seem to me to move strangely for boats," said Jack in a low tone, as if he were talking to himself.

I noticed that a shade of anxiety crossed Jack's countenance as he gazed long and intently at the two objects, which were now nearing us fast. At last he sprang to his feet. "They are canoes, Ralph! whether war-canoes or not, I cannot tell; but this I know—that all the natives of the South Sea Islands are fierce cannibals, and they have little respect for strangers. We must hide if they land here, which I earnestly hope they will not do."

I was greatly alarmed at Jack's speech; but I confess I thought less of what he said than of the earnest, anxious manner in which he said it, and it was with very uncomfortable feelings that Peterkin and I followed him quickly into the woods.

"How unfortunate," said I as we gained the shelter of the bushes, "that we have forgotten our arms!"

"It matters not," said Jack; "here are clubs enough and to spare." As he spoke, he laid his hand on a bundle of stout poles of various sizes, which Peterkin's ever-busy hands had formed, during our frequent visits to the cliff, for no other purpose, apparently, than that of having something to do.

We each selected a stout club according to our several tastes and lay down behind a rock, whence we could see the canoes approach without ourselves being seen. At first we made an occasional remark on their appearance; but after they entered the lagoon and drew near the beach, we ceased to speak, and gazed with intense interest at the scene before us.

We now observed that the foremost canoe was being chased by the other, and that it contained a few women and children as well as men—perhaps forty souls altogether—while the canoe which pursued it contained only men. They seemed to be about the same in number, but were better armed, and had the appearance of being a war-party. Both crews were paddling with all their might, and it seemed as if the pursuers exerted themselves to overtake the fugitives ere they could land. In this, however, they failed. The foremost canoe made for the beach close beneath the rocks behind which we were concealed. Their short paddles flashed like meteors in the water, and sent up a constant shower of spray. The foam curled from the prow, and the eyes of the rowers glistened in their black faces as they strained every muscle of their naked bodies. Nor did they relax their efforts till the canoe struck the beach with a violent shock; then, with a shout of defiance, the whole party sprang, as if by magic, from the canoe to the shore. Three women, two of whom carried infants in their arms, rushed into the woods; and the men crowded to the water's edge, with stones in their hands, spears levelled, and clubs brandished, to resist the landing of their enemies.

The distance between the two canoes had been about half-a-mile, and at the great speed they were going, this was soon passed. As the pursuers neared the shore, no sign of fear or hesitation was noticeable. On they came, like a wild charger—received, but recked not of, a shower of stones. The canoe struck, and with a yell that seemed to issue from the throats of incarnate fiends, they leaped into the water and drove their enemies up the beach.

The battle that immediately ensued was frightful to behold. Most of the men wielded clubs of enormous size and curious shapes, with which they dashed out each other's brains. As they were almost entirely naked, and had to bound, stoop, leap, and run in their terrible hand-to-hand encounters, they looked more like demons than human beings. I felt my heart grow sick at the sight of this bloody battle, and would fain have turned away; but a species of fascination seemed to hold me down and glue my eyes upon the combatants. I observed that the attacking party was led by a most extraordinary being, who, from his size and peculiarity, I concluded was a chief. His hair was frizzed out to an enormous extent, so that it resembled a large turban. It was of a light-yellow hue, which surprised me much, for the man's body was as black as coal, and I felt convinced that the hair must have been dyed. He was tattooed from head to foot; and his face, besides being tattooed, was besmeared with red paint and streaked with white. Altogether, with his yellow turban-like hair, his Herculean black frame, his glittering eyes, and white teeth, he seemed the most terrible monster I ever beheld. He was very active in the fight, and had already killed four men.

Suddenly the yellow-haired chief was attacked by a man quite as strong and large as himself. He flourished a heavy club, something like an eagle's beak at the point. For a second or two these giants eyed each other warily, moving round and round, as if to catch each other at a disadvantage; but seeing that nothing was to be gained by this caution, and that the loss of time might effectually turn the tide of battle either way, they apparently made up their minds to attack at the same instant, for, with a wild shout and simultaneous spring, they swung their heavy clubs, which met with a loud report. Suddenly the yellow-haired savage tripped, his enemy sprang forward, the ponderous club was swung; but it did not descend, for at that moment the savage was felled to the ground by a stone from the hand of one who had witnessed his chief's danger. This was the turning-point in the battle. The savages who landed first turned and fled towards the bush on seeing the fall of their chief. But not one escaped; they were all overtaken and felled to the earth. I saw, however, that they were not all killed. Indeed, their enemies, now that they were conquered, seemed anxious to take them alive; and they succeeded in securing fifteen, whom they bound hand and foot with cords, and carrying them up into the woods, laid them down among the bushes. Here they left them, for what purpose I knew not, and returned to the scene of the late battle, where the remnant of the party were bathing their wounds.

Out of the forty blacks that composed the attacking party only twenty-eight remained alive, two of whom were sent into the bush to hunt for the women and children. Of the other party, as I have said, only fifteen survived, and these were lying bound and helpless on the grass.

Jack and Peterkin and I now looked at each other, and whispered our fears that the savages might clamber up the rocks to search for fresh water, and so discover our place of concealment; but we were so much interested in watching their movements that we agreed to remain where we were—and indeed we could not easily have risen without exposing ourselves to detection. One of the savages now went up to the woods and soon returned with a bundle of firewood, and we were not a little surprised to see him set fire to it by the very same means used by Jack the time we made our first fire—namely, with the bow and drill. When the fire was kindled, two of the party went again to the woods and returned with one of the bound men. A dreadful feeling of horror crept over my heart as the thought flashed upon me that they were going to burn their enemies. As they bore him to the fire my feelings almost overpowered me. I gasped for breath, and seizing my club, endeavoured to spring to my feet; but Jack's powerful arm pinned me to the earth. Next moment one of the savages raised his club and fractured the wretched creature's skull. He must have died instantly; and, strange though it may seem, I confess to a feeling of relief when the deed was done, because I now knew that the poor savage could not be burned alive. Scarcely had his limbs ceased to quiver when the monsters cut slices of flesh from his body, and after roasting them slightly over the fire, devoured them.

Suddenly there arose a cry from the woods, and in a few seconds the two savages hastened towards the fire, dragging the three women and their two infants along with them. One of these women was much younger than her companions, and we were struck with the modesty of her demeanour and the gentle expression of her face, which, although she had the flattish nose and thick lips of the others, was of a light-brown colour, and we conjectured that she must be of a different race. She and her companions wore short petticoats, and a kind of tippet on their shoulders. Their hair was jet black, but instead of being long, was short and curly—though not woolly—somewhat like the hair of a young boy. While we gazed with interest and some anxiety at these poor creatures, the big chief advanced to one of the elder females and laid his hand upon the child. But the mother shrank from him, and clasping the little one to her bosom, uttered a wail of fear. With a savage laugh, the chief tore the child from her arms and tossed it into the sea. A low groan burst from Jack's lips as he witnessed this atrocious act and heard the mother's shriek as she fell insensible on the sand.

The rippling waves rolled the child on the beach, as if they refused to be a party in such a foul murder, and we could observe that the little one still lived.

The young girl was now brought forward, and the chief addressed her; but although we heard his voice and even the words distinctly, of course we could not understand what he said. The girl made no answer to his fierce questions, and we saw by the way in which he pointed to the fire that he threatened her life.

"Peterkin," said Jack in a hoarse whisper, "have you got your knife?"

"Yes," replied Peterkin, whose face was pale as death.

"That will do. Listen to me, and do my bidding quick.—Here is the small knife, Ralph. Fly, both of you, through the bush, cut the cords that bind the prisoners, and set them free! There! quick, ere it be too late!" Jack sprang up and seized a heavy but short bludgeon, while his strong frame trembled with emotion, and large drops rolled down his forehead.

At this moment the man who had butchered the savage a few minutes before advanced towards the girl with his heavy club. Jack uttered a yell that rang like a death-shriek among the rocks. With one bound he leaped over a precipice full fifteen feet high, and before the savages had recovered from their surprise, was in the midst of them, while Peterkin and I dashed through the bushes towards the prisoners. With one blow of his staff Jack felled the man with the club; then turning round with a look of fury he rushed upon the big chief with the yellow hair. Had the blow which Jack aimed at his head taken effect, the huge savage would have needed no second stroke; but he was agile as a cat, and avoided it by springing to one side, while at the same time he swung his ponderous club at the head of his foe. It was now Jack's turn to leap aside; and well was it for him that the first outburst of his blind fury was over, else he had become an easy prey to his gigantic antagonist. But Jack was cool now. He darted his blows rapidly and well, and the superiority of his light weapon was strikingly proved in this combat; for while he could easily evade the blows of the chief's heavy club, the chief could not so easily evade those of his light one. Nevertheless, so quick was he, and so frightfully did he fling about the mighty weapon, that although Jack struck him almost every blow, the strokes had to be delivered so quickly that they wanted force to be very effectual.

It was lucky for Jack that the other savages considered the success of their chief in this encounter to be so certain that they refrained from interfering. Had they doubted it, they would have probably ended the matter at once by felling him. But they contented themselves with awaiting the issue.

The force which the chief expended in wielding his club now began to be apparent. His movements became slower, his breath hissed through his clenched teeth, and the surprised savages drew nearer in order to render assistance. Jack observed this movement. He felt that his fate was sealed, and resolved to cast his life upon the next blow. The chief's club was again about to descend on his head. He might have evaded it easily, but instead of doing so, he suddenly shortened his grasp of his own club, rushed in under the blow, struck his adversary right between the eyes with all his force, and fell to the earth, crushed beneath the senseless body of the chief. A dozen clubs flew high in air, ready to descend on the head of Jack; but they hesitated a moment, for the massive body of the chief completely covered him. That moment saved his life. Ere the savages could tear the chief's body away, seven of their number fell prostrate beneath the clubs of the prisoners whom Peterkin and I had set free, and two others fell under our own hand. We could never have accomplished this had not our enemies been so engrossed with the fight between Jack and their chief that they had failed to observe us until we were upon them. They still outnumbered our party by three; but we were flushed with victory, while they were taken by surprise and dispirited by the fall of their chief. Moreover, they were awestruck by the sweeping fury of Jack, who seemed to have lost his senses altogether, and had no sooner shaken himself free of the chief's body than he rushed into the midst of them, and in three blows equalised our numbers. Peterkin and I flew to the rescue, the savages followed us, and in less than ten minutes the whole of our opponents were knocked down or made prisoners, bound hand and foot, and extended side by side upon the seashore.

## 20

## INTERCOURSE WITH THE SAVAGES—CANNIBALISM PREVENTED—THE SLAIN ARE BURIED AND THE SURVIVORS DEPART, LEAVING US AGAIN ALONE ON OUR CORAL ISLAND.

After the battle was over, the savages crowded round us and gazed at us in surprise, while they continued to pour upon us a flood of questions, which, being wholly unintelligible, of course we could not answer. However, by way of putting an end to it, Jack took the chief (who had recovered from the effects of his wound) by the hand and shook it warmly. No sooner did the blacks see that this was meant to express good-will than they shook hands with us all round. After this ceremony was gone through Jack went up to the girl, who had never once moved from the rock where she had been left, but had continued an eager spectator of all that had passed. He made signs to her to follow him, and then, taking the chief by the hand, was about to conduct him to the bower when his eye fell on the poor infant which had been thrown into the sea and was still lying on the shore. Dropping the chief's hand he hastened towards it, and, to his great joy, found it to be still alive. We also found that the mother was beginning to recover slowly.

"Here, get out o' the way," said Jack, pushing us aside as we stooped over the poor woman and endeavoured to restore her; "I'll soon bring her round." So saying, he placed the infant on her bosom and laid its warm cheek on hers. The effect was wonderful. The woman opened her eyes, felt the child, looked at it, and with a cry of joy, clasped it in her arms, at the same time endeavouring to rise—for the purpose, apparently, of rushing into the woods.

"There, that's all right," said Jack, once more taking the chief by the hand.—"Now, Ralph and Peterkin, make the women and these fellows follow me to the bower. We'll entertain them as hospitably as we can."

In a few minutes the savages were all seated on the ground in front of the bower, making a hearty meal off a cold roast pig, several ducks, and a variety of cold fish, together with an unlimited supply of cocoa-nuts, bread-fruits, yams, taro, and plums—with all of which they seemed to be quite familiar and perfectly satisfied.

Meanwhile we three, being thoroughly knocked up with our day's work, took a good draught of cocoa-nut lemonade, and throwing ourselves on our beds, fell fast asleep. The savages, it seems, followed our example, and in half-an-hour the whole camp was buried in repose.

How long we slept I cannot tell; but this I know—that when we lay down the sun was setting, and when we awoke it was high in the heavens. I awoke Jack, who started up in surprise, being unable at first to comprehend our situation. "Now, then," said he, springing up, "let's see after breakfast.—Hallo, Peterkin, lazy fellow! how long do you mean to lie there?"

Peterkin yawned heavily. "Well," said he, opening his eyes and looking up after some trouble, "if it isn't to-morrow morning, and me thinking it was to-day all this time—Hallo, Venus! where did you come from? You seem tolerably at home, anyhow. Bah! might as well speak to the cat as to you—better, in fact, for it understands me, and you don't."

This remark was called forth by the sight of one of the elderly females, who had seated herself on the rock in front of the bower, and having placed her child at her feet, was busily engaged in devouring the remains of a roast pig.

By this time the natives outside were all astir, and breakfast in an advanced state of preparation. During the course of it we made sundry attempts to converse with the natives by signs, but without effect. At last we hit upon a plan of discovering their names. Jack pointed to his breast and said "Jack" very distinctly; then he pointed to Peterkin and to me, repeating our names at the same time. Then he pointed to himself again and said "Jack," and laying his finger on the breast of the chief, looked inquiringly into his face. The chief instantly understood him, and said "Tararo" twice distinctly. Jack repeated it after him, and the chief, nodding his head approvingly, said "Chuck," on hearing which Peterkin exploded with laughter. But Jack turned, and with a frown rebuked him, saying, "I must look even more indignantly at you than I feel, Peterkin, you rascal, for these fellows don't like to be laughed at." Then turning towards the youngest of the women, who was seated at the door of the bower, he pointed to her; whereupon the chief said "Avatea," and pointing towards the sun, raised his finger slowly towards the zenith, where it remained steadily for a minute or two.

"What can that mean, I wonder?" said Jack, looking puzzled.

"Perhaps," said Peterkin, "the chief means she is an angel come down to stay here for a while. If so, she's an uncommonly black one!"

We did not feel quite satisfied with this explanation, so Jack went up to her and said "Avatea." The woman smiled sadly and nodded her head, at the same time pointing to her breast and then to the sun in the same manner as the chief had done. We were much puzzled to know what this could signify; but as there was no way of solving our difficulty, we were obliged to rest content.

Jack now made signs to the natives to follow him, and taking up his axe, he led them to the place where the battle had been fought. Here we found the prisoners, who had passed the night on the beach, having been totally forgotten by us, as our minds had been full of our guests, and were ultimately overcome by sleep. They did not seem the worse for their exposure, however, as we judged by the hearty appetite with which they devoured the breakfast that was soon after given to them. Jack then began to dig a hole in the sand, and after working a few seconds, he pointed to it and to the dead bodies that lay exposed on the beach. The natives immediately perceived what he wanted, and running for their paddles, dug a hole in the course of half-an-hour that was quite large enough to contain all the bodies of the slain. When it was finished, they tossed their dead enemies into it with so much indifference that we felt assured they would not have put themselves to this trouble had we not asked them to do so. The body of the yellow-haired chief was the last thrown in. This wretched man would have recovered from the blow with which Jack felled him, and indeed he did endeavour to rise during the *mêlée* that followed his fall; but one of his enemies, happening to notice the action, dealt him a blow with his club that killed him on the spot.

While they were about to throw the sand over this chief, one of the savages stooped over him, and with a knife, made apparently of stone, cut a large slice of flesh from his thigh. We knew at once that he intended to make use of this for food, and could not repress a cry of horror and disgust.

"Come, come, you blackguard!" cried Jack, starting up and seizing the man by the arm, "pitch that into the hole. Do you hear?"

The savage, of course, did not understand the command; but he perfectly understood the look of disgust with which Jack regarded the flesh, and his fierce gaze as he pointed towards the hole. Nevertheless, he did not obey. Jack instantly turned to Tararo and made signs to him to enforce obedience. The chief seemed to understand the appeal; for he stepped forward, raised his club, and was on the point of dashing out the brains of his offending subject when Jack sprang forward and caught his uplifted arm.

"Stop, you blockhead!" he shouted. "I don't want you to kill the man!" He then pointed again to the flesh and to the hole. The chief uttered a few words, which had the desired effect; for the man threw the flesh into the hole, which was immediately filled up. This man was of a morose, sulky disposition, and during all the time he remained on the island, regarded us—especially Jack—with a scowling visage. His name, we found, was Mahine.

The next three or four days were spent by the savages in mending their canoe, which had been damaged by the violent shock it had sustained on striking the shore. This canoe was a very curious structure. It was about thirty feet long, and had a high, towering stern. The timbers of which it was partly composed were fastened much in the same way as those of our little boat were put together; but the part that seemed most curious to us was a sort of outrigger, or long plank, which was attached to the body of the canoe by means of two stout cross-beams. These beams kept the plank parallel with the canoe, but not in contact with it, for it floated in the water with an open space between—thus forming a sort of double canoe. This, we found, was intended to prevent the upsetting of the canoe, which was so narrow that it could not have maintained an upright position without the outrigger. We could not help wondering both at the ingenuity and the clumsiness of this contrivance.

When the canoe was ready, we assisted the natives to carry the prisoners into it, and helped them to load it with provisions and fruit. Peterkin also went to the plum-tree for the purpose of making a special onslaught upon the hogs, and killed no less than six of them. These we baked and presented to our friends, on the day of their departure. On that day Tararo made a great many energetic signs to us, which, after much consideration, we came to understand were proposals that we should go away with him to his island; but having no desire to do so, we shook our heads very decidedly. However, we consoled him by presenting him with our rusty axe, which we thought we could spare, having the excellent one which had been so providentially washed ashore to us the day we were wrecked. We also gave him a piece of wood with our names carved on it, and a piece of string to hang it round his neck as an ornament.

In a few minutes more we were all assembled on the beach. Being unable to speak to the savages, we went through the ceremony of shaking hands, and expected they would depart; but before doing so, Tararo went up to Jack and rubbed noses with him, after which he did the same with Peterkin and me! Seeing that this was their mode of salutation, we determined to conform to their custom; so we rubbed noses heartily with the whole party, women and all! The only disagreeable part of the process was when we came to rub noses with Mahine; and Peterkin afterwards said that when he saw his wolfish eyes glaring so close to his face, he felt much more inclined to *bang* than to *rub* his nose. Avatea was the last to take leave of us, and we experienced a feeling of real sorrow when she approached to bid us farewell.

Besides her modest air and gentle manners, she was the only one of the party who exhibited the smallest sign of regret at parting from us. Going up to Jack, she put out her flat little nose to be rubbed, and thereafter paid the same compliment to Peterkin and me.

An hour later the canoe was out of sight; and we, with an indefinable feeling of sadness creeping round our hearts, were seated in silence beneath the shadow of our bower, meditating on the wonderful events of the last few days.

## 21

## SAGACIOUS AND MORAL REMARKS IN REGARD TO LIFE—A SAIL!—AN UNEXPECTED SALUTE—THE END OF THE BLACK CAT—A TERRIBLE DIVE—AN INCAUTIOUS PROCEEDING AND A FRIGHTFUL CATASTROPHE.

Life is a strange compound. Peterkin used to say of it that it beat a druggist's shop all to sticks; for whereas the first is a compound of good and bad, the other is a horrible compound of all that is utterly detestable. And indeed the more I consider it, the more I am struck with the strange mixture of good and evil that exists, not only in the material earth, but in our own natures. In our own Coral Island we had experienced every variety of good that a bountiful Creator could heap on us. Yet on the night of the storm we had seen how almost, in our case—and altogether, no doubt, in the case of others less fortunate—all this good might be swept away for ever. We had seen the rich fruit-trees waving in the soft air, the tender herbs shooting upwards under the benign influence of the bright sun; and the next day we had seen these good and beautiful trees and plants uprooted by the hurricane, crushed and hurled to the ground in destructive devastation. We had lived for many months in a clime, for the most part, so beautiful that we had often wondered whether Adam and Eve had found Eden more sweet; and we had seen the quiet solitudes of our paradise suddenly broken in upon by ferocious savages, and the white sands stained with blood and strewed with lifeless forms, yet among these cannibals we had seen many symptoms of a kindly nature. I pondered these things much, and while I considered them there recurred to my memory those words which I had read in my Bible: "The works of God are wonderful, and His ways past finding out."

After these poor savages had left us we used to hold long and frequent conversations about them, and I noticed that Peterkin's manner was now much altered. He did not, indeed, jest less heartily than before, but he did so less frequently; and often there was a tone of deep seriousness in his manner, if not in his words, which made him seem to Jack and me as if he had grown two years older within a few days. But indeed I was not surprised at this when I reflected on the awful realities which we had witnessed so lately. We could by no means shake off a tendency to gloom for several weeks afterwards; but as time wore away, our usual good spirits returned somewhat, and we began to think of the visit of the savages with feelings akin to those with which we recall a terrible dream.

One day we were all enjoying ourselves in the Water Garden preparatory to going on a fishing excursion, for Peterkin had kept us in such constant supply of hogs that we had become quite tired of pork and desired a change. Peterkin was sunning himself on the ledge of rock, while we were creeping among the rocks below. Happening to look up, I observed Peterkin cutting the most extraordinary capers and making violent gesticulations for us to come up; so I gave Jack a push and rose immediately.

"A sail! a sail—Ralph, look—Jack, away on the horizon there, just over the entrance to the lagoon!" cried Peterkin as we scrambled up the rocks.

"So it is—and a schooner, too!" said Jack as he proceeded hastily to dress.

Our hearts were thrown into a terrible flutter by this discovery, for if it should touch at our island, we had no doubt the captain would be happy to give us a passage to some of the civilised islands, where we could find a ship sailing for England or some other part of Europe. Home, with all its associations, rushed in upon my heart like a flood; and much though I loved the Coral Island and the bower which had now been our home so long, I felt that I could have quitted all at that moment without a sigh. With joyful anticipations we hastened to the highest point of rock near our dwelling and awaited the arrival of the vessel, for we now perceived that she was making straight for the island under a steady breeze.

In less than an hour she was close to the reef, where she rounded-to and backed her topsails in order to survey the coast. Seeing this, and fearing that they might not perceive us, we all three waved pieces of cocoa-nut cloth in the air, and soon had the satisfaction of seeing them beginning to lower a boat and bustle about the decks as if they meant to land. Suddenly a flag was run up to the peak, a little cloud of white smoke rose from the schooner's side, and before we could guess their intentions, a cannon-shot came crashing through the bushes, carried away several cocoa-nut trees in its passage, and burst in atoms against the cliff a few yards below the spot on which we stood.

With feelings of terror we now observed that the flag at the schooner's peak was black, with a Death's-head and cross-bones upon it. As we gazed at each other in blank amazement, the word "pirate" escaped our lips simultaneously.

"What is to be done?" cried Peterkin as we observed a boat shoot from the vessel's side and make for the entrance of the reef. "If they take us off the island, it will either be to throw us overboard for sport or to make pirates of us."

I did not reply, but looked at Jack, as being our only resource in this emergency. He stood with folded arms, and his eyes fixed with a grave, anxious expression on the ground. "There is but one hope," said he, turning with a sad expression of countenance to Peterkin. "Perhaps, after all, we may not have to resort to it. If these villains are anxious to take us, they will soon overrun the whole island. But come, follow me."

Stopping abruptly in his speech, Jack bounded into the woods, and led us by a circuitous route to Spouting Cliff. Here he halted, and advancing cautiously to the rocks, glanced over their edge. We were soon by his side, and saw the boat, which was crowded with armed men, just touching the shore. In an instant the crew landed, formed line, and rushed up to our bower.

In a few seconds we saw them hurrying back to the boat, one of them swinging the poor cat round his head by the tail. On reaching the water's edge he tossed it far into the sea, and joined his companions, who appeared to be holding a hasty council.

"You see what we may expect," said Jack bitterly. "The man who will wantonly kill a poor brute for sport will think little of murdering a fellow-creature. Now, boys, we have but one chance left—the Diamond Cave."

"The Diamond Cave!" cried Peterkin. "Then my chance is a poor one, for I could not dive into it if all the pirates on the Pacific were at my heels."

"Nay, but," said I, "we will take you down, Peterkin, if you will only trust us."

As I spoke, we observed the pirates scatter over the beach, and radiate, as if from a centre, towards the woods and along shore.

"Now, Peterkin," said Jack in a solemn tone, "you must make up your mind to do it, or we must make up our minds to die in your company."

"Oh Jack, my dear friend!" cried Peterkin, turning pale, "leave me; I don't believe they'll think it worth while to kill me. Go, you and Ralph, and dive into the cave."

"That will not I," answered Jack quietly, while he picked up a stout cudgel from the ground.—"So now, Ralph, we must prepare to meet these fellows. Their motto is 'No quarter.' If we can manage to floor those coming in this direction, we may escape into the woods for a while."

"There are five of them," said I; "we have no chance."

"Come, then!" cried Peterkin, starting up and grasping Jack convulsively by the arm; "let us dive. I will go."

Those who are not naturally expert in the water know well the feelings of horror that overwhelm them, when in it, at the bare idea of being held down even for a few seconds—that spasmodic, involuntary recoil from compulsory immersion which has no connection whatever with cowardice; and they will understand the amount of resolution that it required in Peterkin to allow himself to be dragged down to a depth of ten feet, and then, through a narrow tunnel, into an almost pitch-dark cavern. But there was no alternative. The pirates had already caught sight of us, and were now within a short distance of the rocks.

Jack and I seized Peterkin by the arms.

"Now, keep quite still—no struggling," said Jack, "or we are lost!"

Peterkin made no reply; but the stern gravity of his marble features, and the tension of his muscles, satisfied us that he had fully made up his mind to go through with it. Just as the pirates gained the foot of the rocks, which hid us for a moment from their view, we bent over the sea and plunged down together, head foremost. Peterkin behaved like a hero. He floated passively between us like a log of wood, and we passed the tunnel and rose into the cave in a shorter space of time than I had ever done it before.

Peterkin drew a long, deep breath on reaching the surface, and in a few seconds we were all standing on the ledge of rock in safety. Jack now searched for the tinder and torch which always lay in the cave. He soon found them, and lighting the torch, revealed to Peterkin's wondering gaze the marvels of the place. But we were too wet to waste much time in looking about us. Our first care was to take off our clothes and wring them as dry as we could. This done, we proceeded to examine into the state of our larder, for, as Jack truly remarked, there was no knowing how long the pirates might remain on the island.

"Perhaps," said Peterkin, "they may take it into their heads to stop here altogether, and so we shall be buried alive in this place."

"Don't you think, Peterkin, that it's the nearest thing to being drowned alive that you ever felt?" said Jack with a smile. "But I have no fear of that. These villains never stay long on shore. The sea is their home, so you may depend upon it that they won't stay more than a day or two at the furthest."

We now began to make arrangements for spending the night in the cavern. At various periods Jack and I had conveyed cocoa-nuts and other fruits, besides rolls of cocoa-nut cloth, to this submarine cave, partly for amusement, and partly from a feeling that we might possibly be driven one day to take shelter here from the savages. Little did we imagine that the first savages who would drive us into it would be white savages—perhaps our own countrymen! We found the cocoa-nuts in good condition, and the cooked yams; but the bread-fruits were spoiled. We also found the cloth where we had left it, and on opening it out, there proved to be sufficient to make a bed—which was important, as the rock was damp. Having collected it all together, we spread out our bed, placed our torch in the midst of us, and ate our supper. It was indeed a strange chamber to feast in; and we could not help remarking on the cold, ghastly appearance of the walls, and the black water at our side with the thick darkness beyond, and the sullen sound of the drops that fell at long intervals from the roof of the cavern into the still water, and the strong contrast between all this and our bed and supper, which, with our faces, were lit up with the deep-red flame of the torch.

We sat long over our meal, talking together in subdued voices, for we did not like the dismal echoes that rang through the vault above when we happened to raise them. At last the faint light that came through the opening died away, warning us that it was night and time for rest. We therefore put out our torch and lay down to sleep.

On awaking, it was some time ere we could collect our faculties so as to remember where we were, and we were in much uncertainty as to whether it was early or late. We saw by the faint light that it was day, but could not guess at the hour; so Jack proposed that he should dive out and reconnoitre.

"No, Jack," said I; "do you rest here. You've had enough to do during the last few days. Rest yourself now, and take care of Peterkin, while I go out to see what the pirates are about. I'll be very careful not to expose myself, and I'll bring you word again in a short time."

"Very well, Ralph," answered Jack; "please yourself. But don't be long. And if you'll take my advice, you'll go in your clothes; for I would like to have some fresh cocoa-nuts, and climbing trees without clothes is uncomfortable—to say the least of it."

"The pirates will be sure to keep a sharp lookout," said Peterkin; "so, pray, be careful."

"No fear," said I. "Good-bye."

"Good-bye," answered my comrades.

And while the words were yet sounding in my ears, I plunged into the water, and in a few seconds found myself in the open air. On rising, I was careful to come up gently and to breathe softly, while I kept close in beside the rocks; but as I observed no one near me, I crept slowly out and ascended the cliff, a step at a time, till I obtained a full view of the shore. No pirates were to be seen—even their boat was gone; but as it was possible they might have hidden themselves, I did not venture too boldly forward. Then it occurred to me to look out to sea, when, to my surprise, I saw the pirate schooner sailing away almost hull down on the horizon! On seeing this I uttered a shout of joy. Then my first impulse was to dive back to tell my companions the good news; but I checked myself, and ran to the top of the cliff in order to make sure that the vessel I saw was indeed the pirate schooner. I looked long and anxiously at her, and giving vent to a deep sigh of relief, said aloud, "Yes, there she goes; the villains have been balked of their prey this time at least!"

"Not so sure of that!" said a deep voice at my side, while at the same moment a heavy hand grasped my shoulder and held it as if in a vice.

## 22

### I FALL INTO THE HANDS OF PIRATES—HOW THEY TREATED ME, AND WHAT I SAID TO THEM—THE RESULT OF THE WHOLE ENDING IN A MELANCHOLY SEPARATION AND IN A MOST UNEXPECTED GIFT.

My heart seemed to leap into my throat at the words; and turning round, I beheld a man of immense stature and fierce aspect regarding me with a smile of contempt. He was a white man—that is to say, he was a man of European blood, though his face, from long exposure to the weather, was deeply bronzed. His dress was that of a common seaman, except that he had on a Greek skull-cap, and wore a broad shawl of the richest silk round his waist. In this shawl were placed two pairs of pistols and a heavy cutlass. He wore a beard and moustache, which, like the locks on his head, were short, curly, and sprinkled with grey hairs.

"So, youngster," he said with a sardonic smile, while I felt his grasp tighten on my shoulder, "the villains have been balked of their prey, have they? We shall see—we shall see. Now, you whelp, look yonder!" As he spoke, the pirate uttered a shrill whistle. In a second or two it was answered, and the pirate boat rowed round the point at the Water Garden and came rapidly towards us. "Now, go make a fire on that point; and hark'ee, youngster, if you try to run away I'll send a quick and sure messenger after you," and he pointed significantly at his pistols.

I obeyed in silence; and as I happened to have the burning-glass in my pocket, a fire was speedily kindled, and a thick smoke ascended into the air. It had scarcely appeared for two minutes when the boom of a gun rolled over the sea, and looking up, I saw that the schooner was making for the island again. It now flashed across me that this was a ruse on the part of the pirates, and that they had sent their vessel away, knowing that it would lead us to suppose that they had left altogether. But there was no use of regret now. I was completely in their power; so I stood helplessly beside the pirate, watching the crew of the boat as they landed on the beach. For an instant I contemplated rushing over the cliff into the sea; but this, I saw, I could not now accomplish, as some of the men were already between me and the water.

There was a good deal of jesting at the success of their scheme, as the crew ascended the rocks and addressed the man who had captured me by the title of "Captain". They were a ferocious set of men, with shaggy beards and scowling brows. All of them were armed with cutlasses and pistols, and their costumes were, with trifling variations, similar to that of the captain. As I looked from one to the other, and observed the low, scowling brows that never unbent even when the men laughed, and the mean, rascally expression that sat on each face, I felt that my life hung by a hair.

"But where are the other cubs?" cried one of the men with an oath that made me shudder. "I'll swear to it there were three at least, if not more."

"You hear what he says, whelp: where are the other dogs?" said the captain.

"If you mean my companions," said I in a low voice, "I won't tell you."

A loud laugh burst from the crew at this answer.

The pirate captain looked at me in surprise. Then drawing a pistol from his belt, he cocked it and said, "Now, youngster, listen to me. I've no time to waste here. If you don't tell me all you know, I'll blow your brains out! Where are your comrades?"

For an instant I hesitated, not knowing what to do in this extremity. Suddenly a thought occurred to me.

"Villain," said I, shaking my clenched fist in his face, "to blow my brains out would make short work of me, and be soon over; death by drowning is as sure, and the agony prolonged. Yet I tell you to your face, if you were to toss me over yonder cliff into the sea, I would not tell you where my companions are; and I dare you to try me!"

The pirate captain grew white with rage as I spoke. "Say you so?" cried he, uttering a fierce oath.—"Here, lads, take him by the legs and heave him in—quick!"

The men, who were utterly silenced with surprise at my audacity, advanced and seized me; and as they carried me towards the cliff, I congratulated myself not a little on the success of my scheme, for I knew that once in the water I should be safe, and could rejoin Jack and Peterkin in the cave. But my hopes were suddenly blasted by the captain crying out, "Hold on, lads, hold on! We'll give him a taste of the thumb-screws before throwing him to the sharks. Away with him into the boat. Look alive! the breeze is freshening."

The men instantly raised me shoulder-high, and hurrying down the rocks, tossed me into the bottom of the boat, where I lay for some time stunned with the violence of my fall.

On recovering sufficiently to raise myself on my elbow, I perceived that we were already outside the coral reef and close alongside the schooner, which was of small size and clipper-built. I had only time to observe this much when I received a severe kick on the side from one of the men, who ordered me, in a rough voice, to jump aboard. Rising hastily, I clambered up the side. In a few minutes the boat was hoisted on deck, the vessel's head put close to the wind, and the Coral Island dropped slowly astern as we beat up against a head sea.

Immediately after coming aboard, the crew were too busily engaged in working the ship and getting in the boat to attend to me; so I remained leaning against the bulwarks close to the gangway, watching their operations. I was surprised to find that there were no guns or carronades of any kind in the vessel, which had more the appearance of a fast-sailing trader than a pirate. But I was struck with the neatness of everything. The brass-work of the binnacle and about the tiller, as well as the copper belaying-pins, were as brightly polished as if they had just come from the foundry. The decks were pure white and smooth. The masts were clean-scraped and varnished, except at the cross-trees and truck, which were painted black. The standing and running rigging was in the most perfect order, and the sails white as snow. In short, everything, from the single narrow red stripe on her low, black hull to the trucks on her tapering masts, evinced an amount of care and strict discipline that would have done credit to a ship of the Royal Navy. There was nothing lumbering or unseemly about the vessel, excepting, perhaps, a boat, which lay on the deck with its keel up between the fore and main masts. It seemed disproportionately large for the schooner; but when I saw that the crew amounted to between thirty and forty men, I concluded that this boat was held in reserve in case of any accident compelling the crew to desert the vessel.

As I have before said, the costumes of the men were similar to that of the captain. But in head-gear they differed, not only from him, but from each other—some wearing the ordinary straw hat of the merchant service, while others wore cloth caps and red worsted nightcaps. I observed that all their arms were sent below, the captain only retaining his cutlass and a single pistol in the folds of his shawl. Although the captain was the tallest and most powerful man in the ship, he did not strikingly excel many of his men in this respect; and the only difference that an ordinary observer would have noticed was a certain degree of open candour, straightforward daring, in the bold, ferocious expression of his face, which rendered him less repulsive than his low-browed associates, but did not by any means induce the belief that he was a hero. This look was, however, the indication of that spirit which gave him the pre-eminence among the crew of desperadoes who called him captain. He was a lion-like villain, totally devoid of personal fear, and utterly reckless of consequences, and therefore a terror to his men, who individually hated him, but unitedly felt it to be to their advantage to have him at their head.

But my thoughts soon reverted to the dear companions whom I had left on shore; and as I turned towards the Coral Island, which was now far away to leeward, I sighed deeply, and the tears rolled slowly down my cheeks as I thought that I might never see them more.

"So you're blubbering, are you, you obstinate whelp?" said the deep voice of the captain as he came up and gave me a box on the ear that nearly felled me to the deck. "I don't allow any such weakness aboard o' this ship. So clap a stopper on your eyes, or I'll give you something to cry for."

I flushed with indignation at this rough and cruel treatment, but felt that giving way to anger would only make matters worse; so I made no reply, but took out my handkerchief and dried my eyes.

"I thought you were made of better stuff," continued the captain angrily. "I'd rather have a mad bulldog aboard than a water-eyed puppy. But I'll cure you, lad, or introduce you to the sharks before long. Now go below, and stay there till I call you."

As I walked forward to obey, my eye fell on a small keg standing by the side of the mainmast, on which the word *gunpowder* was written in pencil. It immediately flashed across me that as we were beating up against the wind, anything floating in the sea would be driven on the reef encircling the Coral Island. I also recollected—for thought is more rapid than the lightning—that my old companions had a pistol. Without a moment's hesitation, therefore, I lifted the keg from the deck and tossed it into the sea! An exclamation of surprise burst from the captain and some of the men who witnessed this act of mine.

Striding up to me, and uttering fearful imprecations, the captain raised his hand to strike me, while he shouted, "Boy! whelp! what mean you by that?"

"If you lower your hand," said I in a loud voice, while I felt the blood rush to my temples, "I'll tell you. Until you do so, I'm dumb."

The captain stepped back and regarded me with a look of amazement.

"Now," continued I, "I threw that keg into the sea because the wind and waves will carry it to my friends on the Coral Island, who happen to have a pistol but no powder. I hope that it will reach them soon; and my only regret is that the keg was not a bigger one. Moreover, pirate, you said just now that you thought I was made of better stuff. I don't know what stuff I am made of—I never thought much about that subject; but I'm quite certain of this—that I am made of such stuff as the like of you shall never tame, though you should do your worst!"

To my surprise, the captain, instead of flying into a rage, smiled, and thrusting his hand into the voluminous shawl that encircled his waist, turned on his heel and walked aft, while I went below.

Here, instead of being rudely handled, as I had expected, the men received me with a shout of laughter; and one of them, patting me on the back, said, "Well done, lad! You're a brick, and I have no doubt will turn out a rare cove. Bloody Bill there was just such a fellow as you are, and he's now the biggest cut-throat of us all."

"Take a can of beer, lad," cried another, "and wet your whistle after that speech o' your'n to the captain. If any one o' us had made it, youngster, he would have had no whistle to wet by this time."

"Stop your clapper, Jack!" vociferated a third. "Give the boy a junk o' meat. Don't you see he's a'most goin' to kick the bucket?"

"And no wonder," said the first speaker with an oath, "after the tumble you gave him into the boat! I guess it would have broke your neck if you had got it."

I did indeed feel somewhat faint, which was owing, doubtless, to the combined effects of ill-usage and hunger; for it will be recollected that I had dived out of the cave that morning before breakfast, and it was now near midday. I therefore gladly accepted a plate of boiled pork and a yam, which were handed to me by one of the men from the locker on which some of the crew were seated eating their dinner. But I must add that the zest with which I ate my meal was much abated in consequence of the frightful oaths and the terrible language that flowed from the lips of these godless men, even in the midst of their hilarity and good-humour. The man who had been alluded to as Bloody Bill was seated near me, and I could not help wondering at the moody silence he maintained among his comrades. He did indeed reply to their questions in a careless, off-hand tone, but he never volunteered a remark. The only difference between him and the others was his taciturnity and his size, for he was nearly, if not quite, as large a man as the captain.

During the remainder of the afternoon I was left to my own reflections, which were anything but agreeable; for I could not banish from my mind the threat about the thumbscrews, of the nature and use of which I had a vague but terrible conception. I was still meditating on my unhappy fate when, just after nightfall, one of the watch on deck called down the hatchway:

"Hallo, there! One o' you tumble up and light the cabin lamp, and send that boy aft to the captain—sharp!"

"Now, then, do you hear, youngster? the captain wants you. Look alive!" said Bloody Bill, raising his huge frame from the locker on which he had been asleep for the last two hours. He sprang up the ladder, and I instantly followed him, and going aft, was shown into the cabin by one of the men, who closed the door after me.

A small silver lamp which hung from a beam threw a dim, soft light over the cabin, which was a small apartment, and comfortably but plainly furnished. Seated on a camp-stool at the table, and busily engaged in examining a chart of the Pacific, was the captain, who looked up as I entered, and in a quiet voice bade me be seated, while he threw down his pencil, and rising from the table, stretched himself on a sofa at the upper end of the cabin.

"Boy," said he, looking me full in the face, "what is your name?"

"Ralph Rover," I replied.

"Where did you come from, and how came you to be on that island? How many companions had you on it? Answer me, now, and mind you tell no lies."

"I never tell lies," said I firmly.

The captain received this reply with a cold, sarcastic smile, and bade me answer his questions.

I then told him the history of myself and my companions from the time we sailed till the day of his visit to the island—taking care, however, to make no mention of the Diamond Cave. After I had concluded, he was silent for a few minutes; then looking up, he said, "Boy, I believe you."

I was surprised at this remark, for I could not imagine why he should not believe me. However, I made no reply.

"And what," continued the captain, "makes you think that this schooner is a pirate?"

"The black flag," said I, "showed me what you are; and if any further proof were wanting, I have had it in the brutal treatment I have received at your hands."

The captain frowned as I spoke; but, subduing his anger, he continued, "Boy, you are too bold. I admit that we treated you roughly, but that was because you made us lose time and gave us a good deal of trouble. As to the black flag, that is merely a joke that my fellows play off upon people sometimes in order to frighten them. It is their humour, and does no harm. I am no pirate, boy, but a lawful trader—a rough one, I grant you; but one can't help that in these seas, where there are so many pirates on the water and such murderous blackguards on the land. I carry on a trade in sandal-wood with the Feejee Islands; and if you choose, Ralph, to behave yourself and be a good boy, I'll take you along with me and give you a good share of the profits. You see, I'm in want of an honest boy like you to look after the cabin, and keep the log, and superintend the traffic on shore sometimes. What say you, Ralph: would you like to become a sandal-wood trader?"

I was much surprised by this explanation, and a good deal relieved to find that the vessel, after all, was not a pirate; but instead of replying, I said, "If it be as you state, then why did you take me from my island, and why do you not now take me back?"

The captain smiled as he replied, "I took you off in anger, boy, and I'm sorry for it. I would even now take you back, but we are too far away from it. See, there it is," he added, laying his finger on the chart; "and we are now here—fifty miles, at least. It would not be fair to my men to put about now, for they have all an interest in the trade."

I could make no reply to this; so, after a little more conversation, I agreed to become one of the crew—at least, until we could reach some civilised island where I might be put ashore. The captain assented to this proposition; and after thanking him for the promise, I left the cabin and went on deck with feelings that ought to have been lighter, but which were, I could not tell why, marvellously heavy and uncomfortable still.

# 23

## BLOODY BILL—DARK SURMISES—A STRANGE SAIL, AND A STRANGE CREW, AND A STILL STRANGER CARGO—NEW REASONS FOR FAVOURING MISSIONARIES—A MURDEROUS MASSACRE, AND THOUGHTS THEREON.

Three weeks after the conversation narrated in the last chapter I was standing on the quarter-deck of the schooner, watching the gambols of a shoal of porpoises that swam round us. It was a dead calm—one of those still, hot, sweltering days so common in the Pacific, when nature seems to have gone to sleep, and the only thing in water or in air that proves her still alive is her long, deep breathing in the swell of the mighty sea. No cloud floated in the deep blue above, no ripple broke the reflected blue below. The sun shone fiercely in the sky, and a ball of fire blazed with almost equal power from out the bosom of the water. So intensely still was it, and so perfectly transparent was the surface of the deep, that had it not been for the long swell already alluded to, we might have believed the surrounding universe to be a huge, blue, liquid ball, and our little ship the one solitary material speck in all creation floating in the midst of it.

No sound broke on our ears save the soft puff now and then of a porpoise, the slow creak of the masts as we swayed gently on the swell, the patter of the reef-points, and the occasional flap of the hanging sails. An awning covered the fore and after parts of the schooner, under which the men composing the watch on deck lolled in sleepy indolence, overcome with excessive heat. Bloody Bill, as the men invariably called him, was standing at the tiller; but his post for the present was a sinecure, and he whiled away the time by alternately gazing in dreamy abstraction at the compass in the binnacle and by walking to the taffrail in order to spit into the sea. In one of these turns he came near to where I was standing, and leaning over the side, looked long and earnestly down into the blue wave.

This man, although he was always taciturn and often surly, was the only human being on board with whom I had the slightest desire to become better acquainted. The other men, seeing that I did not relish their company, and knowing that I was a protégé of the captain, treated me with total indifference. Bloody Bill, it is true, did the same; but as this was his conduct to every one else, it was not peculiar in reference to me. Once or twice I tried to draw him into conversation, but he always turned away after a few cold monosyllables. As he now leaned over the taffrail, close beside me, I said to him:

"Bill, why is it that you are so gloomy? Why do you never speak to any one?"

Bill smiled slightly as he replied, "Why, I s'pose it's because I hain't got nothin' to say!"

"That's strange," said I musingly. "You look like a man that could think, and such men can usually speak."

"So they can, youngster," rejoined Bill somewhat sternly; "and I could speak too if I had a mind to, but what's the use o' speakin' here? The men only open their mouths to curse and swear, and they seem to find it entertainin'; but I don't, so I hold my tongue."

"Well, Bill, that's true, and I would rather not hear you speak at all than hear you speak like the other men. But I don't swear, Bill; so you might talk to me sometimes, I think. Besides, I'm weary of spending day after day in this way, without a single soul to say a pleasant word to. I've been used to friendly conversation, Bill, and I really would take it kind if you would talk with me a little now and then."

Bill looked at me in surprise, and I thought I observed a sad expression pass across his sunburned face.

"An' where have you been used to friendly conversation?" said Bill, looking down again into the sea. "Not on that Coral Island, I take it?"

"Yes, indeed," said I energetically. "I have spent many of the happiest months in my life on that Coral Island;" and without waiting to be further questioned, I launched out into a glowing account of the happy life that Jack and Peterkin and I had spent together, and related minutely every circumstance that befell us while on the island.

"Boy, boy," said Bill in a voice so deep that it startled me, "this is no place for you!"

"That's true," said I. "I am of little use on board, and I don't like my comrades; but I can't help it, and at any rate I hope to be free again soon."

"Free?" said Bill, looking at me in surprise.

"Yes, free," returned I. "The captain said he would put me ashore after this trip was over."

"*This trip*! Hark'ee, boy," said Bill, lowering his voice, "what said the captain to you the day you came aboard?"

"He said that he was a trader in sandal-wood, and no pirate, and told me that if I would join him for this trip he would give me a good share of the profits, or put me on shore in some civilised island if I chose."

Bill's brows lowered savagely as he muttered, "Ay, he said truth when he told you he was a sandal-wood trader, but he lied when—"

"Sail ho!" shouted the lookout at the masthead.

"Where away?" cried Bill, springing to the tiller; while the men, startled by the sudden cry, jumped up and gazed round the horizon.

"On the starboard quarter, hull down, sir," answered the lookout.

At this moment the captain came on deck, and mounting into the rigging, surveyed the sail through the glass. Then sweeping his eye round the horizon, he gazed steadily at the particular point.

"Take in topsails!" shouted the captain, swinging himself down on the deck by the main-back stay.

"Take in topsails!" roared the first mate.

"Ay, ay, sir–r–r!" answered the men as they sprang into the rigging and went aloft like cats.

Instantly all was bustle on board the hitherto quiet schooner. The topsails were taken in and stowed, the men stood by the sheets and halyards, and the captain gazed anxiously at the breeze, which was now rushing towards us like a sheet of dark blue. In a few seconds it struck us. The schooner trembled, as if in surprise at the sudden onset, while she fell away; then, bending gracefully to the wind, as though in acknowledgment of her subjection, she cut through the waves with her sharp prow like a dolphin, while Bill directed her course towards the strange sail.

In half-an-hour we neared her sufficiently to make out that she was a schooner, and from the clumsy appearance of her masts and sails we judged her to be a trader. She evidently did not like our appearance, for the instant the breeze reached her she crowded all sail and showed us her stern. As the breeze had moderated a little, our topsails were again shaken out; and it soon became evident—despite the proverb, "A stern chase is a long one"—that we doubled her speed, and would overhaul her speedily. When within a mile we hoisted British colours, but receiving no acknowledgment, the captain ordered a shot to be fired across her bows. In a moment, to my surprise, a large portion of the bottom of the boat amidships was removed, and in the hole thus exposed appeared an immense brass gun. It worked on a swivel, and was elevated by means of machinery. It was quickly loaded and fired. The heavy ball struck the water a few yards ahead of the chase, and ricochetting into the air, plunged into the sea a mile beyond it.

This produced the desired effect. The strange vessel backed her topsails and hove-to, while we ranged up and lay-to about a hundred yards off.

"Lower the boat!" cried the captain.

In a second the boat was lowered and manned by a part of the crew, who were all armed with cutlasses and pistols. As the captain passed me to get into it he said, "Jump into the stern-sheets, Ralph; I may want you." I obeyed, and in ten minutes more we were standing on the stranger's deck. We were all much surprised at the sight that met our eyes. Instead of a crew of such sailors as we were accustomed to see, there were only fifteen blacks, standing on the quarter-deck, and regarding us with looks of undisguised alarm. They were totally unarmed, and most of them unclothed. One or two, however, wore portions of European attire. One had on a pair of duck trousers, which were much too large for him, and stuck out in a most ungainly manner; another wore nothing but the common, scanty, native garment round the loins and a black beaver hat; but the most ludicrous personage of all, and one who seemed to be chief, was a tall, middle-aged man, of a mild, simple expression of countenance, who wore a white cotton shirt, a swallow-tailed coat, and a straw hat, while his black, brawny legs were totally uncovered below the knees.

"Where's the commander of this ship?" inquired our captain, stepping up to this individual.

"I is cap'in," he answered, taking off his straw hat and making a low bow.

"You!" said our captain in surprise. "Where do you come from, and where are you bound? What cargo have you aboard?"

"We is come," answered the man with the swallow-tail, "from Aitutaki; we was go for Rarotonga. We is native miss'nary ship; our name is de *Olive Branch*; an' our cargo is two tons cocoa-nuts, seventy pigs, twenty cats, and de Gosp'l."

This announcement was received by the crew of our vessel with a shout of laughter, which, however, was peremptorily checked by the captain, whose expression instantly changed from one of severity to that of frank urbanity as he advanced towards the missionary and shook him warmly by the hand.

"I am very glad to have fallen in with you," said he, "and I wish you much success in your missionary labours. Pray take me to your cabin, as I wish to converse with you privately."

The missionary immediately took him by the hand, and as he led him away I heard him saying, "me most glad to find you trader; we t'ought you be pirate. You very like one 'bout the masts."

What conversation the captain had with this man I never heard; but he came on deck again in a quarter of an hour, and shaking hands cordially with the missionary, ordered us into our boat and returned to the schooner, which was immediately put before the wind. In a few minutes the *Olive Branch* was left far behind us.

That afternoon, as I was down below at dinner, I heard the men talking about this curious ship.

"I wonder," said one, "why our captain looked so sweet on yon swallow-tailed supercargo o' pigs and Gospels? If it had been an ordinary trader, now, he would have taken as many o' the pigs as he required and sent the ship with all on board to the bottom."

"Why, Dick, you must be new to these seas if you don't know that!" cried another. "The captain cares as much for the Gospel as you do (an' that's precious little); but he knows, and everybody knows, that the only place among the southern islands where a ship can put in and get what she wants in comfort is where the Gospel has been sent to. There are hundreds o' islands, at this blessed moment, where you might as well jump straight into a shark's maw as land without a band o' thirty comrades armed to the teeth to back you."

"Ay," said a man with a deep scar over his right eye. "Dick's new to the work. But if the captain takes us for a cargo o' sandal-wood to the Feejees, he'll get a taste o' these black gentry in their native condition. For my part, I don't know, and I don't care, what the Gospel does to them; but I know that when any o' the islands chance to get it, trade goes all smooth and easy. But where they ha'n't got it, Beelzebub himself could hardly desire better company."

"Well, you ought to be a good judge," cried another, laughing, "for you've never kept any company but the worst all your life!"

"Ralph Rover!" shouted a voice down the hatchway; "captain wants you, aft."

Springing up the ladder, I hastened to the cabin, pondering as I went the strange testimony borne by these men to the effect of the Gospel on savage natures—testimony which, as it was perfectly disinterested, I had no doubt whatever was strictly true.

On coming again on deck I found Bloody Bill at the helm, and as we were alone together, I tried to draw him into conversation. After repeating to him the conversation in the forecastle about the missionaries, I said:

"Tell me, Bill: is this schooner really a trader in sandal-wood?"

"Yes, Ralph, she is; but she's just as really a pirate. The black flag you saw flying at the peak was no deception."

"Then how can you say she's a trader?" asked I.

"Why, as to that, she trades when she can't take by force; but she takes by force when she can, in preference. Ralph," he added, lowering his voice, "if you had seen the bloody deeds that I have witnessed done on these decks, you would not need to ask if we were pirates. But you'll find it out soon enough. As for the missionaries, the captain favours them because they are useful to him. The South Sea Islanders are such incarnate fiends that they are the better of being tamed, and the missionaries are the only men who can do it."

Our track after this lay through several clusters of small islets, among which we were becalmed more than once. During this part of our voyage the watch on deck and the lookout at the masthead were more than usually vigilant, as we were not only in danger of being attacked by the natives (who, I learned from the captain's remarks, were a bloody and deceitful tribe at this group), but we were also exposed to much risk from the multitudes of coral reefs that rose up in the channels between the islands—some of them just above the surface, others a few feet below it. Our precautions against the savages, I found, were indeed necessary.

One day we were becalmed among a group of small islands, most of which appeared to be uninhabited. As we were in want of fresh water, the captain sent the boat ashore to bring off a cask or two. But we were mistaken in thinking there were no natives; for scarcely had we drawn near to the shore when a band of naked blacks rushed out of the bush and assembled on the beach, brandishing their clubs and spears in a threatening manner. Our men were well armed, but refrained from showing any signs of hostility, and rowed nearer in order to converse with the natives; and I now found that more than one of the crew could imperfectly speak dialects of the language peculiar to the South Sea Islanders. When within forty yards of the shore we ceased rowing, and the first mate stood up to address the multitude; but instead of answering us, they replied with a shower of stones, some of which cut the men severely. Instantly our muskets were levelled, and a volley was about to be fired when the captain hailed us in a loud voice from the schooner, which lay not more than five or six hundred yards off the shore.

"Don't fire!" he shouted angrily. "Pull off to the point ahead of you!"

The men looked surprised at this order, and uttered deep curses as they prepared to obey; for their wrath was roused, and they burned for revenge. Three or four of them hesitated, and seemed disposed to mutiny.

"Don't distress yourselves, lads," said the mate, while a bitter smile curled his lip. "Obey orders. The captain's not the man to take an insult tamely. If Long Tom does not speak presently, I'll give myself to the sharks."

The men smiled significantly as they pulled from the shore, which was now crowded with a dense mass of savages, amounting probably to five or six hundred. We had not rowed off above a couple of hundred yards when a loud roar thundered over the sea, and the big brass gun sent a withering shower of grape point-blank into the midst of the living mass, through which a wide lane was cut; while a yell, the like of which I could not have imagined, burst from the miserable survivors as they fled to the woods. Amongst the heaps of dead that lay on the sand just where they had fallen, I could distinguish mutilated forms writhing in agony; while ever and anon one and another rose convulsively from out the mass, endeavoured to stagger towards the wood, and ere they had taken a few steps, fell and wallowed on the bloody sand. My blood curdled within me as I witnessed this frightful and wanton slaughter; but I had little time to think, for the captain's deep voice came again over the water towards us: "Pull ashore, lads, and fill your water-casks!" The men obeyed in silence, and it seemed to me as if even their hard hearts were shocked by the ruthless deed. On gaining the mouth of the rivulet at which we intended to take in water, we found it flowing with blood; for the greater part of those who were slain had been standing on the banks of the stream, a short way above its mouth. Many of the wretched creatures had fallen into it; and we found one body, which had been carried down, jammed between two rocks, with the staring eyeballs turned towards us, and his black hair waving in the ripples of the blood-red stream. No one dared to oppose our landing now, so we carried our casks to a pool above the murdered group, and having filled them, returned on board. Fortunately a breeze sprang up soon afterwards, and carried us away from the dreadful spot; but it could not waft me away from the memory of what I had seen.

"And this," thought I, gazing in horror at the captain, who, with a quiet look of indifference, leaned upon the taffrail, smoking a cigar and contemplating the fertile green islets as they passed like a lovely picture before our eyes—"this is the man who favours the missionaries because they are useful to him and can tame the savages better than any one else can do it!" Then I wondered in my mind whether it were possible for any missionary to tame *him*!

# 24

## BLOODY BILL IS COMMUNICATIVE AND SAGACIOUS —UNPLEASANT PROSPECTS—RETROSPECTIVE MEDITATIONS INTERRUPTED BY VOLCANIC AGENCY—THE PIRATES NEGOTIATE WITH A FEEJEE CHIEF—VARIOUS ETCETERAS THAT ARE CALCULATED TO SURPRISE AND HORRIFY.

It was many days after the events just narrated ere I recovered a little of my wonted spirits. I could not shake off the feeling for a long time that I was in a frightful dream, and the sight of our captain filled me with so much horror that I kept out of his way as much as my duties about the cabin would permit. Fortunately he took so little notice of me that he did not observe my changed feelings towards him, otherwise it might have been worse for me.

But I was now resolved that I would run away the very first island we should land at, and commit myself to the hospitality of the natives rather than remain an hour longer than I could help in the pirate schooner. I pondered this subject a good deal, and at last made up my mind to communicate my intention to Bloody Bill; for during several talks I had had with him of late, I felt assured that he too would willingly escape if possible. When I told him of my design he shook his head. "No, no, Ralph," said he; "you must not think of running away here. Among some of the groups of islands you might do so with safety; but if you tried it here, you would find that you had jumped out of the fryin'-pan into the fire."

"How so, Bill?" said I. "Would the natives not receive me?"

"That they would, lad; but they would eat you too."

"Eat me!" said I in surprise. "I thought the South Sea Islanders never ate anybody except their enemies."

"Humph!" ejaculated Bill. "I 'spose 'twas yer tender-hearted friends in England that put that notion into your head. There's a set o' soft-hearted folk at home that I knows on who don't like to have their feelin's ruffled; and when you tell them anything they don't like—that shocks them, as they call it—no matter how true it be, they stop their ears and cry out, 'Oh, that is *too* horrible! We can't believe that!' An' they say truth. They can't believe it, 'cause they won't believe it. Now, I believe there's thousands o' the people in England who are sich born drivellin' *won't believers* that they think the black fellows hereaways, at the worst, eat an enemy only now an' then out o' spite; whereas I know for certain, and many captains of the British and American navies know as well as me, that the Feejee Islanders eat not only their enemies but one another—and they do it not for spite, but for pleasure. It's a *fact* that they prefer human flesh to any other. But they don't like white men's flesh so well as black; they say it makes them sick."

"Why, Bill," said I, "you told me just now that they would eat *me* if they caught me!"

"So I did, and so I think they would. I've only heard some o' them say they don't like white men *so well* as black; but if they was hungry they wouldn't be particular. Anyhow, I'm sure they would kill you. You see, Ralph, I've been a good while in them parts, and I've visited the different groups of islands oftentimes as a trader. And thorough-goin' blackguards some o' them traders are—no better than pirates, I can tell you. One captain that I sailed with was not a chip better than the one we're with now. He was trading with a friendly chief one day aboard his vessel. The chief had swam off to us with the things for trade tied atop of his head, for them chaps are like otters in the water. Well, the chief was hard on the captain, and would not part with some o' his things. When their bargainin' was over they shook hands, and the chief jumped overboard to swim ashore; but before he got forty yards from the ship, the captain seized a musket and shot him dead. He then hove up anchor and put to sea, and as we sailed along the shore he dropped six black fellows with his rifle, remarkin' that 'that would spoil the trade for the next-comers.' But, as I was sayin', I'm up to the ways o' these fellows. One o' the laws o' the country is that every shipwrecked person who happens to be cast ashore, be he dead or alive, is doomed to be roasted and eaten. There was a small tradin' schooner wrecked off one of these islands when we were lyin' there in harbour during a storm. The crew was lost—all but three men, who swam ashore. The moment they landed, they were seized by the natives and carried up into the woods. We knew pretty well what their fate would be; but we could not help them, for our crew was small, and if we had gone ashore they would likely have killed us all. We never saw the three men again. But we heard frightful yelling and dancing and merrymaking that night; and one of the natives, who came aboard to trade with us next day, told us that the *long pigs*, as he called the men, had been roasted and eaten, and their bones were to be converted into sail-needles. He also said that white men were bad to eat, and that most o' the people on shore were sick."

I was very much shocked and cast down in my mind at this terrible account of the natives, and asked Bill what he would advise me to do. Looking round the deck to make sure that we were not overheard, he lowered his voice and said, "There are two or three ways that we might escape, Ralph, but none o' them's easy. If the captain would only sail for some o' the islands near Tahiti we might run away there well enough, because the natives are all Christians; an' we find that wherever the savages take up with Christianity they always give over their bloody ways, and are safe to be trusted. I never cared for Christianity myself," he continued in a soliloquising voice, "and I don't well know what it means; but a man with half-an-eye can see what it does for these black critters. However, the captain always keeps a sharp lookout after us when we get to these islands, for he half-suspects that one or two o' us are tired of his company. Then we might manage to cut the boat adrift some fine night when it's our watch on deck, and clear off before they discovered that we were gone. But we would run the risk o' bein' caught by the blacks. I wouldn't like to try that plan. But you and I will think over it, Ralph, and see what's to be done. In the meantime it's our watch below, so I'll go and turn in."

Bill then bade me good-night and went below, while a comrade took his place at the helm; but feeling no desire to enter into conversation with him, I walked aft, and leaning over the stern, looked down into the phosphorescent waves that gurgled around the rudder, and streamed out like a flame of blue light in the vessel's wake. My thoughts were very sad, and I could scarce refrain from tears as I contrasted my present wretched position with the happy, peaceful time I had spent on the Coral Island with my dear companions. As I thought upon Jack and Peterkin, anxious forebodings crossed my mind, and I pictured to myself the grief and dismay with which they would search every nook and corner of the island in a vain attempt to discover my dead body; for I felt assured that if they did not see any sign of the pirate schooner or boat when they came out of the cave to look for me, they would never imagine that I had been carried away. I wondered, too, how Jack would succeed in getting Peterkin out of the cave without my assistance; and I trembled when I thought that he might lose presence of mind, and begin to kick when he was in the tunnel! These thoughts were suddenly interrupted and put to flight by a bright-red blaze, which lighted up the horizon to the southward and cast a crimson glow far over the sea. This appearance was accompanied by a low growling sound, as of distant thunder, and at the same time the sky above us became black, while a hot, stifling wind blew around us in fitful gusts.

The crew assembled hastily on deck, and most of them were under the belief that a frightful hurricane was pending; but the captain, coming on deck, soon explained the phenomena.

"It's only a volcano," said he. "I knew there was one hereabouts, but thought it was extinct.—Up, there, and furl topgallant sails! We'll likely have a breeze, and it's well to be ready."

As he spoke, a shower began to fall, which, we quickly observed, was not rain, but fine ashes. As we were many miles distant from the volcano, these must have been carried to us from it by the wind. As the captain had predicted, a stiff breeze soon afterwards sprang up, under the influence of which we speedily left the volcano far behind us; but during the greater part of the night we could see its lurid glare and hear its distant thunder. The shower did not cease to fall for several hours, and we must have sailed under it for nearly forty miles —perhaps farther. When we emerged from the cloud, our decks and every part of the rigging were completely covered with a thick coat of ashes. I was much interested in this, and recollected that Jack had often spoken of many of the islands of the Pacific as being volcanoes, either active or extinct, and had said that the whole region was more or less volcanic, and that some scientific men were of opinion that the islands of the Pacific were nothing more or less than the mountain-tops of a huge continent which had sunk under the influence of volcanic agency.

Three days after passing the volcano, we found ourselves a few miles to windward of an island of considerable size and luxuriant aspect. It consisted of two mountains, which seemed to be nearly four thousand feet high. They were separated from each other by a broad valley, whose thick-growing trees ascended a considerable distance up the mountain-sides; and rich, level plains or meadow-land spread round the base of the mountains, except at the point immediately opposite the large valley, where a river seemed to carry the trees, as it were, along with it down to the white, sandy shore. The mountain-tops, unlike those of our Coral Island, were sharp, needle-shaped, and bare, while their sides were more rugged and grand in outline than anything I had yet seen in those seas. Bloody Bill was beside me when the island first hove in sight.

"Ah!" he exclaimed, "I know that island well. They call it Emo."

"Have you been there before, then?" I inquired.

"Ay, that I have, often, and so has this schooner. 'Tis a famous island for sandal-wood. We have taken many cargoes of it already—and have paid for them, too, for the savages are so numerous that we dared not try to take it by force. But our captain has tried to cheat them so often that they're beginnin' not to like us overmuch now. Besides, the men behaved ill the last time we were here, and I wonder the captain is not afraid to venture. But he's afraid o' nothin' earthly, I believe."

We soon ran inside the barrier coral reef, and let go our anchor in six fathoms water, just opposite the mouth of a small creek, whose shores were densely covered with mangroves and tall umbrageous trees. The principal village of the natives lay about half-a-mile from this point. Ordering the boat out, the captain jumped into it, and ordered me to follow him. The men, fifteen in number, were well armed; and the mate was directed to have Long Tom ready for emergencies.

"Give way, lads!" cried the captain.

The oars fell into the water at the word, the boat shot from the schooner's side, and in a few minutes reached the shore. Here, contrary to our expectation, we were met with the utmost cordiality by Romata, the principal chief of the island, who conducted us to his house and gave us mats to sit upon. I observed in passing that the natives, of whom there were two or three thousand, were totally unarmed.

After a short preliminary palaver, a feast of baked pigs and various roots was spread before us, of which we partook sparingly, and then proceeded to business. The captain stated his object in visiting the island, regretted that there had been a slight misunderstanding during the last visit, and hoped that no ill-will was borne by either party, and that a satisfactory trade would be accomplished.

Romata answered that he had forgotten there had been any differences between them, protested that he was delighted to see his friends again, and assured them they should have every assistance in cutting and embarking the wood. The terms were afterwards agreed on, and we rose to depart. All this conversation was afterwards explained to me by Bill, who understood the language pretty well.

Romata accompanied us on board, and explained that a great chief from another island was then on a visit to him, and that he was to be ceremoniously entertained on the following day. After begging to be allowed to introduce him to us, and receiving permission, he sent his canoe ashore to bring him off. At the same time he gave orders to bring on board his two favourites, a cock and a paroquet. While the canoe was gone on this errand, I had time to regard the savage chief attentively. He was a man of immense size, with massive but beautifully moulded limbs and figure, only parts of which—the broad chest and muscular arms—were uncovered; for although the lower orders generally wore no other clothing than a strip of cloth called *maro* round their loins, the chief, on particular occasions, wrapped his person in voluminous folds of a species of native cloth made from the bark of the Chinese paper-mulberry. Romata wore a magnificent black beard and moustache, and his hair was frizzed out to such an extent that it resembled a large turban, in which was stuck a long wooden pin! I afterwards found that this pin served for scratching the head, for which purpose the fingers were too short without disarranging the hair. But Romata put himself to much greater inconvenience on account of his hair; for we found that he slept with his head resting on a wooden pillow, in which was cut a hollow for the neck, so that the hair of the sleeper might not be disarranged.

In ten minutes the canoe returned, bringing the other chief, who certainly presented a most extraordinary appearance, having painted one half of his face red and the other half yellow, besides ornamenting it with various designs in black! Otherwise he was much the same in appearance as Romata, though not so powerfully built. As this chief had never seen a ship before—except, perchance, some of the petty traders that at long intervals visit these remote islands—he was much taken up with the neatness and beauty of all the fittings of the schooner. He was particularly struck with a musket which was shown to him, and asked where the white men got hatchets hard enough to cut the tree of which the barrel was made! While he was thus engaged, his brother-chief stood aloof, talking with the captain, and fondling a superb cock and a little blue-headed paroquet—the favourites of which I have before spoken. I observed that all the other natives walked in a crouching posture while in the presence of Romata. Before our guests left us, the captain ordered the brass gun to be uncovered and fired for their gratification; and I have every reason to believe he did so for the purpose of showing our superior power, in case the natives should harbour any evil designs against us. Romata had never seen this gun before, as it had not been uncovered on previous visits, and the astonishment with which he viewed it was very amusing. Being desirous of knowing its power, he begged that the captain would fire it; so a shot was put into it. The chiefs were then directed to look at a rock about two miles out at sea, and the gun was fired. In a second the top of the rock was seen to burst asunder, and to fall in fragments into the sea.

Romata was so delighted with the success of this shot that he pointed to a man who was walking on the shore, and begged the captain to fire at him, evidently supposing that his permission was quite sufficient to justify the captain in such an act. He was therefore surprised, and not a little annoyed, when the captain refused to fire at the native and ordered the gun to be housed.

Of all the things, however, that afforded matter of amusement to these savages, that which pleased Romata's visitor most was the ship's pump. He never tired of examining it and pumping up the water. Indeed, so much was he taken up with this pump that he could not be prevailed on to return on shore, but sent a canoe to fetch his favourite stool, on which he seated himself, and spent the remainder of the day in pumping the bilge-water out of the ship!

Next day the crew went ashore to cut sandal-wood, while the captain, with one or two men, remained on board, in order to be ready, if need be, with the brass gun, which was unhoused and conspicuously elevated, with its capacious muzzle directed point-blank at the chief's house. The men were fully armed, as usual; and the captain ordered me to go with them, to assist in the work. I was much pleased with this order, for it freed me from the captain's company, which I could not now endure, and it gave me an opportunity of seeing the natives.

As we wound along in single file through the rich, fragrant groves of banana, cocoa-nut, bread-fruit, and other trees, I observed that there were many of the plum and banyan trees, with which I had become familiar on the Coral Island. I noticed, also, large quantities of taro—roots, yams, and sweet potatoes growing in enclosures. On turning into an open glade of the woods, we came abruptly upon a cluster of native houses. They were built chiefly of bamboos, and were thatched with the large, thick leaves of the pandanus; but many of them had little more than a sloping roof and three sides with an open front, being the most simple shelter from the weather that could well be imagined. Within these and around them were groups of natives—men, women, and children—who all stood up to gaze at us as we marched along, followed by the party of men whom the chief had sent to escort us. About half-a-mile inland we arrived at the spot where the sandal-wood grew, and while the men set to work I clambered up an adjoining hill to observe the country.

About midday the chief arrived with several followers, one of whom carried a baked pig on a wooden platter, with yams and potatoes on several plantain leaves, which he presented to the men, who sat down under the shade of a tree to dine. The chief sat down to dine also; but, to my surprise, instead of feeding himself, one of his wives performed that office for him! I was seated beside Bill, and asked him the reason of this.

"It is beneath his dignity, I believe, to feed himself," answered Bill; "but I dare say he's not particular, except on great occasions. They've a strange custom among them, Ralph, which is called *tabu,* and they carry it to great lengths. If a man chooses a particular tree for his god, the fruit o' that tree is tabued to him; and if he eats it, he is sure to be killed by his people—and eaten, of course, for killing means eating hereaway. Then, you see that great mop o' hair on the chief's head? Well, he has a lot o' barbers to keep it in order; and it's a law that whoever touches the head of a living chief or the body of a dead one, his hands are tabued. So in that way the barbers' hands are always tabued, and they daren't use them for their lives, but have to be fed like big babies—as they are, sure enough!"

"That's odd, Bill. But look there," said I, pointing to a man whose skin was of a much lighter colour than the generality of the natives. "I've seen a few of these light-skinned fellows among the Feejeeans. They seem to me to be of quite a different race."

"So they are," answered Bill. "These fellows come from the Tongan Islands, which lie a long way to the eastward. They come here to build their big war-canoes; and as these take two, and sometimes four, years to build, there's always some o' the brown-skins among the black sarpents o' these islands."

"By the way, Bill," said I, "your mentioning serpents reminds me that I have not seen a reptile of any kind since I came to this part of the world."

"No more there are any," said Bill, "if ye except the niggers themselves. There's none on the islands but a lizard or two, and some sich harmless things; but I never seed any myself. If there's none on the land, however, there's more than enough in the water; and that reminds me of a wonderful brute they have here. But come, I'll show it to you." So saying, Bill arose, and leaving the men still busy with the baked pig, led me into the forest. After proceeding a short distance we came upon a small pond of stagnant water. A native lad had followed us, to whom we called and beckoned him to come to us. On Bill saying a few words to him, which I did not understand, the boy advanced to the edge of the pond and gave a low, peculiar whistle. Immediately the water became agitated, and an enormous eel thrust its head above the surface and allowed the youth to touch it. It was about twelve feet long, and as thick round the body as a man's thigh.

"There!" said Bill, his lip curling with contempt; "what do you think of that for a god, Ralph? This is one o' their gods, and it has been fed with dozens o' livin' babies already. How many more it'll get afore it dies is hard to say."

"Babies!" said I with an incredulous look.

"Ay, babies," returned Bill. "Your soft-hearted folk at home would say, 'Oh, horrible! Impossible!' to that, and then go away as comfortable and unconcerned as if their sayin' 'Horrible! impossible!' had made it a lie. But I tell you, Ralph, it's a *fact*. I've seed it with my own eyes the last time I was here; an' mayhap, if you stop awhile at this accursed place and keep a sharp lookout, you'll see it too. They don't feed it regularly with livin' babies, but they give it one now and then as a treat.—Bah, you brute!" cried Bill in disgust, giving the reptile a kick on the snout with his heavy boot that sent it sweltering back in agony into its loathsome pool. I thought it lucky for Bill—indeed for all of us—that the native youth's back happened to be turned at the time, for I am certain that if the poor savages had come to know that we had so rudely handled their god we should have had to fight our way back to the ship. As we retraced our steps I questioned my companion further on this subject.

"How comes it, Bill, that the mothers allow such a dreadful thing to be done?"

"Allow it? the mothers *do* it! It seems to me that there's nothing too fiendish or diabolical for these people to do. Why, in some of the islands they have an institution called the *Areoi,* and the persons connected with that body are ready for any wickedness that mortal man can devise. In fact, they stick at nothing; and one o' their customs is to murder their infants the moment they are born. The mothers agree to it, and the fathers do it. And the mildest ways they have of murdering them is by sticking them through the body with sharp splinters of bamboo, strangling them with their thumbs, or burying them alive and stamping them to death while under the sod."

I felt sick at heart while my companion recited these horrors.

"But it's a curious fact," he continued after a pause, during which we walked in silence towards the spot where we had left our comrades—"it's a curious fact that wherever the missionaries get a footin' all these things come to an end at once, an' the savages take to doin' each other good and singin' psalms, just like Methodists."

"God bless the missionaries," said I, while a feeling of enthusiasm filled my heart so that I could speak with difficulty. "God bless and prosper the missionaries till they get a footing in every island of the sea!"

"I would say Amen to that prayer, Ralph, if I could," said Bill, in a deep, sad voice; "but it would be a mere mockery for a man to ask a blessing for others who dare not ask one for himself. But, Ralph," he continued, "I've not told you half o' the abominations I have seen durin' my life in these seas. If we pull long together, lad, I'll tell you more; and if times have not changed very much since I was here last, it's like that you'll have a chance o' seeing a little for yourself before long."

## 25

## THE SANDAL-WOOD PARTY—NATIVE CHILDREN'S GAMES SOMEWHAT SURPRISING—DESPERATE AMUSEMENTS SUDDENLY AND FATALLY BROUGHT TO A CLOSE—AN OLD FRIEND RECOGNISED—NEWS —ROMATA'S MAD CONDUCT.

Next day the wood-cutting party went ashore again, and I accompanied them as before. During the dinner-hour I wandered into the woods alone, being disinclined for food that day. I had not rambled far when I found myself unexpectedly on the seashore, having crossed a narrow neck of land which separated the native village from a large bay. Here I found a party of the islanders busy with one of their war-canoes, which was almost ready for launching. I stood for a long time watching this party with great interest, and observed that they fastened the timbers and planks to each other very much in the same way in which I had seen Jack fasten those of our little boat. But what surprised me most was its immense length, which I measured carefully, and found to be a hundred feet long; and it was so capacious that it could have held three hundred men. It had the unwieldy outrigger and enormously high stern-posts which I had remarked on the canoe that came to us while I was on the Coral Island. Observing some boys playing at games a short way along the beach, I resolved to go and watch them; but as I turned from the natives who were engaged so busily and cheerfully at their work, I little thought of the terrible event that hung on the completion of that war-canoe.

Advancing towards the children, who were so numerous that I began to think this must be the general playground of the village, I sat down on a grassy bank under the shade of a plantain-tree to watch them. And a happier or more noisy crew I have never seen. There were at least two hundred of them, both boys and girls, all of whom were clad in no other garments than their own glossy little black skins, except the maro, or strip of cloth, round the loins of the boys, and a very short petticoat or kilt on the girls. They did not all play at the same game, but amused themselves in different groups.

One band was busily engaged in a game exactly similar to our blind man's buff. Another set were walking on stilts, which raised the children three feet from the ground. They were very expert at this amusement, and seldom tumbled. In another place I observed a group of girls standing together, and apparently enjoying themselves very much; so I went up to see what they were doing, and found that they were opening their eyelids with their fingers till their eyes appeared of an enormous size, and then thrusting pieces of straw between the upper and lower lids, across the eyeball, to keep them in that position! This seemed to me, I must confess, a very foolish as well as dangerous amusement. Nevertheless, the children seemed to be greatly delighted with the hideous faces they made. I pondered this subject a good deal, and thought that if little children knew how silly they seemed to grown-up people when, they make faces, they would not be so fond of doing it. In another place were a number of boys engaged in flying kites; and I could not help wondering that some of the games of those little savages should be so like to our own, although they had never seen us at play. But the kites were different from ours in many respects, being of every variety of shape. They were made of very thin cloth, and the boys raised them to a wonderful height in the air by means of twine made from the cocoa-nut husk. Other games there were, some of which showed the natural depravity of the hearts of these poor savages, and made me wish fervently that missionaries might be sent out to them. But the amusement which the greatest number of the children of both sexes seemed to take chief delight in was swimming and diving in the sea, and the expertness which they exhibited was truly amazing. They seemed to have two principal games in the water, one of which was to dive off a sort of stage which had been erected near a deep part of the sea, and chase each other in the water. Some of them went down to an extraordinary depth; others skimmed along the surface, or rolled over and over like porpoises, or diving under each other, came up unexpectedly and pulled each other down by a leg or an arm. They never seemed to tire of this sport, and from the great heat of the water in the South Seas, they could remain in it nearly all day without feeling chilled. Many of these children were almost infants, scarce able to walk; yet they staggered down the beach, flung their round, fat little black bodies fearlessly into deep water, and struck out to sea with as much confidence as ducklings.

The other game to which I have referred was swimming in the surf. But as this is an amusement in which all engage, from children of ten to grey-headed men of sixty, and as I had an opportunity of witnessing it in perfection the day following, I shall describe it more minutely.

I suppose it was in honour of their guest that this grand swimming-match was got up, for Romata came and told the captain that they were going to engage in it, and begged him to "come and see."

"What sort of amusement is this surf-swimming?" I inquired of Bill as we walked together to a part of the shore on which several thousands of the natives were assembled.

"It's a very favourite lark with these 'xtr'or'nary critters," replied Bill, giving a turn to the quid of tobacco that invariably bulged out of his left cheek. "Ye see, Ralph, them fellows take to the water as soon a'most as they can walk, an' long before they can do that anything respectably, so that they are as much at home in the sea as on the land. Well, ye see, I 'spose they found swimmin' for miles out to sea, and divin' fathoms deep, wasn't excitin' enough, so they invented this game o' swimmin' on the surf. Each man and boy, as you see, has got a short board or plank, with which he swims out for a mile or more to sea, and then, gettin' on the top o' yon thunderin' breaker, they come to shore on the top of it, yellin' and screechin' like fiends. It's a marvel to me that they're not dashed to shivers on the coral reef, for sure an' sart'in am I that if any o' us tried it, we wouldn't be worth the fluke of a broken anchor after the wave fell. But there they go!"

As he spoke, several hundreds of the natives, amongst whom we were now standing, uttered a loud yell, rushed down the beach, plunged into the surf, and were carried off by the seething foam of the retreating wave.

At the point where we stood, the encircling coral reef joined the shore, so that the magnificent breakers, which a recent stiff breeze had rendered larger than usual, fell in thunder at the feet of the multitudes who lined the beach. For some time the swimmers continued to strike out to sea, breasting over the swell like hundreds of black seals. Then they all turned, and watching an approaching billow, mounted its white crest, and each laying his breast on the short, flat board, came rolling towards the shore, careering on the summit of the mighty wave, while they and the onlookers shouted and yelled with excitement. Just as the monster wave curled in solemn majesty to fling its bulky length upon the beach, most of the swimmers slid back into the trough behind; others, slipping off their boards, seized them in their hands, and plunging through the watery waste, swam out to repeat the amusement; but a few, who seemed to me the most reckless, continued their career until they were launched upon the beach and enveloped in the churning foam and spray. One of these last came in on the crest of the wave most manfully, and landed with a violent bound almost on the spot where Bill and I stood. I saw by his peculiar head-dress that he was the chief whom the tribe entertained as their guest. The sea-water had removed nearly all the paint with which his face had been covered, and as he rose panting to his feet, I recognised, to my surprise, the features of Tararo, my old friend of the Coral Island!

Tararo at the same moment recognised me, and advancing quickly, took me round the neck and rubbed noses, which had the effect of transferring a good deal of the moist paint from his nose to mine. Then, recollecting that this was not the white man's mode of salutation, he grasped me by the hand and shook it violently.

"Hallo, Ralph!" cried Bill in surprise, "that chap seems to have taken a sudden fancy to you, or he must be an old acquaintance."

"Right, Bill," I replied; "he is indeed an old acquaintance." And I explained, in a few words, that he was the chief whose party Jack and Peterkin and I had helped to save.

Tararo having thrown away his surf-board, entered into an animated conversation with Bill, pointing frequently during the course of it to me, whereby I concluded he must be telling him about the memorable battle and the part we had taken in it. When he paused I begged of Bill to ask him about the woman Avatea, for I had some hope that she might have come with Tararo on this visit. "And ask him," said I, "who she is, for I am persuaded she is of a different race from the Feejeeans." On the mention of her name the chief frowned darkly, and seemed to speak with much anger.

"You're right, Ralph," said Bill when the chief had ceased to talk; "she's not a Feejee girl, but a Samoan. How she ever came to this place the chief does not very clearly explain; but he says she was taken in war, and that he got her three years ago, an' kept her as his daughter ever since. Lucky for her, poor girl, else she'd have been roasted and eaten like the rest."

"But why does Tararo frown and look so angry?" said I.

"Because the girl's somewhat obstinate, like most o' the sex, an' won't marry the man he wants her to. It seems that a chief of some other island came on a visit to Tararo and took a fancy to her; but she wouldn't have him on no account, bein' already in love, and engaged to a young chief whom Tararo hates, and she kicked up a desperate shindy. So, as he was goin' on a war-expedition in his canoe, he left her to think about it, sayin' he'd be back in six months or so, when he hoped she wouldn't be so obstropolous. This happened just a week ago; an' Tararo says that if she's not ready to go, when the chief returns, as his bride, she'll be sent to him as a *long pig*."

"As a long pig!" I exclaimed in surprise. "Why, what does he mean by that?"

"He means somethin' very unpleasant," answered Bill with a frown. "You see, these blackguards eat men an' women just as readily as they eat pigs; and as baked pigs and baked men are very like each other in appearance, they call men *long* pigs. If Avatea goes to this fellow as a long pig, it's all up with her, poor thing!"

"Is she on the island now?" I asked eagerly.

"No; she's at Tararo's island."

"And where does it lie?"

"About fifty or sixty miles to the south'ard o' this," returned Bill; "but I—"

At this moment we were startled by the cry of "mao! mao—a shark! a shark!" which was immediately followed by a shriek that rang clear and fearfully loud above the tumult of cries that arose from the savages in the water and on the land. We turned hastily towards the direction whence the cry came, and had just time to observe the glaring eyeballs of one of the swimmers as he tossed his arms in the air. Next instant he was pulled under the waves. A canoe was instantly launched, and the hand of the drowning man was caught; but only half of his body was dragged from the maw of the monster, which followed the canoe until the water became so shallow that it could scarcely swim. The crest of the next billow was tinged with red as it rolled towards the shore.

In most countries of the world this would have made a deep impression on the spectators; but the only effect it had upon these islanders was to make them hurry with all speed out of the sea, lest a similar fate should befall some of the others. But so utterly reckless were they of human life that it did not for a moment suspend the progress of their amusements. It is true the surf-swimming ended for that time somewhat abruptly, but they immediately proceeded with other games. Bill told me that sharks do not often attack the surf-swimmers, being frightened away by the immense numbers of men and boys in the water, and by the shouting and splashing that they make. "But," said he, "such a thing as you have seen just now don't frighten them much. They'll be at it again to-morrow or next day, just as if there wasn't a single shark between Feejee and Nova Zembla."

After this the natives had a series of wrestling and boxing matches; and being men of immense size and muscle, they did a good deal of injury to each other, especially in boxing, in which not only the lower orders but several of the chiefs and priests engaged. Each bout was very quickly terminated; for they did not pretend to a scientific knowledge of the art, and wasted, no time in sparring, but hit straight out at each other's heads, and their blows were delivered with great force. Frequently one of the combatants was knocked down with a single blow, and one gigantic fellow hit his adversary so severely that he drove the skin entirely off his forehead. This feat was hailed with immense applause by the spectators.

During these exhibitions, which were very painful to me, though I confess I could not refrain from beholding them, I was struck with the beauty of many of the figures and designs that were tattooed on the persons of the chiefs and principal men. One figure, that seemed to me very elegant, was that of a palm-tree tattooed on the back of a man's leg, the roots rising, as it were, from under his heel, the stem ascending the tendon of the ankle, and the graceful head branching out upon the calf. I afterwards learned that this process of tattooing is very painful, and takes long to do, commencing at the age of ten, and being continued at intervals up to the age of thirty. It is done by means of an instrument made of bone, with a number of sharp teeth, with which the skin is punctured. Into these punctures a preparation made from the kernel of the candle-nut, mixed with cocoa-nut oil, is rubbed, and the mark thus made is indelible. The operation is performed by a class of men whose profession it is, and they tattoo as much at a time as the person on whom they are operating can bear, which is not much, the pain and inflammation caused by tattooing being very great—sometimes causing death. Some of the chiefs were tattooed with an ornamental stripe down the legs, which gave them the appearance of being clad in tights; others had marks round the ankles and insteps, which looked like tight-fitting and elegant boots. Their faces were also tattooed, and their breasts were very profusely marked with every imaginable species of device—muskets, dogs, birds, pigs, clubs, and canoes, intermingled with lozenges, squares, circles, and other arbitrary figures.

The women were not tattooed so much as the men, having only a few marks on their feet and arms. But I must say, however objectionable this strange practice may be, it nevertheless had this good effect—that it took away very much from their appearance of nakedness.

Next day, while we were returning from the woods to our schooner, we observed Romata rushing about in the neighbourhood of his house, apparently mad with passion.

"Ah!" said Bill to me, "there he's at his old tricks again. That's his way when he gets drink. The natives make a sort of drink o' their own, and it makes him bad enough; but when he gets brandy he's like a wild tiger. The captain, I suppose, has given him a bottle, as usual, to keep him in good-humour. After drinkin' he usually goes to sleep, and the people know it well, and keep out of his way for fear they should waken him. Even the babies are taken out of earshot; for when he's waked up he rushes out, just as you see him now, and spears or clubs the first person he meets."

It seemed at the present time, however, that no deadly weapon had been in his way, for the infuriated chief was raging about without one. Suddenly he caught sight of an unfortunate man who was trying to conceal himself behind a tree. Rushing towards him, Romata struck him a terrible blow on the head, which knocked out the poor man's eye and also dislocated the chief's finger. The wretched creature offered no resistance; he did not even attempt to parry the blow. Indeed, from what Bill said, I found that he might consider himself lucky in having escaped with his life, which would certainly have been forfeited had the chief been possessed of a club at the time.

"Have these wretched creatures no law among themselves," said I, "which can restrain such wickedness?"

"None," replied Bill. "The chief's word is law. He might kill and eat a dozen of his own subjects any day for nothing more than his own pleasure, and nobody would take the least notice of it."

This ferocious deed took place within sight of our party as we wended our way to the beach, but I could not observe any other expression on the faces of the men than that of total indifference or contempt. It seemed to me a very awful thing that it should be possible for men to come to such hardness of heart and callousness to the sight of bloodshed and violence; but, indeed, I began to find that such constant exposure to scenes of blood was having a slight effect upon myself, and I shuddered when I came to think that I too was becoming callous.

I thought upon this subject much that night while I walked up and down the deck during my hours of watch, and I came to the conclusion that if I, who hated, abhorred, and detested such bloody deeds as I had witnessed within the last few weeks, could so soon come to be less sensitive about them, how little wonder that these poor, ignorant savages, who were born and bred in familiarity therewith, should think nothing of them at all, and should hold human life in so very slight esteem!

## 26

### MISCHIEF BREWING—MY BLOOD IS MADE TO RUN COLD—EVIL CONSULTATIONS AND WICKED RESOLVES—BLOODY BILL ATTEMPTS TO DO GOOD, AND FAILS—THE ATTACK—WHOLESALE MURDER—THE FLIGHT—THE ESCAPE.

Next morning I awoke with a feverish brow and a feeling of deep depression at my heart; and the more I thought on my unhappy fate, the more wretched and miserable did I feel.

I was surrounded on all sides by human beings of the most dreadful character, to whom the shedding of blood was mere pastime. On shore were the natives, whose practices were so horrible that I could not think of them without shuddering. On board were none but pirates of the blackest dye, who, although not cannibals, were foul murderers, and more blameworthy even than the savages, inasmuch as they knew better. Even Bill, with whom I had, under the strange circumstances of my lot, formed a kind of intimacy, was so fierce in his nature as to have acquired the title of "Bloody" from his vile companions. I felt very much cast down the more I considered the subject and the impossibility of delivery, as it seemed to me—at least, for a long time to come. At last, in my feeling of utter helplessness, I prayed fervently to the Almighty that He would deliver me out of my miserable condition; and when I had done so I felt some degree of comfort.

When the captain came on deck, before the hour at which the men usually started for the woods, I begged of him to permit me to remain aboard that day, as I did not feel well; but he looked at me angrily, and ordered me, in a surly tone, to get ready to go on shore as usual. The fact was that the captain had been out of humour for some time past. Romata and he had had some differences, and high words had passed between them, during which the chief had threatened to send a fleet of his war-canoes, with a thousand men, to break up and burn the schooner; whereupon the captain smiled sarcastically, and going up to the chief, gazed sternly in his face while he said, "I have only to raise my little finger just now, and my big gun will blow your whole village to atoms in five minutes!" Although the chief was a bold man, he quailed before the pirate's glance and threat, and made no reply; but a bad feeling had been raised, and old sores had been opened.

I had, therefore, to go with the woodcutters that day. Before starting, however, the captain called me into the cabin and said:

"Here, Ralph; I've got a mission for you, lad. That blackguard Romata is in the dumps, and nothing will mollify him but a gift; so do you go up to his house and give him these whale's teeth, with my compliments. Take with you one of the men who can speak the language."

I looked at the gift in some surprise, for it consisted of six white whale's teeth, and two of the same dyed bright red, which seemed to me very paltry things. However, I did not dare to hesitate, or to ask any questions; so gathering them up, I left the cabin, and was soon on my way to the chief's house, accompanied by Bill. On expressing my surprise at the gift, he said:

"They're paltry enough to you or me, Ralph, but they're considered of great value by them chaps. They're a sort o' cash among them. The red ones are the most prized, one of them bein' equal to twenty o' the white ones. I suppose the only reason for their bein' valuable is that there ain't many of them, and they're hard to be got."

On arriving at the house we found Romata sitting on a mat, in the midst of a number of large bales of native cloth and other articles, which had been brought to him as presents from time to time by inferior chiefs. He received us rather haughtily; but on Bill explaining the nature of our errand, he became very condescending, and his eyes glistened with satisfaction when he received the whale's teeth, although he laid them aside with an assumption of kingly indifference.

"Go," said he with a wave of the hand— "go tell your captain that he may cut wood to-day, but not to-morrow. He must come ashore; I want to have a palaver with him."

As we left the house to return to the woods, Bill shook his head.

"There's mischief brewin' in that black rascal's head. I know him of old. But what comes here?"

As he spoke, we heard the sound of laughter and shouting in the wood, and presently there issued from it a band of savages, in the midst of whom were a number of men bearing burdens on their shoulders. At first I thought that these burdens were poles with something rolled round them, the end of each pole resting on a man's shoulder; but on a nearer approach I saw that they were human beings, tied hand and foot, and so lashed to the poles that they could not move. I counted twenty of them as they passed.

"More murder!" said Bill in a voice that sounded between a hoarse laugh and a groan.

"Surely they are not going to murder them?" said I, looking anxiously into Bill's face.

"I don't know, Ralph," replied Bill, "what they're goin' to do with them; but I fear they mean no good when they tie fellows up in that way."

As we continued our way towards the woodcutters, I observed that Bill looked anxiously over his shoulder in the direction where the procession had disappeared. At last he stopped, and turning abruptly on his heel, said:

"I tell ye what it is, Ralph: I must be at the bottom o' that affair. Let us follow these black scoundrels and see what they're goin' to do."

I must say I had no wish to pry further into their bloody practices; but Bill seemed bent on it, so I turned and went. We passed rapidly through the bush, being guided in the right direction by the shouts of the savages. Suddenly there was a dead silence, which continued for some time, while Bill and I involuntarily quickened our pace until we were running at the top of our speed across the narrow neck of land previously mentioned. As we reached the verge of the wood we discovered the savages surrounding the large war-canoe, which they were apparently on the point of launching. Suddenly the multitude put their united strength to the canoe; but scarcely had the huge machine begun to move when a yell, the most appalling that ever fell upon my ear, rose high above the shouting of the savages. It had not died away when another and another smote upon my throbbing ear, and then I saw that these inhuman monsters were actually launching their canoe over the living bodies of their victims. But there was no pity in the breasts of these men. Forward they went in ruthless indifference, shouting as they went, while high above their voices rang the dying shrieks of those wretched creatures as, one after another, the ponderous canoe passed over them, burst the eyeballs from their sockets, and sent the life-blood gushing from their mouths. Oh reader, this is no fiction! I would not, for the sake of thrilling you with horror, invent so terrible a scene. It was witnessed. It is true—true as that accursed sin which has rendered the human heart capable of such diabolical enormities!

When it was over I turned round and fell upon the grass with a deep groan; but Bill seized me by the arm, and lifting me up as if I had been a child, cried:

"Come along, lad; let's away!" And so, staggering and stumbling over the tangled underwood, we fled from the fatal spot.

During the remainder of that day I felt as if I were in a horrible dream. I scarce knew what was said to me, and was more than once blamed by the men for idling my time. At last the hour to return aboard came. We marched down to the beach, and I felt relief for the first time when my feet rested on the schooner's deck.

In the course of the evening I overheard part of a conversation between the captain and the first mate, which startled me not a little. They were down in the cabin, and conversed in an undertone; but the skylight being off; I overhead every word that was said.

"I don't half-like it," said the mate. "It seems to me that we'll only have hard fightin' and no pay."

"No pay!" repeated the captain in a voice of suppressed anger. "Do you call a good cargo all for nothing no pay?"

"Very true," returned the mate; "but we've got the cargo aboard. Why not cut your cable and take French leave o' them? What's the use o' tryin' to kill the blackguards when it'll do us no manner o' good?"

"Mate," said the captain in a low voice, "you talk like a fresh-water sailor. I can only attribute this shyness to some strange delusion, for surely,"—his voice assumed a slightly sneering tone as he said this—"surely I am not to suppose that you have become soft-hearted! Besides, you are wrong in regard to the cargo being aboard; there's a good quarter of it lying in the woods, and that blackguard chief knows it, and won't let me take it off. He defied us to do our worst yesterday."

"Defied us! did he?" cried the mate with a bitter laugh. "Poor, contemptible thing!"

"And yet he seems not so contemptible but that you are afraid to attack him."

"Who said I was afraid?" growled the mate sulkily. "I'm as ready as any man in the ship. But, captain, what is it that you intend to do?"

"I intend to muffle the sweeps and row the schooner up to the head of the creek there, from which point we can command the pile of sandal-wood with our gun. Then I shall land with all the men except two, who shall take care of the schooner and be ready with the boat to take us off. We can creep through the woods to the head of the village, where these cannibals are always dancing round their suppers of human flesh; and if the carbines of the men are loaded with a heavy charge of buck-shot, we can drop forty or fifty at the first volley. After that the thing will be easy enough. The savages will take to the mountains in a body, and we shall take what we require, up anchor, and away."

To this plan the mate at length agreed. As he left the cabin, I heard the captain say:

"Give the men an extra glass of grog, and don't forget the buck-shot."

The reader may conceive the horror with which I heard this murderous conversation. I immediately repeated it to Bill, who seemed much perplexed about it. At length he said:

"I'll tell you what I'll do, Ralph. I'll swim ashore after dark and fix a musket to a tree not far from the place where we'll have to land, and I'll tie a long string to the trigger, so that when our fellows cross it they'll let it off, and so alarm the village in time to prevent an attack, but not in time to prevent us gettin' back to the boat.—So, Master Captain," added Bill with a smile that, for the first time, seemed to me to be mingled with good-natured cheerfulness, "you'll be balked at least for once in your life by Bloody Bill."

After it grew dark, Bill put this resolve in practice. He slipped over the side with a musket in his left hand, while with his right he swam ashore and entered the woods. He soon returned, having accomplished his purpose, and got on board without being seen, I being the only one on deck.

When the hour of midnight approached, the men were mustered on deck, the cable was cut, and the muffled sweeps got out. These sweeps were immensely large oars, each requiring a couple of men to work it. In a few minutes we entered the mouth of the creek, which was indeed the mouth of a small river, and took about half-an-hour to ascend it, although the spot where we intended to land was not more than six hundred yards from the mouth, because there was a slight current against us, and the mangroves which narrowed the creek impeded the rowers in some places. Having reached the spot, which was so darkened by overhanging trees that we could see with difficulty, a small kedge-anchor attached to a thin line was let softly down over the stern.

"Now, lads," whispered the captain as he walked along the line of men, who were all armed to the teeth, "don't be in a hurry, aim low, and don't waste your first shots."

He then pointed to the boat, into which the men crowded in silence. There was no room to row; but oars were not needed, as a slight push against the side of the schooner sent the boat gliding to the shore.

"There's no need of leaving two in the boat," whispered the mate as the men stepped out; "we shall want all our hands. Let Ralph stay."

The captain assented, and ordered me to stand in readiness with the boat-hook, to shove ashore at a moment's notice if they should return, or to shove off if any of the savages should happen to approach. He then threw his carbine into the hollow of his arm, and glided through the bushes, followed by his men. With a throbbing heart I awaited the result of our plan. I knew the exact locality where the musket was placed, for Bill had described it to me, and I kept my straining eyes fixed upon the spot. But no sound came, and I began to fear that either they had gone in another direction or that Bill had not fixed the string properly. Suddenly I heard a faint click, and observed one or two bright sparks among the bushes. My heart immediately sank within me, for I knew at once that the trigger had indeed been pulled, but that the priming had not caught. The plan, therefore, had utterly failed. A feeling of dread now began to creep over me as I stood in the boat, in that dark, silent spot, awaiting the issue of this murderous expedition. I shuddered as I glanced at the water that glided past like a dark reptile. I looked back at the schooner; but her hull was just barely visible, while her tapering masts were lost among the trees which overshadowed her. Her lower sails were set, but so thick was the gloom that they were quite invisible.

Suddenly I heard a shot. In a moment a thousand voices raised a yell in the village; again the cry rose on the night air, and was followed by broken shouts as of scattered parties of men bounding into the woods. Then I heard another shout, loud and close at hand; it was the voice of the captain cursing the man who had fired the premature shot. Then came the order, "Forward!" followed by a wild hurrah of our men as they charged the savages. Shots now rang in quick succession, and at last a loud volley startled the echoes of the woods. It was followed by a multitude of wild shrieks, which were immediately drowned in another hurrah from the men, the distance of the sound proving that they were driving their enemies before them towards the sea.

While I was listening intently to these sounds, which were now mingled in confusion, I was startled by the rustling of the leaves not far from me. At first I thought it was a party of savages who had observed the schooner, but I was speedily undeceived by observing a body of natives—apparently several hundreds, as far as I could guess in the uncertain light—bounding through the woods towards the scene of battle. I saw at once that this was a party who had outflanked our men, and would speedily attack them in the rear. And so it turned out; for in a short time the shouts increased tenfold, and among them I thought I heard a death-cry uttered by voices familiar to my ear.

At length the tumult of battle ceased, and from the cries of exultation that now arose from the savages, I felt assured that our men had been conquered. I was immediately thrown into dreadful consternation. What was I now to do? To be taken by the savages was too horrible to be thought of; to flee to the mountains was hopeless, as I should soon be discovered; and to take the schooner out of the creek without assistance was impossible. I resolved, however, to make the attempt, as being my only hope, and was on the point of pushing off, when my hand was stayed and my blood chilled by an appalling shriek, in which I recognised the voice of one of the crew. It was succeeded by a shout from the savages. Then came another and another shriek of agony, making my ears to tingle, as I felt convinced they were murdering the pirate crew in cold blood. With a bursting heart and my brain whirling as if on fire, I seized the boat-hook to push from shore when a man sprang from the bushes.

"Stop! Ralph, stop! There, now, push off!" he cried, and bounded into the boat so violently as nearly to upset her. It was Bill's voice! In another moment we were on board—the boat made fast, the line of the anchor cut, and the sweeps run out. At the first stroke of Bill's giant arm the schooner was nearly pulled ashore, for in his haste he forgot that I could scarcely move the unwieldy oar. Springing to the stern, he lashed the rudder in such a position as that, while it aided me, it acted against him, and so rendered the force of our strokes nearly equal. The schooner now began to glide quickly down the creek; but before we reached its mouth, a yell from a thousand voices on the bank told that we were discovered. Instantly a number of the savages plunged into the water and swam towards us; but we were making so much way that they could not overtake us. One, however, an immensely powerful man, succeeded in laying hold of the cut rope that hung from the stern, and clambered quickly upon deck. Bill caught sight of him the instant his head appeared above the taffrail. But he did not cease to row, and did not appear even to notice the savage until he was within a yard of him; then dropping the sweep, he struck him a blow on the forehead with his clenched fist that felled him to the deck. Lifting him up, he hurled him overboard, and resumed the oar. But now a greater danger awaited us; for the savages had outrun us on the bank, and were about to plunge into the water ahead of the schooner. If they succeeded in doing so, our fate was sealed. For one moment Bill stood irresolute. Then drawing a pistol from his belt, he sprang to the brass gun, held the pan of his pistol over the touch-hole, and fired. The shot was succeeded by the hiss of the cannon's priming; then the blaze and the crashing thunder of the monstrous gun burst upon the savages with such deafening roar that it seemed as if their very mountains had been rent asunder.

This was enough. The moment of surprise and hesitation caused by the unwonted sound gave us time to pass the point; a gentle breeze, which the dense foliage had hitherto prevented us from feeling, bulged out our sails; the schooner bent before it, and the shouts of the disappointed savages grew fainter and fainter in the distance as we were slowly wafted out to sea.

## 27

## REFLECTIONS—THE WOUNDED MAN—THE SQUALL —TRUE CONSOLATION—DEATH

There is a power of endurance in human beings, both in their bodies and in their minds, which, I have often thought, seems to be wonderfully adapted and exactly proportioned to the circumstances in which individuals may happen to be placed—a power which, in most cases, is sufficient to carry a man through and over every obstacle that may happen to be thrown in his path through life, no matter how high or how steep the mountain may be, but which often forsakes him the moment the summit is gained, the point of difficulty passed, and leaves him prostrated, with energies gone, nerves unstrung, and a feeling of incapacity pervading the entire frame that renders the most trifling effort almost impossible.

During the greater part of that day I had been subjected to severe mental and much physical excitement, which had almost crushed me down by the time I was relieved from duty in the course of the evening. But when the expedition whose failure has just been narrated was planned, my anxieties and energies had been so powerfully aroused that I went through the protracted scenes of that terrible night without a feeling of the slightest fatigue. My mind and body were alike active and full of energy. No sooner was the last thrilling fear of danger past, however, than my faculties were utterly relaxed; and when I felt the cool breezes of the Pacific playing around my fevered brow, and heard the free waves rippling at the schooner's prow, as we left the hated island behind us, my senses forsook me, and I fell in a swoon upon the deck.

From this state I was quickly aroused by Bill, who shook me by the arm, saying:

"Hallo, Ralph, boy! Rouse up, lad; we're safe now! Poor thing! I believe he's fainted." And raising me in his arms he laid me on the folds of the gaff-topsail, which lay upon the deck near the tiller. "Here, take a drop o' this; it'll do you good, my boy," he added in a voice of tenderness which I had never heard him use before, while he held a brandy-flask to my lips.

I raised my eyes gratefully as I swallowed a mouthful; next moment my head sank heavily upon my arm, and I fell fast asleep. I slept long, for when I awoke the sun was a good way above the horizon. I did not move on first opening my eyes, as I felt a delightful sensation of rest pervading me, and my eyes were riveted on and charmed with the gorgeous splendour of the mighty ocean that burst upon my sight. It was a dead calm; the sea seemed a sheet of undulating crystal, tipped and streaked with the saffron hues of sunrise, which had not yet merged into the glowing heat of noon; and there was a deep calm in the blue dome above that was not broken even by the usual flutter of the sea-fowl. How long I would have lain in contemplation of this peaceful scene I know not, but my mind was recalled suddenly and painfully to the past and the present by the sight of Bill, who was seated on the deck at my feet, with his head reclining, as if in sleep, on his right arm, which rested on the tiller. As he seemed to rest peacefully, I did not mean to disturb him; but the slight noise I made in raising myself on my elbow caused him to start and look round.

"Well, Ralph, awake at last, my boy? You have slept long and soundly," he said, turning towards me.

On beholding his countenance I sprang up in anxiety. He was deadly pale, and his hair, which hung in dishevelled locks over his face, was clotted with blood. Blood also stained his hollow cheeks and covered the front of his shirt, which, with the greater part of his dress, was torn and soiled with mud.

"Oh Bill!" said I with deep anxiety, "what is the matter with you? You are ill. You must have been wounded."

"Even so, lad," said Bill in a deep, soft voice, while he extended his huge frame on the couch from which I had just risen. "I've got an ugly wound, I fear; and I've been waiting for you to waken to ask you to get me a drop o' brandy and a mouthful o' bread from the cabin lockers. You seemed to sleep so sweetly, Ralph, that I didn't like to disturb you. But I don't feel up to much just now."

I did not wait till he had done talking, but ran below immediately, and returned in a few seconds with a bottle of brandy and some broken biscuit. He seemed much refreshed after eating a few morsels and drinking a long draught of water mingled with a little of the spirits. Immediately afterwards he fell asleep, and I watched him anxiously until he awoke, being desirous of knowing the nature and extent of his wound.

"Ha!" he exclaimed on awaking suddenly, after a slumber of an hour; "I'm the better of that nap, Ralph. I feel twice the man I was;" and he attempted to rise, but sank back again immediately with a deep groan.

"Nay, Bill, you must not move, but lie still while I look at your wound. I'll make a comfortable bed for you here on deck, and get you some breakfast. After that you shall tell me how you got it. Cheer up, Bill!" I added, seeing that he turned his head away; "you'll be all right in a little, and I'll be a capital nurse to you, though I'm no doctor."

I then left him, and lighted a fire in the caboose. While it was kindling, I went to the steward's pantry and procured the materials for a good breakfast, with which, in little more than half-an-hour, I returned to my companion. He seemed much better, and smiled kindly on me as I set before him a cup of coffee and a tray with several eggs and some bread on it.

"Now, then, Bill," said I cheerfully, sitting down beside him on the deck, "let's fall to. I'm very hungry myself, I can tell you. But—I forgot—your wound," I added, rising; "let me look at it."

I found that the wound was caused by a pistol-shot in the chest. It did not bleed much, and as it was on the right side, I was in hopes that it might not be very serious. But Bill shook his head. "However," said he, "sit down, Ralph, and I'll tell you all about it.

"You see, after we left the boat an' began to push through the bushes, we went straight for the line of my musket, as I had expected. But by some unlucky chance it didn't explode, for I saw the line torn away by the men's legs, and heard the click o' the lock; so I fancy the priming had got damp and didn't catch. I was in a great quandary now what to do, for I couldn't concoct in my mind, in the hurry, any good reason for firin' off my piece. But they say necessity's the mother of invention; so just as I was giving it up and clinchin' my teeth to bide the worst o't and take what should come, a sudden thought came into my head. I stepped out before the rest, seemin' to be awful anxious to be at the savages, tripped my foot on a fallen tree, plunged head foremost into a bush, an' ov coorse my carbine exploded! Then came such a screechin' from the camp as I never heard in all my life. I rose at once, and was rushin' on with the rest when the captain called a halt.

"'You did that a purpose, you villain!' he said with a tremendous oath, and drawin' a pistol from his belt, let fly right into my breast. I fell at once, and remembered no more till I was startled and brought round by the most awful yell I ever heard in my life—except, maybe, the shrieks o' them poor critters that were crushed to death under yon big canoe. Jumpin' up, I looked round, and through the trees saw a fire gleamin' not far off; the light of which showed me the captain and men tied hand and foot, each to a post, and the savages dancin' round them like demons. I had scarce looked for a second when I saw one o' them go up to the captain flourishing a knife, and before I could wink he plunged it into his breast, while another yell, like the one that roused me, rang upon my ear. I didn't wait for more, but bounding up, went crashing through the bushes into the woods. The black fellows caught sight of me, however, but not in time to prevent me jumpin' into the boat, as you know."

Bill seemed to be much exhausted after this recital, and shuddered frequently during the narrative; so I refrained from continuing the subject at that time, and endeavoured to draw his mind to other things.

"But now, Bill," said I, "it behoves us to think about the future, and what course of action we shall pursue. Here we are, on the wide Pacific, in a well-appointed schooner, which is our own—at least, no one has a better claim to it than we have—and the world lies before us. Moreover, here comes a breeze, so we must make up our minds which way to steer."

"Ralph, boy," said my companion, "it matters not to me which way we go. I fear that my time is short now. Go where you will; I'm content."

"Well, then, Bill, I think we had better steer to the Coral Island and see what has become of my dear old comrades, Jack and Peterkin. I believe the island has no name, but the captain once pointed it out to me on the chart, and I marked it afterwards; so, as we know pretty well our position just now, I think I can steer to it. Then, as to working the vessel, it is true I cannot hoist the sails single-handed, but luckily we have enough of sail set already; and if it should come on to blow a squall, I could at least drop the peaks of the main and fore sails, and clew them up partially without help, and throw her head close into the wind, so as to keep her all shaking till the violence of the squall is past. And if we have continued light breezes, I'll rig up a complication of blocks and fix them to the topsail halyards, so that I shall be able to hoist the sails without help. 'Tis true I'll require half-a-day to hoist them, but we don't need to mind that. Then I'll make a sort of erection on deck to screen you from the sun, Bill; and if you can only manage to sit beside the tiller and steer for two hours every day, so as to let me get a nap, I'll engage to let you off duty all the rest of the twenty-four hours. And if you don't feel able for steering, I'll lash the helm and heave-to while I get you your breakfasts and dinners; and so we'll manage famously, and soon reach the Coral Island."

Bill smiled faintly as I ran on in this strain.

"And what will you do," said he, "if it comes on to blow a storm?"

This question silenced me, while I considered what I should do in such a case. At length I laid my hand on his arm and said, "Bill, when a man has done all that he can do, he ought to leave the rest to God."

"Oh Ralph," said my companion in a faint voice, looking anxiously into my face, "I wish that I had the feelin's about God that you seem to have, at this hour. I'm dyin', Ralph; yet I, who have braved death a hundred times, am afraid to die. I'm afraid to enter the next world. Something within tells me there will be a reckoning when I go there. But it's all over with me, Ralph. I feel that there's no chance o' my bein' saved."

"Don't say that, Bill," said I in deep compassion; "don't say that. I'm quite sure there's hope even for you, but I can't remember the words of the Bible that make me think so. Is there not a Bible on board, Bill?"

"No; the last that was in the ship belonged to a poor boy that was taken aboard against his will. He died, poor lad—I think through ill-treatment and fear. After he was gone, the captain found his Bible and flung it overboard."

I now reflected, with great sadness and self-reproach, on the way in which I had neglected my Bible, and it flashed across me that I was actually, in the sight of God, a greater sinner than this blood-stained pirate; for, thought I, he tells me that he never read the Bible and was never brought up to care for it, whereas I was carefully taught to read it by my own mother, and had read it daily as long as I possessed one, yet to so little purpose that I could not now call to mind a single text that would meet this poor man's case and afford him the consolation he so much required. I was much distressed, and taxed my memory for a long time. At last a text did flash into my mind, and I wondered much that I had not thought of it before.

"Bill," said I in a low voice, "'Believe on the Lord Jesus Christ, and thou shalt be saved.'"

"Ay, Ralph, I've heard the missionaries say that before now; but what good can it do me? It's not for me, that; it's not for the likes o' me."

I knew not now what to say, for although I felt sure that that word was for him as well as for me, I could not remember any other word whereby I could prove it.

After a short pause, Bill raised his eyes to mine and said, "Ralph, I've led a terrible life. I've been a sailor since I was a boy, and I've gone from bad to worse ever since I left my father's roof. I've been a pirate three years now. It is true I did not choose the trade, but I was inveigled aboard this schooner and kept here by force till I became reckless and at last joined them. Since that time my hand has been steeped in human blood again and again. Your young heart would grow cold if I—But why should I go on? 'Tis of no use, Ralph; my doom is fixed."

"Bill," said I, "'Though your sins be red like crimson, they shall be white as snow.' Only believe."

"Only believe!" cried Bill, starting up on his elbow. "I've heard men talk o' believing as if it was easy. Ha! 'tis easy enough for a man to point to a rope and say, 'I believe that would bear my weight;' but 'tis another thing for a man to catch hold o' that rope and swing himself by it over the edge of a precipice!"

The energy with which he said this, and the action with which it was accompanied, were too much for Bill. He sank back with a deep groan. As if the very elements sympathised with this man's sufferings, a low moan came sweeping over the sea.

"Hist, Ralph!" said Bill, opening his eyes; "there's a squall coming, lad! Look alive, boy! Clew up the foresail! Drop the mainsail peak! Them squalls come quick sometimes."

I had already started to my feet, and saw that a heavy squall was indeed bearing down on us. It had hitherto escaped my notice, owing to my being so much engrossed by our conversation. I instantly did as Bill desired, for the schooner was lying motionless on the glassy sea. I observed with some satisfaction that the squall was bearing down on the larboard bow, so that it would strike the vessel in the position in which she would be best able to stand the shock. Having done my best to shorten sail, I returned aft, and took my stand at the helm.

"Now, boy," said Bill in a faint voice, "keep her close to the wind."

A few seconds afterwards he said, "Ralph, let me hear those two texts again."

I repeated them.

"Are ye sure, lad, ye saw them in the Bible?"

"Quite sure," I replied.

Almost before the words had left my lips the wind burst upon us, and the spray dashed over our decks. For a time the schooner stood it bravely, and sprang forward against the rising sea like a war-horse. Meanwhile clouds darkened the sky, and the sea began to rise in huge billows. There was still too much sail on the schooner, and as the gale increased, I feared that the masts would be torn out of her or carried away, while the wind whistled and shrieked through the strained rigging. Suddenly the wind shifted a point, a heavy sea struck us on the bow, and the schooner was almost laid on her beam-ends, so that I could scarcely keep my legs. At the same moment Bill lost his hold of the belaying-pin which had served to steady him, and he slid with stunning violence against the skylight. As he lay on the deck close beside me, I could see that the shock had rendered him insensible; but I did not dare to quit the tiller for an instant, as it required all my faculties, bodily and mental, to manage the schooner. For an hour the blast drove us along, while, owing to the sharpness of the vessel's bow and the press of canvas, she dashed through the waves instead of breasting over them, thereby drenching the decks with water fore and aft. At the end of that time the squall passed away, and left us rocking on the bosom of the agitated sea.

My first care, the instant I could quit the helm, was to raise Bill from the deck and place him on the couch. I then ran below for the brandy-bottle, and rubbed his face and hands with it, and endeavoured to pour a little down his throat. But my efforts, although I continued them long and assiduously, were of no avail; as I let go the hand which I had been chafing, it fell heavily on the deck. I laid my hand over his heart, and sat for some time quite motionless; but there was no flutter there—the pirate was dead!

# 28

## ALONE ON THE DEEP—NECESSITY THE MOTHER OF INVENTION—A VALUABLE BOOK DISCOVERED—NATURAL PHENOMENON—A BRIGHT DAY IN MY HISTORY.

It was with feelings of awe, not unmingled with fear, that I now seated myself on the cabin skylight and gazed upon the rigid features of my late comrade, while my mind wandered over his past history and contemplated with anxiety my present position. Alone in the midst of the wide Pacific, having a most imperfect knowledge of navigation, and in a schooner requiring at least eight men as her proper crew! But I will not tax the reader's patience with a minute detail of my feelings and doings during the first few days that followed the death of my companion. I will merely mention that I tied a cannon-ball to his feet, and with feelings of the deepest sorrow, consigned him to the deep.

For fully a week after that a steady breeze blew from the east, and as my course lay west and by north, I made rapid progress towards my destination. I could not take an observation, which I very much regretted, as the captain's quadrant was in the cabin; but from the day of setting sail from the island of the savages I had kept a dead reckoning, and as I knew pretty well now how much leeway the schooner made, I hoped to hit the Coral Island without much difficulty. In this I was the more confident that I knew its position on the chart—which, I understood, was a very good one—and so had its correct bearings by compass.

As the weather seemed now quite settled and fine, and as I had got into the trade-winds, I set about preparations for hoisting the topsails. This was a most arduous task, and my first attempts were complete failures, owing, in a great degree, to my reprehensible ignorance of mechanical forces. The first error I made was in applying my apparatus of blocks and pulleys to a rope which was too weak, so that the very first heave I made broke it in two, and sent me staggering against the after-hatch, over which I tripped, and striking against the main-boom, tumbled down the companion-ladder into the cabin. I was much bruised and somewhat stunned by this untoward accident. However, I considered it fortunate that I was not killed. In my next attempt I made sure of not coming by a similar accident, so I unreeved the tackling and fitted up larger blocks and ropes. But although the principle on which I acted was quiet correct, the machinery was now so massive and heavy that the mere friction and stiffness of the thick cordage prevented me from moving it at all. Afterwards, however, I came to proportion things more correctly; but I could not avoid reflecting at the time how much better it would have been had I learned all this from observation and study, instead of waiting till I was forced to acquire it through the painful and tedious lessons of experience.

After the tackling was prepared and in good working order, it took me the greater part of a day to hoist the main topsail. As I could not steer and work at this at the same time, I lashed the helm in such a position that, with a little watching now and then, it kept the schooner in her proper course. By this means I was enabled, also, to go about the deck and down below for things that I wanted as occasion required; also to cook and eat my victuals. But I did not dare to trust to this plan during the three hours of rest that I allowed myself at night, as the wind might have shifted, in which case I should have been blown far out of my course ere I awoke. I was, therefore, in the habit of heaving-to during those three hours—that is, fixing the rudder and the sails in such a position as that, by acting against each other, they would keep the ship stationary. After my night's rest, therefore, I had only to make allowance for the leeway she had made, and so resume my course.

Of course I was, to some extent, anxious lest another squall should come; but I made the best provision I could in the circumstances, and concluded that by letting go the weather-braces of the topsails and the topsail halyards at the same time, I should thereby render these sails almost powerless. Besides this, I proposed to myself to keep a sharp lookout on the barometer in the cabin; and if I observed at any time a sudden fall in it, I resolved that I would instantly set about my multiform appliances for reducing sail, so as to avoid being taken unawares. Thus I sailed prosperously for two weeks, with a fair wind, so that I calculated I must be drawing near to the Coral Island, at the thought of which my heart bounded with joyful expectation.

The only book I found on board, after a careful search, was a volume of Captain Cook's voyages. This, I suppose, the pirate captain had brought with him in order to guide him, and to furnish him with information regarding the islands of these seas. I found this a most delightful book indeed; and I not only obtained much interesting knowledge about the sea in which I was sailing, but I had many of my own opinions, derived from experience, corroborated, and not a few of them corrected. Besides the reading of this charming book, and the daily routine of occupations, nothing of particular note happened to me during this voyage—except once, when on rising one night, after my three hours' nap, while it was yet dark, I was amazed and a little alarmed to find myself floating in what appeared to be a sea of blue fire! I had often noticed the beautiful appearance of phosphorescent light, but this far exceeded anything of the sort I ever saw before. The whole sea appeared somewhat like milk, and was remarkably luminous.

I rose in haste, and letting down a bucket into the sea, brought some of the water on board and took it down to the cabin to examine it; but no sooner did I approach the light than the strange appearance disappeared, and when I removed the cabin lamp the luminous light appeared again. I was much puzzled with this, and took up a little of the water in the hollow of my hand and then let it run off, when I found that the luminous substance was left behind on my palm. I ran with it to the lamp, but when I got there it was gone. I found, however, that when I went into the dark my hand shone again; so I took the large glass of the ship's telescope and examined my hand minutely, when I found that there were on it one or two small patches of a clear, transparent substance like jelly, which were so thin as to be almost invisible to the naked eye. Thus I came to know that the beautiful phosphoric light, which I had so often admired before, was caused by animals; for I had no doubt that these were of the same kind as the medusa or jelly-fish, which are seen in all parts of the world.

On the evening of my fourteenth day I was awakened out of a nap into which I had fallen by a loud cry, and starting up, I gazed around me. I was surprised and delighted to see a large albatross soaring majestically over the ship. I immediately took it into my head that this was the albatross I had seen at Penguin Island. I had, of course, no good reason for supposing this; but the idea occurred to me, I know not why, and I cherished it, and regarded the bird with as much affection as if he had been an old friend. He kept me company all that day, and left me as night fell.

Next morning, as I stood motionless and with heavy eyes at the helm—for I had not slept well—I began to weary anxiously for daylight, and peered towards the horizon, where I thought I observed something like a black cloud against the dark sky. Being always on the alert for squalls, I ran to the bow. There could be no doubt it was a squall, and as I listened I thought I heard the murmur of the coming gale. Instantly I began to work might and main at my cumbrous tackle for shortening sail, and in the course of an hour and a half had the most of it reduced—the topsail yards down on the caps, the topsails clewed up, the sheets hauled in, the main and fore peaks lowered, and the flying-jib down. While thus engaged, the dawn advanced, and I cast an occasional furtive glance ahead in the midst of my labour. But now that things were prepared for the worst, I ran forward again and looked anxiously over the bow. I now heard the roar of the waves distinctly; and as a single ray of the rising sun gleamed over the ocean, I saw—what! could it be that I was dreaming?—that magnificent breaker with its ceaseless roar—that mountain-top! Yes, once more I beheld the Coral Island!

# 29

## THE EFFECT OF A CANNON-SHOT—A HAPPY REUNION OF A SOMEWHAT MOIST NATURE—RETROSPECT AND EXPLANATIONS—AN AWFUL DIVE—NEW PLANS—THE LAST OF THE CORAL ISLAND.

I almost fell upon the deck with the tumult of mingled emotions that filled my heart as I gazed ardently towards my beautiful island. It was still many miles away, but sufficiently near to enable me to trace distinctly the well-remembered outlines of the two mountains. My first impulse was to utter an exclamation of gratitude for being carried to my former happy home in safety; my second, to jump up, clap my hands, shout, and run up and down the deck, with no other object in view than that of giving vent to my excited feelings. Then I went below for the telescope, and spent nearly ten minutes of the utmost impatience in vainly trying to get a focus, and in rubbing the skin nearly off my eyes, before I discovered that having taken off the large glass to examine the phosphoric water with, I had omitted to put it on again.

After that I looked up impatiently at the sails, which I now regretted having lowered so hastily, and for a moment thought of hoisting the main topsail again; but recollecting that it would take me full half-a-day to accomplish, and that, at the present rate of sailing, two hours would bring me to the island, I immediately dismissed the idea.

The remainder of the time I spent in making feverish preparations for arriving and seeing my dear comrades. I remembered that they were not in the habit of rising before six, and as it was now only three, I hoped to arrive before they were awake. Moreover, I set about making ready to let go the anchor, resolving in my own mind that as I knew the depth of water in the passage of the reef and within the lagoon, I would run the schooner in and bring up opposite the bower. Fortunately the anchor was hanging at the cat-head, otherwise I should never have been able to use it. Now I had only to cut the tackling, and it would drop of its own weight. After searching among the flags, I found the terrible black one, which I ran up to the peak. While I was doing this a thought struck me. I went to the powder-magazine, brought up a blank cartridge, and loaded the big brass gun, which, it will be remembered, was unhoused when we set sail; and as I had no means of housing it, there it had stood, bristling alike at fair weather and foul all the voyage. I took care to grease its mouth well, and before leaving the fore part of the ship, thrust the poker into the fire.

All was now ready. A steady five-knot breeze was blowing, so that I was now not more than quarter of a mile from the reef. I was soon at the entrance; and as the schooner glided quickly through, I glanced affectionately at the huge breaker as if it had been the same one I had seen there when I bade adieu, as I feared for ever, to the island. On coming opposite the Water Garden, I put the helm hard down. The schooner came round with a rapid, graceful bend, and lost way just opposite the bower. Running forward, I let go the anchor, caught up the red-hot poker, applied it to the brass gun, and saluted the mountains with a *bang* such as had only once before broke their slumbering echoes!

Effective although it was, however, it was scarcely equal to the bang with which, instantly after, Peterkin bounded from the bower, in scanty costume, his eyeballs starting from his head with surprise and terror. One gaze he gave, one yell, and then fled into the bushes like a wild cat. The next moment Jack went through exactly the same performance, the only difference being that his movements were less like those of Jack-in-the-box, though not less vigorous and rapid than those of Peterkin.

"Hallo!" I shouted, almost mad with joy. "What ho! Peterkin! Jack! hallo! it's *me*!"

My shout was just in time to arrest them. They halted and turned round, and the instant I repeated the cry I saw that they recognised my voice by both of them running at full speed towards the beach. I could no longer contain myself. Throwing off my jacket, I jumped overboard at the same moment that Jack bounded into the sea. In other moment we met in deep water, clasped each other round the neck, and sank, as a matter of course, to the bottom! We were well-nigh choked, and instantly struggled to the surface, where Peterkin was spluttering about like a wounded duck, laughing and crying by turns, and choking himself with salt water!

It would be impossible to convey to my reader, by description, an adequate conception of the scene that followed my landing on the beach, as we stood embracing each other indiscriminately in our dripping garments, and giving utterance to incoherent rhapsodies, mingled with wild shouts. It can be more easily imagined than described; so I will draw a curtain over this part of my history, and carry the reader forward over an interval of three days.

During the greater part of that period Peterkin did nothing but roast pigs, taro, and bread-fruit, and ply me with plantains, plums, potatoes, and cocoa-nuts, while I related to him and Jack the terrible and wonderful adventures I had gone through since we last met. After I had finished the account, they made me go all over it again; and when I had concluded the second recital I had to go over it again, while they commented upon it piecemeal. They were much affected by what I told them of the probable fate of Avatea, and Peterkin could by no means brook the idea of the poor girl being converted into a *long pig*! As for Jack, he clenched his teeth, and shook his fist towards the sea, saying at the same time that he was sorry he had not broken Tararo's head, and he only hoped that one day he should be able to plant his knuckles on the bridge of that chief's nose! After they had 'pumped me dry,' as Peterkin said, I begged to be informed of what had happened to them during my long absence, and particularly as to how they got out of the Diamond Cave.

"Well, you must know," began Jack, "after you had dived out of the cave, on the day you were taken away from us, we waited very patiently for half-an-hour, not expecting you to return before the end of that time. Then we began to upbraid you for staying so long when you knew we would be anxious; but when an hour passed we became alarmed, and I resolved at all hazards to dive out and see what had become of you, although I felt for poor Peterkin, because, as he truly said, 'If you never come back, I'm shut up here for life.' However, I promised not to run any risk, and he let me go—which, to say truth, I thought very courageous of him!"

"I should just think it was," interrupted Peterkin, looking at Jack over the edge of a monstrous potato which he happened to be devouring at the time.

"Well," continued Jack, "you may guess my consternation when you did not answer to my halloo. At first I imagined that the pirates must have killed you, and left you in the bush or thrown you into the sea; then it occurred to me that this would have served no end of theirs, so I came to the conclusion that they must have carried you away with them. As this thought struck me, I observed the pirate schooner standing away to the nor'ard, almost hull down on the horizon, and I sat down on the rocks to watch her as she slowly sank from my sight. And I tell you, Ralph, my boy, that I shed more tears that time at losing you than I have done, I verily believe, all my life before—"

"Pardon me, Jack, for interrupting," said Peterkin; "surely you must be mistaken in that. You've often told me that when you were a baby you used to howl and roar from morning to—"

"Hold your tongue, Peterkin!" cried Jack.—"Well, after the schooner had disappeared, I dived back into the cave, much to Peterkin's relief, and told him what I had seen. We sat down and had a long talk over this matter, and then we agreed to make a regular, systematic search through the woods, so as to make sure at least that you had not been killed. But now we thought of the difficulty of getting out of the cave without your help. Peterkin became dreadfully nervous when he thought of this; and I must confess I felt some alarm, for, of course, I could not hope alone to take him out so quickly as we two together had brought him in. And he himself vowed that if we had been a moment longer with him that time, he would have had to take a breath of salt water. However, there was no help for it, and I endeavoured to calm his fears as well as I could; 'for,' said I, 'you can't live here, Peterkin,' to which he replied, 'Of course not, Jack; I can only die here, and as that's not at all desirable, you had better propose something.' So I suggested that he should take a good, long breath, and trust himself to me.

"'Might we not make a large bag of cocoa-nut cloth, into which I could shove my head, and tie it tight round my neck?' he asked with a haggard smile. 'It might let me get one breath under water!'

"'No use,' said I; 'it would fill in a moment and suffocate you. I see nothing for it, Peterkin, if you really can't keep your breath so long, but to let me knock you down, and carry you out while in a state of insensibility.'

"But Peterkin didn't relish this idea. He seemed to fear that I would not be able to measure the exact force of the blow, and might, on the one hand, hit him so softly as to render a second or third blow necessary, which would be very uncomfortable; or, on the other hand, give him such a smash as would entirely spoil his figurehead, or mayhap knock the life out of him altogether! At last I got him persuaded to try to hold his breath, and commit himself to me; so he agreed, and down we went. But I had not got half-way through when he began to struggle and kick like a wild bull, burst from my grasp, and hit against the roof of the tunnel. I was therefore obliged to force him violently back into the cave again, where he, rose panting to the surface. In short, he had lost his presence of mind, and—"

"Nothing of the sort!" cried Peterkin indignantly; "I only lost my wind, and if I had not had presence of mind enough to kick as I did, I should have bu'st in your arms!"

"Well, well, so be it," resumed Jack with a smile.—"But the upshot of it was that we had to hold another consultation on the point; and I really believe that had it not been for a happy thought of mine, we should have been consulting there yet."

"I wish we had!" again interrupted Peterkin with a sigh.—"I'm sure, Ralph, if I had thought that you were coming back again I would willingly have awaited your return for months rather than have endured the mental agony which I went through.—But proceed."

"The thought was this," continued Jack—"that I should tie Peterkin's hands and feet with cords, and then lash him firmly to a stout pole about five feet long, in order to render him quite powerless and keep him straight and stiff. You should have seen his face of horror, Ralph, when I suggested this! But he came to see that it was his only chance, and told me to set about it as fast as I could; 'for,' said he, 'this is no jokin', Jack, *I* can tell you, and the sooner it's done the better.' I soon procured the cordage and a suitable pole, with which I returned to the cave, and lashed him as stiff and straight as an Egyptian mummy; and, to say truth, he was no bad representation of what an English mummy would be, if there were such things, for he was as white as a dead man.

"'Now,' said Peterkin in a tremulous voice, 'swim with me as near to the edge of the hole as you can before you dive; then let me take a long breath; and as I sha'n't be able to speak after I've taken it, you'll watch my face, and the moment you see me wink—dive! And oh,' he added earnestly, 'pray don't be long!'

"I promised to pay the strictest attention to his wishes, and swam with him to the outlet of the cave. Here I paused. 'Now, then,' said I, 'pull away at the wind, lad.'

"Peterkin drew in a breath so long that I could not help thinking of the frog in the fable, that wanted to swell itself as big as the ox. Then I looked into his face earnestly. Slap went the lid of his right eye; down went my head, and up went my heels. We shot through the passage like an arrow, and rose to the surface of the open sea before you could count twenty.

"Peterkin had taken in such an awful load of wind that, on reaching the free air, he let it out with a yell loud enough to have been heard a mile off; and then the change in his feelings was so sudden and great that he did not wait till we landed, but began, tied up as he was, to shout and sing for joy as I supported him with my left arm to the shore. However, in the middle of a laugh that a hyena might have envied, I let him accidentally slip, which extinguished him in a moment.

"After this happy deliverance, we immediately began our search for your dead body, Ralph; and you have no idea how low our hearts sank as we set off; day after day, to examine the valleys and mountain-sides with the utmost care. In about three weeks we completed the survey of the whole island, and had at least the satisfaction of knowing that you had not been killed. But it occurred to us that you might have been thrown into the sea; so we examined the sands and the lagoon carefully, and afterwards went all round the outer reef. One day, while we were upon the reef, Peterkin espied a small, dark object lying among the rocks, which seemed to be quite different from the surrounding stones. We hastened towards the spot, and found it to be a small keg. On knocking out the head we discovered that it was gunpowder."

"It was I who sent you that, Jack," said I with a smile.

"Fork out!" cried Peterkin energetically, starting to his feet and extending his open hand to Jack. "Down with the money, sir, else I'll have you shut up for life in a debtor's prison the moment we return to England!"

"I'll give you an I.O.U. in the meantime," returned Jack, laughing, "so sit down and be quiet.—The fact is, Ralph, when we discovered this keg of powder Peterkin immediately took me a bet of a thousand pounds that you had something to do with it, and I took him a bet of ten thousand that you had not."

"Peterkin was right, then," said I, explaining how the thing had occurred.

"Well, we found it very useful," continued Jack, "although some of it had got a little damp; and we furbished up the old pistol, with which Peterkin is a crack shot now. But to continue. We did not find any other vestige of you on the reef, and finally gave up all hope of ever seeing you again. After this the island became a dreary place to us, and we began to long for a ship to heave in sight and take us off. But now that you're back again, my dear fellow, it looks as bright and cheerful as it used to do, and I love it as much as ever.

"And now," continued Jack, "I have a great desire to visit some of the other islands of the South Seas. Here we have a first-rate schooner at our disposal, so I don't see what should hinder us."

"Just the very thing I was going to propose!" cried Peterkin. "I vote for starting at once."

"Well, then," said Jack, "it seems to me that we could not do better than shape our course for the island on which Avatea lives, and endeavour to persuade Tararo to let her marry the black fellow to whom she is engaged instead of making a 'long pig' of her. If he has a spark of gratitude in him, he'll do it. Besides, having become champions for this girl once before, it behoves us, as true knights, not to rest until we set her free; at least, all the heroes in all the story-books I have ever read would count it foul disgrace to leave such a work unfinished."

"I'm sure I don't know or care what your knights in story-books would do," said Peterkin; "but I'm certain that it would be capital fun, so I'm your man whenever you want me."

This plan of Jack's was quite in accordance with his romantic, impulsive nature; and having made up his mind to save this black girl, he could not rest until the thing was commenced.

"But there may be great danger in this attempt," he said at the end of a long consultation on the subject. "Will you, lads, go with me in spite of this?"

"Go with you!" we repeated in the same breath.

"Can you doubt it?" said I.

"For a moment?" added Peterkin.

I need scarcely say that having made up our minds to go on this enterprise, we lost no time in making preparations to quit the island; and as the schooner was well laden with stores of every kind for a long cruise, we had little to do except to add to our abundant supply a quantity of cocoa-nuts, bread-fruit, taro, yams, plums, and potatoes, chiefly with the view of carrying the fragrance of our dear island along with us as long as we could.

When all was ready, we paid a farewell visit to the different familiar spots where most of our time had been spent. We ascended the mountain-top, and gazed for the last time at the rich green foliage in the valleys, the white sandy beach, the placid lagoon, and the barrier coral reef with its crested breakers. Then we descended to Spouting Cliff, and looked down at the pale-green monster which we had made such fruitless efforts to spear in days gone by. From this we hurried to the Water Garden, and took a last dive into its clear waters and a last gambol amongst its coral groves. I hurried out before my companions, and dressed in haste, in order to have a long examination of my tank, which Peterkin, in the fulness of his heart, had tended with the utmost care, as being a vivid remembrancer of me rather than out of love for natural history. It was in superb condition: the water as clear and pellucid as crystal; the red and green seaweed of the most brilliant hues; the red, purple, yellow, green, and striped anemones fully expanded, and stretching out their arms as if to welcome and embrace their former master; the starfish, zoophytes, sea-pens, and other innumerable marine insects, looking fresh and beautiful; and the crabs, as Peterkin said, looking as wide-awake, impertinent, rampant, and pugnacious as ever. It was, indeed, so lovely and so interesting that I would scarcely allow myself to be torn away from it.

Last of all, we returned to the bower and collected the few articles we possessed—such as the axe, the pencil-case, the broken telescope, the penknife, the hook made from the brass ring, and the sail-needle, with which we had landed on the island; also the long boots and the pistol, besides several curious articles of costume which we had manufactured from time to time.

These we conveyed on board in our little boat, after having carved our names on a chip of iron-wood, thus:

**Jack Martin**
**Ralph Rover**
**Peterkin Gay**

This we fixed up inside of the bower. The boat was then hoisted on board and the anchor weighed, which latter operation cost us great labour and much time, as the anchor was so heavy that we could not move it without the aid of my complex machinery of blocks and pulleys. A steady breeze was blowing off-shore when we set sail, at a little before sunset. It swept us quickly past the reef and out to sea. The shore grew rapidly more indistinct as the shades of evening fell, while our clipper bark bounded lightly over the waves. Slowly the mountain-top sank on the horizon until it became a mere speck. In another moment the sun and the Coral Island sank together into the broad bosom of the Pacific.

# 30

## THE VOYAGE—THE ISLAND, AND A CONSULTATION IN WHICH DANGER IS SCOUTED AS A THING UNWORTHY OF CONSIDERATION—RATS AND CATS—THE NATIVE TEACHER—AWFUL REVELATIONS—WONDERFUL EFFECTS OF CHRISTIANITY.

Our voyage during the next two weeks was most interesting and prosperous. The breeze continued generally fair, and at all times enabled us to lie our course; for being, as I have said before, clipper-built, the pirate schooner could lie very close to the wind and make little leeway. We had no difficulty now in managing our sails, for Jack was heavy and powerful, while Peterkin was active as a kitten. Still, however, we were a very insufficient crew for such a vessel; and if any one had proposed to us to make such a voyage in it before we had been forced to go through so many hardships from necessity, we would have turned away with pity from the individual making such proposal as from a madman. I pondered this a good deal, and at last concluded that men do not know how much they are capable of doing till they try, and that we should never give way to despair in any undertaking, however difficult it may seem—always supposing, however, that our cause is a good one, and that we can ask the Divine blessing on it.

Although, therefore, we could now manage our sails easily, we nevertheless found that my pulleys were of much service to us in some things, though Jack did laugh heartily at the uncouth arrangement of ropes and blocks, which had, to a sailor's eye, a very lumbering and clumsy appearance. But I will not drag my reader through the details of this voyage. Suffice it to say that, after an agreeable sail of about three weeks, we arrived off the island of Mango, which I recognised at once from the description that the pirate Bill had given me of it during one of our conversations.

As soon as we came within sight of it, we hove the ship to and held a council of war.

"Now, boys," said Jack as we seated ourselves beside him on the cabin skylight, "before we go further in this business we must go over the pros and cons of it; for although you have so generously consented to stick by me through thick and thin, it would be unfair did I not see that you thoroughly understand the danger of what we are about to attempt."

"Oh, bother the danger!" cried Peterkin. "I wonder to hear you, Jack, talk of danger! When a fellow begins to talk about it, he'll soon come to magnify it to such a degree that he'll not be fit to face it when it comes—no more than a suckin' baby."

"Nay, Peterkin," replied Jack gravely, "I won't be jested out of it. I grant you that when we've once resolved to act, and have made up our minds what to do, we should think no more of danger. But before we have so resolved, it behoves us to look it straight in the face, and examine into it, and walk round it; for if we flinch at a distant view, we're sure to run away when the danger is near.—Now, I understand from you, Ralph, that the island is inhabited by thorough-going, out-and-out cannibals, whose principal law is, 'Might is right, and the weakest goes to the wall?'"

"Yes," said I; "so Bill gave me to understand. He told me, however, that at the southern side of it the missionaries had obtained a footing amongst an insignificant tribe. A native teacher had been sent there by the Wesleyans, who had succeeded in persuading the chief at that part to embrace Christianity. But instead of that being of any advantage to our enterprise, it seems the very reverse; for the chief Tararo is a determined heathen, and persecutes the Christians—who are far too weak in numbers to offer any resistance—and looks with dislike upon all white men, whom he regards as propagators of the new faith."

"'Tis a pity," said Jack, "that the Christian tribe is so small, for we shall scarcely be safe under their protection, I fear. If Tararo takes it into his head to wish for our vessel, or to kill ourselves, he could take us from them by force. You say that the native missionary talks English?"

"So I believe."

"Then, what I propose is this," said Jack. "We will run round to the south side of the island, and cast anchor off the Christian village. We are too far away just now to have been descried by any of the savages, so we shall get there unobserved, and have time to arrange our plans before the heathen tribes know of our presence. But in doing this we run the risk of being captured by the ill-disposed tribes, and being very ill-used, if not—a—"

"Roasted alive and eaten!" cried Peterkin. "Come, out with it, Jack! According to your own showing, it's well to look the danger straight in the face."

"Well, that *is* the worst of it, certainly. Are you prepared, then, to take your chance of that?"

"I've been prepared and had my mind made up long ago," cried Peterkin, swaggering about the deck with his hands thrust into his breeches pockets. "The fact is, Jack, I don't believe that Tararo will be so ungrateful as to eat us, and I'm quite sure that he'll be too happy to grant us whatever we ask; so the sooner we go in and win the better."

Peterkin was wrong, however, in his estimate of savage gratitude, as the sequel will show.

The schooner was now put before the wind, and after making a long run to the southward, we put about and beat up for the south side of Mango, where we arrived before sunset, and hove-to off the coral reef. Here we awaited the arrival of a canoe, which immediately put off on our rounding-to. When it arrived, a mild-looking native, of apparently forty years of age, came on board, and taking off his straw hat, made us a low bow. He was clad in a respectable suit of European clothes; and the first words he uttered, as he stepped up to Jack and shook hands with him, were:

"Good-day, gentlemen. We are happy to see you at Mango. You are heartily welcome."

After returning his salutation, Jack exclaimed, "You must be the native missionary teacher of whom I have heard—are you not?"

"I am. I have the joy to be a servant of the Lord Jesus at this station."

"You're the very man I want to see, then," replied Jack; "that's lucky. Come down to the cabin, friend, and have a glass of wine. I wish particularly to speak with you. My men there"—pointing to Peterkin and me—"will look after your people."

"Thank you," said the teacher as he followed Jack to the cabin; "I do not drink wine or any strong drink."

"Oh! then there's lots of water, and you can have biscuit."

"Now, 'pon my word, that's cool!" said Peterkin; "his *men*, forsooth! Well, since we are to be men, we may as well come it as strong over these black chaps as we can.—Hallo, there!" he cried to the half-dozen of natives who stood upon the deck, gazing in wonder at all they saw, "here's for you;" and he handed them a tray of broken biscuit and a can of water. Then thrusting his hands into his pockets, he walked up and down the deck with an enormous swagger, whistling vociferously.

In about half-an-hour Jack and the teacher came on deck, and the latter, bidding us a cheerful good-evening, entered his canoe and paddled to the shore. When he was gone, Peterkin stepped up to Jack, and touching his cap, said:

"Well, captain, have you any communications to make to your *men*?"

"Yes," cried Jack: "ready about, mind the helm, and clew up your tongue, while I con the schooner through the passage in the reef. The teacher, who seems a first-rate fellow, says it's quite deep, and good anchorage within the lagoon close to the shore."

While the vessel was slowly advancing to her anchorage, under a light breeze, Jack explained to us that Avatea was still on the island, living amongst the heathens; that she had expressed a strong desire to join the Christians; but Tararo would not let her, and kept her constantly in close confinement.

"Moreover," continued Jack, "I find that she belongs to one of the Samoan Islands, where Christianity had been introduced long before her capture by the heathens of a neighbouring island; and the very day after she was taken she was to have joined the church which had been planted there by that excellent body, the London Missionary Society. The teacher tells me, too, that the poor girl has fallen in love with a Christian chief, who lives on an island some fifty miles or so to the south of this one, and that she is meditating a desperate attempt at escape. So, you see, we have come in the nick of time.—I fancy that this chief is the fellow whom you heard of, Ralph, at the island of Emo.—Besides all this, the heathen savages are at war among themselves, and there's to be a battle fought the day after to-morrow, in which the principal leader is Tararo; so that we'll not be able to commence our negotiations with the rascally chief till the day after."

The village off which we anchored was beautifully situated at the head of a small bay, from the margin of which trees of every description peculiar to the tropics rose in the richest luxuriance to the summit of a hilly ridge, which was the line of demarcation between the possessions of the Christians and those of the neighbouring heathen chief.

The site of the settlement was an extensive plot of flat land, stretching in a gentle slope from the sea to the mountain. The cottages stood several hundred yards from the beach, and were protected from the glare of the sea by the rich foliage of rows of large Barringtonia and other trees which girt the shore. The village was about a mile in length, and perfectly straight, with a wide road down the middle, on either side of which were rows of the tufted-topped ti-tree, whose delicate and beautiful blossoms, hanging beneath their plume-crested tops, added richness to the scene. The cottages of the natives were built beneath these trees, and were kept in the most excellent order, each having a little garden in front, tastefully laid out and planted, while the walks were covered with black and white pebbles.

Every house had doors and Venetian windows, painted partly with lamp-black made from the candle-nut, and partly with red ochre, which contrasted powerfully with the dazzling coral lime that covered the walls. On a prominent position stood a handsome church, which was quite a curiosity in its way. It was a hundred feet long by fifty broad, and was seated throughout to accommodate upwards of two thousand persons. It had six large folding-doors, and twelve windows with Venetian blinds; and although a large and substantial edifice, it had been built, we were told by the teacher: in the space of two months! There was not a single iron nail in the fabric, and the natives had constructed it chiefly with their stone and bone axes and other tools, having only one or two axes or tools of European manufacture. Everything around this beautiful spot wore an aspect of peace and plenty; and as we dropped our anchor within a stone's-cast of the substantial coral wharf, I could not avoid contrasting it with the wretched village of Emo, where I had witnessed so many frightful scenes. When the teacher afterwards told me that the people of this tribe had become converts only a year previous to our arrival, and that they had been living before that in the practice of the most bloody system of idolatry, I could not refrain from exclaiming, "What a convincing proof that Christianity is of God!"

On landing from our little boat we were received with a warm welcome by the teacher and his wife, the latter being also a native, clothed in a simple European gown and a straw bonnet. The shore was lined with hundreds of natives, whose persons were all more or less clothed with native cloth. Some of the men had on a kind of poncho formed of this cloth, their legs being uncovered; others wore clumsily fashioned trousers, and no upper garment except hats made of straw and cloth. Many of the dresses, both of women and men, were grotesque enough, being very bad imitations of the European garb; but all wore a dress of some sort or other. They seemed very glad to see us, and crowded round us as the teacher led the way to his dwelling, where we were entertained, in the most sumptuous manner, on baked pig and all the varieties of fruits and vegetables that the island produced. We were much annoyed, however, by the rats: they seemed to run about the house like domestic animals. As we sat at table, one of them peeped up at us over the edge of the cloth, close to Peterkin's elbow, who floored it with a blow on the snout from his knife, exclaiming as he did so:

"I say, Mister Teacher, why don't you set traps for these brutes? Surely you are not fond of them!"

"No," replied the teacher with a smile. "We would be glad to get rid of them if we could; but if we were to trap all the rats on the island, it would occupy our whole time."

"Are they, then, so numerous?" inquired Jack.

"They swarm everywhere. The poor heathens on the north side eat them, and think them very sweet. So did my people formerly; but they do not eat so many now, because the missionary who was last here expressed disgust at it. The poor people asked if it was wrong to eat rats; and he told them that it was certainly not wrong, but that the people of England would be much disgusted were they asked to eat rats."

We had not been an hour in the house of this kind-hearted man when we were convinced of the truth of his statement as to their numbers; for the rats ran about the floors in dozens, and during our meal two men were stationed at the table to keep them off!

"What a pity you have no cats!" said Peterkin; and he aimed a blow at another reckless intruder, and missed it.

"We would indeed be glad to have a few," rejoined the teacher, "but they are difficult to be got. The hogs, we find, are very good rat-killers; but they do not seem to be able to keep the numbers down. I have heard that they are better than cats."

As the teacher said this, his good-natured black face was wrinkled with a smile of merriment. Observing that I had noticed it, he said:

"I smiled just now when I remembered the fate of the first cat that was taken to Rarotonga. This is one of the stations of the London Missionary Society. It, like our own, is infested with rats, and a cat was brought at last to the island. It was a large black one. On being turned loose, instead of being content to stay among men, the cat took to the mountains and lived in a wild state, sometimes paying visits during the night to the houses of the natives; some of whom, living at a distance from the settlement, had not heard of the cat's arrival, and were dreadfully frightened in consequence, calling it a 'monster of the deep,' and flying in terror away from it. One night the cat—feeling a desire for company, I suppose—took its way to the house of a chief who had recently been converted to Christianity, and had begun to learn to read and pray. The chief's wife, who was sitting awake at his side while he slept, beheld with horror two fires glistening in the doorway, and heard with surprise a mysterious voice. Almost petrified with fear, she awoke her husband, and began to upbraid him for forsaking his old religion and burning his god, who, she declared, was now come to be avenged of them. 'Get up and pray! get up and pray!' she cried. The chief arose, and on opening his eyes, beheld the same glaring lights and heard the same ominous sound. Impelled by the extreme urgency of the case, he commenced, with all possible vehemence, to vociferate the alphabet, as a prayer to God to deliver them from the vengeance of Satan! On hearing this, the cat, as much alarmed as themselves, fled precipitately away, leaving the chief and his wife congratulating themselves on the efficacy of their prayer."

We were much diverted with this anecdote, which the teacher related in English so good that we certainly could not have supposed him a native but for the colour of his face and the foreign accent in his tone. Next day we walked out with this interesting man, and were much entertained and instructed by his conversation as we rambled through the cool, shady groves of bananas, citrons, limes, and other trees, or sauntered among the cottages of the natives, and watched them while they laboured diligently in the taro-beds or manufactured the tapa, or native cloth. To some of these Jack put questions, through the medium of the missionary; and the replies were such as to surprise us at the extent of their knowledge. Indeed, Peterkin very truly remarked that "they seemed to know a considerable deal more than Jack himself!"

Among other pieces of interesting information that we obtained was the following, in regard to coral formations:

"The islands of the Pacific," said our friend, "are of three different kinds or classes. Those of the first class are volcanic, mountainous, and wild—some shooting their jagged peaks into the clouds at an elevation of ten and fifteen thousand feet. Those of the second class are of crystallised limestone, and vary in height from one hundred to five hundred feet. The hills on these are not so wild or broken as those of the first class, but are richly clothed with vegetation, and very beautiful. I have no doubt that the Coral Island on which you were wrecked was one of this class. They are supposed to have been upheaved from the bottom of the sea by volcanic agency; but they are not themselves volcanic in their nature, neither are they of coral formation. Those of the third class are the low coralline islands, usually having lagoons of water in their midst. They are very numerous.

"As to the manner in which coral islands and reefs are formed, there are various opinions on this point. I will give you what seems to me the most probable theory—a theory, I may add, which is held by some of the good and scientific missionaries. It is well known that there is much lime in salt water; it is also known that coral is composed of lime. It is supposed that the polypes, or coral insects, have the power of attracting this lime to their bodies, and with this material they build their little cells or habitations. They choose the summit of a volcano, or the top of a submarine mountain, as a foundation on which to build, for it is found that they never work at any great depth below the surface. On this they work. The polypes on the mountain-top, of course, reach the surface first; then those at the outer edges reach the top sooner than the others between them and the centre, thus forming the coral reef surrounding the lagoon of water and the central island. After that, the insects within the lagoon cease working. When the surface of the water is reached, these myriads of wonderful creatures die. Then birds visit the spot, and seeds are thus conveyed thither, which take root and spring up and flourish. Thus are commenced those coralline islets of which you have seen so many in these seas. The reefs round the large islands are formed in a similar manner. When we consider," added the missionary, "the smallness of the architects used by our heavenly Father in order to form those lovely and innumerable islands, we are filled with much of that feeling which induced the ancient king to exclaim, 'How manifold, O Lord, are Thy works! in wisdom hast Thou made them all.'"

We all heartily agreed with the missionary in this sentiment, and felt not a little gratified to find that the opinions which Jack and I had been led to form, from personal observation on our Coral Island, were thus to a great extent corroborated.

The missionary also gave us an account of the manner in which Christianity had been introduced among them. He said: "When missionaries were first sent here, three years ago, a small vessel brought them; and the chief, who is now dead, promised to treat well the two native teachers who were left with their wives on the island. But scarcely had the boat which landed them returned to the ship than the natives began to maltreat their guests, taking away all they possessed, and offering them further violence, so that when the boat was sent in haste to fetch them away, the clothes of both men and women were torn nearly off their backs.

"Two years after this the vessel visited them again, and I, being in her, volunteered to land alone, without any goods whatever, begging that my wife might be brought to me the following year—that is, *this* year; and, as you see, she is with me. But the surf was so high that the boat could not land me; so with nothing on but my trousers and shirt, and with a few catechisms and a Bible, besides some portions of the Scripture translated into the Mango tongue, I sprang into the sea, and swam ashore on the crest of a breaker. I was instantly dragged up the beach by the natives; who, on finding I had nothing worth having upon me, let me alone. I then made signs to my friends in the ship to leave me, which they did. At first the natives listened to me in silence, but laughed at what I said while I preached the Gospel of our blessed Saviour Jesus Christ to them. Afterwards they treated me ill, sometimes; but I persevered, and continued to dwell among them, and dispute, and exhort them to give up their sinful ways of life, burn their idols, and come to Jesus.

"About a month after I landed, I heard that the chief was dead. He was the father of the present chief, who is now a most consistent member of the Church. It is a custom here that when a chief dies his wives are strangled and buried with him. Knowing this, I hastened to his house to endeavour to prevent such cruelty if possible. When I arrived, I found two of the wives had already been killed, while another was in the act of being strangled. I pleaded hard for her, but it was too late; she was already dead. I then entreated the son to spare the fourth wife, and after much hesitation, my prayer was granted; but in half-an-hour afterwards this poor woman repented of being unfaithful, as she termed it, to her husband, and insisted on being strangled, which was accordingly done.

"All this time the chief's son was walking up and down before his father's house with a brow black as thunder. When he entered I went in with him, and found, to my surprise, that his father was *not* dead! The old man was sitting on a mat in a corner, with an expression of placid resignation on his face.

"'Why,' said I, 'have you strangled your father's wives before he is dead?'

"To this the son replied, 'He is dead. That is no longer my father. He is as good as dead now. He is to be *buried alive*.'

"I now remembered having heard that it is a custom among the Feejee Islanders that when the reigning chief grows old and infirm, the heir to the chieftainship has a right to depose his father, in which case he is considered as dead, and is buried alive. The young chief was now about to follow this custom, and despite my earnest entreaties and pleadings, the old chief was buried that day before my eyes in the same grave with his four strangled wives! Oh, my heart groaned when I saw this! and I prayed to God to open the hearts of these poor creatures, as He had already opened mine, and pour into them the light and the love of the Gospel of Jesus. My prayer was answered very soon. A week afterwards the son, who was now chief of the tribe, came to me, bearing his god on his shoulders, and groaning beneath its weight. Flinging it down at my feet, he desired me to burn it!

"You may conceive how overjoyed I was at this. I sprang up and embraced him, while I shed tears of joy. Then we made a fire and burned the god to ashes, amid an immense concourse of the people, who seemed terrified at what was being done, and shrank back when we burned the god, expecting some signal vengeance to be taken upon us; but seeing that nothing happened, they changed their minds, and thought that our God must be the true one after all. From that time the mission prospered steadily; and now, while there is not a single man in the tribe who has not burned his household gods and become a convert to Christianity, there are not a few, I hope, who are true followers of the Lamb, having been plucked as brands from the burning by Him who can save unto the uttermost. I will not tell you more of our progress at this time; but you see," he said, waving his hand around him, "the village, and the church did not exist a year ago!"

We were indeed much interested in this account, and I could not help again in my heart praying to God to prosper those missionary societies that send such inestimable blessings to these islands of dark and bloody idolatry. The teacher also added that the other tribes were very indignant at this one for having burned its gods, and threatened to destroy it altogether; but they had done nothing yet. "And if they should," said the teacher, "the Lord is on our side; of whom shall we be afraid?"

"Have the missionaries many stations in these seas?" inquired Jack.

"Oh yes. The London Missionary Society have a great many in the Tahiti group, and other islands in that quarter. Then the Wesleyans have the Feejee Islands all to themselves, and the Americans have many stations in other groups. But still, my friend, there are hundreds of islands here, the natives of which have never heard of Jesus, or the good word of God, or the Holy Spirit; and thousands are living and dying in the practice of those terrible sins and bloody murders of which you have already heard.—I trust, my friends," he added, looking earnestly into our faces—"I trust that if you ever return to England, you will tell your Christian friends that the horrors which they hear of in regard to these islands are *literally true*, and that when they have heard the worst, the '*half has not been told them;*' for there are perpetrated here foul deeds of darkness of which man may not speak. You may also tell them," he said, looking around with a smile, while a tear of gratitude trembled in his eye and rolled down his coal-black cheek—"tell them of the blessings that the Gospel has wrought *here*!"

We assured our friend that we would certainly not forget his request. On returning towards the village, about noon, we remarked on the beautiful whiteness of the cottages.

"That is owing to the lime with which they are plastered," said the teacher. "When the natives were converted, as I have described, I set them to work to build cottages for themselves, and also this handsome church which you see. When the framework and other parts of the house were up, I sent the people to fetch coral from the sea. They brought immense quantities. Then I made them cut wood, and piling the coral above it, set it on fire.

"'Look! look!' cried the poor people in amazement; 'what wonderful people the

Christians are! He is roasting stones! We shall not need taro or bread-fruit any more; we may eat stones!'

"But their surprise was still greater when the coral was reduced to a fine, soft, white powder. They immediately set up a great shout, and mingling the lime with water, rubbed their faces and their bodies all over with it, and ran through the village screaming with delight. They were also much surprised at another thing they saw me do. I wished to make some household furniture, and constructed a turning-lathe to assist me. The first thing that I turned was the leg of a sofa, which was no sooner finished than the chief seized it with wonder and delight, and ran through the village exhibiting it to the people, who looked upon it with great admiration. The chief then, tying a string to it, hung it round his neck as an ornament! He afterwards told me that if he had seen it before he became a Christian, he would have made it his god!"

As the teacher concluded this anecdote we reached his door. Saying that he had business to attend to, he left us to amuse ourselves as we best could.

"Now, lads," said Jack, turning abruptly towards us, and buttoning up his jacket as he spoke, "I'm off to see the battle. I've no particular fondness for seein' bloodshed; but I must find out the nature o' these fellows and see their customs with my own eyes, so that I may be able to speak of it again, if need be, authoritatively. It's only six miles off, and we don't run much more risk than that of getting a rap with a stray stone or an overshot arrow. Will you go?"

"To be sure we will," said Peterkin.

"If they chance to see us, we'll cut and run for it," added Jack.

"Dear me!" cried Peterkin; "*you* run! I thought you would scorn to run from any one."

"So I would, if it were my duty to fight," returned Jack coolly; "but as I don't want to fight, and don't intend to fight, if they offer to attack us I'll run away, like the veriest coward that ever went by the name of Peterkin. So come along."

# 31

## A STRANGE AND BLOODY BATTLE—THE LION BEARDED IN HIS DEN—FRIGHTFUL SCENES OF CRUELTY, AND FEARS FOR THE FUTURE.

We had ascertained from the teacher the direction to the spot on which the battle was to be fought, and after a walk of two hours, reached it. The summit of a bare hill was the place chosen; for, unlike most of the other islanders, who are addicted to bush-fighting, those of Mango are in the habit of meeting on open ground. We arrived before the two parties had commenced the deadly struggle, and creeping as close up as we dared among the rocks, we lay and watched them.

The combatants were drawn up face to face, each side ranged in rank four deep. Those in the first row were armed with long spears; the second with clubs to defend the spearmen; the third row was composed of young men with slings; and the fourth consisted of women, who carried baskets of stones for the slingers, and clubs and spears with which to supply the warriors. Soon after we arrived, the attack was made with great fury. There was no science displayed. The two bodies of savages rushed headlong upon each other and engaged in a general mélée, and a more dreadful set of men I have never seen. They wore grotesque war-caps, made of various substances and decorated with feathers. Their faces and bodies were painted so as to make them look as frightful as possible; and as they brandished their massive clubs, leaped, shouted, yelled, and dashed each other to the ground, I thought I had never seen men look so like demons before.

We were much surprised at the conduct of the women, who seemed to be perfect furies, and hung about the heels of their husbands in order to defend them. One stout young woman we saw, whose husband was hard pressed and about to be overcome: she lifted a large stone, and throwing it at his opponent's head, felled him to the earth. But the battle did not last long. The band most distant from us gave way and were routed, leaving eighteen of their comrades dead upon the field. These the victors brained as they lay; and putting some of their brains on leaves, went off with them, we were afterwards informed, to their temples to present them to their gods as an earnest of the human victims who were soon to be brought there.

We hastened back to the Christian village with feelings of the deepest sadness at the sanguinary conflict which we had just witnessed.

Next day, after breakfasting with our friend the teacher, we made preparations for carrying out our plan. At first the teacher endeavoured to dissuade us.

"You do not know," said he, turning to Jack, "the danger you run in venturing amongst these ferocious savages. I feel much pity for poor Avatea; but you are not likely to succeed in saving her, and you may die in the attempt."

"Well," said Jack quietly, "I am not afraid to die in a good cause."

The teacher smiled approvingly at him as he said this, and after a little further conversation, agreed to accompany us as interpreter—saying that although Tararo was unfriendly to him, he had hitherto treated him with respect.

We now went on board the schooner, having resolved to sail round the island and drop anchor opposite the heathen village. We manned her with natives, and hoped to overawe the savages by displaying our brass gun to advantage. The teacher soon after came on board, and setting our sails, we put to sea. In two hours more we made the cliffs reverberate with the crash of the big gun, which we fired by way of salute, while we ran the British ensign up to the peak and cast anchor. The commotion on shore showed us that we had struck terror into the hearts of the natives; but seeing that we did not offer to molest them, a canoe at length put off and paddled cautiously towards us. The teacher showed himself, and explaining that we were friends and wished to palaver with the chief, desired the native to go and tell him to come on board.

We waited long and with much impatience for an answer. During this time the native teacher conversed with us again, and told us many things concerning the success of the Gospel among those islands; and perceiving that we were by no means so much gratified as we ought to have been at the hearing of such good news, he pressed us more closely in regard to our personal interest in religion, and exhorted us to consider that our souls were certainly in as great danger as those of the wretched heathen whom we pitied so much if we had not already found salvation in Jesus Christ. "Nay, further," he added, "if such be your unhappy case, you are, in the sight of God, much worse than these savages—forgive me, my young friends, for saying so—for they have no knowledge, no light, and do not profess to believe; while you, on the contrary, have been brought up in the light of the blessed Gospel and call yourselves Christians. These poor savages are indeed the enemies of our Lord; but you, if ye be not true believers, are traitors!"

I must confess that my heart condemned me while the teacher spoke in this earnest manner, and I knew not what to reply. Peterkin, too, did not seem to like it, and, I thought, would willingly have escaped. But Jack seemed deeply impressed, and wore an anxious expression on his naturally grave countenance, while he assented to the teacher's remarks, and put to him many earnest questions. Meanwhile the natives who composed our crew, having nothing particular to do, had squatted down on the deck and taken out their little books containing the translated portions of the New Testament, along with hymns and spelling-books, and were now busily engaged—some vociferating the alphabet, others learning prayers off by heart, while a few sang hymns—all of them being utterly unmindful of our presence. The teacher soon joined them, and soon afterwards they all engaged in a prayer, which was afterwards translated to us, and proved to be a petition for the success of our undertaking and for the conversion of the heathen.

While we were thus engaged a canoe put off from shore, and several savages leaped on deck, one of whom advanced to the teacher and informed him that Tararo could not come on board that day, being busy with some religious ceremonies before the gods, which could on no account be postponed. He was also engaged with a friendly chief, who was about to take his departure from the island, and therefore begged that the teacher and his friends would land and pay a visit to him. To this the teacher returned answer that we would land immediately.

"Now, lads," said Jack as we were about to step into our little boat, "I'm not going to take any weapons with me, and I recommend you to take none either. We are altogether in the power of these savages; and the utmost we could do, if they were to attack us, would be to kill a few of them before we were ourselves overpowered. I think that our only chance of success lies in mild measures. Don't you think so?"

To this I assented gladly; and Peterkin replied by laying down a huge bell-mouthed blunderbuss, and divesting himself of a pair of enormous horse-pistols, with which he had purposed to overawe the natives! We then jumped into our boat and rowed ashore.

On reaching the beach we were received by a crowd of naked savages, who shouted a rude welcome, and conducted us to a house or shed where a baked pig and a variety of vegetables were prepared for us. Having partaken of these, the teacher begged to be conducted to the chief; but there seemed some hesitation, and after some consultation among themselves, one of the men stood forward and spoke to the teacher.

"What says he?" inquired Jack when the savage had concluded.

"He says that the chief is just going to the temple of his god, and cannot see us yet; so we must be patient, my friend."

"Well," cried Jack, rising, "if he won't come to see me, I'll e'en go and see him. Besides, I have a great desire to witness their proceedings at this temple of theirs. Will you go with me, friend?"

"I cannot," said the teacher, shaking his head. "I must not go to the heathen temples and witness their inhuman rites, except for the purpose of condemning their wickedness and folly."

"Very good," returned Jack; "then I'll go alone, for I cannot condemn their doings till I have seen them."

Jack arose, and we, having determined to go also, followed him through the banana-groves to a rising ground immediately behind the village, on the top of which stood the Buré, or temple, under the dark shade of a group of iron-wood trees. As we went through the village I was again led to contrast the rude huts and sheds, and their almost naked, savage-looking inhabitants, with the natives of the Christian village, who, to use the teacher's scriptural expression, were now "clothed and in their right mind."

As we turned into a broad path leading towards the hill, we were arrested by the shouts of an approaching multitude in the rear. Drawing aside into the bushes, we awaited their coming up; and as they drew near, we observed that it was a procession of the natives, many of whom were dancing and gesticulating in the most frantic manner. They had an exceedingly hideous aspect, owing to the black, red, and yellow paints with which their faces and naked bodies were bedaubed. In the midst of these came a band of men carrying three or four planks, on which were seated, in rows, upwards of a dozen men. I shuddered involuntarily as I recollected the sacrifice of human victims at the island of Emo, and turned with a look of fear to Jack as I said:

"Oh Jack! I have a terrible dread that they are going to commit some of their cruel practices on these wretched men. We had better not go to the temple. We shall only be horrified without being able to do any good, for I fear they are going to kill them."

Jack's face wore an expression of deep compassion as he said in a low voice, "No fear, Ralph; the sufferings of these poor fellows are over long ago."

I turned with a start as he spoke, and glancing at the men, who were now quite near to the spot where we stood, saw that they were all dead. They were tied firmly with ropes in a sitting posture on the planks, and seemed, as they bent their sightless eyeballs and grinning mouths over the dancing crew below, as if they were laughing in ghastly mockery at the utter inability of their enemies to hurt them now. These, we discovered afterwards, were the men who had been slain in the battle of the previous day, and were now on their way to be first presented to the gods and then eaten. Behind these came two men leading between them a third, whose hands were pinioned behind his back. He walked with a firm step, and wore a look of utter indifference on his face as they led him along, so that we concluded he must be a criminal who was about to receive some slight punishment for his faults. The rear of the procession was brought up by a shouting crowd of women and children, with whom we mingled and followed to the temple.

Here we arrived in a few minutes. The temple was a tall, circular building, open at one side. Around it were strewn heaps of human bones and skulls. At a table inside sat the priest, an elderly man with a long grey beard. He was seated on a stool, and before him lay several knives, made of wood, bone, and splinters of bamboo, with which he performed his office of dissecting dead bodies. Farther in lay a variety of articles that had been dedicated to the god, and among them were many spears and clubs. I observed among the latter some with human teeth sticking in them, where the victims had been clubbed in their mouths.

Before this temple the bodies, which were painted with vermilion and soot, were arranged in a sitting posture; and a man called a "dan-vosa" (orator) advanced, and laying his hands on their heads, began to chide them, apparently, in a low, bantering tone. What he said we knew not, but as he went on he waxed warm, and at last shouted to them at the top of his lungs, and finally finished by kicking the bodies over and running away, amid the shouts and laughter of the people, who now rushed forward. Seizing the bodies by a leg or an arm, or by the hair of the head, they dragged them over stumps and stones and through sloughs until they were exhausted. The bodies were then brought back to the temple and dissected by the priest, after which they were taken out to be baked.

Close to the temple a large fire was kindled, in which stones were heated red hot. When ready these were spread out on the ground, and a thick coating of leaves strewn over them to slack the heat. On this "lovo," or oven, the bodies were then placed, covered over, and left to bake.

The crowd now ran with terrible yells towards a neighbouring hill or mound, on which we observed the framework of a house lying ready to be erected. Sick with horror, yet fascinated by curiosity, we staggered after them mechanically, scarce knowing where we were going or what we did, and feeling a sort of impression that all we saw was a dreadful dream.

Arrived at the place, we saw the multitude crowding round a certain spot. We pressed forward, and obtained a sight of what they were doing. A large wooden beam or post lay on the ground, beside the other parts of the framework of the house, and close to the end of it was a hole about seven feet deep and upwards of two feet wide. While we looked, the man whom we had before observed with his hands pinioned was carried into the circle. His hands were now free, but his legs were tightly strapped together. The post of the house was then placed in the hole, and the man put in beside it. His head was a good way below the surface of the hole, and his arms were clasped round the post. Earth was now thrown in until all was covered over and stamped down; and this, we were afterwards told, was a ceremony usually performed at the dedication of a new temple or the erection of a chief's house!

"Come, come," cried Jack on beholding this horrible tragedy; "we have seen enough, enough—far more than enough! Let us go."

Jack's face looked ghastly pale and haggard as we hurried back to rejoin the teacher; and I have no doubt that he felt terrible anxiety when he considered the number and ferocity of the savages, and the weakness of the few arms which were ready indeed to essay, but impotent to effect, Avatea's deliverance from these ruthless men.

## ☙ 32 ❧

## AN UNEXPECTED DISCOVERY, AND A BOLD, RECKLESS DEFIANCE, WITH ITS CONSEQUENCES—PLANS OF ESCAPE, AND HEROIC RESOLVES.

When we returned to the shore and related to our friend what had passed, he was greatly distressed, and groaned in spirit; but we had not sat long in conversation when we were interrupted by the arrival of Tararo on the beach, accompanied by a number of followers bearing baskets of vegetables and fruits on their heads.

We advanced to meet him, and he expressed, through our interpreter, much pleasure in seeing us.

"And what, is it that my friends wish to say to me?" he inquired.

The teacher explained that we came to beg that Avatea might be spared.

"Tell him," said Jack, "that I consider that I have a right to ask this of him, having not only saved the girl's life, but the lives of his own people also; and say that I wish her to be allowed to follow her own wishes, and join the Christians."

While this was being translated the chief's brow lowered, and we could see plainly that our request met with no favourable reception. He replied with considerable energy and at some length.

"What says he?" inquired Jack.

"I regret to say that he will not listen to the proposal. He says he has pledged his word to his friend that the girl shall be sent to him, and a deputy even now on this island awaiting the fulfilment of the pledge."

Jack bit his lip in suppressed anger. "Tell Tararo," he exclaimed with a flashing eye, "that if he does not grant my demand it will be worse for him. Say I have a big gun on board my schooner that will blow his village into the sea if he does not give up the girl."

"Nay, my friend," said the teacher gently, "I will not tell him that. We must 'overcome evil with good.'"

"What does my friend say?" inquired the chief, who seemed nettled by Jack's looks of defiance.

"He is displeased," replied the teacher.

Tararo turned away with a smile of contempt, and walked towards the men who carried the baskets of vegetables, and who had now emptied the whole on the beach in an enormous pile.

"What are they doing there?" I inquired.

"I think that they are laying out a gift which they intend to present to some one," said the teacher.

At this moment a couple of men appeared, leading a young girl between them, and going towards the heap of fruits and vegetables, placed her on top of it. We started with surprise and fear, for in the young female before us we recognised the Samoan girl, Avatea.

We stood rooted to the earth with surprise and thick-coming fears.

"Oh my dear young friend!" whispered the teacher in a voice of deep emotion; while he seized Jack by the arm, "she is to be made a sacrifice even now!"

"Is she?" cried Jack with a vehement shout, spurning the teacher aside, and dashing over two natives who stood in his way, while he rushed towards the heap, sprang up its side, and seized Avatea by the arm. In another moment he dragged her down, placed her back to a large tree, and wrenching a war-club from the hand of a native who seemed powerless and petrified with surprise, whirled it above his head, and yelled, rather than shouted, while his face blazed with fury, "Come on, the whole nation of you, an ye like it, and do your worst!"

It seemed as though the challenge had been literally accepted; for every savage on the ground ran precipitately at Jack with club and spear, and doubtless would speedily have poured out his brave blood on the sod had not the teacher rushed in between them, and raising his voice to its utmost, cried:

"Stay your hands, warriors! It is not your part to judge in this matter! It is for Tararo, the chief, to say whether or not the young man shall live or die!"

The natives were arrested; and I know not whether it was the gratifying acknowledgment of his superiority thus made by the teacher, or some lingering feeling of gratitude for Jack's former aid in time of need, that influenced Tararo, but he stepped forward, and waving his hand, said to his people, "Desist. The young man's life is mine." Then turning to Jack, he said, "You have forfeited your liberty and life to me. Submit yourself, for we are more numerous than the sand upon the shore. You are but one: why should you die?"

"Villain!" exclaimed Jack passionately. "I may die, but assuredly I shall not perish alone! I will not submit until you promise that this girl shall not be injured!"

"You are very bold," replied the chief haughtily, "but very foolish. Yet I will say that Avatea shall not be sent away—at least, for three days."

"You had better accept these terms," whispered the teacher entreatingly. "If you persist in this mad defiance, you will be slain and Avatea will be lost. Three days are worth having."

Jack hesitated a moment, then lowered his club, and throwing it moodily to the ground, crossed his arms on his breast and hung down his head in silence.

Tararo seemed pleased by his submission, and told the teacher to say that he did not forget his former services, and therefore would leave him free as to his person, but that the schooner would be detained till he had further considered the matter.

While the teacher translated this, he approached as near to where Avatea was standing as possible without creating suspicion, and whispered to her a few words in the native language. Avatea, who, during the whole of the foregoing scene, had stood leaning against the tree perfectly passive, and seemingly quite uninterested in all that was going on, replied by a single rapid glance of her dark eye, which was instantly cast down again on the ground at her feet.

Tararo now advanced, and taking the girl by the hand, led her unresistingly away; while Jack, Peterkin, and I returned with the teacher on board the schooner.

On reaching the deck we went down to the cabin, where Jack threw himself, in a state of great dejection, on a couch; but the teacher seated himself by his side, and laying his hand upon his shoulder, said:

"Do not give way to anger, my young friend. God has given us three days, and we must use the means that are in our power to free this poor girl from slavery. We must not sit in idle disappointment; we must act—"

"Act!" cried Jack, raising himself and tossing back his hair wildly. "It is mockery to talk of acting when one is bound hand and foot. How can I act? I cannot fight a whole nation of savages single-handed. Yes," he said with a bitter smile, "I *can* fight them; but I cannot conquer them, or save Avatea."

"Patience, my friend: your spirit is not a good one just now. You cannot expect that blessing which alone can ensure success unless you are more submissive. I will tell you my plans if you will listen."

"Listen!" cried Jack eagerly. "Of course I will, my good fellow! I did not know you had any plans. Out with them! I only hope you will show me how I can get the girl on board of this schooner, and I'd up anchor and away in no time. But proceed with your plans."

The teacher smiled sadly. "Ah, my friend, if one fathom of your anchor-chain were to rattle as you drew it in, a thousand warriors would be standing on your deck! No, no; that could not be done. Even now your ship would be taken from you were it not that Tararo has some feeling of gratitude towards you. But I know Tararo well. He is a man of falsehood, as all the unconverted savages are. The chief to whom he has promised this girl is very powerful, and Tararo *must* fulfil his promise. He has told you that he would do nothing to the girl for three days, but that is because the party who are to take her away will not be ready to start for three days. Still, as he might have made you a prisoner during those three days, I say that God has given them to us."

"Well, but what do you propose to do?" said Jack impatiently.

"My plan involves much danger; but I see no other, and I think you have courage to brave it. It is this. There is an island about fifty miles to the south of this, the natives of which are Christians, and have been so for two years or more, and the principal chief is Avatea's lover. Once there, Avatea would be safe. Now, I suggest that you should abandon your schooner. Do you think that you can make so great a sacrifice?"

"Friend," replied Jack, "when I make up my mind to go through with a thing of importance, I can make any sacrifice."

The teacher smiled. "Well, then, the savages could not conceive it possible that for the sake of a girl you would voluntarily lose your fine vessel; therefore, as long as she lies here, they think they have you all safe. So I suggest that we get a quantity of stores conveyed to a sequestered part of the shore, provide a small canoe, put Avatea on board, and you three would paddle to the Christian island."

"Bravo!" cried Peterkin, springing up and seizing the teacher's hand. "Missionary, you're a regular brick! I didn't think you had so much in you!"

"As for me," continued the teacher, "I will remain on board till they discover that you are gone. Then they will ask me where you are gone to, and I will refuse to tell."

"And what'll be the result of that?" inquired Jack.

"I know not. Perhaps they will kill me; but," he added, looking at Jack with a peculiar smile, "I too am not afraid to die in a good cause!"

"But how are we to get hold of Avatea?" inquired Jack.

"I have arranged with her to meet us at a particular spot, to which I will guide you to-night. We shall then arrange about it. She will easily manage to elude her keepers, who are not very strict in watching her, thinking it impossible that she could escape from the island. Indeed, I am sure that such an idea will never enter their heads. But, as I have said, you run great danger. Fifty miles in a small canoe, on the open sea, is a great voyage to make. You may miss the island, too, in which case there is no other in that direction for a hundred miles or more; and if you lose your way and fall among other heathens, you know the law of Feejee —a castaway who gains the shore is doomed to die. You must count the cost, my young friend."

"I have counted it," replied Jack. "If Avatea consents to run the risk, most certainly I will; and so will my comrades also. Besides," added Jack, looking seriously into the teacher's face, "your Bible—our Bible—tells of ***One*** who delivers those who call on Him in the time of trouble; who holds the winds in His fists, and the waters in the hollow of His hand."

We now set about active preparations for the intended voyage: collected together such things as we should require, and laid out on the deck provisions sufficient to maintain us for several weeks, purposing to load the canoe with as much as she could hold consistently with speed and safety. These we covered with a tarpaulin, intending to convey them to the canoe only a few hours before starting. When night spread her sable curtain over the scene, we prepared to land; but first kneeling along with the natives and the teacher, the latter implored a blessing on our enterprise. Then we rowed quietly to the shore and followed our sable guide, who led us by a long détour in order to avoid the village, to the place of rendezvous. We had not stood more than five minutes under the gloomy shade of the thick foliage when a dark figure glided noiselessly up to us.

"Ah, here you are!" said Jack as Avatea approached.—"Now, then, tell her what we've come about, and don't waste time."

"I understan' leetl' English," said Avatea in a low voice.

"Why, where did you pick up English?" exclaimed Jack in amazement. "You were dumb as a stone when I saw you last."

"She has learned all she knows of it from me," said the teacher, "since she came to the island."

We now gave Avatea a full explanation of our plans, entering into all the details, and concealing none of the danger, so that she might be fully aware of the risk she ran. As we had anticipated, she was too glad of the opportunity thus afforded her to escape from her persecutors to think of the danger or risk.

"Then you're willing to go with us, are you?" said Jack.

"Yis, I willing to go."

"And you're not afraid to trust yourself out on the deep sea so far?"

"No, I not 'fraid to go. Safe with Christian."

After some further consultation the teacher suggested that it was time to return, so we bade Avatea good-night; and having appointed to meet at the cliff where the canoe lay on the following night, just after dark, we hastened away—we to row back to the schooner with muffled oars, Avatea to glide back to her prison-hut among the Mango savages.

## 33

## THE FLIGHT—THE PURSUIT—DESPAIR AND ITS RESULTS—THE LION BEARDED IN HIS DEN AGAIN—AWFUL DANGER THREATENED AND WONDERFULLY AVERTED—A TERRIFIC STORM.

As the time for our meditated flight drew near, we became naturally very fearful lest our purpose should be discovered, and we spent the whole of the following day in a state of nervous anxiety. We resolved to go ashore and ramble about the village, as if to observe the habits and dwellings of the people, as we thought that an air of affected indifference to the events of the previous day would be more likely than any other course of conduct to avert suspicion as to our intentions. While we were thus occupied, the teacher remained on board with the Christian natives, whose powerful voices reached us ever and anon as they engaged in singing hymns or in prayer.

At last the long and tedious day came to a close, the sun sank into the sea, and the short-lived twilight of those regions, to which I have already referred, ended abruptly in a dark night. Hastily throwing a few blankets into our little boat, we stepped into it, and whispering farewell to the natives in the schooner, rowed gently over the lagoon, taking care to keep as near to the beach as possible. We rowed in the utmost silence and with muffled oars, so that had any one observed us at the distance of a few yards, he might have almost taken us for a phantom boat or a shadow on the dark water. Not a breath of air was stirring; but fortunately the gentle ripple of the sea upon the shore, mingled with the soft roar of the breaker on the distant reef, effectually drowned the slight plash that we unavoidably made in the water by the dipping of our oars.

A quarter of an hour sufficed to bring us to the overhanging cliff under whose black shadow our little canoe lay, with her bow in the water, ready to be launched, and most of her cargo already stowed away. As the keel of our little boat grated on the sand, a hand was laid upon the bow, and a dim form was seen.

"Ha!" said Peterkin in a whisper as he stepped upon the beach; "is that you, Avatea?"

"Yis, it am me," was the reply.

"All right—Now, then, gently—Help me to shove off the canoe," whispered Jack to the teacher.—"And, Peterkin, do you shove these blankets aboard; we may want them before long.—Avatea, step into the middle: that's right."

"Is all ready?" whispered the teacher.

"Not quite," replied Peterkin.—"Here, Ralph, lay hold o' this pair of oars, and stow them away if you can. I don't like paddles. After we're safe away, I'll try to rig up rowlocks for them."

"Now, then, in with you and shove off!"

One more earnest squeeze of the kind teacher's hand, and with his whispered blessing yet sounding in our ears, we shot like an arrow from the shore, sped over the still waters of the lagoon, and paddled as swiftly as strong arms and willing hearts could urge us over the long swell of the open sea.

All that night and the whole of the following day we plied our paddles in almost total silence and without a halt, save twice to recruit our failing energies with a mouthful of food and a draught of water. Jack had taken the bearing of the island just after starting, and laying a small pocket-compass before him, kept the head of the canoe due south, for our chance of hitting the island depended very much on the faithfulness of our steersman in keeping our tiny bark exactly and constantly on its proper course. Peterkin and I paddled in the bow, and Avatea worked untiringly in the middle.

As the sun's lower limb dipped on the gilded edge of the sea Jack ceased working, threw down his paddle, and called a halt.

"There!" he cried, heaving a deep, long-drawn sigh; "we've put a considerable breadth of water between us and these black rascals, so now we'll have a hearty supper and a sound sleep."

"Hear, hear!" cried Peterkin. "Nobly spoken, Jack!—Hand me a drop of water, Ralph.—Why, girl, what's wrong with you? You look just like a black owl blinking in the sunshine!"

Avatea smiled. "I sleepy," she said; and as if to prove the truth of this, she laid her head on the edge of the canoe and fell fast asleep.

"That's uncommon sharp practice," said Peterkin with a broad grin. "Don't you think we should awake her to make her eat something first? Or perhaps," he added with a grave, meditative look—"perhaps we might put some food in her mouth, which is so elegantly open at the present moment, and see if she'd swallow it while asleep.—If so, Ralph, you might come round to the front here and feed her quietly, while Jack and I are tucking into the victuals. It would be a monstrous economy of time."

I could not help smiling at Peterkin's idea, which indeed, when I pondered it, seemed remarkably good in theory; nevertheless, I declined to put it in practice, being fearful of the result should the victuals chance to go down the wrong throat. But on suggesting this to Peterkin, he exclaimed:

"Down the wrong throat, man! Why, a fellow with half-an-eye might see that if it went down Avatea's throat it could not go down the wrong throat!—unless, indeed, you have all of a sudden become inordinately selfish, and think that all the throats in the world are wrong ones except your own. However, don't talk so much, and hand me the pork before Jack finishes it. I feel myself entitled to at least one minute morsel."

"Peterkin, you're a villain—a paltry little villain!" said Jack quietly as he tossed the hind legs (including the tail) of a cold roast pig to his comrade; "and I must again express my regret that unavoidable circumstances have thrust your society upon me, and that necessity has compelled me to cultivate your acquaintance. Were it not that you are incapable of walking upon the water, I would order you, sir, out of the canoe!"

"There! you've awakened Avatea with your long tongue," retorted Peterkin, with a frown, as the girl gave vent to a deep sigh. "No," he continued, "it was only a snore. Perchance she dreameth of her black Apollo.—I say, Ralph, do leave just one little slice of that yam! Between you and Jack I run a chance of being put on short allowance, if not—yei-a-a-ow!"

Peterkin's concluding remark was a yawn of so great energy that Jack recommended him to postpone the conclusion of his meal till next morning—a piece of advice which he followed so quickly that I was forcibly reminded of his remark, a few minutes before, in regard to the sharp practice of Avatea.

My readers will have observed, probably, by this time, that I am much given to meditation: they will not, therefore, be surprised to learn that I fell into a deep reverie on the subject of sleep, which was continued without intermission into the night, and prolonged without interruption into the following morning. But I cannot feel assured that I actually slept during that time, although I am tolerably certain that I was not awake.

Thus we lay, like a shadow, on the still bosom of the ocean, while the night closed in, and all around was calm, dark, and silent.

A thrilling cry of alarm from Peterkin startled us in the morning, just as the grey dawn began to glimmer in the east.

"What's wrong?" cried Jack, starting up.

Peterkin replied by pointing, with a look of anxious dread, towards the horizon; and a glance sufficed to show us that one of the largest-sized war-canoes was approaching us!

With a groan of mingled despair and anger, Jack seized his paddle, glanced at the compass, and in a suppressed voice commanded us to "Give way!" But we did not require to be urged. Already our four paddles were glancing in the water, and the canoe bounded over the glassy sea like a dolphin, while a shout from our pursuers told that they had observed our motions.

"I see something like land ahead," said Jack in a hopeful tone. "It seems impossible that we could have made the island yet; still, if it is so, we may reach it before these fellows can catch us, for our canoe is light and our muscles are fresh."

No one replied; for, to say truth, we felt that in a long chase we had no chance whatever with a canoe which held nearly a hundred warriors. Nevertheless, we resolved to do our utmost to escape, and paddled with a degree of vigour that kept us well in advance of our pursuers. The war-canoe was so far behind us that it seemed but a little speck on the sea, and the shouts to which the crew occasionally gave vent came faintly towards us on the morning breeze. We therefore hoped that we should be able to keep in advance for an hour or two, when we might perhaps reach the land ahead. But this hope was suddenly crushed by the supposed land, not long after, rising up into the sky, thus proving itself to be a fog-bank!

A bitter feeling of disappointment filled each heart, and was expressed on each countenance, as we beheld this termination to our hopes. But we had little time to think of regret. Our danger was too great and imminent to permit of a moment's relaxation from our exertions. No hope now animated our bosoms; but a feeling of despair, strange to say, lent us power to work, and nerved our arms with such energy that it was several hours ere the savages overtook us. When we saw that there was indeed no chance of escape, and that paddling any longer would only serve to exhaust our strength without doing any good, we turned the side of our canoe towards the approaching enemy and laid down our paddles.

Silently, and with a look of bitter determination on his face, Jack lifted one of the light boat-oars that we had brought with us, and resting it on his shoulder, stood up in an attitude of bold defiance. Peterkin took the other oar and also stood up, but there was no anger visible on his countenance: when not sparkling with fun, it usually wore a mild, sad expression, which was deepened on the present occasion as he glanced at Avatea, who sat with her face resting in her hands upon her knees. Without knowing very well what I intended to do, I also arose and grasped my paddle with both hands.

On came the large canoe like a war-horse of the deep, with the foam curling from its sharp bow, and the spear-heads of the savages glancing in the beams of the rising sun. Perfect silence was maintained on both sides; and we could hear the hissing water, and see the frowning eyes of the warriors, as they came rushing on. When about twenty yards distant, five or six of the savages in the bow rose, and laying aside their paddles, took up their spears. Jack and Peterkin raised their oars, while, with a feeling of madness whirling in my brain, I grasped my paddle and prepared for the onset. But before any of us could strike a blow, the sharp prow of the war-canoe struck us like a thunderbolt on the side and hurled us into the sea!

What occurred after this I cannot tell, for I was nearly drowned; but when I recovered from the state of insensibility into which I had been thrown, I found myself stretched on my back, bound hand and foot, between Jack and Peterkin, in the bottom of the large canoe.

In this condition we lay the whole day, during which time the savages only rested one hour. When night came they rested again for another hour, and appeared to sleep just as they sat. But we were neither unbound nor allowed to speak to each other during the voyage, nor was a morsel of food or a draught of water given to us. For food, however, we cared little; but we would have given much for a drop of water to cool our parched lips. And we would have been glad, too, had they loosened the cords that bound us; for they were tightly fastened, and occasioned us much pain. The air, also, was unusually hot—so much so that I felt convinced that a storm was brewing. This also added to our sufferings. However, these were at length relieved by our arrival at the island from which we had fled.

While we were being led ashore, we caught a glimpse of Avatea, who was seated in the hinder part of the canoe. She was not fettered in any way. Our captors now drove us before them towards the hut of Tararo, at which we speedily arrived, and found the chief seated with an expression on his face that boded us no good. Our friend the teacher stood beside him, with a look of anxiety on his mild features.

"How comes it," said Tararo, turning to the teacher, "that these youths have abused our hospitality?"

"Tell him," replied Jack, "that we have not abused his hospitality, for his hospitality has not been extended to us. I came to the island to deliver Avatea, and my only regret is that I have failed to do so. If I get another chance, I will try to save her yet."

The teacher shook his head. "Nay, my young friend, I had better not tell him that: it will only incense him."

"I care not," replied Jack. "If you don't tell him that, you'll tell him nothing, for I won't say anything softer."

On hearing Jack's speech, Tararo frowned, and his eye flashed with anger.

"Go, presumptuous boy!" he said. "My debt to you cancelled. You and your companions shall die!"

As he spoke he rose and signed to several of attendants, who seized Jack and Peterkin and violently by the collars, and dragging us from the house of the chief, led us through the wood to the outskirts of the village. Here they thrust us into a species of natural cave in a cliff, and having barricaded the entrance, left us in total darkness.

After feeling about for some time—for our legs were unshackled, although our wrists were still bound with thongs—we found a low ledge of rock running along one side of the cavern. On this we seated ourselves, and for a long time maintained unbroken silence.

At last I could restrain my feelings no longer. "Alas! dear Jack and Peterkin," said I, "what is to become of us? I fear that we are doomed to die."

"I know not," replied Jack in a tremulous voice—"I know not. Ralph, I regret deeply the hastiness of my violent temper, which, I must confess, has been the chief cause of our being brought to this sad condition. Perhaps the teacher may do something for us. But I have little hope."

"Ah no!" said Peterkin with a heavy sigh; "I am sure he can't help us. Tararo doesn't care more for him than for one of his dogs."

"Truly," said I, "there seems no chance of deliverance, unless the Almighty puts forth His arm to save us. Yet I must say I have great hope, my comrades; for we have come to this dark place by no fault of ours—unless it be a fault to try to succour a woman in distress."

I was interrupted in my remarks by a noise at the entrance to the cavern, which was caused by the removal of the barricade. Immediately after three men entered, and taking us by the collars of our coats, led us away through the forest. As we advanced we heard much shouting and beating of native drums in the village, and at first we thought that our guards were conducting us to the hut of Tararo again. But in this we were mistaken. The beating of drums gradually increased, and soon after we observed a procession of the natives coming towards us. At the head of this procession we were placed, and then we all advanced together towards the temple where human victims were wont to be sacrificed!

A thrill of horror ran through my heart as I recalled to mind the awful scenes that I had before witnessed at that dreadful spot. But deliverance came suddenly from a quarter whence we little expected it. During the whole of that day there had been an unusual degree of heat in the atmosphere, and the sky assumed that lurid aspect which portends a thunderstorm. Just as we were approaching the horrid temple, a growl of thunder burst overhead, and heavy drops of rain began to fall.

Those who have not witnessed gales and storms in tropical regions can form but a faint conception of the fearful hurricane that burst upon the island of Mango at this time. Before we reached the temple the storm burst upon us with a deafening roar; and the natives, who knew too well the devastation that was to follow, fled right and left through the woods in order to save their property, leaving us alone in the midst of the howling storm. The trees around us bent before the blast like willows, and we were about to flee in order to seek shelter when the teacher ran toward us with a knife in his hand.

"Thank the Lord," he said, cutting our bonds, "I am in time! Now, seek the shelter of the nearest rock."

This we did without a moment's hesitation, for the whistling wind burst, ever and anon, like thunderclaps among the trees, and tearing them from their roots, hurled them with violence to the ground. Rain cut across the land in sheets, and lightning played like forked serpents in the air, while high above the roar of the hissing tempest the thunder crashed and burst and rolled in awful majesty.

In the village the scene was absolutely appalling. Roofs were blown completely off the houses in many cases, and in others the houses themselves were levelled with the ground. In the midst of this the natives were darting to and fro—in some instances saving their goods, but in many others seeking to save themselves from the storm of destruction that whirled around them. But terrific although the tempest was on land, it was still more tremendous on the mighty ocean. Billows sprang, as it were, from the great deep, and while their crests were absolutely scattered into white mist, they fell upon the beach with a crash that seemed to shake the solid land. But they did not end there. Each successive wave swept higher and higher on the beach until the ocean lashed its angry waters among the trees and bushes, and at length, in a sheet of white, curdled foam, swept into the village and upset and carried off, or dashed into wreck, whole rows of the native dwellings! It was a sublime, an awful scene, calculated, in some degree at least, to impress the mind of beholders with the might and majesty of God.

We found shelter in a cave that night and all the next day, during which time the storm raged in fury. But on the night following, it abated somewhat; and in the morning we went to the village to seek for food, being so famished with hunger that we lost all feeling of danger and all wish to escape in our desire to satisfy the cravings of nature. But no sooner had we obtained food than we began to wish that we had rather endeavoured to make our escape into the mountains. This we attempted to do soon afterwards; but the natives were now able to look after us, and on our showing a disposition to avoid observation and make towards the mountains, we were seized by three warriors, who once more bound our wrists and thrust us into our former prison.

It is true Jack made a vigorous resistance, and knocked down the first savage who seized him with a well-directed blow of his fist, but he was speedily overpowered by others. Thus we were again prisoners, with the prospect of torture and a violent death before us.

# 34

## IMPRISONMENT—SINKING HOPES—UNEXPECTED FREEDOM TO MORE THAN ONE, AND IN MORE SENSES THAN ONE

For a long, long month we remained in our dark and dreary prison, during which dismal time we did not see the face of a human being except that of the silent savage who brought us our daily food.

There have been one or two seasons in my life during which I have felt as if the darkness of sorrow and desolation that crushed my inmost heart could never pass away until death should make me cease to feel. The present was such a season.

During the first part of our confinement we felt a cold chill at our hearts every time we heard a footfall near the cave, dreading lest it should prove to be that of our executioner. But as time dragged heavily on we ceased to feel this alarm, and began to experience such a deep, irrepressible longing for freedom that we chafed and fretted in our confinement like tigers. Then a feeling of despair came over us, and we actually longed for the time when the savages would take us forth to die. But these changes took place very gradually, and were mingled sometimes with brighter thoughts; for there were times when we sat, in that dark cavern on our ledge of rock, and conversed almost pleasantly about the past until we well-nigh forgot the dreary present. But we seldom ventured to touch upon the future.

A few decayed leaves and boughs formed our bed, and a scanty supply of yams and taro, brought to us once a day, constituted our food.

"Well, Ralph, how have you slept?" said Jack in a listless tone on rising one morning from his humble couch. "Were you much disturbed by the wind last night?"

"No," said I. "I dreamed of home all night, and I thought that my mother smiled upon me and beckoned me to go to her; but I could not, for I was chained."

"And I dreamed too," said Peterkin; "but it was of our happy home on the Coral Island. I thought we were swimming in the Water Garden. Then the savages gave a yell, and we were immediately in the cave at Spouting Cliff, which, somehow or other changed into this gloomy cavern; and I awoke to find it true."

Peterkin's tone was so much altered by the depressing influence of his long imprisonment that, had I not known it was he who spoke, I should scarcely have recognised it, so sad was it, and so unlike to the merry, cheerful voice we had been accustomed to hear. I pondered this much, and thought of the terrible decline of happiness that may come on human beings in so short a time; how bright the sunshine in the sky at one time, and in a short space bow dark the overshadowing cloud! I had no doubt that the Bible would have given me much light and comfort on this subject if I had possessed one, and I once more had occasion to regret deeply having neglected to store my memory with its consoling truths.

While I meditated thus, Peterkin again broke the silence of the cave by saying, in a melancholy tone, "Oh, I wonder if we shall ever see our dear island more!"

His voice trembled, and covering his face with both hands, he bent down his head and wept. It was an unusual sight for me to see our once joyous companion in tears, and I felt a burning desire to comfort him; but, alas! what could I say? I could hold out no hope; and although I essayed twice to speak, the words refused to pass my lips. While I hesitated Jack sat down beside him and whispered a few words in his ear, while Peterkin threw himself on his friend's breast and rested his head on his shoulder.

Thus we sat for some time in deep silence. Soon after we heard footsteps at the entrance of the cave, and immediately our jailer entered. We were so much accustomed to his regular visits, however, that we paid little attention to him, expecting that he would set down our meagre fare as usual and depart. But, to our surprise, instead of doing so, he advanced towards us with a knife in his hand, and going up to Jack, he cut the thongs that bound his wrists; then he did the same to Peterkin and me! For fully five minutes we stood in speechless amazement, with our freed hands hanging idly by our sides. The first thought that rushed into my mind was that the time had come to put us to death; and although, as I have said before, we actually wished for death in the strength of our despair, now that we thought it drew really near I felt all the natural love of life revive in my heart, mingled with a chill of horror at the suddenness of our call.

But I was mistaken. After cutting our bonds the savage pointed to the cave's mouth, and we marched, almost mechanically, into the open air. Here, to our surprise, we found the teacher standing under a tree, with his hands clasped before him, and the tears trickling down his dark cheeks. On seeing Jack, who came out first, he sprang towards him, and clasping him in his arms, exclaimed:

"Oh my dear young friend, through the great goodness of God you are free!"

"Free?" cried Jack.

"Ay, free!" repeated the teacher, shaking us warmly by the hands again and again—"free to go and come as you will. The Lord has unloosed the bonds of the captive, and set the prisoners free. A missionary has been sent to us, and Tararo has embraced the Christian religion! The people are even now burning their gods of wood! Come, my dear friends, and see the glorious sight!"

We could scarcely credit our senses. So long had we been accustomed, in our cavern, to dream of deliverance, that we imagined for a moment this must surely be nothing more than another vivid dream. Our eyes and minds were dazzled, too, by the brilliant sunshine, which almost blinded us after our long confinement to the gloom of our prison, so that we felt giddy with the variety of conflicting emotions that filled our throbbing bosoms; but as we followed the footsteps of our sable friend, and beheld the bright foliage of the trees, and heard the cries of the paroquets, and smelt the rich perfume of the flowering shrubs, the truth —that we were really delivered from prison and from death—rushed with overwhelming power into our souls, and with one accord, while tears sprang to our eyes, we uttered a loud, long cheer of joy.

It was replied to by a shout from a number of the natives who chanced to be near. Running towards us, they shook us by the hand with every demonstration of kindly feeling.

They then fell behind, and forming a sort of procession, conducted us to the dwelling of Tararo.

The scene that met our eyes here was one that I shall never forget. On a rude bench in front of his house sat the chief. A native stood on his left hand, who from his dress seemed to be a teacher. On his right stood an English gentleman, who I at once, and rightly, concluded was a missionary. He was tall, thin, and apparently past forty, with a bald forehead and thin grey hair. The expression of his countenance was the most winning I ever saw, and his clear grey eyes beamed with a look that was frank, fearless, loving, and truthful. In front of the chief was an open space, in the centre of which lay a pile of wooden idols, ready to be set on fire; and around these were assembled thousands of natives, who had come to join in or to witness the unusual sight. A bright smile overspread the missionary's face as he advanced quickly to meet us, and he shook us warmly by the hands.

"I am overjoyed to meet you, my dear young friends," he said. "My friend and *your* friend, the teacher, has told me your history; and I thank our Father in heaven with all my heart, that He has guided me to this island and made me the instrument of saving you."

We thanked the missionary most heartily, and asked him, in some surprise, how he had succeeded in turning the heart of Tararo in our favour.

"I will tell you that at a more convenient time," he answered, "meanwhile we must not forget the respect due to the chief. He waits to receive you."

In the conversation that immediately followed between us and Tararo, the latter said that the light of the Gospel of Jesus Christ had been sent to the island, and that to it we were indebted for our freedom. Moreover, he told us that we were at liberty to depart in our schooner whenever we pleased, and that we should be supplied with as much provision as we required. He concluded by shaking hands with us warmly, and performing the ceremony of rubbing noses.

This was indeed good news to us, and we could hardly find words to express our gratitude to the chief and to the missionary.

"And what of Avatea?" inquired Jack.

The missionary replied by pointing to a group of natives, in the midst of whom the girl stood. Beside her was a tall, strapping fellow, whose noble mien and air of superiority bespoke him a chief of no ordinary kind. "That youth is her lover. He came this very morning in his war-canoe to treat with Tararo for Avatea. He is to be married in a few days, and afterwards returns to his island home with his bride."

"That's capital!" said Jack as he stepped up to the savage and gave him a hearty shake of the hand. "I wish you joy, my lad!—And you too, Avatea!"

As Jack spoke, Avatea's lover took him by the hand and led him to the spot where Tararo and the missionary stood, surrounded by most of the chief men of the tribe. The girl herself followed and stood on his left hand, while her lover stood on his right, and commanding silence, made the following speech, which was translated by the missionary:

"Young friend, you have seen few years, but your head is old. Your heart, also, is large and very brave. I and Avatea are your debtors; and we wish, in the midst of this assembly, to acknowledge our debt, and to say that it is one which we can never repay. You have risked your life for one who was known to you only for a few days. But she was a woman in distress, and that was enough to secure to her the aid of a Christian man. We, who live in these islands of the sea, know that the true Christians always act thus. Their religion is one of love and kindness. We thank God that so many Christians have been sent here: we hope many more will come. Remember that I and Avatea will think of you, and pray for you and your brave comrades, when you are far away."

To this kind speech Jack returned a short, sailor-like reply, in which he insisted that he had only done for Avatea what he would have done for any woman under the sun. But Jack's forte did not lie in speech-making, so he terminated rather abruptly by seizing the chief's hand and shaking it violently, after which he made a hasty retreat.

"Now, then, Ralph and Peterkin," said Jack as we mingled with the crowd, "it seems to me that, the object we came here for having been satisfactorily accomplished, we have nothing more to do but get ready for sea as fast as we can, and hurrah for old England!"

"That's my idea precisely," said Peterkin, endeavouring to wink; but he had wept so much of late, poor fellow, that he found it difficult. "However, I'm not going away till I see these fellows burn their gods."

Peterkin had his wish, for in a few minutes afterwards fire was put to the pile, the roaring flames, ascended, and amid the acclamations of the assembled thousands, the false gods of Mango were reduced to ashes!

# 35

## CONCLUSION

To part is the lot of all mankind. The world is a scene of constant leave-taking, and the hands that grasp in cordial greeting to-day are doomed ere long to unite for the last time when the quivering lips pronounce the word "Farewell." It is a sad thought, but should we on that account exclude it from our minds? May not a lesson worth learning be gathered in the contemplation of it? May it not, perchance, teach us to devote our thoughts more frequently and attentively to that land where we meet but part no more?

How many do we part from in this world with a light good-bye whom we never see again! Often do I think, in my meditations on this subject, that if we realised more fully the shortness of the fleeting intercourse that we have in this world with many of our fellow-men, we would try more earnestly to do them good, to give them a friendly smile, as it were, in passing (for the longest intercourse on earth is little more than a passing word and glance), and show that we have sympathy with them in the short, quick struggle of life by our kindly words and looks and actions.

The time soon drew near when we were to quit the islands of the South Seas; and strange though it may appear, we felt deep regret at parting with the natives of the island of Mango, for after they embraced the Christian faith, they sought, by showing us the utmost kindness, to compensate for the harsh treatment we had experienced at their hands. And we felt a growing affection for the native teachers and the missionary, and especially for Avatea and her husband.

Before leaving we had many long and interesting conversations with the missionary, in one of which he told us that he had been making for the island of Rarotonga when his native-built sloop was blown out of its course, during a violent gale, and driven to this island. At first the natives refused to listen to what he had to say; but after a week's residence among them, Tararo came to him and said that he wished to become a Christian and would burn his idols. He proved himself to be sincere, for, as we have seen, he persuaded all his people to do likewise. I use the word "persuaded" advisedly, for, like all the other Feejee chiefs, Tararo was a despot, and might have commanded obedience to his wishes; but he entered so readily into the spirit of the new faith that he perceived at once the impropriety of using constraint in the propagation of it. He set the example, therefore; and that example was followed by almost every man of the tribe.

During the short time that we remained at the island repairing our vessel and getting her ready for sea, the natives had commenced building a large and commodious church under the superintendence of the missionary, and several rows of new cottages were marked out; so that the place bid fair to become, in a few months, as prosperous and beautiful as the Christian village at the other end of the island.

After Avatea was married, she and her husband were sent away loaded with presents, chiefly of an edible nature. One of the native teachers went with them, for the purpose of visiting still more distant islands of the sea, and spreading, if possible, the light of the glorious Gospel there.

As the missionary intended to remain for several weeks longer in order to encourage and confirm his new converts, Jack and Peterkin and I held a consultation in the cabin of our schooner—which we found just as we had left her, for everything that had been taken out of her was restored. We now resolved to delay our departure no longer. The desire to see our beloved native land was strong upon us, and we could not wait.

Three natives volunteered to go with us to Tahiti, where we thought it likely that we should be able to procure a sufficient crew of sailors to man our vessel; so we accepted their offer gladly.

It was a bright, clear morning when we hoisted the snow-white sails of the pirate schooner and left the shores of Mango. The missionary and thousands of the natives came down to bid us God-speed and to see us sail away. As the vessel bent before a light, fair wind, we glided quickly over the lagoon under a cloud of canvas.

Just as we passed through the channel in the reef the natives gave us a loud cheer; and as the missionary waved his hat, while he stood on a coral rock with his grey hairs floating in the wind, we heard the single word "Farewell" borne faintly over the sea.

That night, as we sat on the taffrail gazing out upon the wide sea and up into the starry firmament, a thrill of joy, strangely mixed with sadness, passed through our hearts; for we were at length "homeward bound" and were gradually leaving far behind us the beautiful, bright-green coral islands of the Pacific Ocean.

# THE KING OF THE PIRATES

## BEING AN ACCOUNT OF THE FAMOUS ENTERPRISES OF CAPTAIN AVERY, THE MOCK KING OF MADAGASCAR

DANIEL DEFOE

# THE PREFACE

One of the particular Advantages of the following Letters from Captain Avery, is, the Satisfaction they will give the Readers how much they have been impos'd upon in the former ridiculous and extravagant Accounts which have been put upon the World in what has been publish'd already.

It has been enough to the Writers of this Man's Life, as they call it, that they could put any Thing together, to make a kind of monstrous unheard of Story, as romantick as the Reports that have been spread about of him; and the more those Stories appear'd monstrous and incredible, the more suitable they seem'd to be to what the World would have been made to expect of Captain Avery.

There is always a great Deference between what Men say of themselves, and what others say for them, when they come to write Historically of the Transactions of their Lives.

The Publisher of these Letters recommends this Performance to the Readers, to make their Judgment of the Difference between them and the extravagant Stories already told, and which is most likely to be genuine; and, as they verily believe these Letters to be the best and truest Account of Captain Avery's Piracies, that ever has or ever will come to the Knowledge of the World, they recommend them as such, and doubt not but they will answer for themselves in the Reading.

The Account given of Captain Avery's taking the Great Mogul's Daughter, ravishing and murdering her, and all the Ladies of her Retinue, is so differently related here, and so extravagantly related before, that it cannot but be a Satisfaction to the most unconcern'd Reader, to find such a horrible Piece of Villainy as the other was suppos'd to be, not to have been committed in the World.

On the contrary, we find here, that except plundering that Princess of her Jewels and Money to a prodigious Value, a Thing which, falling into the Hands of Freebooters, every one that had the Misfortune to fall into such Hands would expect: But, that excepting this, the Lady was used with all the Decency and Humanity, and, perhaps, with more than ever Women, falling among Pirates, had found before; especially considering that, by Report, she was a most beautiful and agreeable Person herself, as were also several of those about her.

The Booty taken with her, tho' infinitely great in itself, yet has been so magnify'd beyond common Sense, that it makes all the rest that has been said of those Things ridiculous and absurd.

The like Absurdity in the former Relations of this Matter, is that of the making an Offer of I know not how many Millions to the late Queen, for Captain Avery's Pardon, with a Petition to the Queen, and her Majesty's negative Answer; all which are as much true as his being Master of so many Millions if Money, which he nor his Gang never had; and of his being proclaim'd King of Madagascar; marrying the Mogul's Daughter, and the like: And, by the Bye, it was but ill laid together of those who publish'd, that he first ravish'd her, then murder'd her, and then marry'd her; all which are very remarkable for the recommending the Thing to those that read it.

If these Stories are explain'd here, and duly expos'd, and the History of Captain Avery set in a fairer Light, the End is answer'd; and of this the Readers are to be the only Judges: But this may be said, without any Arrogance, that this Story, stripp'd of all the romantick, improbable, and impossible Parts of it, looks more like the History of Captain Avery, than any Thing yet publish'd ever has done; and, if it is not prov'd that the Captain wrote these Letters himself, the Publisher says, None but the Captain himself will ever be able to mend them.

# A FIRST LETTER

You may be sure I receiv'd with Resentment enough the Account, that a most ridiculous Book, entitled, *My Life and Adventures*, had been publish'd in *England*, being fully assur'd nothing of Truth could be contain'd in such a Work; and tho' it may be true, that my extravagant Story may be the proper Foundation of a Romance, yet as no Man has a Title to publish it better than I have to expose and contradict it, I send you this by one of my particular Friends, who having an Opportunity of returning into *England*, has promis'd to convey it faithfully to you; by which, at least, two Things shall be made good to the World; first, that they shall be satisfy'd in the scandalous and unjust Manner in which others have already treated me, and it shall give, in the mean Time, a larger Account of what may at present be fit to be made publick, of my unhappy tho' successful Adventures.

I shall not trouble my Friends with any Thing of my Original and first Introduction into the World, I leave it to you to add from yourself what you think proper to be known on that Subject; only this I enjoin you to take Notice of, that the Account printed of me, with all the Particulars of my Marriage, my being defrauded, and leaving my Family and native Country on that Account, is a meer Fable and a made Story, to embellish, as the Writer of it perhaps suppos'd, the rest of his Story, or perhaps to fill up the Book, that it might swell to a Magnitude which his barren Invention could not supply.

In the present Account, I have taken no Notice of my Birth, Infancy, Youth, or any of that Part; which, as it was the most useless Part of my Years to myself so 'tis the most useless to any one that shall read this Work to know, being altogether barren of any Thing remarkable in it self, or instructing to others: It is sufficient to me to let the World know, as above, that the former Accounts, made publick, are utterly false, and to begin my Account of myself at a Period which may be more useful and entertaining.

It may be true, that I may represent some Particulars of my Life, in this Tract, with Reserve, or Enlargement, such as may be sufficient to conceal any Thing in my present Circumstance that ought to be conceal'd and reserv'd, with Respect to my own Safety; and therefore, if on Pretence of Justice the busy World should look for me in one Part of the World when I am in another, search for my new Kingdom in *Madagascar*, and should not find it, or search for my Settlement on one Side of the Island, when it lies on another, they must not take this ill; for Self-preservation being the supreme Law of Nature, all Things of this Kind must submit to that.

In Order then to come immediately to my Story, I shall, without any Circumlocutions, give you Leave to tell the World, that being bred to the Sea from a Youth, none of those romantick Introductions publish'd had any Share in my Adventures, or were any way the Cause of my taking the Courses I have since been embark'd in: But as in several Parts of my wandring Life I had seen something of the immense Wealth, which the Buccaneers, and other Adventurers, met with in their scouring about the World for Purchase, I had, for a long Time, meditated in my Thoughts to get possess'd of a good Ship for that Purpose, if I could, and to try my Fortune. I had been some Years in the Bay of *Campeachy*, and tho' with Patience I endur'd the Fatigue of that laborious Life, yet it was as visible to others as to myself, that I was not form'd by Nature for a Logwood-Cutter, any more than I was for a Foremast-man; and therefore Night and Day I apply'd myself to study how I should dismiss myself from that Drudgery, and get to be, first or last, Master of a good Ship, which was the utmost of my Ambition at that Time; resolving, in the mean Time, that when ever any such Thing should happen, I would try my Fortune in the Cruising Trade, but would be sure not to prey upon my own Countrymen.

It was many Years after this before I could bring my Purposes to pass; and I serv'd, first, in some of the Adventures of Captain *Sharp*, Captain *Sawkins*, and others, in their bold Adventures in the South Seas, where I got a very good Booty; was at the taking of *Puna*, where we were oblig'd to leave infinite Wealth behind us, for want of being able to bring it away; and after several Adventures in those Seas, was among that Party who fought their Way Sword in Hand thro' all the Detachments of the *Spaniards*, in the Journey over Land, cross the Isthmus of *Darien*, to the North Seas; and when other of our Men gat away, some one Way, some another, I, with twelve more of our Men, by Help of a *Periagua*, gat into the Bay of *Campeachy*, where we fell very honestly to cutting of Logwood, not for Want, but to employ ourselves till we could make off.

Here three of our Men dy'd, and we that were left, shar'd their Money among us; and having stay'd here two Years, without seeing any Way of Escape that I dar'd to trust to, I at last, with two of our Men, who spoke *Spanish* perfectly well, made a desperate Attempt to travel over Land to L— having bury'd all our Money, (which was worth eight thousand Pieces of Eight a Man, tho' most of it in Gold) in a Pit in the Earth which we dug twelve Foot deep, and where it would have lyen still, for no Man knew where to look for it; but we had an Opportunity to come at it again some Years after.

We travell'd along the Sea-shore five Days together, the Weather exceeding hot, and did not doubt but we should so disguise ourselves as to be taken for *Spaniards*; but our better Fortune provided otherwise for us, for the sixth Day of our March we found a Canoe lying on the Shore with no one in her: We found, however, several Things in her, which told us plainly that she belong'd to some *Englishmen* who were on Shore; so we resolv'd to sit down by her and wait: By and by we heard the *Englishmen*, who were seven in Number, and were coming back to their Boat, having been up the Country to an *Ingenio*, where they had gotten great Quantities of Provision, and were bringing it down to their Boat which they had left on the Shore, (with the Help of five *Indians*, of whom they had bought it) not thinking there was any People thereabouts: When they saw us, not knowing who we were, they were just going to fire at us; when I, perceiving it, held up a white Flag as high as I could reach it, which was, in short, only a Piece of an old Linnen Wastcoat which I had on, and pull'd it off for the Occasion; upon this, however, they forbore firing at us, and when they came nearer to us, they could easily see that we were their own Countrymen: They enquir'd of us what we came there for; we told them, we had travell'd from *Campeachy*, where being tir'd with the Hardships of our Fortune, and not getting any Vessel to carry us where we durst go, we were even desperate, and cared not what became of us; so that had not they came to us thus happily, we should have put our selves into the Hands of the *Spaniards*rather than have perish'd where we were.

They took us into their Boat, and afterwards carry'd us on Board their Ship; when we came there, we found they were a worse Sort of Wanderers than ourselves, for tho' we had been a Kind of Pyrates, known and declar'd Enemies to the *Spaniards*, yet it was to them only, and to no other; for we never offer'd to rob any of our other *European* Nations, either *Dutch* or *French*, much less *English*; but now we were listed in the Service of the Devil indeed, and, like him, were at War with all Mankind.

However, we not only were oblig'd to sort with them, while with them, but in a little Time the Novelty of the Crime wore off, and we grew harden'd to it, like the rest: And in this Service I spent four Years more of my Time.

Our Captain in this Pirate Ship was nam'd *Nichols*, but we call'd him Captain *Redhand*; it seems it was a *Scots* Sailor gave him that Name, when he was not the Head of the Crew, because he was so bloody a Wretch, that he scarce ever was at the taking any Prize, but he had a Hand in some Butchery or other.

They were hard put to it for fresh Provisions, or they would not have sent thus up into the Country a single Canoe; and when I came on Board they were so straiten'd, that, by my Advice, they resolv'd to go to the Isle of *Cuba* to kill wild Beef, of which the South Side of the Island is so full: Accordingly we sail'd thither directly.

The Vessel carry'd sixteen Guns, but was fitted to carry twenty two, and there was on Board one hundred and sixty stout Fellows, as bold and as case-harden'd for the Work as ever I met with upon any Occasion whatever: We victual'd in this Place for eight Months, by our Calculation; but our Cook, who had the Management of the Salting and Pickling the Beef, order'd his Matters so, that had he been let alone he would have starv'd us all, and poison'd us too; for as we are oblig'd to hunt the black Cattle in the Island sometimes a great while before we can shoot them, it should be observ'd, that the Flesh of those that are heated before they are kill'd, is not fit to be pickled or salted up for Keeping.

But this Man happening to pickle up the Beef, without Regard to this particular Distinction, most of the Beef, so pickled, stunk before we left the Place, so that we were oblig'd to throw it all away: The Men then said it was impossible to salt any Beef in those hot Countries, so as to preserve it, and would have had us given it over, and ha' gone to the Coast of *New England*, or *New York*, for Provisions; but I soon convinc'd them of the Mistake, and by only using the Caution, *viz.* not to salt up any Beef of those Cattle that had been hunted, we cur'd one hundred and forty Barrels of very good Beef, and such as lasted us a very great while.

I began to be of some Repute among them upon this Occasion, and *Redhand* took me into the Cabin with him to consult upon all Emergencies, and gave me the Name of Captain, though I had then no Command: By this Means I gave him an Account of all my Adventures in the South Seas, and what a prodigious Booty we got there with Captain *Goignet*, the *Frenchman*, and with Captain *Sharp*, and others; encouraging him to make an Attempt that Way, and proposing to him to go away to the *Brasils*, and so round by the Straits of *Magellan*, or *Cape Horn*.

However, in this he was more prudent than I, and told me, that not only the Strength but the Force of his Ship was too small, not but that he had Men enough, as he said very well, but he wanted more Guns, and a better Ship; for indeed the Ship we were in was but a weak crazy Boat for so long a Voyage: So he said he approv'd my Project very well, but that he thought we should try to take some more substantial Vessel for the Business: And says he, if we could but take a good stout Ship, fit to carry thirty Guns, and a Sloop, or Brigantine, he would go with all his Heart.

This I could not but approve of; so we form'd the Scheme of the Design, and he call'd all his Men together, and propos'd it to them, and they all approv'd it with a general Consent; and I had the Honour of being the Contriver of the Voyage. From this Time we resolv'd, some how or other, to get a better Ship under us, and it was not long before an Opportunity presented to our Mind.

Being now upon the Coast of the Island of *Cuba*, we stood away West, coasting the Island, and so went away for *Florida*, where we cruis'd among the Islands, and in the Wake of the Gulph; but nothing presented a great while; at length we spy'd a Sail, which prov'd an *English* homeward bound Ship from *Jamaica*: We immediately chac'd her, and came up with her; she was a stout Ship, and the Captain defended her very well; and had she not been a comber'd deep Ship, being full loaded, so that they could scarce come at their Guns, we should have had our Hands full of her. But when they found what we were, and that, being full of Men, we were resolv'd to be on Board them, and that we had hoisted the black Flag, a Signal that we would give them no Quarter, they began to sink in their Spirits, and soon after cry'd Quarter, offering to yield: *Redhand* would have given them no Quarter, but, according to his usual Practice, would have thrown the Men all into the Sea; but I prevail'd with him to give them Quarter, and good Usage too; and so they yielded; and a very rich Prize it was, only that we knew not what to do with the Cargo.

When we came to consider more seriously the Circumstances we were in by taking this Ship, and what we should do with her, we found, that she was not only deep loaden, but was a very heavy Sailer, and that, in short, she was not such a Ship as we wanted; so, upon long Debate, we resolv'd to take out of her all the Rum, the Indigo, and the Money we could come at, with about twenty Casks of Sugar, and twelve of her Guns, with all the Ammunition, small Arms, Bullets, *&c.* and let her go; which was accordingly done, to the great Joy of the Captain that commanded her: However, we took in her about six thousand Pounds Sterling in Pieces of Eight.

But the next Prize we met, suited us better on all Accounts, being a Ship from *Kingsale* in *Ireland*, loaden with Beef, and Butter, and Beer, for *Barbadoes*; never was Ship more welcome to Men in our Circumstances; this was the very Thing we wanted: We saw the Ship early in the Morning, at about five Leagues Distance, and we was three Days in Chace of her; she stood from us, as if she would have run away for the *Cape de Verd* Islands, and two or three Times we thought she sail'd so well she would have got away from us, but we had always the good Luck to get Sight of her in the Morning: She was about 260 Tun, an *English* Frigat-built Ship, and had 12 Guns on Board, but could carry 20. The Commander was a Quaker, but yet had he been equal to us in Force, it appear'd by his Countenance he would not have been afraid of his Flesh, or have baulk'd using the Carnal Weapon of Offence, *viz.* the Cannon Ball.

We soon made ourselves Master of this Ship when once we came up with him, and he was every Thing that we wanted; so we began to shift our Guns into her, and shifted about 60 Tun of her Butter and Beef into our own Frigate; this made the *Irish* Vessel be a clear Ship, lighter in the Water, and have more Room on Board for Fight, if Occasion offer'd.

When we had the old Quaking Skipper on Board, we ask'd him whether he would go along with us; he gave us no Answer at first; but when we ask'd him again, he return'd, that he did not know whether it might be safe for him to answer the Question: We told him, he should either go or stay, as he pleas'd; Why then, says he, I had rather ye will give me Leave to decline it.

We gave him Leave, and accordingly set him on Shore afterwards at *Nevis*, with ten of his Men; the rest went along with us as Volunteers, except the Carpenter and his Mate, and the Surgeon, those we took by Force: We were now supply'd as well as Heart could wish, had a large Ship in our Possession, with Provisions enough for a little Fleet rather than for a single Ship. So with this Purchase we went away for the *Leeward Islands*, and fain we would have met with some of the *New York* or *New England* Ships, which generally come loaden with Peas, Flower, Pork, *&c.* But it was a long while before any Thing of that Kind presented. We had promis'd the *Irish* Captain to set him on Shore, with his Company, at *Nevis*, but we were not willing till we had done our Business in those Seas, because of giving the Alarm among the Islands; so we went away for St. *Domingo*, and making that Island our Rendezvous, we cruis'd to the Eastward, in Hopes of some Purchase; it was not long before we spy'd a Sail, which prov'd to be a *Burmoodas* Sloop, but bound from *Virginia* or *Maryland*, with Flower, Tobacco, and some Malt; the last a Thing which in particular we knew not what to do with: However, the Flower and Tobacco was very welcome, and the Sloop no less welcome than the rest; for she was a very large Vessel, and carry'd near 60 Tun, and when not so deep loaden, prov'd an excellent Sailer. Soon after this we met with another Sloop, but she was bound from *Barbadoes* to *New England*, with Rum, Sugar, and Molosses: Nothing disturb'd us in taking this Vessel, but that being willing enough to let her go; (for as to the Sugar and Molosses, we had neither Use for them, or Room for them) but to have let her go, had been to give the Alarm to all the Coast of *North America*, and then what we wanted would never come in our Way. Our Captain, justly call'd *Redhand*, or *Bloodyhand*, was presently for dispatching them, that they might tell no Tales; and, indeed, the Necessity of the Method had very near prevail'd; nor did I much interpose here, I know not why, but some of the other Men put him in as good a Way; and that was, to bring the Sloop to an Anchor under the Lee of St. *Domingo*, and take away all her Sails, that she should not stir till we gave her Leave.

We met with no less than five Prizes more here in about 20 Days Cruise, but none of them for our Turn; one of them, indeed, was a Vessel bound to St. *Christopher*'s with *Madera* Wine: We borrow'd about 20 Pipes of the Wine, and let her go. Another was a *New England* built Ship, of about 150 Tun, bound also Home with Sugar and Molosses, which was good for nothing to us; however, we gat near 1000 *l.* on Board her in Pieces of Eight, and taking away her Sails, as before, brought her to an Anchor under the Lee of the Sloop: At last we met with what we wanted, and this was another Ship of about 100 Tun, from *New England*, bound to *Barbadoes*; she had on Board 150 Barrels of Flower, about 350 Barrels of Pease, and 10 Tun of Pork barrell'd up and pickel'd, besides some live Hogs, and some Horses, and six Tun of Beer.

We were now sufficiently provided for; in all those Prizes we got also about 56 Men, who, by Choice and Volunteer, agree'd to go along with us, including the Carpenters and Surgeons, who we oblig'd always to go; so that we were now above 200 Men, two Ships, and the *Burmoodas* Sloop; and giving the other Sloop, and the *New England* homeward bound Ship their Sails again, we let them go; and as to the Malt which we took in the *Burmoodas* Sloop, we gave it the last *New England* Master, who was going to *Barbadoes*.

We gat in all those Ships, besides the Provisions above-mention'd, about 200 Musquets and Pistols, good Store of Cutlasses, about 20 Tun of Iron Shot and Musquet Ball, and 33 Barrels of good Powder, which was all very suitable Things to our Occasions.

We were fully satisfy'd, as we said to one another, now, and concluded that we would stand away to the Windward, as well as we could, towards the Coast of *Africa,* that we might come in the Wind's Way for the Coast of *Brasil;* but our Frigat (I mean that we were first shipp'd in) was yet out upon the Cruise, and not come in; so we came to an Anchor to wait for her, when, behold, the next Morning she came in with full Sail, and a Prize in Tow: She had, it seems, been farther West than her Orders, but had met with a *Spanish* Prize, whither bound, or from whence, I remember we did not enquire, but we found in her, besides Merchandize, which we had no Occasion for, 65000 Pieces of Eight in Silver, some Gold, and two Boxes of Pearl of a good Value; five *Dutch,* or rather *Flemish,* Seamen that were on Board her, were willing to go with us; and as to the rest of the Cargo, we let her go, only finding four of her Guns were Brass, we took them into our Ship, with seven great Jars of Powder, and some Cannon-Shot, and let her go, using the *Spaniards* very civilly.

This was a Piece of meer good Fortune to us, and was so encouraging as nothing could be more, for it set us up, as we may say; for now we thought we could never fail of good Fortune, and we resolv'd, one and all, directly to the South Seas.

It was about the Middle of *August* 1690 that we set forward, and steering E. by S. and E. S. E. for about fifteen Days, with the Winds at N. N. W. variable, we came quickly into the Trade Winds, with a good Offing, to go clear of all the Islands; and so we steer'd directly for *Cape St. Augustin* in the *Brasils,* which we made the 22nd of *September.*

We cruis'd some Time upon the Coast, about the Bay of *All Saints,* and put in once or twice for fresh Water, especially at the Island of St. *John*'s, where we got good Store of Fish, and some Hogs, which, for fresh Provisions, was a great Relief to us: But we gat no Purchase here; for whether it was that their *European* Ships were just come in, or just gone out, we know not, or whether they suspected what we were, and so kept close within their Ports, but in thirteen Days that we ply'd off and on about *Fernambuque,* and about fourteen Days more that we spent in coasting along the *Brasil* Shore to the South, we met not one Ship, neither saw a Sail, except of their Fishing-Boats or small Coasters, who kept close under Shore.

We cross'd the Line here about the latter End of *September,* and found the Air exceeding hot and unwholsome, the Sun being in the *Zenith,* and the Weather very wet and rainy; so we resolv'd to stand away South, without looking for any more Purchase on that Side.

Accordingly we kept on to the South, having tolerable good Weather, and keeping the Shore all the Way in View till we came the Length of St. *Julien,* in the Latitude of 48 Degrees, 22 Minutes South; here we put in again, being the Beginning of *November,* and took in fresh Water, and spent about ten Days, refreshing ourselves, and fitting our Tackle; all which Time we liv'd upon Penguins and Seals, of which we kill'd an innumerable Number; and when we prepar'd to go, we salted up as many Penguins as we found would serve our whole Crew, to eat them twice a Week as long as they would keep.

Here we consulted together about going thro' the Straits of *Magellan;* but I put them quite out of Conceit of making that troublesom and fatieguing Adventure, the Straits being so hazardous, and so many Winds requir'd to pass them; and having assur'd them, that in our Return with *Bat Sharp,* we went away to the Latitude of 55 Degrees 30 Minutes, and then steering due East, came open with the North Seas in five Days Run, they all agreed to go that Way.

On the 20th of November we weigh'd from Port *Julien,* and having a fair Wind at N. E. by E. led it away merrily, till we came into the Latitude of 54, when the Wind veering more Northerly, and then to the N. W. blowing hard, we were driven into 55 Degrees and half, but lying as near as we could to the Wind, we made some Westward Way withal: The 3d of *December* the Wind came up South, and S. E. by S. being now just as it were at the Beginning of the Summer Solstice in that Country.

With this Wind, which blew a fresh Gale, we stood away N. N. W. and soon found ourselves in open Sea, to the West of *America;* upon which we haul'd away N. by E. and N. N. E. and then N. E. when on the 20th of *December* we made the Land, being the Coast of *Chili,* in the Latitude of 41 Degrees, about the Height of *Baldivia;* and we stood out from hence till we made the Isle of St. *Juan Fernando,* where we came to an Anchor, and went on Shore to get fresh Water; also some of our Men went a hunting for Goats, of which we kill'd enough to feed us all with fresh Meat for all the while we stay'd here, which was 22 Days. [*Jan.* 11.]

During this Stay we sent the Sloop out to Cruise, but she came back without seeing any Vessel; after which we order'd her out again more to the North, but she was scarce gone a League, when she made a Signal that she saw a Sail, and that we should come out to help them; accordingly the Frigat put to Sea after them, but making no Signal for us to follow, we lay still, and work'd hard at cleaning our Ship, shifting some of the Rigging, and the like.

We heard no more of them in three Days, which made us repent sorely that we had not gone all three together; but the third Day they came back, tho' without any Prize, as we thought, but gave us an Account that they had chac'd a great Ship and a Bark all Night, and the next Day; that they took the Bark the Evening before, but found little in her of Value; that the great Ship ran on Shore among some Rocks, where they durst not go in after her, but that manning out their Boats, they got on Shore so soon, that the Men belonging to her durst not land; that then they threaten'd to burn the Ship as she lay, and burn them all in her, if they did not come on Shore and surrender: They offer'd to surrender, giving them their Liberty, which our Men would not promise at first; but after some Parly, and arguing on both Sides, our Men agreed thus far, that they should remain Prisoners for so long as we were in those Seas, but that as soon as we came to the Height of *Panama,* or if we resolv'd to return sooner, then they should be set at Liberty; and to these hard Conditions they yielded.

Our Men found in the Ship 6 Brass Guns, 200 Sacks of Meal, some Fruit, and the Value of 160000 Pieces of Eight in Gold of *Chili,* as good as any in the World: It was a glittering Sight, and enough to dazzle the Eyes of those that look'd on it, to see such a Quantity of Gold laid all of a Heap together, and we began to embrace one another in Congratulation of our good Fortune.

We brought the Prisoners all to the Island *Fernando,* where we used them very well, built little Houses for them, gave them Bread, and Meat, and every Thing they wanted; and gave them Powder and Ball to kill Goats with, which they were fully satisfy'd with, and kill'd a great many for us too.

We continu'd to Cruise [*Feb.* 2] hereabout, but without finding any other Prize for near three Weeks more; so we resolv'd to go up as high as *Puna,* the Place where I had been so lucky before; and we assur'd our Prisoners, that in about two Months we would return, and relieve them; but they chose rather to be on Board us, so we took them all in again, and kept on with an easy Sail, at a proper Distance from Land, that we might not be known, and the Alarm given; for as to the Ship which we had taken, and which was stranded among the Rocks, as we had taken all the Men out of her, the People on the Shore, when they should find her, could think no other than that she was driven on Shore by a Storm, and that all the People were drown'd, or all escap'd and gone; and there was no Doubt but that the Ship would beat to Pieces in a very few Days.

We kept, I say, at a Distance from the Shore, to prevent giving the Alarm; but it was a needless Caution, for the Country was all alarm'd on another Account, *viz.* about an 130 bold Buccaneers had made their Way over Land, not at the Isthmus of *Darien,* as usual, but from *Granada,* on the Lake of *Nicaragua* to the North of *Panama,* by which, tho' the Way was longer, and the Country not so practicable as at the ordinary Passage, yet they were unmolested, for they surpriz'd the Country; and whereas the *Spaniards*, looking for them at the old Passage, had drawn Entrenchments, planted Guns, and posted Men at the Passages of the Mountains, to intercept them and cut them off, here they met with no *Spaniards*, nor any other Obstruction in their Way, but coming to the South Sea had Time, undiscover'd, to build themselves Canoes and Periaguas, and did a great deal of Mischief upon the Shore, having been follow'd, among the rest, by 80 Men more, commanded by one *Guilotte*, a *Frenchman*, an old Buccaneer; so that they were now 210 Men; and they were not long at Sea before they took two *Spanish* Barks going from *Guatimala* to *Panama*, loaden with Meal, Coco, and other Provisions; so that now they were a Fleet of two Barks, with several Canoes, and Periaguas, but no Guns, nor any more Ammunition than every one carry'd at first at their Backs.

However, this Troop of Desperadoes had alarm'd all the Coast, and Expresses both by Sea and Land were dispatch'd, to warn the Towns on the Coast to be upon their Guard, all the way from *Panama* to *Lima*; but as they were represented to be only such Freebooters as I have said, Ships of Strength did not desist their Voyages, as they found Occasion, as we shall observe presently: We were now gotten into the Latitude of 10, 11, and 12 Degrees and a Half; but, in our overmuch Caution, had kept out so far to Sea, that we miss'd every Thing which would otherwise have fallen into our Hands; but we were better inform'd quickly, as you shall hear.

Early in the Morning, one of our Men being on the Missen-top, cry'd, A Sail, a Sail; it prov'd to be a small Vessel standing just after us; and as we understood afterwards, did so, believing that we were some of the King's Ships looking after the Buccaneers. As we understood she was a-Stern of us, we shorten'd Sail, and hung out the *Spanish* Colours, separating ourselves, to make him suppose we were cruising for the Buccaneers, and did not look for him; however, when we saw him come forward, but stretching in a little towards the Shore, we took Care to be so much to Starboard that he could not escape us that Way; and when he was a little nearer, the Sloop plainly chac'd him, and in a little Time came up with him, and took him: We had little Goods in the Vessel, their chief Loading being Meal and Corn for *Panama*, but the Master happen'd to have 6000 Pieces of Eight in his Cabin, which was good Booty.

But that which was better than all this to us was, that the Master gave us an Account of two Ships which were behind, and were under Sail for *Lima* or *Panama*; the one having the Revenues of the Kingdom of *Chili*, and the other having a great Quantity of Silver, going from *Puna* to *Lima*, to be forwarded from thence to *Panama*, and that they kept together, being Ships of Force, to protect one another; how they did it we soon saw the Effects of.

Upon this Intelligence we were very joyful, and assur'd the Master, that if we found it so, we would give him his Vessel again, and all his Goods, except his Money, as for That, we told him, such People as we never return'd it any Body: However, the Man's Intelligence prov'd good, for the very next Day, as we were standing South-West, our *Spanish* Colours being out, as above, we spy'd one of the Ships, and soon after the other; we found they had discover'd us also, and that being doubtful what to make of us, they tack'd and stood Eastward to get nearer the Land; we did the like, and as we found there was no letting them go that Way but that we should be sure to lose them, we soon let them know that we were resolv'd to speak with them.

The biggest Ship, which was three Leagues a-Stern of the other, crowded in for the Shore with all the Sail, she could make, and it was easy for us to see that she would escape us; for as she was a great deal farther in with the Land than the other when we first gave Chace, so in about three Hours we saw the Land plain a-Head of us, and that the great Ship would get into Port before we could reach her.

Upon this we stretch'd a-Head with all the Sail we could make, and the Sloop, which crowded also very hard, and out-went us, engag'd the small Ship at least an Hour before we could come up: But she could make little of it, for the *Spanish* Ship having 12 Guns and 6 Patereroes, would have been too many for the Sloop if we had not come up: However, at length, our biggest Ship came up also, and, running up under her Quarter, gave her our whole Broadside; at which she struck immediately, and the *Spaniards* cry'd, *Quarter*, and *Miserecordia*; Upon this, our Sloop's Men enter'd her presently, and secur'd her.

In the Beginning oft his Action, it seems, our *Redhand* Captain was so provok'd at losing the greater Prize, which, as he thought, had all the Money on Board, that he swore he would not spare one of the Dogs, (so he call'd the *Spaniards* in the other Ship) but he was prevented; and it was very happy for the *Spaniards*, that the first Shot the Ship made towards us, just as we were running up to pour in our Broadside, I say, the first Shot took Captain *Redhand* full on the Breast, and shot his Head and one Shoulder off, so that he never spoke more, nor did I find that any one Man in the Ship shew'd the least Concern for him; so certain it is, that Cruelty never recommends any Man among *Englishmen*; no, tho' they have no Share in the suffering under it; but one said, D—n him, let him go, he was a butcherly Dog; another said, D—n him, he was a merciless Son of a B—ch; another said, he was a barbarous Dog, and the like.

But to return to the Prize, being now as certain of the smaller Prize as that we had miss'd the great one, we began to examine what we had got; and it is not easy to give an exact Account of the prodigious Variety of Things we found: In the first Place, were 116 Chests of Pieces of Eight in Specie, 72 Bars of Silver, 15 Bags of wrought Plate, which a Fryer that was on Board would have perswaded us, for the Sake of the Blessed Virgin, to have return'd, being, as he said, consecrated Plate to the Honour of the holy Church, the Virgin *Mary*, and St. *Martin*; but, as it happen'd, he could not perswade us to it; also we found about 60000 Ounces of Gold, some in little Wedges, some in Dust. We found several other Things of Value, but not to be nam'd with the rest.

Being thus made surprisingly rich, we began to think what Course we should steer next; for as the great Ship, which was escap'd, would certainly alarm the Country, we might be sure we should meet with no more Purchase at Sea, and we were not very fond of landing, to attack any Town on Shore. In this Consultation 'tis to be observ'd, that I was, by the unanimous Consent of all the Crew, made Captain of the great Ship, and of the whole Crew; the whole Voyage hither, and every Part of it, having, for some Time before, been chiefly manag'd by my Direction, or at least by my Advice.

The first Thing I propos'd to them all, was, seeing we had met with such good Luck, and that we could not expect much more, and if we stay'd longer in these Seas, should find it very hard to revictual our Ships, and might have our Retreat cut off by *Spanish* Men of war; (five of which we heard were sent out after the other Buccaneers) we should make the best of our Way to the South, and get about into the North Seas, where we were out of all Danger.

In Consequence of this Advice, which was generally approv'd, we stood away directly South; and the Wind blowing pretty fair at N. N. E. a merry Gale, we stood directly for the Isle of *Juan Fernando*, carrying our rich Prize with us.

We arriv'd here the Beginning of *June*, having been just six Months in those Seas. We were surpriz'd, when coming to the Island, we found two Ships at an Anchor close under the Lee of the Rocks, and two little Periaguas farther in, near the Shore; but being resolv'd to see what they were, we found, to our Satisfaction, they were the Buccaneers of whom I have spoken above: The Story is too long to enter upon here; but in short, without Guns, without Ship, and only coming over Land with their Fusees in their Hands, they had rang'd these Seas, had taken several Prizes, and some pretty rich, and had got two pretty handsome Barks, one carry'd six Guns, and the other four; they had shar'd, as they told us, about 400 Pieces of Eight a Man, besides one Thing they had which we were willing to buy of them; they had about 100 Jarrs of Gunpowder, which they took out of a Store Ship going to *Lima.*

If we was glad to meet them, you may be sure they were glad to meet with us, and so we began to sort together as one Company, only they were loth to give over and return, as we were and which we had now resolv'd on.

We were so rich ourselves, and so fully satisfy'd with what we had taken, that we began to be bountiful to our Countrymen; and indeed they dealt so generously with us, that we could not but be inclin'd to do them some Good, for when we talk'd of buying their Gunpowder, they very frankly gave us 50 Jarrs of it *gratis.*

I took this so kindly, that I call'd a little Council among ourselves, and propos'd to send the poor Rogues 50 Barrels of our Beef, which we could very well spare; and our Company agreeing to it, we did so, which made their Hearts glad; for it was very good, and they had not tasted good Salt-beef for a long Time; and with it we sent them two Hogsheads of Rum: This made them so hearty to us, that they sent two of their Company to compliment us, to offer to enter themselves on Board us, and to go with us all the World over.

We did not so readily agree to this at first, because we had no new Enterprize in View; but however, as they sent us Word they had chosen me so unanimously for their Captain, I propos'd to our Men to remove ourselves, and all our Goods, into the great Ship and the Sloop, and so take the honest Fellows into the Fregat, which now had no less than 22 Guns, and would hold them all, and then they might sail with us, or go upon any Adventures of their own, as we should agree.

Accordingly we did so, and gave them that Ship, with all her Guns and Ammunition, but made one of our own Men Captain, which they consented to, and so we became all one Body.

Here also we shar'd our Booty, which was great indeed to a Profusion; and as keeping such a Treasure in every Man's particular private Possession, would have occasion'd Gaming, Quarrelling, and perhaps Thieving and Pilfering, I order'd that so many small Chests should be made as there were Men in the Ship, and every Man's Treasure was nail'd up in these Chests, and the Chests all stow'd in the Hold, with every Man's Name upon his Chest, not to be touch'd but by general Order, and to prevent Gaming, I prevail'd with them to make a Law or Agreement, and everyone to set their Hands to it; by which they agreed, That if any Man play'd for any more Money than he had in his Keeping, the Winner should not be paid whatever the Loser run in Debt, but the Chest containing every Man's Dividend, should be all his own, to be deliver'd whole to him; and the Offender, whenever he left the Ship, if he would pay any Gaming Debts afterward, that was another Case; but such Debts should never be paid while he continu'd in that Company.

By this Means also we secur'd the Ship's Crew keeping together; for if any Man left the Ship now, he was sure to leave about 6000 Pieces of Eight behind him, to be shar'd among the rest of the Ship's Company, which few of them car'd to do.

As we were now all embark'd together, the next Question was, Whither we should go? As for our Crew, we were so rich, that our Men were all for going back again, and so to make off to some of the *Leeward Islands,* that we might get a-Shore privately with our Booty: But as we had shipp'd our new Comrades on Board a good Ship, it would be very hard to oblige them to go back without any Purchace, for that would be to give them a Ship to do them no Good, but to carry them back to *Europe* just as they came out from thence, *viz.* with no Money in their Pockets.

Upon these Considerations we came to this Resolution, That they should go out to Sea and Cruise the Height of *Lima,* and try their Fortune, and that we would stay 60 Days for them at *Juan Fernando.*

Upon this Agreement they went away very joyful, and we fell to work to new rig our Ship, mending our Sails, and cleaning our Bottom. Here we employ'd ourselves a Month very hard at Work; our Carpenters also took down some of the Ship's upper Work, and built it, as we thought, more to the Advantage of Sailing; so that we had more Room within, and yet did not lie so high.

During this Time we had a Tent set up on Shore, and 50 of our Men employ'd themselves wholly in killing Goats and Fowls for our fresh Provisions; and one of our Men understanding we had some Malt left on Board the Ship, which was taken in one of the Prizes, set up a great Kettle on Shore, and went to work to Brewing, and, to our great Satisfaction, brew'd us some very good Beer; but we wanted Bottles to keep it in, after it had stood a while in the Cask.

However, he brew'd us very good Small Beer, for present Use; and instead of Hops he found some wild Wormwood growing on the Island, which gave it no unpleasant Taste, and made it very agreeable to us.

Before the Time was expir'd, our Frigat sent a Sloop to us, which they had taken, to give us Notice that they were in a small Creek near the Mould of the River *Guyaquil,* on the Coast of *Peru,* in the Latitude of 22 Degrees. They had a great Booty in View, there being two Ships in the River of *Guyaquil,* and two more expected to pass by from *Lima,* in which was a great Quantity of Plate; that they waited there for them, and begg'd we would not think the Time long; but that if we should go away, they desir'd that we would fix up a Post, with a Piece of Lead on it, signifying where they should come to us, and wherever it was, East or West, North or South, they would follow us with all the Sail they could make.

A little while after this, they sent another Sloop, which they had taken also; and she brought a vast Treasure in Silver and very rich Goods, which they had got in plundering a Town on the Continent; and they order'd the Sloop to wait for them at the Island where we lay, till their Return: But they were so eager in the Pursuit of their Game, that they could not think of coming back yet, neither could we blame them, they having such great Things in View: So we resolv'd, in Pursuit of our former Resolution, to be gone; and after several Consultations among our selves in what Part of the World we should pitch our Tent, we broke up at first without any Conclusion.

We were all of the Opinion, that our Treasure was so great, that wherever we went, we should be a Prey to the Government of that Place; that it was impossible to go all on Shore, and be conceal'd; and that we should be so jealous of one another, that we should certainly betray one another, everyone for fear of his Fellow, that is to say, for fear the other should tell first. Some therefore propos'd our going about the South Point of Cape *Horne,* and that then, going away to the Gulph of *Mexico,* we should go on Shore at the Bay of *Campeachy,* and from thence disperse ourselves as well as we could, and every one go his own Way.

I was willing enough to have gone thither, because of the Treasure I had left there under Ground; but still I concluded we were (as I have said) too rich to go on Shore any where to separate, for every Man of us had too much Wealth to carry about us; and if we separated, the first Number of Men any of us should meet with, that were strong enough to do it, would take it from us, and so we should but just expose ourselves to be murder'd for that Money we had gotten at so much Hazard.

Some propos'd then our going to the Coast of *Virginia*, and go some on Shore in one Place, and some in another privately, and so travelling to the Sea-Ports where there were most People, we might be conceal'd, and by Degrees reduce our selves to a private Capacity, every one shifting Home as well as they could. This I acknowledge might be done, if we were sure none of us would be false one to another; but while Tales might be told, and the Teller of the Tale was sure to save his own Life and Treasure, and make his Peace at the Expence of his Comrade's, there was no Safety; and they might be sure, that as the Money would render them suspected wherever they came, so they would be examin'd, and what by faltering in their Story, and by being cross-examin'd, kept apart, and the one being made to believe the other had betray'd him, and told all, when indeed he might have said nothing to hurt him, the Truth of Fact would be dragg'd out by Piece-meal, till they would certainly at last come to the Gallows.

These Objections were equally just, to what Nation or Place soever we could think of going: So that upon the whole, we concluded there was no Safety for us but by keeping all together, and going to some Part of the World where we might be strong enough to defend ourselves, or be so conceal'd till we might find out some Way of Escape that we might not now be so well able to think of.

In the Middle of all these Consultations, in which I freely own I was at a Loss, and could not tell which Way to advise, an old Sailor stood up, and told us, if we would be advis'd by him, there was a Part of the World where he had been, where we might all settle ourselves undisturb'd, and live very comfortably and plentifully, till we could find out some Way how to dispose of ourselves better; and that we might easily be strong enough for the Inhabitants, who would at first, perhaps, attack us, but that afterwards they would sort very well with us, and supply us with all Sorts of Provisions very plentifully; and this was the Island of *Madagascar*: He told us we might live very well there. He gave us a large Account of the Country, the Climate, the People, the Plenty of Provisions which was to be had there, especially of black Cattle, of which, he said, there was an infinite Number, and consequently a Plenty of Milk, of which so many other Things was made: In a Word, he read us so many Lectures upon the Goodness of the Place, and the Conveniency of living there, that we were, one and all, eager to go thither, and concluded upon it.

Accordingly, having little left to do, (for we had been in a sailing Posture some Weeks) we left word with the Officer who commanded the Sloop, and with all his Men, that they should come after us to *Madagascar*; and our Men were not wanting to let them know all our Reasons for going thither, as well as the Difficulties we found of going any where else, which had so fully possess'd them with the Hopes of farther Advantage, that they promis'd for the rest that they would all follow us.

However, as we all calculated the Length of the Voyage, and that our Water, and perhaps our Provisions might not hold out so far, but especially our Water, we agreed, that having pass'd Cape *Horn*, and got into the North Seas, we would steer Northward up the East Shore of *America* till we came to St. *Julien*, where we would stay at least fourteen Days to take in Water, and to store ourselves with Seals and Penguins, which would greatly eek out our Ship's Stores; and that then we should cross the great *Atlantick* Ocean in a milder Latitude than if we went directly, and stood immediately over from the Passage about the Cape, which must be, at least, in 55 or 56, and perhaps, as the Weather might be, would be in the Latitude of 60 or 61.

With this Resolution, and under these Measures, we set Sail from the Island of St. *Juan Fernando* the 23d of *September*, (being the same there as our *March* is here) and keeping the Coast of *Chili* on Board, had good Weather for about a Fortnight, [*Octob.* 14.] till we came into the Latitude of 44 Degrees South; when finding the Wind come squally off the Shore from among the Mountains, we were oblig'd to keep farther out at Sea, where the Winds were less uncertain; and some Calms we met with, till about the Middle of *October*, [16.] when the Wind springing up at N. N. W. a pretty moderate Gale, we jogg'd S. E. and S. S. E. till we came into the Latitude of 55 Degrees; and the 16th of *November*, found our selves in 59 Degrees, the Weather exceeding cold and severe. But the Wind holding fair, we held in with the Land, and steering E. S. E. we held that Course till we thought ourselves entirely clear of the Land, and enter'd into the North Sea, or *Atlantick Ocean*; and then changing our Course, we steer'd N. and N. N. E. but the Wind blowing still at N. N. W. a pretty stiff Gale, we could make nothing of it till we made the Land in the Latitude of 52 Degrees; and when we came close under Shore, we found the Winds variable; so we made still N. under the Lee of the Shore, and made the Point of St. *Julien* the 13th of November, having been a Year and seven Days since we parted from thence on our Voyage Outwardbound.

Here we rested ourselves, took in fresh Water, and began to kill Seals and Fowls of several Sorts, but especially Penguins, which this Place is noted for; and here we stay'd, in Hopes our Fregate would arrive, but we heard no News of her; so, at Parting, we set up a Post, with this Inscription, done on a Plate of Lead, with our Names upon the Lead, and these Words;

*Gone to Madagascar, December* 10, 1692.

(Being in that Latitude the longest Day in the Year;) and I doubt not but the Post may stand there still.

From hence we launch'd out into the vast *Atlantick Ocean*, steering our Coast E. by N. and E. N. E. till we had sail'd, by our Account, about 470 Leagues, taking our Meridian Distance, or Departure, from St. *Julian*. And here a strong Gale springing up at S. E. by E. and E. S. E. encreasing afterwards to a violent Storm, we were forc'd by it to the Norward, as high as the *Tropick*; not that it blew a Storm all the while, but it blew so steady, and so very hard, for near 20 Days together, that we were carry'd quite out of our intended Course: After we had weather'd this, we began to recover ourselves again, making still East; and endeavouring to get to the Southward, we had yet another hard Gale of Wind at S. and S. S. E. so strong, that we could make nothing of it at all; whereupon it was resolv'd, if we could, to make the Island of St. *Helena*, which in about three Weeks more we very happily came to, on the 17th of *January*.

It was to our great Satisfaction that we found no Ships at all here, and we resolv'd not by any Means to let the Governor on Shore know our Ship's Name, or any of our Officers Names; and I believe our Men were very true to one another in that Point, but they were not at all shy of letting them know upon what Account we were, *&c.* so that if he could have gotten any of us in his Power, as we were afterwards told he endeavour'd by two or three Ambuscades to do, we should have pass'd our Time but very indifferently; for which, when we went away, we let him know we would not have fail'd to have beat his little Port about his Ears.

We stay'd no longer here than just serv'd to refresh ourselves, and supply our Want of fresh Water; the Wind presenting fair, *Feb.* 2. 1692, we set Sail, and (not to trouble my Story with the Particulars of the Voyage, in which nothing remarkable occur'd) we doubled the Cape the 13th of *March*, and passing on without coming to an Anchor, or discovering ourselves, we made directly to the Island of *Madagascar*, where we arriv'd the 7th of *April*; the Sloop, to our particular Satisfaction, keeping in Company all the Way, and bearing the Sea as well as our Ship upon all Occasions.

To this Time I had met with nothing but good Fortune; Success answer'd every Attempt, and follow'd every Undertaking, and we scarce knew what it was to be disappointed; but we had an Interval of our Fortunes to meet with in this Place: We arriv'd, as above, at the Island on the 13th of *March*, but we did not care to make the South Part of the Island our Retreat; nor was it a proper Place for our Business, which was to take Possession of a private secure Place to make a Refuge of: So after staying some Time where we put in, which was on the Point of Land a little to the South of Cape St. *Augustine*, and taking in Water and Provisions there, we stood away to the North, and keeping the Island in View, went on till we came to the Latitude of 14 Degrees: Here we met with a very terrible Tornado, or *Hurricane*, which, after we had beat the Sea as long as we could, oblig'd us to run directly for the Shore to save our Lives as well as we could, in Hopes of finding some Harbour or Bay where we might run in, or at least might go into smooth Water till the Storm was over.

The Sloop was more put to it than we were in the great Ship, and being oblig'd to run afore it, a little sooner than we did, she serv'd for a Pilot-Boat to us which follow'd; in a Word, she run in under the Lee of a great Head-land, which jetted far out into the Sea, and stood very high also, and came to an Anchor in three Fathom and a half Water: We follow'd her, but not with the same good Luck, tho' we came to an Anchor too, as we thought, safe enough; but the Sea going very high, our Anchor came Home in the Night, and we drove on Shore in the Dark among the Rocks, in spight of all we were able to do.

Thus we lost the most fortunate Ship that ever Man sail'd with; however, making Signals of Distress to the Sloop, and by the Assistance of our own Boat, we sav'd our Lives; and the Storm abating in the Morning, we had Time to save many Things, particularly our Guns, and most of our Ammunition; and, which was more than all the rest, we sav'd our Treasure: Tho' I mention the saving our Guns first, yet they were the last Things we sav'd, being oblig'd to break the upper Deck of the Ship up for them.

Being thus got on Shore, and having built us some Huts for our Conveniency, we had nothing before us but a View of fixing our Habitations in the Country; for tho' we had the Sloop, we could propose little Advantage by her; for as to cruising for Booty among the *Arabians* or *Indians*, we had neither Room, for it or Inclination to it; and as for attacking any *European* Ship, the Sloop was in no Condition to do it, tho' we had all been on Board; for every Body knows that all the Ships trading from *Europe* to the *East-Indies*, were Ships of Force, and too strong for us; so that, in short, we had nothing in View for several Months but how to settle ourselves here, and live as comfortably and as well as we could, till something or other might offer for our Deliverance.

In this Condition we remain'd on Shore above eight Months, during which Time we built us a little Town, and fortify'd it by the Direction of one of our Gunners, who was a very good Engineer, in a very clever and regular Manner, placing a very strong double Palisado round the Foot of our Works, and a very large Ditch without our Palisado, and a third Palisado beyond the Ditch, like a Counterscarp or Cover'd-way; besides this, we rais'd a large Battery next to the Sea, with a Line of 24 Guns plac'd before it, and thus we thought ourselves in a Condition to defend ourselves against any Force that could attempt us in that Part of the World.

And besides all this, the Place on which our Habitation was built, being an Island, there was no coming easily at us by Land.

But I was far from being easy in this Situation of our Affairs; so I made a Proposal to our Men one Day, that tho' we were well enough in our Habitation, and wanted for nothing, yet since we had a Sloop here, and a Boat so good as she was, 'twas Pity she should lye and perish there, but we should send her Abroad, and see what might happen; that perhaps it might be our good Luck to surprise some Ship or other for our Turn, and so we might all go to Sea again: The Proposal was well enough relish'd at first Word, but the great Mischief of all was like to be this, That we should all go together by the Ears upon the Question who should go in her: My secret Design was laid, that I was resolv'd to go in her myself, and that she should not go without me; but when it began to be talk'd of, I discover'd the greatest seeming Resolution not to stir, but to stay with the rest, and take Care of the main Chance, that was to say, the Money.

I found, when they saw that I did not propose to go myself, the Men were much the easier; for at first they began to think it was only a Project of mine to run away from them; and so indeed it was: However, as I did not at first propose to go my self, so when I came to the Proposal of who should go, I made a long Discourse to them of the Obligation they had all to be faithful one to another, and that those who went in the Sloop, ought to consider themselves and those that were with them to be but one Body with those who were left behind; that their whole Concern ought to be to get some good Ship to fetch them off: At last, I concluded, with a Proposal, that who ever went in the Sloop, should leave his Money behind in the common Keeping, as it was before; to remain as a Pledge for his faithful performing the Voyage, and coming back again to the Company; and should faithfully swear that wherever they went, (for as to the Voyage, they were at full Liberty to go whither they would) they would certainly endeavour to get back to *Madagascar*; and that if they were cast away, stranded, taken, or whatever befel them, they should never rest till they got to *Madagascar*, if it was possible.

They all came most readily into this Proposal, for those who should go into the Sloop, but with this Alteration in them, (which was easy to be seen in their Countenances) *viz.* that from that Minute there was no striving who should go, but every Man was willing to stay where they were: This was what I wanted, and I let it rest for two or three Days; when I took Occasion to tell them, that seeing they all were sensible that it was a very good Proposal to send the Sloop out to Sea, and see what they could do for us, I thought it was strange they should so generally shew themselves backward to the Service for fear of parting from their Money; I told them that no Man need be afraid, that the whole Body should agree to take his Money from him without any pretended Offence, much less when he should be Abroad for their Service: But however, as it was my Proposal, and I was always willing to hazard myself for the Good of them all, so I was ready to go on the Conditions I had propos'd to them for others, and I was not afraid to flatter myself with serving them so well Abroad, that they should not grudge to restore me my Share of Money when I came Home, and the like of all those that went with me.

This was so seasonably spoken, and humour'd so well, that it answer'd my Design effectually, and I was voted to go *nemine contradicente;* then I desir'd they would either draw Lots for who and who should go with me, or leave it in my absolute Choice to pick and cull my Men: They had for some Time agreed to the first; and forty Blanks were made for those to whose Lot it should come to draw a Blank to go in the Sloop; but then it was said, this might neither be a fair nor an effectual Choice; for Example, if the needful Number of Officers, and of particular Occupations, should not happen to be lotted out, the Sloop might be oblig'd to go out to Sea without a Surgeon, or without a Carpenter, or without a Cook, and the like: So, upon second Thoughts, it was left to me to name my Men; so I chose me out forty stout Fellows, and among them several who were trusty bold Men, fit for any thing.

Being thus Mann'd, the Sloop rigg'd, and having clear'd her Bottom, and laid in Provisions enough for a long Voyage, we set Sail the 3d of *January* 1694, for the *Cape of Good Hope*. We very honestly left our Money, as I said, behind us, only that we had about the Value of 2000 Pound in Pieces of Eight allow'd us on Board for any Exigence that might happen at Sea.

We made no Stop at the *Cape*, or at St. *Helena*, tho' we pass'd in Sight of it, but stood over to the *Caribbee* Islands directly, and made the Island of *Tobago* the 18th of *February*, where we took in fresh Water, which we stood in great Need of, as you may judge by the Length of the Voyage. We sought no Purchase, for I had fully convinc'd our Men, that our Business was not to appear, as we were used to be, upon the Cruise, but as Traders; and to that End I propos'd to go away to the Bay of *Campeachy*, and load Logwood, under the Pretence of selling of which we might go any where.

It is true, I had another Design here, which was to recover the Money which my Comrade and I had bury'd there; and having the Man on Board with me to whom I had communicated my Design, we found an Opportunity to come at our Money with Privacy enough, having so conceal'd it, as that it would have lain there to the general Conflagration, if we had not come for it our selves.

My next Resolution was to go for *England*, only that I had too many Men, and did not know what to do with them: I told them we could never pretend to go with a Sloop loaden with Logwood to any Place, with 40 Men on Board, but we should be discover'd; but if they would resolve to put 15 or 16 Men on Shore as private Seamen, the rest might do well enough; and if they thought it hard to be set on Shore, I was content to be one, only that I thought it was very reasonable that whoever went on Shore should have some Money given them, and that all should agree to rendezvous in *England*, and so make the best of our Way thither, and there perhaps we might get a good Ship to go fetch off our Comrades and our Money. With this Resolution, sixteen of our Men had three hundred Pieces of Eight a Man given them, and they went off thus; the Sloop stood away North, thro' the Gulph of *Florida*, keeping under the Shore of *Carolina* and *Virginia*; so our Men dropp'd off as if they had deserted the Ship; three of the sixteen run away there, five more went off at Virginia, three at *New York*, three at *Road Island*, and myself and one more at *New England*; and so the Sloop went away for *England* with the rest. I got all my Money on Shore with me, and conceal'd it as well as I could; some I got Bills for, some I bought Molosses with, and turn'd the rest into Gold; and dressing myself not as a common Sailor, but as a Master of a Ketch, which I had lost in the Bay of *Campeachy*, I got Passage on Board one Captain *Guillame*, a *New England* Captain, whose Owner was one Mr. *Johnson* a Merchant, living at *Hackney*, near *London*.

Being at *London*, it was but a very few Months before several of us met again, as I have said we agreed to do. And being true to our first Design of going back to our Comrades, we had several close Conferences about the Manner and Figure in which we should make the Attempt, and we had some very great Difficulties appear'd in our Way: First, to have fitted up a small Vessel, it would be of no Service to us, but be the same Thing as the Sloop we came in; and if we pretended to a great Ship, our Money would not hold out; so we were quite at a Stand in our Councils what to do, or what Course to take, till at length our Money still wasting, we grew less able to execute any Thing we should project.

This made us all desperate; when as desperate Distempers call for desperate Cures, I started a Proposal which pleas'd them all, and this was, that I would endeavour among my Acquaintance, and with what Money I had left, (which was still sixteen or seventeen hundred Pound) to get the Command of a good Ship, bearing a quarter Part, or thereabout, myself; and so having gat into the Ship, and got a Freight, the rest of our Gang should all enter on Board as Seamen, and whatever Voyage we went, or wheresoever we were bound, we would run away with the Ship and all the Goods, and so go to our Friends as we had promis'd.

I made several Attempts of this Kind, and once bought a very good Ship, call'd, *The Griffin*, of one *Snelgrove* a Shipwright, and engag'd the Persons concern'd to hold a Share in her and fit her out, on a Voyage for *Leghorn* and *Venice*; when it was very probable the Cargo, to be shipp'd on Board casually by the Merchant, would be very rich; but Providence, and the good Fortune of the Owner prevented this Bargain, for without any Objection against me, or Discovery of my Design in the least, he told me afterwards his Wife had an ugly Dream or two about the Ship; once, that it was set on Fire by Lightning, and he had lost all he had in it; another Time, that the Men had mutiny'd and conspir'd to kill him; and that his Wife was so averse to his being concern'd in it, that it had always been an unlucky Ship, and that therefore his Mind was chang'd; that he would sell the whole Ship, if I would, but he would not hold any Part of it himself.

Tho' I was very much disappointed at this, yet I put a very good Face upon it, and told him, I was very glad to hear him tell me the Particulars of his Dissatisfaction; for if there was any Thing in Dreams, and his Wife's Dream had any Signification at all, it seem'd to concern me (more than him) who was to go the Voyage, and command the Ship; and whether the Ship was to be burnt, or the Men to mutiny, tho' Part of the Loss might be his, who was to stay on Shore, all the Danger was to be mine, who was to be at Sea in her; and then, as he had said, she had been an unlucky Ship to him, it was very likely she would be so to me; and therefore I thank'd him for the Discovery, and told him I would not meddle with her.

The Man was uneasy, and began to waver in his Resolution, and had it not been for the continu'd Importunities of his Wife, I believe would have come on again; for People generally encline to a Thing that is rejected, when they would reject the same Thing when profer'd: But I knew it was not my Business to let myself be blow'd upon, so I kept to my Resolution, and wholly declin'd that Affair, on Pretence of its having got an ill Name for an unlucky Ship; and that Name stuck so to her, that the Owners could never sell her, and, as I have been inform'd since, were oblig'd to break her up at last.

It was a great while I spent with hunting after a Ship, but was every Way disappointed, till Money grew short, and the Number of my Men lessen'd apace, and at last we were reduc'd to seven, when an Opportunity happen'd in my Way to go Chief-Mate on Board a stout Ship bound from *London* to . . . . . .

[*N. B. In Things so modern, it is no Way convenient to write to you particular Circumstances and Names of Persons, Ships, or Places, because those Things being in themselves criminal, may be call'd up in Question in a judicial Way; and therefore I warn the Reader to observe, that not only all the Names are omitted, but even the Scene of Action in this criminal Part, is not laid exactly as Things were acted; least I should give Justice a Clew to unravel my Story by, which no Body will blame me for avoiding.*]

It is enough to tell the Reader, that being put out to Sea, and being for Conveniency of Wind and Weather come to an Anchor on the Coast of *Spain*, my seven Companions having resolv'd upon our Measures, and having brought three more of the Men to confederate with us, we took up Arms in the middle of the Night, secur'd the Captain, the Gunner, and the Carpenter, and after that, all the rest of the Men, and declar'd our Intention: The Captain and nine Men refus'd to come into our projected Roguery, (for we gave them their Choice to go with us, or go on Shore) so we put them on Shore very civilly, gave the Master his Books, and every Thing he could carry with him; and all the rest of the Men agreed to go along with us.

As I had resolv'd, before I went on Board, upon what I purpos'd to do, so I had laid out all the Money I had left in such Things as I knew I should want, and had caus'd one of my

Men to pretend he was going to ——— to build or buy a Ship there, and that he wanted Freight for a great deal of Cordage, Anchors, eight Guns, Powder and Ball, with about 20 Tun of Lead and other bulky Goods, which were all put on Board as Merchandize.

We had not abundance of Bail Goods on Board, which I was glad of; not that I made any Conscience or Scruple of carrying them away, if the Ship had been full of them; but we had no Market for them: Our first Business was to get a larger Store of Provision on Board than we had, our Voyage being long; and having acquainted the Men with our Design, and promis'd the new Men a Share of the Wealth we had there, which made them very hearty to us, we set Sail: We took in some Beef and Fish, at ——— where we lay fifteen Days, but out of all Reach of the Castle or Fort; and having done our Business, sail'd away for the *Canaries*, where we took in some Butts of Wine, and some fresh Water: With the Guns the Ship had, and those eight I had put on Board as Merchandize, we had then two and thirty Guns mounted, bur were but slenderly Mann'd, tho' we gat four *English* Seamen at the *Canaries*; but we made up the Loss at *Fiall*, where we made bold with three *English* Ships we found, and partly by fair Means, and partly by Force, shipp'd twelve Men there; after which, without any farther Stop for Men or Stores, we kept the Coast of *Africa* on Board 'till we pass'd the Line, and then stood off to St. *Helena*.

Here we took in fresh Water, and some fresh Provisions, and went directly for the *Cape of Good Hope*, which we pass'd, stopping only to fill about 22 Butts of Water, and with a fair Gale enter'd the Sea of *Madagascar*, and sailing up the West Shore, between the Island and the Coast of *Africa*, came to an Anchor over against our Settlement, about two Leagues Distance, and made the Signal of our Arrival, with firing twice seven Guns at the Distance of a Two-Minute Glass between the Seven; when, to our infinite Joy, the Fort answer'd us, and the Long-boat, the same that belong'd to our former Ship, came off to us.

We embrac'd one another with inexpressible Joy, and the next Morning I went on Shore, and our Men brought our Ship safe into Harbour, lying within the Defence of our Platform, and within two Cables length of the Shore, good soft Ground, and in eleven Fathom Water, having been three Months and eighteen Days on the Voyage, and almost three Years absent from the Place.

When I came to look about me here, I found our Men had encreas'd their Number, and that a Vessel which had been cruising, that is to say, Pirating on the Coast of *Arabia*, having seven *Dutchmen*, three *Portuguese*, and five *Englishmen* on Board, had been cast away upon the Northern Shore of that Island, and had been taken up and reliev'd by our Men, and liv'd among them. They told us also of another Crew of *European* Sailors, which lay, as we did, on the Main of the Island, and had lost their Ship and were, as the Islanders told them, above a hundred Men, but we heard nothing who they were.

Some of our Men were dead in the mean Time, I think about three; and the first Thing I did was to call a Muster, and see how Things stood as to Money: I found the Men had been very true to one another; there lay all the Money, in Chests piled up as I left it, and every Man's Money having his Name upon it: Then acquainting the rest with the Promise I had made the Men that came with me, they all agreed to it; so the Money belonging to the dead Men, and to the rest of the forty Men who belong'd to the Sloop, was divided among the Men I brought with me, as well those who join'd at first, as those we took in at the *Cape de Verd*, and the *Canaries*: And the Bails of Goods which we found in the Ship, many of which were valuable for our own Use, we agreed to give them all to the fifteen Men mention'd above, who had been sav'd by our Men, and so to buy what we wanted of those Goods of them, which made their Hearts glad also.

And now we began to consult what Course to take in the World: As for going to *England*, tho' our Men had a great Mind to be there, yet none of them knew how to get thither, notwithstanding I had brought them a Ship; but I, who had now made myself too publick to think any more of *England*, had given over all Views that Way, and began to cast about for farther Adventures; for tho', as I said, we were immensely rich before, yet I abhorr'd lying still, and burying my self alive, as I call'd it, among Savages and Barbarians; besides, some of our Men were young in the Trade, and had seen nothing; and they lay at me every Day not to lie still in a Part of the World where, as they said, such vast Riches might be gain'd; and that the *Dutchmen* and *Englishmen* who were cast away, as above, and who our Mencall'd the *Comelings*, were continually buzzing in my Ears what infinite Wealth was to be got, if I would but make one voyage to the Coast of *Malabar*, *Coromandel*, and the Bay of *Bengale*; nay, the three *Portuguese* Seamen offer'd themselves to attack and bring off one of their biggest Galleons, even out of the Road of *Goa*, on the *Malabar* Coast, the Capital of the *Portuguese* Factories in the *Indies*.

In a Word, I was overcome with these new Proposals, and told the rest of my People, I was resolv'd to go to Sea again, and try my good Fortune; I was sorry I had not another Ship or two, but if ever it lay in my Power to master a good Ship, I would not fail to bring her to them.

While I was thus fitting out upon this new Undertaking, and the Ship lay ready to Sail, and all the Men who were design'd for the Voyage, were on Board, being 85 in Number; among which were all the Men I brought with me, the 15 Comelings, and the rest made up out of our old Number; I say, when I was just upon the Point of setting Sail, we were all surpriz'd just in the Grey of the Morning to spy a Sail at Sea; we knew not what to make of her, but found she was an *European* Ship; that she was not a very large Vessel, yet that she was a Ship of Force too: She seem'd to shorten Sail, as if she look'd out for some Harbour; at first Sight I thought she was *English*; immediately I resolv'd to slip Anchor and Cable and go out to Sea and speak with her, if I could, let her be what she would: As soon as I was got a little clear of the Land, I fir'd a Gun, and spread *English* Colours: She immediately brought too, fir'd three Guns, and mann'd out her Boat with a Flag of Truce: I did the like, and the two Boats spoke to one another in about two Hours, when, to our infinite Joy, we found they were our Comrades who we left in the South Seas, and to whom we gave the Fregate at the Isle of *Juan Fernando*.

Nothing of this Kind could have happen'd more to our mutual Satisfaction, for tho' we had long ago given them over either for Lost, or Lost to us; and we had no great Need of Company, yet we were overjoy'd at meeting, and so were they too.

They were in some Distress for Provisions, and we had Plenty; so we brought their Ship in for them, gave them a present Supply, and when we had help'd them to moor and secure the Ship in the Harbour, we made them lock all their Hatches and Cabins up, and come on Shore, and there we feasted them five or six Days, for we had a Plenty of all Sorts of Provisions, not to be exhausted; and if we had wanted an hundred Head of fat Bullocks, we could have had them for asking for of the Natives, who treated us all along with all possible Courtesy and Freedom in their Way.

The History of the Adventures and Success of these Men, from the Time we left them to the Time of their Arrival at our new Plantation, was our whole Entertainment for some Days. I cannot pretend to give the Particulars by my Memory; but as they came to us *Thieves*, they improv'd in their Calling to a great Degree, and, next to ourselves, had the greatest Success of any of the Buccaneers whose Story has ever been made publick.

I shall not take upon me to vouch the whole Account of their Actions, neither will this

Letter contain a full History of their Adventures; but if the Account which they gave us was true, you may take it thus:

First, that having met with good Success after they left us, and having taken some extraordinary Purchase, as well in some Vessels they took at Sea, as in the Plunder of some Towns on the Shore near *Guyaquil,* as I have already told you, they got Information of a large Ship which was loading the King's Money at *Puna,* and had Orders to sail with it to *Lima,* in order to its being carry'd from thence to *Panama* by the Fleet, under the Convoy of the *Flotilla,* or Squadron of Men of War, which the King's Governor at *Panama* had sent to prevent their being insulted by the Pirates, which they had Intelligence were on the Coast; by which, we suppose, they meant us who were gone, for they could have no Notion of these Men then.

Upon this Intelligence they cruis'd off and on upon the Coast for near a Month, keeping always to the Southward of *Lima,* because they would not fall in the Way of the said *Flotilla,* and so be overpower'd and miss of their Prize: At last they met with what they look'd for, that is to say, they met with the great Ship abovenam'd: But to their great Misfortune and Disappointment, (as they first thought it to be) she had with her a Man of War for her Convoy, and two other Merchant Ships in her Company.

The Buccaneers had with them the Sloop which they first sent to us for our Intelligence, and which they made a little Fregate of, carrying eight Guns, and some Patareroes: They had not long Time to consult, but in short they resolv'd to double man the Sloop, and let her attack the great Merchant-Ship, while the Fregate, which was the whole of their Fleet, held the Man of War in Play, or at least kept him from assisting her.

According to this Resolution, they put 50 Men on Board the Sloop, which was, in short, almost as many as would stand upon her Deck one by another; and with this Force they attack'd the great Merchant-Ship, which, besides its being well mann'd, had 16 good Guns, and about 30 Men on Board. While the Sloop thus began the unequal Fight, the Man of War bore down upon her to succour the Ship under her Convoy, but the Fregate thrusting in between, engag'd the Man of War, and began a very warm Fight with her, for the Man of War had both more Guns and more Men than the Fregate after she had parted with 50 Men on Board the Sloop: While the two Men of War, as we may now call them, were thus engag'd, the Sloop was in great Danger of being worsted by the Merchant-Ship, for the Force was too much for her, the Ship was great, and her Men fought a desperate and close Fight: Twice the Sloop-Men enter'd her, and were beaten off, and about nine of their Men kill'd, several other wounded, and an unlucky Shot taking the Sloop between Wind and Water, she was oblig'd to fall a-Stern, and heel her over to stop the Leek; during which the *Spaniards* steer'd away to assist the Man of War, and pour'd her Broadside in upon the Fregate, which tho' but small, yet at a Time when she lay Yard-arm and Yard-arm close by the Side of the *Spanish* Man of War, was a great Extremity; however, the Fregate return'd her Broadside, and therewith made her sheer off, and, which was worse, shot her Main-mast thro', tho' it did not come presently by the Board.

During this Time, the Sloop having many Hands, had stopp'd the Leak, was brought to rights again, and came up again to the Engagement, and at the first Broadside had the good Luck to bring the Ship's Foremast by the Board, and thereby disabled her; but could not for all that lay her athwart, or carry her by Boarding, so that the Case began to be very doubtful; at which, the Captain of the Sloop, finding the Merchant Ship was disabled, and could not get away from them, resolv'd to leave her a while and assist the Fregate; which he did, and running a Longside our Fregate, he fairly laid the Man of War on Board just thwart his Hawser; and besides firing into her with his great Shot, he very fairly set her on Fire; and it was a great Chance but that they had been all three burnt together, but our Men helpt the *Spaniards* themselves to put out the Fire, and after some Time master'd it: But the *Spaniards* were in such a terrible Fright at the Apprehension of the Fire, that they made little Resistance afterwards, and in short, in about an Hour's Fight more, the *Spanish* Man of War struck, and was taken; and after that the Merchant Ship also, with all the Wealth that was in her: And thus their Victory was as compleat as it was unexpected.

The Captain of the *Spanish* Man of War was kill'd in the Fight, and about 36 of his Men, and most of the rest wounded, which it seems happen'd upon the Sloop's lying athwart her. This Man of War was a new Ship, and with some Alteration in her upper Work, made a very good Fregate for them, and they afterwards quitted their own Ship, and went all on Board the *Spanish* Ship, taking out the Main-mast of their own Ship, and making a new Fore-mast for the *Spanish* Ship, because her Fore-mast was also weaken'd with some Shot in her; this, however, cost them a great deal of Labour and Difficulty, and also some Time, when they came to a certain Creek, where they all went on Shore, and refresh'd themselves a while.

But if the taking the Man of War was an unexpected Victory to them, the Wealth of the Prize was much more so; for they found an amazing Treasure on Board her, both in Silver and Gold; and the Account they gave me was but imperfect, but I think they calculated the Pieces of Eight to be about 13 Tun in Weight, besides that they had 5 small Chests of Gold, some Emeralds, and, in a Word, a prodigious Booty.

They were not, however, so modest in their Prosperity as we were; for they never knew when to have done, but they must Cruise again to the Northward for more Booty, when to their great Surprize, they fell in with the Flotilla or Squadron of Men of War, which they had so studiously avoided before, and were so surrounded by them, that there was no Remedy but they must fight, and that in a Kind of Desperation, having no Prospect now but to sell their Lives as dear as they could.

This unlucky Accident befel them before they had chang'd their ship, so that they had now the Sloop and both the Men of War in Company, but they were but thinly mann'd; and as for the Booty, the greater Part of it was on Board the Sloop, that is to say, all the Gold and Emeralds, and near half the Silver.

When they saw the Necessity of fighting, they order'd the Sloop, if possible, to keep to Windward, that so she might as Night come on, make the best of her Way, and escape; but a *Spanish* Fregate of 18 Guns tended her so close, and sail'd so well, that the Sloop could by no Means get away from the rest; so she made up close to the Buccaneers Fregate, and maintain'd a Fight as well as she could, till in the Dusk of the Evening the *Spaniards* boarded and took her, but most of her Men gat away in her Boat, and some by swimming on Board the other Ship: They only left in her five wounded *Englishmen*, and six *Spanish* Negroes. The five *English* the barbarous *Spaniards* hang'd up immediately, wounded as they were.

This was good Notice to the other Men to tell them what they were to expect, and made them fight like desperate Men till Night, and kill'd the *Spaniards* a great many Men. It prov'd a very dark rainy Night, so that the *Spaniards* were oblig'd by Necessity to give over the Fight till the next Day, endeavouring, in the mean time, to keep as near them as they could: But the Buccaneers concerting their Measures where they should meet, resolv'd to make Use of the Darkness of the Night to get off if they could; and the Wind springing up a fresh Gale at S. S. W. they chang'd their Course, and, with all the Sail they could make, stood away to the N. N. W. slanting it to Seawards as nigh the Wind as they could; and getting clear away from the *Spaniards,* who they never saw more, they made no Stay till they pass'd the Line, and arriv'd in about 22 Days Sail on the Coast of *California,* where they were quite out of the Way of all Enquiry and Search of the *Spaniards.*

Here it was they chang'd their Ship, as I said, and quitting their own Vessel, they went all on Board the *Spanish* Man of War, fitting up her Masts and Rigging, as I have said, and taking out all the Guns, Stores, *&c.* of their own Ship, so that they had now a stout Ship under them, carrying 40 Guns, (for so many they made her carry) and well furnish'd with all Things; and tho' they had lost so great a Part of their Booty, yet they had still left a vast Wealth, being six or seven Tun of Silver, besides what they had gotten before.

With this Booty, and regretting heartily they had not practis'd the same Moderation before, they resolv'd now to be satisfy'd, and make the best of their Way to the Island of *Juan Fernando*; where keeping at a great Distance from the Shore, they safely arriv'd, in about two Months Voyage, having met with some contrary Winds by the Way.

However, here they found the other Sloop which they had sent in with their first Booty, to wait for them: And here understanding that we were gone for St. *Julien*, they resolv'd, (since the Time was so long gone that they could not expect to find us again) that they would have t'other Touch with the *Spaniards*, cost what it would. And accordingly, having first bury'd the most Part of their Money in the Ground, on Shore in the Island, and having revictual'd their Ship in the best Manner they could in that barren Island, away they went to Sea.

They beat about on the South of the Line all up the Coast of *Chili*, and Part of *Peru*, till they came to the Height of *Lima* itself.

They met with several Ships, and took several, but they were loaden chiefly with Lumber or Provisions, except that in one Vessel they took between 40 and 50000 Pieces of Eight, and in another 75000. They soon inform'd themselves that the *Spanish* Men of War were gone out of those Seas up to *Panama*, to boast of their good Fortune, and carry Home their Prize; and this made them the bolder. But tho' they spent near five Months in this second Cruise, they met with nothing considerable; the *Spaniards* being every where alarm'd, and having Notice of them, so that nothing stirr'd Abroad.

Tir'd then with their long Cruise, and out of Hope of more Booty, they began to look Homeward, and to say to one another that they had enough; so, in a Word, they came back to *Juan Fernando*, and there furnishing themselves as well as they could with Provisions, and not forgeting to take their Treasure on Board with them, they set forward again to the South; and after a very bad Voyage in rounding the *Terra del Fuego*, being driven to the Latitude of 65 Degrees, where they felt Extremity of Cold, they at length obtain'd a more favourable Wind, *viz.* at S. and S. S. E; with which, steering to the North, they came into a milder Sea and a milder Coast, and at length arriv'd at *Port St. Julien*, where, to their great Joy, they found the Post or Cross erected by us; and understanding that we were gone to *Madagascar*, and that we would be sure to remain there to hear from them, and withal that we had been gone there near two Year, they resolv'd to follow us.

Here they staid, it seems, almost half a Year, partly fitting and altering their Ship, partly wearing out the Winter Season, and waiting for milder Weather; and having victuall'd their Ship in but a very ordinary Manner for so long a Run, *viz.* only with Seals Flesh and Penguins, and some Deer they kill'd in the Country, they at last launch'd out, and crossing the great *Atlantick Ocean*, they made the *Cape of Good Hope* in about 76 Days, having been put to very great Distresses in that Time for Want of Food, all their Seals Flesh and Penguins growing nauseous and stinking in little less than half the Time of their Voyage; so that they had nothing to subsist on for seven and twenty Days, but a little Quantity of dry'd Venison which they kill'd on Shore, about the Quantity of 3 Barrels of *English* Beef, and some Bread; and when they came to the *Cape of Good Hope*, they gat some small Supply, but it being soon perceiv'd on Shore what they were, they were glad to be gone as soon as they had fill'd their Casks with Water, and gat but a very little Provisions; so they made to the Coast of *Natal* on the South East Point of *Africa*, and there they gat more fresh Provisions, such as Veal, Milk,

Goats-Flesh, some tolerable Butter, and very good Beef: And this held them out till they found us in the North Part of *Madagascar*, as above.

We staid about a Fortnight in our Port, and in a sailing Posture, just as if we had been Wind-bound, meerly to congratulate and make merry with our new-come Friends, when I resolv'd to leave them there, and set Sail; which I did with a Westerly Wind, keeping away North till I came into the Latitude of seven Degrees North; so coasting along the *Arabian* Coast E. N. E. towards the Gulph of Persia, in the Cruise I met with two *Persian* Barks loaden with Rice; one of which I mann'd and sent away to *Madagascar*, and the other I took for our own Ship's Use. This Bark came safe to my new Colony, and was a very agreeable Prize to them; I think verily almost as agreeable as if it had been loaded with Pieces of Eight, for they had been without Bread a great while; and this was a double Benefit to them, for they fitted up this Bark, which carry'd about 55 Tun, and went away to the Gulph of *Persia* in her to buy Rice, and brought two or three *Freights* of that which was very good.

In this Time I pursu'd my Voyage, coasted the whole *Malabar* Shore, and met with no Purchase but a great *Portugal East-India* Ship, which I chac'd into *Goa,* where she got out of my Reach: I took several small Vessels and Barks, but little of Value in them, till I enter'd the great Bay of *Bengale,* when I began to look about me with more Expectation of Success, tho' without Prospect of what happen'd.

I cruis'd here about two Months, finding nothing worth while; so I stood away to a Port on the North Point of the Isle of *Sumatra,* where I made no Stay; for here I gat News that two large Ships, belonging to the Great Mogul, were expected to cross the Bay from *Hugely* in the *Ganges* to the Country of the King of *Pegu,* being to carry the Grandaughter of the Great Mogul to *Pegu,* who was to be marry'd to the King of that Country, with all her Retinue, Jewels, and Wealth.

This was a Booty worth watching for, tho' it had been some Months longer; so I refolv'd that we would go and Cruise off of Point *Negaris,* on the East Side of the Bay, near *Diamond Isle*; and here we ply'd off and on for three Weeks, and began to despair of Success; but the Knowledge of the Booty we expected spurr'd us on, and we waited with great Patience, for we knew the Prize would be immensely rich.

At length we spy'd three Ships coming right up to us with the Wind; we could easily see they were not *Europeans* by their Sails, and began to prepare ourselves for a Prize, not for a Fight; but were a little disappointed, when we found the first Ship full of Guns, and full of Soldiers, and in Condition, had she been manag'd by *English* Sailors, to have fought two such Ships as ours were; however, we resolv'd to attack her if she had been full of Devils as she was full of Men.

Accordingly, when we came near them, we fir'd a Gun with Shot as a Challenge; they fir'd again immediately three or four Guns; but fir'd them so confusedly that we could easily see they did not understand their Business; when we consider'd how to lay them on Board, and so to come thwart them, if we could; but falling, for want of Wind, open to them, we gave them a fair Broadside; we could easily see, by the Confusion that was on Board, that they were frighted out of their Wits; they fir'd here a Gun and there a Gun, and some on that Side that was from us, as well as those that were next to us. The next Thing we did was to lay them on Board, which we did presently, and then gave them a Volley of our Small-shot, which, as they stood so thick, kill'd a great many of them, and made all the rest run down under their Hatches, crying out like Creatures bewitch'd: In a Word, we presently took the Ship, and having secur'd her Men, we chac'd the other two: One was chiefly fill'd with Women, and the other with Lumber. Upon the Whole, as the Grandaughter of the Great

Mogul was our Prize in the first Ship, so, in the second was her Women, or, in a Word, her Houshold, her Eunuchs, all the Necessaries of her Wardrobe, of her Stables, and of her Kitchin; and in the last, great Quantities of Houshold-stuff, and Things less costly, tho' not less useful.

But the first was the main Prize. When my Men had enter'd and master'd the Ship, one of our Lieutenants call'd for me, and accordingly I jump'd on Board; he told me, he thought no Body but I ought to go into the great Cabin, or, at least, no Body should go there before me; for that the Lady herself and all her Attendance was there, and he fear'd the Men were so heated they would murder them all, or do worse.

I immediately went to the great Cabin-door, taking the Lieutenant that call'd me, along with me, and caus'd the Cabin-door to be open'd: But such a Sight of Glory and Misery was never seen by Buccaneer before; the Queen (for such she was to have been) was all in Gold and Silver, but frighted; and crying, and at the Sight of me she appear'd trembling, and just as if she was going to die. She sate on the Side of a kind of a Bed like a Couch with no Canopy over it, or any Covering, only made to lie down upon; she was, in a Manner, cover'd with Diamonds, and I, like a true Pirate, soon let her see that I had more Mind to the Jewels than to the Lady.

However, before I touch'd her, I order'd the Lieutenant to place a Guard at the Cabin-door; and fastening the Door, shut us both in, which he did: The Lady was young, and, I suppose, in their Country Esteem, very handsome, but she was not very much so in my Thoughts: At first, her Fright, and the Danger she thought she was in of being kill'd, taught her to do every Thing that she thought might interpose between her and Danger; and that was to take off her Jewels as fast as she could, and give them to me; and I, without any great Compliment, took them as fast as she gave them me, and put them into my Pocket, taking no great Notice of them, or of her, which frighted her worse than all the rest, and she said something which I could not understand; however, two of the other Ladies came, all crying, and kneel'd down to me with their Hands lifted up: What they meant I knew not at first, but by their Gestures and Pointings I found at last it was to beg the young Queen's Life, and that I would not kill her.

I have heard that it has been reported in *England* that I ravish'd this Lady, and then used her most barbarously; but they wrong me, for I never offer'd any Thing of that Kind to her, I assure you; nay, I was so far from being inclin'd to it, that I did not like her; and there was one of her Ladies who I found much more agreeable to me, and who I was afterwards something free with, but not even with her either by Force, or by Way of Ravishing.

We did, indeed, ravish them of all their Wealth, for that was what we wanted, not the Women; nor was there any other Ravishing among those in the great Cabin, that I can assure you: As for the Ship where the Women of inferior Rank were, and who were in Number almost two hundred, I cannot answer for what might happen in the first Heat; but even there, after the first Heat of our Men was over, what was done, was done quietly, for I have heard some of the Men say, that there was not a Woman among them but what was lain with four or five Times over, that is to say, by so many several Men; for as the Women made no Opposition, so the Men even took those that were next them, without Ceremony, when and where Opportunity offer'd.

When the three Ladies kneel'd down to me, and as soon as I understood what it was for, I let them know I would not hurt the Queen, nor let any one else hurt her, but that she must give me all her Jewels and Money: Upon this they acquainted her that I would save her Life; and no sooner had they assur'd her of that, but she got up, smiling, and went to a fine *Indian* Cabinet, and open'd a private Drawer, from whence she took another little Thing full of little square Drawers and Holes; this she brings to me in her Hand, and offer'd to kneel down to give it me. This innocent Usage began to rouse some Good-Nature in me, (tho' I never had much) and I would not let her kneel; but sitting down myself on the Side of her Couch or Bed, made a Motion to her to sit down too: But here she was frighted again, it seems, at what I had no Thought of; for sitting on her Bed, she thought I would pull her down to lie with her, and so did all her Women too; for they began to hold their Hands before their Faces, which, as I understood afterwards, was that they might not see me turn up their Queen: But as I did not offer any Thing of that Kind, only made her sit down by me, they began all to be easier after some Time, and she gave me the little Box or Casket, I know not what to call it, but it was full of invaluable Jewels. I have them still in my Keeping, and wish they were safe in *England*; for I doubt not but some of them are fit to be plac'd on the King's Crown.

Being Master of this Treasure, I was very willing to be good-humour'd to the Persons; so I went out of the Cabin, and caus'd the Women to be left alone, causing the Guard to be kept still, that they might receive no more Injury than I would do them myself.

After I had been out of the Cabin some Time, a Slave of the Womens came to me, and made Sign to me that the Queen would speak with me again. I made Signs back, that I would come and dine with her Majesty: And accordingly I order'd that her Servants should prepare her Dinner, and carry it in, and then call me. They provided her Repast after the usual Manner, and when she saw it brought in, she appear'd pleas'd, and more, when she saw me come in after it; for she was exceedingly pleas'd that I had caus'd a Guard to keep the rest of my Men from her; and she had, it seems, been told how rude they had been to some of the Women that belong'd to her.

When I came in, she rose up, and paid me such Respect as I did not well know how to receive, and not in the least how to return. If she had understood *English*, I could have said plainly, and in good rough Words, Madam, be easy, we are rude rough-hewn Fellows, but none of our Men should hurt you, or touch you; I will be your Guard and Protection; we are for Money, indeed and we shall take what you have, but we will do you no other Harm. But as I could not talk thus to her, I scarce knew what to say; but I sate down, and made Signs to have her sit down and eat, which she did, but with so much Ceremony, that I did not know well what to do with it.

After we had eaten, she rose up again, and drinking some Water out of a *China* Cup, sate her down on the Side of the Couch, as before: When she saw I had done eating, she went then to another Cabinet, and pulling out a Drawer, she brought it to me; it was full of small Pieces of Gold Coin of *Pegu*, about as big as an *English* Half Guinea, and I think there were three thousand of them. She open'd several other Drawers, and shew'd me the Wealth that was in them and then gave me the Key of the Whole.

We had revell'd thus all Day, and Part of the next Day, in a bottomless Sea of Riches, when my Lieutenant began to tell me, we must consider what to do with our Prisoners, and the Ships, for that there was no subsisting in that Manner; besides, he hinted privately, that the Men would be ruin'd, by lying with the Women in the other Ship, where all Sorts of Liberty was both given and taken: Upon this we call'd a short Council, and concluded to carry the great Ship away with us, but to put all the Prisoners, Queen, Ladies, and all the rest, into the lesser Vessels, and let them go: And so far was I from ravishing this Lady, as I hear is reported of me, that tho' I might rifle her of every Thing else, yet I assure you I let her go untouch'd for me, or, as I am satisfy'd, for any one, of my Men; nay, when we dismiss'd them, we gave her Leave to take a great many Things of Value with her, which she would have been plunder'd of, if I had not been so careful of her.

We had now Wealth enough, not only to make us rich, but almost to have made a Nation rich; and to tell you the Truth, considering the costly Things we took here, which we did not know the Value of, and besides Gold, and Silver, and Jewels, I say, we never knew how rich we were; besides which, we had a great Quantity of Bales of Goods, as well Calicoes as wrought Silks; which being for Sale, were, perhaps, as a Cargo of Goods to answer the Bills which might be drawn upon them for the Account of the Bride's Portion; all which fell into our Hands, with a great Sum in Silver Coin, too big to talk of among *Englishmen*, especially while I am living, for Reasons which I may give you hereafter.

I had nothing to do now but to think of coming back to *Madagascar*, so we made the best of our Way; only that, to make us quite distracted without other Joy, we took in our Way a small Bark loaden with Arack and Rice, which was good Sawce to our other Purchace; for if the Women made our Men drunk before, this *Arack* made them quite mad; and they had so little Government of themselves with it, that I think it might be said, the whole Ship's Crew was drunk for above a Fortnight together, till six or seven of them kill'd themselves; two fell overboard and were drown'd, and several more fell into raging Fevers, and it was a Wonder, in the whole, they were not all kill'd with it.

But, to make short of the Story as we did of the Voyage, we had a very pleasant Voyage, except those Disasters, and we came safe back to our Comrades at *Madagascar*, having been absent in all about seven Months.

We found them in very good Health, and longing to hear from us; and we were, you may be assur'd, welcome to them; for now we had amass'd such a Treasure as no Society of Men ever possess'd in this World before us, neither could we ever bring it to an Estimation, for we could not bring particular Things to a just Valuation.

We liv'd now and enjoy'd ourselves in full Security; for tho' some of the *European* Nations, and perhaps all of them had heard of us; yet they heard such formidable Things of us, such terrible Stories of our great Strength, as well as of our great Wealth, that they had no Thought of undertaking any Thing against us; for, as I have understood, they were told at *London*, that we were no less than 5000 Men; that we had built a regular Fortress for our Defence by Land, and that we had 20 Sail of Ships; and I have been told that in *France* they have heard the same Thing: But nothing of all this was ever true, any more than it was true, that we offer'd ten Millions to the Government of *England* for our Pardon.

It is true, that had the Queen sent any Intimation to us of a Pardon, and that we should have been receiv'd to Grace at Home, we should all have very willingly embrac'd it; for we had Money enough to have encourag'd us all to live honest; and if we had been ask'd for a Million of Pieces of Eight, or a Million of Pounds Sterling, to have purchas'd our Pardon, we should have been very ready to have comply'd with it; for we really knew not what to do with ourselves, or with our Wealth; and the only Thing we had now before us, was to consider what Method to take for getting Home, if possible, to our own Country with our Wealth, or at least with such Part of it as would secure us easy and comfortable Lives; and, for my own Part, I resolv'd, if I could, to make full Satisfaction to all the Persons who I had wrong'd in *England*, I mean by that, such People as I had injur'd by running away with the Ship; as well the Owners, and the Master or Captain, who I set a-shore in *Spain*, as the Merchant whose Goods I had taken with the Ship; and I was daily forming Schemes in my Thoughts how to bring this to pass: But we all concluded that it was impossible for us to accomplish our Desires as to that Part, seeing the Fact of our Piracy was now so publick all over the World, that there was not any Nation in the World that would receive us, or any of us; but would immediately seize on our Wealth, and execute us for Pirates and Robbers of all Nations.

This was confirm'd to us after some Time, with all the Particulars, as it is now understood in *Europe*; for as the Fame of our Wealth and Power was such, that it made all the World afraid of us, so it brought some of the like Sort with our selves to join with us from all Parts of the World; and particularly, we had a Bark, and 60 Men of all Nations, from *Martinico*, who had been cruising in the Gulph of *Florida*, came over to us, to try if they could mend their Fortunes; and these went afterwards to the Gulph of *Persia*, where they took some Prizes, and return'd to us again. We had after this three Pirate Ships came to us, most *English*, who had done some Exploits on the Coast of *Guinea*, had made several good Prizes, and were all tolerably rich.

As these People came and shelter'd with us, so they came and went as they would, and sometimes some of our Men went with them, sometimes theirs staid with us: But by that Coming and Going our Men found Ways and Means to convey themselves away, some one Way, some another. For I should have told you at first, that after we had such Intelligence from *England*, *viz.* that they knew of all our successful Enterprizes, and that there was no Hopes of our returning, especially of mine and some other Men who were known: I say, after this we call'd a general Council to consider what to do; and there, one and all, we concluded that we liv'd very happy where we were; that if any of us had a Mind to venture to get away to any Part of the World, none should hinder them, but that else we would continue where we were; and that the first Opportunity we had we would cruise upon the *English East India* Ships, and do them what Spoil we could, fancying that some Time or other they would proclaim a Pardon to us, if we would come in; and if they did, then we would accept of it.

Under these Circumstances we remain'd here, off and on, first and last, above three Year more; during which Time our Number encreas'd so, especially at first, that we were once eight hundred Men, stout brave Fellows, and as good Sailors as any in the World. Our Number decreas'd afterwards upon several Occasions; such as the going Abroad to Cruise, wandering to the South Part of the Island, (as above) getting on Board *European* Ships, and the like.

After I perceiv'd that a great many of our Men were gone off, and had carry'd their Wealth with them, I began to cast about in my own Thoughts how I should make my Way Home also: Innumerable Difficulties presented to my View; when at last, an Account of some of our Mens Escape into *Persia* encourag'd me. The Story was this: One of the small Barks we had taken, went to *Guzaratte* to get Rice, and having secur'd a Cargo, but not loaded it, ten of our Men resolv'd to attempt their Escape; and accordingly they drest themselves like Merchant-Strangers, and bought several Sorts of Goods there, such as an *Englishman*, who they found there, assisted them to buy; and with their Bales, (but in them pack'd up all the rest of their Money) they went up to *Bassora* in the Gulph of *Persia*, and so travell'd as Merchants with the Caravan to *Aleppo*, and we never heard any more of them, but that they went clean off with all their Cargo.

This fill'd my Head with Schemes for my own Deliverance; but however, it was a Year more before I attempted any Thing, and not till I found that many of our Men shifted off, some and some, nor did any of them miscarry; some went one Way, some another; some lost their Money, and some sav'd it; nay, some carry'd it away with them, and some left it behind them: As for me, I discover'd my Intentions to no Body, but made them all believe I would stay here till some of them should come and fetch me off, and pretended to make every Man that went off promise to come for me, if it ever was in his Power, and gave every one of them Signals to make for me, when they came back, upon which I would certainly come off to them. At the same Time nothing was more certain, than that I intended from the Beginning to get away from the Island, as soon as I could any Way make my Way with Safety to any Part of the World.

It was still above two Years after this that I remain'd in the Island; nor could I, in all that Time, find any probable Means for removing my self with Safety.

One of the Ways I thought to have made my Escape was this: I went to Sea in a Long-boat a fishing, (as we often did) and having a Sail to the Boat, we were out two or three Days together; at length it came into my Thoughts that we might Cruise about the Island in this Long-boat, a great Way, and perhaps some Adventure might happen to us which we might make something of; so I told them I had a Mind to make a Voyage with the Long-boat to see what would happen.

To this Purpose we built upon her, made a State-Room in the Middle, and clapt four Patareroes upon her Gunnel, and away we went, being sixteen stout Fellows in the Boat, not reckoning my self: Thus we ran away, as it were, from the rest of our Crew, tho' not a Man of us knew our own Minds as to whither we were going, or upon what Design. In this Frolick we ran South quite away to the Bay of St. *Angustine*'s, in the Latitude of 24 Degrees, where the Ships from *Europe* often put in for Water and Provisions.

Here we put in, not knowing well what to do next; I thought myself disappointed very much that we saw no *European* Ship here, tho' afterwards I saw my Mistake, and found that it was better for us that we were in that Port first: We went boldly on Shore; for as to the Natives, we understood how to manage them well enough, knew all their Customs, and the Manner of their treating with Strangers as to Peace or War; their Temper, and how to oblige them, or behave if they were disoblig'd; so we went, I say, boldly on Shore, and there we began to chaffer with them for some Provisions, such as we wanted.

We had not been here above two or three Days, but that, early in the Morning, the Weather thick and haizy, we heard several Guns fire at Sea; we were not at a Loss to know what they meant, and that it was certainly some *European* Ships coming in, and who gave the Signal to one another that they had made the Land, which they could easily see from the Sea, tho' we, who were also within the Bay, could not see them from the Shore: However, in a few Hours, the Weather clearing up, wet saw plainly five large Ships, three with *English* Colours, and two with *Dutch*, standing into the Bay, and in about four or five Hours more they came to an Anchor.

A little while after they were come to an Anchor, their Boats began to come on Shore to the usual Watering-place to fill their Casks; and while they were doing that, the rest of the Men look'd about them a little, as usual, tho' at first they did not stir very far from their Boats.

I had now a nice Game to play, as any Man in the World ever had: It was absolutely necessary for us to speak with these Men; and yet how to speak with them, and not have them speak with us in a Manner that we should not like, that was the main Point: It was with a great deal of Impatience that we lay still one whole Day, and saw their Boats come on Shore, and go on Board again, and we were so irresolute all the while, that we knew not what to do; at last I told my Men, it was absolutely necessary we should speak with them, and seeing we could not agree upon the Method how to do it friendly and fairly, I was resolv'd to do it by Force, and that if they would take my Advice, we would place ourselves in Ambuscade upon the Land somewhere, that we might see them when they were on Shore, and the first Man that straggled from the rest we would clap in upon and seize him, and three or four of them if we could. As for our Boat, we had secur'd it in a Creek three or four Miles up the Country, where it was secure enough out of their Reach or Knowledge.

With this Resolution we plac'd ourselves in two Gangs; eleven of us in one Place, and only three of us in another, and very close we lay: The Place we chose for our Ambuscade was on the Side of a rising Ground almost a Mile from the Watering-place, but where we could see them all come towards the Shore, and see them if they did but set their Foot on Shore.

As we understood afterwards, they had the Knowledge of our being upon the Island, but knew not in what Part of it, and were therefore very cautious and wary how they went on Shore, and came all very well arm'd. This gave us a new Difficulty, for in the very first Excursion that any of them made from the Watering-place, there was not less than twenty of them, all well arm'd, and they pass'd by in our Sight; but as we were out of their Sight we were all very well pleas'd with seeing them go by, and being not oblig'd to meddle with them, or show our selves.

But we had not long lain in this Circumstance, but, by what Occasion we knew not, five of the Gentlemen Tarrs were pleas'd to be willing to go no farther with their Companions; and thinking all safe behind them, because they had found no Disturbance in their going out, came back the same Way, straggling without any Guard or Regard.

I thought now was our Time to show our selves; so taking them as they came by the Place where we lay in Ambuscade, we plac'd ourselves just in their Way, and as they were entring a little Thicket of Trees, we appear'd; and calling to them in *English*, told them they were our Prisoners; that if they yielded, we would use them very well, but if they offer'd to resist, they should have no Quarter: One of them looking behind, as if he would show us a Pair of Heels, I call'd to him, and told him, if he attempted to run for it, he was a dead Man, unless he could out-run a Musquet-Bullet; and that we would soon let him see we had more Men in our Company; and so giving the Signal appointed, our three Men, who lay at a Distance, shew'd themselves in the Rear.

When they saw this, one of them, who appear'd as their Leader, but was only the Purser's Clerk, ask'd, Who we were they must yield to? And if we were Christians? I told them, jestingly, We were good honest Christian Pirates, and belong'd to Captain *Avery*, (not at all letting them know that I was *Avery* himself) and if they yielded it was enough; that we assur'd them they should have fair Quarter and good Usage upon our Honour; but that they must resolve immediately, or else they would be surrounded with 500 Men, and we could not answer for what they might do to them.

They yielded presently upon this News, and deliver'd their Arms; and we carry'd them away to our Tent, which we had built near the Place where our Boat lay. Here I enter'd into a particular serious Discourse with them about Captain *Avery*, for 'twas this I wanted, upon several Accounts: First, I wanted to enquire what News they had had of us in *Europe*? and then to give them Ideas of our Numbers and Power as romantick as I could.

They told us, that they had heard of the great Booty Captain *Avery* had taken in the Bay of *Bengale*; and among the rest, a bloody Story was related of *Avery* himself, *viz.* That he ravish'd the Great Mogul's Daughter, who was going to be marry'd to the Prince of *Pegu*; that we ravish'd and forc'd all the Ladies attending her Train, and then threw them into the Sea, or cut their Throats; and that we had gotten a Booty of ten Millions in Gold and Silver, besides an inestimable Treasure of Jewels, Diamonds, Pearls, *&c.* but that we had committed most inhuman Barbarities on the innocent People that fell into our Hands. They then told us, but in a broken imperfect Account, how the Great Mogul had resented it; and that he had raised a great Army against the *English* Factories, resolving to root them out of his Dominions; but that the Company had appeas'd him by Presents, and by assuring him that the Men who did it, were Rebels to the *English* Government, and that the Queen of *England* would hang them all when ever they could be taken. I smil'd at that, and told them, Captain *Avery* would give them Leave to hang him, and all his Men, when they could take them; but that I could assure him they were too strong to be taken; that if the Government of *England* went about to provoke them, Captain *Avery* would soon make those Seas too hot for the *English*, and they might even give over their *East-India* Trade, for they little thought Circumstances Captain *Avery* was in.

This I did, as well to know what Notions you had of us in *England*, as to give a formidable Account of us, and of our Circumstances to *England*, which I knew might be of Use to us several Ways hereafter. Then I made him tell his Part, which he did freely enough; he told us, that indeed they had receiv'd an Account in *England* that we were exceeding strong; that we had several Gangs of Pirates from the *Spanish West-Indies*, that had taken great Booties there, and were gone all to *Madagascar* to join Captain *Avery*; that he had taken three great *East-India* Ships, one *Dutch*, and two *Portuguese*, which they had converted into Men of War; that he had 6000 Men under his Command; that he had twelve Ships, whereof three carry'd 60 Guns a-piece, and six more of them, from 40 to 50 Guns; that they had built a large Fort to secure their Habitations; and that they had two large Towns, one on one Side, one on the other of a River, cover'd by the said Fort, and two great Platforms or Batteries of Guns to defend the Entrance where their Ships rode; that they had an immense invaluable Treasure; and that it was said, Captain *Avery* was resolv'd to People the whole Island of *Madagascar* with *Europeans*, and to get Women from *Jamaica* and the *Leeward Islands*; and that it was not doubted but he would subdue, and make himself King of that Country, if he was let alone a little longer.

I had enjoin'd my Men, in the first Place, not to let him know that I was *Avery*, but that I was one of his Captains; and in the next Place, not to say a Word but just *Ay*, and *No*, as Things occurr'd, and leave the rest to me. I heard him patiently out in all the Particulars above, and when he had done, I told him it was true, Captain *Avery* was in the Island of *Madagascar*, and that several other Societies of Buccaneers and Freebooters were join'd him from the *Spanish West-Indies*; for, said I, the Plenty and Ease of our living here is such, and we are so safe from all the World, that we do not doubt but we shall be twenty thousand Men in a very little Time, when two Ships which we have sent to the *West-Indies* shall come back, and shall have told the Buccaneers at the Bay of *Campeachy*, how we live here.

But, said I, you in *England* greatly wrong Captain *Avery*, our General, (so I call'd myself, to advance our Credit) for I can assure you, that except plundering the Ship, and taking that immense Booty which he got in the great Ship where the Great Mogul's Daughter was, there was not the least Injury done to the Lady, no Ravishing or Violence to her, or any of her Attendance; and this, said I, you may take of my certain Knowledge; for, said I, I was on Board the Ship with our General all the while: And if any of the Princess's Women were lain with, said I, on Board the other Ship, as I believe most of them were, yet it was done with their own Consent and good Will, and no otherwise; and they were all dismiss'd afterwards, without so much as being put in Fear or Apprehensions of Life or Honour.

This I assur'd him, (as indeed it was just) and told him, I hop'd, if ever he came safe to *England*, he would do Captain *Avery*, and all of us, Justice in that particular Case.

As to our being well fortify'd on the Island, and our Numbers, I assur'd them all they were far from thinking too much of us; that we had a very good Fleet, and a very good Harbour for them; that we were not afraid of any Force from *Europe*, either by Land or Water; that it was, indeed, in vain to pretend to attack us by Force; that the only Way for the Government of *England* to bring us back to our Duty, would be to send a Proclamation from *England* with the Queen's Pardon for our General and all his People, if they came in by a certain Time: And, added I, we know you want Money in *England,* I dare say, said I, our General, Captain *Avery,* and his particular Gang, who have the main Riches, would not grudge to advance five or six Millions of Ducats to the Government, to give them Leave to return in Peace to *England,* and sit down quietly with the rest.

This Discourse, I suppose, was the Ground of the Rumour you have had in *England,* That *Avery* had offer'd to come in and submit, and would give six Millions for his Pardon: For as these Men were soon after this dismiss'd, and went back to *England,* there is no Doubt but they gave a particular Account of the Conference they had with me, who they call'd one of Captain *Avery*'s Captains.

We kept these five Men six or seven Days, and we pretended to show them the Country from some of the Hills, calling it all our own, and pointing every Way how many Miles we extended ourselves; we made them believe also that all the rest of the Country was at our Disposal, that the whole *Island* was at our Beck; we told them we had Treasure enough to enrich the whole Kingdom of *England;* that our General had several Millions in Diamonds, and we had many Tuns of Silver and Gold; that we had fifty large Barns full of all Sorts of Goods, as well *European* as *Indian;* and that it would be truly the best Way for *England* to do as they said, namely, to invite us all Home by a Proclamation with a Pardon: And if they would do this, said I, they can ask no reasonable Sum, but our General might advance it; besides, getting Home such a Body of stout able Seamen as we were, such a Number of Ships, and such a Quantity of rich Goods.

We had several long Discourses with them upon these Heads, and our frequent offering this Part to them with a Kind of feeling Warmth, (for it was what we all desir'd) has caus'd, I doubt not, the Rumour of such great Offers made by us, and of a Letter sent by me to the Queen, to beg her Majesty's Pardon for myself and my Company, and offering ten Millions of Money Advance to the Queen for the publick Service: All which is a meer Fiction of the Brain of those which have publish'd it; neither were we in any Condition to make such an Offer; neither did I, or any of my Crew or Company, ever write a Letter or Petition to the Queen, or to any one in the Government, or make any Application in the Case other than as above, which was only Matter of Conversation or private Discourse.

Nor were we so strong in Men or Ships, or any Thing like it. You have heard of the Number of Ships which we had now with us, which amounted to two Ships and a Sloop, and no more, except the Prize in which we took the Mogul's Daughter; (which Ship we call'd, *The Great Mogul*) but she was fit for nothing, for she would neither sail or steer worth a Farthing, and indeed was fit for no Use but a Hulk, or a Guard-Ship.

As to Numbers of Men, they bely'd us strangely, and particularly, they seem'd only to mistake Thousands for Hundreds: For whereas they told us, that you in *England* had a Report of our being six thousand Men, I must acknowledge that I think we were never, when we were at the most, above six hundred; and at the Time when I quitted the Country, I left about one hundered and eight Men there, and no more, and I am assur'd, all the Number that now remains there, is not above twenty two Men, no, not in the whole Island.

Well, we thought, however, that it was no Business of ours at that Time to undeceive them in their high Opinion of our great Strength, so we took Care to magnify ourselves, and the Strength of our General, (meaning myself) that they might carry the Story to *England,* depending upon it, *That a Tale loses nothing in the carrying.* When they told us of our Fort, and the Batteries at the Mouth of the River where our Ships lie, we insinuated, that it was a Place where we did not fear all the Fleets in the World attacking us; and when they told us of the Number of Men, we strove to make them believe that they were much many more.

At length, the poor Men began to be tir'd of us, and indeed we began to be tir'd of them;

for we began to be afraid very much that they would prye a little Way into our Affairs, and that a little too narrowly that Way; so as they began to sollicit their Deliverance, we began to listen to their Importunities: In a Word, we agreed to dismiss them; and accordingly we gave them Leave to go away to the Watering-place, as if they had made their Escape from us; which they did, carrying away their Heads full of all those unlikely projected Things which you have heard above.

In all this, however, I had not the good Luck to advance one Step towards my own Escape; and here is one Thing remarkable, *viz.* That the great Mass of Wealth I had gotten together, was so far from forwarding my Deliverance, that it really was the only Thing that hinder'd it most effectually; and I was so sensible of it, that I resolv'd once to be gone, and leave all my Wealth behind me, except some Jewels, as several of our Men had done already: For many of them were so impatient of staying here, that they found Means to get away, some and some, with no more Money than they could carry about them; particularly, thirteen of our Men made themselves a Kind of Shaloup with a Mast and Sail, and went for the Red Sea, having two Patareroes for her Defence, and every Man a thousand Pieces of Eight, and no more, except that one *Macmow* an *Irishman,* who was their Captain, had five Rubies and a Diamond, which he got among the Plunder of the Mogul's Ship.

These Men, as I heard, gat safe to *Mocca* in the *Arabian* Gulph, where they fetch the Coffee, and their Captain manag'd for them all so well, that of Pirates he made them Merchants, laid out all the Stock in Coffee, and got a Vessel to carry it up the Red Sea to *Sues,* where they sold it to the Factors for the *European* Merchants, and came all safe to *Alexandria,* where they parted the Money again; and then every one separated as they thought fit, and went their own Way.

We heard of this by mere Accident afterwards, and I confess I envy'd their Success; and tho' it was a great while after this that I took a like Run, yet you may be sure I form'd a Resolution from that Time to do the like; and most of the Time that I stay'd after this, was employ'd in picking out a suitable Gang that I might depend upon, as well to trust with the Secret of my going away, as to take with me; and on whom I might depend, and they on me, for keeping one another's Council when we should come into *Europe.*

It was in Pursuit of this Resolution that I went this little Voyage to the South of the Island, and the Gang I took with me prov'd very trusty, but we found no Opportunity then for our Escape: Two of the Men that we took Prisoners would fain have gone with us, but we resolv'd to trust none of them with the real and true Discovery of our Circumstances; and as we had made them believe mighty Things of ourselves, and of the Posture of our Settlement, that we had 5000 Men, 12 Men of War, and the like, we were resolv'd they should carry the Delusion away with them, and that no Body should undeceive them; because, tho' we had not such an immense Wealth as was reported, and so as to be able to offer ten Millions for our Pardon, yet we had a very great Treasure; and, being nothing near so strong as they had imagin'd, we might have been made a Prey, with all our Riches, to any Set of Adventurers who might undertake to attempt us, by Consent of the Government of *England,* and make the Expedition, *No Purchase no Pay.*

For this Reason we civily declin'd them, told them we had Wealth enough, and therefore did not now Cruise Abroad as we used to do, unless we should hear of another Wedding of a King's Daughter; or unless some rich Fleet, or some Heathen Kingdom was to be attempted; and that therefore a new Comer, or any Body of new Comers, could do themselves no good by coming over to us: If any Gang of Pirates or Buccaneers would go upon their Adventures, and when they had made themselves rich, would come and settle with us, we would take them into our Protection, and give them Land to build Towns and Habitations for themselves, and so in Time we might become a great Nation, and inhabit the whole Island: I told them, the *Romans* themselves were, at first, no better than such a Gang of Rovers as we were; and who knew but our General, Captain *Avery*, might lay the Foundation of as great an Empire as they.

These big Words amaz'd the Fellows, and answer'd my End to a Tittle; for they told such Rhodomantading Stories of us, when they came back to their Ships, and from them it spread so universally all over the *East-Indies*, (for they were Outward-bound) that none of the *English* or *Dutch* Ships would come near *Madagascar* again, if they could help it, for a great while, for Fear of us; and we, who were soon after this dwindled away to less than 100 Men, were very glad to have them think us too strong to meddle with, or so strong that no Body durst come near us.

After these Men were gone, we rov'd about to the East Side of the Island, and in a Word, knew not what to do, or what Course to take, for we durst not put out to Sea in such a Bauble of a Boat as we had under us; but tir'd at last, we came back to the South Point of the Island again; in our rounding the Island we saw a great *English*-built Ship at Sea, but at too far Distance to speak with her; and if it had not, we knew not what to have said to her, for we were not strong enough to attack her: We judg'd by her Course, she stood away from the Isle of St. *Maurice* or *Mauritius*, for the *Cape of Good Hope*, and must, as we suppos'd, come from the *Malabar* Coast, bound Home for *England*; so we let her go.

We are now return'd back to our Settlement on the North Part of the Island; and I have singl'd out about 12 or 13 bold brave Fellows, with whom I am resolv'd to venture to the Gulph of *Persia*; twenty more of our Men have agreed to carry us thither as Passengers in the Sloop, and try their own Fortunes afterwards, for they allow we are enough to go together. We resolve, when we come to *Bassaro*, to separate into three Companies, as if we did not know one another; to dress ourselves as Merchants, for now we look like Hell-hounds and Vagabonds; but when we are well dress'd, we expect to look as other Men do. If I come thither, I purpose, with two more, to give my Companions the Slip, and travel as *Armenians* thro' *Persia* to the *Caspian* Sea, so to *Constantinople*; and I doubt not we shall, one Way or other, find our Way, with our Merchandize and Money, to come into *France*, if not quite Home to my own Country. Assure yourself, when I arrive in any Part of Christendom, I will give you a farther Account of my Adventures.

*Your Friend and Servant,*

AVERY.

*The End of the First Letter.*

# A SECOND LETTER

*Sir,*

I wrote my last Letter to you from *Madagascar*, where I had continu'd so long till my People began to drop from me, some and some, and, indeed, I had, at last, but few left; so that I began to apprehend they would give an Account in *Europe*, how weak I was, and how easy it was to attack me; nay, and to make their Peace, might some of them, at least, offer their Service to be Pilots to my Port, and might guide the Fleets or Ships that should attempt me.

With these Apprehensions, I not only was uneasy myself, but made all my Men uneasy too; for, as I was resolv'd to attempt my own Escape, I did not care how many of my Men went before me: But this you must take with you by the Bye, that I never let them imagine that I intended to stir from the Spot myself; I mean, after my Return from the Ramble that I had taken round the Island, of which I have given you an Account; but, that I resolv'd to take up my Rest in *Madagascar* as long as I liv'd; indeed, before, I said otherwise, as I wrote you before, and made them all promise to fetch me away, but now I gave it out that I was resolv'd to live and die here; and therefore, a little before I resolv'd upon going, I set to Work to build me a new House, and to plant me a pretty Garden at a Distance from our Fort; only I had a select Company, to whom I communicated every Thing, and who resolv'd that, at last, we would go altogether, but that we would do it our own Way.

When I had finish'd my new House, (and a mighty Palace you would say it was, if you had been to see it) I remov'd to it, with eight of the Gang that were to be my Fellow adventurers; and to this Place we carry'd all our private Wealth, that is to say, Jewels and Gold; as to our Share of Silver, as it was too heavy to remove, and must be done in Publick, I was oblig'd to leave it behind; but we had a Stratagem for that too, and it was thus:

We had a Sloop, as you have heard, and she lay in our Harbour, 'tis true; but she lay ready to sail upon any Occasion; and the Men, who were of our Confederacy, who were not with me at my Country-house, were twelve in Number: These Men made a Proposal, that they would take the Sloop, and go away to the Coast of *Malabar*, or where else they could speed to their Mind, and buy a Fraight of Rice for the publick Account: In a free State as we were, every Body was free to go wherever they would, so that no Body oppos'd them; the only Dispute at any Time, was about taking the Vessel we had to go in: However, as these Men seem'd only to act upon the publick Account, and to go to buy Provisions, no Body offer'd to deny them the Sloop, so they prepar'd for their Voyage: Just as they were ready to go, one of them starts it to the rest, that it was very hazardous and difficult to run such a Length every now and then to get a little Rice, and if they would go, why should they not bring a good Quantity? This was soon resolv'd; so they agreed, they should take Money with them to buy a good Ship wherever they could find her, and then to buy a Loading of Rice to fill her up, and so come away with her.

When this was agreed, they resolv'd to take no Money out of the grand Stock, but to take such Mens Money as were gone, and had left their Money behind; and this being consented to, truly, my Friends took the Occasion, and took all their own Money, and mine, (being 64 little Chests of Pieces of Eight) and carry'd it on Board, as if it had been of Men that were Prick'd-run, and no Body took any Notice of it. These twelve Men had also now got twelve more with them, under Pretence of manning a Ship, if we should buy one, and in this Pickle away they put to Sea.

We had due Notice of every Thing that was done; and having a Signal given of the Time they resolv'd to go, we pack'd up all our Treasure, and began our March to the Place appointed, which from our Quarters was about forty Mile farther North.

Our Habitation, that is to say, my new House, was about sixteen Miles up the Country, so that the rest of our People could have no Notice of our March, neither did they miss us, at least, as I heard of, for we never heard any more of them; nor can I imagine what Condition or Circumstance they can be in at present, if they are still upon the Place, as, however, I believe some of them are.

We join'd our Comrades, with a great Deal of Ease, about three Days afterwards, for we march'd but softly, and they lay by for us: The Night before we went on Board, we made them a Signal by Fire, as we had appointed to let them know where we were, and that we were at Hand; so they sent their Boat and fetch'd us off, and we embark'd without any Notice taken by the Rest.

As we were now loose, and at Sea, our next Business was to resolve whither we should go; and I soon govern'd the Point, resolving for *Bassaro* in the Gulph of *Persia*, where I knew we might shift for ourselves: Accordingly, we steer'd away for the *Arabian* Coast, and had good Weather for some Time, even till we made the Land at a great Distance, when we steer'd Eastward along the Shore.

We saw several Ships, in our Way, bound to and from the Red Sea, as we suppos'd, and, at another Time, we would have been sure to have spoken with them: But, we had done Pirating; our Business now was, how to get off, and make our Way to some Retreat, where we might enjoy what we had got; so we took no Notice of any Thing by the Way; but, when we was thus sailing merrily along, the Weather began to change, the Evening grew black and cloudy, and threaten'd a Storm: We were in Sight or a little Island, (I know nothing of its Name) under which we might have anchor'd with Safety enough, but our People made light of it, and went on.

About an Hour after Sun-set the Wind began to rise, and blew hard at N. E. and at N. E. by N. and in two Hours Time encreas'd to such a Tempest, as in all my Rambles I never met with the like; we were not able to carry a Knot of Sail, or to know what to do, but to stow every Thing close, and let her drive; and, in this Condition we continu'd all the Night, all the next Day, and Part of the Night after; towards Morning the Storm abated a little, but not so as to give us any Prospect of pursuing our voyage; all the Ease we had, was, that we could just carry a little Sail to steddy the Vessel, and run away before it; which we did at that violent Rate, that we never abated 'till we made Land on the East Side of *Madagascar*, the very Island we came from, only on the other Side of the Island.

However, we were glad we had any Place to run to for Harbour; so we put in under the Lee of a Point of Land that gave us Shelter from the Wind, and where we came to an Anchor, after being all of us almost dead with the Fatigue; and, if our Sloop had not been an extraordinary Sea-boat, she could never have born such a Sea, for twelve Days together, as we were in, the worst I ever saw before or since. We lay here, to refresh ourselves, about twenty Days; and, indeed, the Wind blew so hard all the while, that if we had been dispos'd to go to Sea, we could not have done it; and, being here, about seven of our Men began to repent their Bargain, and left us, which I was not sorry for. It seems, the principal Reason of their looking back, was, their being of those who had left their Money behind them. They did not leave us without our Consent, and therefore our Carpenters built them a Boat, during the three Weeks we stay'd here, and fitted it very handsomely for them, with a Cabin for their Convenience, and a Mast and Sail, with which they might very well sail round to our Settlement, as we suppose they did: We gave them Fire-arms and Ammunition sufficient, and left them furnishing themselves with Provisions; and this, we suppose, was the Boat, tho' with other Men in it, which adventur'd afterwards as far as the *Cape of Good Hope*, and was taken up by a *Portugese* in Distress, by which Means they got Passage for themselves to *Lisbone*, pretending they had made their Escape from the Pirates at *Madagascar*; but we were told, that the *Portuguese* Captain took a good deal of their Money from them, under Pretence of keeping it from his own Seamen; and that when they came on Shore, and began to claim it, he threaten'd them with taking them up, and prosecuting them for Pirates, which made them compound with him, and take about 10000 Dollars for above 120000, which they had with them; which, by the Way, was but a scurvy Trick: They had, it seems, a considerable Quantity of Gold among them, which they had the Wit to conceal from the Captain of the Ship, and which was enough for such Fellows as them, and more than they well knew what to do with; so that they were rich enough still, tho' the *Portugal* Captain was nevertheless a Knave for all that.

We left them here, as I have said, and put to Sea again; and, in about twenty Days Sail, having pretty good Weather, we arriv'd at the Gulph of *Persia*: It would be too long to give you an Account of the particular Fortunes of some of our People after this, the Variety of which would fill a Volume by itself: But, in the first Place, we, who were determin'd to travel, went on Shore at *Bassaro*, leaving the rest of our Men to buy Rice, and load the larger Vessel back to their Comrades, which they promis'd to do; but how far they perform'd I know not.

We were thirteen of us that went on Shore here; from whence we hir'd a kind of Barge, or rather a Bark, which, after much Difficulty, and very unhandy Doings of the Men who we had hir'd, brought us to *Babylon*, or *Bagdat*, as it is now call'd.

Our Treasure was so great, that if it had been known what we had about us, I am of Opinion we should never have troubl'd *Europe* with our Company: However, we gat safe to *Babylon* or *Bagdat*, where we kept ourselves *Incog* for a while, took a House by ourselves, and lay four or five Days still, till we had got Vests and long Gowns made to appear Abroad in as *Armenian* Merchants. After we had got Cloaths, and look'd like other People, we began to appear Abroad; and I, that from the Beginning had meditated my Escape by myself, began now to put it into Practice; and, walking one Morning upon the Bank of the River *Euphrates*, I mus'd with myself what Course I should take to make off, and get quite away from the Gang, and let them not so much as suspect me.

While I was walking here, comes up one of my Comrades, and one who I always took for my particular Friend: I know what you are employ'd in, *said he,* while you seem only to be musing, and refreshing yourself with the cool Breeze. Why, *said I,* what am I musing about? Why, *said he,* you are studying how you should get away from us; but, muse upon it as long as you will, *says he,* you shall never go without me, for I am resolv'd to go with you which Way soever you take. 'Tis true, *says I,* I was musing which Way I should go, but not which Way I should go without you; for tho' I would be willing to part Company, yet you cannot think I would go alone; and you know I have chosen you out from all the Company to be the Partner of all my Adventures.

Very well, *says he,* but I am to tell you now, that it is not only necessary that we should not go all together; but, our Men have all concluded, that we should make our Escape every one for himself, and should separate as we could; so that you need make no Secret of your Design any more than of the Way you intend to take.

I was glad enough of this News, and it made me very easy in the Preparations we made for our setting out: And, the first Thing we did, was, to get us more Cloaths, having some made of one Fashion, some of another; but, my Friend and I, who resolv'd to keep together, made us Cloaths after the Fashion of the *Armenian* Merchants, whose Country we pretended to travel through.

In the mean Time, five of our Men dress'd like Merchants; and, laying out their Money in Raw Silk, and Wrought Silks, and other Goods of the Country, proper for *Europe,* (in which they were directed by an *English* Merchant there) resolv'd to take the usual Rout, and travel by the Caravans from *Babylon* to *Alleppo,* and so to *Scanderoon,* and we staid and saw them and their Bales go off in Boats for a great Town on the *Euphrates,* where the Caravans begin to take up the Passengers; the other six divided themselves, one Half of them went for *Agra,* the Country of the Great Mogul, resolving to go down the River *Hoogly* to *Bengal;* but whither they went afterward or what Course they took, I never knew, neither whether they really went at all or not.

The other three went by Sea, in a *Persian* Vessel, back from the Red Sea to the Gulf of *Mocca,* and I heard of them all three at *Marseilles;* but whither they went afterwards I never knew, nor could I come to speak with them even there.

As for me and my Friend, we first laid out all the Silver we had in *European* Ware, such as we knew would vend at *Ispahan,* which we carry'd upon twelve Camels; and hiring some Servants, as well for our Guide as our Guard, we set out.

The Servants we hir'd were a Kind of *Arab,* but rather looking like the Great Mogul's people, than real *Arabians;* and when we came into *Persia,* we found they were look'd upon as no better than Dogs, and were not only used ill, but that we were used ill for their Sakes; and after we were come three Days into the *Persian* Dominions, we found ourselves oblig'd to part with them; so we gave them three Dollars a Man to go back again.

They understood their Business very well, and knew well enough what was the Reason of it, though we did not. However, we found we had committed a great Mistake in it; for we perceiv'd that they were so exasperated at being turn'd off, that they vowed to be revenged; and, indeed, they had their Revenge to the Full; for the same Day, at Night, they return'd in the Dark, and set eleven Houses on Fire in the Town where we quartered; which, by the Way, had gone near to have cost me my Life, and would certainly have done so, if in the Hurry I had not seiz'd one of the Incendiaries and deliver'd him up to them.

The People were so provok'd at him that was taken that they fell upon him with all possible Fury as the common Incendiary and Burner of the Town, and presently quitted us (for they had before vowed our Destruction) but, as I said, quitted us immediately, and thronged about the Wretch they had taken; and, indeed, I made no Question but that they would have immediately murder'd him (nay, that they would have torn him in Pieces before they parted with him). But after they had vented their Rage at him for some Time with all possible Reproaches and Indignities, they carry'd him before the *Cadi*, or Judge of the Place. The *Cadi*, a wise, grave Man, answered, no, he would not judge him at that Time, for they were too hot and passionate to do Justice; but they should come with him in the Morning, when they were cool, and he would hear them.

It is true this was a most excellent Step of the *Cadi* as to the right Way of doing Justice; but it did not prove the most expedient in the present Occasion, though that was none of his Fault neither; for in the Night the Fellow got out of their Hands, by what Means or by whose Assistance I never heard to this Day; and the *Cadi* fined the Town in a considerable Sum for letting a Man accused of a capital Crime make his Escape before he was adjudged, and, as we call it, discharged according to Law.

This was an eminent Instance of the Justice of these People; and though they were doubly enraged at the Escape of the Fellow, who, without Doubt, was guilty, yet they never open'd their Mouths against the *Cadi*; but acquiesc'd in his Judgment, as in that of an Oracle, and submitted to the national Censure, or Censure according to the Custom of their Nation, which he had pass'd upon them in their publick Capacity for the Escape of the Man.

We were willing to get out of this Place as soon as we could; for we found the Peoples Rage, which wanted an Object to vent itself upon, began to threaten us again: So having pack'd up our Goods, and gotten five ordinary Camel-Drivers for our Servants in the Country, we set out again.

The Roads in *Persia* are not so much frequented, as to be well accommodated with Inns, so that several Times we were oblig'd to lodge upon the Ground in the Way; but our new Servants took Care to furnish us with Lodging; for as soon as we let them know we wanted Rest, and inclin'd to stop, they set up a Tent for us, in so short a Time, that we were scarce able to imagine it possible, and under this we encamp'd, our Camels being just by us, and our Servants and Bales lying all hard by.

Once or twice we lodg'd in publick Inns, built at the King of *Persia*'s Charge: These are fair large Buildings, built square, like a large Inn, they have all of them large Stables, and good Forrage for the Camels and Horses, and Apartments for perhaps two or three hundred People, and they are call'd *Caravansera's*, as being built to entertain whole Caravans of Travellers: On the great Roads to *Tauris* and the Side of *Turky* they are all fortify'd, and are able to entertain five or six Thousand People, and have a Stock to furnish what Number of Men can come with Provisions; nay, it has been known, that whole armies of the *Persians* have on their March been furnish'd with Provisions in one of these *Caravansera's*, and that they have kill'd 2000 Sheep for them in one Night's Time.

In this Manner we travell'd to *Ispahan*, the Capital of *Persia*, where appearing as Merchants, and with several Camels loaden with Merchandize, we pass'd all Possibility of Suspicion, and being perfectly easy, we continu'd here some Time, sold our Cargoes, and would gladly have remitted the Money to other Places, as for *Constantinople* in particular; but we found the *Turks* and *Persians* have no such Thing as an Exchange, by Bills running between them and other Nations, no, nor between one Town and another.

We were invited here by a sudden Accident to have gone Home by the *Caspian* Sea and *Astracan*, so thro' *Muscovy*; but I had heard so much of the Barbarity of the *Russians*, the dangerous Navigation of the *Caspian* Sea by Reason of the Calms and Shoals, the Hazard of being robb'd by the *Tartars* on the River *Wolga*, and the like, that I chose to travel to *Constantinople*, a Journey through Desarts, over Mountains and Wastes, among so many

Sorts of Barbarians, that I would run any Kind of Hazards by Sea, before I would attempt such a Thing again.

It would deserve another History to let you into all the different Circumstances of this Journey; how well I was us'd by some, and how ill by others; nay, how well by some *Mahometans*, how ill by some Christians: But it shall suffice to tell you, that I am at present at *Constantinople*; and, tho' I write this here, I do not purpose to send it to you till I come to *Marseilles* in *France*; from whence I intend to go and live in some inland Town, where, as they have, perhaps, no Notion of the Sea, so they will not be inquisitive after us.

I am, *&c.*

*FINIS.*

# THE OFFSHORE PIRATE

F. SCOTT FITZGERALD

# THE OFFSHORE PIRATE

## I.

This unlikely story begins on a sea that was a blue dream, as colorful as blue-silk stockings, and beneath a sky as blue as the irises of children's eyes. From the western half of the sky the sun was shying little golden disks at the sea—if you gazed intently enough you could see them skip from wave tip to wave tip until they joined a broad collar of golden coin that was collecting half a mile out and would eventually be a dazzling sunset. About half-way between the Florida shore and the golden collar a white steam-yacht, very young and graceful, was riding at anchor and under a blue-and-white awning aft a yellow-haired girl reclined in a wicker settee reading The Revolt of the Angels, by Anatole France.

She was about nineteen, slender and supple, with a spoiled alluring mouth and quick gray eyes full of a radiant curiosity. Her feet, stockingless, and adorned rather than clad in blue-satin slippers which swung nonchalantly from her toes, were perched on the arm of a settee adjoining the one she occupied. And as she read she intermittently regaled herself by a faint application to her tongue of a half-lemon that she held in her hand. The other half, sucked dry, lay on the deck at her feet and rocked very gently to and fro at the almost imperceptible motion of the tide.

The second half-lemon was well-nigh pulpless and the golden collar had grown astonishing in width, when suddenly the drowsy silence which enveloped the yacht was broken by the sound of heavy footsteps and an elderly man topped with orderly gray hair and clad in a white-flannel suit appeared at the head of the companionway. There he paused for a moment until his eyes became accustomed to the sun, and then seeing the girl under the awning he uttered a long even grunt of disapproval.

If he had intended thereby to obtain a rise of any sort he was doomed to disappointment. The girl calmly turned over two pages, turned back one, raised the lemon mechanically to tasting distance, and then very faintly but quite unmistakably yawned.

"Ardita!" said the gray-haired man sternly.

Ardita uttered a small sound indicating nothing.

"Ardita!" he repeated. "Ardita!"

Ardita raised the lemon languidly, allowing three words to slip out before it reached her tongue.

"Oh, shut up."

"Ardita!"

"What?"

"Will you listen to me—or will I have to get a servant to hold you while I talk to you?"

The lemon descended very slowly and scornfully.

"Put it in writing."

"Will you have the decency to close that abominable book and discard that damn lemon for two minutes?"

"Oh, can't you lemme alone for a second?"

"Ardita, I have just received a telephone message from the shore——"

"Telephone?" She showed for the first time a faint interest.

"Yes, it was——"

"Do you mean to say," she interrupted wonderingly, "'at they let you run a wire out here?"

"Yes, and just now——"

"Won't other boats bump into it?"

"No. It's run along the bottom. Five min——"

"Well, I'll be darned! Gosh! Science is golden or something—isn't it?"

"Will you let me say what I started to?"

"Shoot!"

"Well it seems—well, I am up here—" He paused and swallowed several times distractedly. "Oh, yes. Young woman, Colonel Moreland has called up again to ask me to be sure to bring you in to dinner. His son Toby has come all the way from New York to meet you and he's invited several other young people. For the last time, will you——"

"No," said Ardita shortly, "I won't. I came along on this darn cruise with the one idea of going to Palm Beach, and you knew it, and I absolutely refuse to meet any darn old colonel or any darn young Toby or any darn old young people or to set foot in any other darn old town in this crazy state. So you either take me to Palm Beach or else shut up and go away."

"Very well. This is the last straw. In your infatuation for this man.—a man who is notorious for his excesses—a man your father would not have allowed to so much as mention your name—you have rejected the demi-monde rather than the circles in which you have presumably grown up. From now on——"

"I know," interrupted Ardita ironically, "from now on you go your way and I go mine. I've heard that story before. You know I'd like nothing better."

"From now on," he announced grandiloquently, "you are no niece of mine. I——"

"O-o-o-oh!" The cry was wrung from Ardita with the agony of a lost soul. "Will you stop boring me! Will you go 'way! Will you jump overboard and drown! Do you want me to throw this book at you!"

"If you dare do any——"

Smack! The Revolt of the Angels sailed through the air, missed its target by the length of a short nose, and bumped cheerfully down the companionway.

The gray-haired man made an instinctive step backward and then two cautious steps forward. Ardita jumped to her five feet four and stared at him defiantly, her gray eyes blazing.

"Keep off!"

"How dare you!" he cried.

"Because I darn please!"

"You've grown unbearable! Your disposition——"

"You've made me that way! No child ever has a bad disposition unless it's her fancy's fault! Whatever I am, you did it."

Muttering something under his breath her uncle turned and, walking forward called in a loud voice for the launch. Then he returned to the awning, where Ardita had again seated herself and resumed her attention to the lemon.

"I am going ashore," he said slowly. "I will be out again at nine o'clock to-night. When I return we start back to New York, wither I shall turn you over to your aunt for the rest of your natural, or rather unnatural, life." He paused and looked at her, and then all at once something in the utter childness of her beauty seemed to puncture his anger like an inflated tire, and render him helpless, uncertain, utterly fatuous.

"Ardita," he said not unkindly, "I'm no fool. I've been round. I know men. And, child, confirmed libertines don't reform until they're tired—and then they're not themselves—they're husks of themselves." He looked at her as if expecting agreement, but receiving no sight or sound of it he continued. "Perhaps the man loves you—that's possible. He's loved many women and he'll love many more. Less than a month ago, one month, Ardita, he was involved in a notorious affair with that red-haired woman, Mimi Merril; promised to give her the diamond bracelet that the Czar of Russia gave his mother. You know—you read the papers."

"Thrilling scandals by an anxious uncle," yawned Ardita. "Have it filmed. Wicked clubman making eyes at virtuous flapper. Virtuous flapper conclusively vamped by his lurid past. Plans to meet him at Palm Beach. Foiled by anxious uncle."

"Will you tell me why the devil you want to marry him?"

"I'm sure I couldn't say," said Audits shortly. "Maybe because he's the only man I know, good or bad, who has an imagination and the courage of his convictions. Maybe it's to get away from the young fools that spend their vacuous hours pursuing me around the country. But as for the famous Russian bracelet, you can set your mind at rest on that score. He's going to give it to me at Palm Beach—if you'll show a little intelligence."

"How about the—red-haired woman?"

"He hasn't seen her for six months," she said angrily. "Don't you suppose I have enough pride to see to that? Don't you know by this time that I can do any darn thing with any darn man I want to?"

She put her chin in the air like the statue of France Aroused, and then spoiled the pose somewhat by raising the lemon for action.

"Is it the Russian bracelet that fascinates you?"

"No, I'm merely trying to give you the sort of argument that would appeal to your intelligence. And I wish you'd go 'way," she said, her temper rising again. "You know I never change my mind. You've been boring me for three days until I'm about to go crazy. I won't go ashore! Won't! Do you hear? Won't!"

"Very well," he said, "and you won't go to Palm Beach either. Of all the selfish, spoiled, uncontrolled disagreeable, impossible girl I have——"

Splush! The half-lemon caught him in the neck. Simultaneously came a hail from over the side.

"The launch is ready, Mr. Farnam."

Too full of words and rage to speak, Mr. Farnam cast one utterly condemning glance at his niece and, turning, ran swiftly down the ladder.

II.

Five o'clock robed down from the sun and plumped soundlessly into the sea. The golden collar widened into a glittering island; and a faint breeze that had been playing with the edges of the awning and swaying one of the dangling blue slippers became suddenly freighted with song. It was a chorus of men in close harmony and in perfect rhythm to an accompanying sound of oars dealing the blue writers. Ardita lifted her head and listened.

"Carrots and Peas,
Beans on their knees,
Pigs in the seas,
Lucky fellows!
Blow us a breeze,
Blow us a breeze,
Blow us a breeze,
With your bellows."

Ardita's brow wrinkled in astonishment. Sitting very still she listened eagerly as the chorus took up a second verse.

"Onions and beans,
Marshalls and Deans,
Goldbergs and Greens
And Costellos.
Blow us a breeze,
Blow us a breeze,
Blow us a breeze,
With your bellows."

With an exclamation she tossed her book to the desk, where it sprawled at a straddle, and hurried to the rail. Fifty feet away a large rowboat was approaching containing seven men, six of them rowing and one standing up in the stern keeping time to their song with an orchestra leader's baton.

"Oysters and Rocks,
Sawdust and socks,
Who could make clocks
Out of cellos?——"

The leader's eyes suddenly rested on Ardita, who was leaning over the rail spellbound with curiosity. He made a quick movement with his baton and the singing instantly ceased. She saw that he was the only white man in the boat—the six rowers were negroes.

"Narcissus ahoy!" he called politely.

"What's the idea of all the discord?" demanded Ardita cheerfully. "Is this the varsity crew from the county nut farm?"

By this time the boat was scraping the side of the yacht and a great bulking negro in the bow turned round and grasped the ladder. Thereupon the leader left his position in the stern and before Ardita had realized his intention he ran up the ladder and stood breathless before her on the deck.

"The women and children will be spared!" he said briskly. "All crying babies will be immediately drowned and all males put in double irons!" Digging her hands excitedly down into the pockets of her dress Ardita stared at him, speechless with astonishment. He was a young man with a scornful mouth and the bright blue eyes of a healthy baby set in a dark sensitive face. His hair was pitch black, damp and curly—the hair of a Grecian statue gone brunette. He was trimly built, trimly dressed, and graceful as an agile quarter-back.

"Well, I'll be a son of a gun!" she said dazedly.

They eyed each other coolly.

"Do you surrender the ship?"

"Is this an outburst of wit?" demanded Ardita. "Are you an idiot—or just being initiated to some fraternity?"

"I asked you if you surrendered the ship."

"I thought the country was dry," said Ardita disdainfully. "Have you been drinking finger-nail enamel? You better get off this yacht!"

"What?" the young man's voice expressed incredulity.

"Get off the yacht! You heard me!"

He looked at her for a moment as if considering what she had said.

"No," said his scornful mouth slowly; "No, I won't get off the yacht. You can get off if you wish."

Going to the rail be gave a curt command and immediately the crew of the rowboat scrambled up the ladder and ranged themselves in line before him, a coal-black and burly darky at one end and a miniature mulatto of four feet nine at to other. They seemed to be uniformly dressed in some sort of blue costume ornamented with dust, mud, and tatters; over the shoulder of each was slung a small, heavy-looking white sack, and under their arms they carried large black cases apparently containing musical instruments.

"'Ten-*shun*!" commanded the young man, snapping his own heels together crisply. "Right *driss*! Front! Step out here, Babe!"

The smallest Negro took a quick step forward and saluted.

"Take command, go down below, catch the crew and tie 'em up—all except the engineer. Bring him up to me. Oh, and pile those bags by the rail there."

"Yas-suh!"

Babe saluted again and wheeling about motioned for the five others to gather about him. Then after a short whispered consultation they all filed noiselessly down the companionway.

"Now," said the young man cheerfully to Ardita, who had witnessed this last scene in withering silence, "if you will swear on your honor as a flapper—which probably isn't worth much—that you'll keep that spoiled little mouth of yours tight shut for forty-eight hours, you can row yourself ashore in our rowboat."

"Otherwise what?"

"Otherwise you're going to sea in a ship."

With a little sigh as for a crisis well passed, the young man sank into the settee Ardita had lately vacated and stretched his arms lazily. The corners of his mouth relaxed appreciatively as he looked round at the rich striped awning, the polished brass, and the luxurious fittings of the deck. His eye felt on the book, and then on the exhausted lemon.

"Hm," he said, "Stonewall Jackson claimed that lemon-juice cleared his head. Your head feel pretty clear?"

Ardita disdained to answer.

"Because inside of five minutes you'll have to make a clear decision whether it's go or stay."

He picked up the book and opened it curiously.

"The Revolt of the Angels. Sounds pretty good. French, eh?" He stared at her with new interest "You French?"

"No."

"What's your name?"

"Farnam."

"Farnam what?"

"Ardita Farnam."

"Well Ardita, no use standing up there and chewing out the insides of your mouth. You ought to break those nervous habits while you're young. Come over here and sit down."

Ardita took a carved jade case from her pocket, extracted a cigarette and lit it with a conscious coolness, though she knew her hand was trembling a little; then she crossed over with her supple, swinging walk, and sitting down in the other settee blew a mouthful of smoke at the awning.

"You can't get me off this yacht," she raid steadily; "and you haven't got very much sense if you think you'll get far with it. My uncle'll have wirelesses zigzagging all over this ocean by half past six."

"Hm."

She looked quickly at his face, caught anxiety stamped there plainly in the faintest depression of the mouth's corners.

"It's all the same to me," she said, shrugging her shoulders. "'Tisn't my yacht. I don't mind going for a coupla hours' cruise. I'll even lend you that book so you'll have something to read on the revenue boat that takes you up to Sing-Sing."

He laughed scornfully.

"If that's advice you needn't bother. This is part of a plan arranged before I ever knew this yacht existed. If it hadn't been this one it'd have been the next one we passed anchored along the coast."

"Who are you?" demanded Ardita suddenly. "And what are you?"

"You've decided not to go ashore?"

"I never even faintly considered it."

"We're generally known," he said "all seven of us, as Curtis Carlyle and his Six Black Buddies late of the Winter Garden and the Midnight Frolic."

"You're singers?"

"We were until to-day. At present, due to those white bags you see there we're fugitives from justice and if the reward offered for our capture hasn't by this time reached twenty thousand dollars I miss my guess."

"What's in the bags?" asked Ardita curiously.

"Well," he said "for the present we'll call it—mud—Florida mud."

## III.

Within ten minutes after Curtis Carlyle's interview with a very frightened engineer the yacht Narcissus was under way, steaming south through a balmy tropical twilight. The little mulatto, Babe, who seems to have Carlyle's implicit confidence, took full command of the situation. Mr. Farnam's valet and the chef, the only members of the crew on board except the engineer, having shown fight, were now reconsidering, strapped securely to their bunks below. Trombone Mose, the biggest negro, was set busy with a can of paint obliterating the name Narcissus from the bow, and substituting the name Hula Hula, and the others congregated aft and became intently involved in a game of craps.

Having given order for a meal to be prepared and served on deck at seven-thirty, Carlyle rejoined Ardita, and, sinking back into his settee, half closed his eyes and fell into a state of profound abstraction.

Ardita scrutinized him carefully—and classed him immediately as a romantic figure. He gave the effect of towering self-confidence erected on a slight foundation—just under the surface of each of his decisions she discerned a hesitancy that was in decided contrast to the arrogant curl of his lips.

"He's not like me," she thought "There's a difference somewhere." Being a supreme egotist Ardita frequently thought about herself; never having had her egotism disputed she did it entirely naturally and with no detraction from her unquestioned charm. Though she was nineteen she gave the effect of a high-spirited precocious child, and in the present glow of her youth and beauty all the men and women she had known were but driftwood on the ripples of her temperament. She had met other egotists—in fact she found that selfish people bored her rather less than unselfish people—but as yet there had not been one she had not eventually defeated and brought to her feet.

But though she recognized an egotist in the settee, she felt none of that usual shutting of doors in her mind which meant clearing ship for action; on the contrary her instinct told her that this man was somehow completely pregnable and quite defenseless. When Ardita defied convention—and of late it had been her chief amusement—it was from an intense desire to be herself, and she felt that this man, on the contrary, was preoccupied with his own defiance.

She was much more interested in him than she was in her own situation, which affected her as the prospect of a matineé might affect a ten-year-old child. She had implicit confidence in her ability to take care of herself under any and all circumstances.

The night deepened. A pale new moon smiled misty-eyed upon the sea, and as the shore faded dimly out and dark clouds were blown like leaves along the far horizon a great haze of moonshine suddenly bathed the yacht and spread an avenue of glittering mail in her swift path. From time to time there was the bright flare of a match as one of them lighted a cigarette, but except for the low under-tone of the throbbing engines and the even wash of the waves about the stern the yacht was quiet as a dream boat star-bound through the heavens. Round them bowed the smell of the night sea, bringing with it an infinite languor.

Carlyle broke the silence at last.

"Lucky girl," he sighed "I've always wanted to be rich—and buy all this beauty."

Ardita yawned.

"I'd rather be you," she said frankly.

"You would—for about a day. But you do seem to possess a lot of nerve for a flapper."

"I wish you wouldn't call me that."

"Beg your pardon."

"As to nerve," she continued slowly, "it's my one redeemiug feature. I'm not afraid of anything in heaven or earth."

"Hm, I am."

"To be afraid," said Ardita, "a person has either to be very great and strong—or else a coward. I'm neither." She paused for a moment, and eagerness crept into her tone. "But I want to talk about you. What on earth have you done—and how did you do it?"

"Why?" he demanded cynically. "Going to write a movie, about me?"

"Go on," she urged. "Lie to me by the moonlight. Do a fabulous story."

A negro appeared, switched on a string of small lights under the awning, and began setting the wicker table for supper. And while they ate cold sliced chicken, salad, artichokes and strawberry jam from the plentiful larder below, Carlyle began to talk, hesitatingly at first, but eagerly as he saw she was interested. Ardita scarcely touched her food as she watched his dark young face—handsome, ironic faintly ineffectual.

He began life as a poor kid in a Tennessee town, he said, so poor that his people were the only white family in their street. He never remembered any white children—but there were inevitably a dozen pickaninnies streaming in his trail, passionate admirers whom he kept in tow by the vividness of his imagination and the amount of trouble he was always getting them in and out of. And it seemed that this association diverted a rather unusual musical gift into a strange channel.

There had been a colored woman named Belle Pope Calhoun who played the piano at parties given for white children—nice white children that would have passed Curtis Carlyle with a sniff. But the ragged little "poh white" used to sit beside her piano by the hour and try to get in an alto with one of those kazoos that boys hum through. Before he was thirteen he was picking up a living teasing ragtime out of a battered violin in little cafés round Nashville. Eight years later the ragtime craze hit the country, and he took six darkies on the Orpheum circuit. Five of them were boys he had grown up with; the other was the little mulatto, Babe Divine, who was a wharf nigger round New York, and long before that a plantation hand in Bermuda, until he stuck an eight-inch stiletto in his master's back. Almost before Carlyle realized his good fortune he was on Broadway, with offers of engagements on all sides, and more money than he had ever dreamed of.

It was about then that a change began in his whole attitude, a rather curious, embittering change. It was when he realized that he was spending the golden years of his life gibbering round a stage with a lot of black men. His act was good of its kind—three trombones, three saxaphones, and Carlyle's flute—and it was his own peculiar sense of rhythm that made all the difference; but he began to grow strangely sensitive about it, began to hate the thought of appearing, dreaded it from day to day.

They were making money—each contract he signed called for more—but when he went to managers and told them that he wanted to separate from his sextet and go on as a regular pianist, they laughed at him and told him he was crazy—it would be an artistic suicide. He used to laugh afterward at the phrase "artistic suicide." They all used it.

Half a dozen times they played at private dances at three thousand dollars a night, and it seemed as if these crystallized all his distaste for his mode of livlihood. They took place in clubs and houses that he couldn't have gone into in the daytime. After all, he was merely playing to rôle of the eternal monkey, a sort of sublimated chorus man. He was sick of the very smell of the theatre, of powder and rouge and the chatter of the greenroom, and the patronizing approval of the boxes. He couldn't put his heart into it any more. The idea of a slow approach to the luxury of leisure drove him wild. He was, of course, progressing toward it, but, like a child, eating his ice-cream so slowly that he couldn't taste it at all.

He wanted to have a lot of money and time and opportunity to read and play, and the sort of men and women round him that he could never have—the kind who, if they thought of him at all, would have considered him rather contemptible; in short he wanted all those things which he was beginning to lump under the general head of aristocracy, an aristocracy which it seemed almost any money could buy except money made as he was making it. He was twenty-five then, without family or education or any promise that he would succeed in a business career. He began speculating wildly, and within three weeks he had lost every cent he had saved.

Then the war came. He went to Plattsburg, and even there his profession followed him. A brigadier-general called him up to headquarters and told him he could serve his country better as a band leader—so he spent the war entertaining celebrities behind the line with a headquarters band. It was not so bad—except that when the infantry came limping back from the trenches he wanted to be one of them. The sweat and mud they wore seemed only one of those ineffable symbols of aristocracy that were forever eluding him.

"It was the private dances that did it. After I came back from the war the old routine started. We had an offer from a syndicate of Florida hotels. It was only a question of time then."

He broke off and Ardita looked at him expectantly, but he shook his head.

"No," he said, "I'm going to tell you about it. I'm enjoying it too much, and I'm afraid I'd lose a little of that enjoyment if I shared it with anyone else. I want to hang on to those few breathless, heroic moments when I stood out before them all and let them know I was more than a damn bobbing, squawking clown."

From up forward came suddenly the low sound of singing. The negroes had gathered together on the deck and their voices rose together in a haunting melody that soared in poignant harmonics toward the moon. And Ardita listens in enchantment.

"Oh down——
oh down,
Mammy wanna take me down milky way,
Oh down,
oh down,
Pappy say to-morra-a-a-ah
But mammy say to-day,
Yes—mammy say to-day!"

Carlyle sighed and was silent for a moment looking up at the gathered host of stars blinking like arc-lights in the warm sky. The negroes' song had died away to a plaintive humming and it seemed as if minute by minute the brightness and the great silence were increasing until he could almost hear the midnight toilet of the mermaids as they combed their silver dripping curls under the moon and gossiped to each other of the fine wrecks they lived on the green opalescent avenues below.

"You see," said Carlyle softly, "this is the beauty I want. Beauty has got to be astonishing, astounding—it's got to burst in on you like a dream, like the exquisite eyes of a girl."

He turned to her, but she was silent.

"You see, don't you, Anita—I mean, Ardita?"

Again she made no answer. She had been sound asleep for some time.

## IV.

In the dense sun-flooded noon of next day a spot in the sea before them resolved casually into a green-and-gray islet, apparently composed of a great granite cliff at its northern end which slanted south through a mile of vivid coppice and grass to a sandy beach melting lazily into the surf. When Ardita, reading in her favorite seat, came to the last page of The

Revolt of the Angels, and slamming the book shut looked up and saw it, she gave a little cry of delight, and called to Carlyle, who was standing moodily by the rail.

"Is this it? Is this where you're going?"

Carlyle shrugged his shoulders carelessly.

"You've got me." He raised his voice and called up to the acting skipper: "Oh, Babe, is this your island?"

The mulatto's miniature head appeared from round the corner of the deck-house.

"Yas-suh! This yeah's it."

Carlyle joined Ardita.

"Looks sort of sporting, doesn't it?"

"Yes," she agreed; "but it doesn't look big enough to be much of a hiding-place."

"You still putting your faith in those wirelesses your uncle was going to have zigzagging round?"

"No," said Ardita frankly. "I'm all for you. I'd really like to see you make a get-away."

He laughed.

"You're our Lady Luck. Guess we'll have to keep you with us as a mascot—for the present anyway."

"You couldn't very well ask me to swim back," she said coolly. "If you do I'm going to start writing dime novels founded on that interminable history of your life you gave me last night."

He flushed and stiffened slightly.

"I'm very sorry I bored you."

"Oh, you didn't—until just at the end with some story about how furious you were because you couldn't dance with the ladies you played music for."

He rose angrily.

"You have got a darn mean little tongue."

"Excuse me," she said melting into laughter, "but I'm not used to having men regale me with the story of their life ambitions—especially if they've lived such deathly platonic lives."

"Why? What do men usually regale you with?"

"Oh, they talk about me," she yawned. "They tell me I'm the spirit of youth and beauty."

"What do you tell them?"

"Oh, I agree quietly."

"Does every man you meet tell you he loves you?"

Ardita nodded.

"Why shouldn't he? All life is just a progression toward, and then a recession from, one phrase—'I love you.'"

Carlyle laughed and sat down.

"That's very true. That's—that's not bad. Did you make that up?"

"Yes—or rather I found it out. It doesn't mean anything especially. It's just clever."

"It's the sort of remark," he said gravely, "that's typical of your class."

"Oh," she interrupted impatiently, "don't start that lecture on aristocracy again! I distrust people who can be intense at this hour in the morning. It's a mild form of insanity—a sort of breakfast-food jag. Morning's the time to sleep, swim, and be careless."

Ten minutes later they had swung round in a wide circle as if to approach the island from the north.

"There's a trick somewhere," commented Ardita thoughtfully. "He can't mean just to anchor up against this cliff."

They were heading straight in now toward the solid rock, which must have been well over a hundred feet tall, and not until they were within fifty yards of it did Ardita see their objective. Then she clapped her hands in delight. There was a break in the cliff entirely hidden by a curious overlapping of rock, and through this break the yacht entered and very slowly traversed a narrow channel of crystal-clear water between high gray walls. Then they were riding at anchor in a miniature world of green and gold, a gilded bay smooth as glass and set round with tiny palms, the whole resembling the mirror lakes and twig trees that children set up in sand piles.

"Not so darned bad!" cried Carlyle excitedly.

"I guess that little coon knows his way round this corner of the Atlantic."

His exuberance was contagious, and Ardita became quite jubilant.

"It's an absolutely sure-fire hiding-place!"

"Lordy, yes! It's the sort of island you read about."

The rowboat was lowered into the golden lake and they pulled to shore.

"Come on," said Carlyle as they landed in the slushy sand, "we'll go exploring."

The fringe of palms was in turn ringed in by a round mile of flat, sandy country. They followed it south and brushing through a farther rim of tropical vegetation came out on a pearl-gray virgin beach where Ardita kicked of her brown golf shoes—she seemed to have permanently abandoned stockings—and went wading. Then they sauntered back to the yacht, where the indefatigable Babe had luncheon ready for them. He had posted a lookout on the high cliff to the north to watch the sea on both sides, though he doubted if the entrance to the cliff was generally known—he had never even seen a map on which the island was marked.

"What's its name," asked Ardita—"the island, I mean?"

"No name 'tall," chuckled Babe. "Reckin she jus' island, 'at's all."

In the late afternoon they sat with their backs against great boulders on the highest part of the cliff and Carlyle sketched for her his vague plans. He was sure they were hot after him by this time. The total proceeds of the coup he had pulled off and concerning which he still refused to enlighten her, he estimated as just under a million dollars. He counted on lying up here several weeks and then setting off southward, keeping well outside the usual channels of travel rounding the Horn and heading for Callao, in Peru. The details of coaling and provisioning he was leaving entirely to Babe who, it seemed, had sailed these seas in every capacity from cabin-boy aboard a coffee trader to virtual first mate on a Brazillian pirate craft, whose skipper had long since been hung.

"If he'd been white he'd have been king of South America long ago," said Carlyle emphatically. "When it comes to intelligence he makes Booker T. Washington look like a moron. He's got the guile of every race and nationality whose blood is in his veins, and that's half a dozen or I'm a liar. He worships me because I'm the only man in the world who can play better ragtime than he can. We used to sit together on the wharfs down on the New York water-front, he with a bassoon and me with an oboe, and we'd blend minor keys in African harmonics a thousand years old until the rats would crawl up the posts and sit round groaning and squeaking like dogs will in front of a phonograph."

Ardita roared.

"How you can tell 'em!"

Carlyle grinned.

"I swear that's the gos——"

"What you going to do when you get to Callao?" she interrupted.

"Take ship for India. I want to be a rajah. I mean it. My idea is to go up into Afghanistan somewhere, buy up a palace and a reputation, and then after about five years appear in

England with a foreign accent and a mysterious past. But India first. Do you know, they say that all the gold in the world drifts very gradually back to India. Something fascinating about that to me. And I want leisure to read—an immense amount."

"How about after that?"

"Then," he answered defiantly, "comes aristocracy. Laugh if you want to—but at least you'll have to admit that I know what I want—which I imagine is more than you do."

"On the contrary," contradicted Ardita, reaching in her pocket for her cigarette case, "when I met you I was in the midst of a great uproar of all my friends and relatives because I did know what I wanted."

"What was it?"

"A man."

He started.

"You mean you were engaged?"

"After a fashion. If you hadn't come aboard I had every intention of slipping ashore yesterday evening—how long ago it seems—and meeting him in Palm Beach. He's waiting there for me with a bracelet that once belonged to Catherine of Russia. Now don't mutter anything about aristocracy," she put in quickly. "I liked him simply because he had had an imagination and the utter courage of his convictions."

"But your family disapproved, eh?"

"What there is of it—only a silly uncle and a sillier aunt. It seems he got into some scandal with a red-haired woman name Mimi something—it was frightfully exaggerated, he said, and men don't lie to me—and anyway I didn't care what he'd done; it was the future that counted. And I'd see to that. When a man's in love with me he doesn't care for other amusements. I told him to drop her like a hot cake, and he did."

"I feel rather jealous," said Carlyle, frowning—and then he laughed. "I guess I'll just keep you along with us until we get to Callao. Then I'll lend you enough money to get back to the States. By that time you'll have had a chance to think that gentleman over a little more."

"Don't talk to me like that!" fired up Ardita. "I won't tolerate the parental attitude from anybody! Do you understand me?" He chuckled and then stopped, rather abashed, as her cold anger seemed to fold him about and chill him.

"I'm sorry," he offered uncertainly.

"Oh, don't apologize! I can't stand men who say 'I'm sorry' in that manly, reserved tone. Just shut up!"

A pause ensued, a pause which Carlyle found rather awkward, but which Ardita seemed not to notice at all as she sat contentedly enjoying her cigarette and gazing out at the shining sea. After a minute she crawled out on the rock and lay with her face over the edge looking down. Carlyle, watching her, reflected how it seemed impossible for her to assume an ungraceful attitude.

"Oh, look," she cried. "There's a lot of sort of ledges down there. Wide ones of all different heights."

"We'll go swimming to-night!" she said excitedly. "By moonlight."

"Wouldn't you rather go in at the beach on the other end?"

"Not a chance. I like to dive. You can use my uncle's bathing suit, only it'll fit you like a gunny sack, because he's a very flabby man. I've got a one-piece that's shocked the natives all along the Atlantic coast from Biddeford Pool to St. Augustine."

"I suppose you're a shark."

"Yes, I'm pretty good. And I look cute too. A sculptor up at Rye last summer told me my calves are worth five hundred dollars."

There didn't seem to be any answer to this, so Carlyle was silent, permitting himself only a discreet interior smile.

V.

When the night crept down in shadowy blue and silver they threaded the shimmering channel in the rowboat and, tying it to a jutting rock, began climbing the cliff together. The first shelf was ten feet up, wide, and furnishing a natural diving platform. There they sat down in the bright moonlight and watched the faint incessant surge of the waters almost stilled now as the tide set seaward.

"Are you happy?" he asked suddenly.

She nodded.

"Always happy near the sea. You know," she went on, "I've been thinking all day that you and I are somewhat alike. We're both rebels—only for different reasons. Two years ago, when I was just eighteen and you were——"

"Twenty-five."

"——well, we were both conventional successes. I was an utterly devastating débutante and you were a prosperous musician just commissioned in the army——"

"Gentleman by act of Congress," he put in ironically.

"Well, at any rate, we both fitted. If our corners were not rubbed off they were at least pulled in. But deep in us both was something that made us require more for happiness. I didn't know what I wanted. I went from man to man, restless, impatient, month by month getting less acquiescent and more dissatisfied. I used to sit sometimes chewing at the insides of my mouth and thinking I was going crazy—I had a frightful sense of transiency. I wanted things now—now—now! Here I was—beautiful—I am, aren't I?"

"Yes," agreed Carlyle tentatively.

Ardita rose suddenly.

"Wait a second. I want to try this delightful-looking sea."

She walked to the end of the ledge and shot out over the sea, doubling up in mid-air and then straightening out and entering to water straight as a blade in a perfect jack-knife dive.

In a minute her voice floated up to him.

"You see, I used to read all day and most of the night. I began to resent society——"

"Come on up here," he interrupted. "What on earth are you doing?"

"Just floating round on my back. I'll be up in a minute. Let me tell you. The only thing I enjoyed was shocking people; wearing something quite impossible and quite charming to a fancy-dress party, going round with the fastest men in New York, and getting into some of the most hellish scrapes imaginable."

The sounds of splashing mingled with her words, and then he heard her hurried breathing as she began climbing up side to the ledge.

"Go on in!" she called

Obediently he rose and dived. When he emerged, dripping, and made the climb he found that she was no longer on the ledge, but after a second frightened he heard her light laughter from another shelf ten feet up. There he joined her and they both sat quietly for a moment, their arms clasped round their knees, panting a little from the climb.

"The family were wild," she said suddenly. "They tried to marry me off. And then when I'd begun to feel that after all life was scarcely worth living I found something"—her eyes went skyward exultantly——"I found something!"

Carlyle waited and her words came with a rush.

"Courage—just that; courage as a rule of life, and something to cling to always. I began to build up this enormous faith in myself. I began to see that in all my idols in the past some manifestation of courage had unconsciously been the thing that attracted me. I began separating courage from the other things of life. All sorts of courage—the beaten, bloody prize-fighter coming up for more—I used to make men take me to prize-fights; the déclassé woman sailing through a nest of cats and looking at them as if they were mud under her feet; the liking what you like always; the utter disregard for other people's opinions—just to live as I liked always and to die in my own way— Did you bring up the cigarettes?"

He handed one over and held a match for her gently.

"Still," Ardita continued, "the men kept gathering—old men and young men, my mental and physical inferiors, most of them, but all intensely desiring to have me—to own this rather magnificent proud tradition I'd built up round me. Do you see?"

"Sort of. You never were beaten and you never apologized."

"Never!"

She sprang to the edge, poised for a moment like a crucified figure against the sky; then describing a dark parabola plunked without a slash between two silver ripples twenty feet below.

Her voice floated up to him again.

"And courage to me meant ploughing through that dull gray mist that comes down on life—not only overriding people and circumstances but overriding the bleakness of living. A sort of insistence on the value of life and the worth of transient things."

She was climbing up now, and at her last words her head, with the damp yellow hair slicked symmetrically back appeared on his level.

"All very well," objected Carlyle. "You can call it courage, but your courage is really built, after all, on a pride of birth. You were bred to that defiant attitude. On my gray days even courage is one of the things that's gray and lifeless."

She was sitting near the edge, hugging her knees and gazing abstractedly at the white moon; he was farther back, crammed like a grotesque god into a niche in the rock.

"I don't want to sound like Pollyanna," she began, "but you haven't grasped me yet. My courage is faith—faith in the eternal resilience of me—that joy'll come back, and hope and spontaneity. And I feel that till it does I've got to keep my lips shut and my chin high, and my eyes wide—not necessarily any silly smiling. Oh, I've been through hell without a whine quite often—and the female hell is deadlier than the male."

"But supposing," suggested Carlyle, "that before joy and hope and all that came back the curtain was drawn on you for good?"

Ardita rose, and going to the wall climbed with some difficulty to the next ledge, another ten or fifteen feet above.

"Why," she called back "then I'd have won!"

He edged out till he could see her.

"Better not dive from there! You'll break your back," he said quickly.

She laughed.

"Not I!"

Slowly she spread her arms and stood there swan-like, radiating a pride in her young perfection that lit a warm glow in Carlyle's heart.

"We're going through the black air with our arms wide and our feet straight out behind like a dolphin's tail, and we're going to think we'll never hit the silver down there till suddenly it'll be all warm round us and full of little kissing, caressing waves."

Then she was in the air, and Carlyle involuntarily held his breath. He had not realized that the dive was nearly forty feet. It seemed an eternity before he heard the swift compact sound as she reached the sea.

And it was with his glad sigh of relief when her light watery laughter curled up the side of the cliff and into his anxious ears that he knew he loved her.

VI.

Time, having no axe to grind, showered down upon them three days of afternoons. When the sun cleared the port-hole of Ardita's cabin an hour after dawn she rose cheerily, donned her bathing-suit, and went up on deck. The negroes would leave their work when they saw her, and crowd, chuckling and chattering, to the rail as she floated, an agile minnow, on and under the surface of the clear water. Again in the cool of the afternoon she would swim—and loll and smoke with Carlyle upon the cliff; or else they would lie on their sides in the sands of the southern beach, talking little, but watching the day fade colorfully and tragically into the infinite langour of a tropical evening.

And with the long, sunny hours Ardita's idea of the episode as incidental, madcap, a sprig of romance in a desert of reality, gradually left her. She dreaded the time when he would strike off southward; she dreaded all the eventualities that presented themselves to her; thoughts were suddenly troublesome and decisions odious. Had prayers found place in the pagan rituals of her soul she would have asked of life only to be unmolested for a while, lazily acquiescent to the ready, naïf flow of Carlyle's ideas, his vivid boyish imagination, and the vein of monomania that seemed to run crosswise through his temperament and colored his every action.

But this is not a story of two on an island, nor concerned primarily with love bred of isolation. It is merely the presentation of two personalities, and its idyllic setting among the palms of the Gulf Stream is quite incidental. Most of us are content to exist and breed and fight for the right to do both, and the dominant idea, the foredoomed attest to control one's destiny, is reserved for the fortunate or unfortunate few. To me the interesting thing about Ardita is the courage that will tarnish with her beauty and youth.

"Take me with you," she said late one night as they sat lazily in the grass under the shadowy spreading palms. The negroes had brought ashore their musical instruments, and the sound of weird ragtime was drifting softly over on the warm breath of the night. "I'd love to reappear in ten years, as a fabulously wealthy high-caste Indian lady," she continued.

Carlyle looked at her quickly.

"You can, you know."

She laughed.

"Is it a proposal of marriage? Extra! Ardita Farnam becomes pirate's bride. Society girl kidnapped by ragtime bank robber."

"It wasn't a bank."

"What was it? Why won't you tell me?"

"I don't want to break down your illusions."

"My dear man, I have no illusions about you."

"I mean your illusions about yourself."

She looked up in surprise.

"About myself! What on earth have I got to do with whatever stray felonies you've committed?"

"That remains to be seen."

She reached over and patted his hand.

"Dear Mr. Curtis Carlyle," she said softly, "are you in love with me?"

"As if it mattered."

"But it does—because I think I'm in love with you."

He looked at her ironically.

"Thus swelling your January total to half a dozen," he suggested. "Suppose I call your bluff and ask you to come to India with me?"

"Shall I?"

He shrugged his shoulders.

"We can get married in Callao."

"What sort of life can you offer me? I don't mean that unkindly, but seriously; what would become of me if the people who want that twenty-thousand-dollar reward ever catch up with you?"

"I thought you weren't afraid."

"I never am—but I won't throw my life away just to show one man I'm not."

"I wish you'd been poor. Just a little poor girl dreaming over a fence in a warm cow country."

"Wouldn't it have been nice?"

"I'd have enjoyed astonishing you—watching your eyes open on things. If you only wanted things! Don't you see?"

"I know—like girls who stare into the windows of jewelry-stores."

"Yes—and want the big oblong watch that's platinum and has diamonds all round the edge. Only you'd decide it was too expensive and choose one of white gold for a hundred dollar. Then I'd say: 'Expensive? I should say not!' And we'd go into the store and pretty soon the platinum one would be gleaming on your wrist."

"That sounds so nice and vulgar—and fun, doesn't it?" murmured Ardita.

"Doesn't it? Can't you see us travelling round and spending money right and left, and being worshipped by bell-boys and waiters? Oh, blessed are the simple rich for they inherit the earth!"

"I honestly wish we were that way."

"I love you, Ardita," he said gently.

Her face lost its childish look for moment and became oddly grave.

"I love to be with you," she said, "more than with any man I've ever met. And I like your looks and your dark old hair, and the way you go over the side of the rail when we come ashore. In fact, Curtis Carlyle, I like all the things you do when you're perfectly natural. I think you've got nerve and you know how I feel about that. Sometimes when you're around I've been tempted to kiss you suddenly and tell you that you were just an idealistic boy with a lot of caste nonsense in his head. Perhaps if I were just a little bit older and a little more bored I'd go with you. As it is, I think I'll go back and marry—that other man."

Over across the silver lake the figures of the negroes writhed and squirmed in the moonlight like acrobats who, having been too long inactive, must go through their tacks from sheer surplus energy. In single file they marched, weaving in concentric circles, now with their heads thrown back, now bent over their instruments like piping fauns. And from trombone and saxaphone ceaselessly whined a blended melody, sometimes riotous and jubilant, sometimes haunting and plaintive as a death-dance from the Congo's heart.

"Let's dance," cried Ardita. "I can't sit still with that perfect jazz going on."

Taking her hand he led her out into a broad stretch of hard sandy soil that the moon flooded with great splendor. They floated out like drifting moths under the rich hazy light, and as the fantastic symphony wept and exulted and wavered and despaired Ardita's last sense of reality dropped away, and she abandoned her imagination to the dreamy summer scents of tropical flowers and the infinite starry spaces overhead, feeling that if she opened her eyes it would be to find herself dancing with a ghost in a land created by her own fancy.

"This is what I should call an exclusive private dance," he whispered.

"I feel quite mad—but delightfully mad!"

"We're enchanted. The shades of unnumbered generations of cannibals are watching us from high up on the side of the cliff there."

"And I'll bet the cannibal women are saying that we dance too close, and that it was immodest of me to come without my nose-ring."

They both laughed softly—and then their laughter died as over across the lake they heard the trombones stop in the middle of a bar, and the saxaphones give a startled moan and fade out.

"What's the matter?" called Carlyle.

After a moment's silence they made out the dark figure of a man rounding the silver lake at a run. As he came closer they saw it was Babe in a state of unusual excitement. He drew up before them and gasped out his news in a breath.

"Ship stan'in' off sho' 'bout half a mile suh. Mose, he uz on watch, he say look's if she's done ancho'd."

"A ship—what kind of a ship?" demanded Carlyle anxiously.

Dismay was in his voice, and Ardita's heart gave a sudden wrench as she saw his whole face suddenly droop.

"He say he don't know, suh."

"Are they landing a boat?"

"No, suh."

"We'll go up," said Carlyle.

They ascended the hill in silence, Ardita's hand still resting in Carlyle's as it had when they finished dancing. She felt it clinch nervously from time to time as though he were unaware of the contact, but though he hurt her she made no attempt to remove it. It seemed an hour's climb before they reached the top and crept cautiously across the silhouetted plateau to the edge of the cliff. After one short look Carlyle involuntarily gave a little cry. It was a revenue boat with six-inch guns mounted fore and aft.

"They know!" he said with a short intake of breath. "They know! They picked up the trail somewhere."

"Are you sure they know about the channel? They may be only standing by to take a look at the island in the morning. From where they are they couldn't see the opening in the cliff."

"They could with field-glasses," he said hopelessly. He looked at his wrist-watch. "It's nearly two now. They won't do anything until dawn, that's certain. Of course there's always the faint possibility that they're waiting for some other ship to join; or for a coaler."

"I suppose we may as well stay right here."

The hour passed and they lay there side by side, very silently, their chins in their hands like dreaming children. In back of them squatted the negroes, patient, resigned, acquiescent, announcing now and then with sonorous snores that not even the presence of danger could subdue their unconquerable African craving for sleep.

Just before five o'clock Babe approached Carlyle. There were half a dozen rifles aboard the Narcissus he said. Had it been decided to offer no resistance?

A pretty good fight might be made, he thought, if they worked out some plan.

Carlyle laughed and shook his head.

"That isn't a Spic army out there, Babe. That's a revenue boat. It'd be like a bow and arrow trying to fight a machine-gun. If you want to bury those bags somewhere and take a chance on recovering them later, go on and do it. But it won't work—they'd dig this island over from one end to the other. It's a lost battle all round, Babe."

Babe inclined his head silently and turned away, and Carlyle's voice was husky as he turned to Ardita.

"There's the best friend I ever had. He'd die for me, and be proud to, if I'd let him."

"You've given up?"

"I've no choice. Of course there's always one way out—the sure way—but that can wait. I wouldn't miss my trial for anything—it'll be an interesting experiment in notoriety. 'Miss Farnam testifies that the pirate's attitude to her was at all times that of a gentleman.'"

"Don't!" she said. "I'm awfully sorry."

When the color faded from the sky and lustreless blue changed to leaden gray a commotion was visible on the ship's deck, and they made out a group of officers clad in white duck, gathered near the rail. They had field-glasses in their hands and were attentively examining the islet.

"It's all up," said Carlyle grimly.

"Damn," whispered Ardita. She felt tears gathering in her eyes "We'll go back to the yacht," he said. "I prefer that to being hunted out up here like a 'possum."

Leaving the plateau they descended the hill, and reaching the lake were rowed out to the yacht by the silent negroes. Then, pale and weary, they sank into the settees and waited.

Half an hour later in the dim gray light the nose of the revenue boat appeared in the channel and stopped, evidently fearing that the bay might be too shallow. From the peaceful look of the yacht, the man and the girl in the settees, and the negroes lounging curiously against the rail, they evidently judged that there would be no resistance, for two boats were lowered casually over the side, one containing an officer and six bluejackets, and the other, four rowers and in the stern two gray-haired men in yachting flannels. Ardita and Carlyle stood up, and half unconsciously started toward each other.

Then he paused and putting his hand suddenly into his pocket he pulled out a round, glittering object and held it out to her.

"What is it?" she asked wonderingly.

"I'm not positive, but I think from the Russian inscription inside that it's your promised bracelet."

"Where—where on earth——"

"It came out of one of those bags. You see, Curtis Carlyle and his Six Black Buddies, in the middle of their performance in the tea-room of the hotel at Palm Beach, suddenly changed their instruments for automatics and held up the crowd. I took this bracelet from a pretty, overrouged woman with red hair."

Ardita frowned and then smiled.

"So that's what you did! You *have* got nerve!"

He bowed.

"A well-known bourgeois quality," he said.

And then dawn slanted dynamically across the deck and flung the shadows reeling into gray corners. The dew rose and turned to golden mist, thin as a dream, enveloping them until they seemed gossamer relics of the late night, infinitely transient and already fading. For a moment sea and sky were breathless, and dawn held a pink hand over the young mouth of life—then from out in the lake came the complaint of a rowboat and the swish of oars.

Suddenly against the golden furnace low in the east their two graceful figures melted into one, and he was kissing her spoiled young mouth.

"It's a sort of glory," he murmured after a second.

She smiled up at him.

"Happy, are you?"

Her sigh was a benediction—an ecstatic surety that she was youth and beauty now as much as she would ever know. For another instant life was radiant and time a phantom and their strength eternal—then there was a bumping, scraping sound as the rowboat scraped alongside.

Up the ladder scrambled the two gray-haired men, the officer and two of the sailors with their hands on their revolvers. Mr. Farnam folded his arms and stood looking at his niece.

"So," he said nodding his head slowly.

With a sigh her arms unwound from Carlyle's neck, and her eyes, transfigured and far away, fell upon the boarding party. Her uncle saw her upper lip slowly swell into that arrogant pout he knew so well.

"So," he repeated savagely. "So this is your idea of—of romance. A runaway affair, with a high-seas pirate."

Ardita glanced at him carelessly.

"What an old fool you are!" she said quietly.

"Is that the best you can say for yourself?"

"No," she said as if considering. "No, there's something else. There's that well-known phrase with which I have ended most of our conversations for the past few years—'Shut up!'"

And with that she turned, included the two old men, the officer, and the two sailors in a curt glance of contempt, and walked proudly down the companionway.

But had she waited an instant longer she would have heard a sound from her uncle quite unfamiliar in most of their interviews. He gave vent to a whole-hearted amused chuckle, in which the second old man joined.

The latter turned briskly to Carlyle, who had been regarding this scene with an air of cryptic amusement.

"Well Toby," he said genially, "you incurable, hare-brained romantic chaser of rainbows, did you find that she was the person you wanted?"

Carlyle smiled confidently.

"Why—naturally," he said "I've been perfectly sure ever since I first heard tell of her wild career. That'd why I had Babe send up the rocket last night."

"I'm glad you did," said Colonel Moreland gravely. "We've been keeping pretty close to you in case you should have trouble with those six strange niggers. And we hoped we'd find you two in some such compromising position," he sighed. "Well, set a crank to catch a crank!"

"Your father and I sat up all night hoping for the best—or perhaps it's the worst. Lord knows you're welcome to her, my boy. She's run me crazy. Did you give her the Russian bracelet my detective got from that Mimi woman?"

Carlyle nodded.

"Sh!" he said. "She's coming on deck."

Ardita appeared at the head of the companionway and gave a quick involuntary glance at Carlyle's wrists. A puzzled look passed across her face. Back aft the negroes had begun to sing, and the cool lake, fresh with dawn, echoed serenely to their low voices.

"Ardita," said Carlyle unsteadily.

She swayed a step toward him.

"Ardita," he repeated breathlessly, "I've got to tell you the—the truth. It was all a plant, Ardita. My name isn't Carlyle. It's Moreland, Toby Moreland. The story was invented, Ardita, invented out of thin Florida air."

She stared at him, bewildered, amazement, disbelief, and anger flowing in quick waves across her face. The three men held their breaths. Moreland, Senior, took a step toward her; Mr. Farnam's mouth dropped a little open as he waited, panic-stricken, for the expected crash.

But it did not come. Ardita's face became suddenly radiant, and with a little laugh she went swiftly to young Moreland and looked up at him without a trace of wrath in her gray eyes.

"Will you swear," she said quietly "That it was entirely a product of your own brain?"

"I swear," said young Moreland eagerly.

She drew his head down and kissed him gently.

"What an imagination!" she said softly and almost enviously. "I want you to lie to me just as sweetly as you know how for the rest of my life."

The negroes' voices floated drowsily back, mingled in an air that she had heard them singing before.

"Time is a thief;
Gladness and grief
Cling to the leaf
As it yellows——"

"What was in the bags?" she asked softly.

"Florida mud," he answered. "That was one of the two true things I told you."

"Perhaps I can guess the other one," she said; and reaching up on her tiptoes she kissed him softly in the illustration.

Made in United States
Troutdale, OR
03/22/2025

29943056R20433